BRITISH WRITERS

BRITISH WRITERS

JAY PARINI
Editor

SUPPLEMENT XVI

CHARLES SCRIBNER'S SONS
A part of Gale, Cengage Learning

GALE CENGAGE Learning

Detroit • New York • San Francisco • New Haven, Conn • Waterville, Maine • London

British Writers Supplement XVI

Project Editors: Lisa Kumar

Copyeditors: Katy Balcer, Gretchen Gordon, Linda Sanders

Proofreaders: Susan Barnett

Indexer: Wendy Allex

Permission Researcher: Laura Myers

Permissions: Kelly Quin, Tim Sisler, Tracie Richardson

Composition: Gary Leach

Buyer: Cynde Lentz

Publisher: Frak Menchaca

Project Manager: Janet Witalec

Copyright © 2010 by Charles Scribner's Sons

ALL RIGHTS RESERVED. No part of this work covered by the copyright herein may be reproduced, transmitted, stored, or used in any form or by any means graphic, electronic, or mechanical, including but not limited to photocopying, recording, scanning, digitizing, taping, Web distribution, information networks, or information storage and retrieval systems, except as permitted under Section 107 or 108 of the 1976 United States Copyright Act, without the prior written permission of the publisher.

For product information and technology assistance, contact us at
Gale Customer Support, 1-800-877-4253.
For permission to use material from this text or product, submit all requests online at www.cengage.com/permissions.
Further permissions questions can be emailed to
permissionrequest@cengage.com

While every effort has been made to ensure the reliability of the information presented in this publication, Gale, a part of Cengage Learning, does not guarantee the accuracy of the data contained herein. Gale accepts no payment for listing; and inclusion in the publication of any organization, agency, institution, publication, service, or individual does not imply endorsement of the editors or publisher. Errors brought to the attention of the publisher and verified to the satisfaction of the publisher will be corrected in future editions.

EDITORIAL DATA PRIVACY POLICY. Does this publication contain information about you as an individual? If so, for more information about our editorial data privacy policies, please see our Privacy Statement at www.gale.cengage.com.

LIBRARY OF CONGRESS CATALOGING-IN-PUBLICATION DATA

British writers. Supplement XVI / Jay Parini, editor.
   p. cm.
   Includes bibliographical references and index.
   ISBN-13: 978-1-4144-3903-7 (alk. paper)
   ISBN-10: 1-4144-3903-2
   1. English literature--History and criticism. 2. English literature--Bio-bibliography. 3. Commonwealth literature (English)--History and criticism. 4. Commonwealth literature (English)--Bio-bibliography. 5. Authors, English--Biography. 6. Authors, Commonwealth-- Biography. I. Parini, Jay.
   II. Title, PR85.B688 Suppl.
   16 820.9--dc22   [B] 2010004484

The paper used in this publication meets the requirements of ANSI/NISO Z39.48-1992 (Permanence of Paper).

Charles Scribner's Sons
an imprint of Gale, Cengage Learning
27500 Drake Rd.
Farmington Hills, MI 48331–3535

ISBN-13: 978-1-4144-3903-7
ISBN-10: 1-4144-3903-2

Printed in the United States of America
1 2 3 4 5 6 7   14 13 12 11 10

Acknowledgements

Acknowledgement is gratefully made to those publishers and individuals who permitted the use of the following materials in copyright.

BUTLIN, RONALD. Butlin, Ronald. From *Creatures Tamed By Cruelty: Poems in English and Scots and Translations.* Edinburgh University Student Publication Board, 1979. Copyright © Ronald Butlin and EUSPB 1979. Reproduced by permission of the author. / Butlin, Ron. From *The Exquisite Instrument.* The Salamander Press, 1982. © Ron Butlin, 1982. Reproduced by permission. / Butlin, Ron. From *Ragtime in Unfamiliar Bars.* Secker & Warburg, 1985. Copyright © Ron Butlin 1985. Reproduced by permission of the author. / Butlin, Ron. From *Histories of Desire.* Bloodaxe Books, 1995. Copyright © Ron Butlin 1995. All rights reserved. Reproduced by permission of the author.

DARWIN, ERASMUS. Wordsworth, William. From "Lyrical Ballads (1798): The Thorn," in *Lyrical Ballads.* Edited by R. L. Brett and A. R. Jones. Routledge, 2005. Introduction and notes © 1963, 1991 R. L. Brett and A. R. Jones. Preface to Routledge Classic edition © 2005 Nicholas Roe. Reproduced by permission of the publisher. / Wordsworth, William. From "Lyrical Ballads (1798): Lines Written a Few Miles above Tintern Abbey," in *Lyrical Ballads.* Edited by R. L. Brett and A. R. Jones. Routledge, 2005. Introduction and notes © 1963, 1991 R. L. Brett and A. R. Jones. Preface to Routledge Classic edition © 2005 Nicholas Roe. Reproduced by permission of the publisher.

GREIG, ANDREW. Greig, Andrew. From *This Life, This Life: New & Selected Poems 1970-2006.* Bloodaxe Books Ltd., 2006. Copyright © Andrew Greig 1973, 1977, 1982, 1986, 1990, 1994, 2001, 2006. All rights reserved. Reproduced by permission. / *English: The Magazine of the English Association,* v. 2, 1939. Copyright © The English Association 1939. Reproduced by permission. / Greig, Andrew. From *Electric Brae: A Modern Romance.* Faber and Faber, 2002. © Andrew Greig, 1992. All rights reserved. Reproduced by permission of Faber & Faber Ltd. / Greig, Andrew. From *In Another Light.* Weidenfeld & Nicolson, 2004. © Andrew Greig 2004. All rights reserved. Reproduced by permission. / Greig, Andrew.

SOUTAR, WILLIAM. Soutar, William. From *Conflict.* Chapman & Hall Ltd., 1931. Reproduced by permission of the National Library of Scotland. / Soutar, William. From *The Solitary Way: Poems.* The Moray Press, 1934. Reproduced by permission of the National Library of Scotland. / Soutar, William. From *Brief Words: One Hundred Epigrams.* The Moray Press, 1935. Reproduced by permission of the National Library of Scotland. / Soutar, William. From *Poems in Scots.* The Moray Press, 1935. Reproduced by permission of the National Library of Scotland. / Soutar, William. From "Black Day," in *Poems of William Soutar: A New Selection.* Edited by W. R. Aitken. Scottish Academic Press, 1988. William Soutar's Poems, Diaries and Notebooks © 1988 Trustees of the National Library of Scotland. Selection and Introduction © W. R. Aitken 1998. All rights reserved. Reproduced by permission of the National Library of Scotland. / Soutar, William. From "Coorie in the Corner," in *Poems of William Soutar: A New Selection.* Edited by W. R. Aitken. Scottish Academic Press, 1988. William Soutar's Poems, Diaries and Notebooks © 1988 Trustees of the National Library of Scotland. Selection and Introduction © W. R. Aitken 1998. All rights reserved. Reproduced by permission of the National Library of Scotland. / Soutar, William. From "The Gowk," in *Poems of William Soutar: A New Selection.* Edited by W. R. Aitken. Scottish Academic Press, 1988. William Soutar's Poems, Diaries and Notebooks © 1988 Trustees of the National Library of Scotland. Selection and Introduction © W. R. Aitken 1998. All rights reserved. Reproduced by permission of the National Library of Scotland. / Soutar, William. From "A Drunk Man Looks at the Thistle," in *Poems of William Soutar: A New Selection.* Edited by W. R. Aitken. Scottish Academic Press, 1988. William Soutar's Poems, Diaries and Notebooks © 1988 Trustees of the National Library of Scotland. Selection and Introduction © W. R. Aitken 1998. All rights reserved. Reproduced by permission of the National Library of Scotland. / Soutar, William. From "Gin ye had come last Nicht," in *Poems of William Soutar: A New Selection.* Edited by W. R. Aitken. Scottish Academic Press, 1988. William Soutar's Poems, Diaries and Notebooks © 1988 Trustees of the National Library of Scotland. Selection and Introduction © W. R. Aitken 1998. All rights reserved. Reproduced by permission of the National Library of Scotland. / Soutar, William. From "The Whale," in *Poems of William Soutar: A New Selection.* Edited by W. R. Aitken. Scottish Academic

ACKNOWLEDGEMENTS

Press, 1988. William Soutar's Poems, Diaries and Notebooks © 1988 Trustees of the National Library of Scotland. Selection and Introduction © W. R. Aitken 1998. All rights reserved. Reproduced by permission of the National Library of Scotland. / Soutar, William. From "From the Wilderness," in *Poems of William Soutar: A New Selection*. Edited by W. R. Aitken. Scottish Academic Press, 1988. William Soutar's Poems, Diaries and Notebooks © 1988 Trustees of the National Library of Scotland. Selection and Introduction © W. R. Aitken 1998. All rights reserved. Reproduced by permission of the National Library of Scotland. / Soutar, William. From "Day is Dune," in *Poems of William Soutar: A New Selection*. Edited by W. R. Aitken. Translated by w. Scottish Academic Press, 1988. William Soutar's Poems, Diaries and Notebooks © 1988 Trustees of the National Library of Scotland. Selection and Introduction © W. R. Aitken 1998. All rights reserved. Reproduced by permission of the National Library of Scotland. / Soutar, William. From "The Tryst," in *Poems of William Soutar: A New Selection*. Edited by W. R. Aitken. Scottish Academic Press, 1988. William Soutar's Poems, Diaries and Notebooks © 1988 Trustees of the National Library of Scotland. Selection and Introduction © W. R. Aitken 1998. All rights reserved. Reproduced by permission of the National Library of Scotland. / Soutar, William. From "The Return of the Swallow," in *Poems of William Soutar: A New Selection*. Edited by W. R. Aitken. Scottish Academic Press, 1988. William Soutar's Poems, Diaries and Notebooks © 1988 Trustees of the National Library of Scotland. Selection and Introduction © W. R. Aitken 1998. All rights reserved. Reproduced by permission of the National Library of Scotland. / Soutar, William. From "Cosmos," in *Poems of William Soutar: A New Selection*. Edited by W. R. Aitken. Scottish Academic Press, 1988. William Soutar's Poems, Diaries and Notebooks © 1988 Trustees of the National Library of Scotland. Selection and Introduction © W. R. Aitken 1998. All rights reserved. Reproduced by permission of the National Library of Scotland. / Soutar, William. From "Riddles: 2," in *Poems of William Soutar: A New Selection*. Edited by W. R. Aitken. Scottish Academic Press, 1988. William Soutar's Poems, Diaries and Notebooks © 1988 Trustees of the National Library of Scotland. Selection and Introduction © W. R. Aitken 1998. All rights reserved. Reproduced by permission of the National Library of Scotland. / Soutar, William. From "The Children," in *Poems of William Soutar: A New Selection*. Edited by W. R. Aitken. Scottish Academic Press, 1988. William Soutar's Poems, Diaries and Notebooks © 1988 Trustees of the National Library of Scotland. Selection and Introduction © W. R. Aitken 1998. All rights reserved. Reproduced by permission of the National Library of Scotland. / Soutar, William. From "In Time of Tumult," in *Poems of William Soutar: A New Selection*. Edited by W. R. Aitken. Scottish Academic Press, 1988. William Soutar's Poems, Diaries and Notebooks © 1988 Trustees of the National Library of Scotland. Selection and Introduction © W. R. Aitken 1998. All rights reserved. Reproduced by permission of the National Library of Scotland. / Soutar, William. From "In the Time of Tyrants," in *Poems of William Soutar: A New Selection*. Edited by W. R. Aitken. Scottish Academic Press, 1988. William Soutar's Poems, Diaries and Notebooks © 1988 Trustees of the National Library of Scotland. Selection and Introduction © W. R. Aitken 1998. All rights reserved. Reproduced by permission of the National Library of Scotland. / Soutar, William. From "Wintry Beauty," in *Poems of William Soutar: A New Selection*. Edited by W. R. Aitken. Scottish Academic Press, 1988. William Soutar's Poems, Diaries and Notebooks © 1988 Trustees of the National Library of Scotland. Selection and Introduction © W. R. Aitken 1998. All rights reserved. Reproduced by permission of the National Library of Scotland. / Soutar, William. From "To the Future," in *Poems of William Soutar: A New Selection*. Edited by W. R. Aitken. Scottish Academic Press, 1988. William Soutar's Poems, Diaries and Notebooks © 1988 Trustees of the National Library of Scotland. Selection and Introduction © W. R. Aitken 1998. All rights reserved. Reproduced by permission of the National Library of Scotland. / Soutar, William. From "Sic A Hoast," in *Poems of William Soutar: A New Selection*. Edited by W. R. Aitken. Scottish Academic Press, 1988. William Soutar's Poems, Diaries and Notebooks © 1988 Trustees of the National Library of Scotland. Selection and Introduction © W. R. Aitken 1998. All rights reserved. Reproduced by permission of the National Library of Scotland.

SUTTCLIFF, ROSEMARY. *The Times Literary Supplement,* March 27, 1981. Copyright © 1981 by The Times Supplements Limited. Reproduced from *The Times Literary Supplement* by permission.

WAIN, JOHN. Wain, John. From *Weep Before God.* Macmillan & Co Ltd, 1962. Copyright © John Wain 1962. All rights reserved. Reproduced with permission of the author's estate. / Wain, John. From *Letters to Five Artists.* Macmillan, 1969. All rights reserved. Reproduced with permission of the author's estate.

Contents

Contents vii
Introduction ix
Chronology xi
List of Contributors lv

Subjects in Supplement XVI

LASCELLES ABERCROMBIE / Tyler Hoffman 1
JOHN ARBUTHNOT / Christopher Vilmar 15
WILLIAM BOYD / Charlie Samuelson 31
RON BUTLIN / Brian Hoyle 51
JOHN BYROM / Timothy Underhill 71
THOMAS CAMPION / Benjamin Ivry 89
HANNAH COWLEY / Druann Bauer 109
ERASMUS DARWIN / Adam Komisaruk 127
ELIZABETH I, QUEEN OF ENGLAND / Jane Beal 145
ANDREW GREIG / Les Wilkinson 161
PATRICK HAMILTON / Robert Sullivan 177
CHARLES KINGSLEY / Sandie Byrne 193
HENRY MAYHEW / Fred Bilson 209
J.K. ROWLING / Charles Robert Baker 225
WILLIAM SOUTAR / Helena Nelson 241
ROSEMARY SUTCLIFF / Abby Mims 261
CATHARINE TROTTER / Sayanti Ganguly Puckett 277
JOHN WAIN / Dale Salwak 293
MASTER INDEX to Volumes I–VII, Supplements I–XVI, Retrospective Supplements I–II 311

Introduction

The great historian Barbara Tuchman once wrote: "Books are the carriers of civilization. Without books, history is silent, literature dumb, science crippled, thought and speculation at a standstill." The articles in this volume describe and evaluate a wealth of literature in many genres, treating a wide range of British authors, or authors who write in the tradition of British literature. In Supplement XVI we present detailed introductions to authors over many centuries, although a fair number of the articles in this selection focus on writers from the distant past. In each case the articles have been designed to increase the reader's understanding of the subject, and to make the shape of his or her career, its evolution and influence, comprehensible. We hope they will help readers to see, with Tuchman, that books are "the carriers of civilization."

Taken as a whole, this series brings together a range of critical writing on British authors—poets, playwrights, novelists, essayists—who have a considerable reputation in the world of letters. As in previous volumes, the subjects have been chosen for their contribution to the British tradition in literature, and each has influenced intellectual life in the United Kingdom in important ways. Readers will find these essays lively and intelligent, shaped in ways that will interest readers unfamiliar with the work at hand and to assist those who know the work quite well by providing close readings of texts and a sense of the biographical, cultural, and critical context of that production. Bibliographies of work by the subject as well as writing about this author are included.

British Writers was originally an off–shoot of a series of monographs that appeared between 1959 and 1972, the *Minnesota Pamphlets on American Writers*. These pamphlets were incisively written and informative, treating ninety–seven American writers in a format and style that attracted a devoted following of readers. The series proved invaluable to a generation of students and teachers, who could depend on these reliable and interesting critiques of major figures. The idea of reprinting these essays occurred to Charles Scribner, Jr., an innovative publisher during the middle decades of the twentieth century. The series appeared in four volumes entitled *American Writers: A Collection of Literary Biographies* (1974). *British Writers* began with a series of essays originally published by the British Council, and regular supplements have followed nearly each year. The goal of the supplements has been consistent with the original idea of the series: to provide clear, knowledgeable essays aimed at the general reader. These articles often rise to a high level of craft and critical vision, but they are meant to introduce a writer of importance in the history of British or Anglophone literature as well as to provide a sense of the scope and nature of the career at hand for discussion.

The authors of these critical articles are mainly college teachers and scholars. Many of them have published books and articles in their field. As anyone leafing through this volume will see, they have been held to high standards of writing and scholarship. Jargon has been discouraged, except when strictly relevant. Supplement XVI centers on writers from various genres and traditions who have had little sustained attention from critics, although most are well known. William Boyd, Ron Butlin, Andrew Greig, Patrick Hamilton, J.K. Rowling, William Soutar, Rosemary Sutcliff, and John Wain have all been written about in the review pages of newspapers and magazines, often at considerable length, and their work has acquired a substantial following, but their careers have yet to attract significant scholarship. That will certainly follow, but the essays included in this volume constitute a beginning of sorts, an attempt to map out the particular universe of each writer.

Ten classic writers from the distant or more recent past included in this volume are Lascelles Abercrombie, John Arbuthnot, John Byrom, Thomas Campion, Hannah Cowley, Erasmus Darwin, Charles Kingsley, Henry Mayhew, Queen

INTRODUCTION

Elizabeth I, and Catharine Trotter. These are all important authors who, for one reason or another, have yet to be treated in this series. It is time they were included, and we think these articles will interest a fair number of our readers.

As ever, our purpose in these presenting these articles is to bring readers back to the texts under discussion, to help them in their reading by explaining the contours of a particular writer's career, by providing context. These are especially strong and stimulating articles, and they should enable students and general readers to enter into the world of these British writers freshly. Above all, these articles should serve to lengthen the reading list of those wishing to exercise their minds.

—*JAY PARINI*

Chronology

ca. 1342	Birth of John Trevisa and Julian of Norwich
1348	The Black Death (further outbreaks in 1361 and 1369)
ca. 1350	Boccaccio's *Decameron*
	Langland's *Piers Plowman*
1351	The Statute of Laborers pegs laborers' wages at rates in effect preceding the plague
1356	The Battle of Poitiers
1360	The Treaty of Brétigny: end of the first phase of the Hundred Years' War
1362	Pleadings in the law courts conducted in English
	Parliaments opened by speeches in English
1369	Chaucer's *The Book of the Duchess*, an elegy to Blanche of Lancaster, wife of John of Gaunt
1369–1377	Victorious French campaigns under du Guesclin
ca. 1370	John Lydgate born
1371	Sir John Mandeville's *Travels*
1372	Chaucer travels to Italy
1372–1382	Wycliffe active in Oxford
1373–1393	William of Wykeham founds Winchester College and New College, Oxford
ca. 1373	Margery Kempe born
ca. 1375–1400	*Sir Gawain and the Green Knight*
1376	Death of Edward the Black Prince
1377–1399	**Reign of Richard II**
ca. 1379	Gower's *Vox clamantis*
ca. 1380	Chaucer's *Troilus and Criseyde*
1381	The Peasants' Revolt
1386	Chaucer's *Canterbury Tales* begun
	Chaucer sits in Parliament
	Gower's *Confessio amantis*
1399–1413	**Reign of Henry IV**
ca. 1400	Death of William Langland
1400	Death of Geoffrey Chaucer
1408	Death of John Gower
1412–1420	Lydgate's *Troy Book*
1413–1422	**Reign of Henry V**
1415	The Battle of Agincourt
ca. 1416	Death of Julian of Norwich
1420–1422	Lydgate's *Siege of Thebes*
1422–1461	**Reign of Henry VI**
1431	François Villon born
	Joan of Arc burned at Rouen
ca.1439	Death of Margery Kempe
1440–1441	Henry VI founds Eton College and King's College, Cambridge
1444	Truce of Tours
1450	Jack Cade's rebellion
ca. 1451	Death of John Lydgate
1453	End of the Hundred Years' War
	The fall of Constantinople
1455–1485	The Wars of the Roses
ca. 1460	Births of William Dunbar and John Skelton
1461–1470	**Reign of Edward IV**
1470–1471	**Reign of Henry VI**
1471	Death of Sir Thomas Malory
1471–1483	**Reign of Edward IV**
1476–1483	Caxton's press set up: *The Canterbury Tales*, *Morte d'Arthur*, and *The Golden Legend* printed
1483–1485	**Reign of Richard III**
1485	The Battle of Bosworth Field; end of the Wars of the Roses
1485–1509	**Reign of Henry VII**
1486	Marriage of Henry VII and Elizabeth of York unites the rival houses of Lancaster and York
	Bartholomew Diaz rounds the Cape of Good Hope
1492	Columbus' first voyage to the New World
1493	Pope Alexander VI divides undiscovered territories between Spain and Portugal
1497–1498	John Cabot's voyages to Newfoundland and Labrador
1497–1499	Vasco da Gama's voyage to India
1499	Amerigo Vespucci's first voyage to America
	Erasmus' first visit to England
1503	Thomas Wyatt born
1505	John Colet appointed dean of St.

CHRONOLOGY

	Paul's: founds St. Paul's School
1509–1547	**Reign of Henry VIII**
1509	The king marries Catherine of Aragon
1511	Erasmus' *Praise of Folly* published
1513	Invasion by the Scots defeated at Flodden Field
1515	Wolsey appointed lord chancellor
1516	Sir Thomas More's *Utopia*
1517	Martin Luther's theses against indulgences published at Wittenberg
	Henry Howard (earl of Surrey) born
1519	Charles V of Spain becomes Holy Roman Emperor
1519–1521	Magellan's voyage around the world
1525	Cardinal College, the forerunner of Christ Church, founded at Oxford
1526	Tyndale's English translation of the New Testament imported from Holland
1529	Fall of Cardinal Wolsey
	Death of John Skelton
1529–1536	The "Reformation" Parliament
1531	Sir Thomas Elyot's *The Governour* published
1532	Thomas Cranmer appointed archbishop of Canterbury
	Machiavelli's *The Prince*
1533	The king secretly marries Anne Boleyn
	Queen Elizabeth I born
	Cranmer pronounces the king's marriage with Catherine "against divine law"
1534	The Act of Supremacy constitutes the king as head of the Church of England
1535	Sir Thomas More executed
	Thomas Cromwell appointed vicar general of the Church of England
1536	The Pilgrimage of Grace: risings against the king's religious, social, and economic reforms
	Anne Boleyn executed
	The king marries Jane Seymour
1537	The dissolution of the monasteries: confiscation of ecclesiastical properties and assets; increase in royal revenues
	Jane Seymour dies
1538	First complete English Bible published and placed in all churches
1540	The king marries Anne of Cleves
	Marriage dissolved
	The king marries Catherine Howard
	Fall and execution of Thomas Cromwell
1542	Catherine Howard executed
	Death of Sir Thomas Wyatt
1543	The king marries Catherine Parr
	Copernicus' *De revolutionibus orbium coelestium*
1546	Trinity College, Cambridge, refounded
1547	The earl of Surrey executed
1547–1553	**Reign of Edward VI**
1548–1552	Hall's *Chronicle*
1552	The second Book of Common Prayer
ca. 1552	Edmund Spenser born
1553	Lady Jane Grey proclaimed queen
1553–1558	**Reign of Mary I (Mary Tudor)**
ca. 1554	Births of Walter Raleigh, Richard Hooker, John Lyly, and Fulke Greville
1554	Lady Jane Grey executed
	Mary I marries Philip II of Spain
	Bandello's *Novelle*
	Philip Sidney born
ca. 1556	George Peele born
1557	Tottel's *Miscellany*, including the poems of Wyatt and Surrey, published
ca. 1558	Thomas Kyd born
1558	Calais, the last English possession in France, is lost
	Birth of Robert Greene
	Mary I dies
1558–1603	**Reign of Elizabeth I**
1559	John Knox arrives in Scotland
	Rebellion against the French regent
ca. 1559	George Chapman born
1561	Mary Queen of Scots (Mary Stuart) arrives in Edinburgh
	Thomas Hoby's translation of Castiglione's *The Courtier Gorboduc*, the first English play in blank verse
	Francis Bacon born
1562	Civil war in France
	English expedition sent to support the Huguenots
1562–1568	Sir John Hawkins' voyages to Africa
1564	Births of Christopher Marlowe and William Shakespeare
1565	Mary Queen of Scots marries Lord Darnley
1566	William Painter's *Palace of Plea-*

CHRONOLOGY

	sure, a miscellany of prose stories, the source of many dramatists' plots
1567	Darnley murdered at Kirk o'Field
	Mary Queen of Scots marries the earl of Bothwell
	Thomas Campion born
1569	Rebellion of the English northern earls suppressed
1570	Roger Ascham's *The Schoolmaster*
1571	Defeat of the Turkish fleet at Lepanto
ca. 1572	Ben Jonson born
1572	St. Bartholomew's Day massacre
	John Donne born
1574	The earl of Leicester's theater company formed
1576	The Theater, the first permanent theater building in London, opened
	The first Blackfriars Theater opened with performances by the Children of St. Paul's
	John Marston born
1576–1578	Martin Frobisher's voyages to Labrador and the northwest
1577–1580	Sir Francis Drake sails around the world
1577	Holinshed's *Chronicles of England, Scotlande, and Irelande*
1579	John Lyly's *Euphues: The Anatomy of Wit*
	Thomas North's translation of *Plutarch's Lives*
1581	The Levant Company founded
	Seneca's *Ten Tragedies* translated
1582	Richard Hakluyt's *Divers Voyages Touching the Discoverie of America*
1583	Philip Massinger born
1584–1585	Sir John Davis' first voyage to Greenland
1585	First English settlement in America, the "Lost Colony" comprising 108 men under Ralph Lane, founded at Roanoke Island, off the coast of North Carolina
1586	Kyd's *Spanish Tragedy*
	Marlowe's *Tamburlaine*
	William Camden's *Britannia*
	The Babington conspiracy against Queen Elizabeth
	Death of Sir Philip Sidney
1587	Mary Queen of Scots executed
	Birth of Virginia Dare, first English child born in America, at Roanoke Island
1588	Defeat of the Spanish Armada
	Marlowe's *Dr. Faustus*
1590	Spenser's *The Faerie Queen*, Cantos 1–3
	Richard Brome born
1592	Outbreak of plague in London; the theaters closed
	Henry King born
1593	Death of Christopher Marlowe
1594	The Lord Chamberlain's Men, the company to which Shakespeare belonged, founded
	The Swan Theater opened
	Death of Thomas Kyd
1595	Ralegh's expedition to Guiana
	Sidney's *Apology for Poetry*
1596	The earl of Essex's expedition captures Cadiz
	The second Blackfriars Theater opened
ca. 1597	Death of George Peele
1597	Bacon's first collection of *Essays*
1598	Jonson's *Every Man in His Humor*
1598–1600	Richard Hakluyt's *Principal Navigations, Voyages, Traffics, and Discoveries of the English Nation*
1599	The Globe Theater opened
	Death of Edmund Spenser
1600	Death of Richard Hooker
1601	Rebellion and execution of the earl of Essex
1602	The East India Company founded
	The Bodleian Library reopened at Oxford
1603–1625	**Reign of James I**
1603	John Florio's translation of Montaigne's *Essays*
	Cervantes' *Don Quixote* (Part 1)
	The Gunpowder Plot
	Thomas Browne born
	Death of **Queen Elizabeth I**
1604	Shakespeare's *Othello*
ca. 1605	Shakespears's *King Lear*
	Tourneur's *The Revenger's Tragedy*
1605	Bacon's *Advancement of Learning*
1606	Shakespeare's *Macbeth*
	Jonson's *Volpone*
	Death of John Lyly
	Edmund Waller born
1607	The first permanent English colony established at Jamestown, Virginia
1608	John Milton born
1609	Kepler's *Astronomia nova*

xiii

CHRONOLOGY

	John Suckling born
1610	Galileo's *Sidereus nuncius*
1611	The Authorized Version of the Bible
	Shakespeare's *The Tempest*
1612	Death of Prince Henry, King James's eldest son
	Webster's *The White Devil*
	Bacon's second collection of *Essays*
ca. 1613	Richard Crashaw born
1613	The Globe Theatre destroyed by fire
	Webster's *The Duchess of Malfi*
1614	Ralegh's *History of the World*
1616	George Chapman's translation of Homer's *Odyssey*
	Deaths of William Shakespeare, Francis Beaumont, and Miguel Cervantes
ca. 1618	Richard Lovelace born
1618	The Thirty Years' War begins
	Sir Walter Ralegh executed
	Abraham Cowley born
1619	The General Assembly, the first legislative assembly on American soil, meets in Virginia
	Slavery introduced at Jamestown
1620	The Pilgrims land in Massachusetts
	John Evelyn born
	Death of Thomas Campion
1621	Francis Bacon impeached and fined
	Robert Burton's *Anatomy of Melancholy*
	Andrew Marvell born
1622	Middleton's *The Changeling*
	Henry Vaughan born
1623	The First Folio of Shakespeare's plays
	Visit of Prince Charles and the duke of Buckingham to Spain; failure of attempts to negotiate a Spanish marriage
1624	War against Spain
1625–1649	**Reign of Charles I**
1625	Death of John Fletcher
	Bacon's last collection of *Essays*
1626	Bacon's *New Atlantis*, appended to *Sylva sylvarum*
	Dutch found New Amsterdam
	Death of Cyril Tourneur
	Death of Francis Bacon
1627	Ford's *'Tis Pity She's a Whore*
	Cardinal Richelieu establishes the Company of New France with monopoly over trade and land in Canada
	Buckingham's expedition to the Isle of Ré to relieve La Rochelle
	Death of Thomas Middleton
1627–1628	Revolt and siege of La Rochelle, the principal Huguenot city of France
1628	Buckingham assassinated
	Surrender of La Rochelle
	William Harvey's treatise on the circulation of the blood (*De motu cordis et sanguinis*)
	John Bunyan born
	Death of Fulke Greville
1629	Ford's *The Broken Heart*
	King Charles dismisses his third Parliament, imprisons nine members, and proceeds to rule for eleven years without Parliament
	The Massachusetts Bay Company formed
1629–1630	Peace treaties with France and Spain
1631	John Dryden born
	Death of John Donne
1633	William Laud appointed archbishop of Canterbury
	Death of George Herbert
	Samuel Pepys born
1634	Deaths of George Chapman and John Marston
1635	The Académie Française founded
	George Etherege born
1636	Pierre Corneille's *Le Cid*
	Harvard College founded
ca. 1637	Thomas Traherne born
1637	Milton's "Lycidas"
	Descartes's *Discours de la méthode*
	King Charles's levy of ship money challenged in the courts by John Hampden
	The introduction of the new English Book of Common Prayer strongly opposed in Scotland
	Death of Ben Jonson
ca. 1638	Death of John Webster
1638	The Scots draw up a National Covenant to defend their religion
ca. 1639	Death of John Ford
1639	Parliament reassembled to raise taxes
	Death of Thomas Carew
	Charles Sedley born
1639–1640	The two Bishops' Wars with Scot-

CHRONOLOGY

	land
1640	The Long Parliament assembled
	The king's advisers, Archbishop Laud and the earl of Strafford, impeached
	Aphra Behn born
	Death of Philip Massinger
1641	Strafford executed
	Acts passed abolishing extraparliamentary taxation, the king's extraordinary courts, and his power to order a dissolution without parliamentary consent
	The Grand Remonstrance censuring royal policy passed by eleven votes
	William Wycherley born
1642	Parliament submits the nineteen Propositions, which King Charles rejects as annihilating the royal power
	The Civil War begins
	The theaters close
	Royalist victory at Edgehill; King Charles established at Oxford
	Death of Sir John Suckling
1643	Parliament concludes the Solemn League and Covenant with the Scots
	Louis XIV becomes king of France
	Charles Sackville, earl of Dorset, born
1644	Parliamentary victory at Marston Moor
	The New Model army raised
	Milton's *Areopagitica*
1645	Parliamentary victory under Fairfax and Cromwell at Naseby
	Fairfax captures Bristol
	Archbishop Laud executed
1646	Fairfax besieges King Charles at Oxford
	King Charles takes refuge in Scotland; end of the First Civil War
	King Charles attempts negotiations with the Scots
	Parliament's proposals sent to the king and rejected
1647	Conflict between Parliament and the army
	A general council of the army established that discusses representational government within the army
	The Agreement of the People drawn up by the Levelers; its proposals include manhood suffrage
	King Charles concludes an agreement with the Scots
	George Fox begins to preach
	John Wilmot, earl of Rochester, born
1648	Cromwell dismisses the general council of the army
	The Second Civil War begins
	Fairfax defeats the Kentish royalists at Maidstone
	Cromwell defeats the Scots at Preston
	The Thirty Years' War ended by the treaty of Westphalia
	Parliament purged by the army
1649–1660	**Commonwealth**
1649	King Charles I tried and executed
	The monarchy and the House of Lords abolished
	The Commonwealth proclaimed
	Cromwell invades Ireland and defeats the royalist Catholic forces
	Death of Richard Crashaw
1650	Cromwell defeats the Scots at Dunbar
1651	Charles II crowned king of the Scots, at Scone
	Charles II invades England, is defeated at Worcester, escapes to France
	Thomas Hobbes's *Leviathan*
1652	War with Holland
	Death of Richard Brome
1653	The Rump Parliament dissolved by the army
	A new Parliament and council of state nominated; Cromwell becomes Lord Protector
	Walton's *The Compleat Angler*
1654	Peace concluded with Holland
	War against Spain
1655	Parliament attempts to reduce the army and is dissolved
	Rule of the major-generals
1656	Sir William Davenant produces *The Siege of Rhodes*, one of the first English operas
1657	Second Parliament of the Protectorate
	Cromwell is offered and declines the

CHRONOLOGY

	throne
	Death of Richard Lovelace
1658	Death of Oliver Cromwell
	Richard Cromwell succeeds as Protector
1659	Conflict between Parliament and the army
1660	General Monck negotiates with Charles II
	Charles II offers the conciliatory Declaration of Breda and accepts Parliament's invitation to return
	Will's Coffee House established
	Sir William Davenant and Thomas Killigrew licensed to set up two companies of players, the Duke of York's and the King's Servants, including actors and actresses
	Pepys's *Diary* begun
1660–1685	**Reign of Charles II**
1661	Parliament passes the Act of Uniformity, enjoining the use of the Book of Common Prayer; many Puritan and dissenting clergy leave their livings
	Anne Finch born
1662	Peace Treaty with Spain
	King Charles II marries Catherine of Braganza
	The Royal Society incorporated (founded in 1660)
1664	War against Holland
	New Amsterdam captured and becomes New York
	John Vanbrugh born
1665	The Great Plague
	Newton discovers the binomial theorem and invents the integral and differential calculus, at Cambridge
1666	The Great Fire of London
	Bunyan's *Grace Abounding*
	London Gazette founded
1667	The Dutch fleet sails up the Medway and burns English ships
	The war with Holland ended by the Treaty of Breda
	Milton's *Paradise Lost*
	Thomas Sprat's *History of the Royal Society*
	Death of Abraham Cowley
	John Arbuthnot born
1668	Sir Christopher Wren begins to rebuild St. Paul's Cathedral
	Triple Alliance formed with Holland and Sweden against France
	Dryden's *Essay of Dramatick Poesy*
1670	Alliance formed with France through the secret Treaty of Dover
	Pascal's *Pensées*
	The Hudson's Bay Company founded
	William Congreve born
1671	Milton's *Samson Agonistes* and *Paradise Regained*
1672	War against Holland
	Wycherley's *The Country Wife*
	King Charles issues the Declaration of Indulgence, suspending penal laws against Nonconformists and Catholics
1673	Parliament passes the Test Act, making acceptance of the doctrines of the Church of England a condition for holding public office
1674	War with Holland ended by the Treaty of Westminster
	Deaths of John Milton, Robert Herrick, and Thomas Traherne
1676	Etherege's *The Man of Mode*
1677	Baruch Spinoza's *Ethics*
	Jean Racine's *Phèdre*
	King Charles's niece, Mary, marries her cousin William of Orange
1678	Fabrication of the so-called popish plot by Titus Oates
	Bunyan's *Pilgrim's Progress*
	Dryden's *All for Love*
	Death of Andrew Marvell
	George Farquhar born
1679	Parliament passes the Habeas Corpus Act
	Rochester's *A Satire Against Mankind*
	Catharine Trotter Cockburn born
1680	Death of John Wilmot, earl of Rochester
1681	Dryden's *Absalom and Achitophel* (Part 1)
1682	Dryden's *Absalom and Achitophel* (Part 2)
	Thomas Otway's *Venice Preserv'd*
	Philadelphia founded
	Death of Sir Thomas Browne
1683	The Ashmolean Museum, the

CHRONOLOGY

	world's first public museum, opens at Oxford
	Death of Izaak Walton
1685–1688	**Reign of James II**
1685	Rebellion and execution of James Scott, duke of Monmouth
	John Gay born
1686	The first book of Newton's *Principia—De motu corporum*, containing his theory of gravitation—presented to the Royal Society
1687	James II issues the Declaration of Indulgence
	Dryden's *The Hind and the Panther*
	Death of Edmund Waller
1688	James II reissues the Declaration of Indulgence, renewing freedom of worship and suspending the provisions of the Test Act
	Acquittal of the seven bishops imprisoned for protesting against the Declaration
	William of Orange lands at Torbay, Devon
	James II takes refuge in France
	Death of John Bunyan
	Alexander Pope born
1689–1702	**Reign of William III**
1689	Parliament formulates the Declaration of Rights
	William and Mary accept the Declaration and the crown
	The Grand Alliance concluded between the Holy Roman Empire, England, Holland, and Spain
	War declared against France
	King William's War, 1689–1697 (the first of the French and Indian wars)
	Samuel Richardson born
	Death of Aphra Behn
1690	James II lands in Ireland with French support, but is defeated at the battle of the Boyne
	John Locke's *Essay Concerning Human Understanding*
1692	Salem witchcraft trials
	Death of Sir George Etherege
	John Byrom born
ca. 1693	Eliza Haywood born
1694	George Fox's *Journal*
	Voltaire (François Marie Arouet) born
	Death of Mary II
1695	Congreve's *Love for Love*
	Death of Henry Vaughan
1697	War with France ended by the Treaty of Ryswick
	Vanbrugh's *The Relapse*
1698	Jeremy Collier's *A Short View of the Immorality and Profaneness of the English Stage*
1699	Fénelon's *Les Aventures de Télémaque*
1700	Congreve's *The Way of the World*
	Defoe's *The True-Born Englishman*
	Death of John Dryden
	James Thomson born
1701	War of the Spanish Succession, 1701–1714 (Queen Anne's War in America, 1702–1713)
	Death of Sir Charles Sedley
1702–1714	**Reign of Queen Anne**
1702	Clarendon's *History of the Rebellion* (1702–1704)
	Defoe's *The Shortest Way with the Dissenters*
1703	Defoe is arrested, fined, and pilloried for writing *The Shortest Way*
	Death of Samuel Pepys
1704	John Churchill, duke of Marlborough, and Prince Eugene of Savoy defeat the French at Blenheim
	Capture of Gibraltar
	Swift's *A Tale of a Tub* and *The Battle of the Books*
	The Review founded (1704–1713)
1706	Farquhar's *The Recruiting Officer*
	Deaths of John Evelyn and Charles Sackville, earl of Dorset
1707	Farquhar's *The Beaux' Stratagem*
	Act of Union joining England and Scotland
	Death of George Farquhar
	Henry Fielding born
1709	The *Tatler* founded (1709–1711)
	Nicholas Rowe's edition of Shakespeare
	Samuel Johnson born
	Marlborough defeats the French at Malplaquet
	Charles XII of Sweden defeated at Poltava
1710	South Sea Company founded
	First copyright act

CHRONOLOGY

1711	Swift's *The Conduct of the Allies*
	The *Spectator* founded (1711–1712; 1714)
	Marlborough dismissed
	David Hume born
1712	Pope's *The Rape of the Lock* (Cantos 1–2)
	Jean Jacques Rousseau born
1713	War with France ended by the Treaty of Utrecht
	The *Guardian* founded
	Swift becomes dean of St. Patrick's, Dublin
	Addison's *Cato*
	Laurence Sterne born
1714–1727	**Reign of George I**
1714	Pope's expended version of *The Rape of the Lock* (Cantos 1–5)
1715	The Jacobite rebellion in Scotland
	Pope's translation of Homer's *Iliad* (1715–1720)
	Death of Louis XIV
1716	Death of William Wycherley
	Thomas Gray born
1717	Pope's *Eloisa to Abelard*
	David Garrick born
	Horace Walpole born
1718	Quadruple Alliance (Britain, France, the Netherlands, the German Empire) in war against Spain
1719	Defoe's *Robinson Crusoe*
	Death of Joseph Addison
1720	Inoculation against smallpox introduced in Boston
	War against Spain
	The South Sea Bubble
	Gilbert White born
	Defoe's *Captain Singleton* and *Memoirs of a Cavalier*
1721	Tobias Smollett born
	William Collins born
1722	Defoe's *Moll Flanders*, *Journal of the Plague Year*, and *Colonel Jack*
1724	Defoe's *Roxana*
	Swift's *The Drapier's Letters*
1725	Pope's translation of Homer's *Odyssey* (1725–1726)
1726	Swift's *Gulliver's Travels*
	Voltaire in England (1726–1729)
	Death of Sir John Vanbrugh
1727–1760	**Reign of George II**
1728	Gay's *The Beggar's Opera*
	Pope's *The Dunciad* (Books 1–2)
	Oliver Goldsmith born
1729	Swift's *A Modest Proposal*
	Edmund Burke born
	Deaths of William Congreve and Sir Richard Steele
1731	Navigation improved by introduction of the quadrant
	Pope's *Moral Essays* (1731–1735)
	Death of Daniel Defoe
	William Cowper born
	Erasmus Darwin born
1732	Death of John Gay
1733	Pope's *Essay on Man* (1733–1734)
	Lewis Theobald's edition of Shakespeare
1734	Voltaire's *Lettres philosophiques*
1735	Death of **John Arbuthnot**
1736	James Macpherson born
1737	Edward Gibbon born
1738	Johnson's *London*
1740	War of the Austrian Succession, 1740–1748 (King George's War in America, 1744–1748)
	George Anson begins his circumnavigation of the world (1740–1744)
	Frederick the Great becomes king of Prussia (1740–1786)
	Richardson's *Pamela* (1740–1741)
	James Boswell born
1742	Fielding's *Joseph Andrews*
	Edward Young's *Night Thoughts* (1742–1745)
	Pope's *The New Dunciad* (Book 4)
1743	**Hannah Cowley born**
1744	Johnson's *Life of Mr. Richard Savage*
	Death of Alexander Pope
1745	Second Jacobite rebellion, led by Charles Edward, the Young Pretender
	Death of Jonathan Swift
1746	The Young Pretender defeated at Culloden
	Collins' *Odes on Several Descriptive and Allegorical Subjects*
1747	Richardson's *Clarissa Harlowe* (1747–1748)
	Franklin's experiments with electricity announced
	Voltaire's *Essai sur les moeurs*
1748	War of the Austrian Succession

CHRONOLOGY

	ended by the Peace of Aix-la-Chapelle		"The Bard"
	Smollett's *Adventures of Roderick Random*		Burke's *Philosophical Enquiry into the Origin of Our Ideas of the Sublime and Beautiful*
	David Hume's *Enquiry Concerning Human Understanding*		Hume's *Natural History of Religion*
	Montesquieu's *L'Esprit des lois*		William Blake born
1749	Fielding's *Tom Jones*	1758	The *Idler* founded (1758–1760)
	Johnson's *The Vanity of Human Wishes*		Mary Darby Robinson born
	Bolingbroke's *Idea of a Patriot King*	1759	Capture of Quebec by General James Wolfe
	Death of **Catharine Trotter Cockburn**		Johnson's *History of Rasselas, Prince of Abyssinia*
1750	The *Rambler* founded (1750–1752)		Voltaire's *Candide*
1751	Gray's *Elegy Written in a Country Churchyard*		The British Museum opens
	Fielding's *Amelia*		Sterne's *The Life and Opinions of Tristram Shandy* (1759–1767)
	Smollett's *Adventures of Peregrine Pickle*		Death of William Collins
	Denis Diderot and Jean le Rond d'Alembert begin to publish the *Encyclopédie* (1751–1765)		Mary Wollstonecraft born
			Robert Burns born
	Richard Brinsley Sheridan born	**1760–1820**	**Reign of George III**
1752	Frances Burney born	1760	James Macpherson's *Fragments of Ancient Poetry Collected in the Highlands of Scotland*
	Thomas Chatterton born		William Beckford born
1753	Richardson's *History of Sir Charles Grandison* (1753–1754)	1761	Jean-Jacques Rousseau's *Julie, ou la nouvelle Héloïse*
	Smollett's *The Adventures of Ferdinand Count Fathom*		Death of Samuel Richardson
	Birth of Elizabeth Inchbald	1762	Rousseau's *Du Contrat social* and *Émile*
1754	Hume's *History of England* (1754–1762)		Catherine the Great becomes czarina of Russia (1762–1796)
	Death of Henry Fielding	1763	The Seven Years' War ended by the Peace of Paris
	George Crabbe born		Smart's *A Song to David*
1755	Lisbon destroyed by earthquake		Death of **John Byrom**
	Fielding's *Journal of a Voyage to Lisbon* published posthumously	1764	James Hargreaves invents the spinning jenny
	Johnson's *Dictionary of the English Language*		Ann Radcliffe born
1756	The Seven Years' War against France, 1756–1763 (the French and Indian War in America, 1755–1760)	1765	Parliament passes the Stamp Act to tax the American colonies
			Johnson's edition of Shakespeare
	William Pitt the elder becomes prime minister		Walpole's *The Castle of Otranto*
	Johnson's proposal for an edition of Shakespeare		Thomas Percy's *Reliques of Ancient English Poetry*
	Death of Eliza Haywood		Blackstone's *Commentaries on the Laws of England* (1765–1769)
	Birth of William Godwin	1766	The Stamp Act repealed
1757	Robert Clive wins the battle of Plassey, in India		Swift's *Journal to Stella* first published in a collection of his letters
	Gray's "The Progress of Poesy" and		Goldsmith's *The Vicar of Wakefield*
			Smollett's *Travels Through France*

CHRONOLOGY

	and Italy		James Watt and Matthew Boulton begin building steam engines in England
	Lessing's *Laokoon*		
	Rousseau in England (1766–1767)		
1768	Sterne's *A Sentimental Journey Through France and Italy*		Births of Jane Austen, Charles Lamb, Walter Savage Landor, and Matthew Lewis
	The Royal Academy founded by George III	1776	American Declaration of Independence
	First edition of the *Encyclopaedia Britannica*		Edward Gibbon's *Decline and Fall of the Roman Empire* (1776–1788)
	Maria Edgeworth born		Adam Smith's *Inquiry into the Nature & Causes of the Wealth of Nations*
	Death of Laurence Sterne		
1769	David Garrick organizes the Shakespeare Jubilee at Stratford-upon-Avon		
	Sir Joshua Reynolds' *Discourses* (1769–1790)		Thomas Paine's *Common Sense*
			Death of David Hume
	Richard Arkwright invents the spinning water frame	1777	Maurice Morgann's *Essay on the Dramatic Character of Sir John Falstaff*
1770	Boston Massacre		
	Burke's *Thoughts on the Cause of the Present Discontents*		Sheridan's *The School for Scandal* first performed (published 1780)
	Oliver Goldsmith's *The Deserted Village*		General Burgoyne surrenders at Saratoga
	Death of Thomas Chatterton	1778	The American colonies allied with France
	William Wordsworth born		
	James Hogg born		Britain and France at war
1771	Arkwright's first spinning mill founded		Captain James Cook discovers Hawaii
	Deaths of Thomas Gray and Tobias Smollett		Death of William Pitt, first earl of Chatham
	Walter Scott born		Deaths of Jean Jacques Rousseau and Voltaire
1772	Samuel Taylor Coleridge born		
1773	Boston Tea Party		William Hazlitt born
	Goldsmith's *She Stoops to Conquer*	1779	Johnson's *Prefaces to the Works of the English Poets* (1779–1781); reissued in 1781 as *The Lives of the Most Eminent English Poets*
	Johann Wolfgang von Goethe's *Götz von Berlichingen*		
1774	The first Continental Congress meets in Philadelphia		Sheridan's *The Critic*
			Samuel Crompton invents the spinning mule
	Goethe's *Sorrows of Young Werther*		
	Death of Oliver Goldsmith		Death of David Garrick
	Robert Southey born	1780	The Gordon Riots in London
1775	Burke's speech on American taxation		Charles Robert Maturin born
		1781	Charles Cornwallis surrenders at Yorktown
	American War of Independence begins with the battles of Lexington and Concord		
			Immanuel Kant's *Critique of Pure Reason*
	Samuel Johnson's *Journey to the Western Islands of Scotland*		Friedrich von Schiller's *Die Räuber*
	Richard Brinsley Sheridan's *The Rivals* and *The Duenna*	1782	William Cowper's "The Journey of John Gilpin" published in the *Public Advertiser*
	Beaumarchais's *Le Barbier de Séville*		Choderlos de Laclos's *Les Liaisons*

CHRONOLOGY

dangereuses
Rousseau's *Confessions* published posthumously

1783 American War of Independence ended by the Definitive Treaty of Peace, signed at Paris
William Blake's *Poetical Sketches*
George Crabbe's *The Village*
William Pitt the younger becomes prime minister
Henri Beyle (Stendhal) born

1784 Beaumarchais's *Le Mariage de Figaro* first performed (published 1785)
Death of Samuel Johnson

1785 Warren Hastings returns to England from India
James Boswell's *The Journey of a Tour of the Hebrides, with Samuel Johnson, LL.D.*
Cowper's *The Task*
Edmund Cartwright invents the power loom
Thomas De Quincey born
Thomas Love Peacock born

1786 William Beckford's *Vathek* published in English (originally written in French in 1782)
Robert Burns's *Poems Chiefly in the Scottish Dialect*
Wolfgang Amadeus Mozart's *The Marriage of Figaro*
Death of Frederick the Great

1787 The Committee for the Abolition of the Slave Trade founded in England
The Constitutional Convention meets at Philadelphia; the Constitution is signed

1788 The trial of Hastings begins on charges of corruption of the government in India
The Estates-General of France summoned
U.S. Constitution is ratified
George Washington elected president of the United States
Giovanni Casanova's *Histoire de ma fuite* (first manuscript of his memoirs)
The *Daily Universal Register* becomes the *Times* (London)
George Gordon, Lord Byron born

1789 The Estates-General meets at Versailles
The National Assembly (Assemblée Nationale) convened
The fall of the Bastille marks the beginning of the French Revolution
The National Assembly draws up the Declaration of Rights of Man and of the Citizen
First U.S. Congress meets in New York
Blake's *Songs of Innocence*
Jeremy Bentham's *Introduction to the Principles of Morals and Legislation* introduces the theory of utilitarianism
Gilbert White's *Natural History of Selborne*

1790 Congress sets permanent capital city site on the Potomac River
First U.S. Census
Burke's *Reflections on the Revolution in France*
Blake's *The Marriage of Heaven and Hell*
Edmund Malone's edition of Shakespeare
Wollstonecraft's *A Vindication of the Rights of Man*
Death of Benjamin Franklin

1791 French royal family's flight from Paris and capture at Varennes; imprisonment in the Tuileries
Bill of Rights is ratified
Paine's *The Rights of Man* (1791–1792)
Boswell's *The Life of Johnson*
Burns's *Tam o' Shanter*
The *Observer* founded

1792 The Prussians invade France and are repulsed at Valmy September massacres
The National Convention declares royalty abolished in France
Washington reelected president of the United States
New York Stock Exchange opens
Mary Wollstonecraft's *Vindication of the Rights of Woman*
William Bligh's voyage to the South

CHRONOLOGY

      Sea in H.M.S. *Bounty*
      Percy Bysshe Shelley born
1793 Trial and execution of Louis XVI and Marie-Antoinette
      France declares war against England
      The Committee of Public Safety (Comité de Salut Public) established
      Eli Whitney devises the cotton gin
      William Godwin's *An Enquiry Concerning Political Justice*
      Blake's *Visions of the Daughters of Albion* and *America*
      Wordsworth's *An Evening Walk* and *Descriptive Sketches*
      John Clare born
1794 Execution of Georges Danton and Maximilien de Robespierre
      Paine's *The Age of Reason* (1794–1796)
      Blake's *Songs of Experience*
      Ann Radcliffe's *The Mysteries of Udolpho*
      Death of Edward Gibbon
1795 The government of the Directory established (1795–1799)
      Hastings acquitted
      Landor's *Poems*
      Death of James Boswell
      John Keats born
      Thomas Carlyle born
1796 Napoleon Bonaparte takes command in Italy
      Matthew Lewis' *The Monk*
      John Adams elected president of the United States
      Death of Robert Burns
1797 The peace of Campo Formio: extinction of the Venetian Republic XYZ Affair
      Mutinies in the Royal Navy at Spithead and the Nore
      Blake's *Vala, Or the Four Zoas* (first version)
      Mary Shelley born
      Deaths of Edmund Burke, Mary Wollstonecraft, and Horace Walpole
1798 Napoleon invades Egypt
      Horatio Nelson wins the battle of the Nile
      Wordsworth's and Coleridge's *Lyrical Ballads*
      Landor's *Gebir*
      Thomas Malthus' *Essay on the Principle of Population*
1799 Napoleon becomes first consul
      Pitt introduces first income tax in Great Britain
      Sheridan's *Pizarro*
      Honoré de Balzac, Thomas Hood, and Alexander Pushkin born
1800 Thomas Jefferson elected president of the United States
      Alessandro Volta produces electricity from a cell
      Library of Congress established
      Death of William Cowper and Mary Darby Robinson
      Marie Jane Jewsbury and Thomas Babington Macaulay born
1801 First census taken in England
1802 The Treaty of Amiens marks the end of the French Revolutionary War
      The *Edinburgh Review* founded
      Birth of Harriet Martineau
      Death of **Erasmus Darwin**
      England's war with France renewed
      The Louisiana Purchase
      Robert Fulton propels a boat by steam power on the Seine
      Birth of Thomas Lovell Beddoes George Borrow and James Clarence Mangan
1804 Napoleon crowned emperor of the French
      Jefferson reelected president of the United States
      Blake's *Milton* (1804–1808) and *Jerusalem*
      The Code Napoleon promulgated in France
      Beethoven's *Eroica* Symphony
      Schiller's *Wilhelm Tell*
      Benjamin Disraeli born
1805 Napoleon plans the invasion of England
      Battle of Trafalgar
      Battle of Austerlitz
      Beethoven's *Fidelio* first produced
      Scott's *Lay of the Last Minstrel*
1806 Scott's *Marmion*
      Death of William Pitt
      Death of Charles James Fox

CHRONOLOGY

	Elizabeth Barrett born
1807	France invades Portugal
	Aaron Burr tried for treason and acquitted
	Byron's *Hours of Idleness*
	Charles and Mary Lamb's *Tales from Shakespeare*
	Thomas Moore's *Irish Melodies*
	Wordsworth's *Ode on the Intimations of Immortality*
1808	National uprising in Spain against the French invasion
	The Peninsular War begins
	James Madison elected president of the United States
	Covent Garden theater burned down
	Goethe's *Faust* (Part 1)
	Beethoven's Fifth Symphony completed
	Lamb's *Specimens of English Dramatic Poets*
1809	Drury Lane theater burned down and rebuilt
	The *Quarterly Review* founded
	Byron's *English Bards and Scotch Reviewers*
	Byron sails for the Mediterranean
	Goya's *Los Desastres de la guerra* (1809–1814)
	Edward Fitzgerald, Alfred Tennyson born
	Death of **Hannah Cowley**
1810	Crabbe's *The Borough*
	Scott's *The Lady of the Lake*
	Elizabeth Gaskell born
1811–1820	**Regency of George IV**
1811	Luddite Riots begin
	Coleridge's *Lectures on Shakespeare* (1811–1814)
	Jane Austen's *Sense and Sensibility*
	Shelley's *The Necessity of Atheism*
	John Constable's *Dedham Vale*
	William Makepeace Thackeray born
1812	Napoleon invades Russia; captures and retreats from Moscow
	United States declares war against England
	Henry Bell's steamship *Comet* is launched on the Clyde river
	Madison reelected president of the United States
	Byron's *Childe Harold* (Cantos 1–2)
	The Brothers Grimm's *Fairy Tales* (1812–1815)
	Hegel's *Science of Logic*
	Charles Dickens born
	Robert Browning born
	Henry Mayhew born
1813	Wellington wins the battle of Vitoria and enters France
	Jane Austen's *Pride and Prejudice*
	Byron's *The Giaour* and *The Bride of Abydos*
	Shelley's *Queen Mab*
	Southey's *Life of Nelson*
1814	Napoleon abdicates and is exiled to Elba; Bourbon restoration with Louis XVIII
	Treaty of Ghent ends the war between Britain and the United States
	Jane Austen's *Mansfield Park*
	Byron's *The Corsair* and *Lara*
	Scott's *Waverley*
	Wordsworth's *The Excursion*
1815	Napoleon returns to France (the Hundred Days); is defeated at Waterloo and exiled to St. Helena
	U.S.S. *Fulton*, the first steam warship, built
	Scott's *Guy Mannering*
	Schlegel's *Lectures on Dramatic Art and Literature* translated
	Wordsworth's *The White Doe of Rylstone*
	Anthony Trollope born
1816	Byron leaves England permanently
	The Elgin Marbles exhibited in the British Museum
	James Monroe elected president of the United States
	Jane Austen's *Emma*
	Byron's *Childe Harold* (Canto 3)
	Coleridge's *Christabel, Kubla Khan: A Vision, The Pains of Sleep*
	Benjamin Constant's *Adolphe*
	Goethe's *Italienische Reise*
	Peacock's *Headlong Hall*
	Scott's *The Antiquary*
	Shelley's *Alastor*
	Rossini's *Il Barbiere di Siviglia*
	Death of Richard Brinsley Sheridan

xxiii

CHRONOLOGY

1817	Charlotte Brontë born *Blackwood's Edinburgh* magazine founded Jane Austen's *Northanger Abbey* and *Persuasion* Byron's *Manfred* Coleridge's *Biographia Literaria* Hazlitt's *The Characters of Shakespeare's Plays* and *The Round Table* Keats's *Poems* Peacock's *Melincourt* David Ricardo's *Principles of Political Economy and Taxation* Death of Jane Austen Death of Mme de Staël Branwell Brontë born Henry David Thoreau born		George Eliot, **Charles Kingsley** born
		1820–1830	**Reign of George IV**
		1820	Trial of Queen Caroline Cato Street Conspiracy suppressed; Arthur Thistlewood hanged Monroe reelected president of the United States Missouri Compromise The *London* magazine founded Keats's *Lamia, Isabella, The Eve of St. Agnes, and Other Poems* Hazlitt's *Lectures Chiefly on the Dramatic Literature of the Age of Elizabeth* Charles Maturin's *Melmoth the Wanderer* Scott's *Ivanhoe* and *The Monastery* Shelley's *Prometheus Unbound* Anne Brontë born
1818	Byron's *Childe Harold* (Canto 4), and *Beppo* Hazlitt's *Lectures on the English Poets* Keats's *Endymion* Peacock's *Nightmare Abbey* Scott's *Rob Roy* and *The Heart of Mid-Lothian* Mary Shelley's *Frankenstein* Percy Shelley's *The Revolt of Islam* Emily Brontë born Karl Marx born Ivan Sergeyevich Turgenev born	1821	Greek War of Independence begins Liberia founded as a colony for freed slaves Byron's *Cain, Marino Faliero, The Two Foscari,* and *Sardanapalus* Hazlitt's *Table Talk* (1821–1822) Scott's *Kenilworth* Shelley's *Adonais* and *Epipsychidion* Death of John Keats, Elizabeth Inchbald and Napoleon Charles Baudelaire, Feodor Dostoyevsky, and Gustave Flaubert born
1819	The *Savannah* becomes the first steamship to cross the Atlantic (in 26 days) Peterloo massacre in Manchester Byron's *Don Juan* (1819–1824) and *Mazeppa* Crabbe's *Tales of the Hall* Géricault's *Raft of the Medusa* Hazlitt's *Lectures on the English Comic Writers* Arthur Schopenhauer's *Die Welt als Wille und Vorstellung (The World as Will and Idea)* Scott's *The Bride of Lammermoor* and *A Legend of Montrose* Shelley's *The Cenci,* "The Masque of Anarchy," and "Ode to the West Wind" Wordsworth's *Peter Bell* Queen Victoria born	1822	The Massacres of Chios (Greeks rebel against Turkish rule) Byron's *The Vision of Judgment* De Quincey's *Confessions of an English Opium-Eater* Peacock's *Maid Marian* Scott's *Peveril of the Peak* Shelley's *Hellas* Death of Percy Bysshe Shelley Matthew Arnold born
		1823	Monroe Doctrine proclaimed Byron's *The Age of Bronze* and *The Island* Lamb's *Essays of Elia* Scott's *Quentin Durward* Death of Ann Radcliffe
		1824	The National Gallery opened in London

CHRONOLOGY

John Quincy Adams elected president of the United States
The *Westminster Review* founded
Beethoven's Ninth Symphony first performed
William (Wilkie) Collins born
James Hogg's *The Private Memoirs and Confessions of a Justified Sinner*
Landor's *Imaginary Conversations* (1824–1829)
Scott's *Redgauntlet*
Death of George Gordon, Lord Byron

1825 Inauguration of steam-powered passenger and freight service on the Stockton and Darlington railway
Bolivia and Brazil become independent Alessandro Manzoni's *I Promessi Sposi* (1825–1826)

1826 André-Marie Ampère's *Mémoire sur la théorie mathématique des phénomènes électrodynamiques*
James Fenimore Cooper's *The Last of the Mohicans*
Disraeli's *Vivian Grey* (1826–1827)
Scott's *Woodstock*

1827 The battle of Navarino ensures the independence of Greece
Josef Ressel obtains patent for the screw propeller for steamships
Heinrich Heine's *Buch der Lieder*
Death of William Blake

1828 Andrew Jackson elected president of the United States
Births of Henrik Ibsen, George Meredith, Margaret Oliphant, Dante Gabriel Rossetti, and Leo Tolstoy

1829 The Catholic Emancipation Act
Robert Peel establishes the metropolitan police force
Greek independence recognized by Turkey
Balzac begins *La Comédie humaine* (1829–1848)
Peacock's *The Misfortunes of Elphin*
J. M. W. Turner's *Ulysses Deriding Polyphemus*

1830–1837 Reign of William IV
1830 Charles X of France abdicates and is succeeded by Louis-Philippe
The Liverpool-Manchester railway opened
Tennyson's *Poems, Chiefly Lyrical*
Death of William Hazlitt
Christina Rossetti born

1831 Michael Faraday discovers electromagnetic induction
Charles Darwin's voyage on H.M.S. *Beagle* begins (1831–1836)
The Barbizon school of artists' first exhibition
Nat Turner slave revolt crushed in Virginia
Peacock's *Crotchet Castle*
Stendhal's *Le Rouge et le noir*
Edward Trelawny's *The Adventures of a Younger Son*
Isabella Bird born

1832 The first Reform Bill
Samuel Morse invents the telegraph
Jackson reelected president of the United States
Disraeli's *Contarini Fleming*
Goethe's *Faust* (Part 2)
Tennyson's *Poems, Chiefly Lyrical*, including "The Lotus-Eaters" and "The Lady of Shalott"
Death of Johann Wolfgang von Goethe
Death of Sir Walter Scott
Lewis Carroll born

1833 Robert Browning's *Pauline*
John Keble launches the Oxford Movement
American Anti-Slavery Society founded
Lamb's *Last Essays of Elia*
Carlyle's *Sartor Resartus* (1833–1834)
Pushkin's *Eugene Onegin*
Mendelssohn's *Italian Symphony* first performed
Death of Maria Jane Jewsbury

1834 Abolition of slavery in the British Empire
Louis Braille's alphabet for the blind
Balzac's *Le Père Goriot*
Nikolai Gogol's *Dead Souls* (Part 1, 1834–1842)
Death of Samuel Taylor Coleridge

CHRONOLOGY

	Death of Charles Lamb
	William Morris born
1835	Hans Christian Andersen's *Fairy Tales* (1st ser.)
	Robert Browning's *Paracelsus*
	Births of Samuel Butler and Mary Elizabeth Braddon
	Alexis de Tocqueville's *De la Democratie en Amerique* (1835–1840)
	Death of James Hogg
1836	Martin Van Buren elected president of the United States
	Dickens' *Sketches by Boz* (1836–1837)
	Landor's *Pericles and Aspasia*
	Death of William Godwin
1837–1901	**Reign of Queen Victoria**
1837	Carlyle's *The French Revolution*
	Dickens' *Oliver Twist* (1837–1838) and *Pickwick Papers*
	Disraeli's *Venetia* and *Henrietta Temple*
1838	Chartist movement in England
	National Gallery in London opened
	Elizabeth Barrett Browning's *The Seraphim and Other Poems*
	Dickens' *Nicholas Nickleby* (1838–1839)
1839	Louis Daguerre perfects process for producing an image on a silver-coated copper plate Faraday's *Experimental Researches in Electricity* (1839–1855)
	First Chartist riots
	Opium War between Great Britain and China
	Carlyle's *Chartism*
1840	Canadian Act of Union
	Queen Victoria marries Prince Albert
	Charles Barry begins construction of the Houses of Parliament (1840–1852)
	William Henry Harrison elected president of the United States
	Robert Browning's *Sordello*
	Thomas Hardy and John Addington Symonds born
1841	New Zealand proclaimed a British colony
	James Clark Ross discovers the Antarctic continent
	Punch founded
	John Tyler succeeds to the presidency after the death of Harrison
	Carlyle's *Heroes and Hero-Worship*
	Dickens' *The Old Curiosity Shop*
1842	Chartist riots
	Income tax revived in Great Britain
	The Mines Act, forbidding work underground by women or by children under the age of ten
	Charles Edward Mudie's Lending Library founded in London
	Dickens visits America
	Robert Browning's *Dramatic Lyrics*
	Macaulay's *Lays of Ancient Rome*
	Tennyson's *Poems*, including "Morte d'Arthur," "St. Simeon Stylites," and "Ulysses"
	Wordsworth's *Poems*
1843	Marc Isambard Brunel's Thames tunnel opened
	The Economist founded
	Carlyle's *Past and Present*
	Dickens' *A Christmas Carol*
	John Stuart Mill's *Logic*
	Macaulay's *Critical and Historical Essays*
	John Ruskin's *Modern Painters* (1843–1860)
1844	Rochdale Society of Equitable Pioneers, one of the first consumers' cooperatives, founded by twenty-eight Lancashire weavers
	James K. Polk elected president of the United States
	Elizabeth Barrett Browning's *Poems*, including "The Cry of the Children"
	Dickens' *Martin Chuzzlewit*
	Disraeli's *Coningsby*
	Turner's *Rain, Steam and Speed*
	Edward Carpenter and Gerard Manley Hopkins born
1845	The great potato famine in Ireland begins (1845–1849)
	Disraeli's *Sybil*
1846	Repeal of the Corn Laws
	The *Daily News* founded (edited by Dickens the first three weeks)
	Standard-gauge railway introduced

CHRONOLOGY

        in Britain
        The Brontës' pseudonymous *Poems by Currer, Ellis and Action Bell*
        Lear's *Book of Nonsense*
1847 The Ten Hours Factory Act
        James Simpson uses chloroform as an anesthetic
        Anne Brontë's *Agnes Grey*
        Charlotte Brontë's *Jane Eyre*
        Emily Brontë's *Wuthering Heights*
        Bram Stoker and Flora Annie Steel born
        Tennyson's *The Princess*
1848 The year of revolutions in France, Germany, Italy, Hungary, Poland
        Marx and Engels issue *The Communist Manifesto*
        The Chartist Petition
        The Pre-Raphaelite Brotherhood founded
        Zachary Taylor elected president of the United States
        Anne Brontë's *The Tenant of Wildfell Hall*
        Dickens' *Dombey and Son*
        Elizabeth Gaskell's *Mary Barton*
        Macaulay's *History of England* (1848–1861)
        Mill's *Principles of Political Economy*
        Thackeray's *Vanity Fair*
        Death of Emily Brontë
        Birth of Richard Jefferies
1849 Bedford College for women founded
        Arnold's *The Strayed Reveller*
        Charlotte Brontë's *Shirley*
        Ruskin's *The Seven Lamps of Architecture*
        William Thomas Stead born
        Death of Anne Brontë, Thomas Lovell Beddoes and James Clarence Mangan
1850 The Public Libraries Act
        First submarine telegraph cable laid between Dover and Calais
        Millard Fillmore succeeds to the presidency after the death of Taylor
        Elizabeth Barrett Browning's *Sonnets from the Portuguese*
        Carlyle's *Latter-Day Pamphlets*
        Dickens' *Household Words* (1850–1859) and *David Copperfield*
        Charles Kingsley's *Alton Locke*
        The Pre-Raphaelites publish the *Germ*
        Tennyson's *In Memoriam*
        Thackeray's *The History of Pendennis*
        Wordsworth's *The Prelude* is published posthumously
1851 The Great Exhibition opens at the Crystal Palace in Hyde Park
        Louis Napoleon seizes power in France
        Gold strike in Victoria incites Australian gold rush
        Elizabeth Gaskell's *Cranford* (1851–1853)
        Meredith's *Poems*
        Ruskin's *The Stones of Venice* (1851–1853)
        Death of Mary Shelley
1852 The Second Empire proclaimed with Napoleon III as emperor
        David Livingstone begins to explore the Zambezi (1852–1856)
        Franklin Pierce elected president of the United States
        Arnold's *Empedocles on Etna*
        Thackeray's *The History of Henry Esmond, Esq.*
1853 Crimean War (1853–1856)
        Arnold's *Poems*, including "The Scholar Gypsy" and "Sohrab and Rustum"
        Charlotte Brontë's *Villette*
        Elizabeth Gaskell's *Crawford and Ruth*
1854 Frederick D. Maurice's Working Men's College founded in London with more than 130 pupils
        Battle of Balaklava
        Dickens' *Hard Times*
        James George Frazer born
        Theodor Mommsen's *History of Rome* (1854–1856)
        Tennyson's "The Charge of the Light Brigade"
        Florence Nightingale in the Crimea (1854–1856)
        Oscar Wilde born

CHRONOLOGY

1855 David Livingstone discovers the Victoria Falls
Robert Browning's *Men and Women*
Elizabeth Gaskell's *North and South*
Olive Schreiner born
Tennyson's *Maud*
Thackeray's *The Newcomes*
Trollope's *The Warden*
Death of Charlotte Brontë
1856 The Treaty of Paris ends the Crimean War
Henry Bessemer's steel process invented
James Buchanan elected president of the United States
H. Rider Haggard born
1857 The Indian Mutiny begins; crushed in 1858
The Matrimonial Causes Act
Charlotte Brontë's *The Professor*
Elizabeth Barrett Browning's *Aurora Leigh*
Dickens' *Little Dorritt*
Elizabeth Gaskell's *The Life of Charlotte Brontë*
Thomas Hughes's *Tom Brown's School Days*
Trollope's *Barchester Towers*
1858 Carlyle's *History of Frederick the Great* (1858–1865)
George Eliot's *Scenes of Clerical Life*
Morris' *The Defense of Guinevere*
Trollope's *Dr. Thorne*
Rudyard Kipling born
1859 Charles Darwin's *The Origin of Species*
Dickens' *A Tale of Two Cities*
Arthur Conan Doyle born
George Eliot's *Adam Bede*
Fitzgerald's *The Rubaiyat of Omar Khayyám*
Meredith's *The Ordeal of Richard Feverel*
Mill's *On Liberty*
Samuel Smiles's *Self-Help*
Tennyson's *Idylls of the King*
1860 Abraham Lincoln elected president of the United States
The *Cornhill* magazine founded with Thackeray as editor
James M. Barrie born
William Wilkie Collins' *The Woman in White*
George Eliot's *The Mill on the Floss*
1861 American Civil War begins
Louis Pasteur presents the germ theory of disease
Arnold's *Lectures on Translating Homer*
Dickens' *Great Expectations*
George Eliot's *Silas Marner*
Meredith's *Evan Harrington*
Francis Turner Palgrave's *The Golden Treasury*
Trollope's *Framley Parsonage*
Peacock's *Gryll Grange*
Death of Prince Albert
1862 George Eliot's *Romola*
Meredith's *Modern Love*
Christina Rossetti's *Goblin Market*
Ruskin's *Unto This Last*
Trollope's *Orley Farm*
1863 Thomas Huxley's *Man's Place in Nature*
1864 The Geneva Red Cross Convention signed by twelve nations
Lincoln reelected president of the United States
Robert Browning's *Dramatis Personae*
John Henry Newman's *Apologia pro vita sua*
Tennyson's *Enoch Arden*
Trollope's *The Small House at Allington*
Death of John Clare
1865 Assassination of Lincoln; Andrew Johnson succeeds to the presidency
Arnold's *Essays in Criticism* (1st ser.)
Carroll's *Alice's Adventures in Wonderland*
Dickens' *Our Mutual Friend*
Meredith's *Rhoda Fleming*
A. C. Swinburne's *Atalanta in Calydon*
Arthur Symons born
Death of Elizabeth Gaskell
1866 First successful transatlantic tele-

CHRONOLOGY

graph cable laid
George Eliot's *Felix Holt, the Radical*
Elizabeth Gaskell's *Wives and Daughters*
Beatrix Potter born
Swinburne's *Poems and Ballads*

1867 The second Reform Bill
Arnold's *New Poems*
Bagehot's *The English Constitution*
Carlyle's *Shooting Niagara*
Marx's *Das Kapital* (vol. 1)
Trollope's *The Last Chronicle of Barset*
George William Russell (AE) born

1868 Gladstone becomes prime minister (1868–1874)
Johnson impeached by House of Representatives; acquitted by Senate
Ulysses S. Grant elected president of the United States
Robert Browning's *The Ring and the Book* (1868–1869)
Collins' *The Moonstone*

1869 The Suez Canal opened
Girton College, Cambridge, founded
Arnold's *Culture and Anarchy*
Mill's *The Subjection of Women*
Trollope's *Phineas Finn*

1870 The Elementary Education Act establishes schools under the aegis of local boards
Dickens' *Edwin Drood*
Disraeli's *Lothair*
Morris' *The Earthly Paradise*
Dante Gabriel Rossetti's *Poems*
Saki born

1871 Trade unions legalized
Newnham College, Cambridge, founded for women students
Carroll's *Through the Looking Glass*
Darwin's *The Descent of Man*
Meredith's *The Adventures of Harry Richmond*
Swinburne's *Songs Before Sunrise*
William H. Davies born

1872 Max Beerbohm born
Samuel Butler's *Erewhon*
George Eliot's *Middlemarch*
Grant reelected president of the United States
Hardy's *Under the Greenwood Tree*

1873 Arnold's *Literature and Dogma*
Mill's *Autobiography*
Pater's *Studies in the History of the Renaissance*
Trollope's *The Eustace Diamonds*
Dorothy Richardson born

1874 Disraeli becomes prime minister
Hardy's *Far from the Madding Crowd*
James Thomson's *The City of Dreadful Night*

1875 Britain buys Suez Canal shares
Trollope's *The Way We Live Now*
T. F. Powys born
Death of **Charles Kingsley**

1876 F. H. Bradley's *Ethical Studies*
George Eliot's *Daniel Deronda*
Henry James's *Roderick Hudson*
Meredith's *Beauchamp's Career*
Morris' *Sigurd the Volsung*
Trollope's *The Prime Minister*
Death of Harriet Martineau
Birth of Flora Thompson

1877 Rutherford B. Hayes elected president of the United States after Electoral Commission awards him disputed votes
Henry James's *The American*

1878 Electric street lighting introduced in London
Hardy's *The Return of the Native*
Swinburne's *Poems and Ballads* (2d ser.)
Births of A. E. Coppard and Edward Thomas

1879 Somerville College and Lady Margaret Hall opened at Oxford for women
The London telephone exchange built
Gladstone's Midlothian campaign (1879–1880)
Browning's *Dramatic Idyls*
Meredith's *The Egoist*

1880 Gladstone's second term as prime minister (1880–1885)
James A. Garfield elected president of the United States
Browning's *Dramatic Idyls Second Series*

xxix

CHRONOLOGY

Disraeli's *Endymion*
Radclyffe Hall born
Hardy's *The Trumpet-Major*
Lytton Strachey born
1881 Garfield assassinated; Chester A. Arthur succeeds to the presidency
Henry James's *The Portrait of a Lady* and *Washington Square*
D. G. Rossetti's *Ballads and Sonnets*
P. G. Wodehouse born
Lascelles Abercrombie born
Death of George Borrow
1882 Triple Alliance formed between German empire, Austrian empire, and Italy
Leslie Stephen begins to edit the *Dictionary of National Biography*
Married Women's Property Act passed in Britain
Britain occupies Egypt and the Sudan
James Joyce born
1883 Uprising of the Mahdi: Britain evacuates the Sudan
Royal College of Music opens
T. H. Green's *Ethics*
T. E. Hulme born
Stevenson's *Treasure Island*
1884 The Mahdi captures Omdurman: General Gordon appointed to command the garrison of Khartoum
Grover Cleveland elected president of the United States
The *Oxford English Dictionary* begins publishing
The Fabian Society founded
Hiram Maxim's recoil-operated machine gun invented
1885 The Mahdi captures Khartoum: General Gordon killed
Haggard's *King Solomon's Mines*
Marx's *Das Kapital* (vol. 2)
Meredith's *Diana of the Crossways*
Pater's *Marius the Epicurean*
1886 The Canadian Pacific Railway completed
Gold discovered in the Transvaal
Births of Frances Cornford, Ronald Firbank, and Charles Stansby Walter Williams

Henry James's *The Bostonians* and *The Princess Casamassima*
Stevenson's *The Strange Case of Dr. Jekyll and Mr. Hyde*
1887 Queen Victoria's Golden Jubilee
Rupert Brooke born
Haggard's *Allan Quatermain* and *She*
Hardy's *The Woodlanders*
Edwin Muir born
Death of Richard Jefferies
Death of **Henry Mayhew**
1888 Benjamin Harrison elected president of the United States
Henry James's *The Aspern Papers*
Kipling's *Plain Tales from the Hills*
T. E. Lawrence born
1889 Yeats's *The Wanderings of Oisin*
Death of Robert Browning
1890 Morris founds the Kelmscott Press
Agatha Christie born
Frazer's *The Golden Bough* (1st ed.)
Henry James's *The Tragic Muse*
Morris' *News From Nowhere*
Jean Rhys born
1891 Gissing's *New Grub Street*
Hardy's *Tess of the d'Urbervilles*
Wilde's *The Picture of Dorian Gray*
1892 Grover Cleveland elected president of the United States
Conan Doyle's *The Adventures of Sherlock Holmes*
Shaw's *Widower's Houses*
Rebecca West, Hugh MacDiarmid, and J. R. R. Tolkien born
Wilde's *Lady Windermere's Fan*
Death of Alfred Tennyson
1893 Wilde's *A Woman of No Importance* and *Salomé*
Vera Brittain born
Death of John Addington Symonds
1894 Kipling's *The Jungle Book*
Moore's *Esther Waters*
Marx's *Das Kapital* (vol. 3)
Audrey Beardsley's *The Yellow Book* begins to appear quarterly
Shaw's *Arms and the Man*
Death of Christina Rossetti
1895 Trial and imprisonment of Oscar Wilde

CHRONOLOGY

William Ramsay announces discovery of helium
The National Trust founded
Conrad's *Almayer's Folly*
Hardy's *Jude the Obscure*
Wells's *The Time Machine*
Wilde's *The Importance of Being Earnest*
Yeats's *Poems*

1896 William McKinley elected president of the United States
Failure of the Jameson Raid on the Transvaal
Housman's *A Shropshire Lad*
Edmund Blunden and Austin Clarke born

1897 Queen Victoria's Diamond Jubilee
Conrad's *The Nigger of the Narcissus*
Havelock Ellis' *Studies in the Psychology of Sex* begins publication
Henry James's *The Spoils of Poynton* and *What Maisie Knew*
Kipling's *Captains Courageous*
Shaw's *Candida*
Stoker's *Dracula*
Wells's *The Invisible Man*
Death of Margaret Oliphant
Ruth Pitter born

1898 Kitchener defeats the Mahdist forces at Omdurman: the Sudan reoccupied
Hardy's *Wessex Poems*
Henry James's *The Turn of the Screw*
C. S. Lewis born
Shaw's *Caesar and Cleopatra* and *You Never Can Tell*
Alec Waugh born
Wells's *The War of the Worlds*
Wilde's *The Ballad of Reading Gaol*
William Soutar born

1899 The Boer War begins
Elizabeth Bowen born
Noël Coward born
Elgar's *Enigma Variations*
Kipling's *Stalky and Co.*

1900 McKinley reelected president of the United States
British Labour party founded
Boxer Rebellion in China
Reginald A. Fessenden transmits speech by wireless
First Zeppelin trial flight
Max Planck presents his first paper on the quantum theory
Conrad's *Lord Jim*
Elgar's *The Dream of Gerontius*
Sigmund Freud's *The Interpretation of Dreams*
V. S. Pritchett born
William Butler Yeats's *The Shadowy Waters*

1901–1910 Reign of King Edward VII
1901 William McKinley assassinated; Theodore Roosevelt succeeds to the presidency
First transatlantic wireless telegraph signal transmitted
Chekhov's *Three Sisters*
Freud's *Psychopathology of Everyday Life*
Rudyard Kipling's *Kim*
Thomas Mann's *Buddenbrooks*
Potter's *The Tale of Peter Rabbit*
Shaw's *Captain Brassbound's Conversion*
August Strindberg's *The Dance of Death*
Lewis Grassic Gibbon born

1902 Barrie's *The Admirable Crichton*
Arnold Bennett's *Anna of the Five Towns*
Cézanne's *Le Lac D'Annecy*
Conrad's *Heart of Darkness*
Henry James's *The Wings of the Dove*
William James's *The Varieties of Religious Experience*
Kipling's *Just So Stories*
Maugham's *Mrs. Cradock*
Stevie Smith born
Times Literary Supplement begins publishing

1903 At its London congress the Russian Social Democratic Party divides into Mensheviks, led by Plekhanov, and Bolsheviks, led by Lenin
The treaty of Panama places the Canal Zone in U.S. hands for a nominal rent
Motor cars regulated in Britain to a

xxxi

CHRONOLOGY

20-mile-per-hour limit
The Wright brothers make a successful flight in the United States
Burlington magazine founded
Samuel Butler's *The Way of All Flesh* published posthumously
Cyril Connolly born
George Gissing's *The Private Papers of Henry Ryecroft*
Thomas Hardy's *The Dynasts*
Henry James's *The Ambassadors*
Alan Paton born
Shaw's *Man and Superman*
Synge's *Riders to the Sea* produced in Dublin
Yeats's *In the Seven Woods* and *On Baile's Strand*
Frank O'Connor, William Plomer, Edward Upward and John Wyndham born

1904 Roosevelt elected president of the United States
Russo-Japanese war (1904–1905)
Construction of the Panama Canal begins
The ultraviolet lamp invented
The engineering firm of Rolls Royce founded
Barrie's *Peter Pan* first performed
Births of Cecil Day Lewis and Nancy Mitford
Chekhov's *The Cherry Orchard*
Conrad's *Nostromo*
Henry James's *The Golden Bowl*
Kipling's *Traffics and Discoveries*
Georges Rouault's *Head of a Tragic Clown*
G. M. Trevelyan's *England Under the Stuarts*
Puccini's *Madame Butterfly*
First Shaw-Granville Barker season at the Royal Court Theatre
The Abbey Theatre founded in Dublin
Death of Isabella Bird
Patrick Hamilton born

1905 Russian sailors on the battleship Potemkin mutiny
After riots and a general strike the czar concedes demands by the Duma for legislative powers, a wider franchise, and civil liberties
Albert Einstein publishes his first theory of relativity
The Austin Motor Company founded
Bennett's *Tales of the Five Towns*
Claude Debussy's *La Mer*
E. M. Forster's *Where Angels Fear to Tread*
Richard Strauss's *Salome*
H. G. Wells's *Kipps*
Oscar Wilde's *De Profundis*
Births of Norman Cameron, Henry Green, and Mary Renault

1906 Liberals win a landslide victory in the British general election
The Trades Disputes Act legitimizes peaceful picketing in Britain
Captain Dreyfus rehabilitated in France
J. J. Thomson begins research on gamma rays
The U.S. Pure Food and Drug Act passed
Churchill's *Lord Randolph Churchill*
William Empson born
Galsworthy's *The Man of Property*
Kipling's *Puck of Pook's Hill*
Shaw's *The Doctor's Dilemma*
Yeats's *Poems 1899–1905*

1907 Exhibition of cubist paintings in Paris
Henry Adams' *The Education of Henry Adams*
Henri Bergson's *Creative Evolution*
Conrad's *The Secret Agent*
Births of Barbara Comyns, Daphne du Maurier, and Christopher Fry
Forster's *The Longest Journey*
André Gide's *La Porte étroite*
Shaw's *John Bull's Other Island* and *Major Barbara*
Synge's *The Playboy of the Western World*
Trevelyan's *Garibaldi's Defence of the Roman Republic*
Christopher Caudwell (Christopher St. John Sprigg) born

1908 Herbert Asquith becomes prime minister

CHRONOLOGY

David Lloyd George becomes chancellor of the exchequer
William Howard Taft elected president of the United States
The Young Turks seize power in Istanbul
Henry Ford's Model T car produced
Bennett's *The Old Wives' Tale*
Pierre Bonnard's *Nude Against the Light*
Georges Braque's *House at L'Estaque*
Chesterton's *The Man Who Was Thursday*
Jacob Epstein's *Figures* erected in London
Forster's *A Room with a View*
Anatole France's *L'Ile des Pingouins*
Henri Matisse's *Bonheur de Vivre*
Elgar's First Symphony
Ford Madox Ford founds the *English Review*
Ian Fleming born

1909 The Young Turks depose Sultan Abdul Hamid
The Anglo-Persian Oil Company formed
Louis Bleriot crosses the English Channel from France by monoplane
Admiral Robert Peary reaches the North Pole
Freud lectures at Clark University (Worcester, Mass.) on psychoanalysis
Serge Diaghilev's Ballets Russes opens in Paris
Galsworthy's *Strife*
Hardy's *Time's Laughingstocks*
Malcolm Lowry born
Claude Monet's *Water Lilies*
Stephen Spender born
Trevelyan's *Garibaldi and the Thousand*
Wells's *Tono-Bungay* first published (book form, 1909)

1910–1936 Reign of King George V
1910 The Liberals win the British general election
Marie Curie's *Treatise on Radiography*
Arthur Evans excavates Knossos
Edouard Manet and the first post-impressionist exhibition in London
Filippo Marinetti publishes "Manifesto of the Futurist Painters"
Norman Angell's *The Great Illusion*
Bennett's *Clayhanger*
Forster's *Howards End*
Galsworthy's *Justice* and *The Silver Box*
Kipling's *Rewards and Fairies*
Norman MacCaig born
Rimsky-Korsakov's *Le Coq d'or*
Stravinsky's *The Firebird*
Vaughan Williams' *A Sea Symphony*
Wells's *The History of Mr. Polly*
Wells's *The New Machiavelli* first published (in book form, 1911)
Death of Rudyard Kipling

1911 Lloyd George introduces National Health Insurance Bill
Suffragette riots in Whitehall
Roald Amundsen reaches the South Pole
Bennett's *The Card*
Chagall's *Self Portrait with Seven Fingers*
Conrad's *Under Western Eyes*
D. H. Lawrence's *The White Peacock*
Katherine Mansfield's *In a German Pension*
Edward Marsh edits *Georgian Poetry*
Moore's *Hail and Farewell* (1911–1914)
Flann O'Brien born
Strauss's *Der Rosenkavalier*
Stravinsky's *Petrouchka*
Trevelyan's *Garibaldi and the Making of Italy*
Wells's *The New Machiavelli*
Mahler's *Das Lied von der Erde*

1912 Woodrow Wilson elected president of the United States
SS *Titanic* sinks on its maiden voyage
Five million Americans go to the movies daily; London has four hundred movie theaters

xxxiii

CHRONOLOGY

Second post-impressionist exhibition in London
Bennett's and Edward Knoblock's *Milestones*
Constantin Brancusi's *Maiastra*
Wassily Kandinsky's *Black Lines*
D. H. Lawrence's *The Trespasser*
Death of William Thomas Stead
Lawrence Durrell born

1913 Second Balkan War begins
Henry Ford pioneers factory assembly technique through conveyor belts
Epstein's *Tomb of Oscar Wilde*
New York Armory Show introduces modern art to the world
Alain Fournier's *Le Grand Meaulnes*
Freud's *Totem and Tabu*
D. H. Lawrence's *Sons and Lovers*
Mann's *Death in Venice*
Proust's *Du Côté de chez Swann* (first volume of *À la recherche du temps perdu*, 1913–1922)
Barbara Pym born
Ravel's *Daphnis and Chloé*
R.S. Thomas born

1914 The Panama Canal opens (formal dedication on 12 July 1920)
Irish Home Rule Bill passed in the House of Commons
Archduke Franz Ferdinand assassinated at Sarajevo
World War I begins
Battles of the Marne, Masurian Lakes, and Falkland Islands
Joyce's *Dubliners*
Norman Nicholson born
Shaw's *Pygmalion* and *Androcles and the Lion*
Yeats's *Responsibilities*
Wyndham Lewis publishes *Blast* magazine and *The Vorticist Manifesto*
C. H. Sisson, Patrick O'Brian, Henry Reed, and Dylan Thomas born

1915 The Dardanelles campaign begins
Britain and Germany begin naval and submarine blockades
The *Lusitania* is sunk
Hugo Junkers manufactures the first fighter aircraft
First Zeppelin raid in London
Brooke's *1914: Five Sonnets*
Norman Douglas' *Old Calabria*
D. W. Griffith's *The Birth of a Nation*
Gustav Holst's *The Planets*
D. H. Lawrence's *The Rainbow*
Wyndham Lewis's *The Crowd*
Maugham's *Of Human Bondage*
Pablo Picasso's *Harlequin*
Sibelius' Fifth Symphony
John Cornford and Denton Welch born

1916 Evacuation of Gallipoli and the Dardanelles
Battles of the Somme, Jutland, and Verdun
Britain introduces conscription
The Easter Rebellion in Dublin
Asquith resigns and David Lloyd George becomes prime minister
The Sykes-Picot agreement on the partition of Turkey
First military tanks used
Wilson reelected president president of the United States
Henri Barbusse's *Le Feu*
Griffith's *Intolerance*
Joyce's *Portrait of the Artist as a Young Man*
Jung's *Psychology of the Unconscious*
Moore's *The Brook Kerith*
Edith Sitwell edits *Wheels* (1916–1921)
Wells's *Mr. Britling Sees It Through*

1917 United States enters World War I
Czar Nicholas II abdicates
The Balfour Declaration on a Jewish national home in Palestine
The Bolshevik Revolution
Georges Clemenceau elected prime minister of France
Lenin appointed chief commissar; Trotsky appointed minister of foreign affairs
Conrad's *The Shadow-Line*
Douglas' *South Wind*

CHRONOLOGY

Eliot's *Prufrock and Other Observations*
Modigliani's *Nude with Necklace*
Sassoon's *The Old Huntsman*
Prokofiev's *Classical Symphony*
Yeats's *The Wild Swans at Coole*

1918 Wilson puts forward Fourteen Points for World Peace
Central Powers and Russia sign the Treaty of Brest-Litovsk
Execution of Czar Nicholas II and his family
Kaiser Wilhelm II abdicates
The Armistice signed
Women granted the vote at age thirty in Britain
Rupert Brooke's *Collected Poems*
Gerard Manley Hopkins' *Poems*
Joyce's *Exiles*
Lewis's *Tarr*
Sassoon's *Counter-Attack*
Oswald Spengler's *The Decline of the West*
Strachey's *Eminent Victorians*
Béla Bartók's *Bluebeard's Castle*
Charlie Chaplin's *Shoulder Arms*

1919 The Versailles Peace Treaty signed
J. W. Alcock and A. W. Brown make first transatlantic flight
Ross Smith flies from London to Australia
National Socialist party founded in Germany
Benito Mussolini founds the Fascist party in Italy
Sinn Fein Congress adopts declaration of independence in Dublin
Eamon De Valera elected president of Sinn Fein party
Communist Third International founded
Lady Astor elected first woman Member of Parliament
Prohibition in the United States
John Maynard Keynes's *The Economic Consequences of the Peace*
Eliot's *Poems*
Maugham's *The Moon and Sixpence*
Shaw's *Heartbreak House*
The Bauhaus school of design, building, and crafts founded by Walter Gropius
Amedeo Modigliani's *Self-Portrait*
Patricia Beer born

1920 The League of Nations established
Warren G. Harding elected president of the United States
Senate votes against joining the League and rejects the Treaty of Versailles
The Nineteenth Amendment gives women the right to vote
White Russian forces of Denikin and Kolchak defeated by the Bolsheviks
Karel Čapek's *R.U.R.*
Galsworthy's *In Chancery* and *The Skin Game*
Sinclair Lewis' *Main Street*
Katherine Mansfield's *Bliss*
Matisse's *Odalisques* (1920–1925)
Ezra Pound's *Hugh Selwyn Mauberly*
Paul Valéry's *Le Cimetière Marin*
Yeats's *Michael Robartes and the Dancer*
Edwin Morgan born
Rosemary Sutcliff born

1921 Britain signs peace with Ireland
First medium-wave radio broadcast in the United States
The British Broadcasting Corporation founded
Braque's *Still Life with Guitar*
Chaplin's *The Kid*
Aldous Huxley's *Crome Yellow*
Paul Klee's *The Fish*
D. H. Lawrence's *Women in Love*
John McTaggart's *The Nature of Existence* (vol. 1)
Moore's *Héloïse and Abélard*
Eugene O'Neill's *The Emperor Jones*
Luigi Pirandello's *Six Characters in Search of an Author*
Shaw's *Back to Methuselah*
Strachey's *Queen Victoria*
Births of George Mackay Brown and Brian Moore

1922 Lloyd George's Coalition government succeeded by Bonar Law's

CHRONOLOGY

Conservative government
Benito Mussolini marches on Rome and forms a government
William Cosgrave elected president of the Irish Free State
The BBC begins broadcasting in London
Lord Carnarvon and Howard Carter discover Tutankhamen's tomb
The PEN club founded in London
The *Criterion* founded with T. S. Eliot as editor
Kingsley Amis born
Eliot's *The Waste Land*
A. E. Housman's *Last Poems*
Joyce's *Ulysses*
D. H. Lawrence's *Aaron's Rod* and *England, My England*
Sinclair Lewis's *Babbitt*
O'Neill's *Anna Christie*
Pirandello's *Henry IV*
Edith Sitwell's *Façade*
Virginia Woolf's *Jacob's Room*
Yeats's *The Trembling of the Veil*
Donald Davie, Philip Larkin born

1923 The Union of Soviet Socialist Republics established
French and Belgian troops occupy the Ruhr in consequence of Germany's failure to pay reparations
Mustafa Kemal (Ataturk) proclaims Turkey a republic and is elected president
Warren G. Harding dies; Calvin Coolidge becomes president
Stanley Baldwin succeeds Bonar Law as prime minister
Adolf Hitler's attempted coup in Munich fails
Time magazine begins publishing
E. N. da C. Andrade's *The Structure of the Atom*
Brendan Behan born
Bennett's *Riceyman Steps*
Churchill's *The World Crisis* (1923–1927)
J. E. Flecker's *Hassan* produced
Nadine Gordimer born
Paul Klee's *Magic Theatre*
Lawrence's *Kangaroo*
Rainer Maria Rilke's *Duino Elegies* and *Sonnets to Orpheus*
Sibelius' *Sixth Symphony*
Picasso's *Seated Woman*
William Walton's *Façade*
Elizabeth Jane Howard born

1924 Ramsay MacDonald forms first Labour government, loses general election, and is succeeded by Stanley Baldwin
Calvin Coolidge elected president of the United States
Noël Coward's *The Vortex*
Forster's *A Passage to India*
Mann's *The Magic Mountain*
Shaw's *St. Joan*
G. F. Dutton born

1925 Reza Khan becomes shah of Iran
First surrealist exhibition held in Paris
Alban Berg's *Wozzeck*
Chaplin's *The Gold Rush*
John Dos Passos' *Manhattan Transfer*
Theodore Dreiser's *An American Tragedy*
Sergei Eisenstein's *Battleship Potemkin*
F. Scott Fitzgerald's *The Great Gatsby*
André Gide's *Les Faux Monnayeurs*
Hardy's *Human Shows and Far Phantasies*
Huxley's *Those Barren Leaves*
Kafka's *The Trial*
O'Casey's *Juno and the Paycock*
Virginia Woolf's *Mrs. Dalloway* and *The Common Reader*
Brancusi's *Bird in Space*
Shostakovich's *First Symphony*
Sibelius' *Tapiola*
John Wain born

1926 Ford's *A Man Could Stand Up*
Gide's *Si le grain ne meurt*
Hemingway's *The Sun also Rises*
Kafka's *The Castle*
D. H. Lawrence's *The Plumed Serpent*
T. E. Lawrence's *Seven Pillars of Wisdom* privately circulated

CHRONOLOGY

Maugham's *The Casuarina Tree*
O'Casey's *The Plough and the Stars*
Puccini's *Turandot*
Jan Morris born

1927 General Chiang Kai-shek becomes prime minister in China
Trotsky expelled by the Communist party as a deviationist; Stalin becomes leader of the party and dictator of the Soviet Union
Charles Lindbergh flies from New York to Paris
J. W. Dunne's *An Experiment with Time*
Freud's *Autobiography* translated into English
Albert Giacometti's *Observing Head*
Ernest Hemingway's *Men Without Women*
Fritz Lang's *Metropolis*
Wyndham Lewis' *Time and Western Man*
F. W. Murnau's *Sunrise*
Proust's *Le Temps retrouvé* posthumously published
Stravinsky's *Oedipus Rex*
Virginia Woolf's *To the Lighthouse*

1928 The Kellogg-Briand Pact, outlawing war and providing for peaceful settlement of disputes, signed in Paris by sixty-two nations, including the Soviet Union
Herbert Hoover elected president of the United States
Women's suffrage granted at age twenty-one in Britain
Alexander Fleming discovers penicillin
Bertolt Brecht and Kurt Weill's *The Three-Penny Opera*
Eisenstein's *October*
Huxley's *Point Counter Point*
Christopher Isherwood's *All the Conspirators*
D. H. Lawrence's *Lady Chatterley's Lover*
Wyndham Lewis' *The Childermass*
Matisse's *Seated Odalisque*
Munch's *Girl on a Sofa*
Shaw's *Intelligent Woman's Guide to Socialism*
Virginia Woolf's *Orlando*
Yeats's *The Tower*
Iain Chrichton Smith born

1929 The Labour party wins British general election
Trotsky expelled from the Soviet Union
Museum of Modern Art opens in New York
Collapse of U.S. stock exchange begins world economic crisis
Robert Bridges's *The Testament of Beauty*
William Faulkner's *The Sound and the Fury*
Robert Graves's *Goodbye to All That*
Hemingway's *A Farewell to Arms*
Ernst Junger's *The Storm of Steel*
Hugo von Hoffmansthal's *Poems*
Henry Moore's *Reclining Figure*
J. B. Priestley's *The Good Companions*
Erich Maria Remarque's *All Quiet on the Western Front*
Shaw's *The Applecart*
R. C. Sheriff's *Journey's End*
Edith Sitwell's *Gold Coast Customs*
Thomas Wolfe's *Look Homeward, Angel*
Virginia Woolf's *A Room of One's Own*
Yeats's *The Winding Stair*
Second surrealist manifesto; Salvador Dali joins the surrealists
Epstein's *Night and Day*
Mondrian's *Composition with Yellow Blue*
Death of Edward Carpenter and Flora Annie Steel
John Montague, Keith Waterhouse, and Thom Gunn born

1930 Allied occupation of the Rhineland ends
Mohandas Gandhi opens civil disobedience campaign in India
The *Daily Worker*, journal of the British Communist party, begins publishing

CHRONOLOGY

J. W. Reppe makes artificial fabrics from an acetylene base
John Arden born
Auden's *Poems*
Coward's *Private Lives*
Eliot's *Ash Wednesday*
Wyndham Lewis's *The Apes of God*
Maugham's *Cakes and Ale*
Ezra Pound's *XXX Cantos*
Evelyn Waugh's *Vile Bodies*
Birth of Kamau (Edward) Brathwaite and Ruth Rendell

1931 The failure of the Credit Anstalt in Austria starts a financial collapse in Central Europe
Britain abandons the gold standard; the pound falls by twenty-five percent
Mutiny in the Royal Navy at Invergordon over pay cuts
Ramsay MacDonald resigns, splits the Cabinet, and is expelled by the Labour party; in the general election the National Government wins by a majority of five hundred seats
The Statute of Westminster defines dominion status
Ninette de Valois founds the Vic-Wells Ballet (eventually the Royal Ballet)
Coward's *Cavalcade*
Dali's The *Persistence of Memory*
O'Neill's *Mourning Becomes Electra*
Anthony Powell's *Afternoon Men*
Antoine de Saint-Exupéry's *Vol de nuit*
Walton's *Belshazzar's Feast*
Virginia Woolf's *The Waves*
Caroline Blackwood, John le Carré born

1932 Franklin D. Roosevelt elected president of the United States
Paul von Hindenburg elected president of Germany; Franz von Papen elected chancellor
Sir Oswald Mosley founds British Union of Fascists
The BBC takes over development of television from J. L. Baird's company
Basic English of 850 words designed as a prospective international language
The Folger Library opens in Washington, D.C.
The Shakespeare Memorial Theatre opens in Stratford-upon-Avon
Faulkner's *Light in August*
Huxley's *Brave New World*
F. R. Leavis' *New Bearings in English Poetry*
Boris Pasternak's *Second Birth*
Ravel's *Concerto for Left Hand*
Athol Fugard and Peter Redgrove born
Rouault's *Christ Mocked by Soldiers*
Waugh's *Black Mischief*
Yeats's *Words for Music Perhaps*
Geoffrey Hill born

1933 Roosevelt inaugurates the New Deal
Hitler becomes chancellor of Germany
The Reichstag set on fire
Hitler suspends civil liberties and freedom of the press; German trade unions suppressed
George Balanchine and Lincoln Kirstein found the School of American Ballet
Beryl Bainbridge born
Lowry's *Ultramarine*
André Malraux's *La Condition humaine*
Orwell's *Down and Out in Paris and London*
Gertrude Stein's *The Autobiography of Alice B. Toklas*
Peter Scupham and Anne Stevenson born

1934 The League Disarmament Conference ends in failure
The Soviet Union admitted to the League
Hitler becomes Führer
Civil war in Austria; Engelbert Dollfuss assassinated in attempted Nazi coup
Frédéric Joliot and Irene Joliot-Curie discover artificial (induced) radioac-

CHRONOLOGY

tivity
Einstein's *My Philosophy*
Fitzgerald's *Tender Is the Night*
Graves's *I, Claudius* and *Claudius the God*
Toynbee's *A Study of History* begins publication (1934–1954)
Waugh's *A Handful of Dust*
Births of Fleur Adcock, Alan Bennett, Christopher Wallace-Crabbe, and Alasdair Gray

1935 Grigori Zinoviev and other Soviet leaders convicted of treason
Stanley Baldwin becomes prime minister in National Government; National Government wins general election in Britain
Italy invades Abyssinia
Germany repudiates disarmament clauses of Treaty of Versailles
Germany reintroduces compulsory military service and outlaws the Jews
Robert Watson-Watt builds first practical radar equipment
Karl Jaspers' *Suffering and Existence*
Births of André Brink, Dennis Potter, Keith Roberts, and Jon Stallworthy
Ivy Compton-Burnett's *A House and Its Head*
Eliot's *Murder in the Cathedral*
Barbara Hepworth's *Three Forms*
George Gershwin's *Porgy and Bess*
Greene's *England Made Me*
Isherwood's *Mr. Norris Changes Trains*
Malraux's *Le Temps du mépris*
Yeats's *Dramatis Personae*
Klee's *Child Consecrated to Suffering*
Benedict Nicholson's *White Relief*
Death of Lewis Grassic Gibbon
Edward VII accedes to the throne in January; abdicates in December

1936–1952 Reign of George VI

1936 German troops occupy the Rhineland
Ninety-nine percent of German electorate vote for Nazi candidates
The Popular Front wins general election in France; Léon Blum becomes prime minister
Roosevelt reelected president of the United States
The Popular Front wins general election in Spain
Spanish Civil War begins
Italian troops occupy Addis Ababa; Abyssinia annexed by Italy
BBC begins television service from Alexandra Palace
Auden's *Look, Stranger!*
Auden and Isherwood's *The Ascent of F-6*
A. J. Ayer's *Language, Truth and Logic*
Chaplin's *Modern Times*
Greene's *A Gun for Sale*
Huxley's *Eyeless in Gaza*
Keynes's *General Theory of Employment*
F. R. Leavis' *Revaluation*
Mondrian's *Composition in Red and Blue*
Dylan Thomas' *Twenty-five Poems*
Wells's *The Shape of Things to Come* filmed
Steward Conn and Reginald Hill born
Death of John Cornford

1937 Trial of Karl Radek and other Soviet leaders
Neville Chamberlain succeeds Stanley Baldwin as prime minister
China and Japan at war
Frank Whittle designs jet engine
Picasso's *Guernica*
Shostakovich's Fifth Symphony
Magritte's *La Reproduction interdite*
Hemingway's *To Have and Have Not*
Malraux's *L'Espoir*
Orwell's *The Road to Wigan Pier*
Priestley's *Time and the Conways*
Virginia Woolf's *The Years*
Emma Tennant born
Death of Christopher Caudwell (Christopher St. John Sprigg)

1938 Trial of Nikolai Bukharin and other Soviet political leaders

CHRONOLOGY

Austria occupied by German troops and declared part of the Reich
Hitler states his determination to annex Sudetenland from Czechoslovakia
Britain, France, Germany, and Italy sign the Munich agreement
German troops occupy Sudetenland
Edward Hulton founds *Picture Post*
Cyril Connolly's *Enemies of Promise*
du Maurier's *Rebecca*
Faulkner's *The Unvanquished*
Graham Greene's *Brighton Rock*
Hindemith's *Mathis der Maler*
Jean Renoir's *La Grande Illusion*
Jean-Paul Sartre's *La Nausée*
Yeats's *New Poems*
Anthony Asquith's *Pygmalion* and Walt Disney's *Snow White*
Ngũgĩ wa Thiong'o born
Death of **Lascelles Abercrombie**

1939 German troops occupy Bohemia and Moravia; Czechoslovakia incorporated into Third Reich
Madrid surrenders to General Franco; the Spanish Civil War ends
Italy invades Albania
Spain joins Germany, Italy, and Japan in anti-Comintern Pact
Britain and France pledge support to Poland, Romania, and Greece
The Soviet Union proposes defensive alliance with Britain; British military mission visits Moscow
The Soviet Union and Germany sign nonaggression treaty, secretly providing for partition of Poland between them
Germany invades Poland; Britain, France, and Germany at war
The Soviet Union invades Finland
New York World's Fair opens
Eliot's *The Family Reunion*
Births of Ayi Kwei Armah, Seamus Heaney, Michael Longley and Robert Nye
Isherwood's *Good-bye to Berlin*
Joyce's *Finnegans Wake* (1922–1939)
MacNeice's *Autumn Journal*

Powell's *What's Become of Waring?*
Ayi Kwei Armah born

1940 Churchill becomes prime minister
Italy declares war on France, Britain, and Greece
General de Gaulle founds Free French Movement
The Battle of Britain and the bombing of London
Roosevelt reelected president of the United States for third term
Betjeman's *Old Lights for New Chancels*
Angela Carter born
Chaplin's *The Great Dictator*
Bruce Chatwin born
Death of William H. Davies
J. M. Coetzee born
Disney's *Fantasia*
Greene's *The Power and the Glory*
Hemingway's *For Whom the Bell Tolls*
C. P. Snow's *Strangers and Brothers* (retitled *George Passant* in 1970, when entire sequence of ten novels, published 1940–1970, was entitled *Strangers and Brothers*)

1941 German forces occupy Yugoslavia, Greece, and Crete, and invade the Soviet Union
Lend-Lease agreement between the United States and Britain
President Roosevelt and Winston Churchill sign the Atlantic Charter
Japanese forces attack Pearl Harbor; United States declares war on Japan, Germany, Italy; Britain on Japan
Auden's *New Year Letter*
James Burnham's *The Managerial Revolution*
F. Scott Fitzgerald's *The Last Tycoon*
Huxley's *Grey Eminence*
Derek Mahon born
Shostakovich's *Seventh Symphony*
Tippett's *A Child of Our Time*
Orson Welles's *Citizen Kane*
Virginia Woolf's *Between the Acts*
Death of James Joyce

1942 Japanese forces capture Singapore, Hong Kong, Bataan, Manila

CHRONOLOGY

German forces capture Tobruk
U.S. fleet defeats the Japanese in the Coral Sea, captures Guadalcanal
Battle of El Alamein
Allied forces land in French North Africa
Atom first split at University of Chicago
William Beveridge's *Social Insurance and Allied Services*
Albert Camus's *L'Étranger*
Joyce Cary's *To Be a Pilgrim*
Edith Sitwell's *Street Songs*
Waugh's *Put Out More Flags*
Births of Ama Ata Aidoo, Douglas Dunn, Susan Hill, and Jonathan Raban

1943 German forces surrender at Stalingrad
German and Italian forces surrender in North Africa
Italy surrenders to Allies and declares war on Germany
Cairo conference between Roosevelt, Churchill, Chiang Kai-shek
Teheran conference between Roosevelt, Churchill, Stalin
Eliot's *Four Quartets*
Henry Moore's *Madonna and Child*
Sartre's *Les Mouches*
Vaughan Williams' *Fifth Symphony*
Peter Carey, David Malouf, and Iain Sinclair born
Death of **William Soutar**

1944 Allied forces land in Normandy and southern France
Allied forces enter Rome
Attempted assassination of Hitler fails
Liberation of Paris
U.S. forces land in Philippines
German offensive in the Ardennes halted
Roosevelt reelected president of the United States for fourth term
Education Act passed in Britain
Pay-as-You-Earn income tax introduced
Beveridge's *Full Employment in a Free Society*
Cary's *The Horse's Mouth*
Huxley's *Time Must Have a Stop*
Maugham's *The Razor's Edge*
Sartre's *Huis Clos*
Edith Sitwell's *Green Song and Other Poems*
Graham Sutherland's *Christ on the Cross*
Trevelyan's *English Social History*
David Constantine, Craig Raine and W. G. Sebald born

1945 British and Indian forces open offensive in Burma
Yalta conference between Roosevelt, Churchill, Stalin
Mussolini executed by Italian partisans
Roosevelt dies; Harry S. Truman becomes president
Hitler commits suicide; German forces surrender
The Potsdam Peace Conference
The United Nations Charter ratified in San Francisco
The Labour Party wins British General Election
Atomic bombs dropped on Hiroshima and Nagasaki
Surrender of Japanese forces ends World War II
Trial of Nazi war criminals opens at Nuremberg
All-India Congress demands British withdrawal from India
De Gaulle elected president of French Provisional Government; resigns the next year
Betjeman's *New Bats in Old Belfries*
Britten's *Peter Grimes*
Orwell's *Animal Farm*
Russell's *History of Western Philosophy*
Sartre's *The Age of Reason*
Edith Sitwell's *The Song of the Cold*
Waugh's *Brideshead Revisited*
Births of Wendy Cope and Peter Reading
Death of Arthur Symons

1946 Bills to nationalize railways, coal mines, and the Bank of England

CHRONOLOGY

passed in Britain
Nuremberg Trials concluded
United Nations General Assembly meets in New York as its permanent headquarters
The Arab Council inaugurated in Britain
Frederick Ashton's *Symphonic Variations*
Britten's *The Rape of Lucretia*
David Lean's *Great Expectations*
O'Neill's *The Iceman Cometh*
Roberto Rosselini's *Paisà*
Dylan Thomas' *Deaths and Entrances*
Jim Crace and Philip Pullman born

1947 President Truman announces program of aid to Greece and Turkey and outlines the "Truman Doctrine"
Independence of India proclaimed; partition between India and Pakistan, and communal strife between Hindus and Moslems follows
General Marshall calls for a European recovery program
First supersonic air flight
Britain's first atomic pile at Harwell comes into operation
Edinburgh festival established
Discovery of the Dead Sea Scrolls in Palestine
Princess Elizabeth marries Philip Mountbatten, duke of Edinburgh
Auden's *Age of Anxiety*
Camus's *La Peste*
Chaplin's *Monsieur Verdoux*
Lowry's *Under the Volcano*
Priestley's *An Inspector Calls*
Edith Sitwell's *The Shadow of Cain*
Waugh's *Scott-King's Modern Europe*
Births of Dermot Healy, and Redmond O'Hanlon
Death of Flora Thompson,

1948 Gandhi assassinated
Czech Communist Party seizes power
Pan-European movement (1948–1958) begins with the formation of the permanent Organization for European Economic Cooperation (OEEC)
Berlin airlift begins as the Soviet Union halts road and rail traffic to the city
British mandate in Palestine ends; Israeli provisional government formed
Yugoslavia expelled from Soviet bloc
Columbia Records introduces the long-playing record
Truman elected of the United States for second term
Greene's *The Heart of the Matter*
Huxley's *Ape and Essence*
Leavis' *The Great Tradition*
Pound's *Cantos*
Priestley's *The Linden Tree*
Waugh's *The Loved One*
Death of Denton Welch
Ciaran Carson and Zakes Mda born

1949 North Atlantic Treaty Organization established with headquarters in Brussels
Berlin blockade lifted
German Federal Republic recognized; capital established at Bonn
Konrad Adenauer becomes German chancellor
Mao Tse-tung becomes chairman of the People's Republic of China following Communist victory over the Nationalists
Peter Ackroyd born
Simone de Beauvoir's *The Second Sex*
Cary's *A Fearful Joy*
Arthur Miller's *Death of a Salesman*
Orwell's *Nineteen Eighty-four*
Birth of Michèle Roberts
Ron Butlin born

1950 Korean War breaks out
Nobel Prize for literature awarded to Bertrand Russell
R. H. S. Crossman's *The God That Failed*
T. S. Eliot's *The Cocktail Party*
Fry's *Venus Observed*
Doris Lessing's *The Grass Is Sing-*

CHRONOLOGY

ing
C. S. Lewis' *The Chronicles of Narnia* (1950–1956)
Wyndham Lewis' *Rude Assignment*
George Orwell's *Shooting an Elephant*
Carol Reed's *The Third Man*
Dylan Thomas' *Twenty-six Poems*
Births of Sara Maitland, and A. N. Wilson

1951 Guy Burgess and Donald Maclean defect from Britain to the Soviet Union
The Conservative party under Winston Churchill wins British general election
The Festival of Britain celebrates both the centenary of the Crystal Palace Exhibition and British postwar recovery
Electric power is produced by atomic energy at Arcon, Idaho
W. H. Auden's *Nones*
Samuel Beckett's *Molloy* and *Malone Dies*
Benjamin Britten's *Billy Budd*
Greene's *The End of the Affair*
Akira Kurosawa's *Rashomon*
Wyndham Lewis' *Rotting Hill*
Anthony Powell's *A Question of Upbringing* (first volume of *A Dance to the Music of Time*, 1951–1975)
J. D. Salinger's *The Catcher in the Rye*
C. P. Snow's *The Masters*
Igor Stravinsky's *The Rake's Progress*
Peter Fallon born
Andrew Greig born

1952– Reign of Elizabeth II
At Eniwetok Atoll the United States detonates the first hydrogen bomb
The European Coal and Steel Community comes into being
Radiocarbon dating introduced to archaeology
Michael Ventris deciphers Linear B script
Dwight D. Eisenhower elected president of the United States
Beckett's *Waiting for Godot*
Charles Chaplin's *Limelight*
Ernest Hemingway's *The Old Man and the Sea*
Arthur Koestler's *Arrow in the Blue*
F. R. Leavis' *The Common Pursuit*
Lessing's *Martha Quest* (first volume of *The Children of Violence*, 1952–1965)
C. S. Lewis' *Mere Christianity*
Thomas' *Collected Poems*
Evelyn Waugh's *Men at Arms* (first volume of *Sword of Honour*, 1952–1961)
Angus Wilson's *Hemlock and After*
Births of Rohinton Mistry and Vikram Seth
William Boyd born

1953 Constitution for a European political community drafted
Julius and Ethel Rosenberg executed for passing U.S. secrets to the Soviet Union
Cease-fire declared in Korea
Edmund Hillary and his Sherpa guide, Tenzing Norkay, scale Mt. Everest
Nobel Prize for literature awarded to Winston Churchill
General Mohammed Naguib proclaims Egypt a republic
Beckett's *Watt*
Joyce Cary's *Except the Lord*
Robert Graves's *Poems 1953*
Death of Norman Cameron, Dylan Thomas
Birth of Tony Parsons

1954 First atomic submarine, *Nautilus,* is launched by the United States
Dien Bien Phu captured by the Vietminh
Geneva Conference ends French dominion over Indochina
U.S. Supreme Court declares racial segregation in schools unconstitutional
Nasser becomes president of Egypt
Nobel Prize for literature awarded to Ernest Hemingway
Kingsley Amis' *Lucky Jim*

CHRONOLOGY

John Betjeman's *A Few Late Chrysanthemums*
William Golding's *Lord of the Flies*
Christopher Isherwood's *The World in the Evening*
Koestler's *The Invisible Writing*
Iris Murdoch's *Under the Net*
C. P. Snow's *The New Men*
Thomas' *Under Milk Wood* published posthumously
Births of Iain Banks, Louise De Bernières, Romesh Gunesekera, Kevin Hart, Alan Hollinghurst, Hanif Kureishi, and Kazuo Ishiguro

1955 Warsaw Pact signed
West Germany enters NATO as Allied occupation ends
The Conservative party under Anthony Eden wins British general election
Cary's *Not Honour More*
Greene's *The Quiet American*
Philip Larkin's *The Less Deceived*
F. R. Leavis' *D. H. Lawrence, Novelist*
Vladimir Nabokov's *Lolita*
Patrick White's *The Tree of Man*
John Burnside and Patrick McCabe born

1956 Nasser's nationalization of the Suez Canal leads to Israeli, British, and French armed intervention
Uprising in Hungary suppressed by Soviet troops
Khrushchev denounces Stalin at Twentieth Communist Party Congress
Eisenhower reelected president of the United States
Anthony Burgess' *Time for a Tiger*
Golding's *Pincher Martin*
Murdoch's *Flight from the Enchanter*
John Osborne's *Look Back in Anger*
Snow's *Homecomings*
Edmund Wilson's *Anglo-Saxon Attitudes*
Janice Galloway, Philip Kerr and Kate Thompson born

1957 The Soviet Union launches the first artificial earth satellite, *Sputnik I*
Eden succeeded by Harold Macmillan
Suez Canal reopened
Eisenhower Doctrine formulated
Parliament receives the Wolfenden Report on Homosexuality and Prostitution
Nobel Prize for literature awarded to Albert Camus
Beckett's *Endgame* and *All That Fall*
Lawrence Durrell's *Justine* (first volume of *The Alexandria Quartet*, 1957–1960)
Ted Hughes's *The Hawk in the Rain*
Murdoch's *The Sandcastle*
V. S. Naipaul's *The Mystic Masseur*
Eugene O'Neill's *Long Day's Journey into Night*
Osborne's *The Entertainer*
Muriel Spark's *The Comforters*
White's *Voss*
Death of Dorothy Richardson
Birth of Nick Hornby

1958 European Economic Community established
Khrushchev succeeds Bulganin as Soviet premier
Charles de Gaulle becomes head of France's newly constituted Fifth Republic
The United Arab Republic formed by Egypt and Syria
The United States sends troops into Lebanon
First U.S. satellite, *Explorer 1*, launched
Nobel Prize for literature awarded to Boris Pasternak
Beckett's *Krapp's Last Tape*
John Kenneth Galbraith's *The Affluent Society*
Greene's *Our Man in Havana*
Murdoch's *The Bell*
Pasternak's *Dr. Zhivago*
Snow's *The Conscience of the Rich*
Greg Delanty born

1959 Fidel Castro assumes power in Cuba
St. Lawrence Seaway opens
The European Free Trade Associa-

xliv

CHRONOLOGY

tion founded
Alaska and Hawaii become the forty-ninth and fiftieth states
The Conservative party under Harold Macmillan wins British general election
Brendan Behan's *The Hostage*
Golding's *Free Fall*
Graves's *Collected Poems*
Koestler's *The Sleepwalkers*
Harold Pinter's *The Birthday Party*
Snow's *The Two Cultures and the Scientific Revolution*
Spark's *Memento Mori*
Susanna Clarke and Robert Crawford born

1960 South Africa bans the African National Congress and Pan-African Congress
The Congo achieves independence
John F. Kennedy elected president of the United States
The U.S. bathyscaphe *Trieste* descends to 35,800 feet
Publication of the unexpurgated *Lady Chatterley's Lover* permitted by court
Auden's *Hommage to Clio*
Betjeman's *Summoned by Bells*
Pinter's *The Caretaker*
Snow's *The Affair*
David Storey's *This Sporting Life*
Andrew Miller and Ian Rankin born

1961 South Africa leaves the British Commonwealth
Sierra Leone and Tanganyika achieve independence
The Berlin Wall erected
The New English Bible published
Beckett's *How It Is*
Greene's *A Burnt-Out Case*
Koestler's *The Lotus and the Robot*
Murdoch's *A Severed Head*
Naipaul's *A House for Mr Biswas*
Osborne's *Luther*
Spark's *The Prime of Miss Jean Brodie*
White's *Riders in the Chariot*
Jonathan Coe, Meaghan Delahunt and Jackie Kay born

1962 John Glenn becomes first U.S. astronaut to orbit earth
The United States launches the spacecraft *Mariner* to explore Venus
Algeria achieves independence
Cuban missile crisis ends in withdrawal of Soviet missiles from Cuba
Adolf Eichmann executed in Israel for Nazi war crimes
Second Vatican Council convened by Pope John XXIII
Nobel Prize for literature awarded to John Steinbeck
Edward Albee's *Who's Afraid of Virginia Woolf?*
Beckett's *Happy Days*
Anthony Burgess' *A Clockwork Orange* and *The Wanting Seed*
Aldous Huxley's *Island*
Isherwood's *Down There on a Visit*
Lessing's *The Golden Notebook*
Nabokov's *Pale Fire*
Aleksandr Solzhenitsyn's *One Day in the Life of Ivan Denisovich*
Kathleen Jamie born
Death of **Patrick Hamilton**

1963 Britain, the United States, and the Soviet Union sign a test-ban treaty
Birth of Simon Armitage
Britain refused entry to the European Economic Community
The Soviet Union puts into orbit the first woman astronaut, Valentina Tereshkova
Paul VI becomes pope
President Kennedy assassinated; Lyndon B. Johnson assumes office
Nobel Prize for literature awarded to George Seferis
Britten's *War Requiem*
John Fowles's *The Collector*
Murdoch's *The Unicorn*
Spark's *The Girls of Slender Means*
Storey's *Radcliffe*
John Updike's *The Centaur*

1964 Tonkin Gulf incident leads to retaliatory strikes by U.S. aircraft against North Vietnam
Greece and Turkey contend for control of Cyprus

CHRONOLOGY

Britain grants licenses to drill for oil in the North Sea
The Shakespeare Quatercentenary celebrated
Lyndon Johnson elected president of the United States
The Labour party under Harold Wilson wins British general election
Nobel Prize for literature awarded to Jean-Paul Sartre
Saul Bellow's *Herzog*
Burgess' *Nothing Like the Sun*
Golding's *The Spire*
Isherwood's *A Single Man*
Stanley Kubrick's *Dr. Strangelove*
Larkin's *The Whitsun Weddings*
Naipaul's *An Area of Darkness*
Peter Shaffer's *The Royal Hunt of the Sun*
Snow's *Corridors of Power*
Alan Warner born
Death of Ian Fleming

1965 The first U.S. combat forces land in Vietnam
The U.S. spacecraft Mariner transmits photographs of Mars
British Petroleum Company finds oil in the North Sea
War breaks out between India and Pakistan
Rhodesia declares its independence
Ontario power failure blacks out the Canadian and U.S. east coasts
Nobel Prize for literature awarded to Mikhail Sholokhov
Robert Lowell's *For the Union Dead*
Norman Mailer's *An American Dream*
Osborne's *Inadmissible Evidence*
Pinter's *The Homecoming*
Spark's *The Mandelbaum Gate*
J. K. Rowling born

1966 The Labour party under Harold Wilson wins British general election
The Archbishop of Canterbury visits Pope Paul VI
Florence, Italy, severely damaged by floods
Paris exhibition celebrates Picasso's eighty-fifth birthday
Fowles's *The Magus*
Greene's *The Comedians*
Osborne's *A Patriot for Me*
Paul Scott's *The Jewel in the Crown* (first volume of *The Raj Quartet*, 1966–1975)
White's *The Solid Mandala*
Peter Ho Davies born
Death of Frank O'Connor

1967 Thurgood Marshall becomes first black U.S. Supreme Court justice
Six-Day War pits Israel against Egypt and Syria
Biafra's secession from Nigeria leads to civil war
Francis Chichester completes solo circumnavigation of the globe
Dr. Christiaan Barnard performs first heart transplant operation, in South Africa
China explodes its first hydrogen bomb
Golding's *The Pyramid*
Hughes's *Wodwo*
Isherwood's *A Meeting by the River*
Naipaul's *The Mimic Men*
Tom Stoppard's *Rosencrantz and Guildenstern Are Dead*
Orson Welles's *Chimes at Midnight*
Angus Wilson's *No Laughing Matter*

1968 Violent student protests erupt in France and West Germany
Warsaw Pact troops occupy Czechoslovakia
Violence in Northern Ireland causes Britain to send in troops
Tet offensive by Communist forces launched against South Vietnam's cities
Theater censorship ended in Britain
Robert Kennedy and Martin Luther King Jr. assassinated
Richard M. Nixon elected president of the United States
Booker Prize for fiction established
Durrell's *Tunc*
Graves's *Poems 1965–1968*
Osborne's *The Hotel in Amsterdam*
Snow's *The Sleep of Reason*

CHRONOLOGY

Solzhenitsyn's *The First Circle* and *Cancer Ward*
Spark's *The Public Image*
Monica Ali born

1969 Humans set foot on the moon for the first time when astronauts descend to its surface in a landing vehicle from the U.S. spacecraft *Apollo 11*
The Soviet unmanned spacecraft *Venus V* lands on Venus
Capital punishment abolished in Britain
Colonel Muammar Qaddafi seizes power in Libya
Solzhenitsyn expelled from the Soviet Union
Nobel Prize for literature awarded to Samuel Beckett
Carter's *The Magic Toyshop*
Fowles's *The French Lieutenant's Woman*
Storey's *The Contractor*
Death of John Wyndham
Hari Kunzru and David Mitchell born

1970 Civil war in Nigeria ends with Biafra's surrender
U.S. planes bomb Cambodia
The Conservative party under Edward Heath wins British general election
Nobel Prize for literature awarded to Aleksandr Solzhenitsyn
Durrell's *Nunquam*
Hughes's *Crow*
F. R. Leavis and Q. D. Leavis' *Dickens the Novelist*
Snow's *Last Things*
Spark's *The Driver's Seat*
Death of Vera Brittain

1971 Communist China given Nationalist China's UN seat
Decimal currency introduced to Britain
Indira Gandhi becomes India's prime minister
Nobel Prize for literature awarded to Heinrich Böll
Bond's *The Pope's Wedding*
Naipaul's *In a Free State*
Pinter's *Old Times*
Spark's *Not to Disturb*
Births of Kiran Desai, Sarah Kane and Martin McDonagh
Death of Stevie Smith

1972 The civil strife of "Bloody Sunday" causes Northern Ireland to come under the direct rule of Westminster
Nixon becomes the first U.S. president to visit Moscow and Beijing
The Watergate break-in precipitates scandal in the United States
Eleven Israeli athletes killed by terrorists at Munich Olympics
Nixon reelected president of the United States
Bond's *Lear*
Snow's *The Malcontents*
Stoppard's *Jumpers*

1973 Britain, Ireland, and Denmark enter European Economic Community
Egypt and Syria attack Israel in the Yom Kippur War
Energy crisis in Britain reduces production to a three-day week
Nobel Prize for literature awarded to Patrick White
Bond's *The Sea*
Greene's *The Honorary Consul*
Lessing's *The Summer Before the Dark*
Murdoch's *The Black Prince*
Shaffer's *Equus*
White's *The Eye of the Storm*
Death of William Plomer

1974 Miners strike in Britain
Greece's military junta overthrown
Emperor Haile Selassie of Ethiopia deposed
President Makarios of Cyprus replaced by military coup
Nixon resigns as U.S. president and is succeeded by Gerald R. Ford
Betjeman's *A Nip in the Air*
Bond's *Bingo*
Durrell's *Monsieur* (first volume of *The Avignon Quintet*, 1974–1985)
Larkin's *The High Windows*
Solzhenitsyn's *The Gulag Archipelago*

CHRONOLOGY

	Spark's *The Abbess of Crewe*		murdered by left-wing terrorists
	Death of Edmund Blunden, Austin Clarke, and Nancy Mitford		Nobel Prize for literature awarded to Isaac Bashevis Singer
1975	The U.S. *Apollo* and Soviet *Soyuz* spacecrafts rendezvous in space		Greene's *The Human Factor*
			Hughes's *Cave Birds*
	The Helsinki Accords on human rights signed		Murdoch's *The Sea, The Sea*
			Death of Hugh MacDiarmid
	U.S. forces leave Vietnam	1979	The United States and China establish diplomatic relations
	King Juan Carlos succeeds Franco as Spain's head of state		
			Ayatollah Khomeini takes power in Iran and his supporters hold U.S. embassy staff hostage in Teheran
	Nobel Prize for literature awarded to Eugenio Montale		
1976	New U.S. copyright law goes into effect		
			Rhodesia becomes Zimbabwe
	Israeli commandos free hostages from hijacked plane at Entebbe, Uganda		Earl Mountbatten assassinated
			The Soviet Union invades Afghanistan
	British and French SST Concordes make first regularly scheduled commercial flights		The Conservative party under Margaret Thatcher wins British general election
	The United States celebrates its bicentennial		Nobel Prize for literature awarded to Odysseus Elytis
	Jimmy Carter elected president of the United States		Golding's *Darkness Visible*
			Hughes's *Moortown*
	Byron and Shelley manuscripts discovered in Barclay's Bank, Pall Mall		Lessing's *Shikasta* (first volume of *Canopus in Argos, Archives*)
	Hughes's *Seasons' Songs*		Naipaul's *A Bend in the River*
	Koestler's *The Thirteenth Tribe*		Spark's *Territorial Rights*
	Scott's *Staying On*		White's *The Twyborn Affair*
	Spark's *The Take-over*	1980	Iran-Iraq war begins
	White's *A Fringe of Leaves*		Strikes in Gdansk give rise to the Solidarity movement
1977	Silver jubilee of Queen Elizabeth II celebrated		
			Mt. St. Helen's erupts in Washington State
	Egyptian president Anwar el-Sadat visits Israel		
			British steelworkers strike for the first time since 1926
	"Gang of Four" expelled from Chinese Communist party		
			More than fifty nations boycott Moscow Olympics
	First woman ordained in the U.S. Episcopal church		
			Ronald Reagan elected president of the United States
	After twenty-nine years in power, Israel's Labour party is defeated by the Likud party		
			Burgess's *Earthly Powers*
			Golding's *Rites of Passage*
	Fowles's *Daniel Martin*		Shaffer's *Amadeus*
	Hughes's *Gaudete*		Storey's *A Prodigal Child*
1978	Treaty between Israel and Egypt negotiated at Camp David		Angus Wilson's *Setting the World on Fire*
	Pope John Paul I dies a month after his coronation and is succeeded by Karol Cardinal Wojtyla, who takes the name John Paul II	1981	Greece admitted to the European Economic Community
			Iran hostage crisis ends with release of U.S. embassy staff
	Former Italian premier Aldo Moro		Twelve Labour MPs and nine peers

CHRONOLOGY

found British Social Democratic party
Socialist party under François Mitterand wins French general election
Rupert Murdoch buys *The Times* of London
Turkish gunman wounds Pope John Paul II in assassination attempt
U.S. gunman wounds President Reagan in assassination attempt
President Sadat of Egypt assassinated
Nobel Prize for literature awarded to Elias Canetti
Spark's *Loitering with Intent*

1982 Britain drives Argentina's invasion force out of the Falkland Islands
U.S. space shuttle makes first successful trip
Yuri Andropov becomes general secretary of the Central Committee of the Soviet Communist party
Israel invades Lebanon
First artificial heart implanted at Salt Lake City hospital
Bellow's *The Dean's December*
Greene's *Monsignor Quixote*

1983 South Korean airliner with 269 aboard shot down after straying into Soviet airspace
U.S. forces invade Grenada following left-wing coup
Widespread protests erupt over placement of nuclear missiles in Europe
The ?1 coin comes into circulation in Britain
Australia wins the America's Cup
Nobel Prize for literature awarded to William Golding
Hughes's *River*
Murdoch's *The Philosopher's Pupil*

1984 Konstantin Chernenko becomes general secretary of the Central Committee of the Soviet Communist party
Prime Minister Indira Gandhi of India assassinated by Sikh bodyguards
Reagan reelected president of the United States
Toxic gas leak at Bhopal, India, plant kills 2,000
British miners go on strike
Irish Republican Army attempts to kill Prime Minister Thatcher with bomb detonated at a Brighton hotel
World Court holds against U.S. mining of Nicaraguan harbors
Golding's *The Paper Men*
Lessing's *The Diary of Jane Somers*
Spark's *The Only Problem*

1985 United States deploys cruise missiles in Europe
Mikhail Gorbachev becomes general secretary of the Soviet Communist party following death of Konstantin Chernenko
Riots break out in Handsworth district (Birmingham) and Brixton
Republic of Ireland gains consultative role in Northern Ireland
State of emergency is declared in South Africa
Nobel Prize for literature awarded to Claude Simon
A. N. Wilson's *Gentlemen in England*
Lessing's *The Good Terrorist*
Murdoch's *The Good Apprentice*
Fowles's *A Maggot*
Death of Philip Larkin

1986 U.S. space shuttle *Challenger* explodes
United States attacks Libya
Atomic power plant at Chernobyl destroyed in accident
Corazon Aquino becomes president of the Philippines
Giotto spacecraft encounters Comet Halley
Nobel Prize for literature awarded to Wole Soyinka
Final volume of *Oxford English Dictionary* supplement published
Amis's *The Old Devils*
Ishiguro's *An Artist of the Floating World*
A. N. Wilson's *Love Unknown*
Powell's *The Fisher King*
Death of Henry Reed

CHRONOLOGY

1987 Gorbachev begins reform of Communist party of the Soviet Union
Stock market collapses
Iran-contra affair reveals that Reagan administration used money from arms sales to Iran to fund Nicaraguan rebels
Palestinian uprising begins in Israeli-occupied territories
Nobel Prize for literature awarded to Joseph Brodsky
Golding's *Close Quarters*
Burgess's *Little Wilson and Big God*
Drabble's *The Radiant Way*

1988 Soviet Union begins withdrawing troops from Afghanistan
Iranian airliner shot down by U.S. Navy over Persian Gulf
War between Iran and Iraq ends
George Bush elected president of the United States
Pan American flight 103 destroyed over Lockerbie, Scotland
Nobel Prize for literature awarded to Naguib Mafouz
Greene's *The Captain and the Enemy*
Amis's *Difficulties with Girls*
Rushdie's *Satanic Verses*

1989 Ayatollah Khomeini pronounces death sentence on Salman Rushdie; Great Britain and Iran sever diplomatic relations
F. W. de Klerk becomes president of South Africa
Chinese government crushes student demonstration in Tiananmen Square
Communist regimes are weakened or abolished in Poland, Czechoslovakia, Hungary, East Germany, and Romania
Lithuania nullifies its inclusion in Soviet Union
Nobel Prize for literature awarded to José Cela
Second edition of *Oxford English Dictionary* published
Drabble's *A Natural Curiosity*
Murdoch's *The Message to the Planet*
Amis's *London Fields*
Ishiguro's *The Remains of the Day*
Death of Bruce Chatwin

1990 Communist monopoly ends in Bulgaria
Riots break out against community charge in England
First women ordained priests in Church of England
Civil war breaks out in Yugoslavia; Croatia and Slovenia declare independence
Bush and Gorbachev sign START agreement to reduce nuclear-weapons arsenals
President Jean-Baptiste Aristide overthrown by military in Haiti
Boris Yeltsin elected president of Russia
Dissolution of the Soviet Union
Nobel Prize for literature awarded to Nadine Gordimer
Death of Lawrence Durrell

1992 U.N. Conference on Environment and Development (the "Earth Summit") meets in Rio de Janeiro
Prince and Princess of Wales separate
War in Bosnia-Herzegovina intensifies
Bill Clinton elected president of the United States in three-way race with Bush and independent candidate H. Ross Perot
Nobel Prize for literature awarded to Derek Walcott
Death of Ruth Pitter
Death of Rosemary Sutcliff

1993 Czechoslovakia divides into the Czech Republic and Slovakia; playwright Vaclav Havel elected president of the Czech Republic
Britain ratifies Treaty on European Union (the "Maastricht Treaty")
U.S. troops provide humanitarian aid amid famine in Somalia
United States, Canada, and Mexico sign North American Free Trade Agreement
Nobel Prize for literature awarded to Toni Morrison

l

CHRONOLOGY

1994   Nelson Mandela elected president in South Africa's first post-apartheid election
Jean-Baptiste Aristide restored to presidency of Haiti
Clinton health care reforms rejected by Congress
Civil war in Rwanda
Republicans win control of both houses of Congress for first time in forty years
Prime Minister Albert Reynolds of Ireland meets with Gerry Adams, president of Sinn Fein
Nobel Prize for literature awarded to Kenzaburo Õe
Amis's *You Can't Do Both*
Naipaul's *A Way in the World*
Death of Dennis Potter
Death of **John Wain**

1995   Britain and Irish Republican Army engage in diplomatic talks
Barings Bank forced into bankruptcy as a result of a maverick bond trader's losses
United States restores full diplomatic relations with Vietnam
NATO initiates air strikes in Bosnia
Death of Stephen Spender
Israeli Prime Minister Yitzhak Rabin assassinated
Nobel Prize for literature awarded to Seamus Heaney

1996   IRA breaks cease-fire; Sein Fein representatives barred from Northern Ireland peace talks
Prince and Princess of Wales divorce
Cease-fire agreement in Chechnia; Russian forces begin to withdraw
Boris Yeltsin reelected president of Russia
Bill Clinton reelected president of the United States
Nobel Prize for literature awarded to Wislawa Szymborska
Death of Caroline Blackwood

1996   British government destroys around 100,000 cows suspected of infection with Creutzfeldt-Jakob, or "mad cow" disease

1997   Diana, Princess of Wales, dies in an automobile accident
Unveiling of first fully-cloned adult animal, a sheep named Dolly
Booker McConnell Prize for fiction awarded to Arundhati Roy

1998   United States renews bombing of Bagdad, Iraq
Independent legislature and Parliaments return to Scotland and Wales
Booker McConnell Prize for fiction awarded to Ian McEwan
Nobel Prize for literature awarded to Jose Saramago

1999   King Hussein of Jordan dies
United Nations responds militarily to Serbian President Slobodan Milosevic's escalation of crisis in Kosovo
Booker McConnell Prize for fiction awarded to J. M. Coetzee
Nobel Prize for literature awarded to Günter Grass
Deaths of Patricia Beer, Ted Hughes, Brian Moore, and Iain Chrichton Smith

2000   Penelope Fitzgerald dies
J. K. Rowling's *Harry Potter and the Goblet of Fire* sells more than 300,000 copies in its first day
Oil blockades by fuel haulers protesting high oil taxes bring much of Britain to a standstill
Slobodan Milosevic loses Serbian general election to Vojislav Kostunica
Death of Scotland's First Minister, Donald Dewar
Nobel Prize for literature awarded to Gao Xingjian
Booker McConnell Prize for fiction awarded to Margaret Atwood
George W. Bush, son of former president George Bush, becomes president of the United States after Supreme Court halts recount of closest election in history
Death of former Canadian Prime Minister Pierre Elliot Trudeau
Human Genome Project researchers announce that they have a complete

CHRONOLOGY

map of the genetic code of a human chromosome

Vladimir Putin succeeds Boris Yeltsin as president of Russia

British Prime Minister Tony Blair's son Leo is born, making him the first child born to a sitting prime minister in 152 years

Death of Patrick O'Brian Keith Roberts and R.S. Thomas

2001 In Britain, the House of Lords passes legislation that legalizes the creation of cloned human embryos

British Prime Minister Tony Blair wins second term

Margaret Atwood's *The Blind Assassin* wins Booker McConnell Prize for fiction

Kazuo Ishiguro's *When We Were Orphans*

Trezza Azzopardi's *The Hiding Place*

Terrorists attack World Trade Center and Pentagon with hijacked airplanes, resulting in the collapse of the World Trade Center towers and the deaths of thousands. Passengers of a third hijacked plane thwart hijackers, resulting in a crash landing in Pennsylvania. The attacks are thought to be organized by Osama bin Laden, the leader of an international terrorist network known as al Qaeda

Ian McEwan's *An Atonement*

Salman Rushdie's *Fury*

Peter Carey's *True History of the Kelly Gang*

Deaths of Eudora Welty and W. G. Sebald

2002 Former U.S. President Jimmy Carter awarded the Nobel Peace Prize

Europe experiences its worst floods in 100 years as floodwaters force thousands of people out of their homes

Wall Street Journal reporter Daniel Pearl kidnapped and killed in Karachi, Pakistan while researching a story about Pakistani militants and suspected shoe bomber Richard Reid. British-born Islamic militant Ahmad Omar Saeed Sheikh sentenced to death for the crime. Three accomplices receive life sentences.

Slobodan Milosevic goes on trial at the U.N. war crimes tribunal in The Hague on charges of masterminding ethnic cleansing in the former Yugoslavia.

Yann Martel's *Life of Pi* wins Booker McConnell Prize for fiction

Nobel Prize for literature awarded to Imre Kertész

2003 Ariel Sharon elected as Israeli prime minister

Venezuelan President Hugo Chavez forced to leave office after a nine week general strike calling for his resignation ends

U.S. presents to the United Nations its Iraq war rationale, citing its Weapons of Mass Destruction as imminent threat to world security

U.S. and Britain launch war against Iraq

Baghdad falls to U.S. troops

Official end to combat operations in Iraq is declared by the U.S.

Aung San Suu Kyi, Burmese opposition leader, placed under house arrest by military regime

NATO assumes control of peacekeeping force in Afghanistan

American troops capture Saddam Hussein

J.K. Rowling's *Harry Potter and the Order of the Phoenix*, the fifth installment in the wildly popular series, hit the shelves and rocketed up the best-seller lists

Nobel Prize for literature awarded to J. M. Coetzee

Death of C. H. Sisson

2004 NATO admits seven new members—Bulgaria, Estonia, Latvia, Lithuania, Romania, Slovakia, and Slovenia

Terrorists bomb commuter trains in Spain—al–Qaeda claims responsibility

Ten new states join the European Union, expanding it to twenty–five

CHRONOLOGY

members states total

Muslim terrorists attack a school in Beslan, Russia, resulting in over 300 civilian deaths, many of them schoolchildren

George W. Bush is re-elected president of the United States

Allegations of corruption in the election of Ukraine's Viktor Yanukovych result in the “Orange Revolution" and Parliament's decision to nullify the first election results— the secondary run-off election is closley monitored and favors Viktor Yushchenko for president

A massive 9.0 earthquake rocks the Indian Ocean, resulting in a catastrophic tsunami, devastating southern Asia and eastern Africa and killing tens of thousands of people

Alan Hollinghurst's *The Line of Beauty* wins Man Booker Prize for fiction

Death of Thom Gunn

2005 Terrorists bomb three subway stations in London, killing 52 and injuring more than 700

Pope John Paul II dies, marking the end of an era for the Roman Catholic Church. He is succeeded by Pope Benedict XVI

Hurricane Katrina hits the U.S. Golf Coast, devastating cities in Louisianna and Mississippi, and killing over 1,000 people.

J.K. Rowling's *Harry Potter and the Half-Blood Prince* sells over 6.9 billion copies on the first day of release in the U.S. alone

Nobel Prize for literature awarded to Harold Pinter

Deaths of Saul Bellow and Arthur Miller

2006 Former Iraqi President Saddam Hussein is found guilty for crimes against humanity and is executed in Iraq

Ban Ki-moon elected the next UN secretary-general

International Astronomical Union rules that Pluto is no longer seen as a planet

Fleur Adcock wins the Queen's Gold Medal for Poetry

Kamau Brathwaite wins the Griffin Poetry Prize for *Born to Slow Horses*

2007 Oil prices skyrocket as a barrel of crude oil tops ninety dollars

Record-high mortgage foreclosures and a steep decline in the housing market strain financial industries causing multibillion-dollar losses at major banks and investment firms

Seung-Hui Cho opens fire at Virginia Tech University killing 32 and wounding several others before turning the gun on himself

The final volume of J.K. Rowling's *Harry Potter* series, *Harry Potter and the Deathly Hallows*, is released selling over 8.3 million copies in the first twenty-four hours

Nobel Prize for literature awarded to Doris Lessing

2008 Barack Obama is elected the first African-American President of the United States

A 7.9 magnitude earthquake strikes the Sichaun region of China, leaving 4.8 million homeless and over 68,000 dead

Fidel Castro resigns as President of Cuba after a record-breaking 49 years as head of state

Georgia launches a military strike against the defected region of South Ossetia, sparking the start of the short-lived South Ossetia War

2009 United States President Barack Obama orders the closure of all secret prisons and detention camps operated by the CIA, including the Guantánamo Bay facility in Cuba

The World Health Organization declares a flu pandemic of the H1N1 virus, following an initial outbreak of the illness in Mexico

Carol Ann Duffy is the first woman appointed poet laureate of the United Kingdom

Mahmoud Ahmadinejad is confirmed as the winner of a second term as

CHRONOLOGY

president of Afghanistan, following accusations of ballot tampering and other forms of election fraud

Nobel Prize for literature awarded to Herta Müller

2010 Fighting intensifies in Afghanistan, measured by escalating numbers of foreign troops on Afghan soil, multi-country offensives on Afghan cities that are the largest since fighting began in 2001, the capture of the Taliban's top military commander in Karachi, and continued high numbers of civilian deaths in bombings and air strikes intended to target insurgents.

An earthquake of 7.0 magnitude devastates Haiti, killing more than 230,000 people and leaving the capital Port-au-Prince in ruins.

An earthquake in Chile has a magnitude of 8.8, one of the strongest ever measured, but infrastructure holds up sufficiently for recovery relative to the size of the shock, and deaths number fewer than 1,000

Google halts its China search engine, announcing that the company will no longer censor search results as required by Chinese law, and the Chinese government retaliates by enacting a national ban on all Google services.

Deaths of J.D. Salinger and Dick Francis.

List of Contributors

CHARLES ROBERT BAKER. Charles Robert Baker has worked for Bridwell Library at Southern Methodist University for the past twenty-one years. He is the author of dozens of the essays found in *British Writers, American Writers, American Writers Classics* and the *Oxford Encyclopedia of American Literature*. His current projects include a novel set in mid-nineteenth century England and France. **J.K. Rowling**

DRUANN BAUER. Druann Bauer is an Assistant Professor of English at Ohio Northern University where she teaches Restoration/Eighteenth-Century literature and the Romantics. She is currently revising her critical editions of Hannah Cowley's three most popular plays, *The Belle's Stratagem, The Runaway,* and *Who's the Dupe?* Bauer's research is primarily centered around Cowley, but in 2009, she began compiling an annotated bibliography on all secondary research conducted on vampires since Bram Stoker penned *Dracula* in 1897. She earned her Ph.D. in Eighteenth-Century British Literature from the University of Louisiana-Lafayette. **Hannah Cowley**

JANE BEAL. Jane Beal earned her M.A. from Sonoma State University, and a Ph.D. in English literature with specializations in medieval literature, classical mythology, and the literature of the Bible from the University of California–Davis. She is the author of three collections of poetry, as well as numerous works of literary criticsm. She is currently editing the essay collection *Illuminating Moses: A History of Reception,* and is also at work on the academic title *Interpreting Pearl*. **Elizabeth I, Queen of England**

FRED BILSON. Fred Bilson holds B.A. degrees in Philosophy and English and a Masters in Science. He has taught English, Linguistics and Computer Studies at University level, and is researching the phonological structure of Chinese. **Henry Mayhew**

SANDIE BYRNE. Former Fellow and Tutor in English at Balliol College, Oxford. Her publications include a number of articles and books on eighteenth and nineteenth-century fiction and twentieth-century poetry. **Charles Kingsley**

TYLER HOFFMAN. Tyler Hoffman is Associate Professor of English and Associate Dean of the College of Arts and Sciences at Rutgers University–Camden. He has published two books—*Robert Frost and the Politics of Poetry* and *Teaching with The Norton Anthology of Poetry: A Guide for Instructors*—and is completing work on a book on the history and theory of public performance poetry in the U.S. He has published articles on American Civil War poetry, Walt Whitman, Emily Dickinson, Vachel Lindsay, Robert Frost, Wallace Stevens, Elizabeth Bishop, Gary Snyder, Thom Gunn, and the contemporary slam poetry scene. **Lascelles Abercrombie**

BRIAN HOYLE. Brian Hoyle is a lecturer in English and Film Studies at the University of Dundee. He has published articles on a variety of film related topics, including literary adaptation, however, his main area of research is Post-War British Art Cinema. He is currently writing a book on John Boorman and researching one on the composer biopics of Ken Russell. **Ron Butlin**

BENJAMIN IVRY. Benjamin Ivry is the author of biographies of Arthur Rimbaud, Maurice Ravel, and Francis Poulenc. He has translated many books from the French, by authors including André Gide, Jules Verne, and Balthus. His poetry collection, *Paradise for the Portuguese Queen,* appeared in 1998. **Thomas Campion**

ADAM KOMISARUK. Adam Komisaruk is Associate Professor of English at West Virginia University. He studies the literary and cultural history of eighteenth- and nineteenth-century Britain, focusing on attitudes toward sexuality. He has written on William Blake, Lord Byron, "Monk" Lewis, Thomas Rowlandson, Mary Shelley and Mary Wollstonecraft. Among his works in progress is a critical edition of Erasmus Darwin's *Botanic Garden*. **Erasmus Darwin**

ABBY MIMS. Abby Mims has an MFA from University of Californa–Irvine. Her fiction and essays have been featured in *The Santa Monica Review, Other Voices, Swink* and various anthologies. She is currently at work on a collection of essays and a novel. **Rosemary Sutcliff**

HELENA NELSON. Helena Nelson is a lecturer in English and communication at Adam Smith College, Fife. She is the editor and originator of the independent poetry imprint Happen*Stance* Press, and a poetry reviewer

lv

LIST OF CONTRIBUTORS

for several UK magazines. Her poetry collections include *Mr & Mrs Philpott on Holiday at Auchterawe, Starlight on Water,* and *Unsuitable Poems.* **William Soutar**

SAYANTI GANGULY PUCKETT. Sayanti Ganguly Puckett received her doctorate in seventeenth–century British literature and nineteenth–century colonial Indian literature from Oklahoma State University in 2009. She is an assistant professor at Johnson County Community College, and is currently working on a book on the libertine "babus" in nineteenth–century colonial Calcutta. **Catharine Trotter**

DALE SALWAK. Dale Salwak is Professor of English at southern California's Citrus College and a recipient of Purdue University's Distinguished Alumni Award as well as a National Defense Education Act fellowship from the University of Southern California, where he earned his Ph.D. He is the author of numerous books, including *Kingsley Amis: Modern Novelist* and *Teaching Life: Letters From a Life in Literature,* and the editor of *The Wonders of Solitude, Anne Tyler as Novelist, Philip Larkin: The Man and His Work, A Passion for Books,* and *The Life and Work of Barbara Pym.* **John Wain**

CHARLIE SAMUELSON. Charlie Samuelson received his MA in English literature from the University of Cambridge, and completed his undergraduate study of English and French literature at Amherst College. He holds a degree from L'École Normale Supérieure in Paris, and has also attended the Universités de Paris IV and VIII. He lives and works in Boston. **William Boyd**

ROBERT SULLIVAN. Robert Sullivan is Visiting Professor of Literary Studies at the University of Mostar, BiH. He was born in Ireland and educated at universities in the United Kingdom and the United States. He has taught literature in England, Africa, and the U.S., and has been awarded three Fulbright grants to teach in Croatia and Montenegro. He has published two books and numerous essays on literary matters. **Patrick Hamilton**

TIMOTHY UNDERHILL. Timothy Underhill works in the international education division of Cambridge Assessment, a department of the University of Cambridge. He read English at Pembroke College Cambridge, and earned his Ph.D. in 2002 for his research on John Byrom. He is preparing an edition of Byrom's writing and related studies on Byrom and his milieu and on eighteenth-century shorthand and early-modern English palaeography. **John Byrom**

CHRISTOPHER VILMAR. Christopher Vilmar is Assistant Professor of English at Salisbury University. He teaches widely in British literature and culture from the medieval period to the eighteenth century. He has written on Samuel Johnson, John Arbuthnot, and Charlotte Lennox, and his current research interests include satire, philology, political writing, and the novel during the eighteenth century. **John Arbuthnot**

LES WILKINSON. Les Wilkinson is Senior Master at Nottingham High School, England, where he has taught English for more than thirty years and where he has directed a number of major dramatic productions, including his own recent translation of Pirandello's *Sei Personaggi in Cerca d'Autore.* His became interested in Scottish literature at St Andrews University where he studied in the early seventies. He writes occasionally and continues to perform traditional and modern folk music and song. **Andrew Greig**

BRITISH WRITERS

LASCELLES ABERCROMBIE

(1881—1938)

Tyler Hoffman

LASCELLES ABERCROMBIE WAS one of the most prominent of the Georgian poets and playwrights of the second decade of the twentieth century, becoming in his later years a respected literary critic. His poetry, like that of William Wordsworth, whose work he discussed in lectures in the 1930s (these lectures were collected and published by his son posthumously in 1952 as *The Art of Wordsworth*), sought to bring the poet's language nearer to the actual language of day-to-day speech. Perhaps fittingly, his greatest poetic output and success was not in the lyric mode but in the dramatic form, where character is king. Throughout his career, Abercrombie did not shrink from indelicate subject matter, bringing a realism to his artistic project even as he conveyed a sense of the spiritual and emotional value of reality. In revolt against Victorian sentimentality and fin-de-siècle aestheticism, he committed himself to the project of finding nobility, humor, and pathos in the circumstances of ordinary people as they struggle through life. Even as he broke with the traditions of certain literary canons as a result of his modern sensibilities, he insisted on the vital force of tradition, crafting much of his poetry and drama in blank verse, a medium that he felt combined effectively the flexibility of speech-rhythm with the formality of metrical pattern.

Lascelles (the name rhymes with "tassels") Abercrombie was born on January 9, 1881, to an aristocratic family outside Manchester, in Ashton upon Mersey, Cheshire, England. He was the eighth of nine children of William Abercrombie, a stockbroker, and Sarah Ann Heron Abercrombie. He first attended Malvern College in Worcestershire, and in 1900 he enrolled at Owens College, Manchester, to study chemistry, but he was forced to leave school after just two years due to financial setbacks suffered by his family as a result of the Boer War. As a young man seeking to earn a living, he worked briefly as a surveyor and then as a senior journalist and book reviewer) for the *Liverpool Courier,* the *Daily News,* and the *Manchester Guardian.* Abercrombie married Catherine Gwatkin, a Liverpool art student, in 1909, and his relationship with her opened doors for the aspiring poet. Through her, he met Goldsworthy Lowes Dickinson, a scholar at Cambridge, who helped him get his poems and "interludes," or short plays, published in the *Independent Review* and the *Nation.*

EARLY INTERLUDES AND POEMS

One of the interludes published in the *Independent Review,* "Blind" (1907), the first of his poems to be published in a well-known London periodical, captures Abercrombie's early interest in country folk who find themselves in exigent circumstances and react passionately to those circumstances. In the poem an old beggar woman raises her "simple" blind son with one object: when they meet the father who deserted her before the child was born, the son must strangle him. When they finally come across the father, a tramp himself, the mother's love for him is rekindled, but the boy goes into action, killing the father tragically; the mother subsequently is consumed with guilt. "Blind" is a gothic tour de force, an expressive dramatic dialogue in blank verse that predicts a major strain in Abercrombie's work—the intensive examination of marginalized human subjects, who acutely suffer psychological, emotional, and physical distress.

"Blind" was included in Abercrombie's first book of verse, which was issued in 1908 under the title *Interludes and Poems* by the publisher John Lane. In other poems included there, Abercrombie further commits to a dialogic form. "Soul and Body" (first published in the *Nation* on November 30, 1907) stages a conversation between those two entities, with Body reminiscing about the raptures they have experienced together and Soul yearning for a transcendent joy, proclaiming finally the value of "ecstasy," which in later writing Abercrombie would define as a fullness in the consciousness of one's self ("Being supremely and superbly knowing itself for Being" [*The Function of Poetry in the Drama*, p. 115]) and what here is framed as inhabiting a state where there is "no more saying 'I am I'" (*The Poems of Lascelles Abercrombie*, p. 4). The book contains four other metaphysical dialogues: "The New God: A Miracle," "The Fool's Adventure," "An Escape," and "Peregrinus." The interlude "The New God" pictures a newly converted Christian princess, Margaret, who refuses an arranged marriage to a pagan prince. The prince is entranced by her beauty ("your use is to turn mankind from gods, / I Yet must love you" (p. 31), and the princess wants nothing more than to be rid of her beauty and the lust it invokes, praying to God to "Sluice on my beauty shame, and ugly scalds" (p. 34). In the end, God, in a speaking part, answers her prayers, telling Margaret that henceforth she "shalt appear as God, and the glory of God" (p. 35): when the king attempts to facilitate the prince's seduction of his daughter, the two men are reduced to nothingness as the princess' chastity is secured. Abercrombie's philosophical idealism on display in the book led one reviewer, his friend the Georgian poet Edward Thomas, to proclaim the poems "too metaphysical" but at the same time as exhibiting "a wonderful variety" (Thomas, p. 158) in their blank verse. In his Nietzsche-influenced prose published a few years later, *Speculative Dialogues* (1913), Abercrombie continues in this dialectical-metaphysical vein, imagining conversations occurring between such allegorical figures as Famine and Pestilence, Lust and Love, and Time and Eternity.

In 1912, Abercrombie published another collection of poems, *Emblems of Love* (1912), which he thought of as "a book of interludes all dealing from various points of view with Love," one that amounted to a "Treatise of Love" (p. 23). It is divided into three parts representing the progression of secular love: "Discovery and Prophecy"; "Imperfection"; and "Virginity and Perfection." In the opening lyric, "Hymn to Love," he expresses the futility of living without the significance of love. A dramatic poem of five acts, "Vashti" (in "Discovery and Prophesy") features the Persian king Ahaseurus, who replaces Vashti with Esther for refusing to show off her beauty in the banquet hall of the palace; it stands as an example of "sensual, selfish imperfect love" (p. 23) and is in a supple blank verse that captures the vitality of speech. Vashti understands the ways in which women exist for men's enjoyment, as a means to satisfy their lusts:

man
Hath forged in his furnace of desire our beauty
Into that chain of law which binds our lives—
Man, please thyself, and woman, please thou man
(*The Poems of Lascelles Abercrombie*, pp. 157–158)

Her noble resistance to male violence and domination leads to her banishment from the palace, and in her exile she is shown visions by the goddess Ishtar of women through history who mark the progression of woman from loved to love: Helen, Sappho, and finally Theresa, God's bride. In the second part of the book ("instances of how love works on different natures, and some of love's over-growths and mis-shaped growths," as Abercrombie described it) (Thomas, p. 23). Mary in "Mary: A Legend of the '45" (set during the 1745 Second Jacobite Rebellion) experiences love at first sight when she gazes on a rebel's severed head set on a spike at the Scottish Gate at Carlisle. The macabre situation predicts some of the grotesque scenes of suffering in Abercrombie's later work and reveals his ability to imagine the complex inner life of characters different from himself, most especially women. The third part of *Emblems of Love*, which takes on a more mystical cast, culminates in "The Eternal Wedding," a perfection of human love where sexual and spiritual are fused through a "conversation" between "He" and "She."

Abercrombie and his wife moved to the hamlet of Ryton near the village of Dymock in Gloucestershire in 1911, and it was from that rural retreat that he finished work on *Emblems of Love;* it was also where he entered into some of the most important friendships and professional associations of his life. His cottage was called "The Gallows." He resided near the homes of the poets Wilfrid Gibson, Edward Thomas, and, for a time, Robert Frost, who came to England in 1913 and moved his family to Ledington just north of Dymock the following year. While living in Ryton, Abercrombie was thoroughly engaged in literary politics and began to be known as one of the "Georgian" poets. The term "Georgian" was coined by Edward Marsh, a patron of the arts and a classical scholar and translator, in 1912 to describe the new literary sensibility that was emerging in that decade, although he and others took pains to disavow it as a "movement." Rather, it was held that the poets under that banner, in loose confederation, were committed to certain ideals and a thoroughly modern temper (as Abercrombie saw it, "What with modern science, modern philosophy, modern religion, modern politics, and modern business, the present is a time fermenting with tremendous change; the most tremendous of all changes, a change in the idealistic interpretation of the universe" [quoted in Ross, p. 16]). The label, in honor of the reigning monarch at the time, George V, who was crowned in 1910, was intended to signal a clear break from the previous Victorian and Edwardian eras and their romantic arts. Abercrombie's work appeared in all four of Edward Marsh's flagship *Georgian Poetry* anthologies published by Harold Monro.

EARLY PLAYS AND IDYLLS

In his three-act poetic drama *Deborah* (1912), Abercrombie starts down the road of an unwavering realism, setting his action in a fishing village against which the characters explode passionately, and with tragic results. The critic Louis Untermeyer praised the play for its unstinting "unliterary" quality, comparing Abercrombie to the Irish playwright J. M. Synge, who observed that "in a good play every speech should be as fully flavored as a nut or apple, and such speeches cannot be written by any one who works among people who have shut their lips on poetry." (Abercrombie admired Synge for certain effects, but he accused both William Butler Yeats and Synge of creating "shadowy, insubstantial and delicate and only half-human" dramas [quoted in Untermeyer, p. 357]). As with others of Abercrombie's plays, the characters in *Deborah* are dealing with traumatic experience; they are imperfect and halting. In particular, the villagers are suffering from an epidemic of cholera and are waiting for a doctor to come by boat with the skill required to save the lives of their loved ones. Some believe that the pestilence is a plague sent by God as judgment for their sinfulness, that God is "merciless and angry" (*The Poems of Lascelles Abercrombie,* p. 459) against them. They see that the environmental conditions of the village have allowed the epidemic to take hold and that their vulnerable position is as a result of their class position, with one of the townspeople saying that only "nobles" can afford to build houses where sickness and disease do not thrive; however, "there's never choosing for us folks" (p. 456), who must live near their trade. The title character, Deborah, observes that "for us, with lives so hazardous, to love / Is like a poor girl's game of being a queen" (p. 457), and she pleads with her neighbors to allow the doctor to attend to her lover David first when he arrives. Saul refuses and hauls the doctor out of the boat bodily, proceeding to lock him up in his house in an attempt to save his dying boy, Barnaby. When David dies, Deborah seeks revenge on Saul, calling him a murderer; she soon discovers him dead from cholera.

Act 2 opens on a scene in the future, with Barnaby grown into a young man; he has been raised by Deborah, who saved him from the malicious intent of the other villagers, who blamed him for the fact that the doctor was kept from saving their loved ones. Deborah has been saved by Barnaby's presence in her life, and she has encouraged the courtship of Miriam, David's sister, by Barnaby. When Barnaby is about to leave to go to sea, he tells Deborah that he has no intention of returning, as he finds the village too stifling. Miriam refuses to tell him that she is pregnant. In the third act Miriam has delivered a stillborn son and believes the wind howling outside Deborah's cottage is the sound of the Gabriel Hounds hunting after her unchristened baby's soul. Barnaby then returns after a shipwreck and near starvation, but Deborah tells him that he is not welcome, and she blames herself for ruining Miriam's life by stoking her love for Barnaby and thus bringing on her present state of madness. In the end, Miriam, haunted by her fear for her baby's soul, races out the door and into sure death in the flooded marsh; Deborah runs after her, doubtless to meet the same tragic fate. Although Abercrombie's realism is tinged with melodrama, the characters that he represents—in particular the title character—are psychologically nuanced and natural, and significantly shaped by the poet's acute class consciousness; the emotional crises that they experience are portrayed honestly and in a language that fully captures their pain.

In his 1912 critical study of Thomas Hardy (his first published work of literary criticism), Abercrombie reveals something of his own method of characterization, as he reflects on the fact that Hardy's characters

> have in them some weakness, disability, inherited instinct, or perhaps some error in the assertion of their strength, which inevitably becomes the chance for the power of the world finally to assert itself against them. This is more pathetic, because more natural, than any tragic interference from the outside; but Hardy always knows how to mitigate it by an exquisite tenderness, a justice of mercy, towards his own creations.
>
> (p. 31)

He admires Hardy's "great psychological imagination" and his humor, "altogether a property of his rustics" (pp. 33, 46), qualities that lie at the heart of some of the best of Abercrombie's dramatic productions for the page and the stage.

In fiction such writers as Arnold Bennett, John Galsworthy, and H. G. Wells already had made the decision to take a "realist" route, much to the chagrin of Virginia Woolf, who in her essay "Modern Fiction" dubs these writers "materialists," by which she means that "they write of unimportant things; that they spend immense skill and immense industry making the trivial and the transitory appear the true and the enduring" (p. 148). As she argued, they believe in realism for its own sake. Woolf praised Thomas Hardy in particular for giving us not merely a transcript of life but a whole vision of the world and the human lot in it, filtered through the poetic imagination. His, she felt, was realism with a spiritual cast. In much the same way, Abercrombie's dramatic poetry and poetic drama deal with characters as they actually exist, in their rustic and often grotesque milieu, and who achieve symbolic significance. In defiance of romanticism (which Abercrombie decried in some of the poetry of Alfred, Lord Tennyson), he refuses subjects who have been cleansed of the world, somehow abstracted from it, as pure models of heroism; instead, he finds that real life is just as noble—or can be—as any romantic refinement of it. Abercrombie took as his mission to bring an artistic sincerity to the portrayal of contemporary life—even to the disagreeable, brutal facts that are part of that life. As Wilfrid Gibson observed, when Abercrombie "tackles an uncompromisingly realistic theme, he manages to illuminate it with a supernal radiance" (Gibson, p. 212).

Abercrombie preferred drama to fiction, and he was responding in part to the publisher Harold Monro's exhortation of poets of his age to "write us plays, simple, direct, dependent for their beauty, not on outward decoration, but on inward force of the spirit that conceives them." But what form should these plays take? There was prose, but not for Abercrombie. In his article "The Function of Poetry in the Drama" in Monro's *Poetry Review* in March 1912, he mounted a spirited polemical defense of verse drama. Abercrombie argues that the metrical language that characters in verse drama speak is an exaggerated form of language, but one that is perfectly consistent with, indeed natural to, the presentation of heightened, or exaggerated, personality in drama; it is, he claims, a matter of the "exhibition of life intensified, life supposed at a higher pressure than actuality" (p. 109). The fault of the prose play, he finds, is that it seeks merely to imitate life; whereas in a verse drama, while there is imitation so as to keep the experience being staged credible, there is a larger business involved, that of expressing the emotional reality, the "innermost" reality. Verse drama "seeks to imitate in you the *effect* which would be produced if you perceived with certainty and clarity the grand emotional impulse driving all existence," he says (Gibson, p. 112) and the verbal process of that drama—the use of figurative speech and meter—"is inescapably recognizable as *symbolic* of the emotional reality of life" (p. 112). While a prose drama keeps to the imitation of a surface (or material) reality, then, a verse drama penetrates to the spiritual core of existence. Abercrombie's praise of the plays of his fellow Georgians John Drinkwater and Gordon Bottomley echo these sentiments. He commends Drinkwater for his "symbolic method of drama" his synthesis of symbolism and realism, and noted of Bottomley's 1910 play *The Riding to Lithend* that it is admirably shaped not "according to nature, but according to the curves of beauty, into a symbol of life infinitely more powerful than any actuality could do" (quoted in Fisher, p. 297). Abercrombie was critical of the commercial theater of his day, finding it to be sentimental and to involve a merely factual treatment of contemporary social issues, what he termed "naturalism."

In keeping with his realist attitude, Abercrombie's work abandons Victorian rhetoric and other linguistic ornament: he adopts rather a colloquial diction, one that is far from the precincts of the traditionally "poetic" in line with a poetry that steadfastly avoids traditionally poetic subject matter. In February 1914, Abercrombie published a pamphlet titled *Poetry and Contemporary Speech* in which he insists on the importance of a poet's diction, the "magic" a poet can work with "the secondary suggestive power of words" (pp. 3–4). He notes that the poetry of the Elizabethan era was so vital because it "was so intimately in touch with common *speech*" unafraid of the slang of its time; as he finds, "the original element of poetic expression is the *spoken word*" (p. 7.). He would have agreed with the modernist poet Ezra Pound, who famously said that the new poetry must be "direct, free from emotional slither" and employ a sparer, more vivid language without endless adjectives. Pound did not see the two poets as being on the same page, though, and he disparaged Abercrombie publicly for his view that poetry should return to a Wordsworthian simplicity, for his preference for the simple word to the Flaubertian "mot juste." He even went so far as to challenge Abercrombie to a duel. As the story goes, Abercrombie, given choice of weapon, proposed humorously that they pelt each other with unsold copies of their own books. The affair ended in laughter, but Pound did view Abercrombie's call for simplicity as "stupidity." Abercrombie and the Georgian poet Rupert Brooke first became acquainted when Harold Monro asked Brooke in September 1912 to write a defense of Abercrombie's poetry for *Poetry Review* against Pound's attack.

Abercrombie's poetic priorities are expressed clearly in his one-act play *The Sale of Saint Thomas* (1911; he later expanded it with another five acts), which was his contribution to the first issue of *Georgian Poetry* (*Georgian Poetry 1911–1912*). It is a blank-verse drama that stages the fear and uncertainty that Thomas, a runaway slave, has upon being tasked with the job of going to India as a missionary. He worries about the impending sea voyage and its dangers, believing that he is "precious," and therefore should safeguard himself, because Christ resides in him. In the poem Abercrombie does not shrink from the grossness and barbarity of life. The ship's captain paints a scene of the way strangers to India are tortured for the king's pleasure, and he describes in realistic detail the nastiness of the insects that will inflict Thomas on his arrival:

And there be flies in India will drink
Not only blood of bulls, tigers, and bears,
But pierce the river-horses' creasy leather,
Ay, worry crocodiles through their cuirasses
And prick the metal fishes when they bask.
You'll feel them soon, with beaks like sturdy pins,
Treating their stinging thirst with your best blood.

(*The Poems of Lascelles Abercrombie*, p. 119)

Thomas muses that it is "folly" to think that one man can Christianize an entire country, and he does not look forward to such torments of the flesh. Doubting his mission, he tells the ship's captain that he will not make the journey, but at that point Thomas' master appears and tells the captain that Thomas will go on the voyage. Assessing Thomas' carpentry skills, they agree to a price. The final speech of the slave master clarifies the lesson of the poem: that fear is not a deadly sin, but rather prudence is, that one must be willing to take risks and make forays beyond the limit of the self in the service of God and spirit, "search[ing] into the sacred darkness lying / Outside thy knowledge of thyself" (p. 125). Gibson judged *The Sale of Saint Thomas* to be Abercrombie's greatest poem, one that embodies his salient gospel—namely, "that man must endeavour towards the attainment of a conscious realization of the palpable and visible glory of the universe in its integrity, that, in doing so, he may re-create it on the spiritual plane as a celestial palace for the habitation of his soul" (p. 213).

Abercrombie's own review of *Georgian Poetry 1911–1912* in the *Manchester Guardian* (January 6, 1913) contends that the Georgians' break with Victorianism is "in manner as well as matter," and he salutes the Georgian "determination to undertake new duties in the old style," not to be "merely revolutionary" (p. 5). This appeal to tradition represents a fundamental view of the Georgian poets, who, like Frost, were "content with the old-fashioned way to be new" (Frost, p. 741). Marsh fought with D. H. Lawrence about the use of free verse (Marsh was adamantly opposed to it), and Gibson proudly declared that Abercrombie liberated blank verse from "the restrictive and academic devitalization of melodious, but too pedantically precise, Victorian practice" (p. 212). The literary project at hand was the renovation of the tradition, not the wholesale rejection of it. That they were not jettisoning the tradition, Abercrombie explains in the *Guardian,* is seen in the fact that the anthology is dedicated to the poet laureate Robert Bridges, "the man who has kept the classical tradition of English poetry nobly alive and vivid among us" (p. 5). Insisting that the Georgians do not constitute a school or movement, Abercrombie does say that the poetry under that name must be "able to accept the significance of its own time without refusing, or trying to refuse, the unalterable traditional nature of its art" (p. 5). He singles out Gibson's working-class poetry about such matters as unemployment, poverty, illness, and domestic violence for special praise: it is, he observes, a poetry "dealing frankly and uncompromisingly with familiar workaday life, using a language which is charged indeed with the race of common speech, but serenely indifferent to the supposed requirements of customary ornament, effecting the transformation of reality into art" (p. 5).

In June 1914 Abercrombie published a review of Frost's new book, *North of Boston,* in the *Nation,* giving himself an opportunity to expound further on the Georgian aesthetic. In it he discusses at length Frost's theory of "the sound of sense," or intonation, in versification. As Frost explains in his letters to and conversations with Abercrombie, "the sound of sense" is vital in the effort to renew poetry in the modern period. It is not enough to write in meter, although that is, for Frost, a required element: one must skillfully break human tones of voice across a meter both to avoid singsong and to invest the poetry with passionate thoughts and feelings, with humane values and beliefs. Abercrombie praises Frost's poems for "their determination to deal unequivocally with everyday life in New England," for "utilizing the traits and necessities of common life, the habits of common speech, the minds and hearts of common folk" (p. 262). It is clearly his unstinting realism that constitutes a large part of his appeal for Abercrombie, who further contends that Frost "stands out against tradition" on the basis of "a peculiar adaptation ... of the pattern of blank verse" (p. 262), an adaptation that Abercrombie himself undertook. As he finds, Frost's dramatic dialogues and soliloquies sound like talk, and "psychological idylls" like "The Housekeeper," which deals with inherited lunacy, represent the horror that exists in the world. It is not surprising that Abercrombie and others would seek to promote to Marsh the inclusion of Frost in one of the *Georgian Poetry* anthologies, though to no avail, as Marsh insisted that all of the poets appearing there be British. For his part, Frost in letters to friends endorsed in particular *The Sale of Saint Thomas* and *The End of the World,* two of Abercrombie's dramatic works that are like Frost's own in *North of Boston* outgrowths of a vivid psychological imagination.

Abercrombie's blank-verse play *The End of the World,* which first appeared in the second issue of *New Numbers,* a quarterly magazine that featured the work of the Georgians Abercrombie, Gibson, Drinkwater, and Brooke exclusively and lasted just four issues (1914–1915), was featured in the 1915 issue of *Georgian Poetry,* and John Drinkwater produced *The End of the World* for the Birmingham Repertory Theatre's 1914 season (in *The Poems of Lascelles Abercrombie,* pp. 420–449). In it Abercrombie recounts with grim humor the reactions of country people to a rumor of the coming apocalypse. As the first act opens we are in a pub, with two men in heated conversation: Huff, a farmer, is complaining about his lot (a laborer, Shale, has run off with his wife) and is straightaway interrupted by Sollers, a wainwright, who taunts him for always complaining. As they contend, a wandering dowser tells them that a comet visible in the sky is about to collide with the earth; he preys on the gullibility of the whole cast of characters. And we learn all there is to know about these characters as they express themselves in light of the news. Shale returns Mrs. Huff to her husband as if she is nothing to him, so that he will not be tried harshly by God on the day of Judgment. The jealous Huff welcomes the destruction as God's vengeance on Shale and his wife for the harm they have done him ("What else could pay / For all my wrong but a blow of blazing anger / Striking down to shiver the earth, and change / Their strutting wickedness to horror and crying?"; p. 430). Sollers laments the coming cataclysm, since he has spent his life learning a trade and all for nothing, even as the barkeep, Vine, eagerly anticipates it, because his dead wife, whom he did not love, would have enjoyed seeing such a spectacular display and will be denied the chance to see it. For the smith Merrick it turns all of life

meaningless: the end of the world is the "the end of a joke" (p. 438), a terrible joke played by God on all of us. As the play unfolds, Huff finally wonders, "What good has my goodness been to me?" (p. 440) and regrets his lack of daring, the very thing Shale has shown ("he's had a stirring sense of what he is"; p. 441). When Shale returns Mrs. Huff to her husband and then acts to take her back when the end of the world does not occur (it is only one of Huff's hayricks on fire), we get a clear sense of the poet's progressive stance toward women and the gender politics that guides much of his work. Mrs. Huff responds to her ill treatment with rage:

They thinking I'd be near one or the other
After this night! Will I be made no more
Than clay that children puddle to their minds,
Moulding it what they fancy?

(p. 448)

She refuses to be a pawn in a man's game and is perhaps the only character in the comedy who is not subject to our laughter.

Like Frost, Marsh thought highly of the play, calling it "a sublime work," and claiming that "in its fusion of poetry and comedy there has been nothing like it" (quoted in Ross, p. 132). But there was criticism of Abercrombie's play, too, in particular over its unflinching realism. The lines featuring frogs being crushed under cartwheels were, according to D. H. Lawrence, "nasty efforts at cruelty":

When I was young
My mother would catch us frogs and set them down,
Lapt in a screw of paper, in the ruts,
And carts going by would quash 'em; and I'd laugh,
And yet be thinking, "Suppose it was myself
Twisted stiff in huge paper, and wheels
Big as the wall of a barn treading me flat!"

(*The Poems of Lascelles Abercrombie,* p. 432)

Lawrence felt that the violence of the passage was gratuitous, and the spirit of the play "mean and vulgar" (quoted in Ross, p. 130). Of Abercrombie, he speculated that something was "going bad in his soul," that his feelings were "corrupt and dirty": he "is determined above all things not to be sentimental. Not one of his rustics shall show a glimmer of decent feeling; and they … become rigid in their conventional baseness" (p. 130). He objected precisely to Abercrombie's realism, what he regarded as simply realism-for-realism's-sake. In fact, though, Abercrombie allows us to feel deeply for these country folk, and though we may laugh at them at times, we are also encouraged to sympathize with their injuries and with their situation, one that has them questioning the very purpose of life.

In the fourth issue of *New Numbers*, Abercrombie's one-act drama *The Staircase* made its debut, a play that is richly gothic in its realism (in *The Poems of Lascelles Abercrombie*, pp. 383–400). The curtain opens on a man building a new staircase in a run-down house to replace the rotting stairway that his father died falling down. He builds it with the hope that a woman he loves will return home. The woman turns out to be the child of a girl who was forced to leave the house in shame after becoming pregnant. When the woman does return, with a baby in her arms, she is with a lover who is a fugitive from the police for having set a fire and killed a child in the process. The man building the staircase tries to persuade the woman to leave her lover, who is the father of her baby, but she refuses to do so, admitting to being an accomplice to murder and going off with him to jail when the police catch up to them. The man is bewildered at her choice not to stay with him, but the audience can see why she chooses as she does: she has a low opinion of the man who has stayed at home, yearning and never daring anything. As with other plays of this period, Abercrombie praises deeds of bravery and decision that make life worth having lived.

The flawed characters of *The Staircase* find their match in *The Adder* (in *The Poems of Lascelles Abercrombie,* pp. 365–382), a verse drama published by Monro in *Poetry and Drama* (the successor to *Poetry Review*) in March 1913; it is a play about illicit sex and its after-effects. The play features two charcoal-burners talking in the woods; one of them is named Seth, a man with an illegitimate daughter that his sister has raised and that he has kept distant from him, as he is ashamed of the sinfulness that led to her birth; the other is Newby, an old man who serves as Seth's foil. The two begin their conversation by referring to a squire in town who has come home to die, having been ravaged by venereal disease in London; it is against this backdrop that Seth's story of sexual depravity unfurls. We learn that Seth keeps an adder in his hut as a charm to protect him from the terrors lurking in the woods, and he tells Newby that he nourishes the snake with his mind; the snake is meant to stand as a symbol of his fall from innocence into sin. When Seth's sister dies, his daughter comes looking for him, and Seth is consumed with fear, fear of his own sexual sinfulness as represented by her. He describes the wicked, lecherous life he led that brought the baby into existence and how he has been reformed, saved by the Lord. His goal has been to keep his daughter from knowing him and from knowing evil, shutting her completely off from life; as a result, though, the girl does not know what sin is and does not know how to ward against it. In the end, she touches the snake and is bitten by it; her father lets her die, believing that he is protecting her from a world filled with evil. The play is yet another of Abercrombie's allegories of the need to make the most of life, not to live in fear of it and so fail to embrace it fully; it is another version of the lesson of Saint Thomas.

The first issue of *New Numbers* earlier the same year included Abercrombie's "The Olympians" (in *The Poems of Lascelles Abercrombie*, pp. 340–356), a poem that treats a classical theme—the death of the gods—and stands as a type of what he referred to as a "metaphysical" idyll, an idyll being a narrative poem treating an epic, romantic, or tragic theme. It features a peasant mother and her son in conversation in ancient Crete, at a time when the pagan era was ending and the Christian era just dawning. The two are talking in their hut about the mother's trade of "corpse-tending." As someone who prepares corpses for burial, she should be ashamed of her work, her son says. In defense, she seeks to ennoble her trade, claiming that she restores to man his pride in dressing him for death, restoring to him his dignity. When an old man comes to their door with a bundle the size of a dead baby, the woman suspects some wickedness on his part, wondering how he came by this dead baby and whether he strangled it. The man wants to know if the woman will "eat" the dead one's sins—an easy task, she thinks, as she imagines a dead infant could accumulate but few. The deceased turns out to be none other than Zeus, however, and the old man carrying the bundle is Apollo; the woman vows never to play the undertaker again, having eaten the sins of Zeus. Abercrombie was fascinated with the moment in the world's history when paganism gave way to Christianity, and he worked to represent that epic shift on a human scale. As the human-seeming Apollo tragically allows, "Our world / Required us and we were. A change has come" (p. 354).

The third issue of *New Numbers* ran what Abercrombie called the "mixed" idyll, "The Innocents" (in *The Poems of Lascelles Abercrombie,* pp. 280-284), another poem that hearkens back to the beginning of the Christian era. In the first lines of the poem, we see a widowed farm woman in ancient Palestine still glowing with her love for her dead husband and for their son, who remains with her. When she reaches the house from the farm, she feels something is amiss: as she comes to find, her boy has been speared in the breast by Herod's soldiers and lies dead on the floor. The woman's mother, who was at the time in the house with the child, says that one of the soldiers lamented what he had done, crying in the house afterward and saying, "I can't do things like this" (p. 283). The human tragedy for all involved is brought out in this horrible recounting. The boy's mother renounces her faith in God when she realizes that her boy has been slaughtered in an effort to eradicate the newborn Christ; she yearns for him in desperate tones— "I do not want Messiah: / I want my boy, my little nimble boy, / Warm and living and laughing"—and pathetically cries, "We did not need / Messiah to change the world for us: the world / Would have been ours, we would have made it ours" through love (p. 283). As with his earlier self-published idyll *Mary and the Bramble* (1910), where the Virgin Mary on a walk becomes entangled in thorns that dig into her out of jealousy of her future fame and immortality, a woman suffers for Christ's sake. The metaphysical poem bears the rhetorical mark of a work that Abercrombie greatly admired, Thomas Hardy's epic-drama of the Napoleonic Wars, *The Dynasts* (1903–1908), with Hardy's symbolic supernatural "Spirit of the Years," which contemplates and comments on earthly events, transformed into the "Spirit of Life."

POSTWAR POETRY AND DRAMA

Abercrombie did not see action in World War I as a result of his poor eyesight, although many of his friends fought. However, he did serve as a munitions examiner in Liverpool to help pay the bills. Marsh helped him out financially, too, obtaining for him a civil list pension. When Brooke was killed in the war, Abercrombie wrote an elegy, "R. B." (in *Twelve Idyls and Other Poems*) saluting that poet's power to transform the world into radiance: "where he past / He shone; he brought with him a golden place" (p. 15). Abercrombie was named as one of the beneficiaries of Brooke's estate, along with the poets Wilfrid Gibson and Walter de la Mare.

During the war Abercrombie continued to write poetry with realist matter and in a realist manner. In the 1918–1919 issue of *Georgian Poetry,* Marsh included Abercrombie's *Witchcraft: New Style,* a horribly sardonic short play. In it a slatternly woman enters a tavern, fills up her ale bottle, and confronts a crowd of jeering men. We discover that her husband has left her and that she possesses a powerful witchcraft to get him back: she defiantly claims to "have hold of his mind" (p. 298). Later that evening, the men witness the husband running down the street to her, with a bloody foot, tattered clothes, and foam at the mouth: he is bewitched and in her complete control. Abercrombie recast another witch poem, "At Endor" (originally titled "Witch at Endor" and then "Witchcraft: Old Style"), at about the same time (1919). In it, a dialogue in alternating iambic runs between the ghost of a character named Samuel, which the witch has conjured forth, and the witch herself. The ghost bemoans his disturbance from the world of the dead and the mastery of the witch's sorcery over him: "My will is thy Jehovah now," she asserts (p. 293), taunting Samuel that God has deserted him, but he steadfastly refuses to desert his faith. The two poems together suggest that the only power permitted women in the world is through the black arts.

Published for the first time in 1923 in a periodical called *The Chapbook* was Abercrombie's idyll "Ham and Eggs," a poem in iambic tetrameter (reminiscent of Jonathan Swift's parodic "Description of a City Shower"), which presents a sordid window onto the oldest of professions, refusing to look away from the social realities of poverty and prostitution that existed in England at the time. It begins with a sickening description of the polluted sky over a factory town and goes on to paint a crass commercial scene, with boats disgorging military troops on leave who are enticed immediately by the lusty amusements on shore. The brothels serve ham and eggs; they are "frowsy within, dingy without" (p. 322); the prostitutes stand in the doorways trying to attract customers. One of the prostitutes and an old lady who plays the piano in the brothel, only because she must earn a living, are at odds over the business that occurs there. At one point, the prostitute asks the old lady how she looks, and the disapproving old lady retorts, "You look like what you are" (p. 325), refusing her any illusions. Eventually, the prostitute secures a customer, gets him drunk, and takes him upstairs. She picks his pockets while he makes love to her; they are interrupted when a girl comes to the door with the news that the prostitute's mother has died. The prostitute leaves, vowing never to return, but the old lady at the piano knows the painful social truth that "another one will come to take her place," and she keeps on playing. The idyll has an elegiac intensity to it and is designed to arouse our profound pity.

Abercrombie's 1922 idyll "Ryton Firs" (first published in the *Chapbook*) does another kind of eulogizing, this time of the forests in Ryton before they are cleared and the trees in them harvested for mine props during World War I. In the poem, which the poet dedicates to his three sons, he begins, "Dear boys, they've killed our woods: the ground / Now looks ashamed, to be shorn so bare" (*The Poems of Lascelles Abercrombie,* p. 333). When the poem was published in *Georgian Poetry 1920–1922,* it was without the prelude. The speaker imagines the starvation of the hills stripped bare in elegiac stanzas, but then shifts register, recreating an image of a former time when the trees stood tall. Abercrombie compares the despoliation of the idyllic woods to what the war has wrought: "Ryton Firs, like Europe, fell" (p. 333). As he imagines, we have suffered terribly the loss of innocence and beauty in the world—a theme that runs throughout the poet's stark realism.

In the 1920s Abercrombie also wrote and published two stage plays. In *The Deserter* (1927) he portrays the difficult situation of a woman named Martha who has hastened the death of her sick husband by poisoning him. Her husband, Peter, had been in debt to another man in town, Luther, and had promised his wife to him upon his death in satisfaction; his wife is regarded as just another one of his "belongings." Luther has insinuated himself into the heart of Martha's young daughter and goes so far as to tell her that he will be her father someday in the future. Knowing this, the wife sends letters to her lover, a soldier, asking him to return from war so that they can be married as soon as her husband dies and before the creditor, Luther, can lay claim to her. Her lover deserts his unit and comes to her, but he regrets his decision even before he finds out the full circumstances; he blames Martha for turning him into a deserter. *The Deserter* uses the modern situation of the war to weave a tragic story of the lengths to which a woman will go to control her fate and the recriminations that occur when a man is forced to choose between duty and love; in the play, Abercrombie extends to his crippled characters a justice of mercy in the style of Hardy.

In 1923 his three-act play *Phoenix* sets the action farther afield, in a town on the coast of northern Greece sometime before the Trojan War. Phoenix is a prince who after going out on his first hunt and killing a lion comes home to find his father, the aged king (Amyntor), with a young concubine (Rhodope), bought for his pleasure from pirates; his jealous mother, the queen, attempts to use Phoenix to lure the woman from Amyntor. As in the case of much of Abercrombie's work, the drama relies subtly but firmly on a gender and class politics that shapes the options available to the characters. Amyntor has been sexually reinvigorated by Rhodope and is eager to spend all his time gratifying his desire for her ("I will be now nothing but my own pleasure. I've been merely senseless duty until now" p. 506). Rhodope chafes under the watchful eye of the queen, and she refuses to be made into the king's pet. She offers up resistance when he claims on her behalf that she "never lived till now," that it was he who brought her to life, that she only exists "because my love can dream you" (pp. 508–509)—she dismisses his conceits as an old man's fantasies. The queen tricks her son into making sexual advances on Rhodope and tricks her husband into not revealing to Phoenix his relationship with Rhodope. In the process, Rhodope makes clear her dissatisfaction with Amyntor and feels strongly her own powerlessness as a woman: "What a simple harmless world it would have been / If they had made it with no men in it" (p. 522). Amyntor cheapens Rhodope when he appears to have lost her to Phoenix, in stark contrast to his earlier high talk of love: he calls Rhodope an object to be bought and sold and berates her for her wantonness, as he is reduced to misery and shame. When the queen's ruse is discovered, she becomes the target of the prince's scorn, and he vows to leave the palace forever; however, she defends herself, claiming that she has been ill-used and as a wife had no other recourse. The play—described in its subtitle as a "tragicomedy"—is about the debasement of love and does what Aristotle says tragedy should do, that is, arouse the emotions of pity and fear. We feel sympathy for the plights of these characters, despite their obvious flaws, and yet we are also roused to laughter, as their foibles and delusions imitate (in exaggerated form) our own.

In 1928 Abercrombie published *Twelve Idyls and Other Poems*. Among the newer poems to appear in this volume was "The Death of a Friar," composed in heroic couplets. In the poem the bland dying of the friar is turned magnificent when the queen of Heaven, Mary, the mother of God, appears and the friar experiences the ardor of spiritual exaltation. It is about as far from Abercrombie's earlier realism as one could get, reaching back to his early metaphysical strain.

In 1930 *The Poems of Lascelles Abercrombie* appeared as part of the Oxford Poets series of the Oxford University Press. He was only the second poet to be so honored while still living, the other being the poet laureate Robert Bridges (1844–1930). The book includes all of his poems except the full five-act version of *The Sale of Saint Thomas*, which was published later the same year.

LITERARY CRITICISM

During his later life, Abercrombie held prestigious academic posts at the University of Liverpool (1919–1922), the University of Leeds (1922–1929), the University of London (1929–1935), and Oxford University (1935–1938). During these years, he devoted himself primarily to teaching and to the writing of literary criticism, and he developed in that criticism theories of art that relied on his knowledge of a wide range of philosophers and critics, from Aristotle and Francis Bacon to Immanuel Kant and Benedetto Croce. In his criticism, he was focused on the aspects and function of poetry (as a type of literature), or as he put it in one of his scholarly works, "what poetry is in fact—the things it does and the way it does them" (*The Theory of Poetry*, p. 13).

As Abercrombie held, literature is "the expression of imaginative experience, valued simply as such and significant simply as such, in the communicable state given by language which employs every available and appropriate device" (*The Idea of Great Poetry*, p. 161). By this formulation he meant that it is not enough simply to regard a work of literature as the expression of the author's mind (or mood or temperament), to focus exclusively on the subjective aspect, which would lead to romanticism; nor is it enough to regard a work of literature as a method of representing things to the reader, to focus exclusively on the objective aspect, which would

11

lead to realism. Rather, he says, "Literature exists not only in expressing a thing; it equally exists in the receiving of the thing expressed" (*Principles of Literary Criticism,* p. 34). The author of a poem communicates "pure experience," that is, experience valued for its own sake and not based on its truth value. It does not matter what the subject matter of literature is, only that "the experience which lived in the author's mind ... live again in the reader's mind" (p. 34). The author must use words that imitate his experience by making them a symbol of his own experience, since experience cannot be directly transferred from one mind to another.

In *Principles of Literary Criticism* (1932), Abercrombie reveals the extent to which his aesthetic theory is indebted to Aristotle, whose implicit refutation of Plato in his *Poetics* hinges on his sense that the art of poetry imitates not the external world but the imaginative inspiration that the poet has received based on his experience of the world. This technique, he asserts, is true in realism as well: poetry never intends to create a copy of nature, but "to imagine life as it might be" (p. 87), to imitate the poetic impulse in poetic language. Elsewhere, Abercrombie traces the development of Aristotelian aesthetic theory through history, and argues that the function of poetry is implied in "the profoundest aphorism ever contributed to the theory of art—Bacon's assertion that in poetry we have 'the shows of things submitted to the desire of the mind'" (*An Essay towards a Theory of Art,* p. 102). Kant, too, stands in the Aristotelian line, and in his theory the Baconian "desires of the mind" becomes "the desire for a representation of the purpose of things" (p. 135); poetry for Kant represents things as purposive, or moral, without representing any distinct purpose (as it likewise does for Shelley); it renders experience coherent and, thus, significant. Finally, Croce stresses the value of what Abercrombie refers to as "pure intuition, of experience accepted for its own sake" (pp. 135–136). The question of the reality of experience does not arise; the issue for Croce is about satisfaction with the experience itself, simply as such. According to Croce's expressionist theory, art is to be understood first as experience, then as intuition—or the inner vision of an image. Where Abercrombie and Croce part ways is over the importance of the communication of that inner vision to the reader.

It is through a symbolic language that such communication between author and reader is made possible, and Abercrombie writes at length about the semantic and phonetic properties of words and their functions. As he states in *The Theory of Poetry* (1924; republished in America combined with *The Idea of Great Poetry* in 1926), the poet "must, out of the subtly adjusted sound and sense of words, contrive such a texture of intensities and complexities of meaning, of unsuspected filaments of fine allusion and suggestion, as will enable those gossamers to capture and convey into our minds just those fleeting, gleaming qualities of experience which elude the hold of every-day straightforward language" (p. 85). He goes on to explain that the "magical" words of the poet exhibit an incantatory power with the ability to "create in us, over and over again, the complete and many-colored sense of a notably individual experience: the poet's experience" (p. 185). In *Principles* he breaks down the expressive and representative language of the poet into its parts, explaining that language is both meaning and sound and that the power of literature to communicate resides in sentences (syntax of the sense; rhythm of the sound) and individual words (imaginative value of the sense; syllabic quality of the sound). He also draws a clear distinction between diction and poetic form: "The aspect of language which symbolizes the substance of the originating experience we may call its *diction;* the aspect which symbolizes the unity of the substance in a single act of comprehensive attention we call the *form* of a piece of literature" (p. 50). Form gives coherence to experience and thereby gives experience meaning and significance.

In *The Theory of Poetry,* Abercrombie further insists that words are uniquely derived from a poet's individual mind, and he remarks on the poet's "power of using words so as to produce a sort of enchantment" (p. 181)—"a power not merely to charm and delight, but to kindle our minds into unusual vitality, exquisitely aware both of things and the connexion of things" (p. 181). Abercrombie lashes out at Victorianism in the form of Algernon Charles Swinburne for what he perceives as that poet's "language without meaning," "for the art of poetry is simply the art of electrifying language with extraordinary meaning. Art without matter is not art at all" (p. 93). His view that language must both convey ideas and enact within us through those ideas sensuous and emotional experiences lies at the heart of his theory. Abercrombie advocated throughout his career as a literary critic (beginning in 1914 with *Poetry and Contemporary Speech*) the use of ordinary language in poetry, believing as he did that "it is the common words that have the finest triumphs in poetry, because they necessarily have the greatest suggestive power behind them" (p. 109): a poetic vocabulary should be drawn "from the rough and tumble of everyday speech" (p. 109), which with its fresh turns of phrase and slang keep the language alive. He hails Elizabethan poetry for that very quality, for keeping the accent and idiom near to "the language of people talking" (p. 111).

Abercrombie also worked to achieve that quality of talk in his own prosodic arrangements, going to great lengths to demonstrate how the rhythms of verse communicate experience (that is, re-create the poet's experience of reality) in the reader. In *The Theory of Poetry* he explains that there is "a very great range in the degree of mutual accommodation possible between speech rhythm and pattern rhythm in metre," concluding that "on the whole, the history of English prosody shows a progressive absorption of more and more varieties of speech rhythm into metrical forms of one kind or another" (p. 136). He instances John Milton and William Shakespeare as more or less breaking with the lockstep of meter in fruitful ways, and he clearly has them in mind as models in his own practice of versification.

Apart from these technical considerations, great poetry, Abercrombie believed, requires three things: a range of subject matter; "intellectual form"; and vivid characterization. Of the first of these, Abercrombie observes that "we could not call poetry great which did not face the whole fact of man's life in this world, its wickedness and misery as well as its nobility and joy" (p. 278), the whole gamut of human experience. Of the second item, Abercrombie notes that the form that a poem takes expresses the "peculiar unity of significance" (p. 62) that the matter has achieved in the poet's mind, that all passages of a poem must be read in the context of all the others, making for an integrated whole. And third, he finds that "the art of poetry, in its widest sense, can do nothing more impressive than the creation of human character" (p. 274). A poetry that is truly great relies on "the greatness of the living symbolism of vividly personal figures" (p. 285) that the poet creates, figures like Milton's Satan, Homer's Achilles, and Shakespeare's Hamlet. It is in these representative personalities, and not in abstract ideas, that we experience the full force and pleasure of significance. The performance of Abercrombie's own plays and poetry are guided by these criteria.

ASSESSMENT

Lascelles Abercrombie died on October 27, 1938, in London. Upon his death, his friend the poet Wilfrid Gibson eulogized him in print, saying that Abercrombie had not yet been given his due as a poet, noting the tendency in most obituaries "to stress the professorial activities at the expense of those of the creative writer" (p. 211). Wilson insisted on correcting the record, claiming that "first and foremost, he was a great poet" (p. 211), even though he did not gain wide renown, mostly, as Gibson believes, because his "was hardly the anthologist's game," with most of his poetry not of the lyric variety; moreover, Gibson claims that Abercrombie's work is "not easy of appreciation," that it demands that we "have our wits about us" when we read him as we seek to interpret his "large and transcendental gestures." Juxtaposing him favorably to contemporary modernists, Gibson makes the vigorous case that Abercrombie's difficulty was not merely "modish," that it was "never ineptly incoherent" and had none of the modernists' pretentious obscurity. He hails Abercrombie's rich and ranging vocabulary as well as his masterful control of "rhythmical incantation," his ability to transmute reality into art and to impress upon us the sorrows and endurances of life. Indeed, Gibson claims for Abercrombie the mantle of epic poet: "Epic poetry exhibits life in some great symbolic attitude. It cannot strictly be said to symbolize life itself, but always some manner of life." This judgment chimes with what Abercrombie himself said of Hardy's *The Dynasts,* a poem "dramatic in manner" but with all "the emotional scope and imaginative reverberation of epic" (all references to Gibson in this section, p. 212) and is as true.

Selected Bibliography

WORKS OF LASCELLES ABERCROMBIE

POETRY

Interludes and Poems. London: John Lane, 1908.

Mary and the Bramble. Privately printed, 1910

The Sale of Saint Thomas. Act 1. Ryton, Dymock, U.K.: Privately printed, 1911.

Emblems of Love. London: John Lane, 1912.

Deborah. London: John Lane, 1913.

Speculative Dialogues. London: Martin Secker, 1913.

Four Short Plays. London: Martin Secker, 1922.

Phoenix. London: Martin Secker, 1923.

Twelve Idyls and Other Poems. London: Martin Secker, 1928.

The Poems of Lascelles Abercrombie. London: Oxford University Press, 1930.

The Sale of Saint Thomas, in Six Acts. London: Martin Secker, 1930.

Lyrics and Unfinished Poems. Edited by Wilfred Wilson. Newtown, Wales: Gregynog Press, 1940.

Vision and Love. London: Arts Research, 1966.

CRITICISM

Thomas Hardy: A Critical Study. London: Martin Secker, 1912.

"The Function of Poetry in the Drama," *Poetry Review.* March 1912: 107–118.

"Victorians and Georgians," *Manchester Guardian* No. 20722 (January 6, 1913):5.

Review of "North of Boston" by Robert Frost, *London Times* (May 28, 1914):262.

Review of "North of Boston" by Robert Frost, *Nation* Vol. XV, No. II (June 13, 1914):423–424.

The Epic. London: Martin Secker, 1914.

Poetry and Contemporary Speech. London: The English Association (Pamphlet No. 27), 1914.

An Essay Towards a Theory of Art. London: Martin Secker, 1922.

Principles of English Prosody. London: Martin Secker, 1923.

The Theory of Poetry. London: Martin Secker, 1924.

The Idea of Great Poetry. London: Martin Secker, 1925.

The Theory of Poetry. New York: Harcourt Brace, 1926.

Romanticism. London: Martin Secker, 1926.

Progress in Literature. Cambridge, U.K.: Cambridge University Press, 1929.

Colloquial Language in Literature. Oxford: Clarendon Press, 1931.

Poetry: Its Music and Meaning. London: Oxford University Press, 1932.

Principles of Literary Criticism. London: Victor Gollancz, 1932.

The Art of Wordsworth. Edited by Ralph Abercrombie. London: Oxford University Press, 1952.

BIOGRAPHICAL AND CRITICAL STUDIES

Cooper, Jeffrey. *A Bibliography and Notes on the Works of Lascelles Abercrombie.* Hamden, Conn.: Archon Books, 1969.

Fisher, Esther Safer. "Lascelles Abercrombie—Playwright." *Modern Drama* 23, no. 3: 297–308 (September 1980).

Frost, Robert. "Introduction to E. A. Robinson's 'King Jasper.'" *King Jasper.* New York: Library of America, 1995.

Gibson, Wilfrid. "Lascelles Abercrombie." *English* 2, no. 10 (1939): 211–213.

Jones, Llewellyn. "Lascelles Abercrombie." In his *First Impressions: Essays on Poetry, Criticism, and Prosody.* New York: Knopf, 1925; Freeport, N.Y.: Books for Libraries Press, 1968.

Parker, Rennie. *The Georgian Poets: Abercrombie, Brooke, Drinkwater, Gibson, and Thomas.* Plymouth: Northcote House, 1999.

Ross, Robert H. *The Georgian Revolt, 1910–1922: Rise and Fall of a Poetic Ideal.* Carbondale: Southern Illinois University Press, 1965.

Thomas, R. George, Ed. "Edward Thomas to Gordon Bottomley" in *Letters from Edward Thomas to Gordon Bottomley.* London: Oxford University Press, 1968.

Untermeyer, Louis. "Deborah: Mr. Abercrombie's Verse Drama of Life among Fisher Folk," *New York Times Book Review* (June 15, 1913):357.

Woolf, Virginia. *The Common Reader: First Series.* New York: Harcourt, [1925], 1953.

JOHN ARBUTHNOT

(1667—1735)

Christopher Vilmar

AT SOME POINT during the winter of 1713–1714, a group of men, called by the poet William Cowper "the most celebrated collection of clever fellows this country ever saw," began to meet in the rooms of Dr. John Arbuthnot at St. James's Palace on Pall Mall in London. Alexander Pope, the member who oversaw the publication of many of their works, imagined the friends—who called themselves the "Scriblerus Club"—"walking arm in arm down to posterity," and most readers familiar with Arbuthnot know him as a friend to the more famous members of the club: Pope, Jonathan Swift, and John Gay. But during his life Arbuthnot himself was the club's most prominent member—in addition to his fame as author of the political satire known as the *John Bull* tracts, he was a scientist and a member of the Royal Society, a physician to two queens and a member of the royal household, a politician admired for his morality and upright dealings, and a warm man noted for his friendship and love of family. The novelist William Makepeace Thackeray called Arbuthnot "one of the wisest, wittiest, most accomplished, gentlest of mankind," (pp. 159–160), and only by placing his many publications in the context of his professional honors and his exuberant and rich life can a full sense of his genius be obtained.

CHILDHOOD, EDUCATION, AND EARLY YEARS IN LONDON

Twenty-six miles south of Aberdeen, Scotland, in the heart of Kincardineshire, lies the estate of Arbuthnott. During the seventeenth century, the Lord of Arbuthnott gave the parish estate to a relative, Alexander Arbuthnott. The new priest, a Scottish Episcopalian, married Margaret Lammy on April 4, 1666. In the parish register for April 29, 1667, the following entry marks the birth of his son: "Alexander Arbuthnott, Parson of Arbuthnott, had one son baptized named John." The baby was likely several days old when the sacrament was given.

Little is known of Arbuthnot's early years. He had four brothers and four sisters, and another half brother from his father's second marriage. As the eldest son of a priest, he would have had the opportunity to read widely under his father's supervision in the household library. The subjects that formed the reading of an educated clergyman—theology and divinity, classical literature, and history—were ones in which John later excelled.

Arbuthnot matriculated at Marischal College, at the University of Aberdeen, in 1681. His course of study was traditional, consisting of grammar, logic, and rhetoric, conducted in the classical languages. It also included a year of "natural philosophy," or modern science as developed in the work of thinkers like Francis Bacon, René Descartes, and later Isaac Newton. The new science rejected abstract questions to focus on empirical observation of the world, and it applied mathematical reasoning to the solution of ordinary problems. Arbuthnot probably learned these subjects from the lectures of David Gregory and Archibald Pitcairne, both of whom remained in contact with Arbuthnot in later years and were interested in science as well as medicine and philosophy. Arbuthnot graduated in 1685 at the age of eighteen.

Arbuthnot's activities during the years immediately after graduation are obscure, but the death of Charles II in 1685 and the coronation of his brother James, who was openly and aggressively Catholic, precipitated a series of events that led to the Revolution of 1688. Parliament invited the Protestant William of Orange and his wife, Mary, to take the English throne, and James abdicated and fled to France. In Scotland, Presbyterians seized the opportunity to reassert their primacy in church affairs. Arbuthnot's father refused to conform to the Presbyterians just as he had refused to take the oath of allegiance to William and Mary required by the new government, and these refusals were strong proofs of his allegiance to the deposed Stuart king, James—an allegiance known as Jacobitism, from "Jacobus," the Latin form of the name "James." Arbuthnot's brother joined the Jacobite uprising against the new settlement in 1689, and as his friend Lord Chesterfield remembered after his death, Arbuthnot was himself "a Jacobite by prejudice, and a Republican by reflection and reasoning" (Stanhope, p. 1412). In later life Arbuthnot appears to have been able to examine his own politics with a measure of that detachment and objectivity found in his later writings on politics. As a young man, however, he may have been more vehement in his allegiances; after the death of the elder Arbuthnott in 1691, authorities refused to allow his sons to raise a monument over his tomb, possibly fearing that the rebellious brothers would inscribe it with pro-Stuart sentiments.

With the death of Alexander, the brothers scattered southward to England and France in search of their fortunes. By the early 1690s, Arbuthnot was living in London opposite the Royal Exchange. There he published his first book, *Of the Laws of Chance* (1692). This work is largely a translation from a treatise in Dutch by Christiaan Huygens on the laws of mathematical probability. It draws examples from gambling on cards, which was one of Arbuthnot's favorite pastimes. He added little to the book, but one original contribution was an application of Huygens' analytical techniques to the popular English card game Hazard. This book is the first example of a kind of writing in which Arbuthnot excelled: the treatment of difficult and technical subjects in a way that makes them accessible to a broad readership.

After this early demonstration of his skill as a mathematician and familiarity with contemporary research in mathematics, Arbuthnot was introduced to the small circle of prominent intellectuals who formed the Royal Society. This body, formed in 1660 for the advancement of scientific knowledge, included minds famous for literature and philosophy as well as science, medicine, and mathematics. The breadth of Arbuthnot's knowledge secured him a place in the company of men like the mathematician Newton and the Scots astronomer Edmond Halley. It was probably through such connections that he was recommended as a tutor to a young noble going up to Oxford, where he was entered as a fellow commoner at University College, Oxford, on October 6, 1694.

There, Arbuthnot quickly made the acquaintance of the master of his college, Dr. Arthur Charlett, with whom he corresponded for many years. It is likely that through Charlett and his old teacher David Gregory, who had been appointed the Savilian Professor of Astronomy at Oxford, Arbuthnot was introduced to the society of others who shared his diverse intellectual interests. That many Oxford men were also Tories would have made a political fellow traveler like Arbuthnot still more welcome.

In the company of other eager scholars, Arbuthnot must have progressed quickly in his studies. In 1696, after his pupil had begun to show signs of mediocrity and lack of interest, Arbuthnot wrote to Charlett that he was "resolved on some other course of life" (Ross, p. 104). He then wrote to the University of St. Andrews asking to be examined as a candidate for a medical degree. The request was answered, somewhat tardily, in August, when the University Senate agreed to let him sit the examination. He defended his theses in September and took his degree. In a letter to Charlett, George Hamilton, principal of St. Andrews, described Arbuthnot as "a gentleman of great merit, that has acquit himself extraordinarily well both in his private and his public trials in solemn meetings of several professors and Doctors of Medicine towards his promotion." (quoted in Aitken, p. 19).

The seven theses were published that same year in a journal as *Theses Medicae de Secretione Animali* (Medical Theses on the Secretion of Animals). Animal secretion, or the operation and circulation of bodily fluids, was at the forefront of medical science. On these questions Arbuthnot employed the "iatromechanical" method of his former teachers Gregory and Pitcairne. Iatromechanics treated the body as a machine and tried to reduce its operations to mathematical regularity so that better cures could be discovered through scientific experimentation. Though still primitive compared to modern medicine, this approach represented a significant advance over older methods. By going north for his medical training, Arbuthnot bypassed the dated teaching that predominated in English medical study.

Arbuthnot returned to London and busied himself with the establishment of his medical practice. He remained conversant socially with members of the Royal Society and other learned men, and intellectually with the latest ideas. His friends persuaded him to print some objections he had to a new book, which was to become the first clash in the long antagonism between Arbuthnot and the Cambridge scholar and antiquarian Dr. John Woodward.

In 1695 Woodward had published a book, *An Essay Towards a Natural History of the Earth and Terrestrial Bodies ... With an Account of the Universal Deluge, and of the Effects That It Had upon the Earth*. In it he attempted to prove that the biblical Flood was caused by the overflow of water from a cavity deep inside the earth; that the present geography of the earth had been formed by the settling of sediments raised during this overflow; and that fossils were skeletons sunk into various strata by gravity. This thesis sounds more far-fetched today than it did at the time, when many of the greatest scientists struggled to reconcile their discoveries with scriptural history.

Arbuthnot, therefore, confined his objections to the methods and conclusions of Woodward, which he satirized in his *Examination of Dr. Woodward's Account of the Deluge* (1697). He begins by explaining that his remarks are made in the spirit of scientific disagreement, not personal animosity. To ensure that Woodward's book is not misrepresented by him, he quotes from it at length. In the next section Arbuthnot arrives at his substantial objections, often in the form of mathematical proofs. Finally, he places passages from Woodward next to those of an earlier geographer, Nicolaus Steno, so that their similarities can be discussed. He does not accuse Woodward of plagiarism, but rather of overstating his conclusions or failing to provide enough evidence. Throughout the examination Arbuthnot is fair and judicious, even excusing simple mistakes in order to address the more book's more fundamental errors.

Those expecting the fiery disagreements of much eighteenth-century satire (or current debate about science and religion) will be disappointed to find that the satire of the *Examination* is finally quite mild. Against the tendency to spin out systematic explanations from too little evidence, Arbuthnot recommends empirical observation and mathematical reasoning. As a result his conclusion is cordial, from one scientist to another: "if he takes off the objections I have proposed, I'll promise him, I cannot be in the least disposed to cavil; only I cannot forbear to wish that people were more diligent in observing, and more cautious in system-making" (*Miscellaneous Works*, vol. 2, p. 234). Instead of cutting personal attacks on Woodward, Arbuthnot takes a kind of muted delight in holding him to higher scientific standards than those to which he has held himself.

As the seventeenth century drew to a close, it must be supposed that Arbuthnot devoted much of his time to his medical practice, but the clearest picture of him during this period can be had from his scientific work. Halley deputized Arbuthnot to act in his place as clerk to the Royal Society in February 1699. That Arbuthnot was felt to have the qualifications to work closely with the best scientific minds in England speaks much about his familiarity with current topics of research.

His next book, *An Essay on the Usefulness of Mathematical Learning* (1701), was meant to promote university study of its subject. Written as a letter addressed to the students of Oxford, it urges them to study mathematics by listing the many practical benefits of doing so. Arbuthnot sums up these advantages under three heads:

First, he says, "mathematics make the mind attentive to the objects it considers." "The second advantage ... is a habit of clear, demonstrative, and methodical reasoning." And "thirdly, mathematical knowledge adds a manly vigor to the mind, frees it from prejudice, credulity, and superstition" (Aitken, pp. 410–412). Given the general nature of these claims, Arbuthnot lists specific cases where math has an immediate and practical application: astronomy, optics, navigation, warfare, mechanics, business, civil affairs and politics, and last—but not least, given his love of cards and wagers—gambling. He sets out a practical course of study in the foundations of mathematics, so that the student can undertake more advanced training as occasions require. Arbuthnot makes a compelling case for a subject that seems at first to be far removed from the needs or interests of ordinary life. As in his best political satires, the *Essay* reveals his talent for making a rigorous argument accessible to ordinary readers.

PHYSICIAN-EXTRAORDINARY TO THE QUEEN

Arbuthnot married Margaret, whose maiden name is unknown, in 1702—the same year that King William died, Anne was crowned queen, and the War of the Spanish Succession (1701–1714) was getting under way. During the reign of Anne, Arbuthnot was preferred at court and honored elsewhere. His career reached its maturity and his success in all areas was nearly total. In the course of a single decade, he became a celebrated and much-sought-after physician, an influential political figure at court, an honored scientist, and the creator of an enduring symbol of the English nation.

Arbuthnot was elected a fellow of the Royal Society in November 1704. Also elected at this time was Anne's husband, Prince George, along with several members of his household. This joint election established one point of connection with the royal family. During the following April, Arbuthnot accompanied the Queen to the University of Cambridge, where he was one of three men presented with honorary medical degrees.

In the summer Arbuthnot published a work of antiquarian studies, *Tables of the Grecian, Roman, and Jewish Measures, Weights, and Coins, Reduc'd to the English Standard* (1705). A second edition, given the new title *Tables of Ancient Coins, Weights, and Measures,* appeared in 1727. It was reprinted a number of times during the decades that followed and even translated into Latin in 1754. The first edition was dedicated to Prince George by his "dutiful servant Jo: Arbuthnott, M.D." In the preface to the second edition, Arbuthnot confessed an awareness of the work's defects, and admitted that he had written it when he had little time for serious scholarship. The book itself contains many digressions on little-known aspects of the classical world, and it ranges beyond the measurements and currencies mentioned in the title to include ancient medicine, trade, and climate. The book was too specialized to attract a general readership, but among the educated it was very successful. Though outdated now, in its time it was much in vogue, and schoolmasters and pupils alike cribbed from it well into the nineteenth century.

Arbuthnot probably gained favor by dedicating his book to Prince George, and his former teacher David Gregory, who was also in service to George, may also have helped to secure him a position as royal physician. One of Arbuthnot's letters suggests that he had entered their service as early as 1703, when he was said to have treated Anne's children. Tradition likewise has it that Arbuthnot treated Prince George during a visit to Epsom earlier in the same year, 1705, that Anne appointed him as physician-extraordinary on October 30.

If Arbuthnot had little time for writing during the years preceding his *Tables,* he probably had less after being appointed to the royal household, when his duties began to compete with other commitments. Prince George asked him to assist a committee of the Royal Society charged with obtaining the astronomical tables gathered by John Flamsteed since his appointment as Astronomer Royal decades earlier. Other scientists, including Newton and Halley, wanted access to the charts, which Flamsteed refused to surrender. Arbuthnot tried to arbitrate between the two parties but was not able to resolve the dispute without much bitterness and enmity on both sides. Arbuthnot was also asked to serve later on a committee to decide whether Newton or the German philosopher Gottfried Leibniz had invented calculus. Naturally enough, the Englishmen on the committee quickly decided in favor of their countryman.

Arbuthnot also became involved in the political pamphleteering over the proposed union between England and Scotland. William of Orange had conceived of the union, but after his death the proposal moved forward slowly under great opposition from the Scots. Arbuthnot wrote *A Sermon Preach'd to the People at the Mercat Cross of Edinburgh; on the Subject of the Union* (1706). Taking as his text an apocryphal verse, "Better is he that laboreth, and aboundeth in all things, than he that boasteth himself and wanteth bread" (Ecclesiasticus 10:27), Arbuthnot accused Scotland of being too hasty and proud in its objections. He argued that Scotland would prosper economically from the union, and would avoid the immorality of pride and idleness. His concluding description of Scotland transformed by its participation in the grandeur and industry of its southern neighbor was meant to allay the fears of both opportunists and patriots. Arbuthnot captures one strain of Scots sentiment, the desire to modernize the nation and improve its economy, and expressed the view that ultimately prevailed when the two nations signed the Act of Union in 1707.

These efforts, along with his loyal and amiable service as the queen's doctor, steadily improved his position at court until he wielded considerable, if indirect, influence over affairs. He quickly became one of Anne's favorites. His rise mirrored in some respects the political fortunes of the Tory party. The Duke of Marlborough, a great general who won many victories over France, and the duke's wife, Sarah, a close friend and advisor of the queen, were Whigs with intimate ties to the government led by Sidney Godolphin. Though the Whigs remained in power until 1710, many, including Anne, became disenchanted with England's involvement in the war abroad and what was perceived as Whig corruption at home. Anne began to resent the Duke and his wife and the Whig government, and she increasingly placed her trust in Tories such as Robert Harley, Earl of Oxford, and Abigail Hill, one of the ladies of her bedchamber. Anne trusted her intimacy with Arbuthnot to such an extent that when she secretly married Hill to Samuel Masham in 1707, she held the ceremony in Arbuthnot's palace apartments. In December, moreover, Arbuthnot was elected honorary fellow of the College of Physicians in Edinburgh.

Arbuthnot's political star continued to rise. In late 1709 he became physician-in-ordinary to Anne. He was understood to be her favorite physician and was close with many in her government. Arbuthnot, in fact, was on excellent social terms with the Whigs as well as the Tories. During 1710, his political acumen was tested as he remained near the center of events while his Tory friends were swept into power.

At the beginning of 1710, the Tory minister Dr. Henry Sacheverell was impeached for preaching a sermon critical of the Godolphin ministry and its prosecution of the war. The Tories, backed by the High Church party as well as the London mob, were able to topple the Whig government and bring Oxford and the Tories into power. In this change, both Arbuthnot and Jonathan Swift were important figures. Swift wrote extensively in support of the Tories, and Arbuthnot's influence on affairs was less tangible but also considerable. During this time Arbuthnot was described by Peter Wentworth as "a very cunning man, and not much talked of, but … what he says is as much heard as any that give advice now" (quoted in Aitken, p. 24).

During these political upheavals Arbuthnot continued to pursue his other interests. In April 1710 he was elected a fellow of the Royal College of Physicians. He also published a paper titled "An Argument for Divine Providence, Taken from the Constant Regularity Observed in the Births of Both Sexes" (1710) in which he attempted to answer age-old questions about the existence of God and divine providence using applied statistics. By looking at the official records of births and deaths between 1629 and 1710, he showed that the number of male births invariably outnumbered those of females. This statistical unlikelihood of this pattern, he argued, was evidence that God intervened in human affairs to ensure the survival of the species. In a scholium added after the work, he also argued that these statistics proved that polygamy was contrary to the laws of nature as well as of God.

The book is characteristic of Arbuthnot's scientific work, using mathematical reasoning to address political and religious questions, but also ultimately more interested in the mathematical facts than in the conclusions drawn from them. Arbuthnot's orderly arrangement of the data was used by other writers to draw different, less circumspect conclusions. Some argued that the calculations were not simply one indication of providence, but incontrovertible proof of God's existence. Bernard Mandeville, on the other hand, used these numbers to argue that war was nature's way of reducing the disproportionately large male population. Arbuthnot's book is of little consequence as science today, but it does give a sense of the kinds of questions that occupied scientific minds at the beginning of the eighteenth century.

THE POLITICAL SATIRE OF JOHN BULL

Between March and July 1712, Arbuthnot published five pamphlets anonymously. When they were later collected together into a single work, they became known as *The History of John Bull*. In his biased *History of England* (1870), Thomas Babington Macaulay, a nineteenth-century Whig, called *John Bull* "the most ingenious and humorous political satire in the language" (pp. 129–130). The collected pamphlets are commonly considered to be Arbuthnot's finest and most important literary work.

The pamphlets satirize many aspects of English politics during the time between 1702 and 1713. The main plot of the work is a satiric treatment of the events that occurred during the War of the Spanish Succession, especially the various Tory attempts that were made to bring the war to an end. But various domestic issues are also woven into the allegory, such as the events leading up to the Act of Union, the continuing agitation of religious factions and of Jacobites who were antagonistic to England, and squabbling between various ministers and factions in the British government. The five parts are loosely connected by the plot, but each one is also meant to stand alone as a serious look at current affairs. The currency of each pamphlet's references to figures and events is part of the book's sly humor and political meaning. Though the book was wildly popular among all classes of readers, it was generally understood that full enjoyment of its allusive humor was left to those who read it with detailed knowledge of the political events to which it refers.

The first pamphlet, *Law Is a Bottomless-Pit*, was published on March 4, 1712, as negotiations for peace were under way at Utrecht. This installment summarizes the events of the war up to this point. "John Bull," or England, finds it necessary to join with "Nicolas Frog," the Dutch, in a "lawsuit" against "Philip Baboon," whose last name is a pun on Bourbon, now "Lord Strutt" of Spain on the death of the elder "Strutt," Charles II of Spain. The lawsuit was made necessary when Philip agreed to buy his liveries from "Lewis Baboon," Louis XIV of France, instead of from Bull and Frog. The suit represents the War of the Spanish Succession, which began when the French intervened to help Philip to the throne of Spain.

Bull is described as "in the main" an "honest, plain-dealing fellow, choleric, bold, and of a very constant temper" (p. 9), hardworking, and wealthy, but also prone to be cheated due to his carelessness. The early success of his lawsuit makes him forget his clothing business and resolve to become a lawyer. Bull is encouraged by his lawyer, "Hocus," or Marlborough, but when he discovers that Hocus has been carrying on an affair with his wife, he gives vent to his anger in an outburst against "Mrs. Bull," the Godolphin ministry. The two fight violently, and Mrs. Bull dies of her wounds. Bull remarries, to "a sober, country gentlewoman" (p. 16) who represents the Tory government under Harley. The second Mrs. Bull urges Bull to give up the lawsuit, which they resolve to do after she helps him examine his "Attorney's Bill," the war debt, and discovers how great the cost of it has been. But they also discover that the deceased Mrs.

Bull left behind a curse that would bring down Bull if he came to terms with Strutt. She also left behind instructions for the care of their daughters Polemia, Discordia, and Usuria—respectively war, political faction, and usury or financial corruption. Because neither Bull nor his new wife can circumvent the curse, they continue the suit, against their better judgment. The first pamphlet ends with Bull "gaping and staring, like a man in a trance" (p. 20).

By leaving the plot unfinished, Arbuthnot left himself the opportunity to write further about the ongoing peace negotiations. The second pamphlet, *John Bull in His Senses,* appeared on March 18, and the new title suggests a certain cautious optimism about the sensible progress of British affairs. It begins with the discovery of "Mrs. Bull's Vindication of the Indispensable Duty of Cuckoldom" (p. 25), an argument that parodied the arguments Whigs had used to attack Sacheverell using marriage as a metaphor for the relationship between Mrs. Bull as the government and John Bull as both monarch and people. At root was the question of political authority, which Sacheverell argued required passive obedience to king and ancient constitution, while the Whigs felt such a question was a matter of social contract subject to renegotiation at any time.

As sustained political satire, this first chapter is one of the finest in the entire work, but as the short second chapter sharply demonstrates, Arbuthnot was not content with a simple division of the parties into right and wrong sides. He divides the nation's wives into "Hits" and "Devotos," contractual Whigs and constitutional Tories, but pointedly notes that the Hits were often loyal while the Devotos were no strangers to marital infidelity. Arbuthnot's approach to politics, as these chapters demonstrates, is clear-sighted, pragmatic, and fair-minded. Instead of encouraging political divisiveness, he examines political realities.

The remaining chapters of the second pamphlet include further satire of the peace negotiations as they unfold among Bull, Frog, and Lewis Baboon, especially on the confusion in the Bull household and the double-dealing between Frog and Baboon. The characters of the three daughters Polemia, Discordia, and Usuria are each described in a lengthy portrait, and Arbuthnot is unsparing in his satire of the immorality and irrationality that drives international war, politics, and finance.

The third pamphlet, *John Bull Still in His Senses,* appeared on April 17. Arbuthnot covers his trail on the title page by stating that it was "published by the Author of the *New Atalantis,*" or Delarivier Manley, and in the preface the putative author is Sir Humphrey Polesworth, but in spite of these ruses Arbuthnot was generally understood to be the author. The majority of the pamphlet concerns, as Sir Humphrey intimates, the publication of papers "that concerned *John Bull*'s relations and domestic affairs" (p. 47) and that he hopes will "serve to make the history of the law-suit more intelligible" (p. 47). By widening the scope of its satire to include the causes of contemporary events, the story of John Bull takes on some of the qualities of an actual history.

Among the new characters introduced in this pamphlet are Bull's "Mother," the Church of England; his sister "Peg," or Scotland; and her lover "Jack," who represents Calvinist Presbyterianism. Bull and Peg had been divided by tawdry intrigues since childhood. Mother Bull attempts to conciliate between the two but is foiled by Peg's announcement that she has fallen in love with Jack. With these disagreements, Arbuthnot satirizes the religious and political antagonisms that divided England and Scotland during the century leading up to the Act of Union. His moderation and balanced views are nowhere more evident than in his treatment of Peg, whose Scottish pride and independence are the center of the zany comedy but are never treated with contempt or malice. In fact, Arbuthnot is quick to point out that Bull shares the familial vanity and irrationality. The final chapters relate the meeting of Bull; Frog; "Esquire South," or Austria; and Lewis Baboon at the "Salutation Tavern," or Utrecht, to negotiate the end of the lawsuit. These negotiations break down due to the greed of Frog, the pretended incapacities of Lewis, and the insane ambitions of South. Arbuthnot seems genuinely to have wished that the Church of England could mitigate domestic conflicts, just as he undoubtedly hoped that Utrecht would bring a lasting peace. Yet his talent for comedy and burlesque makes all this political strife uproariously funny.

The fourth installment, *An Appendix to John Bull Still in His Senses,* is the shortest of the five and was published on May 9. Much of the story involves further religious satire and thus is rightly a continuation of the third part. Arbuthnot was mainly concerned to write a parodic history of religious controversies leading up to the bill against Occasional Conformity (1711) and he shows the complicity of "Yan Ptschirnsooker," Bishop Gilbert Burnet, with Jack, as the two form various schemes to subvert Bull. Burnet is given a Dutch surname to suggest Whig complicity with Holland after 1688. Indeed, the fourth pamphlet ends with Bull in conference with "Don Diego Dismallo," a figure who represents a conglomerate of prominent Whigs who were paying court to Anne in an attempt to ingratiate their way back into her favor. Like the others, this part of the story is generally inconclusive.

The final installment, *Lewis Baboon Turned Honest, and John Bull Politician,* was advertised as the "Fourth Part of Law Is a Bottomless-Pit." It appeared on July 31 and takes the settlement of Utrecht up through the negotiations over the port of Dunkirk. The main subject of the pamphlet is the continued wrangling at the Salutation Tavern, which degenerates into a cacophony of shouting. After this breakdown in the peace talks, Bull tries unsuccessfully to square his accounts with Frog and finds his family once again in an "uproar" over whether his "nephew," the Elector of Hanover and later George I, would inherit Bull's estate. These events precipitate Bull's private dealings with Baboon, and thus his turning "politician." Bull decides to call off the lawsuit at any price, but when Frog and South discover that he will receive "Ecclesdown Castle," or Dunkirk, from Lewis, they plot to prevent it. Thus Arbuthnot concludes the allegory with the suspicion that England has spent enormous sums for the aggrandizement of Holland and Austria, who are determined to block even a modest return to England for its investments of money and manpower.

The most important addition to the fifth part is the expansion of Sir Humphrey Polesworth's role, from a mere keeper of Bull's papers to the "Office of Historiographer to John Bull" (p. 93). Sir Humphrey mentions both classical historians and Grubstreet hack writers as models for his work, a major innovation in form: it combines the Tory preference for writing "secret histories" that gossiped about and satirized the hidden acts of those in power with the Whig "annals" that recounted the public acts of the war and celebrated its heroes. By casting the story in the intensely personal terms of a neighborhood history, Arbuthnot discovered a way to make the calculations of international politics accessible to a wide audience. At times the resulting text is difficult to understand, but its low humor is always amusing. The allusions to historical events are balanced against the immediate comedy of neighbors who cannot get along.

A key to the satire of *John Bull* was published in 1712, *A Complete Key to the Four Parts of Law is a Bottomless-Pit,* and its brisk sales (it went through six editions) were testament not only to the immediate success of the pamphlets but also to the desire to understand them more fully. Arbuthnot had remained more or less detached from the extremes of either party, avoiding the rhetorical excesses that his friend Swift fell into when he wrote Tory propaganda. As a result, *The History of John Bull* was read with interest and appreciation by both country Tories and town Whigs. Over time, many continuations and rebuttals to *John Bull* were written, by writers zealous for both parties, and Bull gradually came to be regarded as an enduring symbol of the British nation.

Later in 1712, Arbuthnot published a shorter political satire, elaborately titled *Proposals for Printing a Very Curious Discourse, in Two Volumes in Quarto, Intitled* ΘΕΥΔΟΛΟΓΙΑ ΠΟΛΙΤΙΚΗ; *or, A Treatise of the Art of Political Lying, with an Abstract of the First Volume of the Said Treatise,* written as a faux proposal for a two-volume work that was soon to be published. Arbuthnot discusses the language of popular political journalism and its tendency to propagate and publicize lies. His approach is not political, but rhetorical and philosophical—if the lie is a necessary tool of political rhetoric, then it is an art, as the title suggests, that must be mastered by the practical politician. Thus Arbuthnot begins his discussion in *The Art of Political Lying* with a look at the soul's propensity for falsehood, examines the utility and morality of political lies, and develops a taxonomy that classifies the different kinds of lies, the types of liars, and the rhetorical, social, and even physical aspects of lying. In this work's few pages, Arbuthnot demonstrates his familiarity with a great deal of technical scientific and philosophical literature. In his usual, somewhat desultory manner, he is able to apprehend how various branches of learning intersect to illuminate a single topic. Even as brief as it is, *The Art of Political Lying* shows how quickly and easily Arbuthnot could bring together his knowledge of many subjects in light, witty satire.

The years of Arbuthnot's life that are known in the greatest detail are described in his friend Swift's *Journal to Stella,* a record of events (published posthumously in 1766) during the final years of Anne's reign, when the queen's health was an issue of national and international importance. Arbuthnot was much consulted. Naturally, his diagnoses became subject to intense scrutiny. Perhaps as a way of counterbalancing these political pressures, Arbuthnot cultivated the acquaintance of young, brilliant minds. He met the philosopher George Berkeley during the latter's first visit to London in 1713, and he sent letters of introduction on Berkeley's behalf to various influential friends. Berkeley described Arbuthnot during this period thus: "He is the Queen's domestic physician, and in great esteem with the whole Court, a great philosopher, and reckoned the first mathematician of the age, and has the character of uncommon virtue and probity" (quoted in Aitken, p. 55). This praise exaggerates Arbuthnot's skill as a mathematician, but it does suggest that, unlike many of his Tory friends, he had survived the political fallout after Anne's death with his reputation for goodness and his wide friendships intact.

THE MEMOIRS OF MARTINUS SCRIBLERUS

In the winter of 1713 Arbuthnot's eminent Tory friends gathered privately to form a small club. The Scriblerus Club, as it became known, included Robert Harley, Jonathan Swift, John Arbuthnot, Alexander Pope, John Gay, and Thomas Parnell, and occasionally Bishop Francis Atterbury and William Congreve. The indirect influence of the club was felt by the members for the rest of their lives, as the evidence of their correspondence shows, and they remained nostalgic for its convivial warmth and intellectual stimulation.

The club served as a place where these important and busy men might enjoy intellectual fellowship during their leisure hours. But they also proposed for themselves a variety of literary ambitions, building on one of Pope's earlier ideas for a review that showered the worst books of the time with mock praise and lambasted the best with mock criticism. But this project was never accomplished, and indeed few books can be traced directly to the collaborative authorship of the club.

The correspondence of the members is filled with tantalizing hints about a planned "life of Scriblerus." According to Pope, this mock biography of their namesake, Martinus Scriblerus, was "to have ridiculed all the false tastes in learning, under the character of a man of capacity enough, that had dipped into every art and science, but injudiciously in each" (quoted in Aitken, p. 57). One begins to suspect, given the infrequency of casual references in their letters, that this planned biography was something of an inside joke meant to recall the pleasures of their conversations together, rather than a serious undertaking.

But in June 1714, the following summer, Arbuthnot mentions real work on the book and urges Swift to "remember Martin": "The ridicule of medicine is so copious a subject that I must only here and there touch it. I have made [Scriblerus] study physic from the apothecary's bills, where there is a good plentiful field for a satire upon the present practice" (Ross, p. 179). The topic and the method was one Arbuthnot would return to again, in the 1724 pamphlet. Swift replied: "To talk of Martin in any hands but yours, is a folly. You everyday give better hints than all of us together could do in a twelve-month" (Ross, p. 182). He continues: "The hints you mention, relating to medicine, are admirable; I wonder how you can have a mind so degagé in a court where there are so many million of things to vex you" (Ross, p. 182). From this letter it is clear that Arbuthnot had managed to steal himself away from his obligations at court long enough to make some substantial progress on the life of Scriblerus. It is also clear that Swift greatly admired Arbuthnot's satiric talents. In another letter, he wrote: "Go on for the sake of wit and humor, and cultivate that vein which no man alive possesses but yourself, and which lay like a mine in the earth, which the owner for a long time never knew of" (Ross, p. 195).

But in spite of all this work and encouragement, *The Memoirs of Martinus Scriblerus* remained unfinished during the active years of the club. Anne's death and the question of the Hanoverian succession undoubtedly absorbed some of the group's attention and energies. From the correspondence it can be surmised that some of the book was complete within a relatively short time, but it is difficult to determine which authors contributed to the different sections, or when those sections were completed. The satire of several learned subjects is unmistakably the work of Arbuthnot, and as his letter above implies it was well under way before Anne's death. But the travels of Scriblerus in the sixteenth chapter contain the basic outline of Swift's *Gulliver's Travels* (1726), which was not completed for a decade, while the sections on critics and criticism suggest later satires on which Pope and Arbuthnot collaborated. At any rate, the book was not published until 1741, when it appeared in the second volume of Pope's collected prose.

Martin is the son of Dr. Cornelius Scriblerus, a German whose learning is great but misguided in nearly every instance. Cornelius hopes that his son will be an intellectual prodigy and model himself on the classical virtues. His reverence for the ancient Greeks and Romans leads him into absurdity as he tries to plan his son's gestation, birth, and childhood according to classical principles so that everything will be propitious to "the generation of children of wit" (p. 96). In accordance with these great expectations, Cornelius devises a plan for Martin's education that is as intricate as it is impractical. Among the rules that Cornelius lays down are the methods and times of Martin's breastfeeding, the choice of his schoolfellows, and the manner of his instruction in such subjects as physical exercise, music, rhetoric, logic, metaphysics, criticism, medicine, and law. Having been prevented by his father from learning his catechism like a normal child, Martin consults freethinkers and deists about the soul and concludes against the truths of revealed religion. Even his first romantic involvement is turned upside down, and he finds himself in a love triangle with a pair of conjoined twins.

The *Memoirs* contain touches of broad humor, such as the resolution of Martin's romantic woes in the famous "double marriage," which confines the two husbands to a highly impractical kind of chastity with regard to one of their respective sister-wives. Like the humor in the *John Bull* pamphlets, this kind of impish joking was intended to appeal to a broad audience. Other sections, however, like the plan for Martin's education or the technical details of the book's ridicule of various modern sciences, are necessarily meant for a smaller, more learned audience. This inherent difficulty of the book remains the biggest obstacle to the modern reader, and this is perhaps what led Samuel Johnson to proclaim of the *Memoirs,* "no man could be wiser, better, or merrier, by remembering it" (Boswell, p. 48).

MISCELLANEOUS SATIRES

The death of Anne in 1714, however, was of much greater importance to the club than Scriblerian trifling. Of Anne, whom he attended in her final days, Arbuthnot wrote: "I believe sleep was never more welcome to a weary traveler than Death was to her" (Ross, p. 200). On her deathbed Anne gave the staff of the lord treasurer's office to the Duke of Shrewsbury, a Whig, who immediately intervened to ensure the peaceful ascension of the Hanoverian George I to the throne. This event must have been met with mixed feelings by Arbuthnot and his Tory friends. While they must have sighed with relief that the nation was not plunged into another civil war, none of them could have been pleased to learn that their friend Oxford was forced out of office and that they would be left to shift for themselves. Swift returned to Ireland, and Pope to his translation of Homer. Arbuthnot lost his place in the royal household and many of his other minor positions, but he was not left destitute. He retained his connections with many noble families and other wealthy Londoners, many of whom were his patients.

The smooth transfer of power to the House of Hanover foiled any Jacobite hopes that the exiled Stuarts might regain the throne, but there were various Jacobite murmurings and uprisings in the years and decades that followed. Because of their known Jacobite leanings, Oxford, Henry St. John, Viscount Bolingbroke, and James Butler, Duke of Ormonde, were tried for treason in 1715. Bolingbroke and Ormonde fled to France to join James the Pretender, and Oxford was imprisoned for several years. Later in 1715, the Pretender tried to help the Scottish Earl of Mar in his rebellion against the Hanoverians. Arbuthnot's brother was among the Earl's forces, and Arbuthnot himself was under suspicion from this connection and his own known Jacobitism. He was not detained or formally accused—in fact, like the other members of the club he seems to have spent these years more or less pleasantly and productively.

Arbuthnot's next work, the *To the Right Honourable the Mayor and Aldermen of the City of London: The Humble Petition of the Colliers, Cooks, Cook-Maids, Blacksmiths, Jackmakers, Braziers, and Others,* was published in 1716. This brief sheet pretends to be a petition (from the groups mentioned) to the mayor and aldermen of London. They write to complain about the "catoptrical victuallers," a group of "virtuosi" or scientists who are "disaffected to the government and to the trade and prosperity of the kingdom" (Aitken, p. 375). By using magnifying glasses and mirrors, or the science of catoptrics, these scientists were attempting to replace the old-fashioned use of fire with new inventions of their own making. The trades mentioned in the title, all of which rely on fire for their livelihoods, are a clever mask for attacking the impracticality of schemes hatched by early scientists. It is ironic, of course, that fire is manifestly superior to refracted sunlight for these tasks, but if the ordinary tradespeople are superior to the scientists in this point of common sense, they are also afraid of technological innovation. This lighthearted look at the application of science and the popular reactions to it combines Arbuthnot's scientific understanding with his satiric wit and displays his generosity to and sympathy for points of view not necessarily his own.

Toward the end of 1716 Arbuthnot collaborated with Gay and Pope on a new play, *Three Hours After Marriage*. The plot of this piece, such as it is, concerns the marriage of Dr. Fossile, an antiquarian, to Mrs. Townley, a sophisticate who immediately introduces two rivals, Plotwell and Underplot, into his house. For the rest of the play Townley tries to hide her past from Fossile, including her former liaisons with both of the rivals, who are maneuvering to resume their former intimacies with the new wife. The characters are stock, to some extent, like the absentminded husband or the foppish would-be lovers, but Fossile is thought to be a lampoon on Arbuthnot's old enemy Woodward, while Sir Tremendous is Pope's antagonist, the critic John Dennis. Arbuthnot is thought to have chiefly written those parts of the play that deal with Fossile's knowledge of antiquarianism and other scientific subjects. The play was a considerable success by contemporary standards, with a run of seven nights in January 1717.

LATER CAREER AND DEATH

Arbuthnot published little, insofar as can be known with any certainty, for several years. He may have written some short pieces of medical satire in a controversy over the treatment of smallpox. Much of his time, however, was spent with his wife and children, and the rest was divided between practicing medicine and leisurely visits with family and friends. He collected political news and gossip and put this information at the disposal of friends who used it for financial speculation. He bought stocks, and though he was involved in the market crash that became known as the South Sea Bubble, he was more prudent than many investors and survived its collapse.

In 1722, when Atterbury was brought to trial by Robert Walpole, Arbuthnot joined Pope in giving aid to their old friend. Walpole was working to remove his political enemies from power while safeguarding the nation against further Jacobite unrest, which continued to be a serious threat to stability. In spite of the efforts of his friends, Atterbury was banished. Arbuthnot, however, was not much affected by such affiliations, and he was appointed second censor of the College of Physicians that year.

In his pamphlet *Reasons Humbly Offer'd by the Company Exercising the Trade and Mystery of Upholders, Against Part of the Bill for the Better Viewing, Searching, and Examing Drugs, Medicines, &c.* (1724), Arbuthnot took up the old dispute between doctors and apothecaries over who was best suited to prescribe drugs to the sick. He pretended to write on behalf of the undertakers, who complained that their business would suffer if the apothecaries were prevented from writing prescriptions and therefore boosting the mortality rate. Arbuthnot argues that a decline in funerals would affect the prosperity of the kingdom, and his undertaker persona argues that anything good for business is good for England.

Another political satire appeared later in the same year, *A Poem Address'd to the Quidnunc's, at St. James's Coffee-House London. Occasion'd by the Death of the Duke of Orleans* (1724). The title was shortened to *The Quidnunckis* when it was reprinted in 1727. In this dialogue between Master Travers and an India merchant, the former seeks news about the death of the regent of France to learn how it will affect politics at home in England and abroad. The merchant responds by telling him of a tribe of monkeys who live on the banks of the Ganges. In this beast fable, the monkeys are like the British public, who forget to pay attention to the present because they are consumed by fears of an uncertain future. Though generally uninspired, the poem shows Arbuthnot continuing to examine the sociological effects of political gossip and news.

Arbuthnot became ill in September 1725, with a cyst in the bowels that was considered life-threatening. He recovered by winter, however, and spent much of his time working on a revision of his earlier antiquarian book, published as *Tables of Ancient Coins, Weights, and Measures* in 1727. Swift returned to London from Ireland in March 1726. There he rejoined his old friends Pope and Gay, who like Arbuthnot had connections with the Prince of Wales. The doctor, who remained a skillful courtier, introduced Swift to Princess Caroline. The reunion of old friends led to further collaboration and in the last years of his life Arbuthnot's pen was very active, with him writing or helping to write a number of works.

On October 5, 1727, Arbuthnot was chosen an elect of the College of Physicians, and thirteen days later he delivered the Harveian Oration. This lecture series had been instituted to commemorate the work of William Harvey, whose discovery of the circulation of blood was the most important medical advance of the seventeenth century. The lectureship was the highest honor that could be bestowed on a British physician. Arbuthnot begins his oration in the usual manner by tracing the rise of scientific medicine in the face of superstition. He urged that medical research using modern methods be continued: recommending the use of microscopes to study disease, the collection of data on climate and its effect on health, and the use of autopsies to learn more about the human body. The lecture, which had been given in Latin, was published soon after as *Oratio Anniversaria Harvaeana* (1727).

Pope claimed that Arbuthnot had a hand in the writing of *Peri Bathous; or, The Art of Sinking in Poetry,* which was published in the "last" volume of the Pope-Swift *Miscellanies* in 1728. Its subject, the ridicule of the defectiveness of modern (mostly Whig) poetry, was certainly one Arbuthnot was familiar with and one he had taken up in other works. But in one of his letters, Pope mentions that Arbuthnot "had grown quite indolent" (quoted in Ross, p. 79) in regard to it, and modern scholars generally believe that he probably supplied little more than conversational hints that Pope later fleshed out in the actual writing.

It is certain that Arbuthnot wrote some of the mock footnotes that Pope added to his *Dunciad Variorum* (1729), as did Swift. Many of these notes contain remarks on the poem written by Martinus Scriblerus, and they continue the satire on learning begun in earlier works like the *Memoirs*. The Scriblerians were well read in classical literature but were opposed to the kind of precise and meticulous scholarship practiced by men like Richard Bentley and Lewis Theobald. They believed that these new scholars made unjustified corrections to the texts they edited and that they buried literature under loads of commentary that either obscured or misrepresented its meaning. The Scriblerians mocked these practices by making Scriblerus oblivious to the irony and humor of the *Dunciad*. His penchant for literal-mindedness and his fascination with the pedantic details of the text lead him to misread the poem in ways that are hilariously wrongheaded.

The scholarship of Bentley and Theobald was subjected to further satire in an appendix of the *Dunciad Variorum,* a mock scholarly treatise by Arbuthnot (pp. 369–374) written in Latin titled *Virgilius Restauratus* (1729). The irony of this work, also putatively by Scriblerus, is in its subject: it sets out to correct the first two books of Virgil's *Aeneid*. Since Virgil was thought to be the most correct poet of antiquity and the *Aeneid* his most perfect poem, the mere fact that Scriblerus would try to improve upon it is a cardinal sin against Scriblerian preferences. His notes are self-evident proof that he is a tasteless bumbler. The real bite of the satire is in its ad hominem attack on Bentley's arrogance, abrasiveness, and self-importance, since not even the learned Arbuthnot could rival his scholarship.

In the last years of the 1720s, Arbuthot's wife, Margaret, became ill, and her health steadily worsened. She died of an apoplexy on May 3, 1730, and was buried in the Church of St. James's, Picadilly. His oldest son died the following year. Arbuthnot was much grieved by these losses. Triumph followed tragedy, however, as Arbuthnot was called to kiss the hand of Caroline on May 21, 1730, to commemorate his second preferment as personal physician to a queen of England.

Though in steadily worsening health himself Arbuthnot returned again to the abuse of political language in *A Brief Account of Mr. John Ginglicutt's Treatise Concerning the Altercation or Scolding of the Ancients* (1731). Like *The Art of Political Lying,* this work is a mock prospectus for an imaginary book. The author claims to prove that "the calling of names is a true Greek and Roman eloquence" (Aitken, p. 383), finding classical precedents for the most vulgar political insults. He admits that these examples are offensive to Christian morality, but finds examples of such language used by priests, popes, and even saints. Traditional British vulgarity is defended as a safeguard of political liberty and an inviolable part of national politics. Though the satire is witty at times, and carries the unexceptionable moral that such behavior is condemned by Christian ethics, even friends like Pope felt that this work was lackluster and uneven.

Another medical treatise appeared in May 1731, *An Essay Concerning the Nature of Aliments, and the Choice of Them, According to the Different Constitution of Human Bodies*. Arbuthnot promoted an attention to diet as a way of securing health. The book was once again meant for a popular audience, and in it he adopts a tone of vigorous common sense: "what we take in daily by pounds," or food, "is at least of as much importance as of what we take seldom, and only by grams and spoonfuls," or medicine. (quoted in Beattie, p. 360). To the second edition, subtitled *To Which Is Added, Practical Rules of Diet in the Various Constitutions and Diseases of Human Bodies,* Arbuthnot added diet advice. It went through many editions throughout Europe.

Arbuthnot's last satire, the "Epitaph on Francis Charteris" (1732), appeared simultaneously and anonymously in both the *London Magazine* and the *Gentleman's Magazine*. Charteris was notoriously immoral, and the "Epitaph" is notable for being Arbuthnot's only departure from the amused detachment of his other satires. Lewdness, fraud, whore-mongering, and rape are among the vices that Arbuthnot condemns Charteris for having practiced. Even in direct condemnation, however, Arbuthnot is morally severe rather than cruel. There is also a political dimension to these attacks, since Charteris had connections with the government of Walpole, so that the personal crimes are also meant as a reflection on the general corruption of the ministry.

In his final medical work, *An Essay Concerning the Effects of Air on Human Bodies* (1733), Arbuthnot studied the influence of air and climate on health. He reasoned that, like food, air was another substance that humans ingest in great quantities. Given how little was actually known about respiration at the time, Arbuthnot made many shrewd guesses about its operations. He also anticipated modern sociology by postulating that climate played a great role in the development of human cultures. Yet true to his religious beliefs, he also felt that people could exercise a certain amount of control over the environment because they were free to follow their own ideas.

Arbuthnot remained undecided about these kinds of questions. In his final work, the poem *Know Yourself* (1734), he explains some of the reasons for his intellectual reserve. The poem begins by asking: "What am I? how produced? and for what end?" (Aitken, p. 436). A mechanical examination of the human body and its workings is balanced by inquiries into the divine qualities of the soul. After dismissing various philosophical and scientific theories that claim to explain human nature, Arbuthnot borrows his conclusion from Pascal: faith can secure divine grace, which helps perfect what has been made imperfect by sin. As Arbuthnot recommends in the conclusion, "Let humble thoughts thy wary footsteps guide, / Regain by meekness what you lost by pride" (p. 439). This rather humble sentiment, one of the last written by a man who was a politician as well as a scientist and an author, is notable for its dual faith in reason and in revelation. Like Pascal before him, Arbuthnot relied equally on both.

Arbuthnot's final years were not all spent in reflection, however. He remained fascinated by the world of finance, investing in stocks, often unsuccessfully. But during this time his health steadily worsened. In the months before his death, he sent letters to Swift and Pope assuring them of his friendship and his expectations of a quiet, peaceful end. He died on February 27, 1735, at the age of sixty-eight, and was buried at St. James's Church in Piccadilly with his wife.

Eulogies written by his contemporaries praised Arbuthnot for his knowledge, morality, and pleasant demeanor. Lord Orrery wrote: "Although he was justly celebrated for wit and learning, there was an excellence in his character more amiable than all his other qualifications" (quoted in Aitken, p. 164). Though some mistook his social complaisance as the sign of an inferior mind, his closest friends agreed with Swift that Arbuthnot had the greatest intellect among the Scriblerians. Chesterfield corroborates this claim: "His imagination was almost inexhaustible, and whatever subject he treated, or was consulted upon, he immediately overflowed with all that it could possibly produce" (p. 1411).

In his *Life of Pope* (1781), the great critic Samuel Johnson described Arbuthnot's character thus: "Arbuthnot was a man of great comprehension, skilful in his profession, versed in the sciences, acquainted with ancient literature, and able to animate his mass of knowledge by a bright and active imagination; a scholar with great brilliancy of wit; a wit, who, in the crowd of life, retained and discovered a noble ardor of religious zeal" (p. 46). In *The Life of Johnson*, James Boswell records that Johnson also praised Arbuthnot as being, "among the eminent writers of Queen Anne's reign ... the first man among them. He was the most universal genius, being an excellent physician, a man of deep learning, and a man of much humour" (p. 225).

This "universal genius" is the quality that is most difficult to appreciate without knowing something of how Arbuthnot's works fit into the fabric of his life, and the most likely to be misunderstood by modern readers. His writings, though successful at the time and respectable today, give glimpses of it. His works reveal his familiarity with life in all its forms as well as his understanding of many professions and sciences, but he carries all this knowledge lightly and his wit animates even the most technical discussions. His social successes also indicate something further about its character. Arbuthnot was intimate with several kings and queens; the highest aristocrats in the nation; politicians, generals, and financiers; the ablest scientists and most talented writers of the time. He was also a Scot at a time when national rivalries and prejudices were fierce. To be an outsider and yet to move gracefully among such different groups of people and to please them all, as Arbuthnot did, required him to be cosmopolitan and polished to an extraordinary degree. He understood himself and his place in the complicated hierarchy of his acquaintances so well that he was able to please many different companions and preserve his reputation as a gentleman with all of them. He earned the professional respect and personal regard of people as different as Queen Anne and Queen Caroline, Flamsteed and Halley, Swift and Pope, Chesterfield and Bolingbroke. Finally, the best qualities of his social genius were deepened in the intimacy that he shared with his family. The breadth of these many qualities is indeed that of a universal genius, and John Arbuthnot was one of the last great examples of the Renaissance gentleman whose scholarship and manners were equally accomplished and graceful.

Selected Bibliography

WORKS OF JOHN ARBUTHNOT

INDIVIDUAL WORKS

Of the Laws of Chance. London: B. Motte, 1692.

An Examination of Dr. Woodward's Account of the Deluge. London: C. Bateman, 1697.

An Essay on the Usefulness of Mathematical Learning, in a Letter from a Gentleman in the City to His Friend in Oxford. Oxford: A. Peisley, 1701.

Tables of the Grecian, Roman and Jewish Measures, Weights, and Coins, Reduc'd to the English Standard. London: R. Smith, 1705. Revised, *Tables of Ancient Coins, Weights, and Measures, Explain'd and Exemplify'd in Several Dissertations.* London: J. Tonson, 1727.

A Sermon Preach'd to the People at the Mercat Cross of Edinburgh on the Subject of the Union. Edinburgh: n.p., 1706.

"An Argument for Divine Providence, Taken from the Constant Regularity Observed in the Births of Both Sexes." *Philosophical Transactions* 27: 186–190 (1710).

An Appendix to John Bull Still in His Senses; or, Law Is a Bottomless-Pit. London: J. Morphew, 1712.

John Bull in His Senses. London: J. Morphew, 1712.

John Bull Still in His Senses. London: J. Morphew, 1712.

Law Is a Bottomless-Pit. London: J. Morphew, 1712.

Lewis Baboon Turned Honest, and John Bull Politician. London: J. Morphew, 1712.

A Complete Key to Law is a Bottomless Pit, and the St. Alban's Ghost. (Variously attributed to Arbuthnot, Jonathan Swift, and William Wagstaffe). London: 1712.

Proposals for Printing a Very Curious Discourse, in Two Volumes in Quarto, Intitled ΩΕΥΔΟΛΟΓΙΑ ΠΟΛΙ-ΤΙΚΗ; or, A Treatise of the Art of Political Lying, with an Abstract of the First Volume of the Said Treatise. London: J. Morphew, 1712.

To the Right Honourable the Mayor and Aldermen of the City of London: The Humble Petition of the Colliers, Cooks, Cook-Maids, Blacksmiths, Jack-makers, Brasiers, and Others. London: J. Roberts, 1716.

Three Hours After Marriage. A Comedy. (With John Gay and Alexander Pope.) London: B. Lintot, 1717.

Reasons Humbly Offer'd by the Company Exercising the Trade and Mystery of Upholders, Against Part of the Bill for the Better Viewing, Searching, and Examining Drugs, Medicines, &c. London: J. Roberts, 1724.

A Poem Address'd to the Quidnunc's, at St. James's Coffee-House London. Occasion'd by the Death of the Duke of Orleans (1724). London: 1724.

Oratio Anniversaria Harvaeana. London: J. Tonson, 1727.

Virgilius Restauratus: Seu Martini Scribleri Summi Critici Castigationum in Aeneidum Specimen. In Alexander Pope, *Dunciad Variorum.* London: A. Dodd, 1729. Pp. 99–103.

A Brief Account of Mr. John Ginglicutt's Treatise Concerning the Altercation or Scolding of the Ancients. London: J. Roberts, 1731.

"An Epitaph on Francis Charteris." *London Magazine,* April 1732, and *Gentleman's Magazine,* April 1732.

An Essay Concerning the Nature of Aliments, and the Choice of Them, According to the Different Constitutions of Human Bodies. London: J. Tonson, 1731. Revised, with the added subtitle, *To Which Is Added, Practical Rules of Diet in the Various Constitutions and Diseases of Human Bodies.* 2 vols. London: J. Tonson, 1732.

"An Essay of the Learned Martinus Scriblerus, Concerning the Origin of Sciences. Written to the Most Learned Dr.——. F. R. S., from the Deserts of Nubia." In *Miscellanies in Prose and Verse,* vol. 3, by Jonathan Swift and Alexander Pope. London: C. Bathurst, 1732.

An Essay Concerning the Effects of Air on Human Bodies. London: J. Tonson, 1733.

Know Yourself. London: J. Tonson, 1734.

The Memoirs of Martinus Scriblerus. In *The Works of Mr. Alexander Pope, In Prose,* vol. 2. London: J. and P. Knapton, C. Bathurst, and R. Dodsley, 1741.

COLLECTED WRITINGS AND CORRESPONDENCE

The Miscellaneous Works of the Late Dr. Arbuthnot. 2 vols. Glasgow: J. Carlisle, 1751.

The Life and Works of John Arbuthnot. Edited by George A. Aitken. Oxford: Clarendon Press, 1892. Reprint, New York: Russell and Russell, 1968.

Memoirs of the Extraordinary Life, Works, and Discoveries of Martinus Scriblerus. Edited by Charles Kerby-Miller. New Haven, Conn.: Yale University Press, 1950. Reprint, Oxford: Oxford University Press, 1988.

The History of John Bull. Edited by Alan W. Bower and Robert A. Erickson. Oxford: Clarendon Press, 1976.

The Correspondence of John Arbuthnot. Edited by Angus Ross. Munich: Wilhelm Fink, 2006.

BIOGRAPHICAL AND CRITICAL STUDIES

Ahrens, Rüdiger. "The Political Pamphlet, 1660–1714: Pre- and Post-Revolutionary Aspects." *Anglia* 109, nos. 1–2): 21–43 (1991).

Aitken, George A. "Life of Arbuthnot." In *Life and Works of John Arbuthnot.* Edited by George A. Aitken. Oxford: Clarendon Press, 1892. Reprint, New York: Russell and Russell, 1968. Pp. 1–188. (Includes criticism and bibliography.)

Beattie, Lester M. *John Arbuthnot, Mathematician and Satirist.* Cambridge: Harvard University Press, 1935.

Bellhouse, D. R. "A Manuscript on Chance Written by John Arbuthnot." *International Statistical Review* 57, no. 3: 249–259 (December 1989).

Boswell, James. *The Life of Samuel Johnson.* Edited by David Womersley. London: Penguin, 2008.

Condren, Conal. *Satire, Lies, and Politics: The Case of Dr. Arbuthnot.* Basingstoke and London: Palgrave Macmillan, 1997.

Erickson, Robert A. "Situations of Identity in the *Memoirs of Martinus Scriblerus.*" *Modern Language Quarterly* 26:388–400 (1965).

Johnson, Samuel. "The Life of Pope." In *The Lives of the Most Eminent English Poets; With Critical Observations on Their Works.* Vol. 4. Edited by Roger Lonsdale. Oxford, U. K.: Oxford University Press, 2006. Pp. 1-93.

Korkowski, Eugene. "Scriblerus' Sinking Opera: *Peri Bathous* XIII." *Literature and Psychology* 24:80–88 (1974).

Koster, P. J. "Arbuthnot's Use of Quotation and Parody in His Account of the Sacheverell Affair." *Philological Quarterly* 48:201–211 (1969).

Laprevotte, Guy. "Note on Arbuthnot's Use of Official Documents in *The History of John Bull.*" *Multiple Worlds, Multiple Words: Essays in Honor of Irène Simon.* Edited by Hena Maes-Jelinek, Pierre Michel, and Paulette Michel-Michot. Liège: Université de Liège, 1987. Pp. 153–159.

Lewis, Peter E. "Dramatic Burlesque in *Three Hours after Marriage.*" *Durham University Journal* 33: 232–39 (1972).

Macaulay, Thomas Babington. *The History of England from the Accession of James the Second.* Vol. 8. London: Longman, Greens, 1870.

Mondschein, Dee, trans. "Virgilius Restauratus: A Translation." *Scriblerian and the Kit-Cats* 33, no. 2:182–88 (spring 2001).

Reynolds, Richard. "*Three Hours After Marriage*: Love on Stage." *Eighteenth-Century Life* 1, no. 1:19–20 (1974).

Rogers, Pat. "Dr. Arbuthnot and His Family." *Notes and Queries* 51, no. 4: 387–389 (December 2004).

Ross, Angus. "Biographical Introduction." In *The Correspondence of John Arbuthnot.* Edited by Angus Ross. Munich: Wilhelm Fink, 2006. Pp. 28–93. (Also includes criticism of letters, pp. 407–489.)

Shoesmith, Eddie. "The Continental Controversy over Arbuthnot's Argument for Divine Providence." *Historia Mathematica* 14: 133-46 (1981).

Shuttleton, David E. "'A Modest Examination': John Arbuthnot and the Scottish Newtonians." *British Journal for Eighteenth-Century Studies* 18, no. 1: 47–62 (spring 1995).

Stanhope, Philip Dormer, Earl of Chesterfield. *The Letters of Philip Dormer Stanhope, Earl of Chesterfield, with his Characters.* Vol. 3. Edited by John Bradshaw. London: Swan Sonnenschein, 1892.

Steensma, Robert C. *Dr. John Arbuthnot.* Boston: Twayne, 1979.

Thackeray, William Makepeace. *The English Humorists of the Eighteenth Century.* Edited by Stark Young. Boston: Ginn, 1911.

Thomas, Claudia Newel. "John Arbuthnot." In *British Prose Writers, 1660–1800.* First series. Edited by Donald T. Siebert. Detroit: Gale, 1991. Pp. 29–40.

WILLIAM BOYD
(1952—)

Charlie Samuelson

A GHANAIAN-BORN writer of Scottish origin, William Boyd has, since the late 1970s, exercised his talents as novelist, short story writer, journalist, screenwriter, and director. He is primarily regarded as a novelist—and, more specifically, a comic novelist, although his later novels move away from the predominantly humorous cast of his early work. Exotic settings further characterize his oeuvre, as well as specific concerns with British expatriates, the visual arts, Africa, and France. Many of his novels are historical fiction, flooded with accurate research. At a philosophic level, a sense of life's fundamental contingency—of chance's unrivaled dominance over individual destinies—is evident in most of his fiction. His lucid and unsentimental prose has frequently been compared to that of Evelyn Waugh. Unlike Waugh, however, Boyd has yet to achieve a considerable following within academic circles. This is possibly the consequence of his being dubbed a "popular" writer, a reflection both of his fiction's accessibility and of its strong sales, notably in Europe. Boyd's fundamental interest lies in his characters, whom he categorically refuses to judge. It is possible that this interest in characters at a microcosmic level has negated the kind of overarching political message favored by today's critics. Regardless, though, Boyd is a prolific, serious writer, who has succeeded both at creating a diverse oeuvre and at maintaining a distinct voice.

"*I am not an autobiographical writer*" (*Bamboo*, p. 1), Boyd often insists. Indeed, the connection between his life and his work is considerably more tenuous than it is for many of his contemporaries. Much to Boyd's distaste, reviewers often attribute this disconnect to the relative stability of his life. While Boyd's life does seem largely free of unusually traumatic occurrences, the distance between his personal and his professional life moreover marks a deliberate, even courageous—certainly unmodish—artistic choice.

BIOGRAPHY

William Murray Andrew Boyd was born on March 7, 1952 in Accra, Ghana. His father, Alexander Boyd, was a successful medical doctor, whose portrait Boyd draws in the highly moral, even self-righteous character of Dr. Murray in *A Good Man in Africa* (1981). Apparently the likeness is so strong that Ken Saro-Wiwa, the Nigerian author and activist, easily recognized him. Boyd's mother was a schoolteacher, and he has two sisters. Little information is available on other members of Boyd's family, with the exception of his paternal grandfather and his great-uncle. These two brothers served together in World War I, prompting Boyd's fascination with this war.

The family lived around Accra until 1963, when they moved to Ibadan, Nigeria. Although Boyd considers his time in Africa as relatively idyllic, growing up there and only infrequently visiting the United Kingdom instilled in him a sense of permanent exile. Boyd has harshly questioned his early relationship with Africa: "We were," he writes, " 'colonial brats.' Lazy, self-regarding, pleasure-seeking and utterly incurious about the country we were living in" (*Bamboo*, p. 7). The Biafran War, however, challenged this deliberate ignorance about things African. Boyd frequently recounts an anecdote in which he and his father accidently drove through a military roadblock, only to have the soldiers raise their rifles. A sense, then, of a world at peace becoming one in turmoil characterizes Boyd's African childhood.

WILLIAM BOYD

In September 1961, nine-year-old William left for prep school in northern Scotland. He candidly evokes his nine years at Gordonstoun in a short memoir published in *School Ties* (1985). Although he offers only minor criticism of the prep school, the secondary school is another story entirely. Boyd describes himself and his peers as "unreflecting snobs," "racist," misogynist, and "politically naïve"—in sum, "not the best set of values with which to re-join the world" (p. 25).

Following his graduation from Gordonstoun, Boyd spent the 1971 academic year at the Université de Nice, where he fell in love with France and matured considerably. He describes his time in Nice as "wholly formative": "It was in Nice that I learned to speak French and where, for the first time, I lived alone and found myself" (*Bamboo*, p. 89). Because of a British postal strike that prevented, for some time, his receiving money, Boyd lived very frugally.

He thereafter returned to Scotland, taking up studies at the University of Glasgow and eventually earning an honors M.A. in English and Philosophy. His considerable productivity was already evident: he was the theater and film critic for the university newspaper; he wrote a play, much poetry, and his first novel, *Is That All There Is?*, an unpublished autobiographical account of his time in France. Shortly before leaving Glasgow, he married Susan, to whom each of his books is dedicated. Susan Boyd, never explicitly discussed in his literature, has worked as an editor and writer for various magazines including *Harper's Bazaar*.

In 1975 the couple moved to Oxford, where Boyd began reading for a D.Phil. in English at Jesus College. His unpublished dissertation, "Philosophical Influences on the Poetry and Prose of P. B. Shelley," led him to certain figures later prominent in his writing, notably Jean-Jacques Rousseau. At Oxford, Boyd wrote two unpublished novels: *Against the Day*, an experimental account of the Biafran War, and *Truelove at 29*, "a thriller about a poet" (*The Dream Lover*, p. 5). After completing his dissertation, he worked as a lecturer at St. Hilda's College, Oxford, and as a teacher of English as a foreign language.

While at Oxford, Boyd began to publish his fiction. "Next Boat to Douala," a story featuring Morgan Leafy, was published by Alan Ross in the August 1978 issue of *London Magazine*. After placing stories in various magazines, Boyd attempted, in 1979, to publish a collection of stories (eventually titled *On the Yankee Station*). In a letter to the publishing house Hamish Hamilton, Boyd lied, claiming that he also had written a novel about Morgan's adventures. Christopher Sinclair-Stevenson agreed to publish Boyd's stories—on condition that he would also publish Boyd's then-unwritten novel. *A Good Man in Africa* was the stunning product of three months of extreme diligence.

Boyd's professional journalism also took off during his Oxford years. From 1981 to 1983 he was the television critic for the *New Statesman*, writing a weekly column. He also regularly contributed (often disparaging) book reviews to the *Sunday Times*. Also while at Oxford, the first of his screenplays, *Good and Bad at Games*, appeared on BBC Channel 4. In 1982 Boyd become a fellow of the Royal Society of Literature.

In 1983 he resigned his Oxford lectureship, and the Boyds moved to the now-swanky London neighborhood of Chelsea, where Boyd continued to write novels and screenplays. He estimates that one in three of his screenplays has been filmed—"*not bad going for a screenwriter*" (*Bamboo*, p. 425). Boyd the novelist professes to enjoy the human contact that filmmaking fosters; no longer is his working day solitary. His numerous screen credits include adaptations of his own novels and works by Evelyn Waugh, Joyce Cary, and Mario Vargas Llosa. In 1998 he took the biggest leap in his film career, for the first time directing one of his own screenplays, *The Trench*.

Asked if he considered himself as much a screenwriter as a novelist, Boyd's response was simple: "No, I consider myself a novelist" (*Bamboo*, p. 427). Throughout his novel-writing career, Boyd has attempted to work eight-hour days. He writes drafts in longhand and knows that he has finished a novel when roughly five notebooks are complete. As of August 2009 he has published nine novels, four collections of short stories, one "monograph," and an impressive amount of journalism, nearly half of which he collects in *Bamboo* (2005).

Various aspects of his earlier life have resurfaced in his adulthood. France, notably, continues to play an important role in both his private life and his career. In 1985 Boyd appeared on the popular television program *Apostrophes*, where Bernard Pivot, its legendary host, promised personally to reimburse any reader who was not satisfied by *An Ice-Cream War*—prompting impressive sales and celebrity status. In 1991 the Boyds bought a small house in the Dordogne, where they preside over a vineyard. The French government compensated Boyd's literary efforts by making him, in 1998, a *chevalier* in the Ordre des Arts et des Lettres, before promoting him, in 2005, to *officier*.

Africa too has continued to exercise an influence over Boyd's life. Most notably, he met Ken Saro-Wiwa in 1986. Boyd remained in contact with Saro-Wiwa until shortly before his untimely and unjust death in 1995. Boyd's disgust at the Nigerian government's treatment of Saro-Wiwa prompted the most politically active moments of his life. He also regularly reviews literature pertaining to Africa.

In 1998 Karen Wright of *Modern Painters* revived Boyd's interest in the visual arts, inviting him to contribute to the magazine and, shortly thereafter, to join its editorial board. Boyd has since been an avid art critic, an expert in postwar British art with a distaste for abstract art and an especial fondness for portraiture. The comic high point of his involvement with the arts occurred with the 1998 publication of *Nat Tate: An American Artist, 1928–1960*. Tate did not exist; the monograph, however, was presented as if it were factually accurate. Much of the New York art world purported to think Tate's legacy unfairly neglected—until the *Telegraph* exposed the "monograph" as a complete hoax.

Finally, Boyd is the recipient of many honors. In 2005 he was given the honorary title of commander of the British Empire. He also holds honorary degrees from the universities of St. Andrews, Stirling, Glasgow, and Dundee.

Boyd concludes an interview with *Le Magazine Littéraire* by refuting any notion that he has achieved all he desires. "When I started wanting to be a writer ... the goal was to realize that ambition. Now that I am a writer, the goal is to continue. I have written, in twenty years of novelistic activity, eight novels. As I will, in twenty years, be seventy, will I write eight more novels between now and then?"

A GOOD MAN IN AFRICA

A Good Man in Africa (1981), Boyd's first published novel and winner of the Whitbread First Novel Award and the Somerset Maugham Award, tells the story of Morgan Leafy, first secretary at the British Commission in the fictional African state of Kinjanja. Morgan inaugurates a long line of Boyd's antiheroes, protagonists characterized by their ravenous sexual appetites, self-obsession, general feelings of dissatisfaction, and uncanny ability to get themselves into situations that spiral far beyond their control. Morgan does, however, stand alone; the freckled, overweight *fonctionnaire* is the most vulgar and angry protagonist Boyd has yet to imagine.

Boyd's prose remains, throughout the novel, fixed in Morgan's mind. The decision to follow his thoughts is all the more remarkable given their illogical, monomaniacal nature. "Confronted by ... logic, he decided to be unreasonable" (p. 40) serves as a terse summation of Morgan's mental processes, and Boyd relentlessly—and humorously—gives them free reign. After Morgan refuses, for example, to copulate with Priscilla because he has gonorrhea, a "sudden flash of prophetic inspiration" leads him to realize that "the price you paid for being good was simply quite out of proportion, preposterously over-valued" (p. 178). By constraining the reader to Morgan's thoughts, Boyd has the reader move with Morgan, and to some extent, one falls into sympathizing with his self-congratulation. While the reader can hardly be as generous to Morgan as Morgan is to himself, Boyd's achievement resides in the intimacy that develops between a morally questionable protagonist and the reader, an endearment that functions almost despite itself.

Boyd subjugates everything in the novel to Morgan—even its exotic setting. Morgan describes Kinjanja as "some immense yeast culture ... festering uncontrolled, running rampant in the ideal growing conditions" (p. 10). Hardly a sensitive description of Africa: here Boyd uses the setting both as a platform on which Morgan's insensitivity can manifest itself and as a means of foregrounding the way Morgan's own story will soon be "festering uncontrolled."

In fact, Boyd's intricate plot provides the "ideal growing conditions" for this festering. Throughout the novel, Morgan often has "the dangerous assumption" that "things couldn't get much worse" (p. 252). And dangerous this assumption is, both for Morgan and for Boyd's later protagonists: things never stop getting worse. Be it in driving around with his boss's dead maid in his trunk, or tackling a visiting poet that his servant mistakes for a local god, Morgan is tested by the intricate plot far more than he—or the reader—could possibly imagine.

By fusing the detestable but subtly endearing Morgan with the often absurd plot, Boyd allows for his signature comedy. Although the novel's depiction of nearly every character as self-interested, insensitive, and unjust would suggest a dark vision, *A Good Man in Africa* is notable for its general levity of tone. For example, it is difficult to understand the novel as a dark portrait of neocolonialism when Morgan is referring to his boss's wife as "the Fat Bitch, or the Old Bag" (p. 18).

In sum, Morgan, the plot, and the comedy are all outrageous; their uniqueness, however, lies in the pathos of Morgan that emerges alongside this absurdity. It is easy to laugh at him, and Boyd provides many opportunities to do so. Yet, when Boyd writes that "he closed his eyes, squeezed them tight shut but the tears seeped through, fat and hot, trickling down his fat hot cheeks" (p. 294), one sympathizes with Morgan—even if he is in the midst of attempting to corrupt the novel's only morally untainted character. The novel makes use of slapstick comedy and an outrageous plot, but it is, fundamentally, the first of many novels built around a "very human heart"—or around a strange but "good man."

AN ICE-CREAM WAR

Winner of the John Llewellyn Rhys Memorial Prize and short-listed for the Booker Prize, *An Ice-Cream War* (1982) is Boyd's first historical novel. Set during World War I, it employs six protagonists: the rebellious and *"different"* (p. 49) Felix Cobb; his sociable but sexually eccentric brother, Gabriel; Gabriel's young wife, Charis; Erich von Bishop, a German farmer; von Bishop's stoic, unexpressive wife Liesl; and Walter Smith, a simpleminded American obsessed with his "Decorticator," a machine for stripping the usable fiber from sisal plants.

A descendant of Joseph Heller's *Catch-22, An Ice-Cream War* portrays war as replete with an absurdity that wavers between the humorous and the harrowing. Boyd sets his novel in what historians consider to be a neglected theater of the war, and the retreat of German troops under General von Lettow-Vorbeck from present-day Tanzania through to Mozambique and into Zambia represents verifiable fact. The inefficiency of the characters' roles in the war, however, does not. After the Armistice, Felix realizes that "he had never fired a shot in anger," begging the question, "What kind of war was it where this sort of absurdity could occur?" (p. 398). Characters indeed spend far less time combating the enemy than they do combating themselves; Gabriel, for example, spends most of the war justifying to himself his desire to remain at a German hospital. When Boyd more directly describes warfare, he often invokes absurdity, as when a British commander accidently kills his Portuguese ally by sneezing and causing Stokes guns to fire. Yet the line between humorous absurdity and sheer horror is nebulous. If it seems absurd that Temple cannot "come to terms" with the disappearance of his Decorticator (p. 276), absurdity moves into horror when the Germans unearth the remains of Temple's dead daughter and "set" the "tiny skull" on a wooden cross (p. 275), or when the deranged intelligence officer Bilderbeck executes troops too scared to engage in combat.

Yet to understand Boyd's novel only as a satirical depiction of war neglects the care—even the twisted love—for his characters that dominates his novels, and *An Ice-Cream War* is as much the story of the Cobbs and the von Bishops as it is that of wartime East Africa. Each of the many protagonists begins the novel as naive, falsely confident, as Felix underscores when he tells Gabriel, "they can't have a war. I'm going to Oxford" (p. 53). The sense of certainty in their initial predicaments—Boyd introduces Charis with the concise "Charis loved Gabriel" (p. 83)—eventually gives way to ambiguous relationships. Indeed, nothing goes as planned for the novel's protagonists, stripping them of their initial naïveté. While Boyd's thwarting of his characters' expectations can ring comically, he nevertheless intersperses, amid the light tone that comedy furnishes, moments of high drama—notably, Charis' suicide. Intermingling comedy with drama keeps drama from seeming overly melodramatic; more importantly, though, such intermingling portrays the characters' lives as a gray scale wherein the distance between the serious and the light, the important and the unimportant—even that between love and indifference—becomes highly suspect.

Of Boyd's first three novels, *An Ice-Cream War* is the least insistently comic, and its serious notes suggest there is more at stake for Boyd in this project. But what is at stake is never explicitly stated, because the characters all retain a crippling disability: they cannot express themselves. Characteristically, Boyd offers little resolution at the novel's end; he writes of Felix and Temple's parting, "There was a pause. They didn't know each other very well" (p. 415). Contrary to what the reader expects in this final glimpse of two protagonists, the conclusion of the novel reiterates the theme of miscommunication or noncommunication that characterizes both the lives of the characters and, on a larger scale, the war. It seems neither purely melodramatic nor purely humorous that, even in the throes of desperation, these characters who lose so much still cannot communicate with each other.

STARS AND BARS

Published in 1984, *Stars and Bars* recounts the adventures, mostly in the Deep South, of Henderson Dores, an English art appraiser recently arrived in New York. Middle-aged and polite, Henderson has "a grumble of a deep insidious kind": he "isn't happy with the personality he's been provided with, thank you very much" (p. 11). Through a series of bizarre adventures, he will eventually acquire not a new personality but "a moment of true liberation": he happily comes to fit in by becoming "just another fucking weirdo" (p. 333).

Henderson initially diagnoses his problem as extreme shyness, an inability to assert his will. Despite his desire to vacation with his mistress, he instead finds himself traveling with his ex-wife's fourteen-year-old daughter Bryant—who then encrusts herself on Henderson's business venture, the valuation of various paintings in the mansion of the eccentric millionaire Loomis Gage.

Henderson's initial passivity becomes all the more evident when contrasted with the extraordinarily willful—or, deranged—cast of secondary characters that surrounds him. The inhabitants of the Gage mansion are the most memorable: among others, Beckman, an amateur particle physicist with a blinking problem who pretends he served in Vietnam; and Shanda, the alcoholic, pregnant former pageant girl who only understands Henderson when he imitates her accent.

In Henderson's mind, the differences between him and the secondary characters are symptomatic of Anglo-American differences. He understands "the way most of his countrymen were shy" as "an ethnic trait, a racial configuration" (p. 16). Conversely, secondary characters often resemble American stock characters: a smarmy, pedophiliac evangelical preacher and the overly sensitive young professional who reminds Henderson "how I value our friendship" (p. 35) serve as examples of a rather stereotypical understanding of America. The superficiality of Henderson's cross-cultural understanding is perhaps explicable in what he calls his "horrible fear of depths" (p. 118).

While the novel does not push beyond a certain superficiality, it nevertheless manipulates Henderson's experience into startlingly ridiculous comedy. Henderson will correctly observe, "Someone up there is having fun at my expense" (p. 278). It is indeed "fun" when, for example, Henderson, "deriving the capacity to *act*" (p. 291) drugs Bryant to prevent her from eloping with Duane, a thirty-five-year-old incapable of fixing Henderson's car and obsessed with hard rock music. Boarding a plane back to New York with Bryant, Henderson pretends that she is "retarded," and that, when she drunkenly moans "Duane," she confusedly means "train" (p. 307).

Finally, it is arguable that the experience of this polite Englishman in a land of lunatics does more than merely strike comic notes. "In the setting of this bizarre household," what once seemed "outrageous" becomes "*de rigueur* rather" (p. 291), and the ridiculous and outlandish serve, at least for Henderson, to question the frontiers and pertinence of "normalcy." It is only through Henderson's recognition of the ubiquity of the abnormal—through, even, his embracing the eccentric in himself—that he can develop a sense of confidence, even of security. What Henderson thinks of his own southern accent could be applied to much of the novel: "It was a little overdone, he admitted, but like an orchestra tuning up, he had to get in key" (pp. 140–141). Once Boyd "gets in key," the comedy resurges; and once Boyd and Henderson get even more "in key," something indefinite but reaffirming does: Henderson comes to embrace himself.

THE NEW CONFESSIONS

Although *The New Confessions* (1987) stands alongside *Any Human Heart* as Boyd's most ambitious novel, it is also among the few not to win any awards. Like *An Ice-Cream War*, it is a historical novel, covering nearly the entirety of the twentieth century, with especial emphases on the Great War, Weimar Germany, and the McCarthy era. The novel, however, avoids as many historical events as it explores—despite John James Todd's presence in Berlin, Hitler's rise is ignored—thereby suggesting the infeasibility of reading it as Boyd's treatise on modern history.

As its title indicates, *The New Confessions* is the only Boyd novel to draw insistently on a literary forebear. Jean-Jacques Rousseau's *Confessions,* Todd informs the reader, were to "become my life" (p. 208). In 1997 Boyd explained Rousseau's appeal to him, writing that "the key to Rousseau's abiding fascination in the modern age" emanates from his being "one of the great characters of history, an absorbing psychological case study" (*Bamboo,* p. 172). Current Rousseau criticism argues that the *Confessions* have a literary interest not because of the various persecutions that tormented Rousseau but instead because of the constant flux in distance that readers feel between themselves and Jean-Jacques—and similar flux marks the reader's relationship to Todd. Despite the many faults of both men (betrayals, impulsiveness, sheer mistakes), the colorful, unusual, and extremely candid character of each remains strikingly constant and disturbingly gripping.

Basic biographical similarities between Rousseau and Todd help to cement the comparison. Both men's mothers die during their births, the first of their many "misfortunes" (p. 1). Both men abandon their children; both feel—and are—unjustly persecuted. Even Todd's name, "John James," is a rather literal translation of Jean-Jacques.

Biographical similarities are nevertheless less telling than structural ones. For the premiere of his film *Confessions: Part I,* the avant-garde Todd employs three screens, and this presentation serves as an apt metaphor for the form of his confessions. Always, in the center screen, is the present, a compelling tale of adventure, love, and frustration. Simultaneously, though, knowledge of Todd's past leads to a sense of its intrusion on present actions. Further, each chapter concludes with a flash-forward to the aging Todd, which reminds the reader that Todd writes retrospectively of his past. The past and the future therefore function as the two "side screens," never far off, that frame Todd's present.

In a sense, then, Boyd's novel is a translation—maybe a vulgarization—of Rousseau's work. Yet, even in Boyd's reliance on Rousseau, there are important differences. Notably, of course, Boyd's work is fictional. That Todd's confessions are fictional implies a constant undercurrent—characteristic of Boyd—of irony. Although the reader is invited to bask in the colorful portrait Boyd draws of Todd, it would be difficult to consider him a social philosopher. Furthermore, unlike Rousseau, Todd fails: he never completes his "great immortal document" (p. 307), the film of the *Confessions*.

But does Todd fail? Like Morgan Leafy, he is proof of Boyd's subtle ability to lead the reader to embrace a seemingly unlikable, even repellent character. Furthermore, it is impressive, even touching, how Boyd has Todd, despite his many shortcomings, address his weaknesses. Todd complains of a "dangerous tendency in my character: the long view, the long term, rarely attracts me" (p. 76). Fascinatingly, though, the narrative's rhythmic, artistic, and diligent pacing contradicts this rampant inconstancy. Inaugurating the importance that mathematics will have in Boyd's later work is Todd's repeated (and scientifically valid) assertion that "life at its basic level, the quantum physicists tell us, is deeply paradoxical and fundamentally uncertain" (p. 569). In his art, however, Todd searches for "control, total control" (p. 176). While Todd remains convinced that life's fundamental uncertainty has dominated his past, it is nevertheless true that in writing, Todd—to an important extent—undoes his credo by resisting, through the pacing, unity, and consistency of the novel, the uncertainty that has dominated his life.

Paradoxical, then, is the narrator's attempt both to write life's contingency and to describe his life retrospectively. Boyd opposes the two notions, and the novel gains from their opposition. Boyd underscores the richness of his characterization of Todd through this characterization's seeming ability to trump life's contingency. John James lives through trials, some of which are historically significant and some of which are purely personal, but from his confessions something richer than a philosophic notion emerges: an identity. One so round that it is, necessarily, "new."

BRAZZAVILLE BEACH

Winner of the James Tait Black Memorial Prize and arguably Boyd's strangest novel, *Brazzaville Beach* (1990) is Hope Clearwater's account of her past. Her story centers on "two sets of strange and extraordinary events" (p. 5): her relationship with her mathematician husband, from its inception through his "insanity" and up to his suicide; and her discovery, at the fictional African research center Grosso Arvore, that the chimpanzees are methodically murdering each other. Hope is loosely modeled on Jane Goodall, and the African intrigue on the chimpanzee wars in 1970s Tanzania.

The novel's technique is radical. Referring to herself, Hope intermingles the first and the third person, generally using the first person to refer to her time with her husband and the third for her adventures in Africa, although this neat delineation eventually collapses. She also includes thirty sections, set off by italics, that relate aspects of her stories to scientific concepts, generally in mathematics and physics. Appearing without chapter breaks, the various means of recounting her story fuse together into a hot body of remembrance, which she hopes to "evaluate" through the act of writing: "I have to make sense of what has taken place before I can start my life in the world, as it were" (p. 5). Ironically, though, Hope "makes sense" of her own past through reflections that have an inverse, dizzying effect on the reader. To adopt the novel's terms, there is no formula for its organization; story lines do not necessarily alternate, and the use of pronouns varies. Instead, the structure of the novel seeks to demonstrate the cornerstone of Hope's philosophy: the prominence of what physicists call "noise," or that which is "completely random and unpredictable" (p. 62).

"Disorder," Hope recalls her husband as saying, *"is not simply handed down a chain, some of it is always being handed back again"* (p. 84). Hope's intermingling of the two story lines invites comparison between them, and it is through this comparison that the subtlety of Boyd's technique emerges. The novel debunks the myth of the peaceful primate, suggesting by analogy that human violence—as seen in the civil

war raging around Grosse Arvore—is somehow genetic. The juxtaposition of the two main story lines even suggests that one should question Hope's trustworthiness. Shortly into her marriage, "the thought came to her, unbidden, unwelcome, that perhaps her husband was going insane" (p. 112). The parallels between her husband's research and her own leave the reader wondering, in a manner recalling Henry James's "The Turn of the Screw," if Hope is also "insane." When she presents her findings to her superior, he rejects them: "So there was no other witness," he says, and Hope responds, "For God's sake, I'm not on trial" (p. 132). While the novel later suggests that Hope is trustworthy, the reader's persistent difficulty in identifying benevolent, admirable, or trustworthy characters creates a sense of uneasiness that extends the theme of uncertainty beyond the novel's rhetoric and into the core of the experience of reading it.

Thematic discussion of the novel, however, does it only partial justice. *"He was trying to comprehend happenstance,"* Hope recalls of her husband, *"and write the book of the unruly world we lived in"* (p. 62). It would perhaps be an exaggeration to hold *Brazzaville Beach* up as "the book of the unruly world," although the world it describes is, without question, characterized by life's precariousness. At the most superficial level, the novel possesses, to adopt Hope's phrase, "a kind of validity" by virtue of her ability to "enchant" (p. 395). It introduces a character whose unique means of understanding the world is dominated by her obsession with life's uncertainties. More compelling, though, than the existence of these uncertainties are her particular means of "evaluating" them. Recalling her period as a wartime hostage, Hope writes, "Coming to a halt had brought me to my senses: no wistful fantasy could be constructed around our present circumstances" (p. 303). Yet, in the novel, Hope rarely "comes to a halt"; she relives the experiences of her past and, despite her initial desire "to say: enough, slow down, give me a break" (p. 5), she instead provides the opposite: a voluptuous, tangled, and fast-paced narrative. Although she claims to be evaluating her past, her reflections on herself are not as clear as those of her immediate predecessor, John James Todd. In fact, more than any other Boydian protagonist, Hope resists the reader. Boyd's antiheroes tend to have moral shortcomings but effect an eventual endearment; Hope, however, is likable but aloof, distant. The Socratic epigram that both opens and closes the novel—"the unexamined life is not worth living"—functions less as a motto by which Hope lives than as a teasing invitation to the reader: an invitation to try to pierce a character and a novel denser and more ambiguous than anything else Boyd has written.

THE BLUE AFTERNOON

Winner of the Sunday Express Book of the Year Award and the Los Angeles Times Book Award, *The Blue Afternoon* (1993) begins and ends with Kay Fischer, an architect in 1930s Los Angeles. Her life is in shambles: her baby has died, prompting her divorce, and her former boss fires her and then steals her work. She is approached by Dr. Salvador Carriscant, an elderly man claiming to be her father. She eventually discovers that, around the turn of the century, Carriscant was Manila's most prestigious surgeon. The heart of the novel lies in Carriscant's recounting of his past to Kay, which Kay then transcribes for the reader. Carriscant's adventures intermingle the story of his love for Delphine Sieverance with a series of unsolved murders in which Salvador may or may not be involved. The novel, then, could be called Boyd's first love story and his only murder mystery.

Boyd divides the novel into three sections: Kay narrates the first and the third in the first person, while the lengthy second section employs the third person to describe Salvador's adventures. True to her profession, Kay serves as the novel's architect: "In architecture, as in art," she writes, everything "must be shaped and styled with intense concentration and focus. One inch ... can make all the difference between something perfect and something botched" (p. 34). Kay's pragmatism conflicts with the exotic, fantastical nature both of Salvador's claims to paternity and of his story itself. Short, though, of overwhelming Salvador's narrative, Kay's presence functions as a layer of security for the reader: we trust the story all the more because Kay too overcomes her difficulties in finding it credible. In concluding the novel's first part, Kay insists on the veracity of her story; and this insistence, when coupled with the precise but somewhat desperate character with which she is identified, largely explains the presence of what some consider a seventy-page preamble to the novel: "in the end this is Salvador Carriscant's story and I have had to trust the teller, as we all must in these circumstances, but what follows is, I believe, as close to the truth as anyone could come" (p. 69).

As in *Brazzaville Beach,* there are important correlations between the two levels of the story. Within Salvador's story, for example, his reactions to his colleague and friend Pantaleon's determination to build the world's first working "aero-mobile" mimic Kay's growing belief in this story: "For the first time he sensed that Pantaleon's dream was not a deluded fantasy after all," he thinks; "the fellow might actually be on to something" (p. 177). The novel, then, foregrounds the notion that out of incredulity comes a growing trust. And the trust is most significant in its eventual fruit: a faith, persistent despite considerable obstacles, in love. In fact, the conceit that Kay transcribes the novel moves her not only from incredulity to belief, but also from a scientific and ascetic coldness to an embrace of love as "a real presence in ... messy, crazy life" (p. 324). At one level, then, the novel is her—and the reader's—leap of faith.

At another level, however, it is Salvador's story—and perhaps primarily so. It is a story of an *amour impossible*. The various secondary characters that surround Salvador—and even Salvador himself—are manipulative and self-interested. Yet, despite human failings—even despite a sense of what Salvador calls "life's impermanency and transience" (p. 200)—love remains as an ideal worth pursuing. Neither Salvador nor Kay solve the murders, and Salvador is not able to spend his life with Delphine. But the ambiguity as to who perpetrates the murders—as well as the extent to which Salvador manipulates Kay—recede before his unambiguous love for Delphine. "He was loved," Kay writes of her father, "and his life was therefore good. And therefore I envy him" (p. 324).

By insisting on the power of love—a power so strong that it overcomes Kay's skepticism and survives Salvador and Delphine's years of separation—*The Blue Afternoon* is Boyd's most optimistic novel. Granted, Boyd heavily qualifies what may otherwise seem a hokey message: the strength of Salvador's love does not negate that bad things happen because people act maliciously. Boyd's earlier novels tend to fuse a levity of tone with a largely dark vision. Salvador and Kay's novel, however, provides the opposite: the prose, though accessible, is less humorous and lighthearted, but its final note is considerably more optimistic. The novel therefore can seem more conclusive than Boyd's others; Kay, in fact, takes her leave with a finality that Boyd never attempts in his other novels: "and I know the answer" (p. 324).

ARMADILLO

The "armadillo," defined in the epigram as a "little armed man," of *Armadillo* (1998) is Lorimer Black, born Milomre Bloçj. Lorimer is a "loss adjuster," the person sent by insurance companies to attempt to soften claims to compensation. Boyd recounts the majority of the novel in the third person, all the while interspersing segments of Lorimer's diary, entitled "The Book of Transfiguration." Like the italicized passages in *Brazzaville Beach,* these entries concisely present either a short anecdote or an idea. Boyd does not present them in their chronological order (he begins with entries 379 and 144) to suggest that the "transfiguration" that Lorimer undergoes is as much a movement backward as it is forward—an exploration of his discontents that takes him well into his past. "The Book of Transfiguration" systematically highlights Lorimer's central interests: his insomnia; the French romantic poet Gérard de Nerval; the enigmatic B-list actress Flavia Malinverno; the theory behind insurance, especially that of his petulant boss; a traumatic experience on LSD;

his passion for armor, medieval and ancient; and his upbringing in an immigrant family.

In many respects *Armadillo* signals Boyd's return to his original turf, and the novel more closely resembles *A Good Man in Africa* and *Stars and Bars* than it does those more chronologically proximate to it. As with Henderson and Morgan, Boyd surrounds Lorimer with an extremely eccentric secondary cast of characters, from the rock star David Watts, convinced that the devil resides on his cheek, to the self-obsessed, slobbish womanizer Torquil Helvoir-Jayne, who latches on to Lorimer. When Boyd combines Lorimer's relative passivity with this strange entourage, a lighthearted and absurd comedy emerges—one that has not been so prominent since *Stars and Bars*. Ridiculous things happen to Lorimer, and Lorimer, in turn, behaves absurdly. In the novel's climactic scene, for example, Lorimer heads to the emergency room—his destination because he has fixed an ancient Greek helmet to his head.

More subtle aspects of Boyd's earlier novels also find their way into Lorimer's story. Like Morgan and Henderson, Lorimer is sarcastic, and when the humor does not lie in the plot's absurdity, it is tangible in his endless quibbles. Complaining about others' reactions to his insomnia, Lorimer reflects, "An admission of constipation did not engender proud boasts of regular bowel movements" (p. 26). Likewise, a sense of irresolution colors the novel, even through its final pages. Despite his sarcasm and his sense of life's contingency, Lorimer grows more comfortable with himself; he even comes to embrace a past from which he has run, willing—at least before Flavia—to re-become "Milo." This "transfiguration," the result of the upheaval of every element of his life—familial, professional, romantic—leads him to notice that "he was beginning to sound like David Watts" (p. 359). In other words, Lorimer, in embracing himself, moves, again like Henderson and Morgan, toward pronounced eccentricity.

While the basic frame of *Armadillo* recalls Boyd's early novels, Lorimer nevertheless possesses certain distinct qualities. He is one of relatively few Boydian protagonists capable of empathy: *"I don't think I am a cold person, on the contrary I am too warm and this, in fact, may be my problem"* (p. 13). His capacity for empathy would, in theory, contradict the lightheartedness of the novel's comedy because, unlike the protagonists in other novels, Lorimer does not seem to deserve what happens to him. At the same time, however, Lorimer's humanity renders the novel more subtle, making it seem less exaggerated, improbable, or outrageous. Lorimer also latches on to the English language as a means of substantiating his process of assimilation. The prose, therefore, pushes farther than those of other Boyd novels; the language moves into a more complex, obviously pondered, exactitude.

In sum, then, Lorimer picks up on notions that have obsessed Boyd throughout his career, and does so in means subtly but not extremely different. The result is a certain directness. He invents, for example, the concept of *"zemblanity,"* or *"the opposite of serendipity, the faculty of making unhappy, unlucky and expected discoveries by design"* (pp. 234–235). This notion, taken up under various names in nearly each of Boyd's novels, has never been stated so clearly. Boyd has moved back from the far reaches of the planet to London, from the exotic to something akin to what Lorimer notices in petty crimes court: "life's niggles and gripes, not real problems—the snagged nail syndrome, the minor toothache disturbance, the sprained ankle effect." Lorimer will say of this scene, "It was all too tawdry" (p. 257). The measure of the novelist, however, is his ability to render the mundane compelling, exciting, rich, and touching—and this is Boyd's achievement vis-à-vis Lorimer.

ANY HUMAN HEART

Winner of the Prix Jean Monnet, *Any Human Heart* (2002) is the fictional diary of Logan Gonzago Mountstuart, whose life spans the quasi-entirety of the twentieth century. Although reviews of the novel were uncharacteristically mixed, many—including Boyd himself—consider it to be his masterpiece. The novel both investigates Boyd's interest in life's contingency and furiously ingratiates itself into various moments of history. Most interestingly, though, it explores how best to enliven a character in his weaknesses and his strengths. If characterization has always been the heart of Boyd's novels, there is no subtler, more moving example than that of Logan.

The ten divisions of Logan's journal roughly demarcate the stages of his long life. A "Preamble" covers his infancy in Uruguay and his Birmingham childhood; his "School Journal" his time at Abbeyhurst College; his "Oxford Journal" his time at university; his "First London Journal" his two marriages; his "Second World War Journal" his spying on the Duke of Windsor in the Bahamas and his incarceration in Switzerland; his "Post-War Journal" his grief at the untimely deaths of his wife and daughter; his "New York Journal" his stint as manager of an art gallery; his "African Journal" his professorship in Nigeria during the Biafran War; his "Second London Journal" his extreme poverty and (naive) involvement with a branch of the revolutionary Baader-Meinhof Group; and, finally, his "French Journal," which chronicles his last days in a cottage in the fictional village of Pays du Lot, situated in the French Pyrénées region.

The generally brief journal entries recount the turns of his life and his mind. Occasionally, an older Logan supplements the entries with a "Note in Retrospect." Logan also includes several "Memoranda," accounts of the various conspiracies that he either uncovers or thinks he does. An anonymous editor supplies brief introductions to each of the diary's "sections" and explanations for chronological gaps in Logan's record keeping. This anonymous editor also inserts explanatory footnotes and even compiles a lengthy index at the end of the book. The editor's interventions testify to the irregularity—and thus the "humanness"—of Logan's diaries while also somewhat ironically suggesting that he is a "historical" figure.

The novel's form allows for Boyd's most direct treatment of his belief in life's contingency. The lack of dominating retrospection distances *Any Human Heart* from *The New Confessions* and allows the reader to experience unexpectedness with Logan. There is no better example of life's brutal randomness than Logan's discovery, upon returning from wartime captivity, that his wife and daughter have died in one of the bombing missions that plagued wartime London. Through experiencing surprise with Logan, the reader gets an acute, perhaps disturbing sense of life's fundamental insecurity: "Feelings of depression; feelings of frustration; feelings of emptiness in the face of all this randomness—done down by the haphazard, yet again" (p. 295), Logan writes. This form leaves Boyd open to charges of evasiveness, even of forgetfulness; jumping and running, the narrative occasionally ignores threads it has previously germinated.

As always, however, it would be dangerous to place too much weight on philosophical notions underlying the novel. Logan writes that "abstraction leaves me cold—there has to be something with a human connection in a painting, otherwise all we are talking about is form, pattern and tone—and it's simply not enough for a work of art" (p. 85). In this vein, "contingency" as an abstract principle is, in its lack of "human connection," "simply not enough" for substantial discussion of the novel's importance.

A similar insufficiency applies to the novel's reliance on history. Boyd's ability to intertwine many of history's most prominent figures into Logan's narrative is remarkable: Virginia Woolf, the Duchess of Windsor, James Joyce, and Pablo Picasso all make appearances. The danger, though, would be to understand Logan as one of his final editors does, when Logan tells him about the famous writers he has met: "As the names tripped off my tongue I could see his eyes widening and I felt more and more like a museum piece, someone to be pointed out … " (p. 379). The inclusion of this secondary cast of real and influential men and women suggests, to some extent, that Logan's life is exceptional. The power, however, of Boyd's characterization is his ability to render Logan both exceptional and unexceptional; to apply Marlow's famous formulation in *Lord Jim,* Logan is "one of us" despite his moving in elite, historically significant circles.

To state the problem otherwise, Boyd does not pretend that a novelistic protagonist ought to be divorced from the historically influential; but therein does not lie his sole, or even predominant, interest.

This interest, instead, is tangible in Logan's roundness. E. M. Forster famously defines the "round character" as one capable of surprising in a credible manner, and Logan epitomizes this. Throughout his life, he constantly evolves, often contradicting, almost negating, earlier "Logans." "The true *journal intime*," he writes, "doesn't try to posit any order or hierarchy, doesn't try to judge or analyse: I am all those different people—all these different people are me" (p. 7). An elderly Logan reflects, "I can see no connection between that schoolboy and the man I am now. What a morose, melancholy, troubled soul I was. That wasn't me, was it?" (p. 464). It is beyond question that Logan contradicts himself. He is alternately optimistic and pessimistic, without there necessarily being substantial reason for the change. He can be extremely caring, providing companionship to a former lover throughout her battle with cancer—and extremely selfish, essentially ignoring that his father is dying. He can be argumentative and he can be resigned; he can be smug or humble.

That Logan can be so many things, and all this credibly, is an achievement, and the scale of this versatility is evident in his ostensible inability to recognize himself at various stages of his life. What unites him throughout the novel—perhaps all that unifies his portrait—is his Loganness. As his friend Ben says to him, "I don't care, Logan. You live your life and I'll live mine. I won't judge you—just as long as you're happy. I'd hope you'd do the same for me" (p. 169). Logan has moments of what would traditionally be identified as "moral weakness"—but, the novel implies, who doesn't? The power and precision, the tenor and the evocativeness of Logan's portrayal of himself (and Boyd's of Logan) are without parallel in Boyd's oeuvre, and Logan's novel represents Boyd's most complex exploration of the aspect of the novel that most interests him: characterization.

RESTLESS

Winner of the Costa Novel Award, *Restless* (2006) is the story of Ruth Gilmartin's discovery, during the summer of 1976, that her seemingly domestic mother was a World War II spy. The novel alternates between Ruth's retrospective memories of the summer, relayed in the first person, and her mother's account of her wartime activities, which she compiles and hands to her daughter in segments.

Her mother, she discovers, is not only Sally Gilmartin but also Eva Delectorskaya, a young woman recruited by British intelligence in 1939 Paris. Eva spends the first years of the war spreading falsified news stories in Europe and then in America. Her time in the United States chronicles Britain's extensive pre–Pearl Harbor propaganda campaign, aimed at getting the United States to join the Allied war effort and, it seems, a moment in history that has been (deliberately) overlooked. Through Eva's compelling story, Boyd draws more heavily on the spy novel subgenre than he has previously done—although Logan dabbles in the world of espionage. Her story, however, is not only one of espionage; it is also one of love and betrayal, for which the profession provides an unusual backdrop.

Shortly into Eva's career as a spy, Lucas Romer, her superior, explains to her "rule number one": "Don't trust anyone" (p. 56). Eva nonetheless becomes infatuated with Romer, despite an outward ability "to switch her feelings off" (p. 168). After a disastrous mission to New Mexico during which she is nearly murdered, she realizes that her lover, Romer, has betrayed her—and his country. She sees that Romer has manipulated his knowledge of her: "He *knew* her, he knew completely what she would do in that situation" (p. 247). She thus resorts to an underground life, "covert, fearful, always watchful, always restless, always watching, suspecting" (p. 273).

She only reveals her secret so as to enlist her daughter's help in confronting her demons. While Ruth offers few insights into her mother's story, she does have recourse to an Oxford professor who speculates that Romer was a Soviet double agent. If, however, Ruth's role in clarifying aspects of her mother's story is questionable, her presence is essential to Boyd's novel. She provides the story with much-needed credibility: "The story of Eva Delectorskaya was too textured, detailed and precise," she writes, "to be the product of a mind convulsed with fantastical re-invention, let alone on the verge of senile dementia" (p. 181). Beyond insisting on the veracity of her mother's story, Ruth also becomes a surrogate through which her mother exercises what she learned as a spy, thus rendering this improbable past more credible. Her mother, she realizes, "had used me almost in the same way Romer had tried to use her. I realised that, all this summer, my mother had been carefully running me, like a spy" (p. 311). Ruth, therefore, comes to testify to the spy-like aspects of her mother's character that she has chosen to adopt as well as to the long-lasting, devastating effects of her former career: paranoia. "What duplicities are still fizzing in your brain? Will you ever have a quiet life, will you ever truly be at rest?" (p. 311).

Surprisingly, Boyd also has Ruth normalize or render quasi-quotidian aspects of the spy profession. Ruth constantly reflects on "how little we actually, really, know of our parents' biographies ... unless we take the trouble to dig deeper" (p. 33). Does this truism—certainly one in the Boydian cosmos—render pasts as incredible as that of Eva Delectorskaya somehow normal? Even the paranoia that plagues her mother is also evident in Ruth: she experiences "some atavistic motherly anxiety" (p. 34) when, waiting to fetch her son from school, she imagines that he will not appear. Indeed, links between Ruth's and Eva's emotional registers strongly suggest that *Restless* is not only a spy novel; instead, Boyd manipulates aspects of the genre to highlight what Ruth calls "a very human reaction to the human condition" (p. 58).

Yet the world of espionage, true as it can be to elements of the human condition, is also ridiculous. And this ridiculousness, which, in characteristic manner, Boyd invokes with an ironic tone, also marks the fruit of Ruth's presence in the novel. Ruth wonders, for example, if her former boyfriend's brother and his companion are working for radical German terrorists—only to learn they are being investigated for "aggressive begging." Drunk, she distastefully asks one of her Iranian students if there are Iranian secret agents in Oxford. The spy world, then, becomes not only "human" but also Ruth's absurd adult playground, invented to escape life's tedium.

Romer's guiding principle is that "false information can be just as useful, influential, as telling, transforming or as damaging as true information" (p. 72). The test of Boyd's most commercial novel will lie in his dissemination of false information, the ultimate question being, do his characters render pathetic what, even for Boyd, is a very unlikely story?

SHORT FICTION

Throughout his career as a novelist, Boyd has also been writing short fiction. Although his short fiction—perhaps due to the genre's place in today's market—has attracted neither the audience nor the critical reception that his novels have, his three collections of stories (the fourth, *The Dream Lover,* merely combining the first two) and his one fictive biography evidence many of the concerns apparent in his novels and stand in their own right as a diverse, somewhat experimental body of work.

"The stories in *The Dream Lover*," writes Boyd, "are as much a part of my writing life—and help explain who I am as a writer of fiction—as my novels" (p. 8). The twenty-four stories, sixteen of which appeared in 1981 as *On the Yankee Station* and the remaining nine of which appeared in 1995 as *The Destiny of Nathalie 'X,'* (one story is repeated) were for the most part previously published in a diverse array of magazines, including *London Magazine* and *Granta*. Notable in both collections is how little the stories have in common: Boyd ranges from a crazed man convinced that the two sides of his brain do not communicate to two lengthy accounts of a British student's experiences in Nice; from an African shooting a French film in Los Angeles to a World War I Austrian soldier battling depression. Both collections are also directly relevant to his novels: *Yankee Station,* a collection of sixteen stories, includes two stories about Morgan Leafy, and *Nathalie 'X'* one about Logan Mountstuart (then "Mountstewart").

While the prose always remains comprehensible, Boyd permits himself, in both collections, a level of stylistic experimentation—or affectation?—that his novels would never take up. The themes remain distinctly Boydian—fidelity, obsession, Africa, France, and art, for example—but Boyd profits from the "freedom" of the shorter genre: "freedom to change habits, to experiment, to take risks, to try out different voices, to fracture narrative ..." (p. 7). The result of such experimentation is, frequently, a reigning ambiguity, and the sense of uncertainty that plagues the lives of his many characters is transmitted to the reader by way of a reigning uncertainty about each story. Without explicitly indentifying them, Boyd also weaves several historical figures—Fernando Pessoa and Ludwig Wittgenstein, among others—into his collections.

Fascination (2004) comprises sixteen stories, ten of which were previously published, mostly in the *New Yorker*. Unlike his other collections, *Fascination* has no direct ties to his novels. As in the earlier collections, however, the settings and tones of the stories vary dramatically: from a young man selling fake steroids in contemporary Eastbourne (U.K.) to a boy who, escaping his mother's infidelity, nourishes a friendship with Georges Braque. Similar distinctively Boydian themes reappear: dissatisfaction, adultery, art and eccentricity. Most striking, though, are the unconventional narrative forms on which Boyd draws. "Adult Video" is presented as a DVD, with Edward manipulating the technology's ability to run forward and back, quickly and slowly through his life; "Lunch" as a series of menus; and "Incandescence" as various interviews that together form a portrait of Alex's time with his ex-girlfriend's family. Even the more seemingly conventional stories frequently employ double narratives, where Boyd juxtaposes a fictional present with his character's past.

The range of narrative structures, most of which, it seems, Boyd judges too audacious to include in his novels, often leads to a considerable amount of uncertainty. It is not, for example, clear in "Visions Fugitives" exactly who narrates each of the various segments of a story that defies chronology. The collection, therefore, contradicts the narrator of "The View from Yves Hill," who claims, "only in fiction is everything about other people explained. Only in our fictions is everything sure and certain" (p. 106). Ambiguity and uncertainty are themes Boyd belabors in his novels; but the brevity of the form allows his short fiction to underscore said ambiguity and leave it—quite often—as the dominant impression that a story offers. Regardless, though, ambiguity relies on the reader's latching on to characters, and it is the measure of Boyd's talent as writer of short fiction that, in few words, he creates characters sufficiently interesting for the reader to become attached and sufficiently mysterious for the reader to continue wondering about them.

The black sheep of Boyd's short fiction—if not of his oeuvre—is *Nat Tate: An American Artist, 1928–1960* (1998). Ostensibly a monograph, it ignores detailed analyses of Tate's work and instead traces the story of his short life, from his childhood through his brief period of fame as an abstract expressionist and his suicide. Most of the information that Boyd cites comes from Logan Mountstuart's journals, with Boyd even transposing lengthy passages into Logan's "New York Journal" in *Any Human Heart,* published four years later. Beyond merely serving as evidence of the amount of toil Boyd put into Logan, *Nat Tate* also serves as an investigation into the nature of reality. Verisimilitude has always had a particularly important place in Boyd's writing, and from the beginning of his career, Boyd has intermingled fact with fiction. Never, however, does he do so more prominently than in *Nat Tate* and *Any Human Heart,* and, unlike in the latter, nothing in the presentation of *Nat Tate* suggests that it is a work of complete fabrication. Boyd's success at flexing his muscles—at rendering determinably credible his ability to fuse the fictional and the historical—is tangible in the reaction that the monograph received. The biography is fictional. The photographs that Boyd includes are ones he had collected throughout his life; the drawings are his own. In on the secret of

Tate's fictitiousness were, notably, David Bowie (whose 21 Publishing published the "monograph"), Gore Vidal, and Picasso's biographer John Richardson. On 1 April 1998 Bowie invited much of the New York art world to the Manhattan studio of the pop artist Jeff Koons, where he read dramatic excerpts from the monograph.

Apparently, many in the crowd pretended already to know of Tate's existence; some even claimed to have met him. Several days after the New York premiere, the *Telegraph* exposed the monograph as a hoax. While Boyd and the monograph's publishers have insisted that it was not intended to expose the pretentiousness of New York's art world, it most certainly did so. Standing quite alone in his oeuvre, *Nat Tate* provides substantial evidence of, among other things, Boyd's knowledge of the art world; his penchant for satire and humor; and his ability to create a fictive story that is extremely credible. However, because much of the value of the work lies in the reaction it elicited and not in what its pages contain, it does not stand with his novels as a literary monument.

FILMS

"As I began to write and publish novels," writes Boyd, *"I always hoped that this would encourage a door to open to the world of cinema"* (*Bamboo,* p. 425). The "door opened" in 1982, when the newly founded Channel 4 commissioned non–film writers to write scripts. Since *Good and Bad at Games,* Boyd has written *"some three dozen scripts,"* (p. 425), about a third of which have been made into films, either for the cinema or for British television. The films, however, have not been greeted with much applause, in terms of either popular or academic response. Nevertheless, as with his novels and stories, they encompass an extraordinary variety of settings, genres, and styles, thereby testifying to Boyd's impressive work ethic and to his versatility.

Good and Bad at Games (1983) is the first of two films to deal with the public school experience. In 1985 Boyd published it alongside *Dutch Girls* and a memoir about his time at public school as *School Ties*. *Good and Bad at Games* is a dark portrayal of the trauma incurred by public school hazing—and its persistence years after the fact. The film is remarkably faithful to the experience that Boyd outlines in his memoirs, incorporating the sexism, racism, and violence inherent in the public school experience. While *Dutch Girls* (1985) also explores the public school experience, it instead offers a lighthearted, playful look at adolescent sex. Starring a young Colin Firth, the film follows a Scottish public school's field hockey team during a trip to Amsterdam, where the various players do not find hockey to be the main sport.

Shortly after *Dutch Girls,* Boyd began to adapt the fiction of others. He vehemently dislikes the term "adaptation," arguing that the generic constraints of film render it impossible—and irrelevant—for a film to be faithful to its parent novel; it nevertheless seems that each of his screenplays is, at least in spirit, faithful to the original work. *Scoop* (1987), an adaptation of Evelyn Waugh's farcical and satirical novel, is the story of a young man mistakenly identified as a war correspondent and thereafter sent to Ishmaelia, a fictionalized African nation. Also set in Africa is *Mister Johnson* (1990), an adaptation of Joyce Cary's novel of the same name. Set in the 1920s, the film treats the life of an intelligent but flawed African who, enamored of England, attempts to earn his living within the colonial administration. The film succeeds at presenting a complex and nuanced portrait of the relationships between colonists and their subjects, and Maynard Eziashi's portrayal of Mr. Johnson earned him a Berlin Silver Bear.

The year 1990 also saw the realization of *Tune in Tomorrow* (a.k.a. *Aunt Julia and the Scriptwriter*), adapted from Mario Vargas Llosa's novel. The film won the director Jon Amiel both the Audience Award and the Critics Award at the 1990 Deauville Film Festival. The story of a young man's (Keanu Reeve) affair with his (nonbiological) aunt and the influence a radio playwright exercises over their romance, the film combines simple and lighthearted comedy with an ironic, self-referential take on the act of storytelling. Finally, Boyd returns to Waugh in *Sword of Honour* (2001), a four-hour adaptation of the famous trilogy for Britain's Channel 4 and winner of several RTS (Royal Television Society) awards. A largely autobiographical story of Waugh's wartime pursuits as they take him around Europe and Africa, the film explores Guy Crouchback's (Daniel Craig) initial infatuation and then growing disillusion with the British military as well as his struggle with Catholicism.

In 1988 Boyd began to adapt his own fiction; and, to date, he has adapted his three most comic novels: *Stars and Bars* (1988), *A Good Man in Africa* (1994), and *Armadillo* (2001). *Stars and Bars* stars Daniel Day-Lewis as Henderson Dores and includes, among others, a young Joan Cusak as Henderson's mistress. Like the novel, the film is an outlandish comedy that pits an uptight and stereotypically English Henderson against a deranged and equally stereotypical cast of American southerners. Because of infighting at Columbia Pictures, the film never got a traditional release. In *A Good Man in Africa,* Colin Friels plays Morgan Leafy, and Sean Connery Dr. Alex Murray, and, as in the novel, everything goes wrong for Morgan. The film, however, serves as evidence of the subtlety of Boyd's novel; although the plots of the film and the novel are extremely similar, the film fails to get the viewer to empathize with Morgan and thus flounders before the book's power. In 2001, BBC 1 commissioned a three-hour *Armadillo*. Starring James Frain as Lorimer Black, the novel is a dark comedy that takes the viewer through many of London's quite varied neighborhoods. As in the novel, Black finds himself at the center of a massive insurance fraud—before becoming its unlikely victim.

Since *School Ties,* Boyd has written four original screenplays. His most mainstream film, *Chaplin* (1992), is the story of the man behind the legend. He shares scriptwriting credit with Bryan Forbes and William Goldman; Boyd credits the latter with all scenes featuring an elderly Chaplin. Nominated for three Academy Awards, the film casts a largely sympathetic look at Chaplin's rise from extreme poverty to his unparalleled success in a newly emergent Hollywood. The film also chronicles Chaplin's love affairs with several young girls and his eventual expulsion from the United States.

Boyd shares the screenwriting credits for *Man to Man* (2005) with Michel Fessler, Fred Fougea, and Régis Wargnier. The French Wargnier directed the film, earning himself a Berlin Golden Bear. Although the film opened the 2005 Berlin Film Festival, it was never released in the United States or the United Kingdom. Set in the late nineteenth century, the plot involves several British scientists who capture two African pygmies and bring them to Scotland. The scientists are bent on proving that the pygmy functions as a link in the evolutionary chain that stretches from chimpanzees through to the white man. In the course of their research, however, Dr. Dodd (Joseph Fiennes) begins to notice his subjects' humanity, and eventually sets out, much to the displeasure of his cohorts, to prove their equal stature to white men.

Also appearing in 2005, *A Waste of Shame: The Mystery of Shakespeare and His Sonnets* stars Rupert Graves as William Shakespeare in a film that attempts both to humanize the legendary writer and to posit a hypothesis as to the identities of the figures evoked in his sonnet sequences. Boyd asserts that the young man evoked in his sonnets is Master William Herbert (Tom Sturridge) and that the "dark lady" (Indira Varma) may well have been a local prostitute. The film also suggests that Shakespeare died after contracting syphilis from the young woman in question.

Finally, Boyd took the most significant leap in his film career in 1999, for the first time directing one of his own screenplays. *"The Trench,"* writes Boyd, "can sit on the shelf with my novels because, although it's a huge collaboration, it's exactly as I hoped it would be" (*Bamboo*, p. 442). The film capitalizes on Boyd's profound interest in the Great War by following the life of several privates and their sergeant in the forty-eight hours prior to the 1916 Battle of the Somme. Daniel Craig stars as the sergeant and was awarded a British Independent Film Award for Best Actor. Boyd composed the rest of the cast, including Paul Nicholls and Julian Rhind-Tutt, of young and relatively inexperienced actors in an attempt to underscore more accurately how young the frontline soldiers of the time were.

JOURNALISM AND CONCLUSION

Boyd begins *Bamboo* (2005) with an apt question: "When did I find the time to write these hundreds of thousands of words alongside the main business of my writing life: novels and screenplays?" (p. xv). Representing, according to his estimates, forty percent of his total journalism, *Bamboo* functions as testament to a startling work ethic and a versatile, curious intellect.

Faced with roughly three decades of journalism, Boyd imposes "a rough criterion of choice" (p. xvi): the included journalism is to shed light on his literature. This light can be factual, as when Boyd explains that *Stars and Bars*'s Luxora Beach is modeled on Tallapoosa, Georgia. At other times, however, it is more profound. Boyd's review, for example, of a biography of Rousseau elaborates his understanding of Rousseau's "abiding fascination in the modern age" (p. 172).

Like Logan Mountstuart's journal, Boyd divides the collection into overarching categories that represent his principal interests: "Literature," "Art," "Africa," "Film," "Television," and the more loosely unified "People and Places." Also like Logan's journals, the collection represents a tonal range, moving from often biting literary reviews for the *Sunday Times* to highly emotional pieces on, among others, Saro-Wiwa and Sarah Raphael; from a humorous piece on translation to stoical, calm theorizing on short fiction. Boyd's impressive range, both in terms of the subjects he treats and his means of treating them, recalls the Henry James epigraph that introduces Logan's novel: "Never say you know the last word about any human heart."

As with Logan, the various divergent strands nevertheless come together to form, as Boyd writes, an "intellectual portrait, I suppose" (p. xv). And, contrary to Logan's or John James Todd's reflections on their own lives, Boyd realizes that "it's never quite so haphazard a journey as you think" (p. xvi).

There is, however, an important difference between the Boyd who resurfaces in *Bamboo* and many of his novelistic protagonists. His protagonists tend to be somewhat dislikable and later become endearing despite morally problematic qualities. Yet Mr. Boyd has never been unlikable—quite the contrary, in fact.

Selected Bibliography

WORKS OF WILLIAM BOYD
(All citations in this article refer to the most widely accessibly paperbacks, published, through *Fascination*, by Penguin and thereafter by Bloomsbury.)

Novels
A Good Man in Africa. London: Hamilton, 1981; Harmondsworth, U.K.: Penguin, 1982.

An Ice-Cream War. London: Hamilton, 1982; Harmondsworth, U.K.: Penguin, 1983.

Stars and Bars. London: Hamilton, 1984; Harmondsworth, U.K.: Penguin, 1985.

The New Confessions. London: Hamilton, 1987; London: Penguin, 1988.

Brazzaville Beach. London: Sinclair-Stevenson, 1990; London: Penguin, 1991.

The Blue Afternoon. London: Sinclair-Stevenson, 1993; London: Penguin, 1994.

Armadillo. London: Hamilton, 1998; London: Penguin, 1999.

Any Human Heart. London, Hamilton, 2002; London: Penguin, 2003.

Restless. London: Bloomsbury, 2006.

Short Fiction
On the Yankee Station, and Other Stories. London: Hamilton, 1981; Harmondsworth, U.K.: Penguin, 1982. Expanded ed., Penguin, 1988.

The Destiny of Nathalie 'X.' London: Sinclair-Stevenson, 1995; Harmondsworth, U.K.: Penguin, 1996. (One story, "Alpes Maritimes," is reprinted from *On the Yankee Station* with few changes.)

Nat Tate: An American Artist, 1928–1960. Cambridge, U.K.: 21 Publishing, 1998.

Fascination. London: Hamilton, 2004; London: Penguin, 2005.

The Dream Lover. London: Bloomsbury, 2008. (Re-collects stories from *On the Yankee Station* and *The Destiny of Nathalie 'X.'*)

Films
Good and Bad at Games. Written by William Boyd. Directed by Jack Gold. Channel Four Television, 1983.

Dutch Girls. Written by William Boyd. Directed by Giles Foster. London Weekend Television, 1985.

Scoop. Written by William Boyd. Novel by Evelyn Waugh. Directed by Gavin Millar. London Weekend Television, 1987.

Stars and Bars. Screenplay by William Boyd. Directed by Pat O'Connor. Columbia, 1988.

Mister Johnson. Written by William Boyd. Novel by Joyce Cary. Directed by Bruce Beresford. Avenue Pictures, 1990.

Tune in Tomorrow (U.K. title: *Aunt Julia and the Scriptwriter*). Written by William Boyd. Novel by Mario Vargas Llosa. Directed by Jon Amiel. Odyssey and Polar Entertainment, 1990.

Chaplin. Screenplay by William Boyd, Bryan Forbes, and William Goldman. Books by David Robinson and Charles Chaplin. Story by Diana Hawkins. Directed by Richard Attenborough. Carolco Pictures, Canal+, RCS Video, and Lambeth Productions, 1992.

A Good Man in Africa. Screenplay by William Boyd. Directed by Bruce Beresford. Capitol Films, Polar Entertainment, South African Breweries, and Southern Sun, 1994.

The Trench. Screenplay by William Boyd. Directed by William Boyd. Arts Council of England, Blue PM, Bonaparte, British Screen, Canal+, Galatée, Portman Entertainment, and Skyline Films, 1999.

Sword of Honour. Screenplay by William Boyd. Novels by Evelyn Waugh. Directed by Bill Anderson. TalkBack Productions, 2001.

Armadillo. Screenplay by William Boyd. Directed by Howard Davies. A&E, BBC, 2001.

A Waste of Shame: The Mystery of Shakespeare and His Sonnets. Screenplay by William Boyd. Directed by John McKay. BBC, 2005.

Man to Man. Written by William Boyd and Régis Wargnier. Screenplay by Michel Fessler and Fred Fougea. Directed by Régis Wargnier. Vertigo, Skyline Films, France 2 Cinéma, France 3 Cinéma, Boréales, TPS Star, Imaginarium, 2005.

OTHER WORKS

School Ties. London: Hamilton, 1985. Harmondsworth, U.K.: Penguin, 1985.

Bamboo: Nonfiction 1978–2004. London: Hamilton, 2005. Published in the United States as *Bamboo: Essays and Criticism.* New York: Bloomsbury, 2007.

BIOGRAPHICAL STUDIES

(There are very few scholarly articles and books directly pertaining to Boyd. While perhaps not seminal works, they are all included here.)

Dunn, Douglass. "Divergent Scottishness: William Boyd, Allan Massie, Ronald Frame." In *The Scottish Novel Since the Seventies: New Visions, Old Dreams.* Edited by Gavin Wallace and Randall Stevenson. Edinburgh: Edinburgh University Press, 1993. Pp. 149–169.

Elices, Juan F. *The Satiric Worlds of William Boyd: A Case Study.* Europäische Hochschulschriften. Bern: Peter Lang, 2006.

Lázaro, Luis Alberto. "El nuevo destino de William Boyd." *Revista Canaria de Estudios Ingleses* 35: 47–59 (1997).

Reymond, Jacqueline. "Paratexte et échec des formules dans *Brazzaville Beach* de William Boyd." *Études Britanniques Contemporaines* 1:45–61 (1992).

Rivas, Christina. "Alteridad y aliedad: Reflexiones sobre identidad y marginalidad en *A Good Man in Africa* de William Boyd." *Revista Canaria de Estudios Ingleses* 39:323–338 (1999).

Vinet, Dominique. "Intertextualité et jeu de lois dans *The New Confessions* de William Boyd." *Études Britanniques Contemporaines* 7:17–28 (1995).

———. "William Boyd: L'échouage du récit dans l'épilogue." *Études Britanniques Contemporaines* 10: 37–53 (1996).

REVIEWS AND INTERVIEWS

Blau, Eleanor. "New Territory for Explorer in Fiction." *New York Times,* May 21, 1983, sec. 1, p. 29. (Interview with particular relevance to *An Ice-Cream War.*)

Clements, Toby. "A Writer's Life." *Daily Telegraph,* August 26, 2006, p. 12. (Interview with particular relevance to *Restless.*)

Cox, Tom. "William Boyd: The Magician of Realism." *Daily Telegraph,* April 16, 2002, p. 17. (Interview.)

Decker, Jacques de. "William Boyd ou la vie en examen." *Le Magazine Littéraire,* November 1, 2002, pp. 98–103. (Interview; citation in article is author's translation.)

Dibock, Barry. "Condemned by His Own Success, How Does William Boyd Keep Producing Bestselling Novels?" *Sunday Herald,* October 1, 2006, p. 24. (Interview and review of *Restless.*)

Foden, Giles. "Heart of the Matter: Giles Foden Sifts the Many Selves of William Boyd." *Guardian,* April 20, 2002, p. 9. (Review of *Any Human Heart.*)

Gillmor, Don. "Boyd's Subtle *Blue Afternoon* Moves at the Pace of a Mystery." *Globe and Mail,* February 12, 1994. (Review of *The Blue Afternoon.*)

Glover, Fi. "The Book That Changed My Life." *New Statesman,* May 25, 2009, p. 52. (Review of *Any Human Heart.*)

Guinness, Daphne. "Tapping Into His Female Side." *Sydney Morning Herald,* October 14, 2006, p. 39. (Interview with particular relevance to *Restless.*)

Huck, Peter. "A Good Man in Print." *Sydney Morning Herald,* February 9, 1991, p. 49. (Interview with particular relevance to *Brazzaville Beach.*)

Kakutani, Michiko. "William Boyd's Reverberations with Rousseau." *New York Times,* April 27, 1988, sec. C, p. 24. (Review of *The New Confessions.*)

———. "Living Among Mathematicians and Apes." *New York Times,* May 31, 1991, sec. C, p. 29. (Review of *Brazzaville Beach.*)

———. "Love at the Busy Intersection of Public and Private." *New York Times,* April 11, 1995, sec. C, p. 18. (Review of *The Blue Afternoon.*)

Lyall, Sarah. "Raising Obscurity to an Art, a Book Gives a Painter Undue Fame." *New York Times,* April 9, 1998, sec. E, p. 1. (Review of *Nat Tate: An American Artist, 1928–1960.*)

Scott, A. O. "As Ill Luck Would Have It." *New York Times,* November 22, 1998, sec. 7, p. 10. (Review of *Armadillo.*)

Yardley, Jonathan. "The Great War Goes to East Africa: *An Ice-Cream War.*" *Washington Post,* March 20, 1983, p. 3. (Review of *An Ice-Cream War.*)

RON BUTLIN

(1949—)

Brian Hoyle

THE SCOTTISH POET, novelist, and short story writer Ron Butlin is one of the best-kept secrets in contemporary British literature. Over his four-decade career as a writer he has, in his own words, been "constantly undiscovered and rediscovered." He emerged as a promising poet in the mid-1970s, won the Scottish Arts Council Book Award three years running (twice for poetry, once for prose) in the early 1980s, yet by the late 1990s his debut novel, *The Sound of My Voice* (1987), was being discussed as a "lost classic." However, since the 1990s Butlin's international reputation has grown considerably. He has won yet more awards and been named the *makar* (poet laureate) of the city of Edinburgh. While at the time of this writing Butlin may be set to be rediscovered once again, a wide popular readership has always eluded him. Rather, he remains something of a critic's favorite and a "writer's writer." Figures as diverse as Edwin Morgan, Douglas Dunn, Irvine Welsh, and Ian Rankin have championed his work and helped it to at least begin to reach the wider audience it wholly deserves.

The following critical overview of Butlin's career to date draws from reviews, published interviews, and appreciations by other writers in order to give as nuanced an introduction to Butlin's work as possible. Lizzie MacGregor at the Edinburgh Poetry Library also provided invaluable assistance to this essay. The text owes its greatest debt, however, to the author's personal interviews with Ron Butlin. All unattributed quotations are taken from those conversations.

BIOGRAPHICAL AND CAREER OVERVIEW,

Ron Butlin was born in Edinburgh on November 17 1949, but spent (most of) his first eleven years in the village of Hightae and the next five in the town of Dumfries. His difficult relationship with his father is reflected in much of his work. At the age of sixteen he left school and moved to London. While there he supported himself with a variety of odd jobs, including working as a lyricist with a pop band (called Tangerine Peel), a barnacle scraper on Thames barges, and a footman attending embassies and country houses. Finally, in the early 1970s, Butlin returned to Scotland, where, after a year working as a life model in the Edinburgh College of Art, he attended Edinburgh University to study philosophy and history from 1971 to 1977. It was at this time that Butlin began writing poetry, although at first he never thought of taking up writing as a profession.

In the early to mid-1970s, Butlin and two other aspiring poets, Brian McCabe and Andrew Greig, now also notable Scottish writers, gave readings under the collective name "The Lost Poets." As Butlin remembers, in an essay recalling the group for the *Edinburgh Review,* "The Lost Poets were formed ... as a way of making some money, selling some books and pulling women. In none of these were we particularly successful" (p. 86). Later, Liz Lochhead joined them, and the Lost Poets produced one short collection, which featured several of Butlin's early poems. As Butlin remembers, it was "an attempt to recoup our finances. Maybe we should have tried T-shirts" (p. 88).

Despite their lack of commercial success, Butlin notes that this was a formative experience for him as a writer:

The ear is a much better critic than the eye. Through reading my work day after day, and listening to the others, I came to find my own voice and to be increasingly sensitive to what I wrote. Also, from well before The Lost Poets were "founded" and right up to the present we have met and read each others' work and made helpful comments. Without this, I know I would never have written the way I have.

(p. 88).

Following on from this, Butlin produced a pamphlet of twenty-three poems in both English and Scots titled *Stretto* (1976), which established him as a Scottish poet of great promise. Subsequently, Butlin published several more volumes of poems: *Creatures Tamed by Cruelty* (1979), which placed highlights from *Stretto* alongside new pieces and a significant early poem; *The Exquisite Instrument* (1982) was a series of free translations from Chinese poets, which won him the first of his three consecutive Scottish Arts Council Book Awards; *Ragtime in Unfamiliar Bars* (1985), which was Butlin's first collection of original material written entirely in English (which not only won the Scottish Arts Council Book Award for poetry but was also a Poetry Book Society recommendation); *Histories of Desire* (1995); and in 2005, *Without a Backward Glance,* a career-spanning volume containing work from all the previous volumes (with the exception of *The Exquisite Instrument*) as well as some new and previously uncollected poems. In 2008 Butlin was selected to succeed Valerie Gillies as the official *makar (*poet laureate) of the city of Edinburgh. He was commissioned to write poems on subjects such as "The Gathering of the Clans," "The Clipper Yacht Race," "Poetry in St. Andrew's Garden," "Vibrant Edinburgh," and "The Homecoming." Butlin has said that he was delighted at such an honor and accepted it immediately.

In the early 1980s Butlin also turned his hand to fiction. As of 2009 he had written three volumes of short stories and three novels. His first published work of fiction was *The Tilting Room* (1983), a collection of surreal and often harrowing stories that drew favorable comparisons to the work of Franz Kafka and won him a second Scottish Arts Council Book Award, this time in the fiction category. This was followed by what is almost certainly Butlin's best-known work, his debut novel, *The Sound of My Voice.* Originally published in 1987, the novel, which uses an unusual but highly effective second-person narration to chart the mental disintegration of an alcoholic executive, did not receive much attention at first, but it gained a new lease on life in subsequent years when was publicly championed by authors such as Irvine Welsh, and it went on to win international awards. Butlin's second novel, *Night Visits* (1997), is arguably his finest. However, the novel was barely marketed or reviewed, and it sold as few as eighty-seven copies upon its initial release.

Setbacks such as these caused Butlin to consider giving up prose altogether in 2002. Thankfully, he did not hold himself to this resolution, and he soon began to write fiction with a renewed energy. In the next few years, he produced two acclaimed volumes of short stories: *Vivaldi and the Number 3* (2004) and *No More Angels* (2007). In between these two volumes, Butlin completed his third novel, *Belonging* (2006), which he also adapted for BBC Radio 4's popular "Book at Bedtime" slot. Butlin has at times been a writer in residence at Edinburgh University and at the University of Stirling, as well as novelist in residence at St. Andrews University. He also gives readings of his work across Britain and Europe, sometimes in collaboration with his wife, the novelist and short story writer Regi Claire.

Perhaps unsurprisingly for a writer who puts so much emphasis on the musicality of language (and whose love of classical music permeates his work), Butlin has also forged successful creative partnerships with composers such as Lyell Cresswell (b. 1944) and the late Edward Harper (1941–2009); Harper's acclaimed Second Symphony includes a setting of poem ("Them! Not Us!") specially written by Butlin for the occasion alongside ones by William Barnes and Walt Whitman. Butlin has also written several opera libretti for Cresswell, including *Good Angel, Bad Angel* (2005), a one-act, hour-long chamber opera based on Robert Louis Stevenson's short story "Markheim," and *The Perfect Woman* (2008), a shorter chamber opera commissioned as part of Scottish Opera's high-profile "Five:15" project, in which writers such as Butlin, Alexander McCall Smith, and Ian Rankin collaborated with composers such as Cresswell, Nigel Osbourne, and Craig Armstrong on a series of fifteen-minute operas. The brevity of these acclaimed pieces and the resourceful economy of their staging is in keeping with the precision and economy that are among Butlin's chief virtues as a writer.

CREATURES TAMED BY CRUELTY *AND EARLY POEMS*

Although it is often counted as his first major volume, *Creatures Tamed by Cruelty* (1979) contains enough of Butlin's output from the 1970s that the reviewer Carl MacDougall suggested it could be considered "his Collected [early] Poems" (p. 43). It contains around fifty-five poems of greatly varying length, which are divided between poems in English, poems in Butlin's native Scots, and various translations. While Butlin later chose to write exclusively in English, the early verse, to quote Edwin Morgan's introduction to *Creatures Tamed by Cruelty,* show him trying "different approaches and styles," with varying degrees of success, while "learning about his craft" (p. 7).

The centerpiece of this volume is Butlin's earliest published work; an ambitious Scots poem titled "The Wonnerfu Walrd O John Milton." This eight-part, 150-odd-line parody of Milton's *Paradise Lost* was self-published in 1974 and featured calligraphy by Brian McCabe. Although this poem reached a comparatively larger audience when it was included in *Creatures,* Butlin notes that his privately printed, handwritten edition of this poem was the only volume of poetry he made money on until *Without a Backward Glance* in 2005.

The second part of the poem, a witty "Invocation to Milton," mocks the style, heroic register, and erudition of Milton's blank-verse epic with what Colin Nicholson calls "a jester's irreverence" (p. 38):

Blin Milton poet, git tae it man!
Gies something guid tae chow upon
—shair, a decasyllabic line impresses
specially when it's got five stresses
risin and faain on thae even beats

we caa accentuated feets.
Ye were awfae clever maist o the time
—But what a pity ye didnae rhyme!

(*Creatures,* p. 49)

Although Butlin's poetic voice would mature over subsequent years in a number of ways, many of his virtues are already present in this earliest poem, as are the elements of his work some critics see as defects. First, there is the undoubted playfulness and humor of the piece, apparent in lines such as "Then God gied him a right fou blast o The Divine Look / an tell him tae get the Hell, which he did" (*Creatures,* p. 50). Humor has always played an important part in Butlin's work, which may come as a surprise to those who are only familiar with *The Sound of My Voice,* the surface of which is relentlessly grim. But if one needs to go beneath the surface to find the comic elements in that novel, playfulness and humor would later resurface to become one of the defining qualities of Butlin's mature works such as *Vivaldi and the Number 3*.

Second, "The Wonnerfu Walrd O John Milton" admirably demonstrates Butlin's interest in the nuances of language and the musicality of words. Take, for example, this pun-laden description of Satan:

He's real fast mover,
Whit a groover! Hoover-sexed,
He picks up every bit o fluff!
He's so far oot yin meenit that he's oot o sicht the next
Yin warld's too much for him but a thoosand's no enough!

(*Creatures,* p. 49)

The bold rhymes and pop song–like rhythm of the first two lines quoted above segue admirably into the extended assonance of the longer, more prosy final lines, with the multiple repetitions of "o" and "oo." What is even more impressive in this piece is the way form is linked to content. The rhythm and rhyme, combined with the slangy resister and the jocular tone, (the coarse but clever pun on "Hoover-sexed / He picks up every bit of fluff"), admirably reflect, in a few lines, the charisma and eloquently populist rhetoric Milton put into the mouth of his inadvertent hero, Satan. This leads us to the third quality of Butlin's writing: its considerable intelligence. Butlin's interest in and wide knowledge of art, philosophy, literature, and, perhaps most importantly, music, come through in almost all of his writing, but it is never forced or precious. On the contrary, as Sorley MacLean notes in his introduction to *Stretto,* "Butlin can be very clever, but the best poems in this book ... do not strike one as clever. There is no strain after ingenuity or image ... the poems are the expression of a man who can think and feel and to whom poems come because they must" (*Stretto,* p. 1). Or, as Ian Rankin succinctly puts it in his introduction to *No More Angels,* Butlin always "wears his learning lightly" (p. xv).

However, British tastes are often suspicious of cleverness, particularly when it is worn lightly, and several commentators have accused Butlin of being too clever by half. For example, Christopher Rush, in his review of *Creatures,* damns with not-so-faint praise. He calls the poem "witty, cerebral, thought-provoking" and says that "Butlin is undoubtedly highly intelligent, mentally alert, knowledgeable, and moves, Ariel-like, through a welter of abstractions as if it were all a game" (p. 46), but he does so as a means of criticizing it. He goes on to say that he prefers "Milton's high seriousness to Butlin's comic treatment of it, however serious he might believe the core of his poem to be. For all ... its dazzling wit, its allusiveness, its bathos, its ironies, its word-play, its clever rhymes, it fails to impress me as being of literary importance" (p. 46).

Rush is also critical of Butlin's use of this dialect in the Milton poem, which he finds too "conversational." However, he argues that a "much more authentic and effective" (p. 47) use of Scots can be found in some of Butlin's slightly later poems collected in *Stretto.* Among the best of these is "In Memoriam Jimi Hendrix." The poem is worth quoting in full:

Haudin the breadth an hecht o the universe
(the Deil at his richt haun, God at his left),
His fingers were gropin amang stars
Fer the sichtless quasars
That boomed inside his heid.
Yin meenit ran a lifespan an back
As his hauns thrummled wi the years

Yin weirdless keek an the world couped...
An we're left whisperin tae ourselves
Hou yince the planets circled us.

(*Creatures,* p. 47)

Poems such as this one have justly been called "metaphysical" (Rush, p. 47), and if the exact meaning of the poem is somewhat (consciously) enigmatic, the combination of sound and image are remarkable. (Sound is paramount in Butlin's poems, and meaning is often allowed to "look after itself" [Nicholson, p. 37]). It is this rich combination of sound and image that Butlin seems to strive for in all his writing, be it poetry or prose. It is perhaps for this reason that some of his poems have been described as "prosy," while his prose is often usually poetic. Each of Butlin's poems (and indeed stories and novels), he says, "starts with a word, a phrase, maybe just a particular sound or image in my head, and then it evolves from there."

Butlin says that these early poems first came to him in Scots and therefore were developed and written in it. It is partly for this reason that Butlin has been reluctant to translate these poems into English, despite requests from publishers to do so. The other reason for this reluctance comes from the possible loss of meaning and nuance that almost inevitably comes from translating a poem into another language. For example, the word "thrummled" seems particularly hard to translate, as it has connotations of fumbling, but also, aptly, recalls "strummed"

By 1979 it became clear to several Scottish critics that Butlin, much to their chagrin, was moving away from Scots toward English. In her review of *Creatures,* Ruth McQuillian reluctantly agreed that "the real achievement of this collection must surely be the group of English poems" (p. 37), rather than those in dialect. Butlin is less regretful, and he told Colin Nicholson that while he sees this period as "a very necessary thing to go through," he thinks that Scots "wasn't, finally, appropriate for [his] writing purposes" (p. 38). He continues:

I wasn't sure where I was going [but...] In the sudden discovery, or re-discovery, of the whole sound-world of the Scots language I had known and felt as a child, I was able to draw on an emotional life and point of view that I recognised as mine ... I couldn't sustain [it] for long, but it released in me what appeared to be a kind of humour, a lack of self-consciousness ... I think that the Scots language put me in touch with parts of myself that English couldn't reach. And, Scots having opened them out, then English can get to them.

(p. 38)

Butlin's poetry can be technically complex, but he never allows himself to be a slave to form, preferring to bend certain rules and play with formal conventions, as in "A Bit Sonnet," a sonnet about sonnets (in Scots) that features only the first octave, as the poet gives up before the final sestet. Jürg Joss notes that a poem such as "How Seagulls Move" shows Butlin's ability to "adapt the form of a poem to its specific meaning" (p. 38). Here, Butlin plays with the fourteen-line structure of a sonnet, while at the same time paying careful attention to line length and the arrangement of the words on the page, giving it the visual quality of a concrete poem; here, "the birds suggest Pythagoras as easily as they appear to move," says Carl MacDougall (p. 47):

Three gulls move circlewise,
one between the other two
and yet again
one between the other two
and their graceful paths close-bounded
trace such surface-tumbling curves
as would confuse the proofs
of circlewise Pythagoras
for planets move in harmony
and seagulls circle easily.
I will consider how seagulls move,
then, holding the sun in my hands,
I watch the earth go spinning into the distance
—and consider how seagulls move.

(*Creatures,* p. 15)

THE EXQUISITE INSTRUMENT

Despite the collection's winning Butlin his first of several Scottish Arts Council Book Awards, *The Exquisite Instrument* is perhaps his least known work. None of the poems in this volume appeared in the career-spanning collection *Without a Backward Glance,* but this was due to their complex origins and is not a comment on their quality. *The Exquisite Instrument* consists of loose translations of works by several eighth-century Chinese poets and by the twentieth century poet Wen I-to. Butlin, who does not read Mandarin, generally began with very literal word-for-word translations of the original poems and then freely adapted them into his own versions. He explained to Colin Nicholson that in some instances, such as the translations from Wen I-to, he tried to keep the original poet's "rhyme and careful scansion" (p. 38), but other poems are completely his own; for instance, in "This Embroidery," he says, the poet Yuan Chen has provided "only the original situation of an elegiac setting; the man laying out the clothes of a dead woman" (p. 38):

I have laid your clothes out on our bed;
Smoothing the lace, the silk and satin finery
Seam by seam.
Only a mess of coloured thread
Remains to fold away;
This embroidery you said was part-dream
And part-imaginary.
You would have finished it next spring.
These chalkmarks are clouds, and these—men fishing.

(*The Exquisite Instrument,* p. 14)

In this respect, these are neither translations in the proper sense nor are they entirely original works (Butlin prefers to call them "imitations"). However, Butlin finds both an economy of expression and a musicality in his source material that admirably compliments his own poems. For example, the final piece in the collection, "Climbing the Stork Pagoda," taken from an eighth-century original by Wang Zin-Huai, is a superb imitation of Ch'an Buddhist poetry of enlightenment:

You can see the white sun setting behind the mountains,
and the yellow river disappearing into the ocean.
—But if you wish to see more, you must climb higher:
You will see the white sun setting behind the mountains,
and the yellow river disappearing into the ocean.

(p. 29)

However, the volume manages to avoid charges of orientalism, and other poems in the collection, particularly those derived from Wen I-to, an outspoken, American-educated member of the Crescent Moon Society who was assassinated by the Kuomintang in 1946, have an altogether earthier tone, as in this example from "Deadwater":

The toads have a place where they squat in the ditch;
They breathe-out, they breath-in and they wait: one
    starts,
The rest belch in chorus, and the air is soon rich
With their rancid rhetorical farts.

(p. 16)

RAGTIME IN UNFAMILIAR BARS *AND* HISTORIES OF DESIRE

If the title of *The Exquisite Instrument* was partly referring to the Chinese language and the oriental poets' masterful ability to "play" it, *Ragtime in Unfamiliar Bars* (1985) begins to confirm Butlin's mastery of the English language. "A Gentle Demolition" takes up John Donne's metaphor of love as a contract in "Woman's Constancy" and applies it to a modern-day separation. "Descriptions of the Falling Snow" works as a lyric poem and a parody of one. "Argentina 1978" is a fine contribution to the long list of Scottish poems about football. The surreal "Preparation for a Sea Voyage" demonstrates Butlin's gift for creating strong visual images:

It was like this: we made the spare oars
from wax; the ropes from weed;
smoke we gathered into sails, and the prow
was once the concentration of a cat.

(*Ragtime*, p. 29)

The title poem is one of the longest in the collection and worthy of particular attention. Taking the form of an interior monologue by a thwarted composer who teaches the piano to children while he labors on his magnum opus, "Ragtime in Unfamiliar Bars" is a tour de force of verbal invention and one of Butlin's finest and most enjoyable works. It begins:

I'm teaching Peter how to play a suite
in the style of J. S. Bach complete
with grace notes. He suspects I improvise
the rules myself; I sit back, close my eyes
and bid him conscientiously repeat
each dreary trill. This exercise
can kill at least ten minutes. "To modulate:
all keys and accidentals should relate
in your imagination *before* you play ...

(*Ragtime*, p. 37)

The poem continues in this way for eighteen stanzas, and Butlin somehow conspired to makes it seem effortless, as in this segment, where the pupil's mother inquires about her son's progress:

... Last week she asked: "I'm sure
Peter's coming on a dream ...
Has he begun on Brahms? Bach can be
so very dull at twelve, I'd hate to see
him bored. One does not like to interfere,
of course, but *Brahms!*" An hour's walk from here
my "Oratorio Profane" for three
hundred voices, children's choir
and pre-recorded tape rots in piles
upon the floor. De-structured parables
inter-cut Ecclesiastes; the last
words of Christ are Man's first—a vast
anti-fugue upon the syllables
"Lama Sabachthani" cast
in twelve equal parts to symbolise
the tribes of Israel and the Serial cries
of Master Schönberg wandering the Late
Romantic wilderness ...

(*Ragtime*, pp. 38–39)

Jürg Joss stresses that this poem can create great difficulty for the reader, whose eyes want to stop at the end of each line or stanza, but cannot due to Butlin's constant use of "run-ons" (p. 40). If read aloud, the run-ons also encourage one to read the poem more like a piece of prose, and Butlin is confident enough to allow his extremely elaborate rhymes get somewhat buried.

Joss also argues that "the poem neatly fits a traditional ragtime rhythm" (p. 42), in the mold of Scott Joplin. However, the subject of the poem is classical music, "thus the combination of form (ragtime) and theme (classical music) makes then poem mimetic of its own title" (p. 42).

The volume concludes with a sequence of six very personal poems about Butlin's family. Three of these: "Inheritance," "Claiming My Inheritance," and "My Inheritance," form a loose triptych. The emphasis in these is perhaps more on emotion more than form (although that is always a consideration), and stylistically, these works are far freer than, say, the collection's title poem. For example, in the final part, "My Inheritance," the rhythm and rhyme schemes are irregular, and several part-rhymes are employed:

Since my father's death I've managed to disgrace
a dozen hearts and beds, making each a court
where I might love and talk of love, yet still support
whatever sinecures most pleasantly debase
that love into allegiance. Courtly etiquette
could make my servitude appear as *politesse*
Well practised passion, warmth. I needed nakedness
to show my feelings, even to myself—to let myself
  go.
                                       (*Ragtime*, p. 49)

While reviewers such as Alexander Hutchinson are ambivalent about whether these poems are too clever to be wholly moving (Butlin uses allusions to *The Odyssey* to reflect on the ten years that have elapsed since his father's death), Hutchinson admits that "confessions" such as these have "real impact" (p. 175).

These final poems, which draw so fruitfully from Butlin's personal life, seem to point ahead to Butlin's next collection, *Histories of Desire* (1995), where the opening poems recall a holiday at Linton and the excitement and uncertainty of a new relationship:

Our first weekend together: a night without much
  sleep,
a morning's levitation over hills and cold rain.
The visitors' book lies open. We flip the pages back
to catch sight of a world before we'd met,
then pause uncertain what to write …
Your scent, the colour of the scarf you wear,
our closeness—these are not memories.
Once we've signed the book and put the date we'll
  leave
and Linton Kirk stand empty.
How far into the future can I reach to take your hand?
                                       (*Histories*, p. 13)

If there is an affinity in subject and theme between this poem and the "Inheritance" poems that conclude *Ragtime*, the style here is even more pared down. Butlin's insistence on the "right number of words" is never more apparent than in this collection of around forty poems (one third of which are ten lines or fewer). Indeed, as Robyn Marsack notes, the entire volume, which represents Butlin's poetic output from 1985 and 1995, "bears the signs of a rewarding deliberation [with] each poem carrying its weight" (p. 15).

While foreign travel and locations still play an important part in this collection ("Budapest: All Wars Are Civil Wars" and "African Sunlight" are standouts), the interest in Scotland and what it means to be Scottish (Butlin's cultural inheritance) is more to the fore than ever. Marsack observes that "Advertisement for a Scottish Servant" acerbically dissects "the hovering presence of Scottish male expectations" (p. 15), while "Edinburgh: A Place of My Own" gives a voice to the many dispossessed and homeless "residents" of the nation's capital. But Butlin puts forward his views on the subject most succinctly in the first part of a poem titled "Letting the Demons Speak":

… the Scottish Tao: say nothing
until you're sure it is too late;
do nothing until you're sure there's nothing
can be done. The Scottish Way is—no way.
                                       (*Histories*, p. 48)

This unusual four-part poem turns something ordinary (a Chinese takeaway) into some extraordinary by imagining an exchange where "two Scottish men, two Chinese men / twelve hundred years apart, sit down together / to let the demons speak" (*Histories*, p. 48). It is also one of the most successful examples of Butlin realizing his avowed ambition to try to find the "universal" in his writing. The critic Amanda Hooton has noted that the presence of Butlin's dog, Anja, helps in no small way to achieve this ambitious aim. For example, Butlin describes the dog as existing in "Anja-Time," where "that metaphysics of pure greed complemented / by complete forgiveness, repeats one life / over between sleeps" (p. 48). As pensive and philosophical as this poem is, the presence of the dog ensures that it is always playful and never allowed to become too serious. For example, when Butlin writes:

Once upon a time she visited the Eastern Pearl:
Its door pushed open, she entered no longer walking
upon the surface of the earth ...

(*Histories*, p. 49)

Butlin's register makes this seem like an almost mystical experience, in which someone has transcended time and gravity (and perhaps it is). However, it is also just a description of a dog entering a Chinese restaurant in Edinburgh, and as Hooton notes, Anja "no longer walking / upon the surface of the earth," in more "prosaic terms," simply means "choking on her lead" (p. 16).

Like *Ragtime*, *Histories* concludes with an extended sequence of poems about Butlin's family, in this case, "Ryecroft," a series of eight short pieces about the death of Butlin's mother in 1991. As Robyn Marsack notes, these moving poems center "round a slowly vanishing presence which is both hers and that of a house. What has to be dismantled, let go of, and what we try to keep hold of: these emotional delusions have no season" (p. 15). Yet although these poems are personal, they also achieve the universal resonance that Butlin often strives for, both in their sorrow—

My mother died much slower than expected:
I saw her, talked, held her hands, sat,
held her hands, kissed goodbye
and left the nursing home. That visit lasted seven
  months.

(*Histories*, p. 54)

—and in their strange but haunting juxtaposition of the mundane (clearing out his mother's house) and the philosophical, as in the segment entitled "The Rats":

Their sky was laid out in planks with hardly a Rizla-
  paper's gap
between each tongue and groove. Underneath,
a sea of black without tide, night without day;
where the floor was badly wormhold stars began. Is
  this
the rats' astronomy? Does the rate of wood decay
when set against the lifespan of a rat allow
a glimpse of the eternal?

(*Histories*, p. 57)

There is also a grace note, says Marsack, as "Butlin presents us with a charming, self-contained image: a bath abandoned in a field" (p. 15):

... claw footed
White-lipped, porcelain-plungered, fully stretched
For the reading of detective novels in;
Ocean-going, and of Jurassic proportions
All but extinct in this designer world.
...
The sun had a perfect view of me the day
I first climbed in, trying it for size.

(*Histories*, p. 59)

Although some new poems were included at the end of *Without a Backward Glance* in 2005, as of 2009 Butlin had not published a full volume of new poetry since *Histories of Desire*. But the new works in that 2005 volume, such as "A Recipe for Whisky" and "The Circle Dante Wasn't Shown," demonstrate Butlin in fine form. In 2009, he also continued to write poems in his capacity as Edinburgh *makar*. Butlin says that these "official" poems involve a rather different writing process than his usual one. He usually begins with a sound or image and allows it to develop organically. He may start with only a sentence, which comes into his head like a piece of music, but once it becomes too long to remember he writes it down. He then begins to develop it. With the *makar* poems, he says, he is first given the subject to write upon. He then tries to "to take ownership of the topics and then write as best I can from the heart (if that doesn't sound too pretentious!)." In the early 2000s, says Butlin, he has found himself "tending more towards prose," although he hopes that it is not at the expense of his poetry. Moreover, since Butlin argues that much of his]fiction is "argued strongly through image, rather than through narrative and character alone ... the poetry sometimes finds its way in."

RON BUTLIN

THE TILTING ROOM

Butlin's first volume of stories, *The Tilting Room*, appeared in 1983 but it was not the product of a conscious decision to move from poetry to prose (he was working on the poems in *Ragtime* concurrently). Rather, it came from Butlin's preferred method of "going with the flow," and stories began to emerge, often in the voice of a character, alongside the poems.

In terms of his prose writing, Butlin has said that the majority of his influences are not British and that he preferred the work of Americans such as F. Scott Fitzgerald and Flannery O'Connor and European writers like Kafka. However, Butlin has also spoken of his great affection for Charles Dickens and Scottish writers such as Robert Louis Stevenson. And while Butlin did not set out to write "Scottish" fiction, the stories in *The Tilting Room* embrace these international influences without losing their inherent Scottishness. Kafka is perhaps the dominant influence on the collection (aside from the tone, many of the stories seem to have a central or Eastern European setting), but several critics have also aligned the collection with the Scottish gothic tradition, as typified by Stevenson's *Strange Case of Dr. Jekyll and Mr. Hyde* (1886).

Jürg Joss has usefully compared Butlin's story "The Child and the Man" to Stevenson's most famous story in its engagement with the "typically Scottish theme of the divided self" (p. 60), and it is not the only story worthy of such a comparison. What is so disturbing about this story, and what perhaps makes it so typically Scottish, is the peculiar nature of this divided self. Here, the Jekyll half is Paul, a boy barely in his teens, who is raised by his "debauched" aunt after both his parents are killed suddenly in an accident. The Hyde figure manifests itself as the spirit of the boy's father, which enters him on the night his aunt seduces him:

> over the next few months she introduced me to many kinds of intimacies. She began taking me to her bed sometimes where I would have to lie close beside her in the darkness. Then one night she said I wasn't to be afraid but she was going to make me grow big and tall like my father. I became afraid. But soon I felt a strange thrilling and shivering sensation run all over me for the first time—and this I took to be the spirit of my father being raised within me.
>
> (*The Tilting Room*, p. 73)

What unsettles even more than the incestuous relationship is the matter-of-fact tone Butlin employs to describe it, which is often alarmingly casual: "when I was fourteen I fell in love for the last time and, considering the way aunt Vera brought me up, it's nothing short of miraculous that I fell in love at all. She used the word 'love' when ever we were in bed together saying, 'you love me John, don't you' (John was my father's name)" (p. 73).

Almost all the stories in the collection share this dispassionate tone, even when describing incidents of unspeakable violence, such as when Paul rapes and then kills his girlfriend, Margaret, at the "instigation" of his dead father:

> Then my father became serious: this is not the woman you love, he said. "Yes she is, she is," I stammered. She was staring at my face and looking far into the distance; she was very frightened. The tears were streaming down my cheeks as I held her, my hands on her shoulders. "I love you, can't you understand," I pleaded.
>
> Then my father began gripping her shoulders more tightly in my hands. He must have been very strong because he lifted her up off her feet and threw her onto the ground. This is not the woman you love, he said, look at her. And though her face was all dirt and blood I said yes it is, this is Margaret whom I love. Then he picked up a stone in my hand and struck her face with it, and still I said I recognise her because I love her so deeply. Again and again he struck her until at last I could no longer recognise her, then he stopped. Do you know who she is? he asked. No, I answered. Come with me, he said.
>
> We went home. The house was empty. My aunt was out.
>
> (pp. 80–81)

The writing is typically skillful. The lack of speech marks around the father's words subtly imply that they are only audible inside Paul's head, while his own vain protests are at first spoken aloud, before these speech marks also disappear. The sudden switch to "we" also has sinister implications. It is as if Paul has stopped struggling and has come to accept his father's presence inside him. The abuse he suffers at the hands of his aunt, combined with the lack of paternal (and maternal) love and guidance, have corrupted the rights-of-passage of Paul's adolescence beyond measure. Even his breaking voice becomes a sign of his father's increasing dominance: "I keep hearing myself differently, my voice is changing all the time—it is my father's voice speaking more and more" (p. 81).

Death never lessens a father's ability to damage a son's life in Butlin's work. On the contrary, dead fathers exert a palpable influence over the narrators of all three of Butlin's novels, and feature in numerous stories and poems. Butlin sees this as a characteristic of Scottish literature. When the interviewer Susan Mansfield remarked that boys and men in his stories "typically have problematic relationships with their fathers," Butlin dryly retorted: "Yes. I'm Scottish. Say no more ... My relationship with my father was pretty terrible. He was a very sad, disappointed man who didn't get any treatment for what was clearly chronic depression. And he was only too happy to share his unhappiness with the rest of us. It was very difficult" (2007, p. 4).

What is also remarkable about this collection is Butlin's assurance in his handling of narrative voice. At their best, these stories are dramatic monologues worthy of Robert Browning, and although most of them are written in the first person, each voice seems quite distinct from the last. However, it soon becomes clear that all of the stories are connected in two key ways. First, from the opening lines of the first story, "Journal of a Dead Man"—"I am called Samuel, but I am not a Jew. Would the Germans believe that? I am afraid of the Germans, they do terrible things my father told me about" (p. 11)—a general sense of horror and despair pervades the volume. Second, and more importantly, all of the narrators seem to be in some way unbalanced or disturbed.

As Nicholson notes, there is a constant "blurring of the edges of what is real and what is not" (p. 39) throughout the collection. This merging of reality and fantasy is often so effective that critics have had trouble deciphering the exact events of some of the stories (sometimes because they defy conventional logic and summary). For example, as Joss points out, the title story approaches the theme of the divided self in "a rather intriguing way with respect to both the story's narrative and its subject matter" (p. 56) by having the narrator essentially step outside himself halfway through telling his circular story and start to narrate in the second person to rather unsettling effect. If the majority of the stories are dramatic monologues, "The Tilting Room" is a "hybrid of dramatic monologue and interior monologue" (p. 57), and its intriguing shift into second-person narration prefigures the stylistic tour de force of Butlin's debut novel, *The Sound of My Voice*.

THE SOUND OF MY VOICE

Butlin's first novel is perhaps its author's most "enduring" work, says Andrew Greig (p. 20), although it seems to have been "undiscovered and rediscovered" as often as Butlin himself. The story of the novel's eventual attainment of cult status is too long and complicated to discuss in complete detail here. But suffice to say that despite being largely ignored by critics both on its original publication in 1987 and its subsequent 1994 reprint, the novel has doggedly refused to fade into obscurity, and the 2002 reissue from Serpent's Tail, with a forward by Irvine Welsh, received overwhelmingly favorable reviews. Butlin has said he is very grateful for the part Welsh played in resurrecting the novel, and he is certain that having Welsh's name on the cover of the new edition helped greatly in the decision to republish it. Welsh's introduction is in fact a reprint of a short article he wrote for the *Village Voice* in 1997. When asked to pick a "lost classic," Welsh chose Butlin's novel, which he called "one of the greatest pieces of fiction to come out of Britain in the '80s" (p. 23).

The novel tells the story of Morris Magellan, an executive at Majestic Biscuits, a company in Scotland in the 1980s. To outward appearances Morris is living the Thatcherite middle-class dream. He has a good job, a caring wife, two children, and a nice suburban home. However, Morris is also an alcoholic. Over an extraordinarily controlled narrative, lasting little more than one hundred pages, Butlin charts his protagonist's decline into oblivion, where, feeling his pain at last, there is a chance he might begin to heal. It is a testament to the novel's power that it not only withstands comparisons with Malcolm Lowry's *Under the Volcano* (1938) in its depiction of alcoholism, but that it may actually surpass it as a stylistic achievement. Butlin's great coup in this respect was the unusual decision to write the entire novel in the second person.

The effect of this is quite startling, and it is impossible to think of the novel working any other way. For example, when Morris says "You keep trying [to be yourself], like an actor learning his lines, in the belief that eventually, if you work hard enough, you will play the part of 'Morris Magellan' convincingly" (*The Sound of My Voice*, 2002, p. 20), we realize, as John Burns notes, that "everything in [his] life is kept at a distance" (p. 36), including himself. Also, as Welsh and others have noted, the second-person narration has the effect of drawing the reader into the story and, "yet simultaneously, and strangely, producing a sense of distance. It's as if the reader becomes the central character, yet has no control over his actions. This control, of course, rests with the drug" (Welsh, p. 23).

Butlin remembers that the writing of the novel began with writing the sentence, "You are thirty-four years old and already two-thirds destroyed" (p. 20), and he assumed it would turn out as a short story. However, he found that the words kept coming, and soon he had enough material for a short novel. Although he maintains that he writes what "comes to him," Butlin also stressed that the great economy of his work is the result of discipline and careful editing. Early versions of all his novels were substantially longer than the published versions, and every scene is slowly refined until only the essentials remain. But in *The Sound of My Voice*, Butlin even pares down these essentials. As Morris' addiction seems to become more severe, Butlin leaves out increasing amounts of information, brilliantly mirroring Morris' blackouts, time slips, and disintegrating short-term memory:

You turned and rushed back to the house—choking, bent almost double.

The cocktail cabinet was locked and the key missing. Where was it?

The door was glass-fronted. You could hardly breathe. Inside you could see a large bottle of gin. Your fingers slid across the glass panel; you were on your knees trying to prise open the door. Where was the key?

There were three bottles: gin, brandy and vodka. Standing behind the clear glass. And no key. You were choking, retching almost.

A moment later, the gin tasted like liquid oxygen. The pressure lifted immediately and you could breathe again. It was like surfacing; you took deep gulps of air.

Then you looked round to see Mary come in.

"Oh no, Morris! No!" she cried out.

...

"I just needed one drink, that was all. I couldn't breathe." You added: "It's all right now."

"One drink!" she exclaimed. "Morris, you've drunk nearly half the bottle. And there's blood all over your—"

She started to cry again.

Half a bottle? No, not quite. But your hands and arms were covered in blood from smashing the glass front of the cocktail cabinet.

(pp. 38–39)

The first two chapters of the novel "are almost a short story" in their own right, suggests John Burns (p. 36). Here, Morris briefly explains his difficult relationship with his father. This short prologue does not, however, offer any easy psychological explanation for Morris' drinking. Maybe Morris does drink because his father did not love him. But if this is a cause of his alcoholism, it is not *the* cause. Morris provides a far more terrifying explanation of why he drinks: "At home your wife and children ... love you and need you. You know all this, and know that it is not enough" (p. 20). The picture Butlin paints of

Morris is of an intelligent, witty, and sensitive man "whose mind is moving too quickly, sharply, and restlessly for the banalities of bourgeois life" (Welsh, p. 23).

Morris' job, marketing biscuits (that is, cookies), is undeniably banal and unsatisfying; his work, and the Thatcherite ideal Morris has unwillingly signed up to, are brilliantly satirized in Butlin's description of Morris' thoughts after an office party:

> Mary must have taken off your jacket and shoes before putting the top blanket over you. An understanding woman. A night out for the biscuit-men and their wives—could anyone have endured that sober? Not that many seemed to be trying. You needed to be drunk to feel normal with all those publicity-biscuits walking round in high heels, cardboard and tassels. The launching of a new line: British biscuits—famous historical characters covered in chocolate, and each with its own particular flavour. Wrapped in Union Jack foil. Patriotic. Educational.
>
> No wonder you had felt sick—a Newton, two Shakespeares, a Nell Gwyn, a Drake and a Margaret Thatcher. But no one seemed to notice.
>
> After a short sleep you were feeling better and could move your head without bending the room in the same direction. The bed was horizontal.
>
> (p. 22)

Without stressing the point, Butlin uses biscuits as a metaphor for all that is wrong with Morris' life and with the time in which he lives. Like the product he helps sell, his job is insubstantial, and bad for his health, and the artificial sweetness of his life literally makes him feel nauseous. Similarly, the farcical new line of biscuits reduces genius (Newton, Shakespeare) to a cheap consumer product and elevates the dubious achievements of Thatcher to the level of greatness.

Due to the unusual nature of the second person narrative, contemporary reviewers were quick to compare *The Sound of My Voice* to Jay McInerney's *Bright Lights, Big City* (1984), another novel about addiction written in the second person. Butlin had not read McInerney's novel at the time, but later did and found the similarity to be purely superficial. "They're really quite different," he noted, "in terms of their milieu and the character." (McInerney's unnamed protagonist is a fact checker at a literary magazine who gets caught up in the hedonistic excesses of the New York yuppie set and becomes a cocaine addict.) Furthermore, had reviews looked at the title story in Butlin's collection *The Tilting Room*, they would have seen that he had experimented with the second person before.

Welsh is particularly keen to separate Butlin's novel from McInerny's, arguing that Butlin's is the greater and more daring achievement. He writes that:

> Unlike the New York- and London-based antiheroes of the yuppie novel, Morris does not emerge as a mere victim of '80s excess ... with perhaps one eye on the clock, hoping to meet Ms. Right and acquire the two kids and the suburban home that will straighten everything out. He already has all this and it hasn't straightened out anything ... So Morris becomes a far more terrifying ghost at the feast of '80s consumerism than your stock McInerney-Amis character could ever be.

For Welsh, what is genuinely laudable about *The Sound of My Voice* is the fact that it "ruthlessly and skilfully subverts ... that tiresome but omnipresent fictional journey where the hero slays his demons" (p. 23).

It is hard to disagree with Welsh's assessment of *The Sound of My Voice* as one of the great British novels of the 1980s. And after some twenty years, the novel began to gain the recognition it deserves. Following the novel's translation into French in 2004, it won two prestigious awards for Best Foreign Novel, the Prix Mille Pages in 2004 and the Prix Lucioles in 2005. It was subsequently adapted for the stage (in 2008), listed among the "100 Best Scottish Books" by a panel of Scottish academics and writers for World Book Day in 2005. However, there is a danger that Butlin will become known for this one novel at the expense of his other work, for while *The Sound of My Voice* is an astonishingly confident debut, Butlin's second novel, *Night Visits,* as Roderick Watson asserts in his overview of twentieth-century Scottish literature, is perhaps "even more powerful, and equally sinister in its exploration of family loss, past pain, repression, and obsession" (p. 287).

RON BUTLIN

NIGHT VISITS

Like its predecessor, the novel *Night Visits* (1997) opens with the death of a father. Here, however, the dead man's son is a ten-year-old, named Malcolm, and the bereavement forces Malcolm's mother to move them to Edinburgh, where they live in the large family house that her sister, Fiona, a pious and repressed spinster, has converted into a nursing home for the elderly. Again the story is simple and the novel's brilliance all in the telling. This time, Butlin's coup is to tell the story from two points of view: both Aunt Fiona's (relayed in the third person) and Malcolm's, which is again a voice in the second person.

One of the many remarkable things about *Night Visits* is the fact that this use of the second person does not seem to be a mere repetition of *The Sound of My Voice*. Indeed, the narrative voices of these novels share only two superficial similarities: the repeated use of the word "you" and the fact that a trauma has caused both Morris and Malcolm to look at themselves from the outside. Otherwise, these voices are no more related than they would be if Butlin had used the first person, and reading these novels one gets the sense of how underused and versatile second-person narration is.

For young Malcolm, the trauma of discovering his dead father causes him to see "the world only through his reflection's eyes" (p. 1). At this life-changing moment, Butlin shifts from the third person, "Suddenly his mother was standing in the doorway; staring, white-faced. She screamed" (p. 4) to the second, "You can still hear your mother's screams but as they are on the *outside* now, they can no longer hurt you" (p. 5). As Douglas Gifford notes, Malcolm's "self- and community-excluding extremity is motivated by complex desires—to protect himself, to keep his father in limbo, to arrest time. Butlin empathises with the boy as well as any writer dealing with the pain of adolescent trauma I've read, and shows the reflections of that pain in the eyes of his mother, unable to reach him" (p. 15).

However, this is only half the story, and, Gifford says, "What makes his achievement special ... is the way warped adolescent yearning is interwoven with a very different and repressed yearning, that of Malcolm's puritan aunt ... whose inner life rages with guilt and suppressed desire" (p. 15). Butlin introduces the character of Aunt Fiona with typical economy:

What had she done wrong?

If she kept holding the Bible she would be safe.

Her slightest movement rubbed her body against her nightdress, against the sheet. Temptation.

Temptation, and then sin. Wickedness.

(p. 6)

Butlin is aware that this character belongs to a long tradition of similarly tortured and repressed women in British literature. For example, Gifford compares Fiona (favorably) to "George Friel's Miss Partridge of *Grace and Miss Partridge,* and George Mackay Brown's Mrs McKee of *Greenvoe*" (p. 15), and parallels could also be drawn between Fiona's character and her dwelling and that of Brian Moore's title character in *Judith Hearne* (1955). And these are not the only familiar elements. The Edinburgh setting, the large house, the strange elderly men and women who live in it are more classic ingredients of the Scottish gothic novel, and *Night Visits* is certainly cast in what Roderick Watson describes as the "God-haunted Scottish tradition of Stevenson and Hogg" (p. 288). However, part of the novel's greatness comes from its ability to play with these familiar ingredients. Knowledge of these other works simply does not prepare the reader for Butlin's twist in the tale—Fiona's sexual longing for her ten-year-old nephew:

You touch one of the buttons in the middle.

"That's a good boy." She leans closer to you, pressing the button against your fingers. "Does it feel loose?"

"No."

"Let's make sure." Without her having taken a step she seems to be even closer. She's breathing quite loudly and, with one quick movement, she has undone the button ...

"Now, you fasten it up for me. Properly. Can't have your favourite aunt going around like something the cat dragged in."

What does she want you to do that for? Can't she fasten her own buttons? Her hands are trembling, maybe she's getting cold. If she stood still, you could do it quicker, but she's started shivering, making it much harder for you. She must be really cold. She'll be angry if you don't hurry up. The white material's so slidy underneath, the button-hole and the button keep slipping apart. Also, she keeps pressing nearer; as if trying to help, but really making it harder.

You've finished, at last.

"Clever boy. Did you like doing that for me?"

Like it? You like that she's not being snappy and angry anymore.

"Good boy. That's our secret then ..."

(2003, pp. 100–101)

What is also remarkable about the book is the fact that Butlin does not judge his characters for their actions. Fiona is perhaps more sinned against than sinner. As Roderick Watson has argued, *Night Visits* is Butlin's "vision of Scottish Presbyterian bourgeois hell," but it is "lightened only by his deeply sympathetic understanding of his characters' fear and grief and their need for peace and closure from old abuses in the past" (p. 288). This comes through in the events of the final pages, which almost deserve to be called miraculous, and ultimately offer more hope for redemption than *The Sound of My Voice*.

Here, Malcolm smashes the stained-glass window above the front door to the house with his hands. At first he bleeds and screams, until suddenly:

Malcolm's hand had stopped bleeding. He unclasped his fingers and there, lying on his palm, was his dad's toy yacht ...

The closer his father had come to the moment of death the tighter he would have grasped this yacht. It was time its voyage continued ...

... almost imperceptibly at first, the boat drifted forwards. He blew a little harder ...

And all at once it was gone. He stared at the point where it had vanished, then cautiously reached out to touch the ocean.

When he turned round a moment later he saw his mother and Aunt Fiona coming down the stairs, his mother with her arm about his aunt's shoulders. Their adult unhappiness, their adult weariness were caught in the sunlight streaming through the broken window. Already he could feel the sun's warmth soothing him, like the touch of someone's hand.

He got to his feet, and began to make his way up towards them.

(2003, p. 150)

This description of the toy boat miraculously floating away, coupled with a shift back to the third person, implies that Malcolm has come to an understanding and acceptance of his father's death. Indeed, the description of the boat brings the novel full circle as it recalls the father's dying vision of the boat on the very first page, creating a literal communication between father and son:

He'd been dreaming about that small boat, the tiny metal yacht his father had made for him more than forty years ago. On the wall directly opposite there was a picture of swans flying over a stretch of river. He had dreamt of being on the yacht and drifting easily downstream ...

He was never to see them disappear. Nor the trees, the line of low hills or the river itself. Only the small yacht remained, having come to rest in the palm of his hand.

(Prologue, unnumbered)

Furthermore, these first and last passages, which are essentially the prologue and epilogue of the novel, both end with paragraphs that are separated from the main text and not indented, again bringing the novel full circle. These two passages both hint at the possibility of some sort of human contact, with the father leaving the boat as a kind of message to his son, and Malcolm climbing the stairs to bring the warmth he now feels to his mother and aunt. Finally, as Roderick Watson suggests, the novel is more "compassionate ... than its Gothic aspects ... might at first suggest" (p. 288).

RON BUTLIN

VIVALDI AND THE NUMBER 3

Upon its initial publication, *Night Visits* sold fewer than one hundred copies, and while it has been republished, it has yet to find even the cult audience *The Sound of My Voice* has begun to enjoy. Given such critical neglect, it is hardly surprising that Butlin grew disillusioned and considered giving up writing fiction. Around 2002, "Sheaves of short stories and the guts of a new novel were bundled into a bag and pushed to the back of a cupboard" (Mansfield, 2007, p. 4). However, during this difficult time, Butlin did not entirely stop telling or inventing stories, and he recalled for Kenneth Walton that "regular sessions I have over Chinese carry-outs and wine with musical friends" (p. 17) led to the idea to write a series of short stories that played with the lives of the great composers. If this sounds like a rather rarified project, "brow distinction is [soon] blown away," says the critic Tom Adair (p. 13), and the resulting collection, *Vivaldi and the Number 3* (2004), is nothing short of a revelation. One of the most unusual and original works in English-language fiction since the 1990s, the first seventeen "impossible" stories combine genuine biographical details from the lives of Vivaldi, Beethoven, Bach, Mozart, Brahms, and numerous others with surreal flights of fancy that see Haydn asked to appear on *The Jerry Springer Show* and Bach's house inundated with computers sent to him by well-wishers. If *The Tilting Room* drew comparisons to Kafka, *Vivaldi*, in its invention, erudition, and economy, is closer to Jorge Luis Borges.

Sometimes the surreal encounters stem from little-known biographical details. For example, the story that sees Beethoven terrorized by a "super-bigot" taxi driver in Edinburgh draws from the fact that the city was the composer's "El Dorado" (*Vivaldi*, p. 194). Although he had never visited Edinburgh, he was commissioned to write settings of Scottish folk songs and "cleaned up in a big way" (p. 194). While knowledge of the lives and works of these composers is not a prerequisite to appreciating this collection, it is an enormous help. To this end, Butlin includes his own concise biographical sketches at the end of the book to help the uninitiated. However, with hindsight, he admits that he should have placed them at the start of each story so that the reader could see how the stories played with, but were firmly rooted in, the facts.

The book is also alive with Butlin's rediscovery of the joys of writing. His style has never been so relaxed. Unlike his previous three works of fiction, each of which was a stylistic tour de force of narrative voice, here he generally works in the third person, employing simple syntax and an often conversational register. Take for example, the opening sentences of "Vivaldi Learns a New Skill," which admirably illustrates the economy, wit, surreal invention, and originality of the collection: "It's been only two weeks since Vivaldi learned to walk on water, a real time saver in Venice. But for a man who normally writes a concerto faster than anyone who can copy it, he's been slow to master this new skill" (p. 17)

While Butlin admits that "doing this book cheered me up no end" (Black, p. 11), not all the stories are this jocular. On the contrary, what gives these stories weight and places some of them up with Butlin's very best work is the careful balance of tone. As Murrough O'Brien notes: "Everything is mingled in Butlin's world—past and present, dream and waking, with daring and deftness. It is not so much that the comic becomes tragic, as that a bubble of lightness somehow carries up with it a heavy stone of sorrow" (p. 33). Tom Adair similarly detects "terminal ripples" of *The Tilting Room* that run through the new stories as a "sober and undulant presence plucking the hairs on the back of the neck" (p. 13).

For example, the elegiac "Tchaikovsky Decides Which World He Belongs To" recounts the composer's alleged suicide by drinking cholera-infected water:

> Tchaikovsky has come to a decision. With his Sixth Symphony completed, he will allow himself a few days more. He has given the world his dreams and his art, and he will finish by giving it everything. His decision will bring lasting peace. Dramas of love and death set to a precise choreography are only a brief release. The rest is a terrifying chaos of the heart.

One last ballet then, with himself as creator, performer, director and audience. It will end as every day has ended: he returns to an empty house, a solitary bed. To dreams he wakes from with his face covered in tears.

He will pretend it is the attractive young man who is offering him the final glass from his tray. His last indulgence.

(p. 110)

Butlin briefly moves away from composers in the penultimate section of his book and puts the time he spent reading philosophy to good use in stories that move Seneca to the Southside of Edinburgh or picture Nietzsche running a failing chicken farm: "Given his Theory of Eternal Recurrence he'd been hoping for a nice little earner: chickens-and-eggs, eggs-and-chickens until the end of time … But no" (p. 163). Yet Butlin saves what is perhaps the most moving story for the end. In "Nadia Boulanger Has the Last Word," Butlin conspires to have the souls of the forgotten women composers Hildegard von Bingen, Elizabeth-Claude Jacquet de la Guerre, Fanny Mendelssohn, Clara Schumann, and Lili Boulanger (the only woman to win the Prix-de-Rome) gather around the deathbed of Lili's older sister, Nadia Boulanger, "the greatest teacher of composition in the history of Western music" (p. 189). (If Alma Mahler seems conspicuously missing from the group in the story, it is probably because she is the subject of her own story earlier in the volume.) This story ends this excellent volume on a note of gentle humor and quiet dignity.

NO MORE ANGELS

Around the same time as he began writing *Vivaldi and the Number 3,* Butlin also produced a novella of about sixty pages titled *Coming on Strong* for publication online. This story of a teenager from a small town in Scotland who leaves school and moves to Edinburgh, where he experiences the hardships of sleeping rough before finding a job as a footman, is one of Butlin's most enjoyable pieces. This story appeared, in slightly altered form as "Alice Kerr Went with Older Men," the final tale in Butlin's third collection, *No More Angels* (2007). Like the stories in *Vivaldi*, it is written in a simple style, and Butlin's renewed love of writing is palpable throughout. And again, humor is to the fore:

In less than two minutes he'd be in Environmental Studies. In less than two minutes he'd be sitting next to Alice Kerr. Steve's whole body went rigid. All-over lust …

He stared out the boys' locker room window: he had to think about something else, something depressing. Quick. The bell was about to ring. Something really depressing: Scotland's not qualifying for the World Cup? Those planes going into the Twin Towers? Blair? Bush? The Iraq War? The melting ice caps? The threatened rainforests?

Anything but Alice Kerr; her long black hair, her short black skirt, her slow sexy smile.

He shut his eyes: *the Twin Towers, the threatened rainforests …*

(*No More Angels*, p. 147)

This story provides a rather lighthearted coda to the collection, which at times threatens to match the horrors of *The Tilting Room*. The reviewer Madeleine Brettingham, sensing that Butlin had returned the darker themes of his earlier work, even joked that *No More Angels* "includes such cheery and uplifting tales as "How the Angels Fly In," about a man showing two guests around the house where he murdered his parents" (p. 38). However, several of the stories brilliantly reconcile that horror with the vibrant humor of *Vivaldi and the Number 3*. The two stories involving an old widow named Lily Williams are particularly memorable and have subsequently become a mainstay of Butlin's live readings. In "Not Dead Yet Lily?," the old woman contends with "constant neighbourly visits about nothing in particular, except to check she hadn't died in her sleep" (*No More Angels,* p. 17) and she slowly begins to crack. First, she "discovers the relish of bad language" (*No More Angels,* p. 17):

In a short time the *bloodys* had given way to *hells,* and the *hells* to *damns*—but getting into *fucks* had been her big breakthrough. It was after the postman went by a couple of days ago: *No letters, well fuck him!* she'd thought, then announced,

'Fuck him! Fuck him! Fuck him!' to the clock, the empty armchair and a whole clutch of wedding photographs.

(p. 18)

As funny as this is, like the best stories in *Vivaldi and the Number 3,* there is also more than a hint of sadness. The fact that Lily finds swearing so liberating speaks volumes about her frustration and the mention of the wedding photos allude to happier times and the loneliness of her existence. Finally, she goes into the garden and begins to dig a hole, which attracts an inquisitive, but well-meaning neighbour:

> The bush came out more easily than she'd expected, almost first pull, making her stagger a couple of steps backwards. She threw it to one side then picked up the spade again.
>
> 'You really should be resting in weather like this, Mrs Williams. What are you doing?'
>
> Before she could stop herself she'd replied, 'Digging my fucking grave. At my age what the fuck else would I be doing?'

(*No More Angels,* p. 20)

As Susan Mansfield suggests, *No More Angels* "is certainly Butlin on top form" (2007, p. 4) and the fact that the collection came only three years after *Vivaldi,* with a novel between them, confirmed that Butlin's career was in resurgence.

BELONGING

Although Butlin's third novel, *Belonging,* was published in 2006, between *Vivaldi* and *No More Angels,* it provides a useful conclusion to this examination of his work. The novel involves a more complex narrative than any of his previous work, so it is worth summarizing in some detail: Jack McCall, a Scotsman with a gift for fixing things, but no real ambitions, takes a job as a handyman in an Alpine ski resort, accompanied by his partner, Anna, a difficult, even slightly disturbed woman, who nevertheless wants to marry Jack and have children. The resort is empty until a wealthy man arrives with a much younger woman, who appears to be his daughter until "the man put his arm round her in a most unfatherly way" (p. 2). Soon after their arrival, the man slips on a frozen balcony and dies. Only the young woman, Thérèse, saw what happened. Jack and Anna try to comfort Thérèse through the subsequent investigation, but eventually Jack's affections shift, and he abandons Anna for Thérèse on the day they are due to return home to Scotland. The new couple drifts down to Spain, where they meet Thérèse's mother and stepfather. Here, Jack is told that the man Thérèse was with at the chalet was her real father and that the shock of discovering this inadvertently caused his death. The couple then go farther south and meet up with Charlie and Toni, a couple who have dropped out and live in a shack near a remote village. Jack and Thérèse stay on in this area despite an increasing strain in their relationship. Eventually Jack discovers that Thérèse is having an affair with another dropout, an American named Marshall. Soon after this discovery, Marshall and Thérèse are killed in a fire. What at first seems to be either murder or a terrible accident soon transpires to be double suicide. More confused and aimless than ever, Jack stays near the site of Thérèse's death until Anna tracks him down. Although their relationship is as volatile as it ever was, the two eventually reconcile. At the end of the novel they are drifting just as they were at the start.

With three deaths, plenty of sexual intrigue, international locations, and more conventional first-person narration, *Belonging* is Butlin's first "page turner," said Carrie O'Grady in a review for the *Guardian* (p. 17). However, Butlin is adamant that the novel does not mark a conscious attempt to write an accessible, commercially viable novel, and further examination of the novel bears him out. While it is certainly Butlin's most instantly accessible work, and while it initially seems looser in construction than its predecessors (although it is only 240 pages, it is by far Butlin's longest novel, longer than his first two put together) and less overtly "literary," these impressions are misleading.

The key to this false impression is the character of Jack, who is a far cry from the typical Butlin narrator. Morris Magellan, Malcolm, and many of the characters of *The Tilting Room,*

No More Angels, and *Vivaldi* are unbalanced, extraordinary in some way, or both. Jack, however, seems to be "a fairly normal bloke" (O'Grady, p. 17). The reader even discovers that, as Andrew Greig points out, the "worst thing that happens in Jack's childhood is when it becomes clear that, though a competent pianist, he is no prodigy" (p. 20). In short, there is nothing particularly special about him, and so his narration, by extension, seems rather ordinary.

One is made more acutely aware of this when one compares him to the two women he is involved with in the novel. Thérèse is extreme enough to almost sleep with her real father in order to rekindle their relationship, and she is passionate enough to kill herself along with her lover. Anna fakes suicide twice in order to show Jack "how devastated [he'd] feel to lose her," and she lies about being pregnant; she is "dishonest," "ghastly" and "awful," but she is also the "liveliest" character, says Allan Massie (p. 15). Either one of these women is closer to one's impression of the "typical" Butlin narrator than Jack is. On the other hand, Massie thinks that Jack is a "bore" and calls him "an inadequate narrator; [whose] voice seems more often the author's own than his" (p. 15).

However, a closer examination of the text shows that Jack is perhaps not as far removed from the typical, disturbed Butlin narrator as he at first seems. Take for example his description of his feelings after the death of Thérèse and Marshall:

> I lay there wide awake and pictured her and Marshall touching, kissing, whispering to each other. I imagined myself stopping the flames and rekindling them at will, watching the fire blaze up into their faces, scorching into their flesh all the rage I felt. If I wanted, I could shout to them, I could rouse them to the danger they were in. Or I could look on, say nothing and watch them burn.
>
> (p. 166)

Yes, Jack is *more* ordinary, *more* like us than the average Butlin narrator, but he is nevertheless confused, even disturbed. His fantasises would not be out of place in *The Tilting Room*. Therefore, by extension, Butlin is perhaps saying that we are *all* like this.

Another admirer of the novel, Butlin's friend and contemporary Andrew Greig, calls it "a very odd book that haunts long after it's done" as well as an "unusual and profoundly pessimistic vision" (p. 20). Greig also writes that he is disturbed by Jack, who for him lacks not only a sense of romantic commitment but also any "political, class or familial sense of connection" (p. 20). Greig sees him as "an outsider who, in a more alarming retake on Camus, doesn't even see himself as an outsider; a lost soul who doesn't know it. Love isn't going to sort him and his world out, nor will self-knowledge, therapy or political action" (p. 20).

Jack, who is, by his own admission, "happy drifting" (p. 46), is ultimately as withdrawn from the people around him as Morris is. For all the sex in the novel, he is as afraid and incapable of intimacy as Aunt Fiona in *Night Visits*. But unlike these other characters, he does not have an excuse. He is neither an addict nor a zealot. He can't even bring himself to leave Anna, and the novel's final sentences—"I slip my arm around Anna's waist. We continue walking. The day burns hotter at every step we take" (p. 241)—seem devoid of hope and redemption.

Without ever forcing it, *Belonging* becomes Butlin's most pointed statement on the impossibility of genuine communication between people. Many of the characters in the novel, not least Jack and Thérèse, communicate in a broken mishmash of French, English, and Spanish. Anna and Jack may speak the same language, but she is always deconstructing his words, telling him what they "really" meant. As Butlin says, "The fact that Jack could understand only the most easily recognizable Spanish words for bomb, deaths, and so forth [on the radio] underlined the helplessness of any given individual in our times." Finally, the more one reads *Belonging*, the more one senses that it is as much a masterwork of control and narrative voice as any of its predecessors. It may also be Butlin's bleakest work.

ASSESSMENT

It can be hard to reconcile Butlin's work, in its bleakness and horror, with the man himself, who is quiet, modest, and amusing. He is also a meticulous craftsman, who gives every word on the page careful consideration. Put simply, Butlin has put quality before quantity. While he would never reject a popular audience for one of his books, he never writes a book in the hope that it would be popular. Butlin has rejected many offers to write in recognizable genres, such as detective stories or science fiction, preferring to concentrate on what is more personally meaningful.

And while this may have cost him in some respects, it has earned him the admiration of many of his peers. Numerous Scottish writers who have enjoyed far greater commercial success and popular recognition than Butlin credit him as an inspiration and an influence. Ian Rankin once described seeing Ron Butlin selling volumes of poetry from a satchel in a student union bar at Edinburgh University in 1978 as "the epiphany which turned him against poetry as a career" He thought to himself, "if I want to be a full-time writer, I'd better choose a different form" (Mansfield, 2009, p. 43).

Butlin's obscurity stands as a reminder that a good deal of world-class contemporary poetry and fiction goes largely unnoticed. There are few contemporary British writers whose works are as ripe for, and as thoroughly deserving of, rediscovery.

Selected Bibliography

WORKS BY RON BUTLIN

OPERA LIBRETTI
Good Angel, Bad Angel (2005).
The Perfect Woman (2008).

POETRY
Stretto. Introduction by Sorley MacLean. Edinburgh: Outline Arts, 1976.
Creatures Tamed by Cruelty. Edinburgh: Edinburgh University Student Publications Board, 1979.
The Exquisite Instrument. Edinburgh: Salamander Press, 1982.
Ragtime in Unfamiliar Bars. London: Secker and Warburg, 1985.
Histories of Desire. Newcastle Upon Tyne, U.K.: Bloodaxe Books, 1995.
Without a Backward Glance: New and Selected Poems. Manchester: Barzan, 2005.

PROSE
The Tilting Room. Edinburgh: Canongate, 1983. (Stories.)
The Sound of My Voice. Edinburgh: Canongate, 1987. (Novel.)
The Sound of My Voice (Second Edition). Edinburgh: Black Ace, 1994. (Novel.)
The Sound of My Voice (Third Edition). London: Serpents Tail, 2002. (Novel.) (All quotations from this edition)
Night Visits. Edinburgh: Scottish Cultural Press, 1997. (Novel.)
Night Visits (Second Edition). London: Serpent's Tail, 2003. (Novel.) (All quotations from this edition)
Vivaldi and the Number 3. London: Serpent's Tail, 2004. (Stories.)
Belonging. London: Serpent's Tail, 2006. (Novel.)
No More Angels. London: Serpent's Tail, 2007. (Stories.)

CRITICAL AND BIOGRAPHICAL STUDIES

Adair, Tom. "Everything to Declare About Artistic Genius." *Scotsman,* July 24, 2002, p. 13.

Black, Edward. "Boswell's Diary." *Scotsman,* June 14, 2004, p. 11.

Brettingham, Madeleine. "*No More Angels,* Ron Butlin." *Times Educational Supplement,* September 7, 2007, p. 38.

Burns, John. "Parables for Our Time." *Cencrastus,* no. 32:36–37 (spring 1988).

Butlin, Ron. "The Lost Poets." *Edinburgh Review,* no. 95:86–88 (spring 1996).

Cooper, Neil. "Raise Your Glass to the Revival of a Lost Classic." *Glasgow Herald,* May 20, 2008, p. 16.

Gifford, Douglas. "Travels with his Aunt: *Night Visits.*" *The Scotsman,* August 16, 1997, p.15.

Greig, Andrew. "The Disturbed Love Life of a Perpetual Drifter, with No Happy Ever After." *Independent Extra,* October 25, 2006, p. 20.

Hooton, Amanda. "Tales of Desire from a True Romantic." *The Scotsman,* November 4, 1995, p. 16.

Hutchinson, Alexander. "*Ragtime in Unfamiliar Bars.*" *Chapman 43–44* 8, no. 6:174–176 (spring 1986).

Joss, Jürg. "A Man of Sorrow Acquainted with Grief: The Work of Ron Butlin." Master's Thesis, University of Zurich, 1991.

MacDougall, Carl. "*Creatures Tamed by Cruelty* by Ronald Butlin." *Akros,* no. 46:45–52 (April 1981).

McQuillian, Ruth. "New Poetry Review." *Lines Review,* no. 71: 34–38 (December 1979).

Mansfield, Susan. "A Voice from the Gloom." *Scotsman,* August 27, 2007, p. 4.

———. "Poetry: Stanza Festival." *Scotsman,* March 25, 2009, p. 43.

Marsack, Robyn. "Haunting Collections Invoke Ghosts of Times Past." *Scotland on Sunday,* November 26, 1995, p. 15.

Massie, Allan. "Too Cold to Care." *Scotsman,* August 12, 2006, p. 15.

Morgan, Edwin. "Introduction to *Creatures Tamed by Cruelty.*" Edinburgh: Edinburgh University Student Publications Board, 1979, pp. 7-8.

Nicholson, Colin. "'Widdershins This Life o' Mine': Ron Butlin's Writing." *Cencrastus,* no. 24:34–40 (autumn 1986).

O'Brien, Murrough. "Books: Paperbacks." *Independent on Sunday,* August 1, 2004, p. 33.

O'Grady, Carrie. "Brewing Up a Storm: Carrie O'Grady Is Happy to Welcome Back a Singular Voice: Ron Butlin's *Belonging.*" *Guardian,* September 30, 2006, p. 17.

Royle, Nicholas. "Brief Encounters." *Time Out,* October 16, 2002, p. 59.

———. "The Books Interview: Ron Butlin." *The Independent,* August 10, 2002, pp. 16-17.

Rush, Christopher. "Younger Writers in Scotland." *Akros* 15, no. 45:7–50 (December 1980).

Walton, Kenneth. "Revealed: The Weird World of Composers." *Scotsman,* May 31, 2004, p. 17.

Watson, Donna. "Are These the Best 100 Scottish Books Ever?: The Hunt Is On for Top Read." *Daily Record,* March 4, 2005, p. 60.

Watson, Roderick. *The Literature of Scotland: The Twentieth Century*. London: Palgrave Macmillan, 2007.

Welsh, Irvine. "Forward to *The Sound of My Voice.*" London: Serpent's Tail, 2002, pp. vii–ix.

JOHN BYROM

(1692—1763)

Timothy Underhill

JOHN BYROM WROTE one of the eighteenth century's most popular songs and one of its most famous hymns, a richly detailed sequence of diaries, an influential manual of shorthand, and a substantial, heterogeneous body of poetry. His work includes epistles, epigrams, paraphrases, translations, and dialogues, and its subject matter ranges from expositions of church festivals to political propaganda, from coterie-based anecdote to promulgations of mystical and counter-Enlightenment thought. There is an idiosyncratic and intriguing voice behind all these, the exploration of which is still in its infancy.

BIOGRAPHICAL OVERVIEW

Scion of a prosperous dynasty of linen mercers and property owners, Byrom was born on February 29, 1692 in Manchester, then a small but rapidly expanding trading town, in the county of Lancashire in northwest England, the seventh child (of nine) and second son of Edward Byrom (1656–1711) and Dorothy Allen (1659–1729). While most of what we know of his life relates to periods in London and Cambridge, his proudly maintained regional identity holds particular importance with regard to his political verse, and partly explains tendencies to see himself as an outsider in some of the more urbane circles he inhabited. His earliest formal, classically based education took place in the neighboring county town of Chester. Subsequently he lodged with relatives in London, where at fifteen he entered Merchant Taylors' School, then primarily a day school in the heart of the city area. He matriculated as a pensioner at Trinity College, Cambridge, in April 1709, gaining a scholarship the following month. Having fulfilled statutory requirements he obtained his B.A. degree toward the beginning of 1712 and was elected to a minor fellowship in 1714 and to a major fellowship the following year, when he gained his M.A.

At Cambridge his extracurricular interests in music and modern languages flourished, and he came to the attention of a wider literary public, contributing two prose essays about dreams to the *Spectator* in 1714 under the pseudonym "John Shadow." Praised by "Mr. Spectator" for their originality, these have been argued to anticipate aspects of Freud's dream theories. It was probably from a miscellaneous batch of writing submitted simultaneously that a "Copy of Verses" (entitled "A Pastoral" in his *Miscellaneous Poems*) made its way into the *Spectator* soon afterward. In this, Byrom's best-known verse to his contemporaries, the shepherd Colin laments the absence of his beloved Phebe and his consequent suffering, deprived of her transformative powers on his perception of the joys of nature. (Phebe has often been claimed, though improbably so, to represent a daughter of his college's master, the great classicist Richard Bentley, whom Byrom revered and actively supported in years to come.) The "Pastoral" was imitated, parodied, and even Latinized, its fame stemming from a lightly comic undercutting of pastoral convention in a distinctive stanza form. Ostensible adjectival triteness ("Sweet Musick," "agreeable Sound," ll. 49, 56) might render its popularity strange to us, but silent reading of the printed poem today makes it easy to overlook the key context explaining that fame. These were the lyrics to "a good pastoral song" (*Private Journal and Literary Remains,* vol. 1, p. 25), a text for performance where mood, and perhaps irony, was dictated by choice of major or minor key, and where the coaxing out of nuances and subtleties depended on a performer's decisions over stress, pause, or speed. Several musical settings of it circulated—one of these by no less a figure than William Croft—and over twenty years later it was still being performed by singers of note.

The religious controversialist William Warburton (1698–1779) thought Byrom "too devout to cultivate poetry, otherwise he would have excelled in it" (p. 54). Putting aside Warburton's sarcasm at perceived pious aloofness, this recognition of unfulfilled potential is incisive: limited "cultivation" explains why Byrom's early reputation as a poet was not sustained. It was not simply in the sense that much of his output was unpolished and extempore, but also because he never steadfastly attempted to forge a literary career for himself. While maintaining contacts on the fringes of London's literary circles into the 1730s, he distanced himself from those he regarded as hacks. If at times in his life verse writing seems to have verged on being a personal obsession, especially given his views of its didactic and propagandistic potential, it was never seriously contemplated, nor available, as a vocation.

Edward Byrom intended that university should prepare his son for the Anglican church. But matters did not run to plan. Principled misgivings about the requisite formal oaths, combined with a newfound disinclination to enter the priesthood, had a major impact on the course of Byrom's career, and his nonjuror sympathies and Jacobitism (that is to say, loyalty to the exiled Stuart royal succession) ruled him out of establishment posts and preferment. He took up medicine instead, and while still a nonresident college fellow, studied anatomy in Montpellier, France, in the winter of 1717–1718. Since he never obtained an M.D., the (disclaimed) "Doctor" regularly adjoining his name carried more the ring of a courtesy title. He treated some patients in Manchester in the earlier 1720s, but there is evidence suggesting problems with his early practice. After some prevarication he abandoned medicine as a career, but maintained a lay interest, as shown, for example, in religiously founded opposition in both verse and prose to the newly introduced practice of inoculation.

At the time of his marriage in 1721 to his cousin Elizabeth Byrom (1700–1778), his unsettled circumstances weighed heavily on the minds of his relatives, who were soon alarmed by his decision to concentrate on his "Universal English Short-hand," a writing system he invented between 1715 and 1723, to which he made subsequent refinements. Understanding Byrom's shorthand and its milieu is crucial to the study of surviving documents by him and his circle. Facilitating speed, secrecy, and space-saving, it had manifold applications. Its promotion was a preoccupation for much of the rest of his life; contrary to some accounts, it was not abandoned when he inherited money on his elder brother's death in 1744. Initial attempts to launch it via subscription publication foundered embarrassingly, and Byrom turned instead to giving personal tuition for a five-guinea fee, a sum beyond all but the professional and leisured classes. He accrued over three hundred pupils, mainly during regular visits to London and Cambridge, where young men at the Inns of Court and colleges were his target markets. The liveliest diary sections of his *Private Journal and Literary Remains* were written during these visits. Eminent "Byromites" included the physician and philosopher David Hartley, the playwright brothers Benjamin and John Hoadly, the hymn writer John Newton, the evangelists Charles and John Wesley, and the prime minister's son Horace Walpole. Through shorthand Byrom strengthened his contacts in London's medical and scientific communities; he was elected a fellow of the Royal Society in 1724. Despite two further subscription campaigns, and obtaining a parliamentary act in 1742 to secure copyright and a teaching monopoly, he was unable to establish his system as the vehicle for recording the nation's institutional memory and hence ensure its longevity. Even so, as a quasi-phonotypic method it was an influential precursor of Pitman's shorthand.

Byrom died in Manchester on September 26, 1763, after a lengthy illness (its nature not established). He was survived by his wife and three of their six children, Elizabeth ("Beppy"), Edward ("Tedy"), and Dorothy ("Dolly"), who were instrumental in the posthumous publication of his *Universal English Short-hand* and *Miscellaneous Poems,* neither of which were finalized or sanctioned by him.

FAMILIAR AND COTERIE VERSE

In an unfinished ars poetica of sorts, "An Epistle to a Friend On the Art of English Poetry," elements of which might be read autobiographically, Byrom cautions a shorthand pupil and aspiring poet against becoming "an artificial Fool" (l. 72). Poetry should not be exploited cynically for advancing public reputation; rather, the poet's mission is "At once to profit, and to pleasure Friends" (l. 356). Here Byrom envisages a familiar or coterie audience for poetry, much of his own presupposing a particular reader (or listener). The most obvious examples are his numerous verse letters. In moods by turn amiable, spluttering, nit-pickingly allusive or expansively discursive, the topics they treat range from domestic life to recondite scriptural exegesis. Of those included in his *Miscellaneous Poems,* "many ... were written rather for private, than for public Perusal" (p. i). The editors probably obscured or removed the epistolary contexts of numerous other pieces therein. Others remained in manuscript, many probably now lost to us.

Although most were in five-beat (iambic) couplets, a significant number used the distinctive stanzas of four rhymed couplets of four-beat triple meter made famous by his "Pastoral." To avoid confusion these might conveniently be styled "Byromics." Usually the meter has been termed anapestic tetrameter—with substitutions and variations such as omission of the initial foot's first syllable—but Byrom and some contemporaries thought of it as dactylic. He often exploited triple meter's potential for the comic, poking self-conscious fun at his own methods in poems such as *Tunbridgiale,* where a bluff, writerly presence disarmingly draws attention to the act of composition/narration itself in lines such as: "You put up your Horse, for Rhyme sake, at the *Crown*" (l. 18); "So, to fill up the Stanza—I wish you Goodnight" (l. 24); and "Compare 'em—let's see—to the *De'el's Arse o'Peak*"

(l. 62). (Later editors' more polite substitution of "Derbyshire Peak" in the last example deprives us of the original's colloquial force; it pays to go back to earlier print or manuscript texts wherever possible.) Byrom did not deem triple meter inherently lightweight, though, and sometimes its use effects a peculiar tension with his subject matter, a tension that jarred particularly for later critics. He experimented with "our sort of verse" (*Remains,* vol. 1, p. 70) for religious poems too. A notable success in this connection was his "Divine Pastoral," an expanded verse paraphrase of Psalm 23 which was to become a popular hymn.

Byromics effectively became his signature form for much convivial, network-centered writing, and as such they were often a vehicle for relating news: his verse letters were real letters. A typical example is the sparky "To Henry Wright, of Mobberley, Esq," about bidding for Nicolas Malebranche's portrait at a London saleroom. (Auction records verify the events described: Byrom did indeed pay three pounds five shillings for this, Lot 1.) The concluding stanza links Byrom's associational world of shorthand with that of an informal group he established for discussing the philosopher's work:

And now, if some evening when you are at leisure,
You'll come and rejoice with me over my treasure,
With a friend or two with you, that will in free sort
Let us mix metaphysicks and short-hand and port,
We'll talk of his book, or what else you've a mind,
Take a glass, read or write, as we see we're inclin'd.
Such friends and such freedom! What can be more clever?
Huzza! Father Malebranche and short-hand for ever!
(ll. 89–96)

Wright, and his circle to whom it was read aloud, would have recognized in such poems an oblique, playful gesturing toward a tradition of verse epistles influenced by the Roman poet Horace. Likewise, in the first six stanzas of "A Letter to R.L., Esq., on his Departure from London," Byrom's close friend Ralph Leycester, recipient of epistles over five decades, was expected to enjoy Byrom's undermining of another classical genre popular at the time, the Ovidian heroic epistle, in which the tragic lover bemoans separation from the beloved. For all the fun of the Byromics, with their rhyme-supplying bathos ("All Ways have I try'd the sad Loss to forget, / I have saunter'd, writ Short-hand, eat Custard, *et. cet.*"), such subversion is not a negative act. With the very slightest of (mock) erotic tinting, it works to affirm a strong bond, and its bluster and exaggeration do not obscure the fact that sadness at Leycester's absence is heartfelt, an absence causing a disruption to Byrom's bearings from which only the act of verse writing can give respite. Byrom's "Letter to R.L." is endorsed "Richard's [coffeehouse], / Monday Night / May 24, 1725"—another example of writing to the occasion, with the remaining stanzas relating news about the procession to the gallows "thro' a *Holborn* of Heads" (l. 56) of the thief-taker Jonathan Wild, whose trial he and Leycester had attended, perhaps as unofficial shorthand writers.

Byrom's diary for 16 May 1725 casts some light on the transmission of poems in the circle in which he and Leycester moved:

> I stayed at home all day, turned the Beau's Head into my verses, at the end transcribed what I had done, about twelve stanzas; ... we all went to Meyer's [coffeehouse]; he [Lucas] told me they had read my verses there about Figg, Mr. Roberts had read them well, the only thing that was said was that "fluted" came in for rhyme; we went home with Mr. C., though Mr. Leycester proposed going to a tavern; we had a bottle of white and a bottle of red, ... we stayed till past twelve. I repeated my verses about the Beau to them, which they liked, and Mr. Clarke took a copy of my epigram upon Handel and Bononcini, and the old one of St. George and the Dragon, would have had a copy of the Beau, but I excused myself for that.
>
> (*Remains,* vol. 1, p. 135)

The entry highlights contexts of spoken delivery and transmission via manuscript (and hence potentially fugitive status—nothing is known of the George and the Dragon epigram) and is interestingly corroborated by Leycester's shorthand diary for the same day. Both show the need to approach such work by locating it outside the confines of printed page and instead recovering its coterie basis. The poem recited here was the "Dissection of a Beau's Head," based on Joseph Addison's *Spectator* number 275 satirizing male foppery, which Byrom "turn[ed] ... into my sort of verses" (*Remains,* vol. 1, p. 134) as a disciplined exercise in paraphrase for both personal stimulation and to amuse his friends. For all their occasional fillers and painfully stretched comic rhymes ("Residence is"/"Essences," ll. 9–10), the Byromics proceed with gusto, a deft act of versifying working simultaneously to transform and, crucially, preserve. Adhesion to his source, including its peremptory conclusion, is striking, making the few omissions or embellishments all the more pointed. For example, he interpolates a gibe at contemporary operamania in supplementing Addison's billet-doux and dance tunes with "Op'ra Songs" (l. 20), in so doing glancing at man-about-town Leycester. (Addison's reference to sonnets and musical instruments inside the beau's head is one of the few details in the original not actually picked up; Byrom avoids imputing beauism to poetry and musicianship per se.)

The "verses about Figg" were Byromics about a veritably gladiatorial prizefight which the friends had recently attended; these gained a much wider audience by later inclusion in the sixth volume of Robert Dodsley's canon-shaping *Collection of English Poems* (1748–1758). What would seem to be a slight on line 14's "fluted" is perfectly justified, but criticism Byrom would have taken in his stride. Also referred to in the diary entry is Byrom's famous epigram on the disputes by rival camps of fans of the composers George Frideric Handel and Giovanni Buononcini. With the ardent Handelian Leycester, Byrom had recently attended one of the earliest performances of Handel's *Guilio Cesare* but remained hostile to opera (as he increasingly was to stage performance). Albeit sometimes (mis-)used as evidence of his philistinism, the epigram proved one of his most quoted pieces, a likely source for Lewis Carroll's belligerent enantiomorph brothers:

Some say, compar'd to Bononcini,
That Mynheer Handel's but a Ninny;
Others aver, that he to Handel
Is scarcely fit to hold a Candle:

Strange all this Difference should be,
'Twixt Tweedle-dum and Tweedle-dee!

Here some key aspects of Byrom's coterie verse are epitomized: reliance on recitation for effect (a distorted "cändel" rhyme would emphasize the recently naturalized mynheer's origins); its fundamentally occasional basis; and a bluff, unpretentious idiom used for debunking ends.

ENTHUSIASM *AND OTHER COUNTER-ENLIGHTENMENT POEMS*

Expounded in poems ranging from short epigrams to verse essays of hundreds of lines, Byrom's theology is at odds with what might once have been expected from writer in a so-called Age of Reason. It belongs, rather, to a broadly defined counter-Enlightenment that pitched itself against the spread of a Newtonian physico-theology based on evidence of design in the natural world. Byrom used poetry to attack the assumptions behind this trend and to advocate a more mystical approach, one striving for an apprehension of spiritual truths beyond the intellect's reach, seeing humankind's right purpose as a union of the soul with God. At the risk of oversimplifying the developments over three decades in the thinking behind them, three important recurring, interrelated strands in Byrom's counter-Enlightenment poetry can be summarized: first, a critique of the role of reason, evidence, and academic learning in relation to belief; second, a revaluation of the nature and place of religious enthusiasm; and third, advocacy of a heart-centered faith and perception of truth as a new birth in the soul (hence an opposition voiced through a number of his later poems to doctrines of predestination and Calvinism). In engaging with these areas Byrom placed himself beyond the pale in the eyes of contemporaries both orthodox and otherwise, some of whom looked askance at what they perceived as an outlook not just eccentrically misguided but subversive, even blasphemous; one of Byrom's main targets, Warburton, lamented that Byrom was "a fine genius, but fanatical even to madness" (p. 54).

The cause for much of this hostility was the influence exerted on Byrom by the religious writer William Law (1686–1761). Byrom sought out Law in person soon after the publication in 1729 of his devotional work *A Serious Call to a Devout and Holy Life,* and Law, who called him "my most beloved of friends, and best of poets" (*Remains,* vol. 2, p. 614), was to become something of a spiritual mentor to him for the remainder of his life. The *Serious Call* is famous as a proto-evangelical manual that profoundly affected Samuel Johnson and John Wesley; while Byrom greatly admired it, in his own case its message about a widening gulf between nominal and practical Christianity was more a confirmation of existing views than a stimulus for conversion. Of far more importance to his poetry came to be the thinking behind Law's increasingly mystical publications of the late 1730s onward. Byrom's assorted verse paraphrases of elements of those, together with a host of other poems permeated by Law's ideas, were works he undertook as Law's "Laureate" (*Remains,* vol. 2, p. 588).

The two most notable were the mid-century verse essays *An Epistle to a Gentleman of the Temple* and *Enthusiasm*. Both manifest his veneration for his "Master," who deeply appreciated them and involved himself in seeing them into print. When a review in a French journal sniffed at the *Epistle* for doing little more, in its view, than versifying Law, Byrom took it as an "agreeable" compliment, for "to copy true ideas that appear to be grand, simple, salutary, was the intention of the verse" (*Remains,* vol. 2, p. 518). Byrom told Law "I may be jealous ... that the verse will drop for want of its support—it wants to cling like ivy to an oak" (vol. 2, p. 521). But this was work of promulgation, not parasitism. Neither of these poems are by any means simple paraphrases of Law nor totally dependent on him. Despite some sweeping verdicts by earlier hostile commentators to the contrary, much of Byrom's counter-Enlightenment verse is in any case independent of Law's texts. Praising Law in the *Epistle,* Byrom exclaims:

Master, I call him; not that I incline
To pin my Faith on any One Divine;
But, Man or Woman, whosoe'er it be,
That speaks true Doctrine, is a *Pope* to me.

(ll. 413–418)

Provocatively feminist in its time, the phrase "Man or Woman" signals Byrom's absorption in a wide range of traditions of continental religious and mystical writing, notably that of the Flemish mystic Antoinette Bourignon. (Two of Byrom's translations from Bourignon appeared in the Wesley brothers' early Methodist devotional collection *Hymns and Sacred Poems* [1739] under the titles "Farewell to the World" and "Renouncing All for Christ.") In this connection Byrom seems to have been significantly more catholic, eclectic, and adventurous in his reading than Law. This allowed him in turn to inform Law's own thinking, even if his friend could be skeptical about his tastes.

Their mutual reverence for the seventeenth-century German theosophist Jakob Böhme (or Behmen as he was then more usually known in England) was one that strengthened a rift with the early Methodists. For John Wesley the otherwise pleasurable experience of reading Byrom's *Miscellaneous Poems* was marred by their incorporation of ideas drawn from Böhme. Byrom immersed himself in Böhme's writing, arranging the reprinting of an earlier translation of his *Way to Christ* in Manchester in 1752, and promulgating aspects of Behmenist thought through pieces such as his thirty-one stanzas of "A Poetical Version of a Letter, from Jacob Behmen, to a Friend." These poems are simplified and selective in their appropriation. While making use of metaphors of fire, heat, and flame in conveying his messages about inner light, Byrom generally avoids the more complex cabalistic symbolism and imagery of Böhme's esoteric cosmology that can render Law's later writing so challenging and obscure.

For Byrom the crucial area of Böhme's thinking—filtered through Law—lay in an interpretation of the fall and redemption which he used to counter some fashionable interpretations of Scripture in his own time. This he communicated in poems such as "On the True Meaning of the Scripture Terms 'Life' and 'Death' When Applied to Men," "On the Fall of Man," "On the Ground of True and False Religion," and, at most length, the *Epistle,* which in places paraphrases or alludes to Law's Behmenist text *The Spirit of Prayer*. Adam's fall was for Byrom and Law a falling from divine nature in a self-willed act rather than one of disobedience to arbitrary command. Through his "Death to his pristin, *Spirit-life* divine" (l. 155) Adam instantly fell into earthly physicality:

He *dy'd* to Paradise, and, by a Birth
That shoul'd not have been rais'd, he *liv'd* to Earth;
Fell into bestial Flesh, and Blood, and Bones.

(ll. 35–37)

It is through Christ, the second Adam, working within the soul that we are redeemed:

There is within us a *celestial Birth;*
A Life that waits the *Efforts of our Mind,*
To raise itself within this *outward Rind.*
This *Husk of ours,* this stately *stalking Clod,*
Is not the Body that we have from *God.*

(ll. 344–348)

Byrom wrote the *Epistle* to contrast this outlook with Bishop Thomas Sherlock's figurative, legalistic reading of the Fall, a reading he felt moved toward deism and undermined the importance of grace:

Without acknowledging that *Adam dy'd,*
Scripture throughout is, in Effect, deny'd;
All the whole Process of *Redeeming Love,*
Of *Life,* of *Light,* and *Spirit from above,*
Loses, by Leaning's piteous Pretence
Of *Modes,* and *Metaphors,* its real Sense:
All the glad Tidings, in the Gospel found,
Are sunk in empty and unmeaning Sound.

(ll. 373–80)

This suspicion of "Learning" is echoed by many of Byrom's later poems.

A sense of the distance Byrom had traveled by his fifties under Law's (and others') influence is gained by juxtaposing "The Pond," written not long before their first meeting, with the more obviously substantial *Enthusiasm,* begun in the 1740s and published in 1752. The former was based on a short parable in Law's *Serious Call* about a man so obsessed with maintaining and extending his large pond that he lives in perpetual thirst, until he falls into it only to be drowned. It can be linked with a body of moralizing verse fables that Byrom wrote for younger audiences, such as "The Three Black Crows," a comic tale about the dangers of inaccurately transmitted gossip. (Through later dissemination in school readers and reciters, both poems had a performance life lasting well into the nineteenth century.) When Byrom read it to him, Law jokingly "desired I would not put the whole book into verse, for then it would not sell in prose" (*Remains,* vol. 1, p. 337). In dramatizing Law's two-sentence prose paragraph in over fifty couplets, Byrom introduces direct speech and an element of humor, as well as showing how covetousness is linked to cruelty, and he gives it a more obviously contemporary pertinence in embellishing it with imagery of landscape design and financial accounting. A conclusion to his listeners provides an analogy not explicit in his source between the pond and a mishandled estate; the man represents a self-seeking squire who lives contrary to ideals of benevolence and is contemptuous of the poor. There is an Augustan flavor to the piece with its choice of epigraph from Horace's *Satires;* Byrom locates a classical parallel to endorse the act of amplifying Law's source text. Like many other sinners depicted in the *Serious Call,* the pond-builder is, by implication, sinful because he fails to act in accordance with reason and hence God (never mentioned in the poem); he manifests one of the forms of behavior that Byrom castigates in *Enthusiasm.* But the latter, with its recondite title-page epigraph from the mystical theologian Dionysius, is far from Augustan, and by the time it appeared, Byrom, following Law, had come to place reason and religion in opposition.

A verse essay of slightly over four hundred lines, prefaced by a prose letter to "a Friend in Town," *Enthusiasm* is Byrom's assertion of a creative, imaginative psychology, highlighting the vital role played by the "Fire within the human Soul" (l. 273). Through it he aimed at rehabilitating a word that had long carried negative associations of the fanatically zealous and superstitious. It seems to have gestated for a decade before it was printed and owes much to Law in that parts of it paraphrase or use as a springboard some sections within Law's rejoinder to the vilification of his and others' "enthusiasm" by Joseph Trapp; this rejoinder appeared in 1740 as "Some Animadversions upon Dr. Trap's late Reply," an appendix to Law's *An Appeal to All That Doubt.* But *Enthusiasm* was by no means completely dependent on the "Animadversions" and its immediate context. The decision to print it is best seen against a wider backdrop of subsequent attacks from both press and pulpit on groups such as Quakers and Methodists by those suspicious of their stress on personal religious experience and emotion. These were groups with whom Byrom, as "a friend of God's people in every denomination" (*Remains,* vol. 2, p. 645*n*) in the words of the Moravian Francis Okely, maintained active, if sometimes strained, contact.

Picking up on the "common Cant" (l. 7) of anti-enthusiast polemic, *Enthusiasm*'s opening traps unwary readers into assuming that they have embarked on something along similar lines:

Fly from *Enthusiasm*—It is the Pest,
Bane, Poison, Frensy, Fury—and the rest.

(ll. 1–2)

But it swiftly shows that his agenda is far removed from the dismissive "Clamour" that makes us

fly from what we almost know we want;
A deeper Sense of *something* that should set
The Heart at Rest

(ll. 8–10)

as Byrom moves into three verse paragraphs in which enthusiasm, "Thought enkindled to an high Degree" (l. 76), is displayed as a driving, universal energy. He extends Law's definition of enthusiasm in his *Appeal* as a "*kindling* of the Will, Imagination, and Desire" (p. 306), celebrating this energy through which matter is governed by mind:

'Tis *Will, Imagination,* and *Desire*
Of thinking Life, that constitute the Fire,
The Force, by which the strong Volitions drive,
And form the Scenes to which we are alive.
...
Imagination, trifling as it seems,
Big with Effects, its own Creation teems.

We think our Wishes and Desires a Play,
And sport important Faculties away:
Edg'd are the Tools with which we trifle thus,
And carve out deep Realities for us.

(ll. 23–27, 37–42)

It is in such sections that *Enthusiasm* is significant for prefiguring aspects of Romanticism in ways that are at a remove from the ideas of those mid-eighteenth century poets sometimes classed as "pre-romantic." Byrom portrays imagination, which comes to be analogized with God, as an active, not passive, faculty: we create the "deep Realities" rather than merely perceive them. But his concern is spiritual and ethical rather than aesthetic, with the last third of the poem demonstrating that enthusiasm is the essence of everyone's humanity and that our minds enjoy freedom of choice in exercising this for good or ill. When rightly directed, by means of the indwelling holy spirit, the enthusiastic imagination is our salvation, that of the "true regenerated Soul" (l. 337). Realization of "God within the Heart of Man" (l. 350) results in a universal loving benevolence "that no Distinction knows / Of *System, Sect,* or *Party, Friends,* or *Foes*" (ll. 345–346).

Enthusiasm's central section closely versifies Law's argument that there are sinful and worldly forms of enthusiasm too, the concept not being confined to religious faith; all of us belong to a "Species of Enthusiasts" (l. 250), and opposition to "true religious Earnestness" (l. 89) is itself just the enthusiastic behavior of one species. While not directly named, Warburton features as exemplar of the enthusiasm of misdirected learning. Byrom significantly extends Law's allusions to the combative methods of Warburton's mammoth *Divine Legation* (1737–1741), in a trenchant passage of forty lines infused with an almost Pope-like wit, both in their criticism (Warburton is made to seem like one of Pope's dunces) and, for Byrom, a more than usually assured handling of pause and caesura, mocking the arrogance of the *"Clarissimus Enthusiast"* (l. 156) buoyed up by mere "Conjecture, tinsel'd with its own Applause" (l. 164). Stung—but intrigued—by Byrom's taunting, Warburton initiated a formal correspondence between them,

formal in the sense that both sides knew their letters would be circulated more widely. He paid his adversary the tribute that it was the first time he had ever replied to one his many public abusers, Byrom being "the only honest man of that number" (*Remains,* vol. 2, p. 524). His first letter neatly summarizes their fundamental differences: "You would convince men of the truth of the Gospel by inward feelings; I, by outward facts and evidence" (*Remains,* vol. 2, p. 523). In Byrom's eyes, Warburton irreligiously reduces Scripture to historical record, whereas to him Scripture is a book of the heart, with the process of God's illumination working within us, rather than being something rationally demonstrable through external evidence. This is the difference underlying more sustained criticism of Warburton in several other poems, such as the series of six "Familiar Epistles to a Friend," all attacking one of his sermons, where Byrom bemoans the way that "Learning, History, and critic Sense" (Letter 3, l. 16) has attempted to supplant the role of revelation. Both here and in "A Stricture on the Bishop of Gloucester's *Doctrine of Grace*" he coins the word *"Bibliolatry"* (ll. 62, 48) to condemn Warburton's approach.

By contrast, Byrom's psychology of rightly directed enthusiasm is one antithetical to any emphasis on reason. Hence the anti-intellectual strain in many poems, stressing that what we know is emotional, not rational, and that God's influence is direct, not analogical. Through them he argues that reason is a woefully inadequate basis for religion, and that those according it primacy amongst the faculties of insight are solipsists. This is one line of attack in "Remarks on Dr. Middleton's Examination ... ," at just over a thousand lines Byrom's lengthiest poem. In the course of dissecting recently published views about prophecy by the classicist Conyers Middleton, it shows freethinkers to be constrained by a subjective idealism. (Middleton is also an unnamed target in a central passage in *Enthusiasm.* There Byrom probably relished an opportunity afforded by Law's source text to have a dig at a man "seiz'd with classic Rage" [l. 91] because of long-standing resentments grounded in the university politics of his twenties.) Other poems argue that through its promotion of pride in the self, human reason is effectively proof of our fallen nature.

Byrom's critique of reason is usually at its most effective when he deploys simple metaphor, as in "Thoughts on the Constitution of Human Nature ... ," a take on Plato's allegory of the charioteer of the soul in *Phaedrus,* with the substitution of stagecoach for chariot. Coach-driver Reason may be thought to guide the "Body Coach, of Flesh and Blood" (l. 2) as it is drawn along by passions, yet

They, who are loud in human Reason's Praise,
And celebrate the Drivers of our Days,
Seem to suppose, by their continual Bawl,
That Passions, Reason, and Machine, is all;
To them the Windows are drawn up, and clear
Nothing that does not outwardly appear.

(ll. 19–24)

The "Thoughts" show Byrom's opposition to the philosopher John Locke's denial of innate ideas and notion of the mind as a tabula rasa. He wants to open the coach's windows and look inside: "What *Spirit* drives the willing Mind within?" (l. 42). The gulf between poems such as this and the writings of modernist rationalism and deism is illustrated by the opening of "A Penitential Soliloquy":

What! tho' no Objects strike upon the Sight!
Thy sacred Presence is an *inward* Light!
What! tho' no Sounds should penetrate the Ear!
To list'ning Thought the Voice of Truth is clear!
Sincere devotion needs no outward Shrine;
The Center of an *humble* Soul is thine!

(ll. 1–6)

Pointedly reworking the climax of Addison's celebrated ode on the creation, "The Spacious Firmament on High" (1712), the stanza epitomizes Byrom as counter-Enlightenment poet: he is thinking about the soul's center in us, not Addison's external firmament, and his concern is not for Addison's sense-dependent ear of Reason but for the "*inward* Light" and a heart-centered faith.

POLITICAL WRITING

Even though he frequently adopts an irenic and ecumenical stance, Byrom was ever the controversialist, and no stranger to a world of intrigue and invective, as shown by his involvement in disputes with the likes of Trapp, Warburton, and Sherlock. Two instances of his earlier pamphleteering have been discovered. In 1720 the vice chancellor's court at Cambridge charged him with defamation for publishing *A Review of the Proceedings Against Dr. Bentley* under the pseudonym "N.O." This was mainly an attack on the wrangling of Bentley's adversaries taking place against a backdrop of Whig-influenced demands for a rigorous visitation of the university. More subversively, later that decade he was behind a satirical farrago called *A Collection of Curious Papers,* designed to ridicule measures against northeastern clergy by the Erastian Whig bishop Samuel Peploe. Simultaneously he involved himself in politically influenced machinations at the Royal Society, and at the turn of the decade worked assiduously at the forefront of a successful campaign to persuade Parliament to throw out the Manchester Workhouse Bill, which he feared would result in the consolidation of an ascendant Whig, low-church power base in the region. While the density of topical and local allusion renders Byrom's responses to these and similar episodes, both in prose and verse, opaque to all but specialists today, their existence needs factoring into any overview of his life and work, putting to rest a once prevalent view that he was somehow indifferent to or aloof from the world of politics. Such a view may be tempting given the quietist implications of his religious verse. But the origins of his counter-Enlightenment writing are not divorceable from his links with the nonjuring schism, and hence Jacobitism.

Byrom's famous epigram on the Stuart versus Hanoverian succession was once conventionally quoted to illustrate a prevaricating or cautiously equivocating outlook, to be seen as a political equivalent of that on Handel versus Buononcini:

God bless the King, I mean the Faith's Defender;
God bless—no Harm in blessing—the Pretender;

But who Pretender is, or who is King,
God bless us all—that's quite another Thing.

But in fact this carries anything but the insouciant tone of "Careless Content," Byrom's fine alliterative invigoration of the topos of the contented mind rising above transient fashions, whose speaker's advice is to remain aloof or go with the flow, to "swing what Way the Ship shall swim, / Or tack about, with equal Trim" (ll. 23-24) as the wisest means of self-preservation. For rather than representing a noncommittal stance, some balanced weighing up of sides, the epigram would have been Jacobitical to its contemporary readers (or hearers), its staged act of bemusement provocative in merely suggesting that doubt might linger over Hanoverian-Whig claims to the succession.

We find a similar approach toward the end of Byrom's boldest and most assured political poem, "The Contrast Between Two Executed Lords." These archly sequenced stanzas were written in the wake of the public beheading of Lords Kilmarnock and Balmerino for their involvement in the 1745 Jacobite rebellion. The opening depiction of the former's behavior at the scaffold, with its stress on public penitence and "offended Majesty," ingeniously traps the reader into assumptions that a pro-Hanoverian, anti-Jacobite pen is working to draw a pious contrast with Balmerino's stubborn immorality. The description at the end of the third stanza of renegade Kilmarnock being composed "reluctantly" hence comes as a jolt, striking us with fuller force as we realize that the contrasting exemplar Balmerino is actually being positioned for our approval:

The OTHER—firm, and steady in the Cause
Of injur'd Monarchs, and of ancient Laws,
By change of Conduct never stain'd his Fame,
Child, Youth, and Man, his Principles the same:
How greatly generous his last Adieu!
...
Scorning, when past through Life with Conscience clear,
In Death to play the Hypocrite—and fear:
His Head adorned with the *Scottish* Plaid,
His Heart confiding upon God for Aid,

He, as a Guest, invites his welcome Fate,
Gallant, Intrepid, Fearless, and *Sedate.*

(ll. 25–29, 35–40)

The conclusion briefly plays with the illusion of impartiality reminiscent of the "God bless the king" epigram, but Byrom's loyalties emerge clear in the triumphant assertion that Balmerino might be accorded the status of "valiant Martyr" (l. 48). This is hardly a call to arms in support of the Jacobite cause, but nor is it the nostalgic "Charlie o'er the Waterism" that pervades some Jacobite verse by others later in the century. Far from being secondary witness discourse about the world of politics, this is verse that participates in that world: it works as propaganda in its implication that less significant Jacobite rebels might be accorded martyr status likewise for courageously adhering to perceived moral and religious imperatives.

Understanding the original publication context of such writing is essential to grasping this purpose. Like much of Byrom's other 1740s political verse it was first printed in the Tory-Jacobite newspaper *Adams's Weekly Courant,* to which Byrom regularly contributed poems, epigrams, and, probably, prose commentary during a dispute with Whig journalists on the rival *Manchester Magazine;* some of this was also conducted in London-based periodicals. A selection of pieces from both sides—albeit selected by the Tory-Jacobite camp—appeared in the anthology *Manchester Vindicated* (1749). (Work continues on establishing attributions, though the full extent of Byrom's contribution will probably never be clear.) Protracted and often bitter, this dispute stemmed from an anti-Jacobite crackdown by government forces in the aftermath of the Young Pretender's incursion in the region in late 1745. (Byrom attended a levee where they briefly met.) One grisly triggering event was the fate of two young Jacobite Manchester Regiment soldiers, one of them the eldest son of Byrom's friend Thomas Deacon; after execution in London their heads were sent to Manchester to be impaled on spikes outside the Exchange. A defiant act of obeisance to his son's rotting head by Deacon, already a controversial figure as nonjuror bishop of the "British Orthodox Church," precipitated vituperative pulpit and press attacks. Byrom defended Deacon and his supporters in his writing for the *Courant* and became embroiled in broader public discourse about the nature of martyrdom. Incensed by the church's interference in this "fierce Dispute of secular Affairs" (l. 322) through its promulgation of "Bigotries of State" (l. 324), in 1747 he distributed a separately printed *Epistle to a Friend; Occasioned by a Sermon Intituled The False Claims to Martyrdom Consider'd,* 430 lines condemning political sermonising against the Manchester rebels:

O Divine Sermon! little understood,
If they who preach thee, not content with Blood,
Justly perhaps, perhaps * * * * * * * * shed,
(Do Thou determine, Judge of Quick and Dead)
By this devoted Earth's all transient Scene
Measure the glories of eternal Reign;
Adjust it's martyr'd Ranks, and seem to fear,
Lest Heav'n should err—and *Jacobites* be there.

(ll.33–40)

The poem goaded the presbyterian minister Josiah Owen into attacking Byrom as "the Master-Tool of the [Jacobite] Faction" on the very title page of a pamphlet attacking Deacon. It was deliberately excluded from the *Miscellaneous Poems,* probably on account of the risk of opening old wounds. Once again, Byrom uses a pretence of the noncommittal, here craftily hinging on "perhaps, perhaps ... ," with asterisks employed in a mock gesture of censorship of the daring concept that the executions might have taken place "unjustly," in effect emphasizing that viewpoint. Byrom employs a similar technique comically in another *Courant* poem, which also circulated as a separate broadside, *A Genuine Dialogue Between a Gentlewoman at Derby and Her Maid Jenny....* This can profitably be read against a wider context of prosecutions of Jacobite seditious words cases in the law courts. Hyphen ellipses are used as a flimsy pretence of masking dangerous labels of calling the Young Pretender "Prince" or "Royal Highness," manifestly absurd in what purports to be a *"Dialogue":*

Mrs. Good! this is you that did not call him K—g;
And is not P—e, ye Minx, the self-same Thing?
Jen. You are so hasty, Madam! with your Snarles—
Wou'd you have me call the Gentleman plain Ch—s?
Mrs. P—*Ch*—*s* again! —speak out your Treason Tales;
His R—l H—s, *Ch*—*s,* the P—of W—s!

(ll. 33–38)

Simultaneously they convey a sense of the need for whispering Jenny's "secret Views" (l. 73) in the Young Pretender's favor, views to which, by strong implication at the end of the poem, her mistress is in due course converted.

This dialogue format is also employed in a series of unusual pieces by Byrom wholly or partly in Lancashire dialect, which are likewise informed by events after the Jacobite rebellion of 1745. It seems likely that the three printed posthumously in *Miscellaneous Poems* belonged to a wider set which has not survived (or yet surfaced), and that they were influenced by the recent successful dialect publication of his countryman John Collier (or "Tim Bobbin"). Byrom's editor felt obliged to concede that they might baffle general readers—the second edition of his poems duly provides a translation—but the dialect is actually far from impenetrable, especially in any animated reading aloud, and more accessible than Collier's. In two exchanges between the landowning justice of the peace Sir John Jobson and the weaver Harry Homespun we glimpse dialect's potential as a language of social protest, asserting a cherished identity under threat. As in his better-known *Courant* poem, "Tom the Porter," Byrom's sympathies lie very much with the poorer members of society here, who, because they do not have any real stake in the country, are indifferent to any perceived threat of invasion by Jacobites:

Sir J. But, *Harry,* to see Fire and Sword advance!
To have such enemies as *Rome* and *France!*
Shou'd not this move alike both Rich and Poor,
To drive impending Ruin from their Door?
H. As for the Rich, Sur John, *I conno' tell*
But for the Poor, I'll onser for mysel;
If Fire shid come, I ha' nout for it to brun, ...

(ll. 17–23)

Along with Byrom's other *Courant* verse, the dialogues condense arguments relating to allegiance, succession, and usurpation treated in the prose essays in the rival journalism. They show how debates on religio-political turmoil of seventeenth-century England lived well into the eighteenth, debates underlying the faction and contention that were so influential in determining the course of Byrom's own life.

BYROM'S DIARY: THE PRIVATE JOURNAL AND LITERARY REMAINS

The relative richness of known biographical detail about Byrom is largely owing to the twelve-hundred-odd pages of his *Private Journal and Literary Remains*. Printed in four parts between 1854 and 1857 under the somewhat nominal editorship of Richard Parkinson, and based on manuscripts until then known only to family members and descendants, it stayed relatively neglected for over a century, notwithstanding Adolphus William Ward's view that it should "rank among the popular works of English biographical literature" (vol. 1, p. iv). Ironically, relatively little of what Parkinson seems to have intended as "literary remains" came to be printed, and his plans in the 1840s to publish Byrom's daily memoranda from boyhood to old age were never borne out: at the time of *Remains*'s first diary entry Byrom was a man of thirty, and only mere scraps of diary-type writing are presented for his final nineteen years. In fact a large proportion of *Remains* is devoted to correspondence, which is often cut into the diary sequences. The most significant tranche of it consists of nearly two hundred mostly news-packed letters from Byrom when in London or Cambridge to his wife back at home in Manchester, at least a quarter of them abridged, revealing a strongly companionate and affectionate bond with his "dear, dear love," "dear partner," "good girl," "sweetheart," and "Valentine." (Aside from these, the most important correspondence in *Remains* is that with Law and Warburton. As for the rest, more is material written to, rather than by, Byrom.)

Readers new to *Remains* need to be clear that it is a mediated, nineteenth-century text, one which is selective, lacunate, and at some remove from Byrom's original writing in ways going far beyond imposition of later conventions of house style and layout. Similar charges might be leveled against any print edition, particularly one of a diary; and transformation of shorthand into longhand inevitably introduces yet another layer of distortion. But in contrast with those of William Byrd, Samuel Pepys, and Dudley Ryder—to cite the three other notable early modern shorthand diary writers with whom Byrom might most appropriately be compared and contrasted—it is unfortunate that we cannot gain a better purchase on his diaries as material entities, with the attendant documentary indicators and clues afforded about composition processes, because virtually all the manuscripts behind *Remains* were destroyed at the end of the nineteenth century. This also frustrates any assessment of the labors of his inadequately recognized transcriber, Sarah Bolger. Some recent research, however, shows that her considerable skill in deciphering was not infallible; as well as cases of slips with individual shorthand words, some entire passages simply proved too elusive for her. Evidence has also emerged of a diary entry's becoming telescoped by extensive internal cutting of complete sentences and paragraphs before transformation into print. It is tempting to assume that such treatment, and likewise the subsequent manuscript destruction, betokens censorship of the controversial or salacious—the reason why *Remains* casts little if any light on Byrom's sexuality, say—and to make the related assumption that shorthand was employed because Byrom wished to keep things hidden. But, disappointingly, what stayed unprinted in the evidence mentioned was the reverse of scandalous. More pragmatic reasons for cutting are likelier, such as deciphering difficulties and, more mundanely, exigencies of publishing costs and deadlines.

While these are concerns that thwart any conclusive analysis of Byrom's methods and style as diarist, *Remains* nevertheless furnishes abundant material for a provisional overview. It does not make sense to identify any overriding "theme," although Byrom's recording of progress—or lack of it—with his shorthand projects affords something of a unifying narrative thread across many entries, should one be sought. Byrom also used diaries to record food he consumed (of perennial interest to him before and after a move to lacto-vegetarianism in his forties), to register the names of pupils and attendees at meetings and clubs, to transcribe or copy letters, and to transcribe verse. They also furnish a record of his intellectual curiosity and growth, or at least pretensions, instanced especially by frequent detailing of the fruits of his book-buying *"cacoethes"* (*Remains,* vol. 1, p. 564). Recording of these types of detail was not done in any methodical way, though—just one reason why citing any single diary entry as typical would be problematic, for Byrom was no creature of set routines, whether in the pattern of his daily life or in his methods of journalizing. In general there is no predictability to the length of an entry nor to its level of detail, and he operated on no fixed recording schedule, sometimes writing shortly after (or during) events mentioned, at other times writing several days up retrospectively. By turns peremptory, elliptical, or impromptu, and frequently juxtaposing the (apparently) trivial with the intellectual ("Chestnuts, 100 roasted; sat up till three reading Goropius") (vol. 1, p. 431), relatively little in *Remains*'s diary sections is stylistically embellished, and description is scant. This is not to say that Byrom's diary writing is artless: any diary is, after all, a constructed form, and in his habit of composing some entries from separately kept loose notes Byrom, like Pepys, reveals that writing "this diurnal nonsense" (vol. 1, p. 336) could also be less a spontaneous act and more a studied labor of love than it might at first appear.

We do not know when Byrom began writing a diary (the terms "diary" and "journal" are used synonymously here). But it may be telling that he mentions the practice of monitoring the day's activities before going to sleep—in order to amend future conduct—in the opening sentence of his first appearance in print, in the first of his essays on dreams. Here "John Shadow" inverts the advice, recommending morning scrutiny of the night's dream activity and coining the word "Noctuary" for a written repository for such scrutiny. While only rarely does he record his own dreams, the long-established idea of diary-keeping as a means to personal analysis, here attributed to Pythagoras, is something that seems to have been one motivating factor for Byrom's own, though it was never the key one. His has sometimes been categorized as a "religious journal," yet the term is inadequate for a text far removed from the tradition of seventeenth- and eighteenth-century chronicling to record God's providence. A far simpler sense of diary-as-confessional emerges in entries such as a record of a meeting with his tailor—"Tuesday, [26th]: Mr. Whitehead half after eight, and I was cross-ish, qu. [query] it was wrong my behaviour to him, and others upon occasion, very wrong, the complaining and fault-finding way not suitable to a sinner" (vol. 2, p. 132)—or frustrations at repeated failure to adhere to resolutions about early rising: "the coffee tasted very good after my fasting since morning, that is, since twelve or one o'clock—fine morning indeed, you idle rogue!" (vol. 1, p. 174). The diary's therapeutic role as confidant emerges especially during a period of absence from his family in London in 1737, when his composure is undermined by dilemmas over a revamped shorthand subscription, and he uses it as an audience for misgivings about the direction in which he finds himself being pushed. There are also instances of more formal direct address to God; for example, reference to indecision over a case of smallpox contains a plea that God should forgive medical errors he had made, and his entry on his wife's thirty-seventh birthday constitutes a prayer for her and their children. On his own birthday in 1728 he considers making the diary a more meditative medium, duly appending to the account of that day's events a paragraph on the necessity for maintaining cheerfulness, a favorite theme. But any plan to compose regular extended contemplations was promptly abandoned. While they are significant, such moments of piety and reflection were never the raison d'être for Byrom's diary habit, and he never set out to lay bare candidly a full inner life.

The notion of the single "Private Journal" of *Remains*'s title is misleading. With the marked exception of some of the sequences of London-based entries for the mid-1720s and later 1730s, so much is intermittent or fragmentary, with any overall sense of journal continuum being something of an illusion achieved by editorial extraction of significantly different types of diary entry within significantly different types of manuscript book. It is more appropriate to think of Byrom's *diaries*—in the plural—as semi-disparate modes of journalizing rather than constituting any organically conceived, developing single "work." There is a wealth of difference between his bustling, detailed, and lengthy accounts of his coffeehouse- and tavern-based social life and contact-forging in London in 1725, for example, and the brief, peremptory entries he made in Manchester in September that year when back home with his family ("Tuesday … : stayed at home till about four") (vol. 1, p. 179). Putting aside the possibility of subsequent editorial telescoping, the shortness of some entries should not be taken as evidence that a day was uneventful or deemed unworthy of recording—in fact, this might just as well indicate quite the reverse: "hurry worry from one place and body to another, I have not time to take down matters" (vol. 1, p. 459), he complains during frenetic politicking over the Workhouse Bill affair. Brevity (or silence) can hold its own eloquence too: the simple statement about brother Edward's parentage, birth and death dates on the very day of his death seems cold in its matter-of-factness, but it might equally be read as a choked marking of the loss of a bond too close to need expressing.

By contrast, elsewhere Byrom finds more time on his hands to give glimpses of more expansive thought process. Take 5 June 1729, where ideas are hatched distinguishing between enlightenment and inner light, in a mulling over of implications of the previous evening's discussion with what seems to have been a group of heterodox freethinkers at the Rose Tavern. Byrom, tellingly, rises late, is oblivious to one morning caller, puts off another, receives and transcribes a letter from a publisher about a project to decipher the shorthand sermons of a proto-Seventh-day Adventist, and then proceeds to the Devil Tavern

> to enquire for any of my acquaintance, but none there; dined there alone upon a mackerel. Pits's notion of a man's right to his person and property, and to judge of his own happiness, runs in my head much, there being something very clever in his way of talking upon it. Thoughts after dinner. Is there not in all or most words an inward and an outward meaning? The body! and the shadow! When truth rises in the mind at first it makes a long shadow, but when it is vertical, and shines perpendicularly through us, little or no shadow. Baptism! Does it not signify doctrine, and the outward way of professing that we believe the doctrine? so that a man may be baptised himself; but to make this baptism appear to others, or rather his profession of it appear to others, he is baptised by water. There is thought! or principle! and the maxim to show it or promote it,—the substance, and the form.
>
> (vol. 1, pp. 366–367)

Probably written up at more than one stage during the course of the day (or the one following), the appeal of such entries lies in their merging of the metaphysical and the quotidian: thereafter he visits a friend at a regular coffeehouse haunt, attends a club before a Royal Society meeting, briefly comments on his purchase ("1s. 6d.") of Conyers Place's *Essay towards the Vindication of the Visible Creation,* and later joins some acquaintances for supper ("beef steaks") (vol. 1, pp. 366–367). In such accounts Byrom was building a storehouse of detail to trigger memories in both the short- and long-term future, as he explains when justifying resumption of his diary after a period of desuetude:

> I find that though what I set down in this kind of journal is nonsense for the most part, yet that these nonsenses help to recollect times and persons and things upon occasion, and serve at least to some purpose as to writing shorthand; therefore I must not, I think, discontinue it any longer, but only, if I have a mind, omit some trifling articles; though when I consider that it is the most trifling things sometimes that help us to recover more material things, I do not know that I should omit trifles; they may be of use to me, though to others they would appear ridiculous; but as nobody is to see them but myself, I will let myself take any notes, never so trifling, for my own use.
>
> (vol. 1, p. 229)

In *Remains* we find captured a socialized self aware of his privileged status as witness to the discourse and behavior of other people he finds remarkable. These embraced both well-known public or professional figures and a host of lesser-known and often obscure writers, clergymen, freethinkers, scholars, aristocrats, tradespeople, and eccentrics (sometimes several of these combined), knowledge of whose existence to us today would otherwise be restricted to baptism and burial records. In "A Hint to a Young Person ... ," gnomic verses that repeat the advice about noctuarizing, Byrom stresses the value of preserving "Things or facetious, or sublime" (l. 20) gleaned in conversation, concluding that Socrates is known to posterity only because of the endeavor of an amanuensis, his (alleged) "Short-Hand Youth" (l. 39). Journalizing was a way for him to practice what he preached, and elements of *Remains* should be seen in the context of a vogue for collecting *ana* (anecdotes) or table talk. In places, Byrom's love of conversation, for which he was celebrated, leads him to use his diary not just as a record of it but a substitute for it, something we find too in his correspondence with Elizabeth: "My dear, I ramble on, it being somewhat like talking with thee" (vol. 2, p. 22). At times a down-to-earth style in which the diary becomes almost a listener, grows endearingly digressive, even on the most trivial level: in "thence (bought an ink horn 4d.) to Richard's" (vol. 1, p. 588) the mid-phrase interruption neatly enacts a straying from a main purpose, with an implied stopping-off at a shop along the way to a coffeehouse. Similarly, sudden parenthesized remembrance, instead of more studied retrospective word amendment, suggests spontaneity in thought and rapidity in communicating: "Somebody joined us of our acquaintance, I forget who, and Sir John Bland afterwards, (it was Dr. Hooper,) who told of his having had the gout" (vol. 2, p. 94). Byrom strikes an almost comic note of the informally spoken in such cases, as he does in his frustrated forehead-tapping to recollect a name, in writing that seems to transcribe his own speaking aloud: "I saw Mr.—what's his name? my scholar in Figtree Court—Robyns" (vol. 2, p. 118).

In recording others' conversation himself, often with a view to then summarizing it retrospectively, shorthand's potential to fix the moment could come into its own, as in his record of a confabulation between Hartley and the mathematician Roger Paman on April 15, 1737, partly laid out as if a direct transcript. Byrom never claimed that his shorthand system would allow for verbatim accuracy in taking down "ordinary" speech (very different from coping with the more measured pace of delivered speech such as sermons), and it seems clear that in order to keep up with his companions he had to omit much. Despite the likely selectivity and unpreventable lacunae, the shorthand here still gives us a moment of hearing eighteenth-century men of science in informal converse in an era long before mechanized sound inscription. The record is remarkable less for the wide-ranging subject matter touched on (including infinitesimal calculus, "ancient" versus "modern" poetry, and the relative value of different academic disciplines across time) than for the way that conversation, captured as it is happening, with its colloquialisms, trailings, and interruptions, begins to be made an actuality for us.

POSTHUMOUS REPUTATION

By the first half of the nineteenth century Byrom had gained a minor niche within the canon of English verse, mainly through representation in Alexander Chalmers's influential *English Poets* series. But Leslie Stephen's assumption by that century's end that "an answer might reasonably be expected" of students facing the exam question " 'Who was John Byrom?' " (p. 74) became hopelessly optimistic in the twentieth-century academy. Byrom's verse was usually treated—if it was treated at all—as an embarrassing and unfortunate diversion. Heavily context-dependent, mired in specific allusion to long-forgotten or arcane controversies, often awkward and cumbrous in diction and syntax, his verse was at a distinct remove from newer canons of verbal icons. Neither did it help that Byrom failed to fit comfortably with some standard narratives and labels in literary history. While there were exceptions to this neglect—Eric Rothstein, for example, believed that Byrom's was "the only genuinely interesting body of eighteenth-century religious verse" (p. 228)—comprehensive consideration was practically nonexistent and has remained so. If occasionally surfacing in anthologies, usually through the Christmas day hymn "Christians awake" (better known in later redactions that removed its original Geneva-Bible influenced diction and mystical dimension), for much of the twentieth century Byrom sank into marginalized obscurity. There is no modern edition of his diaries, letters, and other prose, and the most recent edition of his poems—that by Adolphus William Ward, his most informed and appreciative commentator—is now over a century old. No wonder, then, that in a step toward broadening the canon of eighteenth-century poetry in the 1970s Dennis Davison issued a more challenging take on Stephen's question: "dare one really resurrect such forgotten names as Byrom ... ?" (p. 6).

Attempting a resurrection is far less daring today, given the continuing remapping of the eighteenth century to take account of previously neglected authors, explanatory models for writing, and liminal forms and genres. As cross-disciplinary work too on Britain's "long eighteenth century" has broadened considerably since the 1970s, so Byrom's writing has become more recognized as a significant source for investigations in areas as diverse as the intersection of manuscript and print cultures, the dissemination of popular scientific knowledge, and the reception of continental mysticism. But it is far more than an information repository to be mined for evidence and citation, and now merits a place in what David Fairer, surveying developments in eighteenth-century literary studies, calls a "conversation with new accents" (p. ix).

Selected Bibliography

WORKS OF JOHN BYROM

POETRY

Tunbridgiale, a Poem: Being A Description of Tunbridge. In a Letter to A Friend at London. London: W. Meadows, 1726.

A Full and True Account of an Horrid and Barbarous Robbery, Committed on Epping-Forest, upon the Body of the Cambridge Coach. In a Letter to M.F. Esq. London: J. Roberts, 1728.

An Epistle to a Friend; Occasioned by a Sermon Intituled, The False Claims to Martyrdom Consider'd: A Sermon Preach'd at St. Anne's Church, Manchester, November 2, 1746. Being the Sunday After All-Saints Day, By Benj. Nichols, M.A. Assistant-Curate of the Said Church and Chaplain to the Right Honourable the Earl of Uxbridge. London: M. Cooper, 1747.

An Epistle to a Gentleman of the Temple. Occasioned by Two Treatises Just Published, Wherein the Fall of Man is Differently Represented; Viz. I. Mr Law's Spirit of Prayer, II. The Bishop of London's Appendix. Shewing, That, According to the Plainest Sense of Scripture, the Nature of the Fall is Greatly Mistaken in the Latter. London: R. Spavan, 1749.

Enthusiasm; a Poetical Essay. In a Letter to a Friend in Town. London: W. Owen, 1752.

Miscellaneous Poems. 2 vols. Manchester: J. Harrop, 1773. (All quotations from Byrom's poems in the present article are to this edition, apart from those from "To Henry Wright, of Mobberley, Esq" [quoted from the second edition of his poems: 2 vols., Leeds: James Nichols, 1814] and *An Epistle to a Friend ...* , quoted from the edition cited above.)

The Poems of John Byrom. Edited by Adolphus William Ward. 3 vols. in 5 parts. Manchester: Chetham Society, 1894–1913. (The fullest edition, with much useful annotation and valuable appendixes of correspondence and notebook material, but sometimes textually insecure.)

PROSE

Papers on dreams, under the pseudonym "John Shadow." *The Spectator* 586 (August 27, 1714) and 593 (September 13, 1714). Reprinted in *The Spectator*. Edited by Donald F. Bond. Oxford: Clarendon, 1965. Vol. 5, pp. 3–6, 29–31.

A Review of the Proceedings Against Dr. Bentley, in the University of Cambridge: In Answer to a Late Pretended Full and Impartial Account, &c. With Some Remarks upon Serjeant Miller's Account of That University; Wherein the Egregious Blunders of That Gentleman Are Briefly Set Forth. London: E. Moor, 1719.

A Collection of Curious Papers, Containing First, A New Method of Reasoning, by the B—p of C—r. Secondly and Thirdly, Two Essays by an Admirer of His L—p, ... The Fourth Proves the Method to be Inconclusive. [Leeds?]: Printed for the Author, [c. 1727]. (Cowritten with Thomas Cattell and Thomas Deacon.)

Manchester Vindicated: Being a Compleat Collection of the Papers Lately Published in Defence of that Town, in the Chester Courant. Chester: Eliz. Adams, 1749. (Includes contributions by Byrom.)

The Universal English Short-Hand; or, The Way of Writing English, in the Most Easy, Concise, Regular, and Beauti-

ful Manner, Applicable to Any Other Language, but Particularly Adjusted to Our Own. Manchester: Joseph Harrop, 1767.

JOURNALS AND CORRESPONDENCE

The Private Journal and Literary Remains of John Byrom. Edited by Richard Parkinson. Transcribed by Sarah Bolger. 2 vols. in 4 parts. Manchester: Chetham Society, 1854–1857. (Cited as *Remains* in the preceding essay.)

Selections from the Journals & Papers of John Byrom. Edited by Henri Talon. London: Rockliff, 1950. (A useful selection, based on the texts in *Remains*.)

TRANSLATION

The Immortality of the Soul. A Poem. Book the First. Translated from the Latin. London: W. Owen, 1754. (A translation of *De Animi Immortalitate Book 1* by Isaac Hawkins Browne, 1754.

MANUSCRIPTS AND ITEMS OWNED BY BYROM

Chetham's Library, Manchester, is the most significant repository of manuscripts by Byrom. It also holds a collection of nearly three thousand books and manuscripts that he owned.

[Wheatley, B. R.] *A Catalogue of the Library of the Late John Byrom, Esq., M.A., F.R.S., Preserved at Kersall Cell, Lancashire*. [London]: [Compton & Ritchie], 1848.

CRITICAL AND BIOGRAPHICAL STUDIES

Davie, Donald. "Dr Byrom of Manchester, FRS." In *The Eighteenth-Century Hymn in England*. Cambridge, U.K.: Cambridge University Press, 1993. pp. 11–25.

Hancox, Joy. *The Queen's Chameleon: The Life of John Byrom. A Study of Conflicting Loyalties*. London: Jonathan Cape, 1994. (A controversial reading.)

Hobhouse, Stephen. *William Law and Eighteenth Century Quakerism: Including Some Unpublished Letters and Fragments of William Law and John Byrom*. London: George Allen & Unwin, 1927.

Hoole, Elijah. *Byrom and the Wesleys*. London: William Nichols, 1864.

Hoyles, John. *The Edges of Augustanism: The Aesthetics of Spirituality in Thomas Ken, John Byrom, and William Law*. The Hague: Martinus Nijhoff, 1972.

Rogal, Samuel J. "John Byrom." In *Critical Survey of Poetry: English Language Series*. Edited by Frank N. McGill. Englewood Cliffs, N.J., and Epping, U.K.: Bowker, 1982. Vol. 1, pp. 391–399.

Stephen, Leslie. "John Byrom." In *Studies of a Biographer*. London: Duckworth, 1898. Vol. 1, pp. 74–104.

Thomson, W. H. *The Byroms of Manchester. A Unique Collection of Deeds and Wills*. 3 vols. Manchester: the Author, [1959–1968].

Underhill, Timothy. " 'What Have I To Do with the Ship?': John Byrom and Eighteenth-Century Manchester Politics, with New Verse Attributions." In *Early Modern Manchester (Manchester Region History Review* 19). Edited by Craig Horner. Manchester: MCRH, 2008. Pp. 95–119.

———. "John Byrom's Shorthand: An Introduction." *Transactions of the Lancashire and Cheshire Antiquarian Society* 104: 61–91 (2008).

OTHER SOURCES

Davison, Dennis, ed. *The Penguin Book of Eighteenth-Century English Verse*. Harmondsworth, U.K.: Penguin, 1973.

Fairer, David. *English Poetry of the Eighteenth Century, 1700–1789*. London: Longman, 2003.

Law, William. *An Appeal to All that Doubt, or Disbelieve the Truths of the Gospel, Whether they be Deists, Arians, Socinians, or Nominal Christians. In which, the true Grounds and Reasons of the whole Christian Faith and Life are Plainly and Fully Demonstrated. To which are added, some Animadversions upon Dr. Trap's Late Reply*. London: W. Innys, 1742.

Owen, Josiah. *Jacobite and Nonjuring Principles, Freely Examined: In a Letter to the Master-Tool of the Faction at Manchester*. Manchester: R. Whitworth, 1747.

Rothstein, Eric. *Restoration and Eighteenth-Century Poetry 1660–1780*. Boston, London, and Henley: Routledge & Kegan Paul, 1981.

Warburton, William. *Pope's Literary Legacy: The Book-Trade Correspondence of William Warburton and John Knapton with Other Letters and Documents, 1744–1780*. Edited by Donald W. Nichol. Oxford: Oxford Bibliographical Society, 1992.

THOMAS CAMPION
(1567—1620)

Benjamin Ivry

THOMAS CAMPION, A Renaissance English poet, composer, writer of masques, and physician, enjoys a unique status in English culture as the author of both music and words for dozens of masterful lute songs. W. H. Auden claimed: "Thomas Campion is the only man in English cultural history who was both a poet and composer" (Auden, p. 9). While this is not strictly true, since the World War I veteran Ivor Gurney (1890–1937) was also an accomplished poet and composer, Campion nonetheless unifies the two arts of literature and music more concretely and endearingly than anyone before or since. A doctor by profession, Campion repeatedly insisted that his songs and other writings were avocations, products of his free time. Nevertheless, through the quality of his work, Campion's achievement provides a professional and highly accomplished link between Elizabethan and Jacobean writers. Campion's contemporaries include the poet, courtier, and soldier Sir Philip Sidney (1554–1586), who influenced his work; the playwright and poet Ben Jonson (1572–1637); and the Jacobean poet and preacher John Donne (1572–1631).

Campion also produced treatises on poetry and music, respectively, in his *Observations in the Art of English Poesie* (1602) and *A New Way of Making Fowre Parts in Counter-point* (circa 1610). Sometimes overlooked are Campion's extensive writings in Latin, especially his *Epigrammatum* (*Epigrams*), making him one of the rare English poets, along with George Herbert, John Milton, and Walter Savage Landor, who produced significant work in both Latin and English. Campion's epigrams, often inspired by the precedent of the Roman poet Martial (Marcus Valerius Martialis, c. 40 C.E.–c. 103 C.E.), reflect both his lifelong interest in medicine as well as abortive early studies in law, a profession he never ultimately practiced. A devotee of condensed forms like ayres and epigrams, Campion's intense expression within these modest dimensions is formidable. To dismiss Campion as a miniaturist, as some critics have done, is a serious underestimation of his work. Although writing with affection, Auden termed Campion a "minor poet" and classed him as a personal favorite along with the obscure nineteenth-century bard of Dorset dialect William Barnes (1801–1886). Yet the scholars Edward Lowbury, Timothy Slater, and Alison Young (1970) more aptly liken Campion's artistry to the great painter of miniatures Nicholas Hilliard (c. 1547–1619), whose powerfully concentrated artworks are masterworks despite their diminutive form. Few would think of dismissing later creators like Emily Dickinson (1830–1886) or Anton Webern (1883–1945), who worked on comparably small scales, because of the brevity of their works.

LIFE

Thomas Campion was born in London on February 12, 1567. His parents, John and Lucy Campion, died when he was still a boy, leaving enough money for Thomas and a stepbrother to be sent to Cambridge University. The fact that Campion's parents left enough money to pay for his education set him apart from other future colleagues among lutenists and composers, who usually came from more modest and less-educated backgrounds. Campion did not ultimately graduate from Cambridge, but he did meet many fellow students who became noted writers, like the pamphleteer and poet Thomas Nashe (1567–1601) and the scholar Gabriel Harvey (c. 1545–1630). During Campion's studies at Cambridge he mastered Latin, and around one-third of his subsequent writings were in that language. At a time when Shakespeare's "small Latine and lesse Greeke," according to Ben Jonson, was common among writers, Campion's classical erudition was unusual.

In 1586, Campion enrolled at Gray's Inn, one of the London Inns of Court, the professional associations to which English barristers must belong (beginning in medieval times and continuing into the present) in order to start their careers. Yet apparently Campion never practiced law but benefited instead from the lively social atmosphere of Gray's Inn to perform in plays and masques. More than mere amateur entertainments, these festivities were sometimes attended by Queen Elizabeth herself. Such masques, in which music, dance, and acting combine in a courtly entertainment, were popular in sixteenth- and seventeenth-century Europe. Stage designs and costumes added further excitement to the events, which usually offered allegorical figures praising the show's patrons. In 1602 Campion began medical studies at the University of Caen in France, and by the age of forty, he was a doctor in London. Medicine was Campion's lifelong profession, and he considered his songs, masques, and other writings for which he is remembered today to be avocational activities.

Even so, he was writing songs before he received his medical degree. Campion's first published works were five songs appended to a 1591 edition of Sir Philip Sidney's "Astrophel and Stella," a notable pioneering English sonnet sequence probably dating from the 1580s. Campion's songs in the 1591 volume were grouped in a section of "Poems and Sonets of Sundrie Other Noblemen and Gentlemen." This first edition printed by Thomas Newman included ten of Sidney's songs, a preface by Thomas Nashe, and poetry by, apart from Campion, Samuel Daniel (1562–1619) and Edward de Vere, 17th Earl of Oxford (1550–1604). The text was notoriously error-ridden and untrustworthy, and not until 1598 would "Astrophel and Stella" appear in an authoritative edition. Nevertheless it proved a landmark for young Campion's burgeoning literary career.

Some biographers have suggested that in the same year of his first publication, 1591, Campion may have been present during the siege of Rouen, an episode during which Queen Elizabeth I of England aided King Henry IV of France with money and troops, which were led by the Earl of Essex, in order to combat troops sponsored by the Catholic League of France, an extremist group determined to eradicate French Protestants. The reason that some writers feel Campion may have been present is that in his Latin poem "In Barnum" (1619) Campion described in some detail the actions during this siege taken by the poet-playwright Barnabe Barnes (c. 1569–1609), who certainly accompanied Essex to Dieppe in 1591.

Despite the sometimes sketchy subsequent details of Campion's life, we know that around 1594 he left Gray's Inn. The following year, 1595, Campion's first collection of poems, *Thomae Campiani Poemata,* was published in Latin. This collection of over 120 epigrams also contained other poems, from elegies to an unfinished epic. Campion somewhat mysteriously acquired musical mastery, since there is no record of his having pursued formal studies of music. Instead, he just began composing accompanying melodies for his lyrics. In 1597, he published a dedicatory poem in the composer and lutenist John Dowland's *First Book of Songs or Ayres,* thereby expressing his personal interest in a new art form, combining poetry and music, without himself being a virtuoso lutenist like Dowland. Dowland's collection was the first English publication in this genre, and by 1601, Campion had produced enough of his own work to publish twenty-one songs, as well as a short treatise on songwriting, in Philip Rosseter's *Book of Ayres* (1601). Rosseter (1567/68–1623) was a composer who also served as lutenist for King James I from 1603 until his death in 1623. Campion remained close to Rosseter and eventually named Rosseter his sole heir.

Indeed, the dedicatory page in Rosseter's *Book of Ayres* shows Campion's friend to have served in the role of "onlie begetter," as Shakespeare called Mr. W. H., the dedicatee of his *Sonnets,* or an intermediary recipient of creative works positioned between the artist and the public. Rosseter explains that Campion's songs are "made at his vacant hours, and privately emparted to his friends," thereby introducing them as an amateur's fancy rather than a full-time musician's professional efforts. Rosseter adds that Campion underestimates his own songs and "neglects these light fruits as superfluous blossomes of his deeper Studies," but Rosseter managed to convince him to publish some, joined together with some of Rosseter's own work. Critics have debated exactly what Campion might have felt his "deeper studies" to be (some suggest his Latin poems, but he might also have considered his professional medical activities to be "deeper" than occasional songs).

The dedicatee of Rosseter's *Book of Ayres* was Sir Thomas Monson (1565–1641), a politician and supporter of King James I. Among Monson's other positions of authority was as court patron of the lieutenant of the Tower of London, which would later land him in difficulties when it was alleged that the courtier and poet Sir Thomas Overbury, who died in 1613 as a prisoner in the Tower, had in fact been poisoned. Monson was arrested, and Campion testified in his favor, helping to obtain his release.

Rosseter's *Book of Ayres* dedication explains that the

> manie particular favours which I have heard Master Campion (with dutifull respect often acknowledge himselfe to have received from you) have emboldned mee to present this Booke of Ayres to your favourable iudgement, and gracious protection; especially because the first ranke of songs are of his owne composition, made at his vacant houres, and privately emparted to his friends, whereby they grew both publicke, and (as coine crackt in exchange) corrupted: some of them both words and notes unrespectively challenged by others. In regard of which wronges, though his selfe neglects these light fruits as superfluous blossomes of his deeper Studies, yet hath it pleased him upon my entreaty, to grant me the impression of part of them, to which I have added an equall number of mine owne.
>
> (Davis, 1970, p. 14)

In the same collection's preface addressed "To the reader," (reproduced in Davis, 1970, p. 15) Campion (almost certainly the author of the essay that follows) begins with a comparison that is essential for appreciating his artistry: "What Epigrams are in Poetrie, the same are Ayres in musicke, then in their chief perfection when they are short and well seasoned." For Campion, the power of a literary work (such as the epigrams of Martial, which he much admired) or a well-wrought song does not depend on its length. Campion declares at the outset of his literary and musical career that epigrammatic works can strive for "perfection" and their brevity adds to, rather than detracts from, their artistic rank.

One year later, in 1602, Campion published his "Observations in the Art of English Poesie," a plea for writing English verse in classical meters, decrying in particular the use of rhyme in poetry of his day. Another poet, Samuel Daniel (1562–1619), the author of the lovely sonnet "Care-charmer Sleep, son of the sable Night," retorted with a 1603 "Defense of Rhyme," observing that Campion's metric theories were not new, however much they reveal about Campion's approach to writing.

Around this time Campion's inheritance was running out, and he needed to find a remunerative profession. Campion had already decided against working in the legal profession. Seeing professional musicians among his friends and acquaintances scrambling desperately for a living, he instead chose the field of medicine. By 1602 Campion was studying at the University of Caen, France, and he was around forty by the time he was actually practicing medicine in London. Soon, however, his literary fame would catch up with his practical careerism.

By 1605 Campion had already won enough esteem as a writer to be included in a formidable list that appears in *Remains of a Greater Worke Concerning Britaine* by the antiquarian and historian William Camden (1551–1623), who wrote: "If I would come to our own time, what a world I could present to you out of Sir Philipp Sidney, Ed. Spenser, Samuel Daniel, Hugh Holland, Ben. Jonson, Th. Campion, Mich. Drayton, George Chapman, John Marston, William Shakespeare and other most pregnant witts of thes times, whom succeeding ages may iustly admire" (Camden, p. 344). As a "pregnant witt," despite the requirements of his new profession, in 1607 Campion found time to create *Lord Hay's Masque,* an entertainment commissioned by the court of King James I. A Scottish nobleman and one of King James's favorites, James Hay was the 1st Earl of Carlisle (c. 1590–1636).

Despite Hay's status as "prime favorite" (as King James, who historians generally accept was gay or bisexual, deemed him), James arranged for Hay to wed a wealthy heiress, Honoria Denny, the only daughter of Edward, Lord Denny, later Earl of Norwich. *Lord Hay's Masque* was the first such entertainment that Campion created. Others, which would be performed in 1613, were even more auspicious: *The Lord's Masque* for the wedding of Princess Elizabeth to Frederick Count Palatine; and *The Squire's Masque* (also called *The Somerset Masque*), for the marriage of Robert Carr, Earl of Somerset and a new favorite of King James's, to Lady Frances Howard.

Campion's participation in courtly life made a reaction in verse mandatory when Henry Frederick, Prince of Wales (1594–1612), King James's eldest son and heir, suddenly died of typhoid fever at age eighteen. Campion's poem *Songs of Mourning: Bewailing the Untimely Death of Prince Henry* (1613) is described as being "worded" to music by the prince's music teacher, an Englishman named James Cooper (c. 1575–1626) who had adopted the foreign-sounding professional name of "Giovanni Coperario."

Campion's creative reputation was solidly established, and around this time—certainly no later than 1616—he published a musical treatise, *A New Way of Making Fowre Parts in Counterpoint.* With no further need of an "onlie begetter" or introducer, he also published *Two Bookes of Ayres* (circa 1613) containing further accomplishments in song. In 1617, Campion's legacy as a song composer was rounded off with his *Third and Fourth Booke of Ayres,* dedicated to Sir Thomas Monson and his son, John Monson, respectively. The author's name in the printed version of the *Third and Fourth Booke of Ayres* is spelled "Campian" instead of Campion, a variant that is not surprising, given the quiddities of free-form Elizabethan spelling of the English language.

Campion's dedication to Sir Thomas Monson was particularly significant, as Monson had just been released from prison after being implicated in the poisoning of Sir Thomas Overbury. Campion was involved in this complex intrigue because he personally carried a payment to Monson from Sir Jervis Elwes, who had purchased the office of lieutenant of the Tower of London; Elwes subsequently used this office to help Robert Carr and Lady Frances Howard—for whom Campion would create *The Squire's Masque*—to murder Overbury, who had opposed the marriage between Carr and Lady Frances. Although Campion was clearly an unwitting pawn in all these events, Carr and Frances were ultimately imprisoned and Elwes hanged. Like Campion, Monson eventually convinced authorities that he had nothing to do with the poisoning; while Monson bided his time in prison, Campion was allowed to make supervised medical visits to tend to the health of his jailed friend.

In 1619, as a relief from these harrowing incidents, Campion published his *Thomae Campiani Epigrammatum Liber Secundus* (*The Epigrams of Thomas Campion, Book 2*), a new presentation of his 1595 collection with omissions and additions, thereby beginning and ending his literary career with Latin writings. On March 1, 1620, Campion died at age fifty-two, perhaps fatigued by the terrors of the Overbury Affair. It has been suggested that he died of the plague, because he was buried promptly—as plague victims tended to be—on the day of his death, at the church of St. Dunstan-in-the-West, Fleet Street. Yet from 1609 until 1625, the plague was in remission in England; instead, 1620 saw a spread of plague in Germany and Holland. Campion had never married, and he left his modest assets of just over £20 to his friend Philip Rosseter.

SONGS

The thematic integrity of Campion's songs runs strikingly through all of his work. In his first published work, of the five songs added to a 1591 edition of Sir Philip Sidney's "Astrophel and Stella," the fifth, "Canto Quinto," identifies medical symptoms with grief caused by love. Before Campion's own medical studies, and also before the English physician William Harvey (1578–1657) became the first to correctly describe the human circulatory system in 1616 (a theory not published until 1628), Campion was discussing in verse blood clots in veins ("In everie vaine that leaves such clods behind"). Campion may have read books on the circulatory system by Harvey's teacher, the Italian anatomist Hieronymus Fabricius (Girolamo Fabrizio). Wherever Campion's medical information derived from, in "Canto Quinto" he was clearly thinking like a physiologist by the time of his first public poems:

A daie, a night, an houre of sweete content
Is worth a world consum'd in fretfull care.
Unequall Gods! in your Arbitrement
To sort us daies whose sorrowes endles are!
And yet what were it? as a fading flower:
To swim in blisse a daie, a night, an hower.
What plague is greater than the griefe of minde?
The griefe of minde that eates in everie vaine,
In everie vaine that leaves such clods [clots] behind,
Such clods behind as breed such bitter paine,
So bitter paine that none shall ever finde
What plague is greater than the griefe of minde.

(reproduced in Davis, 1970, p. 10)

The diagnosis of blood circulating as a metaphor of love is repeated in Campion's 1601 *Booke of Ayres,* in song 14:

Blame not my cheeks, though pale with love they be;,
The kindly heate unto my heart is flowne
To cherish it that is dismaid by thee,
Who art so cruell and unsteedfast growne:
For nature, cald for by distressed harts,
Neglects and quite forsakes the outward partes.
But they whose cheeks with careles blood are stain'd,
Nurse not one sparke of love within their harts;
And, when they woe, they speake with passion fain'd,
For their fat love lyes in their outward parts:
But in their brests, where love his court should hold,
Poor Cupid sits and blowes his nailes for cold.

(reproduced in Davis, 1970, p. 38)

Later in the same collection, song 16 compares gradual involvement in love to the increased blood flow that results in male sexual arousal:

Mistris, since you so much desire
To know the place of Cupids fire,
In your faire shrine that flame doth rest,
Yet never harbourd in your brest;
It bides not in your lips so sweete,
Nor where the rose and lillies meete,
But a little higher, but a little higher:
There, there, O there lies Cupids fire.
Even in those starrie pearcing eyes,
There Cupids sacred fire lyes;
Those eyes I strive not to enioy,
For they have power to destroy.
Nor woe I for a smile, or kisse,
So meanely triumph's not my blisse;
But a little higher, but a little higher,
I climbe to crowne my chast desire.

(Davis, 1970, p. 38)

The highly personal, individuated tone of Campion's songs is enhanced by the fact that they were expressly intended to be performed by a solo voice and single accompanying instrument, unlike many songs of the time, whose composers offer alternate versions to be sung in madrigal form by multiple voices. The single-voiced Campion song is a more private and intimate matter, investigating personal obsessions rather than a vehicle for the expression of social unity. One such individuated theme is Campion's repeated evocation of having sex with someone who pretends to be asleep, or who is indeed asleep. Modern-day psychiatrists have diagnosed this penchant as somnophilia, or "Sleeping Beauty syndrome." In Campion's pre-Freudian world, this theme assigns lovemaking to the realm of the unconscious, as a kind of dream experience. Song 8 from *A Book of Ayres* depicts such a scene:

It fell on a sommers day,
While sweete Bessie sleeping laie
In her bowre, on her bed,
Light with curtaines shadowed;
Jamy came: shee him spies,
Opning halfe her heavie eies.
Jamy stole in through the dore,
She lay slumbring as before;
Softly to her he drew neere,
She heard him, yet would not heare;
Bessie vow'd not to speake,
He resolv'd that dumpe to breake.

THOMAS CAMPION

First a soft kisse he doth take,
She lay still, and would not wake;
Then his hands learn'd to woo,
She dreamp't not what he would doo,
But still slept, while he smild
To see love by sleepe beguild.
Jamy then began to play,
Bessie as one buried lay,
Gladly still through this sleight
Deceiv'd in her owne deceit,
And, since this traunce begoon,
She sleepes ev'rie afternoone.

(Davis, 1970, p. 38)

This romantic scene is evoked once again in song 11 from Campion's *Second Book of Ayres* ("Sweet, exclude mee not, nor be divided"), which reminds the listener: "Women are most apt to be surprised / Sleeping, or sleepe wisely fayning." Years later, in Campion's second book of epigrams (*Thomae Campiani Epigrammatum Liber Secundus,* 1619), the same theme resurfaces in epigrams 60 and 61. In epigram 60, "In Lycium et Clytham" (On Lycius and Clythia), the youth Lycius sees the maiden Clytha stretched out in sleep:

> Stealthily he came near her and taking her by the cheeks, he put a small kiss on her sweet little lips. When he saw that she was motionless, he planted more, ever sweeter, and gradually harder. She remained as inert as if she was in her tomb. The boy smirked and tried to achieve the ultimate pleasure; still the coy girl did not budge, but tolerated all his ploys. What kind of sleep was this?

And epigram 61, "In Eosdem" (On the Same), continues the scene: "Lycius keeps smiling because his Clytha sleeps. In her slumbers Clytha smiles even more" (epigrams translated from the Latin by the present author).

Yet for Campion, rather than the quasi-necrophiliac fetish of somnophilia, penetrating a sleeping beauty may reflect a higher aspiration. Song 13 from the *Third and Fourth Booke of Ayres* ("Awake, thou spring of speaking grace, mute rest becomes not thee") states that "The fayrest women, while they sleepe, and Pictures equall bee" (reproduced in Davis, 1970, p. 148). Becoming one with a sleeping "artwork" thus becomes a way of unifying with aesthetic creation.

Others of Campion's loving tableaux resort to obscene allusions with the license that is frequently seen in Elizabethan and Jacobean literature. Act 3, scene 2 of Shakespeare's *Hamlet* mentions "country matters," referring to sex with a pun on a vulgar four-letter slang term, which dates back to Middle English, for a female body part. Similarly, in song 3 of *A Booke of Ayres,* Campion introduces Amarillis, the "wanton countrey maid." In this highly characterful song, Campion's swain begins by stating, "I Care not for these ladies," and it is unclear if the singer rejects all ladies. Subsequent verses make it clear he is only objecting to ladies who play hard to get:

I care not for these Ladies,
That must be woode and praide:
Give me kind Amarillis,
The wanton countrey maide.
Nature art disdaineth,
Her beautie is her owne;
Her when we court and kisse,
She cries, forsooth, let go:
But when we come where comfort is,
She never will say no.
If I love Amarillis,
She gives me fruit and flowers:
But if we love these Ladies,
We must give golden showers;
Give them gold that sell love,
Give me the Nutbrowne lasse,
Who, when we court and kisse,
She cries, forsooth, let go:
But when we come where comfort is,
She never will say no.
These Ladies must have pillowes,
And beds by strangers wrought,
Give me a Bower of willowes,
Of mosse and leaves unbought,
And fresh Amarillis,
With milke and honie fed,
Who when we court and kisse,
She cries, forsooth, let go:
But when we come where comfort is,
She never will say no.

(reproduced in Davis, 1970, p. 22)

In the enticingly idyllic scene-painting of this song, Amarillis, fed on milk and honey, is like an inhabitant of Cockaigne (*The Land of Cokaygne,* an anonymous fourteenth-century Middle English poem from Ireland, may be among the sources for this song). Yet despite this evocation of a paradisiacal land, Campion is fully aware that inner life can be hell, as in song 9 of *A Book of Ayres* (1601):

The Sypres curten of the night is spread,
And over all a silent dewe is cast.
The weaker cares by sleepe are conquered;
But I alone, with hideous griefe agast,
In spite of Morpheus charmes, a watch doe keepe
Over mine eies, to banish carelesse sleepe.
Yet oft my trembling eyes through faintnes close,
And then the Mappe of hell before me stands,
Which Ghosts doe see, and I am one of those
Ordain'd to pine in sorrowes endles bands,
Since from my wretched soule all hopes are reft
And now no cause of life to me is left.
Griefe, ceaze my soule, for that will still endure
When my cras'd bodie is consum'd and gone,
Bear it to thy blacke denne, there keepe it sure,
Where thou ten thousand soules doest tyre upon:
But all doe not affoord such foode to thee
As this poore one, the worser part of mee.

(reproduced in Davis, 1970, p. 33)

This Dantesque vision of eternal torment is not merely doleful, as the motto of the song composer John Dowland (1563–1626) proclaims: "Semper Dowland semper dolens" [Always Dowland, always doleful]. The psychic torments of the damned as evoked by Campion are close to the infernal landscapes of the Early Netherlandish painter Hieronymous Bosch (1450–1516). One way to avoid these "horrours of the deepe / And terrours of the Skies" (reproduced in Davis, 1970, p. 43) as Campion describes them in song 18 of the same collection, is by ethical conduct. In this song, virtuous behavior is detailed with such concision that the final quatrain seems to prefigure Emily Dickinson (1830–1886) in its hymn-like concentration:

The man of life upright,
Whose guiltlesse hart is free
From all dishonest deedes,
Or thought of vanitie,
The man whose silent dayes,
In harmeles joys are spent,
Whom hopes cannot delude,
Nor sorrow discontent,
That man needs neither towers
Nor armour for defence,
Nor secret vautes to flie
From thunders violence.
Hee onely can behold
With unafrighted eyes
The horrours of the deepe
And terrours of the Skies.
Thus, scorning all the cares
That fate, or fortune brings,
He makes the heav'n his booke,
His wisedome heev'nly things,
Good thoughts his onely friendes,
His wealth a well-spent age,
The earth his sober Inne
And quiet Pilgrimage.

Another solution for escaping mental horrors and terrors is to find a reciprocal love, as expressed in the words and boldly confident, striding melody of song 11 from *A Book of Ayres* (1601):

Faire, if you expect admiring,
Sweet, if you provoke desiring,
Grace deere love with kind requiting.
Fond, but if thy sight be blindnes,
False if thou affect unkindnes,
Flie both love and loves delighting.
Then when hope is lost and love is scorned,
Ile bury my desires, and quench the fires that ever yet
  in vaine have burned.
Fates, if you rule lovers fortune,
Stars, if men your powers importune,
Yield reliefe by your relenting:
Time, if sorrow be not endles,
Hope made vaine, and pittie friendles,
Helpe to ease my long lamenting.
But if griefes remaine still unredressed,
I'le flie to her againe, and sue for pitie to renue my
  hopes distressed.

(reproduced in Davis, 1970, p. 33)

If the lover's suit does indeed fail, Campion is well aware of the pains of unreciprocated love, as detailed in song 17 from his *Third and Fourth Booke of Ayres,* accentuated by a poignant, pleading melody that earnestly argues with the recalcitrant lover, as do the emotionally persuasive words. To emphasize the slow-moving time spent waiting for a lover, the tune unusually repeats words from the poem, about the "long, long houres" spent at her door:

Shall I come, sweet Love, to thee
When the ev'ning beames are set?
Shall I not excluded be?
Will you finde no fained lett?
Let me not, for pitty, more,
Tell the long houres at your dore.
Who can tell what theefe or foe,
In the covert of the night,
For his prey will worke my woe,
Or through wicked foule despight:
So may I dye unredrest,
Ere my long love be possest.
But to let such dangers passe,
Which a lovers thoughts disdaine,
'Tis enough in such a place
To attend loves joyes in vaine.
Doe not mocke me in thy bed,
While these cold nights freeze me dead.

(reproduced in Davis, 1970, p. 152)

As a remedy for the frozen stasis of unrequited love, the last line of the above-mentioned song 11 emphasizes what might be termed a need for speed. Campion's lovers move hastily, whether in joy or fury, as in song 13 from *A Booke of Ayres* (1601): "See where she flies enrag'd from me, / View her when she intends despite, / The winde is not more swift then shee ..." (reproduced in Davis, 1970, p. 37). In his introduction to *Two Bookes of Ayres* (circa 1613) Campion defines songs as ideally "like quicke and good Epigrammes in Poesie," (reproduced in Davis, 1970, p. 55) with the term "quicke" expressing both liveliness and sensuality, as in a later song, number 24 ("Faine would I wed a faire yong man that day and night could please mee" [reproduced in Davis, 1970, p. 193]), from his *Third and Fourth Booke of Ayres* (1617): "Maids are full of longing thoughts that breed a bloudlesse sicknesse, / And that, oft I heare men say, is onely cur'd by quicknesse" (reproduced in Davis, 1970, p. 193).

This impatience for physical fulfillment can also extend to desiring speedy salvation, or spiritual joy. In one of Campion's most moving works, song 11 from *Two Bookes of Ayres,* the accompanying lute melody is spare and deliberate, in distinct contrast to the singer's urgent yearning for his "spright" (a lovelier-sounding synonym for the modern word "spirit") to ascend to heaven:

Never weather-beaten Saile more willing bent to shore,
Never tyred Pilgrims limbs affected slumber more,
Than my wearied spright now longs to flye out of my troubled brest.
O come quickly, sweetest Lord, and take my soule to rest.
Ever-blooming are the joyes of Heav'ns high paradice,
Cold age deafes not there our eares, nor vapour dims our eyes;
Glory there the Sun outshines, whose beames the blessed onely see:
O come quickly, glorious Lord, and raise my spright to thee.

(reproduced in Davis, 1970, p. 70)

Using music as a vehicle of speed, Campion aspires to a paradise of acuter perceptions. By reaching for such sensory evolution, listeners and readers too may grow closer to the divine. In his 1602 treatise "Observations in the Art of English Poesie," Campion notes that "it is generally agreed that man excels all other creatures, in reason, and speech: and in them by how much one man surpasseth an other, by so much the neerer he aspires to a celestiall essence" (reproduced in Davis, 1970, p. 291). Part of the emotional depth of Campion's songs is their earnest striving for this celestial essence, matched by full awareness of the potential sufferings of hellish torments.

As Campion explains in his prefatory note to his *Fourth Booke* of songs, his songs are utilitarian, not merely decorative. They are potential remedies, concoctions of a doctor who practices the healing arts, of which music is one. Like a magical spell cast to win a lover's affection (song 18, *Third Booke,* "Thrice tosse these Oaken ashes in the ayre" [reproduced in Davis, 1970, p. 154]) Campion in the aforementioned prefatory note compares songwriting to the work of an apothecary, a medical professional who formulates and dispenses healing substances to patients: "The Apothecaries have Bookes of Gold, whose leaves, being opened, are so light as that they are subject to be shaken with the least breath; yet rightly handled, they serve both for ornament and use. Such are light Airs" (reproduced in Davis, 1970, p. 168).

MASQUES

English court masques of the Elizabethan and Jacobean periods blend music, dance, costumes, scenic effects, and allegorical drama, the full effect of which has been increasingly explored in scholarship since the 1970s. Rich in panoply and design, as well as in music and poetry, masques are an ultimate fusion of the arts, much as Campion himself fused the arts of music and poetry in his songs. Unfortunately, of Campion's own masques, only fragments of the music and designs have survived, so they must principally be studied from the printed texts in which Campion himself often strives to describe the stage effects, costumes by Inigo Jones and other noted designers, and especially the instrumentation of his musical effects. While such descriptions are necessarily incomplete, they can give a good general sense of his accomplishments as a writer of masques, then an important entrée to court life for any poet or composer.

The lifelong bachelor Campion was repeatedly called upon in his masques to celebrate weddings. He did so with his usual convincing talents for occasional verse. Just as his songs of mourning for King James' eldest son, Henry Frederick, Prince of Wales (1594–1612), ring true, so the fervor of Campion's masque writing offers a convincing series of intense aesthetic celebrations for the marriages of a series of King James's favorites to rich noblewomen. This formality in elegies may have been influenced by French authors of the funeral oration genre in the generations before Jacques-Bénigne Bossuet (1627–1704), who often wrote in verse. The allegories in Campion's *Lord Hay's Masque* (1607), his first effort in the genre, may also have been influenced by a French precedent, *Le Mascarade du duc de Longueville,* a court ballet created in 1565 by Jean Antoine de Baïf (1532–1589). *Lord Hay's Masque* offers an allegory of marriage as a "golden dreame" of the creation of the universe, with homage rendered to King James as Apollo the sun-giver who brought about the marriage. With costumes, sets, and stage effects designed by Inigo Jones, the masque was prominently performed on Twelfth Night, January 6, 1607, in the Great Hall of Whitehall Palace.

Jones's stage design included a Grove of Diana with nine golden trees, with a Bower of Flora on the right and a House of Night on the left. In one scene of stage magic, owls and bats flew around on wires. At one point, the golden trees split apart to reveal the nine principal masquers, representing nine knights of Apollo, while torchbearers were intended to represent the nine Hours of the night. *Lord Hay's Masque* featured music by several composers including Campion, which was performed by consorts of twelve instruments, ten instruments, and an ensemble of cornets. Only scant details of the musical arrangements survive, so the text has special importance to readers today.

Some of Campion's metaphors in *Lord Hay's Masque* may strike the modern readers as oddly provocative, at least unconsciously, such as a dedication in which the marriage of James Hay to Honora Denny is compared to the ancient Scythian custom of mixing soldiers' blood in a bowl and drinking the admixture as a ritual of unification. The wedding arranged by King James, says Campion, does likewise "these bloods devided mixe in one." After this reference to a pagan blood ritual, Campian next praises James as ruler of Scotland and England in a Latin poem that also skirts the unseemly, at least to a modern reader. "Atque, maritali natas violare parentem / Complexu quis non cogitat esse scelus?" (Who doesn't consider it a crime for a father to rape his daughter in marital embrace?) asks Campion, hastening to add that King James, by uniting two countries, can do this, creating a "wonderful marriage" in which he is "father and husband" (reproduced in Davis, 1970, p. 208) both.

Presenting King James as a ruler who transcends the common moral order may be read by scholars of gender study as an allusion to the ruler's well-known bisexuality, yet it seems highly unlikely that Campion would have dared any such overt allusion in a court entertainment. Instead, the lasting emotional message of *Lord Hay's Masque* is of sincere celebration, in which even trees dance for joy at the newlyweds' nuptial bliss. The author adds an ironic, modest epigram (in Latin) to conclude his masque, disarmingly reminding his reader of his status as a medical professional dabbling in a field outside his full-time area of expertise: "'Why do you get mixed up in prosody? Do theatrical meters befit an ingrained healer?' Phoebus, you are a composer, doctor, and famed poet, and pleasure heals the suffering when art permits. Believe me, whoever has no taste for cultivated verse also lacks innate medical ability and learning." (present author's translation).

Campion's next effort in this genre, *The Lord's Masque,* was performed in the Chapel Royal, Whitehall, on February 14, 1613, celebrating the wedding of King James's eldest daughter Elizabeth of Bohemia (1596–1662) and Frederick V, Elector Palatine (1596–1632). This international Protestant alliance was underlined by Campion, whose masque, according to Walter R. Davis, associated "fertility with political order while relating both to the Roman roots of European civilization" (*The Works of Thomas Campion,* p. 232). *The Lord's Masque* opens on the scene of a forest with a cave. Orpheus confronts Mania, the "Goddesse of madnesse," and her cohorts, Twelve Franticks, are described as if they are denizens of London's Bethlem Royal Hospital (Bedlam)—a place the English nobility would visit from time to time, to gape at the mentally ill as a form of entertainment. Campion's Franticks include the "Selfe-lover, the melancholicke-man full of feare, the Schooleman overcome with phantasie, the over-watched Usurer, with others that made an absolute medly of madnesse" (p. 250). However the Franticks' "madde" music is becalmed by a "very solemn ayre, which they softly played, while Orpheus spake," (p. 251) clearly an allegory for music's healing powers.

In the printed version of *The Lord's Masque,* Campion praises at length the stage design and special effects by Inigo Jones, whose "whole invention shewed extraordinarie industrie and skill," singling out for particular kudos the way onstage "Starres mooved in an exceeding strange and delightfull maner" (p. 254). Yet Campion mainly focuses on the glorious marriage, which is further feted in a Latin hymn near the end of the masque, which proclaims: "Additur Germaniae / Robur Britannicum: ecquid esser par potest?" (May German power be added to British strength; can anything rival it?).

Campion's *Caversham Entertainment* (reproduced in Davis, 1970) was written two months later, in April 1613, to entertain Queen Anne on her way to Bath, England, a place she regularly visited in order to receive treatment for the gout. *The Caversham Entertainment* begins with the queen being addressed by a "Cynick," who appears from a bower with his hair "blacke and disordered, stucke carelessly with flowers" (p. 235). The Cynick calls his sylvan dwelling a "place of silence; heere a kingdome I enjoy without people; my selfe commands, my selfe obeys" (p. 235). This misanthrope in a kingdom of solitude seems to echo the protagonist of Shakespeare's *Timon of Athens,* a play of uncertain date which, according to one theory, may have been written before 1608. The Cynick is quickly tamed by arguments from a "fantastick Traveller" and newly civilized, he asserts: "I am conquered by reason, and humbly ask pardon for my error; henceforth my heart shall honour greatnesse, and love societie" (p. 237).

The Squire's Masque (or *The Somerset Masque*) (reproduced in Davis, 1970) was performed at the Banqueting Room of Whitehall on December 26, 1613, offering the newlyweds Robert Carr, 1st Earl of Somerset, and Frances Carr, Countess of Somerset, the "fruite of *Peace and Joy* ... in a Perpetuall Spring." Peace and Joy defeat the false opinions personified by Error, which swirled around the couple, who played main roles in the notorious Overbury murder case. Offered in homage to the king, the queen, and the prince as a "triple majestie," *The Squire's Masque* did not benefit from the stage designs of Inigo Jones, who was in Italy when it was staged. Instead Campion worked with a different, less inspired, designer, the Florentine architect Constantine de' Servi (1554–1622).

In one song, Campion offers observations directly aimed at the noble couple, with echoes of Shakespeare's sonnets, in which a beautiful young man is encouraged to have offspring:

Some friendship betweene man and man prefer,
But I th' affection betweene man and wife.
What good can be in life,
Whereof no fruites appeare?
...
How can man Perpetuall be,
But in his owne Posteritie?

(reproduced in Davis, 1970, pp. 274–275)

Campion's masque-writing days ceased with the imprisonment of his friend Sir Thomas Monson, which understandably estranged Campion from court life. His efforts in this genre remain highlights of Jacobean creativity.

LATIN POEMS AND EPIGRAMS

Fully one-third of Campion's writings were in Latin, including poems and epigrams, and this important portion of his work remains the least thoroughly studied. In his otherwise excellent 1967 edition of Campion's works, Walter H. Davis includes only a small proportion of the author's Latin writings with original texts and translations. Readers and students seeking a fuller picture must consult earlier editions like Percival Vivian's 1909 volume *Campion's Works* for the full Latin texts, but without translations. As of 2009, a complete translation of Campion's Latin works was available only online at the Web site "The Latin Poetry of Thomas Campion (1567–1620)," a useful hypertext critical edition by Dana F. Sutton of the University of California, Irvine.

Campion's Latin writings comprise two books of epigrams and one of elegies, as well as two long poems, "Umbra" ("Shadow") and "Ad Thamesin" ("To the Thames"), the latter work belatedly celebrating the 1588 defeat of the Spanish Armada. In 1595, *Thomae Campiani Poemata* was published, followed by an augmented second edition of the same work, *Thomae Campiani Epigrammatum Liber Secundus,* as well as "Umbra" and *Elegiarum Liber* in 1619. Eighteen Latin elegies by Campion survive, as do 453 epigrams. Campion also wrote "De Pulverea Coniuratione" ("On the Gunpowder Plot"), a long Latin poem divided into two books about the failed 1605 attempt by English Catholics to kill King James I and a majority of the Protestant aristocracy by blowing up London's Houses of Parliament.

"Ad Thamesis" is heavily influenced by Ovid's *Ars Amatoria* and *Metamorphoses,* as well as Virgil's *Aeneid.* Walter R. Davis has aptly observed that "Ad Thamesis" is best classified as an

> epic fragment, derived ultimately from the infernal of Tasso's *Gerusalemme Liberata,* Book IV ... and, like its progenitor, it possesses many features unusual in traditional epic poetry ... Campion here deserves much more than Tasso the accusation of having composed a set of scenes or madrigals rather than a whole poem. Yet it must be alleged that the purpose of the poem is not to present the defeat of the Armada but to place it in its proper epic frame by relating it to the broadest of human concerns.
>
> (p. 359)

"Umbra" tells the tragic story of Iole and her son Melampus, focusing yet again on one of Campion's favorite themes of sexual attraction as an unconscious state, with efforts made to achieve sexual congress with a passively sleeping object of affection. In "Umbra," when Iole rejects the sexual overtures of Apollo, he violates her when she is asleep; she goes mad and dies after giving birth. Her son, Melampus, is also sexually victimized, by Morpheus—the god of dreams in Greek mythology who, according to Ovid, was the son of Hypnos, the god of sleep. When Morpheus fails to seduce Melampus, he arranges for a lovely ghost to visit the boy in a dream. On waking and realizing the apparition was fleeting, Melampus dies of grief. Amid luxuriant descriptions of a valley rich in plant life, including roses and violets, the message in "Umbra" is that nature's loveliness can be a deceptive, harmful trap.

"De Pulverea Coniuratione" cannot be precisely dated, although one of its epigrams refers to John Donne as a doctor of theology, a degree that Donne is known to have received in 1615, so it is reasonable to assume it was completed after this year. In this historical epic, Campion presents the Gunpowder Plot's leaders, the Roman Catholics Robert Catesby (1573–1605) and Sir Thomas Percy (c. 1560–1605), amid such dramatic scenes as a Jesuit priest telling the Devil that Parliament should be blown up. The vehement anti-Catholic sentiment in "De Pulverea Coniuratione" may be one reason why it was long neglected, until the edition by Lindley and Sowerby was published in 1956. Lindley and Sowerby point out that unlike Campion's English poetry, "De Pulverea Coniuratione" is strongly influenced by Edmund Spenser's "The Faerie Queene."

The Latin elegies of Campion are strongly influenced by Ovid, and indeed he is called a new Ovid by the Elizabethan poet and clergyman Charles Fitzgeoffrey (1576–1638), whose own modestly titled 1601 collection of Latin epigrams, *Affaniae* (Trivial Chatter), addresses Campion in order to praise his elegies: "O you to whose genius Latin Elegy is indebted, as much as she was earlier to her Ovid!" In a 1974 essay, "The Latin Poems of Thomas Campion," J. W. Binns writes:

> Campion's mood in his love elegies is one of lightness and detachment, the result of his easy and graceful style, which derives above all from Ovid ... the atmosphere of Campion's elegies is that of Ovidian love elegy, somewhat cynical, portraying a love that is concerned with physical beauty and attraction rather than a spiritual and transcendent love ... From Ovid too derive the mythological figures whom Campion uses as studied *exempla* in his love elegies
>
> (pp. 10–11).

In contrast to these learned works, in Campion's Latin epigrams, as his early editor Percival Vivian (1909) notes, he "frequently resorts to degrees of obscenity unusual even in that age" (p. xxxvi). Nonetheless Campion's Latin epigrams were highly valued by his contemporaries, and indeed he was esteemed as an author of epigrams second only to the *Epigrammata* of Thomas More (1478–1535), which were published in Basel in 1520. Typical for the highly personal tone of Campion's writings, even in Latin, he often identifies himself as a doctor in his epigrams. In book 1, epigram 167, "Ad Labienum" (To Labienus), he reminds a friend:

> Tres novit, Labiene, Phoebus artes,
> Ut narrant veteres sophi; peraeque
> Quas omnes colui, colamque semper:
> Nunc omnes quoque musicum, et poetam
> Agnoscunt, medicumque Campianum.
> (Translation (by contributor): Labienus, as wise men of old relate, Apollo knew three arts which I myself have exercised, and always will. Now everyone knows that Campion is a musician, poet, and doctor.)

These medical responsibilities clearly included warning patients against overindulgence, as some vehement antismoking epigrams testify, such as number 51, "In Tabaccam" (On Tobacco)—"Cum cerebro inducat fumo hausta tabacca stuporem, / Nonne putem stupidos quos vapor iste capit?" (which translates, "Since inhaled tobacco fumes cause brain stupor, should I not consider addicts of this vapor to be morons?")—and number 121, "In Lausum" (On Lausus):

> Lausus ut aeterna degit sub nube tabaccae,
> Coniux ardenti sic sua gaudet aqua:
> Vir fumum, haec flammam bibit; infumata maritus
> Tanquam perna olim, frixa sed uxor erit.
> (Translation: Lausus lives under an eternal cloud of tobacco, while his wife relishes fire-water. He imbibes smoke, she imbibes fire. One day the husband will be a smoked ham, and his wife fried.)

Likewise, readers are warned against the perils of obesity, both in this life and the next, in epigram number 49, "In Turbonem" (On Turbo): "Turbo, deos manes celsi tu pondere gressus / Tota in se terres ne sua tecta ruant" (that is: Due to your overbearing weight, Turbo, the gods of the Underworld worry that your footstep will make the roof [of Hell] cave in).

There are also sensitive psychological diagnoses, as in the epigram no. 101, "To Pontilianus," in which the suicide of a wealthy young man, who was not afflicted by any apparent misfortune, is attributed to "inertia" (*desidia*), which made him "nauseated with life ... nothing inspired him." Campion is also highly critical of medical colleagues who prescribe a then-fashionable remedy of *aurum potabile* (potable gold), which the Swiss physician and alchemist Paracelsus (born Phillip von Hohenheim, 1493–1541) claimed to have concocted. In epigram 6, "De Auro Potabili" (On Potable Gold), he writes:

Pomponi, tantum vendis medicabilis auri,
Quantum dat fidei credula turba tibi;
Evadunt aliqui, sed non vi futilis auri:
Servantur sola certius ergo fide
(Pomponius, you manage to hawk that medicinal gold insofar as the credulous mobs puts its faith in you. Some are cured, but not by this futile gold. Surely they are saved by their belief alone.)

In other epigrams, Campion strives to import a classical sensibility, akin to his beloved Martial. Variant sexuality is fully explored, and rudely mocked, much like Martial, as in Campion's epigram number 123 from book 2, "In Fuscinum" (On Fuscinus):

Contrectare tuos nequeam, Fuscine, puellos
Non myrrham, non si thura, rosasque cacent.
Pro turpi est quicquid facilis natura negavit;
Si faciem demas, nec placet ipsa Venus.
(Fuscinus, may I be unable to fondle your small boys, if they fail to defecate a blend of myrrh, incense, and roses. Whatever is forbidden by compliant Nature may be seen as dishonorable—Venus herself would fail to please, were her face missing.)

Latin also provided a means for Campion, as for many English writers before or since, to discuss private—even "obscene," as Vivian termed them—matters with the cloak of learnedness. An epigram from book 2, number 139A—"In Se" (On Himself)—refers frankly to the writer's sexual organs and their functioning in a way that could only be alluded to at the time in English; such allusion occurs, for instance, in lightly suggestive songs like number 14 from the *Second Booke of Ayres* ("Pin'd I am, and like to die").

THEORETICAL WRITINGS

In 1602, Campion published a prosody manifesto, "Observations in the Art of English Poesie," defending the use of quantitative meters in English. Used by classical Greek and Roman poets, quantitative verse is made up of long and short syllables, the duration of which is determined by the amount of time required for pronunciation. Because English is a highly accentual language, the disregard for accents in quantitative verse generally makes it seem unsuitable for use in English. Nevertheless, in "Observations in the Art of English Poesie," Campion tries to find agreements between the quantity of classical meters and English-language stress patterns. Historians of prosody generally see "Observations" as an example of a theory, already outdated by 1602, that advocates the imitation of classical verse in English.

In its second chapter, Campion's "Observations" declares the "unaptness of rhyme in poesie," which ought "sparingly to be used, lest it should offend the ear with tedious affectation" Campion criticizes what he calls the "childish titillation of rhyming." Poets of the day commonly employed rhyme, as did Campion himself, who nonetheless complains that the "facilitie and popularitie of Rime creates as many Poets as a hot sommer flies" (reproduced in Davis, 1970, p. 294). Campion was not attacking rhyme per se, but rather the automatic, platitudinous, and overfamiliar rhymes seen in mediocre writings. As Campion states in his dedication, "the vulgar and unarteficiall custome of riming hath, I know, deter'd many excellent wits from the exercise of English Poesy" (reproduced in Davis, 1970, p. 291). For Campion, to be inartificial, or lacking artifice, is a pejorative term. Vulgar and facile rhymes, he argues, deter better minds from expressing themselves in verse. With his typical verve, Campion even alludes to Philip Sidney's story in his *Apologie for Poetrie* (1595), in which Ireland's rats are destroyed by rhyming incantation, or " rhymed to death, as is said to be done in Ireland." Campion revises this conceit, finding in rhyme a potential mortal danger for men, not just rats, referring to those who misuse rhyme as able to "extempore (as they say) rime a man to death" (reproduced in Davis, 1970, pp. 292–293).

In addition to a lively polemic tone, there is common sense in Campion's "Observations," such as how rhyme "enforceth a man oftentimes to abjure his matter and extend a short conceit beyond all bounds of arte." In a vivid metaphor, Campion likens the requirements of rhyme to a Procrustean bed, or arbitrary standard to which exact conformity is forced: "Me thinks the Poet handles his subject as tyrannically as *Procrustes* the thiefe his prisoners whom when he had taken, he used to cast upon a bed, which if they were too short to fill, he would stretch them longer, if too long, he would cut them shorter" (reproduced in Davis, 1970, pp. 295–296).

There was quick, powerful objection to "Observations" in the form of Samuel Daniel's "A Defence of Rhyme" (1603), which dismisses Campion's discussion of quantitative meters as offering nothing new. Indeed, Campion's prosodic ideas are mainly drawn from *Brevissima Institutio* (1540), the most popular Latin grammar textbook of the time, by William Lilye, or Lily (c. 1468–1522). Reflective of the extreme care and attention that Campion paid to word selection, his "Observations," although his arguments proved less than influential, is a product of his intense interest in blending music and poetry.

Unlike Campion's "Observations," generally seen by critics as backward-looking and retrograde, his *A New Way of Making Fowre Parts in Counter-point* (c. 1614) offers progressive theories about musical matters, such as the fundamental bass, cadences and tonality, and the major-minor octave scale. *A New Way of Making Fowre Parts* has strong parallels with another influential music treatise, *Rules How to Compose* (written before 1617), by Campion's friend and colleague Giovanni Coprario (John Cooper (c. 1570–1626). In his 2003 volume pairing these works by Campion and Coprario, Christopher Wilson convincingly points out that Campion's ideas follow historical German music theory rather than available Italian precedents. As such, *A New Way of Making Fowre Parts* points forward as a prototype of the early modern harmony tutor.

In his dedication to Prince Charles, later King Charles I of England (r. 1625–1649) in *A New Way of Making Fowre Parts,* Campion once again brings up his principal profession, medicine: "Why should I, being by profession a Physition, offer a worke of Musicke to his Highnesse?" He cites the precedent of Galen of Pergamum (129 CE–200 CE), the noted Roman physician of Greek origin, author of *De pulsibus,* a treatise on the pulse reproduced in Venice around 1550. According to Campion, Galen "became so expert a Musition, that he could not containe himselfe, but needes he must apply all the proportions of Musicke to the uncertaine motions of the pulse" (reproduced in Davis, 1970, p. 323). Galen was indeed a pioneer in diagnosing maladies through irregularities in the pulse. Yet Campion's view of Galen as a "musition" offering "far-fetchd Doctrine" is part of a larger Renaissance conceit following Eryximachus, the doctor who speaks in Plato's *Symposium,* likening concordant harmony and rhythm in music to the way medicine finds agreement between divergent elements of the body.

CAMPION'S POSTERITY

Soon after Campion's death in 1620, the genres of masques and lute songs both became old-fashioned, and his works in these media were consequently neglected. The Puritan movement in England frowned on secular music, especially licentious love lyrics, although Campion's poetry did continue to appear in seventeenth-century commonplace books, suggesting a certain enduring domestic popularity, regardless of the favors and fashions of the court. It is untrue, however, as some writers allege, that Campion disappeared entirely, as his songs were included in such volumes as a 1739 anthology compiled by the important English psalmodist William Tans'ur (c. 1699–1783). His treatises remained even more available, thanks to the London publisher and bookseller John Playford (1623–1686), whose *A Breefe Introduction to the Skill of Musick* (1654, followed by several editions in the following decades) included Campion's *New Way of Making Fowre Parts in Counter-point*. Likewise, in 1815, Campion's "Observations in the Art of English Poesie" was reproduced in volume 2 of of Joseph Haslewood's *Ancient Critical Essays upon English Poets and Poesy*. Such examples effectively counteract the oft-stated claim that Campion and his works entirely disappeared from public view during the eighteenth and early nineteenth centuries.

Nevertheless, it was not until 1887, when Arthur Henry Bullen (1857–1920) an editor and publisher specializing in sixteenth- and seventeenth-century literature, published *Lyrics from the Song-books of the Elizabethan Age,* followed in 1889 by *The Works of Dr. Thomas Campion,* that a generous selection of Campion's works were again more fully available. Although his editions are now dated, Bullen was a firm advocate of Campion's artistic excellence, noting that "there are no sweeter lyrics in English poetry than are to be found in Campion's song-books" (p. xxi) and opined that Campion was "at once an eminent composer and a lyric poet of the first rank" (p. xi). Yet the authoritative literary historian and critic George Saintsbury, in his *Seventeenth-Century Lyrics* (1892), opined that "no competent judge ... would dream of setting such men as Campion, Carew, Herrick, Lovelace, and others on a par, as men of general literary faculty, with Swift, Pope, Thomson, even Gray" (p. xv).

The aesthete and poet John Gray (1866–1934), a friend of Oscar Wilde who served as a model for Wilde's character Dorian Gray, edited a deluxe selection of Campion's songs in 1896, decorated by the artist and designer Charles Ricketts (1866–1931). Celebrating Campion's joyous love songs, Victorian gay men like Gray and Ricketts sensed an emotional and sensual freedom in the Elizabethan arts world that was absent in society of their own time. The British song composer Henry Erskine Allon (1864–1897), son of the Nonconformist pastor Henry Allon (1818–1892), must have sensed a comparable unfettered liberty in Campion's texts; the younger Allon published his own new setting of six poems by Campion in 1894.

A more authoritative edition of Campion's works appeared in 1909 from the Oxford University Press, edited by Sir Sylvanus Percival Vivian (1880–1958), who also served as longtime registrar general of the United Kingdom. Full appreciation of both the words and music of Campion's songs had to wait until the turn-of-the-century revival of authentic early music performance by the English music antiquarian and scholar Arnold Dolmetsch (1858–1940), whose *Interpretation of the Music of the XVII and XVIII Centuries* (1915) introduced long-neglected Elizabethan composers to a wide readership. Dolmetsch himself had begun playing the lute in the late 1880s, and W. B. Yeats (1865–1939) asked him for advice on a suitable instrument to accompany the "chaunting of verse," while the writer and tenor James Joyce (1882–1941) stated that he planned to travel through southern England singing old English songs while playing his Dolmetsch lute. Among Dolmetsch's most avid readers was the American Ezra Pound, whose "Donna mi prega," his 1928–1934 translation of a poem by Guido Cavalcanti, is dedicated to Campion and Henry Lawes.

When Pound, who fancied himself a composer, produced an opera, *Le Testament,* inspired by François Villon, the critic Virgil Thomson claimed in a 1926 review that Pound's opera was the "finest poet's music since Thomas Campion." This judgment reflected not just Thomson's unreliable taste—Pound's music did not even begin to approach Campion's in quality—but also the continuing underestimation of Campion as a composer in the 1920s, although his lyrics were widely admired. T. S. Eliot wrote in his 1933 study *The Use of Poetry and the Use of Criticism* that, after Shakespeare, Campion is the "most accomplished master of rhymed lyric of his time" (p. 29).

An exception to the general neglect of Campion's music was the highly original Anglo-Welsh composer and music critic Peter Warlock (born Philip Arnold Heseltine, 1894–1930) who edited and wrote about Elizabethan and Jacobean songs, including Campion's, from the 1920s onward. While a few pioneering lutenists such as Suzanne Bloch (1907–2002), Diana Poulton (1903–1995), and Walter Gerwig (1899–1966) gave recitals that included Campion, not until the mid-twentieth century, when lutenists such as Joseph Iadone (1914–2004) and Desmond Dupré (1916–1974) performed with singers like the tenor Hugues Cuénod (born 1902) and countertenor Alfred Deller (1912–1979), were Campion's songs widely heard in concert halls and on records.

A useful new *Works of Thomas Campion* (1967) was edited by Walter R. Davis, who dedicated his book to yet another modern performer of early music, the conductor Noah Greenberg (1919–1966). Davis's wide-ranging edition, which remains the most complete volume of Campion's works in English as of 2009, also offers a small fraction of Campion's abundant Latin writings in the original, as well as in English translation. Readers are still awaiting a complete modern edition of Campion's works that includes the Latin writings as well as those in English, and this remains a priority for the future of Campion studies.

In a 1947 lecture on Shakespeare, W. H. Auden termed Campion a minor artist, ranking him alongside A. E. Housman and Claude Debussy, because he is "idiosyncratic, keeps to one thing, does it well, and keeps on doing it" (in Kirsch, 2002, p. 166) In 1973, in a preface to his selection of Campion's songs, Auden persisted in classing Campion as a minor poet "for whom one feels a particular personal affection," (p. 14) and in the same volume, the poet and critic John Hollander pointed to the "limitations of [Campion's] poetic chamber music," grudgingly adding that as a composer, he is "idiomatic and graceful, seldom tactless but seldom inspired" (p. 17). By contrast, the influential American poet Robert Creeley (1926–2005) admired Campion wholeheartedly as a writer as well as an inspiration for his own poetry.

While John Donne will doubtless continue to be more studied and admired, poets of today, following Creeley's example, may continue to find Campion's works not just beautiful but also inspiring. Continued investigations by today's leading musicians, including tenors like Peter Pears (1910–1986) and Ian Partridge (born 1938) have brought Campion's songs to a wider range of listeners, through performances and recordings. Since the late twentieth century, CD recordings have made a fuller understanding of Campion's range of achievement available to a wider audience. As a composer and poet, Campion remains unique and unsurpassed.

Selected Bibliography

WORKS BY THOMAS CAMPION

Modern editions and translations, listed in chronological order:

"Observations in the Art of English Poesie." In *Ancient Critical Essays upon English Poets and Poesy,* vol. 2, edited by Joseph Haslewood et al. London: Printed by Harding and Wright for Robert Triphook, 1815.

The Works of Dr. Thomas Campion. Edited by A. H. Bullen. London: Chiswick Press, 1889.

The Lyric Poems of Thomas Campion. Edited by Ernest Rhys. London: J. M. Dent, 1896.

Fifty Songs. Chosen by John Gray. London: Ballantyne Press, 1896. (Deluxe edition designed by Charles Ricketts.)

"Lords' Masque." In *English Masques.* Edited by Herbert Arthur Evans. London: Warwick, 1897.

Songs and Masques: With "Observations in the Art of English Poesy." Edited by A. H. Bullen. London: Bullen, 1903.

"Observations in the Art of English Poesy." In *Elizabethan Critical Essays.* Edited by George Gregory Smith. Oxford: Oxford University Press, 1904.

Campion's Works. Edited by Percival Vivian. Oxford: Clarendon, 1909.

Fourth Booke of Ayres. Edited by Edmund H. Fellowes. London: Stainer & Bell, 1926.

The Works of Thomas Campion: Complete Songs, Masques, and Treatises with a Selection of the Latin Verse. Edited by Walter R. Davis. Garden City, N.Y.: Doubleday, 1967.

"The Lords' Masque (1613)." Edited by I. A. Shapiro. In *A Book of Masques: In Honour of Allardyce Nicoll.* Cambridge, U.K.: Cambridge University Press, 1967.

Third Booke of Ayres. Edited by Edmund H. Fellowes, revised by Thurston Dart. London: Stainer & Bell, 1969.

The Discription of a Maske in Honour of the Lord Hayes, 1607. Edited by David Greer. Menston, U.K.: Scolar Press, 1970.

The Description of a Maske Presented at the Marriage of the Earle of Somerset, 1614. Edited by David Greer. Menston, U.K.: Scolar Press, 1970.

Selected Songs of Thomas Campion: Selected and Prefaced by W. H. Auden. With an introduction by John Hollander. Boston: David Godine, 1973.

Ayres & Observations: Selected Poems of Thomas Campion. Edited by Joan Hart. Cheadle, U.K.: Carcanet Press, 1976.

Four Hundred Songs and Dances from the Stuart Masque: With a Supplement of Sixteen Additional Pieces. Edited by Andrew J. Sabol. Providence, R.I.: Brown University Press, 1978.

First Book of Ayres: Thomas Campion. Transcribed and edited by David Scott. New York: Galaxy Music, 1979.

Second Book of Ayres: Thomas Campion. Transcribed and edited by David Scott. New York: Galaxy Music, 1979.

De Puluerea Coniuratione [On the Gunpowder Plot]. Edited by David Lindley, with translation and additional notes by Robin Sowerby. Leeds, U.K.: Leeds Studies in English, 1987.

"The Latin Poetry of Thomas Campion (1567–1620)." Compiled and translated by Dana F. Sutton. 1997. Rev. version, May 23, 1999, http://www.philological.bham.ac.uk/campion/ (A searchable hypertext critical edition.)

"A New Way of Making Fowre Parts in Counter-point," by Thomas Campion, and "Rules How to Compose," by Giovanni Coprario. New ed. Edited by Christopher Wilson. Aldershot, U.K.: Ashgate, 2003.

CRITICAL AND BIOGRAPHICAL STUDIES

Alexander, Gavin. *Sidney's "The Defence of Poesy" and Selected Renaissance Literary Criticism*. London: Penguin Classics, 2004.

Auden, W. H. Preface to *Selected songs of Thomas Campion?*. Boston: David Godine, 1973.

Auden, W. H. *Lectures on Shakespeare*. Edited by Arthur C. Kirsch. Princeton, N.J.: Princeton University Press, 2002.

Bellany, Alastair. *The Politics of Court Scandal in Early Modern England: News Culture and the Overbury Affair, 1603–1660*. Cambridge, U.K.: Cambridge University Press, 2002.

Bentley, Gerald Eades. *The Jacobean and Caroline Stage*. 7 vols. Oxford: Clarendon Press, 1941–1968.

Bergeron, David M. *English Civic Pageantry 1558–1642*. Columbia: University of South Carolina Press, 1971.

———. *Twentieth-Century Criticism of English Masques, Pageants, and Entertainments:1558–1642*. San Antonio, Tex.: Trinity University Press, 1972.

Berringer, Ralph. "Thomas Campion's Share in *A Booke of Ayres*." *PMLA* 58 (1943):938–948.

Bevington, David M., and Peter Holbrook, eds. *The Politics of the Stuart Court Masque*. Cambridge, U.K.: Cambridge University Press, 1998.

Binns, J. W. "The Latin Poems of Thomas Campion." In *The Latin Poetry of English Poets*. London: Routledge, 1974.

Bradner, Leicester. *Musae Anglicanae: A History of Anglo-Latin Poetry, 1500–1925*. London: Oxford University Press, 1940.

Camden, William. "Remaines of a Greater Worke Concerning Britaine" in *Remains Concerning Britain*. London: John Russell Smith, 1870, p. 344.

Cerasano, S. P., and Marion Wynne-Davies. *Gloriana's Face: Women, Public and Private, in the English Renaissance*. Detroit: Wayne State University Press, 1992.

Chambers, E. K. *The Elizabethan Stage*. Oxford: Clarendon Press, 1951.

Cooper, Helen. "Location and Meaning in Masque, Morality, and Royal Entertainment." In *The Court Masque*. Edited by David Lindey. Manchester, U.K.: Manchester University Press, 1984.

Coprario, Giovanni. *Rules How to Compose: A Facsimile Edition of a Manuscript from the Library of the Earl of Bridgewater Now in the Huntington Library, San Marino, California*. Edited and with an introduction by Manfred F. Bukofzer. Los Angeles: Ernest E. Gottlieb, 1952.

Coren, Pamela. "In the Person of Womankind: Female Persona Poems by Campion, Donne, Jonson." *Studies in Philology* 98, no. 2 (spring 2001):225ff.

Curran, Kevin. "Erotic Policy: King James, Thomas Campion, and the Rhetoric of Anglo-Scottish Marriage." *Journal for Early Modern Cultural Studies* 7, no. 1 (spring–summer 2007):55–77.

———. "James I and Fictional Authority at the Palatine Wedding Celebrations." *Renaissance Studies* 20, no.1 (2006):51–67.

Davis, Walter R. "Melodic and Poetic Structure: The Examples of Campion and Dowland." *Criticism* 4 (1962):89–107.

———. "A Note on Accent and Quantity in *A Booke of Ayres*." *MLQ* 22 (1961):32–36.

———. *The Works of Thomas Campion*. New York: Norton, 1970.

———. *Thomas Campion*. Boston: Twayne, 1987.

DeNeef, A. Leigh. "Structure and Theme in Campion's 'The Lords Masque.'" *Studies in English Literature* 17 (1977):95–103.

Dolmetsch, Arnold. *The Interpretation of the Music of the XVII and XVIII Centuries, Revealed by Contemporary Evidence*. London: Novello, 1915.

Doughtie, Edward. *English Renaissance Song*. Boston: Twayne, 1986.

———. "Sibling Rivalry: Music vs. Poetry in Campion and Others." *Criticism* 20 (1978):1–16.

Eldridge, Muriel Tilden. *Thomas Campion: His Poetry and Music 1567–1620*. New York: Vantage Press, 1971.

Feldman, Martha. "In Defense of Campion: A New Look at His Ayres and Observations." *Journal of Musicology* 5 (spring 1987):226–256.

Fenyo, Jane K. "Grammar and Music in Thomas Campion's 'Observations in the Art of English Poesie.'" *Studies in the Renaissance* 17 (1970):46–72.

Gazzard, Hugh. "'Many a herdsman more disposde to morne': Peele, Campion, and the Portugal Expedition of 1589." *Review of English Studies* 2006 57(228):16–42.

Gömöri, George. "'A Memorable Wedding': The Literary Reception of the Wedding of the Princess Elizabeth and Frederick of Pfalz." *Journal of European Studies* 34, no. 3 (2004):215–224.

Green, Barclay. "Quantitative Verse, Bookselling, and Thomas Campion's 'Observations in the Art of English Poesie.'" *Rocky Mountain E-Review of Language and Literature* 61, no. 1 (spring 2007).

Greer, David. "Campion the Musician." *Lute Society Journal* 9 (1967):7–16.

Gullans, Charles. "Campion, Virgil, Horace, and Propertius." *Seventeenth-Century News* 46 (1988):9–17.

Hamlin, Hannibal. *Psalm Culture and Early Modern English Literature.* Cambridge, U.K.: Cambridge University Press, 2004.

Hollander, John. "Introduction." In *Selected Songs of Thomas Campion,* edited by W. H. Auden, pp. 15–27. Boston: David R. Godine, 1973. (Revised and expanded into chapter 4 of his *Vision and Resonance,* pp. 71–90.)

———. *The Untuning of the Sky: Ideas of Music in English Poetry 1500–1700.* Princeton, N.J.: Princeton University Press, 1961.

———. *Vision and Resonance: Two Senses of Poetic Form.* Oxford: Oxford University Press, 1975.

Ing, Catherine. *Elizabethan Lyrics: A Study of the Development of English Metrics and Their Relation to Poetic Effect.* London: Chatto & Windus, 1951.

Jorgens, Elise Bickford. *The Well-Tun'd Word: Musical Interpretations of English Poetry, 1597–1651.* Minneapolis: University of Minnesota Press, 1982.

Kastendieck, Miles Merwin. *England's Musical Poet: Thomas Campion.* New York: Russell, 1963.

Kenny, Elizabeth. "The Uses of Lute Song: Texts, Contexts, and Pretexts for 'Historically Informed' Performance." *Early Music* 36, no. 2 (2008):285–300.

Kneidel, Gregory. "Samuel Daniel and Edification." *SEL Studies in English Literature 1500–1900* 44, no. 1 (winter 2004):59–76.

Kogan, Stephen. *The Hieroglyphic King: Wisdom and Idolatry in the Seventeenth-Century Masque.* Rutherford, N.J.: Fairleigh Dickinson University Press, 1986.

Lanier, Douglas. "Fertile Visions: Jacobean Revels and the Erotics of Occasion." *SEL Studies in English Literature 1500–1900* 39, no. 2 (spring 1999):327–356.

Leapman, Michael. *Inigo: The Troubled Life of Inigo Jones, Architect of the English Renaissance.* London: Headline, 2003.

Lees-Milne, James. *The Age of Inigo Jones.* London: B. T. Batsford, 1953.

Lewis, C. S. *English Literature in the Sixteenth Century, Excluding Drama.* Oxford: Clarendon Press, 1954.

Limon, Jerzy. *The Masque of Stuart Culture.* Newark: University of Delaware Press, 1990.

Lindley, David, ed. *The Court Masque.* Manchester, U.K. Manchester University Press, 1984.

———. *Thomas Campion.* Leiden: E. J. Brill, 1986.

Lowbury, Edward, Timothy Salter, and Alison Young. *Thomas Campion, Poet, Composer, Physician.* London: Chatto & Windus, 1970.

MacDonagh, Thomas. *Thomas Campion and the Art of English Poetry.* Dublin: Hodges, Figgis, 1913.

Maynard, Winifred. *Elizabethan Lyric Poetry and Its Music.* Oxford: Clarendon Press, 1986.

McCabe, Ellen Thompson. "Thomas Campion." In *The Age of Milton: An Encyclopedia of Major Seventeenth-Century British and American Authors.* Edited by Alan Hager. Santa Barbara, Calif.: Greenwood, 2004.

McColley, Diane Kelsey. *Poetry and Music in Seventeenth-Century England.* Cambridge, U.K.: Cambridge University Press, 1997.

McElwee, William Lloyd. *The Murder of Sir Thomas Overbury.* London: Faber & Faber, 1952.

McKerrow, R. B. "The Use of So-Called Classical Metres in Elizabethan Verse." *MLQ* 4 (1901):172–180 and 5 (1902):5–13, 148–149.

Nicoll, Allardyce. *Stuart Masques and the Renaissance Stage.* London: G. C. Harrap, 1937.

Orgel, Stephen. *The Illusion of Power: Political Theatre in the English Renaissance.* Berkeley: University of California Press, 1975.

Orrell, John. *The Theatres of Inigo Jones and John Webb.* Cambridge, U.K.: Cambridge University Press, 1985.

Pattison, Bruce. *Music and Poetry of the English Renaissance.* London: Methuen, 1948.

Peacock, John. *The Stage Designs of Inigo Jones: The European Context.* Cambridge, U.K.: Cambridge University Press, 1995.

Peltz, Catherine W. "Thomas Campion, an Elizabethan Neo-Classicist." *Modern Language Quarterly* 11 (1950):3–6.

Playford, John. *An Introduction to the Skill of Musick.* Ridgewood, N.J.: Gregg Press, 1966.

Price, David C. *Patrons and Musicians of the English Renaissance.* Cambridge, U.K.: Cambridge University Press, 1981.

Ratcliffe, Stephen. *Campion: On Song.* Boston: Routledge & Kegan Paul, 1981.

Ravelhofer, Barbara. *The Early Stuart Masque: Dance, Costume, and Music.* Oxford: Oxford University Press, 2006.

Richardson, David A. "The Golden Mean in Campion's Airs." *Comparative Literature* 30 (spring 1978):108–132.

Reyher, Paul, *Les Masques anglais: Étude sur les Ballets et la vie de coeur en Angleterre (1512–1640).* Paris: Librairie Hachette et Cie, 1909.

Ryding, Erik S. "Collaboration Between Campion and Rosseter?" *Journal of the Lute Society of America* 19 (1986):13–28.

———. *In Harmony Framed: Musical Humanism, Thomas Campion, and the Two Daniels.* Kirksville, Mo.: Sixteenth Century Journal Publishers, 1993.

Sabol, Andrew J., ed. *A Score for "The Lord's Masque" by Thomas Campion.* Hanover, N.H.: Brown University Press, 1993.

Saintsbury, George. *Seventeenth-Century Lyrics.* London: Rivingtons, 1903.

Schleiner, Louise. *The Living Lyre in English Verse from Elizabeth Through the Restoration.* Columbia: University of Missouri Press, 1984.

Short, R. W. "The Metrical Theory and Practice of Thomas

Campion." *Publications of the Modern Language Association of America* 59 (1944):1003–1018.

Spink, Ian. *English Song: Dowland to Purcell.* London: Batsford, 1974.

Spring, Matthew. *The Lute in Britain: A History of the Instrument and Its Music.* Oxford: Oxford University Press, 2001.

Steele, Mary Susan. *Plays and Masques at Court During the Reigns of Elizabeth, James, and Charles.* New York: Russell & Russell, 1986.

Sternfeld, Frederick W. "A Song from Campion's *Lord's Masque.*" *Journal of the Warburg and Courtauld Institutes* 20 (1957):373–375.

Stevens, John E. *Music and Poetry in the Early Tudor Court.* London: Methuen, 1961.

Thompson, Guy Andrew. *Elizabethan Criticism of Poetry.* 1914. Reprint, Whitefish, N.Y.: Kessinger, 2007.

Thompson, John. *The Founding of English Metre.* New York: Columbia University Press, 1961.

Vickers, Brian. *English Renaissance Literary Criticism.* Oxford: Oxford University Press, 2003.

Walls, Peter. *Music in the English Courtly Masque, 1604–1640.* Oxford: Clarendon Press, 1996.

Warlock, Peter. *The English Ayre.* Oxford: Oxford University Press, 1926.

———. *English Ayres, Elizabethan and Jacobean.* Oxford: Oxford University Press, 1932.

Weiner, Seth. "Spenser's Study of English Syllables and Its Completion by Thomas Campion." In *Spenser Studies: A Renaissance Poetry Annual 3.* Edited by Patrick Cullen and Thomas P. Roche, Jr., pp. 3–56. Pittsburgh: University of Pittsburgh Press, 1982.

Welsford, Enid. *The Court Masque: A Study in the Relationship Between Poetry and the Revels.* New York: Russell & Russell, 1962.

Wilson, Christopher. "Number and Music in Campion's Measured Verse." *John Donne Journal of America* 25 (spring 2006):267–289.

———. "Some Musico-Poetic Aspects of Campion's Masques." In *The Well Enchanting Skill: Music, Poetry, and Drama in the Culture of the Renaissance.* Edited by J. Caldwell, E. Olleson, and S. Wollenberg, pp. 91–106. Oxford: Clarendon Press, 1990.

———. *Words and Notes Coupled Lovingly Together: Thomas Campion, a Critical Study.* New York: Garland, 1989.

Woodfill, Walter L. *Musicians in English Society from Elizabeth to Charles I.* New York: Da Capo, 1969.

HANNAH COWLEY

(1743—1809)

Druann Bauer

HANNAH COWLEY, THE author of *The Belle's Stratagem* (1782), was the dominant female voice writing for the English stage in the 1780s. *The Belle's Stratagem* ranks fourth in total performance dates for new plays produced during the last quarter of the eighteenth century. Jeffrey Cox and Michael Gamer, the editors of the *Broadview Anthology of Romantic Drama* (2003), call Hannah Cowley "arguably the London stage's premier practitioner of comedy and farce" (p. xxii). Her plays were standard repertory pieces throughout the eighteenth and nineteenth centuries, and they are still being staged in the twenty-first century; they have consistently been included in anthologies for over two hundred years. As a group, these dramas reveal much about England during the last twenty-five years of the eighteenth century, and they remain timeless because they address universal concerns such as a woman's role in society and the nature of patriotism.

LIFE

Hannah Parkhouse Cowley was the daughter of Hannah Richards and Philip Parkhouse of Tiverton in Devonshire, who was educated to take holy orders. However, family finances dictated otherwise, so as an alternative career, Parkhouse chose to become a bookseller. Hannah was born on March 14, 1743, in Tiverton.

As the daughter of a bookseller, Cowley belonged to the middle class. Since there was no formal education for women at that time, she, like other women in her situation, had to be self-taught or tutored by family members. She was lucky to have an educated man for a father. Philip Parkhouse was knowledgeable in classical literature, and he tutored his daughter. She dedicated her poem *The Maid of Arragon* (1780) to him. Cowley's lack of a thorough education, however, shows in her work. She refers to Greek mythological figures and inserts French expressions that were in vogue during her time period, but otherwise, her visible learning is slight. According to Frederick M. Link in *The Plays of Hannah Cowley,* Cowley knew "little or no Latin, Greek, or French, and considered an interest in politics 'unfeminine'" (p. v).

Hannah was about twenty-five when she married Thomas Cowley in 1772. Her husband made fifty pounds per year in the Stamp Office and supplemented that income with an additional fifty pounds he received for writing play reviews for the *Gazetteer*. Thomas Cowley later became a soldier for the East India Company, earning yet another small salary. He went to India in 1783 and died there, a captain, in 1797, twenty-five years after their marriage. Hannah remained in London, raising their three children. Cowley and her husband had one son, Thomas, and two daughters, Mary Elizabeth and Frances. Mary died in 1789, at the age of seventeen.

CAREER

At the time of Cowley's retirement in 1795, she had written a total of thirteen plays, eleven of which were published. Cowley wrote for the stage for eighteen years, composing nine comedies, a farce, an interlude, and two tragedies. Judith Stanton, in a study of women dramatists in England between 1660 and 1800, composed a list of the fifty-three most popular plays staged during that period, and seven of those were plays by Cowley. Three of Cowley's plays were among what Stanton determined to be in the top fifteen most popular works for the stage: *Who's the Dupe?* (1779) is seventh on the list, with twenty-one years on stage; *The Belle's Stratagem* (1780) is eighth, with twenty years on stage; and *The Runaway* (1776) is fourteenth, with eleven years on stage. In *The London Stage, 1776–1800: A Critical Introduction*, Charles Hogan ranks *The Belle's Stratagem* eleventh of the twelve main-pieces most frequently acted from 1776 to 1800 (it takes fourth place for new plays produced), and *Who's the Dupe?*, acted 126 times during this time period, ranks twelfth in the list of after-pieces (eleventh for new pieces).

Cowley's plays were very successful during the late eighteenth century despite the fact that she borrowed plotlines, settings, characters, and themes dating back to the Restoration. In many of her plays, Cowley takes stock characters and molds them into multidimensional, realistic characters. She then writes brilliant dialogue. Additionally, Cowley restructures old plots and makes them more manageable. Cowley's plotlines are never very serious, and when the dialogue assumes a dark tone, she ridicules it or quickly ends the scene and introduces one that is highly humorous. She also infuses her scenes with great spirit and vitality, largely through her manipulation of dialogue. Her ability to write witty dialogue that features stichomythia (verbal fencing) keeps the pace of her plays moving swiftly.

In addition to manipulating old plotlines to better suit her contemporary audiences, Cowley also frequently changes the sex of her leading characters, making them women. She implements this strategy in *The Runaway* with Bella, and as Cowley became more self-assured as a playwright, her female characters in subsequent plays simultaneously were drawn progressively stronger and more opinionated. The anonymous editors of *The Works of Mrs. Cowley: Dramas and Poems* (1813) write that "women are generally made the Leading Characters. Her favorite idea of female character is—a combination of the purest innocence of Conduct with the greatest vivacity of Manners, in the mind of a woman who, like Lady Bell Bloomer in *Which Is the Man?*—is mistress of her whole situation, and cannot be surprised'" (p. x).

Cowley's comedies evolved to suit changing times and theater tastes. Of the three plays to be discussed in this present essay, *The Runaway* is largely sentimental, although it includes elements of traditional comedy and farce. *Who's the Dupe?* is a farce, but one that can be labeled a *petite pièce* because it illustrates many of the elements found in five-act comedies, such as a well-constructed plot and multifaceted characters (rather than one-dimensional types). And finally, *The Belle's Stratagem* is a combination of sentimental and "laughing comedy," such as her contemporary Oliver Goldsmith crafted in *She Stoops to Conquer* (1773). Cowley was most successful as a comedic writer; her tragedies are forgettable, as is her poetry.

Cowley also owes the success she enjoyed during her lifetime as a playwright to her business acumen. She was able to assess what the public wanted to see and then deliver it, as illustrated by her ever-changing writing style and her topical themes. Cowley's plays, especially *The Belle's Stratagem*, are didactic works that concern themselves with social issues and themes, such as city versus country, resistance against patriarchy, female friendships, a woman's role in society, and patriotism.

THE RUNAWAY

The story of how Hannah Cowley became a playwright, which has often been repeated, was first told in the preface to *The Works of Mrs. Cowley* (1813). The editors of the collection write that in 1776 Cowley was watching a play with her husband, who was enjoying the performance, when she remarked, probably in a fit of pique (several contemporary reports on Cowley include mention of a volatile temperament), that she could do better. "So delighted with this? said she to him—why I could write as well myself!" She answered his responding laugh by getting up the following morning and sketching out the first act of *The Runaway* (p. viii).

The Runaway opened at Drury Lane on February 15, 1776. It was performed for a total of seventeen nights in the 1775–1776 season. *The Runaway* was the only new main piece produced that season, as well as the last main piece staged by the eminent producer and theater manager David Garrick prior to his retirement. By eighteenth-century London stage standards, it was a huge success. Cowley earned over £500 for this play from benefit night alone (publishing profits of £100 not included), which was five times her husband's annual salary. Benefit nights were a typical source of income for playwrights. Stage producers, such as Garrick, allowed playwrights to collect the total proceeds from designated performance dates in the first season. The longer a play ran, the more benefit nights (up to three) a playwright could earn.

The Runaway is a fast-paced play filled with comic characters, sentimentalism, didactic lessons, and sprightly dialogue. Cowley's didacticism covers a variety of subjects: she ridicules marriages based on financial gain rather than on love, she praises patriotism, she warns her female audience of the dangers of an education that exceeds acceptable limits, she advocates resistance against patriarchy, and she subtly criticizes contemporary society's tendency to oversentimentalize. Another message found in several of Cowley's plays is that the city is evil and the country represents purity and simplicity, but that country dwellers lack knowledge of social graces. In *The Runaway,* Bella dislikes Lady Dinah's presence in their country home because they are forced to maintain city manners and dress. She complains, "Hang this Lady Dinah—one's forc'd to be so dress'd, and so formal!—In the country we should be all shepherds and shepherdesses—Meadows, ditches, rooks, and court-manners, are the strangest combination!" (1.2.1–3).

In *The Runaway,* Cowley utilizes her plot to play on the audience's love for sentimentalism, as well as to convey her overtly didactic messages. When the play opens, young George Hargrave has fallen in love with an incognita at a masked ball, yet he is separated from her before he can discover her name or residence. As a result, he has returned to his family's country home, feeling dejected and restless. His listlessness is quickly overcome, however, when he discovers that his sister is secretly in love with his best friend, Sir Charles Seymour, and that his father has invited the "antiquated" Lady Dinah to his home. George concludes that his father wishes to marry Lady Dinah, and he gleefully ridicules the woman whom he assumes will be his stepmother, stating that he is overcome by her "excessive propriety and decorum" (1.1.56).

Lady Dinah's character is harshly drawn throughout the play. She is made to appear pompous, egotistical, and sexually aggressive. Cowley leads the reader to believe that these faults are caused by Lady Dinah's excessive education, a criticism frequently seen in Cowley's plays. When the audience first encounters her, Lady Dinah tries to impress George by commending him on his education: "To you, Sir, who have been so long conversant with the fine manners of the Antients [sic], the frivolous custom of tea-drinking must appear ridiculous" (1.2.6–8). Lady Dinah then commends George's education to his father. Mr. Hargrave, however, is actually more concerned with George's lack of interest in hunting than in his education. Lady Dinah is completely unaware that her attempts at seduction are failing.

In act 1, we also discover that Harriet has misinterpreted her brother George's remarks and believes that her love for Sir Charles Seymour is not returned, after George jokingly tells Harriet that Seymour is on the point of marriage. Cowley uses the romance between Seymour and Harriet to gently criticize lovers' tendencies to be overemotional, at the same time that she includes such sentimentalism in *The Runaway* to please part of her audience: Seymour and Harriet almost do not unite in a happy marriage due to their excessive lamentations and vivid imaginations. It ultimately takes two pragmatists, George and Bella, to bring them together.

Cowley soon introduces her audience to Mr. Drummond, George's godfather, who has come to ask a favor. He has discovered a young girl on the run from her uncle, her guardian, who is trying to force her into a loveless marriage based on wealth. The girl, Emily, who wishes to keep her family's identity a secret, took refuge at a widow tenant's of Mr. Drummond. But Drummond feels Emily should be removed from such a "situation highly dangerous" (1.2.82), because he has seen the widow encouraging Emily to weep freely—that is, crying for the sake of enjoying a good cry—and such exaggerated sentimentalism upsets him.

Emily is soon revealed to be George's incognita from the ball, and now she has landed in his home, where no other man will vie for her attention. Everything seems to be working in George's favor; he even has his godfather's approval, which is important because we later learn that George will inherit Drummond's considerable fortune. The audience is soon made aware, however, that Lady Dinah, a "forty-thousand-pounder" (her annual income), is not at the Hargrave home for an impending marriage with the *elderly* Mr. Hargrave, but for one with *young* George Hargrave. George is blissfully in the dark about his future, as he pursues his romantic interest in Emily. We discover in act 2 that Emily reciprocates George's feelings, although she only alludes to her attraction, calling George "the Man who, *that once,* possess'd himself of my tenderest wishes" (2.2.9–10).

The noticeable attraction between the two young lovers causes Lady Dinah to become jealous, so she begins to establish her rights to George by informing her maid, Susan, that she will soon marry him, knowing that her maid will spread the information throughout the household. The maid is naturally shocked at this May-December union and expresses her disbelief. The scene's humor lies in Lady Dinah's response to the maid's blundering attempts to cover her amazement.

Lady Dinah's announcement is quickly followed by the development of another plot complication. Sir Charles Seymour arrives at the Hargrave home and reveals to George that he loves Harriet. George feels injured because he was not in Seymour's confidence earlier on this subject, so he decides to punish Seymour by implying that Harriet loves another. Bella is coerced into going along with the duping, and for the next two acts, Seymour and Harriet avoid each other, lament over their loss, and make a sentimental spectacle out of themselves.

In act 3, the pace of *The Runaway* picks up. First, we are shown more of Bella's character. She is revealed to be logical and witty. Her repartee with her cousin George is some of Cowley's best dialogue. He teases her about her attraction for Lord Belville, who is currently touring Europe. Bella denies her attraction, because rumors are circulating that Belville has found a foreign mistress. Cowley draws Bella as a strong, pragmatic woman, and one not likely to accept infidelity. Unlike Harriet and Emily, who spend their free time mooning over their unobtainable lovers, Bella does not. Although Bella does not play a large role in this play, she is significant because she is Cowley's first strong female, serving as the prototype for later characters such as Elizabeth and Charlotte in *Who's the Dupe?* and Letitia Hardy in *The Belle's Stratagem*.

The play reaches its climax in act 4, when George is informed that he is the one intended for Lady Dinah, Harriet and Seymour discover that there is no real obstacle to their love, and Lady Dinah and Susan (Lady Dinah's servant) put their plot to dispose of Emily into action. George feels the sorrow that Harriet and Seymour experienced earlier, when he learns that Lady Dinah is actually *his* intended, and he turns to Drummond for assistance. Drummond delivers most of Cowley's didactic and sentimental lines in *The Runaway*. He is a champion for marriages based on love, so when George tells him that he has proposed to Emily and is determined to marry her despite his father's interference, Drummond responds with this sentimental speech: "Bravo—I like to see a man romantic in his love, and in his friendships—the virtues of him who is not an enthusiast in those noble passions, will never have strength to rise into fortitude, patriotism, and philanthropy" (4.3.17–20).

Patriotism is another theme that runs throughout Cowley's plays; patriotic fever was wholly raging in England during Cowley's writing career. There was a popular enthusiasm for the military successes of the Seven Years' War; by 1760, the British empire was extended "beyond the dreams of seventeenth-century Englishmen" (Paul Langford, *A Polite and Commercial People: England 1727–1783,* p. 340); George II had died in 1760, leaving much hope regarding the heir to the throne, George III; and finally, there was discontent, and later war, in the English colonies of North America. In *The Runaway,* Cowley emphasizes her own patriotism in her description of the perfect male: "He must be *English,* and an *English*-Man. / To Nature, and his Country, false and blind" (Epilogue l.12–13). Many of Cowley's patriotic passages in *The Runaway* are delivered by Mr. Drummond: Perhaps the best example is found near the end of the play, when Mr. Morley arrives to claim his niece, Emily, and he criticizes her dead father for choosing the profession of soldier. Drummond angrily responds in defense of his country.

Morley's arrival, rather than patriotism, however, is the primary concern of the character George in this play. George hopes to secure Emily as his wife, and he is willing to give up his fortune if necessary. Morley will not listen to any of Emily's pleading. He has come to escort her to the home of her fiancé, Baldwin, so that *they* may be married. Baldwin's annual income is £5,000, and this financial position brings him Mr. Morley's approval. When George realizes that Morley will not be swayed, he decides to abduct Emily from her uncle's carriage and take her to France, where they can be married.

George does indeed kidnap Emily in the coach, but she faints. In a chivalrous gesture, George returns with Emily, depositing her at Mr. Drummond's. One characteristic of sentimental comedy of Cowley's era is that virtue must be rewarded. The repentant rake figure (George) shows his character's nobility when we see him making a choice between his own personal interests and adhering to an ideal. In *The Runaway,* when George decides not to abduct Emily after she faints in the carriage, and when instead he brings her home, his nobility becomes clear. This decision to return home means he will be forced to return her to her guardian, and he will lose his true love, but he acts in this ethical way because Emily is not willing to disobey her guardian, which not only goes against her upbringing but would separate her from her own inheritance.

This resistance against patriarchy is another element that appears prominently in Cowley's plotlines that deal with unmarried young ladies. In *Female Playwrights and Eighteenth-Century Comedy: Negotiating Marriage on the London Stage,* Misty Gale Anderson addresses the position held by young women in late-eighteenth-century society, where, says Anderson, women's bodies were connected to both economics and society. In a newly evolving consumer-oriented society in eighteenth-century England, marriage was viewed more as a financial arrangement than as a love match. This economic focus can be attributed to both the Industrial Revolution of the late eighteenth century and the English law of primogeniture, which held that the eldest male heir inherited everything. Therefore, when men chose a bride they wanted one who would bring a large dowry, as well as one who was a virgin—the husband must be assured that the male children produced inside the marriage were actually his, because the oldest of these males would inherit all of his holdings. In plays written by men of the era, the dominant patriarchal order was reestablished when the comedy ended in a marriage. According to Anderson, women writers, in order to be read, needed to align themselves with this established plotline, and so they did, but that they questioned the standard marriage ending through the vehicle of comedy, where irony and contradictions can be appreciated by an audience (p. 3). Indeed, Cowley writes ironically. She questions the marriage market, the role of subservient woman, and a woman's need for a man, in the way that her plays end in marriage—but a marriage that best suits the woman, not necessarily the man. For instance, in *The Runaway,* George Hargrave is willing to reject his own inheritance in order to marry Emily, but Emily is not willing to give up hers. These contradictions show Cowley's willingness to write realistically about complicated subjects such as marriage and the rights of women.

In the final act of *The Runaway,* Lady Dinah's treachery is fully exposed and she is sent packing. George and Emily receive unanimous approval for their wedding, the wedding of Harriet and Seymour is blessed by Mr. Hargrave, and Bella is informed that Belville is at Dover and is headed her way. *The Runaway* ends with all of these anticipated weddings, and as in all of Cowley's romances, the women manage to not only marry the men they love, but they marry financially secure men as well.

WHO'S THE DUPE?

Who's the Dupe? was the third play that Cowley wrote (after *Albina, Countess Raimond*, which was not produced until later in 1779) but her second one to be performed. It opened on April 10, 1779, and became one of her most enduring pieces, despite the fact that it was a farce, considered by theater critics to be the lowest form of comedy. Audiences did not have that bias—they loved it. It was performed continuously for twenty-one years, and is still popular in the twenty-first century.

The success of *Who's the Dupe?* can be attributed to several factors. Cowley selected a popular group of actors and actresses to perform in her play when it opened in London in 1779. John Palmer and James Aickin played Granger and Sandford, respectively, in the original production. Priscilla Hopkins (who was later married to the actor William Brereton) played Elizabeth until the end of the century. Mr. Doiley was created by William Parsons, and the role remained his until his retirement in 1794. Thomas King was the original Gradus, and in her newspaper "Advertisement," Cowley acknowledges him for taking on a role that he did not necessarily desire. Since Gradus provides much of the comic element in the play, it was important to select the right actor, and Cowley's tribute to King in her published play suggests that audiences approved of him in the role.

Several other elements make *Who's the Dupe?* a superior play. Cowley followed the basic principles of farce for this drama, but she avoided the heavy exaggeration of characterization and pace. The play moves swiftly, but not to the point that we feel we are observing, or reading, it in fast forward. And although Gradus and Doiley are exaggerated characters, they are still highly believable—in general, Cowley's complex, highly interesting, characters are perhaps her greatest skill as a playwright. In *Who's the Dupe?*, Cowley's heroines, Elizabeth and Charlotte, are resourceful, strong, and determined. Cowley's ability to write witty dialogue also serves to make *Who's the Dupe?* one of the best plays written in the late eighteenth century and one that can still be performed today.

When the action in *Who's the Dupe?* begins, it quickly becomes evident that the play will not only be a light criticism of pedants but a didactic treatise against forced marriages and the importance Englishmen place on the acquisition of wealth, themes seen earlier in *The Runaway* and later in *The Belle's Stratagem*. Sandford and Granger, two friends, meet after a short separation and exchange news. Granger bemoans his financial state. As the younger son who only inherited £5,000, he has already spent all of his money and cannot coerce his older brother into giving him more. He now looks to marriage with Elizabeth Doiley, the daughter of a wealthy merchant, as his answer.

But Granger's plan of marrying Elizabeth appears to be blocked when Sandford informs him that Mr. Doiley has selected a husband for his daughter—Gradus, the pedant. According to Sandford, Mr. Doiley, who was brought up poor and uneducated, "swears he'll have a Man of LARNING [sic] for his Son. His caprice makes him regardless of fortune; but Elizabeth's Husband must have Latin at his fingers' ends, and be able to teach his Grandsons to sputter in Greek" (1.1.73–76). Although Granger lacks in book learning, he is street savvy, and he decides that Gradus shall not rob him of Elizabeth. Meanwhile, Elizabeth is of the same mind, and she has sent a letter to Granger asking him to visit her. As Elizabeth enjoys breakfast with her father, we see that father and daughter actually love each other; they joke and call each other names. However, father and daughter are both stubborn and each wishes to have his/her own way in regard to Elizabeth's marriage. From act 1, scene 2, on, the audience is anticipating who will win the battle of wills.

In *Early Women Dramatists: 1550–1800*, Margarete Rubik claims that in *Who's the Dupe?* Cowley introduced the first of her "witty, resourceful heroines, who are so rare in the dramas of her female contemporaries" (p. 168). Actually, however, the first witty (although not resourceful) Cowley heroine is Bella in *The Runaway*, who likes to exchange verbal barbs with family members. With Elizabeth and Charlotte (Elizabeth's cousin) in *Who's the Dupe?*, Cowley adds the characteristic of resourcefulness to her female depictions. Charlotte demonstrates her resourcefulness and quick thinking in act 1, scene 2, when she interrupts the breakfast of Elizabeth and Mr. Doiley to announce that Mrs. Taffety, the gownmaker, is upstairs in Elizabeth's dressing room. The visitor is actually Granger, but an announcement of *that* guest would only antagonize Mr. Doiley. Charlotte's quick thinking is needed again almost immediately when Gradus arrives shortly after Granger, and Mr. Doiley wishes to bring him up to meet Elizabeth. A fast pace must be maintained throughout a farce in order to keep the laughter rolling in the audience; Cowley here maintains this fast pace with a true "chase" scene. With Granger and Elizabeth cornered in her dressing room, in true farcical fashion, Elizabeth and Charlotte try to hide Granger by dressing him as a woman. The undermining of gender roles that this cross-dressing suggests is explored from another perspective in Andrew Effenbein's study "Lesbian Aestheticism on the Eighteenth-Century Stage," where he uses examples from Cowley's comedy *The Town Before You* (1795) to argue that Cowley depicts lesbian relationships in her plays, Effenbein is the only critic to read Cowley's strong females as inherently lesbian, although other critics have noted Cowley's proclivity for depicting strong bonds between her female characters.

Cowley's male characters are never as strong, or as interesting, as her female ones. In *Who's the Dupe?*, Gradus is a stock character. He is a pedant with little interest in anything outside books. When he is introduced to Elizabeth, he tries to woo her in his own bookish way: "Madam!—(*bows*)—hem—permit me—this honour—hem—believe me, Lady, I have more satisfaction in beholding you, than I should have in conversing with Graevius and Gronovius" (1.3.56–58).

While this indication of his education thrills Mr. Doiley, Elizabeth is considerably less impressed. Mr. Doiley complains of the money wasted on educating his daughter in "Dancing, her French, her Tambour, her Harpsicholl, her Jography, her Stronomy" (1.3.79–80). Gradus agrees, and laments the passage of a time when women could neither read nor write. Of course, although Elizabeth does not have an abundance of book learning, she has enough ingenuity and wit to escape marriage with Gradus. The audience is aware of this irony, and this audience awareness is what ultimately makes the scene humorous.

Elizabeth and Charlotte devise a plan that will dupe Mr. Doiley into allowing Elizabeth to marry Granger. Gradus will also be duped into playing along with the plan. Charlotte sends Gradus to Sandford for a makeover, and the women prepare for Mr. Doiley's reaction when he sees the "new and improved" Gradus.

In act 2, Sandford returns with Gradus, who is dressed up in "sattins and tassels, and spangles and foils" (2.2.1–2). Elizabeth enters and pretends to be both overwhelmed and overjoyed by the transformation. When Mr. Doiley sees the foppish Gradus, however, he starts back in shock. Stage directions indicate that Mr. Doiley is "behind," so we can assume he is hiding, so that he might overhear the conversation. Elizabeth leads Gradus into damaging his chances with Mr. Doiley by remarking, "But I am convinced now—I am sure all this is put on—in your heart you are still Mr. Gradus" (2.2.48–49). One of the funniest scenes follows, with Gradus protesting that learning is "a vile Bore!" and that he is fixed on his resolution not to return to his college ways. He insults Mr. Doiley when he says, "I have learn'd that the acquisitions of which your Father is so ridiculously fond, are useless lumber—that a man who knows more than his neighbours, is in danger of being shut out of society—or, at best, of being invited at dinner once in a twelve-month, to be exhibited like an antique Bronze—or Porridge-pot from Herculaneum" (2.2.51–55). The statement that a man who knows more than his neighbors will be shut out of society seems to be Cowley's comment on pedantry.

When Mr. Doiley can tolerate no more of what he perceives as a betrayal by Gradus, he jumps out and confronts him. As Elizabeth expects, Gradus tries to placate Mr. Doiley by assuring him that he can toss off this new look and manner of speech. Both Sandford and Elizabeth indicate their disgust with Gradus, so he finds himself caught between two opposing forces, or as Gradus so humorously puts it, "I stand reeling between two characters, like a Substantive between two Adjectives" (2.2.114–115).

Cowley then takes a few minutes to flesh out Mr. Doiley's character and allows the audience to see him not simply as a ridiculous merchant, but as a man who has been scarred by his past. Mr. Doiley explains why having a learned son-in-law is so important to him. He recounts an incident in his past to Sandford. For fifteen years he attended the parish meetings and never once stood up to talk. Finally, he had an opportunity to take a seat as alderman, but first it was necessary that he stand up to speak. He could not do it. The audience is drawn to Mr. Doiley, and they better understand the relationship between Mr. Doiley and Elizabeth—they love each other *and* they love squabbling with each other. The love Elizabeth feels for her father will not allow her to intentionally hurt him. When he is ultimately duped, Elizabeth never lets him become aware of his duping. This humanizing of her characters is one of Cowley's remarkable talents.

One of the funniest scenes in *Who's the Dupe?* is what might be called, in our time, the "Pedants' Quiz Bowl." Old Doiley has decided to give his daughter Elizabeth to the smarter of her two suitors, and he requires them to demonstrate their knowledge of ancient languages. Granger knows none, but he has been studying the English dictionary, searching for polysyllabic words. The humor in the scene is generated by Gradus, as he becomes aware that he, as well as Old Doiley, is being duped. One of the goals of a farce is laughter, but in most farces, the humor is generated by the situation, not by the dialogue; however, in this scene, Cowley manages to make both situation *and* dialogue humorous, a remarkable feat for any writer of farce.

The contest is brief, but hilarious. Gradus asks Granger to choose his weapons: Hebrew, Greek, Latin, or English. Before Granger can grasp the opportunity to converse in English, Mr. Doiley out rules it, demanding Greek. Mr. Doiley is not impressed with Gradus' Greek, however, because to Mr. Doiley, everything sounds like the word "pantry" and he jokes, "*Panta, tri pantry!* Why, that's all about the Pantry. What, the old Grecians lov'd Tid-bits, may hap—but that's low! aye, Sandford!" (2.2.333–334). When it is Granger's turn, he hesitates, then in desperation, links together words he discovered while exploring the dictionary. Of course, it is gibberish, but to the uneducated Mr. Doiley, it sounds impressive. Gradus' reaction is hilarious because he is almost speechless when he realizes that Mr. Doiley is totally unaware that he has been hoodwinked.

The "quiz bowl" scene was not only written to be humorous: Cowley also utilizes the play to satirize both pedantry and forced marriages. In "The Rise of Social Comedy in the Eighteenth Century," Dougald MacMillan notes that as the eighteenth century drew to a close, comedies became more serious but not more sentimental. Instead, playwrights reintroduced satire in the comedies of the period—although not the harsh satire of Restoration comedy, which frequently made the cuckold or the fop the butt of the joke. Late eighteenth-century satire criticized manners or social institutions, and it was meant to be instructive, not purely entertaining. In *Who's the Dupe?*, the satire is particularly directed at forced marriages. At the conclusion of the "quiz bowl" scene, Mr. Doiley tells Elizabeth that Granger will be her husband. She appears to meekly accept: "Sir, in obedience to the commands of my *Father*—" (2.2.386), but we understand the hidden meaning of "commands of my *Father*." The only commands Elizabeth obeys are those of her heart. This is a common theme that runs throughout Cowley's plays—that a woman must follow her heart and not be forced into a loveless marriage. At the same time—and again, as in other Cowley plays—while both heroines of *Who's the Dupe?*, Elizabeth and Charlotte, marry the men they love, they also marry financially sound men. Gradus, upon losing Elizabeth, asks for Charlotte's hand. The audience sees throughout the play that Gradus truly prefers Charlotte and that he only pursues Elizabeth for her money. When Gradus follows his heart and asks for Charlotte's hand, he is rewarded for his sentimental spirit. Mr. Doiley tells Charlotte he will "throw in a few Hundreds, that you mayn't repent your Bargain" (2.2.403). The play ends with plans for marriage; Mr. Doiley is satisfied he has triumphed over Elizabeth; and Elizabeth possesses, but keeps to herself, the knowledge that she has duped not one, but two, members of the "smarter" sex.

Who's the Dupe?, like most popular entertainment, did not always receive critical praise. The editors of her *Works* felt that Cowley owed the public an apology for writing a farce. *Who's the Dupe?*, they said, "is the only instance in which she [Cowley], descended to Farce, but, with the utmost flow of Humour, she will be found to have by no means sunk herself with her Subject; her mind is always perceived paramount to the vulgarity or the folly she is describing" (p. x). Literary snobbery notwithstanding, *Who's the Dupe?* ranks as Cowley's second most popular play, behind *The Belle's Stratagem*.

THE BELLE'S STRATAGEM

Cowley borrowed from the past, both for characterizations and plotlines, when she wrote her best plays. Margarete Rubik has called *The Belle's Stratagem* (1780) a throwback to "the Restoration motif of the resourceful, active heroine, who disguises herself as a loose woman to attract the rake, and is in control of all the intrigues" (p. 169). Cowley was at the height of her creative ability when she wrote *The Belle's Stratagem*, and paradoxically, in her depiction of the imaginative, self-sufficient heroine Letitia Hardy, she has drawn a woman who is very atypical of the late eighteenth century. Letitia fits more closely the mold of a Restoration female, or one who might live in the early twentieth century—but in any case, not in 1780. This complex, and interesting, creature named Letitia Hardy is what primarily draws audiences time and time again to *The Belle's Stratagem*. Contemporary, as well as later, reaction to the play was mixed, largely owing to Letitia's antics: Victorian audiences saw Letitia as a disgrace to femininity. In the prefatory remarks to the play that appeared in the 1849 edition of *Davidson's Shilling Volume of Cumberland's Plays,* the editors called her a "boisterous vulgar hoyden" (p. A3).

The Belle's Stratagem was popular, and remains so, for many more reasons than just a feisty female character. Cowley opened her play with a cast that featured audience favorites, she returns with her didactic message about what makes a happy marriage, and she includes a subplot that questions a wife's traditional role in marriage. She also adds crowd-pleasing elements such as songs and a masquerade ball. Finally, the audience is treated to popular stock characters such as the rakish Courtall, the gossipy widow Mrs. Racket, the sentimental Saville, and the dashing Doricourt. In the introductory remarks to the first published edition of the play, the editors of the 1822 *Oxberry's New English Drama* say, "We … have no hesitation in attributing to the comedy of the *Belle's Stratagem* the praise of wit, invention, a knowledge of life, and of the stage, spirited dialogue, and a story replete with incident and interest" (pp. 4–5).

The play was well cast; everyone fit their part, but then Cowley wrote for certain actors. Her "types" show up frequently throughout her plays. Therefore, when the play opened in 1780, and Saville and Courtall, played by James Aicken and Thomas Robson, respectively, took the stage, the audience expected to see Aicken play a blunt, honest man, and Robson play a scoundrel. Their suppositions were quickly affirmed when Courtall recounts his recent visit with his country cousins. He paints a critical picture of them: "After waiting thirty minutes, during which there was a violent bustle, in bounced five sallow damsels, four of them maypoles;—the fifth, Nature, by way of variety, had bent in the Æsop style" (1.1.23–25).

Cowley quickly establishes that Courtall is cruel and self-centered, and the audience is put on notice that he will probably create trouble. Doricourt, the hero, has been on his European tour, and he returns home with an elevated opinion of everything French. His friend Saville attempts to correct his new beliefs, and Cowley uses Doricourt's reason for choosing French servants to spout her patriotic ideas: "A Frenchman neither hears, sees, nor breathes, but as his master directs; and his whole system of conduct is compris'd in one short word, *Obedience!* An Englishman reasons, forms opinions, cogitates, and disputes" (1.3.22–24); therefore, according to Cowley, an Englishman makes a poor servant. Cowley closes the scene with an additional bit of patriotic flag-waving: when Saville begins to appear worried that Doricourt has lost his love for his own country, Doricourt responds, "I have never yet found any man whom I could cordially take to my heart, and call Friend, who was not born beneath a British sky, and whose heart and manners were not truly English" (1.3.94–96). Misty G. Anderson suggests that Cowley was exploiting the sympathies of her audiences by playing on the idea of individual liberty fostered during the Enlightenment. With her excessively patriotic dialogue, she claims that Cowley's goal was to "make Englishness the ultimate aphrodisiac" (2002, p. 6).

Aside from serving as a venue for expounding patriotic values, this scene also sets up Saville as a foil to Doricourt. Saville is serious; Doricourt is jaded, but frivolous, and he has a cavalier attitude toward life. When asked about his fiancée, Letitia Hardy, Doricourt dismisses her with, "Why, she's *only* a fine girl; complexion, shape, and features; nothing more" (1.3.52–53). Doricourt's father pledged him to Letitia when he was just a child, and Doricourt is honorable enough to fulfill the promise. Doricourt tells Saville that although Letitia "has not inspir'd me with violent passion, my honour secures her felicity" (1.3.77–78). According to Doricourt, Letitia lacks "zest" and "poignancy" (1.3.62), and his attitude indicates that, once they are married, Letitia will be but a minor inconvenience in his life.

Doricourt's indifferent attitude toward marriage is juxtaposed against Saville's sentimental one. Doricourt mentions the recent marriage of the Touchwoods, and Saville reveals that he felt some passion for Lady Frances Touchwood when she was single. Saville's acknowledgment of the dashing of his dreams is spoken as a true sentimentalist: "You know I never look'd up to her with hope, and Sir George is every way worthy of her" (1.3.84–85).

In *The Belle's Stratagem,* the theme of city versus country arises in the Sir George–Lady Frances subplot and in the speeches of auxiliary characters. When the play opens, we see Cowley's image of uncouth country come to town. Courtall is telling Saville about his female country cousins, recently arrived in London: "They came from the farthest part of Northumberland, had never been in town, and in course were made up of rusticity, innocence, and beauty" (1.1.20–21). But although the country may fail to instill proper etiquette, the city also has its disadvantages. In the subplot of *The Belle's Stratagem,* the newly married Sir George Touchwood wishes to keep his country wife, Lady Frances, innocent of city evils. He deliberately marries a country woman because he dislikes the artificiality of the city, and he believes that, as a simple woman from the country, Lady Frances will grant him complete control over her likes and dislikes. He tells Doricourt, "Lady Frances despises high life so much from the ideas I have given her, that she'll live in it like a salamander in fire" (2.1.14–16). Sir George, however, does not want to take any chances with his new wife, so he attempts to isolate her from the sights of London and from its people.

Intertwined with serious discussions of English manners and marriages is the introduction of comedy via the character of Flutter, a nincompoop who means no harm but, nevertheless, does much damage to almost everyone with whom he comes into contact. His biggest flaw is that he confuses everything he hears, and when he retells a tale, it takes on an entirely different meaning. Flutter provides much of the comedy in *The Belle's Stratagem,* with some assistance from the witticisms of Mrs. Racket.

Mrs. Racket serves as both comedian and social commentator. Through her, Cowley criticizes contemporary marriage practices. Mrs. Racket explains the way of the world to Letitia, saying, "He is the prettiest fellow you have seen, and in course bewilders your imagination; but he has seen a million of pretty women, child, before he saw you; and his first feelings have been over long ago" (1.4.134–137). She then advises Letitia to be happy with what she *does* have: "If you have no reason to believe his heart pre-engaged, be satisfied; if he is a man of honour, you'll have nothing to complain of" (1.4.140–142). When Letitia asks if that is all she can expect out of marriage, Mrs. Racket matter of factly tells her, "When you have fretted yourself pale, my dear, you'll have mended your expectation greatly" (1.4.145–146).

Letitia will not be swayed by Mrs. Racket's worldview, which insinuates that most marriages are simply tolerated or marked by indifference. Another of Letitia's strong character traits is creativity, and determined to "touch his heart, or never be his wife" (1.4.138–139), Letitia plans to attract Doricourt's attention by repulsing him. She informs her father of her plans: "Why, Sir—it may seem a little paradoxical; but, as he does not like me enough, I want him to like me still less, and will at our next interview endeavour to heighten his indifference into dislike" (1.4.207–209).

While Cowley's Doricourt-Letitia main plot is designed primarily for comedy, her subplot, involving the Touchwood marriage, is largely didactic in nature. Mrs. Racket and her friend Miss Ogle symbolize female solidarity, and therefore they represent a threat to the happiness of Sir George, who wishes to keep his wife perpetually by his side and under his control. These two women initiate Lady Frances into fashionable society, but more importantly, they awaken her desire for self-determination.

Later that afternoon, back at the Hardy residence, Letitia is preparing to entertain Doricourt. She has enlisted Mrs. Racket's help in her plot to make herself appear ignorant and lacking in social graces. Here, as in Cowley's other plays, we see women working together to achieve their desired goals, which is usually the acquisition of a husband. Mrs. Racket agrees to help Letitia, even though she is not sure the plan is a good one.

With the arrival of the evening, everyone gathers at the masquerade, and the climax of the play occurs. Mrs. Racket instructs Lady Frances to avoid spending too much time alone with her husband, and as a result of her compliance with this suggestion, Lady Frances is exposed to Courtall's treachery. Saville enters with a known prostitute, Kitty Willis, who he has dressed as Lady Frances. He intends to have her exchange places with Lady Frances moments before Courtall tries to whisk Lady Frances away from the masquerade.

Doricourt's eagerness to escape marriage is further strengthened with the appearance of a masked lady (who is in fact Letitia). She sings a song about shaking off a sense of dullness, grasping "all the gifts that Pleasure sends," (4.1.166) and touching a man's feelings. Letitia and Doricourt then converse, and their conversation is slightly outside the bounds of propriety, which further excites Doricourt's interest.

The action changes swiftly to the abduction of Lady Frances. Cowley delivers a didactic message to the audience through the lectures of Saville, who throughout the evening has been shadowing Lady Frances. When Lady Frances asks him why he is so concerned for her welfare, Saville answers, "Goodness will ever interest; its home is Heaven: on earth 'tis but a Wanderer. Imprudent Lady! why have you left the side of your Protector? Where is your Husband?" (4.1.210–212). He then warns her, "Lady! there are dangers abroad—Beware!" (4.1.218–219). Unfortunately, Lady Frances does not "beware," because she is too innocent to understand the danger she has exposed herself to by separating from her husband.

Cowley incorporates the Courtall seduction into her play in order to address another of her persistent themes: resistance against patriarchy. In her portrayal of the Touchwood marriage, Cowley implies that a man and woman should have some independence from each other but that a husband is ultimately responsible for the care of his wife, and that a wife should know when to obey her husband. In other words, Lady Frances should not have gone sightseeing with Mrs. Racket, and Sir George should not have left his wife alone at the masquerade. It is a compromise, but it is the type of compromise that Cowley often makes in her plays, for she takes a conservative approach to female liberation, allowing her women to express their individuality but not to the point that they will disturb the social order. As with all of Cowley's couples, Sir George and Lady Frances reaffirm their love for each other, and the play ends with their marriage on firmer ground. As a playwright, Cowley had to criticize marriage customs from within tight restrictions and still be entertaining—not an easy task. Early in her career Cowley used humor often to soften her didactic messages. In *The Belle's Stratagem,* when Doricourt wants to get out of his engagement, he comically feigns madness. Some of Cowley's best comedic moments can be found in act 5 of *The Belle's Stratagem,* when Cowley brings the Doricourt-Letitia misconceptions to an end. Doricourt pretends to be insane, and Mr. Hardy pretends to be dying. Even Letitia keeps up her pretense until the last moment. Villers suggests that Letitia not reveal her "masquerade-lady" identity to Doricourt until he marries her, and they devise a plan that will hasten the marriage. Mr. Hardy is to feign a severe illness that places him on his deathbed. They hope that Doricourt, out of a sense of duty, will agree to marry Letitia so that Mr. Hardy can "go out of the world in peace" (5.1.43).

In the final scene, Doricourt enters the Hardy residence and pretends to be insane: "There! there she darts through the air in liquid flames! Down again! Now I have her—Oh, she burns, she scorches!—Oh! she eats into my very heart!" (5.5.45–47). Mrs. Racket cuts Doricourt's ranting short by ridiculing him, and although he attempts to leave, Doricourt's sense of honor stays him and he agrees to marry Letitia. His acceptance of his fate, however, is not flattering to his fiancée: "Oh, aye, any where; to the Antipodes—to the Moon—Carry me—Do with me what you will" (5.5.76–77). With a dramatic sweep, Letitia enters, masked, and reminds Doricourt that she said she would appear when he least expected it. Misunderstandings begin to be cleared up when Doricourt accuses her of being Jennett's lover. She denies the allegations, which leads Doricourt to turn to Flutter, who sputters, "Who, she? O Lard! no—'Twas quite a different person that I meant.—I never saw that Lady before" (5.5.192–193). The realization that his beloved has been snatched from him by misunderstandings and a forced marriage causes Doricourt to explode. His anger increases when Mr. Hardy, appearing to be in perfect health, walks into the room. Doricourt then turns to his masked love and asks her to reveal her face. Letitia realizes that her future happiness depends on Doricourt's reaction to her subterfuge, but once she removes her mask, she is reassured when Doricourt utters, "Rapture! Transport! Heaven!" (5.5.222).

Cowley shows that Letitia has experienced emotional and intellectual growth during her campaign to win Doricourt. Once she has identified herself as his true wife, she refuses to behave submissively, as she might have in the past. When Villers attempts to protect Letitia by accepting responsibility for the plot against Doricourt, Letitia demonstrates her new sense of maturity by taking the responsibility upon herself. She also comments on her new attitude: "I will not allow that [Villers to accept responsibility]. This little stratagem arose from my disappointment, in not having made the impression on you I wish'd" (5.5.225–226). Doricourt's response reveals Cowley's belief that marriages can be successful if men and women throw off their masks and be themselves: "You shall be nothing but yourself—nothing can be captivating that you are not" (5.5.236–237). Doricourt's recognition that Letitia is more than just a sexual object, that she has a mind, is also an important Cowley message. Jean Gagen is among the critics who have noticed Cowley's positive portrayal of women, writing in "The Weaker Sex: Hannah Cowley's Treatment of Men in Her Comedies of Courtship and Marriage" that "Cowley glorifies these women who are independent and resourceful, intelligent and well educated without becoming pedantic, and completely undeterred by the authority that men attempt to impose on them in the choice of their mates" (p. 115).

Cowley closes *The Belle's Stratagem* with somewhat typical didacticism, in Doricourt's embrace of patriotism and his permanent disavowal of his love for foreign women and manners. But Cowley's tendency toward flag-waving and moralizing did in fact decrease as her career progressed.

COWLEY'S COMEDIC WRITING STYLE

Critics have always noted the likenesses between Cowley's plays and Restoration comedy, and more specifically, her habit of borrowing characterizations and plotlines from Restoration writers. In her introduction to *The Belle's Stratagem*, collected in the 1808 edition of *The British Theatre*, the playwright Elizabeth Inchbald emphasizes that the play's setting, costumes, and topics of conversation are those that would be found in a Restoration play: "the mention of powder worn by the ladies, their silk gowns, and other long exploded fashions, ... gives a certain sensation to the reader, which seems to place the work on the honourable list of ancient dramas" (p. 5). Inchbald's examples reference just a few of Cowley's "borrowings." The title of *The Belle's Stratagem*, for instance, is a reference to George Farquhar's late Restoration comedy *The Beaux' Stratagem* (1707).

In *The Belle's Stratagem*, Cowley pits Doricourt against Letitia in several verbal duels. The duel of wits between belle and beau is a device typical of Restoration comedy, of which the best example in Cowley's 1782 play is the masquerade ball scene, where Doricourt is trying to seduce the masked Letitia but is totally unaware of her identity. In an attempt to gain this knowledge, he engages in a verbal exchange—but it is an exchange that, significantly, she starts. In *The Laughing Tradition: Stage Comedy in Garrick's Day* (1980), Richard Bevis explains that Cowley's contemporary Arthur Murphy uses the same type of exchange as a plot device in a three-act farce titled *No One's Enemy but His Own*, and that Murphy, too, borrowed his ideas from the Restoration—in this case, the playwrights George Etherege and William Wycherley. Like Etherege and Wycherley, Murphy incorporates illicit affairs and gossip in his play, and Murphy even lifts the names of Restoration comedy characters. In these approaches, however, both Cowley and Murphy are simply following an established stage tradition of "borrowing."

As in most Restoration comedies, Cowley also incorporates fops, fools, and gallants. Flutter, in *The Belle's Stratagem*, is Cowley's combination fop and fool, for his outward appearance is more important to him than his intelligence, and he displays this lack of intelligence in most of his verbal exchanges, by either revealing what he should keep secret or by mangling the retelling of a story. Cowley crafts two gallants for *The Belle's Stratagem*: Doricourt and Courtall. Courtall bears more resemblance to a Restoration rake than does Doricourt, for Courtall's love intrigue involves not only seduction but sexual assault. He plans to cuckold Sir George Touchwood by kidnapping his wife and bringing her to his bedroom, where he plans not to seduce but rather to "use" her. No gentleman, Courtall informs all of his drinking buddies of his plans, boasting cavalierly that, after the abduction and (in modern terms) the rape, he will post her name in his books at his favorite club.

Doricourt is Cowley's less rakish gallant: Like a Restoration gallant, he is independently wealthy, well-bred, handsome, and witty. And unlike a Restoration rake, he is only somewhat promiscuous. He does hint at his sexual experiences while in France, but unlike Courtall, who is ill-bred, Doricourt does not reveal names. Even before we meet him, we are told by Courtall of Doricourt's Restoration-like prowess with women and of his great sense of fashion taste.

Cowley was equally indebted to her contemporaries for her stage devices and plot ideas. In act 2 of *The Belle's Stratagem*, Cowley includes an auction scene that features some unscrupulous "antique" dealers. The depiction of antique dealers was a common scene in eighteenth-century comedy. In 1752, Samuel Foote's play *Taste*, for instance, satirized the dealers of fake antiquities, who flourished along with their trade. Cowley may also owe a debt to Foote for the infatuation with Gallic culture expressed by Doricourt. In 1756, Foote wrote *The Englishman Returned from Paris*, which features a proud and foolish Englishman who, like Doricourt, loves everything French and is satirized for his obsession. But the two plays share something else in common: both involve a complication that hinges on money and marriage. In Foote's play, Lucinda must marry Buck if she wishes to inherit. If she refuses, she will inherit less. If Buck refuses Lucinda, he must settle twenty thousand pounds on her. In *The Belle's Stratagem,* a marriage contract signed by their fathers when Doricourt and Letitia were young stipulates that if either rejects the marriage, they must turn over a sizeable portion of their wealth to the other.

The Belle's Stratagem not only borrows plot devices from contemporary plays but it also follows the direction many plays were taking, which was a gradual movement away from the sentimental. Many of the playwrights who influenced Cowley's creative spirit not only rejected but ridiculed sentimental comedy, preferring what Oliver Goldsmith referred to as "laughing" comedy, in which the exhibition of man's failings would be accomplished through humor rather than through weeping sentimentality. Richard Sheridan's influence on Cowley's plays was perhaps especially important. Ernest Bernbaum, in *The Drama of Sensibility,* calls Sheridan's style "high comedy," claiming that he returned to the "earliest type of sentimental comedy, in which … one of the plots was comic and the other sentimental" (p. 253), and Cowley likewise relegates the sentimental to the subplot. Her main plots are largely comedic with little of the didactic present. In her Ph.D. dissertation on Hannah Cowley, Joyce East claims that the duping ploy used in *The Runaway* keeps the sentimental from overpowering the comedy. Other examples of the way Cowley adroitly intersperses the sentimental with the humorous in *The Runaway* occurs when Sir Charles' sentimental dialogue begins to become oppressive in act 3 and Cowley inserts a humorous scene between two servants, Susan and Jarvis, or the play's farcical moment involving the drunk Justice.

Cowley and Sheridan share other similarities in their writing styles. Their stories are largely romantic with happy endings (usually marriage); both utilize humorous characters who stem from the traditional comedic mode; both alter or recombine earlier works to form new plays; and both enjoy incorporating the double entendre and "asides" into their plays. The scenes from Sheridan's *The School for Scandal* are filled with asides, for example, especially in the first scene of act 4, when Charles Surface's uncle, Sir Oliver, keeps close to the audience, letting them into his state of mind. And Cowley wrote *The Belle's Stratagem* in 1780, just three years after *The School for Scandal*. And as in Sheridan's play, *The Belle's Stratagem* frequently resorts to asides in order to increase the humor of a situation or to further develop a character. When the gallant Doricourt visits the newlywed Sir George Touchwood, the two men verbally fence with each other. Doricourt wishes to meet Sir George's wife, and Sir George, who fears Doricourt's attractiveness, wishes to avoid the encounter. Cowley includes asides in this scene to show the audience what each is thinking:

SIR GEORGE: Introduce!—oh, aye, to be sure—I believe Lady Frances is engaged just now—but another time. (*Aside.*) (How handsome the dog looks to-day!)

DORICOURT: Another time!—but I have no other time. 'Sdeath! this is the only hour I can command this fortnight!

SIR GEORGE: (ASIDE.) (I am glad to hear it, with all my soul.) So then, you can't dine with us to-day? That's very unlucky.

(2.1.26–32)

DRAMAS AND POETRY

Cowley also pursued an interest in poetry, although her poetic talent was weak. Her longer poetic pieces include *The Maid of Arragon: A Tale* (1780), *The Scottish Village; or, Pitcairne Greene* (1786), and *The Siege of Acre: An Epic Poem* (1801; revised 1810). She was the "Anna Matilda," who carried on a questionably romantic poetical correspondence with "Della Crusca" (Robert Merry) in the pages of the *World; or, Fashionable Advertiser*. Cowley's poetry was first published in this newspaper, although by 1788 she had published a collection titled *The Poetry of Anna Matilda: Containing "A Tale for Jeal-*

ousy," "The Funeral," Her Correspondence with Della Crusca, and Several Other Poetical Pieces.

An example of her poetry in this collection provides its own testimony as to why her poetic works are not regularly anthologized. In "Address to Two Candles" collected in *Poetry of Anna Matilda,* Cowley recounts a recent incident in her life. She had removed some candles from the window, but when she realized that it was dark outside, she replaced them. Here are two stanzas of the eight-stanza poem:

Burn—lucid tapers! fiercer burn!
Refine each ray to purer light,
Pervade the circumambient air
And pierce the closest robe of Night!
Why *faintly* glow your spiral fires,
Whilst Charity invokes your beams?
Why, inauspicious to my prayer,—
Still faint and fainter are your gleams?

(1788, p. B3)

Perhaps the best critique of her poetic ability is expressed by Frederick Link in the introduction to his *The Plays of Hannah Cowley*: "She left behind a fairly substantial body of work. Her poems are forgettable, and have been forgotten" (p. xliii).

Cowley retired from the stage in 1795 following the production of *The Town Before You.* Her recent plays were not receiving the acclaim granted to her early works, and as she writes in her preface to that year's published edition *The Town Before You,* she had grown disgruntled with the public's demand for physical comedy over character development and brilliant dialogue—her forte. She writes: "The combinations of interest, the strokes which are meant to reach the heart, we are equally incapable of tasting. Laugh! Laugh! Laugh! Is the demand: Not a word must be uttered that looks like instruction, or a sentence which ought to be remembered" (p. x). In her retirement, Cowley returned to Tiverton, where, one morning each week, she held an open house for women only that was said to be well attended. On March 11, 1809, she died at the age of sixty-six of a liver ailment. At the time of her death, her son had become a lawyer and her only surviving daughter was living in India, married to the Reverend Dr. Brown, provost of the College of Calcutta.

The performances of Cowley's plays did not end with her death or in the eighteenth century. Cowley's more popular plays continued to be regularly performed on the London and provincial stages into the nineteenth century. They were also performed in the United States throughout the same time period. *The Belle's Stratagem* continues to draw audiences. In 2003, it was performed by the Prospect Theater Company at the West End Theatre in New York City. The *New York Times* reviewer Hampton Wilborn called it a "delightful discovery" and labeled Letitia Hardy the "prototype of the liberated woman." The director Davis McCallum then took the play to San Francisco, where it ran for one month at the Angus Bowman Theatre as part of the Oregon Shakespeare Festival's 2005 season. New York City's Juggernaut Theater Company in 2003 launched a campaign to promote female playwrights from the seventeenth and eighteenth centuries, offering free play readings and discussions of plays by five female playwrights, including Cowley's *The Belle's Stratagem.* But modern interest in Cowley has not been found solely in large cities. In 2008, the American Players Theater in Spring Green, Wisconsin, included *The Belle's Stratagem* on its summer repertoire lineup

Selected Bibliography

WORKS OF HANNAH COWLEY

PLAYS BY PREMIERE DATE
The Runaway, comedy (1776)
Who's the Dupe?, farce (1779)
Albina, Countess Raimond, tragedy (1779)
The Belle's Stratagem, comedy (1780)
The School for Eloquence, interlude (1780)
The World As It Goes, comedy (1781), and *Second Thoughts*

HANNAH COWLEY

Are Best, comedy (1781; a rewrite of *The World As It Goes*)

Which Is the Man?, comedy (1782)

A Bold Stroke for a Husband, comedy (1783)

More Ways Than One, comedy (1784)

School for Graybeards, comedy (1786)

The Fate of Sparta, tragedy (1788)

A Day in Turkey, comedy (1792)

The Town Before You, comedy (1795)

First Editions of Individual Published Plays

The Runaway, A Comedy: As It Is Acted at the Theatre-Royal in Drury-Lane. London: Printed for the author; And Sold by Mr. Dodsley, in Pall-Mall; Mr. Becket, and Mr. Cadell, in the Strand; Mr. Longman, in Pater-Noster-Row; and Carnan and Newbery, in St. Paul's Church-Yard, 1776.

Who's the Dupe? A Farce: As It Is Acted at the Theatre-Royal in Drury-Lane. London: Printed For J. Dodsley, L. Davis, W. Owen, S. Crowder, T. Longman, T. Cadell, T. Becket, and Messrs. Carnan and Newbery, 1779.

Albina, Countess Raimond; A Tragedy, By Mrs. Cowley; As it is Performed at the Theatre-Royal in the Haymarket. London: Printed by T. Spilsbury for J. Dodsley, R. Faulder & others, 1779.

The Belle's Stratagem, A Comedy, As Acted at the Theatre-Royal in Covent-Garden. London: Printed for T. Cadell, in the Strand, 1782.

Which Is the Man? A Comedy, As Acted at Theatre-Royal in Covent-Garden. London: C. Dilly, 1783.

A Bold Stroke for a Husband, A Comedy, As Acted at the Theatre Royal, in Covent Garden. London: Printed by M. Scott for T. Evans, 1784.

More Ways Than One, A Comedy, As Acted at the Theatre Royal in Covent Garden. London: Printed by J. Davis for T. Evans, 1784.

A School for Greybeards; or, the Mourning Bride: A Comedy, In Five Acts. As Performed at the Theatre Royal, Drury-Lane. London: Printed for G. G. J. & J. Robinson, 1786.

The Fate of Sparta; or, The Rival Kings. A Tragedy. As it is Acted at the Theatre-Royal in Drury-Lane. London: Printed for G. G. J. & J. Robinson, 1788.

A Day in Turkey; or, The Russian Slaves. A Comedy, As Acted at the Theatre Royal, in Covent Garden. London: Printed for G. G. J. & J. Robinson, 1792.

The Town Before You, A Comedy, As Acted at the Theatre-Royal, Covent-Garden. London: Printed by G. Woodfall, for T. N. Longman, Paternoster-Row, 1795.

Poetry

The Maid of Arragon. London: L. Davis, et al., 1780.

The Scottish Village; or, Pitcairne Green. London: G. G. J. & J. Robinson, 1786.

The Poetry of Anna Matilda. Containing "A Tale For Jealousy," "The Funeral," Her Correspondence with Della Crusca, and Several Other Poetical Pieces. London: John Bell, 1788.

The British Album: Containing the Poems of Della Crusca [Robert Merry], Anna Matilda [Hannah Cowley], Arley, Benedict, the Bard [Edward Jerningham], Which Were Originally Published Under the Title of "The Poetry of the World." 3rd ed. Dublin: B. Dornin, 1790. (There are at least four British and one American editions of this collection.)

"Written by Mrs. Cowley, on Reading the Verses of Lady Manners to Solitude." In *Poems By Lady Manners.* London: John Booth, et al., 1794.

The Siege of Acre: An Epic Poem in Six Books. London: J. Debritt, 1801. Revised 1810.

"Invocation to Horror." In *Gothic Readings: The First Wave, 1764–1840.* Edited by Rictor Norton. London: Leicester University Press, 2000. Pp. 230–232.

Collected Works

Works of Mrs. Cowley: Dramas and Poems. 3 vols. London: Wilkie and Robinson, 1813. (Vol. 1 includes the [anonymous] editors' preface, pp. v–xxi.)

The Plays of Hannah Cowley. Edited by Frederick M. Link. 2 vols. New York: Garland, 1979.

Works of Mrs. Cowley: Dramas and Poems. Brown University Women Writers Project (http://www.wwp.brown.edu).

Hughes, Derek, ed. *Eighteenth-Century Women Playwrights.* Vol. 5. London: Pickering & Chatto, 2001. (Includes *The Runaway, The Belle's Stratagem, A Bold Stroke for a Husband,* and *The Town Before You.*)

Selected Individual Plays in Anthologies

The Belle's Stratagem. In *The British Theatre; or, A Collection of Plays, Which Are Acted at The Theatres Royal, Drury Lane, Covent Garden, and Haymarket.* Edited by Elizabeth Inchbald. Vol. 19. London: Longman, 1808.

The Belle's Stratagem. In *The New English Drama.* Edited by William Oxberry. Vol. 28.. Boston: Wells and Lilly, 1822. (With prefatory remarks by Oxberry.)

The Belle's Stratagem. In *Davidson's Shilling Volume of Cumberland's Plays: With Remarks, Biographical and Critical.* Vol. 1. London: G. H. Davidson, 1849.

The Belle's Stratagem. In *Other Eighteenth Century: English Women of Letters 1660–1800.* Edited by Robert W. Uphaus and Gretchen M. Foster. East Lansing, Mich.: Colleagues, 1991.

The Belle's Stratagem. In *Meridian Anthology of Restoration and Eighteenth-Century Plays by Women.* Edited by Katharine M. Rogers. New York: Penguin, 1994.

Who's the Dupe? In *Broadview Anthology of Restoration and Eighteenth-Century Literature in English.* Edited by Noel Chevalier, David Oakleaf, and Joyce Rappaport. Peterborough, Ont.: Broadview, 2001.

The Belle's Stratagem. In *Broadview Anthology of Restoration and Early Eighteenth-Century Drama*. Edited by J. Douglas Canfield and Maja-Lisa Von Sneidern. Peterborough, Ont.: Broadview, 2001.

A Bold Stroke for a Husband. In *Broadview Anthology of Romantic Drama*. Edited by Jeffrey N. Cox and Michael Gamer. Peterborough, Ont.: Broadview, 2003.

The Belle's Stratagem. In *Major Voices: 18th Century Women Playwrights*. Edited by Michael Caines. New Milford, Conn.: Toby Press, 2004.

CRITICAL AND BIOGRAPHICAL STUDIES

Anderson, Misty Gale. "Laughing Between the Lines: Women Writers and Comic Texts in England, 1662–1801." Ph.D. diss., Vanderbilt University, 1995.

———. *Female Playwrights and Eighteenth-Century Comedy: Negotiating Marriage on the London Stage*. New York: Palgrave, 2002.

Bernbaum, Ernest. *The Drama of Sensibility: A Sketch of the History of English Sentimental Comedy and Domestic Tragedy, 1696–1780*. 1915. Reprint, Gloucester, U.K.: Peter Smith, 1958.

Bevis, Richard. *The Laughing Tradition: Stage Comedy in Garrick's Day*. Athens: University of Georgia Press, 1980.

Cowley, Hannah. Preface to *Albina, Countess Raimond*. London: T. Spilsbury, et al., 1779.

———. Preface to *The Town Before You*. London: Longman, 1795.

———. Introduction to *Albina*. In *Bell's British Theatre*. Vol. 29. London: George Cawthorn, 1797.

Cox, Jeffrey N., and Michael Gamer, eds. Introduction to *The Broadview Anthology of Romantic Drama*. Peterborough, Ont.: Broadview, 2003.

Donkin, Ellen. *Getting into the Act: Women Playwrights in London, 1776–1829*. London: Routledge, 1995.

East, Joyce. "Dramatic Works of Hannah Cowley." Ph.D. diss., University of Kansas, 1979.

———. "Mrs. Hannah Cowley, Playwright." In *Eighteenth-Century Women and the Arts*. Edited by Frederick M. Keener and Susan E. Lorsch. New York: Greenwood, 1988. Pp. 67–76.

Effenbein, Andrew. "Lesbian Aestheticism on the Eighteenth-Century Stage." *Eighteenth-Century Life* 25:1–16 (winter 2001).

Gagen, Jean. "Hannah Cowley." In *Dictionary of Literary Biography,* 3rd series. Vol. Vol. 89: *Restoration and Eighteenth-Century Dramatists*. Edited by Paula R. Backscheider. Detroit: Gale, 1989. Pp. 82–105.

———. "The Weaker Sex: Hannah Cowley's Treatment of Men in Her Comedies of Courtship and Marriage." *University of Mississippi Studies in English* 8:107–116 (1990).

Genest, John. *Some Account of the English Stage*. London: C. Chapple, 1808.

Hogan, Charles Beecher. *London Stage, 1776–1800: A Critical Introduction*. Carbondale: Southern Illinois University Press, 1968.

Link, Frederick M., ed. Introduction to *The Plays of Hannah Cowley*. Vol 1. New York: Garland, 1979. Pp. v–xlvi.

Macmillan, Dougald. "Rise of Social Comedy in the Eighteenth Century." *Philological Quarterly* 41:330–338 (1962).

Rogers, Katharine M., ed. *Meridian Anthology of Restoration and Eighteenth-Century Plays by Women*. New York: Penguin, 1994.

Rubik, Margarete, ed. *Early Women Dramatists: 1550–1800*. New York: St. Martin's, 1998.

Schneider, Ben Ross, Jr. *Index to The London Stage: 1660–1800*. Carbondale: Southern Illinois University Press, 1979.

Spencer, Jane. "Adapting Aphra Behn: Hannah Cowley's *A School for Greybeards* and *The Lucky Chance*." *Women's Writing: The Elizabethan to Victorian Period* 2, no. 3:221–234 (1995).

Stanton, Judith Phillips. "Statistical Profile of Women Writing in English from 1660–1800." In *Eighteenth-Century Women and the Arts*. Edited by Frederick M. Keener and Susan E. Lorsch. New York: Greenwood, 1988. Pp. 247–254.

———. "'This New-Found Path Attempting': Women Dramatists in England, 1660–1800." In *Curtain Calls: British and American Women and the Theatre, 1660–1820*. Edited by Mary Anne Schofield, and Cecilia Macheski. Athens: Ohio University Press, 1991. Pp. 325–354.

Uphaus, Robert W., and Gretchen M. Foster, eds. *The "Other" Eighteenth-Century: English Women of Letters, 1660–1800*. East Lansing, Mich.: Colleages, 1991.

Wilborn, Hampton. "The Days of Bons Mots and Arranged Marriages." *New York Times,* October 7, 2003. P. 5.

ERASMUS DARWIN

(1731—1802)

Adam Komisaruk

ALTHOUGH HIS REPUTATION has been eclipsed by that of his grandson Charles, Erasmus Darwin boasted one of the most versatile minds in eighteenth-century Britain. As a practicing physician, prolific inventor and essayer of natural history, he left an impression on nearly every branch of scientific knowledge, especially zoology. Darwin's literary *magnum opus,* and the synthesis of his myriad interests, was the epic poem *The Botanic Garden*; its themes were continued in his chronicle of human society, *The Temple of Nature.* Darwin also composed significant prose works on such subjects as botany, medicine and education.

BIOGRAPHY

Erasmus Darwin was born on December 12, 1731 at Elston, Nottinghamshire, the youngest of Robert and Elizabeth Darwin's seven children. His father was a barrister, antiquarian, and all-around "person of curiosity" who in 1718 discovered the first known fossil of a Jurassic reptile, *Plesiosaurus dolichodeirus* (Royal Society, p. 963). The young Erasmus, called "Mus" or "Rasee," was inclined toward poetry, scientific inquiry, and getting into scrapes: he once sustained serious injuries while playing with gunpowder. He attended Chesterfield School, St. John's College (Cambridge), and the Edinburgh Medical School, eventually affecting the title (but not, it appears, earning the degree) of MD. Eschewing the glamour of London, he hung out his medical shingle in Nottingham, then Lichfield. "Fond of sacrificing to both Bacchus and Venus" in his salad days, he came to repudiate alcohol and, in 1757, married seventeen-year-old Mary "Polly" Howard ("Biographical Memoirs," p. 458).

In the 1760s Darwin began his three-decade association with what would become the Lunar Society, an informal coterie of industrialists and natural philosophers who met at Birmingham every month on the Monday afternoon nearest the full moon. They included, at various points, the businessman Matthew Boulton, who built an ironworks near Birmingham; Richard Lovell Edgeworth, an inventor and the father of the novelist Maria Edgeworth; the chemist James Keir; Joseph Priestley, who discovered oxygen and ammonia; the Derbyshire geologist John Whitehurst; James Watt, who designed an improved steam engine; and Josiah Wedgwood, manufacturer of the exceptional pottery that bears his name today. The creative synergy of the Lunar circle represented the eighteenth-century industrial revolution at its most advanced yet. For example, Wedgwood made his pottery out of minerals unearthed by Whitehurst, colored it with pigments ground in a horizontal windmill of Darwin's devising, then shipped the finished pieces along a canal network for whose construction Darwin had petitioned the government, with the Boulton-built Watt engine powering the boats. Darwin's productivity in this period (one of his cannier inventions was a speaking machine consisting of a wooden mouth, leather lips, and a silk vocal cord vibrated by a bellows) suggests how invigorating he found the collaborative enterprise that would inform his mature writings.

Polly died of a gall bladder disease in 1770, leaving Darwin to raise their three young sons. He fathered two illegitimate daughters by his housekeeper, Mary Parker, and was devastated when his son Charles, a star medical student not yet twenty, succumbed to an infection contracted in the autopsy chamber. His creativity unbowed, he drew up plans for an electrotherapy machine and a pantograph that could copy writing, adding to the artificial bird and the canal lift he had invented earlier in the 1770s. In 1781 he married Elizabeth Pole, mother of four from a previous marriage, who would bear him seven more children. As a love offering he had built a botanic garden that would come to symbolize his newest intellectual pursuit. Inspired by rustic pleasures, Darwin embarked on a massive translation of Linnaeus, whose taxonomy of plants was already gaining traction in England. *A System of Vegetables* was published around 1783, *The Families of Plants* in 1787; both were credited simply to "a Botanical Society at Lichfield." To disseminate his Linneaean findings to a popular audience, Darwin decided to "inlist Imagination under the banner of Science" (*Botanic Garden* 1.iii). His first major poem, *The Loves of the Plants*, wittily employed metaphors of human courtship to describe the reproductive cycles of hundreds of different flowers. The radical Joseph Johnson published it in 1789 after a five-year hesitation by Darwin, who asked that his own name be left off the title page to protect his medical reputation. Reception of *The Loves* was enthusiastic. Darwin wrote a sequel, *The Economy of Vegetation*, this time singing the praises of British industry as a dance of supernatural creatures. The two volumes were bound together and released under the title *The Botanic Garden* in 1792, with *The Economy* as Part I and *The Loves* as Part II. Johnson was the publisher, and would be of all Darwin's subsequent works; the Swiss artist Henry Fuseli designed some of the illustrations; William Blake worked as one of the engravers.

Had he contributed nothing but the resplendent *Botanic Garden,* Darwin's place in the literary pantheon of his day would probably have been secure. His final decade, however, was to prove a fertile one. He wrote a moderately progressive *Plan for the Conduct of Female Education, in Boarding Schools* for the benefit of his daughters, Susanna and Mary Parker, who had recently opened such an institution in the Derbyshire town of Ashbourne; it was distributed privately in 1794, and published by Johnson in 1797. *Zoonomia; or, The Laws of Organic Life* (Part I, 1794; Parts II and III, 1796) was Darwin's massive treatise on the biological functions of animals, notable chiefly for its proto-evolutionary theory. Where the Linnaean texts had focused on the classification and the *Botanic Garden* on the sex lives of plants, *Phytologia; or, The Philosophy of Agriculture and Gardening* (1800) surveyed their entire physiology, as well as the harnessing of those processes for human advantage. Published posthumously, *The Temple of Nature; or, The Origin of Society* (1803) celebrated the ways that species and civilizations alike come into existence.

Darwin expired on 18 April 1802, most likely of a lung infection. He did not live to see the birth of Charles Robert, one of his twenty-seven grandchildren, whose voyage aboard the HMS *Beagle* was only twenty-nine years away.

THE BOTANIC GARDEN: THE LOVES
OF THE PLANTS

The Loves of the Plants consists of four cantos, alternating with three prose dialogues in which an unnamed author and bookseller debate the nature of poetry. There are also annotations in which Darwin expounds on scientific topics of particular interest to him.

Like all Darwin's poems, *The Loves of the Plants* is written in the venerable form known as heroic couplets (rhymed iambic pentameter). Its style is grandiose rather than grand. To readers, the presence of epic conventions—the invocation to the muse, the description of familiar things by means of stylized epithets, the extended similes, the "machinery" of supernatural interlopers—may have called to mind Homer, Virgil, and Milton less than the tongue-in-cheek tone of Alexander Pope's *The Rape of the Lock* (1712-1717). Darwin's machinery even comes from the same source as Pope's—the mythology of the Rosicrucians, a mystic order allegedly founded by Christian Rosenkreuz in the late fifteenth century. According to this system, a different kind of spirit inhabits each of the four elements: the gnomes preside over earth; sylphs, air; nymphs, water; and salamanders, fire.

Linnaeus distinguished over twenty thousand classes of flowers according to the number, shape, position, and size of their "parts of fructification" (their male organs or stamens, and their female organs or pistils) (*Botanic* 2.217n). Darwin's technique is to catalog roughly a hundred of them, each with a poetical description (rarely more than a dozen lines) supplemented by a scientific footnote (often considerably longer, and distinct from the "additional notes" that end the volume). The unique reproductive mechanism of each flower is allegorized as some permutation of human lovers. The balm (genus *Melissa*) has one pistil and four stamens, two of which stand higher than the other two; Darwin therefore personifies "Melissa" as a lovely maiden with two knights and two squires vying for her attentions. The lichen, because it grows on barren rocks and has no discernible flower, practices "clandestine marriage":

Retiring LICHEN climbs the topmost stone,
And drinks the aerial solitude alone.—
Bright shine the stars unnumber'd *o'er her head*,
And the cold moon-beam gilds her flinty bed;
While round the rifted rocks hoarse whirlwinds breathe,
And dark with thunder sail the clouds *beneath*.—
The steepy path her plighted swain pursues,
And tracks her light step o'er the imprinted dews;
Delighted Hymen gives his torch to blaze,
Winds round the crags, and lights the mazy ways;
Sheds o'er their *secret* vows his influence chaste,
And decks with roses the admiring waste.
(*Botanic* 2.45–46: 1.347–358)

Botanical sexuality, however, forms only one layer of this elaborate narrative. A passage on the rubia or madder herb (cultivated for red pigment) leads to a discussion of dyeing fabric in a cauldron, which reminds Darwin of Aeson's resurrection by the enchanted waters of Medea, which occasions a note on "the efficacy of warm bathing in retarding the progress of old age" (*Botanic* 2.50n). Observing air bladders in the leaves of the ulva or sea lettuce, Darwin ponders similar structures in the haddock, the eggs of chickens, and the faulty diving bell in which its own inventor, John Day, drowned. From mythology to geology, from music to the abolition debate, Darwin leaves scarcely a disciplinary stone unturned. For all his concern with taxonomy, his transitions from subject to subject seem governed more often by stream of consciousness than by system.

This digressive tendency characterizes Darwin's entire corpus. It could be written off as the product of a restless mind were there not a serious point to be made about it. Darwin subscribes to a radical materialism—the belief that the laws of matter govern all operations of the universe. The mind itself is a machine that exists on the same continuum as the body. The English philosopher John Locke had held that we form no ideas except through the evidence of the five senses. In the eighteenth century David Hartley elaborated how these simpler ideas undergo a sort of chain reaction to form complex ones—a theory that came to be known as associative psychology. Darwin does more than make this argument: he enacts it. Digression is a fitting, even necessary, mode to describe a world in which there is no phenomenon not potentially connected to every other. Dreams seem to interest Darwin because they exemplify the associative process: as he says in a passage accompanying Fuseli's famous image *The Night-Mare*, "the WILL presides not in the bowers of SLEEP" (*Botanic* 2.127: 3.74). When one is asleep, the "painful desire to exert the voluntary motions" produces the sensation of an incubus, or nightmare, pressing on one's body (*Botanic* 2.128n). For Darwin, however, even the monstrous can become a thing of wonder—just as poisonous plants such as the foxglove or poppy, he reminds us, can be medicinal if taken in moderation.

THE BOTANIC GARDEN: THE ECONOMY OF VEGETATION

The Economy of Vegetation is the longer, better-organized and more accomplished half of *The Botanic Garden*. Like *The Loves of the Plants,* it consists of four cantos narrated primarily by the Goddess of Botany. Although it lacks the prose "interludes" of *The Loves,* its "philosophical notes" are more extensive. Darwin devotes each canto to one of the four elements with its corresponding Rosicrucian entity, describing the natural phenomena peculiar to that element and the human inventions that have harnessed, employed, or emulated them. Thus, in the first canto (fire) we find disquisitions on lightning and the electrical experiments of Benjamin Franklin; in the second (earth), the precipitation of limestone and the Venus de Medici; in the third (water), natural springs and the use of controlled flooding in Chinese agriculture; in the fourth (air), the chemistry of wind changes and the balloon launches of the Montgolfier brothers.

Darwin both reviews and gives an original cast to the leading scientific controversies of his day. What he gets wrong, therefore, is often as suggestive as what he gets right. One such debate concerns the nature of combustion. According to followers of Georg Ernst Stahl (1659–1734), combustion occurred when a heated substance released an impurity called phlogiston into the air. Antoine-Laurent de Lavoisier (1743–1794) debunked the phlogiston theory by demonstrating that, instead, the air added something—oxygen—to the heated substance. Darwin notices, however, that Lavoisier's own theory of heat (which we now understand as the kinetic energy of molecules) involves the flow of a mysterious mass called calorique, essentially phlogiston under a different name. Thus, the pressing question for Darwin concerns not the existence of phlogiston but its nature and the number of its varieties; he finds it "not yet determinable whether heat and light be different materials, or modifications of the same materials" (*Botanic* 1.52n).

Another subject of interest to Darwin is geology, about which there were two major schools of thought in the eighteenth century. Neptunism, a theory advanced by Abraham Gottlob Werner (1749–1817), held that all rocks were sedimentary, precipitated from the ocean, and that volcanoes were caused by burning coal beds. Under the auspices of James Hutton (1726–1797) it was supplanted by Plutonism or Vulcanism, the theory that rocks are formed by heat in the bowels of the earth. As usual, however, Darwin develops his own synthesis of the two. A passage on volcanoes reads as follows:

GNOMES! as you pass'd beneath the labouring soil,
The guards and guides of Nature's chemic toil,
YOU saw, deep-sepulchred in dusky realms,
Which Earth's rock-ribbed ponderous vault o'erwhelms,
With self-born fires the mass fermenting glow,
And flame-wing'd sulphurs quit the earths below.
(*Botanic* 1.98: 2.271–276)

Thus, although Darwin inclines toward the Plutonist camp, he misrepresents the "subterranean fires"—which are in fact the result of pressure—as a kind of spontaneous combustion (*Botanic* 1.107n).

Darwin's politics reflect a sympathy, common to the left-leaning thinkers of the Lunar circle, with the revolutionary fervor of the late eighteenth century. He hails the march of liberty from America (which Benjamin Franklin helped electrify both scientifically and politically) to Ireland (which achieved parliamentary independence in 1782) to France (whose rebellion against the strictures of monarchism and Roman Catholicism is usually dated to 1789). He condemns slavery, albeit on sentimental grounds that can sidestep questions of economic justice. Thus, his discussion of the famous abolitionist cameo manufactured by Wedgwood—an image of a supplicating slave beneath the motto "Am I Not a Man and a Brother?"—overlooks Wedgwood's own dubious relationship to labor, including his authoritarian factory-management style and use of raw materials from Australian penal colonies. Darwin even flirts with vegetarianism, positing the "destruction of other living animals" as "contributing less to the sum of general happiness" (*Botanic* 1.33n). Such inclinations were radical enough to draw the derision of the conservative weekly *The Anti-Jacobin,* which in April 1798 published "The Loves of the Triangles" by one "Mr. Higgins" (probably George Canning, John Hookham Frere, and George Ellis, politicians who helped found the journal). This rather accurate parody—describing the amours of geometric forms—skewers what it regards as Darwin's overwrought poetics, middlebrow erudition, and reckless revolutionism at one stroke:

Yet why, ELLIPSIS, at thy fate repine?
More lasting bliss, securer joys are thine.

Though to each fair his treacherous wish may stray,
Though each, in turn, may seize a transient sway,
'Tis thine with mild coercion to restrain,
Twine round his struggling heart, and bind with endless chain.
Thus, happy France! in thy regenerate land,
Where TASTE with RAPINE saunters hand in hand;
Where, nursed in seats of innocence and bliss,
REFORM greets TERROR with fraternal kiss....

("Loves," lines 124–133)

Though sometimes branded atheistical in his day, Darwin hardly wants spiritual curiosity. Like the work of William Warburton, William Blake, and Richard Payne Knight, *The Economy* eschews sectarianism and advances a syncretic mythology that stresses the harmony of different symbolic traditions. Most of these traditions, Darwin argues, borrow their imagery from the natural world: "From having observed the gradual evolution of the young animal or plant from its egg or seed; and afterwards its successive advances to its more perfect state, or maturity; philosophers of all ages seem to have imagined, that the great world itself had likewise its infancy and its gradual progress to maturity" (*Botanic* 1.8n). Likewise, the transmigration or immortality of the spirit is an idea that probably comes from the "perpetual circulation of matter in the growth and dissolution of vegetable and animal bodies" (*Botanic* 1.122n). Thus, the gods of all religions are essentially fertility gods; sex itself is a sacrament. In one inspired passage, Darwin pays tribute to the winged child Eros or Cupid (a primordial life-giver rather than the lewd prankster of the popular imagination) as represented on the Portland Vase, a first-century Roman urn of which Wedgwood had made an exquisite copy.

A PLAN FOR THE CONDUCT OF FEMALE EDUCATION

Darwin's boarding-school manual contains forty short chapters, the last of which is a suggested bibliography for various disciplines. Sprinkled throughout are advertisements for his daughters' Ashbourne Hall (including a fee schedule and garden-view frontispiece) and for his own scientific writings. The principle on which the plan operates may be stated simply: "strength of mind join'd with strength of body" (*Plan*, p. 118). To foster these twin strengths, Darwin prescribes a liberal-arts curriculum (literature, the English and Romance languages, world and natural history, geography, arithmetic, botany, chemistry, mineralogy) coupled with moral instruction, deportment coaching, and a regimen of exercise and amusement. He also makes recommendations concerning proper ventilation of the schoolhouse; dress; diet; and the prevention and treatment of bad posture, lisping, stammering (Darwin's own affliction), squinting, muscular tics, chilblains, and rheumatism.

A recurring theme in Darwin's work is the centrality of pleasure to human development. Education is no exception. Games will facilitate children's mastery of grammar and geography; natural history lessons may employ Thomas Bewick's popular "account of quadrupeds, with woodprints of the animals, and amusing tale-pieces to the sections" (*Plan*, p. 24). Ever the empiricist, Darwin suggests that applying abstract concepts to the observable world will itself be pleasurable to children: basic money-management lessons can bring mathematical principles to life, and "the various arts and manufactories, which adorn and enrich this country, should occasionally be shewn and explain'd to young persons, as so many ingenious parts of experimental philosophy; as well as from their immediately contributing to the convenience of life, and to the wealth of the nations, which have invented or established them" (*Plan*, p. 43).

The *Plan* is not altogether free of the prejudices for which Mary Wollstonecraft, in *A Vindication of the Rights of Woman* (1792), faulted other educational theorists such as John Locke and Jean-Jacques Rousseau. There is no shame in being a learned lady, Darwin insists; still,

> The female character should possess the mild and retiring virtues rather than the bold and dazzling ones; great eminence in almost any thing is sometimes injurious to a young lady; whose temper and disposition should appear to be pliant rather than robust; to be ready to take impressions rather than to be decidedly mark'd; as great apparent strength of character, however excellent, is liable to

alarm both her own and the other sex; and to create admiration rather than affection.

(*Plan,* p. 10)

Accordingly, young women should acquire traditional "accomplishments" (skill in music, art, dancing, embroidery), though not to the point of vanity or to the exclusion of deeper learning (*Plan,* p. 12). Aesthetic tracts by Edmund Burke and William Hogarth should teach them about beauty—not so much how to judge its universal standards (a capacity defined as "taste") as how to conform to those standards themselves (*Plan,* p. 25). A graceful suppleness of form is preferred; physical exercise should help girls grow tall but not too "robust and muscular" (*Plan,* p. 68). In all, the destiny for which Darwin seems to be preparing women is a domestic one. Although Wollstonecraft admittedly glorifies the roles of wife and mother, she emphasizes the cultivation of reason as the key to their fulfillment, whereas Darwin emphasizes the cultivation of "charms" (*Plan,* p. 32).

ZOONOMIA

Zoonomia (pronounced ZOH-a-NOH-mi-a) draws its title from the Greek words for "animal" and "laws." At nearly 1,400 pages, it is Darwin's longest prose work and no less than an attempt to "reduce the facts belonging to ANIMAL LIFE into classes, orders, genera, and species; and, by comparing them with each other, to unravel the theory of diseases" (Z 1.1). Part I covers such matters as the origin of our ideas, the nature of the will, the ways in which the will may be compromised (sleep, drunkenness, disease, etc.) and the function of the bodily systems (circulatory, digestive, etc.)—a kind of *Aristotle's Physics* or *Gray's Anatomy* for the late eighteenth century. Part II, then, is its *Merck Manual* and Part III its *Physician's Desk Reference*—taxonomies, respectively, of diseases and their treatments.

Part I of *Zoonomia* begins by dividing the natural world into "two essences or substances; one of which may be termed spirit, and the other matter. The former of these possesses the power to commence or produce motion, and the latter to receive and communicate it" (Z 1.5). No metaphysician, however, Darwin pursues the materialist hypothesis as far as possible, attributing passive and active "motion" alike to physiological causes. Thought itself works like a muscle: "external objects" "irritate" our "organs of sense," whose "animal motions or configurations" constitute our ideas (Z 1.21). (These ideas actually reside in the brain, or "sensorium," rather than in the peripheral organs; still, "we have no other inlets to knowledge but our perceptions" (Z 1.28). When the original objects are absent, our imagination can duplicate the motions they previously stimulated. From the recapitulation of concrete ideas we may also form abstractions (e. g., sweetness from sugar) or combinations that we have not experienced per se (e.g., the monster Caliban from "the nastiness and gluttony of a hog, the stupidity and obstinacy of an ass, with the fur and awkwardness of a bear" [Z 1.133]).

Pleasure tends to be sought and pain avoided. Any motion that results from "desire" or "aversion" is "voluntary," says Darwin, "whether we have the power of restraining that action, or not" (Z 1.420). Thus, sneezing and vomiting are "voluntary" because they help to expel an "offending cause" (Z 1.424). Although his own terminology is not consistent even within *Zoonomia,* Darwin's radical redefinition of "volition" construes the entire created world as interconnected through the pursuit of pleasure. Humans still hold pride of place in this great chain of being; for instance, we can occupy ourselves with "the means of procuring future bliss, or of avoiding future misery," whereas beasts live only in the present (Z 1.59). Still, the difference between the kingdoms seems to lie with the extent of their volition and not the kind. In one striking passage, Darwin defines plants as "inferior or less perfect animals," with analogous anatomical structures (roots for milk ducts, leaves for lungs, seeds for eggs, etc.) that recognize "agreeable" and "disagreeable sensation" (Z 1.102–103). His argument concerning vegetable reproduction—that it is driven by the very "sensation of love" rather than "mechanical attraction"—is more audacious than that in his largely allegorical *Loves of the Plants* (Z 1.106).

One of the most important questions that Darwin takes up in *Zoonomia* had persisted since at least the time of Aristotle: How does an organism grow to maturity? According to the doctrine of "preformation," the germ (egg or sperm) cell already contained a miniature version of the organism (called a "homunculus" in the case of humans), which needed only to increase in size. Adherents of "epigenesis," on the other hand, held that an adult organism developed through the progressive differentiation of originally undifferentiated cells. In his long thirty-ninth chapter, "Of Generation," Darwin sides firmly with the epigenesists: "the fetus or embryon is formed by apposition of new parts, and not by the distention of a primordial nest of germs, included one within another, like the cups of a conjurer" (Z 1.506). He situates himself within a subsidiary debate, however, more common to the preformationists: that between the "spermatists" ("animalculists") and the "ovists," who held that all embryonic material comes, respectively, from the sperm and the egg. Darwin's conclusion is that the male parent contributes the entire embryo, the female only its "apparatus for nutriment and for oxygenation" (Z 1.488). In the third edition of 1801, Darwin significantly revises these findings, acknowledging that both male and female "generative secretions," called "formative fibrils" and "formative molecules" respectively, must mingle to shape the embryo (4th American ed. 1818, based on 3rd London ed. of 1801, 1.426).

What drives the development of the organism is, once again, pleasure and pain—the "animal appetencies" (Z 1.532). Darwin believes "the primordium, or rudiment of the embryon, as secreted from the blood of the parent, to consist of a simple living filament ... endued with the capability of being excited into action by certain kinds of stimulus" (Z 1.496). "By the pleasurable sensations attending those irritations, and by the exertions in consequence of painful sensations," this material achieves a "new organization, or accretion of parts" with "new kinds of irritability," and so on (Z 1.499, 1.496). This process continues outside the womb, as "all the parts of the body endeavour to grow, or to make additional parts to themselves throughout our lives" (Z 1.500). Likewise, anticipating the late-nineteenth-century formulation that "ontogeny recapitulates phylogeny" (i.e., the development of the individual organism mirrors in miniature the history of the species), Darwin postulates all creatures as having developed, diversified and intermingled from a "single living filament" (Z 1.493). Over the life cycle of the frog, the tadpole grows legs and loses its tail; so over evolutionary time has the original "filament" variously shot forth the human foot, the eagle's talon, and the tiger's claw. Evidence for "the gradual formation and improvement of the animal world" includes not only these anatomical parallels but also vestigial structures such as the "teats of all male quadrupeds, to which no use can be now assigned" (Z 1.512).

Darwin even accepts the contention, credited to the English philosopher David Hume, "that the world itself might have been generated, rather than created; that is, it might have been gradually produced from very small beginnings, increasing by the activity of its inherent principles, rather than by a sudden evolution of the whole by the Almighty fire" (Z 1.513). In so doing, however, Darwin affirms rather than negates a divine presence in whom this chain of being terminates: "What a magnificent idea of the infinite power of THE GREAT ARCHITECT! THE CAUSE OF CAUSES! PARENT OF PARENTS! ENS ENTIUM [Being of beings]!" (Z 1.513). Darwin's God is rather like that of the Deists, a cosmic watchmaker by whom the universe is first "endued with animality" and then allowed "to improve by its own inherent activity ... delivering down those improvements by generation to its posterity, world without end!" (Z 1.509).

In the course of discussing how all natural phenomena are interlinked through cause and effect, Darwin differentiates "proximate causes," "remote causes," "proximate effects," and "remote effects." For example, when we look at a sunrise, the light rays are the remote cause, the energy of the nervous system the proximate cause, the excitement of the optic nerve the proximate effect, and the pleasurable or painful sensation the remote effect; these four operations together constitute our "sensitive idea" of the sunrise (Z 1.536). In Part II of *Zoonomia,* Darwin applies the same logic to nosology, or the classification of diseases. He acknowledges that tracts on this subject have been written before but hopes to clear up some of their confusion. Proximate causes, he says, are the proper basis for such a system; they allow us best to understand the behavior of known diseases, discover new ones, and cure both.

Darwin identifies four "classes" of diseases: those of "irritation," "sensation," "volition," and "association." He subdivides each class into "orders": "increased," "decreased," or (in some cases) "retrograde" actions. Each order includes several "genera" according to the bodily system involved (muscular, digestive, excretory, etc.), and each genus includes numerous "species" of individual diseases. For example, since *stranguria* (slow and painful urination) is defined not by the remote cause (a bladder stone or inflammation) but by the proximate cause of the discomfort (the extraordinary effort to discharge the urine), Darwin places it in Class II ("Diseases of Sensation"), Order I ("Increased Sensation"), Genus I ("With Increased Action of the Muscles"), Species 11—alongside other species of increased muscular activity such as sneezing, panting, hiccupping, and even childbirth (Z 2.168). An oil-and-laudanum enema is recommended. *Scorbutus* (scurvy), Darwin says, is a circulatory impairment arising from excessive salt in the diet (in fact it is an impairment of tissue formation arising from a vitamin C deficiency); it therefore belongs to Class I ("Diseases of Irritation"), Order II ("Decreased Irritation"), Genus I ("With Decreased Action of the Sanguiferous [blood-carrying] System"), Species 15— kin to hemorrhage, hemorrhoids, heart palpitations, and abnormal menstruation (Z 2.6).

Darwin's catalog of diseases includes some surprising entries. Among these are emotional afflictions such as *erotomania* ("sentimental love"), *nostalgia* (homesickness), *sympathia aliena* ("pity"), *spes religiosa* ("superstitious hope"), *lethi timor* ("fear of death"), and *orci timor* ("fear of hell"); character flaws such as *superbia stemmatis* ("pride of family"), *ambitio* ("inordinate desire of fame"), and *credulitas* (gullibility); as well as biological inevitabilities such as *desiderium pulchritudinis* ("loss of beauty") and *catameniae periodus* ("periods of menstruation") (Z 2.317–19, 2.369, 2.419). The cures are equally idiosyncratic. For *maeror* ("grief"), Darwin prescribes "the Christian doctrine of a happy immortality"; for *paupertatis timor* ("fear of poverty"), the keeping of a budget and the study of mathematics; for *ira* ("anger"), the forbearance of "loud oaths, violent upbraidings, or strong expressions of countenance, or gesticulations of the arms, or clenched fists" (Z 2.317, 2.372, 2.380).

Part II of the *Zoonomia* frequently refers to the "Articles of the Materia Medica," which constitute Part III. Here Darwin classifies medicines into the "Nutrentia," or natural substances that help the body reach and maintain its proper level of activity (as animal products, vegetables, water and air); "Incitantia," or general stimulants (as certain narcotics, heat, the passions, and exercise); "Secernentia," which stimulate secretion (as expectorants and diuretics); "Sorbentia," which stimulate absorption (sulfuric acid to reduce sweating, mercury preparations to treat ulcers); "Invertentia," which invert the order of natural motions (emetics, "fear and anxiety"); "Reverentia," which restore this order (enemas, suppositories, calmatives); and "Torpentia," which retard motion ("mucilages," "silence, darkness," cold air and warm baths) (Z 2.657–658, 2.745, 2.761).

THE TEMPLE OF NATURE

Though not so ambitious as *The Botanic Garden* or *Zoonomia,* from which it occasionally plagiarizes, Darwin's last major work may be regarded as a recapitulation and synthesis of his entire career. As its alternate title (*The Origin of Society*) suggests, *The Temple of Nature* seeks to trace human civilization back to the primordial affinities of organic matter. Its four cantos chronicle the emergence of complex systems from simpler ones ("Production of Life," "Reproduction of Life,"

"Progress of the Mind," "Of Good and Evil"), and so vindicate Darwin's universe as having "been from the beginning in a perpetual state of improvement" (*Temple,* p. 61).

Many techniques of *The Temple* are familiar from *The Botanic Garden:* the heroic couplets and epic diction; the supernatural machinery (here borrowed not from the Rosicrucian doctrine but from the Eleusinian mysteries, an agrarian ritual of ancient Greece); the elaborate allegories of scientific processes; and (notwithstanding his too-modest claim that he "does not pretend to instruct by deep researches of reasoning ... simply to amuse") the "philosophical notes" in which Darwin holds forth on subjects as wide ranging as magnetism, phonetics, sexual reproduction, and aesthetic taste (*Temple,* p. 5).

The huge desert temple of Darwin's title is located in the "cradle" of Eurasian society—"near the banks of the Mediterranean, as probably in Syria, the site of Paradise, according to the Mosaic history" (*Temple,* p. 9n). There presides the hundred-handed, hundred-breasted goddess Nature, with her female procession of Graces, Loves, and Nymphs performing their devotions. The hierophant or high priestess Urania, muse of astronomy, instructs Darwin's own muse in the history of Nature's ways; reminiscent of the late books of *Paradise Lost,* these long speeches constitute the bulk of the poem.

Having thus set the scene, Darwin has Urania describe the creation of the universe by "God the first cause":

Ere Time began, from flaming Chaos hurl'd
Rose the bright spheres, which form the circling
  world;
Earths from each sun with quick explosions burst,
And second planets issued from the first.
Then, whilst the sea at their coeval birth,
Surge over surge, involved the shoreless earth;
Nursed by warm sun-beams in primeval caves
Organic Life began beneath the waves.
(*Temple* 12: 223; 13: 227–234)

Heat, gravity and irritability (all of which Darwin persists in referring to as the movement of different kinds of "ethereal fluid") give rise to "Repulsion," "Attraction," and "Contraction" respectively (*Temple,* p. 13n). From the action of these forces on primordial matter comes "the first specks of animated earth": specks join to form threads; threads join ends to form rings; rings lengthen into tubes; tubes evolve into ducts, veins, glands, then more complex organs (*Temple* 13: 1.248). Once the nervous system is established, "Sensation," "emotions," "Volitions," and "Reason" follow (*Temple* 14: 1.270–275).

What the forces of nature give, they also take away; rather than live forever, each organism soon "reverts to elements by chemic strife" (*Temple* 21: 2.8). Yet "new life rekindles, ere the first expires," ensuring that "the long line of being never ends" (*Temple* 21: 2.14, 2.20). This reproduction is at first asexual:

Unknown to sex the pregnant oyster swells,
And coral-insects build their radiate shells;
Parturient Sires caress their infant train,
And heaven-born Storge weaves the social chain;
...
In these lone births no tender mothers blend
Their genial powers to nourish or defend;
No nutrient streams from Beauty's orbs improve
These orphan babes of solitary love;
Birth after birth the line unchanging runs,
And fathers live transmitted in their sons; ...
(*Temple* 23: 2.89–92, 2.103–108)

Storge (rhymes with "corgi") is Greek for parental love; Darwin implies (inaccurately) an etymological connection to the stork, which feeds its young by regurgitation. It is worth pausing here to emphasize the importance of the "domestic affections," as they were more commonly known, to eighteenth-century British thought. Although Darwin's culture did not of course invent the parent-child bond, it did see an unprecedented explosion in the philosophical, scientific, and creative literature on this subject, as well as a redefinition of "family" itself around the nuclear rather than the more outlying relations. The home was the rehearsal space for an effective citizenry, a state in miniature (just as the state was a family writ large). In the intimate sphere, one cultivated the capacity for fellow-feeling—variously called "sensibility," "sentiment," or "sympathy"—that stitched together the entire social fabric. In contrast to its present-day association with reason or common sense, "sensibility" was believed to originate with the five senses; literal and figurative "feeling" were intertwined (as we sometimes speak of a person being "sensible" of heat or cold). Darwin theorizes that since incubating, seeing, touching, and nursing a child all stimulate "the glandular system ... into greater natural action," they are all pleasurable (*Temple,* p. 73). From this pleasure arises the "affection from the parent to the progeny," which "existed before animals were divided into sexes, and produced the beginning of sympathetic society" (*Temple,* p. 73).

From the powers of affection and desire, Darwin continues, sprang sexual dimorphism itself:

Increasing wants the pregnant parents vex
With the fond wish to form a softer sex;
Whose milky rills with pure ambrosial food
Might charm and cherish their expected brood.
The potent wish in the productive hour
Calls to its aid Imagination's power,
O'er embryon throngs with mystic charm presides,
And sex from sex the nascent world divides,
With soft affections warms the callow trains,
And gives to laughing Love his nymphs and swains;
Whose mingling virtues interweave at length
The mother's beauty and the father's strength.

(*Temple* 23–24: 2.113–124)

The emergence of a distinct, lactiferous female allows the mammalian child to learn "Ideal Beauty from its Mother's breast" and so accelerates the stirrings of "Sentimental Love" ("the desire or sensation of beholding, embracing, and saluting a beautiful object") (*Temple* 37: 3.176, 37n). From the desire to duplicate pleasurable sensations comes the faculty of "Imitation," the next event in "Association's endless course" (*Temple* 39: 3.278). The re-creation of a sensory object as an idea is the most basic kind of imitation. The more complex kinds, which distinguish humans from the beasts, include the acquisition of language (which imitates ideas), of the arts and sciences (which imitate natural forms) and, ultimately, of social affection or "sympathy" (which imitates the ideas "we believe to exist in the minds of the persons whom we commiserate or congratulate") (*Temple,* p. 43n). Manifestations of the lattermost range from the trivial ("sympathetic" yawning) to the exalted (the invention of a "moral plan") (*Temple* 43: 3.483).

Darwin admits to having his own powers of sympathy, and even his faith, tested by a "warring world" that appears to him "one great Slaughter-house" for man, animal, and vegetable alike (*Temple* 48: 4.66). Fortunately he finds abundant consolation. From the music of Handel, to Isaac Newton's and William Herschel's disquisitions on astronomy, to Thomas Savery's water-raising and Richard Arkwright's cotton-spinning inventions, to the "patriot heroes" who "guard the freedom of the immortal Press"— human endeavor testifies again and again to the rightness of creation (*Temple* 52: 4.273, 4.286). Death is omnipresent but bestows a secret blessing by helping to keep populations at sustainable levels; besides, no living thing dies but that it decomposes to fuel the phoenix-like reconstitution of new forms. Considering that man owes his very atoms to the organic matter (inanimate as well as animate) of ages past, it is all the more appropriate that he should feel a kinship with the rest of the universe:

man should ever be the friend of man;
Should eye with tenderness all living forms,
His brother-emmets, and his sister-worms.
...
Unmeasured beds of clay, and marl, and coal,
Black ore of manganese, the zinky stone,
And dusky steel on his magnetic throne,
In deep morass, or eminence superb,
Rose from the wrecks of animal or herb;
These from their elements by Life combined
Form'd by digestion, and in glands refined,
Gave by their just excitement of the sense
The Bliss of Being to the vital Ens.

(*Temple* 55: 4.426–428, 4.438–446)

Heaven hears the devotions of the celebrant and her train as Darwin concludes the poem, confident of the eventual triumph of "Virtue's beams" over the "guilty heart," over tyranny, and over "Death's tremendous gloom" (*Temple* 56: 4.501, 506, 503).

ERASMUS DARWIN

INFLUENCE ON WILLIAM BLAKE (1757–1827)

Virtually unknown as a poet during his lifetime, Blake was a commercial engraver by trade. His services to *The Botanic Garden* were recommended by Darwin's publisher, Joseph Johnson. Of the ten plates in the 1791 *Economy of Vegetation*, Blake engraved at least five: four views of the Portland Vase, most likely modeled on one of Wedgwood's copies, and "The Fertilization of Egypt," after a design by Fuseli (the 1795 edition added another Fuseli/Blake illustration titled "Tornado"). The striking "Fertilization," which accompanies Darwin's passage on monsoons, depicts the jackal-headed god Anubis standing astride the banks of the Nile. His palms pressed together and arms held aloft, he communes with the six-pointed Dog Star, Sirius, whose annual rise coincides with the flood season. In Fuseli's original pencil sketch, a ghostly figure is visible in the background, presumably one of Darwin's water nymphs bidding the delta to yield up its bounty. Blake thoroughly reworks this figure into a threatening, bearded god with enormous wings, outstretched arms and lightning bolts darting from his fingertips; in Blake's mythological works, where he frequently appears, he is dubbed Urizen ("your reason"). Urizen symbolizes the perverted rationality that manifests itself throughout human existence (including, in Blake's view, the stern lawgiver God of Judeo-Christian tradition). The material world is his province because, unlike the realm of pure spirit, it is "finite & corrupt" (Blake, p. 39). Blake therefore appears—in what would not be the first instance of his subverting the texts he was hired to illustrate—to parlay Darwin's celebration of Nature's glories into a critique of mental tyranny. He drives home the point with a few other additions to Fuseli's design: some pyramids on Anubis' right evoke the Egyptian captivity (where Urizen seems more of an architect than a liberator) as well as the confines of Newtonian geometry; on the left, an Egyptian musical instrument called a sistrum lies on the ground, as if the poetic spirit that might prophesy truth to power has been abandoned.

Darwin's influence on Blake was not limited to their direct collaboration. One of Blake's first works, the unfinished satire *An Island in the Moon* (c. 17846–1785), pokes fun at the intellectual pretensions of the Lunar Circle with such characters as "Inflammable Gass" (possibly Joseph Priestley, discoverer of oxygen) and "Etruscan Column" (possibly Josiah Wedgwood, whose Staffordshire pottery works was called "Etruria") (Blake, pp. 449–450). Numerous floral motifs adorn *The Book of Thel* (1789), *Songs of Innocence and of Experience* (1789/1794) and *Visions of the Daughters of Albion* (1793)—early examples of the "illuminated" books where Blake etched both words and images into metal plates, then hand-watercolored each print. Vegetable love in Blake, however, is rarely so uncomplicated as in Darwin: the innocent eroticism suggested by arching vines and waking buds seems scarcely to blossom before it is blighted by jealousy, shame, and moral hypocrisy. Blake's view becomes even more jaundiced in the mature prophecies *Vala; or, The Four Zoas* (1797), *Milton* (c. 1804–1811), and *Jerusalem* (c. 1804–1820), where sexuality itself is a symptom of a spiritual existence confined in matter and governed by self-interest. In these poems Blake sometimes employs pagan fertility symbols like those depicted on the Portland Vase; whereas Darwin associates them with the primal creative impulse, Blake sees a fallen state of consciousness that, knowing only itself, breeds upon itself. Even Darwin's *storge* (and its adjective, "storgous") becomes a term of opprobrium in Blake, who regards domestic ideology (and sentimentalism generally) as bourgeois and an aggrandized form of self-love. In the mythic vision of *Milton,* Storge is the name of a river that runs past the "Mundane Egg" or "Mundane Shell," Blake's image (also appropriated from antiquity) for a material world closed off from eternity (Blake, pp. 97, 112).

INFLUENCE ON WILLIAM WORDSWORTH (1770–1850)

In March of 1798, the future poet laureate wrote to his publisher, Joseph Cottle, asking to borrow a copy of Darwin's *Zoonomia. Lyrical Ballads,* a groundbreaking volume on which Wordsworth collaborated with Samuel Taylor Coleridge, appeared that September. Darwin's influence is apparent throughout the collection, most famously in the poem "Goody Blake and Harry Gill." This ballad concerns a poor Dorsetshire spinster who, lacking enough firewood for the winter, steals twigs from a neighboring hedge. The owner, a vigorous young farmer, apprehends her in the act; she prays that he may "never more be warm," a curse he carries with him forever after (*Lyrical Ballads* 57: 100). Darwin's nearly identical story, attributed to true newspaper accounts from Warwickshire, illustrates *"Mania mutabilis"* ("Mutable madness")—one of the Class-III "Diseases of Volition" in *Zoonomia* (Z 2.317). Similarly, Darwin's entry for *"Erotomania"* ("Sentimental love") mentions the case of the Reverend James Hackman, executed in April 1779 for jealously murdering the singer Martha Ray (Reay) at a Covent Garden playhouse; the victim, grandmother to Wordsworth's young ward Basil Montagu, was the likely analogue for the heroine Martha Ray in "The Thorn" in *Lyrical Ballads* (Z 2.317). In Wordsworth's version, Martha is the jilted lover and possibly an infanticide; she spends her days on a mossy hillside by a hawthorn shrub and muddy pond, crying "Oh woe is me! oh misery!" as the "loquacious narrator" speculates obsessively as to the reason why (*LB* 72: 66; 8). Indeed, as he explains in an endnote, Wordsworth is interested not in Martha Ray's idée fixe about her loved ones but the narrator's about Martha Ray. "Ruth" was added to the *Lyrical Ballads* in the second edition of 1800; here, a Somerset woman is reduced to madness and beggary when her husband abandons her for the American wilds that bore him. For Darwin, a "maniacal idea, or hallucination" usually betokens some physical distress, such as a postpartum infection or a toothache, and should be treated accordingly; Wordsworth posits a similar psychosomatic continuum, although his logic generally seems to run from mental causes to bodily effects rather than vice versa (Z 2.358).

Other parallels may be noted. Like the interludes to *The Loves of the Plants,* the preface to *Lyrical Ballads* (added to the 1800 edition, expanded in the 1802) explores the question: What is the difference between poetry and prose?

Darwin locates the singularity of poetic language chiefly in the visual imagery, however idiosyncratic and "improbable," that it deploys (*Botanic* 2.74). Wordsworth admits that the poetry has a special power, deriving from the metrical patterns that produce variety amid regularity ("similitude in dissimilitude"); in its fidelity to the "real language of men," however, good poetry does not differ essentially from prose (*LB*, pp. 265, 241). Still, both agree that the chief duty of the practitioner is, by arousing the passions, to give the reader pleasure. Indeed, the *Lyrical Ballad* "Lines Written in Early Spring" advances the very Darwinian hypothesis that the pursuit and repetition of pleasurable feeling drives the motions of all living things:

Through primrose-tufts, in that sweet bower,
The periwinkle trail'd its wreathes;
And 'tis my faith that every flower
Enjoys the air it breathes.
The birds around me hopp'd and play'd:
Their thoughts I cannot measure,
But the least motion which they made,
It seem'd a thrill of pleasure.
The budding twigs spread out their fan,
To catch the breezy air;
And I must think, do all I can,
That there was pleasure there.

(*LB* 69: 9–20)

It is not difficult to see, as Darwin's *Temple of Nature* explains, how in human beings the capacity for pleasure gives rise to interpersonal affinities (including the domestic affections, a frequent Wordsworthian theme) and hence to the social compact. In Wordsworth, the hope of such connections is never abandoned, though frequently disappointed. The betrayed lover, the orphaned child and the ostracized vagrant are as common a sight as (according to the famous *Lyrical Ballad* "Tintern Abbey") the "little, nameless, unremembered acts / Of kindness and of love"; even "Lines Written in Early Spring" is framed by a "lament" about "What man has made of man" (*LB* 114: 35–36; 69: 23–24). Still, Wordsworth would not be Wordsworth without a powerful insistence on the interdependency of God, Nature, and the human soul. If there is a difference from Darwin, it lies primarily with Wordsworth's transcendence of the materialist argument. Works such as *The Prelude* (1805/1850) pulsate with the influence of northern England's Lake District and its sublime landscape; yet the finite, created *objects* of nature ultimately present an impediment to the infinite, creative *spirit* of nature that Wordsworth ties back to the poetic mind itself.

INFLUENCE ON SAMUEL TAYLOR COLERIDGE (1772–1834)

"Dr. Darwin possesses, perhaps, a greater range of knowledge than any other man in Europe, and is the most inventive of philosophical men," wrote Coleridge to his friend Josiah Wade after a visit to Derby in January 1796 (*Collected Letters* 1.177). Something of a polymath himself, Coleridge also admired Darwin's success at "combining weighty performances in literature with full and independent employment" (*Collected Works* 7.225). On the balance, however, his assessment of the good doctor was far from favorable on either aesthetic or ideological grounds. To begin with, Darwin's stylized allegories in heroic couplets represented the antithesis of the "real language of men" to which the *Lyrical Ballads* paid tribute. *The Botanic Garden* "absolutely nauseate[d]" Coleridge with its "downright simpleness, under the affectation of simplicity, prosaic words in feeble metre, silly thoughts in childish phrases, and ... preference of mean, degrading, or at best trivial associations and characters"; "it was written with all the industry of a Milliner or tradesman, who was anxious to dress his ideas in silks & satins and by collecting all the sonorous & handsome-looking words" (*CL* 1.216, *CW* 7.75, *CW* 7.19n). *The Temple of Nature* he described as "claiming to be poetical for no better reason, than that it would be intolerable in conversation or in prose" (*CW* 7.30). While these compositions themselves were like "the Russian palace of ice, glittering, cold and transitory," Coleridge feared that the *"dulcia vitia"* or "seductive faults" of Darwin's literary tribe "might reasonably be thought capable of corrupting the public judgement for half a century, and require a twenty years war, campaign after campaign, in order to dethrone the usurper and re-establish the legitimate taste" (*CW* 7.20, 7.74, 7.746–75).

A more serious objection was philosophical. Throughout his career, Coleridge painstakingly theorized the origin and association of ideas. For a materialist like Darwin, the mind was a machine that received, linked and recombined the data of the senses. Coleridge argued for something the "natural philosophers" denied—the existence of innate ideas: "A considerable Length of Time is necessary to teach the use of Motion: but before [man] could have learnt this, he must have perished from want of Food.... Who was present to teach him that the Pains which he felt proceeded from the want of Food or that opening his Mouth & chewing were the means of rendering useful what by accidental[ly] stretching out his hand he had acquired?" (*CW* 1.103). Although Coleridge appreciated the importance of material causes and effects, he rejected the position that the mind was incapable of originating anything, which would reduce organic life to a collision of billiard balls. He distinguishes between what the Middle Ages called *natura naturans* ("nature naturing") and *natura naturata* ("nature natured"); between that which creates and that which is created; between subject and object; between activity and passivity. (What Darwin calls "active" motions would still be material and therefore, by Coleridge's definition, passive.) Thought involves a relationship between the two terms in each of these pairs—what Coleridge, in his magnum opus the *Biographia Literaria,* likens to a "water-insect" that *"wins* its way up against the stream, by ... now resisting the current, and now yielding to it" in "alternate pulses" (*CW* 7.124).

For Coleridge, moreover, innate ideas require the existence of the divine, working in and through the mind. Despite his own spiritual eclecticism—fleetingly pantheist, later Unitarian, finally Trinitarian—he never forgives Darwin his "infidelity" (*CL* 1.177). While Darwin was not technically an atheist, such is Coleridge's persistent label for one who "degrades the Deity into ... a clock-work-maker" and the creation of the universe into "the bursting of a *barrel of gunpow-*

der"; who believes that in the earth's early "state of Fluidity ... the Elements might [concur] unthinkingly to produce Man" and that man "progressed from an Ouran Outang state—so contrary to all History, to all Religion, nay, to all Possibility" (*CL* 4.760; *CW* 5.401, 1.1016–102; *CL* 4.5746–575). For Coleridge, such a belief does not even rise to the level of an hypothesis or supposition (i.e., a "placing-below," a foundational principle that already exists); he prefers his own coinage, "hypopoesis" or "suffection" (i.e., a "making-below," a foundational principle that is simply fabricated) (*CL* 4.760). To be sure, the cosmologies of the two poets are not without similarities. *The Rime of the Ancient Mariner*, Coleridge's greatest contribution to the otherwise Wordsworth-dominated *Lyrical Ballads*, may be regarded as obliquely Darwinian in its glorification of "happy living things"—from the albatross that the mariner wantonly kills to the "watersnakes" that he spontaneously blesses (*LB* 21: 274, 265). In "The Aeolian Harp" Coleridge speaks likewise of

the one Life within us and abroad,
Which meets all motion and becomes its soul,
A light in sound, a sound-like power in light,
Rhythm in all thought, and *joyance every where*—
Methinks, it should have been impossible
Not to love all things in a world so fill'd; ...

(*CW* 16.233: 26–31)

It is important to note, however, that Coleridge does not end the latter poem on this note. Instead, his conscience—in the person of his wife, Sara Fricker—recommends a more "meek" and "humbl[e]" Christianity, rebuking him for what he fears have been his impious, idle and, one might say, Darwinian speculations (*CW* 16.234: 53, 52).

INFLUENCE ON MARY SHELLEY (1797–1851)

Mary Wollstonecraft Godwin spent the summer of 1816 at Villa Diodati, near Lake Geneva, Switzerland. Her companions included Percy Bysshe Shelley (her eventual husband and the father of her two, eventually four children, only one of whom would survive its parents); George Gordon, Lord Byron; Dr. John Polidori (Byron's physician); and Clara Mary Jane "Claire" Clairmont (Mary's half-sister, Byron's lover and possibly Shelley's also). Their ghost story writing game, which Byron proposed to pass the time during a spell of dreary weather, is well known. What is less well known is that Mary's "waking dream" of 16 June 1816, whose "grim terrors" yielded her famous contribution, was touched off in part by talk of Erasmus Darwin (Shelley, p. 10). The introduction to the third edition (1831) of *Frankenstein; or, The Modern Prometheus* explains:

> Many and long were the conversations between Lord Byron and [Percy] Shelley, to which I was a devout but nearly silent listener. During one of these, various philosophical doctrines were discussed, and among others the nature of the principle of life, and whether there was any probability of its ever being discovered and communicated. They talked of the experiments of Dr. Darwin, (I speak not of what the Doctor really did, or said that he did, but, as more to my purpose, of what was then spoken of as having been done by him), who preserved a piece of vermicelli in a glass case, till by some extraordinary means it began to move with voluntary motion. Not thus, after all, would life be given. Perhaps a corpse would be re-animated; galvanism had given token of such things: perhaps the component parts of a creature might be manufactured, brought together, and endued with vital warmth.
>
> (Shelley, p. 8)

As Shelley herself suspects, the "vermicelli" anecdote appears nowhere in Darwin's writings: she may be thinking of the algae *Conferva fontinalis* or the protozoon *Vorticella* (both from the discussion of "spontaneous vitality" in *The Temple of Nature*, note 1); or of the tapeworm, *Vermes tenia* (an instance of asexual generation from *Zoonomia*, chapter 39). What is certain, however, is that Darwin's meditations on organic life affected hers profoundly.

In general, isolating the vital principle was an occupation that Darwin left to others. He was not convinced by the Italian physician Luigi Galvani's hypothesis of "animal electricity"—a fluid that coursed through the body to stimulate the muscles and could be short-circuited to do so even after death. (Although Shelley leaves unspecified the means by which Dr. Victor Frankenstein awakens his creature, her reference to "galvanism" shows that contemporary electrical experiments were very much on her mind.) More interesting to Darwin was the question of how extant life was propagated. In order to advance toward an ever more perfect state, he maintained, an organism needed not simply to subdivide itself but to reproduce sexually. Darwin further argued that the characteristics of an organism could be determined by the imagination of one or more of its parents, which impresses itself upon the embryo at the moment of conception. From the father tended to come the sex; from the mother, more superficial traits such as aspect or hair color. In the case of "monstrous births," any "new conformations, or new dispositions of parts in respect to each other" (e.g., a misplaced mouth) also came from the father; any "deficiencies" or "redundancies of parts" (e.g., a missing or extra limb), from the mother—not her imagination but the amount of food and oxygen her womb supplied (Z 1.520). Moreover, Darwin revised his theory of generation for the third edition of *Zoonomia,* concluding that the male "fibrils" were responsible for the "essential" organs (e.g., the brain or heart), the female "molecules" for the rest; monstrous births therefore could occur when some independent parts developed fully and others did not (Z 1.427).

How we read Shelley's complex debt to Darwin depends largely on what we think of the intriguing, problematic figure of Victor Frankenstein himself. His entire saga might be warning against "disturb[ing], with profane fingers, the tremendous secrets of the human frame" (Shelley, p. 55). (Recall that Prometheus, his antecedent, was the Titan damned for stealing fire from the gods; his name means "foreknowledge.") His creature may be monstrous because it is the fruit of asexual reproduction, because it is in a state of arrested rather than organic development, because it bears the stamp of its father's own disordered imagination, because it contains a dearth of either the masculine or feminine principle, or because it contains a surfeit of one of these principles. The outcome might have been less tragic if Victor had achieved greater harmony within his own breast, if he had welcomed the intimate society of another person, or even if he had invited such a person to share in his scientific enterprise. As yet another alternative, one might argue that the creature is not monstrous at all, or at least does not begin that way—that it is instead a highly functional organism capable of both reason and sympathy and Victor's error that he reacts to it with neither.

INFLUENCE ON CHARLES DARWIN (1809–1882)

Charles Robert Darwin's father, Robert Waring Darwin, was Erasmus Darwin's son; and his mother, Susannah Wedgwood, was Josiah Wedgwood's daughter. In his late teens he read *Zoonomia,* of which his mentor at Edinburgh University, the physician Robert Grant, also spoke highly. He was a staunch creationist, however, through the time of his South Seas voyages (1831–1836); and it was not until well after his return to England that, poring over the voluminous notes he had assembled there, he began to formulate his theory of evolution (for which he always preferred the terms "transmutation" or "descent"). Some of the central tenets of *The Origin of Species* (1859) and *The Descent of Man* (1871) echo those of his famous grandfather. Just as *Zoonomia* traces all organic life to a "single living filament," for example, so does *The Descent* argue that

> the close resemblance of the embryo of man to that, for instance, of a dog—the construction of his skull, limbs, and whole frame, independently of the uses to which the parts may be put, on the same plan with that of other mammals—the occasional reappearance of various structures, for instance of several distinct muscles, which man does not normally possess, but which are common to the Quadrumana [four-handed creatures]—and a crowd of analogous facts—all point in the plainest manner to the conclusion that man is the co-descendant with other mammals of a common progenitor.... In the dim obscurity of the past we can see that the early progenitor of all the Vertebrata must have been an aquatic animal, provided with branchiae [gills], with the two sexes united in the same individual, and with the most important organs of

the body (such as the brain and heart) imperfectly or not at all developed.

(pp. 676, 679)

The two Darwins have other arguments in common: that living creatures engage in a perpetual struggle for survival; that their competition for sexual primacy is one important aspect of this struggle; that they improve through the generations; that they adapt to their environment; and that these mechanisms do not preclude but confirm the presence of a benevolent God. Erasmus' fundamental error, however, is to assume that the "forms or propensities" that a creature acquires during its lifetime can be "transmitted to [its] posterity"—for example, the elephant's long trunk comes from the "perpetual endeavour" of reaching for food (Z 1.506, 1.508). Charles posited instead a process of "natural selection" whereby the traits most favorable to survival are inherited—thus, random mutations produce both long- and short-trunked elephants; the former survive to breed while the latter starve. In this respect, Erasmus anticipates Charles less than he does Jean-Baptiste Lamarck (1744–1829), the French naturalist whom Charles sought to refute. As the German scientist Ernst Krause put it, "The elder Darwin was a Lamarckian, or, more properly, Jean Lamarck was a Darwinian of the older school" (p. 133).

In February of 1879, the scientific journal *Kosmos* published a festschrift marking Charles' seventieth birthday; it concluded with an essay on Erasmus by Krause. Later that year, Krause expanded the essay; William Dallas translated it from German into English; Charles himself wrote a long "Preliminary Notice" documented by some of Erasmus' correspondence and other uncollected material; Charles' daughter Henrietta edited it significantly at his request; and John Murray published the whole as a book. The second edition of 1887 bore the title *The Life of Erasmus Darwin by Charles Darwin*. Chatty and brisk, the *Life* treads lightly over its subject's scientific arguments, allowing that "Although Dr. Darwin indulged largely in hypotheses, he knew full well the value of experiments"; it quotes approvingly an observation from *The Botanic Garden* that "Extravagant theories ... are not without their use; as they encourage ... the investigation of ingenious deductions to confirm or refute them" (*Life*, pp. 35–36). It praises Erasmus' medical prowess, "his great originality of thought, his prophetic spirit both in science and in the mechanical arts," and his strength of character (*Life*, p. 60). Several pages are also devoted to an indignant rebuttal of Anna Seward's 1804 *Memoirs of the Life of Dr. Darwin*, which claimed that Erasmus reacted callously to the possible suicide of his son (also named Erasmus) in 1799.

Selected Bibliography

WORKS OF ERASMUS DARWIN

MAJOR WORKS AND EDITIONS

A System of Vegetables. Translation of *Systema vegetabilium* by Carl von Linné. 2 vols. London: Leigh & Sotheby, 1783.

The Families of Plants. Translation of *Genera plantarum* by Carl von Linné. 2 vols. London: J. Johnson, 1787.

Zoonomia; or, The Laws of Organic Life. 2nd ed., corrected, of Part I (1st ed. of Part I pub. Johnson, 1794.); 1st ed. of Parts II and III. 2 vols. London: J. Johnson, 1796. (Reprint, New York: AMS, 1974.) (Abbreviated Z.)

A Plan for the Conduct of Female Education, in Boarding Schools. 1794. London: J. Johnson, 1797.

The Botanic Garden, a Poem. In Two Parts. Part I: Containing The Economy of Vegetation. Part II: The Loves of the Plants. With Philosophical Notes. 4th ed. 2 vols. London: J. Johnson, 1799. (1st ed. of Part II pub. Johnson, 1789; reprint, Oxford: Woodstock Books, 1991. 1st ed. of Parts I and II pub. Johnson, 1792; reprinted, Yorkshire, U.K.: Scolar Press, 1973; reprinted, New York: Garland Press, 1978.)

Phytologia; or, The Philosophy of Agriculture and Gardening. London: J. Johnson, 1800.

The Temple of Nature; or, The Origin of Society. London: Jones & Co., 1825. (1st ed. pub. London: Johnson, 1803. Reprinted, New York: Garland Press, 1978; reprinted, edited by Martin Priestman, College Park, MD: Romantic Circles, 2006 [http://www.rc.umd.edu/editions/darwin_temple/]).

COLLECTED WORKS

The Essential Writings of Erasmus Darwin. Edited by Desmond King-Hele. London: MacGibbon & Kee, 1968.

The Collected Writings of Erasmus Darwin. Edited by Martin Priestman. 9 vols. Bristol, U.K.: Thoemmes Continuum, 2004.

The Collected Letters of Erasmus Darwin. Edited by Desmond King-Hele. New York: Cambridge University Press, 2007.

ARCHIVES

Darwin's papers and correspondence are held at the Fitzwilliam Museum, Cambridge, UK; at University College, London; at the Birmingham Central Library, Birmingham City Archives (correspondence with Matthew Bolton and letters to James Watt); at the British Library (letters to Charles Francis Greville); at the Natural History Museum, London (letters to Jonas Dryander and Joseph Banks); and at the Royal Society of Medicine, London (letter to William Withering). The Royal Society, London, holds his essays read at that institution; the Wellcome Library, also in London, his medical notes. There is one commonplace-book of poems in a private collection.

OTHER

In the text, prose works are identified by (volume or section, if applicable, and) page number, with "n" representing a footnote, e.g., "p. 42," "2.42," "42n." Poetical works are identified by (volume, if applicable, and) page number; then, following a colon, by (canto, if applicable, and) line number(s), e.g., "2: 36–39," "2.145–146: 3.347–350."

CRITICAL AND BIOGRAPHICAL STUDIES

Coffey, Donna. "Protecting the Botanic Garden: Seward, Darwin and Coalbrookdale." *Women's Studies* 31, no. 2:141–164 (2002).

Damon, S. Foster. *A Blake Dictionary: The Ideas and Symbols of William Blake.* Rev. ed. Hanover, N.H.: University Press of New England, 1988.

Fulford, Tim. "Coleridge, Darwin, Linnaeus: The Sexual Politics of Botany." *Wordsworth Circle* 28, no. 3:124–130 (1997).

Hassler, Donald. *Erasmus Darwin.* New York: Twayne, 1973.

Heringman, Noah. *Romantic Rocks, Aesthetic Geology.* Ithaca, N.Y.: Cornell University Press, 2004.

Holmes, Richard. *Coleridge: Early Visions.* New York: Viking, 1990.

———. *Coleridge: Darker Reflections, 1804–1834.* New York: Pantheon, 1999.

King, Amy M. *Bloom: The Botanical Vernacular in the English Novel.* New York: Oxford University Press, 2003.

King-Hele, Desmond. *Erasmus Darwin.* New York: Scribners, 1964.

———. *Doctor of Revolution: The Life and Genius of Erasmus Darwin.* London: Faber & Faber, 1977.

———. *Erasmus Darwin and the Romantic Poets.* New York: St. Martin's Press, 1986.

———. "Disenchanted Darwinians: Wordsworth, Coleridge, and Blake." *Wordsworth Circle* 25, no. 2:114–118 (1994).

———. *Erasmus Darwin: A Life of Unequalled Achievement.* London: DLM, 1999.

Mahood, M. M. *The Poet as Botanist.* New York: Cambridge University Press, 2008.

Matlak, Richard. "Wordsworth's Reading of *Zoonomia* in Early Spring." *Wordsworth Circle* 21, no. 2:76–81 (1990).

McGavran, James. "Darwin, Coleridge, and 'The Thorn.' " *Wordsworth Circle* 25, no. 2:118–122 (1994).

McLane, Maureen N. *Romanticism and the Human Sciences: Poetry, Population, and the Discourse of the Species.* Cambridge, U.K., and New York: Cambridge University Press, 2000.

McNeil, Maureen. *Under the Banner of Science: Erasmus Darwin and His Age.* Manchester, U.K., and Wolfeboro, N.H.: Manchester University Press, 1987.

Mellor, Anne. *Mary Shelley: Her Life, Her Fiction, Her Monsters.* New York: Routledge, 1989.

Packham, Catherine. "The Science and Poetry of Animation: Personification, Analogy, and Erasmus Darwin's *Loves of the Plants.*" *Romanticism* 10, no. 2:191–208 (2004).

Page, Michael. "The Darwin Before Darwin: Erasmus Darwin, Visionary Science and Romantic Poetry." *Papers on Language and Literature* 41, no. 2:146–169 (2005).

Porter, Dahlia. "Scientific Analogy and Literary Taxonomy in Darwin's *Loves of the Plants.*" *European Romantic Review* 18, no. 2:213–221 (2007).

Richardson, Alan. *British Romanticism and the Science of the Mind.* Cambridge, U.K., and New York: Cambridge University Press, 2001.

———. "Erasmus Darwin and the Fungus School." *Wordsworth Circle* 33, no. 3:113–116 (2002).

Seligo, Carlos. "The Monsters of Botany and Mary Shelley's *Frankenstein.*" In *Science Fiction: Critical Frontiers.* Edited by Karen Sayer and John Moore. New York: St. Martin's Press, 2000.

Smith, C. U. M., and Robert Arnott, eds. *The Genius of Erasmus Darwin.* Burlington, Vt.: Ashgate, 2005.

Teute, Frederika. "The Loves of the Plants; or, the Cross-Fertilization of Science and Desire at the End of the Eighteenth Century." In *British Radical Culture of the 1790s.* Edited by Robert M. Maniquis. San Marino, Calif.: Huntington Library, 2002. Pp. 63–89.

Trott, Nicola. "Wordsworth's Loves of the Plants." In *1800: The New Lyrical Ballads.* Edited by Nicola Trott and Seamus Perry. New York: Palgrave, 2001. Pp. 141–168.

Uglow, Jenny. *The Lunar Men: Five Friends Whose Curiosity Changed the World.* New York: Farrar, Straus and Giroux, 2002.

WORKS BY OTHER EIGHTEENTH- AND NINETEENTH-CENTURY AUTHORS

"Biographical Memoirs of the Late Dr. Darwin." *Monthly Magazine* 13, no. 87 (1802): 457–463.

Blake, William. *The Complete Poetry and Prose of William Blake.* Rev. ed. Edited by David V. Erdman. Commentary by Harold Bloom. New York: Anchor, 1988.

Brown, Thomas. *Observations on the Zoonomia of Erasmus Darwin, M.D.* London: J. Johnson, 1798.

Coleridge, Samuel Taylor. *Collected Letters of Samuel Taylor Coleridge.* Edited by Earl Leslie Griggs. 6 vols. Oxford: Clarendon Press, 2002. (Abbreviated *CL.*)

———. *The Collected Works of Samuel Taylor Coleridge.* Edited by J. Engell, W. Jackson Bate et al. 16 vols. Princeton, N.J.: Princeton University Press, 1969–2001. (Of the volumes referenced here, vol. 1 contains the religious and political lectures, vol. 5 the literary lectures, vol. 7 the *Biographia Literaria,* and vol. 16 the poetical works. Abbreviated *CW.*)

Darwin, Charles. *The Descent of Man, and Selection in Relation to Sex.* 1871. Reprinted 1879. Edited by James Moore and Adrian Desmond. New York: Penguin, 2004.

———. *The Life of Erasmus Darwin.* Edited by Desmond King-Hele. New York: Cambridge University Press, 2003.

Krause, Ernst. *Erasmus Darwin.* Translated by W. S. Dallas. Preliminary Notice by Charles Darwin. London: John Murray, 1879.

"The Loves of the Triangles." In *Poetry of the Anti-Jacobin.* London: J. Wright, 1799. Pp. 108–129.

Royal Society. *Philosophical Transactions.* Vol. 30. London: W. and J. Innys, 1720.

Seward, Anna. *Memoirs of the Life of Dr. Darwin.* London: J. Johnson, 1804.

Shelley, Mary Wollstonecraft. *Frankenstein.* (1831 ed.) Edited by Maurice Hindle. New York: Penguin, 2003.

Wordsworth, William. *Complete Poetical Works.* Edited by Thomas Hutchinson. Revised by Ernest De Selincourt. New York: Oxford, 1936. (Abbreviated *WW.*)

Wordsworth, William, and Samuel Taylor Coleridge. *Lyrical Ballads.* Edited by R. L. Brett and A. R. Jones. New York: Routledge, 1988. (Abbreviated *LB.*)

ELIZABETH I, QUEEN OF ENGLAND

(1533—1603)

Jane Beal

ELIZABETH I, QUEEN of England is well remembered as one of the greatest monarchs ever to rule the British Empire. However, she was not much recognized for her powerful writing and her influence as a patron of the arts in Renaissance England. Publication of editions of her collected works and translations now make it possible to evaluate her literary legacy in the context of her historical roles: extraordinary woman, great monarch, powerful writer, accomplished translator, and influential patron. As a writer, Elizabeth I authored many fine poems, prayers, letters, and speeches. As a multilingual translator, she enjoyed working with Christian texts about faith and classical texts on governance.

AN EXTRAORDINARY WOMAN

By the time she ascended the throne of England at the age of twenty-five, Elizabeth had been shaped by experiences that made her into a truly extraordinary woman. Socially, she was a princess: the privileged daughter of King Henry VIII. However, because her father divorced her mother in highly suspicious and scandalous circumstances, she was declared a bastard. Both her half brother Edward and her half sister Mary ascended to the throne of England before she could, and only their deaths permitted her to become queen. Emotionally and psychologically, Elizabeth was complex. She certainly loved her father, but his decisions marred her life in many ways. Her family, as well as the turbulent times in which she lived, compelled her to endure significant personal loss and suffering.

Intellectually, Elizabeth was a rigorously trained, humanist scholar. It seems that Elizabeth took refuge from the world and its troubles in the disciplines of learning. She was well versed in the liberal arts, modern European languages, Latin, and Greek, Protestant theology, and works on the art of governing well. Spiritually, Elizabeth was a devout Christian. She was raised as a Protestant, but for a brief period during the reign of her sister Mary, she put on an outward show of Catholicism to preserve her life and keep the peace with her sister, the queen. When Elizabeth herself became queen, and the governor of the Church of England, she wanted conformity from her people: Catholics were not to be persecuted; radical Protestants were not to be encouraged. This position was political for the sake of peace. Spiritually, Elizabeth's Christian faith was both dynamic and profound, as her writings attest, and it seems that her desire was for her people to experience Christianity meaningfully in their souls and social practices, as she did.

In order to understand Elizabeth's social position, it is important to consider her life in the context of a royal family. Elizabeth was born on September 7, 1533. She was an instant disappointment to her parents, King Henry VIII and Anne Boleyn, who were hoping for a boy child who could inherit the throne of England. Despite her apparently unfortunate gender, Elizabeth was recognized as princess and heir apparent to the throne—that is, until she was three years old.

When Elizabeth was just beginning to walk and talk and understand a little bit about the world, her mother, Queen Anne, was executed by her father, King Henry, on charges of adultery, incest, and treason. While five men were accused of committing adultery with the queen, including her own brother, only one confessed to it—and

ELIZABETH I, QUEEN OF ENGLAND

that under severe torture. Meanwhile, King Henry was the one who had engaged in multiple affairs throughout the years of his marriage to Anne, including the affair he was having with Jane Seymour while Anne was locked in the Tower of London. Historians surmise that Anne's multiple miscarriages after the birth of Elizabeth—and thus the inability to produce a living male heir to Henry's throne—further incited Henry's decision to accuse her. Englishmen at the time were appalled and protested the queen's innocence in the face of Henry's obviously dark motives, but she was beheaded with a Spanish sword in the Tower of London on May 19, 1536.

As a result, Elizabeth no longer held a title as princess but rather was declared an illegitimate child of King Henry, who then married Jane Seymour. In this, her father was following a familiar pattern. His first marriage had been to Catherine of Aragon, the mother of his first surviving child, also a daughter, Mary. When Henry divorced Catherine to marry Elizabeth's mother, Anne, he declared Mary illegitimate, too. Henry's third wife, Jane, did give him the son, Edward VI, whom he was hoping for. But Edward was sickly.

When Jane Seymour died shortly after the birth of Edward, Henry married Anne of Cleves. The marriage lasted six months; then it was annulled. Henry then married Catherine Howard, a woman who had been a lady-in-waiting to Anne of Cleves. Henry was thirty years older than Catherine Howard. They were married less than two years, after which Catherine was accused of adultery and beheaded. Henry then married Catherine Parr, who, miraculously, outlived him.

During these tumultuous years in the personal and political life of Henry VIII, Elizabeth was growing up. She turned ten years old soon after her father married Catherine Parr, the last of his wives, on July 12, 1543. Elizabeth had been cared for up to that point by Kat Ashley, her governess and lifelong friend, who also taught Elizabeth to write English, Latin, and Italian.

William Grindal became Elizabeth's tutor at age eleven, and he taught her French and Greek. When Elizabeth was thirteen, Grindal died, and Roger Ascham took his place. Her training with Ascham was in the seven liberal arts—grammar, dialectic, rhetoric, arithmetic, music, geometry, and astronomy—as well as additional learning from the secular humanist perspective emanating from Italy.

In addition to language and liberal arts studies, at which she clearly excelled, Elizabeth was accomplished in needlework, intricate figure-dancing, and the playing of the lute (a stringed instrument) and the virginal (a precursor of the modern piano). By the time Elizabeth finished her academic studies and courtly training at age seventeen, her brilliance and accomplishment were undeniable; she was clearly one of the best-educated and most talented women of the Renaissance.

Her studies nonetheless were continually interrupted by tragedy. When she was thirteen years old, Elizabeth's father, Henry VIII, died. Her half brother Edward, at age nine, succeeded to the throne. Edward died from an illness at the age of fifteen. According to his father's will, the next in line to inherit would have been Edward's eldest sister, Mary, and then his next eldest sister, Elizabeth. However, at this time, all of England was in an uproar over religion, which complicated matters.

Essentially, King Henry had separated himself from the Catholic Church and declared himself the supreme head of the Anglican Church when the pope refused to grant an annulment of his marriage to Catherine of Aragon and when the pope further refused to acknowledge his marriage to Anne Boleyn. Henry's separation from the Catholic Church had the advantage of unifying the Anglican Church with the English state, which meant that the money (and thus, to some extent, the power) that used to go to Rome now stayed in Canterbury. Furthermore, Henry had dispossessed the monasteries, and their wealth now went to the Crown.

However, this decision created a major division in the country and in Henry's own family. His oldest daughter, Mary, was raised as a Catholic; his younger children, Elizabeth and Edward, were raised as staunch Protestants. When Edward died, a power struggle ensued between the Protestant nobles of Henry's court

ELIZABETH I, QUEEN OF ENGLAND

and the Catholic supporters of Mary, who was ultimately to take the throne. So Lady Jane Grey took it instead, but only for nine days, after which Mary was crowned queen of England several days after her father's death. Queen Mary worked hard to undo Protestant reforms and restore Catholic power in England, with the result that the country was torn apart by religious infighting.

Once Mary was queen, and married to King Philip of Spain, Elizabeth was relegated to the household of her stepmother, Catherine Parr, who secretly married Thomas Seymour four months after King Henry died. (Thomas was actually the older brother of Jane Seymour, Henry's third wife—which is how Elizabeth's "uncle," the brother of her first stepmother, became her "stepfather," the husband of her last stepmother.) Scandalously, the forty-year-old Thomas Seymour began sexually pursuing the fifteen-year-old Elizabeth in his wife's house—and got caught by that same wife in an "embrace" with Elizabeth. Accusations flew. Elizabeth was sent away from the house. A year later, in 1548, Catherine Parr died. And a year after that, Thomas Seymour was accused of conspiring to overthrow Queen Mary, and his private misbehavior became a matter of public investigation.

Among other things, the government investigated whether Thomas Seymour had sought to marry Elizabeth and whether or not the two of them had shared a sexual relationship. Elizabeth was compelled to write a letter to Edward Seymour, Lord Protector of the Commonwealth, defending herself—and her friend Kat Ashley—against all defamation of her character. She concluded by saying:

> there goeth rumors abroad which be greatly against mine honor and honesty, which above all else things I esteem, which be these: that I am in the Tower and with child by my lord admiral [Thomas Seymour]. My lord, these are shameful slanders, for the which besides the great desire I have to see the king's majesty, I shall most heartily desire your lordship that I may come to the court after your first determination, that I may show myself as I am.
> (*Elizabeth I: Collected Works*, p. 24)

In other words, Elizabeth was well-prepared to show herself as she was: not pregnant. As it turned out, Elizabeth was not named a coconspirator in the plot to overthrow Queen Mary, and her life was spared. Thomas Seymour, however, was executed in the Tower of London.

Five years later, in 1554, when Elizabeth was twenty, the Protestants of England rebelled against Mary, but they were not successful. Elizabeth was interrogated at court and then imprisoned in the Tower. It was the same Tower where her own mother had been imprisoned and executed years before and where, only a month before, the Lady Jane Grey had been executed as well after being found guilty of treason for briefly taking the throne when Mary was next in line by Henry's decree. Later in her life, Elizabeth would remember her time in the Tower as the most oppressive and terrifying experience of her life. Queen Mary eventually released Elizabeth, but she was kept under house arrest at Woodstock for the next year.

In 1555, Elizabeth was allowed to return to court. Three years later, in 1558, the childless Queen Mary became ill and died. Elizabeth became queen of England, and she ruled the country for almost forty-five years thereafter.

A GREAT MONARCH

Elizabeth I is remembered as one of the greatest monarchs ever to rule England for many reasons, few of them traditional. She was not ambitious to conquer or control foreign territories, unlike previous English monarchs or contemporary European princes. In fact, when offered the crown of the Netherlands, she declined it, and her military interventions in Europe were primarily defensive of Protestant allies and responsive to threats from the Spanish empire. Nor did she amass great wealth or give birth to heirs to the throne of England. She certainly encouraged positive representations of herself in art, in pageantry, and in literature; she was popular among her people from her youth, and she cultivated that popularity well into her old age. But her legacy consists, in large part, in her great ability to govern her country with a balanced and even hand.

ELIZABETH I, QUEEN OF ENGLAND

Elizabeth faced many challenges during her reign as queen of England. These challenges were religious, marital, and political in nature. Born into an era of reformation, Elizabeth inherited a country that was religiously divided between Catholics and Protestants. Partially on account of this division, her marriage was always a political question, never merely a personal one. She was continually encouraged by her parliament and her people to marry, particularly advantageously, but marriage alliances proved untenable for her. International political maneuvering shaped her reign as well. One of the greatest crises of her reign was the threat posed to her by Mary, Queen of Scots, a Catholic who claimed the right to England's throne. Another was the planned invasion of England by Spain. Finally, Elizabeth had to contend with the reality that she did not have an heir of her own body to ascend the throne, and so the question of succession caused great anxiety in her government, though perhaps not in Elizabeth herself.

Elizabeth had inherited the religious division in her country from her father, Henry VIII. In 1533, Henry VIII had been excommunicated by the Roman Catholic pope because of Henry's decision to divorce his wife Catherine of Aragon and marry Elizabeth's mother, Anne. The separation of England from Rome was complete by the next year. In 1536, Henry VIII dissolved the monasteries and seized the wealth of the Catholic Church remaining in England. Henry had already declared himself the Supreme Head of the Church of England, thus establishing the Anglican Church as a separate entity from the Catholic Church. On the continent, meanwhile, Protestants began to be persecuted, and by 1543, the first Protestants were burned by the Inquisition.

After Henry's death, when his son assumed the throne of England, Edward had followed in his father's staunchly Protestant footsteps, assuring that Protestant theology was taught by the Anglican Church and that Protestant nobility remained in power in England. However, when Edward died and Mary assumed the throne, her reign was that of a devout Catholic who was determined to restore England to Catholicism and reconcile her people to the pope. When Mary married another devout Catholic, Philip II of Spain in 1554, she further committed herself and her country to a Catholic course. Indeed, in her zeal for restoration, Mary began burning English Protestants in 1555.

When Elizabeth became queen following the death of her sister Mary, it was therefore imperative that the new queen establish a religious settlement in the country. In 1559, the Acts of Supremacy and Uniformity accomplished religious peace in England. This peace was often threatened, both from within the country and from without it, but it endured. Four years later, in 1563, the approval of the Thirty-nine Articles of Religion fully articulated the beliefs that would govern the Anglican Church, and in the same year, John Foxe's "Actes and Monuments," also known as the "Book of Martyrs," provided a popular history of Protestants who had suffered for their faith. The cultural shift in England toward religious moderation was felt throughout the country and internationally as well.

For Elizabeth, her government, and her country, the necessity for religious peace in England meanwhile heavily influenced consideration of all potential suitors for the queen's hand in marriage. It was vitally important to the English court and parliament that Elizabeth wed a noble or royal Protestant, a Catholic willing to convert, or, if no one more suitable could be found, a Catholic strongly supportive of the religious settlement in England. As the years went on, however, it became apparent that Elizabeth's people were strongly against any marriage to a foreign Catholic power, and this greatly affected Elizabeth's marriage negotiations over time.

Initially, Elizabeth's advisers and her parliament had urged her to marry, primarily because they wished Elizabeth to bear the heir to the throne and secure the dynastic succession. In addition, there was discomfort with Elizabeth's gender: it was at times difficult for her male subordinates to acknowledge her authority; the fact that Elizabeth was also the governor of the Anglican Church, when Christian bishops of her day believed that women could not serve as priests, further complicated matters. But Elizabeth herself was in no hurry to marry.

ELIZABETH I, QUEEN OF ENGLAND

Elizabeth's attitude toward marriage appeared to be one of infinite patience. In her reply to a petition from her parliament to marry, Elizabeth affirmed that she was not inclined to marriage, but that God might well direct her to that state, and if she felt so directed, she would choose a husband who had as great a care for the preservation of the realm as she had. However, she also said that if it were up to her, her marble tombstone would declare that she lived and died a virgin queen:

> now that the Publick Care of governing the Kingdom is laid upon me, to draw upon me also the Cares of marriage may seem a point of inconsiderate Folly. Yea, to satisfie you, I have already joyned myself in marriage to an Husband, namely, the Kingdom of England … And to me it shall be a Full satisfaction, both for the memorial of my Name, and for my Glory also, if when I shall let my last breath, it be ingraven upon my Marble Tomb, "Here lieth Elizabeth, which Reigned a Virgin, and died a Virgin."
>
> (*Elizabeth I: Collected Works*, pp. 59–60)

Elizabeth spoke rhetorically of being married to England more than once, expressing her view of England as her true husband and the English people as her children. Nonetheless, she did entertain several marriage proposals, many of them seriously, and she even contracted a marriage alliance late in life, although it was not consummated.

The first marriage proposal that Elizabeth refused came from her brother-in-law, Philip II of Spain, who requested her hand immediately following the death of Queen Mary and Elizabeth's ascension to the English throne. Elizabeth waited a few months to give her answer, however, and the delay enabled her to work on England's diplomatic relationship with France in the interim, since the prospect of an alliance between England and Spain put pressure on France. In the end, she rejected the king on the grounds of his Catholicism and on the basis of his previous marriage to her sister. But this means of using a potential marriage alliance for short-term political gains at home and abroad while withholding the final commitment to a marriage proved to be an important strategy for the queen for the remainder of her reign. From 1563 to 1567, for instance, Elizabeth kept a possible marriage alliance to Charles, the archduke of Austria, in open negotiations. In the end, after four years, Elizabeth rejected him because Charles was Catholic, and if Elizabeth had married him, the marriage would have offended her people and caused division, perhaps even civil war, in her country. Elizabeth's other suitors included James, the earl of Arran, from Scotland; Eric, the king of Sweden; and when she was in her forties, Francis, the duke of Alençon. In 1581, Elizabeth actually signed a marriage contract with Francis, even though he was half her age. Francis, however, died in 1584 of fever in the Netherlands. Francis was the first of her suitors to come in person to woo her, and Elizabeth's extant correspondence with him suggests she had become sincerely fond of him; his death made her grieve. After the death of Alençon, there were no more suitors. But throughout this time, none of Elizabeth's noble or royal wooers was as dear to her as Robert Dudley, her Master of the Horse, whom she created earl of Leicester.

Contemporaries believed that Elizabeth and Robert were born on the same day in the same year. The two knew each other from the time Elizabeth was eight years old, and they became friends in the schoolroom when they were educated together by royal tutors. Robert married Amy Robsart during the reign of Edward VI; both Elizabeth and Edward attended the wedding. During the reign of Elizabeth's sister, Mary, Elizabeth and Robert were both imprisoned in the Tower of London at the same time. Although they were heavily guarded, and it is unlikely that they had much personal interaction, they could certainly see one another on an almost daily basis. After Elizabeth was freed and became queen, she made Robert Master of the Horse. In this role, Robert had rooms in Elizabeth's palace and spent much time in attendance on her. He organized Elizabeth's public appearances, her progresses through the country, and her personal entertainment. In the early years of Elizabeth's reign, this intimacy provoked gossip and scandal.

If Elizabeth's relationship with Robert looked suspicious, even immoral in the eyes of her counselors, her people, and the international courts of Europe, the situation became even worse when Robert's wife, Amy, was found dead at the foot of the stairs in her house with a broken neck. Scholars have since found it likely that Amy was suffering from breast cancer that weakened her bones, which could have led to a stress fracture and an accidental death. However, many people suspected that Robert had had his wife killed in order to make way for his ambitious desire to marry Elizabeth. Robert himself thought someone had murdered his wife. Had Elizabeth married Robert as she seemed to have been considering, she would have implicated herself in Amy's death, at least in the minds of many people.

Robert Dudley proposed marriage to Elizabeth multiple times over the next several years. She never accepted his proposal, although it is clear that Robert loved her and that, especially in the early years of her reign, she returned that love. When he died, she locked herself in her rooms and would not come out for hours, even days. When she died, her counselors found a letter from Robert, marked "his last letter" in her own script, in her treasure box. Their feelings for each other may have changed over the years from passion to appreciation, but the relationship between Elizabeth and Robert clearly maintained some constancy throughout their lifetimes.

Her decision not to marry her friend had multiple reasons. A marriage to Robert had no political advantage; his only wealth and status came from her. As queen, Elizabeth seems to have felt that she was obligated to marry advantageously for the sake of England if she were to marry at all. Certainly she also realized that the power dynamics in her relationship with Robert would be changed by marriage, since Elizabeth would be in a subordinate position of a wife even if she remained the reigning queen of England. Perhaps Elizabeth was hesitant to marry Robert because of his sexual relationships with other women, including one with Lady Dudley Sheffield, which produced a son named Robert. Indeed, in 1578, when it became apparent that Elizabeth would not marry Robert, Robert married Lettice Devereux, the countess of Essex, and Elizabeth apparently hated her.

But Elizabeth's hesitancy about marriage also certainly had deep roots in her personal history and psychology. Robert said that even from the time she was eight years old, she had insisted she would never marry; she was eight when her stepmother Catherine Howard was sent to the Tower of London and beheaded on charges of adultery. Was it at this time that Elizabeth learned of the manner and causes of her own mother's death? People may have talked in her hearing when Catherine went to the block of how Anne Boleyn had been similarly executed, especially since Catherine was Anne's cousin.

Whatever fear Elizabeth might have felt in learning about the manner of her mother's death at her father's direction and the implications for her own future marital relationship, however, cannot have been the only factor that influenced her. Elizabeth also was a devoted scholar, who, at age twelve, translated a work for her stepmother Catherine Parr, which imagined the human soul as the bride of Christ. Did Elizabeth consider her own soul to be married to Christ? Did she privately consider herself to be already married in this way? Some of her prayers reflect this possibility.

The abusive pursuit she suffered as a young woman of fifteen at the hands of Thomas Seymour might also have left her uninclined toward the sexual aspects of marriage. Seymour's execution, partially for reasons having to do with her, could not have provided her much consolation and may have provoked feelings of undeserved guilt instead. Elizabeth had a lifelong hesitancy about ordering the execution of traitors, which suggests the strength of her personal morality but may also reflect on some of her early life experiences with injustice.

Some scholars have suggested that Elizabeth was afraid of losing her life or her power, either by marrying or bearing children or enduring the machinations of those who would move to strike against her once she acknowledged her heir to the throne. Perhaps all of these inner factors, when thrown together with the outer factors, simply meant that Elizabeth would ultimately decline every proposal of marriage she received—except the last. Certainly she only had to look

ELIZABETH I, QUEEN OF ENGLAND

north to Scotland in the life of her cousin, Mary Stuart, to see a moral parable unfolding, one with clear implications for her own life and decisions. Indeed, Mary handled her decisions about marriage very differently than Elizabeth did, with unfortunate consequences.

Mary was the daughter of James V, the king of Scotland, and Mary of Guise. After her father's death, she was crowned queen of Scotland at the age of one. Initially, the Scots agreed with Henry VIII that Mary would be the wife of Edward VI. However, Henry's aggression toward Scotland alienated the Scottish nobles, and Mary was sent to France at the age of five, where she was raised and married the dauphin in 1558 at the age of fifteen. When her father-in-law, Henry II, died, she and her husband were crowned queen and king of France.

Only two years later, her husband died of an ear infection, and her mother, who had been acting as regent in Scotland, also died. Mary returned to Scotland as queen of the country. At the age of twenty-two, she hastily married her nineteen-year-old cousin, Lord Darnley. Darnley was not a good man. When Mary was six months pregnant, Darnley and other Scottish nobles dragged Mary's secretary away from her service and murdered him in her sight, possibly intending Mary to miscarry from the shock. By the next year, Lord Darnley himself was murdered, and Mary was hastily wed to James Hepburn, the earl of Bothwell. The Scottish nobles forced Mary to abdicate in favor of her son. She was twenty-four years old. She was imprisoned but managed to escape to England, where she presented a major problem to Elizabeth: Mary had a viable claim to the throne of England, being the granddaughter of Henry VIII's sister, and she was a devout Catholic. Mary's existence was thus a rallying point for those discontent in Elizabeth's kingdom, especially those Catholics who wished to dissolve their allegiance to their Protestant monarch. In consequence of this, Mary lived as a prisoner until she was executed at the age of forty-four, after being charged and convicted of plotting to kill Elizabeth I and usurp her throne.

King Philip II of Spain presented another challenge to Elizabeth's rule. Philip was outraged at the execution of Mary, his fellow Catholic monarch, and he determined that Elizabeth, a Protestant who had been excommunicated by the pope, should no longer rule in England. Elizabeth and Philip had already experienced military conflict in the Netherlands, and in 1588, Philip's Spanish Armada began to move across the Channel with the intention of invading England. When the Spanish Armada was defeated by a combination of Spanish mismanagement, English maneuvering, and bad weather, many in England took it as a sign of God's divine favor resting on Elizabeth.

In the latter part of her reign, Elizabeth also suffered treachery in the person of Essex, the stepson of Robert Dudley. Essex became one of her favorites, but he was also presumptuous and failed to listen to some of Elizabeth's direct orders, especially her orders about military campaigns in the Netherlands and Ireland. He planned a short-lived rising against the queen, which resulted in his execution in 1601, a final grief to her.

In 1603, Elizabeth died without naming an heir to her throne. The ring signifying her royal authority had to be cut from her hand; it had grown into her flesh. Upon her death, the English government quickly asked Mary's son James to take the crown, which he did, thus becoming the king of both Scotland and England.

A POWERFUL WRITER

Educated, articulate, and elegant, Elizabeth generally shaped her prose to persuasive ends and her verses to commemorative effects. She wrote abundantly in three major prose genres: speeches, letters, and prayers. The first two genres were certainly for a public audience; so was the third, although ostensibly Elizabeth's prayers were first for her private use. Elizabeth also wrote some poetry; her poetry is often occasional, linked to Elizabeth's memories of key experiences in her lifetime.

Elizabeth's earliest surviving poems are associated with her imprisonment at Woodstock between 1554 and 1555. She wrote a ten-line poem on the subject of fortune, noting how "innocents were enclosed" while "those that death had well deserved" were set free. She reputedly wrote a couplet with a diamond in a glass windowpane: "Much suspected by me, / Nothing proved can be" (*Elizabeth I: Collected Works,* p. 46). The verses were preserved in the books of John Foxe and of the chonicler Raphael Holinshed.

Another short poem, the first line in Latin and the next four lines in English, was an ironic response to Roman Catholic priests who placed her under examination during Mary's reign. It particularly addressed the theological divide between Protestants and Catholics over the transubstantiation of the Eucharist. Elizabeth's poem quotes the words of Jesus in Latin: *hoc est corpus meum* (this is my body). The message of the poem thereafter is that Elizabeth believes this to be true, but her belief in Christ's words does not commit her to a Catholic understanding of transubstantiation.

Elizabeth wrote a four-line poem on the last leaf of her French psalter, perhaps about 1565. In it, Elizabeth says that no outward deformity is half as ugly as the inward deformity of a "suspicious mind." The poem is signed "your loving mistress, Elizabeth R." Some scholars have suggested that Elizabeth wrote this about Robert Dudley when she was offended by him. Whether the suspicious mind in question is Elizabeth's or Robert's is difficult to discern. As with Elizabeth's other poems, double and even opposite meanings are made possible by the deliberate obscurity of her phrasing.

Another poem inspired by a troubled relationship is "The Doubt of Future Foes," written about 1571. When the Catholic Mary, Queen of Scots, fled from Scotland into England in 1568, the threat she posed to Elizabeth's Protestant realm made Elizabeth mark the occasion with this poem, the opening lines of which read: "the dread of future foes / exiles my present joy." This poem was more frequently included in anthologies than any of Elizabeth's other verses; it was particularly praised in George Puttenham's book *The Art of English Poesie* (1589).

Elizabeth also wrote poems in exchange for poems with four men: Sir Thomas Henage, a gentlemen of the privy chamber, about 1572; Paul Milissus, the poet laureate of the court of Emperor Maximilian II, about 1577; Sir Walter Raleigh; and King Philip II of Spain in the spring of 1588 when Spain and England were on the verge of war. When Elizabeth and her navy defeated the Spanish Armada in December 1588, she wrote a victory song, which like that of Miriam and Moses when they left Egypt during the Exodus particularly acknowledges God's intervention and help. The poem, which is made up of three six-line stanzas, invites God to listen and to look down on Elizabeth, the "handmaid" of the lord, and instructs Elizabeth's own soul to ascend to the holy place. Alluding to the fiery pillar and the cloud that led the Israelites through the wilderness after the Exodus, Elizabeth thanks God for preserving his "turtledove," a term of loving affection used in the Song of Solomon and used in Elizabeth's poem to refer to her own spirit.

Six years before the defeat of the Spanish Armada, in 1582, Elizabeth had seen Alençon, the one man to whom she became engaged (but did not in the end marry), for the last time before his death in Europe. About this time, Elizabeth wrote a poem known as "On Monsieur's Departure," which, although apparently not exchanged with Alençon in their correspondence, certainly seems to concern him. In three stanzas, the queen expresses frustration in love, especially in these lines: "I love, and yet am forced to seem to hate … let me live with some more sweet content / or die, and so forget what love e'er meant" (*Elizabeth I: Collected Works,* p. 303).

The frustrated love poem contrasts with the last poem Elizabeth was known to have written, twenty-seven stanzas in French, originally composed around 1590: a meditation on her soul's salvation. The poem contains Elizabeth's allegorical reflections on the spiritual struggles of her soul, the help she has received from God, and the roles of imagination, reason, understanding, will, and memory (all internal faculties of the soul) as well as justice and mercy in her soul's pilgrimage. It is easy to see the influence of her early translations, such as "The Mirror of the Sinful Soul" (discussed below) on her lifelong meditations on her soul's relationship to God.

Like her poetry, Elizabeth's speeches commemorate occasions, but unlike her poetry, her orations were quite public and reached a large audience both at the time she spoke them and at later times when they were copied, printed, and circulated in her court and throughout the country. Some of her speeches were copied by scribal listeners at the time she gave them; others were written in advance or even after the occasion of speaking, which resulted in multiple versions of key speeches. So although it is not always possible to determine what the queen actually said, it is certainly possible to read in the extant speeches what people thought and believed she said. In the case of speeches with more than one version, comparison may reveal Elizabeth's revisionary thinking.

Two of Elizabeth's most famous speeches came in the latter part of her reign: her "Speech to the Troops at Tilbury" (the authenticity of which has sometimes been questioned) and her "Golden Speech" to her last parliament. Each of these speeches is clearly situated in a specific historical moment as are others, such as those responding to parliamentary petitions urging her to execute Mary, Queen of Scots. Elizabeth's speeches clearly demonstrate Elizabeth's self-fashioning of her own image in her public, historic context.

Elizabeth's humanist education, which drew on classical Roman tradition and medieval university training, emphasized the power of rhetoric: the art of persuasion. Certainly Elizabeth's speeches demonstrate her ability to persuade, but they also reveal her inclination to obfuscate when the occasion called for it. A number of her speeches to her early parliaments, for example, are careful negotiations of the nobles' demands that she marry. Her speeches alternately assert her authority, affirm her willingness to cooperate, and call for a delay of decision or action, or sometimes undertake all these goals at once.

Elizabeth was an effective and well-trained orator whose speeches usually accomplished their intended effect. When the queen spoke, she typically spoke in English, although she famously addressed learned university Englishmen extemporaneously in Latin on at least one occasion (September 28, 1592), and of course she spoke to her international visitors in their native languages when she wanted to do so on many other occasions.

Her versatility in the art of speaking was well-matched by her versatility in the art of letter writing. Elizabeth wrote over one hundred letters in her lifetime that have been copied and preserved to this day. The letters are of different types, including dedicatory epistles prefacing her translations, such as those to Queen Catherine Parr, King Henry VIII, and her brother, King Edward VI; ostensibly personal but obviously not private correspondence with her family members (for instance, her sister, Queen Mary), her royal servants, and her noble advisors (for example, Robert Dudley, William Cecil, Walter Raleigh), and later the international suitors seeking her hand in marriage; and diplomatic letters exchanged with other sovereigns, such as Mary, Queen of Scots, and King Philip of Spain, and King James of Scotland, negotiating their agreements and disagreements. These letters clearly reveal not only Elizabeth's rhetorical skill but also the most pressing concerns of her life in relation to others.

Although each of Elizabeth's letters are typically addressed to one person, her letters had a larger audience than the addressee, since they were often read by her own advisers, by the recipient's advisers, by the servants who copied them, and even by later generations to whom they were handed down. Elizabeth easily wrote letters not only in English but also in Latin, French, and Italian. When read in chronological order with explanatory notes, the letters constitute an autobiographical record of Elizabeth's life in the world, her memories of her experiences, and her emotional, intellectual, and spiritual responses to those experiences.

While Elizabeth's letters give the sense of her outer life, her prayers reveal the nature of her inner life. Certainly Elizabeth composed and articulated some of her prayers for public or ceremonial occasions, such as the two prayers she prayed when she was imprisoned in the Tower of London, a prayer she prayed at Bristol when a treaty was concluded between England and Spain in 1574, and the prayers she prayed on the defeat of the Spanish Armada in 1588, the sailing of the Cadiz expedition in 1596, and the sailing of the Azores expedition in 1597. But the majority of her prayers survive in her three private prayer books, each known by a separate title: "The Private Prayers of Elizabeth I at Court, 1563"; "Queen Elizabeth I Prayers and Verses, 1569"; and her late "Prayer Book, 1579–1582."

The "Private Prayers" survive in a small volume that is entirely in Latin and includes both scriptural verses and prayers written by Elizabeth in its first section. Interestingly, the second section of the book is Elizabeth's commonplace book, while the third section consists of lists of civil and ecclesiastical offices. The whole was published in London in 1563. The first three prayers are designated as collects, the next two as prayers of thanksgiving, and a final prayer as a petition for wisdom in administering the kingdom and the commonwealth of England. Each prayer begins by addressing God by his names and qualities: "sovereign Lord, omnipotent God, Father of mercies, God of all grace," "most good and most great Savior Jesus Christ, son of the living God," "eternal God, Creator and accomplisher of all things." In these direct addresses, readers can hear the echo of the liturgy of the Anglican Church, which was so much a part of Elizabeth's life of faith.

In 1569, J. Day published a second volume of Elizabeth's prayers, *Christian Prayers and Meditations in English, French, Italian, Spanish, Greek, and Latin,* which contained eighteen prayers, one poem, and Psalm 101 rendered into stanzas in French by the Protestant poet Clément Marot. One of the most beautiful prayers in the collection is composed in French and known as the "Morning Prayer" and begins: "My God, my Father, and my Savior, as Thou now send us Thy sun upon the earth to give corporeal life to the creatures, and vouchsafe also to illumine my heart and understanding by the heavenly light of Thy Holy Spirit, that I neither think nor say nor do anything unless to serve and please Thee" (*Elizabeth I: Collected Works,* p. 144). Elizabeth reportedly began most mornings with this prayer, and it is interesting to meditate on how it may have shaped her interior life and her consequent actions of the world.

The multilingual nature of these prayers suggests that Elizabeth maintained her mental flexibility and fluency through a prayer life practiced in the languages of many cultures. Moreover, Elizabeth's publication of prayers various languages once again demonstrated her learning to her country and to international courts.

The prayers in the 1569 collection not only include the queen's morning and evening prayers, but also record prayers of thanksgiving, confession, and petition, especially for the ability to administer well the kingdom of England. One Greek prayer was intended to be prayed by the subjects of the queen on her behalf, and it is the only prayer not written in the first person, feminine voice of Elizabeth. The Greek prayer includes this request: "direct Thy handmaid, Elizabeth our queen, and illumine her soul with a light of Thine unbounded wisdom, that she may honor Thy name through her whole life with true service and piety." The prayer emphasizes the fact that Elizabeth's sovereignty was contingent upon virtue and on total devotion to the sovereignty of God, it indicates that the people should serve her with zeal and humility, and it requests that God give Elizabeth a long life on earth along with the ability to defend the realm from all enemies. It ends with a request that Elizabeth obtain eternal life "in accordance with Thy boundless mercy, through the blood of Thy only begotten Son, the undefiled Lamb who died upon the cross to redeem us." Since the prayer was written in Greek, it seems likely that only the learned would be able to pray it on behalf of their sovereign.

The third prayer book of Elizabeth was copied out by her by hand. It was a tiny volume, measuring two inches wide by three inches long, with gold clasps, each inset with a ruby, and containing two miniatures: one of Elizabeth and one of Francis, that is François Hercule de Valois, duc d'Alencon, to whom she was engaged to be married before his death. (A facsimile exists today, though the original has gone missing.) Elizabeth's third book contained six prayers: the first in English, the second in French, the third in Italian, the fourth in Latin, the fifth in Greek, and the last in English again. At some level, the ordering of the prayers indicates which languages were nearest to Elizabeth's heart: her mother tongue, English; French, the first language of the man to whom she was betrothed; Italian, which she loved; Latin, the language of learning, which she translated so often; and lastly Greek, the language of the new humanist learning and the original language of the New Testament of the Bible. The number of the prayers, six, corresponds to the number of days in the week, minus either the Sabbath or Sunday, when Elizabeth would pray many prayers in church.

In each prayer, Elizabeth emphasizes one of her identities in relationship to God. In the English prayer, she is the handmaid of God. In the French prayer, she twice refers to herself as the mother of the children God has given her in England and from the persecuted Church abroad. In the Italian prayer, she calls "Emperor," "Father," and "Greatest Shepherd"; she is correspondingly his servant, his daughter, and his sheep. The prayer specifically asks God to wash her in the fountain of life and hide her in the shelter of his wings. Indeed, the allusions to the Psalms in her prayers are consistent. For example, she often voices her contrition in the words of Psalm 51: "Create in me a clean heart, O God, and renew a right spirit within me."

In the Latin prayer, Elizabeth identifies herself as queen and asks, like King Solomon, for wisdom to judge God's people in righteousness and his poor in justice. She also asks, in the words of Paul, to be dressed in the full armor of God as, in effect, a spiritual warrior-queen. Her meditation in this prayer on God's word, and her description of the intimate roles it plays in her inner and outward life of faith, is full of beauty and passion. The Greek prayer is shorter than the Latin. In the Greek prayer, Elizabeth first focuses on penitence but then notes the many examples from scripture of sinners who repented and so became God's friends. In this prayer, therefore, Elizabeth sees herself as a forgiven sinner who becomes the friend of God.

The final English prayer sums up the themes of Elizabeth's prayer life in general, and it includes expressions of thanksgiving, contrition, and petition, but at one point it focuses specifically on the request that God help her to remember God. The prayer concludes with the hope that Elizabeth herself will one day be "translated into immortality" because of the merit of God's son, Jesus Christ. In all, the prayer book is a fascinating study in Elizabeth's life of faith in her later years, a faith nourished not only through her devotional prayers, but also through her many translations.

AN ACCOMPLISHED TRANSLATOR

As a child and young woman, Elizabeth pursued a humanist program of studies, most likely alongside her brother, Prince Edward, under the tutelage of various educated men, including William Grindal (her Latin tutor), Roger Ascham (her second Latin and first Greek tutor), and Battista Castiglione (her Italian tutor). She may have studied French with Jean Bellemain. She practiced her linguistic skills in a circle of educated women, which included her governess Kat Ashley and her stepmother Catherine Parr, and in various translation projects, which she undertook with the intention of giving the results as gifts.

Her first translation, made in 1544 when she was twelve, was of Marguerite of Navarre's *Le miroir de l'âme pecheresse*. Elizabeth's mother, Anne Boleyn, once owned a copy of the book, which she obtained when she was working in the service of Marguerite in France, and Elizabeth may have made her translation from that edition. When she completed her translation, Elizabeth gave it as a New Year's gift to Queen Catherine Parr.

Elizabeth rendered the original French poem into English prose and called it "A Glass of the Sinful Soul." As Elizabeth wrote in an introductory letter to the queen, the work concerns the soul, who "doth perceive how of herself and of her own strength she can do nothing that is good or prevaileth for her salvation, unless it be through the grace of God, whose mother, daughter, sister, and wife by the Scriptures she proveth herself to be." The work was a significant early accomplishment, and it was published by John Bale in Germany in 1548. In 1568 and 1570, James Cancellar republished it; in 1582, Thomas Bentley included it in his anthology *Monument of Matrons*.

In 1545, Elizabeth translated Queen Catherine Parr's *Prayers or Meditations,* originally composed in English, into Latin, French, and Italian as a New Year's gift for her father, King Henry VIII, and her stepmother Queen Catherine. Latin and French were two languages Henry used for foreign diplomacy, while Italian was a language Queen Catherine enjoyed. Queen Catherine had originally derived her English meditations from Thomas à Kempis's *De imitatione Christi,* and her changes to the Catholic original reflect her Reformed sentiments.

Elizabeth's translation consisted of a dedicatory letter in Latin to Henry VIII, in which she declared her intentions:

> Which work, since it is pious, and by the pious exertion and great diligence of the most illustrious queen has been assembled in English, and on that account may be desired by all and held in greater value by your Majesty: it was thought by me the most suitable thing that this work, which is most worthy because it was indeed an assemblage by a queen as subject matter for her king, be translated into other languages by me, your daughter, who by this means would be indebted to you not only as an imitator of your virtues but also as an inheritor of them.
>
> (*Elizabeth I: Collected Works*, p. 10)

There then follow 183 short thoughts and prayers, a prayer for the king, and a prayer to be said for men who are entering into war. Elizabeth's work certainly demonstrates her proficiency in foreign languages as well as the focus of the meditations of her heart, which clearly concerned the right relationship of her soul to God and her relationship to her parents, especially the king.

Also in 1545, Elizabeth translated the first chapter of John Calvin's *Institution de la religion chrestienne* from French into English. She relied on the 1541 version, not the later one produced in 1545, when composing her translation. How she obtained a copy of this book is not known. Perhaps Jean Bellemain, then in residence at the court and a correspondent of Calvin's, encouraged Elizabeth to translate part of it. He may have also aided her with the quality of the French.

Elizabeth dedicated the chapter to Queen Catherine. In her dedicatory letter, composed in French, Elizabeth begins by noting that humanity has invented arts and sciences to preserve the memory of things worthy of commemoration, and she argues that the "invention of letters" is the most "spiritual, excellent, and ingenious." She goes on to point out that the scriptures exemplify this truth because "God by his Word and Scripture can be seen, heard, and known for who He is, inasmuch as it is permitted and necessary for our salvation." Elizabeth notes that no image made by a painter, engraver, or sculptor could represent God the way the scriptures do; she thus affirms Reformed, evangelical sentiments even before the major iconoclasms of the Renaissance and Reformation.

Discussing her translation technique in the letter, Elizabeth asserts that she has translated *mot pour mot* or word for word. An analysis of her translation by the editors Janel Mueller and Joshua Scodel shows that her claim is largely accurate. She makes few errors, but she sometimes produces unidiomatic English prose in her faithfulness to the French (e.g., "it must that" for *il fault que*). She also reduces Calvin's emphatic doublets to one powerful word. The translation emphasizes the supremacy of the scriptures as a means of revealing God's truth and God himself. It begins by asserting that wisdom consists of knowing God and knowing oneself; it concludes by admitting that we cannot fully know God, since he does not fully reveal himself to us, unless it be in "the face of his Christ."

In 1547, Elizabeth translated Bernadino Ochino's "Che cosa è Christo," an Italian sermon she rendered into Latin, for her younger brother, Edward, who had by this date become the ten-year-old king of England. Ochino was a Franciscan monk from Siena who later joined the Capuchins in 1534 and became their vicar general. He was a firm believer in the doctrine of justification by faith. After being summoned to appear before the Inquisition in Rome, he went to Geneva instead and then to England. He became a prebendary of Canterbury Cathedral and received a pension from the young Protestant king Edward VI, a situation that ended when the Catholic Queen Mary ascended the English throne. His sermon very much emphasizes themes similar to those in "The Mirror of the Sinful Soul."

In her dedicatory letter to Edward, composed in Latin, Elizabeth expresses her desire to offer "the greatest things" to her brother and claims, "although I am surpassed by others in resources, I am outdone by no one in love and goodwill." She observes that since the subject of the sermon is Christ, the reading of it will be "profitable (*utilis*) and fruitful (*fructuosa*)." Her letter dates from the end of December, clearly suggesting that this translation was another New Year's gift.

The sermon is a thematic one (not an explication of the particular Bible passage), and the theme is straightforward: "what Christ is and why he came into the world." It begins:

> If a little sheep did not know at Shepherd, a soldier his captain, a servant his lord; if someone did not recognize his friend, his wife, his brother or his own parent, indeed, none of himself, this would be a crass and pernicious ignorance. But not to know Christ is an ignorance of so much more crass and pernicious in as much as he is to us not only a good Shepherd, best captain, most pious lord, true friend, sweet spouse, loving brother, and dear Father, but, indeed, nearer to us than our own soul.
> (*Elizabeth I: Translations, Vol. I*, p. 305)

The sermon takes time to compare and contrast Christ and Moses. It examines Christ's relationship with people as depicted in the New Testament, such as Mary Magdalene, the disciples on the road to Emmaus, the apostles, and so on. Ochino notes the roles Christ played in each relationship. It describes Christ's major actions and what motivated them. The sermon concludes with a prayer that Christ will make the listeners "sharers in His true light."

In 1563, Elizabeth produced her Latin *Sententia*: a collection of 259 brief, wise sayings. These may have had their origin in a collection of 100 sayings Elizabeth produced earlier and dedicated to her father, as James Montague, the bishop of Winchester, suggested in 1616 (though such a collection of 100 sayings is no longer extant). Elizabeth divides her 259 Latin sentences into six categories: on rule, on justice, on mercy, on counsel, on peace, and on war. Her sources include biblical and classical authors, the Church fathers and medieval ecclesiastics as well as Erasmus. Notably, her first sentence boldly affirms the divine right of kings: "Quae sunt potestes a Deo ordinate. Rom. 13" ("the powers that be are ordained of God").

The collection was very much a statement of her learning and fitness to rule, a statement made both to the nobility of England and to the international courts of Europe. The sentences show a transition in Elizabeth's focus as well. As she herself claimed in a speech to her parliament in 1566, she "studied nothing else but divinity" until she became queen, but afterward she concentrated on that which was helpful "for government." Indeed, Elizabeth's next three translations were from classical sources and pertained to rule.

In about 1567, the queen translated Seneca's 107th moral epistle from Latin to English for her godson, John Harington. The letter's conclusion is particularly robust: "the greatest heart is it that bequeaths to God his part; and he, of base and bastardly mind, that wrestles a pluck with the world's order, conceives thereof an evil opinion, and seeks rather to amend God than himself" (*Elizabeth I: Translations, 1544–1589*, p. 421). Her choice of a letter with such didactic content relates to her previous work, the *Sententia*, as well as her instructive corpus of translations in general. The internal rhyme, alliteration, and parallelism in the last sentence show Elizabeth's fine style in translation. The fact that she changed the Roman philosopher Cicero's plural "gods" to her own English singular "God" shows her willingness to adapt the Latin her own convictions and purpose.

In about 1579, Elizabeth translated one of Cicero's letters (the sixth one in his second book from *Epistulae ad familiares*). Its focus on balancing the requirements of friendship with the requirements of the political realm is obviously pertinent to Elizabeth's relationships to many other people during her reign. Then, in about 1589, Elizabeth translated a choral ode from "Hercules Oetaeus," which was attributed to Seneca during the Renaissance. It is a meditation on the vagaries of Fortune, a theme Elizabeth treats in other letters, prayers, and poems. A few years later, around 1592, Elizabeth translated Cicero's speech "Pro Marcello." This speech expresses Cicero's gratitude to Caesar for his pardon of the Marcellus, a senator who had offended Caesar during the civil war.

In the last decade of her life, Elizabeth made three more significant translations of Latin works. In 1593, she translated all five books of the ancient philosopher Boethius' *De consolatione philosophiae* ("Consolation of Philosophy") from Latin into English. In so doing, she followed in the footsteps of two previous English translators of this most famous work of Boethius: King Alfred the Great and Geoffrey Chaucer. Finally, in 1598, she translated two works from Latin into English: Desiderius Erasmus's Latin version of Plutarch's *De curiositate* and lines 1–178 of Horace's *De arte poetica*.

AN INFLUENTIAL PATRON

Elizabeth I was not only an extraordinary woman, a great monarch, a powerful writer, and an accomplished translator, but she was also an influential patron of the arts. Her patronage was directly responsible for financing or rewarding artists who painted her portrait for her public, composed music for her court, performed plays in her presence, wrote poetry in her honor, and produced books of various kinds commemorating her reign. Her person was indirectly responsible for inspiring an even wider circle of artists who, without direct payment, wrote for or about Elizabeth and thereby helped establish her legacy.

Elizabeth's patronage was fostered in her court culture. The development of this aesthetic court culture began with Elizabeth's progress through London the day before her coronation, when her people created for her five symbolically rich pageants, including one in which the allegorical virtues of Pure Religion, Love of Subjects, Wisdom, and Justice vanquished Rebellion and Folly. After Elizabeth was crowned, she continued to sponsor the arts. For example, her Master of the Horse, Robert Dudley, was responsible for arranging many complex and expensive entertainments for the queen, especially during her summer progresses through England to visit her nobles. But of course, her patronage extended beyond summer entertainments; it influenced Renaissance painting, music, drama, and literature, among other things, in England throughout her lifetime and afterward.

Elizabeth is justly famous for the many portraits of her that were painted throughout her life by such men as William Scrots, Levina Teerlinc, Federico Zuccaro, William Segar, John Betts the Younger, George Gower, Marcus Gheeraerts the Elder and the Younger, Isaac Oliver, William Rogers, and Nicholas Hilliard and his workshop. Many of the portraits have symbolic and allegorical significance. Elizabeth was also a patron of musicians. Many court composers wrote music for Elizabeth I, who herself was an accomplished musician who enjoyed listening and dancing to music and was appreciative of works both secular and sacred. Her favorite composer was William Byrd (1543–1623), but others whose work she supported included Jane Pickering, Thomas Morley, John Dowland, Richard Allison, Daniel Bachiler, John Tavener, and Thomas Lupo. Music composed for Elizabeth could be either secular or sacred.

Along with painting and music, Elizabeth was a great patron of Renaissance drama in England. Shakespeare's company performed plays for her, including *The Merry Wives of Windsor* and *A Midsummer Night's Dream*. Elizabeth may have even inspired some of Shakespeare's characters, including Portia from the *Merchant of Venice* (whose problems with her many suitors look very much like a retrospective commentary in the Jacobean period on Elizabeth's marital challenges only a few short years before). Other Renaissance dramatists working in this period and enjoying the possibilities of the performance culture Elizabeth fostered included Christopher Marlowe and Ben Jonson.

Elizabeth's great influence on Renaissance literature is well recognized to this day. Edmund Spencer immortalized his monarch in his long allegorical poem "The Faerie Queene." Sir Walter Raleigh, Sir Philip Sidney, and Ben Jonson wrote verses in her honor. Especially later in her life, and after her death when her godson King James ruled, Elizabeth was praised in Renaissance literature as Cynthia, the goddess of the moon, the hunt, and, of course, virginity.

Elizabeth I had such a profound impact on the history, culture, and arts in the England of her day that her time period has come to be known as the Elizabethan Age. In fact, she has more often been viewed as a great queen and patron than as a great writer and translator. But as new editions of her complete works and translations are published, scholars have the opportunity to reevaluate Elizabeth's significant literary contributions in her time. For even into the modern era, Elizabeth I continues to be a felt presence in film, fiction, and historical memory: beloved, controversial, and inspiring.

Selected Bibliography

EDITED EDITIONS OF THE WORKS OF ELIZABETH I

Marcus, Leah, Janel Mueller, and Mary Beth Rose, eds. *Elizabeth I: Collected Works*. Chicago: University of Chicago Press, 2000.

Mueller, Janel, and Joshua Scodel, eds. *Elizabeth I: Translations, 1544–1589*. Chicago: University of Chicago Press, 2009.

Mueller, Janel, and Joshua Scodel, eds. *Elizabeth I: Translations, 1592–1598*. Chicago: University of Chicago Press, 2009.

Mueller, Janel, and Leah Marcus, eds. *Elizabeth I: Autograph Compositions and Foreign Language Originals*. Chicago: University of Chicago Press, 2003.

Perry, Maria. *The Word of a Prince: A Life of Elizabeth I from Contemporary Documents*. Woodbridge, U.K.: Boydell Press, 1990.

Pryor, Felix. *Elizabeth I: Her Life in Letters*. Berkeley: University of California Press, 2003.

CRITICAL AND BIOGRAPHICAL STUDIES

Bassnett, Susan. *Elizabeth I: A Feminist Perspective*. Oxford: Berg, 1988.

Berry, Philippa. *Of Chastity and Power: Elizabethan Literature and the Unmarried Queen*. London and New York: Routledge, 1989.

Doran, Susan, and Thomas Freeman, eds. *The Myth of Elizabeth*. New York: Palgrave Macmillan, 2003.

Farrell, Kirby, and Kathleen Swaim, eds. *The Mysteries of Elizabeth I: Selections from English Literary Renaissance*. Amherst: University of Massachusetts Press, 1978. Reprint, 2003.

Forster, Leonard. *The Icy Fire: Five Studies in European Petrarchism*. London: Cambridge University Press, 1969.

Foster, Brett. "The Continuing Reign of Queen Elizabeth I." *Common Review* 7, no. 2:32–41 (fall 2008).

Gift of Music, "Great Music from the Court of Elizabeth I." Classical Communications Ltd., 2003. (CD)

Levin, Carole. *The Heart and Stomach of the King: Elizabeth I and the Politics of Sex and Power*. Philadelphia: University of Pennsylvania Press, 1994.

Loades, David. *Elizabeth I*. London and New York: Hambledon, 2003.

Montrose, Louis. *The Subject of Elizabeth: Authority, Gender, and Representation*. Chicago: University of Chicago Press, 2006.

Ronald, Susan. *The Pirate Queen: Queen Elizabeth I, Her Pirate Adventurers, and the Dawn of Empire*. New York: HarperCollins, 2007.

Strong, Roy. *Gloriana: The Portraits of Queen Elizabeth I*. London: Pimlico, 2003.

Stump, Donald, and Susan Felch, eds. *Elizabeth I and Her Age*. New York and London: W. W. Norton, 2009.

Summit, Jennifer. "'The Arte of a Ladies Penne': Elizabeth I and the Poetics of Queenship." In *Reading Monarch's Writing: The Poetry of Henry VIII, Mary Stuart, Elizabeth I, and James VI/I*. Edited by Peter C. Herman. Tempe: Arizona Center for Medieval and Renaissance Studies, 2002. Pp.79–108.

Teague, Francis. "Elizabeth I: Queen of England." In *Women Writers of the Renaissance and Reformation*. Edited by Katharina Wilson. Athens: University of Georgia Press, 1987. Pp. 522–547.

———. "Queen Elizabeth in Her Speeches." In *Gloriana's Face: Women, Public and Private, in the English Renaissance*. Edited by S. P. Cerasano and Marion Wynne Davies. Detroit: Wayne State University Press, 1992. Pp. 63–78.

ANDREW GREIG

(1951—)

Les Wilkinson

ANDREW GREIG WAS born on September 23, 1951, in Bannockburn, a location significant in Scottish history and Scottish consciousness as the battlefield where Robert the Bruce defeated the forces of Edward II in a decisive engagement and ensured that Scottish independence, so long fought for, became a reality. Given Greig's birthplace, it was perhaps inevitable he would develop a strong sense of what it means to be Scots. The family moved during his childhood to Anstruther in Fife, a small rural and fishing community, where his father worked as a doctor. Educated at Waid Academy and Edinburgh University, he worked for a short time as an advertising copywriter until he could afford to make a living as a writer, depending for a period on writer's bursaries, workshops, and appointments as writer in residence at both Edinburgh and Glasgow universities and as Scottish-Canadian Exchange Fellow in the early 1980s. His first poetry collection, *White Boats,* was published in 1973. His second publication, *Men on Ice* (1977), which focused on an imagined experience of climbing, brought him an invitation to take part in an expedition to conquer the Mustagh Tower, one of the "unclimbable" peaks of the Himalayas. This led to him becoming a climbing writer of considerable repute, chronicling this expedition and also a second to the Northeast Ridge of Everest a year later. He continued to publish poetry, but in 1992 he published his first novel, *Electric Brae.* In 2001 his life was threatened by a colloid cyst, which required delicate brain surgery and the insertion of a stent into his temple, an experience reflected in his novel *In Another Light* (2004); his 2006 nonfiction publication (the nearest thing to an autobiography), *Preferred Lies: A Journey to the Heart of Scottish Golf,* is centered around his awakened passion for golf once his climbing days were over. He is married to the novelist Lesley Glaister. Having lived in different areas of Scotland including Orkney, Peebles, and South Queensferry, he has settled near Sheffield in England.

POETRY

Andrew Greig's poetic voice can perhaps best be described in his own words in a quotation from the poem "Wordscape: Elegy for Angus":

words bared to the bone
words weighted like rocks
split raw from the vein.

(*This Life, This Life*, p. 51)

Although Greig's literary reputation is based primarily on his novels, the main themes of his writing are apparent in his poetry: accounts of vivid experience, adventurous and emotional, recounted with clarity and honesty. His admiration for his father, and the effect on his work of his father's death, is a recurrent theme in his writing. An early version of his novel *That Summer* (2000) is evident in the verse sequence *A Flame in Your Heart* (1987), cowritten with a former partner, Kathleen Jamie, herself an accomplished poet and academic.

Greig's earliest collection of poems, *White Boats,* is characterized by a heavily Scottish theme, depicting an outdoor, rural life of (among others) fishermen and poachers who seek solace in whisky at the end of a dangerous day. There is no romanticism in the way Scotland is portrayed: an emotionless viewpoint is established where "The night turns over without effort / without interest" ("Maxwell"). His next collection, *Men on Ice* (1977) is an imaginative insight into what drives men to climb mountains, all the more impressive because at this stage Greig was no more than an armchair mountaineer himself: his experiences as a climber were to be in the future, but this collection was the catalyst that brought those experiences about. The sequence begins with three friends caught on a mountain, facing certain death, each preparing in their own way for the end of their lives, before they are rescued by the mysterious Zen Climber who leads them to safety and narcotic awareness of themselves. The three protagonists, Axe-Man, Grimpeur, and Poet (the latter a representation of Greig himself) are very different in their outlook and temperaments, and indeed the dynamics of the sequence depend upon this. Axe-Man is the hedonistic hard man:

Life is a glorious tit:
I've wanted to feel it, I felt it—...
Now I've sucked it dry
and I'm ready to die

whereas Grimpeur is more aspirational in his outlook: "O / but my powers / were made to be extended." ("Grimpeur's Explanation"; *This Life, This Life,* p. 30). The relationship between the three depends on mutual trust but is disguised by ironic banter, and as such it anticipates the relationships Greig will find between real mountaineers in his nonfiction work.

Surviving Passages (1982) is a collection of single poems worked at greater length than those in *White Boats*. "Confessions of an Airman" examines the mind of a World War II fighter pilot whose psychology is not unlike that of the eponymous flyer in William Butler Yeats's "An Irish Airman Foresees His Death" and who, like Greig's mountaineers, only feels truly alive when close to death, described as his "sudden girl-friend" who as yet has only brushed his cheek with her lips. "In the Tool Shed" describes a young boy listening to the exotic stories told by an old gardener; the boy is mesmerized by the words the old man uses to describe his adventures in the jungle and the Congo, but he also confuses them with the language of gardening: azaleas, zebras, and the Zambesi are equally resonant in his mind, as are orchids, oranges, and orangutans.

The gardener becomes a witch doctor, reminding us how childhood experience resonates into adulthood. "Portobello Beach," a short sequence of poems describing two lovers in an out-of-season seaside café, offers an analysis of Greig's relationship with Scotland, "the half-cut / ragged fingernail / on the outflung arm of Europe,") (*This Life, This Life,* p. 59) which moves him to both affection and despair. The café becomes for him a symbol of the nation, and like many Scots before him he feels contradictory impulses toward his native land: " - How can we ever leave? / - How can we ever stay?" (*This Life, This Life,* p. 60).

A Flame in Your Heart (1986) is a poem sequence that charts a wartime relationship between an airman and a young woman from a different social class who have by accident in a pub; Greig's contribution sees their faltering and growing love from the man's point of view. The relationship reaches a point where the two are clear that they intend to spend their lives together ("My roots / are in our future" *This Life, This Life,* p. 69). The poem proceeds through several images of foreboding until the final sequence, recounted with bleak objectivity describes the final three seconds of Len's life, as he is struck by shrapnel that tears into his thigh and stomach, spilling his intestines into a tangle with his oxygen tube and radio leads before his plane explodes and he enters "the fire he became." The sequence offers a more accessible narrative than other poem sequences and delivers a powerful impact.

The Order of the Day (1990) offers a number of poems based upon experiences from Greig's first Himalayan expedition; then in *Western Swing* (1994) we encounter the friends Axe-Man, Grimpeur, and Poet again in another free-flowing sequence, this time in quest of a knife and its sheath. The list of characters is expanded to include the Heretical Buddha, who replaces the Zen Climber as the guide to enlightenment, and Stella, a patient who breaks out of a mental hospital to join the quest. That "Bud" and "Stella" are both brands of beer should alert us to the tone of the poem, which is filled with puns, pastiche, parody, and lines from sources as diverse as T. S. Eliot, Hugh MacDiarmid, and modern pop lyrics. Greig makes us aware of these two poets as points of reference when Stella requests the poet to bring "thistles from Brownsbank and roses from the Bostonian's garden." Brownsbank was the cottage where MacDiarmid lived the final years of his life; the Bostonian is an allusion to Eliot. Sustained allusions to *The Waste Land,* and indeed the sequence's very structure, invite comparisons with Eliot's poem, with the quest for the knife mirroring the grail quest theme in Eliot. There is also a brilliant sustained parody of MacDiarmid's style employing "synthetic" Scots. The whole is a fantastic poetic journey embracing Tibet, Pakistan, Morocco, and Scotland, and drawing important comparisons between them all; Axe-Man's hedonism remains unquenched—"Sod it, we're all going to die" ("A Carry Out Episode"; *This Life, This Life,* p. 140)—but the whole expresses a positive morality embedded in pithy aphorisms: "It's whit ye dae when naebody's lookin' that counts" (p. 142) and Bud's final advice:

*Don't buy
what can be bought—
it's rubbish.
Without expectation, aid all living things.
And my opinion of life remains
Probably the least interesting thing about it.*
(*This Life, This Life,* p. 156)

By the end of the poem, Poet has come to realize that life in the mountain villages of Pakistan is no different from what it was in Scotland a hundred years ago. Looking around his boyhood home (Anstruther) with Bud at the end of the poem, he has an awareness of the continuity and flux of the generations who have lived there, of death and renewal. The final poem of the sequence, an echo of Eliot's "Hollow Men" in tone and structure, accepts human insignificance and the impermanence of life, but encourages us to live in expectation of having to account for how we have lived our lives. The whole is an exhilarating epic journey, bristling with wit and verbal invention.

Greig's poetry since *Western Swing* has returned to shorter lyrics and observations, in the style and voice of *Surviving Passages*. A number of poems explore his developing relationship with his wife, such as "Lucky" or "That Summer." (*This Life, This Life,* pp. 165, 173, respectively) In "Scotland," (p. 173) he proclaims a manifesto for his homeland, urging Scots to forget their self-pity and sense of having fallen on hard times and instead to walk unaided towards the newly born twenty-first century, greeting it with a clear head and open heart. Another important poem from 2006 deals with his relationship to his dead father, a constant source of inspiration to him: in "From the Royal College of Surgeons of Edinburgh," (*This Life, This Life,* 198) he remembers his father, and in particular his father's reliance on his hands to diagnose a patient's illness in his work as a general medical practitioner:

*On good days it seemed my fingertips
could see through skin, and once inside
had little lamps attached, that showed
exactly how and where to go.*

Greig remembers that those skillful, healing hands are now no more than ash, but his father's confidence in working blind—seeing and healing through touch, without vision, inspire him with confidence:

*... We need
to believe we are not working blind;
with his eye open in my mind
I open the notebook and proceed.*

Like Seamus Heaney in his famous poem "Digging," Greig finds inspiration in his father's distinctive skills to achieve excellence in his own field—writing.

SUMMIT FEVER

The offer to join an expedition into the Himalayas to conquer the summit of the Mustagh Tower was made casually, in the kitchen of the house Greig shared with Kathleen Jamie, by the almost legendary Scottish mountaineer Mal Duff—the enigmatic leader of the expedition who fascinated Greig and who becomes the focal character in the later stages of the resulting book *Summit*

Fever, which appeared in 1985. Greig was invited to accompany the expedition as a writer, to record all that he saw; he would have access to the journals and diaries of the expedition's members; his part would be to write a book about what happened. The book he produced benefits greatly from its dual point of view: that is, first, it was written by someone who was very much part of the climbing team and who made a valuable contribution as a mountaineer to the success of the expedition; and second, it was written by someone who was new to the experience of Himalayan climbing and who therefore saw events through fresh eyes. Above all, Greig was fascinated by what drives such a group of men and women—the "shuffling dossers" to whom the book is dedicated—to do what they do; in the course of the expedition he comes to realize that "to call mountaineering a sport or a pastime is like calling monastic life a hobby" (p. 45).

But before Greig could embark on the expedition, he had to learn to climb, and the early passages of the book describe his first lessons with Mal Duff in Glencoe, where he seesaws between terror and exhilaration. He finds the total concentration on the next handhold a liberating experience from the cares of the world. It is in Glencoe that he first becomes aware of the fatalism of mountaineers; when he hears of the death on the Matterhorn of Brian Sprunt, someone Duff had intended to accompany them to the Mustagh Tower, while climbing with Sandy Allen, who will become a member of the team, he realizes that underlying the camaraderie of the climbing community is a sense of the fragility of life, which makes it all the more important to live it to the full.

The expedition sets off; Greig describes its members and their relationships (including his own) with meticulous honesty, particularly regarding his own self-consciousness as the "writer" on the expedition, slightly mistrusted by some of its members. The company has its tensions, particularly when the members realize that the expedition is drastically underfunded and it is likely a number of them will have drop out—before Duff returns to Scotland to raise more funding. The situation does give rise to a wonderful comic sequence in the book, when expedition members aim to liquidize their assets in the bank in Skadu, the last town in rural Pakistan before their walk-in to the mountain begins—"a simple operation, you might think"—which turns into "a total epic," (p. 83) a three-and-a-half-hour encounter with third-world bureaucracy leading to frustration, disbelief, and a final sense of triumph when the transaction is accomplished.

The expedition party moves on, and Greig spends an idyllic week in the village of Askole, where he feels a profound admiration for the simplicity of a way of life he finds less medieval than Neolithic: villagers plow with wooden plowshares drawn by oxen; they weave baskets from branches. They may be poor, but there is no unemployment, as everyone has a role to play in the functioning of the society of the village, and although there is private property, it is held by wide communal family groups rather than by individuals. Is such a village a pit or a paradise? Greig asks. His answer is that the chickens there may be scrawny, but at least they are not battery hens.

From Askole the walk-in continues to Base Camp; his first views of the Karakoram find Greig overwhelmed by the "austere, crazed, magnificently indifferent presence" (p. 145) of the mountains. He describes their impact as a blow to the chest, and as his time among them continues he comes to realize the insignificance of human life—his life—to their vast impersonality, a thought he finds an immense relief: whatever our self-important race is led to by its leaders with their potential to destroy life itself, these high peaks on the roof of the world will remain.

The final stage of the book deals with the painstaking preparations from Base Camp in provisioning the higher camps for the final assault on the peak. Tensions between the climbers persist; the pairings are based on absolute trust, rather like a marriage, but that does not preclude bickering. It is in this context that Greig comes to admire the mountaineers and see them as inspired by a vocation: for them there is only climbing and preparing to climb, just as the thing that gives meaning to his own life is writing. Here, as they sort out their equipment and prepare for the final ascent, he understands his companions fully: they may be "shuffling dossers" in "civilised" contexts, but they are also experts in their chosen field. They are ordinary men with human failings, but in this environment their persistence, courage, and the fact they have faced death many times endows them with a spiritual resonance.

Greig contributes to the success of the expedition by taking supplies across the glacier as high as Camp 2—the highest point he will reach, a tremendous achievement for someone on his first Himalayan expedition, and as high as he wants to go. The tension of the crucial chapter as to whether the expedition will succeed is masterfully controlled as he constantly switches narrative perspective from himself at Base Camp to the support climbers, Sandy Allen and Jon Tinker, at Camp 2—which is 3,000 feet below the summit—and Mal Duff and Tony Brindle on their climb from Camp 4 at 22,000 feet to the summit, 1,860 feet above. The tension is palpable as Greig waits for overdue radio contact, and the euphoria strangely muted when Duff calls in to report that he and Brindle are sitting on the summit. The next day Allen and Tinker also achieve the summit. They are the only four people to have done this since the Joe Brown–Tom Patey expedition in 1956, yet Greig notes their triumph (in which he has had a part) "changed nothing at all. Except us" (p. 249)

The book celebrates the diversity of all the members of the expedition—their quirks and their foibles, as well as their strengths and heroism—but it is Duff who comes across as the character who has fascinated Greig most. Greig refers to a verse by the Marquis of Montrose (1612–1650) that is one of Duff's favorite quotations:

He either fears his fate too much
Or his deserts are small,
That dares not put it to the touch
To win or lose at all.

(quoted on p. 243)

He concludes that Montrose must have had a climber's mentality: "That's why death isn't tragic for those who decide that, win or lose, life merits the gamble" (p. 243). Excess of life, not the lack of it, is what drove Duff, who died in his sleep on Everest thirteen years after the events described in Greig's book. *Summit Fever* is a fitting tribute to a man who Greig admired so much.

ELECTRIC BRAE

Greig's first novel, *Electric Brae,* appeared in 1992 and is very much in the modern Scottish tradition: an allusion is made to William McIlvanney's *Docherty* (1975), and the gritty realism of that author's work is present here, together with the influence of Iain Banks.

The story is told by Jim Renison, a climber who finances his hobby by working on the oil rigs (a biographical detail borrowed from Sandy Allen, a member of the Mustagh expedition). Early in the novel he meets Graeme, who becomes his climbing companion, and he also meets an art student who is ten years younger than he—Kim, an unpredictable and potentially unstable girl of Polish Scottish descent. The novel goes on to explore the relationship of these three central characters together with Lesley, Graeme's partner at the outset of the tale.

Jim follows Kim and her friend Joan to an archaeological dig in Orkney, where he develops a plan to climb the Old Man of Hoy, a remarkable sea stack and an established climbing challenge. Kim and Jim become lovers; he is totally overwhelmed by her. Although there is no commitment on either side, the relationship continues, through her years as a student in Edinburgh to her first art exhibition. Jim buys a house in Dunbar, on the east coast of Scotland, and he creates a studio for Kim on the top floor, which he makes available for her use. Significantly, the room has a lock on the door and he never enters it without her permission. The relationships develop to the point where Jim, Kim, Graeme, and Lesley go to Orkney together so that the men can climb the Old Man of Hoy. Jim sees this as an idyllic period, although in retrospect it is fraught with tensions he was unaware of at the time. On the morning they are to set out for the climb, Graeme leaves without explanation, to Jim's confusion. The reason soon becomes clear:

he and Lesley have argued over his increasing fascination with Kim. This feeling is reciprocated, and Kim begins a relationship with Graeme; Lesley leaves for the United States. After a while, however, Kim realizes she still has strong feelings for Jim, and she proposes a relationship with "the two people I love most in the world" which they christen the Golden Triangle. The unstable triangle causes tension between the two men— "It wasn't an experiment in living, just something we were trapped in" (p. 157)—as shown on a climb in Glencoe through the dangerous Disappearing Gully, and it eventually breaks up; Jim goes to recover from his despair to stay with Joan, now a fish farmer on Orkney. He considers a relationship with her, but an attempt to climb the Old Man solo (in order to aggravate Graeme) ends in him falling and injuring himself badly. As a result, he leaves Orkney.

The final movement of the narrative takes place after a gap of several years. Graeme, like Jim, has gone to stay with Joan to recover from losing Kim, but unlike his friend, he develops a stable relationship with her and the two become lovers. Lesley has formed a lesbian relationship with Tess, one of Kim's friends; Kim, now a successful artist, is seeing Keith, an Edinburgh doctor; Jim has formed a stable relationship with a single parent, Ruth. He forms a strong bond with Ruth's daughter, Mary, and he feels sufficiently free of Kim to contemplate having children with Ruth. A happy ending is in sight, as Jim anticipates, until Kim decides she wants to sleep with her two former lovers before marrying Keith. She becomes pregnant and does not know which of them is the father. Jim's relationship with Ruth ends, as she decides to marry Mary's father; when Graeme receives the news of Kim's pregnancy, including the uncertainty of paternity, he sets out to climb the Old Man alone and is killed in the attempt. At his funeral, Kim's unstable mental condition is clear; she will spend the rest of her life in and out of mental institutions. Jim and Lesley undertake to look after her child when it is born, with the issue of paternity—that is, whether Graeme or Jim is the father of Kim's daughter— simply left unresolved and accepted as an irrelevance.

The novel is certainly complex and full (perhaps too full) of incident and character. The narrative technique is no less ambitious: it is developed in three sections, and each is told in retrospect in a mixture of first- and third-person narrative by Jim: the first section finds Jim alone in his home with an unidentified child whose parentage is not explained. The narrative device around which the first section is centered is a tray of objects, such as would be employed in the parlor game known as Kim's Game, and as Jim picks up and discards each object in turn, it reminds him of a stage of his story. The narrative frame in the second section revolves around a game of paper, scissors, stone, which Jim is playing with "the bairn" as he drives to pick up Lesley from Prestwick Airport. The final section finds Jim sitting in Kim's studio in his house, reading her letters. The device of telling the story in retrospect allows Jim to anticipate events as an omniscient narrator, pointing up ironies that we will later come to realize as the plot develops.

A theme of the novel is Jim's quest to find out who he is: Kim's first question to him in an Aberdeen bar is, "So who are you then?" (p. 11) She is attracted to him because he is "puzzled at the edge of his group, part but not part of it. *Adrift* was the word." (p. 16) Jim believes he will find meaning in his life through his love for Kim, but his relationship with Ruth leads him to see meaning through children, and it is through his relationship with Irina, "the bairn" who may or may not be his daughter, that he finds himself. She is the child of the three of them ("It makes no odds who the dad is"), and before she is born Jim realizes, "I've aye known who I am. I'm the child of my mother and my father and my country. And now I'm the parent of a child to be. That's the centre. That's where the compass point digs in. The circumference is as wide as you want to make it" (p. 309).

When Jim says he is "a child of his country" he is drawing attention to a major aspect of the novel, which deals with what it means to be Scots in a country that, Greig feels, is losing its identity. Jim's speech (but not his prose) is peppered with Scots colloquialisms and vocabulary. Jim comments on his own language: "We'll say 'yea' and 'aye' and 'yeah' in the same conversation, alternate between 'know' and 'ken', 'bairn' and 'wean' and 'child' and not even know why ... We're a small country with blurry boundaries" (p. 56). A small country Scotland may be, but Greig ensures we see almost all of it in the course of the novel, from Jim's east coast towns of Dunbar and Eyemouth to the highlands of Glencoe, the islands of Orkney and Shetland, the very different city environments of Edinburgh and Glasgow, and the housing development in Plean where Kim grew up. The novel's enigmatic title comes from the name of a hillside in Scotland where an optical illusion leads the traveler to think he is climbing on a road that is in fact descending: in this novel, nothing is what it seems and all appearances turn out to be deceptive. But there is more to being Scots than just geography: Jim is aware of differences of outlook with Graeme because Graeme is a west coast man, beside whom Jim is "a marshmallow in comparison" (p. 254). He cannot fully understand Lesley, he feels, because she is English, a race that even walks differently: they "look around as though the world was theirs and ready to be made something of. And us lot, we walk and keek about as if it's something we maun thole" (p. 256). He feels he cannot be separated from his identity as a Scot; in a typically poetic image, he says it cannot be extricated from himself any more than you could fillet the backbone out of a fish and expect it still to swim.

If the novel is fixed firmly geographically, it is also equally fixed in history. The course of the novel roughly covers the period of Margaret Thatcher's years in office as prime minister (1979–1989), during which Graeme's initial political passions gradually diminish as he feels Scotland increasingly marginalized by the Thatcher government, in particular after the referendum of 1979 that failed to deliver a Scottish Assembly at that time. References to the Falklands War (1982), the Miners' Strike (1984), the Chernobyl nuclear disaster (1986), and other key events of the decade serve to establish a time frame for the events in the narrative.

A major aspect of the novel is its exploration of the influence of fathers upon their offspring. Jim is frequently reminded of his father in his own mannerisms and through the skills he has learned from his father's hands (a recurrent theme in Greig's work); Graeme has inherited his crippled father's passion for the mountains; and the memory of witnessing her father's suicide is seen by Kim (and others) as a factor in precipitating her own mental illness and instability as a person.

In many ways, the novel continues to explore through fiction some of the ideas raised in *Summit Fever:* Greig is still interested in what drives human beings, whether it be to climb mountains or to create art: here Jim is the mountaineer and Kim the artist, both with a need to define themselves thorough their respective activities, to the extent that Kim will deliberately not take her medication, even though she knows that it will precipitate mental illness, because it will interfere with her creative processes. The scenes with the climbing "crowd," particularly the wake after Graeme's funeral, owe much to the atmosphere of the Clachan Inn described in *Summit Fever.*

THE RETURN OF JOHN MACNAB

If *Electric Brae* had a tragic cast, then Greig's next novel is a comedy of life-asserting heartiness. As the title suggests, *The Return of John Macnab* (1996) owes a great deal to John Buchan's 1925 novel *John Macnab,* in which three world-weary prominent London figures decide to remedy their condition by setting themselves three poaching challenges in the Highlands to bring excitement back in to their lives: under the fictitious name of John Macnab, each will poach a fish or other animal from a different Highland estate. For Greig, Buchan's novel provides the inspiration for three friends to carry out a similar sequence of feats in modern Scotland, and as a result the two works share a similar structure. The social background of his protagonists is very different, however: Buchan's "heroes" are two Conservative cabinet ministers (one the attorney general, a senior law officer) and the head of an eminent merchant bank, whereas Greig's protagonists are Neil, a recently widowed copy editor, from whose point of view the story is largely seen; Murray, a left-wing joiner; and Alastair, a former member of the Special Forces, who (reminiscent of Graeme in *Electric Brae*) is in an open marriage but unsure of his wife's fidelity. There are other differences, too, as there have been great social changes in Scotland in the seventy-one years between the two novels. In 1925, the three Highland estates targeted were owned by a family of "old blood," the Radens; a nouveau-riche family; and an American archaeologist and his son. In 1996, they are owned by an Arab aristocrat, a Dutch business consortium, and the royal family, as the last estate to be targeted is Balmoral, the Queen's Highland residence, with the Prince of Wales in residence. A key feature driving the political agenda for Murray Hamilton, the neo-Trotskyite of the group, is the publicity they can gain for the issue of land rights through putting forth their challenge; unlike Buchan's aristocrats, they are more politically correct when it comes to blood sports and only tranquillize the Balmoral stag.

Another change in Greig's novel is the inclusion of Kirsty Fowler, who becomes central to the whole "Macnab" enterprise and brings a hard-headed realism to the wilder fantasies of the male characters. She is also a liberated modern woman, an equal of the men, who enjoys a sexual encounter with the Moroccan owner of the first estate targeted and brings him in to the conspiracy; ultimately, she forms a strong sexual relationship with Neil, and together they go off into the sunset at the end of the novel, heading for a new adventure together. Sexual issues also provide comedy in the relationship between Alistair and his wife, Jane: his fear of flying and marital problems are solved simultaneously when he and his wife deliver a brace of poached grouse to the terrace of the first estate by hang glider and immediately resume sexual relationships in the bushes where they crash-land.

Greig solves the problem of the potential lack of tension in the plot by setting the final challenge on the Balmoral estate. Up until now, the Macnabs have only been in fear of gamekeepers and the courts: now, they are viewed as potential terrorists who pose a security risk to the royal family, and their lives are in real danger as Special Forces scramble to protect the heir to the throne. Previously, Alistair's military language and behavior have been amusing, but now there is a real military threat, of which the protagonists are largely unaware. The unlikely relationship of Jim McIvor, the down-to-earth Highland policeman, and Ellen Stobo, the secret services operative, perhaps reassures us that the outcome will be happy, but the Special Forces' decision to mount a "shoot to kill" policy (a very real political issue at the time of publication, following the shooting of terrorists by British Special Forces in Gibraltar) maintains tension until the outcome is resolved. The inclusion of a real person, the Prince of Wales, as a minor character with a speaking role blurs the boundaries between the real world and the fictitious world of the novel, and adds to the lighthearted mood of the ending. As with Buchan's original, a great deal of the enjoyment generated by Greig's novel comes from the atmospheric descriptions of the locations in which it is set: both novelists have an intimate knowledge of the Highlands and capture accurately not only its landscape in all its changing features but also the atmosphere of the hills and the Highland towns and villages, with their slower pace and different outlook on life.

WHEN THEY LAY BARE

Greig's third novel *When They Lay Bare* (1999) is once again radically different from anything else he had written. Set in the Scottish Borders, it draws on the history of the region's lawless past and family feuds, its landscape, its mythology, and its ballad tradition to produce a gripping narrative that twists and turns. Its evocation of a sense of place is one of the novel's major achievements.

There are two plots to the novel that develop simultaneously: in the present, a mysterious young woman arrives on the estate of Sir Simon Elliot and squats in a cottage there. She reveals something of her disturbed past, in and out of Children's Homes, to Simon's son, David, who despite himself (and despite his sexless engagement to Jo, a Canadian academic) feels an attraction for her. Local people come to recognize her as Marnie, the daughter of Simon's lover, for whose murder he stood trial in the past: the verdict of the trial was "not proven," a verdict unique to Scots law, which acquits a prisoner not because he is found innocent but because, in a jury's eyes, he has not been proven guilty. It becomes clear that the woman perceived as Marnie is determined to understand the circumstances of her mother's death, and her presence discomforts not only the Elliot family but also Tat, the factor of the estate, and his wife. Through intuition, she pieces together how the relationship developed between Simon and Jinny, her mother, a free spirit and an impoverished Lauder (a rival Border family in history) who has come to camp with her husband in their caravan on the Elliot estate after claiming in jest that it is rightfully Lauder land. Simon is attracted to Jinny and suddenly he feels his ordinary existence ripped apart by passion he had never expected. Jinny tells him she fears she is pregnant, but when he visits her caravan he sees evidence that her period has arrived. Shortly after, she gives birth to Marnie, and tells Simon the baby is her husband's child. Both try to end the relationship, Simon aware that divorce will reduce his estate, and for a while they succeed in doing so, but relationships begin again and Jinny becomes pregnant with Simon's child. They meet at Lauder Brig (bridge), over the dark gorge of the Liddie Falls, where Jinny falls to her death. The trial verdict has hung on whether Jinny fell or whether she was pushed by Simon Elliot: the closing stages of the novel reveal that she deliberately stepped out in a suicidal act.

Simultaneously, the novel develops the plot in the present: though feared initially, Marnie gradually insinuates herself with David, Tat, and Tat's wife, Annie. Eventually, Simon invites her to join himself, David, and Jo for a meal at the Big House; the evening is pleasant enough, and the young trio go to the village pub, where only Tat's intervention saves them from injury in a barroom brawl. They return to Marnie's cottage, where Simon passes out in his Land Rover after too much alcohol—and hashish cookies. Jo and Marnie become lovers, and the engagement with David is broken. Simon goes to Edinburgh to settle half his estate on the daughter of his late lover, and he dies in the flat he used to share with her. Once she has learned the truth about Jinny's fate, and realized that Marnie is in fact Simon's daughter (through a deception Simon never realizes), the mysterious woman prepares to leave the glen. Her identity is revealed in an unexpected twist, which has nevertheless been carefully prepared for (and which it would be wrong for the critic to reveal). She seduces David before she goes, and with his seed in her womb, pushes him over the Lauder Brig to his death in the same location where Jinny died; that done, she disappears into the mist.

The plot is complex, constantly shifting between time periods, and here Greig develops his technique of employing different viewpoints even further, giving each a distinct voice. We see events primarily from Marnie's point of view, but also from that of Simon Elliot and David, his son. Tat, the factor, has a distinctively Scottish voice, rich in Scots idiom and vocabulary, and what he witnesses as an ever-present watcher fills in narrative gaps of which the central characters could not be aware. Significantly, however, we hear no voices from the past: in particular, we do not hear Jinny's voice. She remains seen only from the subjective viewpoint of others as her story is constructed from Simon and Tat's recollections and Marnie's speculations.

The language of the Scottish Borders is present in Tat's speech; its geography permeates the novel, even if its locations are fictitious. Indeed, the Border lands become a symbol not only of the blurred division between England and Scotland that existed in former times, but between fact and fiction, past and present, this world and the ballad world, the real and the imagined.

An important narrative device in the novel is a collection of "Corbie Plates": nine decorated plates that tell the story of the ballad "The Twa Corbies" in a series of pictures reminiscent of Chinese willow pattern plates. Border ballads such as "Lord Randall" and "Barbara Allen" are in the background of the novel from the first chapter, and their fatalism pervades it, but Greig prints "The Twa Corbies" as a preface, and all the key elements of this ballad about two crows feasting on the body of a dead knight are incorporated into the narrative: David is a blond-haired "knight" who has a faithful hound called Hawk and a lady fair (significant reference is made to Jo's blond crew cut); other allusions include the dike behind which the knight's body is found and the crows that pick out the eyes of a disabled sheep. In some ways, Tat can be identified with the omniscient, detached first-person narrator of the ballad tradition; like the "I" of the ballad's first line, who overhears the crows' dialogue while walking alone, he is an observer, a watcher. The plates themselves have a mysterious power to help Marnie understand the past and also intuit the future; when she studies them, a distinctive voice speaks to her, indicated by italics in the text: *"The plates are neutral and ambiguous as oracles. You read into them what you need to, sure that is their only power"* (p. 183).

The strong sense of fatalism and the supernatural is developed further by what Marnie refers to as "Spook"—"hidden science, the connections we can't quite grasp that tilt our lives one way rather than another ... Everything is connected, nothing truly disappears" (p. 162). The historical tension between the Elliot and Lauder families is played out again in the novel; Jinny believes "the past and the future were all laid out just beyond the range of our sight ... Everything disappears and nothing ends ... *It all comes back in time. I certainly intend to*" (p. 89). And indeed, she appears to do so: David sees someone who could be Jinny (despite her death many years before) in the novel's opening stages, and toward its end Tat encounters her ghost, which discourages him from interfering in the fated meeting between Marnie and David that will ultimately bring David's death. Although "the woman who called herself Marnie" rejects Spook at the close, the strong sense of fatalism has been established: David's death at the Liddie Falls was predestined by his vivid childhood experience at the same spot, and "he knows, he absolutely knows, that he will die there" (p. 34). The novel's tension comes also from a sense of claustrophobia, perhaps as a result of its small number of characters, despite the fact that much of its action happens outdoors.

THAT SUMMER

Greig's next novel, *That Summer,* followed quickly, appearing in 2000. As previously noted, it is essentially a reworking of the earlier poem sequence *A Flame in Your Heart,* and indeed it incorporates not only incidents described in the poems but also key sentences and phrases, a characteristic that emphasizes not only the colloquial style of the original poems but also the poetic nature of Greig's prose, as quotations from the previous work sit wholly unobtrusively in the new.

That Summer is an intense novel: it focuses on a narrow range of characters and examines in detail the development of a relationship between Len Westbourne and Stella Gardam during the course of the Battle of Britain in the summer of 1940. Chapter headings constantly remind us of the novel's restricted time scale—late June to mid-October—which seems extremely short in comparison to the experiences that are crammed into it and the development of the characters during such a short scope: by the end of the novel, Len feels himself "a veteran at twenty-two, antique and scarred by careless handling" (p. 244).

The novel is narrated chiefly by the alternating voices of Len and Stella, describing how Len first meets Tad, a Polish pilot in his squadron, and Stella meets Maddy, a nurse, on a bus. The four meet at a dance and then arrange a subsequent date in a pub. Whereas Tad and Maddy's relationship appears sexual from the outset, Len and Stella's moves more slowly. Initially, they appear mismatched, Len from a rural "peasant" background (in Tad's words), a white-collar worker who began flying for the sheer exhilaration it brings, and Stella, whose university education had led her toward teacher training until the war intervened and she trained as a radar operator.

Len is sexually inexperienced; Stella had a former lover at university. Their relationship is halting and hesitant, but their experiences both together and apart strengthen their bond. When Len is on leave after being wounded in action, they consummate their relationship during an idyllic weekend in his aunt's cottage. But the war is never far away: Stella's radar unit is bombed, Len loses comrades, and for both of them killing becomes personal. Len is concussed while trying to get his plane airborne during a raid on his airfield, and he goes on leave to Scotland; simultaneously, on a visit to London with Stella, Maddy is killed during an air raid on a dance hall. Although he had treated his relationship with Maddy lightly, Tad becomes increasingly morose and dies when failing to complete a forbidden victory roll over the airfield on his return from a mission. Almost inevitably, Len is killed in the final stage of the Battle of Britain, leaving Stella pregnant. This is not a cause for regret or shame on her part, however, but an affirmation of life in a world where she feels surrounded by the dead of the war.

In addition to the two principal voices, there is a third, which dispassionately narrates the progress of the Battle of Britain from a historical perspective, beyond the experience of those caught up in fighting it. This narrator also has access to fictional documents, such as Len's letters and his diary, as well as photographs of the two lovers and the official report of Tad's death, which all add a sense of reality to the narrative. Additionally this voice begins the novel with a view of the "ghosts" or airmen returning to a now-disused airfield, and it ends it with an account of Stella's life until her death long after the war.

Len is no hero: significantly, the most important engagements of the battle for air supremacy are fought when he is on leave in Scotland. Some of the most striking writing in the novel comes in the descriptions of the intense panic of aerial combat, with Len's earliest experiences narrated in short sentences in the present tense, giving a sense of the immediacy of the experience and the need to be simultaneously aware of one's own aircraft, the target, the attacking enemy, and one's comrades. As the summer continues, Len becomes increasingly hardened to the job of killing, and although Tad's words are true—that it's the flying he likes, not the shooting—one sequence where he describes shooting down a Heinkel, dispassionately observing a pilot decapitated by one of his shells, shows how hardened he has become. He finds himself only excited by sex and killing, yet he never loses his sense of panic when going into action, even at the end of the novel as one of the squadron's most experienced pilots.

For all that the novel is about war, and despite the fact that three of its four principal characters die as a result of war (along with many other minor characters, including not only members of the squadron but also Stella's father, working as an air raid warden), the story's key theme is to affirm life and love. War gives both Len and Stella an exaggerated sense of the transience of life. As Stella reflects on a train journey: "How can anyone love in wartime? I thought. It's stupid. But then I looked around the train again and saw that everyone on it was going to die, sooner or later. How can we love in the face of that? Then again, how can we not? Wartime is like real life but more so" (pp. 113–114).

One important section of the novel takes place away from the war, when Len is walking in the mountains of Scotland (and when indeed the aerial battle over southern England is at its most crucial stage). At first this seems anomalous, but it is in fact central to Greig's purpose: while he is in the timelessness of the hills, where the war does not reach him, Stella is in London, amid the air raids. The episode gives us two important images: one of Len, lost in the mist, "peering in blindness as he searches for his destination,"(p. 204) and the other of the hut where he has slept, which the dispassionate third-person narrative voice of this section points out is largely unchanged since his visit. Nothing changes the mountains; they are impervious to the transience of human history, while men seek their destinies blindly, trusting that they are moving in the right direction.

ANDREW GREIG

IN ANOTHER LIGHT

After his lifesaving brain surgery in 2001 came *In Another Light* (2004), possibly Greig's best novel to date. Its narrative structure interweaves two separate plots, carried forward by alternating sections in each chapter throughout the novel.

The first strand deals with Sandy Mackay, a thirty-year-old Scotsman who is sailing out to Penang in the 1930s to take up the position of head of the maternity hospital there. On the voyage he meets characters who influence his life: Alan Hayman, an American water engineer; Philip Marsden, who becomes his bridge partner and who Sandy later realizes is an intelligence officer; and the Simpson sisters, Adele and Ann. Adele is married to Trent, the chief medical officer of Penang, but at Alan's request Sandy draws her away so that Alan can flirt with Ann's sister. Both sisters flirt with Sandy, however, and when on the final night before docking he finds himself kissing one of them on the dark afterdeck, it is not clear to the reader (nor perhaps to Sandy) which it is. Once in Penang, the relationship with the Simpson sisters continues, and Sandy is drawn in to their social circle. He establishes his reputation a successful obstetrician, but he is also drawn into intelligence operations against his will by Marsden. Although it is clear that Ann is still attracted to him, he becomes increasingly closer to Adele, who has been appointed by her husband as Sandy's multilingual secretary at the maternity hospital, and they begin an affair. Sandy soon realizes that this has become public knowledge, and during the final of a billiards competition between Trent and himself, Trent tells him that Adele is pregnant—something he finds surprising, given his own low sperm count. Realizing the baby is almost certainly his, Sandy is unnerved and loses the match. That evening, he is badly beaten as he returns home, and as he recovers, he is caught in compromising circumstances with Adele—a situation that he realizes has been contrived. As a result, he loses his post on the grounds of "gross moral turpitude," together with his residency permit. Initially, he feels that Adele is being kept from him as a prisoner of her family, but it gradually occurs to him that she may have been manipulating him throughout: she has used him to become pregnant and may have contrived the setup that lost him his job. In a final attempt to communicate with her, he sends her a secret message concealed in a domino via her youngest sister, Emily, but the message is unanswered.

The second narrative strand develops as Sandy's son, Eddie, recovering from a brain operation, discovers a box of his father's memorabilia labeled "Penang": a runner-up trophy in a billiards competition, a single domino, a Buddha. His mother's chance remark that Sandy had been forced to leave Penang because of an affair leads him on a trail to discover more. Meanwhile, Eddie has taken up a post in Orkney, researching renewable energy, where he begins a sexual relationship with Mica, an Orcadian writer who has returned reluctantly to the island to care for her terminally ill father. What begins as sex develops into an attraction that prevents Eddie from realizing his colleague, Ellen, is attracted to him and that results in him being badly beaten by the fisherman Kipper Johnson, who is also involved with Mica. When Mica becomes pregnant, Eddie is at first elated, but when she tells him she cannot be sure of the baby's paternity and intends to have an abortion, he cannot forgive her and ends the relationship. Meanwhile, Eddie's research into his father's past leads him to Mrs. Cunninghame, an elderly Edinburgh widow who says she is a cousin of the Simpson sisters. While examining records in London, Eddie meets Roo, a woman many years his junior, who helps him in his researches and discovers further facts about his father's Penang residency. He is attracted to Roo, and when the two meet with Mica in London, the two women seem to get on well. All is not what it seems, however: further revelations lead Eddie to realize that Mrs. Cunninghame is in fact Emily Simpson, Adele's youngest sister, who did not pass on his father's final message to his lover. Moreover, he has been manipulated by the old woman, partially for her amusement as she approaches death, through the agency of Roo (who is revealed as the grandchild of Ann Simpson and Alan Hayman) and Mica. Eddie's narrative ends in Orkney, reconciled with Mica, as "pals at the very least … feeling our way back to the world" (p. 388).

The relationship between the two narratives is handled masterfully: they develop independently, and gradually we realize the significance of objects introduced in one story during the course of the other. Eddie's story is developed as a first-person narrative in the past tense; Sandy's is in the third person and in the present tense, which has the effect of bringing the period further removed in time into the foreground. Sandy's narrative is not revealed as Eddie discovers it, which allows narrative tension to develop as the reader is often in possession of more information than Eddie in his quest to understand the significance of the clues he discovers. For example, we already know the significance of a photograph he discovers in a Penang newspaper, because we have witnessed the incident it depicts one hundred or so pages earlier in the novel. The experiences of father and son do run parallel, however: both are drawn by spirited women into attractions that blind them to the fact that another, steadier, and potentially more loyal woman is in love with them; both are faced with a situation in which they may be the father of a child of uncertain paternity; both are beaten up because of their love lives; ultimately, both are manipulated by the three Simpson sisters without being aware of it. Increasingly, Eddie becomes aware of the similarity of their character: at the novel's end he realizes that in searching for his dead father he has found out about himself rather than his parent. Father and son are both fond of quoting poetry: Sandy quotes William Butler Yeats, Walt Whitman, and John Milton; Eddie alludes to Hugh McDiarmid, Philip Larkin, T. S. Eliot, and Alistair Reid.

The similarity between the two narratives does not end there. Both are played out in an island environment, in restricted communities where it is difficult to have secrets and where one's private business becomes common knowledge in no time at all. Both islands are fully realized, particularly through Greig's description of the differences in the quality of the light on them (hence the relevance of the novel's title): in Penang the light is hazy, but in Orkney mornings are "still and clean-bright, like salt had scoured the light" (p. 138). Because the days are so short in an Orcadian winter, Eddie is all the more attuned to the light there: "a faint mist rose from the flat, electric-blue water, where the low sun and its long, butter-yellow reflection dazzled my eyes" (p. 261). Moreover, we are not allowed to forget the intolerable heat of Penang, where the sweat inside Sandy's shoes makes them squelch as he walks, nor the bitter cold of winter in Orkney, as Eddie hunches up to preserve his warmth in his father's old coat.

The theme of father-child relationships that runs throughout Greig's work is perhaps most fully developed here, not only between Sandy and Eddie but also in the relationship between Mica and her dying father and between Sandy and his father, a saddler from Brechin, a small Scottish coastal town. Indeed, it is Sandy's father's words to him on his final evening before leaving for Penang—"Dae weel, Eck. Dae richt" (Sandy translates this: "Do well, Alec, Do right")—that form the moral core of the novel: deciding exactly what it means to "dae richt" is a problem both father and son have to contend with ("Exactly what? Exactly how?" asks Sandy; p. 165), as they struggle to find their separate answers in the very different historical and social contexts in which they live.

There are clear autobiographical elements in the novel: Sandy, like Greig's father, had died seventeen years before his son's illness, and both fathers visit their sons in the "blue shadowlands" of unconsciousness in intensive care; both fathers describe how their hands can "see" under the skin of a patient (see Greig's poem quoted above); both Eddie's mother and Greig's are suffering from the early stages of dementia. Perhaps most important, Eddie shares the preoccupation at coming to terms with mortality that has marked all Greig's work, more particularly since his colloid cyst. Eddie is aware of the importance of "another ordinary day in that brief break from not-being that we call life" (p. 277), and at the novel's end affirms a credo similar to that voiced by Stella in *That Summer*: "How are we to live in the face of the sure and certain knowledge we will lose parents, friends, lover, the whole shebang and caboodle? Wholeheartedly. Of this one thing I am sure" (pp. 381–382).

ROMANNO BRIDGE

Greig's 2008 novel, *Romanno Bridge,* is, as always, a very different novel from those that have preceded it, despite its being a sequel. It is a thriller in which we meet again the quartet of friends who were John Macnab in the 1996 novel. John Buchan remains a primary narrative inspiration, but the plot involves the kind of quest typical of Dan Brown's *Da Vinci Code* (2003): here, the Macnabs are following clues from a mysterious set of rings passed down by the Moon Runners, guardians of the true Stone of Destiny, the stone on which all Scottish monarchs were crowned at Scone until it was plundered by Edward I and taken to Westminster Abbey. Based to some extent on fact—the Stone was stolen by Scottish Nationalists and many today still believe the one recovered and returned to England to be a copy—the novel allows for the kind of daring escapade typical of its predecessor, for example when Alasdair Sutherland and Murray Hamilton rappel down into an empty Westminster Abbey at night to check the identity of the Stone in King Edward's throne.

If the plot is an improved version of Dan Brown's work, there is also a villain out of James Bond: a sinister, emotionless hit man, Adamson, working for an anonymous antiquarian who wants the Stone for himself. Adamson's sadism is truly chilling, and although his character clearly belongs to the genre, the effect he has on people we have come to identify with is profound. There is violence, too, that had not been portrayed in *The Return of John Macnab,* which leaves men dead and Murray Hamilton seriously wounded.

One intriguing aspect of the novel is how it ties in as a sequel. Almost a third of the book has passed before Kirsty and Neil meet on Romanno Bridge in the episode described in the final pages of *Macnab.* The same scene is repeated in this novel almost word for word, with a few subtle changes, so that we have a sense of continuity of action, interlinking the two novels masterfully.

However fantastic the plot, the action is played out against a backdrop of clearly realized Scottish locations, many of which are real: Romanno Bridge itself, just outside of Peebles (Greig's home for many years), for instance, and the Tibetan Buddhist monastery in Eskdale where Kirsty meets Leo Ngatara, the New Zealand rugby player. Typically, too, relationships develop into love: While Kirsty and Neil realize that their passion has cooled to friendship, they remain firm friends as they find new partners with whom they hope to find "the real thing," and the reader's old friends from the previous novel, Jim McIver and Ellen Stobo, settle down as a couple in the Highlands to enjoy retirement together, despite their differences of outlook.

PREFERRED LIES

Preferred Lies, published in 2006, is a work of nonfiction that charts the recovery of Greig's health after his life-threatening cyst and the operation he underwent to relieve the pressure on his brain—a recovery that he achieved through taking up golf again, a sport he had abandoned years earlier in life for mountaineering. The book is structured around a series of accounts of golf rounds on courses all around Scotland, ranging from a remote, privately owned course on Orkney to the home of golf, the Old Course at St Andrews. He plays with his father's friends in his childhood home of Anstruther, and with Mal Duff's widow in Aberdour; the account of each round—often a hole-by-hole commentary—is followed by a brief essay, and the whole reveals a great deal about Greig's life, his relationships, and his beliefs: it is, in fact, an autobiography by other, less conventional, means. Particularly fascinating is his experience with the group calling themselves "Fairway to Heaven," who seek to find spiritual enlightenment through playing golf. Skeptical at first, Greig warms to their friendship and finds real value in the experience of playing with them. At the end of the book, he is restored to health physically and mentally, no longer feeling provisional about himself as he had immediately after the brain operation: golf allows him to celebrate not being dead.

CONCLUSION

In his author statement on the British Council Web site, Andrew Greig declares: "I write to feel more truly alive, and hope that readers might find themselves the same. My belief is that loss is inevitable and renewal is possible." It is a statement which gives a prospective reader a sense of what to expect from an encounter with this richly varied writer—poet, travel writer and novelist—whose sense of identity as a Scot is a strong element in his work, and whose need to feel alive through vivid experience is clear, whether he is describing crossing an ice field where his chances of survival are less than 50 percent or playing a round of golf. Publishers often claim their writers are "the leading poets/novelists of their generation." In Greig's case this is no mere fluff, but, as the contributor hopes to have demonstrated, a view that bears substance.

Selected Bibliography

WORKS OF ANDREW GREIG

POETRY

White Boats. With Catherine Lucy Czerkawska. Edinburgh: Garret Arts, 1973.

Men on Ice. Edinburgh: Canongate, 1977.

Surviving Passages. Edinburgh: Canongate, 1982.

A Flame in Your Heart. With Kathleen Jamie. Newcastle upon Tyne, U.K.: Bloodaxe, 1986.

The Order of the Day. Newcastle upon Tyne, U.K.: Bloodaxe, 1990.

Western Swing: Adventures with the Heretical Buddha. Newcastle upon Tyne, U.K.: Bloodaxe, 1994.

Into You. Newcastle upon Tyne, U.K.: Bloodaxe, 2001.

This Life, This Life: New and Selected Poems 1970–2006. Tarset, U.K.: Bloodaxe, 2006.

NOVELS

Electric Brae. Edinburgh: Canongate, 1992. Reprint, London: Faber and Faber, 2002. (References are to the 2002 edition.)

The Return of John Macnab. London: Headline, 1996.

When They Lay Bare. London Faber and Faber, 1999.

That Summer. London Faber and Faber, 2000.

In Another Light. London: Weidenfeld and Nicholson, 2004.

Romanno Bridge. London: Quercus, 2008.

NONFICTION

Summit Fever. London: Hutchinson, 1985. Rev. ed., Edinburgh: Canongate Books, 1997. (References are to the revised edition.)

Kingdoms of Experience: Everest, the Unclimbed Ridge. London: Hutchinson, 1986.

Preferred Lies: A Journey into the Heart of Scottish Golf. London: Weidenfeld and Nicholson, 2006.

CRITICAL AND BIOGRAPHICAL STUDIES

Relatively little criticism has been published on Andrew Greig's work, but the following article is perceptive:

Corbett, John. "The Stalking Cure: John Buchan, Andrew Greig, and John Macnab." *ScotLit* 30 (spring 2004).

PATRICK HAMILTON

(1904—1962)

Robert Sullivan

PATRICK HAMILTON PUBLISHED his first novel at the age of twenty-one and went on to publish eleven others. Although recognized by his peers and contemporaries as a significant novelist in the English tradition of Charles Dickens and George Gissing, he was for a time much better known as a playwright, and it was certainly the success of his plays *Rope* (1929; filmed by Alfred Hitchcock) and *Gaslight* (1938; also adapted for film) that made his name as well as a significant amount of money for the relatively young author. However, with success and prosperity came both the need and the ability to drink to excess, to the extent that at one stage during the postwar years he was drinking three bottles of black-market whiskey a day. He lived a peripatetic existence, oscillating between his first wife and his second, both of whom, while intolerant of each other, catered to his bouts of alcoholic malaise. A pattern emerged within this arrangement that saw him leave London with all its temptations where he lived with his second wife Lady Ursula Stewart ("La") and repair to the country, either Henley-on-Thames or Norfolk, where his first wife, Lois Martin, would offer the pastoral solace needed for his convalescence and where he could write. While on a visit to see his sister in London in 1932 he was very badly injured by a drunk driver, and this set back both his confidence (he was badly scarred) and writing momentum for a time. It may also have exacerbated his heavy drinking. It was in Sheringham, Norfolk, that Patrick Hamilton died of kidney failure and cirrhosis of the liver on September 23, 1962. He was working—when he could work—on two manuscripts just before his death, a novel titled "The Happy Hunting Grounds," on the elusive nature of happiness, and an autobiographical memoir called "The Memoirs of a Heavy-Drinking Man."

After his death, his work was neglected for some time, a neglect that stems not from the quality of his fiction but from the simple fact that he never belonged to any literary clique. Although for a time he considered himself a "Marxist"—he even wrote a dystopian fiction, *Impromptu in Moribundia* (1939), from a Marxist position—he was unknown to other left-leaning members of the so-called Auden generation; and although known and to an extent admired by the Communist Party of Great Britain (his pet parrot was named for its leader, Harry Pollit), Hamilton was not a "joiner," as his brother put it. The fact that he left school at age fifteen and never attended university (especially Oxford or Cambridge) is also a crucial factor in his remoteness from other writers of his generation. He has been an unduly forgotten writer and deserves the attention that he is now getting.

Anthony Walter Patrick Hamilton was born on March 17 (St. Patrick's Day), 1904, in the family home, Dale House, in Hassocks, Sussex. The family moved shortly thereafter—the first of many, many moves—to First Avenue, Brighton. Patrick joined a sister, Helen Dorothea Elisa, known as "Lalla" to family and friends, born in 1898, and a brother, Arthur Douglas Bruce, born in 1900. It is a sign of the Hamiltons' literary connections that Bruce took his first name from his godfather, Arthur Conan Doyle. They were indeed a literary family, in that each member would publish books, and Lalla would go on to make a modest name for herself in the theater. His brother, Bruce, published ten detective novels and two nonfiction works, one of which was the memoir of his better-known brother. It is to this biographical memoir, titled *The Light Went Out* (1972), that we owe a great deal of our knowledge of Patrick Hamilton's life and convictions. There is also the voluminous correspondence between the two brothers after Bruce had left England to teach in Barbados, letters that document Patrick's ideas for novels, his insecurities, and his battle with alcoholism. The brothers were born into an upper-middle-class family that was comfortably off. Bernard Hamilton, the paterfamilias, was the recipient of an inheritance of one hundred thousand pounds on his twenty-first birthday—an enormous sum in 1884—and this allowed him to indulge himself to an even greater extent than he had hitherto, with frequent visits to the continent and, closer to home, to sample the pleasures of London nightlife. It was on one of these visits that Bernard Hamilton met a young prostitute who soon became his first wife. Inevitably, the marriage lasted a very short time, and after they separated the young woman threw herself under a train at Wimbledon Station, a scenario that could have appeared in one of Bernard's novelistic melodramas. One would do well to mark these traits of the monocle-wearing Bernard Hamilton (Patrick has his most villainous character, Ralph Gorse, sport a monocle), because excessive drinking, a penchant for prostitutes, and the wish to become a successful author were genetic habits that his son Patrick would inherit.

The more Patrick's father became estranged from the family, the more his mother Nellie (née Ellen Hockley) took control of the children's lives, most particularly that of her youngest son, Patrick, who was her favorite and remained so right up until her death. The relationship was perhaps too close and lent itself to a pattern of conflicted sexuality in Hamilton's relationship with other women later in life, especially those that might promise a lasting bond. A letter to his mother in 1930 when he was twenty-six years old and had just married Lois Martin—remarking that no woman could ever come between them—betrays a peculiar psycho-biographical position that seemed to disallow Patrick Hamilton to fully give himself to another woman. The marriage was never consummated, according to his brother, Bruce. Patrick Hamilton, seemingly, could not lead a fully sexual and marital life until after his mother's death. It was not until 1948, when he had an affair with Lady Ursula Stewart, that Patrick confessed to his brother his achievement of sexual satisfaction. He was forty-four years old.

In his unfinished "Memoirs of a Heavy-Drinking Man," Hamilton is on record as to how he remembers women in his early life as possibly having a detrimental effect on his psychological growth; and it could very well have been these early experiences—both his father's eccentric behavior and his mother's chronic possessiveness—that was to lead to a pattern in his fiction wherein men are teased and tempted and suffer under women, but where men, in their turn, seek their revenge on them. For every long-suffering Bob, the waiter in his 1929 novel, *The Midnight Bell,* or the exasperated George Harvey Bone in *Hangover Square* (1941), there is a Ralph Gorse who achieves his pleasure from defrauding and torturing (sometimes literally) women. And the fuel that feeds these battles of the sexes is always alcohol. These early experiences that may have caused Hamilton's conflicted sexuality could only have been exacerbated by his school experiences. His mother withdrew him from his prep school, Colet Court, when she heard that the boys there indulged in masturbation, and his short period at Westminster as a boarder resulted in his first homoerotic affair when he became enamored of a younger classmate. Given permission by his mother to leave school at fifteen, much to his father's chagrin, Patrick was able to come to a compromise with Bernard, that he would follow his father's wishes and enroll in a business college, but only if he was allowed to take lodgings on his own. Bernard agreed, but issued military-style regulations that Patrick was ordered to follow.

Despite these rules and regulations Patrick was now independent and exploring London, particularly Hammersmith, an area that was to feature importantly in his fiction. Another life-changing breakthrough came when his sister, Lalla, who had formed a theatrical partnership with a man with the unlikely name of Vane Sutton Vane (he was to become her first husband), invited Patrick to work with them. Although many of his tasks were of a menial nature, this period nevertheless allowed Patrick the experience of the workings of the theater and especially how simple sets and small casts might be put to good use, ingredients that mark Hamilton's two best-known plays *Rope* and *Gaslight*. More important, the enormous success of Sutton Vane's 1923 play *Outward Bound* allowed him and Lalla to subsidize her younger brother, who was by now living with them. After a short time at the business college in London that Bernard had insisted upon (in any case, he was now off on one of his jaunts to France), Patrick found rooms for himself and began around 1923 to contemplate the life of a writer.

THE FIRST THREE NOVELS

Of his three early novels, *Monday Morning* (1925), *Craven House* (1926), and *Twopence Coloured* (1928), *Craven House* is by far the best and was a particular favorite of Hamilton's, who had it reissued with some revisions in 1943. Dealing with the claustrophobic existence of boardinghouse life, it bears comparison with a much later novel, *The Slaves of Solitude* (1947), on the same theme. The other two novels are out of print. *Monday Morning* is a typical first novel by a very young man—Hamilton had not yet turned twenty when he completed it—the events of which are shaped by recent occurrences in the young author's life. It centers on his stay at the White House Hotel in Earls Court Square, and particularly Hamilton's infatuation (the first of many) with a young woman named Maruja. She was the daughter of a Peruvian diplomat, and when on holiday from her boarding school she would occasionally visit her brother Carlos (Charles), who also lodged at the hotel and with whom Patrick was on friendly terms. As even Hamilton himself realized some years later, he was more entranced with the idea of "yearning" for an idealistic love, even if unattainable, than any real desire for sexual fulfillment. Indeed, it may well have been that Hamilton was experimenting with an adolescent love affair in order to help him jettison the shackles of the smothering maternal love from which he had recently escaped. In any case, Anthony, Hamilton's fictional alter ego, and Diane, Maruja's counterpart, are led to an eventual and unlikely happy ending, unlike the actual events on which the novel is based.

With working titles such as "Immaturity," "Adolescence," among others, *Monday Morning* belongs to the realm of the bildungsroman and can be fruitfully compared with a novel such as F. Scott Fitzgerald's *This Side of Paradise* (1920). Hamilton's time with his sister in the theater served as fodder for his third novel, *Twopence Coloured*, the title supplied by his editor Michael Sadlier and meant to suggest the "tawdriness and cheapness" behind the scenes. There is evidence that Hamilton was unsure of this book, thinking it "devilishly long" and "amorphous," but Sadlier encouraged him to carry on and finish it. It seems now that this was a mistake. Hamilton made good use of his theater experience, here and there, in other novels, but the subject matter as he treated it here could not sustain a novel of some four hundred pages. It was written at a furious pace and now seems like an excursus into Hamilton's development as a novelist. It is no doubt for this reason that along with his first novel it is the most neglected of his books.

Craven House is Hamilton's most Dickensian book, and it is evident for most of the early parts of the novel that he was building up a repertoire of characters that he would call upon, with variations, in his later fiction. His experience staying in various "guesthouses" enabled him to study the peculiar social dynamic of boardinghouse life that would serve him so well in the writing of *Craven House* and *The Slaves of Solitude*. As well as presenting—for the most part eccentric—individuals, these novels also portray a microcosm of English society and, in *Craven House* particularly, the breakdown of pre–World War I social hierarchies. The novel opens in the year 1911, when Major Wildman (the name is an ancestral one in the Hamilton family) and his son "Master Wildman" (forenames are rarely used in Hamilton's boardinghouse world) arrive at Miss Hatt's boardinghouse on the outskirts of London. During the first few chapters we meet the motley crew of fellow boarders; there are Mr. and Mrs. Spicer, longtime friends of Miss Hatt; Mrs. Nixon and her daughter Elsie; and the "below stairs" help, Audrey Custard (the maid) and Edith (the cook). The first chapter is a deft summary of the nightly rituals of each before bed, including "Mac" the parrot. Gradually we begin to see under the genteel surface of the establishment. Mr. Spicer, who from time to time announces that he is going on a "tramp," leads a double life when he visits West End pubs and consorts with prostitutes. We learn that Mrs. Nixon is a veritable sadist, who beats her daughter Elsie: the latter is, like Dickens' Pip, being "brought up by hand," and just as Mrs. Joe in *Great Expectations* has what is known as her "Tickler," so does Mrs. Nixon have "The Stick." As he matures (a good deal of the early chapters follow a school life close to Hamilton's own), Master Wildman becomes a match for Mrs. Nixon, and indeed encourages Elsie to confront her mother on several occasions until she is finally able to become independent. Major Wildman dies of a stroke (this was about the time that Bernard Hamilton suffered a stroke while in France), World War I breaks out, and Master Wildman leaves school to take a job in London. Elsie, by now an attractive young woman, has become more enamored of Master Wildman, so much so that she is nervously attentive to his every movement: "Elsie is always there to have a chat with him, and her concerned eyes follow him about the room, as though he is looking about for a rope to hang her with" (p. 134). This is Hamilton beginning to hit his compositional stride!

As it turns out, Elsie has an acquaintance named Miss Cotterell, and Master Wildman succumbs to her allure. She is the prototype for many of Hamilton's spellbinders who, at times unintentionally, inflict pain on their male counterparts. He is so smitten that he decides to make himself more eligible (in an unconvincing narrative turn) by writing a play, which is taken up by a well-known actor and becomes a success. However, although he attends dances with Miss Cotterell and Elsie, there is little hope for him as Miss Cotterell has a love interest who works abroad. By now things between Mrs. Nixon, Elsie, and Master Wildman have reached boiling point. He persuades Elsie to "bob" her hair, and when Mrs. Nixon shreds the dress Elsie has made for going to dances, Master Wildman buys her a new one, which causes a climactic confrontation when Elsie challenges her mother, symbolically breaking The Stick into two pieces. This defiance echoes another when the maid Audrey "answers back," and the "dismantling" of the status quo that has reigned for so many years at the house in Keymer Gardens has begun. Mrs. Spicer has found a letter from a "lady" named Catherine Tillotson in Mr. Spicer's pocket and goes berserk, punching her husband in the face: "Mr. Spicer limply requests not to be punched in the face. Mrs. Spicer again punches him in the face and looks at him in another silence. 'My dear,' protests Mr. Spicer. 'I think you're Upset'" (p. 201). This is the beginning of a "violent" turn in the novel, if we do not count the violence brought to bear on Elsie by her mother. The latter now sends for her son "Jock"—a protofascist-type bullyboy, the first of many in Hamilton's fiction—in the hope of quelling Elsie's insurrection.

It is the confrontation between Jock and Master Wildman that precipitates the final unraveling of the household, and the denouement is brought about by an unlikely source. Miss Hatt has had enough, and her smoldering frustration (what with servants answering back and young men almost coming to fisticuffs!) becomes a violent outburst in a scene that oscillates between humor and high farce. During what proves to be their last supper ensemble, Mr. Spicer becomes the recipient of her wrath and is threatened with a leg of mutton, much to the bewilderment of a non–English speaking Russian guest who has recently arrived. The next evening after she recovers from what is described by her guests as a "nervous breakdown," Miss Hatt decides to sell the house and thus everyone must go their own way, in particular Master Wildman to West Kensington and Elsie to North London The movers come to "dismantle" Craven House, and this is described in such a way as to suggest the dismantling of what the house stood for, as the end of an era. The novel seems to reach a firm closure as the door closes on Craven House for the last time. However, Hamilton adds an upbeat, if sentimental and unlikely conclusion, when Master Wildman is somehow driven to revisit the empty house and finds Elsie there. In a scene reminiscent of the end of Dickens' *Great Expectations,* when Pip finds Estella in the ruined garden of Satis House, so too here Master Wildman declares his love for Elsie in the ruined house, and both of them leave with the implication that they will never be parted again.

THE SLAVES OF SOLITUDE

There are signs in *Craven House* that Patrick Hamilton was beginning to find his own peculiar voice, but the inadequacies of that novel are evidenced by comparing it with *The Slaves of Solitude,* a much later book on a similar theme. It is a much darker book, and although it seems for a while that it will offer an uplifting ending like *Craven House,* this is ultimately denied. The novel is set in 1943 at the time of the London blitz, when many people moved out of the city to safer surroundings, in this case the town of "Thames Lockdon," which is modeled on Henley-on-Thames. It was to Henley that Hamilton would frequently escape from his flat in London and all its concomitant temptations, and seek the relative peace of Henley both to recover and do his writing. When the novel opens we meet the unfortunately named Miss Roach, a one-time schoolmistress now working for a publishing company in London, who because of the bombing has taken up residence in the Rosamund Tea Rooms, a guesthouse in Thames Lockdon. She is thirty-nine years old but "she might have been taken for forty-five," and she has "given up 'hope' years ago" (p. 8). Some time ago an older man in her office had taken an interest in her, but she had turned him down.

There was a time not long ago when Miss Roach was at least content, if not happy, at the guesthouse, but now there was something "hellish" about it, and a certain Mr. Thwaites presides in that hell. He is a bully who tortures his victims with his peculiar English usage, an admirer of Hitler, and Miss Roach's nemesis. Why he chooses to concentrate his venom on Miss Roach is never fully explained, but her liberal and even left-wing opinions and her admiration for the Russian people are thorns in Mr. Thwaites' side: "He had therefore come practically to identify Russia with Miss Roach; and in the same way as Russia gnawed at him, he gnawed at Miss Roach" (p. 18). The latter is only relieved when two fellow boarders, Mrs. Barratt and Miss Steele, occasionally come to her aid. There is also Mrs. Payne, who runs the guesthouse and who had converted it from its original purpose as a tearoom; Sheila the maid; and Mr. Prest, who sits at his own table and keeps to himself, preferring the company of the various people he meets in London pubs. The daily routine continues for some time in what is described as an "orgy of ennui," until this awful equilibrium is upset by two "outsiders" who enter the social dynamic of the house and between them bring about the destruction of the status quo.

Lieutenant Pike is an American who is billeted in Thames Lockdon and who takes his meals at the guesthouse. He and Miss Roach strike up a friendship that verges on romance, with talk even of marriage, and his open nature, what Miss Roach calls his "inconsequence," helps bring her out of her daily dooms. A great deal of his inconsequential nature is due to the amount of whiskey he consumes, and he persuades Miss Roach to join him at the River Sun pub on several occasions. Unlike *Craven House,* there is a great deal of alcohol consumed in this book, and it serves as the catalyst for the dramatic outcome. (By this time—1946–1947—Hamilton was himself drinking heavily and a great deal of the novel was actually written in his sickbed.) The other figure who contributes to the breakup of the Rosamund Tea Rooms is a German woman with an uncertain past named Vicki Kugelmann. She is introduced to the guesthouse by Miss Roach and takes a room there. It does not take long for Miss Roach to discover that the manipulative Vicki is not the friend she thought she was, because not only does she form an alliance with Mr. Thwaites (she too has fascist tendencies), but also flirts with Pike the American. Miss Roach slowly but surely begins to hate Miss Kugelmann and comes to identify her with German aggression: "Were not all the odours of Vicki's spirit—her slyness, her insensitiveness—the heaviness, ugliness, coarseness, and finally cruelty of her mind—were not all these the spiritual odours which had prevailed in Germany since 1933, and still prevailed?" (p. 177).

Miss Roach has the above thoughts while lying in bed after a particularly drunken night when the Lieutenant had taken her and Vicki to a country inn for dinner. Another series of binges takes place over the Christmas period, when the Lieutenant brings a bottle of gin to the house, and the day after that, Boxing Day, when he brings a bottle of whiskey. Things get badly out of hand when Mr. Thwaites suggests that Miss Roach's cool behavior is because of her rivalry with Vicki over Lieutenant Pike; but the last straw comes when he suggests that Miss Roach is having a sexual liaison with a young man whom she sees occasionally in the town, a young man who is soon to join the armed forces and whose mother had asked her to meet from time to time. She confronts Mr. Thwaites on the stairs, and in a fit of rage lashes out at him, "half to strike Mr. Thwaites, half to throw the filthy suggestion out of her way" (p. 268). In any case, he is off balance, with his hands in his pockets, and falls down—and as fate would have it he falls ill the next day and has to be taken to hospital. The illness turns out to be peritonitis and Mr. Thwaites dies, forcing the guilt-ridden Miss Roach to seek out a doctor who convinces her that there could be no causal connection between her "push" and Mr. Thwaites's demise. She has also had the good news that her aunt has bequeathed her five hundred pounds in her will, so that the extreme happiness that Miss Roach had felt in being guiltless in the cause of Mr. Thwaites's death is now compounded by the fact that she will have enough money to seek out a new flat and move back to London, away from the claustrophobia of the Rosamund Tea Rooms and the accusing stare of Vicki Kugelmann. This happiness endures, despite the fact that she has met Mr. Prest, who, because of his frequenting of various pubs, is able to disabuse her of any remaining affection she might have for Lieutenant Pike. Pike apparently is well known throughout "pub land" for picking up women and frequently making proposals of marriage. It also turns out that owing to a wartime shortage of actors Archie Prest has found a position at his old profession and is playing a pantomime at the Theatre Royal, Wimbledon, to which he invites Miss Roach.

Since she is going to London anyway, she agrees to attend the performance, and it is here after watching Mr. Prest at this theater, far away from the life-denying environment of the Rosamund Tea Rooms, that the novel "almost" comes to an optimistic close: "There was an extraordinary look of purification about the man—a suggestion of reciprocal purification—as if he had just at that moment with his humour purified the excited children, and they, all as one, had purified him" (p. 314). So too does Miss Roach feel "purified," and the novel seems about to end on this cathartic note. But by this time in his career Hamilton's vision had become much darker than it was in 1927 when he chose a happy ending for his other boardinghouse book. When Miss Roach returns to her room alone in an expensive hotel, we are given a glimpse of her trying to get to sleep as her mind ranges over "this thing, and then that matter, and then this thing again, until at last she put out the light, and turned over, and adjusted the pillow, and hopefully composed her mind for sleep—God help us, God help all of us, every one, all of us" (p. 327).

This closure to the novel is reminiscent of how Melville ends his story "Bartleby the Scrivener"—"Ah, Bartleby, Ah Humanity"—with its suggestion that Bartleby stands in for the sadness of humanity as a whole. Hamilton's ending suggests that people like Miss Roach must learn, inevitably, to live and die alone.

THE LONDON TRILOGY

The three novels *The Midnight Bell* (1929), *The Siege of Pleasure* (1932), and *The Plains of Cement* (1934) were published as a trilogy by Constable in 1935 with the title *Twenty Thousand Streets Under the Sky,* the title alluding perhaps to a more urban version of Jules Verne. As with most of Hamilton's fiction, the genesis of the story finds its roots in his life at this time. During the period when he was finishing *Twopence Coloured,* Hamilton was making frequent forays into the West End of London, particularly the seamier quarters of Soho, and he was already molding his experience into a new fiction. The generic interest in "servants and harlots" that he mentioned in a letter to his brother became fatally particular when Patrick met one Lily Connolly, or "Connerly," as she misspelled her own name. It is likely that Hamilton met Lily in one of the pubs he frequented at this time, and just as the fictional Jenny who meets Bob in the Midnight Bell and leads him on a merry chase, slowly depleting the eighty pounds he has saved, so too did Lily Connolly cost Patrick Hamilton both a great deal of money and peace of mind.

The Midnight Bell opens with Bob the waiter dreaming that he is at sea, and the novel ends with him going back to sea, a closure that suggests a redemptive purification after his sordid interlude with the prostitute Jenny. In the room next to him, Ella the barmaid is also slowly awakening to the start of her day in the bar below. This little world has its "regulars," its characters, those habitués who attend every evening and who are marked by their particular eccentricities. Significantly, there is Mr. Eccles, Ella's admirer who is to feature largely in the third volume of the trilogy, which deals with Ella's story. Mr. Eccles is a kind of linguistic torturer, a monster of innuendo and double entendre. Into this predictable if eccentric little world walk Jenny Maple and her friend, both of whom are recognized immediately for what they are. When Bob serves them and learns that the sick Jenny must go back out on the streets again because she is short of her rent, he lends her ten shillings on the promise of seeing her again. Thus begins an obsession that is punctuated by broken promises, missed appointments, and the inexorable evaporation of Bob's savings. Like his counterpart Bone in *Hangover Square,* Bob is continually left waiting on corners or in pubs for his Jenny to keep one of her appointments, and again like Bone he sets off again in pursuit with the aid of the public telephone box. In these two novels, and in other Hamilton fictions, the London telephone box is figured as a cross between a confessional and a torture chamber: "The door of the box closed upon Bob. Enclosed from the rush and noise of a still visible world, he faced in silence, communion with his own problems" (p. 160"). Jenny finally does keep one of her appointments, and there is an interlude in the novel of pure tenderness and pastoral bliss, a moment when the deceitful and manipulating Jenny seems to offer a ray of sincere hope to the by-now-obsessed Bob. He has persuaded her to leave the streets of the West End of London and go with him for a few hours to the rural environment of Hampstead Heath. Although only a short journey from London's gritty center, this is a different, seemingly magical, place where they are both transformed into the innocent children of a prelapsarian world. This is a crucial section of the novel and forms a kind of fulcrum on which both Bob's and Jenny's futures hang in the balance: "He was appalled by his own innocence and hers—with her blue eyes and the flower held out. She was innocent. His own purity made her pure. He took her hand. He kissed that. His emotion rose" (p. 111).

After this interlude, Bob makes Jenny promise that she will meet him that evening at the Midnight Bell and not fail to turn up like all the other times. But it seems that Jenny Maple is congenitally incapable of keeping a promise, and she lets down a brokenhearted Bob once again. In one last throw of the dice Bob gambles on the idea that if he can get Jenny away from "the plains of cement," he might yet possess her. He withdraws the last of his eighty pounds from the bank and plans a week with Jenny in Brighton. In order that she will not have to sell her wares elsewhere, he gives her twenty-five pounds, and he is to meet her on Boxing Day at Victoria Station. Inevitably, "Jenny did not come. At last he rose, dragged his bag to the cloakroom, received a slip in exchange for it, and went into the Buffet. He ordered a double whisky" (p. 210). As do many of Hamilton's protagonists, Bob decides to get purposefully, "theatrically," drunk, has the balance of his savings stolen, and ends up disconsolate and disillusioned in a cheap rooming house. In the morning, as he walks over Westminster Bridge, Bob has a Wordsworthian moment, suitably framed in the book's most poetic prose: "He reached Westminster Bridge.

Big Ben pointed to a quarter to eight. The glorious sun smote the astonished day. Not a cloud in the sky. The river, full to the brim, sped quickly by ... flowing out to the sea—flowing out to the sea ..." (p. 220). And so at the novel's end Bob returns to the sea from whence he came.

THE SIEGE OF PLEASURE

When Bob comes to the full realization of his plight at the end of *The Midnight Bell*, and he remarks that Jenny could not be entirely blamed, that circumstances helped make her what she was, he points to the theme of the next novel in the trilogy. *The Siege of Pleasure* chronicles how the once-innocent Jenny—the "Treasure," she is called by her genteel employers—is corrupted by circumstances, but it also suggests how her "ignorance, her shallowness, her scheming self-absorption, her vanity, her callousness" (p. 329) predisposes her to such a fate. Like most of Hamilton's abused women, she contributes a great deal to her own downfall. At about half the length of *The Midnight Bell*, this novel is by far the shortest of the trilogy, the action taking place over a few days, and crucially one night and the morning that follows. After the "Prologue," when the narrative proper opens, we are introduced to a Jenny who is perfectly respectable and who has just been engaged as household help and cook to three elderly siblings, two sisters and a brother, who live in the London suburb of Chiswick. After her interview and first day of catering to Bella, Marion, and Robert, it is decided that Jenny will come to live with them and save her the daily trip from Camden Town. For the few days that Jenny Maple works for them they are in domestic bliss, and Hamilton captures beautifully the social dynamic of the household and the various tensions that persist between its geriatric inhabitants. After the second day, Jenny leaves the house, having arranged to return the next day, Saturday, which was to be the first of her "live-in" arrangement. This was not to come to pass, as Jenny Maple's life was to take a totally different turn.

Jenny has arranged to meet her old friend Violet, of whom she is secretly ashamed. One of Violet's traits that particularly annoys Jenny is her friend's penchant for picking up "Boys"—"Environed by Boys, the depths of the Black Hole of Calcutta would have awakened few misgivings in Violet" (p. 260)—and this evening would be no exception. It is not long before the two young women attract the attention of two young gallants, Rex and Andy. Jenny is at first reluctant, but she soon warms to the effects of port and Andy's flattery, and besides there is the attraction of his car. He promises her a position as a "mannequin" with a friend of his, and fed by Andy's adulation Jenny continues to drink more port, finally succumbing, as many of Hamilton's characters do, to the effects of alcohol. (A working title for the novel was "A Glass of Port.") When the by-now-intoxicated foursome move to another "pub," Jenny's forlorn boyfriend Tom, who she was supposed to meet sometime earlier, tracks her down. He pleads with her to go home so that she will be fit the next day for her newly found job, but what was before a cool indifference toward Tom now becomes cruel disdain. The merry group is now joined by a young man even more intoxicated than themselves and who is fond of yodeling. Hamilton, who had much experience of such things, captures very well the drunken, idiotic banter that ensues. It is decided that they will take Andy's car for a drive, and persuaded to go faster by the others—particularly by the now-hopelessly-drunk Jenny, who is in the front seat—he ends up hitting a cyclist. It is the vulgar but honest Violet who persists in yelling at the driver to stop, but he does not do so and the narrative cuts to the next chapter, "The Morning After." Jenny has woken up in a strange bed, in a strange flat, in Richmond on the outskirts of London. Slowly and painfully the events of the night before dawn on her: her first experience of intoxication, her shameful treatment of Tom, her new employment for which she will inevitably be late, and, most crucially, the (possibly fatal?) accident. It turns out that she has come home with the handsome young man who was fond of yodeling. He, accustomed to hangovers, makes her breakfast and promises to drive her to her new job in Chiswick, but not before they have a few whiskey and sodas to help repair the ravages of the night before. At first scandalized by such an idea, Jenny is persuaded by the impressive young gentleman and soon succumbs once more to alcohol's medicinal effects.

It takes little after this for the nameless gentleman to persuade Jenny to spend the day with him rather than fulfill her obligations to the three elderly siblings, who by now (in a separate chapter) have given up on their "treasure's" arrival. What it takes for Jenny's first "professional" engagement is ten pounds and the promise of lunch at a posh restaurant. It is at this juncture that we witness the metamorphosis of Jenny Maple, the home help, into the Jenny that we meet in *The Midnight Bell*.

THE PLAINS OF CEMENT

The third volume of the trilogy is devoted to Ella's story, particularly her brief liaison with Mr. Eccles, the regular customer at "The Midnight Bell," a pub. For a time it seems that in Ella, Hamilton has created a totally upright and benign female character. In contrast to Jenny in the previous volume, Ella is described as being "virtuous" and "homely," but then Jenny Maple started out that way, and as Ella's story progresses we see a different, more predatory side of her. As the novel opens, Mr. Eccles happens to be the first customer on this particular night at the Midnight Bell. He is a master of the ambiguous utterance, has the ability to twist the meaning of everything Ella says, and on this particular occasion persuades Ella to go with him to a matinee at the theater on her afternoon off. The opening conversation between the two of them is the beginning of a linguistic struggle that endures throughout their short "engagement," one in which she endeavors to extract meaning from Mr. Eccles' enigmatic pronouncements while he continues to obfuscate them. Ella is transformed by her experience at the theater and the fact that she is also to have dinner afterward. After being wined and dined, she realizes that despite her "plainness" she has, like all Hamilton's young women, a certain power over the male species. During their next meeting, Ella begins to rationalize her feelings toward Mr. Eccles (she cannot bring herself to utter "Ernest," his first name), moving from a feeling close to abhorrence to one of compromise and conjugal possibility: "In fact why shouldn't she marry him? He was wealthy, he was kind, he had every appearance of being her slave, [at this moment] he was even good-looking" (p. 408). It is only a matter of time until Mr. Eccles makes the ultimate move in this "contest" of move and countermove, meaning and ulterior meaning. Hamilton's prose here is typical of the deftly handled ironic mode of the novel as a whole: "It was next Thursday evening, in the darkness of a secluded bench in Regent's Park, that Mr. Eccles ... finally planted his standard on the subdued heights of his painful manoeuverings and self-consciousness, and kissed her" (pp. 413–414).

Ella is intelligent enough to realize that the contract she is contemplating entering into is one of expediency, and as their intimacy grows she cannot help but have misgivings concerning this consummate artist of arch gaucherie. In another moment of fine humorous writing, Hamilton presents Mr. Eccles in all his awful intimacy: "'You little Puss!' said Mr. Eccles. 'You make me want to Squeeze you!' Ella's soul went faint. Puss! Squeeze! If he had searched through the entire awful vocabulary of archness he could not have alighted upon two expressions which nauseated her more" (p. 423). The whole affair had been so surreptitious, so gradually matter-of-fact and verbally confusing, that Ella has to ask herself how it had all happened. She is conscious that her relationship with Mr. Eccles is economically determined, and if it is economics that drives Ella into the elderly arms of Mr. Eccles—she earns twenty-two shillings per week, of which she gives her mother ten—it is also economics that for a time offers her an escape. Her dreadful stepfather is a taciturn bully of a man, but who, ironically enough, might set Ella free by way of a legacy of three hundred pounds if he succumbs to a dangerous illness. However, Mr. Prosser makes a miraculous recovery and another possibility to go to India as a nanny also falls through, leaving her to face her fate with the indefatigable Mr. Eccles. But even this possibility, horrible as it seemed to her, is denied Ella. In a fit of pique, Mr. Eccles utters the words that both of them have been suppressing, that Ella was after his money, and Ella's pride will not allow her to see him again. Shortly after Ella decides to write Mr. Eccles a letter of rejection she coincidently bumps into Bob, who has now left the Midnight Bell and is about to go back to sea. There is a great deal of irony in the fact that Bob is still suffering the torment of his love for Jenny and Ella her love for Bob, and that it is Bob who serves notice on Mr. Eccles by fulfilling Ella's request to post her letter. There is a kind of editorial coda to the main narrative that summarizes the ordinariness of Ella's story, but also its profound pathos: "But at about half-past ten that night, John, the new waiter ... coming up tired to bed after a hard day's work ... listened, and heard the barmaid weeping" (p. 511).

HANGOVER SQUARE

Hangover Square (1941) is arguably Patrick Hamilton's best novel. In its style it differs from all his other books, mainly because the narrative is filtered through the consciousness (and sometimes semiconsciousness) of its protagonist, George Harvey Bone. It is the closest that Hamilton comes to a modernist approach to narrative technique, a strategy that he more than once denigrated. For example, early in the novel George reflects this way on the name of Netta Longdon, the object of his obsessive desire: "Netta. The tangled net of her hair—the dark net—the brunette. The net in which he was caught—netted ... Nets. Fishing nets. Mermaid's nets. Bewitchment. Syrens—the unearthly beauty of the sea. Nets. Nest. To nestle. To nestle against her. Rest. Breast. In her net. Netta" (p. 27). Not quite stream of consciousness in the mode of James Joyce, but an associative technique that Hamilton never attempted before or after. As far as the content of the novel is concerned, it is right at the center of Hamilton's aesthetic of alcohol-driven calamity, with one character or another drinking or drunk on practically every page—certainly every chapter. As with the other novels, there are biographical strands that went into the making of *Hangover Square*, the very title derived from a joke that Hamilton shared with his brother, Bruce, about Hanover Square in London. In his memoir, *The Light Went Out*, Bruce recalls a time when his younger brother suffered from a malady he called his "dead" periods, when he felt disassociated from his surroundings. It was no doubt this memory—George Harvey Bone remembers on the first page of the novel how his "dead" periods began as a schoolboy—and very likely Hamilton's more recent experiences of alcoholic blackouts that led him to invent the affliction that periodically visits Bone. The other, more contemporaneous, biographical strand was Hamilton's obsession with a young Irish actress named Geraldine Fitzgerald, who became the model for Netta.

The novel opens on Christmas Day 1938, a short time after Neville Chamberlain's visit to Munich, and closes on September 3, 1939, at the outbreak of World War II. These dates are significant because as well as telling of the personal "agony" of George Harvey Bone (many chapters have epigraphs from John Milton's *Samson Agonistes*), the novel is also concerned with broader political and historical concerns. On the first page we are introduced to Bone, who is visiting his aunt and who has just suffered one of his dead moods, "as though a shutter had fallen ... had come over his brain as a sudden film, induced by a foreign body, might come over the eye" (p. 15). Throughout the novel he will suffer these sudden withdrawals from reality more and more frequently, more than once attributing them to his heavy drinking. When he enters this "mood" or alternate reality, he tries to remember one thing he has to do, and that is to kill Netta Longdon. When in full consciousness of his predicament, he is his own best analyst: "You might say he wasn't really 'in love' with her: he was 'in hate' with her. It was the same thing—just looking at his obsession from the other side" (p. 29).

Shortly after the opening of the novel Bone is on his way to London to join Netta and her drinking companion Peter, a fascist who has been in prison twice, once for killing a man while driving his car drunk. Netta's attraction to him is part of her attraction to fascism in general: she is physically attracted to Hitler and likes to look at pictures of marching men in uniform. Secretly she despises Peter as an individual, but admires what he represents. As for Bone, he is so much in Netta's thrall, and her disdain for him so comprehensive, that even when she insults him, which is almost all the time, he is grateful for the recognition. One evening, while frequenting one of his many pubs, Bone meets an old friend named Johnnie Littlejohn. Johnnie represents a much happier past for Bone, a time before he fell under the tortuous spell of Netta. It also happens that Johnnie works for Eddie Carstairs, who is in the theater business and who is someone Netta is very much interested in, so that it is a great opportunity for George to impress Netta by taking Johnnie to a pub that he knows she frequents. He hopes now to show how well connected he is and how he has genuine friends. The three of them get drunk and agree to go to Brighton to see a performance that Johnnie's company is producing, but the next day Johnnie calls Bone to cancel the trip. He says he has had enough of heavy drinking, and besides he did not like Netta Longdon, who "wore her attractiveness not as a girl should, simply, consciously, as a happy crown of pleasure, but rather as a murderous utensil with which she might wound indiscriminately right and left" (p. 104). However, Netta agrees to go alone to Brighton with Bone provided he will finance the trip and also some of her outstanding debts. She persuades him to go ahead of her, and an ecstatic, not to mention gullible, George Harvey Bone sets out to find a hotel and await the object of all his desire and the source of all his unhappiness.

Netta arrives, but with Peter and another young fascist type, all three of them drunk. At the hotel where Bone has reserved rooms for him and Netta, she goes to bed with the young "bully boy," and Bone suffers the humiliating experience of hearing their activity in his room next to theirs. He is forced to leave the room and walk though the night, and when he returns next morning they have left him to pay the bill. In one of his "moods" again, he resolves to go back to London and kill Netta and Peter, but he "clicks" out of this state once again and cannot remember what it was he had to do. Later, on the pretense of going with him to Maidenhead (she really wants to go to Brighton to meet up with Johnnie Littlejohn and the Carstairs connection), Bone advances her more money and they plan to meet the next day. The childlike Bone is now at the zenith of all his hopes and desires, but of course Netta lets him down and goes on her own to Brighton. Now convinced that his only friend, Johnnie Littlejohn, has connived with Netta, he falls from a buoyant would-be lover to an abject fool. Bone now gets very drunk and decides to go to Brighton himself to confront his old friend and the woman who has ruined his life. It turns out that not only does Johnnie have no designs on Netta Longdon—"that bitch," he responds when George confronts him—but Bone is also feted by Carstairs and company, and taken back to his room by Eddie Carstairs in his Rolls Royce. At peace at last, he goes back to London on September 3, 1939, just in time for the "blackout" of the city against possible German bombing. Bone then enters one of his own blackouts and remembers what he has to do. Armed with a bottle of gin and his golf club, he arranges to meet Peter at Netta's flat, where he strikes Peter dead and then drowns Netta in her bath. Simultaneously, the radio is announcing the outbreak of war. All Bone has to do now is get to Maidenhead, that place which for him represents a kind of prelapsarian Eden. However, Maidenhead does not fulfill its promise as the enchanted land he once knew as a child, as he points out in his suicide note to the coroner: "Dear Sir, I am taking my life, as coming to Maidenhead was not of any use. I thought it would be alright if I came here, but I am wrong" (p. 280). He also makes a plea for someone to look after the cat he had adopted at his hotel and which he allowed to sleep in his room. George Harvey Bone's epitaph as it appears in the newspaper, along with headlines about the war, is pathetically brief given the tortuous existence he has just ended: "SLAYS TWO. FOUND GASSED. THINKS OF CAT" (p. 281).

PATRICK HAMILTON

THE GORSE TRILOGY

By the time Patrick Hamilton came to write his trilogy of novels on the villainous activities of Ralph Ernest Gorse (1951, 1953, 1955) he was having less, if any, West End "adventures" on which to base his fiction, and although he was not entirely out of ideas, as his brother had predicted, his lifestyle—most particularly the state of his health—made it difficult to sustain his output. However, although not calling on his recent past experiences, there are still many autobiographical elements—even if disguised—in the Gorse books. It is as if in this late work—*Unknown Assailant* was to be the last novel Hamilton would complete—he was attempting to come to terms, even if indirectly, with his own demons.

Ralph Ernest Gorse was born in 1903 (one year before Hamilton) and attends Rodney House school in Brighton, patently modeled on Hamilton's own Holland House, and like Hamilton he frequents the County Cricket Ground. Gorse has a liking for the theater and played "bit parts" in his youth; we learn that he would have made a good novelist; he wears a ring with a crest similar to that of the Hamilton crest; he sports a monocle later in his life, like Bernard Hamilton; and he even pretends to have attended the same public school, Westminster, as his creator. More significantly, Gorse has a penchant for tying up young women, and we read that he is friendly with prostitutes, but only on a social basis. He appears to be asexual, and his gratification in abusing women (women are his primary target) has more to do, it seems, with revenge on the female species. One of the issues raised about the trilogy, particularly since we rarely if ever witness Gorse engage in any reflective moments, is the lack of any explication of motive. But one might as well ask about the motivation of Netta Longdon in *Hangover Square*. Like Gorse, Netta is less interested in financial gain as she is in power, the sadistic satisfaction of manipulating another human being. This is evident in Gorse's case by the very fact that, despite the intricate machinations he works to realize his confidence tricks, the monetary gain is paltry. Gorse is in it for the pleasure.

The first novel, *The West Pier*, is set in Brighton just before World War I, when Gorse is about ten years old. While still at school he is suspected of tying up a young girl in the County Cricket Ground, and in another incident he steals a flashlight from a fellow schoolboy's locker and plants it on a young Jewish boy who is then falsely accused. The narrative then jumps to three years after the war, when the teenager Gorse is with two of his school acquaintances (he has no "friends"), Ryan and Bell. They pick up two working-class girls on the West Pier, one very plain and the other, Esther Downs, quite beautiful. Ryan and Esther are attracted to one another, and Gorse sees an opportunity for double mischief; he takes both Ryan and Esther into his "confidence" in order to drive them apart, while at the same time impressing Esther by his invented family history and by taking her for drinks at the posh Metropole Hotel. Like most of Hamilton's working-class girls, Esther would like to marry a "gentleman," and she as well as Gorse is capable of double-dealing and rationalizing her unfair treatment of Ryan. After cleverly driving a wedge between Esther and Ryan by means of poisoned letters, Gorse is able to persuade Esther to invest her savings in the purchase of a motorcar, which they will then resell for a profit. Again, like Jenny Maple and other young women in Hamilton's fiction, motorcars are the ultimate seductive trap. Gorse, having now extracted all of Esther's sixty pounds in savings, takes her to a country pub for lunch and then, on the pretence of going to the toilet, abandons her and leaves her to pay the bill with her last three pounds. As he drives off in the car he will now sell for a profit in London, we read: "Gorse, as he drove, was deeply delighted by the superbly easy success of this—his first serious enterprise in his main profession in life—that of defrauding women" (p. 244).

In the second volume of the trilogy, *Mr. Stimpson and Mr. Gorse,* the next woman that Gorse will defraud is Mrs. Plumleigh-Bruce. She is the widow of a colonel and an arrogant snob, and she humiliates her Irish maid, Mary, by indulging in an "Oirish" accent. She enjoys the attention of men, particularly Mr. Stimpson and Major Parry, who meet her frequently in the saloon bar of the Friar pub. It is here in January 1928 (Gorse would now be twenty-five years old) that he encounters Mrs. Plumleigh-Bruce, who is at the bar awaiting her two drinking companions. Immaculately dressed and now sporting a monocle, Gorse is easily able to impress Mrs. Plumleigh-Bruce and immediately sees her as an easy mark for his next confidence trick. He manages to impersonate the character of a successful young businessman, fond of horse racing, and who had done his bit in the war. It is only a matter of time before he ingratiates himself into the company of the three denizens of the Friar and is able to exploit their weaknesses, particularly Mr. Stimpson and his object of desire, Mrs. Plumleigh-Bruce. The former is "a snob, a social climber, a businessman, a boaster, and a subterraneously lecherous man" (p. 263). As for Mrs. Plumleigh-Bruce, she is a vain, snobbish, greedy woman, who for social reasons suffers the company of men, but secretly abhors the notion of physical contact with them: "Mrs. Plumleigh-Bruce disliked men physically almost as much as she disliked the working-class spiritually" (p. 332). This predilection makes Gorse all the more appealing, because he makes it clear that if any union were to take place between them it would be purely platonic, given his own asexual nature. After exploring the particular flaws in his victims' characters, Gorse goes on to exploit them. Mrs. Plumleigh-Bruce's weaknesses are obvious, and she is a "sitting bird" from the very beginning. In Mr. Stimpson's case, it is the habit of visiting prostitutes while in London that will be his downfall. Gorse, who is popular with prostitutes, lures Stimpson into a trap in London after getting him hopelessly drunk and conniving with a French prostitute named Odette. Now he has Mr. Stimpson in his power, especially with regard to his matrimonial chances with Mrs. Plumleigh-Bruce.

Gorse, who has now added an illustrious general (General Gorse of Assandrava) to his family tree, will now play on Mrs. Plumleigh-Bruce's snobbery and vanity in order to complete his business with her. As is his custom, he begins by building confidence and trust, investing small sums to gain the final large amount, in this case Mrs. Plumleigh-Bruce's five hundred pounds. He is now driving a fancy car and (he says) has bought the posh house in which he has been living. Known only to Gorse and the housekeeper at Gilroy Road, both the car and the house belong to a Mr. Ronald Shooter, who has been on an extended trip to Europe. After spending some days at an expensive hotel in London with Mrs. Plumleigh-Bruce (albeit in separate rooms, but nevertheless part of his plan to compromise her reputation) Gorse springs his trap. He tells Mrs. Plumleigh-Bruce that he is presently strapped for cash and he will lose the car they have been traveling in—a ploy similar to that wrought on Esther in *The West Pier*—unless he can come up with five hundred pounds immediately. He suggests that she drive the car back up to Reading ahead of him and await him in his newly acquired fancy house. How could she lose? She would have the car as security, and besides, her future husband would not abandon his recently bought property. She gives him the money and sets off for Reading, where upon her arrival at Gilroy Road, the housekeeper, Mrs. Burford, disabuses her of the true ownership of the house and the car. Mrs. Plumleigh-Bruce is of course absolutely distraught, but there is further, supererogatory, punishment in store for her. Hamilton has the jilted Mr. Stimpson run off with Mary, Mrs. Plumleigh-Bruce's long-suffering Irish maid, and even Major Parry no longer finds her "desirable": "She had become less desirable because two other men, Gorse and Stimpson, had made it plain that they had no desire for her" (p. 500). Cruel and unusual punishment indeed.

UNKNOWN ASSAILANT

The third, shortest, and weakest of the trilogy (Hamilton was by now dictating the novel from his sickbed) is another tale of female incredulity, duplicity, and punishment. It is now 1933, and unknown to her the story that Ivy Barton reads in the newspaper at the beginning of the narrative, about a young woman being tied to a tractor and robbed of twenty pounds by an "unknown assailant," has been committed by her very recent acquaintance. Now going under the pseudonym of "The Honourable Gerald Claridge," Gorse meets Ivy at the Marlborough, the Chelsea pub in which she works as a barmaid. She thinks him a gentleman, and, as often in Hamilton's fiction, class is an instigator of trust. Ivy is ripe for Ralph Ernest Gorse's trickery, but so too is her father, whose vanity makes him also vulnerable to Gorse's class position and his posh "friends," including a Lord Lyddon, who is involved in theater. On the pretense of getting investments for a theater project that Lord Lyddon is involved with, he persuades the latter to open a joint bank account with him. Having taken Mr. Barton and an overwhelmed Ivy backstage at the theater, he is able to manipulate Mr. Barton into investing two hundred pounds, with a check made out to Lord Lyddon, which of course draws no suspicion and which Gorse is able to access. But he is not finished with the Barton family just yet—Ivy, too, must be taught a lesson. On the pretense of going to visit an aunt in the country prior to him and Ivy making wedding plans, Gorse, who has suggested that Ivy withdraw her life savings of fifty pounds from the Post Office, drives her to a hilly wooded area from which they might be able to see his imaginary aunt's house. He would then indulge himself in one of his secret passions: "He liked to tie women up in order to get the impression that they were at his mercy, and he also liked to be tied up by women and to feel that he was at theirs" (p. 577). An editorial "statement," that perhaps betrays Patrick Hamilton's own sexual predilections, enjoins the reader not to think of this as a perversion, but to regard it as a normal, if exaggerated, aspect of sexual behavior.

The novel ends in a most peculiar coda-like way, when Ivy is rescued by Stan Bullitt, a young telegram delivery boy who arranges for her to stay with his grandmother for some days until she can travel to Bradford to stay with her aunt. She feels great relief: "For she was going to her aunt, whom she loved, and she was not going to return to her father, whom she hated and dreaded unutterably" (p. 598). The last pages read like a rather urgent denouement, as if Hamilton knew that he must finish quickly. They were the last published sentences he ever wrote.

Selected Bibliography

WORKS OF PATRICK HAMILTON

NOVELS

Monday Morning. London: Constable, 1925.

Craven House. London: Constable, 1926. Reprint, London: Black Spring Press, 2008 (edition quoted in this essay).

Twopence Coloured. London: Constable, 1928.

The Midnight Bell. London: Constable, 1929.

The Siege of Pleasure. London: Constable, 1932.

The Plains of Cement. London: Constable, 1934.

Twenty Thousand Streets Under the Sky: A London Trilogy [contains *The Midnight Bell, The Siege of Pleasure,* and *The Plains of Cement*]. London: Constable, 1935. Reprint, London: Hogarth Press, 1987 (edition quoted in this essay).

Impromptu in Moribundia. London: Constable, 1939.

Hangover Square. London: Constable, 1941. Reprint, London: Penguin, 2001 (edition quoted in this essay).

The Slaves of Solitude. London: Constable, 1947. Reprint, 2006 (edition quoted in this essay).

The West Pier. London: Constable, 1951.

Mr. Stimpson and Mr. Gorse. London: *Constable,* 1953.

Unknown Assailant. London: Constable, 1955.

The Gorse Trilogy [contains *The West Pier, Mr. Stimpson and Mr. Gorse,* and *Unknown Assailant*]. London: Black Spring Press, 2007 (edition quoted in this essay).

SELECTED STAGE PLAYS

Rope. Premiered 1929. (Although denied by Hamilton, no doubt based on the infamous murder case in which two privileged Chicago socialites, Nathan Leopold and Richard Loeb, murdered Loeb's young cousin because they thought themselves superior beings, "Supermen," in the Nietzschean sense. Hamilton had been reading *Thus Spake Zarathustra* during this time.)

Gaslight. Premiered 1938. (Of all Hamilton's work, this "Victorian" melodrama garnered him the greatest financial reward. It ran for over four years on Broadway and was filmed several times. Its central device of the menacing lowering and heightening of the gaslight was borrowed from his brother's novel *To Be Hanged.*)

The Duke in Darkness. 1942. (What Hamilton himself called a "cloak and sword" drama set in sixteenth-century France, this play was a commercial flop, even though it starred the up-and-coming Michael Redgrave. Many missed the antifascist allegorical plane of the play.)

The Man Upstairs. 1953. (Hamilton's last written play. Despite attracting the attention of Orson Welles, who had thought at one time of filming *Gaslight,* this play was another commercial failure.)

SELECTED RADIO PLAYS

Money with Menaces. 1937. (A play dealing with delayed revenge; an anonymous caller subjects a newspaper magnate who had bullied him at school to menacing phone calls, including the suggestion that he has kidnapped the magnate's daughter.)

To the Public Danger. 1939. (Hamilton welcomed the invitation to write this play as part of the British Home Office road safety campaign and, particularly, the campaign's emphasis on the perils of drunk driving. Hamilton himself was badly injured by a drunk driver in 1932, and he features the motorcar as a dangerous weapon in more than one of his novels. This play follows very closely the drunken accident depicted in *The Siege of Pleasure*.)

Caller Anonymous. 1952. (Again the telephone is the instrument of torture, as it is in some of Hamilton's novels, when a young woman is subjected to seemingly motiveless harassment.)

FILMS BASED ON HAMILTON'S WORKS

Gaslight. 1944. Directed by George Cukor and starring Ingrid Bergman, Charles Boyer, and Joseph Cotton. (There are various adaptations, but this is the classic version, for which Bergman won an Oscar.)

Hangover Square. 1945. Directed by John Brahm and starring Laird Cregar, George Saunders, and Linda Darnell. (Described by one critic as perhaps the worst adaptation of a novel ever made, this version of the novel has George Harvey Bone as a classical composer in thrall to a music-hall artiste.)

Rope. 1948. Directed by Alfred Hitchcock, with writing credits to Patrick Hamilton (play) and Hume Cronyn (adaptation).

Twenty Thousand Streets Under the Sky. 2005. (Excellent BBC adaptation of the London trilogy. Available on DVD.)

BIOGRAPHICAL STUDIES

French, Sean. *Patrick Hamilton*: *A Life*. London: Faber and Faber, 1993. (Supplies a useful list of all the Hamilton family publications.)

Hamilton, Bruce. *The Light Went Out*: *The Life of Patrick Hamilton*. London, Constable, 1972.

Jones, Nigel. *Through a Glass Darkly*. London: Black Spring Press, 2008.

CRITICAL STUDIES

There is no full-length study of Hamilton's writings, although both French and Jones give detailed analyses of most, if not all, the work. Short commentary is available in the following critical works:

Allen, Walter. *Tradition and Dream*. London, Hogarth Press, 1986.

Croft, Andy. *Red Letter Days: British Fiction in the 1930s*. Lawrence and Wishart, 1990.

Lucas, John, ed. *The 1930s: A Challenge to Orthodoxy*. Hassocks, U.K.: Harvester, 1978.

BOOK REVIEWS

French, Sean. "The lost genius." *The Guardian* (http://www.guardian.co.uk/stage/2007/jun/07/theatre), June 7, 2007.

Lodge, David. "Boarding-house blues." *The Guardian* (http://www.guardian.co.uk/books/2007/feb/17/fiction.featuresreviews3), February 17, 2007.

McKie, Robin. "A warm view of a dark novelist." *The Observer* (http://www.guardian.co.uk/books/2008/jul/27/biography), July 27, 2008.

Sinclair, Iain. "Pulped fictions." *The Guardian* (http://www.guardian.co.uk/film/2005/mar/12/books.featuresreviews), March 12, 2005.

Stevens, Andrew. "Welcome back, Patrick Hamilton." *The Guardian* (http://www.guardian.co.uk/books/booksblog/2007/apr/16/welcomebackpatrickhamilton), April 16, 2007.

CHARLES KINGSLEY

(1819—1875)

Sandie Byrne

Charles Kingsley was born on June 12, 1819, the eldest of six children of the Reverend Charles Kingsley, then curate of Holne in Devon, and Mary Lucas, the daughter of a judge and plantation owner in Barbados, where she was born. Though there had been money on each side of the family, on Mary's side from the profits of slave labor, there was little left by the time the couple had married, and Charles Kingsley, Sr., had taken the cloth at the relatively late age of thirty-five. His subsequent clerical appointments took the family to Nottinghamshire, Lincolnshire, North Devon, and Chelsea, in London.

LIFE

As a child, Charles Kingsley, Jr., was both nervous and delicate, and he had a lifelong stutter. In 1831 he went with a younger brother, Herbert, to a prep school in Bristol, where he was a witness to a seminal event in his life and the politics of the day: the riots that took place in Bristol in 1831 following the defeat of Prime Minister Earl Grey's Reform Act, which would have dissolved some of the "rotten" parliamentary boroughs and have improved the fairness of parliamentary elections. In 1832 the brothers were sent to Helston Grammar School in Cornwall, run by the Reverend Derwent Coleridge, son of the Romantic poet Samuel Taylor Coleridge. At school, Kingsley's early interest in natural history and geology was encouraged and developed.

In 1837, with the family living in London, Kingsley entered King's College, London. Long hours of study bore fruit, and in 1838 he went up to Magdalene College, Cambridge. Although both shy and suffering from a weakness of lungs exacerbated by smoking, Kingsley found happiness and fellowship in physical pursuits at Cambridge, particularly hunting, rowing, and boxing, and he tended to alternate periods of athleticism with periods of intense study. A last-ditch effort gained him a first-class degree in classics in 1842. He was ordained in February and in the following July was appointed to the curacy of Eversley Church in Hampshire. For a time, he held the post of clerk in orders at the parish of St. Luke's in Chelsea, but feeling that this was a sinecure, he resigned it, even though its loss left him £200 annually (a not inconsiderable sum at the time) worse off. Through his brother-in-law he gained the curacy of Pimperne in Dorset, but he returned to Eversley in May 1844 as rector, a post he held until his death, though he did delegate some of his parish work to a curate, his son-in-law, William Harrison. A school he founded in Eversley in 1853 remains to this day.

Kingsley had met his future wife, Frances Eliza Grenfell, in July 1839, and they were married in January 1844. The delay was caused by family opposition while Kingsley's financial security was unsecured. During the period of their understanding and engagement the couple exchanged letters that reveal the extent of their physical attraction and desire for one another. Kingsley's awakened sexuality was strong, and he retained an interest in the body, and especially masculine physique and physicality, and an aversion to the creed of celibacy as godliness for the rest of his life. The narrative voices of his fiction often stress the idea that since the human form is a product of the divine, made in God's image, then physical contact with the human body is contact with the divine.

In the summer following his marriage, Kingsley began to correspond with Frederick Denison Maurice, professor of English and history at King's College, London, and author of *The*

Kingdom of Christ (1838), whose writing was perhaps the most important influence in his life and who became godfather of the Kingsley's second child, a son named Maurice. With Maurice and others, Kingsley founded the Christian Socialist movement, and with them began to write for the movement's periodicals, *Politics of the People* and the *Christian Socialist*. Kingsley lamented the demise of the latter publication in a poem, "On the Death of a Certain Journal" (collected in *Poems by Charles Kingsley,* 1908, pp. 302–303, and also available online at http://www.archive.org/stream/poems00king#page/n1/mode/2up).

In 1848, through Maurice's recommendation, Kingsley was made a part-time tutor of English at the then-new Queen's College for women, in London, but he relinquished this post when he suffered from the first of several breakdowns of health and retired to the Devon coast for a prolonged rest. His work in the districts affected by the cholera epidemic of 1849 led to his being asked to speak to the House of Commons on the subject of sanitary reform. In 1859, Kingsley preached before Queen Victoria and before the court at Windsor Castle and was appointed chaplain to the queen. The following year he was appointed as Regius Professor of History at the University of Cambridge, and in 1861 he became private tutor to the Prince of Wales. He resigned his chair in 1869 and was appointed canon at Chester that year and then at Westminster in 1873. Money problems, however, forced him to continue to write and to tour. He visited the West Indies in 1870 and the United States in 1874, but the latter seems to have proved too much for him, and a dangerous illness of his wife's led him to neglect his own health. He died on January 23, 1875. The dean of Westminster offered a burial place in the Abbey for Kingsley, but he was buried in the churchyard of Eversley.

Although he is primarily remembered as an author and founder of the Christian Socialist movement, Kingsley was interested in pursuits other than intellectual or spiritual. He was a passionate amateur naturalist and loved the outdoor life, so much so that he would compose his writings and sermons out of doors.

ALTON LOCKE

Kingsley denied the suggestion that the source for his first novel, *Alton Locke: Tailor and Poet: An Autobiography* (1850), was the writing of Henry Mayhew, insisting that he had had ample opportunity in his father's parishes to see for himself the sufferings of the poor. Nonetheless, it seems likely that Kingsley's novel was influenced by Mayhew's multivolume work *London Labour and the London Poor* (1851), which began as a series of newspaper articles published between 1849 and 1850 in which Mayhew exposed the systematic exploitation of jobbing and indentured tailors: the meager pay; the iniquitous fines levied and stoppages made from that pay; the unsanitary and dangerous working conditions. The *Morning Chronicle* had published a series of letters by Mayhew, including one on December 18, 1849, that cited a report by the tailors on their conditions of employment. A letter from Kingsley to a barrister friend asking for a copy of Mayhew's letter suggests that the report provided an incident for *Alton Locke,* the spread of typhus through a coat that had been used to cover the corpses of those who had died from the disease (see *Charles Kingsley: His Letters and Memories of His Life,* vol. 1, p. 24). Characteristically, Mayhew had reported without any emotive language that tailors in cold, damp, crowded conditions often covered themselves with the cloth that they were stitching. Equally characteristically, Kingsley employs highly colored and highly emotive language for the episode in both his novel and pamphlet. Also influential on *Alton Locke* was the historian and essayist Thomas Carlyle, who appears in the novel as Saunders (Sandy) MacKaye, Alton Locke's guide to the underworld of sweat labor. The novel was written when the Chartist movement was at its height, that is, when Parliament was to be presented with a petition to be signed by millions of workingmen demanding that it act on six points: universal male suffrage; equal electoral districts; secret ballots; annual parliaments; abolition of the property qualification for becoming a member of Parliament; and payment for members of Parliament.

Kingsley may have based his hero on actual people, such as the working-class poet Gerald

Massey and the Chartist poet Thomas Cooper. Born into the lower middle class, Alton Locke descends the social scale almost to the bottom. He moves from a repressively religious upbringing inflicted by his widowed mother to the privations and misery of a tailor's apprentice, to becoming an autodidact, to participation in public protest, to the craft of poetry, to the life of a jobbing journalist. He also moves in political terms. His revolutionary fervor is born out of outrage, and he is initiated into radical politics by a coworker, John Crossthwaite. He begins to write poetry: at first, highly colored Romantic imaginings of Pacific Islanders and buccaneering corsairs; later, political protest in his own voice. When the tailor who employs Crossthwaite and Locke dies, his son converts the business to a "show-shop" in which are sold cheaper ready-to-wear clothes, and he requires his workers to do piecework at home, thus cutting their already meager wages. Crossthwaite and Locke take part in a protest, are betrayed to their employer by their coworker Jemmy Downes, and are summarily dismissed. Downes has become a "sweater"—someone who employs bonded labor, cheating those workmen of their pay by an iniquitous and inhumane system of fines, and keeping them, often almost naked, in conditions from which they cannot escape.

Each day, on his way to and from the sweatshop, Alton goes into a secondhand bookshop run by Sandy Mackaye and reads a few pages of the books that he cannot afford to buy and that, because they are not religious tracts, his mother forbids him. The enlightened and generous Mackaye begins to lend him books. When Mrs. Locke discovers the books, she ejects Alton from the house and family, and Mackaye offers him a home. In spite of this education and his intellectual powers, the rigid social hierarchy of the day keeps Alton in the "station" into which he born. His lot in life is contrasted with that of his cousin, George, who, with money behind him, is strong and healthy where Alton is weak and stunted. George can go to the University of Cambridge, where Alton is denied a formal education; he can court the woman with whom Alton has fallen in love, Lillian Winnstay, where Alton cannot even visit her; and he can have access to the products of culture denied to Alton and others of his rank. George will not exert himself to help Alton, but through him Alton meets Lord Lynedale, Dean Winnstay, and the Winnstay's guest, the philanthropic Christian Eleanor Staunton. Through the dean, Alton's poems are published, but the dean requires that Alton take out the more overtly political sections, which Alton feels is a self-betrayal.

Participation in a rally that becomes a riot leads to Alton Locke's imprisonment, but his release comes in time for him to witness the finalization of the great petition of the Charter that is to be presented to parliament in 1848. Sandy Mackaye's warning that the leadership of Chartism has been infiltrated by unscrupulous rogues, and his conviction that the Charter will not be accepted, prove all too true, and the movement ends in chaos and disorder. In London, Alton meets Jemmy Downes, the man who had betrayed him to the wealthy tailor; he is taken to see Jemmy's wife and child, lying dead under the clothes they had been stitching, and is unable to prevent Jemmy from killing himself. Alton becomes ill and is nursed by John Crossthwaite and Eleanor Staunton. He learns that the coat sewn by Jemmy's wife and child was infected with typhus, which has killed George and ruined the beauty of his widow, Lillian.

Alton now realizes that he loves Eleanor but that she is above him. Having lost her husband, Lord Ellerton, Eleanor is using his fortune to relieve the poor. A dream-vision leads Alton to a more moderate Christian reformist outlook which suggests that the ordinary should be represented not by the ordinary but by the extraordinary. Thus, radical ideals are rejected in favor of a reformed version of the status quo: a hierarchical, monarchical society with an established church. The salvation of the working people, he acknowledges, is in Christ, and the true Charter of the working people is the Bible. Bequeathed money by Mackaye on condition that they leave England, Alton and Crossthwaite take a ship for America, but as they arrive, Alton dies.

In a semidelirium, Alton Locke has a dream in which he mutates from one life-form to another: from a polyp that has no sense of individual existence to a tribesman. In one way, the dream is about Alton's desire for Lillian, who at every stage finds him wanting, and about his fear and envy of George, who at every stage preys upon him. In a more important sense, however, the dream is about evolution, and it provides a vehicle for Kingsley to articulate ideas about the relationship between physical and moral or spiritual development.

Tailoring is more than the incidental profession of the novel's hero. The narrative makes extensive uses of the extended metaphor of cloth that suggests the fabric of society; tailoring equals reshaping; clothes equal trappings, vainglorious adornment, and concealment. (Alan Raunch notes that the metaphor is possibly borrowed from Carlyle's major text, *Sartor Resartus,* meaning "the tailor re-tailored," which was serialized in *Fraser's Magazine* in 1833–1834.) It is of course heavily and bitterly ironic that the makers of the clothing of the rich, which is bought and discarded as fashion dictates, are often nearly naked.

YEAST

Yeast: A Problem (1851) was Kingsley's first published work of fiction, initially published in parts in *Fraser's Magazine* from 1848. Owing to Kingsley's need for a break from city life and work, *Yeast* was not published as a complete novel until 1851. Kingsley's preface to the fourth edition of *Yeast* spoke of improvements that had taken place in the twelve years since the novel was first published. The lot of agricultural laborers has been improved, he writes, by free trade, which increases their food without decreasing their employment. Those laborers are also said to have been taught greater self-help and independence by the imposition of the new Poor Law; self-help, which, the author writes, he hopes will not be destroyed by the indiscriminate almsgiving that he finds is the fashion among the gentry. He suggests that rather than giving money directly to the poor, benefactors should contribute to more systematic forms of relief, such as improvement of housing conditions, but he notes that in most parts of the country conditions remain bad and the apathy of the better-off remains disgraceful. In spite of this apathy, Kingsley finds that the morality and behavior of Englishmen has improved in his lifetime and is continuing to improve, and he is hopeful of a better future. That future will include God-fearing, Christian, and enlightened aristocrats, gentry, landlords, and other leaders of men who will set an upstanding example for, act as patrons to, and govern wisely those born to be their subordinates. The world he imagines is in no sense a utopia of equality and egalitarianism.

Although the living conditions of the laboring poor are, as always, a major theme in Kingsley's work, *Yeast* also addresses what Kingsley sees as the failure of neo-Anglicanism. While praising the ideals of the original movement, Kingsley identifies its failure as that of compromise—compromise between mutually opposed beliefs. Neo-Anglicanism, he writes damningly, is the religion of the smooth man who is adapted to the maxims of the market, which, Kingsley says, leaves him at liberty to supplant others by all the despicable but lawful methods of that market.

Kingsley illustrates the conditions of the rural poor and the laboring poor by creating a central protagonist who is gradually made aware, and painfully aware, of them. Although the novel contains some melodrama, hackneyed situations, and purple passages, its central protagonists, though symbolic, are not entirely straightforward stock characters. Lancelot Smith is both mentally lazy and ardent; painfully self-conscious and sensitive, yet in some ways blinkered; unsure and easily led, yet determined. He veers between a desire to live a pious, thoughtful, and enlightened life, and an enjoyment of hard drinking and hard riding to hounds, which save him from the constant nagging chorus of unstoppable thought. Colonel Bracebridge is a seemingly bluff and hearty fox-hunting man, yet he is kindly, intelligent, and not insensitive. Argemone Lavington (an argemone is a prickly poppy), the object of Lancelot's desire, stately and statuesque, is initially a beautiful, haughty mass of arrogant self-delusion and temporary "manias," which include High Church Tractarianism, while her younger sister, Honoria, is a childish, waiflike, yet stalwart helper of the poor and sick. Argemone, however, develops as a character, selflessly nurses the sick during an epidemic of typhus, and dies of the disease. Tregarva, a young Cornish gamekeeper, becomes the lens through which we observe social injustice in rural areas.

For twenty-first-century readers, *Yeast* has perhaps too many slightly coy narratorial interventions, too many passages that read like apologias and tracts, and too naked an agenda for the condemnation of Catholicism and the fear that Catholicism is infiltrating the Anglican Church. The influence of Carlyle, particularly Carlyle's *Past and Present* (1843) is evident throughout the novel, perhaps to the detriment of the action. *Yeast* also has a structural problem in that once Colonel Bracebridge has committed suicide and Argemone Lavington dies, the plot falls rather flat, and the underpinning philosophy of muscular Christianity, always present, becomes the focus. The mysterious Barnakill who then appears ends the novel by introducing Lancelot to, and adopting him as a kind of apostle in, a new philosophy of Low Church ethics and Christian Socialist action.

In spite of these aspects that made *Yeast* a less successful and less popular novel than *Alton Locke,* it can be read as more than a period piece or entry in the Kingsley canon. Passages of description, such as that of the hunting scene at the beginning of the novel, are both vivid and evocative. In Lancelot Smith, Kingsley creates a hero who, initially raw and even perhaps risible, gains assurance and authority in stating the arguments for direct action and against complacency and apathy. In his speech against "shams," Lancelot is represented with a moving and convincing passionate sincerity. In spite of his antipathy to Catholicism and High Church Anglicanism, Kingsley shows himself to be less of an extremist than some of his contemporaries, in, for example, the statements in *Yeast* about science. The narrator of *Yeast* declares that the study of science and the analysis of the physical world in purely scientific terms is not incompatible with religion, provided the scientist acknowledges that that world was created by God. Kingsley was a friend and correspondent of Thomas Henry Huxley, who recorded that he could write more fully and openly to this man of the church than to anyone else other than his wife. Six years after the publication of *Yeast,* Kingsley was to chide another friend, Philip Henry Gosse, for his denial of what we would now call the scientific theory of evolution. Gosse's *Omphalos* (1857) asserted that the Earth was much younger than geologists suggested, that its creation was exactly as recorded in the biblical book of Genesis, and that God had created the fossils then being disinterred and planted them in the rocks at that time. Kingsley wrote that if this were so, we make God "tell a lie" (letter quoted in Gosse, pp. 280–281).

The first of Kingsley's historical novels, *Hypatia: New Foes with an Old Face* (1853), was based on the life of a martyr, the female Neoplatonist philosopher Hypatia of Alexandria. Although Hypatia was a pagan murdered by Christians, Kingsley makes her struggle and death analogous to a contemporary inter-Christian religious conflict. The "new foe" is Catholicism, specifically the Oxford movement and its leaders, John Henry Newman and E. B. Pusey. Kingsley's novel opposes a fanatical ascetic, celibate, monkish Christianity and a more worldly but rational and tolerant version typified by Bishop Synesius.

Kingsley was not the first author to appropriate the life and legend of Hypatia for religious and philosophical polemic, as the historian Maria Dzielska reminds us in her 1995 study *Hypatia of Alexandria*: Enlightenment writers drawing on fifth- and tenth-century sources represented her as a victim of intolerant closed minds. John Toland's 1720 essay "Hypatia, or the History of a Most Beautiful, Most Virtuous, Most Learned and in Every Way Accomplished Lady; Who was Torn to Pieces by the Clergy of Alexandria, to Gratify the Pride, Emulation, and Cruelty of the Archbishop Commonly, Though Undeservedly, Titled St. Cyril" represented Hypatia as a martyr. Sixteen years later, Voltaire included an account in his *Examen important de milord Bolingbroke ou le tombeau fantatisme,* ascribing the murder to fear and mistrust of Hypatia's Hellenistic ideas about rational Nature and freethinking. Adriano Petta and Antonino Colavito treat Hypatia as the first martyr of Reason in their *Hypatia, Scientist of Alexandria* (2004), as does Michael Deakin in his *Hypatia of Alexandria: Mathematician and Martyr* (2007). Hypatia's life and death still fascinate, and still generate fictional versions (for example, Brian Trent's 2005 "novel of ancient Egypt," *Remembering Hypatia*). There has consistently been opposition to these adoptions of Hypatia, just as there was to Kingsley's representation. Initially, John Toland's essay evoked a riposte by Thomas Lewis in 1721 that relegated (in the terms of the day) Hypatia from scientist and philosopher to mere schoolmistress.

Although there have been many incarnations of the literary legend of Hypatia from its origins in the fifth century all the way through to twentieth- and twenty-first-century feminist periodicals that bear Hypatia's name, the source for Kingsley may have been Edward Gibbon's *Decline and Fall of the Roman Empire* (1776), in which the murder of the rationalist by the superstitious contributes to the argument that the rise of Christianity contributed to the fall of Rome. Kingsley may also have read Charles Leconte de Lisle's long dramatic poem *Hypatie* (1847), although it is the revised version of that poem in 1874 that finds Christianity culpable; de Lisle's play *Hypatie et Cyrille* (1857) came too late to influence Kingsley's novel.

Kingsley's Hypatia is young, beautiful, learned, and influential, but she is unconvincing as a Neoplatonist and she tends, in her contempt for Christianity in general and monks in particular, towards the intolerance of the fictionalized prefect of Alexandria, Cyril. The novel depicts the struggle of a young monk, Philammon, to resist the idealist, rationalist philosophy that Hypatia teaches. Initially warned off by Cyril, he attends a lecture, is convinced and converted, and becomes Hypatia's most ardent devotee and friend. We learn that although Hypatia is nominally a worshipper of the Hellenistic pantheon, she is profoundly moral in a rather Christian-ascetic way, and she is profoundly religious in a way that transcends the worship of any specific deity. An irritant to the scheming prefect Orestes and the dogmatic fundamentalist Cyril, she is cut down much as legend shows Thomas à Beckett cut down, by deranged fanatics, in a church.

WESTWARD HO!

Westward Ho! or, The Voyages and Adventures of Sir Amyas Leigh, Knight of Burrough in the County of Devon, in the Reign of Her Glorious Majesty Queen Elizabeth (1855) is a novel that uses sixteenth-century conflicts to reflect on those of the mid-nineteenth century. It dramatizes contemporary fears of a strengthened Catholic presence following the Catholic Emancipation Act of 1848 and the restoration of a Catholic English church hierarchy in 1850. Based on the travelogues and adventures of Elizabethan seamen and adventurers such as Richard Hawkins, the novel begins in 1575, when its hero, Amyas Leigh, at fifteen, is stirred by the tales of exploration, fighting, and plunder he hears from the sea dog John Oxenford. Two years later, Amyas is able to go to sea with Francis Drake, and we follow him to the Caribbean, to South America, and back to England to fight the Spanish Armada. He falls in love with the beautiful white-skinned Ayacanora, found wandering in the forest as a child, worshipped by the native Indians as a daughter of the sun, and assumed by Amyas to be a descendant of the Incas. Though sorely tempted to remain with her, Amyas returns to his duties and responsibilities as a fighting man and subject of the queen.

Having captured a Spanish ship on which is imprisoned the Devonshire white witch Lucy Passmore, Amyas learns the fate of the object of his youthful adoration, Rose Salterne. Persuaded to marry a Spaniard, Don Guzman Maria Magdalena Sotomayor de Soto, Rose, attended by Lucy, was taken to the West Indies, where Eustace, a Jesuit, had tried to persuade her husband that she remained a heretic whose heart was still in England and with Amyas. As soon as Don Guzman was out of the way, Rose was kidnapped and taken to Spain, where she was tried by the Inquisition, found guilty of heresy and witchcraft, and burned, together with Amyas' brother,

Frank. Lucy, also tried and tortured, was flogged and sentenced to imprisonment. Amyas peremptorily hangs the monks who allowed the burnings, and he vows that for ever after he will show no quarter to any Spaniard. Though saved by Amyas and his crew, and nursed by Ayacanora, Lucy dies before they reach England. Ayacanora is revealed to be the long-lost daughter of John Oxenhope, abandoned in the forest by her Spanish stepfather.

Back in England, Ayacanora gradually learns to be an Englishwoman, and Amyas, though proud of her, keeps aloof because she had a Spanish mother, and he declares that she shall not let a drop of Spanish blood poison his children. He keeps a promise to his mother to remain in England peacefully for a year, but he takes arms again to fight the Spanish Armada, in a ship given the name *Vengeance*. The English fight valiantly, the Armada is defeated, and the fleet turns homeward, but Amyas, who has been knighted, has encountered the ship that carries Don Guzman, and so he pursues it, along the coast of England and around the coast of Scotland, for sixteen days. Then the Spanish ship hits a rock and sinks; a lightning bolt hits Amyas, and he is blinded. In his blindness he has a vision of the dead Don Guzman, and he realizes that Don Guzman did love Rose and did not intend to leave her to the Inquisition. Don Guzman tells him that Rose and Frank have forgiven him, that their fight was just, but that it is time to be friends. Realizing that not all Spaniards are evil, Amyas returns home and marries Ayacanora.

Kingsley's English sailors are bluff and rough, but honorable and in good fellowship with all ranks, whereas the Spaniards are represented as arrogant, vain, sly, and untrustworthy. Despotism and cruelty engender mutiny among the Spanish ships, while the English seamen loyally and doggedly follow their captains into and out of every scrape. The Spaniards use galley slaves to power their vessels, whereas the English ships are crewed by willing freemen.

Although the novel had been begun before Britain entered the Crimean War, by the time it was published, the Anglo-Spanish fight could be taken as a model for the Anglo-Russian. The plausibility of this assumed analogy would have been intensified by the publication of a pamphlet, written by Kingsley with the same patriotic and even xenophobic message, "Brave Words for Brave Soldiers and Sailors" in the same month as *Westward Ho!* and given at his request to troops at Sebastopol.

Westward Ho! is a stirring adventure story that for many years was among the favorite fictions of schoolboy readership. The novel gave its name to a town (the only one in the United Kingdom to include an exclamation mark) sited to the west of Northam and north of Bideford, on the Devon coast.

HEREWARD THE WAKE

In his final novel, *Hereward the Wake: Last of the English* (published serially in *Good Words* in 1865 and then in book form in 1866), Kingsley went further back in time to find another episode of opposing forces, races, and outlooks in English history. This time, the Norman conquerors of England filled the role played by the Spanish who threatened to invade in *Westward Ho!*—that is, the role of the wily, cruel, and devious foreigner, while the role of honorable, courageous, pugnacious and rough, but fundamentally decent Englishman (who would in the sixteenth century have actually been Saxon-Danish-Norman) is given to the "native" Hereward, himself representative of the races that had driven out the Celts from the British Isles. Like *Westward Ho!*, *Hereward* is strongly anti-Catholic. Although the Saxon Hereward is the hero of the story, the Anglo-Saxon clergy are pilloried.

The story of the life of Hereward, the semilegendary eleventh-century leader of the Anglo-Saxon, or Anglo-Danish, resistance to the Norman conquerors, is narrated in the twelfth-century *Gesta Herewardi,* which Kingsley knew from the 1839 edition published by Thomas Wright. The birth date and parentage of Hereward are not known, but his parentage is sometimes ascribed to an Edith and Leofric of Bourne, or to Leofric, Earl of Mercia, and Lady Godiva, as in Kingsley's version.

The novel has a prelude that introduces the fenlands as a mythic landscape, a setting as fit for mythic and heroic events as the Highlands, and that praises the lowlanders as having the virtues of manliness and the quality of not knowing when they are beaten, which leads to a summary of recent history—the settlement of the Danelaw. This becomes an extended idealized description of the landscape so that the land stands vividly in the mind of the reader as a magical, a jewel worth fighting for.

Hereward enters the novel as a heedless and wild young man, a leader of a gang of young thugs whose misdeeds culminate in an assault and robbery of a cleric. His parents are outraged, and his father, at the king's court, demands that Hereward be outlawed. Hereward leaves the fens with the enigmatic Martin Lightfoot as attendant, and he spends time first in Scotland, in the far north of Britain, then in Cornwall, in the far southwest of England, and then in Ireland, where he has the kind of adventures attributed to the iconic hero of myth and gains a hero's sword, called "Brain-biter," and a magic suit of armor.

Hereward is in St. Omer when he hears of the battles of Stamford Bridge and Hastings, and the loss of England. In 1069 he returns to his old home in Bourne, which has been claimed and occupied by Normans, and he leads what is left of the household in throwing out the invaders. He is proclaimed lord by the men of the estate, and the war arrow, divided into four, is sent around, to summon men to fight. Hereward, now reformed, serious, and pledged to wreak vengeance on the killers of his people, is knighted, and after fulfilling an oath he has taken in France, he returns to England with his wife, Torfrida, and their daughter, to raise an army. He becomes a wise leader, and Torfrida, once a sorceress but now devoutly pious, helps him to become truly Christian. In order to obtain the help of a Danish army, Hereward has to let them plunder, and in order to save his native fen and the abbey of Crowland, he gives them Peterborough. He has to watch the city and cathedral burn.

The towns of the fenlands begin to fall to Hereward's forces, but William the Conqueror lays siege to the fenland island of Ely where Hereward has his stronghold. Hereward goes out in disguise as a poor potter, evades two scheming witches, kills some Norman servants who torment him, confronts William the Conqueror, and escapes. Both men recognize something in the other: William perceives Hereward's strength and ability; Hereward perceives William's greatness as soldier and king.

William's forces are close to storming Ely, but with the help of Torfrida, and her stratagem of burning the reeds in the fen, Hereward drives them away. One of Torfrida's rejected past suitors convinces William that she is a witch, and during the absence of Hereward an old enemy arranges for an amnesty to be offered if Torfrida is handed over for burning. The monks of Ely betray their countrymen, but Hereward arrives back just in time, and he, Torfrida, and their men get away.

Hereward and his loyal men disappear into the greenwood, to live a free life as outlaws, and in time they come to prefer the hardships of the forest to the comforts of houses. The narrative approvingly describes the way of life of the outlaws as consisting of hard knocks and good humor, of rules kept strictly but with fair play, and it explicitly equates these values with those of an English public school. Hereward becomes a proto–Robin Hood, hating both the Conqueror and his soldiers and the clerics who are complicit with them. He and his men continue to harry the Normans and to continue to refuse to consider themselves beaten, but winter is difficult in the forest; Torfrida and Hereward grow apart; and a letter from Hereward's old flame, Alftruda, breeds jealousy.

Hereward loves Torfrida but has a terrible fascination for Alftruda. Torfrida joins Hereward's mother at Crowland Abbey and enters the convent (although she cannot take the veil without the consent of her husband). Hereward returns all her property, including the magic armor. She sends it back, but he never wears it again. Soon after, he loses Brain-biter. Despondent and guilty, Hereward tells his men to accept the king's amnesty, and he himself rides to Winchester and announces himself to be the king's man. Hereward is reinvested with his lands, a political marriage is arranged for his daughter (who has to be dragged to the altar), and Hereward marries Alftruda. Without Torfrida's civilizing influence, he begins to degenerate and become the drunken lout he once was. He is imprisoned, a broken man. Though he is rescued by his men, they are away when Norman knights surround Hereward and, after a tremendous fight, kill him. Torfrida comes for his body, and soon after burying it, dies.

THE WATER-BABIES

The "land-baby" in Kingsley's 1863 children's book *The Water-Babies: A Fairy-tale for a Land-Baby* (first published in *Macmillan's Magazine* in 1862) was Kingsley's youngest son, Grenville Arthur, to whom the story is dedicated, together with "all other good boys." The first water-baby of the story is Tom, who begins as a chimney sweep's boy to the harsh and cruel Mr. Grimes. Tom becomes lost in the chimneys of a great house and comes out of a fireplace into a room that to him seems miraculously clean and white—and in whose white bed sleeps a white and gold girl, Ellie. Ellie's frightened cries bring servants and then her father. Tom runs away, through a wood, across a moor, and down a steep cliff. Exhausted, he is allowed to rest in the barn of a cottage school, but he can't sleep. Having seen Ellie, he longs to be clean, and in a feverish stupor he makes his way to a stream, into which he sinks.

Tom has been followed by "the Irishwoman," who is revealed to be the Queen of the Fairies and who instructs the fairies that they must not show themselves to Tom yet. Tom is washed clean, but he has to wash away the habits of his earthly past before he can become a real water-baby. He teases animals, steals, and gorges on sea lollipops before having hard lessons at the hands of Mrs. Bedonebyasyoudid, Mrs. Doasyouwouldbedoneby, Mother Carey (all of whom are in fact, the Queen of the Fairies), and Ellie, who has become a water-baby and been given a pair of wings.

When his lessons are over, and he has given up his nasty ways, Tom is given a test. He must learn to do things he doesn't want to do but that are right. He has to go to the other end of nowhere and rescue Mr. Grimes, who, having drowned, is being punished for his way of life by being himself put to climbing chimneys and who has become stuck. After a number of adventures, Tom finds Grimes and, conquering his resentment, saves him. He is now a fully fledged water-baby, but he is allowed to return to the world and, we are told, becomes a man of science.

The opening of *The Water-Babies* with its description of a loveless, godless, comfortless life, is an indictment of the conditions of child labor in the nineteenth century, and in particular of the ill treatment of climbing boys before the Chimneysweeps Act of 1864. Tom has no better ambition than to grow up to be just like his master. He is without any sense of morality because he has not been taught any. The central section of the story introduces some of the newly current ideas of Kingsley's time about animal behavior and evolution, allowing Tom to discover the wonders and diversity of the natural world and to see the process of evolution in reverse. This comes in an episode (prefigured in *Alton Locke*'s chapter 36, "Dreamland") in which Tom meets the Doasyoulikes who, without regulations on their behavior, are gradually devolving into apes, and are hunted and shot.

Ultimately, however, the novel becomes a story of moral development and redemption. Although it is not explicitly stated, the adult reader understands that when Tom lets himself fall into the stream in which he has been cooling his feet, and falls asleep and dreams, that he has died, and thus the story is in a sense an apologia for an all-too-prevalent occurrence at the time, infant mortality. The narrative voice insists, in one of its many direct addresses, that Tom's nature is not essentially bad and that boys are not naturally cruel; they can learn to behave well. The opposition of dirt and cleanliness, white and black, recurs throughout the story, and the soiling is as much moral as physical. Initially Tom has never washed and is entirely black. In his delirium, he hears church bells and becomes convinced that he must be clean in order to go inside. At the end of the story, the narrator recommends hard work and cold water. Since the time of its publication, *The Water- Babies* has been reprinted in countless different editions, many with whimsical or fantastical illustrations.

THE SAINT'S TRAGEDY

The Saint's Tragedy: or, The True Story of Elizabeth of Hungary, Landgravine of Thuringia, Saint of the Roman Calendar (1848) was published with a preface by Kingsley's fellow Christian Socialist F. E. Maurice. It was Kingsley's only published play, a verse drama in blank verse and tetrameter quatrains whose rhyme scheme varies from a stanza with two rhymed and two unrhymed lines, to *abab* and *aabb*.

The story is set in thirteenth-century Germany. The saint of the title is Elizabeth of Hungary, but her life is the starting point for a representation of the Middle Ages as a period of grossness, barbarity, and brutality. From Kingsley's introduction to the play we would infer that it might be called an "anti-romance," whose function is to dispel the myth of the medieval period as a time of pastoral values, chivalry, and idealism; it is an antidote to the nineteenth-century medievalism found for example in the novels of Sir Walter Scott and later appearing in Tennyson's *Idylls of the King* and the paintings of the Pre-Raphaelite brotherhood. Paradoxically, however, *The Saint's Tragedy* inspired works by Pre-Raphaelite artists Dante Gabrielle Rossetti and John Millais. The introduction also states the play's function as a dispeller of another idea that Kingsley abhors, the idea that ascetic abstinence, especially from human physical relations, is glorious. Kingsley writes in his introduction that his book will have done its work if it deters one person from following the example of those who preach that family ties are carnal and degrading. It will also have done its work if it incites one Protestant to recognize in the saints of the Middle Ages people who themselves were of the same faith, though without knowing it. They are of the same faith because they were witnesses against what he calls the two Antichrists of the age: the caste system of feudalism and those illusory things that Catholicism (which he refers to as popery) substitutes for Christ.

In Kingsley's version of her life, Elizabeth is torn between her love of her husband (whom Kingsley calls Lewis rather than Ludwig) and her desire to dedicate her virginity and life to Christ. Elizabeth and Lewis come under the influence of the ascetic monk Conrad of Marpurg, the pope's commissioner for the suppression of heresy, and Elizabeth vows herself in obedience and duty to him. He enforces a strict life of humility, mortification of the flesh, and self-examination. Elizabeth even questions her own good deeds, asking whether they are committed for the good of those who benefit from them or to earn herself a place in heaven. She angers her husband's courtiers by selling all that she owns and giving away as much as she can from the castle to feed the poor. When Lewis is killed on crusade, Elizabeth is thrown out of the castle without her children or her money, and she is locked out of the convent by the monks, who fear reprisals. When her children are restored to her, she determines to keep them, even when Conrad persuades her uncle, a worldly bishop, to let her enter a convent and tries to persuade her to leave behind all earthly ties. Elizabeth is about to consent when she decides instead that she can do more good within the world. She lives a life barren of comfort and tormented by the penances inflicted on her at the instruction of Conrad, who is determined to make a saint of her. He even refuses her the pleasure of giving.

Elizabeth dies and is canonized, and reports of signs and miracles begin to circulate. Conrad is triumphant as the creator of a saint, but he begins to wonder whether the misery he caused Elizabeth was justified or whether it was for his own pride. In the final scene of the play, a heretic is preaching against the clergy and for reformation when Conrad arrives, and he is killed by the mob.

NONFICTION

Kingsley lectured and gave sermons on subjects ranging from scripture to sanitation to science, many of which were published singly or in collections. An abiding theme in both his fiction and nonfiction was his virulent hatred of the Catholic Church. An acrimonious public exchange with John Henry Newman began with a comment made by Kingsley in a review of a work by Newman's brother-in-law, James Anthony Froude, *History of England* (1856–1870). Discussing Froude's treatment of Catholicism in the reign of Elizabeth I, Kingsley cited a sermon that Newman had given while he was still an Anglican, "Wisdom and Innocence" (1844), and remarked: "Truth for its own sake has never been a virtue of the Roman clergy. Father Newman informs us that it need not, and on the whole ought not, to be" (in *Charles Kingsley: His Letters and Memories,* p. 216).

The first of Kingsley's full-length anti-Catholic publications, "Why Should We Fear the Romish Priests?" appeared in the same year as *Yeast.* Further antagonistic correspondence led to a battle of pamphlets. Newman published "Mr. Kingsley and Dr. Newman: A Correspondence on the Question Whether Dr. Newman Teaches That Truth Is No Virtue." Kingsley responded with his own pamphlet, "'What, Then, Does Dr. Newman Mean'? A Reply to a Pamphlet Lately Published by Dr. Newman." His accusations against Newman's teachings and way of life led to Newman's *Apologia Pro Vita Sua* (1865).

The Christian Socialists envisaged socialism as the ideal of a cooperative rather than competitive economic structure. The unrests of the "hungry forties" came to a head in the Chartist convention of April 10, 1848, when thousands of working people gathered at Kennington Common, London. The establishment fear of "the mob" was extreme, troops were drafted in, under the command of the Duke of Wellington, and thousands of special constables were deployed to control the crowd. Ludlow, Maurice, and Kingsley decided that they must persuade the men to behave peacefully, so Kingsley wrote an address to "the workmen of England," signed by "A Working Parson," which they put on placards to be distributed throughout London. *Workmen of England* urged the workers to strive toward things nobler than the parliamentary reforms demanded by the Charter and announced at the end that those who wished to be free must become wise, since then they would be fit to be free (reprinted in Kingsley, *Letters and Memories,* vol. 1). In the event, the crowd was far smaller than expected, the Charter had fewer signatories than expected, and a number of them were said to be fictitious. The result was more or less the end of Chartism as a movement, though not of reform. Kingsley and his friends founded a periodical aimed at workingmen, *Politics for the People,* of which seventeen weekly issues were published. The tone of *Workmen of England* became that of Kingsley's political writing thereafter.

Kingsley's tract *Cheap Clothes and Nasty* (1850), was published under the pseudonym of Parson Lot. As the second of the Christian Socialists' pamphlet series, it continues the advocacy of the tailors voiced in *Alton Locke.* "Parson Lot" begins by attacking "Mammon." Citing Mayhew's articles on the condition of working tailors in the *Morning Chronicle* of December 14 and 18, 1849, he dares the fashionably dressed to listen to the conditions in which their clothes are made. Distinguishing between the diminishing "honorable trade," which pays for wages, and the burgeoning dishonorable "slop-shops," which pay the workers a fraction of their profits, he moves from the representation of the plight of the tailors to shaming their customers, declaring that no one should call himself a Christian, and indeed that no man should call himself a man, who would buy clothes from a "slop-shop." Damningly, he points out that government contract work is the worst paid of all. Parson Lot's plan of action for the future is the kind of cooperative venture, cutting out the masters and middlemen (the sweaters) and the fierce competition that has depressed prices and thus wages, that Kingsley would advocated through fictional characters in *Alton Locke.*

One of Kingsley's most innovative works of nonfiction was *Glaucus: or, The Wonders of the Shore* (1855), one of the earliest books specifically designed to introduce natural history to young readers. Although this was before the publication of Darwin's *On the Origin of Species* (1859) and *The Descent of Man* (1871), Kingsley was aware of theories of evolution, and his understanding of and support for them are evident in *Glaucus*. It is also evident that he sees no conflict between his belief in the evolution of species and his creationism.

POETRY

Kingsley's works of prose fiction were studded with poems and songs, either sung or quoted by protagonists or interspersed with the narrative without comment. He also wrote poems that stood alone, however. In addition to the verse drama *The Saint's Tragedy* and the long narrative poem, *Andromeda,* he published a number of short poems that became staples of anthologies in the nineteenth and early twentieth centuries. Those poems are far less widely read today, but even so, a number of Kingsley's lines have entered the language as aphorisms, including: "Men must work, and women must weep, and the sooner it's over, the sooner to sleep," from "The Three Fishers" (from *Alton Locke,* p. 279); "Be good, sweet maid, and let who will be clever," from "A Farewell" (*Andromeda and Other Poems* (London: John W. Parker, 1858, p. 64), and "And every dog his day," from "Young and Old" (in *The Water-Babies,* p. 334).

In addition to publishing his own poetry, Kingsley brought working-class poets to the attention of the reading public in reviews such as "Burns and His School" in the *North British Review* (1851). He also turned his attention toward more canonical and established poets, however. He wrote disapprovingly of Percy Bysshe Shelley's alleged unmanliness and sensuality, which he attributed to Shelley's having written in the heat of passion ("Thoughts on Shelley and Byron," in *Literary and General Lectures and Essays,* 1880). Kingsley's distaste for what he called Shelley's insincerity might suggest that his own poems would be more distanced and cool, and to an extent this seems so. They are not clearly autobiographical, nor passionately expressed, though they can be melodramatic. Some of the preoccupations of the novels continue into the poetry, in particular, the representation of Catholicism as repressive and life-denying, which is reiterated in "In an Illuminated Missal."

The modes of Kingsley's shorter verses are lyrical and pastoral, and many have a ballad-like structure and theme, though as we might expect, given Kingsley's classical education, many include classical references. His *Collected Poems* of 1872 (reprinted as *Poems by Charles Kingsley,* 1908; page references are to the 1908 volume) range from poems of place, such as "Airley Beacon," to devotional verses such as "Child Ballad" and hymnlike calls to the church-militant, such as "The Day of the Lord." While a number are set in an unspecified past and use archaic language, others, such as "The Swan-Neck," in the voice of the lover of Harold Godwinson, Edith Swan-neck (p. 285), dramatize specific events in history as imagined by Kingsley. "The Longbeards' Saga" (p. 288), which introduces some unlikely Norse tribesmen to fifth-century Alexandria in *Hypatia,* is written in a short, five-syllable line that perhaps mimics the alliterative half line with two strong stresses of Old English poetry:

*O*ver the *camp*-fires
Drank I with *her*oes
Men of the *Long*beards
*Cun*ning and *an*cient
(emphasis added)

In contrast, the mini-epic "Andromeda" was written in the unusual and complex form of dactylic hexameters. These consist of lines of six feet, each of the first five feet of which is a dactyl (a long followed by two short syllables) or a spondee (two long syllables), and the last foot is of two syllables, either a spondee (two long syllables) or trochee (one long followed by one short syllable):

*O*ver the /*sea, past*/ *Crete,* on the/ *Sy*rian /*shore* to the /*south*ward,
Dwells in the / *well*-tilled / *low*land a / *dark*-haired / *Aeth*iop / *peo*ple
(emphasis added to mark stressed syllables)

Kingsley's nature poetry emphasizes the land and its flora and fauna as the creation of God and as things that identify the presence of God in life. "Dartside" (p. 277) speaks of the spirit that is in nature. "The Poetry of a Root-Crop" (p. 232) uses striking imagery in which a frozen field lies under a surplice, gazing patiently at the sky like a marble effigy of a nun.

Perhaps the best-known and most widely anthologized of Kingsley's poems is the ballad-like "The Sands of Dee," (p. 273), with its varied refrain, archaisms, and haunting tale of Mary, who drowns while bringing the cattle in but is still heard calling them home.

RECEPTION

The novel *Yeast* was attacked on grounds of both its literary value and political import. The *Quarterly Review* in particular was suspicious of its alleged revolutionary intent, inferring from its title "a suggestion that it is meant to ferment in the minds of the people and prepare them to *rise* under the heat of the Socialist oven" (vol. 89, 1851, p. 277). John Parker, the publisher *of Fraser's Magazine,* insisted that his sales had suffered from the poor critical reception of *Yeast,* and he was disinclined to publish *Alton Locke*. Thanks in part to an intercession by Carlyle, however, Chapman Hall took the novel, which is now regarded as essential reading for anyone interested in Victorian social-problem fiction.

In addition to disapproving literary reviews, Kingsley was also the recipient of clerical disapprobation, and he was briefly banned from preaching in London after speaking on Socialist and Chartist issues from the pulpit. His work quickly became popular, however, and his novels went through many editions in his lifetime. His personality gained many admirers, even among those who disagreed with his ideas or politics. These included Elizabeth Barrett Browning; the feminist critic Cora Kaplan has suggested, for instance, that Browning may have used Kingsley's description of working-class and underclass life in her 1856 lyric novel *Aurora Leigh*.

The term "muscular Christianity" is often associated with Kingsley and was coined by T. C. Sandars in a review of Kingsley's 1857 novel *Two Years Ago* (*Saturday Review,* February 21, 1857, p. 176). Kingsley's style of writing is often described as muscular or masculine, and he professed admiration for strong and aggressive men such as the explorer of Australia and later governor of Jamaica, John Eyre, as well as for the rajah Sir James Brooke of Sarawak, to whom, with George Augustus Selwyn, bishop of New Zealand, *Westward Ho!* is dedicated. Kingsley describes these two in terms of the type of English virtue—"at once manful and godly, practical and enthusiastic, prudent and self-sacrificing"—that he says he has tried to depict in his novel and that the two men had exhibited "in a form even purer and more heroic" than exhibited by the Elizabethan heroes and adventurers whom he had fictionalized (*Westward Ho!,* p. 1). Kingsley is probably best remembered today, however, for *The Water-Babies,* as well as for *Hereward the Wake,* which has been published in a number of versions marketed as children's fiction and also adapted for television in a sixteen-part series for the BBC.

Some of the attitudes represented in Kingsley's published and unpublished work, in particular his comments about the Irish and his defense of John Eyre's killing of hundreds of black Jamaicans following the riot of 1865, can offend and alienate readers of today—as they did some people, including friends of Kingsley's, even at the time. His work was popular in his lifetime, and some remains in print to this day. Perhaps his very diversity acted against him, however, and his enthusiasms and drive sometimes led to a greater focus on the didactic function than on the structure and organization of his work. He was not always the first to intervene in the causes he espoused in his writing. Nonetheless, that writing sometimes has a powerful mythic resonance and can stand with the best of the Victorian social-problem fictions.

Selected Bibliography

WORKS OF CHARLES KINGSLEY

FICTION
Alton Locke: Tailor and Poet. London: Chapman Hall, 1850; New York: Harper, 1850.

Yeast: A Problem. London: Parker, 1851; New York: Harper, 1851.

Hypatia: or, New Foes with an Old Face. London: Parker, 1853; New York: Lowell, 1853.

Westward Ho! or, The Voyages and Adventures of Sir Amyas Leigh, Knight of Burrough in the County of Devon, in the Reign of Her Glorious Majesty Queen Elizabeth. London: Macmillan, 1855; Boston: Ticknor and Fields, 1855.

The Heroes: or, Greek Fairy Tales for My Children. Illustrated by Charles Kingsley. Cambridge, U.K.: Macmillan, 1855; Boston: Warner, 1855.

Two Years Ago. Cambridge, U.K.: Macmillan, 1857; Boston: Ticknor and Fields, 1857.

The Water-Babies: A Fairy Tale for a Land-Baby. London and Cambridge: Macmillan, 1863; Boston: Burnham, 1864.

Hereward the Wake: Last of the English. London and Cambridge, U.K.: Macmillan, 1866; Boston: Ticknor and Fields, 1866.

POEMS AND VERSE DRAMA

The Saint's Tragedy: or The True Story of Elizabeth of Hungary, Landgravine of Thuringia, Saint of the Romish Calendar. London: Parker, 1848; New York: International, 1855.

Poems. Boston: Ticknor and Fields, 1856.

Andromeda and Other Poems. London: Parker, 1858; Boston: Ticknor and Fields, 1858.

Collected Poems. London: Macmillan, 1872.

Prose Idylls, New and Old. London: Macmillan, 1873.

Poems by Charles Kingsley. New York: J. F. Taylor, 1908. (Reprint of the 1872 *Collected Poems.* Available online at *http://www.archive.org/stream/poems00king#page/n1/mode/2up.*)

NONFICTION

Cheap Clothes and Nasty [as "Parson Lot"]. Tracts by Christian Socialists 2. London: William Pickering, 1850.

Who Are the Friends of Order? A Reply to Certain Observations in a Late Number of "Fraser's Magazine" on the So-Called "Christian Socialists." London: Lumley, 1852.

Phaethon; or, Loose Thoughts for Loose Thinkers. Cambridge, U.K.: Macmillan, 1852; Philadelphia: Hooker, 1854.

Glaucus: or The Wonders of the Shore. Cambridge: Macmillan, 1855; Boston: Ticknor and Fields, 1855.

The Massacre of the Innocents. London: Jarrold, 1859.

Miscellanies. London: Parker, 1859.

New Miscellanies. Boston: Ticknor and Fields, 1860.

Hints to Stammerers, by a Minute Philosopher. London: Longman, 1864.

"What, Then, Does Dr. Newman Mean?" A Reply to a Pamphlet Lately Published by Dr. Newman. London and Cambridge, U.K.: Macmillan, 1864.

The Hermits. London: Macmillan, 1868; Philadelphia: Lippincott, 1868.

The Two Breaths. London: Jarrold, 1868.

The Address on Education, Read before the National Association for the Promotion of Social Science, at Bristol, on the 1st of October, 1869. London: National Education League, 1869.

Women and Politics. London: London National Society for Women's Suffrage, 1869.

At Last: A Christmas in the West Indies. London and New York: Macmillan, 1871.

Plays and Puritans, and Other Historical Essays. London: Macmillan, 1873.

Town Geology. London: Strahan, 1872; New York: Appleton, 1873.

Health and Education. London: Isbister, 1874; New York: Appleton, 1874.

Charles Kingsley: His Letters and Memories of His Life. Edited by F. E. Kingsley. 5th ed. 2 vols. London: n.p., 1877.

Letters to Young Men on Betting and Gambling. London: King, 1877.

Literary and General Lectures and Essays. London: Macmillan, 1880.

Madam How and Lady Why: or, First Lessons in Earth Lore for Children. London: Bell and Daldy, 1870; New York: Macmillan, 1885.

True Words for Brave Men: a Book for Soldiers' and Sailors' Libraries. London: Kegan Paul, 1878; New York: Whittaker, 1886.

CORRESPONDENCE AND MANUSCRIPTS

The papers and manuscripts of Charles Kingsley are widely distributed. The British Library holds correspondence and other papers, and the Bodleian Library has letters and sermons, but other archives are housed at, among other places, Charterhouse School, Harvard University, Magdelene College, Cambridge, McGill University, the New York Public Library, Princeton University, and the Wellcome Library.

BIOGRAPHICAL AND CRITICAL STUDIES

Alderson, David. *Mansex Fine: Religion, Manliness, and Imperialism in Nineteenth-Century British Culture.* Manchester, U.K., and New York: Manchester University Press, 1998.

Baldwin, Stanley E. *Charles Kingsley.* Ithaca, N.Y.: Cornell University Press, 1934.

Barker, Charles. "Erotic Martyrdom: Kingsley's Sexuality Beyond Sex." *Victorian Studies* 44, no. 3:465–488 (spring 2002).

Beer, Gillian. *Darwin's Plots: Evolutionary Narrative in*

Darwin, George Eliot, and Nineteenth-Century Fiction. London: Routledge and Kegan Paul, 1983.

Brown, William Henry. *Charles Kingsley: The Work and Influence of Parson Lot.* Manchester, U.K.: Co-Operative Union, 1924.

Carpenter, Humphrey. "Parson Lot Takes a Cold Bath: Charles Kingsley and *The Water-Babies*." In his *Secret Gardens: A Study of the Golden Age of Children's Literature.* Boston: Houghton Mifflin, 1985. Pp. 23–43.

Cazamian, Louis Francois. *The Social Novel in England 1830–1850: Dickens, Disraeli, Mrs. Gaskell, Kingsley.* Translated by Martin Fido. London and Boston: Routledge and Kegan Paul, 1973.

Childers, Joseph W. "Industrial Culture and the Victorian World." In *The Cambridge Companion to the Victorian Novel.* Edited by Deirdre David. Cambridge, U.K.: Cambridge University Press, 2001. Pp. 77–96.

Chitty, Susan. *The Beast and the Monk: A Life of Charles Kingsley.* London: Hodder and Stoughton, 1974; New York: Mason and Charter, 1974.

Colloms, Brenda. *Charles Kingsley: The Lion of Eversley.* London: Constable; New York: Barnes and Noble, 1975.

Cunningham, Valentine. *Everywhere Spoken Against: Dissent in the Victorian Novel.* Oxford: Clarendon Press, 1975.

———. "Soiled Fairy: *The Water-Babies* in Its Time." *Essays in Criticism* 35, no. 2:121–148 (April 1985).

Downes, David Anthony. *The Temper of Victorian Belief: Studies in the Religious Novels of Pater, Kingsley, and Newman.* New York: Twayne, 1972.

Fasick, Laura. "The Seduction of Celibacy: Threats to Male Sexual Identity in Charles Kingsley's Writings." In *Mapping Male Sexuality: Nineteenth-Century England.* Edited by Jay Losey and William D. Brewer. Madison, N.J.: Fairleigh Dickinson University Press, 2000. Pp. 215–232.

Gallagher, Catherine. "The Tailor Unraveled: The Unaccountable 'I' in Kingsley's *Alton Locke: Tailor and Poet.*" In her *The Industrial Reformation of English Fiction: Social Discourse and Narrative Form, 1832–1867.* Chicago: University of Chicago Press, 1985. Pp. 88–110.

Gosse, Edmund. *The Naturalist of the Sea-Shore: The Life of Philip Henry Gosse.* London: Heinemann, 1897.

Haley, Bruce. *The Healthy Body and Victorian Culture.* Cambridge, Mass.: Harvard University Press, 1978.

Jay, Elisabeth. *Faith and Doubt in Victorian Britain.* Basingstoke, Hampshire, U.K.: Macmillan, 1986.

Klaver, J. M. I. *The Apostle of the Flesh: A Critical Life of Charles Kingsley.* Brill's Studies in Intellectual History, vol 140. Leiden and Boston: Brill, 2006.

Martin, R. B. *The Dust of Combat: A Life of Charles Kingsley.* London: Faber and Faber, 1959.

Morris, Kevin L. "John Bull and the Scarlet Woman: Charles Kingsley and Anti-Catholicism in Victorian Literature." *Recusant History* 23, no. 2:190–218 (October 1996).

O'Gorman, Francis. "'More interesting than all the books, save one': Charles Kingsley's Construction of Natural History." In *Rethinking Victorian Culture.* Edited by Juliet John and Alice Jenkins. London: Macmillan, 2000. Pp. 146–161.

Paradis, James G. "Satire and Science in Victorian Culture." In *Victorian Science in Context.* Edited by Bernard Lightman. Chicago: University of Chicago Press, 1997. Pp. 143–175.

Pope-Hennessy, Una. *Canon Charles Kingsley: A Biography.* New York: Macmillan, 1949.

Rauch, Alan. "The Tailor Transformed: Kingsley's *Alton Locke* and the Notion of Change." *Studies in the Novel* 25, no. 2:196–213 (1993).

———. *Useful Knowledge: The Victorians, Morality, and the March of Intellect.* Durham, N.C.: Duke University Press, 2001.

Rosen, David. "The Volcano and the Cathedral: Muscular Christianity and the Origins of Primal Manliness." In *Muscular Christianity: Embodying the Victorian Age.* Edited by Donald E. Hall. Cambridge, U.K.: Cambridge University Press, 1994. Pp. 17–44.

Smith, Sheila, and Peter Denman. "Mid-Victorian Novelists." In *The Victorians.* Edited by Arthur Pollard. New York: Peter Bedrick, 1987. Pp. 239–285.

Stitt, Megan P. *Metaphors of Change in the Language of Nineteenth-Century Fiction: Scott, Gaskell, and Kingsley.* Oxford: Clarendon Press, 1998.

Uffelman, Larry K. *Charles Kingsley.* Boston: G. K. Hall, 1979.

HENRY MAYHEW

(1812—1887)

Fred Bilson

HENRY MAYHEW WAS born on November 25, 1812, in St. James's Parish, Piccadilly, London, the fourth of seven sons of Joshua Mayhew and Mary Fenn; in all they had ten daughters and seven sons. Mayhew left no letters or papers, and although there are anecdotes about his childhood and early career, there is no contemporary biography. For these reasons, it is difficult to piece together a coherent picture of his life. What later biographers have determined, however, was that Mayhew's father, a prosperous London solicitor, was a tyrannical and repressive man. The story goes that if any of his sons returned home after midnight, he would find himself locked out. Joshua Mayhew would throw the young man a coin out of the window with the suggestion that he find a bed somewhere else.

Henry Mayhew was sent to Westminster School, a solid academic establishment near Westminster Abbey. Here, on one occasion, says E. P. Thompson in his introduction to *The Unknown Mayhew,* the young scholar was discovered reviewing his Greek grammar during the school service in the abbey. Threatened with a flogging, which he considered unjust, Mayhew ran away from school. The review was apparently successful; he finished at the top of his class in the examination that followed, although he was previously at the bottom of the class in the subject. As Thompson says, it is "an anecdote which illustrates both his indolence and his capacity for concentration" (p. 11).

Mayhew was sent to sea as a midshipman, and he then joined a lawyer's office as a trainee. This venture proved to be a total failure. At the age of twenty-one, with a small allowance (a pound sterling a week, or the equivalent of five U.S. dollars) from his father, he settled down to life in London, where during the 1830s and 1840s he worked as a journalist and dramatist, often in collaboration with his brother Augustus Mayhew (1826–1875). He wrote three plays in the 1830s and also edited a magazine, *Figaro in London,* from 1835 until it ceased publication in 1839. Magazines came and went at that time; the exception to this rule was the magazine *Punch* that Mayhew founded with a group of his friends in 1841.

In 1844, at the age of thirty-two, Mayhew married Jane Jerrold (1826–1880), the eighteen-year-old daughter of his friend and colleague from *Punch,* the playwright Douglas Jerrold (1803–1857). Henry and Jane had two children. The marriage was apparently not happy, but Victor Neuberg is incorrect in suggesting (in his introduction to the 1985 volume *Henry Mayhew: London Labour and the London Poor*) that Jane is not listed as a member of his household in the 1851 census.

Mayhew was declared bankrupt in 1846 following the failure of a newspaper he had started; as a result he was disinherited by his father. He never fully recovered financially from the experience. In the personal realm, moreover, he was a difficult man, he quarreled bitterly with several people including his wife's father, and he was the victim of unfriendly gossip. In particular, it has been suggested that the fact that he spent several periods in Germany means that he was escaping his creditors, but that explanation is unlikely. Men escaping their creditors in Mayhew's era went to France, where the living was cheaper, and they did not take their sons with them, as Mayhew did. A more probable scenario is that he was living in a spa, taking a course of treatment for his health. In the portrait of him that appears in the original edition of his most substantial work, the three-volume collection of journalism published in 1851 as *London Labour and the London Poor* (p. 2), made from a daguerrotype, he seems to be a man in his late fifties, obese and in poor health. Actually he is thirty-nine.

As a writer, however, Mayhew had a strong commercial sense, and he was painstaking about the presentation of his books. He was careful to have his publishers get good illustrators, and he gave them full credit. He had a clear awareness of the readers he was aiming at, and he believed in giving them all the information he could. One of his devices was to fill his title page with information about the book's content; the full title of *The Story of the Peasant-Boy Philosopher* (1854) is forty words long, and there is also an epigraph from Sir Isaac Newton on the title page. Seeing a niche for himself in the publishing market, he aimed many of his books at the younger reader. Later, he would produce books describing life in Germany.

Almost certainly, Mayhew taught himself shorthand as Charles Dickens did—otherwise, it is difficult to explain the apparent accuracy of transcription in the interviews with working-class Londoners collected as *London Labour and the London Poor*. As in Dickens' case, the method would have been Gurney's shorthand. Invented in 1750, Gurney's is simple to learn and has the advantage that anyone who knows the system can read anybody else's notes, which is not always the case with more modern systems. Mayhew often worked by dictating his copy to a shorthand-taker, to his wife, or even to the printer. Such dictation would not have made sense if he had written his copy up in longhand, but it does make sense if he was reading from his own shorthand notes. It also implies that he composed aloud, which may help account for the marked fluency of his writing.

Mayhew's prose is beautifully clear. He was a writer of prodigious energy; his investigations were rigorous, and his writing is full of detailed observation. These qualities contributed to making him one of the great scientific writers of his age. His investigations into the life of the London poor were written originally in response to a commission from the radical newspaper the *Morning Chronicle* and continued in *London Labour and the London Poor*. They marked a great advance in sociology, establishing a rigid methodology in social investigation. The descriptions of the laboring poor and the city's destitute underclass in these works are documentary in genre; when he writes about a sawyer, for example, he does not present a "realistic" account but rather an editing of the realistic to enable him to foreground the sawyer. The sawyer speaks in his own language and becomes the subject, not the object, of the encounter. The background contextualizes the sawyer in the world of work, and in the world of family and social relationships. After the publication of *London Labour and the London Poor*, Mayhew continued to write for another twenty years but without similar achievement. He died on July 25, 1887.

PUNCH

Mayhew and an engraver, Ebenezer Landells, originated the idea of *Punch* magazine, and he invited Douglas Jerrold, William Makepeace Thackeray, and Mark Lemon to the initial meetings to discuss the new venture. Mayhew and Thackeray in particular both wrote comic works and had a serious interest in science; Bernard Lightman explores the apparent paradox of this combination of interests in his 1997 volume, *Victorian Science in Context,* and finds it typical of many Victorian writers.

The name of the weekly magazine probably arose from a pun. ("The paper needs Lemon—like punch," the drink which is a mixture of sweet and sour flavors.) Once he'd hit on the name, Mayhew also decided to adopt as a graphic signature the figure of Mr. Punch, a puppet in a traditional street show for children. In the classic story of the show, Punch is condemned to hang. He outwits the hangman by pretending he doesn't know how to put his head in the noose; the hangman puts his own head in the noose to show him how to do it, and Punch triumphantly hangs the hangman with a cry of "That's the way to do it!" In traditional performances, Punch has a dog called Toby, who sits at the side of the action while it is played out.

All of these elements feature in both the text and the graphics of the magazine. Mayhew was later to say of the costermongers (street traders) that even when they were illiterate, they would often buy the first copy of any new magazine and take it along to the beer shop to have someone read it to them. He probably judged that to have a consistent graphic thumbprint would help sales of later issues, and the appearance of Punch would trigger happy memories in his readers. His scheme seems to have been an inspiration. For over 150 years, until the magazine finally closed down in 2002, the wrapper of the magazine, later the front cover, always featured a graphic of Punch and his dog.

The first issue, which Mayhew and his collaborators published on July 17, 1841 (which is viewable in digitized form online), was entirely different from what the magazine later became. First of all, the content was radical. The leading editorial called for prison reform; it also advocated the abolition of capital punishment, noting that Punch had already got rid of the hangman. Much of the content of the first issue is unintelligible now, but perhaps that is a sign of its strength. Although there are timeless pieces, like a rather charming song in praise of tea, most of the magazine is firmly located in the context of the day.

The magazine's main political commentary is presented in the form of a dialogue between Punch and his Stage Manager, in which Punch announces he is now a member of Parliament. He does have a wooden head, he admits, but so do many other politicians. Despite the political commentary, Punch is not firmly committed to any one party. He is a radical, not a Whig—the outgoing Whig government is the government that introduced the workhouse system that is part of the oppression of the poor. Mayhew was to become increasingly disillusioned with some of the measures introduced by the Whigs, as the discussion of the question of Free Trade below will show.

Along with political slapstick, other articles in early issues parody the arts, the theater, and the opera. The reader of *Punch* was certainly offered value for money spent; the physical magazine is an impressive example of how much writing was necessary to provide the volume the market demanded. But the magazine failed to reach a viable circulation, and in 1842 it was sold to a firm of printers who decided to drop Mayhew, possibly because he was too radical, and to appoint Lemon as editor. In a patronizing gesture, Mayhew was named "suggestor-in-chief"; presumably he would contribute ideas but not necessarily be paid for them. The new focus of the magazine was to be comic writing, and over time *Punch* gradually came to be viewed as the house journal of the comfortable English middle classes. Douglas Jerrold objected to the new editorial emphasis, writing in a letter to Dickens in 1846, "I am convinced that the world will get tired (at least I hope so) of this eternal guffaw at all things. After all, life has something serious in it" (cited in E. P. Thompson and Eileen Yeo, *The Unknown Mayhew,* p. 16).

Gradually, Mayhew severed his connection with *Punch* and his relationship with Lemon deteriorated. He claimed Lemon owed him money. Lemon, for his part, wrote Mayhew out of the history of the magazine, so that Mayhew was not even mentioned in the jubilee edition review of the magazine's history. When Mayhew's obituary appeared in the London *Times* in 1887, long after Lemon's death in 1870, someone wrote in to contest that Mayhew had ever been editor of *Punch*.

THE GREATEST PLAGUE OF LIFE

In 1847, Henry and Augustus Mayhew published a comic novel titled *The Greatest Plague of Life*. On the surface the story details the household troubles of the middle-class lady Caroline, but it also offers a serious critique of the employer-servant relationship. Despite the fact that it centers on a woman, the book reads as though it was designed for a male readership; it is not at all feminist in tone.

The Greatest Plague was published in London by David Bogue and in Philadelphia by Carey and Hart. The American edition is available online. The book's title was a comic exaggeration in itself, and it was provided, at least in the American edition, with a title page (or more accurately a front wrapper cast like a title page) whose language satirizes the title pages of the sentimental novels of the period; the title in full reads:

"THE
GREATEST PLAGUE
OF LIFE,"
OR
THE ADVENTURES OF A LADY IN SEARCH OF
A
GOOD SERVANT.
BY
ONE WHO HAS BEEN "ALMOST WORRIED TO
DEATH."

This is displayed like a theater poster, with screaming large-point capitals, and at the eye-catching center of the page is displayed the added attraction, "With illustrations / BY GEORGE CRUIKSHANK"—again with the second line in capitals. The American publishers follow this with the price, 37½ cents; some small print inside tells us the book without plates could be had at 25 cents.

A Cruikshank plate opposite the true title page is one of his best. Caroline, the distraught lady, is seen in her morning room, surrounded by more than a dozen diminutive, busy figures suggestive of fairies but that are actually servants creating havoc. There is also a true title page by Cruikshank with a drawing showing Caroline interviewing the Irish maid Norah Connor, who is a central character in the story.

Cruikshank had illustrated Dickens' *Oliver Twist* (1838), but by the time of *The Old Curiosity Shop* (1841) he had severed his connection with the author. They had quarreled because Cruikshank had claimed to have contributed ideas for the plot of *Oliver Twist*. Cruikshank and the Mayhews may have enjoyed devising a volume whose presentation heavily suggested that this would be a book within the world of Dickens. However, it does not read at all like Dickens, principally because there are no grotesque characters like the odious Quilp of *The Old Curiosity Shop*. The grotesqueness in Dickens is both physical and moral, and it was tempting to writers of the time to imitate it, but ultimately it leaves the reader with a feeling of detachment, an inability to make an appropriate response. In fact, even Dickens' friend Anthony Trollope was driven in the end to protest. In *The Warden* (1855), Trollope parodies this feature of the work of Dickens, whom he memorably dubs Mr. Popular Sentiment.

Mayhew prefers to use narrative techniques that are closer to those of the stage, building to a series of situational climaxes and avoiding excesses of histrionics.

The Greatest Plague of Life has considerable drive and vigor, moving through a series of set pieces and using a number of theatrical techniques. When we meet Caroline, she is living in a boardinghouse, and she addresses us in one of those soliloquies that in the theater manage the initial exposition: "'Here am I', (I said to myself,) ... 'without an establishment that I can call my own,—positively driven from my home,—obliged to sell my elegant furniture at a sacrifice of five hundred and eighty pounds and odd,—glad to take refuge in the venal hospitality of a boarding house!! in G—ldf—rd St—t." It is all the fault of servants. "Ever since we first commenced housekeeping, I cannot say the creatures have let me know one day's perfect peace" (p. 14).

Determined to write a book on the subject, she calls on "Mr. B——e" on "Fleet-street" (Mayhew's publisher, David Bogue) and tells him of her plan. He is not impressed. Does she know the work of Dean Swift? No, she replies, but as "Mr. Dean Swift" cannot have been a wife and mother "it will not, in any way, clash with the one I purpose." He still demurs and explains, "domestic troubles don't go off at all in the trade; the public seem to have lost all taste for them. Now, if you could work up any horrible fact ... there is a great demand with us for lady poisoners just now" (p. 17). He finally consents to take the book when she waives her fee, and he gives her a letter to George Cruikshank, whom she visits.

The plot revolves on situational comedy of a high order, moving with pace and showing variety in the voices of its characters. There are obviously private jokes in here; when Caroline lays much emphasis on how neat and tidy Cruikshank's house is, the reader may begin to suspect irony. Throughout, Caroline demonstrates an amusing naïveté, as in the reference to Jonathan Swift. Describing Bogue, she says, "He has got my eldest girl's hair and my second boy's eyes (the one being gold-colored, and the other blue)" (p. 16). Caroline tells her prospective the publisher that she is not sure that Cruikshank will be the right choice for illustrator, because "he would be too funny for a work of so serious a character" (p. 17), and there is an important clue here to the subtext of the novel, and to its social observations. In all the catastrophes that befall her, she never sees her situation as comic.

She sets to work on her book and describes how on her wedding night she arrived at her new home to find the maid, Mary, had collapsed drunk in the kitchen, and the sheets she was supposed to be airing had all burned to cinders so there was not even enough left to make cloths for cleaning glasses. Nor is there any food in the house. Yet Mary is given another chance and another, until finally she has to go. It is the first of a series of set pieces, culminating in Caroline fleeing her home and her husband putting the furniture up for auction without reserve, disgusted at having to live in a big house without a wife or a servant to wait on him. Much of the work's humor lies in the sheer size of the disasters that befall Caroline and in the reaction of Caroline's husband to her constant complaints; the book's original middle-class readers would recognize in the story an exaggeration of incidents they had themselves experienced with their own servants. Yet the Mayhews are making a larger point by way of this novel; we often treat comically that which we fear most deeply, and the employer-servant relationship was a central problem of Victorian social life, containing several contradictions.

Caroline's life cannot function, she cannot manage her house, without paid help. The house is too big, too difficult to clean; but she cannot move to a smaller house because of her social status. Her servants need the work, because the alternative would be destitution or a return to an overcrowded and squalid family home in the country. So the employer and the servant enter into a relationship in which they mutually exploit each other. Caroline employs only one servant at a time, a maid of all work who doubles as a plain cook. Caroline expects the maid to work from early in the morning to late at night and to be in the house at all times except when sent on an errand; generally, the maid will be required to do a great deal of hard work for which she has not been trained. In return, the maid will receive a small wage (perhaps six pounds sterling, or the equivalent of thirty dollars a year) along with her bed and meals.

The contradictions of the system are highlighted in Caroline's encounter with the Irish maid Norah Connor, who appears in the drawing on Cruikshank's title page. Underneath the humor that Norah's character brings to the story, the authors show her serious intention and her emerging social awareness. At first when Norah arrives, all seems well. She strikes Caroline as

> such a nice, hard-working body—always cleaning up or doing something ... and positively working like a galley-slave from morning till night for me ... she was so quick over her work, that after I had made her scrub all the house ... and clean all the paint, and take up and beat all the carpets ... I was hard put to it to find some odd jobs to keep her fully employed; for I had no idea of paying servants the wages I did to support them in idleness.
>
> (pp. 44–45)

In return, Norah seems quite content living on potatoes and the scraps in the larder. But Caroline's husband, Edward, reacts in a way that annoys her; "when I had finished getting the house to rights ... my husband, in his blessed ignorance, supposed it to be all Miss Norah Connor's doing" (p. 45). Caroline decides that she will get Norah, in addition to everything else, to do the laundry (she has been paying four pence each, or eight cents, for someone to launder Edward's shirts). In return Norah may have an extra pint of beer on washdays.

Finally, Norah rebels. Caroline takes note that the housemaid is acting overfamiliar, and the reader can see that the servant is attempting to redraw the boundaries between Caroline and herself. She will not, in addition to everything else, be a parlor maid and fetch things for Caroline. So when Caroline rings for her, announcing, "I want a glass of water to drink, Norah," the maid replies, "You want to drink a glass of wather? ... Well, I've no objection. Drink away, darlin'!!" The knockabout continues. Caroline says she wants Norah to bring her a glass, and Norah asks if she means "a glass wid nothin' in it ...?" The maid then winks in understanding, and adds, "Oh, go along wid you—wanting a drop on the sly, now!" (p. 46).

Norah is portrayed by the authors as Caroline sees her, with an exaggerated accent, in a stereotypical way that allows the employer to see the servant as less than human. In this light, Caroline is more able to ignore the contradictions of a system where she is forced to get as much as she can while giving as little as possible in return. Caroline is not by definition a bad employer in this context; she is not morally corrupt, but the system has hardened her and driven her to save every penny she can, to exploit Norah to the full (and then claim the credit for Norah's labor because she has to supervise her and direct her). At the same time, the system makes Norah sly and resentful—and when Caroline asks for the glass of water, Norah uses a technique known to the oppressed everywhere, the practice of feigned incomprehension. In the end it works, and Caroline goes off to her bedroom in tears

The relationship sours, and Norah, like all the other servants, must go. On the morning she leaves, Caroline gives her a tip of five shillings (a dollar twenty-five)—or perhaps half that amount; she cannot quite remember—and then describes the way that Norah "for a quarter-of-an-hour at least ... stood on the door-step" calling her former employer "outlandish" endearments such as "her mavourneen and macree"—Irish words that mark her otherness; Caroline is dismissive of Norah's human distress, saying blithely that she was "sobbing away ... as though she really *had* got ... a heart to break" (p. 55). In her turn, however, Caroline, too, is the victim of the social order. It is ironic that she feels sympathy for Edward, alone in a big house without a wife or servant to wait on him. She accepts the way in which society sees the function of a woman as being to wait upon men, either as wife or as servant, and she cannot see how that reduces her as a woman. The Mayhew brothers followed this publication up in 1848 with another novel in the same persona called *Whom to Marry.*

LETTERS IN THE MORNING CHRONICLE

In 1849 a London daily newspaper, the *Morning Chronicle,* commissioned Mayhew and two other journalists to write a series of articles on the condition of the poor. The work that Mayhew did on this theme for the paper, subsequently continued in *London Labour and the London Poor,* is unique in its perception and its detail.

In the 1851 London census, Mayhew listed his occupation not as journalist but as author of "social philosophy," and he was clearly attempting in his work at the time to give a full sociological description of the poor. His technique was to interview a series of informants, sometimes seeing them more than once, and to prompt them with a series of questions covering their life history, the work they did, their relations to customers or employers, and their social life. When he wrote up the interviews, he removed his prompts; as Anne Humpherys points out, that makes his reports different in structure to reports in government publications, for example. He almost never indicates his informant's accent; when he does so, it is to indicate otherness, as when a German street musician says "ze" for "the." He normalizes sentence patterns to standard English, while retaining original trade terms and individual turns of expression. In this way, he refuses to give the reader any opportunity to stereotype the informants in the way that Caroline stereotypes Norah Connors in *The Greatest Plague.*

For example, in an article titled "The Experience of a Scotsman," Mayhew talks to a man who, though poor, is not destitute and is content with his lot. The informant is a cabinetmaker—that is, a woodworker who makes furniture. The report is part of a thorough investigation of the cabinetmaking industry. Mayhew is always careful to describe the organization of a trade, and here he gives a careful taxonomy of cabinetmakers' specializations. General cabinetmakers make every description of furniture except chairs and bedsteads, "from the smallest comb-tray to the largest bookcase," an informant tells Mayhew. "If he can't do whatever he's put to, he must go" (in Thompson and Yeo, *The Unknown Mayhew*, p. 433). Fancy cabinet makers make light, portable items—ladies' work boxes, portable writing desks. Finally there are chair makers and bedstead makers. Mayhew gives a detailed catalog of the various items of furniture made, and demonstrates that furniture-making is highly skilled work:

> The foreman gives him a sketch of the article he has to make, and points out the materials [that are] to be used in its construction. The journeyman then measures, saws and cuts the wood to the shape required, and is expected to do so with the greatest economy of stuff ... [and ensure] the best portion shall occupy the most prominent part ... or, in the language of the trade "he must put the best side to London."
>
> (in Thompson and Yeo, p. 441)

He is also responsible for cutting out all parts of the piece and for assembling them.

Mayhew's informant for this report is "[a] good-looking man ... with a hardly perceptible Scotch accent" (p. 448) who is a general cabinet-maker of the best class. He gives an account of his upbringing in Scotland, where his mother was a laundress, and says "a cabinet maker without some education is a very poor creature" (p. 448) After serving his apprenticeship, he had come to look for work in London about a dozen years before Mayhew met him.

> I went from place to place for three weeks, asking for work ... At last I called at Mr—'s and met with the master himself. He asked where I'd worked last and I said at Mr—'s of—, and at Mr—'s of Carlisle. "Very respectable men," said he, "I haven't a doubt of it, but I never heard their names before." And then he asked me some more questions, and called his foreman and said, "R—, we want hands; I think you might put on this young man; just try him." So I was put on, and was there four or five years.
>
> (pp. 448–449)

Mayhew's technique allows the Scotsman to speak in his own voice and to preserve the subtly different register that the master uses. Any tradesman would be able to read the subtext of this encounter and would have shared many of the Scotsman's experiences, including the month without earning a penny tramping from place to place asking for work. He would know what sort of questions the master asked ("How would you use this piece of timber? What is chamfering? Show me your tools.") He would understand the etiquette of the "putting on." The master does not take the young man on personally; he recommends his foreman to do so. The foreman will be responsible for supervising the new recruit and deciding if he should stay on. Finally, he would understand why the Scotsman stayed on for four or five years, nearly half his time in London. As things were at the time, a tradesman could not better himself by changing his employer, because all employers paid very much the same depressed wages.

The cabinet maker also describes the comradeship that existed between the craftsmen: "I had many little things to learn in London ways ... I've asked many a good London man for his opinion, and had it given to me as a man should give it. I do the same myself now. A good workman needn't be afraid; he won't be hurt" (p. 449). Mayhew often describes the ways in which men working together help each other, indicating that sharing skills does not disadvantage the men—work itself is not competitive.

The Scotsman reports what his earnings have been over two months or so; possibly he had been asked by Mayhew at an early interview to keep a record. He works by the piece—that is he negotiates a price for each piece of furniture he makes, rather than being paid a weekly wage—and he averages about one pound fifteen shillings a week (about eight U.S. dollars at the time). He is proud that his wife does not have to work and look for employment stitching up clothes: "An average of near 35 s[hillings] is it? Well, no doubt I make that all the year round. I can keep a wife and child comfortably. I wouldn't hear of my wife working for a slop tailor. I'd rather live on bread and water myself than see it. Slop means slavery" (p. 449).

Commenting on their social life, Mayhew reports that up to fifteen years previously, the cabinetmakers as a class had generally been heavy drinkers, but they were now much more temperate. "The masters won't have tipplers," says one of them. They try to live near their work and go home for every meal. They only go to the theater infrequently, except where there is a family, since family groups traditionally go to the theater together, but they are members of literary societies and "great attenders at lectures." "I don't know a card-player among us," one of them told Mayhew (p. 443).

In another report, in the *Morning Chronicle* letters, titled "Interview with a Woman Doing the Worst Paid Convict Work," Mayhew was investigating those who lived by doing outwork by the piece for tailors—that is, collecting cut-out pieces of material and stitching them into garments at home. Mayhew deliberately sought out a woman doing the lowest-paid work, stitching up convict's uniforms. She was at home, but hiding, fearing a visit from a woman who had lent her a shilling and wanted it back. "On a chair without a back was a tray with a cup of hot, milkless tea and a broken saucer with a few potatoes on it. It was the poor soul's dinner. Some tea-leaves had been given her and she had boiled them up again to make something of a meal. She had not even a morsel of bread" (in Thompson and Yeo p. 166). Out of her small earnings (only a few cents a day at best) she must pay for the thread she uses and for candles. "The other day I had to sell a cup and saucer for a half penny in order to get me a candle to work with," she reports (p. 167). She faces having to compete with younger women who can see better than she (she says she is "turned of 70"; p. 168) What she would like most in life is a shawl. The reference to her as a "poor soul" is a rare expression of personal feeling by Mayhew in response to the sheer misery he encounters.

The work engages the reader on a variety of levels, including the understanding of a subtext found in the details. In many of the descriptions of the women who do piecework making up clothes, there are references to the cost of thread and candles, for example. Why candles? Because many of these women must sit up late after the day's work in the house is finished and do their piecework then; the reader can visualize thousands of desperate women carrying on until the candle gutters out, women who are also praying the piece-master will bring some work the next time he calls and not simply say, "Nothing for you today."

RECEPTION

Douglas Jerrold wrote in a letter to his friend Mrs. Cowden Clarke in February 1850: "Do you devour those marvellous revelations of the inferno of misery, of wretchedness, that is smouldering under our feet? ... I am very proud to say these papers [are by] Henry Mayhew, who married my girl. He will cut his name deep" (cited in Thompson and Yeo, p. 9) Mayhew's work prompted a change in the way the Victorian reader saw the poor. To begin with, he knocks away most of the conventional explanations of poverty: the poor are not necessarily unskilled, he demonstrates, and they are not necessarily made poor by drink (although some certainly spend a great deal on beer, it does not prevent them from earning).

More subtly, Mayhew suggests, the poor are not poor because of the moral wickedness of their employers. This perspective was in direct conflict with what such radicals as Dickens had previously suggested. In *The Life and Adventures of Nicholas Nickleby* (1839), for example, Dickens had presented a pair of philanthropic employers, the Cheeryble brothers, who use their position to benefit their employees by paying them generously. With Ebenezer Scrooge, in *A Christmas Carol* (1843), Dickens presents a counterexample. Scrooge is an employer who is miserly both to himself and to his clerk. After he is haunted by three spirits who show him the harmfulness of the man he has become, however, Scrooge has a change of heart and becomes a Cheeryble. The implication is that if employers behave decently, all will be well.

Mayhew's interviews illustrated, by contrast, that employers were bound by economic constraints just as much as workers were—that there was a limit to what an employer personally could do to improve the lives of his employees. His interviews also sometimes showed that there was a limit to what philanthropy could accomplish in alleviating poverty. Mayhew's letters in the *Morning Chronicle* had a profound effect not only on writers such as Dickens and on the Christian Socialists, who included Charles Kingsley, but also on the public mood more generally; some readers demanded a more serious approach and a deeper analysis of society: What, then, was the cause of poverty? If it was not lack of skill, drink, the malice of employers, or overpopulation, where was it to be located?

Mayhew's reports indicated that one source of ruin for the working class could be found in the technological advances of the era. The livelihood of sawyers, for instance—whose work involved cutting timber into planks, or cutting hardwood into veneers (thin plates of wood that are glued to cheaper timber such as plain pine to make more elegant surfaces)—was undermined by the introduction of machinery in the form of steam-driven saws. A forty-nine-year-old sawyer with thirty-five years in the trade told Mayhew, "I can recollect when I could save more money in a week than I can now earn in the same time … Often [in the old days] when I've been going along … with my saw on my back, a timber merchant or a cabinet-maker would hail me, and cry … 'do you want any work, my man?'" (in Thompson and Yeo, p. 399). "'It's no use emigrating,' says another man. 'Let a man go where he will, machinery pursues him … I have paid one shilling and ten pence [fifty cents] for a quartern loaf before now, and I could get it much easier than I can now'" (p. 403). But even the machines are in trouble, Mayhew is told, and "can't hardly raise the price of the coals to get their fires up" (p. 403). The reason is the fall in prices from six pence a foot for cutting veneers to one penny a foot. "Machinery's very powerful, sir, but competition is much stronger" (p. 403).

Mayhew clearly agreed that competition is also part of the problem, observing that "overproduction drives down wages" (p. 464). He reasoned that, faced by an increase in production elsewhere that leads to a fall in prices, a manufacturer is driven to produce and sell more items if he is to cover costs. In the cabinetmaking trade, the established masters of Mayhew's day were faced with the fact that linen stores were beginning to sell furniture, which they bought from the sweatshops in the East End of London. This caused the prices of furniture generally to fall. In response, the masters tried to make more furniture, forcing their men to do more work for the same wage. Since getting more work out of any given number of men is the same as artificially increasing the number of workmen the employer has, the law of supply and demand then enabled the employers to cut wages. In other words "overwork makes underpay" (p. 465), said Mayhew. Further, since workmen cannot easily reduce their expenditure, they tend to work more to try to make up for the loss in wages—in other words "underpay makes overwork" (p. 467).

Mayhew also became increasingly suspicious of Britain's movement toward a free-trade policy that allowed goods from abroad into the United Kingdom without a tariff. Free trade had substantially reduced costs, especially the cost of foodstuffs—for instance, bread became much cheaper than it previously had been. But Mayhew found that many of his informants were suffering from the new trade policy—for example, the sawyer who found it harder to buy bread at the new lower price, because his wages had been reduced so much. In fact, many employers used the fact that bread was cheaper as an excuse for lowering wages. Additionally, the introduction of free-trade policy had triggered the overproduction that led to lower wages.

The *Morning Chronicle* as a Liberal newspaper was firm in its support of free trade, and it deleted some of Mayhew's copy that was critical of the policy. Further, the paper published a letter in the same format as the one Mayhew used praising a particular tailors' shop that was known as an employer of sweated labor. Mayhew asked the *Chronicle* to publish a disclaimer saying he was not the author of this letter, but the editors refused, and Mayhew severed his connection with the paper—with a great deal too much being said on both sides for the breach ever to be healed.

HENRY MAYHEW

LONDON LABOUR AND THE LONDON POOR

London Labour and the London Poor appeared in installments from 1851 through March 1852, in blue paper wrappers, a deliberate imitation of official "blue books." Blue books are purely factual reports commissioned by the government and examining some item of social interest where legislation might be required (hours worked in the coal industry, or education in Wales, for two examples). Mayhew intended this comparison—he referred to the work as a blue book written by one man.

He took to publishing letters from his readers together with his replies on the inside of these wrappers. Bernard Taithe has analyzed the resulting dialog and finds Mayhew to be a pioneering, serious investigator. In particular Taithe exposes the falsity of the suggestion made at the time that Mayhew was a sensationalist and just another author of lurid crime reports.

When, in March 1852, relations with the printer of the installments broke down, the work was published in book form, a full work of reference in two volumes titled *London Labour and the London Poor: A Cyclopaedia of the Condition and Earnings of Those That* Will *Work, Those That* Can Not *Work, and Those That* Will Not *Work*. The emphases on "will," "can not," and "will not" in the title are Mayhew's; he appears to be moving (as Patricia Ingham suggests in *The Language of Gender and Class*), towards the notion that the working class splits into the respectable poor and an underclass.

"THE DUSTMEN"

The suggestion that there is an underclass is near the surface in an account titled "The Dustmen" (found at pp. 218–249 in Neuberg's edition of *London Labour and the London Poor*). This report represents the best of investigative journalism, involving both a good deal of research out on the street and a good deal of time in the Reading Room of the British Museum. The "dustmen" described by Mayhew are the men who patrolled the streets of London with carts and took away the "dust" from any householder who summoned them. Wise householders gave the dustman a tip, so that the workmen would call every day. The "dust" that the dustmen collected was household waste, but it was not garbage in the modern sense. Mostly it was the ash left from the coal fires that were found in every home; most other rubbish was burned on a fire, and this added to the dust.

When Mayhew came to investigate how the service was organized, he met a wall of silence. He could identify some of the dust contractors; they were the men who had agreements with the parishes, the local government bodies, to remove the dust from their areas. But the contractors refused to talk to Mayhew, and they threatened their workmen with dismissal if they talked to him. In fact, Mayhew managed to interview several of the workers despite this threat. Mayhew begins his research with statistics that are publicly available.

He reports that where previously the dust contractors had paid the parishes for the right to remove the dust, they now demanded a fee to take it away. Dust was (for reasons described below) a very profitable commodity, although its value had diminished in the years prior to the time of Mayhew's investigation. Mayhew quotes figures for one small parish showing that dust collection had earlier produced an income of £450 annually *from* the contractor, but that dust collection in the parish had come to represent an expenditure of £250 per annum *to* the contractor. Altogether, Mayhew calculates, £30,000–£40,000 was paid out for collecting dust across the whole of London. Yet the post office directory listed only nine tradesmen calling themselves "dustmen," and the number listed as "scavengers" amounted to ten. "These figures are obviously incomplete," comments Mayhew, in an understatement (Neuberg, p. 221). He estimates, with the help of a man who knows the trade, that the number of dust contractors is probably closer to eighty or ninety.

Mayhew next sets to work to calculate how much business there actually is. He knows the amount of coal that comes into London, and by supposing that 25 percent of the coal is left as ash, he then calculates the amount of ash that needs to be collected. He next calculates the number of men necessary to shift that amount of ash—it comes to about 1,880, roughly equal to the number of men who deliver the coal in the first place. Why then have the contractors gone to such lengths to make their business almost invisible? To find the answer, Mayhew looks next at how the dust is treated.

The contractor has the dust taken to a depot where it is piled up into a "hill." He appoints a "hill master," who is responsible for sifting it. Some items that are sifted out belong to the contractor; for example, he claims the broken bricks and oyster shells, which are used for "hardcore" (in building house foundations or roads); he also claims rope, old shoes, rags, and bones, which go to the chandler. These items are sorted out and piled up by the children of the men who collect the dust and women who work sifting the hill. The children might be as young as five years old, and they spend all their time on the hill. If coins and jewelry are found in the dust, the jewelry is sold to traders and the money, together with the coins, is split half to the hill master and half to the workers.

The dust is sifted by the women whose menfolk work the carts. Each has a metal sieve, and a couple of men (casual hires) go around with a shovel filling each sieve with dust. The dust sieves out into two grades—a fine powder called "soil" and a coarse powder called "brieze." In earlier days, the soil would have been sold to farmers whose land was marshy; the soil would have been mixed in so that the land drained better and gave a better crop of corn. Farmers would have paid up to £1 a bushel for it. Since the enactment of free-trade policies, however, prices for corn had fallen, and farmers had turned to cattle raising. The price of dust-based soil had dropped to one eighth of the old level; it was now only used to dress clover. The only other people who still bought soil as an agricultural amendment were those setting up in the countryside just outside London as market gardeners. The rest of the dust—both brieze and unsold soil—went down the river on barges to brick fields in North Kent, where it was mixed with clay to make bricks and was also used to fill gaps in the kilns where the bricks were baked. But the diminished value of soil offers Mayhew an explanation of the reluctance of the contractors to continue paying the parishes for the right to collect the dust.

Because a whole family works in the dust-handling operation, Mayhew calculates the average earnings for a typical family, including the pennies the children earn, at about one pound eight shillings if they work a full week or a pound a week average all the year round. They spend a lot of the earnings on beer. Their only social life is to go to the pub (the men always take their women), where they drink a great deal of beer, smoke a few pipes of tobacco, and sing what they call a "jolly chorus" or two. They never go to church or to any of the lectures the cabinetmakers frequent. They are illiterate and have no interest in politics. Sometimes they make up a party to go to the theater, sitting in the cheapest seats and enjoying melodramas with "plenty of murdering scenes" (p. 241). They live this way year by year, totally content with life on the hill, claiming it is a very healthy life and pointing to the vast age some dustmen have reached.

"As for [their] morals," Mayhew writes, "it may easily be supposed that they are not of an over-strict character." He lays the responsibility for this on the masters, one of whom says, "They do my work, and that's all I want with them, and all I care about" (p. 244). For every dustman who is married, Mayhew calculates, twenty simply live with their women; the men remain faithful because of the amount the women are able to earn—about half of what a man makes.

This is a curious passage in two ways. First, there is an assumption that the very poor will not have a moral code; if the dustmen find anything valuable while collecting the dust, the master assumes, they will keep it rather than bringing it into the yard. Stereotypically, a dustman is a thief. Second, the attitude of the men to their women does not show a lack of moral code, but rather the existence of a nonstandard moral code. Mayhew quotes one of them describing his life with his woman, Sall: "I just like a pot or two of good heavy [beer] and a song and then I tumble in with my Sall, and I'm as happy as here and there ... That there Sall of mine's a stunner, a regular stunner ... an out-and-outer and worth half a dozen of the other sifters" (p. 247). This rather rhapsodic account is subversive of his claim that this is an amoral culture, and, unusually, Mayhew represents the dustman's London dialect (edited out here), possibly in an attempt to distance himself from the suspicion of sympathy.

Finally, Mayhew calculates the earnings of the contractors, taking the total earnings for the operation over all contractors at about £150,000 a year, from parish contracts and the sale of "brieze" at the new low price of two shillings and six pence (sixty cents) a bushel. He estimates average annual earnings for the contractors at £800 (four thousand U.S. dollars). This is what the contractors have concealed—the sheer size of their wealth as compared to their employees' poverty.

In his report, Mayhew states that some parishes now insist that the contractors must pay their men at an improved rate of pay of eight pence per day. He also notes, "With the exception of Bermondsey, there are no parishes that remove their own dust" (p. 220), as though that were an obvious way forward. Both these developments would mean interfering in the operation of the market, but this is the logic of all that Mayhew has to say.

"THE MUD-LARKS"

In a section of *London Labor and the London Poor* titled "The Mud-Larks," Mayhew directly addresses the question of whether poverty is a direct cause of crime, and whether the very poorest who live on the edge of destitution may be described as worthy. The people known as "mud-larks" are scavengers who wade sometimes waist deep in the mud left by the Thames where it is tidal. They collect all sorts of scraps—pieces of coal that they sell to the poor at one penny a bucket, old ends of rope, copper nails. They work practically naked in all weathers, and Mayhew calculates they earn about three pennies a day. Though there are a few old people who work as mud-larks, they are mostly quite young children. Many of them grow up to become thieves or prostitutes, and Mayhew describes a gang structure within which systematic theft of bread or bacon from shops is organized. Occasionally, a mud-lark ends up in the House of Correction. One of Mayhew's informants had done seven days there for theft; he swept the dust from an empty coal barge, and tells Mayhew that he liked it much better than mud-larking, because "he wore a coat and shoes and stockings ... and was never afraid of going to bed with nothing [to eat] at all—as he often had to do while at liberty" (p. 210).

Mayhew focuses on one mud-lark, J.C., a boy of fourteen who had been in the business three years. Originally, his family had been quite secure; his father was a warehouseman, and one year his mother had managed to save four pounds ten shillings (twenty-two dollars and fifty cents U.S.). Then the father had switched trades and become a coal handler; because he was hired at pubs each day, he became a heavy drinker, often leaving his family without any money. One night he slipped down between two barges while drunk, was badly injured, and died three years later "in a hopeless state." The neighbors collected one pound five shillings (six dollars) for the widow; she went into business as a greengrocer "and got on well for five years," says the boy (p. 215). She even sent J.C to school.

The grocery business came to ruin, however. The potato blight destroyed much of her stock, and two customers died owing money she could not recover. J.C. began work as a mud-lark "because his clothes were too bad for him to look for anything better" (p. 215), which is the answer to Thomas Carlyle. He frequently cut his feet on glass or nails hidden in the mud, went home to dress them, and then returned to the river to carry on working, because if the tide came in before he got back, he could end up earning nothing for the day. He then became ill with ague (probably from malaria, which was endemic in the Thames estuary until the 1920s); later all the other members of the family went down with fever as well, and for long periods one or other of them could not work.

They lived from hand to mouth; J.C.'s older sister sold fish on the street, and his mother had occasional work cleaning. But they are a very warm, supportive family. They tell Mayhew that when J.C. drove a copper nail into his foot, his mother carried him to the doctor every day on her back, and the mother tells warmly of how proud he was when he could put meat on the table (p. 216). In the end, Mayhew intervenes to help the family. He persuades a friend to take the oldest girl on as a servant, and he finds J.C. a job with a printer. At the time of writing, they are doing well, and the money J.C. brings home has enabled his mother to open another shop. "This simple story requires no comment," says Mayhew, "[and shows] how often the poor boys reared in the gutter are thieves, merely because society forbids them being honest lads" (p. 218).

Had this been a work of fiction, the reader might have protested the remorseless piling on of disasters that this family experienced, but in the context of Mayhew's almost clinical analysis, it becomes clear that many families could tell a similar tale. If Victorian literature is sometimes melodramatic, it only reflects Victorian life as it was.

THE MORMONS

Mayhew's interest in the Church of Jesus Christ of the Latter-day Saints, a religious group more often known as the Mormons, was first aroused during a visit to Liverpool as part of his research for the *Morning Chronicle*. One of the explanations for poverty in Britain suggested that poverty was the result of overpopulation and that the solution lay in government-sponsored emigration to the British colonies, especially to Australia or New Zealand. Mayhew was adamant that this explanation was incorrect and that it distracted attention from the real causes; furthermore, his working-class contacts hated the idea of such emigration, because they saw it as a form of transportation, a punishment for convicts (banishment) that was in force until 1868.

The cost of emigration was in general borne by the emigrants themselves, and Mayhew knew how appalling conditions were on the emigrant ships. In the course of his investigation in Liverpool, he learned that the Mormons maintained an missionary agency there to assist the emigration of new members of the church to the Mormon community in the United States, where the church had been founded around 1830. During 1849 no fewer than twenty-five hundred Mormon converts had left for the Salt Lake Valley, and since 1840 the total emigrating had been between thirteen thousand and fourteen thousand.

This was a significant trend, and Mayhew set himself to write about it, in a book that was published in 1851 as *The Mormons, or Latter-day Saints: With Memoirs of the Life and Death of Joseph Smith, the "American Mahomet."* Of course, vast numbers of English and Irish people left for Canada and the United States during the same period (about twenty thousand a month "in the fine season," when the Atlantic crossing was best accomplished) but the Mormons carried out a structured emigration of well-off farmers and mechanics that was professionally directed. To explain the Mormon emigration scheme, Mayhew had first to set it in the context of the Mormon Church, and there was no reliable account of that church in existence.

Mayhew's principal informant for the book was Orson Pratt. The man who supervised the Mormon emigration from Liverpool, he was one of the "quorum of twelve apostles" of the Latter-day Saints and was in charge of the Mormon mission to Britain at the time. Pratt had previously been one of the Mormon pioneers on the trail to Utah, and like Mayhew, he had scientific interests. Mayhew's resulting study of the Mormons is encyclopedic, full of facts and containing many original documents. It is illustrated with plates and illustrations of good quality, and Mayhew promised in his preface that these would include "views of remote places not hitherto portrayed, and representations of events in a wild and very partially settled country ... drawn from the rude sketches or minute descriptions of persons to whom the spots were familiar and who were in many cases eye-witnesses of the incidents depicted" (p. iii).

The Mormon Church, Mayhew explains, originated in the visions of Joseph Smith, "a great impostor or a great visionary—perhaps both" (p. 13), which led Smith in 1823 to discover in New

York State a cache containing a new set of scriptures written on gold in Egyptian hieroglyphics. These he deciphered with the help of a pair of spectacles so large that he could only use one lens at a time, and he published the results as the *Book of Mormon* in 1830. One of Joseph Smith's revelations was that the Native Americans were the descendants of a group of Jews who had left Jerusalem just before it was destroyed by the Babylonians, and the book contained new revelations from God, especially designed for the Americans.

Honesty as a reporter compels Mayhew to summarize all the evidence against the truth of Smith's story, including the fact that the story contained in the Book of Mormon appears to be plagiarized from a contemporary novel and that neither the gold plates nor the magic spectacles were ever publicly produced. But he is more interested in the light the incident throws on the nature of religious belief, especially among the Protestant churches. He focuses on Smith's distress at the conflicting claims of these churches, each of which disparaged the others. By implication, if these churches had shown more tolerance of each other, Mormonism might never have arisen.

Mayhew's primary interest is in the sociology of the church and the way its structure reflects the experience of its members. In seeking converts, Joseph Smith and other Mormons insisted that the Millennium, the end of the world we know, was due instantly. Every appearance of a comet or an unnatural birth among animals was a sign that the end of the world was coming and that it was essential to join the true church now. One appeal of the church seemed to be that those who accepted the invitation felt an enormous relief and a total conviction that they had made the right choice.

The second appeal was the strong social cohesion within the Mormon membership, which was increased by their treatment at the hands of nonbelievers, especially when they began to try to set up their own community. (The social cohesion, incidentally, did not imply any particular friendly comradeship among the Saints, Mayhew points out; they could be a fractious and quarrelsome lot.) Determined to find their Zion, a place where they might live together, a group of Mormons settled first in Independence, Missouri, and Mayhew quotes Joseph Smith's rapturous account of the country: "the beautiful rolling prairies lay spread around like a sea of meadows. The timber is a mixture of oak, hickory, black walnut, elm, cherry, honey locus, mulberry, coffee bean, hackberry, box, elder and bass wood ... The soil is rich and fertile, from three to ten feet deep ... a rich, black mould, intermingled with clay and sand" (p. 52). The list of the trees is hypnotic, and to the British reader it would have been, like the Mormon Church itself, a mixture of the familiar (oak, elm, cherry) and the exotic (honey locus, hackberry, bass wood).

From the first, the Mormons encountered opposition from the local population, which increased in intensity as time went on. Mayhew details the escalation of the persecution of the Saints. Smith himself was tarred and feathered by a mob led by local preachers of other denominations, and in the end, one group of Mormons was massacred by a detachment of the U.S. Army; and the remainder were stripped of all their property. Mayhew offers a careful analysis of why this happened, locating the origin of the persecution in rumors spread by some former Mormons who had been expelled from the church, accusing them of communism and sharing their wives between them. These rumors were readily believed. Further, "[t]he superiority [the Mormons] assumed gave offence ... they talked so imprudently of their determination to possess the whole State and [exclude all who were not Mormons] that a party was secretly formed against them" (p. 60). Finally, they openly advocated freeing the black slaves.

The reaction among the Mormons to the persecution they encountered was to disregard the authority of the State of Missouri, and even of the federal government of the United States, and to rely on themselves for their own protection. When they moved on to Illinois, they mounted armed guards on each wagon train and refused to tell people as they passed who they were. They formed a new settlement at Commerce, Illinois, which was later to be incorporated as the city of Nauvoo (meaning "the beautiful"). It was by 1841 home to fifteen thousand Mormons, "a pre-eminently industrious, frugal and pains-taking people," says Mayhew. "They felt the advantages of co-operation" (p. 102). Joseph Smith was the leader of this community, and it is clear that Mayhew's view of him has undergone a change in the course of this unfolding of the Mormon story, just as Smith himself has undergone a change: from half-crazed visionary to a skilled and competent leader of men and a general in charge of a well-trained militia he has raised himself.

In 1844, however, Joseph and his brother Hyram were kidnapped by Marshalls from Missouri and taken back to that state for trial. On June 27, 1844, they were lynched by a mob. The presidency of the Mormons passed from Smith to Brigham Young, who led the Saints' move to Utah and founded an independent State of Deseret, of which he was appointed governor by the U.S. president Millard Fillmore. One important development in Mormon thinking after the murder of Joseph Smith was a belief that the Mormons in other parts of the United States or in Europe should be called home to join the main community in Deseret. Nowhere else could Mormons really be safe, they felt, and they needed the biggest population they could get.

Great care and expense were therefore devoted to the emigration schemes. The Mormons did not want to share a ship with other emigrants, and so they maintained their own vessels for crossing, in which the conditions aboard the ships would be sanitary, and passengers would carry twenty-five pounds of extra provisions per head above the legal minimum. The provisions were of excellent quality. The ships were segregated, with English and Scots emigrants bunking separately (there were no Irish Mormons). (Mayhew offers is an interesting footnote which suggests that at the time he was writing the Mormons were considering a plan to send their ships directly to California via Panama or Cape Horn rather than to New Orleans as the current practice was, cutting out the rigors of the journey up the Mississippi and minimizing contact with nonbelievers on the way.) Clearly, no government-run emigration scheme could match this level of provision, which was, nonetheless, not much more than what was needed to see the passengers through.

There is a productive tension in Mayhew's account of the Mormons; he is too much of a rationalist to accept their belief system, but he is clearly almost envious of the life in Deseret as Orson Pratt describes it. Mayhew writes of communities where there are no business centers and no shops, not even a barber's. "Every one chose to shave himself, and no one had time to shave his neighbour" (p. 312). In essence, Deseret is a community based on production, not trade, and Mayhew can hear its siren song.

The Mormons was Mayhew's last work of any substance. He died in obscurity, and after his death he was virtually forgotten. The revival of his reputation began in the 1940s as *London Labour and the London Poor* was mined by those in search of nostalgia; later its intellectual importance was reestablished, especially by Anne Humpherys and E. P. Thompson. Additionally, Mayhew's considerable output of comic work is becoming better known as more of his work becomes available online.

Selected Bibliography

WORKS BY HENRY MAYHEW

The Wandering Minstrel: A Farce. London: John Miller, 1834

What to Teach and How to Teach It: So That the Child May Become a Wise and Good Man. Part 1: *The Cultivation of the Intellect.* London: William Smith, 1842.

The Good Genius That Turned Everything into Gold; or, The Queen Bee and the Magic Dress. With Augustus Mayhew. London 1847. London: David Bogue, 1847.

The Greatest Plague of Life; or, The Adventures of a Lady in Search of a Good Servant. With Augustus Mayhew. London: David Bogue, 1847.

Whom to Marry or How to Get Married: By One Who Has Refused "Twenty Excellent Offers" At Least. London: David Bogue, 1848.

The Image of His Father; or, One Boy Is More Trouble Than a Dozen Girls. With Augustus Mayhew. London: H. Hurst, 1848.

HENRY MAYHEW

Acting Charades; or, Deeds Not Words: A Christmas Game to Make a Long Evening Short. With Augustus Mayhew. Illustrated by Henry George Hine. London 1850. (Drama.) London: David Bogue, 1850.

1851; or, The Adventures of Mr. and Mrs. Sandboys and Family Who Came up to London to "Enjoy Themselves" and to See the Great Exhibition. London: David Bogue, 1851.

London Labour and the London Poor. 3 vols. London: George Woodfall, 1851. Expanded ed., 4 vols. London: Griffin Bohn, 1861–1862.

The Mormons, or Latter-day Saints: With Memoirs of the Life and Death of Joseph Smith, the "American Mahomet." With Douglas Mackay. London: Office of the National Illustrated Library, 1851.

The Story of the Peasant-Boy Philosopher; or, "A Child Gathering Pebbles on the Sea Shore." London, George Routledge, 1854.

Living for Appearances. With Augustus Mayhew. London: James Blackwood, 1855.

The Wonders of Science; or, Young Humphry Davy. London: David Bogue, 1855.

The Rhine and Its Picturesque Scenery. 2 vols. Illustrated by Myles Birket Foster. London: David Bogue, 1856.

Young Benjamin Franklin; or, The Right Road Through Life. With illustrations by John Gilbert and Edmund Evans. London: Bryce, Griffin, 1861.

The Criminal Prisons of London and Scenes of Prison Life. Completed by John Binny. Griffin, Bohn, 1862.

German Life and Manners as Seen in Saxony at the Present Day. 2 vols. London: William H. Allen, 1864.

The Magic of Kindness; or, the Wondrous Story of the Good Huan. With Augustus Mayhew. London: Cassel, Petter and Galpin, 1869.

Mont Blanc: A Comedy. With Athol Mayhew. London: privately printed, 1874.

AS EDITOR

The Shops and Companies of London, and the Trades and Manufactories of Great Britain. London 1865.

London Characters: Illustrations of the Humour, Pathos, and Peculiarities of London Life. With illustrations by W. S. Gilbert et al. London: Chatto and Windus, 1874.

MODERN EDITIONS

Neuberg, Victor, ed. *Henry Mayhew: London Labour and the London Poor.* Harmondsworth, U.K.: Penguin 1985. (Selections from the original, in one volume.)

Thompson, E. P., and Yeo, Eileen eds. *The Unknown Mayhew: Selections from the* Morning Chronicle, *1849–50.* London Merlin Press 1971.

BIOGRAPHICAL AND CRITICAL STUDIES

Chapman, Raymond. *Forms of Speech in Victorian Fiction.* London: Longman, 1994.

Chase, Karen, and Michael Levenson. *The Spectacle of Intimacy: A Public Life for the Victorian Age.* Princeton, N.J.: Princeton University Press, 2000.

Green, Bryan S. "The Role of the Impartial Spectator in Mayhew's *London Labour and the London Poor.*" *Journal of Contemporary Ethnology* 31, no. 2:99–134 (2002).

Himmelfarb, Gertrude. *The Idea of Poverty: England in the Early Victorian Age.* New York: Knopf, 1983.

Humpherys, Anne. *Travels into the Poor Man's Country: The Work of Henry Mayhew.* Athens: University of Georgia Press, 1977. (Includes selections from the *Morning Chronicle* letters and biographical information about Mayhew.)

Ingham, Patricia. *The Language of Gender and Class: Transformation in the Victorian Novel.* London: Routledge, 1996.

Jerrold, Walter. *Douglas Jerrold and "Punch."* London: Macmillan, 1910.

Lightman, Bernard, ed. *Victorian Science in Context.* Chicago: University of Chicago Press, 1997.

Taithe, Bernard, ed. *The Essential Mayhew: Representing and Communicating the Poor.* London: Rivers Oram Press, 1996.

Tolson, Andrew. "Social Surveillance and Subjectification: The Emergence of 'Subculture' in the Work of Henry Mayhew." *Cultural Studies* 4, no. 2:113–127 (1990).

J. K. ROWLING

(1965—)

Charles Robert Baker

THE PARENTS OF J. K. Rowling (pronounced "rolling"), Peter James Rowling and Anne Volant, were eighteen years old when they met aboard a train in London in 1964. Peter, the son of Ernie and Kathleen Rowling, shopkeepers in Dorset, and Anne, the daughter of Stan, an engineer turned hospital mail carrier, and Frieda Volant, had boarded the train in King's Cross Station as strangers but when they arrived at their destination, Arbroath, on the east coast of Scotland, a journey of over five hundred miles that took close to nine hours in those days, they had become quite attached to each other. They shared the same purpose in making the long trip; both were hoping to find satisfying careers in the Royal Navy and were reporting to their posting in Scotland. The couple decided after several months that the demands of such a life were not for them and they opted out of the service; they both preferred a more settled existence in a rural area. Further complicating the possibility of careers in the navy was the fact that Anne was pregnant.

The teenaged couple returned to their parents' homes and made preparations for the next, unexpected, phase of their young lives. Peter's father, who had been a machine-tool setter before becoming a grocer, advised his son to seek work in mechanical engineering. Peter's application for work was accepted by the enormous Bristol Siddeley factory at Filton in the West Country and he began his apprenticeship on their assembly line. The wedding of Peter and Anne, who had only weeks before they celebrated their twentieth birthdays, took place in All Saint's Parish Church, a massive Victorian edifice located near Anne's parent's home in North London, on March 14, 1965. Anne was five months pregnant.

CHILDHOOD AND EARLY EDUCATION

The Rowlings settled in the Gloucester County city of Yate, located about ten miles northeast of the Bristol Siddeley factory. Their first home was a modest, one-story cottage at 109 Sundridge Park, located in an area surrounded by open fields. Anne Rowling was admitted to the Cottage Hospital at 240 Station Road, Yate, in late July 1965 and on July Joanne Rowling was born. Another daughter, Dianne, was born nearly two years later, on June 28, 1967, in the home on Sundridge Park. In the meantime, the village atmosphere of Yate had succumbed to the urban, industrial sprawl that grew from Bristol, and Peter Rowling, who had completed his apprenticeship and was on a firmer financial footing, sought a better area in which to raise his family. He found what he was looking for in the town of Winterbourne, four miles from Yate, and bought a three-bedroom, gray stone house at 35 Nicholls Lane.

Peter Rowling worked long hours at Bristol Siddeley assembling Pegasus engines for use in Harrier fighter planes, therefore most of the responsibility for raising Jo and Dianne fell to their mother. And although Mr. Rowling only saw his daughters just before bedtime, if he arrived home early enough, and on weekends, he was a devoted and loving father who played with them and read them their favorite stories. When four-year-old Jo was confined to bed with the measles, her father spent hours sitting at her bedside entertaining her with the exploits of Mr. Toad, Bader, Mole, and Rat as he read to her from Kenneth Grahame's *The Wind in the Willows*. The event and the story made such an impression on Jo that two years later she wrote a tale of her own, "Rabbit," whose title character also suffered from the same illness.

J. K. ROWLING

Anne Rowling was an outgoing woman who made friends easily; one of her closest was Ruby Potter, who with her husband, Graham, and their two young children, Ian and Vikki, lived close by at 29 Nicholls Lane. Anne Rowling and Ruby Potter were both dedicated and voracious readers of historical romances, primarily those of Victoria Holt. They also read to their children from the books of Enid Blyton, James Barrie, Edith Nesbit, and, Jo's favorite, Richard Scarry, and encouraged their imaginative play by allowing access to their wardrobes for costume games. Jo, being the eldest of the four Rowling and Potter children, was their natural leader, and it was she who set the tone for their activities, a favorite of which was pretending to be witches and wizards. Jo, Dianne, and Vikki would don appropriately sinister costumes and run about on brooms, and Ian would become a wizard by wearing a long overcoat backward and putting on a pair of toy eyeglasses.

In the autumn following her fifth birthday, Jo Rowling began her formal education at St. Michael's Church of England school. She made the necessary adjustment from being the eldest in her circle of friends and their acknowledged leader to being one of the youngest in her class. And although she enjoyed the school, her teachers, and her new friends, she looked forward to the end of the school day when she would find her mother and Mrs. Potter waiting outside to walk her and Vikki home. Her time at St. Michael's lasted only four years; Peter Rowling, in his almost obsessive quest to provide an idyllic setting for himself and his family, found, on an outing with his wife in 1974, what he thought would suit the purpose in the village of Tutshill, located just across the recently opened Severn Bridge from Bristol, on the border between England and Wales. Tutshill is wedged between the Wye and Severn rivers and offers spectacular views of each; immediately to the north stands the awe-inspiring Forest of Dean: thirty thousand acres of ancient oaks and ageless myths. The couple made an offer on a quaint stone cottage for sale at the edge of the village, quickly sold their house in Winterbourne, and established themselves in their new home, Church Cottage.

Jo and Dianne were enrolled in Tutshill Church of England Primary School.

Being uprooted from the comfortable familiarity of school and friends, particularly Ian and Vikki Potter, was difficult for nine-year-old Jo. But an even greater difficulty was in the person of Jo's teacher, Mrs. Sylvia Morgan. Mrs. Morgan was a strict disciplinarian of the "spare the rod and spoil the child" type. On the first day of class in the autumn of 1974, Jo and her classmates were subjected to a sorting process Mrs. Morgan called the "daily ten." The purpose of this process was to identify academically advanced students and place them in an area of the classroom apart from those who required special attention. Jo's score on her first daily ten test was low and she was assigned a desk on the far right-hand side of the classroom among the other underachievers. She did, however, take advantage of opportunities to improve her class rank and eventually earned a desk on the left-hand side of the classroom, but in doing so she paid the price exacted of all clever students: the loss of some friends who resented her being smarter than they.

Nine-year-old Jo Rowling was the epitome of a "bookish" child. Shy, hopeless at sports, her rather plain face dominated by a pair of National Health eyeglasses, Rowling depended upon books to be her loyal, entertaining, and nonjudgmental companions. *The Chronicles of Narnia* by C. S. Lewis provided just the sort of escape from drabness, and hope for a better world, that any child could want, but the book that was perhaps the most influential in forming the imagination of the writer Rowling was to become was a children's fantasy novel published by the University of London in 1946, *The Little White Horse* by Elizabeth de Beauchamp Goudge (1900–1984). *The Little White Horse* tells the story of an ordinary, red-haired, thirteen-year-old orphan named Maria Merryweather who, upon the death of her father in 1842, travels from London with her governess, Miss Heliotrope, and Wiggins, an obnoxious dog, to the Merryweather family estate, Moonacre Manor in far western England, which is presided over by her cousin and now guardian, Sir Benjamin Merryweather. Upon arriving in Moonacre Valley, which is accessed by means of a door in a stone and a secret tunnel, Maria discovers that she is none other than the princess of the valley and that it is her destiny to set right all that has gone wrong in the enchanted land. In her quest, Maria encounters such colorfully named characters as Loveday Minette, Marmaduke Scarlet, and Monsieur Cocq de Noir, along with animals with special abilities: Wrolf the lion, Serena the rabbit, Zachariah the cat, and Periwinkle, Maria's pony. The imaginative and descriptive powers exhibited by Goudge earned *The Little White Pony* the 1946 Carnegie Medal.

In her second year at Tutshill, Rowling was taught by the school's deputy headmaster, Mr. John Morgan, husband of the dreaded Sylvia. Fortunately for the ten-year-old girl and her classmates, Mr. Morgan's style of teaching was in marked contrast to that of his wife's. Although he too was a strict disciplinarian, Mr. Morgan maintained order in his classroom and taught the prescribed curriculum without resorting to fear tactics and humiliation. Indeed, such was his reputation in the school that underclass students looked forward to the day when they would finally escape the storm that was Mrs. Morgan and advance into the relative calm of Mr. Morgan.

The Rowlings were a working-class family and as such it would have been a financial difficulty to send their eldest daughter to a private school. Therefore, in the autumn of 1976, Jo Rowling was enrolled in the Tutshill area state school, Wyedean Comprehensive School. Being a state school, Wyedean did not require an entrance examination to be passed or tuition fees to be paid. Ken Smith was Wyedean's headmaster during Rowling's time there, and he oversaw a body of students, faculty, and staff that was socially integrated, representing a mixture of various backgrounds: rural and urban; lower-, middle-, and upper-middle class.

Wyedean Comprehensive was indeed comprehensive in its curriculum; courses ranged from language arts, sciences, history, geography, and mathematics to gymnastics and instruction in the practical arts such as woodworking and metalworking. Rowling endured the demands of all Wyedean had to offer, and it soon became evident that her preference and her talent leaned toward the arts and away from all else. Chemistry was particularly difficult for Rowling. Nevertheless, the school's chemistry master, John Nettleship, played an important role in her family's life. When Dianne Rowling followed her sister to Wyedean in 1978, Anne Rowling, always a very active woman, decided that now that her daughters could, for the most part, look after themselves, she needed something to fill her days. There was a position open in Wyedean's chemistry department and Mrs. Rowling applied. After interviewing with Nettleship and his wife, Shirley, the department's chief technician, Mrs. Rowling was turned down in favor of a more experienced applicant. That person, however, soon tired of the job, quit suddenly, and Mrs. Rowling was hired. In most cases, the idea of having one's mother working at one's school—always about, and in constant communication with one's teachers and friends—would be abhorrent, but the Rowlings were a very tight-knit family and Anne's extended presence in her daughters' lives was welcomed by all concerned. Mrs. Rowling had a marvelous sense of humor, was an accomplished guitarist, and she entered into all activities with boundless enthusiasm and energy. Her youthful and exuberant enjoyment of life made the threesome of Anne, Jo, and Dianne appear to be three sisters rather than a mother and her two daughters.

Jo Rowling was an average student at best in most of her subjects; where she excelled was in English. Her creative writing exercises made her instructors sit up and take notice of the shy girl who rarely took part in class discussions. Perhaps the most influential English teacher Rowling encountered at Wyedean was a young feminist named Lucy Shepherd. The state comprehensive school system in England in the mid 1970s was a magnet that attracted young, enthusiastic teachers who were eager to present new methods; Lucy Shepherd was one of these. Shepherd displayed an openness and genuineness that encouraged trust between student and teacher. She cared deeply about her subject and expected the highest quality work, work that must be precise, well organized, and perfectly structured. Lucy Shepherd was the perfect role model for an impressionable young girl, whether that young girl chose teaching or writing or both as a profession.

Another role model was placed into Rowling's hands at the age of fourteen, when her aunt presented her with a copy of Jessica Mitford's 1960 autobiography, *Hons and Rebels*. As peacefully charming as Tutshill must have been for Peter Rowling and his wife, it must have been mind-numbingly boring for a creative teen-aged girl. *Hons and Rebels* opened Rowling's mind to the great world beyond the Severn River and to the possibilities of escape, adventure, self fulfillment, and romance. Unicorns and magical cats and protective lions were all very entertaining, and Jane Austen's structured society and happy endings (Rowling had read *Emma* over and over again) were the perfect fuel for adolescent daydreams; Jessica Mitford, who not only held romantic ideals but more importantly acted upon them, became, for Rowling, a realistic role model. Rowling had found a kindred spirit.

Jessica Mitford was born in 1917 into a wealthy, eccentric family of minor aristocrats in Gloucestershire who embraced the rising European political movement: Fascism. Indeed, one of Jessica's sisters, Unity, developed a warm, personal friendship with Adolf Hitler and was so distraught when war was declared against him that she attempted suicide by shooting herself in the head; she was not successful. Another sister, Diana, married the notorious British Fascist Sir Oswald Mosley and, like Unity, enjoyed Hitler's company. Jessica rebelled against her family's politics by embracing communism and supporting the labor movement. At the age of nineteen, Jessica met and fell in love with her second cousin, Esmond Romilly. Romilly, who was a nephew of Winston Churchill, shared Jessica's worldview. In fact, when they met, Romilly was recovering at home from dysentery, which he had contracted in Madrid while defending that city from the forces of General Francisco Franco. Although he had seen nearly all of his fellow volunteers slain in that ill-fated defense, Romilly was anxious to get back to the front lines, this time as a reporter, after his recovery. Jessica eloped with him; they married in Bayonne, France, on May 18, 1937, and led a hand-to-mouth nomadic life throughout Spain, France, and finally the United States. They were living in America when Great Britain declared war on Germany; Romilly immediately went to Canada and enlisted in the Royal Canadian Air Force to battle Hitler. He was killed in action when his plane was shot down over the North Sea returning from a bombing raid over Berlin in November of 1941. He was twenty-three. *Hons and Rebels* taught Rowling that a life of rebellion, idealism, courage, service, sacrifice, and romance was possible and very exciting, but it does not always lead to a happy ending. In the meantime, Rowling's rebellions, constricted as they were by the conventional, conservative, and confining Tutshill, amounted to nothing more outrageous than sneaking a smoke while leaning out of her upstairs bedroom window and speeding about the countryside with her friend Seán Harris in his turquoise Ford Anglia.

When Jo Rowling was fifteen, something that had been quietly at work within her vivacious mother asserted itself and demanded to be recognized. Friends and family had noticed Anne Rowling's diminishing abilities; she had difficulty lifting a teapot, a cup would slip from her hand and crash on the floor, a feeling of needles and pins in her fingers would prevent her from completing a piece on her guitar. In 1980, when Anne was thirty-five, her occasional clumsiness and passing tingling sensations were diagnosed and given their proper name: multiple sclerosis. Anne's particular strain of this neurological disease was especially virulent and it was not long before she could not do her work in the chemistry department; soon, she required a walker to move about Church Cottage and a wheelchair to navigate outside the home. Throughout, Anne Rowling maintained her ebullient spirits, doing what housework she could and reading what little information there was at that time about her disease. And although the Rowlings were not a religious family and did not attend church services, Anne, on her good days, made her way to St. Luke's Church next door to do volunteer work with the cleaning crew. Nevertheless, she was above all a practical woman who knew there was little hope for her;

on April 23, 1983, she thought it prudent to make her last will and testament.

It was at this time that Jo Rowling began to show a seriousness of purpose in her life; the shy, average student became, through effort not expended before, a very popular young woman among her peers and a remarkable pupil who was determined to impress her teachers by taking part in the classroom and always having her hand raised to answer a question correctly. Rowling applied herself diligently to her studies and showed exceptional abilities in English, French, and German. Outside the classroom, Seán Harris's friendship and his dependable, though battered, Ford Anglia made it possible for Rowling to escape for a while the pressures of school and the quiet grief that was ever present in Church Cottage, and find fun and entertainment in the pubs, cinemas, discos, and theaters of Bristol, Bath, Cardiff, and Newport. So grateful was Rowling to Harris that she dedicated her second Harry Potter novel, *Harry Potter and the Chamber of Secrets,* to him: "For Seán P. F. Harris. Getaway driver and foul-weather friend." The old Ford Anglia was not forgotten; it plays an important role in the Potter stories.

UNIVERSITY OF EXETER AND LIFE IN LONDON

Perhaps no one was more surprised than Rowling herself when her transformation into a sought-after companion and serious scholar was awarded in her final year at Wyedean by being elected head girl by faculty and students. Such was her self-confidence now at eighteen that Rowling decided to take the bold act of sitting the entrance examinations to the University of Oxford. There was never any doubt that Jo and Dianne would continue their education at university level; Peter and Anne Rowling, who did not have the opportunity to continue their studies, knew firsthand how difficult it was to get on in life without a university degree. The grades Rowling earned on her exams were impressive: two A levels in English and French and one B level in German. They were certainly good enough for admittance to Oxford, but there was a problem with Rowling's educational background. The University of Oxford rarely, if ever, accepted even the most academically gifted students from state schools; therefore, Rowling was turned down.

It was decided that Rowling would enter the University of Exeter, and in the autumn of 1983, after seven years in Wyedean Comprehensive, she made the journey southwest to the ancient town of Devon and the university that stood on a steep hill above it. It was also decided, mainly by her parents, that Rowling would seek a degree in French, the logic behind that being the idea that it would result in obtaining a rewarding career as either a bilingual secretary or translator. Rowling's disappointment must have been profound; the popular head girl from a provincial state school, who had hoped to pursue her interests among the ancient and awe-inspiring architecture and the radical and freethinking student body and faculty of the University of Oxford, found herself instead stuck in a brand-new (Exeter was chartered in 1955), nondescript, comparatively conservative school. She did, however, relish the newfound freedom that living away from home allowed, and she dove deeply into what social life Exeter had to offer. The Wyedean head girl whose delight it was to display her academic abilities nearly completely disappeared; in her place was a stylish young woman who spent most of her time practicing her guitar, drawing in her sketchbook, writing stories for her own and her friends' amusement, and pursuing a personal reading program that ran the gamut from Charles Dickens to Ian Fleming. She haunted the stack of Exeter's six-hundred-thousand-volume campus library and eventually racked up an impressive tab of £50 in overdue fines. Her presence in lectures and tutorials was erratic at best; she was to be found in the Black Horse Pub or the Devonshire House coffee bar more often than in a classroom. Academically, Rowling did the absolute bare minimum required to remain in the university. However, she did progress well enough to be eligible to spend her third year living and working in France. It was a degree requirement that offered Rowling the choice of teaching English in a French school, attending a French college, or working in a

French business. Rowling opted for the teaching position, and for the 1985–1986 academic year she lived in an apartment in Paris that she shared with an Italian, a Spaniard, and a Russian. When she returned to Exeter for her final year, Rowling managed to put aside her old habits and concentrate enough effort on her dissertation and final exams to squeak by; she was granted a degree in French in 1987.

Church Cottage was becoming increasingly gloomy as Rowling's mother's condition worsened. Additionally, Tutshill had nothing to offer a young woman with no practical work experience and a degree in French. Therefore, Rowling took a secretarial course and moved in with some friends in the Clapham district of London. It was a time of boring, meaningless existence for Rowling, who moved from one temporary job to another to make ends meet. She found release from the daily tedium by using every spare moment she could find to work on her fiction. Ever since writing "Rabbit" when she was six, Rowling found pleasure and escape by putting her imagination on paper. It was during her time in Clapham that she began the first of two novels aimed at an adult audience. Those two novels may never be published; if they were, they would perhaps be merely curiosity pieces. But their literary merit, or lack of it, is of no importance. What is important is that these two works proved to Rowling that she had the skills, drive, desire, and discipline to complete an arduous and intensely private project.

Not all of Rowling's jobs were stultifyingly dull; she spent a period of time working as a secretary and translator in the African Research Department at Amnesty International's headquarters in London. Here Rowling's rather sheltered life and her worldview as shaped by a quiet upbringing in England's West Country exploded, as she discovered firsthand man's inhumanity to man. She transcribed and translated letters and testimonies of political prisoners and torture victims, researched accounts of kidnappings, executions, and rapes, and filed and cross-referenced photos of individuals and entire families who had disappeared from their villages. The accounts of horror from those seeking help, some of whom were Rowling's coworkers, were unrelenting, and Rowling suffered from hideous nightmares. Instead of being crushed by the weight of the experience, Rowling found great hope and comfort in her discovery that for every victim of horrific outrages there are scores of people willing to join together in collective action and come to their aid. Rowling, to this day, is a generous supporter of Amnesty International, and she spoke at length about how working for that organization was one of the greatest formative experiences of her life, in her commencement address at Harvard University in 2008.

INSPIRATION ON A DELAYED TRAIN

As fulfilling as it was, working for Amnesty International barely paid Rowling's portion of the rent. A boyfriend from the University of Exeter who had settled in Manchester encouraged Rowling to join him there. She took the train from London to Manchester one weekend in June 1990 to look into the practicality of such a move. The visit was not what she had hoped it would be; they argued over the suitability of apartments they inspected and Rowling took the train back to London very discouraged. In the midst of her doubts and fears, during a forty-minute train delay, an idea for a story established itself in her imagination. Doubly frustrated by the motionless train and her lack of pen and paper, Rowling struggled to retain the rush of creative energy until she finally arrived at her Clapham apartment and began to fill her notebook with the outline of a novel about a boy traveling by train to a school for wizards.

Rowling eventually moved to Manchester and worked secretarial jobs for the University of Manchester and the chamber of commerce. But the disagreements with her boyfriend continued and escalated. Rowling would escape from the hateful atmosphere of the apartment and find a quiet table in a coffee bar or pub where she could work undisturbed on her novel. Here the boy's school began to take shape; it was an enormous castle she placed in the wilds of Scotland and named Hogwarts School of Witchcraft and Wizardry. She began to populate Hogwarts: the first person she named was Ron Weasley, a boy she based on her friend Séan Harris. Then came the school's gamekeeper, a giant named Hagrid. This sort of environment called for ghosts, therefore, Nearly Headless Nick and Peeves were created, followed by the school's headmaster, Professor Dumbledore. The boy traveling aboard the Hogwarts Express she named Harry Potter.

In mid-December 1990, Rowling returned to Church Cottage to stay with her family for part of the Christmas holiday; she left on Christmas Eve to spend Christmas Day with her boyfriend and his family. On December 30, Anne Rowling lost her ten-year battle against multiple sclerosis. After the funeral, Rowling packed up a few sentimental mementos of her mother and returned to a life in Manchester that had become increasingly unbearable. That misery was multiplied when thieves broke into the apartment and took with them those few tangible connections with her mother. Rowling decided it was time to leave the boyfriend, Manchester, indeed, England itself.

TEACHING IN PORTUGAL AND FIRST MARRIAGE

An advertisement in the *Manchester Guardian* hinted at an escape route for Rowling; the Encounter English School in Porto, Portugal, needed qualified English teachers. Rowling applied, interviewed, and was hired. She arrived in Porto in November 1991 and was housed by the school in a large apartment that she shared with two other new teachers, young British women in their twenties. The work was not demanding, and the hours—it was a night school where classes were taught from 5 p.m. until 10 p.m.—were ideal for allowing Rowling time to work on her novel. As in England, Rowling found the atmosphere in coffee bars conducive to her creativity, and she would spend a good portion of each morning writing in Porto's Café Majestic. At night, after the last class of the day, Rowling would go out with her roommates and others for drinks. In March 1992, during such an outing at a bar named Meia Cava, Rowling was introduced to a young journalism student named Jorge Arantes. Flirting quickly advanced to intimacy, and soon Rowling was pregnant. The couple decided not to terminate and, indeed, planned a summer trip to England so that Rowling could introduce Arantes to her father and sister and share her happiness with them and her friends. But she miscarried and the journey was cancelled.

Rowling and Arantes, who at this time were living with Arantes's mother, chose to ignore their grief and the growing evidence of their incompatibility; when Arantes proposed marriage on August 28, 1992, Rowling accepted. They were married in a civil service on October 16, after Arantes had completed his mandatory eight-month service in the Portuguese army. She was twenty-seven and soon to become pregnant again; he was twenty-four and jobless. Jessica Isabel Rowling Arantes was born on July 27, 1993, to parents who were poor, jealous and possessive of each other, and who had increasing difficulty in controlling their tempers. Anger and frustration consumed both of them, the situation become hopeless and Rowling's friends and coworkers encouraged her to leave Arantes. Acting on their advice, and what she knew in her heart to be true, Rowling admitted to Arantes that she did not love him. He responded by dragging her out into the street in front of his mother's house, slapping her hard, and slamming the door on her. The next morning, November 18, 1993, Rowling returned with a friend and a policeman, and they prevailed upon Arantes to allow Rowling to collect her belongings and the baby. Such was Rowling's fear of Arantes's temper that she and Jessica went into hiding, moving from one friend's apartment to another in order not to be traced. After two weeks of this, arrangements were made for them to escape to England.

LIFE STRUGGLES IN SCOTLAND

Once safely in England, with her four-month-old daughter, some clothes, a little money, and the first three chapters of her novel, Rowling was faced with the question of where to go next. Her London friends had moved elsewhere, and her father, who had sold Church Cottage and remarried, did not welcome her. Rowling turned to her sister Dianne—who was then a nurse living in

Edinburgh, Scotland, with her husband of two months, Roger Moore, a restaurateur and co-owner of Nicolson's Cafe—for advice. It was decided that Rowling would move to Edinburgh to be near Dianne but that she would establish herself in her own residence apart from the newlyweds. To accomplish this, Rowling, in December 1993, applied for public assistance and was granted income support and a housing benefit in the amount of £69 per week. With her sister's help, Rowling was able to pull together the bare necessities and create a home for herself and Jessica at 7 South Lorne Place in the Edinburgh suburb of Leith. It would be their home for the next three years. The poverty she endured, supplemented by occasional temporary secretarial jobs, was soul-suffocating, and she eventually went into counseling to combat the ever-deepening depression that threatened her. To make things worse, Arantes managed to find her, and he suddenly appeared in Leith demanding his rights as a husband and a father. Fortunately, Rowling was successful in obtaining a restraining order against Arantes and he returned to Porto. Rowling filed for divorce in August 1994.

A PERSONAL RECOVERY, AN AGENT, AND A PUBLISHER

For her first eighteen months in Leith, Rowling eked out an existence that had little chance of changing; she was caught in the often inescapable trap of poverty and depression. She spent her days sitting in her small apartment caring for Jessica, taking her out in her stroller, and stopping in for a cup of coffee at Nicolson's. Throughout this low time, however, she never gave up on her novel. By the winter of 1995, Rowling had recovered enough self-esteem to look into the possibility of teaching again. She was disappointed to learn that her experience with Encounter English did not qualify her for a position in Scotland; she needed to find a way to go back to school and earn a Postgraduate Certificate of Education. Someone (Rowling will not name the person) came forward at this time with generous financial support. That, and a grant from the Scottish Office of Education and Industry, made it possible for Rowling to enter the one-year certification program in August 1995 at Moray House in Edinburgh. More good news came to Rowling that summer in the form of a final decree of divorce. Now, no longer under the shameful cloud of dependence on welfare, freed from a jealous and sometimes violent husband, and buoyed by the possibility of a teaching career, Rowling set about to find an agent who would sell her novel.

Rowling thumbed through the list of literary agents she found in a copy of *Writers' and Artists' Yearbook* in the Edinburgh Central Library, chose two in London, and mailed off a summary and three chapters to each. One agency refused her work immediately and the other, the Christopher Little Literary Agency, would have done the same had it not been for a curious office manager and personal assistant to Mr. Little, Bryony Evens. Little's agency did not accept works of literature written for children, and Rowling's submission was placed in the rejection basket to be returned. Evens, however, read through it, became intrigued, and passed it along to freelance reader Fleur Howle. The two women then urged Little to read it for himself. Soon afterward, Rowling received an envelope from Little's agency that she assumed contained another letter of rejection and was surprised to find that it held a request to see the rest of the work. After agreeing to a few minor changes in the manuscript, Rowling received a contract offer. The agency then set to work to find a publisher; it was not an easy task. Several publishing houses refused the novel, but Barry Cunningham, who had recently begun a children's book division at Bloomsbury, felt strongly that although it was a rather long book for the children's market, the story was so compelling he was sure young readers would not lose interest. Cunningham offered £1500 to Little, and Little advised Rowling to accept. Rowling made the journey to London by train for a lunch meeting with Little and Cunningham, agreed to the terms, and received a check for one half of Bloomsbury's advance (the other half was given to her six months later as per the contract). Before boarding the train home, Rowling stopped in a Hamley's toy shop and bought a celebratory toy for Jessica. Although she was elated that her work of five years was finally going to be published, she felt sure that what Cunningham had told her, that no one ever makes money from children's books, was true. And although she was nearing completion of a sequel, Rowling returned to Edinburgh certain that her future lay in teaching.

Rowling graduated from Moray House in July 1996 and was awarded the Postgraduate Certificate of Education. She took a teaching job offered by Leith Academy near her South Lorne Place apartment, and she is remembered as a good and popular teacher. During her first year at Leith Academy, Rowling learned of an arts grant available to writers. She submitted her proposal to the Scottish Arts Council and was awarded the highest possible amount, £8000. Although she continued her practice of writing in longhand at Nicolson's, she used a portion of the grant to purchase a computer with word-processing capabilities to make it easier to produce professional work. Meanwhile, prepublication work continued for Rowling, Little, and Cunningham. Very little of Rowling's original manuscript required editorial changes, but Little and Cunningham were concerned about the author's name. They believed that boys would not be drawn to a book written by a woman, even if the hero of the book was a boy wizard-in-training. It was agreed that the name should contain two initials and a surname; Rowling, who had no middle name, offered her own first initial and that of her beloved grandmother, Kathleen, and on June 26, 1997, *Harry Potter and the Philosopher's Stone* by "J. K. Rowling" was published by Bloomsbury.

Bloomsbury's children's literature division was barely two years old when it published Rowling's book. Uncertain as to how well their unknown author's curious tale would be received, Bloomsbury cautiously printed only five hundred hardbound copies. They were equally cautious in expending funds to promote and publicize the book. However, the biographical information that accompanied review copies immediately caught the imagination of the book critic Eddie Gibbs. On June 29, 1997, Gibbs's piece "Tales from a Single Mother" appeared in the *Sunday Times*. Gibbs praised the book as imaginative and humorous and declared that comparisons to the work of Roald Dahl were entirely justified. But, perhaps, more importantly, Gibbs expanded Bloomsbury's targeted age group, nine- to thirteen-year-olds, to include adult readers. This caught the attention of the American market, particularly the editorial director of Scholastic Books, Arthur A. Levine. Levine read the book, saw a great deal of his childhood self in its title character, and entered into the fierce bidding war determined to win American publication rights. Christopher Little, who was in New York to oversee the negotiations on behalf of his client, telephoned Rowling to announce that within just a few days of its British debut, *Harry Potter and the Philosopher's Stone* (renamed *Harry Potter and the Sorcerer's Stone* for the American market) had been bought by Levine for the remarkable amount of $100,000. News of an unknown author receiving such a large amount of money for a children's book created the sort of "rags to riches" curiosity that the media thrives upon. Soon there were favorable reviews appearing in the British press, but the focus of the reviews was as much on Rowling's amazing personal struggle to succeed as it was upon the magical adventures of her hero. Following Gibbs's piece there were "Harry Potter Rides to Author's Rescue" by Nigel Reynolds in the July 7, 1997, issue of the *Daily Telegraph;* "First Attempt at Fantasy Becomes a £100,000 Reality" by Tania Thompson in the next day's *The Scotsman;* and "Coffee in One Hand, Baby in Another—A Recipe for Success" by Judith Woods published in *The Scotsman* on November 19, 1997. But whatever the focus, the press created an enormous interest in both the book and its author. After one year, *Harry Potter and the Philosopher's Stone* had sold seventy thousand copies in the United Kingdom alone.

With her bank account suddenly and unexpectedly swollen, Rowling was able to quit teaching; she devoted herself to writing full-time and she moved herself and her daughter to a much nicer and safer Edinburgh neighborhood, purchasing a roomy upper apartment in Hazelbank

Terrace. In September 1998, five-year-old Jessica was enrolled in the Craiglockhart Primary School. Few of her neighbors and the other parents at Craiglockhart recognized Rowling as being the author whose book their children were excitedly reading; those who knew respected her privacy.

HARRY'S STORY BEGINS

As *Harry Potter and the Philosopher's Stone* opens, we meet Vernon Dursley, who takes pride in his normalcy. Everything about his life is perfectly normal: his wife, Petunia; their son, Dudley; their home (number four, Privet Drive) in Surrey; his job as director of Grunnings, a company that makes drills—all are quite ordinary. Dursley is a large, thick-necked bully who fears, despises, and becomes enraged by anything that challenges his concept of how things should be. So on this particular morning he becomes unnerved when he sees and hears several odd things that are about to change his life forever. As he leaves his house for work, he sees a cat that appears to be studying a map; as he drives away, he sees the cat in his rearview mirror staring at the Privet Drive road sign. Nearing town and his office, Dursley is further discomfited by the sight of several people dressed in brightly colored cloaks. At lunchtime, Dursley, who has had a normal morning in his office, crosses the road to buy a bun. As he forces his way through a crowd of cloaked persons, he is momentarily stunned to overhear broken bits of their conversation regarding the Potters and their son, Harry. When Dursley leaves his office building later that evening, he stumbles into a tiny old man in a violet cloak who, in celebratory excitement, hugs Dursley around the waist and declares that even a "Muggle" (a nonmagical human) like Dursley has reason to rejoice now that "You-Know-Who" has gone at last. When he arrives home, he sees the same cat he saw that morning now sitting on the Dursley's garden wall. Dursley is further unnerved when he watches reports on the evening news of strange occurrences throughout England: countless owls flying in broad daylight, shooting stars falling like rain. No longer able to contain his concerns, Dursley, who is tyrannical toward all except his wife, timidly asks if she has heard from her sister lately. Petunia angrily asks why he wants to know, and he explains that he wonders if any of the day's strange happenings might have something to do with what her refers to as "*her* crowd." Petunia ignores the suggestion, and Dursley falls asleep that night convinced that even if his sister-in-law, her husband, and their infant son, Harry, are somehow involved, the ordinary, normal life at Number Four Privet Drive could not possibly be affected.

What Dursley did not know—indeed, what the entire Muggle world did not know—was that there had been a decisive wizards war the night before. For the previous twenty years, a profoundly powerful and evil wizard—who is called "Lord Voldemort" by his followers, the Death Eaters, and "You-Know-Who" by those who fear and oppose him—had been recruiting like-minded wizards in an effort to take complete control of the wizarding world. The forces of the Ministry of Magic and the Order of the Phoenix united to defeat Voldemort, but he has proven to be invincible. During the darkest days of the war, a prophecy was discovered that foretold the existence of the one person who could destroy Voldemort; it would be a child born in late July whose parents had defied the evil wizard at least three times. Voldemort learned that there were two candidates who met the requirements: Neville Longbottom, born on July 30, 1980, whose parents, Frank and Alice Longbottom, were members of the Order of the Phoenix and had stood up to Voldemort several times; and Harry Potter, born on July 31, 1980, to equally defiant members of the Order of the Phoenix, James and Lily Potter. On October 31, 1981, Voldemort appeared at the treacherously revealed hiding place of the Potters, a house in the town of Godric's Hollow; he killed James instantly but was willing to spare Lily if she would give up Harry. Lily refused and was agonizingly slain protecting her son. Her sacrifice, however, instilled in Harry a special defense, for when Voldemort aimed a killing curse at the child it backfired, destroying Voldemort's power and physical form. The fifteen-month-old Harry Potter survived the chaos and carnage with nothing more than a lightning bolt–shaped scar on his forehead. From that moment on, he will be the most famous person in the wizarding world: he is the boy who defeated Lord Voldemort; he is the boy who lived.

As the Dursleys sleep, a wizard appears at their garden wall; he is Professor Albus Dumbledore, headmaster of Hogwarts School of Witchcraft and Wizardry. The cat who has sat upon the garden wall most of the day transforms itself into Professor Minerva McGonagall, the deputy headmistress of Hogwarts. They await the arrival of Rubeus Hagrid, groundskeeper and gamekeeper at Hogwarts. Hagrid appears flying out of the night sky on a motorcycle, clutching a bundle of blankets. Within the blankets is a sleeping baby, Harry Potter, whom Hagrid had been sent to rescue before anyone else discovered him amid the ruins of the house in Godric's Hollow. Dumbledore has decided it would be in the child's best interest if he were raised by his only relatives, the Dursleys, but when he reaches his eleventh birthday he will be invited to enter the wizarding world and attend Hogwarts. The baby and a letter of explanation are left on the Dursley's doorstep.

The next ten years of Harry's life are purely Dickensian: the Dursleys ignore Dumbledore's letter, tell Harry that his parents died in a traffic accident, force him to live in a closet under the staircase, give him just enough food and clothing, and never pass up an opportunity to torment and abuse him. Throughout it all, Harry maintains a firmness of character and goodness of heart worthy of David Copperfield or Oliver Twist. Hagrid appears at the Dursley's on Harry's eleventh birthday; he tells Harry the truth about his parents and how he came to have the scar, but most surprising, he tells Harry he is a wizard. Harry is doubtful; he finds it hard to believe that he, an abused and neglected boy, could be anything so special. But Hagrid insists, and Harry remembers instances when he was able to do inexplicable things when he was frightened or angry: disappearing from Dudley and a gang of tormentors; making his hair grow back overnight after receiving a humiliating haircut from Aunt Petunia; and causing a glass wall in the reptile house at the zoo to vanish, thereby releasing a boa constrictor to frighten Dudley, then hearing the snake speak his thanks as he made his escape to Brazil.

The next morning, Hagrid takes Harry to a parallel world within the heart of London that is accessed by means of a magical wall behind an invisible pub, the Leaky Cauldron. He has brought Harry here so that the boy can buy his school supplies for Hogwarts: such things as a cloak, assorted robes, a pointed hat, books of spells, a cauldron, and a wand. Hagrid dispels Harry's worries about how to pay for all this by informing him that James and Lily Potter were quite well off and they left Harry a considerable fortune in a wizard bank overseen by goblins. As a birthday present, Hagrid buys Harry a snowy white owl, explaining that owls come in quite handy for delivering mail. They return to the Muggle world, take the underground to Paddington Station, eat some hamburgers there, and separate—Hagrid back to Hogwarts and Harry back to the Dursleys, who have been sufficiently cowed to leave Harry alone.

One month later it is time for Harry to travel to Hogwarts. He arrives at King's Cross Station and, per Hagrid's instructions, seeks out platform number nine and three-quarters. He finds platforms nine and ten without difficulty, but there does not appear to be one in between. Fortunately a mother whose children are also going to Hogwarts explains to Harry that to reach platform nine and three-quarters, one must run at the brick barrier between nine and ten. Harry does so and emerges in another King's Cross Station where dozens of students are boarding the brilliantly red Hogwarts Express.

On board the train, Harry is surprised to find that he is very well known, and Rowling quickly introduces his future friends and foes to the reader. Of the friends there is, first and foremost, Ron Weasley, the youngest son of an old, respected wizarding family. Ron has five brothers, who are either returning to Hogwarts with him or have graduated and gone out into the wizarding world. Ron is a first-year like Harry but, thanks to his brothers, he knows quite a lot about what to expect at Hogwarts and is happy to share his knowledge with Harry. Ginny is the youngest Weasley child, she will enter Hogwarts the following year and play a very important role in Harry's life. Arthur Weasley, the patriarch, is a kindhearted, gentle man who struggles to support his large family with his Ministry of Magic salary. Arthur's wife, Molly, is the sort of mother every child longs for; she is sweet-natured, thoughtful, and endlessly forgiving. The Weasleys will become a loving and protecting family for Harry in the following novels. Hermione Granger is another first-year whose friendship will prove invaluable. She is surprised to have received an invitation to attend Hogwarts and to learn that she is one of only a few Muggle-born witches. Hermione is brilliant and loquacious. She seems to know everything, and what she does not know she learns quickly. She is also amazingly brave, loyal, and resourceful. Although Harry and Ron initially try to avoid her, because they are put off by her braininess and her insistence on strictly following school rules, a friendship forms, and she dramatically comes to their rescue time and time again.

Rowling makes a clear distinction between those characters who are of pure wizard bloodlines and those who are not. The Weasley family is presented as being pure-blood, but since they are firm believers in the equality of magical and nonmagical peoples, they are considered by some to be blood traitors. Harry, regardless of the fact that he was born of a wizard and a witch, is not a pure-blood since his mother had nonmagical parents; therefore, Harry is deemed a half-blood. Hermione is the lowest of the blood purity order, being Muggle-born, and is subjected to the nasty slur "mudblood." The pervading blood prejudice is the foundation of the Harry Potter novels. The battle line has been drawn between Voldemort and his Death Eaters, who, rather like proponents of Nazi Germany's Final Solution, want to restore blood purity by gaining control of the government and imprisoning those they deem impure and defective, and Professor Dumbledore and his supporters who strive to defeat such evilness.

Meanwhile, Ron introduces Harry to some of the enjoyable aspects of the magical world, such as treats like Bertie Bott's Every Flavor Bean, Drooble's Best Blowing Gum, chocolate frogs (which come with a collectible wizard or witch card), and licorice wands. Ron is dumbfounded to learn Harry knows nothing about quidditch, a sport played on flying broomsticks, which Ron declares to be the best game in the world. This train compartment orientation is interrupted by the arrival of three boys: Draco Malfoy and his two thuggish lackeys, Crabbe and Goyle. Draco is the son of Lucius Malfoy, a reputed Death Eater who changed sides after Voldemort's seeming defeat, claiming to have been bewitched by the evil wizard. Draco is a vile, hateful boy who warns Harry that consorting with the wrong sort, meaning Ron and Hermione, could lead to trouble. Harry rebuffs him by asserting that he is quite capable of selecting his own friends. Draco coldly responds by telling Harry to watch his step or he could suffer his parents' fate.

When they finally arrive at Hogwarts, the first order of business for first-years is the assignment of a house. There are four houses within Hogwarts: Gryffindor, Hufflepuff, Ravenclaw, and Slytherin. The assignments are made by means of the Sorting Hat, an old, frayed pointed hat that not only speaks and sings but is able to explore the depths of a student's heart and mind and choose the house best suited. Harry, Ron, and Hermione are assigned to Gryffindor, a house for those who are brave, daring, and chivalrous. Draco, Crabbe, and Goyle are assigned to the house for those who use their cunning to get what they want by all means possible, Slytherin.

Hogwarts School is an enormous castle filled with magical elements: stairways that change direction at will, portraits that talk and whose subjects can move from one frame to another, and resident ghosts. Gryffindor's resident ghost is Sir Nicholas de Mimsy-Porpington, known as Nearly Headless Nick because of someone's botched job of trying to behead him in the fifteenth century. Classes at Hogwarts are similar to those taught in an ordinary school except for the subject matter. Hogwarts students learn such things as care of magical creatures, herbology, charms, potions, divination, defense against the dark arts, and flying on broomsticks. Harry is surprised to find that he excels at flying, a talent that earns him a place on the Gryffindor quidditch team. One thing perplexes Harry, however—he can not understand why his potions professor, Severus Snape, displays such an intense hatred of him.

Rumors of Voldemort's return have spread since his disappearance ten years earlier. The rumor becomes fact when Harry encounters him in the Forbidden Forest. Harry is there in the dead of night serving out a detention by helping Hagrid hunt down whatever it is that has been killing unicorns. Alone, Harry comes upon a creature drinking the blood of a fallen unicorn, and he is rescued by the intervention of Firenze, a centaur. Firenze makes it clear to Harry that the creature who attacked him was Voldemort, who is just managing to stay alive on unicorn blood. With the help of Hermione and Ron, Harry pieces together clues that reveal to him that Voldemort, or what is left of him, is after something hidden in Hogwarts: the Philosopher's Stone, which can create an immortality elixir. Through bravery, intelligence, and sacrifice, Harry, Hermione, and Ron thwart Voldemort, but his essence escapes—not, however, before causing Harry enough pain to render him senseless.

When Harry regains consciousness three days later, he finds he is in the Hogwarts hospital ward being cared for by the school nurse, Madam Pomfrey. Professor Dumbledore comes to visit Harry and brings him gifts from his fellow classmates, but, most welcome of all, he brings comfort and some answers and the news that Hermione and Ron are well and safe. Soon the school year ends, and Harry returns to the Dursleys for the summer break. This is the pattern, with some exceptions, followed in the next six Harry Potter novels as the young wizard in training learns more about himself and his destiny.

It had always been Rowling's intention to tell the story of her bespectacled, dark-haired young wizard in seven volumes, one for each year of his life from age eleven to eighteen. When she had accomplished this, she gave her loyal readers a glimpse into the future lives of her characters in an epilogue to the seventh volume, *Harry Potter and the Deathly Hallows* (2007). It is remarkable that as the subject matter in each volume grew increasingly dark and frightening, and as the page numbers increased from 309 in the first volume to nearly three times that in volume 5, readers could not get enough of Harry's story and clamored for more.

HARRY MANIA

In its first year of publication, *Harry Potter and the Philosopher's Stone* sold approximately seventy thousand copies in the United Kingdom alone; the United States edition, published in June 1999, sat atop the *New York Times* bestseller list for fiction in August of that year and remained in or near that position through 2000, when the newspaper decided to create a separate list of best sellers in the children's market. *Harry Potter and the Chamber of Secrets* realized even greater sales when it was released in the United Kingdom in July 1998 and the United States in June 1999, but its success was outdone by *Harry Potter and the Prisoner of Azkaban,* published in both countries in 1999. In 2000, Bloomsbury and Scholastic agreed upon a marketing strategy that proved successful for sales of the next four books in the series; beginning with *Harry Potter and the Goblet of Fire,* the books would be released simultaneously worldwide at midnight on the day of publication. Book dealers were strongly urged to abide by this and, indeed, were threatened with delayed or cancelled shipments of future Potter books if they were found to have sold copies prematurely. Booksellers around the globe stirred up a frenzy of anticipation by holding special late-night hours and inviting customers to participate in presale celebrations that appealed to children as well as adults: look-alike contests, games and giveaways, live music, readings of Harry's previous adventures by costumed characters, and dramatic countdowns to midnight. Bloomsbury, in an effort to attract older readers, printed two different covers: one to appeal to children and another one for teens and adults. The strategy worked; crowds filled bookshops, long lines formed outside, and sales soared into the millions within the first twenty-four hours of each book's release.

Hollywood was quick to see the lucrative possibilities in bringing Harry to the screen, and in 1997, soon after the publication of the first book, David Heyman, representing Warner Bros., approached Christopher Little. It would be two years before a deal was struck. Rowling was insistent that she have a say in all aspects of the film, demanding that it maintain all the Britishness of the stories and not become Americanized. When all was agreed upon, the film rights for the first four books were sold to Warner Bros. for $1 million, and the search was on for actors and locations. Daniel Radcliffe, Emma Watson, and Rupert Grint were chosen to portray Harry, Hermione, and Ron, and sites throughout England were selected to represent portions of Hogwarts. (There was an early hint of the sort of controversies that were yet to come when Canterbury Cathedral refused to serve as a filming location, because of what the church saw as Rowling's glorification of witchcraft and sorcery.) The movie was a tremendous success, grossing close to $1 billion in ticket sales worldwide and garnering three Academy Award and seven British Academy of Film and Television Arts Award nominations. "Harry mania" ensued: the marketplace was flooded with Harry Potter–themed items—everything from bookmarks to broomsticks, candy to clothing, board and video games, bed linens, shampoo, and countless other products. All this has made the single mother living on public assistance one of the world's wealthiest women; it has also put her under the microscope and made her vulnerable to attacks.

CONTROVERSIES

Soon after the publication of *Harry Potter and the Prisoner of Azkaban,* a reporter discovered its author had once been Mrs. Jorge Arantes. Arantes was tracked down in Porto, and he agreed to sell his story for £15,000. Perhaps because he freely confessed to being a drug addict, his version of the love-hate relationship with his former wife and his claim to having been instrumental in creating the first Harry Potter novel did little damage to Rowling's glowing public reputation. Arantes, who continues to pop up now and then with his claims of authorship, never did receive the £15,000, since he breached the exclusivity clause in the newspaper's contract.

Another, perhaps more serious, controversy for Rowling arose about the same time as Arante's story, when the American author Nancy Stouffer claimed that Rowling had based her works on Stouffer's 1984 stories "The Legend of Rah and the Muggles" and "Larry Potter and His Best Friend Lilly." In 2002, Rowling, Scholastic, and Warner Bros. filed for a declaratory judgment that such was not the case. The court ruled in Rowling's favor, fined Stouffer $50,000, and dismissed her subsequent appeal. And in 2007 Rowling and Warner Bros. filed a lawsuit to prevent publication of a Web site Harry Potter lexicon in book form, which they felt was a copyright violation. The court again sided with Rowling, blocking publication of the book as it was but allowing a modified version to be released.

Worldwide popularity comes with a price, and, no doubt, controversies and problems such as these will continue to pursue Rowling. Battles over authorship and intellectual property have been fought for centuries. To this day, the question of the true authorship of the works of Shakespeare arouses fierce debate among scholars. But Rowling faces some controversies and challenges that defy easy solution or legal settlement—such as when churches, school boards, radio talk show hosts, and public libraries occasionally mount their soapbox to condemn the author and her work for a variety of reasons.

SECOND MARRIAGE AND PHILANTHROPY

Rowling married Neil Michael Murray, an Edinburgh anesthetist who is six years her junior and who bears a remarkable resemblance to Harry Potter, on December 26, 2001, in the library of their palatial home, Killiechassie House, in Perthshire, Scotland; they have another home in Kensington, London. The couple has two children: David Gordon Rowling Murray, born on March 24, 2003, and Mackenzie Jean Rowling Murray, born on January 23, 2005.

In addition to winning nearly every award given for children's literature, Rowling has had honorary doctorates bestowed upon her by Dartmouth College, Harvard University, St. Andrew's University, the universities of Edinburgh, Aberdeen, and her alma mater, Exeter, and others. Prince Charles presented Rowling with the Order of the British Empire in 2001, and the French president Nicolas Sarkozy presented her with the Légion d'Honneur in 2009.

One of Rowling's first opportunities to share the wealth generated by the success of her Harry Potter stories came in 2001 when the British antipoverty organization Comic Relief asked her for a contribution. She responded by writing two booklets, supposed to be the work of wizards and found in the library at Hogwarts—*Fantastic Beasts and Where to Find Them* and *Quidditch through the Ages*—and assigning Comic Relief all the profits from sales. She created a similar book in 2007, *The Tales of Beedle the Bard,* for the benefit of an organization she cofounded in 2005, the Children's High Level Group, a charity that campaigns for the rights of children across Europe, particularly eastern Europe. The profits from sales were assigned to CHLG, but there was a special edition, handwritten and illustrated by Rowling, that was put up for auction at Sotheby's London on December 13, 2007. It was estimated that the book would be sold for between £30,000 and £50,000, but Amazon.com astonished the book world by producing the winning bid of £1,950,000. The money from that sale was given to a charity within CHLG, the Children's Voice.

Rowling established the Volant Charitable Trust to help combat poverty and social injustice in 2000. Single motherhood is another of her concerns, and she contributes her money and time to the One Parent Families organization as well as the Multiple Sclerosis Society, another subject close to her heart. Doctors without Borders, International Book Aid, and several other causes benefit from Rowling's munificence. But perhaps the greatest and most surprising gift J. K. Rowling has given to the world is resurgence in the simple pleasure of reading. To be able to hold the imagination of children and adults who demand instant gratification and whose attention spans are shortening, and have them read intricately plotted books that are several hundred pages long, is nothing less than magical.

Selected Bibliography

WORKS OF J. K. ROWLING

Harry Potter and the Philosopher's Stone. London: Bloomsbury, 1997; published in the United States as *Harry Potter and the Sorcerer's Stone*. New York: Scholastic, 1998.

Harry Potter and the Chamber of Secrets. London: Bloomsbury, 1998; New York: Scholastic, 1998.

Harry Potter and the Prisoner of Azkaban. London: Bloomsbury, 1999; New York: Scholastic, 1999.

Harry Potter and the Goblet of Fire. London: Bloomsbury, 2000; New York: Scholastic, 2000.

Fantastic Beasts and Where to Find Them, by Newt Scamander. London: Bloomsbury, 2001; New York: Scholastic, 2001.

Quidditch Through the Ages, by Kennilworthy Whisp. London: Bloomsbury, 2001; New York: Scholastic, 2001.

Harry Potter and the Order of the Phoenix. London: Bloomsbury, 2003; New York: Scholastic, 2003.

Harry Potter and the Half-Blood Prince. London: Bloomsbury, 2005; New York: Scholastic, 2005.

Harry Potter and the Deathly Hallows. London: Bloomsbury, 2007; New York: Scholastic, 2007.

Tales of Beedle the Bard. London: Bloomsbury, 2008; New York: Scholastic, 2008.

CRITICAL AND BIOGRAPHICAL STUDIES

Abanes, Richard. *Harry Potter and the Bible: The Menace Behind the Magick*. Camp Hill, Pa.: Horizon Books, 2001.

Boyle, Fiona. *A Muggle's Guide to the Wizarding World: Exploring the Harry Potter Universe*. Toronto: ECW Press, 2004.

Fraser, Lindsey. *Conversations with J. K. Rowling*. New York: Scholastic, 2001.

———. *Telling Tales: An Interview with J. K. Rowling*. London: Mammoth, 2000.

Gaines, Ann Graham. *J. K. Rowling: A Real-Life Reader Biography*. Bear, Del.: Mitchell Lane, 2002.

Giselle, Liza Anatol, ed. *Reading Harry Potter: Critical Essays*. Westport, Conn.: Praeger, 2003.

Granger, John. *The Hidden Key to Harry Potter: Understanding the Meaning, Genius, and Popularity of Joanne*

Rowling's Harry Potter Novels. Allentown, Pa.: Zossima Press, 2002.

———. *Looking for God in Harry Potter*. Wheaton, Ill.: Tyndale House, 2004.

Heilman, Elizabeth E., ed. *Harry Potter's World: Multidisciplinary Perspectives*. New York: Routledge, 2003.

Highfield, Roger. *The Science of Harry Potter: How Magic Really Works*. New York: Penguin, 2003.

Hill, Mary. *J. K. Rowling*. New York: Welcome Books, 2003.

Kirk, Connie Ann. *J. K. Rowling: A Biography*. Westport, Conn.: Greenwood Press, 2003.

———. *The J. K. Rowling Encyclopedia*. Westport, Conn.: Greenwood Press, 2006.

Kronzck, Allan Zola, and Elizabeth Kronzck. *The Sorcerer's Companion: A Guide to the Magical World of Harry Potter.* New York: Broadway Books, 2001.

McCarthy, Shaun. *J. K. Rowling*. Chicago: Raintree, 2004.

Neal, Connie. *The Gospel According to Harry Potter: Spirituality in the Stories of the World's Most Famous Seeker*. Louisville, Ky.: Westminster John Knox Press, 2002.

Nel, Philip. *J. K. Rowling's Harry Potter Novels: A Reader's Guide*. New York: Continuum, 2001.

Shapiro, Marc. *J. K. Rowling: The Wizard Behind Harry Potter*. New York: St. Martin's, 2000.

Smith, Sean. *J. K. Rowling: A Biography*. London: Michael O'Mara Books, 2001.

Want, Robert S. *Harry Potter and the Order of the Court: The J. K. Rowling Copyright Case and the Question of Fair Use*. N.p.: NationsCourts.com, 2008.

Whited, Lana A., ed. *The Ivory Tower and Harry Potter: Perspectives on a Literary Phenomenon*. Columbia: University of Missouri Press, 2002.

Wiener, Gary, ed. *Readings on J. K. Rowling*. San Francisco, Calif.: Greenhaven Press, 2004.

WILLIAM SOUTAR

(1898—1943)

Helena Nelson

THE MOST PROLIFIC period for William Soutar, both in poetry and prose, was the final thirteen years of his life, during which he was confined to bed. The crippling condition of ankylosing spondylitis, which had increasingly affected the poet's lower limbs and back since his twenties, incapacitated him completely by the age of thirty-two. He was unable to walk; he could not even turn his head with any degree of ease. His arms and hands, however, did sterling duty: he accomplished an extraordinary amount of written work. There were many hundreds of poems (in both Scots and English), epigrams, riddles, bairn-rhymes, diaries, thirty-three dream journals, commonplace books, the memory and learning aids that he called "Vocable Verses," notes on his reading, and, of course, extensive correspondence.

When Soutar finally died (not as a result of the spinal condition but from tuberculosis), a notebook was found under his pillow. Later published as *The Diary of a Dying Man* (1991), it recorded the wry thoughts and observations of his last months in meticulous handwriting. Left-hand margins were used for subheadings and sometimes pictures. It was the work of a gifted poet and unique diarist. On Wednesday, October 6, 1943 (just over a week before his death), he wrote:

> I am scarcely touched by regret or anxiety; but derive even an element of satisfaction from being able to stand back and watch myself busied or idling under the shadow of a doom which is but rarely remembered. So much can wither away from the human spirit and yet the great gift of the ordinary day remains; the stability of the small things of life which yet in their constancy are the greatest. All the daily kindness; the little obligations; the signs of remembrance in the homely gifts: these do not pass, but still hearten the body and spirit to the verge of the grave.
>
> (*The Diary of a Dying Man,* pp. 35–37)

Soutar felt reasonably confident that some of his poetry would "become part of the literature of our time" (*Diary,* p. 8). He had secured public and literary regard as a Scottish poet; he had published ten books of verse (though several were privately funded); he had the esteem and friendship of Hugh MacDiarmid (Christopher Grieve; 1892–1978), who remains perhaps the most famous Scottish poet of the twentieth century. However, much of Soutar's prose writing—in particular the letters—has never been made available other than in library archives. It remains open to question whether Soutar's full status as a writer and poet has been asserted, for reasons that an examination of his life and work may help to explain.

EARLY YEARS

William Soutar was born on Thursday, April 28, 1898, to parents from working-class backgrounds. Though from farming stock, the poet's father, John Soutar, was a highly regarded craftsman—a master joiner who moved to Perth, Scotland, a thriving town on the River Tay, in 1895. John Soutar married Margaret Smith in June 1887. Both parents were practicing Christians. Margaret was a member of the strict Auld Licht congregation (sometimes known as the Secessionists). John Soutar, who had been a member of the Free Church, joined his wife's sect, and it was in this environment of formal Presbyterian belief that young Soutar was raised.

The poet entered the world as a large and healthy baby. In the introduction to his selected volume of Soutar's diaries, *Diaries of a Dying Man* (1945; rev. ed., 1988), Alexander Scott quotes Soutar himself on the circumstances: "I was a genuine twelve-and-a-half pounder. 'Nurse,' exclaimed the worthy Dr. McAulay: 'fetch me a pinafore and we'll pack him off to school'" (p. 9). William was to be Margaret's only natural child, a source of affection and pride to both parents. He was, by all accounts, a spirited little boy, frequently up to mischief and the recipient of many a "skelp" (smack) at school. One of Soutar's late poems, "Black Day," may have autobiographical resonance (though he had no brother):

A skelp frae his teacher
For a' he cudna spell:
A skelp frae his mither
For cowpin owre the kail. [upsetting the soup]
A skelp frae his brither
For clourin his braw bat: [dirtying his fine bat]
And a skelp frae his faither
For the Lord kens what.

(*Poems of William Soutar*, pp. 92–93)

That humorous reference to "the Lord" reflects the Soutar household, in which prayers were a daily obligation. The poet, though he did not subscribe to the Christian faith in later life, continued to draw on biblical imagery, while the diet of prayer book, hymns, and Bible informed his sense of song and rhythm.

He was brought up to like poetry, too, and since his mother wrote verse, he knew from the start that such a vocation was a possibility. Then there were Scots riddles exchanged with other children, and a great-grand-uncle recited a verse alphabet to him when he was no more than five years old: he was raised in a culture naturally rich in rhythm and cadence.

Soutar went to school locally. The spoken language of the playground was Perthshire Scots; the Soutar household spoke a more "proper" version of Scots, though standard English was the schoolroom medium for reading and writing. Like many children in Scotland, Soutar grew up with the ability to move between registers and dialects without even thinking about it.

He was a confident young man who excelled in football (soccer). He was also capable of spirited rebellion. In 1911, when he and his classmates heard about a miners' strike, they decided to act in sympathy and marched out of the school singing and shouting. Recalled by continued sounding of the school bell, half the rebels lost their nerve and ran back. Soutar and his friend James Armstrong decided they too would return to the fold, but with dignity. They strode back at the head of a boldly singing formation.

Young Soutar also became secretary of his church Bible class, though services often bored him; Alexander Scott, his biographer, records Soutar's recollection of his Sabbath mood as one of "often restless, and irritable and incipient revolt" (*Still Life*, p. 7).

In 1912, he went to the local grammar school, Perth Academy, which he attended until 1916. He experienced the usual teenage passions, including one for a girl called Daisy, whose black garb reflected the fact that her father had recently died. She would continue to appear in Soutar's dreams decades later, just as women in black clothes would continue to seem attractive to him. He also fell in love with literature, thanks to an inspirational English teacher, George McKinlay, himself a poet. Soutar was writing poems himself by now, and was soon published in the school magazine.

In summer of 1915, McKinlay left teaching to join the military forces in World War I—he was killed in action in August 1917, the year Soutar himself started active naval service on HMS *Eclipse*. He enjoyed his time at sea, especially the companionship. Unlike other well-known "war poets" such as Rupert Brooke, Siegfried Sassoon, and Wilfred Owen, Soutar was not an officer: he took up arms as an Ordinary Seaman from a working family. He was never in great danger, although he witnessed the surrender of the German fleet. He did have an episode of food poisoning, however, which may or may not have contributed to later health problems.

By 1918 Soutar was experiencing the first symptoms of the illness that would change his life—he had pain in his feet and arches, sufficient to warrant the use of crutches. He regarded this as a temporary affliction. With the cessation of hostilities, Soutar (still far from well) was demobilized, unaware that anything was seriously wrong. Enthusiastic about the prospect of a new life as a student back in Scotland, he matriculated in medicine at Edinburgh University. Within two weeks he had changed his mind and transferred to the arts faculty, with the intention of taking honors English and thus gaining more time for reading and writing. His feet were better at this point, but he was experiencing severe pain in his hip and leg. Assuming it was neuritis, he was treating the problem with massage.

Poetry remained a central interest. His first contribution to the university's undergraduate magazine, *The Student,* was published on May 21, 1919, barely a month after his matriculation. Strongly influenced by John Keats and Percy Bysshe Shelley (as were most young poets at that time), Soutar started on a long poem ("Hestia—or the Spirit of Peace") with a view to winning the University Poetry Prize. His mini-epic did not win; his ambitions outpaced his performance. Those ambitions, nevertheless, were intense. Alexander Scott, in *Still Life,* quotes the young poet's own words: "'To have written one true poem,' [Soutar] proclaimed dramatically, 'yea, to have written but one line of fire is recompense enough for life itself'" (p. 23).

Study of literature led Soutar first to John Donne and the metaphysical poets, then to Scots verse—not just Robert Burns but also the medieval Scottish *makars,* namely John Barbour, William Dunbar, and Robert Henryson. He loved William Wordsworth and Geoffrey Chaucer, too. Less to his liking were novels and the Anglo-Saxon component of the curriculum. Not one for holding back his opinions, he wrote an article in the student magazine in which he argued that Anglo-Saxon studies should be optional. That part of the curriculum nonetheless remained compulsory (despite Soutar's letter to the well-known literary scholar and Professor of English Literature in the university, Herbert Grierson).

Soutar therefore attended the classes he liked and opted out of those he did not. He led a lively social life and liked to dress well. He read poetry, not prose. His skills in Anglo-Saxon, needless to say, were negligible. His final year as a student also saw increasing debility: the stiffness and pain he was now experiencing in his spine could not be ignored. He began a vegetarian diet, but that did not help his health.

In January 1923 he also started to keep a written record of his dreams: it was to be the first of thirty-three volumes completed over the next twenty years. By July, the poet was lucky to scrape an M.A. with third-class honors. The degree award was certainly not an accurate reflection of his intellectual ability: it did, however, have some connection with his unusually intense dedication to poetry. Further evidence of this was the fact that in the February of his final undergraduate year, Soutar's first collection of verse, *Gleanings by an Undergraduate,* saw the light of day.

GLEANINGS BY AN UNDERGRADUATE

Gleanings by an Undergraduate, a slender collection of thirty poems, was published anonymously in 1923, with Soutar's father footing the bill. Editorial acknowledgements credit the *Scotsman* (the Edinburgh newspaper), *Great Thoughts, Northern Numbers,* and the *Scottish Chapbook.* Soutar had, therefore, been placing poems in the leading Scottish publications of his time, and one of these, *Northern Numbers* (and subsequently the *Scottish Chapbook*), had already brought him to the attention of the poet and editor Christopher Grieve. Though only six years older than Soutar, Grieve was already proving himself an accomplished figure in the world of Scottish letters, working as a journalist and writing verse, short stories, and critical studies, with a self-belief second to none. He readily numbered Soutar in the group of mainly younger poets who were to revive the creative life of the nation (soon Grieve would coin the term "the Scottish Renaissance"), commenting that young Soutar was already within the first fifty best contemporary poets in Scotland. Grieve and Soutar had met in person in summer of 1922, got on very well, and Grieve had remarked favorably on *Gleanings.*

Regrettably, however, this first volume does little to suggest that Soutar was gifted with much more than optimism. Alexander Scott describes "De Profundis, or The Spirit of Despair" as "a kind of lukewarm melting-pot of romantic metal, in which partially-dissolved fragments of Swinburne, Coleridge, Tennyson, Arnold and Rossetti jostle together" (*Still Life,* p. 39). The criticism is fair. What we see here is a young poet, compulsively romantic, hugely influenced by nineteenth-century styles. There were hundreds of young poets writing like this. The task for each of them was to find an individual, distinctive voice. Soutar had not yet done that: he was writing in the English of Keats, and the stylistic features that characterized his verse were what would soon come to be dubbed (with critical distaste) "Georgian." Not that far away, however, in another part of the United Kingdom, modernism was starting to make its presence felt, and Christopher Grieve (soon to experience his own rebirth using the name "Hugh MacDiarmid") was anything but parochial.

Despite the restrictiveness of the archaic diction, the inversions, and the rhetoric in *Gleanings,* furthermore, Soutar's first published volume is noteworthy in that these are promising apprentice pieces. The use of form is confident and skilled. In places ("The Dying Agnostic" and "Ointment") there is lyrical simplicity of some note. Perhaps the most interesting poem is "The Street, November 11th" (*Gleanings,* p. 24), which evokes a particular moment in Edinburgh (the commemoration of the eleventh hour of the eleventh day of the eleventh month in 1918 when World War I officially ended). The military gun, fired from the ramparts of the Castle, alerted the street crowd to two minutes of silence, an annual observance then only a few years old. Soutar's poem peoples the street with a "proud procession," the ghosts of the remembered dead. But it is not the imaginary soldiers who make the poem; it is the precise visual detail and evocation of a kind of "frozen moment," something to which Soutar was to return again and again:

The clash of traffic, and innumerable feet
Shuffling along the wide grey pavement:
A news-boy's cry above the steady bleat
Of gaunt kerb-vendors; and the street
Tapering into the chill November haze.

Here we can see the careful placing of detail, the lack of fuss, the celebration of ordinary life that will later characterize the best of Soutar's work.

After graduating, Soutar—still in hope of improving his health—went for a vacation in Birsay on mainland Orkney, staying with an old friend. Kept inside by the persistent rain, he studied Thomas Percy's *Reliques of Ancient Poetry* (1765), apparently his first introduction to traditional ballads. He also started work on a second volume of his own poetry, *Conflict,* though it would not be until 1931 that this volume was published.

He returned home for X-rays and further massage. Meanwhile, he applied and was accepted for teacher training at Moray House College in Edinburgh. He never took up the position. Another medical consultation led to a diagnosis of extreme osteoarthritis of the spine, possibly caused by an earlier infection (perhaps the food poisoning back in the navy). The treatment was to be monthly injections (a vaccine prepared from the sufferer's stools) and more massage. Soutar seems to have experienced something of a turning point, no doubt connected to the final acceptance that his troubling health condition was something he was going to have to live with. Over a decade later, he recalled this moment in his diary:

> There are moments in every life when the life within us seems to decide. Thus it spoke in me, after I had learned the nature of my trouble, when suddenly I halted in the dusk beside the pillars of West St George's, Edinburgh, and stood for a moment bareheaded saying over to myself "Now I can be a poet." It is life's recognition of itself and a salute to the necessity centred at the core of life: and out of this recognition is born a rock of acceptance on which the selfhood can retain its peace within all the changeableness that daily darkens with doubts and vain imaginings.
>
> (*Diaries,* p. 59)

WRITING IN SCOTS

Meanwhile, Soutar's friend Chris Grieve had been sharing his thoughts in the *Scottish Chap-*

book on the poetic use of "the Doric," or Lowland Scots. At first Grieve had been strongly opposed to the idea of writing in Scots. Like many literary writers he felt distaste for the vogue of Robert Burns imitation, often employed for sentimental verse, (jokingly dubbed the "Canny Sandy" style). However, he was keen to revive the Burns spirit, which combined rich use of Scots with intense national ardor. Grieve began to feel that the vernacular, if used in a new and modernist way, held potential. He published a couple of poems in what he was to call "synthetic Scots," plundering the Scots dictionary to combine archaic and modern terms. At first the poems were said to be by "a friend," then he credited them to "Hugh MacDiarmid." Finally, Grieve openly declared his identity as MacDiarmid, and under this name he went on to become the foremost Scots modernist and self-proclaimed leader of the Scottish Renaissance.

Soutar was both amused and intrigued by Grieve's thinking. While having an unparalleled regard for his friend's unique talent, he could see that Grieve got carried away on his own "high horse," bolstered by the simple fact of being a leader in very small country. Soutar's own serious poetry was in English, but he began to experiment with writing in Scots, and this allowed a new voice to emerge, a more humorous, whimsical self. In 1924, Soutar commenced a careful study of Burns from cover to cover. The following year, Grieve (now publicly Hugh MacDiarmid) published his own first collection of poems: *Sangshaw*. This was groundbreaking work: some believe MacDiarmid never surpassed these early melodic lyrics in Scots. Soutar still thought "the big things which Scotsmen have to do yet in literature must be done in English" (*Still Life*, p. 57), but he very much admired *Sangshaw*. It may well have been the most important influence of his life.

Soutar did not undertake anything lightly. He had always been intensely interested in language and was an avid word collector. He was in the habit of creating what he called "vocable verses," rhyming stanzas containing four difficult or uncommon words in a way that would assist understanding and memory. Now he extended this activity to archaic Scots words. He was still skeptical about whether Scots could be used to create a national literature that would hold its own in the world, but it occurred to him that introducing children to the old words might accomplish a revival.

In 1927, the Soutar household changed dramatically. Soutar's parents adopted Evelyn, the orphaned niece of a cousin of Mrs. Soutar's who had lived in Australia: she arrived just before her sixth birthday. William Soutar liked children, and he liked Evelyn. He enjoyed introducing a child to Scots words, and language became a bond between the two of them. In 1928 he began writing the first of many "bairnrhymes," or nursery rhymes—strongly rhythmical pieces, easy to recite or learn, with a poignantly child's-eye view on the world.

The first of these was "Coorie in the Corner." To "coorie doun" is to crouch down (it carries the connotation of cowering, but also comfort). As soon as English moves into Scots, the "gh" in words like "night," "might," "sight," and so forth becomes "ch," a soft sound at the back of the throat, which shortens the preceding vowel. "Coorie in the Corner" also incorporates the colloquial Scots "chappin" for "knocking" (Scots mainly drops the "g" at the end of an "ing" participle, while "all" becomes "a" and "wall" is pronounced "wa"). Instead of "window," we find "winnock"; "greet" is the familiar word for "cry" or "weep" in Scots; "ava" means "at all"; and a "goloch" is an earwig. The soft "ch" and open vowels create a sound scheme very different from the English:

Coorie in the corner, sitting a' alane,
Whan the nicht wind's chappin
On the winnock-pane:
Coorie in the corner, dinna greet ava;
It's juist a wee bit goloch
Rinning up the wa'.

(*Poems of William Soutar*, p. 63)

Immediately, the natural speaking voice is obvious. The tone is humorously affectionate—and the central character, though jokingly approached—is a small child, isolated by his own fear and alliteratively nicknamed according to his behavior, "Coorie in the Corner." One can imagine Soutar reading this to little Evelyn, and similarly picture her shivery delight at the "wee bit goloch." A more haunting undercurrent is in the word "alane" (alone)—the whole concept of isolation was to prove pivotal in Soutar's later verse.

In May 1928 Soutar penned his first fully successful adult poem in Scots, "The Gowk." In traditional ballad quatrains, the gowk (cuckoo) lures the narrator with promises of gifts ("fairins"). Its shelter, it claims, is made of diamonds and emeralds; its eyes are rubies. The narrator's father and mother arm themselves with sticks and stones. The bird is slain, but the only "fairin" left to the poet is its death. The last lines summon a tone of bitter disappointment, as the narrator slinks away like a thief:

It had nae siller for a croun
Nae rubies for its een;
But a' the cramasy ran doon
Whaur aince its breist had been.
I look't; an' there was nane tae see
The fairin I had taen:
I hung it on a roden-tree
An' left it a' alane.

(*Poems of William Soutar*, p. 198)

The language is simple, easily accessible to a Scots speaker and far from impenetrable to any reader of English. The only "synthetic" or archaic word here is "cramasy," a word MacDiarmid had brought into use in "The Bonnie Broukit Bairn" (in *Sangshaw*). It means "crimson," from "cramoisie," or crimson velvet—which here is a synonym for blood.

"The Gowk" presents a distinctive poetic voice. The poem also provides a medium in which Soutar could write both personally (this was a man too frail to support himself, whose father and mother literally made his life possible) and at the same time with objective distance. "Gowk" is the word not only for a cuckoo but for an idiot or fool. The poem may be about many things, but one of them is the glittering promise of the poetic calling—the desire to possess something that can be admired from a distance but never wholly "owned." That "gowk" was to continue as a pervasive symbol in the poet's later writing.

Meanwhile, although Soutar's mental life was active, his physical state was deteriorating. In December 1928, his cousin Mollie Soutar arrived on vacation from Surrey. Soutar liked her and flirted with her, and she featured (literally) in his dreams. It was his able-bodied friend Bill Mackenzie, however, who took her out and pursued a relationship that later led to marriage. Soutar was aware of the need to stand back. His fate was to be an onlooker in a world where other people fell in love and got married; other people went to dances and parties.

In February 1929 he was seriously ill with pneumonia. He did not recover fully until mid April, and the decline in his health proved permanent. Acute pain in his right groin led to a diagnosis of arthritis of the right hip. He also suffered tonsillitis, sciatica, and extreme difficulty in moving one leg.

By early 1930, Soutar had lost not only his health and any prospect of marriage but also his faith in Jesus Christ as a divine savior (although Christ the man would continue to be important to him). Even writing poetry was proving difficult. An operation was carried out to straighten his right leg. It was unsuccessful. Soon the left leg was even more painful. The treatment (artificial sunlight, massage, and sour milk) did not work. On November 3 an attempt to get up caused such agony that it was the last. From this point, until his death thirteen years later, Soutar was confined to one room.

THE ROOM

Soutar's father adapted the downstairs dining room for his invalid son, extending it from a little square to a fairly spacious rectangle, with one wall a window onto the garden. Glass-fronted bookcases were built into the walls, and seats for visitors were positioned at the foot of the bed. From this restricted space, the poet continued an ambitious program of reading and study, while building one of the most varied and unusual poetic oeuvres of his day.

On the one hand, he continued to write poems and epigrams in formal English, his style becoming less ornate and mannered as he continued; on the other, there were the various styles and forms he pursued in Scots. In 1931, he finished his longest poem, "The Auld Tree" (it had commenced as an experiment in "synthetic Scots"). At the same time he continued with his "bairnrhymes" or poems for children, some of these continuing the ballad style he had employed in "The Gowk." As time went on, he exploited the comic aspects of his bairnrhymes in poems he called "whigmaleeries"—grotesque or whimsical verse, frequently touched with a paradoxical combination of humor and sadness. In this regard, he was working in the tradition of medieval *makars*, the amusing beast fables of Robert Henryson, the bizarre comedy of the unknown author of "Kynd Kittock," and the energy and earthy disrespect of Chaucer. He wrote riddles in Scots, too, further evidence of an active and intensely playful mind.

There is no doubt that Soutar experienced the dark side of isolation and inner loneliness, situated as he was in such a small physical space. How could it be otherwise? His natural resilience, however, kept him remarkably sane and intensely interested in what was going on, not only in the locality (he was very much interested in the day-to-day life of the town in which he lived) but in political movements (communism, pacifism, nationalism) and international literary initiatives. Though a very different character from Grieve/MacDiarmid, Soutar continued to reflect on the role of poetry, and how it could appropriately serve a new Scotland. He passionately wanted to play his part, and he believed that "the stark beauty of the ballads and the courage of Knox" (*Diaries*, p. 8) represented the way forward.

When "The Auld Tree" (dedicated to Hugh MacDiarmid), was published in *The Modern Scot* in 1931, it brought Soutar new literary friends and visitors, as well as a reputation for being one of the foremost proponents of the Scottish Renaissance movement. He himself was less convinced. In his diary of June 1932, he remarked wryly: "I write one poem at any length in the Doric—and immediately *The Glasgow Herald* salutes me as a wee Apollo—the potential saviour of the Vernacular" (*Diaries*, p. 16)

Though perhaps the most "modernist" of his works, with its panoply of characters, elaborate symbolic narrative, and "in" references, "The Auld Tree" also has a medieval flavor to it. Its rhyming tetrameter couplets are not a million miles from Dunbar, though it feels self-consciously wrought. It presents as a vision and a dream, commencing with an evocation of Yggdrasil, the mythological tree whose roots hold earth, heaven, and hell together. The poet finds himself sitting in its branches with all the great Scots *makars:* Burns, Dunbar, Henryson. Burns is holding forth about the difficulty of being a poet and the comfort of feeling at home with one's peers. But there is a problem in today's Scotland, says Burns. If no modern *makar* takes over the song, the country will die.

Then the vision changes: the great tree disappears and the poet finds himself in a lonely place on the Eildon hills in the Scottish Borders. The ancient hero William Wallace appears and escorts the poet to the Eildon Tree where according to the Border ballads the first great Scottish bard, Thomas the Rhymer (or True Thomas), met the Queen of the Fairies. A two-headed snake is wrapped around the tree trunk. Wallace lifts his sword and cleaves the snake in two; one half flees to the north, the other south to Ireland. With his second stroke, he fells the tree. With the third, he strikes into the earth itself, which opens in apocalyptic fashion, exposing fire, the grinding of bones, the rattling of chains, and the wails of women. The poet loses consciousness.

When he comes around, he is alone on the hill. He sees Wallace's great sword buried in the ground, illumined by the moon. Magically it twists, stretches, and shrinks back, transformed into a thistle.

A third man appears; he has glowing eyes and he is singing: it is no other than Hugh MacDiarmid, author of "A Drunk Man Looks at the Thistle." He shakes the thistle, so that all the seed heads fly on the wind. Day dawns, and the plant has turned into a young, green tree full of birds caroling a song the poet cannot name—but the poet is singing too in Scots, and his words are prophetic:

"Daw on o' day that winna düne:"
I sang: *"or Scotland stands abüne*
Her ain deid sel'; and sterkly steers
Into the bairn-time o' her years."

(Poems of William Soutar, p. 207)

This is the vision that is to carry him forward—the green tree, the golden dawn, Scotland going proudly forward into her own young future or "bairn-time."

"The Auld Tree" is a complicated poem. In terms of vision, Soutar may be emulating William Blake, but he does not carry Blake's conviction: the symbolism is too obvious, the message too propagandist. The language, furthermore, is difficult to contend with, dense with unfamiliar words. There are some lovely singing lines, but in general this is a scholar's poem, not a song for "everyman." And it was the latter that Soutar really wanted to achieve.

What Soutar chiefly admired in MacDiarmid were his singing lines; he suspected his overt desire to appear "clever." All the same, he had equal misgivings about what he saw as the merely lyric impulse: "life demands more from a man," he wrote in his diary on August 29, 1932, "than a handful of lyrics. My life's purpose is to write poetry—but behind the poetry must be the vision of a fresh revelation for men: if one cannot help men to find bread for the body then the greater the obligation to give food for the mind. Art is for all—and the greatest art proves it" (*Diaries,* p. 21).

Lured (not unlike MacDiarmid) by the aspiration to great "vision," Soutar was wary of the personal in poetry, nervous about sentiment and self-indulgence. This is, without doubt, why he chose not to publish some of his lyrics in his lifetime, though for a contemporary reader many of his personal pieces have a power that a discursive poem like "The Auld Tree" cannot begin to command.

"Gin ye had come last nicht" ("If you had come last night"), for example, written in spring of 1933, reveals open yearning, partly as a result of a sensual dream recorded in the dream diary.

If the woman of his dream had come to him in actuality, instead of merely as "ae thocht" (a thought), everything would have been different:

Gin ye had come last nicht
Wi' the thochts o' ye that cam',
Ye wudna noo be what ye are
Nor I be what I am.
Gin ye had come last night,
Whan my thocht was but ae thocht,
It wud hae been anither sang
That you an' I had wrocht.

(Poems of William Soutar, p. 217)

The lyric is intensely personal. However, it has universal poignancy far beyond its immediate source, something that Soutar may have underestimated. This is certainly "art for all"—there is nothing intellectually remote about it and the effect is timeless. The lyric form is masterful, too: the two opening lines of each stanza are simple trimeter lines. Then the third is metrically longer, creating a melancholy pause as it extends into a fourth poetic "foot," before pulling back again into sad reality at the end of the first stanza with its final trimeter line. The tone at the start is elegiac—the sorrow hinging on "if," the thing that never happened and the sense of loss associated with that.

But it changes in the second stanza: here it is not just tender regret, but something grimmer—suppressed rage, perhaps, or sexual force. There is no feeling that the narrative voice is weak or emasculated: the fey promise, the feeling of betrayal is all transferred to the absent lover. And that lover could be anyone, at any time, in any place, and in any culture.

CONFLICT

Restricted to one room for thirteen years, Soutar continued to publish, making very deliberate distinctions between the different types of verse he was authoring. His second book, dedicated to his father, was *Conflict* (1931), the collection he had started to work on while on holiday in Orkney back in 1923 when he could still walk. Even nine years later, many of the poems included in this volume were early ones, and typical of his early style, though some more recent ones used a more open, free-verse method, showing the influence of D. H. Lawrence, a poet Soutar admired far more than T. S. Eliot (for whom he had but slight regard). *Conflict* was all English poetry. (Soutar never mixed poems in English and Scots in any publication during his lifetime.)

The volume was praised in an understated way by the *Times Literary Supplement* in London. In Scotland, however, he was lauded highly and compared with the metaphysical poets. He himself, eighteen months later, was much more self-critical and rightly so. Had *Conflict* been his final publication, Soutar's status would have been minor indeed, and its public praise says little for Scottish critics at that time. Though it included "The Thoughts of God," a poem Thomas Moult had selected for *The Best Poems of 1930,* this (like much else in the volume) was derivative and inflated in its rhetoric. There are pieces here of interest ("The Tryst" and "The Stately Palace," for example), which evoke a fey spirit closer to Walter de la Mare than Hugh MacDiarmid, but they are easy to miss when set beside such heavy-handed poems as "On a Cold, Dead Beauty," quoted here in full:

When mindful that thy frory maidenhead
Now wantons, in this uberous repose,
I deem it sin that thou art but a bed
Unto the charnel grass and the wilding rose.

(*Conflict,* p. 28)

Of course, Soutar was not the only poet enmeshed in language such as this, torn between its dangerous attractions and the desire for something new. The 1930s represented something of a turning point: it was a case of either abandoning the archaic second-person-singular with its accompanying verb forms and possessives ("thou liest," and so forth) or being relegated to the status of a "Georgian" dust-gatherer. The transition must, nonetheless, have proved more difficult for those regularly involved in Christian prayer and worship, where "thee" and "thou" remained regular and intimate forms of address for God. Biblical diction, with its own beauties, was one way of summoning a "special" voice for poetry.

But the trend in poetry was toward the speaking voice, not the written one, and at the same time national beliefs were becoming increasingly secular. It was in Scots that Soutar was best able to summon a natural conversational tone. It was, after all, the language he spoke himself. One epigrammatic quatrain in *Conflict* sums up what would have happened had he ceased writing at this point—and Soutar in epigram mode is crisp, direct, and wholly engaging. "Epitaph on a Potential Poet who learned the meaning of every word in the English Dictionary" speaks truly indeed:

Ten years he labour'd till his mind was stor'd;
Then turn'd to greet experience with a word:
But, ere his hand had written half a whit,
He met a truth and left no word of it.

(*Conflict,* p. 15)

SEEDS IN THE WIND

Conflict certainly reads like the book of a man who had swallowed a dictionary. Much more encouraging and original was *Seeds in the Wind* (1933), subtitled *Poems in Scots for Children* and dedicated to Evelyn. It was to be the most successful of Soutar's books in Scots, with a second (enlarged) edition in 1943 and another posthumous volume in 1948. The collection represented innocent delight, entertainment, and sheer joie de vivre, but it was also a considered literary move—Soutar's contribution to the Scottish Renaissance movement. Alexander Scott quotes a crucial letter to Grieve in 1931, in which Soutar states his philosophy:

If the Doric is to come back alive ... it will come on a cock-horse. How are you going to get it into the schools otherwise? ... I fancy, the best beginning would be in bairn-rhymes of six or eight lines which contain no more than one or two uncommon words ... we should thereby begin a sort of vaccination with the Doric; the children will grow up with it in their blood—they would have the vocabulary to build on.

(*Still Life,* p. 116)

Though containing many "bairn-rhymes of six or eight lines" ("Coorie in the Corner" among them), *Seeds in the Wind* also included Soutar's ballad "The Gowk" (hardly a children's poem); "Ae Simmer's Day," another haunting lyric that could appeal to any age; and a lengthy allegorical ballad, "The Whale." Here the eponymous leviathan swallows the narrator-poet, who finds himself in a beautiful country, illumined with a weird red light. The place is full of mythical animals, one of which is the unicorn. It has lived there, like a thing unborn, since the days of Noah's Ark. The poet is struck with grief at the thought of his own land deprived of its unicorn—"I was wae for my ain land / Twin'd o' its unicorn" (p. 212). The phrasing is deliberate—the possessive "its" confirms that the unicorn belongs to Scotland. The poet leaps onto its back and rides out of the whale into the light, but no sooner is he back on land than day is dawning. The snow-white unicorn gallops off sans rider up Arthur's Seat, the steep hill in the heart of Edinburgh. The poem ends on a note of glory and triumph:

It steppit thru the siller air,
For day was at the daw;
An' what had been a bluid-reid baest
Was noo a baest o' snaw.
Or lang, my fit was by the Forth
Whaur I had stude afore;
But the unicorn gaed his ain gait,
An' as he snoov'd owre Arthur's Sate
I heard the lion roar.

(*Poems of William Soutar,* p. 213)

The unicorn is a key symbol for Soutar. It represents Scotland itself, its energy and rebirth, and it moves confidently—"snoov'd" suggests a steady, graceful gait. It is also the spirit of poetry—rare, impossible to tame, but always somewhere in the hills. To some extent he identified the symbol with himself too: lonely, proud, unmated, wayward.

THE SOLITARY WAY

Soutar's next volume of verse, *The Solitary Way* (1934), would have the unicorn as an emblem on the front cover. Designed by his old friend James Finlayson, this image would appear on all subsequent publications by the poet.

The collection of English verse, dedicated to Finlayson, mixed successful and blatantly flawed poems. Once more, Soutar was critical of his own work. Reflecting on newly delivered copies of the book in his diary in June 1934, he remarked: "Looking at this handful of lyrics of unequal quality one is tempted to question if they are worth all the bother of publication. Yet a glimpse of life may be reflected here and there which might have been unrecorded by any other intelligence" (*Diaries*, p. 45).

Although "thees" and "thous" are diminished in this volume (the newest poems use "you"), diction remains fairly ornate, and features such as the accented final syllable (for example, "thoughtéd" and "unbowéd") and words like "twas" and "ere" stand out awkwardly. There are clear echoes of literary influences—shades of Joyce Kilmer, for example, in "I think no heaven shall ever be / More lovely than this flowery lea" ("The Lea," *The Solitary Way,* p. 33). But the underlying thought is interesting, not least when we read with an awareness of Soutar's circumstances. The volume is divided into two sections, "Search" and "Solitariness." During his "Search," the poet's mind or spirit soars across the universe, sleeping and waking. There is a sense of galactic out-of-body experience in the first half of the volume, vast travel and scope of thought—a complete antithesis to real bodily limitation. The section concludes with "Return," the last two lines of which read: "And under quiet stars I come / Bearing my broken armour home" (*The Solitary Way,* p. 39).

In the second section, the poet deals with solitude, a central theme in his life and work. He is preoccupied not only with personal isolation (though this gives added resonance to the work) but also the essential insularity of man. In "Solitariness" he talks of the moment when you (not "thou" this time) realize "You are alone, and utterly alone," but this is not a black thought: "Like a solitary leaf / A bird on the bare bough sings to the sun" (*The Solitary Way,* p. 43). In this loosely rhymed poem of uneven meter, the last line—that bird on the bare bough—sings on the page in completely natural, open language.

The most remarkable poem, though, is probably the concluding one, "From the Wilderness." It draws on the gospel story of Christ's self-imposed exile to the desert, preparing himself in solitude for the task he was about to take on. Soutar amalgamates this with Christ's subsequent isolation in the grave (from which, of course, he also returned). The identification is clearly personal. In one sense, Soutar had died to the world, having been confined to the "grave" of his own small room:

He knew the hour of nothingness when the hand
Is empty, and empty is the heart;
And the intelligence, with its keen dart
Of reasonable speech, slays its own pride.

(*Poems of William Soutar*, p. 7)

In a metaphorical sense, Soutar had also been reborn. Through enforced isolation, he had won an "inheritance which was not his before," no less than

... his own self;
Which yet had been only a flower of stone
Had he not brought it back into the world again.

(*Poems of William Soutar*, p. 7)

The question was, what was he to do with that "self" and where would it take him?

BRIEF WORDS: ONE HUNDRED EPIGRAMS *AND* POEMS IN SCOTS

Soutar had printed epigrams before: they suited his wit and his liking for a trenchant turn of phrase. Now, in *Brief Words: One Hundred Epigrams* (1935), he published a whole book of them. Many are neat and entertaining; many are simply brief poems, often elegiac in tone (some of these were already included in previous volumes of verse). There are a good number of epitaphs, too—some witty, others serious. Alexander Scott felt Soutar lacked the savagery for a good epigrammatist. Certainly he is wry, not cutting, though the book makes for lively, varied, accessible reading. Soutar took out second-person singular archaisms when he revised the manuscript, and the result is cleaner and more direct. Some tiny pieces work beautifully. For example, there is "Improviso":

Upon my five-wired fence the blackbirds sit
Making a live and lyric stave of it.

(*Brief Words,* p. 25)

Here he captures the visual imagery of musical notation at the same time as the actual picture of the fence he could see through his bedroom window. It is vivid, simple, and unerring. Other pieces teeter slightly between elegance and moralizing, as in "Lovers' Epitaph" (*Brief Words,* p. 47):

You lovers who are young, if you should pass
Beside these lovers lying under grass,
Hear me who speak to you in words of stone:
The love we give is all the love we own.

Soutar's main claim to fame does not rest on his epigrams. Nevertheless, the work does reveal much about the man, and these are certainly the fragments of a person who knows his trade. He concludes with "For a Sundial." The tone here is unmistakably Soutar, though not Soutar at his best:

Hold not the hour,
Loving what you have lost;
Only the gifted hour can be your guest:
Gladly accept the flower and the frost:
The sun goes down and shadows are at rest.

(*Poems of William Soutar,* p. 56)

This tenet was important to him. Perhaps that is why he is laboring the point with the telltale negative imperative (again a feature of pulpit diction). And the last line, though peaceful and consolatory, is nothing compared to the tender phrasing in his 1942 lullaby, "Day Is Düne": "Lully, lully, my ain wee deerie, / The darg is owre and the day is düne" (*Poems of William Soutar,* p. 110).

Poems in Scots, however, was also published in 1935, and it is impossible not to feel the sea change when Soutar moves from English into Scots. Immediately, even in lesser pieces, he becomes more alliterative and onomatopoeic. It is as if Lowland Scots is a music to which his ear is attuned, unlike English where he is nearly always on his best and most formal behavior. The volume, nevertheless, mingles strong poems with some that certainly failed to impress Scottish reviewers. It included "The Auld Tree," for example, which is perhaps what led to the charge of having mined John Jamieson's Scots dictionary to the point of disaster. This was, of course, a matter of no inconsiderable literary politics. Some (like MacDiarmid) believed in the revival of the old words and their mingling with the new; others regarded this as a self-conscious literary mannerism, having no connection with the natural spoken language.

Two things need to be borne in mind here. First, Soutar had, quite literally, studied every word in the Scots dictionary, ticking them neatly in black pen as he worked his way through, and marking the ones he had used in poems or "Vocable Verses." Some people would (not unreasonably) regard this as obsessive. Second, and equally important, Soutar's Scots poems are *not* drenched in archaic Scots. Some are very contemporary, accomplishing the occasional introduction of an archaic (but beautiful) word without any sense of jarring. What we are seeing here is a poet developing the art of writing in Scots and learning how to manage it.

The volume includes two lyrics that must be numbered among his finest and most lasting: "Song" and "The Tryst." The latter poem, a dream that could be real, uses a few Scots words that might not be familiar to every reader ("luely" for "softly," "kent" for "knew," "caller" for "cool," "sinder'd" for "sundered," "bane" for "bone," "waukrife" for "wakeful," "smool'd" for "slipped away," "daw" for "dawn," "simmer" for "summer"), but almost all can be guessed or intuited:

O luely, luely, cam she in
And luely she lay doun:
I kent her be her caller lips
And her breasts sae sma' and roun'.
A' thru the nicht we spak nae word
Nor sinder'd bane frae bane:
A' thru the nicht I heard her hert
Gang soundin' wi my ain.

It was about the waukrife hour
Whan cocks begin to craw
That she smool'd saftly thru the mirk
Afore the day wud daw.
Sae luely, luely, cam she in
Sae luely was she gaen;
And wi' her a' my simmer days
Like they had never been.

(*Poems of William Soutar,* pp. 208–209)

The melody of the words is timeless. The poet recognizes his true love by her cool, fresh lips and small breasts: it is as though he has never seen her before but knows her at the instant. All night, they cling together without speaking a word. Just before dawn, she glides away through the darkness—and then the heartbreaking final stanza recalls the tenderness of her arrival ("Sae luely, luely, cam she in" before turning it to pain: "Sae luely was she gaen"). The last line reads the same in Scots or English: "Like they had never been." This is the sort of art that is "for all."

A HANDFUL OF EARTH

Soutar's 1936 collection *A Handful of Earth* comprises only forty-four poems, ten of which are epigrammatic cinquains (five-line stanzas). Soutar himself found his advance copies disappointing: he identified too great a similarity of feeling between many of the poems. He was right that the accumulated poems achieve a disappointing flatness, not really because of their similarity but because the pulpit voice gets through too often and so do stretches of opaque imagery or ornate writing. Here, for example, is the end of "The Return of the Swallow":

O happy mood;
O happy, happy mood in which we are
Bodies that stare
As time's wing cleaves a wave-crest of life's flood.

(*Poems of William Soutar,* p. 10)

The final line (and climax) fails to create a successful image; even enunciating the words is challenging. Some poems in *A Handful of Earth* are incontestably weak. However, there also strong ones. "A Desire During Illness" is very beautiful; "The Arch" combines epigrammatic spareness with visual clarity; and "Cosmos," one of Soutar's best English poems, holds its own with the best of his work in Scots:

There is a universe within this room
Where, through the half-swung shutters,
The sundering day has thrust
A wall of light between the darkened walls:
And on and on and on monotonously
The ticking tongue of time stutters
Across the silence and the dust
Which falls, drifted in little worlds,
From gloom to gloom.
(*Poems of William Soutar,* p. 28)

Here the poet is wholly in control of form and aural intensity. Anyone can hear that clock ticking, see the dust drifting through the light. Inside this particular space, furthermore, there is a sense of the vast within the small, another dimension just behind this one. The room is familiar; the sense of it is strange.

RIDDLES IN SCOTS

By the late 1930s, political changes were moving Britain inexorably toward a second war with Germany. Soutar became convinced that pacifism was the only choice for any true socialist. He was a regular reader of the pacifist John Middleton Murry's magazine, the *Adelphi.* Unfortunately, his lifelong friend James Finlayson was moving in a very different direction: he had developed an intense nationalistic interest in the "Pict Party," an obsession that Soutar found absurd. The friendship broke down.

The riddles collected in 1937 as *Riddles in Scots* (1937) must have been a welcome distraction for Soutar, though they are more five-finger exercises than poems. Here is LVII (a candle):

It has an e'e but canna see:
It stands richt tipper-taed:
It can mak a man get up and rin;
Yet we chain it wi' a threed.
(*Poems of William Soutar,* p. 121)

All the riddles rhyme and scan, all were in Scots. The internal twist of each is neatly handled and fun to guess. They also took Soutar back to his roots (he remarks in his diary that riddles were probably his first introduction to verse). Though not poems in the truest sense, they conform with his sense of playfulness, and even with the idea of something that can only be guessed—never openly stated.

IN THE TIME OF TYRANTS *AND* BUT THE EARTH ABIDETH

It was a troubled time, both in Europe and in the Soutar household as the poet became increasingly frail. *In the Time of Tyrants* was privately printed in 1939 in an edition of 110 signed copies, prefaced with an introductory note about pacifism. Perhaps Soutar's best "war poem" (or more properly antiwar poem) is in this slender volume—"The Children." It uses repetition and varied line length to achieve a haunting focus. Here are the final stanzas:

Silence is in the air:
The stars move to their places:
Silent and serene the stars move to their places:
But from earth the children stare
With blind and fearful faces:
And our charity is in the children's faces.
(*Poems of William Soutar,* p. 27)

Although war had been declared, following the German invasion of Poland, Soutar continued to hang on to his pacifist beliefs. He was reading studies of Lenin by Stalin, as well as some of Lenin's own works. He was also writing extensively in Scots, and in 1940 he completed sixteen poems, fifty-two riddles, sixteen bairn rhymes, and eleven whigmaleeries.

During 1941, sensing his own mortality, he assembled four manuscript collections: "Lyrics in Scots," "Whigmaleeries," "Theme and Variation," and "Hide and Seek." These were not published during his lifetime. His final published work was *But the Earth Abideth* (1943), a lengthy poem in seventy-three sections, of which only the last has the ring of true poetry. It fails in much the same way as does W. H. Davies' long poem *The Song of Love* (1926): the title alone signals a return to biblical diction. Soutar, like Davies, planned a "climactic" work, one that would sum up his life's beliefs. The result was numerous forgettable quatrains. *But the Earth Abideth* is a rhyming sermon, on which Alexander Scott's acerbic comment is all too correct: "A voice crying 'Woe! Woe!' through seventy-three successive poems may warn, but it also wearies" (*Still Life,* p. 157).

While focusing on the "great work," the real achievement had been going on in the background. In 1942, there were forty-six more poems in Scots, sixty-nine bairnrhymes, and forty-two whigmaleeries, as well as riddles and occasional pieces. It was the flowering of a unique talent. But the poet was dying.

In July 1943, he was diagnosed with tuberculosis. He began his *Diary of a Dying Man,* which he concealed underneath his pillow. He ceased to write new verse and instead concentrated on putting his manuscripts in order. He assembled a revised and enlarged version of *Seeds in the Wind* (1943; the collection of bairnrhymes in Scots that first appeared in 1933) and a collection in English, *The Expectant Silence* (1944). He listed titles for two proposed collections in Scots, "*Yon Toun*" and "*Local Habitation.*" He commenced, but did not complete, a prose work titled "*From a Notebook,*" which was to have been a series of revised entries from his diary.

POSTHUMOUS PUBLICATIONS

The revised *Seeds in the Wind,* published in 1943 not long after the poet's death, was well-received. *The Expectant Silence* was printed the following year: it included all the poems from *In the Time of Tyrants,* as well as an additional group of poems Soutar had assembled before his death under the title "The Signature of Silence." The poet believed these to be the best of his lyrics in English, though it is seriously open to question whether this collection would have assured his place in the canon. Soutar here demonstrates that he has learned to avoid excess, but at a cost. Here, for example, is the final stanza from "In Time of Tumult" (*Poems of William Soutar,* p. 16):

Heart! Keep your silence still
Mocking the tyrant's mock:
Thunder is on the hill;
Foam on the rock.

Stating what is clearly apparent in nature is not enough to win readers' hearts, while "The Unicorn" (though it rehearses one of Soutar's most potent symbols) is so quietly stated that it could be missed completely. Negative imperatives ("Fear not the boasts ... / Fear not the threats") mar "In the Time of Tyrants," as does the obviousness of what has been said before elsewhere—and better:

All that the hand may touch;
All that the hand may own;
Crumbles beyond time's clutch
Down to oblivion.

(*Poems of William Soutar,* p. 19)

"Nightmare" is more interesting, but it is another three-stanza poem in quatrains—easy to miss among a dozen similar-looking poems. Overall, there is simply not enough contrast of tone and form, and lovely lines, such as the opening stanza of "Wintry Beauty" (*Poems of William Soutar,* p. 36), which celebrates "The clean anatomy of tree and hill; / The honesty of stone," create expectations that the poem as a whole does not fulfill. "The Permanence of the Young Men" and "The Children" are modestly effective war poems that might perhaps win Soutar minor-poet status in an English verse anthology (thought he did not make it into Philip Larkin's 1973 anthology, *The Oxford Book of Twentieth Century English Verse*), while "The Mystery" and "Benediction" have fascinating thoughts about silence itself (a motif word for Soutar), but again, their abstractions are overwhelmed by the multiplicity of quatrains and the predictable plod of the meter.

The final poem is an envoi: it sums up Soutar's considered view on poetry, his belief that simplicity was the key. In "To the Future," he predicts an unborn poet who will write in a way that children and "common" people can understand, with

Such a sure simpleness
As strength may have;
Sunlight upon the grass:
The curve of the wave.

(*Poems of William Soutar,* p. 22).

This echoes his diary entry of Wednesday August 28, 1935:

> The cry of the writer to-day ought to be: "How can I achieve simplicity?" Perhaps at no other time in history has it been more difficult to be simple. ... But may we not learn from nature ... that simplicity of structure is the secret of survival (and by simplicity is not meant bareness—but directness, clean-cutness, harmoniousness; the smooth action of a bone in its socket, which is not without much subtle adaptation). Let us but seek to make thought and impression fit thus—so that a poem may be as communicative as a gesture.
>
> (*Diaries*, p. 63)

The desire for simplicity was one possible reaction to modernist intellectualism, an instinct closer to W. H. Davies than T. S. Eliot, closer to Robert Louis Stevenson than Hugh MacDiarmid. Soutar remarked of MacDiarmid's *Scots Unbound* (1932) that "the 'thocht' in the lengthier poems confounds the poetry" (*Diaries*, p. 145). The same is true for some of Soutar's own lengthy poems. The downside of his plainer work, however (in the English language at least), was that it restricted him to a kind of weary uniformity, an ordinariness that made him look like a backwoods versifier.

Soutar was not a minor poet. However, the evidence of his worth is only dispersedly apparent in the single collections published during and just after his death. He was not widely anthologized at this point, and most of his books had been printed at his own (or his father's) expense. Much of his best work was still in manuscript form when he died. The task of creating a collected volume that would do him justice was taken on by MacDiarmid—but alas, this simply compounded the problem.

WILLIAM SOUTAR: COLLECTED POEMS

After the death of his son, John Soutar handed over papers and manuscripts to his son's learned friend, Hugh MacDiarmid, who agreed to edit the collected poetic work. Eventually a volume appeared, though it was a lengthy process: *William Soutar: Collected Poems* was published in 1948. In the prefatory essay (written in 1944),

MacDiarmid damned with faint praise. While deeming *Seeds in the Wind* a "minor classic," he took pains to emphasize the word "minor." He remarked on "the extent to which [Soutar] devoted himself to extremely short poems, and to trifling oddments like his riddles and epigrams" and put this down to "his bedridden state" (*William Soutar: Collected Poems,* p. 17). Even while praising Soutar's use of Scots as "idiomatically authentic," he observed that "the movement of his verse is almost always too tame—the Scots Muse has a wilder music and a far more complicated and unexpectable (sic) movement" (p. 17), though he regarded "The Auld Tree" as something of an exception. Soutar was, he suggested, permanently at risk from platitude and sententiousness.

Though this was not the whole truth, there was some truth in it, and the criticism was the more dangerous for that. Perhaps MacDiarmid had spent too long wrestling with the large quantities of Soutar's English quatrains: he certainly proved unequal to the gargantuan task of making sense of the poet's extensive oeuvre. Oddly, he suggested that the best work in Scots was written early on and that latterly Soutar had been working mainly in English. This seems to have been completely inaccurate. MacDiarmid did make one interesting and worthwhile point, however: that Soutar's ability to combine the poetic and the comic was remarkable and unusual.

In ordering the contents, MacDiarmid placed lyrics in Scots first (but certainly not in order of composition), then bairn rhymes and riddles. He included a section on epigrams (not those previously published). He divided lyrics in English into sections according to date of composition, though it is difficult to find where each section starts and ends. He had a section ("Theme and Variation") of poems written in response to or as "versions" of other poems; and finally he included "Poems from the Diaries" and a glossary of Scots words. Since many of the lyrics are short, there are often two or more to a page, with the consequence that the volume feels cluttered. There is evidence of some editorial confusion, too: "The Singing Bush," a noteworthy English lyric, appears twice, in separate sections and in two versions.

It was clearly a difficult task for MacDiarmid, not least because of Soutar's own classifications, grouping his poems in sections, but with some of the epigrams among the English lyrics, the whigmaleeries separated from poems in Scots, and so on. MacDiarmid had many undoubted talents, but editorial skill was not among them.

As soon as the volume was published there was an outcry among Soutar's friends and supporters. Though the volume comprised over one thousand items, many previously unpublished, it completely omitted (among other things) the entire contents of Soutar's best-known books in Scots (*Seeds in the Wind* and *Poems in Scots*). Bearing in mind that MacDiarmid had singled out "The Auld Tree" for praise in his preface, it seems hard to believe he had done this intentionally. However, it was suggested by some that he had deliberately omitted the poet's strongest work in order to make his own achievement more singular.

At best, the *Collected Poems* muddied the waters of Soutar's reputation. Although it did include much excellent work (and some poems to this day not published elsewhere), it certainly failed to include some of the best Scots lyrics. The whole skirmish did little to raise Soutar's status as a poet, and the *Collected Poems* was quickly remaindered.

THE SOUTAR STORY CONTINUES

Meanwhile, Soutar's reputation as a tragic literary hero lived on. Alexander Scott made a selection from the diaries, published with a biographical introduction as *Diaries of a Dying Man* in 1954. He followed this with an excellent critical biography, *Still Life,* in 1958; this was the first volume to advance a balanced and well-informed assessment of the work, though even here, Scott found it difficult to decide Soutar's ultimate literary status.

Another scholar, W. R. Aitken, advanced Soutar's cause significantly with the publication of selected work, *Poems in Scots and English,* in 1961. This was by far the best volume of Soutar to date: 144 poems attractively presented with a biographical introduction, a note on pronunciation, a glossary, and poems grouped according to Soutar's own classifications but this time in chronological order. Aitken also included, as an appendix, the original poems from which Soutar had taken inspiration for the versions in "Theme and Variation."

In 1988, this selection was revised and substantially expanded to include 582 poems, in a volume titled *Poems of William Soutar: A New Selection*. The appendix of sources to the "Theme and Variation" poems was dropped, but Aitken included two sets of Scots poems that Soutar had been compiling just before his death—"Yon Toun" and "Local Habitation." The latter comprises mainly whigmaleeries about local characters. The former affords a fascinating insight into how Soutar's writing was progressing before he died. It accomplishes an astonishing variety of tone, from the haunting elegy of "Ballad" to the tale of Alistair McAllister who died of hiccupping ("The Prodigy"). There is a sense of strength in the verse—a sinewy, masterful poet wholly in control of his craft. There are quatrains aplenty here, too, but they never dwindle into ordinariness: meter becomes rhythm, and rhythm corresponds with tone and sound. In poems like "Backlands," Soutar accomplishes the simplicity he sought and failed to find in English. The expanded Aitken selection remains the best and most comprehensive source of Soutar's work, though it is nothing like a complete collection.

In 2000, another selection of Soutar's poems was published: *Into a Room: Selected Poems of William Soutar,* with a biographical and critical introduction by Carl MacDougall and Douglas Gifford. This time there was a bold attempt not just to rescue Soutar from relative obscurity but to hail him as "one of the greatest poets Scotland has produced" (*Into a Room,* p. 7). The prefatory essay argues that it is time to rescue Soutar from the shadow of Hugh MacDiarmid and place him back in the Scottish *makar* and ballad tradition where he belongs. The real "renaissance," these writers suggest, is a personal one—from innocence to experience, via the many forms the poet chose to pursue. The selection of 139 poems mingles forms and languages and offers some single lyrics the space of a whole page—a welcome improvement. Linguistic barriers are alleviated by footnote glossaries. There is, however, no attempt to present the poems chronologically or to give dates.

Into a Room confirms the continuing interest in William Soutar as a leading twentieth-century Scottish poet. The introduction makes reference to the many musicians (including Benjamin Britten) and folksingers who have set his work to music over past decades. Dramatists too have been inspired by his life and work: Joy Hendry (who was also responsible for the publication of Soutar's final diary) has written both stage and radio plays about him; Tom Fleming performed a one-man show about Soutar, *The Quiet Room;* and Ajay Close's *The Keekin-Gless,* a drama about Soutar's life and work, was performed by a youth theater group at Perth Theatre in summer 2009.

Even for Soutar's followers, however, it is hard to place his absolute significance. He was a hugely prolix poet, and the majority of his poems are not remarkable. It seems reasonable to suggest that the lack of a normal, interactive life allowed him so much time with pen and paper that he simply kept producing verse, not all of which, by any means, was poetry. In summer 1988, *Chapman,* the Edinburgh-based poetry journal, published an issue devoted to Soutar. It included a number of interesting essays, some by people who had known the poet personally. There were also some unpublished extracts from the diaries, as well as nineteen unpublished poems. None of these nineteen poems would convert a new reader to the cause

Nevertheless, there is no doubt that Soutar completed twenty or thirty outstanding poems, distinguished by a quality of timelessness and universality that is exceptionally rare. W. R. Aitken, Soutar's best editor, suggests that "it is on the bairnrhymes, so deservedly popular, on the unique excellence of the whigmaleeries, and on the high achievement of his other poems and lyrics in Scots that Soutar's reputation is securely established" (*Poems of William Soutar,* p. xi). It is true that Soutar's finest and most original work is in Scots. In his native tongue he is never less than interesting, and at his best he is unrivalled.

For the contemporary non-Scottish reader, however, this presents a challenge. Though there are a small number of first-rate poems by Soutar in English, it is absolutely necessary to read his work in Scots. It was the language he spoke; it was the language of the tradition in which he was at home.

Today, just as during Soutar's lifetime, the issue of reading and writing in Scots is political. In schools in the United Kingdom, standard English has long been asserted as the lingua franca for teaching and learning; Scots (at one time the language of court and government in Scotland) has been consigned to a lesser status and is mainly used in speech rather than in writing, while Highland Gaelic has receded mainly to the islands off the West Coast.

Soutar wanted the richness of Lowland Scots to be brought back into common and literary use through primary education, starting with the bairn rhymes he loved. *Seeds in the Wind* was a successful volume, but it did not win the battle of equal status for Scots and English in literature and education; nor did it create everyday familiarity with the Scots words he employed. This issue remains a continuing struggle, hard fought by contemporary writers who choose to work in Scots and by some Scottish publishers (notably Black and White Publishing's Itchy Coo imprint) who continue to create attractive texts in Scots for children. The fact that Soutar's best work is in Scots is certainly one reason that he is less well-known, even in Scotland, than he should be.

Lowlands Scots is far from impenetrable. Once the basic transitions are mastered (night = nicht, of = o, and so forth), it is a question of consulting a glossary or online dictionary for some of the magnificently onomatopoeic words in which Soutar delighted. Picking up connotations is more complex, but in Soutar's case recurring words start to build their own network of association across the poems. For example, "smool'd" is the poet's word for "slipped," but it has connotations of softness and dreaminess—that sense of the uncertain reality between dream and waking. This is a poet who draws full strength from simple repetition, even inside a single lyric—so that key words become quickly familiar, building resonance as they recur. His elegiac lyrics have a timeless quality that is uniquely haunting; his more droll, comical pieces have an inexplicable habit of sticking in the mind. They seem slight—and yet they are not slight—they are not like anything else in literature.

Soutar's comic poem about the cough that was, in real truth, the harbinger of his own death illustrates this. He uses the Scots word "hoast" for cough (a word enunciated from the back of the throat, where a cough begins). "Sic" is the hard-edged Scots word for "such"; "dout" is "suspect" and "on the trot" is just what it suggests. Each end-stopped line creates its own heaving pause, wheezing back into life with the next line:

Sic a hoast hae I got:
Sic a hoast hae I got:
I dout my days are on the trot;
Sic a hoast hae I got.

(*Poems of William Soutar*, p. 194)

All poets look for diction and form to suit their individual talent. Soutar found his in Scots; for him there was "nae ither gait" ("The Makar," *Poems of William Soutar*, p. 253). Here he can ring the changes with an intensity and strangeness not unlike Emily Dickinson, treading his own perilous edge between life and death. As final witness to that fact, here is "Song," the haunting lament first published in *Poems in Scots*, 1935. The surreal central image is a broken bridge (brig), under which water is silent. As the remains of ancient Babylon blow past in dust (stour), the poet invites the reader to go down with a song—down in water too deep for any thirst (drouth), dark enough (wan eneuch) to drown in, salty or sweet (saut, or seelfu'). The reader should hear the plangent assonance in the "oo" sound of "soun," "doun," "mouth," and "drouth":

Whaur yon broken brig hings owre;
Whaur yon water maks nae soun';
Babylon blaws by in stour:
Gang doun wi' a sang, gang doun.

Deep, owre deep, for onie drouth:
Wan eneuch an ye wud droun:
Saut, or seelfu', for the mouth;
Gang doun wi' a sang, gang doun.
Babylon blaws by in stour
Whaur yon water makes nae soun':
Darkness is your only door;
Gang doun wi' a sang, gang doun.

(p. 225)

Selected Bibliography

WORKS OF WILLIAM SOUTAR

Diaries

Diaries of a Dying Man. Edited by Alexander Scott (the poet's biographer). Edinburgh: W. & R. Chambers, 1954. New ed., revised by W. R. Aitken, reissued as Canongate Classic 36. Edinburgh: Canongate, 1988.

The Diary of a Dying Man. Edited by Joy Hendry. Edinburgh: Chapman, 1991. (With a foreword by Hendry and an introduction by W. R. Aitken. Of special interest for its selected facsimile pages, allowing a view of the poet's handwriting and page formats.)

Poetry

Gleanings by an Undergraduate. (Published anonymously at John Soutar's expense.) Paisley, Scotland: Alexander Gardner, 1923.

Conflict. London: Chapman and Hall, 1931.

Seeds in the Wind: Poems in Scots for Children. Edinburgh: Grant & Murray, 1933; new ed., rev. and enl., London: Andrew Dakers, 1943.

The Solitary Way. Edinburgh: Moray Press, 1934.

Brief Words: One Hundred Epigrams. Edinburgh: Moray Press, 1935.

Poems in Scots. Edinburgh: Moray Press, 1935.

A Handful of Earth. Edinburgh: Moray Press, 1936.

Riddles in Scots. Edinburgh: Moray Press, 1937.

In the Time of Tyrants. Privately printed, 1939.

But the Earth Abideth. London: Andrew Dakers, 1943.

The Expectant Silence. London: Andrew Dakers, 1944.

William Soutar: Collected Poems. Edited and with an introductory essay by Hugh MacDiarmid. London: Andrew Dakers, 1948. (Though presented as a definitive collection commissioned by the poet's father after his death and comprising over one thousand poems, some of them not previously published, the collection omitted

Soutar's long poems and several of his strongest and best-known lyrics. As a result, it caused a public outcry and its status was undermined.)

Poems in Scots and English. Selected by W. R. Aitken. Edinburgh: Oliver and Boyd, 1961.

Poems of William Soutar: A New Selection. Edited by W. R. Aitken. Edinburgh: Scottish Academic Press, 1988. (A revised and greatly expanded edition of *Poems in Scots and English*)

A Bairn's Sang and Other Scots Verse for Children. Edited by Tom Hubbard. Edinburgh: Mercat Press, 1999.

Into a Room: Selected Poems of William Soutar. Edited with an introduction by Carl MacDougall and Douglas Gifford. Argyll, Scotland: Argyll Publishing, 2000.

CRITICAL AND BIOGRAPHICAL STUDIES

Bold, Alan. *MacDiarmid: Christopher Murray Grieve, A Critical Biography.* London: Paladin, 1990. (Includes some background on Soutar.)

Dunn, Douglas, ed. *The Faber Book of Twentieth-Century Scottish Poetry.* London: Faber, 1992.

Fitt, Matthew, and James Robertson, eds. *The Smoky Smirr o Rain. A Scots Anthology.* Dundee: Itchy Coo, 2003.

Hendry, Joy. *Gang Doun wi a Sang. A Play About William Soutar.* Edinburgh: Diehard, 1995.

Hendry, Joy, ed. *Chapman 53* (1988). (Edition mainly focused on William Soutar, including nineteen unpublished poems, extracts from journals, and correspondence, with essays on various aspects of the poet's life and work by Duncan Glen, Forbes MacGregor, Christopher Whyte, W. R. Aitken, and Tom Scott.)

Moult, Thomas, ed. *The Best Poems of 1930.* London: Cape, 1930.

Scott, Alexander. *Still Life.* Edinburgh: Chambers, 1958. (Critical biography.)

ROSEMARY SUTCLIFF

(1920—1992)

Abby Mims

A POET, A minstrel, a magician with words—these are just a handful of phrases used to describe the classic storyteller Rosemary Sutcliff. Born in Sussex, England, on December 14, 1920, to a naval family, she began writing during World War II, despite the aftereffects of severe childhood arthritis and familial pressure to remain a miniature portrait artist. Critics note that her art training served to strengthened her eye for detail and the ability to paint words onto the page. Sutcliff produced more than fifty books during the next forty years, and her work has been translated into fifteen languages. She is best known for her novel *The Eagle of the Ninth* (1954), which chronicles the life of a Roman solider, Marcus Flavius Aquila. The book sold over one million copies, was produced as a BBC miniseries and a radio play, and was optioned to become a major motion picture. *Eagle* was the first volume of her popular Roman Trilogy, which also includes *The Silver Branch* (1957) and *The Lantern Bearers* (1959), and over the course of the next three decades Sutcliff would continue to trace the descendants of Marcus through wars, strife, love, and loss from Roman times through the Dark Ages.

Sutcliff is primarily a children's writer (despite penning a few novels explicitly for adults), yet much of her body of work is enjoyed by children and adults alike. Her adaptation of the Robin Hood and King Arthur legends are among her most popular works. Equally impressive, however, are her many historical novels, steeped in extensive research, a passion for storytelling, and a desire to impart the themes of love, loyalty, duty, faith, and courage to children. Using the customs and ceremonies of varied ancient time periods, from the Bronze Age to the Dark Ages to Medieval England, impart she does, while giving readers an action-packed story line, the smells and sights of battle, the beauty of ancient landscapes, and thoroughly developed characters. Many commentators have mentioned that despite her own physical limitations, her vivid and physical depictions of battle are exceptionally fluid, causing the reader to feel and nearly hear the crash of swords and fallen soldiers. She has an ability not only to accurately capture the strategies and complex battle formations of warring factions but also to portray the violence and bloodshed of war without crossing into the gratuitous. As Joan V. Marder writes,

> We are today cushioned from the elements, but Rosemary Sutcliff can make us feel the famine that lurked at winter's end, the threat of wolves making each winter night dangerous. We can feel the narrow boundaries, the constriction of the tribal world, or the stretching of the known world under the Roman Empire.
>
> (p. 139)

In her novels, Sutcliffe returned to several themes over time: the plight of the outcast, the rites of passage from child to adult (or more specifically boy to man), and the play of light versus dark in individuals and civilization as a whole. In terms of the outcast, many of her warriors or young soldiers have either physical or emotional deficiencies that separate them from their tribes, societies, or families. Often they are alienated from their people either as a choice, like Aquila in *The Lantern Bearers,* or from a physical deformity, whether it be Marcus' war injury in *The Eagle of the Ninth* or the withered arm the warrior Drem is born with in *Warrior Scarlet* (1958). She titles one book simply *The Outcast* (1955) which chronicles the life of Beric, a boy brought up among a people not his own, having been cast out by the society of his birth because of fear of his differences; he eventually becomes a trusted servant of the conquering army. These young men are left to fight their way back into their tribe or society and, failing that, to create a new way of life independent from the one they have formerly known. In light of Sutcliff's own physical limitations and struggles to create a life as a writer despite her family's disapproval, one can understand why this theme appears time and again in her novels.

Given that nearly all her main characters are some kind of warrior or soldier from the ancient past, much has been made of Sutcliff's preoccupation with soldiering. It is an obsession she herself has never been quite able to explain. In a 1986 interview with the historian Raymond H. Thompson she mused,

> It always seems to be a fighting man that appeals to me. I don't know why: I'm not a butch character. Somebody once said to me, "Perhaps you'll be a soldier in another life." I heard myself saying, "No thank you, I have had enough of soldiering." Perhaps it was something I remembered. I know that I was really quite startled when I heard my own voice saying this.
>
> (p. 14)

Indeed, there is some kind of wistful knowing in her stories, a long-lost connection to those men on the battlefield. Her heroes, although different from one another, tend to be cut from the same cloth: brave but not reckless; loyal, stoic, thoughtful, and able to overcome their difficulties, although it is never easy. They are rarely anything but common men striving to serve their people, their families, and themselves.

Often too her protagonists have to make some kind of unbearable choice in order to fully cross the line from childhood to adulthood, as evidenced in *Simon* (1953), who must choose between his loyalty to friendship or to country in order to become a man; or in *Knight's Fee* (1960) as Randal sacrifices his closest friend in order to achieve knighthood. Through these rites of passage, we can also see the great influence of Rudyard Kipling on Sutcliff's work—she held him in the highest esteem and completed a biography, *Rudyard Kipling,* in 1960. Sutcliff was never shy about admitting her reliance on Kipling's style and his influence on the stories she created. She points to the Mowgli tales as a prime example of loyalties divided and unbearable choices made, thereby causing the hero to be reborn as an adult. Despite many examples of direct use of Kipling's signs and symbols over the span of her career, it cannot be said that Sutcliff writes any kind of poor imitation of him; it is better stated that she uses some of the same building blocks in order to create something new and wholly her own.

The theme of light versus dark is so pervasive on an individual and societal level in Sutcliff's work that there is almost no need to parse it out volume by volume. It seems as though Sutcliff's characters are always working to keep the light alive in order to stem the coming dark tide and, in terms of Britain, the Dark Ages themselves. Invaders are always just over the horizon, whether it be the Roman advance in *The Eagle of the Ninth* or the Saxon invasion of Britain in *Dawn Wind* (1961). Individuals either represent the light, such as Artos and Medraut in *Sword at Sunset* (1963), or the darkness, via villains like Modred in *Road to Camlann* (1981); in some cases they present a mix of both elements, demonstrated by Aquila's inner conflict in *The Lantern Bearers*. No matter the outcome of these inner and outer battles, those left standing must somehow join together and coexist, living together in some semblance of peace. This struggle of light against dark, aside from being the heart of legends through the ages, is also quite Kiplingesque with regard to his protagonists and the ways in which he acknowledges that Britain was settled by many peoples who learned to live together to create a new nationality.

Sutcliff is said to have written nearly every day of her life, sometimes producing eighteen hundred words a day in small script on a single sheet, writing three longhand drafts of every novel before penning the copy she sent to her publisher. She used large notebooks to sketch out the details of her novels and her historical research, from which she would create an outline of two to three thousand words. Many of her ideas for her novels got their start from the literature and experiences of her childhood; others came from her love of Sussex Downs and her fascination for the continuity of history and the way the land had been inhabited since the Dark Ages; still others simply came organically. Sutcliff is also known as something of a pioneer in terms of the way history in fiction is presented to children. She never pandered or wrote down to her audience, instead creating characters and situations her readers could directly relate to. Her work manages to avoid the usual trap of sentimentality found in much children's literature, and Sutcliff instead balances gritty realism with subtlety and plausibility. In addition to winning a Carnegie Medal for *The Lantern Bearers* in 1960, an OBE in 1975, and being named a Commander of the British Empire in 1992, she was also awarded the Children's Rights Workshop "Other Award" in 1978 for her feminist and sympathetic account of the life of Boudicca in *Song of a Dark Queen*. As John Rowe Townsend notes, "For Rosemary Sutcliff, the past is not something to be taken down from the shelf and dusted. It comes out of her pages alive and breathing and now" (p. 199).

BIOGRAPHY

Flannery O'Connor once said, "Anybody who has survived his childhood has enough information about life to last him the rest of his days." This sentiment could not be truer of writer Sutcliff, who contracted Still's Disease, a form of juvenile arthritis, before the age of three. She would suffer its aftermath in the form of joint and bone damage for the duration of her life, as pain management and hope for remission were all that could be done to manage the disease when she was a child. As a result, by her early teens Sutcliff had lived most of her life in hospitals or nursing homes and was often confined to bed rest. If that were not enough to bear, Sutcliff also had to weather an overbearing and controlling mother along with the constant relocation of her family owing to her father's military career.

For some, this set of circumstances might have stifled their sense of spirit or imagination, but for Sutcliff it was quite the opposite. She was kept distracted and entertained by a large family of eclectic relatives, among them her British uncles who went to India to build the railroads and returned with stories of war, strife, and the exotic. Given that her father (George Ernest Sutcliff) was a British officer, the family traveled to varied locales ranging from Malta to London, Chatham Dockyard, and North Devon. Sutcliff's disability and the constant relocation of her family resulted in an early form of homeschooling for the writer, and her mother (Nessie Elizabeth Lawton Sutcliff) kept her mind active by reading to her constantly. She was regaled with the tales of Kipling, Beatrice Potter, and Charles Dickens along with Norse, Saxton, and Celtic legends. Strangely, despite this vast exposure to literature, Sutcliff herself did not learn to read until the age of nine; she was known to note that Kipling himself did not learn to read until that same age. He remained one of the great influences in her childhood and eventually on her writing career. In her memoir, *Blue Remembered Hills: A Recollection* (1983), Kipling is presented as a kind of kindred spirit. When she was a very young girl, she was a given a medication for her arthritis that contained arsenic and caused her to hallucinate fairly severely. In the corners of her room she saw several animals: a blank panther, wolves, and snakes. She had no way of identifying what these animals were at the time, considering that she was too young to have ever seen them, and it was not until she read Kipling's Jungle Books that she realized what it was she had seen. After that, not only was she unafraid of these animals, she actively sought comfort in Kipling's works.

After a prolonged period of hospital and nursing home stays for her condition, and several military relocations, Sutcliff's family settled for a time in North Devon, where she was able to return to a regular academic environment. However, she felt lonely and isolated most of the time, despite her belief that attending a public school, as opposed to being placed in a specialized one, was far better for her emotional state. Given that she was often taken out of school for weeks or months at a time for stays in children's hospitals (and once she was too old for that, nursing homes among the very old and infirm) in an attempt to repair the damage Still's had done to her joints and bones, she had little chance to form meaningful bonds with her peers.

This pain and suffering obviously shaped Sutcliff as a child and formed her early desire to be a writer. She goes into great detail about the difficult aspects of her childhood in *Blue Remembered Hills,* yet one is left feeling as though Sutcliff spent very little time feeling sorry for herself. There are moments of deep loneliness and frustration, but they are always countered by the positives she finds in every environment. Writing about her constant hospital stays, Sutcliff comments, "The sense of utter powerlessness; no control over one's own destiny from whether one would or would not have an injection to whether one would or would not eat the egg custard ... but there were the good things, too ... we had fun together. We formed friendships" (p. 90). She also attributes her stays in Princess Elizabeth hospital with providing the pinnacle of her inspiration to become a writer—it was there that she read a book titled *Emily of the New Moon,* a coming-of-age tale of a Canadian girl whose father had died and who longed to become a writer. (Years later she searched for the book and discovered it had been written by L. M. Montgomery, who also penned *Anne of Green Gables.*)

Despite her voracious appetite for reading and learning, she left primary schooling at the age of fourteen and went on to enroll in the Bideford Art School (art, painting in particular, was the only subject she excelled in at the time). She could also walk rather well by that point and was able to leave behind the push-carriage of her childhood, something she described as an uncomfortable "coffin on wheels" (*Blue Remembered Hills,* p. 48). Sutcliff's mother never allowed her a wheelchair, believing only in her rehabilitation, often forcing her daughter to walk several painful miles a day to build her strength. Several years after her mother died, Sutcliff procured a wheelchair, and reveled in the flexibility it allowed her. She entered Bideford as its youngest student; most of her classmates were at least eighteen. The next three years of her life were focused solely on cultivating her artistic abilities, and she had few social interactions aside from a brief and intense crush on her cousin Edward when she was seventeen. She excelled in the arts, and it was her ambition for a time to become the first woman president of the Royal Academy.

Sutcliff turned eighteen in 1939, just before World War II broke out. Her cousin was sent off to fight and would eventually marry a woman from South Africa. During the early months of the war she painted tapestries that were sent to prisoner-of-war camps and hospitals, but she soon began to focus on professional miniature painting. Sutcliff would rather have worked on larger canvases with oils, but it was the opinion of her parents and her headmaster that she would excel in this genre. And she did for a time, painting miniatures of children (her least favorite subjects, loath as they were to sit still) and fulfilling commissions for portraits of men away at war and those who had fallen. In those early years she painted a "subject miniature" of a knight in fifteenth-century armor, titled *Spirit of England.* It was chosen to hang in the Royal Academy, much to the delight of Sutcliff's family.

She claims her first urges to write came during the middle of the war, as she began to tire of miniatures, something she never had a real passion for in the first place. She writes, "I took to miniature painting without a completely whole heart, on the advice of my elders and betters. Generally speaking, I do not think that one should ever take another person's advice in the things of life that really matter, but follow the dictates of the still small something in one's innermost self" (*Blue Remembered Hills,* p. 118). She goes on to note that she always felt "cramped" as a miniature painter, and with writing, she was allowed utter expansiveness, a canvas with no discernible edges. She hid her primary efforts from everyone, particularly her mother, whom she knew would have no faith in her daughter's ability and would try to stifle her efforts. As she describes her early work, in particular a story called "Wild Sunrise," the themes and story lines Sutcliff would eventually build her career upon, those of Roman invasions and the British Empire's trials and tribulations, are immediately evident.

She further explains that her first efforts were stories "not quite for adults, but not quite for children either" but mainly for "my own delight."

(*Blue Remembered Hills,* p. 120). She continued to write throughout the war, and soon after it ended came up with a book for children retelling of some of the Saxon and Celtic legends she had heard as a child. She sent off the collection of stories to a close friend, who by chance came into contact with an editor at Oxford University Press. Although Oxford did not ultimately publish her manuscript, they proposed she write a series of children's books based on the legend of Robin Hood. As Sutcliff says, "And that was how it all began" (*Blue Remembered Hills,* p. 122).

Despite her burgeoning writing career, Sutcliff struggled in her personal life. She had not had much interest in men after her cousin married in 1944, but around the time she began to write the *Robin Hood* series she became interested in a family friend, Rupert King, who, it turned out, was already married. This did not stop Sutcliff from embarking on a lengthy emotional affair with him, much to the chagrin of her father. She had always been in her father's favor for most of her life, and his disapproval was not lost on Sutcliff, who turned to her mother for support. This in turn created much tension in the Sutcliff household because she was still living with her parents, who watched this man Rupert come and go, all the while breaking their daughter's heart. Sutcliff writes about this period of her life in some detail in the last chapters of her memoir, noting that while she understood King could never be faithful to just one woman, they were very much in love. The final break came when, after years of waiting for his divorce to become final, King told her that he had actually met another woman whom he planned to marry. Sutcliff is not subtle here about how the lingering effects of her childhood disease might have dissuaded King from choosing her, in that ultimately he did not have the ability to take care of someone who was physically limited.

Despite the pain his choice must have caused her, she notes that afterward, her writing became much deeper and more layered, and she credits this experience with granting her an ability to write in ways she otherwise would not have. And write she did. While waiting for final acceptance from Oxford of *The Chronicles of Robin Hood,* she began another book for children, *The Queen Elizabeth Story,* which she also submitted to Oxford. Both books were eventually accepted and published in 1950.

The conclusion of *Blue Remembered Hills* hints that perhaps Sutcliff meant to write another volume of autobiography; however, none was ever completed. She continued to live with her parents for the rest of their lives. Her mother died in the 1960s and she and her father relocated to Sussex. Even given her increasing handicaps, she traveled during those years to Greece and other countries. When her father died in the 1980s, she moved to Arundel and lived with a housekeeper and two dogs, to whom she was very attached. She was writing the morning she died unexpectedly on 22 July 1992. She had recently finished the second draft of a new novel, *Sword Song,* which was published posthumously in 1997.

EARLY FICTION

With her first half-dozen books, Sutcliff established herself primarily as a children's writer of historical fiction. Early works such as *The Chronicles of Robin Hood* (1950), *The Queen Elizabeth Story* (1950), *The Armourer's House* (1951), and *Brother Dusty-Feet* (1952) were praised for their easy appeal to children, although at times critics noted that her voice was perhaps a tad precious or condescending and others have since commented that not much of her future potential is evident in these pages. These books tended to be rather thin on themes and lessons per se; they were designed more to entertain than to teach children about history. Her next book, *Simon* (1953), is perhaps where Sutcliff broke through to a new level of children's novel and began to find her voice. *Simon* is the story of two young men and the way their childhood friendship is destroyed by the English Civil War. The novel has a distinctly epic flavor and plays on a central Sutcliff theme, one in which characters are forced to choose between duty and personal inclination. Her protagonist, Simon, must choose between his duty to his father and Parliament and his friendship with a Loyalist and, in the process, separate fully from his parents to become an adult. Although not her most successful attempt at transcribing history into fiction, *Simon* demonstrates Sutcliff's ability to immerse herself in the details of historical events, in this case bringing to life the final campaign of the English Civil War. She also makes a break from her earlier work by replacing mere pageantry with timeless themes that emerge through her rendering of battles, troop movements, and characters' internal motivations. Her characterizations are further deepened through use of local Devonshire dialects and writing Simon as a hero who survives a crisis of faith and emerges a well-balanced man. This depth and breadth was such a departure from Sutcliff's first fictional forays, the critics took note. As Margaret Meek writes of *Simon*, "No one who had read the early novels would have foreseen that Miss Sutcliff could describe the beating of a deserter, the battle of Torrington and the harsh discomfort of the sick and wounded so evocatively that the waste, pain, misery, glory and excitement of war are held together in a plot compellingly detailed and yet fast moving" (pp. 28–29).

Perhaps Sutcliff's most important departure in *Simon* is that she moves from the world of childhood to larger themes of loyalty and personal choice, so that her young and adolescent readers are pushed farther to understand the complexities of war and, ultimately, life. Meek notes that with *Simon*, Sutcliff became a writer for the "discriminating" child reader, one who demands respect and is constantly challenged by the stories she provides.

MAJOR WORKS: THE ROMAN TRILOGY

Sutcliff's Roman Trilogy, comprising *The Eagle of the Ninth, The Silver Branch,* and *The Lantern Bearers,* catalogs the trials and tribulations of Marcus Flavia Aquila and his successors. The setting is the twilight period of British history, as the Romans were evacuating Britain and before the coming age of Christianity. In the case of *The Eagle of the Ninth,* Sutcliff claimed that the story was based very loosely on actual events occurring in 117 C.E., when the Ninth Roman Legion, stationed near York, went out to quell a Caledonian uprising and was never heard from again. In the early 1900s, she said, a featherless legionary eagle statue was found near the site. Historians dispute her account, stating that although there was such a legion, it departed England in later years, and that the statue was not necessarily a legionary totem. Whatever the historical truth may be, Sutcliff combined her own sense of history and imagination to create a novel that set her apart from other children's novelists.

Set in Britain in 127 C.E., *Eagle* is essentially the story of Marcus Aquila's struggles as his promising military career is halted by a battlefield injury and he seeks to solve the mystery surrounding the disappearance of his father and the Legion of the Ninth. The novel opens with Marcus' early life on his father's farm, where he dreams of becoming a Roman centurion like his father. He achieves his dream, only to be permanently wounded in his first battle, and he is forced to retire. When his mother remarries and he is essentially left without an immediate family, he seeks refuge with his Uncle Aquila in Rome. In the time he spends there, he falls in love with a neighbor girl, Cottia, and is impressed with a brave slave, Esca, whom he buys and eventually becomes close friends with. Although his uncle tells Marcus he can stay on as long as he to needs to, Marcus becomes restless and is determined to solve the mystery of his father's vanished legion while simultaneously reclaiming the totem of the legion from the Celts. The standard of any Roman legion was a bronze or silver eagle, carried on a staff. Because Marcus' father was a first cohort commander, the eagle was his responsibility, and retrieving it would restore his father's honor. Before he sets out to reclaim it, Esca agrees to travel with him as his friend. Thus Marcus grants Esca his freedom, and they find an abandoned wolf cub who rounds out their self-made tribe.

When Marcus and Esca reach their intended destination, they learn that the Ninth Legion was outnumbered in an ill-fated battle, losing almost one thousand soldiers as they fought. Nearly half the remaining men mutinied, and Marcus' father led the rest into battle; he was the last man bravely standing when the Celts killed him. Given the shame the mutiny of the Ninth caused, Marcus cannot restore their reputation, but he retrieves the eagle statue and clears his father's name upon his return to Britain. Critics have noted that this journey was crafted with much dedication by Sutcliff, and that "each incident has a bold outline, fire-clear details, and is told with passion and skill" (Meek, p. 39).

In her 1987 interview with Thompson, Sutcliff observed that many do not find Marcus the warmest of her heroes, that he is a bit "prickly," but she points out that this may be because so many horrible things have happened to him: his father's death, his mother's remarriage, and being cast out of the legion, along with his obsessive need to find out what happened to his father's troops. However, by the end of the story, as he is forced to deal with his flaws and worst fears, he finds a certain kind of happiness, which eventually leads to his successful reclaiming of the eagle and settling down in Rome. Many have noted Sutcliff's ability to crawl inside her characters, giving them a rich interior life, and Marcus is no exception. During the early stages of his journey, Marcus struggles with his own fears and insecurities:

> And yet for Marcus the tension had not snapped into relief. Perhaps if he had never seen the new heron's feather on an old war spear it might have done.... somewhere deep beneath his thinking mind the instinct for danger had remained with him ever since.... "Am I being every kind of fool?" Marcus wondered. "Am I going to be laughed at so long as my name is remembered in the Legion as the man who doubled the guard for two days because of a bunch of feathers, and then turned out his cohort to repel a herd of milch-cows?"
>
> (pp. 32–33)

Sutcliff employs this universal theme of belonging or finding one's place in the world throughout Marcus' story, which is something all children can relate to. In a sense, none of the main characters here quite fit in society. Marcus is an orphan, Esca a former slave, and the wolf cub has been separated from his pack and needs a family. Ultimately, however, all three find their way in life: Esca is now a free man, the cub is released back into the wild, and the government grants Marcus a full pension and his own farm in return for his heroic deeds. Sutcliff masterfully pulls together these parallel journeys as she weaves a convincing and suspenseful story that provides readers with authentic details of a distant time, while teaching the lessons of self-acceptance, loyalty, and how we as humans are dependent on one another.

The second installment of Sutcliff's Roman trilogy, *The Silver Branch,* takes place during a time of great political turmoil in Britain during the third century. Two descendents of Marcus Aquila—Justin, a junior army surgeon, and Flavius, a young centurion, who are cousins—meet in Albion, where Justin has recently been stationed. Justin is burdened with the fact that his father does not approve of his choice of career, wishing Justin had become a soldier instead of a doctor; as a result, Justin is shy, often stutters, and is unsure of himself. Once he forms an alliance with Flavius, however, he is able to overcome these shortcomings, and together the two men attempt to unearth the source of the governmental strife and injustice that is happening all around them. Their sleuthing reveals a corrupt and self-serving finance minister, but when the emperor himself is murdered, they must flee the city and go into hiding, eventually realizing that the future of a civilized and united Britain is suddenly at stake. The two remain on the run as outcasts in hiding for several years, forming an alliance with a loyal band of underground resistance members. Through the efforts of the resistance, the ideals and order of the Roman Empire emerge triumphant. While there is more fighting in this volume than in the previous book (and even more in the third), there are also elements of comic relief via the emperor's court jester, who wears a tail, calls himself a hound, and sleeps curled up beside his masters. It is he who carries the hollow branch to which are affixed silver bells, which symbolizes the precarious position of Roman emperors stationed in Britain during that time.

Sutcliff employs some of the same themes in *The Silver Branch* that we have seen in *Simon* and *The Eagle of the Ninth,* demonstrating that public excellence is an extension of private virtues; that is, those who do not have a strong sense of right and wrong are doomed to fall, and those who do must carry that good faith into the future. Here, Roman peace is threatened both by the uncontrollable destructiveness of the Saxon barbarians and the dark-hearted individuals who threaten the stability of the Roman order. The pure-hearted young men who fight against them, like Justin and Flavius, are led by a fragile shaft of light contained in their hearts that they must follow to emerge triumphant.

The journey of Marcus Aquila's family continues in *The Lantern Bearers*. Critics applauded Sutcliff's efforts with this novel: she was awarded the Carnegie Medal for Children's Fiction in 1960. It was recognized as a leap forward for Sutcliff in terms of the more sophisticated young adult reader and demonstrated a use of Kiplingesque literary devices, including her successful efforts in establishing a continuity of characters from one volume of fiction to the next. For example, although Aquila, the protagonist of *The Lantern Bearers,* is left behind on the small island where he was born at the end of the novel, Sutcliff uses the symbol of a heavy signet ring, complete with a flawed emerald and the imprint of a dolphin, to carry forth his legacy. The ring first appears in *The Eagle of the Ninth* and reappears in *The Silver Branch, The Lantern Bearers, Frontier Wolf, Sword at Sunset, Dawn Wind, The Shield Ring,* and *Sword Song,* linking a series of books that were written over a period of thirty-five years. Sutcliff also uses this novel to introduce King Arthur into her Roman-Saxon series; he appears as Arto the Bear, a little boy glimpsed by Aquila as he lights a beacon while watching the last of the British legion sail from his island home.

In *The Lantern Bearers,* Aquila is a young legionnaire and descendant of Marcus Flavius Aquila who, during the return of British troops to Italy at the end of the fifth century, deserts the army to defend his native land. Saxon barbarians are invading, and Aquila cannot stop them from killing his father and kidnapping his sister. He too is eventually taken prisoner and suffers greatly knowing his sister has been taken by the Saxons. After many years he finds her living in a Saxon village, married to a Saxon, with whom she has borne a child. Although she ultimately aids Aquila in escaping his captors, she remains with the Saxons because her life is now among them. Aquila then joins a group of literal "lantern bearers" who fight to preserve the last traces of the Roman way of life under the rule of the Prince of Britain, Ambrosius. The Saxons are eventually overthrown and Ambrosius is crowned king, giving Aquila new hope for his people.

Thematically, the play of light and dark that reappears in many of Sutcliff's works seeps into every aspect of *The Lantern Bearers* as Aquila struggles against the darkness within himself and in the world around him. The lantern itself symbolizes the fall of the Roman Empire, a civilization, a way of life. The light is what is valued or treasured by her heroes and what they must fight to save and leave as a legacy for the generations to come; the dark is the coming destruction that threatens to eradicate that legacy. For Aquila an internal battle is also at play because he shuts out the light in his heart after his loyalties have been betrayed. Yet when the darkness is closing in around him as his beloved homeland is being destroyed, he is forever changed by a deep realization that the only defense against such darkness is the light men carry within them. Keeping this light intact is indeed the only way for men to feel compassion for others and to value what is dear, and if a man is left without the love of friends and family, public success is hollow at best. Sutcliff ties this into the fall of Rome as a whole, for without their civilization, the only common bond the men left share are their common ideals and the hope that they can rise above their own sense of vengeance and learn to live in peace with each other. As Aquila states at the end of the novel, "I wonder if they will remember us at all, those people on the other side of the darkness" (p. 279).

RITES OF PASSAGE: FROM BOY TO MAN

In between the books of her Roman trilogy, Sutcliff produced three volumes that focus on perhaps her most important and universal theme (not to mention one that most young readers can relate to): How does one find one's place in the world, and mature from a child to an adult? Although these themes are evident in much of Sutcliff's work, including the Roman trilogy, in *The Shield Ring* (1956), *Warrior Scarlet* (1958), and *Knight's Fee* (1960), Sutcliff employs several guises in guiding her protagonists toward adulthood, including the details of the physical landscape, a triumph over a physical or emotional handicap, and the blending of several cultures and peoples that eventually forms a new society.

The Shield Ring concerns itself with the legend of a group of Norsemen (Vikings) who defended themselves against King William the Conqueror's troops for thirty years before finally defeating them. Sutcliff studied place and local legend "not only as a scholar, but as an artist whose eye can select the details, which, combined with intensity of narration, bring alive the fells, lakes and rock ledges as the tale unfolds" (Meek, pp. 51–52). The landscape itself serves as a "shield ring," or stronghold, at the foot of the Cumberland Fells, which hides a secret valley inside a wild terrain that the Vikings are able to use as protection from their enemies. Against this dramatic background, Sutcliff tells us the story of Bjorn, a young man unsure of his strength and courage who wants to prove his bravery. The narrative is told from two points of view, that of Bjorn and that of Frytha, a Saxon girl who found safe haven in the valley after the Normans destroyed her home. They become fast friends in this time of violence and insecurity, which eventually leads to a more mature kind of love by the end of the tale.

During their thirty years of defiance, this tribe of people harvest, sing, and tell stories in order to keep the rich traditions of their ancestry intact, yet they are always on guard for a Norman attack. Although Bjorn is gradually finding his place in the tribe by honing his skill as a singer and a harpist, he longs to do something more for his people. When the opportunity arises for him to act as a scout to determine the size and location of the coming Norman army, he agrees, yet he is haunted by the possibility of capture and torture. His greatest fear is that if he is caught, he will succumb to his captors, reveal the path to the secret valley, and his people will be conquered. He puts this fear aside and sets out on his heroic journey. In making the transition from boy to man, he secures his place in the world.

Warrior Scarlet operates on some of the same principles, yet this particular hero is handicapped, left without the use of his right arm from birth. Sutcliff set up a challenge for herself by setting this novel in the Bronze Age, during the age of the heroic Golden People, in a time before written record. Critics agree that she succeeded, pointing to the details of cooking and other aspects of daily life in the various tribes she describes. Her hero, Drem, a favorite of the author and readers alike, is one of her most sympathetic and powerful characters. In order to secure his place in the tribe, when Drem reaches age fifteen he is expected to kill a wolf in a ritual battle in order to receive his "warrior scarlet," or medal of acceptance. Failure means banishment among the Neolithic people, who are the servants of the tribe. As a nine-year-old he realizes the near impossibility of this future task when he overhears his grandfather and mother expressing doubts about his abilities. Once he understands the enormity of the task, he begins working twice as hard as his peers to achieve this goal. Sutcliff does not fall into the trap of sentimentality however; she has Drem fail his test with the tribe and be sent to live among the "dark people." He is reborn when he eventually does kill a wolf, but this happens outside his tribe of origin. This success does not grant him the ultimate prize of running with his own pack, so instead he learns to live within the one he is given, providing the reader with a much richer and realistic life lesson. As Meek writes of Drem's observations, "He comes to realize that although his world had been 'a harsh one in which the pack turned on the weakest hound, in which little mercy was asked or given,' the real achievement is to face the fear, to carry the disability, to save one's life by risking it entirely" (p. 61).

In *Knight's Fee* the theme of overcoming great obstacles to become accepted as a man continues through the story of a Randal, a boy who is born into difficulty as the bastard of a Breton man-at-arms and a Saxon woman who abandons him at birth. Sutcliff again sets her story in Norman England, but now we are in the eleventh century, after the Norman Conquest. Randal is a "dog-boy" who cares for the castle hounds and lives among them in kennels while being brutalized by a cruel lord. In contrast to Drem or Marcus, Randal's disability is spiritual rather than physical given his abandonment as a baby. He has lived on the margins of society ever since, lying and stealing in order to survive; he must overcome his bitterness and anger in order to connect with others and become a man. The story focuses on this journey and on his friendship with Bevis, whom he ultimately must sacrifice after an arduous seven-year journey to knighthood. With this volume too it seems Sutcliff owes a great debt to Kipling in that the novel is nearly a sequel to Kipling's Norman stories centering on Sir Richard Dalyngridge. The critic Hilary Wright notes that it is "the same post-Conquest period, the same small Sussex manor, the same old Norman knight, close to his stern but kindly overlord, each with his glimmering gown of chain mail, nut-shaped helmet and notable sword" (p. 96).

THE ARTHURIAN LEGENDS

Sword at Sunset (1963) was Sutcliff's first foray into adult fiction, yet the book begins three days after her young adult novel *The Lantern Bearers* ends. The point of view shifts from Aquila in *Lantern Bearers* to King Arthur, yet Aquila remains a character in *Sword at Sunset*, a kind of continuity Sutcliff did not normally use. She also penned this novel in a first-person point of view, a method of narration Sutcliff had never attempted before. She is said to have been inspired to write about King Arthur and his famous quests from the books she was exposed to as a child, the prose of Sir Thomas Malory and the writer Trelawney Dayrell Reed, whom she discovered around the age of eighteen. Reid wrote the *Battle for Britain in the Fifth Century* and *The Rise of Wessex*, which dealt with the Dark Ages and the possibility of a historical Arthur, a subject that intrigued Sutcliff immensely. As she commented in an interview, "A legendary hero almost always has a basis in a real person, around whom bits of legend and bits of other peoples' stories gather and collect, rather like amber collecting little bits of paper. I was convinced there was a real man in the middle somewhere" (Thompson, p. 111).

The process of writing *Sword at Sunset* was like no other Sutcliff had experienced. In total, it took her three false starts and a switch from third person to first in her various drafts before she could fully engage the novel. After she started, the character possessed her at some level. She admitted to being quite obsessed during the writing of the novel, sometimes staying up until two or three in the morning working on it, then waking at six a.m. to pick up where she left off, often going back to reread passages she had no recollection of writing. After eighteen months at this pace, she finished the book, yet had trouble returning to a woman's perspective after inhabiting Arthur's skin so entirely. She reported that she had never been so absorbed in the writing of a book before or after.

Although the novel focuses on Artos the Bear's (Arthur's) personal development, Sutcliff juxtaposes it within the larger struggle to maintain a civilized Britain. Artos has essentially spent his life helping his uncle, King Ambrosius, fight off the steady tide of Saxon tribesman who have attacked Britain since the Roman army departed. The battles have been raging for nearly twenty years, and Britain is practically overwhelmed; recent victories and Ambrosius' crowning as king is only a delaying measure. The king and Artos fight on, hoping that the longer they hold out, the more of their culture will survive. *Sword at Sunset* is a vision of the legendary King Arthur as the man he might have been, and through his personal strife Sutcliff paints a poignant, bittersweet tale. The bonds and joy of comradeship and victory that fill Artos' early years with his cavalry are eroded away over time by betrayal, weariness, and the foreshadowing of inevitable defeat. However, Artos cannot let go of his dream of a Britain united against the invaders. Taking a chance, he and his remaining cavalry stake everything on one last, climactic battle at Badon Hill.

It is here that Sutcliff opens her story as King Artos lies wounded after the Saxons have been defeated. She then tells us his life story in flashback, bringing the reader back periodically to Badon to give us the smell of smoke in the aftermath of battle, the sound of passing troops. We see Artos, a young cavalry commander in his uncle's army, as he begins to form a group of soldiers to force a band of Saxons known as the Sea Wolves to the end of Britain and into the ocean. The three hundred soldiers he gathers become known as the Artos Companions (Knights of the Round Table), and they are sworn to serve until death or such time as Artos releases them from his service. Yet before he can officially form his cavalry, he is drugged and seduced by Ygerna, who, unknown to him, is his half-sister; she is taking revenge on their father for having abandoned her and her mother. By seducing Artos and later giving birth to his child Modred, she seals Artos' fate and achieves revenge. After Bedwyr (combining the role of Bedivere and Lancelot) enters the story and Artos marries Guenhumara (Guinevere) to gain much-needed troops, the key elements of the legend are all in place: the fight against the Saxons, Guenhumara's infidelity, and the sin of incest that leads to Artos' downfall.

Many of Sutcliff's earlier themes—light versus dark, the role of the outcast, the pilgrimage from boy to man—are present here, but the critic Barbara Talcroft also focuses on her use of three other elements in *Sword at Sunset:* the Goddess, the Sacrificial King, and the Maimed King. Talcroft sees the Goddess as a woman or a symbol of a woman who appears in Sutcliff's stories to legitimize her hero's ascent to power or kingship. For Artos, the goddess appears in three different ways: Ygerna, with whom he unwittingly commits incest; Guenhumara, whom he marries; and the Virgin Mary, in the form of the moon daisy worn by Artos and his companions as they go into battle. Artos then becomes the maimed king after he realizes he has committed incest; that shame leaves him impotent and leaves the child of this union, Modred, damaged and maimed as well. Despite his later marriage and daughter with Guenhumara, he cannot escape this curse—his daughter is sickly and dies, while Guenhumara commits adultery and eventually joins a nunnery, leaving Artos further separated from the goddess and his land. This leads to his final act as sacrificial king, as he dedicates himself to his people and his land, eventually dying for them. This theme can also be seen in *The Lantern Bearers,* when King Ambrosius first declares his allegiance to Britain, and later in *Sword at Sunset,* when he falls ill with cancer and chooses to die while hunting a stag.

Given its complex themes, beautiful writing, and masterful and creative retelling of King Arthur's story, *Sword at Sunset* remains one of the most celebrated historical novels about this mythical hero.

A NOD TO SIR THOMAS MALORY

Critics have written frequently of Sutcliff's Arthurian novels, noting that the four following *Sword at Sunset,* including *Tristan and Iseult* (1971), *The Light Beyond the Forest* (1979), *The Sword and the Circle* (1981), and *The Road to Camlann* (1981), follow in the tradition of Sir Thomas Malory. Malory's *Morte Darthur* (1485) itself is drawn from the writings of a thirteenth-century Cistercian monk. Many have deplored the various unsuccessful attempts at rewriting these legends, the hack jobs and poor imitations that pale in comparison to Sutcliff's retellings. Her novels maintain that "vital spark" that Malory himself brought to the page, and one cannot imagine a higher compliment for Sutcliff. While maintaining much of Malory's style and language, Sutcliff also manages to retell for children these sometimes tragic and violent stories in a way that does not cut out the tales' essential core.

Although some scholars believe that the story of Tristan and Iseult may have originated outside the original King Arthur legends, it is generally thought that their tragic love was the model for the ill-fated romance of Queen Guinevere and Sir Lancelot. In Sutcliff's version, the story is epic and tragic, and the link to King Arthur is the inclusion of Tristan's uncle, King Marc of Cornwall, who eventually becomes one of King Arthur's enemies. Sutcliff's *Tristan and Iseult* was nominated for a Carnegie Medal in 1972, and critics applauded Sutcliff for choosing a legend so intertwined with British culture and for once again making the epic form believable and real. Tristan is sixteen when he leaves home to seek adventure, traveling to his mother's native land of Cornwall, where he meets his uncle, King Marc, with whom he bonds intensely. The king charges him with the task of going out into the world to find him a queen. In Ireland, Tristan manages to slay a dragon and win enough favor to be given the beautiful princess Iseult in return. However, before he can present his uncle with a queen, the two fall desperately in love, although Iseult must still marry the king. Unable to deny themselves one another, their affair is discovered by King Marc, and he banishes Tristan from the country. Although Tristan eventually finds another woman to marry (also named Iseult), his feelings for her can never match those of his first love. The two lovers are reunited only in death, when King Marc atones for his banishment of Tristan by having the queen and his nephew buried together.

In *The Sword and the Circle,* Sutcliff takes us back to the boyhood of the great King Arthur and his cohorts, setting the stage for the rest of her official Arthurian trilogy, *The Light Beyond the Forest* and *The Road to Camlaan.* (She actually weaves the story of Tristan and Iseult into a chapter in *The Sword and Circle,* presenting it here as a story being told to the knights and Queen Guinevere by a traveling harpist, thus foreshadowing her tragic affair with Lancelot.) The novel opens with the traditional Arthurian myth, wherein the young knight pulls the sword Excalibur from the stone, and in accessing its powers, becomes king and wins the hand of Guinevere. Critics praised her retelling of the Arthur story here, noting that she uses a balanced measure of complex, Homerian language tempered with a simplicity that makes it accessible to children. This accessibility is perhaps Sutcliff's finest accomplishment in her treatment of these great legends: as Ann Evan writes, "The tension is never allowed to slacken, and yet there is time to laugh at a pompous ass of a knight being unhorsed backwards, time to ponder the sad truth that even in the Dark Ages a man could be torn apart because he loved his best friend's wife" (*Times Literary Supplement,* March 27, 1981).

In *The Light Beyond the Forest,* Sutcliff whittles down the some of the medieval romance of the tale and focuses on four core characters, Sir Lancelot, Sir Galahad, Sir Percival, and Sir Bors, and their quest for the Holy Grail. This does not mean she abandons all the trappings of the era; the book is rife with angels, demons, magic forests, witchcraft, and the like. It should be noted that the quest for the Holy Grail (a mythical cup thought to be used by Christ and his disciples at the Last Supper, and later to catch a few drops of Christ's blood at the crucifixion) is one laced with traditional Roman Catholic theology, and with it, an overlay of patriarchy. The knights' reliance on priests and monks and their perceived direct contact with God might say more about Catholic influence in the thirteenth century than they do about the author's personal religious beliefs. Much of the quest also has to do with sexual transgressions, for a knight must put all his desires aside and focus solely on this holy quest, and only the purest man will succeed. Sutcliff follows Malory's lead in writing about this aspect of the tale in that nearly all the female characters act as distractions and temptresses who seek to keep the knights from achieving their goals.

She shifts among all four knights throughout the novel but focuses in particular on Sir Lancelot because he has committed perhaps the greatest sin against his king, that of having an affair with Queen Guenevere. After overcoming many obstacles, Sir Lancelot finally reaches the castle where the Grail is kept, but because he is unable to give up his love for the queen, he is paralyzed upon entry. He is forced to watch as the other three knights are permitted to enter and touch the Grail, even drink from it. In the end, it is Sir Galahad the Pure who becomes king of the mythical land where the Grail resides, but only after overcoming many tests of his character, including battles with other knights and ogres who represent different kinds of sin.

In the final and perhaps most masterful of the trilogy, *The Road to Camlann*, we follow King Arthur on his last adventures up until his death. It is a story of intrigue and cruelty, describing the manifestation of Arthur's early sins and his ultimate confrontation with Mordred, the son he fathered through his incestuous relationship with Ygerna. Modred has infiltrated the Knights of the Round Table and undermines the men's trust and loyalty toward one another, ultimately destroying the values on which the allegiance is based. It is a profoundly sad, yet inevitable end to the glory of King Arthur and his court. With that demise, Sutcliff focuses the novel on the tragic love between Sir Lancelot and Queen Guinevere, bringing to life their passion and the restrained and courtly ways in which it must continue to be expressed. The story culminates with Arthur and Modred's final battle in Dover, where the hatred that has fueled Modred's life culminates in his final act against his father, as he strikes the blow that causes his death.

CONCLUSION

In the decade that followed the publication of *The Road to Camlann* in 1981, Sutcliff published a dozen or so more books, a handful of plays, and her memoir, *Blue Remembered Hills*. She left behind her knights for a time to write picture books as well, while also tackling an interpretation of the *Iliad* for children. *Black Ships Before Troy* (1993) and *The Wanderings of Odysseus* (1995) render these complex adventures simply and elegantly, touching on the main plot points of the Cyclops, the Island of the Dead, and Circe, while maintaining the continuity of the narrative. She revisited adult literature with *Blood and Sand* (1987) and collaborated on a stage version of *The Eagle of the Ninth* with Mary Rensten.

Sutcliff is said to have written every day of her life, and she was writing the day she died in 1992. Several manuscripts were finished at that time, and one, *The Sword Song*, was published posthumously in 1997. In it, she returns to the Norse world that she first visited in *The Shield Ring*.

Sword Song's protagonist, Bjarni, is banished for five years from Rafnglas, a Viking settlement in the Lake Country of present-day England. He is ordered to leave his home after flying into a rage and killing a man who had kicked his dog. Bjarni becomes a mercenary swordsman, attaching himself to various historical Viking leaders as they raid and fight throughout the Hebrides, Orkney Islands, and northern Scotland. Shipwrecked in Wales, he is rescued by and in turn rescues the healer Angharad, whom he eventually marries and brings back to his home country. Though critics consider the book rougher and slightly more episodic than her earlier works, they nevertheless agree it is "vintage Sutcliff" and yet another stirring tale we are lucky to count among her varied works.

Sutcliff has left us with over fifty books, spanning the Bronze Age to the thirteenth century, and they remain timeless classics for both children and adults. As she is often quoted as saying, "My books are for children of all ages, from nine to ninety," and indeed, it seems as though Sutcliff never lost her own sense of childlike wonder and with it, created a legendary catalog of writing for all of us to enjoy.

Selected Bibliography

WORKS OF ROSEMARY SUTCLIFF

NOVELS FOR CHILDREN
The Chronicles of Robin Hood. London: Oxford University Press, 1950.
The Queen Elizabeth Story. London: Oxford University Press, 1950.
The Armourer's House. London: Oxford University Press, 1951.
Brother Dusty-Feet. London: Oxford University Press, 1952.
Simon. London: Oxford University Press, 1953.

The Eagle of the Ninth. London: Oxford University Press, 1954.

The Outcast. London: Oxford University Press, 1955.

The Shield Ring. London: Oxford University Press, 1956.

The Silver Branch. London: Oxford University Press, 1957.

Warrior Scarlet. London: Oxford University Press, 1958.

The Bridge-Builders. Oxford: Blackwell, 1959.

The Lantern Bearers. London: Oxford University Press, 1959.

Knight's Fee. London: Oxford University Press, 1960.

Beowulf. London: Bodley Head, 1961.

Dawn Wind. London: Oxford University Press, 1961.

The Hound of Ulster. London: Bodley Head, 1963.

The Mark of the Horse Lord. London: Oxford University Press, 1965.

The Chief's Daughter. London: Hamish Hamilton, 1967.

The High Deeds of Finn McCool. London: Bodley Head, 1967.

A Circlet of Oak Leaves. London: Hamish Hamilton, 1968.

The Witch's Brat. London: Bodley Head, 1970.

Tristan and Iseult. London: Bodley Head, 1971.

The Truce of the Games. London: Hamish Hamilton, 1971.

The Capricorn Bracelet. London: Oxford University Press, 1973.

The Changeling. London: Hamish Hamilton, 1974.

We Lived in Drumfyvie. With Margaret Lyford-Pike. Glasgow and London: Blackie, 1975.

Blood Feud. London: Oxford University Press, 1976.

Shifting Sands. London: Hamish Hamilton, 1977.

Sun Horse, Moon Horse. London: Bodley Head, 1977.

Song for a Dark Queen. London: Pelham, 1978.

The Light Beyond the Forest. London: Bodley Head, 1979.

Frontier Wolf. London: Oxford University Press, 1980.

The Sword and the Circle. London: Bodley Head, 1981.

The Road to Camlann. London: Bodley Head, 1981.

Eagle's Egg. London: Hamish Hamilton, 1981.

Bonnie Dundee. London: Bodley Head, 1983.

Flame-Coloured Taffeta. Oxford: Oxford University Press, 1986.

The Roundabout Horse. London: Hamish Hamiltion, 1986.

A Little Dog Like You. London: Orchard, 1987.

Little Hound Found. London: Hamish Hamilton, 1989.

The Shining Company. London: Bodley Head, 1990.

Black Ships Before Troy: The Story of The Iliad. London: Frances Lincoln, 1993.

Chess-Dream in a Garden. Cambridge, Mass.: Candlewick Publishers, 1993.

The Minstrel and the Dragon Pup. Cambridge, Mass.: Candlewick Publishers, 1993.

The Wanderings of Odysseus. London: Frances Lincoln, 1995.

Sword Song. London: Bodley Head, 1997.

Novels for Adults

Lady in Waiting. London: Hodder & Stoughton, 1956.

The Rider of the White Horse. London: Hodder & Stoughton, 1959.

Sword at Sunset. London: Putnam, 1963.

The Flowers of Adonis. London: Hodder & Stoughton, 1969.

Blood and Sand. London: Hodder & Stoughton, 1987.

Nonfiction

Houses and History. London: Batsford, 1960.

Rudyard Kipling. London: Bodley Head, 1960.

Heroes and History. London: Batsford, 1965.

A Saxon Settler. London: Oxford University Press, 1965.

Blue Remembered Hills: A Recollection. London: Bodley Head, 1983; New York: Farrar, Straus & Giroux, 1983.

PLAYS AND SCREENPLAYS

The New Laird. Radio play. Broadcast May 7, 1966.

Ghost Story. Screenplay with Stephen Weeks and Philip Norman, 1975.

Mary Bedell. Stage play. Produced London, 1986.

The Eagle of the Ninth. Stage play with Mary Rensten.

CRITICAL AND BIOGRAPHICAL STUDIES

Davis, Lavinia R. "In Ancient Britain." *New York Times Book Review,* January 9, 1955, p. BR24.

Eccleshare, Julia. "Obituary, Rosemary Sutcliff." *Independent,* July 27, 1992.

Evan, Ann. "The Real Thing." *Times Literary Supplement,* March 27, 1981, p. 341.

Garside-Neville, Sandra. "Rosemary Sutcliff: An Appreciation." Historical Novel Society. Available online (http://www.historicalnovelsociety.org/solander%20files/rosemary_sutcliff.htm).

Marder, Joan V. "The Historical Novels of Rosemary Sutcliff." In *Good Writers for Young Readers: Critical Essays.* Edited by Dennis Butts. St. Albans, U.K.: Hart-Davis Educational, 1977. Pp. 138–141.

Meek, Margaret. *Rosemary Sutcliff.* London: Bodley Head, 1962.

Payne, Robert. "Britain's Warrior King." *New York Times,* May 26, 1963, p. 300.

Talcroft, Barbara L. *Death of the Corn King: King and Goddess in Rosemary Sutcliff's Historical Fiction for Young Adults.* Metuchen, N.J., and London: Scarecrow Press, 1995.

Townsend, John Rowe. "Rosemary Sutcliff." In *A Sense of Story: Essays on Contemporary Writers for Children.* London: Longman, 1971. Pp. 193–199.

Wright, Hilary. "Shadows on the Downs: Some Influences of Rudyard Kipling on Rosemary Sutcliff." *Children's Literature in Education* 12, no. 2:90–102 (summer 1981).

INTERVIEW

Thompson, R. H. "Interview with Rosemary Sutcliff." *Avalon to Camelot* 2, no. 3:11–14 (1987). Available online (http://www.lib.rochester.edu/camelot/intrvws/sutcliff.htm).

COLLECTIONS

Rosemary Sutcliff Papers, de Grummond Collection, McCain Library and Archives, USM Libraries, The University of Southern Mississippi, 1966. The collection contains a manuscript and two typescripts for the radio play *The New Laird*. The program was taped April 4, 1966, and broadcast from Edinburgh on May 17, 1966 as part of the Stories from Scottish History series. The collection also includes a small red composition book, full of research notes which Sutcliff eventually used to write *The Red Dragon, The Lantern Bearer,* and *The Amber Dolphin.*

CATHARINE TROTTER

(1679—1749)

Sayanti Ganguly Puckett

CATHARINE TROTTER WAS a successful playwright during the Restoration period who, although neglected in the nineteenth century and for most of the twentieth, has received substantial critical attention from modern feminist scholars. In addition to producing plays and a novella, Trotter stands out among her contemporary women writers as the author of philosophical works that are remarkable in their firm understanding of complex theological issues. Trotter had five plays performed on the stages of London between 1695 and 1706. Eminent men of her time such as William Congreve, William Wycherly, Thomas Burnet, and John Locke were her correspondents. A staunch feminist, Trotter's works did much to argue for a better position for women in Restoration society, which granted women very few rights. The female characters in Trotter's plays are strong, intelligent, courageous, and high principled, illustrating Trotter's concern with raising women's status. She insisted in all her writings that women were not mere emotional creatures but were also capable of great rational thought, selfless acts of courage, and the capacity to provide unwavering friendship and support to each other. It is through her work that we are better able to understand the position of women in general, and women writers in particular, who lived and worked during the Restoration era.

Trotter found mention in several contemporary works that dealt with the lives of writers and poets. She earned an entry in Gerard Langbaine and Charles Gildon's *The Lives and Characters of the English Dramatick Poets*, published in 1699, and this entry emphasizes her talent, her chastity, her beauty, and her wit. Thomas Whincorp included her in his *List of All the Dramatic Authors* and praised her for her inclination toward philosophical matters. She is also mentioned favorably in *A Comparison Between the Two Stages* (1702), where she is praised for being the author of *The Fatal Friendship*. In spite of such positive attention, however, Trotter, not surprisingly for a woman playwright during the Restoration, received criticism too. Along with fellow women playwrights Delariviere Manley and Mary Pix, Trotter was parodied in a 1697 play titled *The Female Wits; or, The Triumvirate of Poets at Rehearsal*. In her works *The New Atlantis* (1709), *Memoirs of Europe* (1710), and *The Adventures of Rivella* (1714), Delariviere Manley, Trotter's erstwhile friend and collaborator, accused Trotter of prudery and hypocrisy.

BIOGRAPHY

Most of what we know of Trotter's life comes from Thomas Birch's *The Works of Mrs. Catharine Cockburn, Theological, Moral, Dramatic, and Poetical*, which was published posthumously in 1751. Birch wrote that Trotter had commenced helping him in putting this edition together, but her death prevented her from becoming its editor (Clark, p. 36). This volume included biographical information as well as Trotter's correspondence.

Catharine Trotter was born in London, probably in 1674, to Captain David Trotter and his wife, Sarah, who were both Scottish. There is some dispute about the year of Trotter's birth. The headstone on Trotter's grave points to the year 1679 as that of her birth because the inscription describes her as "in the 70 year of her age" on May 11, 1749 (Kelley, p. 1). But further research has also turned up a baptism entry for "Katherine Trotters, daughter of David Trotters, gentleman, and his wife, Sarah" on August 29, 1674 in the Register of St. Andrew, Holborn (Kelley, p. 1). Charles II sent Captain Trotter, a captain in the navy, to Tangiers, but Captain Trotter died of the plague in Scandaroon (Iskenderun, Turkey) in 1684. The purser of the ship absconded with a considerable portion of Captain Trotter's property. Additionally, the goldsmith who was in possession of a substantial share of Captain Trotter's finances went bankrupt, leaving the Trotter family destitute. On her mother's side, Trotter was related to Lord Bellenden and the earls of Perth and Lauderdale. Although she was related to aristocracy, the Trotter family was left impoverished by Captain Trotter's death, and there is nothing to indicate that the Trotters received much financial aid from their wealthy kinsmen. Sarah Trotter and her two daughters became largely dependent on a pension paid by the crown, and these funds stopped after Charles II's death and the succession to the throne of James II in 1685. Years later, Sarah Trotter petitioned Queen Anne about the pension that had been discontinued during James II's reign. Queen Anne reinstated the pension, but its payment remained sporadic (Kelley, p. 4).

Trotter was largely self-taught, although she had "some assistance in the study of the Latin grammar and Logic" (Birch, p. 5). Additionally, she "gave very early marks of her genius, and was not past her childhood when she surprised a company of her relations and friends with extempory verses on an incident which had fallen under her observation in the street" (Birch, p. 5). At the age of twenty-two, Trotter spent some time in Kent at the home of her patron, Lady Sarah Piers. She then visited her sister and brother-in-law, Dr. Inglis, in Salisbury, Wiltshire. It was at Wiltshire that she became friends with Bishop Burnet, his wife, and Bishop Burnet's relative, George Burnet. Upon leaving Salisbury, Trotter went to Ockham Mills in Surrey, where she became a companion to a Mrs. de Vere. Trotter's sojourn at Ockham Mills was significant in two ways. It was here that she renounced her Catholic faith and joined the Church of England, and it was here that she was courted by a clergyman named Mr. Fenn, whom Trotter rejected in favor of her future husband, Patrick Cockburn. Trotter did not seem to have been in a hurry to get married. In 1705 she had written thus to George Burnet regarding marriage: "As I had never had thought toward it but for one, and there are many obstacles against that, I believe I shall end my days as I am. Indeed, I have always been very fearful of putting my happiness entirely in the power of anyone" (Clark, p. 42). Yet in 1708 Trotter, aged twenty-nine, married the Reverend Patrick Cockburn and moved to Nayland, Suffolk, where he was a curate. In 1713 Patrick Cockburn was given the curacy of St. Dunstan's in the West, but he lost this position by his refusal to take the oath of abjuration when George I came to the throne.

Upon losing his position, Cockburn became a Latin teacher at a school in Chancery Lane, but the family, which included four young children, lived under difficult financial circumstances for the next thirteen years, and Trotter produced no literary works during this difficult period. In an unsent letter to Alexander Pope, Trotter wrote, "Being married in 1708, I bid adieu to the muses and so wholly gave myself up to the cares of a family, and the education of my children, that I scarce knew whether there was any such thing as books, plays, or poems stirring in Great Britain" (Morgan, p. 29). In 1726, however, Cockburn's father, the Scottish cleric John Cockburn, and the Lord Chancellor Peter King, persuaded him to take the oath, and Cockburn became minister at the Episcopal St. Paul's Chapel in Aberdeen, Scotland. His wife returned to writing, producing *A Letter to Dr. Holdsworth, Occasioned by his Sermon Preached before the University of Oxford* and *A Defence of Mr. Locke's Essay of Human Understanding*. Explaining her return to literary activity, she wrote, "My young family was grown up to have less need of my assistance; and beginning to have some taste of polite literature, my inclination revived with my leisure" (Birch, vol. 1, p. xi). In 1737 the Cockburns moved to Long Horsley in Northumberland and remained there till Patrick Cockburn's death in January 1749. Trotter, who suffered from asthma and fading eyesight, died on 11 May 1749, aged seventy, and was survived by three children. She was buried in the churchyard at Long Horsley beside her husband and daughter, Grissel, who had died in 1742.

CATHARINE TROTTER

EARLY SUCCESSES

One of Trotter's earliest poems was written in 1693 to Bevil Higgons (later Lord Lansdowne) upon his recovery from smallpox. Higgons, who was "greatly esteemed at that time for his wit and poetical talents" had written the prologue to William Congreve's *The Old Batchelor* (Morgan, p. 24), and Edmund Gosse infers that it was her acquaintance with Higgons that later led to introductions to Congreve as well as John Dryden. Trotter continued her acquaintance with Congreve, who was later to give her sage advice on her play *The Revolution of Sweden*. The year 1693 also saw the publication of *The Adventures of a Young Lady,* which she anonymously contributed to a collection published by Samuel Briscoe titled *Letters of Love and Gallantry and Several Other Subjects, All Written By Ladies.* A panegyric to Lord Marlborough titled "On his Grace the Duke of Marlborough's Return from his Expedition into Germany, after the battle of Blenheim" was published in 1704. This was followed in 1706 by "On his Grace the Duke of Marlborough, after his victory at Ramellies."

THE ADVENTURES OF A YOUNG LADY

Trotter's first successful work was a novella, *The Adventures of a Young Lady,* also known as *Olinda's Adventures*. After its anonymous publication in 1693, editions were published in 1718 and 1724 under Trotter's name. In *The Works of Mrs. Catharine Cockburn,* Birch describes the heroine Olinda thus: "Olinda, like Mrs. Trotter, is a wit and something of a beauty in adolescence, a fatherless child living with a prudent mother who is anxious to marry her off advantageously, and a solicitor of favors from noble or wealthy connections" (Clark, p. 39). This work is epistolary in nature and the letters are written by Olinda mainly to Cleander, a platonic friend. *Olinda's Adventures* recounts Olinda's encounters with various suitors, none of whom she marries at the end of the novella.

The heroine, albeit young, is mature and able to carry herself with dignity as she handles different situations with different suitors. Her first lover is a tradesman named Berontus, who receives Olinda's mother's permission to court her daughter even though Olinda does not have any feelings for him. Berontus, however, loses his fortune and the match is broken up; the tradesman finally marries an heiress for her fortune. The next suitor is an old Dutchman, and the next a young army man; Olinda takes revenge on him after he attempts to slander her. Finally, Olinda meets and falls in love with Cloridon, her deceased father's friend and a powerful, wealthy, but married man. When Cloridon is sent to Flanders, Olinda finds another suitor, Antonio, who tries to convince Olinda that Cloridon has been unfaithful to her. The heroine's visits to Bath and the theater bring another suitor, Orontes, who proposes marriage with Olinda's mother's permission. The wedding is only averted because Cloridon provides Olinda with an allowance that allows her to live an independent life as a single woman. Olinda's last letter is addressed to Cloridon, and she asks him to desist from pursuing her because he is a married man. Cloridon's wife dies at the end of the novella, however, leaving him free to claim Olinda for himself.

Although only thirteen, Olinda is not an innocent, unable to take care of herself. She writes her letters with a wry and sarcastic sense of humor, often making fun of her more worldly suitors. Even though young and not very wealthy, she does not allow men to manipulate her into sexual relationships or marriage. She asserts self-control and reason when she feels that her emotions may tempt her into a disadvantageous position with Cloridon. Far from being a passive victim, Olinda breaks the stereotype by being a strong and self-sufficient young woman who successfully manipulates several difficult situations and turns them to her benefit. Although the novella moves from one suitor to the next, it is not simply a boring sequence of courtships. Olinda's suitors are very different from one another and come from different classes and backgrounds, providing a variety of characters that makes for an entertaining read.

The male characters in *Olinda's Adventures* are not presented in a flattering light. The Dutch suitor, for example, is far older than Olinda and is a lascivious man who maintains another mistress. Antonio is sly and duplicitous, and even Cloridon, who manages to capture Olinda's heart, is not altogether attractive in his efforts to control and seduce her. On the whole, the men are vain, unappealing lovers, and Olinda's sharp insight into their real motives allows her to paint them as comic caricatures, far removed from the witty and alluring rakes of Restoration comedy. As in Trotter's plays, marriage is not depicted in *Olinda's Adventures* as a profitable undertaking for women. The married Cloridon proves to be a seducer who is unfaithful to his wife. In a letter to her niece, Anne Hepburn, Trotter warned her against allowing "humour or passion [to] sway [her] in so important an affair" as marriage, advising that "rational motives will secure the most lasting happiness." Trotter leaves Olinda a single woman at the end of the novella, indicating her awareness of and dissatisfaction with the inequality written into the marriage laws of her time (Kelley, p. 64). *Olinda's Adventures* presents an attractive, mature young girl whose self-reliance, morality, and rationality allows her to fruitfully negotiate the many sexual and moral pitfalls that are placed in her way to find an ending that permits her to remain her own mistress on her own terms.

AGNES DE CASTRO

Catharine Trotter is now best known for her plays, specifically her tragedies, of which *Agnes De Castro* was the first. Trotter's four tragedies and one comedy mirror some of the issues that she was concerned with in *Olinda's Adventures*. As with the novella, the plays explore the need to use reasoned judgments to govern human behavior. Additionally, Trotter presents strong, chaste, and rational women who form strong attachments to each other. The women in the plays, much like Olinda, face complex moral and ethical dilemmas that they often negotiate by relying on their morality and reason.

Agnes de Castro was performed at the Theatre Royal in Drury Lane in December 1695. It was based on a novel of the same name that Aphra Behn had written, probably in 1688. Behn's work, in its turn, had been a translation of the French *Agnes de Castro, nouvelle portugaise* by Jean-Baptiste de Brilhac. Trotter's play, which was considerably different from Behn's translation, was dedicated to the Earl of Dorset, who was the lord chamberlain, and Delariviere Manley wrote a poem celebrating its publication. It featured a prologue written by no less a personage than the noted playwright William Wycherley, which requested the audience to refrain from mocking and criticizing the play's authoress.

The play begins with the villainess Elvira, the Prince of Portugal's former mistress before his marriage, expressing her jealousy of the Princess Constantia. Alvaro, Elvira's brother and a favorite of the king, is in love with Agnes. From a letter shown to her by a lady-in-waiting, Elvira further learns that the prince is also in love with Agnes, and it is from the prince's secret passion for Agnes that the tragedy rises. The scene then shifts to the Princess Constantia, who laments her husband's lack of affection for her and guesses that he might be in love with someone else. The lady-in-waiting, Bianca, shows her the prince's love poems addressed to Agnes, but the evidence of a rival resigns the princess to her fate and she expresses no anger toward Agnes. When Agnes is shown the letter, she is astonished by it, having had no prior knowledge of the prince's feelings for her. Agnes, desiring only "a Quiet, though Poor, freedom," refuses to marry Alvaro, who petitions to the king to further advance his suit with Agnes (Kelley, p. 248). When Agnes refuses the king's orders to marry his favorite, the king gives Alvaro permission to marry Agnes without her consent and by force. He sends the prince away to further facilitate Alvaro's plans. Frustrated in her initial failure to cause a rift between Agnes and Constantia, Elvira writes another letter, supposedly from Agnes, in which she assents to a secret rendezvous with the prince. The second letter temporarily achieves its purpose by creating tension between Constantia and Agnes, and Constantia retires, asking to be left alone. Constantia soon restores her trust in Agnes, however, and Elvira's second attempt too fails.

Elvira finally plans to kill Agnes by her own hand but mistakenly stabs Constantia, whom she believes is Agnes. Enraged at her mistake, Elvira stabs herself in the arm. Agnes comes upon the scene and hears Elvira confessing that she had been the writer of the letter that had caused Constantia to believe that Agnes had been false to her friend. Finding the dying Constantia, Agnes picks up the dagger to kill herself but faints instead. After she is found holding the dagger, she is proved guilty of murdering Constantia and sentenced to be executed. Alvaro, still in love with Agnes, hires kidnappers to bring Agnes to him, but the kidnappers accidentally meet with the returning prince, who brings Agnes back to the royal court.

Maddened by her crime, Elvira stabs the lady-in-waiting, Bianca, who reveals all of Elvira's crimes. Agnes decides to leave the court, but the prince declares his love for her and persuades her to stay. She hesitantly agrees to stay but names her conditions: she will stay only if he will desist from courting her and also prevent Alvaro from making any more advances to her. Alvaro, who had been hiding in the room and had overheard the conversation between Agnes and the prince, now steps out and attempts to kill the prince but accidentally stabs Agnes instead. The prince kills Alvaro and attempts to kill himself but is prevented from doing so by the warder Lorenzo. The play ends with the king reminding his grieving son that he must consider his duties to his country over his personal loss.

Agnes de Castro concludes with an epilogue, which in the first stage production was spoken by the well-known actress Mrs. Verbruggen, who wore breeches for the occasion. She requested the audience to applaud the play in the hope that the favorable response would prompt the authoress to reveal her identity. Indeed, *Agnes de Castro* was favorably received.

The play is remarkable for the nobility for its two main female characters. Although Elvira tries every trick she can think of to cause a division between Agnes and Constantia, the bond of feminine friendship between them is never in any serious danger. Agnes and Constantia remain women of incontrovertible virtue who meet their tragic ends because they are envied and desired by others far less honorable than they. Elvira herself is significant because she is the only female villain in all of Trotter's works. The play highlights the idea that one's life is often controlled by those who share it, and that an untimely and undeserved end may be met through no fault of one's own. As in *Olinda's Adventures*, marriage is not portrayed in a favorable light. The prince, a married man, falls in love with Agnes, and Agnes herself views marriage as a form of bondage from which she would rather remain free. *Agnes de Castro* is interesting in the complex emotions that it presents. Often the characters suffer from conflicting feelings, which gives them depth. At one point, Alvaro, for example, ruminates about the love he feels for Agnes and his hatred of her for having consistently refused his suit. Constantia too doubts Agnes briefly before renewing her faith in Agnes' character and their friendship. *Agnes de Castro* is a lively play with some action and swordplay on stage. Additionally, the play is neat and tight in its construction and moves at a fast pace, which makes it well suited for production on stage.

THE FATAL FRIENDSHIP

In April or May 1698 Thomas Betterton's company produced Trotter's second tragedy, *The Fatal Friendship,* at Lincoln's Inn Fields. The play is dedicated to Princess Anne of Denmark, later Queen Anne of England. Trotter maintained that her intention in this play was "to discourage Vice, and recommend a firm unshaken Virtue" (Kelley, p. 91). *The Fatal Friendship* was prefaced by four poems that highly praised it. Bevil Higgons, who praised Trotter for her morality, her talent, and her delicacy, wrote the first poem. P. Harmon, who compared Trotter to Congreve and George Granville, also applauded the morality of her second tragedy. Trotter's patron Lady Sarah Piers penned the third poem and, like Higgons and Harmon, praised Trotter for putting virtuous characters on stage. The final poem, anonymous though clearly written by a man, praised Trotter for the strength of her female characters.

The Fatal Friendship is set in France. The story revolves around Gramont and Felicia, who are secretly married and have a baby son. Felicia's brother Bellgard wishes her to marry the elderly, wealthy, oppressive Count Roquelaure, Gramont's father. Bellgard is also attempting to arrange a match between Gramont and the rich widow Lamira. Gramont, who had been serving as a soldier, is imprisoned for having killed his general's son but is set free by his friend Castalio, who is then imprisoned. Gramont needs money to ransom his friend, but Roquelaure only promises to give him money if he marries Lamira. Gramont further hears that pirates have kidnapped his baby son, and in his desperate need for money he commits bigamy by secretly marrying Lamira but refuses to consummate the marriage. Lamira understands on their wedding night that her husband is in love with someone else, but she pays the ransom to free Castalio who, unknown to Gramont, is in love with Lamira.

Lamira realizes that Gramont loves Felicia, but she does not realize that they are married. In a meeting with Felicia, she tells Felicia of her marriage with Gramont and falsely tells Felicia that Gramont has consummated the marriage. Lamira's disclosure prompts Felicia to tell Bellgard of her marriage to Gramont. Felicia and Gramont manage a private meeting in which the misunderstanding between them is cleared up and Felicia forgives Gramont. In the meanwhile, Lamira offers Felicia money to give up her prior claims on Gramont, but Felicia refuses this offer. Gramont confesses his marriage to Castalio and begs Castalio to kill him, which he refuses to do. At this point, Bellgard enters and seeks a duel with Gramont in order to avenge his family's honor. In the duel, Gramont accidentally stabs and kills Castalio and then kills himself. As he is dying, he receives news from a messenger that Roquelaure has relented and has agreed to care for Felicia and their baby. Lamira, who acknowledges Felicia's love for Gramont, takes refuge in a convent.

Of Trotter's five plays, *The Fatal Friendship* was the only one that Thomas Birch included in *The Works of Mrs. Catharine Cockburn, Theological, Moral, Dramatic, and Poetical.* Birch commented, "This tragedy met with great applause, and is still thought the most perfect of her dramatic performances" (Clark, p. 80). Charles Gildon agreed, admitting in his *Lives and Characters,* "I need say nothing of this play, the town has prevented my approbation; ... I can only add that I think it *deserv'd* the Applause it met with, which every Play that has the Advantage of being Clapt cannot get from the severer and abler judges" (Clark, p. 80). But Trotter met with criticism too. James Beattie commented that Trotter was "at eighteen a greater adept in love matters than unmarried women of her age ought to be" (Kelley 2002, p. 29). She also had later detractors such as Jane Williams, who commented in her *Literary Women of England* (1861):

The tragedy thus applauded does not contain a single line of real poetry, and does contain certain indecorous allusions, which would not be tolerated either on the stage or elsewhere in modern times.... his tragedy, having been deemed by contemporary critics the best of Catharine Trotter's dramatic compositions, leaves the reader little cause to join in Dr. Birch's regret that want of space enforced the omission of the other four plays from his edition of her works

(Williams, pp. 183–184).

The Fatal Friendship is largely a domestic tragedy involving private individuals. Its tragedy rises more out of the circumstances in which the characters find themselves rather than any inherent flaws in their natures. Its theme of forced marriages and the troubles that such marriages caused was a common one during the Restoration, having been featured in many plays of the period. The play's focus on the attainment of money is another prominent feature of Restoration plays. William Congreve's play *The Way of the World,* which opened two years later, for example, revolved around a plot to attain money. In *The Fatal Friendship,* Gramont, having stabbed himself, laments,

Oh, what a wretch was I, that could not wait
Heaven's time, the providence that never fails
those who dare trust it. Durst I have been honest,
One day had changed the scene, and made me happy.

(act 5, scene 1, in Morgan, p. 206)

With Gramont's death, which could have been avoided, Trotter suggests that humans must desist from taking their lives into their own hands and leave the ordering of their lives to fate.

The play remains suspenseful to the end because most of the characters have secrets that they cannot share with others, causing them to speak in a restrained fashion and leaving their fates hanging without coming to a resolution until the end of the play. Felicia and Lamira are less active than the women in Trotter's other works because *The Fatal Friendship* largely focuses on the codes of behavior that govern the way men act. It is noticeable, however, that even though men remain the focus of this play, they, especially Gramont, do not always act in a reasonable and responsible manner. In keeping with the male characters in some of her other plays, Trotter depicts Gramont as a man who is given to emotions and hasty actions rather than reasoned judgments. The other men in the play are unappealing as well. Roquelaure is tyrannical, the General is dishonest, and Bellgard is blind to his sister's wishes and a hypocritical schemer. Trotter thus highlights the helpless situation of women such as Felicia, whose brothers and fathers attempt to control their lives, and points out that women are bound to suffer in a world where they are largely dependent on and controlled by men who try to arrange their lives arbitrarily without considering their wishes.

THE UNHAPPY PENITENT

First performed at Drury Lane in February 1701, *The Unhappy Penitent* was dedicated to Charles Montague, Lord Halifax, who was a great patron of the theater. It featured a poem comparing Trotter to Katherine Phillips (poetic name: Orinda) as well as Aphra Behn (Astrea) composed by Lady Sarah Piers, and in her dedication Trotter examines and discusses some of the leading poets of her time including John Dryden, Thomas Otway, and Nathaniel Lee. Trotter's dedication is thus an astute piece of criticism in which she perceptively points out the strengths of other playwrights writing for the stage during her time. In publicly giving voice to her opinions, Trotter was signaling her desire to be taken as an equal with poets such as Dryden, Otway, and Lee. Furthermore, she cites various sources such as the poet and critic Nicolas Boileau to illustrate the depth and variety of her reading and knowledge. In this dedication Trotter clearly states that drama should be more than merely entertaining; it must strive to instruct. She is not sure that the misfortunes of love are weighty enough to serve as the subject of a great tragedy: "I have ventured to propose a Doubt whether Love be a proper subject for it; it seems to me not Noble, not Solemn enough for Tragedy" (Clark, p. 87).

The Unhappy Penitent is set in the fifteenth-century French court of King Charles VIII. Charles's marriage to Margarite of Flanders had been fixed in their childhood, but Charles is hesitant to marry Margarite because he has not seen her recently. Instead, he is in love with Ann of Brittany, marriage to whom, as Charles's advisers point out, would also bring a better political alliance. Echoing the friendship between Agnes and Constantia in *Agnes de Castro,* Ann and Margarite remain friends even though Margarite is engaged to Charles and Ann is in love with him. Like *The Fatal Friendship, The Unhappy Penitent* features a controlling brother in the form of the Archduke of Austria, Margarite's brother. Quarrelling with Charles, the archduke pressures Margarite to marry the Duke of Lorrain. Margarite herself is in love with the Duke of Lorrain and is initially hesitant to develop her relationship with Lorrain because of her prior commitment to Charles.

Meanwhile, the Duke of Brittany, who is also in love with Margarite, slanders her as a woman of ill repute and Charles's cast'off mistress, but Ann helps Margarite prove her innocence. Ann advises Margarite to approach Charles and candidly discuss their engagement so that they can reach a solution that would suit them both, reminding her that developing a relationship with Lorrain would be wrong and duplicitous because of Margarite's prior commitment to Charles. A true friend to Margarite, Ann also reprimands Charles, whom she loves, for his neglect of Margarite. Charles is persuaded to see the error of his ways and decides to honor his commitment to Margarite and marry her. Upon hearing of her impending marriage to Charles, Lorrain urges Margarite to marry him, and like Gramont and Felicia in *The Fatal Friendship,* Margarite and Lorrain marry secretly. Unaware of the marriage and desirous of breaking off Margarite's relationship with Lorrain, Ann's father writes a letter, supposedly from Charles, implying that Charles and Margarite had consummated their relationship. Lorrain and the archduke give credence to the letter and heavily censure Margarite. Margarite is unable to defend herself because she fears that Charles will kill Lorrain if he finds out the truth. Unaware of her father's forged letter, Ann is initially enraged at Margarite, but their friendship triumphs, and Ann agrees to speak to Charles. Margarite promises to enter a convent if her name is cleared. The confusion is eventually cleared up; Margarite leaves her husband and enters the convent as she had promised, leaving Charles and Ann free to marry.

The Unhappy Penitent bears similarities to *Agnes de Castro* as well as *The Fatal Friendship*. The theme of feminine friendship that was so important in *Agnes de Castro* is revisited in this play in the friendship between Ann and Margarite. Although in love with Charles, Ann does not hesitate to take him to task for neglecting his betrothed, giving proof that, as a true friend, she is willing to preserve Margarite's honor to the detriment of her own interests. Like Agnes and Constantia, Ann and Margarite too are noble, high-minded, and virtuous ladies. As in *The Fatal Friendship,* the secret marriage in this play is doomed. Trotter implies that acting hastily in order to secure one's private desires is blameworthy, and instead suggests that humans, especially those who hold positions of authority, must be guided by their reason. Trotter's principled ladies are infelicitously matched with men who resemble the male characters in her other works in their selfishness and controlling natures. Like Bellgard, Felicia's brother in *The Fatal Friendship,* the Archduke of Austria, Brittany, and Lorrain single-mindedly strive to gain their personal ends with no consideration of the desires of the women who share their lives. Trotter again emphasizes the suffering of women in a patriarchal world in which women play insignificant roles and have no rights.

King Charles is an exception to the general portrait of men that Trotter draws in this play. Although initially hesitant to marry Margarite, he is ultimately led to honor his engagement to her, and it is only fitting that he marries the principled and disciplined Ann. Ann of Brittany not only lives her life according to the highest codes of honor but also inspires Charles to become responsible and honorable. Yet Ann's strict adherence to the moral code gives her less depth than some of Trotter's other female characters. Her perfection robs her of humanity, and she remains a flat character with whom women in the audience would have found it difficult to identify. Although high-minded, Margarite is a more recognizable figure who makes mistakes, repents, and imposes the punishment upon herself that she had promised.

THE REVOLUTION OF SWEDEN

Betterton's company at the Queen's Theatre in Haymarket performed Trotter's final tragedy, *The Revolution of Sweden,* on 11 February 1706, and it ran for six nights. Betterton himself played a role in the play, and the noted actress Elizabeth Barry appeared as Constantia. Trotter's play was based on René Aubert de Vertot's *History of the Revolution in Sweden. The Revolution of Sweden* is Trotter's most blatantly feminist play. It is dedicated to Lady Harriet Godolphin, daughter of the Duke and Duchess of Marlborough, and lauds her as someone who

> might incite some greater Geniuses among us to exert themselves, and change our Emulation of a Neighboring Nation's Fopperies, to the commendable Ambition of Rivalling them in their illustrious Women; Numbers we know among them, have made considerable Progress in the most difficult Sciences, several have gain'd the Prizes of Poesie from their Academics, and some have been chosen Members of their Societies.
>
> (Williamson, p. 168)

In her dedication Trotter declares, "the play incites the audience to a particular virtue, 'a disinterested and resolute Care of the Publick Good,' and the two heroines represent this value" (Williamson, p. 191). In keeping with her declaration, her first heroine, Christina, fights on the side of the rebelling Swedes as they rise to expel the Danes from Sweden. The other heroine, Constantia, also keeps the interests of the country uppermost in her mind. The play ends with high praise for both heroines, who subordinate themselves, their emotions, and their relationships with their husbands for the welfare of their country.

The historical background for the play is the seventeenth-century Swedish rebellion against the Danes led by Gustavus Adolphus. His friend, Count Arwide, husband to Constantia, joins Gustavus in his rebellion. Christina's husband is Beron, a traitor from the Swedish side. Her husband's defection causes the noble and patriotic Christina to disguise herself as her nephew, Fredage, and fight in the Swedish army. The disguised Christina fights valiantly, but she is captured by the Danes and taken back to their camp, where she meets Beron. In the battle, the Danes also capture Constantia, who, though married to Arwide, is courted by the Danish viceroy. Constantia engages in moral and political debates with the Danes asserting in Lockeian terms that the Danes' misrule gave the Swedes the right to rebel. In the meanwhile, Arwide learns of his wife's capture and arrives at the viceroy's palace and offers himself as the ransom to set Constantia free.

Beron and the viceroy take advantage of Arwide and dupe him into signing a pact that Arwide mistakenly believes will be advantageous to the Swedes but is in fact beneficial to the Danes. Constantia incorrectly presumes that Arwide has been purposefully disloyal to the Swedes. More battles are fought which result in victory for the Swedes, and the two women are set free. Upon her release, the nationalistic-minded Constantia informs Gustavus of her husband's betrayal. The Swedish Senate tries Arwide, finds him guilty, and condemns him to death. The traitor Beron declares his repentance and rejoins the Swedish side, bringing his wife with him. Christina knows the part Beron played in duping Arwide into signing the pact, and she is able to expose her husband. In return, Beron stabs Christina. The play ends with Arwide praising his patriotic wife for her virtue, and the dying Christina is extolled for her courage.

Trotter had sent a draft of her play to Congreve (who had retired from writing for the stage at this point) for his advice, and it is worthwhile to quote some of his responses in detail. Congreve wrote:

> I think the design in general very great and noble; the conduct of it very artful, if not too full of business, which may either run into length or obscurity. But both of those ... you have skill enough to avoid. You are the best judge whether those of your own sex will approve as much of the heroic virtue of Constantia and Christina, as if they had been engaged in some *belle passion*. In the second act, I would have that noise, which generally attends so much the fighting on the stage, provided against; for those frequent alarms and excursions do much to disturb an audience ... in the fourth act it does not seem to me to be clear enough, how Constantia comes to be made free, and to return to Gustavus.... This act is full of business; and intricacy, in the fourth act, must by all means be avoided. The last act will have many harangues in it, which are dangerous in a catastrophe, if long, and not of the last importance.
>
> (Hodges, p. 212)

From the finished draft of the play, it becomes clear that Trotter did not follow most of Congreve's advice. *The Revolution of Sweden* was not a success. Trotter added a second preface to the published version of the play in which she defended her work, claiming that many of its detractors were criticizing the play without having even seen it. It is undeniable that the plot is difficult to follow, sometimes dull, and very noisy. There are a lot of long patriotic speeches that are, at times, tedious and do not hold the reader's attention. *The Revolution of Sweden* is primarily a political play. Trotter's dedication to the daughter of the Whig Duke and Duchess of Marlborough points to her own Whiggish sympathies. Many of Constantia's speeches are based on John Locke's contract theory of government as expounded in his *Two Treatises of Government,* in which Locke defended overthrowing James II and limiting the authority of the king.

Constantia was not a character in Trotter's source material, but Trotter included her in the play to highlight women's intelligence and their capacity to grasp and expound political theory in a perceptive, reasonable, and rational manner. Trotter puts most of the political speeches in Constantia's mouth to show that women can indeed play a valuable role in politics, a sphere primarily dominated by males even though a queen sat on the British throne. Constantia and Arwide's love is not romantic, and Constantia holds her duties to her country above her love for her husband, as evidenced by her denouncement of Arwide when she believes him a traitor. Like many of the men in Trotter's plays, Arwide is emotional, hasty, and irrational and Beron is a tyrannical and brutish husband. Christina is significant because she is the only female character in Trotter's play who cross-dresses, which allows Trotter to explore female courage. The two heroines of this play are among Trotter's strongest, most intelligent, and most courageous, permitting her to laud feminine bravery and intelligence and to scrutinize women's role in politics.

LOVE AT A LOSS

Trotter tried her hand at comedy only once. *Love at a Loss* explores some of the prevailing concerns of her plays and examines feminine friendships, the institution of marriage, and lack of women's agency in choosing partners. As in most of her tragedies, the action of the comedy revolves around women, their actions, their choices, and their relationships with their lovers.

Love At A Loss; or, Most Votes Carry It was performed at the Drury Lane Theatre on 23 November 1701. It is dedicated to Lady Sarah Piers, and Trotter makes excuses for the play, mentioning that she is not a talented writer of comedies and that she did not exert herself fully in writing this play, having written it in her hours of leisure. The play features three pairs of lovers who face various complex predicaments: Lesbia and Beaumine, Miranda and Constant, and Lucilia and Phillabell. The opening speech of this play is a conversation between Lucilia and her maid Lysetta, who are discussing how they might recover some love letters that Lucilia had written to the foolish fop, Cleon. Engaged to Phillabell, whom she truly loves, Lucilia is concerned on the eve of her marriage that the letters will fall into Phillabell's hands. Lesbia is engaged to the rake Beaumine, who has grown cold toward her since she allowed him to seduce her. His neglect causes her to fear that she has a rival. Lesbia has another suitor, Grandfoy, with whom she has had a previous acquaintance, and Grandfoy wishes to marry her even though he knows she is not chaste. Lesbia is not unwilling to marry Grandfoy, but she does to wish to lose her reputation and hence hopes that the revelation of Beaumine's unfaithfulness to her will free her of her engagement to him, leaving her free to marry Grandfoy. Lesbia gives Grandfoy a ring that Beaumine had given her and pretends to be greatly distraught at its loss. The third heroine, Miranda, is a flirt, in contrast to her lover Constant, who, as his name suggests, is faithful to her and genuinely loves her. Miranda enjoys her independence and continuously teases Constant by refusing to marry him. Unaware that Beaumine is engaged to Lesbia, Miranda begins a flirtation with Beaumine.

A conversation between Miranda and Lesbia makes Miranda aware that Beaumine is Lesbia's lover. True to her friend, Miranda agrees to take part in a plot that will expose Beaumine's disloyalty to Lesbia. Unfortunately, Constant misunderstands Miranda's motives and mistakenly believes that Miranda is in love with Beaumine. Constant candidly speaks to Miranda about her relationship with Beaumine, and Miranda decides to relinquish her freedom and marry Constant, for whom she does truly care. Meanwhile, one of Lucilia's letters to Cleon that speaks of her dissatisfaction with her impending marriage falls into Phillabell's hands. Unaware that this letter had been written as part of a ruse to keep Cleon quiet about the other letters, Phillabell is greatly distressed by his belief that Lucilia has been unfaithful to him. Lysetta, the maid, saves the day with her quick thinking, claiming that it was she who had forged the letters to Cleon. As part of the plan, Lysetta arranges to have Phillabell find her in the act of composing another of these letters using Lucilia's name. This prompts him to believe that Lucilia is innocent, and he is greatly relieved. Lesbia now has two lovers, both of whom wish to marry her: Grandfoy and Beaumine, who has had a change of heart and now wishes to honor his engagement to her. The vote that decides who she will marry is the basis for the subtitle of this play: "Most Votes Carry It." Lesbia's friends vote, and Beaumine wins by a narrow margin. Trotter's condemnation of libertinism is reflected in a speech by Beaumine in which he repents his former rakish way of life.

Love at a Loss, which was not a success, is primarily concerned with the quandaries faced by the three heroines, and the plot works out the manner in which these problems are solved. The three heroines, and Lysetta to a lesser degree, remain the focus of most of the play and share most of the dialogue. The firm female friendships of Trotter's tragedies are also present in this play. Miranda and Lesbia plot together to expose Beaumine, and Lysetta willingly takes the blame for writing the letters so that Lucilia may be exonerated from all blame and dishonor on the eve of her wedding. The vote that decides whom Lesbia will marry is significant in several ways. First, it is disturbing, because the reader cannot help but feel Grandfoy, who loses the vote, would make a more caring husband than Beaumine. Second, it underscores women's vulnerability in choosing their husbands: it seems an arbitrary matter of luck and fate as to whether a woman ends up with a good or a bad husband. Third, it emphasizes that one must go beyond one's personal desire and honor larger social responsibilities by fulfilling contracts. And finally, the vote represents a pro-marriage and an anti-libertinism stance.

Beaumine is a rake in the mold of George Etherege's great Restoration rake Dorimant, although he is not as charming, witty, or attractive as Dorimant. He claims to be reformed by the end of the play and makes a speech about treating wives with love and care, but it is difficult to put much stock in his supposed transformation. Constant and Phillabell are two of Trotter's more considerate male figures. They prove to be better lovers than Beaumine and some of the male characters in her tragedies by genuinely caring for their beloveds and wishing to marry them.

Trotter had written a revised version of *Love at a Loss* titled *The Honourable Deceivers; or, All Right at the Last,* but this manuscript has been lost. However, a letter dated May 1739 does survive in which Trotter writes about the changes she wished to make to a comedy. Considering that she had only written one comedy, it is presumed that she was referring to *Love at a Loss* (Kelley, p. 93). *Love at a Loss* was not performed during the nineteenth century but it was during the twentieth. The Wild Iris Theatre Company put up two productions at the Battersea Arts Centre in London in 1993 and 1994, which were both successful.

A DEFENCE OF THE ESSAY OF HUMAN UNDERSTANDING, WRITTEN BY MR. LOCK

The first of Trotter's writings on John Locke's essay, and the first to bring wide praise for her abilities as a writer of philosophical texts, the *Defence* was published in 1702. Locke's *Essay Concerning Human Understanding* had been published in 1690 and had received much criticism from churchmen such as Edward Stillingfleet, bishop of Worcester, and Thomas Burnet, the master of Charterhouse. Trotter's defense of Locke, which begins with a letter to Locke, focuses on morality, ethics, and the motivations that prompt ethical behavior. Trotter undertakes to answer Burnet's criticisms of Locke and does so in a logical and organized manner. Trotter supported Locke's assertion that humans are not born with an innate sense of the moral but that such an understanding is arrived at by using reason that has been granted to humans by God. Moral laws, she asserts, are understood only when humankind uses reason to deliberate on actions and come to an understanding of right and wrong.

Trotter also addresses Locke's "law of nature." She understands this law as defining the nature of humankind, and asserts that one must understand the fundamental nature of man to gain a perspective on good and evil. Trotter again emphasizes the use of reason to reflect on the nature of man, without which we would be unable to gain an understanding of good and evil, because such an understanding stems from an understanding of ourselves and our actions. Then Trotter asserts that it is only through using our faculty of reason to understand ourselves that we may gain an understanding of the nature of God. Additionally, Trotter discusses the matter of conscience. Locke had been criticized for his claim that conscience was not innate but rather arrived at after the exercise of the faculty of reason. Trotter defended Locke's view, pointing out that moral judgments are not made immediately and also that there are different standards of morality in various cultures, which would not be the case if conscience were innate. Thus, in all her arguments, Trotter follows Locke's lead and places the utmost importance on the faculty of reason.

Trotter's *Defence* is proof of her intelligence, her ability to follow arguments to their logical end, and her perspicacity in grasping complex moral and ethical issues. Trotter initially had the work published anonymously because she feared that it would not be taken seriously if it was revealed that it had been written by a young woman of twenty-three. Locke himself was grateful to Trotter for her defense and sent his cousin, Peter King, to Trotter with a gift of books and a letter in which he stated:

> Give me leave therefore to assure you, that as the rest of the world take notice of the strength and clearness of your reasoning, so I cannot but be extremely sensible that it was employed in my defence. You have herein not only vanquished my adversary, but reduced me also absolutely under your power ...
>
> (Kelley, p. 166)

A very accomplished analytical work, Trotter's *Defence* also attracted the attention of the philosopher Gottfried Wilhelm Leibniz. The question of morality, which was one of the central issues of Locke's writing, was one that Trotter was concerned with and addressed in many of her plays. It is therefore not surprising that Trotter was disturbed by the criticisms leveled at Locke and undertook, albeit anonymously, to defend him. For a young woman with no background in ethical and philosophical issues, *Defence of the Essay of Human Understanding, written by Mr. Lock* is indeed a formidable achievement.

DISCOURSE CONCERNING A GUIDE IN CONTROVERSIES

Bishop Burnet wrote the preface for *Discourse Concerning a Guide in Controversies,* which was published in 1707. As a young woman, Trotter had converted to Catholicism, probably under the influence of her mother's cousin, the Earl of Perth. This piece of writing announced her reconversion to the Church of England. The *Discourse* contained a critique of some of the principles of the Roman Catholic Church. In the preface, Burnet praises Trotter for the "strength and clearness of the reasoning" (Kelley, p. 148). In the *Discourse,* Trotter discounts the view that traditional authority, such as that wielded by churchmen and the king, cannot ever be wrong. She maintains that humans should not have to obey the dictates of the Church and its officials if such dictates clash with one's personal reading of the Scriptures. As evidence, she points out that various bishops may read the Scriptures in a diverse number of ways, which weakens the notion that, as authority figures, they are infallible. She refutes the idea that rank within the Church guarantees infallibility, and writes that those who hold positions within the Church form only a "human constitution" and hence may make mistakes in interpreting the Scriptures; in such cases congregations should no longer follow the dictates of those Church officials (Kelley, p. 149). Trotter asserts that the Scriptures do not state that the Church is infallible, and therefore the Scriptures do not ask Christians to blindly follow the Church. She recommends instead that individuals look to the Scriptures for guidance and follow their own conscience.

In the *Discourse,* Trotter makes an argument that is similar to the argument in her *Defence* of John Locke. She contends that humans must themselves be accountable for their spiritual well-being, just as she had stated in the *Defence* that one must come to an understanding of morality by exercising one's reason. To the charge that being skeptical of the Church is tantamount to being skeptical of the Scriptures, Trotter answers that such reasoning is false because it only proves that the "authority of Church and Scripture are equally uncertain" (Kelley, p. 150). She then goes on to defend the infallibility of the Scriptures, saying that they were accepted by the first Christians only because they were convinced of the veracity of the facts contained in the Scriptures. The doctrines of the Church, by contrast, were not infallible because they had been altered over the course of the years.

Trotter's *Discourse* met with approval from Thomas Burnet of Kemney, who had also corresponded with Locke. Burnet, who did not approve of Trotter's Catholicism, had tried repeatedly to draw her into a theological debate, but until this point she had desisted firmly from being drawn into such a discussion. The *Discourse* is a significant piece of writing because it candidly states many of Trotter's religious beliefs and clearly states her return to the Church of England. Furthermore, it is an additional expression of her support of Locke and the principles of the Whigs, who also questioned traditional authority. It is in keeping with her other works in its denial of dogma and emphasis on rational morality as a guide to human behavior. In the *Discourse,* Trotter again gives proof of her firm grasp of theological issues and ability to discuss them in a logical and analytical fashion.

A LETTER TO DR. HOLDSWORTH, OCCASIONED BY HIS SERMON PREACHED BEFORE THE UNIVERSITY OF OXFORD: ON EASTER-MONDAY, CONCERNING THE RESURRECTION OF THE SAME BODY, 1726

Holdsworth had preached his sermon on Easter Monday in 1720, but Trotter's letter to him in defense of Locke came in 1726 because Trotter had not known of the existence of Holdsworth's sermon till 1726. In 1727 Holdsworth replied to Trotter in *A Defence of the Doctrine of the Resurrection of the Same Body, in Two Parts. In the First of which, the Character, Writings, and Religious Principles of Mr. Lock are Distinctly Considered; And, in the Second, the Doctrine of the Resurrection of the Same Body is at large Explained and Defended, against the Notions and Principles of that Gentleman.* Trotter penned a reply to Holdsworth but was unable to find a publisher for it. Hence, it appeared for the first time in Birch's edition of her collected works. Trotter's two pieces are dealt with together here.

Holdsworth had accused Locke of disallowing the resurrection and of challenging the notion of the Trinity, and Trotter's defense is centered on these two points. She questions whether the resurrected body was exactly the same in physical composition as the dying body. Trotter points out that Locke had not denied the possibility of resurrection of the body; he had merely stated that God's entire will in the matter might not have been revealed. Throughout the letter, Trotter tries to define what exactly is meant by the word "same," hoping that an agreement regarding the meaning of the word as it applies to the condition of the resurrected body would help in solving the controversy. As in the *Discourse,* she challenges that idea that the doctrines of the Church, which had been subjected to change over the years, should constitute infallible articles of faith. As with her previous writings, she again lays great emphasis on the use of an individual's reason to arrive at personal articles of faith. Trotter refutes the charge that Locke had denied the resurrection. Indeed, she asserts that, far from such a denial, Locke had "very frequently and earnestly expresse[d] his belief of the last judgment, the resurrection of the dead, and that the dead shall rise again with their bodies" (Kelley, p. 174).

Her second defense concerns the Trinity. This was a more difficult undertaking since Locke himself had been evasive about his notion of the Trinity, causing him to be accused of atheism and Unitarianism. Trotter bases her defense on the fact that Locke had not specifically written about the Trinity, and hence could not be definitely accused of not being a believer. She defends Locke on the score that he did believe in Christ's divinity by quoting several passages from his *Reasonableness of Christianity* and by associating Locke's use of the term "Son of God" with the manner in which it had been used by great churchmen such as Archbishop Tillotson.

In the *Letter,* Trotter continues her unyielding support of John Locke and reaffirms her position that humankind should use reason to understand and interpret the Scriptures. She writes in a calm and collected tone and reiterates her interest in philosophical, ethical, and theological issues. Trotter boldly steps into spheres that had so far mainly been dominated by men, and she enters it on an equal footing by giving ample proof of her ability to exercise the supposedly "manly" faculty of reason.

CONCLUSION

Trotter was a radical, bold, and intellectual writer of her time who did not shrink from asserting the rights of women. Far from submitting to the unequal conditions under which women of her times suffered, Trotter openly sought intellectual parity for Restoration women. In many of her plays, she inserted women who were far superior to the men, thereby challenging the notion that women should have no rights and should be guided by male caretakers such as fathers, brothers, and husbands. A reexamination of her work illustrates her progressive stance and her radical thinking. Trotter valued the faculty of reason and strove to show through her works that one must use reason to guide one's actions. Trotter believed in reforming the stage and consciously tried to write plays that not merely pleased the theatergoers but also instructed them. In many of her plays, she illustrated the manner in which honoring one's commitments to society must take precedence over satisfying one's own desires. Trotter's duties as a wife and mother prevented her from making any literary or philosophical contributions for a considerable period of time, and hence it is surprising that she ultimately managed to put forth a substantial amount of work of very high quality. Writing for the Restoration stage was not an easy task because women playwrights often had to suffer criticism and attacks on their reputations. Yet Trotter remained relatively unscathed, with contemporary writers and critics referring to her wit, her beauty, and her chastity. A true female intellectual, in many significant ways Trotter was an important precursor of Mary Wollstonecraft as well as the nineteenth-century feminists to follow.

Selected Bibliography

WORKS OF CATHARINE TROTTER

Novella
The Adventures of a Young Lady (a.k.a. *Olinda's Adventures*). Published anonymously in *Letters of Love and Gallantry and Several Other Subjects, All written By Ladies.* Vol 1. London: Printed for Sam. Briscoe, 1693. Republished under Trotter's name in 1718 and 1724.

Plays
Agnes de Castro. First performed at the Theatre Royal in Drury Lane, December 1695. London: Printed for H. Rhodes, R. Parker, and S. Briscoe, 1696.

The Fatal Friendship. First performed at Lincoln's Inn Fields, April or May 1698. London: Printed for Francis Saunders, 1698.

The Unhappy Penitent. First performed at Drury Lane, February 1701. Printed for William Turner & John Nutt, 1701.

Love at a Loss; or, Most Votes Carry It. First performed at Drury Lane Theatre, 23 November 1701. London: Printed for William Turner, 1701.

The Revolution of Sweden. First performed at The Queen's Theatre in Haymarket, 11 February 1706. London: Printed for James Knapton & George Strahan, 1706.

Philosophical Writings
A Defence of the Essay of Human Understanding, written by Mr. Lock. London: William Turner, 1702.

A Discourse Concerning a Guide in Controversies. London: Printed for A. J. Churchill, 1707.

A Letter to Dr. Holdsworth Occasioned By His Sermon Preached before the University of Oxford: On Easter-Monday, Concerning the Resurrection of the Same Body. London: Printed for Benjamin Motte, 1726.

Collections, Facsimiles, and Editions
The Works of Mrs. Catharine Cockburn, Theological, Moral, Dramatic, and Poetical, Several of them now first printed.

Revised and published, with an Account of the Life of the Author, By Thomas Birch. 2 vols. London: J. & P. Knapton, 1751. Facsimile ed., London: Routledge/Thoemmes Press, 1992.

The Female Wits: Women Playwrights on the London Stage 1660–1720. Selected by Fidelis Morgan. London: Virago, 1981. (Includes *The Fatal Friendship.*)

The Plays of Mary Pix and Catharine Trotter. Edited with an introduction by Edna L. Steeves. 2 vols. New York: Garland, 1982.

Catharine Trotter Cockburn: Philosophical Writings. Edited by Patricia Sheridan. Peterborough, Ont.: Broadview Press, 2006.

Catharine Trotter's The Adventures of a Young Lady *and Other Works.* Edited by Anne Kelley. Aldershot, U.K., and Burlington, Vt., Ashgate, 2006.

CRITICAL AND BIOGRAPHICAL STUDIES

Anderson, Julie Nell Aipperspach. "Performance of Authorship: Contexts of Authorship and Audience in the Plays of Delarivier Manley, Catharine Trotter, and Mary Pix." Ph.D. dissertation, Texas A&M University, 2002.

Clark, Constance. "The Female Wits: Catharine Trotter, Delarivière Manley, and Mary Pix—Three Women Playwrights Who Made Their Debuts in the London Season of 1695–96." Ph.D. dissertation, City University of New York, 1984.

Gagen, Jean. *The New Woman: Her Emergence in English Drama, 1600–1730.* New York, Twayne [1954].

Gosse, Edmund. *Catharine Trotter: The Precursor of the Blue-stockings.* London: Adlard, 1916.

Hodges, John Cuynus; Congreve, William. *Letters & Documents.* 1964.

Kelley, Anne. *Catharine Trotter: An Early Modern Writer in the Vanguard of Feminism.* Hampshire, U.K.: Ashgate, 2002.

MacCarthy, Bridget G. *The Female Pen.* Vol. 1, *Women Writers: Their Contribution to the English Novel, 1621–1744.* Ireland: Cork University Press, 1944.

Troost, Linda, ed. *Eighteenth-Century Women: Studies in Their Lives, Work, And Culture.* New York: AMS Press, 2008.

Williams, Jane. *The Literary Women of England.* London: Saunders, Otley, 1861.

Williamson, Marilyn L. *Raising Their Voices: British Women Writers, 1650–1750.* Detroit: Wayne State University Press, 1990.

JOHN WAIN
(1925—1994)

Dale Salwak

THE IMPRESSIVE BODY of work in fiction, poetry, journalism, travel writing, radio, television and stage drama, criticism, autobiography, and biography that John Wain produced between 1955 and 1994 ensured his position, as many critics had predicted, as a modern man of letters. Three of his works merited distinguished literary recognition: Wain received the Somerset Maugham Award for *Preliminary Essays* (1958); the James Tait Black Memorial Prize (1974) for *Samuel Johnson;* and the Whitbread Best Novel Award (1982) for *Young Shoulders.* In 1984 he was also made a CBE (Commander of the British Empire) for services to literature. Respected as an intelligent, learned man who was seriously concerned with the issues of his time and fully dedicated to the writer's craft, Wain made a sustained and determined effort to speak on abiding philosophical concerns to a wider range of readers than that addressed by many of his modernist predecessors and postmodern contemporaries. These concerns included the dignity of human beings and the value of reason, moderation, common sense, moral courage, and intellectual self-respect in the midst of an oftentimes cruel, indifferent, cynical, and increasingly commercialized world. Add to this a stoic honesty, a gentleness, a quiet caring toward his treatment of people, and we have the portrait of a man who from the 1950s on developed an ever more deep, serious, and intelligent insight into and understanding of contemporary English society.

EARLY LIFE

John Barrington Wain was born to Arnold A. Wain, a prosperous dentist, and Anne Turner on March 14, 1925, at Stoke-on-Trent, Staffordshire, an industrial city known for its pottery and coal mining. When Wain was three years old the family took up residence in Penkhull, one of the city's better-off, middle-class districts, and it was here, surrounded by a manufacturing complex of kilns and factories, that Wain would spend his formative years.

Wain's family was not especially scholarly, but they regularly discussed ideas and events and the house never lacked for books. As Wain makes clear in his autobiography, *Sprightly Running* (1982), this and the other particular circumstances of his childhood and adolescence were important influences on his development as a writer, for without them he would have perceived and written about a very different world. These influences arose from three social and historical aspects of his surroundings: the dwindling countryside, advancing industrialism, and the social tensions inherent in being brought up in a family more comfortably circumstanced than the largely working-class residents of industrial Stoke-on-Trent.

From his earliest years, Wain was deeply attracted to rural landscapes and immersed himself in the natural world at every opportunity This kinship with the English countryside developed into a reverence for all created life, almost a pantheism that would eventually make stuffy rooms or heavy clothes—anything that was unnatural or confining—anathema to him.

On holidays, Wain and his family traveled to the coast and hills of North Wales, a region that would remain important to him for many reasons, not least of which was his marriage, at age thirty-four, to a Welsh woman, Eirian Jones. His feeling for Wales—for the independence of its people, for the mountains and the sea—is recorded in his novel *A Winter in the Hills* (1970).

In this and other writings, Wain examines the idea that the natural world, unlike so much of urban life, is the embodiment of order and permanence. Indeed, the tension between the repressiveness of society and the dream of liberation in the natural world became a significant unifying theme in Wain's work. Through his early childhood experiences Wain learned to be open to the beauty of nature, cognizant of its order, and reverent about its liberating spirit.

A second major influence from his early years was the experience of living in an industrial city. His exposure to the hardships faced by the workers and to the depredations of advancing industrialism gave him a deep knowledge of the people and their problems, all of which he depicts with sympathy and humanity in his fiction. The increasing grimness of these surroundings left an indelible imprint, as he records in *Sprightly Running*. For example, the Sutton—a housing estate for slum clearance in the valley—gave him "the perpetual sense of living in a beleaguered garrison" (p. 4). With its growing depersonalization and factory towns, the scene was for Wain filled with menace: "Hedges were slashed; trees had their branches torn off and their bark carved and stripped away; every pool where a few sticklebacks had managed to breed was swept by a thousand nets until the last survivor had been carried away to die in a stifling jam-jar" (p. 4). From his early comic fiction onward, the erosion of dignity and decency concomitant with industrialism is among his most powerful themes.

A third powerful influence from Wain's youth was his understanding of the tensions and, frequently, torments associated with being a minority in a devoutly class-conscious society. Wain's early education at Froebel's Preparatory School (1931–1934) and at Newcastle-under-Lyme High School (1934–1942) made him realize that life was competitive and a perpetual effort to survive. He found himself surrounded and outnumbered by people who resented him for being better off than they. Houses in Penkhull were often suspected of being snobbish, and Wain had to prove continually that he was not. His contact with older children, schoolboy bullies, and authoritarian schoolmasters was such that he acquired a certain defensiveness and the knowledge that the world was a dangerous place. This knowledge made its way into his work, which is imbued with a sense of the difficulty of survival in an intrusive, demanding, and often unjust society. Bullies figure prominently among Wain's worst characters, and his most dystopian settings are always totalitarian in one way or another. No wonder, then, that Wain's writings so often hinge on the use and abuse of power.

Wain's response to these injustices as he grew into adolescence was to turn to humor, debate, and music as well as reading and writing. These defenses also became an important influence in his later work. He developed his verbal agility and wit and used it to lampoon both authorities and fellow students, knowing that humor was the surest way of spotlighting whatever was boring, absurd, or reprehensible in a given situation. It was a talent that often saved him in school and that he honed to razor-sharpness as his writing career unfolded. As for his musical tastes, Wain spoke often of his lifelong enthusiasm for the trumpet playing of Bill Coleman, and he admitted that Percy Brett, the black jazz musician in *Strike the Father Dead* (1962), was created with Coleman in mind.

Accompanying this interest was a growing attraction to serious writing and reading. Wain had known he wanted to become an author since he was nine years old. But his earliest literary efforts were more critical than imaginative; not until his middle twenties did his desire to be a creative writer fully emerge. Thus he began by writing pastiche and parody, composing novels in his exercise books that focused on a private eye named Smellum Owte, a protagonist who owed much to Sherlock Holmes and Edgar Allan Poe's C. Auguste Dupin. In 1939 Wain published his first piece—an article titled "To the Riviera," about a trip to France—in his school magazine, *The Fire Sky*.

Wain matched his writing with voracious reading of prose and verse. His early interest in the novels of Charles Dickens, Tobias Smollett, Daniel Defoe, Arnold Bennett and others in the tradition of the English novel influenced his later literary style. Like these predecessors, Wain would go on to approach his characters through the conventional, straightforward narration of the realist, and, like theirs, his concerns were social and moral. By fourteen he had also read many of the English poets he would years later write about, including Shakespeare as well as the Romantics and the Victorians. He also began at this time to read Samuel Johnson—the eighteenth-century literary giant whose life and works came to serve as a moral and intellectual touchstone for Wain and the one writer to have the most profound and lasting effect on Wain's academic and creative career. In short, by the time he finished high school and was going up to university, Wain had entered into that calling which he continued to pursue until his death— the life of a man of letters.

In 1942 Wain entered St. John's College, Oxford, to study English. He completed his degree (a first) in 1946, and then accepted a Fereday Fellow. He remained at Oxford until 1949, when he took a post as lecturer in the Department of English at Reading University. He resigned in 1955 to become a full-time writer, eventually settling in Wolvercote, on the edge of Oxford. The period from 1942 to 1955 is when he grew, with remarkable speed, into the world of literature and scholarship. He discovered strength in his work. As the prevailing social and political conditions in England and Europe became more complex and ill defined, he found new motivation from productive work, from the sense that he had skills and knowledge that were needed and so could respect himself. When World War II came, he was spared service because of a detached retina and turned his full energies to his studies. At Oxford, hours of reading helped to lay the foundation of his intimate, lifelong familiarity with Samuel Johnson—in whom he found reflected his own "sense of stoical resistance against hopeless odds" (*Sprightly Running*, p. 101).

Also sustaining to Wain were friends and mentors he might talk with and learn from— friends with penetrating minds and broad-ranging sensibilities. These associates included C. S. Lewis, his tutor, from whom he learned and developed assertion, proof, illustration, and metaphor—necessities for surviving as Lewis' pupil. Charles Williams helped to encourage Wain's love of verse. He was always willing to praise what a student did genuinely well, and this stimulated Wain to write and to consider more closely the kind of poetry he himself wished to write. Another formative influence was Philip Larkin, whose determination to write impeccably was an inspiring example. Still another was Kingsley Amis, whose work on a first novel, *Lucky Jim* (1954), encouraged Wain to attempt writing his own novel in his spare time. In 1953 Frederick Warburg accepted *Hurry on Down* for publication, and its unexpected success quickly established Wain as one of Britain's promising new writers.

THE ANGRY YOUNG MEN

Wain came of age as a novelist during the period of cultural and political upheaval in Britain after World War II. In the immediate postwar period, writers such as Aldous Huxley, Graham Greene, Evelyn Waugh, C. P. Snow, and Anthony Powell, among others, who had made their reputations before the war, continued to be the major literary voices. Most of them had come from upper- or upper-middle-class homes and been educated in private schools, then at Oxford or Cambridge; not surprisingly, their novels were likely to revolve around fashionable London or some other privileged locale. Their satire tended to be confined to the intellectual life as well as the social predicaments of the upper middle class. The characters' status, occupations, even their temperaments, varied little from book to book.

But as Britain struggled to redefine itself in the aftermath of World War II and the consequent political turmoil, writers too fought to find a voice appropriate to the changed circumstances of an emergent postwar society. With the exception of the playwright Christopher Fry and the novelist Angus Wilson, however, few signs pointed toward the development of any new fictional voices to express or comment on the current world order. Some critics remarked that the novel, as a literary form, was probably dead.

It appeared that the genre was very much alive when three astonishingly assured, inventive, and frequently funny first novels finally surfaced. John Wain's *Hurry on Down* (1953), Iris Murdoch's *Under the Net* (1954), Kingsley Amis' *Lucky Jim* (1954), and others soon to come (including John Braine's *A Room at the Top* [1957] and Alan Sillitoe's *Saturday Night and Sunday Morning* [1958]) signaled a shift in Britain's intellectual and imaginative universe. These writers represented a literary movement that resisted the technical innovations in fiction and poetry especially predominating between the wars, a literary tradition that had found full flower in the work of James Joyce, Virginia Woolf, and other writers of the *nouveau roman*. Wain and his contemporaries, unlike their modernist predecessors, saw themselves as serious writers who had grown increasingly impatient with narrative methods intended to represent reality as the disordered, frequently disjointed mélange of perceptions and memories viewed through the lens of the mind. Wain and his fellow writers were interested not in testing the limits of expression but in having their books read and understood—an approach that they developed early in their careers and followed assiduously. The likelihood of readers shutting books out of boredom and frustration was an ever-present dread underlying many of their critical observations. They were, indeed, *conscious* artists wedded to the principles of good narrative rather than the lure of verbal pyrotechnics.

Because their fiction reflected a determination to speak to a wider range of readers than their modernist predecessors had, the works reflected a faith in the common reader's ability to recognize and respond to traditional concerns. Thus these writers would aim for both physical and philosophical reality, and they would adapt the techniques of Charles Dickens, Tobias Smollett, and Henry Fielding, whose ability to bring immense variety and fullness to their work without reverting to obscurity or stylistic excess proved appealing. With entertaining, episodic plots, realism, and clear, unadorned style, these novels reminded readers of the conventional picaresque tale—a convention as old as the novel itself.

Along with their style, what was unmistakable was the new voice and vision these writers represented. A few socially minded critics saw in them an attempt to articulate, realistically and comprehensively, highly relevant, contemporary concerns: the social frustrations and aspirations of many average Britons, including the condition of the working and lower middle classes after the war; a discontent that the welfare state had not reached far enough in eliminating remaining class privileges and inequalities; an implicit criticism of the traditional British class structure; a distaste for the profit motive; a mockery of the old bases of morality and the old definitions of "gracious living"; and a loathing of all forms of pretentiousness.

Thus, their politically disillusioned heroes—or antiheroes, as it became fashionable to call them—were seen as apt spokesmen for the post-Romantic, post-Freudian age, which, having witnessed an economic depression and several wars, had rediscovered the fact of humanity's limitations. At the mercy of life's unpredictability and inequities, these fumbling antiheroes are sometimes capable of aspiration and insight but not often strong enough to overcome an entrenched social order and carve out the destiny they desire. Frequently they are dreamers, tossed about by events and pushed about by threats to their way of life. In their search for social readjustment, there is discernible in all of these characters a vague discontent, sometimes anger, and a yearning for someone or something out of their reach. On occasion their sense of disenchantment with the realities of their situation becomes so great that they express a desire not to live at all.

Perhaps most attractive to readers was the fact that these novels also offered good entertainment, providing comic relief for a reading public weary of self-absorbed, tormented, alienated artists and tired of despairing about the future of a world seemingly bent on self-destruction. Implied in the satire infused in these novels was a criticism of some of the cultural values that had been passed on to an unwilling postwar society. Because Amis, Wain, and Murdoch seemed to express similar concerns about social and cultural values, had attended Oxford, and taught for a time at provincial universities, critics soon identified them as a trio of rebellious young writers; indeed, here was the "movement" that had been missing from literature for several decades. Here were the so-called Angry Young Men.

After the 1950s, the angry young men moved so far from one another that few critical generalizations truly apply to them. The most we can say is that they harnessed their considerable novelistic skills to promote clarity, honesty, and reason in their fiction, and that they distrusted excessive emotion and technical experimentalism for its own sake. Wain grew into a genuine man of letters as he continued to produce work of high standard while staying on the fringes of the academic world, as a professor of poetry at Oxford in 1973 and by writing criticism and biography. From here on the record of Wain's life is essentially the record of his writings.

NOVELIST

John Wain was a painfully honest novelist who was always, to varying degrees, transforming autobiography into fiction. His purpose, however, was artistic, not confessional, and he shaped his material accordingly. As Wain himself stated, his intention was both pure and simple: to express his own feelings honestly and to tell the truth about the world he knows. All of his best novels—*Hurry on Down, Strike the Father Dead, A Winter in the Hills, The Pardoner's Tale,* and the trilogy, *Where the Rivers Meet*—convey the message that life is ultimately tragic, but they do so in very different ways. Day-to-day survival is difficult, suffering is inevitable, and the comic mask conceals pain and anguish. Only occasionally is this somber picture relieved by idealism, by some unexpected gesture of compassion or tenderness.

HURRY ON DOWN

Wain's first and still best-known novel, *Hurry on Down* (1953), is a comical examination of the difficulties of surviving in a demanding, sometimes fearsome world. The protagonist, Charles Lumley, is a drifter, seeking to compromise with or to escape from boredom, class lines, hypocrisy, and the conventional perils of success. Although the novel addresses serious moral issues, the plot remains lively thanks to Wain's sharp, inventive wit. His comedy exposes, exaggerates, and criticizes to advocate whatever is reasonable in social behavior and to promote the value and dignity of the individual.

Like the main characters in Amis' *Lucky Jim,* Braine's *Room at the Top,* and Sillitoe's *Saturday Night and Sunday Morning,* Wain's hero is a product of the postwar British welfare state. As an alienated youth on his own for the first time, Lumley feels that neither his upbringing nor his Oxford education has prepared him for making a satisfactory living. His central obsession is to avoid whatever is phony in life, so he naturally finds the world he lives in detestable and rebels against whatever he perceives to be commonplace.

Formally, *Hurry on Down* has the characteristic features of the picaresque novel: a plot that consists of a loosely strung series of short and often comic adventures; an opportunistic and pragmatic antihero who seeks to make a living through his wits; and characters that are mainly satirical stock figures. Unlike the eighteenth-century picaro, however, who is selfish and often cruel, Lumley is simply disconnected, a well-intentioned, lower-middle-class underachiever who distrusts the world of privilege and compromises just enough to live comfortably. His salvation is his sense of humor, which makes it possible for him to make light of some distressful and even disastrous situations. Lumley's character is revealed in his response to repeated assaults on his fundamental decency and sympathy for other people. He himself doesn't change much in spite of the many different guises he assumes—again, in the picaresque tradition—as window cleaner, drug runner, hospital orderly, chauffeur, and the like.

Lumley's true nature shines through immediately with the description at the opening of the novel of a conflict with his landlady. He is presented as the adaptable antihero who takes his fate into his own hands, a jack-of-all-trades, a skilled manipulator, an adept deceiver. Lumley's ingenuity is the focus here, not his mere struggle for survival. At the same time, Wain is developing Lumley's individual personality. In this first scene Lumley is established in the role he will play throughout the narrative—that of a put-upon young man who tries to cope with the workaday world by outwitting it.

Characterization is a vehicle for the novel's satiric edginess, and people who judge others and define themselves by the traditional class structure are the main targets for ridicule. Surrounding the hero is a host of lightly sketched, two-dimensional stock figures, all of whom behave predictably. Here Wain limits himself primarily to caricature: the proletarian girl, the American, the entrepreneur, the middle-class couple, the artist. In the tradition of Tobias Smollett and Charles Dickens, Wain brings these characters to life by emphasizing their eccentricities and by telegraphing his attitude toward them through the selection of specific bodily and facial characteristics. The comedy, then, functions to manipulate our moral judgment so that we sympathize with Lumley and his plight.

Another convention of eighteenth-century fiction Wain employs is the intrusive narrator. The active role of this fictive puppet-master accounts for the distance between the reader and the events of the novel; his exaggerations, his jokes, and his philosophizing ensure against taking Lumley's fate too seriously. In later novels, Wain's narrative stance changed as his vision deepened.

The comedy technique of *Hurry on Down* is sustained through the novel's resolution, in which Lumley is offered a three-year contract as a radio scriptwriter and falls in love with Veronica. Readers may understandably roll their eyes at "perfect" endings to novels, but the unrealistic resolution to this novel does not prove off-putting: it is clear from the beginning that this is a comic tale that depends upon unrealistic turns and crass exaggeration. The rightness of the ending seems like a fitting conclusion to all the comic wrongness that has preceded it.

The entertaining plot, engaging theme, and elements of farce and satire all went into making *Hurry on Down* a noteworthy novel by a promising young writer. In assessing these strengths, critics recognized that because this was the work of a beginning novelist, it had the characteristic vitality of a young man's book. Wain wrote it in bursts of enthusiasm over a three-year span, during which there were frequent pauses. The result was a novel whose focus changes several times. In spite of its flaws, the authenticity in its descriptions of the commercial scene of the 1950s conveyed relevant contemporary themes to an audience starved for stories about their changed and changing world, and more than fifty years later, it still retains its freshness and verve.

STRIKE THE FATHER DEAD

In his fifth novel, *Strike the Father Dead* (1962), Wain extended his artistic vision with a more penetrating, more deeply pondered book that fulfills many of the promises inherent in Wain's earlier work. Here he leaves picaresque conventions behind and instead integrates plot, theme, character, and setting to tell the story of a son who severs parental ties in order to make his own way in life as a jazz pianist. Wain examines the foibles of his fellow human beings and the motives of an indignant parent, using wit and sarcastic humor to lighten this otherwise serious-minded study of the nonconformist's need to assert his individuality.

The plot is arranged in an elaborate, seven-part time scheme. Parts 1 and 6 take place sometime late in 1957 or early 1958; part 2 takes place in the prewar years; and the other divisions follow chronologically up to the last, which is set in 1958. The scene shifts mainly back and forth between a provincial university town and the racier, black-market-and-jazz side of London.

The story is narrated from the first-person points of view of four characters. The central figure, Jeremy Coleman, is a talented young jazz pianist who rebels against his father and the academic establishment in search of personal and artistic self-expression. Alfred Coleman, Jeremy's father and a professor of classics, is an atheist devoted to duty and hard work. Eleanor, Alfred's sister and foster mother to Jeremy, is devoted to him and finds comfort in innocent religiosity. Percy Brett, a black American jazz musician, offers Jeremy his first real parental leadership. With Brett's help Jeremy escapes from his oppressive existence, and once he has the opportunity to develop his passion for music, his formerly shrinking personality expands like a flower in full bloom as he finds his new identity and new way of life.

Strike the Father Dead marks the considerable distance Wain had traveled artistically since *Hurry on Down,* especially in the thorough rendering of each character and scene. Readers end up knowing Jeremy quite well because what we learn about him comes not only from his own narration but also from the accounts of others. With its four central characters, *Strike the Father Dead* represents a larger range for Wain. Each interior monologue is a revelation; the language is personal, distinctive, and descriptive, giving each character a fully realized voice and a fully human face.

Essentially a bildungsroman, this is a novel that recounts the youth and young manhood of a sensitive protagonist who is attempting to learn about the world, discover its meaning and patterns, and develop and clarify a philosophy of life. The two major settings play a vital role in this process. *Strike the Father Dead* moves between two contemporary realms—the provincial one of rigidity and repression, represented by Alfred; and another one of creativity, diversity, and freedom, represented by London and Paris. The first stifles Jeremy; the second exhilarates him. Jazz is central to this new life. For Jeremy, jazz means beauty, love, growth, freedom, and ecstasy—the very qualities he finds missing in Alfred's numb, disciplined world.

Although Jeremy does become successful in *Strike the Father Dead,* that success is somewhat bittersweet. In breaking free of the confinement he feels in his home circumstances, Jeremy loses something as well: innocence, boyhood, nature, and the secure, predictable life. Opportunities beyond the sheltered academic life wait for Jeremy. But with life in the broader world comes a developing awareness of injustice, deprivation, and suffering. These concerns become focal points in Wain's subsequent novels, as he increasingly seeks to define character and dilemma more objectively and with greater moral responsibility.

A WINTER IN THE HILLS

Set in North Wales, *A Winter in the Hills* (1970) expresses, more vividly than any other of his novels, Wain's feelings for a provincial setting he perceives as defined by cohesion, deep-rooted loyalties, and resistance to changes from outside. It is also Wain's most ambitious portrayal of the pain inflicted by the forces of contemporary alienation and sheer loneliness. The novel is also colored by Wain's sympathy for the underdog, his respect for human decency and dignity, and his affirmation of life in the face of these struggles.

On the surface, *A Winter in the Hills* may seem to be chiefly a novel of character, detailing the continuously developing personality of a middle-aged scholar of literature and linguistics, Roger Furnivall. Wain keeps the third-person narrative gaze steadily on Roger through several months that constitute a time of crisis in his life. He struggles doggedly against a complex of adverse circumstances, always in search of a purpose. Outwardly, he justifies his visits to his friend Gareth Jones as a way of improving his idiomatic Welsh. Inwardly, he is searching for personal involvement, a human reason for being in the district. He is also carrying considerable guilt over his brother's suffering and death, and he finds himself in conflict with Dic Sharp, a capitalist bully and the book's villain. In the end, however, these difficulties help to propel Roger into a more active engagement with contemporary life; he is ultimately drawn out of his private grief when he realizes he is helping not only Gareth but also an entire community.

Wain uses the perpetually shifting Welsh landscape to reveal and reflect the protagonist's emotions and mental states. Roger's walk in the rain down country roads, as he attempts to resolve his bitterness and disappointment at his girlfriend Beverley's rejection, is persuasive because Roger's anxiety has been built up gradually and artistically, like the brewing storm itself. Similarly, the sketches of evening descending onto the Welsh hills, their rocks and timber and vast expanses of green aglow with fading sunlight, help to convey the pastoral potential for harmony and sharpen Roger's longing for happiness when everyone seems determined to deny it to him.

A major theme of the book is the invasion of the peaceful sanctuary of Wales by rootless outsiders who have no real concern for its inhabitants. The corrupt sophistication that characterizes these invaders contrasts sharply with the unspoiled simplicity and honesty of the best of the native Welsh depicted in the novel. The inevitable result of this invasion is the decline of the town—its economic insecurity and its struggle to resist an encroaching materialism characterized by greed and tyranny as the rich callously drive the poor to the brink. Through Roger's point of view, Wain expresses his outrage at the pressures—economic, political, and cultural—that seek to destroy the Welsh and, by implication, all minority enclaves attempting to maintain their way of life. Thus, *A Winter in the Hills* is more than a novel about one human being's transformation from loneliness and alienation to mature and selfless love; it is also a powerful inquiry into what represents the "good" life in a contemporary setting threatened by the encroachments of bureaucracy and materialism.

THE PARDONER'S TALE

If *A Winter in the Hills* ended on at least a cautiously optimistic note, no such positive outlook is to be found in *The Pardoner's Tale* (1978), Wain's most somber novel. In none of his other works are his characters so lonely, so frustrated, or so obsessed with thoughts of impermanence, squandered opportunities, and death. The novel is really a novel-within-a-novel: the framing narrative is a third-person account about Giles Hermitage, an established novelist and bachelor living in an English cathedral town; and the internal story is the novel Hermitage is writing, in which Gus Howkins, an aging Londoner contemplating divorce, is the central character. While working on the novel, Hermitage meets a local woman and her daughter, the Chichester-Redferns, and the interplay between his life and that of his character, Howkins, drives the brisk-paced plot.

If there is one protagonist in Wain's novels with whom he closely identifies, it is clearly Giles Hermitage, a highly idiosyncratic man with very recognizable weaknesses: discouragement comes easily to him, and excessive drinking is his way of easing his social and spiritual pain. The root cause of his suffering is loneliness. Like Wain's earlier heroes, especially Roger Furnivall in *A Winter in the Hills,* Hermitage is very much a modern man, quite literally a "hermit" of his "age": vague in his religious and humanitarian aspirations; rootless and alienated from the social life of the community in which he lives; and initially weak and confused in his relationships with women. Plagued by anxiety, depression, and a sense of inner emptiness, he seeks peace of mind under conditions that increasingly work to deprive him of it. Add to these issues his ever-growing urge toward self-destruction, and the reader begins to recognize in this novel a truly modern pulse. Hermitage is lost in a social landscape that is increasingly foreign to him and no longer makes sense.

Hermitage tries to make sense of his confusion through his writing, by stepping into what he calls "the protecting circle of art" (p. 228). His writing is autobiographical, personal, subjective. Howkings, the hero of Hermitage's novel, is a mask for himself; Hermitage creates a character who mirrors his own predicament, and the agonies the character undergoes enable Hermitage to express his deepest feelings about life—an exact parallel to what Wain is doing in his own book. In Hermitage, Wain presents a character who is attempting to create a new order out of the chaos of his life.

The other characters in *The Pardoner's Tale* bear more than a passing resemblance to some in other Wain novels. Here Mrs. Chichester-Redfern is the manipulator. Although Dic Sharp is more ruthless than she is, she nevertheless seeks to exploit Hermitage out of purely selfish motives.

Wain reveals Mrs. Chichester-Redfern's character gradually and subtly. Seen through Hermitage's eyes, she is at first merely a seventy-year-old stranger; over time she shows herself to be innocent yet calculating, the victim of a husband who deserted her; she is grasping for answers to some vital questions about her own experiences. She summons Hermitage under the pretense of wanting to gain insight into herself and her history, and from these conversations, it becomes clear that she, like Hermitage, is confronted and dislocated by personal loss. Also like Hermitage, she wants to come to some understanding of her unhappiness through the medium of art. As it turns out, however, her true motive is revenge: she implores Hermitage to write a novel with her husband portrayed as a character who suffers acute pain and loss. Then, she says, "there will be that much justice done in the world" (p. 183).

The principal tension of this novel is simple and classic: the life force confronting the death force. Just as Mrs. Chichester-Redfern, with her focus trained exclusively on the immutable past, represents the death force, her daughter Diana is the vital, life-giving presence. Diana is an abrasive, liberated, sensual, innately selfish modern young woman who stands in positive contrast to the stasis of her mother; Diana is splashes of color, while her mother is only gray. The younger woman is earthy and fulfilled, content with her music (playing the guitar satisfies her limited need for proficiency), her faith (which in her mind takes care of any and all questions of morality) and her sexuality (which she enjoys as a matter of course). Diana goes from one affair to another, not in search of love (she claims she can't love anybody) but out of habit. Diana defines the human quest for meaning in simple, direct terms—the fulfillment of a man's or woman's emotional requirements. To her, love does not mean self-sacrifice; instead, love is synonymous with need.

The social and spiritual backdrop of *The Pardoner's Tale* bears all the colors of the archetypal world of Wain's other fiction: random, atomized, lonely, and contradictory in hue. In this milieu, wasted lives, debased sexual encounters, and destroyed moral intelligences yield a tragic pattern of futility and sterility, of isolation from the community, estrangement from those who used to be intimate, and loneliness in the midst of an unruly universe.

WHERE THE RIVERS MEET

Where the Rivers Meet (1988), *Comedies* (1990), and *Hungry Generations* (1994) collectively make up Wain's final, deeply personal trilogy called *Where the Rivers Meet,* set in the city and the university of Oxford between the 1930s and the mid-1950s. He wrote the novels, he explained, out of a desire to preserve an Oxford that had been fading from sight for over thirty years. The huge, somewhat mellow trilogy spans fifty years and charts the life of Peter Leonard, son of an Oseney Town innkeeper. Peter's intelligence leads to his becoming a history don at Episcopus College; in contrast, his brother, Brian, is a mechanic and racing adviser at the MG factory in Cowley. The first novel in the series introduces Peter and takes him through his undergraduate years at Oxford during the late 1920s and early 1930s. The second begins in 1933, with his appointment as a fellow, and ends after World War II. The last book in the series was published a few weeks after Wain died in May 1994 and covers Peter Leonard's life from 1947 to 1956. The trilogy ends with the death of Leonard's son in a motor-racing crash and Leonard's thoughts on the Russian invasion of Hungary in 1956.

In a sense, *Where the Rivers Meet* is a nostalgic portrait of an Oxford that began to disappear after the Morris car-making plant opened there in the late 1920s, eventually destroying the city's old rural character and ultimately turning it into an industrial wasteland. Wain draws upon impressions gathered from more than thirty years of his own experience at the university and within the community. All this is woven into a tapestry that blends town history with descriptions of academic formalities and ceremonies as they were practiced in the decade before the war. Other threads include a panorama of country and urban life in Oxford and London in the 1940s and a chronicle of facts that reveal much about the attitudes toward and responses to World War II.

The title of the trilogy, Wain explains in the preface to the last volume, refers both to the confluence of two rivers—the Cherwell and the Thames—and to the city's dual nature as "an international center of learning and ideas and a hub of business and industry for the English Midlands" (*Hungry Generations*, p. x). This theme also parallels the lives of its two central characters, Peter and Brian Leonard, as it shapes their personal development as well as their careers.

In these novels, Wain describes with tangible and finite detail the Oxford he valued and knew so well, from the smells and sounds of a pub in the 1930s to the web of cobblestone streets to the elaborate rules of etiquette the dons were expected to follow. These descriptive details breathe life into larger themes: the university's humanistic tradition and tumultuous years of the 1940s; the events unfolding on the world stage during and after the war. References to the evils of nazism, to sympathy for the Irish, to the philosophies of Albert Camus, Jean-Paul Sartre, and Samuel Beckett are simply Wain speaking through Peter Leonard, who shares many of Wain's social, political, and academic values. Peter's transformation from pessimist to optimist mirrors Wain's own path and represents a kind of affirmation because he adapts and endures.

LITERARY CRITICISM

John Wain called literary criticism a "useful" art. He believed that the best criticism provides a means of preserving a sense of the past literary traditions against which present works may be measured. In his own criticism, he intentionally set out to persuade and influence his readers and, characteristically, believed that there was an overtly moral purpose to literary criticism, defining it as "the discussion, between equals, of works of literature, with a view to establishing common ground on which judgments of value can be based" (*Preliminary Essays*, p. 187). A central concern across his critical writings is that the connection between literature and life must be clear and direct, and consequently all writing that works obliquely, relying too heavily on symbolism, figurative language, or obscure narrative structures should be distrusted. Wain's critical essays and reviews, like his fiction, were written not for an exclusive, erudite clique but for as broad an audience of reasonably intelligent readers as he could possibly reach.

Wain's first collection of criticism, *Preliminary Essays* (1957), exhibits the author's wide-ranging literary interests. Ovid, Restoration comedy, William Wordsworth, Alfred, Lord Tennyson, Robert Browning, Gerard Manley Hopkins, A. E. Housman, Arnold Bennett, contemporary poetry—all are embraced by a sensibility whose interests are aligned with those of the popular reader he extols. Wain's perceived readers are ordinary people who bring their common sense to a book in order to mine insights from the way characters act, think, and feel. Such readers are eager to experience someone else's imaginative attempt to make sense of the world and are willing to read carefully and think deeply in order to comprehend it.

The preface to *Preliminary Essays* establishes the guiding critical concerns of the book. Wain explains that it is called "preliminary" because it is in many respects the record of the opening phase of an apprenticeship. It takes a long time to learn to become a critic, he points out, and this collection represents "only" the first ten years of his mature analytical engagement with literature. Addressed to an audience that is "uncorrupted with literary prejudices" (p. x), Wain's tone is direct and conversational as he asks of literature those rather basic questions that intelligent readers have always pondered: Are the emotions honest? Is the work unified? Is the vision of life embedded in the work of art coherent and substantial, clear and powerful enough to shape our own perceptions and responses in significant ways? In "The Quality of Arnold Bennett," for example, Wain says that Bennett was undervalued by postwar critics. He places Bennett's work in the tradition of Daniel Defoe, with its clear linear chronology and its wealth of social observations—to which Wain's own fiction owes something—and praises one of Bennett's best-known novels, *The Old Wives' Tale* (1908), for its honesty.

A House for the Truth (1972) has proven to be one of Wain's most popular and successful critical collections. In his analysis of others, Wain asserts many of the commitments and approaches reflected in his own fiction including his commonsense insistence on clarity itself. His standard for effective fiction, he says, is "convincingness" (p. 2), a quality that derives from writing whose method is practical and businesslike and whose subject matter is believable and accessible. Wain singles out George Orwell, Samuel Johnson, Flann O'Brien, and Boris Pasternak as his "moral heroes," to use his term. Like them, he believes in the abiding virtues of selfless individualism and steadfast integrity. In addition to citing a thematic kinship with these authors, Wain discusses the technical artistry of their works with the enthusiasm and the detail of a craftsman holding in his hands a piece that is finely and lovingly shaped into a timeless, classic whole. Certainly this is the kind of artistic "truth" to which the book's title refers.

Wain's comments on the nature of poetry and the obligations of the poet in *Professing Poetry* (1977) remain consistent with the views on criticism and the novel he expressed in *A House for the Truth*. The nine lectures in this book were given in the first three years of Wain's five-year term as professor of poetry at Oxford (1973–1978). All nine lectures are linked with a commentary intended to convey "the unique nature of the Oxford chair [and] the special atmosphere that surrounds it" (p. viii). Wain's purpose in the series is twofold: to criticize those contemporary poets who have abandoned what he sees as essential parts of the English poetic tradition and whom he compares to left-wing political protesters; and to praise those poets who consciously adhered to an antimodernist tradition: Edward Thomas, Emily Dickinson, the younger W. H. Auden, William Empson, and Philip Larkin. Poetry, Wain suggests in this collection, is not to be chaotic, but clarifying and admired.

"Let me be specific," he says. "The years since 1960 have seen a mass turning-away from the notion of poetry as an art that used to have something in common with music, and towards a more or less improvisatory style which aims at one of two objectives: either to stimulate the ravings of a drug-addict, or to inculcate very simple political and social messages." Such poetry, Wain observed, represents "the deliquescence"—in other words, the dissolution—of a formerly solid tradition (p. 38). Further on he again complains about the decadence of contemporary verse, noting that "Form, which used to hold the precious liquor of a poem as a jug holds milk, is broken for no other purpose than to allow the milk to spill on to the ground. Verbal nuance and literary allusion are rejected as 'élitist,' the implied directive being that what all cannot achieve no one must.... Form is communication. It is a system of signals between writer and reader" (p. 38). Thus he reminds everyone that while true poems originate in the most personal feelings of their authors and touch the most personal feelings of their readers, the language and syntax must be fundamentally comprehensible in order to carry meaning to the reader; poetry that focuses purely on emotion to the detriment of communication is poetry that fails.

SAMUEL JOHNSON

Besides novels and criticism of fiction and poetry, Wain's broad-ranging writing repertoire included works of biography and autobiography. Of all his nonfiction, however, *Samuel Johnson* (1974) is deemed by many critics to be his best and most lasting work. In this monumental biography, many facets of Wain's writing credo are reflected clearly and forcefully.

"Nobody can write the life of a man," Wain quotes Johnson, "but those who have eaten and drunk and lived in social intercourse with him" (p. 352). Wain came as close to that as possible. For over thirty years he read Johnson's *Lives of the Poets* every year, never failing to find something new of interest and amusement in the pages. Wain saw Johnson's life from the inside and, indeed, could be considered a kind of twentieth-century version of his biographical subject: Wain himself was born in the same district and the same middle-class status as Dr. Johnson, went to the same university, and made his living in Grub Street. His love for and appreciation of the works and life of Johnson grew steadily during his undergraduate years at Oxford.

Then in 1958 the American scholar Edmund Wilson presented Wain with a large, ledger-like manuscript book with blank, green-tinted pages. Wain treasured it; he made part of it into an alphabetical section and divided another part into the years of Johnson's life. From 1958 on, Wain continued to make notes about people, places, and events in Johnson's life, and record his own unanswered questions about them. Wain was attracted to writing the biography for several reasons. Not only would it give him an opportunity to express his admiration for the man, but more important, it offered a new formal challenge. As admiring of Boswell's *Life* as he may have been, that account was anecdotal and limited; it lacked the coherence and the objectivity of a straight narrative, and so Wain determined that he would call upon his own talents as a novelist and dramatist to bring the man alive. Then in 1969, finding himself between novels, he felt the time was right to begin. After months of reading—much of it in Oxford's Bodleian Library, where Johnson had also worked—Wain managed to fill in some of the gaps and started to address his questions. In 1972 he began writing, and the book was published two years later.

Wain begins the biography by introducing the premise that Johnson had not yet been accorded his rightful reputation. He believed that Johnson, for the most part, had traditionally been thought of as a "stupid old reactionary," rather than as a deeply humanitarian man who felt compassion for the poor and outcast (pp. 13, 14). Wain points to Boswell's sentimental-romantic Toryism as one source of this distorted picture; a second was the tendency of Johnsonian scholars to write for each other rather than a broader public. Wain's stated goal for the study, therefore, was to present a portrait of Johnson "as he actually was instead of as he is thought of" (p. 14).

Samuel Johnson, Wain asserted, is a popular biography addressed to the intelligent general reader. He did not claim that he had come up with new material or explanations. In fact, he intentionally avoided reading modern studies of Johnson while writing his book because he felt it was important to draw his impressions directly from eighteenth-century sources. Some critics chided Wain for not acknowledging his sources more directly; the absence of footnotes, they said, meant that differences of scholarly opinion and reliance upon secondary sources were hidden from all but the specialists. Other critics claimed that the volume was a substantial work of synthesis of modern material and established sources. But as Wain explained in his preface, scholars had already been adequately catered to by previous biographies; this book was for popular readers.

Samuel Johnson is both an account of Johnson—his life, times, and works—and an implicit statement of Wain's own views on the state of twentieth-century England. It comprises thirty chapters divided among six main parts, each a major epoch of Dr. Johnson's life: "In the Midlands," "Grub Street," "The Dictionary Years," "True, Evident and Actual Wisdom" (the years of Johnson as legendary conversationalist), "Turtle and Burgundy" (Johnson's comfortable years with Hester Thrale), and "An Honourable Peace." Thus Wain covers all of the great moments of Johnson's career.

Wain begins with a portrait of Johnson's early life in Lichfield, and we see Dr. Johnson's monumental intellectual energy, his deeply passionate nature, his poverty, and his career defeats. Wain also explains Johnson's lifelong feelings of guilt, attributing it to his implacable mother. We learn that poverty compelled him to leave Oxford without a degree. We see him fail in his efforts first as a school usher and then as a school proprietor-teacher. Eventually, however, he was hired to write for the *Gentleman's Magazine,* a development that inspired him to move to London, where he emerged into English literary life. There, in Grub Street, he talked and wrote, researched, attacked the politically powerful Whigs, defended the traditionalist Tories, and lived his life.

In London Johnson met and married Elizabeth "Tetty" Porter, but the happiness brought by the union was short lived. Financial pressures forced him to work as a parliamentary reporter. Then he had the idea of preparing an edition of Shakespeare. When this proposal was frustrated, he undertook the preparation of a dictionary of the English language. This project attracted a number of wealthy supporters, and for a time he was content. In later years, his wife deceased, Johnson turned to Boswell and Hester Thrale for companionship. Throughout it all, Wain recounts Johnson's diseases of the body and torments of the soul.

The preceding summary of the biography's organizational structure gives some indication of how Wain used his novelist's art to establish a sense of the passage of a long and productive life; the book is a chronicle, in a sense, a narrative that also reflects on the events and forces that impact the personal history as it unfolds. Also like his novels, Wain's characterization is strong, vivid, and original; his portrait of the scholar, critic, and professional curmudgeon has an appealing depth and vitality. Wain adds nuance and authenticity by recounting some incidents in Dr. Johnson's own speech patterns, which, like Johnson's writing, is grounded in vivid and concrete detail. Likewise, Wain's descriptive powers create a strong physical image of Johnson—with his huge limbs and weight, his awkwardness and ugliness, his gross appetite and flashpoint angers. Wain chooses incidents, facts, and details that make his subject materialize before us in all his power, versatility, and passion.

Wain's sense of the cultural, historical, and social background is equally powerful. We see the Lichfield market on the September afternoon of Johnson's birth; the English countryside of 1728, through which Johnson rode to go up to Oxford; and the London of a decade later, when the child of the provinces finally faced the metropolis. Wain's even and unaffected writing style is, in its sympathy and intelligence, a splendid testament to the delight in people, art, and life, the originality, and the directness that characterized the Augustan literary giant himself.

Wain does not stop with description or even re-creation. He is also concerned with the large shadow Johnson continues to cast on the moral landscape of England. Wain tries to make Johnson relevant to modern life and repeatedly uses him as a standard against which to compare contemporary literary and intellectual endeavors. Wain's recurrent interpretive comments are undeniably conservative. He characterizes eighteenth-century England as socially stable and intellectually fruitful, and he stresses its moral superiority to the twentieth century's chaos and angst. It is clear that Wain sees eighteenth-century provincial life as a time of dignity, pride, and self-sufficiency, qualities he believes are lacking in his own age. Like Johnson, Wain defends the value of reason and moderation, common sense, moral courage, and intellectual self-respect; also like Johnson, he decries their absence in the society around him.

Wain's loving esteem for the man and his work is palpable. The biography is written with sympathy for Johnson's suffering, with awe for his intellect, and with admiration for his stoicism. Wain was personally involved—the book was written out of a lifetime's interest in the subject—and there is perhaps no finer way to praise its level of achievement than to say that it makes us feel for Johnson what Wain felt for him.

Two more critical works are noteworthy. In the final year of his life Wain produced *Dear Shadows,* a collection of essays on people he had known who had passed on (from Richard Burton to Marshall McLuhan to his own father), and *Johnson Is Leaving*—a study of the last days of Dr. Johnson's life.

POETRY

In 1953 the BBC hired Wain as editor of Third Programme (*New Reading*), a fifteen-minute weekly radio program that introduced promising young writers to an estimated audience of one hundred thousand listeners. It was a brief stint (six months), but Wain set about establishing what he described as a policy of "consolidation"—characteristic reaction against modernism and a return to traditional forms—that would guide his choice of writers to feature on the show. Among them were Kingsley Amis, A. Alvarez, Robert Conquest, Donald Davie, Thom Gunn,

D. J. Enright, John Holloway, Elizabeth Jennings, and Philip Larkin, most of whom wrote both poetry and fiction.

In 1956 an anthology called *New Lines* brought many of these British poets, including Wain, to wider attention. A distinctive feature common to their verse was a rejection of the passion and romantic rhetoric of Dylan Thomas, whose voice had dominated the early part of the decade. They paid greater attention to formal structure and drew their subjects and language from a perception of the everyday in which life is orderly, people are usually polite, and human emotions are fundamentally decent and usually controlled. Because of their similarities in content and form, the poets came to be known among literary journalists as "The Movement." Wain and the other poets saw their writing as an alternative to the symbolic, highly allusive poetry of T. S. Eliot and others. In a movement away from obscurity and excess of style, the Movement poets espoused and practiced precision, lucidity, and craftsmanship. They concentrated on honesty of thought and feeling, on a conversational tone, and a disciplined, formal verse to project what one critic called a "businesslike" intention to communicate with the reader.

Wain's early verse in *Mixed Feelings: Nineteen Poems* (1951) may be appreciated for its direct, commonsense approach. He avoids extremes or excessive stylistic experimentation. For example, in a six-poem sequence called "Who Speaks My Language?" Wain describes the obstacles that ambiguous language, the generation gap, money, and unfamiliar themes can create and how such difficulties derail the reader's understanding and appreciation of the work.

Wain's range and technique advanced with each succeeding volume of verse. Some of the poems in *A Word Carved on a Sill* (1956), such as "Poem Feigned to Have Been Written by an Electronic Brain" convey an almost journalistic immediacy along with wit. In "The Bad Thing," by contrast, Wain achieves a study of depressive states similar to his novelistic treatment in *The Pardoner's Tale*.

Wain's development continued with the looser, more declamatory poems of *Weep Before God* (1961), considered by critics to be one of Wain's most impressive collections. Commentators found a range and rhythm in "Poem Without a Main Verb" (a riddling poem), "Anniversary" (an autobiographical reflection), and "Brooklyn Heights" (a topographical meditation) that was more adventurous and expressive than Wain's earlier poetic work. In "Anecdote of 2 a.m." he is direct and unsentimental; in "A Song About Major Eatherly," more public and topical as he ponders the troubled later career of an American pilot involved in the nuclear attack on Japan in 1945. In "A Boisterous Poem About Poetry," Wain writes about the dehumanizing influence of science, with its all-consuming emphasis on the mechanical and industrial: "Metal hates flesh, / Hates everything that has a beating heart" (VI, ll. 5–6). From this cold, human-hating material we make our human-hating machines.

After *Weep Before God,* Wain found powerful material in politics and social commentary. What separated him from his contemporaries was a moral dignity that was crystalline and a diction that was very much in the manner of his beloved eighteenth century. The later poems embody, in a more compact form, many of the feelings and attitudes that are expressed in his novels; frequently, poems question or even satirize the institutions and prejudices of modern society. As in his novels, Wain is chiefly concerned in his verse with human efforts to seek happiness and self-fulfillment.

The search for peace and contentment is the subject of *Wildtrack,* a long philosophical poem published in 1965. Wain employs a considerable variety of meter, including blank verse, terza rima, a free sestina, a sonnet, couplets and mock dance-lyric, to glide freely from the past to the present, from the public to the personal, in an almost epic quest for happiness and human interdependence.

In 1969 Wain published *Letters to Five Artists*. He stated in the preface that, with one exception, the five constituent poems were written not only to stand by themselves but also to be seen together as a larger work. Wain decried the sea of contemporary violence in which the world seemed to be drowning: "The poet ... is a lyrical recorder who must make others lament and weep over, not understand, such violence" (p. 143). He also declared that a human life can never be seen "except as an inextricable scrambling of private and public" (p. 9). Hence, the theme of this volume echoes *Wildtrack,* with "its inward-looking Night-self and outward-looking Day-self that together constitute the human personality" (p. 9). The basic rhythm of the poems is iambic pentameter, showing the influence of traditional English verse, and Wain directed the poems at five artist acquaintances who inspired him: the painter Victor Neep, poets Elizabeth Jennings and Anthony Conran, sculptor Lee Lubbers, S.J., and jazz trumpeter Bill Coleman. Each was a personal friend of Wain's and also a visionary whose imagination, he suggested, presents to the world a light that guides the poet and the reader toward recognition—of himself, of the artists, and of the world.

Feng: A Poem (1975) is a sequence of poems set in northern Europe during the early Middle Ages, but the reality they explore is that of our own time and place. In a prefatory note, the author explained that the design of the work came from the *Historia Danica* of Saxo Grammaticus—from which Shakespeare borrowed the plot for *Hamlet.* In the original story, Horwendil, father of Amleth, kills the King of Norway in single combat. Feng, Horwendil's brother, poisons him and marries Gerutha, his queen. Amleth feigns madness; Feng tries but fails to trick him out of the guise by means of a beautiful woman. The prince voyages to England, returns and kills Feng, and settles down to an active reign.

Unlike Shakespeare, who concentrates on Amleth (Hamlet), Wain focuses on the inner life of Feng, a sick and delusional person who seizes power and then has to live with the consequences; Wain thus highlights the contrast between natural innocence and human depravity. The victory of human goodness and love over violence, as well as the implicit value of human interaction, are Wain's major poetic themes, just as they were in his fiction. As Wain explained, "The artist's function is always to humanize the society he is living in, to assert the importance of humanity in the teeth of whatever is currently trying to annihilate that importance" (*House,* p. 23). The artist must rise above violence and brutality and affirm the enduring decency of humankind's higher nature.

CONCLUSION

Anyone familiar with the work and talents of John Wain could not but sense an enormous feeling of loss at his sudden death from a stroke on May 24, 1994, at John Radcliffe Hospital in Oxford. He was sixty-nine years old. Five years later one of his three surviving sons, William, recast a Web site (www.smallersky.com) dedicated to the work and the life of his father. Ultimately what Wain stood for, writes his son, was "resilience, tolerance, our common humanity, the producing of art in the most trying of circumstances, and happiness in the familiar and extraordinary things of life." Indeed, if there is one conclusion we can come to about Wain as a writer, it's that he was true to his credo of art as a clarifying rather than an obscuring force, and that he was one of the most accomplished and versatile of England's writers. Although his voice was silenced, he left behind a significant body of work that will stand up to reading and rereading for generations to come.

Selected Bibliography

WORKS OF JOHN WAIN

Novels and Short Stories

Hurry on Down. London: Secker & Warburg, 1953, 1978; New York: Viking Press, 1965. Published in the United States as *Born in Captivity.* New York: Knopf, 1954.

Living in the Present. London: Secker & Warburg, 1955; New York: Putnam, 1960.

The Contenders. London: Macmillan; New York: St. Martin's Press, 1958.

A Travelling Woman. London: Macmillan; New York: St. Martin's Press, 1959.

Nuncle, and Other Stories. London: Macmillan; New York: St. Martin's Press, 1960.

Strike the Father Dead. London: Macmillan; New York: St. Martin's Press, 1962.

The Young Visitors. London: Macmillan; New York: Viking Press, 1965.

Death of the Hind Legs, and Other Stories. London: Macmillan; New York: Viking Press, 1966.

The Smaller Sky. London: Macmillan, 1967.

A Winter in the Hills. London: Macmillan; New York: Viking Press, 1970.

The Life Guard: Stories. London: Macmillan, 1971; New York: Viking Press, 1972.

The Pardoner's Tale. London: Macmillan, 1978; New York: Viking Press, 1979.

King Caliban and Other Stories. London: Macmillan, 1978.

Lizzie's Floating Shop. London: Bodley Head, 1981.

Young Shoulders. London: Macmillan. Published in the United States as *The Free Zone Starts Here.* New York: Delacorte Press, 1982.

Manhood. Cheltenham, Gloucestershire, U.K.: Nelson Thornes, 1986.

Where the Rivers Meet. London: Hutchinson, 1988.

Comedies. London: Hutchinson, 1990.

Hungry Generations. London: Hutchinson, 1994.

POETRY

Mixed Feelings: Nineteen Poems. Reading, Berkshire, U.K.: Reading University School of Art, 1951.

A Word Carved on a Sill. London: Routledge; New York: St. Martin's Press, 1956.

A Song About Major Eatherly. College Park, Md.: Qara Press, 1961. Reprinted in *Weep Before God,* 1961.

Weep Before God: Poems. London: Macmillan; New York: St. Martin's Press, 1961.

Wildtrack: A Poem. London: Macmillan, 1965; New York: Viking Press, 1966.

Letters to Five Artists. London: Macmillan, 1969; New York: Viking Press, 1970.

The Shape of Feng. London: Covent Garden Press, 1972.

Feng: A Poem. London: Macmillan, 1975; New York: Viking Press, 1975.

Poems for the Zodiac. Roxburghshire, Scotland: Pisces Press, 1980.

Thinking About Mr. Person. Beckenham, Kent, U.K.: Chimaera Press, 1980.

Poems: 1949–1979. London: Macmillan, 1981.

The Twofold. Hayes, Middlesex, U.K.: Bran's Head Books, 1981.

Mid-Week Period Return. Stratford-upon-Avon, U.K.: Celandine Press, 1982.

Open Country. London: Hutchinson, 1987.

LITERARY CRITICISM, BIOGRAPHY, MEMOIR

Preliminary Essays. London: Macmillan; New York: St. Martin's Press, 1957.

Gerard Manley Hopkins: An Idiom of Desperation. London: Oxford University Press; Folcroft, Pa.: Folcroft Editions, 1959. Reprinted in *Essays on Literature and Ideas,* 1963.

Sprightly Running: Part of an Autobiography. London: Macmillan, 1962; New York: St. Martin's Press, 1963.

Essays on Literature and Ideas. London: Macmillan; New York: St. Martin's Press, 1963.

The Living World of Shakespeare: A Playgoer's Guide. London: Macmillan; New York: St. Martin's Press, 1964.

Arnold Bennett. New York: Columbia University Press, 1967.

A House for the Truth: Critical Essays. London: Macmillan, 1972; New York: Viking Press, 1973.

Samuel Johnson. London: Macmillan, 1974, 1980; New York: Viking Press, 1975.

Professing Poetry. London: Macmillan, 1977; New York: Viking Press, 1978.

The Seafarer. Translation from the Anglo-Saxon. Warwickshire, U.K.: Greville Press, 1980.

Dear Shadows: Portraits from Memory. London: John Murray, 1986.

EDITED VOLUMES

Contemporary Reviews of Romantic Poetry. London: Harrap; New York: Barnes and Noble, 1953.

Interpretations: Essays on Twelve English Poems. London: Routledge, 1955, 1972; New York: Hillary House, 1957.

International Literary Annual. London: John Calder, 1958, 1959; New York: Criterion Books, 1959, 1960.

Fanny Burney's Diary. London: Folio Society, 1961.

Anthology of Modern Poetry. London: Hutchinson, 1963.

Pope. New York: Dell, 1963.

Thomas Hardy's "The Dynasts." London: Macmillan, 1965; New York: St. Martin's Press, 1966.

Selected Shorter Poems of Thomas Hardy. London: Macmillan; New York: St. Martin's Press, 1966.

Selected Stories of Thomas Hardy. London: Macmillan; New York: St. Martin's Press, 1966.

Shakespeare: Macbeth: A Casebook. London: Macmillan, 1968.

Shakespeare: Othello: A Casebook. London: Macmillan, 1971.

Johnson as Critic: London and Boston: Routledge, 1973.

Samuel Johnson: Lives of the English Poets: A Selection. London: Dent, 1975; New York: Dutton, 1975.

Johnson on Johnson: A Selection of the Personal and Autobiographical Writings of Samuel Johnson (1709–1784). London: Dent; New York: Dutton, 1976.

An Edmund Wilson Celebration. London: Phaidon. Also

published as *Edmund Wilson: The Man and His Work*. New York: New York University Press, 1978.

The New Wessex Selection of Thomas Hardy's Poetry. With Eirian Wain. London: Macmillan, 1978.

Personal Choice: A Poetry Anthology. Newton Abbot, U.K., and North Pomfret, Vt.: David and Charles, 1978.

Anthology of Contemporary Poetry. London: Hutchinson, 1979. *Everyman's Book of English Verse*. London: Dent, 1981.

The Oxford Library of English Poetry. 3 vols. Oxford: Oxford University Press, 1986.

The Oxford Library of Short Novels. 3 vols. Oxford: Clarendon, 1990.

The Journals of James Boswell. London: Heinemann, 1991.

Drama

The Take-Over Bid (radio), 1963.

The Young Visitors (television), 1967.

Dr. Johnson Out of Town (radio), 1974.

Harry in the Night: An Optimistic Comedy (stage), 1975.

Assassination (radio), 1976.

You Wouldn't Remember (radio), 1978.

A Winter in the Hills (radio), 1981.

Frank (radio), 1982.

Young Shoulders (television), 1984. With Robert Smith.

The Mathematic Triangle (radio), 1991.

Johnson Is Leaving: A Melodrama (radio), 1992.

BIBLIOGRAPHIES

Gerard, David. *John Wain: A Bibliography*. London: Mansell; Westport, Conn.: Meckler Corporation, 1987; Westport, Conn.: Greenwood Press, 1988.

Salwak, Dale. *John Braine and John Wain: A Reference Guide*. Boston: G. K. Hall, 1980.

COLLECTIONS

The bulk of John Wain's papers, including published books, articles, reviews, poems and interviews as well as archival materials (chiefly broadcast scripts, transcripts, and a few items of correspondence) are held at the University of Reading. Additional correspondence is held at the University of Maryland and the Lilly Library Manuscript Collections at Indiana University.

CRITICAL AND BIOGRAPHICAL STUDIES

Bode, Carl. "The Redbrick Cinderellas." *College English* 20:332, 334–337 (April 1959).

Edwards, J. A., ed. *John Wain: Poet, Novelist, Critic: Exhibition Catalog*. Reading: University of Reading Library, 1977.

Firchow, Peter, ed. "John Wain." In his *The Writer's Place: Interviews on the Literary Situation in Contemporary Britain*. Minneapolis: University of Minnesota Press, 1974. Pp. 313–330.

Gindin, James J. "The Moral Center of John Wain's Fiction." In his *Postwar British Fiction: New Accents and Attitudes*. Berkeley and Los Angeles: University of California Press, 1962. Pp. 128–144.

Hatziolou, Elizabeth. *John Wain: A Man of Letters*. London: Pisces Press, 1997.

Heptonstall, Geoffrey. "Remembering John Wain." *Contemporary Review* 266:144–147 (1995).

Leader, Zachary, ed. *The Letters of Kingsley Amis*. London: HarperCollins, 2000.

Leader, Zachary. *The Life of Kingsley Amis*. London: Jonathan Cape; New York: Pantheon, 2006.

Leader, Zachary, ed. *The Movement Reconsidered: Essays on Larkin, Amis, Gunn, Davies, and Their Contemporaries*. Oxford: Oxford University Press, 2009.

Lehmann, John, "The Wain-Larkin Myth." *Sewanee Review* 66:578–587 (autumn 1958).

Mellown, Elgin W. "Steps Toward Vision: The Development of Technique in John Wain's First Seven Novels." *South Atlantic Quarterly* 17: 330–342 (summer 1969).

O'Connor, William Van. "John Wain: The Will to Write." *Wisconsin Studies in Contemporary Literature* 1:35–49 (winter 1960).

Rabinovitz, Rubin. "The Novelists of the 1950's: A General Survey." In his *The Reaction Against Experiment in the English Novel, 1950–1960*. New York: Columbia University Press, 1967.

Salwak, Dale. "John Wain: Man of Letters." In his *Interviews with Britain's Angry Young Men*. San Bernardino, Calif.: Borgo Press, 1984. Pp. 67–81.

Taylor, D. J. *After the War: The Novel and English Society Since 1945*. London: Chatto and Windus, 1993.

Wilson, Colin. *The Angry Years: The Rise and Fall of the Angry Young Men*. London: Robson Books, 2007.

MASTER INDEX

The following index covers the entire British Writers series through Supplement XVI. All references include volume numbers in boldface roman numerals followed by page numbers within that volume. Subjects of articles are indicated by boldface type.

A. *Couleii Plantarum Libri Duo* (Cowley), **II:** 202
A. D. Hope (Hart), **Supp. XII:** 123
"A. G. A. V." (Blunden), **Supp. XI:** 45
A la recherche du temps perdu (Proust), **Supp. IV:** 126, 136
A la recherche du temps perdu (Raine), **Supp. XIII:** 173–175
A Laodicean (Hardy), **Retro. Supp. I:** 112, 114
"A Propos of Lady Chatterley's Lover" (Lawrence), **IV:** 106; **VII:** 91
"Aaron" (Herbert), **Retro. Supp. II:** 179
Aaron's Rod (Lawrence), **VII:** 90, 94, 106–107; **Retro. Supp. II:** 230
Abaft the Funnel (Kipling), **VI:** 204
"Abasement of the Northmores, The" (James), **VI:** 69
Abbas, King of Persia (Godwin), **Supp. XV:** 124
"Abbé Delille and Walter Landor, The" (Landor), **IV:** 88*n*, 92–93
Abbess of Crewe, The (Spark), **Supp. I:** 200, 201, 210
"Abbey Mason, The" (Hardy), **Retro. Supp. I:** 119
Abbey Theatre, **VI:** 212, 218, 307, 309, 316; **VII:** 3, 6, 11
Abbey Walk, The (Henryson), **Supp. VII:** 146, 147
Abbot, The (Scott), **IV:** 39
Abbott, C. C., **V:** 379, 381
ABC Murders, The (Christie), **Supp. II:** 128, 130, 135
"ABC of a Naval Trainee" (Fuller), **Supp. VII:** 69
Abercrombie, Lascelles, Supp. XVI: 1–14
"Abomination, The" (Murray), **Supp. VII:** 273
Abyssophone (Redgrove), **Supp. VI:** 236
Abdelazer; or, The Moor's Revenge (Behn), **Supp. III:** 27, 36; **Retro. Supp. III:** 6
Abercrombie, Lascelles, **II:** 247
"Abercuawg," **Supp. XII:** 284, 287
Aberdeen Free Press, **Supp. XII:** 203
"Abernethy" (Dunn), **Supp. X:** 77
"Abiding Vision, The" (West), **Supp. III:** 442
Abinger Harvest (Forster), **VI:** 411, 412; **Supp. II:** 199, 223
"Abir" (Jamie), **Supp. XIV:** 129
"Abject Misery" (Kelman), **Supp. V:** 244
Ableman, Paul, **Supp. IV:** 354

Abolition of Man, The (Lewis), **Supp. III:** 248, 255, 257
Abortive (Churchill), **Supp. IV:** 181
About a Boy (Hornby), **Supp. XV:** 133, 140–141
About a Boy (screenplay, Hornby), **Supp. XV:** 144
About Love: Poems (Montague), **Supp. XV:** 217, 219
About the House (Auden), **Retro. Supp. I:** 13
"About Two Colmars" (Berger), **Supp. IV:** 85
"Above the Dock" (Hulme), **Supp. VI:** 134, 136
"Abraham Men" (Powys), **VIII:** 250
Abridgement of the History of England, An (Goldsmith), **III:** 191
Abridgement of the Light of Nature Pursued, An (Hazlitt), **IV:** 139
Abroad: British Literary Traveling Between the Wars (Fussell), **Supp. IV:** 22
Absalom and Achitophel (Dryden), **II:** 292, 298–299, 304; **Retro. Supp. III:** 54–55, 58, 62, 63–64, 66–75, 77, 79
"Absalom, My Son" (Warner), **Supp. VII:** 380
"Absence" (Jennings), **Supp. V:** 218
"Absence" (Thompson), **V:** 444
"Absence, The" (Thomas), **Supp. XII:** 287–288
"Absence, The" (Warner), **Supp. VII:** 373
Absence of War, The (Hare), **Supp. IV:** 282, 294, 297–298
"Absences" (Larkin), **Supp. I:** 277; **Retro. Supp. III:** 208
Absent Friends (Ayckbourn), **Supp. V:** 2–3, 10, 13, 14
Absent in the Spring (Christie), **Supp. II:** 133
Absentee, The (Edgeworth), **Supp. III:** 154, **160–161**, 165
"Absent–Minded Beggar, The" (Kipling), **VI:** 203
"Absent–Mindedness in a Parish Choir" (Hardy), **VI:** 22
Absolute Friends (le Carré), **Retro. Supp. III:** 229
Abstract of a Book Lately Published, A: A Treatise of Human Nature . . . (Hume), **Supp. III:** 230–231
Absurd Person Singular (Ayckbourn), **Supp. V:** 2, 5–6, 9
"Abt Vogler" (Browning), **IV:** 365, 366, 370

Abuses of Conscience, The (Sterne), **III:** 135
Academy (periodical), **VI:** 249
"Academy, The" (Reid), **Supp. VII:** 331
Academy Notes (Ruskin), **V:** 178
Acceptable Sacrifice, The (Bunyan), **II:** 253
Acceptance World, The (Powell), **VII:** 347, 348, 350
"Access to the Children" (Trevor), **Supp. IV:** 504
"Accident, The" (Beer), **Supp. XIV:** 4, 5
Accident (Bennett), **VI:** 250
Accident (Pinter), **Supp. I:** 374, 375; **Retro. Supp. I:** 226
"Accident" (Scupham), **Supp. XIII:** 228
Accidental Man, An (Murdoch), **Supp. I:** 227
Accidental Woman, The (Coe), **Supp. XV:** 51, 52, 53, 54, 56–57
"Accidents" (Adcock), **Supp. XII:** 9
"Accompanist, The" (Desai), **Supp. V:** 65
"According to His Lights" (Galsworthy), **VI:** 276–277
"Account, The" (Cowley), **II:** 197
Account of Corsica, An (Boswell), **III:** 236, 239, 243, 247
Account of the European Settlements in America, An (Burke), **III:** 205
Account of the Growth of Popery and Arbitrary Government, An (Marvell), **I:** 207–208, 219; **Retro. Supp. II:** 266–268
Account of the Life of Dr. Samuel Johnson . . . by Himself, An (Johnson), **III:** 122
Account of the Life of Mr. Richard Savage, An (Johnson), **Retro. Supp. I:** 142
Account of the Seminary That Will Be opened on Monday the Fourth Day of August at Epsom in Surrey, for the Instruction of Twelve Pupils in the Greek, Latin, French, and English Languages, An (Godwin), **Supp. XV:** 117
Account of the Settlement at Port Jackson, **Supp. IV:** 348
Account Rendered (Brittain), **Supp. X:** 45
Ace of Clubs (Coward), **Supp. II:** 155
"Aceldama" (Delanty), **Supp. XIV:** 78
Achilles (Gay), **III:** 55, 66, 67
Achilles in Scyros (Bridges), **VI:** 83
"Achronos" (Blunden), **Supp. XI:** 45
Ackroyd, Peter, Supp. VI: 1–15
"Acid" (Kelman), **Supp. V:** 245

311

Acis and Galatea (Gay), **III:** 55, 67
Acre of Land, The (Thomas), **Supp. XII:** 283
"Across the Estuary" (Nicholson), **Supp. VI:** 216
"Across the Moor" (Adcock), **Supp. XII:** 8
Across the Plains (Stevenson), **V:** 389, 396
"Act, The" (Harrison), **Supp. V:** 161–162
Act of Creation, The (Koestler), **Supp. I:** 37, 38
Act of Grace (Keneally), **Supp. IV:** 347
"Act of Reparation, An" (Warner), **Supp. VII:** 380
Act of Terror, An (Brink), **Supp. VI: 55–56,** 57
Act of Worship, An (Thompson), **Supp. XIV:** 291
Act Without Words I (Beckett), **Supp. I:** 46, 55, 57
Act Without Words II (Beckett), **Supp. I:** 46, 55, 57
Actaeon and Diana (Johnson), **I:** 286
Acte (Durrell), **Supp. I:** 126, 127; **Retro. Supp. III:** 85
Actions and Reactions (Kipling), **VI:** 204
Acton, John, **IV:** 289, 290; **VI:** 385
"Actor's Farewell, The" (Conn), **Supp. XIII:** 81
"Acts of Restoration" (Fallon), **Supp. XII:** 107
"Ad Amicam"sonnets (Thompson), **V:** 441
"Ad Labienum" (Campion), **Supp. XVI:** 100
Ad Patrem (Milton), **Retro. Supp. II:** 272
"Ad Thamesin" (Campion), **Supp. XVI:** 99
Adam and Eve and Pinch Me (Coppard), **VIII:** 85, 88, 89, 91–93
"Adam and Eve and Pinch Me" (Coppard), **VIII:** 90
Adam and Eve and Pinch Me (Rendell), **Supp. IX:** 189, 195
Adam and the Sacred Nine (Hughes), **Supp. I:** 357, 363
Adam Bede (Eliot), **V:** xxii, 2, 191–192, 194, 200; **Retro. Supp. II:** 104–106
"Adam confesses an infidelity to Eve" (Constantine), **Supp. XV:** 72
"Adam Pos'd" (Finch), **Supp. IX:** 68
"Adam Tempted" (Thomas), **Supp. XII:** 290
Adams, Henry, **VI:** 65
Adam's Breed (Hall), **Supp. VI:** 120, 122, 128
"Adam's Curse" (Yeats), **III:** 184; **VI:** 213
"Adam's Dream" (Muir), **Supp. VI:** 207–208
"Adapting *Nice Work* for Television" (Lodge), **Supp. IV:** 373, 381
Adcock, Fleur, **Supp. XII: 1–16**
"Ad Thamesin" (Campion), **Supp. XVI:** 99
"Adders' Brood" (Powys), **VIII:** 248, 249
Addison, Joseph, **II:** 195, 200; **III:** 1, 18, 19, **38–53,** 74, 198; **IV:** 278, 281, 282

"Additional Poems" (Housman), **VI:** 161
"Address to the Deep" (Jewsbury), **Supp. XIV:** 161
Address to the Deil (Burns), **III:** 315, 317
Address to the Irish People, An (Shelley), **IV:** 208; **Retro. Supp. I:** 245
"Address to the Ocean" (Jewsbury), **Supp. XIV:** 152, 153
"Address to the Unco Guid" (Burns), **III:** 319
"Address to Two Candles" (Cowley), **Supp. XVI:** 123
"Addy" (Blackwood), **Supp. IX:** 12
Adéle: Jane Eyre's Hidden Story (Tennant), **Supp. IX:** 239
Adelphi, **Supp. XIII:** 191
Adelphi (Cowper), **Retro. Supp. III:** 39–40
Adepts of Africa, The (Williams, C. W. S.), see *Black Bastard, The*
"Adieu to Fancy" (Robinson), **Supp. XIII:** 204
"Adina" (James), **VI:** 69
Administrator, The (MacNeice), **VII:** 401
Admirable Bashville, The (Barker), **VI:** 113
Admiral Crichton, The (Barrie), **Supp. III:** 6, 9, **14–15**
Admiral Guinea (Stevenson), **V:** 396
"Admonition on a Rainy Afternoon" (Nye), **Supp. X:** 203
Adolphe (Constant), **Supp. IV:** 125, 126, 136
Adonais (Shelley), **I:** 160; **VI:** 73; **IV:** xviii, 179, 196, 205–206, 207, 208; **Retro. Supp. I:** 255
Adonis and the Alphabet (Huxley), **VII:** 206–207
Adonis, Attis, Osiris: Studies in the History of Oriental Religion (Frazer), **Supp. III:** 175, 180
Adoption Papers, The (Kay), **Supp. XIII:** 99, 100, 102–103, 108
"Adoption Papers, The" (Kay), **Supp. XIII:** 102–103
Adored One, The (Barrie), **Supp. III:** 5, 9
Adorno, Theodor, **Supp. IV:** 29, 82
"Adrian and Bardus" (Gower), **I:** 54
"Adult Video" (Boyd), **Supp. XVI:** 44
"Adultery" (Gunn), **Retro. Supp. III:** 125
"Advanced Lady, The" (Mansfield), **VII:** 172
Advancement of Learning, An (Hill, R.), **Supp. IX:** 122
Advancement of Learning, The (Bacon), **I:** 261–265; **II:** 149; **IV:** 279
Advantages Proposed by Repealing the Sacramental Test, The (Swift), **III:** 36
"Adventure of Charles Augustus Milverton, The" (Doyle), **Supp. II:** 173
"Adventure of Charles Wentworth" (Brontë), **V:** 118–119
"Adventure of the Abbey Grange, The" (Doyle), **Supp. II:** 168, 173, 176
"Adventure of the Blanched Soldier, The" (Doyle), **Supp. II:** 168
"Adventure of the Blue Carbuncle, The" (Doyle), **Supp. II:** 173

"Adventure of the Bruce–Partington Plans, The" (Doyle), **Supp. II:** 170, 175
"Adventure of the Copper Beeches, The" (Doyle), **Supp. II:** 168
"Adventure of the Creeping Man, The" (Doyle), **Supp. II:** 165
"Adventure of the Devil's Foot, The" (Doyle), **Supp. II:** 167, 176
"Adventure of the Empty House, The" (Doyle), **Supp. II:** 160
"Adventure of the Engineer's Thumb, The" (Doyle), **Supp. II:** 170
"Adventure of the Golden Pince–Nez, The" (Doyle), **Supp. II:** 175
"Adventure of the Illustrious Client, The" (Doyle), **Supp. II:** 169
"Adventure of the Lion's Mane, The" (Doyle), **Supp. II:** 168–169
"Adventure of the Missing Three–Quarter, The" (Doyle), **Supp. II:** 165, 171
"Adventure of the Norwood Builder, The" (Doyle), **Supp. II:** 169, 170, 173
"Adventure of the Retired Colourman, The" (Doyle), **Supp. II:** 172
"Adventure of the Second Stain, The" (Doyle), **Supp. II:** 175, 176
"Adventure of the Six Napoleons, The" (Doyle), **Supp. II:** 170–171, 174–175
"Adventure of the Speckled Band, The" (Doyle), **Supp. II:** 165–166
"Adventure of the Sussex Vampire, The" (Doyle), **Supp. II:** 169
"Adventure of the Three Garridebs, The" (Doyle), **Supp. II:** 165
"Adventure of Wisteria Lodge, The" (Doyle), **Supp. II:** 168
Adventure Story (Rattigan), **Supp. VII:** 316–317
Adventures Aboard the Maria Celeste (Carey), **Supp. XII:** 52
Adventures in the Skin Trade (Thomas), **Supp. I:** 182
Adventures in the Skin Trade, and Other Stories (Thomas), **Retro. Supp. III:** 335, 348
Adventures of a Young Lady, The (Trotter), **Supp. XVI:** 279–280, 281
Adventures of Caleb Williams, The (Godwin), **III:** 332, 345; **IV:** 173
Adventures of Covent Garden, The (Farquhar), **II:** 352, 354, 364
Adventures of Eovaai, Princess of Ijaveo, The (Haywood), **Supp. XII:** 135, 141–142, 146
Adventures of Ferdinand Count Fathom, The (Smollett), see *Ferdinand Count Fathom*
Adventures of Harry Richmond, The (Meredith), **V:** xxiii, 228, 234
Adventures of Johnny Walker, Tramp, The (Davies), **Supp. XI:** 93
Adventures of Peregrine Pickle, The (Smollett), see *Peregrine Pickle*
Adventures of Philip on His Way Through the World, The (Thackeray), **V:** 19, 29, 35, 38
Adventures of Robina, The (Tennant), **Supp. IX:** 239

Adventures of Roderick Random, The (Smollett), *see Roderick Random*
Adventures of Sir Launcelot Greaves, The (Smollett), *see Sir Launcelot Greaves*
Adventures of the Black Girl in Her Search for God, The (Shaw), **VI:** 124, 127, 129
Adventures of Ulysses, The (Lamb), **IV:** 85
"Adventurous Exploit of the Cave of Ali Baba, The" (Sayers), **Supp. III:** 340
"Advertisement for a Scottish Servant" (Butlin), **Supp. XVI:** 57
Advice: A Satire (Smollett), **III:** 152n, 158
Advice to a Daughter (Halifax), **III:** 40
"Advice to a Discarded Lover" (Adcock), **Supp. XII:** 5
Advice to a Son (Osborne), **II:** 145
Advocateship of Jesus Christ, The (Bunyan), *II:* 253
A. E. Housman (Gow), **VI:** 164
A. E. Housman: A Divided Life (Watson), **VI:** 164
A. E. Housman: An Annotated Handlist (Sparrow), **VI:** 164
AE. *See* Russell, George William
"Ae Simmer's Day" (Soutar), **Supp. XVI:** 250
"Aeaea" (Burnside), **Supp. XIII:** 17
Ælfric of Eynsham, Abbot, **Retro. Supp. II:** 297–298
Aeneid (tr. Douglas), **III:** 311
Aeneid, The (tr. Dryden), **Retro. Supp. III:** 78
Aeneid (tr. Surrey), **I:** 116–119
Aeneid of Virgil, The (tr. Day Lewis), **Supp. III:** 118
Aeneids of Virgil, Done into English Verse, The (Morris), **V:** 306
Aeneis (Dryden), **II:** 290, 293, 297, 301
"Aerial Views" (Malouf), **Supp. XII:** 221
Aeschylus, **IV:** 199
"Aesculapian Notes" (Redgrove), **Supp. VI:** 234
Aesop (Vanbrugh), **II:** 324, 332, 336
"Aesop and Rhodopè" (Landor), **IV:** 94
Aesop's Fables (Behn), **Supp. III:** 37
"Aesthetic Apologia, An" (Betjeman), **VII:** 357–358
"Aesthetic Poetry" (Pater), **V:** 356, 357
Aethiopian History (Heliodorus), **I:** 164
Affair, The (Snow), **VII:** xxi, 324, 329–330
"Affection in Education" (Carpenter), **Supp. XIII:** 43–44
"Affliction" (Herbert), **II:** 125, 127; **Retro. Supp. II:** 179
"Affliction" (Vaughan), **II:** 187–188
Affliction (Weldon), **Supp. IV:** 531, 532–533
"Affliction of Childhood, The" (De Quincey), **IV:** 152–153, 154
"Afon Rhiw" (Thomas), **Supp. XII:** 290
African Elegy, An (Okri), **Supp. V:** 359
"African Socialism: Utopian or Scientific?" (Armah), **Supp. X:** 2
African Stories (Lessing), **Supp. I:** 240, 243

"African Sunlight" (Butlin), **Supp. XVI:** 57
African Witch, The (Cary), **VII:** 186
"African Woman Today, The" (Aidoo), **Supp. XV:** 7, 9
"After a Childhood away from Ireland" (Boland), **Supp. V:** 36
"After a Death" (Stevenson), **Supp. VI:** 254
"After a Journey" (Hardy), **VI:** 18; **Retro. Supp. I:** 118
"After an Operation" (Jennings), **Supp. V:** 214
"After a Romantic Day" (Hardy), **Retro. Supp. I:** 118
After Bakhtin (The Art of Fiction: Illustrated from Classic and Modern Texts) (Lodge), **Supp. IV:** 366–367
"After Civilization" (Carpenter), **Supp. XIII:** 38
"After Closing Time" (Dunn), **Supp. X:** 69
"After Dunkirk" (Lewis), **VII:** 445
"After Eden" (MacCaig), **Supp. VI:** 187
After Hannibal (Unsworth), **Supp. VII:** 357, 365–366
"After Her Death" (Stevenson), **Supp. VI:** 254
After Julius (Howard), **Supp. XI:** 138, 139, 142–144, 145, 147, 148
After Leaving Mr. Mackenzie (Rhys), **Supp. II:** 388, **392–394**, 400
After London; or, Wild England (Jefferies), **Supp. XV:** 173–176
"After Long Ages" (Carpenter), **Supp. XIII:** 38
"After Long Silence" (Yeats), **VI:** 212in-line"After Lucretius" (Burnside), **Supp. XIII:** 26
After Magritte (Stoppard), **Supp. I:** 443, 444–445, 447, 451; **Retro. Supp. II:** 346–347
After Many a Summer (Huxley), **VII:** xviii, 205
"After Rain" (Thomas), **Supp. III:** 406
After Rain (Trevor), **Supp. IV:** 505
"After Seeing Actors Rehearsing in the Cimetière du Père Lachaise" (Jamie), **Supp. XIV:** 131
After Strange Gods (Eliot), **VI:** 207; **VII:** 153
After the Ark (Jennings), **Supp. V:** 217
After the Ball (Coward), **Supp. II:** 155
After the Dance (Rattigan), **Supp. VII:** 310–311, 312, 318
After the Death of Don Juan (Warner), **Supp. VII:** 376, 377
"After the funeral" (Thomas), **Supp. I:** 176, 177; **Retro. Supp. III:** 341–342
"After the Irish of Aodghan O'Rathaille" (Boland), **Supp. V:** 36
"After the Swim" (Dutton), **Supp. XII:** 93
"After the Vision" (Warner), **Supp. XI:** 298
"After the War" (Dunn), **Supp. X:** 70–71
"After Viewing *The Bowling Match at Castlemary, Cloyne 1847*" (Delanty), **Supp. XIV:** 67–68

"After Viking" (Burnside), **Supp. XIII:** 14
After–Dinner Joke, The (Churchill), **Supp. IV:** 181
"Afterflu Afterlife, The" (Ewart), **Supp. VII:** 42–43
Aftermath, The (Churchill), **VI:** 359
"Afternoon" (Conn), **Supp. XIII:** 71
"Afternoon" (Larkin), **Retro. Supp. III:** 207
"Afternoon Dancing" (Trevor), **Supp. IV:** 503–504
"Afternoon in Florence" (Jennings), **Supp. V:** 210
Afternoon Men (Powell), **VII:** 343–345
Afternoon Off (Bennett), **VIII:** 27
"Afternoon Visit" (Conn), **Supp. XIII:** 74
"Afternoons" (Larkin), **Supp. I:** 281
"Afterthought, An" (Rossetti), **V:** 258
"Afterwards" (Hardy), **VI:** 13, 19; **Retro. Supp. I:** 119
Against a Dark Background (Banks), **Supp. XI:** 1, 12–13
"Against Absence" (Suckling), **II:** 227
"Against Coupling" (Adcock), **Supp. XII:** 5
"Against Dryness" (Murdoch), **Supp. I:** 216, 218, 219, 221
Against Entropy (Frayn), *see Towards the End of Morning*
"Against Fruition" (Cowley), **II:** 197
"Against Fruition" (Suckling), **II:** 227
Against Hasty Credence (Henryson), **Supp. VII:** 146, 147
Against Religion (Wilson), **Supp. VI:** 297, **305–306**, 309
"Against Romanticism" (Amis), **Supp. II:** 3
"Against the Sun" (Dutton), **Supp. XII:** 88, 94
Against Venomous Tongues (Skelton), **I:** 90
Agamemnon (Seneca), **II:** 71
Agamemnon (Thomson), **Supp. III:** 411, 424
Agamemnon, a Tragedy Taken from Aeschylus (FitzGerald), **IV:** 349, 353
Agamemnon of Aeschylus, The (tr. Browning), **IV:** 358–359, 374; **Retro. Supp. III:** 30
Agamemnon of Aeschylus, The (tr. MacNeice), **VII:** 408–409
Agate, James, **Supp. II:** 143, 147
Age of Anxiety, The (Auden), **VII:** 379, 388, 389–390; **Supp. IV:** 100; **Retro. Supp. I:** 11
Age of Bronze, The (Byron), **IV:** xviii, 193
Age of Indiscretion, The (Davis), **V:** 394
Age of Iron (Coetzee), **Supp. VI:** 76, **85**
Age of Longing, The (Koestler), **Supp. I:** 25, 27, 28, 31–32, 35
Age of Reason, The (Hope), **Supp. VII:** 164
Age of Shakespeare, The (Swinburne), **V:** 333
Age of the Despots, The (Symonds), **Supp. XIV:** 249, 255–256

Age of the Rainmakers, The (Harris), **Supp. V:** 132
Agents and Patients (Powell), **VII:** 345–346
Aglaura (Suckling), **II:** 226, 238
Agnes Grey (Brontë), **V:** xx, 129–130, 132, 134–135, 140–141, 153; **Supp. IV:** 239; **Retro. Supp. I:** 52, 54–55
Agnes De Castro (Trotter), **Supp. XVI:** 280–281, 284
"Agnes Lahens" (Moore), **VI:** 98
Agnostic's Apology, An (Stephen), **VI:** 289
"Agonies of Writing a Musical Comedy" (Wodehouse), **Supp. III:** 451
"Agnus Dei" (Nye), **Supp. X:** 202
Ah, But Your Land Is Beautiful (Paton), **Supp. II: 353–355**
"Ah, what avails the sceptred race" (Landor), **IV:** 88
"Ahoy, Sailor Boy!" (Coppard), **VIII:** 97
Aidoo, Ama Ata, **Supp. XV: 1–14**
Aids to Reflection (Coleridge), **IV:** 53, 56
Aiken, Conrad, **VII:** 149, 179; **Supp. III:** 270
Aimed at Nobody (Graham), **Supp. VII:** 106
Ainger, Alfred, **IV:** 254, 267
Ainsi va la monde (Robinson), **Supp. XIII:** 202, 205
Ainsworth, Harrison, **IV:** 311; **V:** 47
"Air" (Traherne), **Supp. XI:** 267
Air and Angels (Hill), **Supp. XIV:** 116, 125
"Air and Angels" (MacCaig), **Supp. VI:** 185
"Air Disaster, The" (Ballard), **Supp. V:** 33
Air Show, The (Scupham), **Supp. XIII:** 224–225
"Aire and Angels" (Donne), **II:** 197
"Airley Beacon" (Kingsley), **Supp. XVI:** 204
Airship, The (Caudwell), **Supp. IX:** 35
"Aisling" (Delanty), **Supp. XIV:** 67
"Aisling" (Muldoon), **Supp. IV:** 418–419
"Aisling Hat, The" (McGuckian), **Supp. V:** 286, 288, 289
Aissa Saved (Cary), **VII:** 185
"Akbar's Bridge" (Kipling), **VI:** 201
Akerman, Rudolph, **V:** 111
Akhenaten Adventure, The (Kerr), **Supp. XII:** 198
Akhmatova, Anna, **Supp. IV:** 480, 494
"Al Som de l'Escalina" (Eliot), **VII:** 152
Alaham (Greville), **Supp. XI:** 110, 120
Alamanni, Luigi, **I:** 110–111
Alamein to Zem–Zem (Douglas), **VII:** xxii, 441
Alarcos (Disraeli), **IV:** 306, 308
Alaric at Rome (Arnold), **V:** 216
"Alas, Poor Bollington!" (Coppard), **VIII:** 94–95
"Alaska" (Armitage), **VIII:** 5
Alastair Reid Reader, An: Selected Poetry and Prose (Reid), **Supp. VII:** 333, 336
Alastor (Shelley), **III:** 330, 338; **IV:** xvii, 195, 198, 208, 217; **Retro. Supp. I:** 247

Albatross, and Other Stories, The (Hill), **Supp. XIV:** 118–119
"Albatross, The" (Hill), **Supp. XIV:** 115, 118–119
"Albergo Empedocle" (Forster), **VI:** 399, 412
Albert's Bridge (Stoppard), **Supp. I:** 439, 445
Albigenses, The (Maturin), **VIII:** 201, 207, 208
"Albinus and Rosemund" (Gower), **I:** 53–54
Albion! Albion! (Hill, R.), **Supp. IX:** 111
"Albion & Marina" (Brontë), **V:** 110
Albion and Albanius (Dryden), **II:** 305
Album, The (Jewsbury), **Supp. XIV:** 157
Album Verses (Lamb), **IV:** 83, 85
Alcazar (Peele), see *Battle of Alcazar, The*
Alcestis (Euripides), **IV:** 358
Alchemist, The (Jonson), **I:** 304–341, 342; **II:** 4, 48; **Retro. Supp. I:** 163
"Alchemist in the City, The" (Hopkins), **V:** 362
Alchemist's Apprentice, The (Thompson), **Supp. XIV:** 286, 291, 292–293
"Alchemy of Happiness, The" (Kureishi), **Supp. XI:** 163
Alcott, Louisa May, **Supp. IV:** 255
Aldington, Richard, **VI:** 416; **VII:** xvi, 36, 121
Aldiss, Brian, **III:** 341, 345; **Supp. V:** 22
Aldous Huxley (Brander), **VII:** 208
Alentejo Blue (Ali), **Supp. XIII:** 6–10, 11
Alexander, Peter, **I:** 300n, 326
Alexander, William (earl of Stirling), **I:** 218; **II:** 80
"Alexander and Zenobia" (Brontë), **V:** 115
Alexander Pope (Sitwell), **VII:** 138–139
Alexander Pope (Stephen), **V:** 289
Alexander Pope as Critic and Humanist (Warren), **II:** 332n
Alexander's Feast; or, The Power of Musique (Dryden), **II:** 200, 300, 304; **Retro. Supp. III:** 77
Alexanders saga, **VIII:** 237, 242
Alexandria: A History and Guide (Forster), **VI:** 408, 412
Alexandria Quartet (Durrell), **Supp. I:** 94, 96, 97, 98, 100, 101, **104–110**, 113, 122; **Retro. Supp. III:** 83, 85, 87, 88–90, 91, 92, 95
"Alfieri and Salomon the Florentine Jew" (Landor), **IV:** 91
"Alford" (Crawford), **Supp. XI:** 78–79
Alfred (Thomson and Mallet), **Supp. III:** 412, 424–425
Alfred Lord Tennyson: A Memoir (Tennyson), **IV:** 324, 338
Alfred the Great of Wessex, King, **Retro. Supp. II:** 293, 295–297
Algernon Charles Swinburne (Thomas), **VI:** 424
Ali, Monica, **Supp. XIII: 1–12**
Ali the Lion: Ali of Tebeleni, Pasha of Jannina, 1741–1822 (Plomer), **Supp. XI:** 225
Alice (Potter, D.), **Supp. X:** 228, 230–233

Alice Fell (Tennant), **Supp. IX:** 235, 236
Alice in Wonderland (Carroll), see *Alice's Adventures in Wonderland*
"Alice Kerr Went with Older Men" (Butlin), **Supp. XVI:** 66
Alice Sit-by-the-Fire (Barrie), **Supp. III:** 8, 9
Alice's Adventures in Wonderland (Carroll), **V:** xxiii, 261–265, **266–269,** 270–273
Alice's Adventures Under Ground (Carroll), **V:** 266, 273; see *Alice's Adventures in Wonderland*
"Alicia's Diary" (Hardy), **VI:** 22
"Alien, The" (Delanty), **Supp. XIV:** 74
Alien (Foster), **III:** 345
"Alien Corn, The" (Maugham), **VI:** 370, 374
Alien Sky, The (Scott), **Supp. I:** 261–263
"Alien Soil" (Kincaid), **Supp. VII:** 221, 229
All About Mr. Hatterr (Desani), **Supp. IV:** 445
"All Alone" (Robinson), **Supp. XIII:** 212
"All blue and bright, in glorious light" (Brontë), **V:** 115
"All Catches Alight" (Larkin), **Retro. Supp. III:** 204
"All Day It Has Rained" (Lewis), **VII:** 445
All Day on the Sands (Bennett), **VIII:** 27
"All Flesh" (Thompson), **V:** 442
All Fools (Chapman), **I:** 235, 238, 244
All for Love (Dryden), **II:** 295–296, 305; **Retro. Supp. III:** 79
All for Love (Southey), **IV:** 71
All Hallow's Eve (Williams, C. W. S.), **Supp. IX:** 281, 282, 284, 285
"All Legendary Obstacles" (Montague), **Supp. XV:** 212, 215, 216
All My Eyes See: The Visual World of G. M. Hopkins (ed. Thornton), **V:** 377n, 379n, 382
All My Little Ones (Ewart), **Supp. VII:** 36
All on a Summer's Day (Inchbald), **Supp. XV:** 155
All Ovid's Elegies (Marlowe), **I:** 280, 291, 293
"All philosophers, who find" (Swift), **IV:** 160
All Quiet on the Western Front (Remarque), **VII:** xvi
All Religions Are One (Blake), **III:** 292, 307; **Retro. Supp. I:** 35
"All Roads Lead to It" (Scupham), **Supp. XIII:** 228
"All Saints: Martyrs" (Rossetti), **V:** 255
"All Souls Night" (Cornford), **VIII:** 112
All That Fall (Beckett), **Supp. I:** 58, 62; **Retro. Supp. I:** 25
All the Conspirators (Isherwood), **VII:** 310
"All the hills and vales along" (Sorley), **VI:** 421–422
"All the Inventory of Flesh" (Raine), **Supp. XIII:** 164
All the Usual Hours of Sleeping (Redgrove), **Supp. VI:** 230
All the Year Round (periodical), **V:** 42

"All Things Ill Done" (Cameron), **Supp. IX:** 23–24
"All Things Will Die" (Tennyson), **Retro. Supp. III:** 321
All Trivia (Connolly), **Supp. III:** 98
"All Washed Up" (Jamie), **Supp. XIV:** 138
All What Jazz: A Record Diary, 1961–1968 (Larkin), **Supp. I:** 286, 287–288; **Retro. Supp. III:** 200
"All Wraiths in Hell are single" (Constantine), **Supp. XV:** 70
Allan Quatermain (Haggard), **Supp. III:** 213, 218
"Allegiance, An" (Wallace-Crabbe), **VIII:** 315
Allegory of Love: A Study in Medieval Tradition (Lewis), **Supp. III:** 248, 249–250, 265
Allen, John, **IV:** 341, 349–350, 352
Allen, Walter Ernest, **V:** 219; **VI:** 257; **VII:** xvii, xxxvii, 71, 343
Allestree, Richard, **III:** 82
Allott, Kenneth, **IV:** 236; **VI:** xi, xxvii, 218
Allott, Miriam, **IV:** x, xxiv, 223n, 224, 234, 236; **V:** x, 218
All's Well That Ends Well (Shakespeare), **I:** 313, 318; **Retro. Supp. III:** 275
All You Who Sleep Tonight (Seth), **Supp. X:** 283–284, 288
"Allusion to the Tenth Satire of the Second Book of Horace" (Rochester), **II:** 259
Almayer's Folly (Conrad), **VI:** 135–136, 148; **Retro. Supp. II:** 70–71
Almeria (Edgeworth), **Supp. III:** 158
Almond Tree, The (Stallworthy), **Supp. X:** 293–294
"Almond Tree, The" (Stallworthy), **Supp. X:** 293–294, 302
"Almswoman" (Blunden), **Supp. XI:** 42
"Aloe, The" (Mansfield), **VII:** 173–174
Alone (Douglas), **VI:** 293, 294, 297, 304, 305
"Along the Terrace" (Conn), **Supp. XIII:** 74–75
Alpers, Antony, **VII:** 176
"Alphabetical Catalogue of Names . . . and Other Material Things Mentioned in These Pastorals, An" (Gay), **III:** 56
Alphabetical Order (Frayn), **Supp. VII:** 60
"Alphabets" (Heaney), **Retro. Supp. I:** 131
Alphonsus, King of Aragon (Greene), **VIII:** 139–140
Alps and Sanctuaries (Butler), **Supp. II:** 114
"Alps in Winter, The" (Stephen), **V:** 282
Alroy (Disraeli), **IV:** 296, 297, 308
"Altar, The" (Herbert), **II:** 128
"Altar of the Dead, The" (James), **VI:** 69
"Altarwise by owl-light" (Thomas), **Supp. I:** 174–176; **Retro. Supp. III:** 340–341
Alteration, The (Amis), **Supp. II:** 12–13
"Alternative to Despair, An" (Koestler), **Supp. I:** 39
Althusser, Louis, **Supp. IV:** 90

Alton, R. E., **I:** 285
Alton Locke (Kingsley), **V:** vii, xxi, 2, 4; **VI:** 240
Alton Locke: Tailor and Poet: An Autobiography (Kingsley), **Supp. XVI:** 194–196, 201, 203, 204, 205
"Altruistic Tenderness of LenWing the Poet, The" (Cameron), **Supp. IX:** 19
Altus Prosator (tr. Morgan, E.), **Supp. IX:** 169
Alvarez, A., **II:** 125n
Alvíssmál, **VIII:** 231
Amadeus (Shaffer), **Supp. I:** 326–327
Amadis of Gaul (tr. Southey), **IV:** 71
Amado, Jorge, **Supp. IV:** 440
Amalgamemnon (Brooke-Rose), **Supp. IV:** 99, 110–111, 112
Amaryllis at the Fair, A Novel (Jefferies), **Supp. XV:** 176–178
Amateur Emigrant, The (Stevenson), **V:** 389, 396
"Amateur Film-Making" (Fuller), **Supp. VII:** 73
Amateur Poacher, The (Jefferies), **Supp. XV:** 166–168
Amazing Marriage, The (Meredith), **V:** 227, 232, 233, 234
Ambarvalia: Poems by T. Burbidge and A. H. Clough, **V:** 159–160, 161, 170
Ambassadors, The (James), **VI:** 55, 57–59; **Supp. IV:** 371
"Amber Bead, The" (Herrick), **II:** 106
Amber Spyglass, The (Pullman), **Supp. XIII:** 150, 151, 153, 157–158
Amberley, Lady, **V:** 129
"Ambiguities" (Fuller), **Supp. VII:** 73
Ambition and Other Poems (Davies), **Supp. XI:** 102
"Ambitious Squire, An" (Jefferies), **Supp. XV:** 169–170
Ambler, Eric, **Supp. IV:** 1–24
Amboyna (Dryden), **II:** 305
"Ambulances" (Larkin), **Retro. Supp. III:** 207
"Ambush" (Conn), **Supp. XIII:** 72
Amelia (Fielding), **III:** 102–103, 105; **Retro. Supp. I:** 81, 89–90
"Amen" (Rossetti), **V:** 256
Amendments of Mr. Collier's False and Imperfect Citations (Congreve), **II:** 339, 340, 350
America. A Prophecy (Blake), **III:** 300, 302, 307; **Retro. Supp. I:** 39, 40–41
America I Presume (Lewis), **VII:** 77
American, The (James), **VI:** 24, 28–29, 39, 67
"American Boy" (Gunn), **Retro. Supp. III:** 129
"American Dreams" (Carey), **Supp. XII:** 54, 55, 56
American Ghosts and Other World Wonders (Carter), **Supp. III:** 91
American Journal of Religious Psychology, **Supp. XIII:** 44
American Notes (Dickens), **V:** 42, 54, 55, 71
American Scene, The (James), **VI:** 54, 62–64, 67
American Senator, The (Trollope), **V:** 100, 102

American Visitor, An (Cary), **VII:** 186
American Wake (Delanty), **Supp. XIV:** 67–69–71, 72, 75
"American Wife, The" (O'Connor), **Supp. XIV:** 226
"Americans in My Mind, The" (Pritchett), **Supp. III:** 316
"Ametas and Thestylis Making Hay-Ropes" (Marvell), **II:** 211
Aminta (Tasso), **II:** 49
"Amir's Homily, The" (Kipling), **VI:** 201
Amis, Kingsley, **Supp. II:** 1–19; **Supp. IV:** 25, 26, 27, 29, 377; **Supp. V:** 206
Amis, Martin, **Supp. IV:** 25–44, 65, 75, 437, 445
"Among All Lovely Things My Love Had Been" (Wordsworth), **IV:** 21
Among Muslims: Everyday Life on the Frontiers of Pakistan (Jamie), **Supp. XIV:** 129, 135, 144
"Among School Children" (Yeats), **VI:** 211, 217
Among the Believers: An Islamic Journey (Naipaul), **Supp. I:** 399, 400–401, 402
Among the Cities (Morris, J.), **Supp. X:** 183
"Among the Ruins" (Malouf), **Supp. XII:** 220
Among the Walls (Fallon), **Supp. XII:** 102
"Among Those Killed in the Dawn Raid was a Man Aged a Hundred" (Thomas), **Retro. Supp. III:** 345
Amores (tr. Marlowe), **I:** 276, 290
Amoretti and Epithalamion (Spenser), **I:** 124, 128–131
Amorous Cannibal, The (Wallace-Crabbe), **VIII:** 319, 320–321
"Amorous Cannibal, The" (Wallace-Crabbe), **VIII:** 319
Amorous Prince, The; or, The Curious Husband (Behn), **Supp. III:** 26
"Amos Barton" (Eliot), **V:** 190
"Amour de l'impossible, L'" (Symonds), **Supp. XIV:** 252
Amours de Voyage (Clough), **V:** xxii, 155, 156, 158, 159, 161–163, 165, 166–168, 170
Amphitryon; or, The Two Sosias (Dryden), **II:** 296, 305
"Ample Garden, The" (Graves), **VII:** 269
Amrita (Jhabvala), **Supp. V:** 224–226
"Amsterdam" (Murphy), **Supp. V:** 326
Amusements Serious and Comical (Brown), **III:** 41
"Amy Foster" (Conrad), **VI:** 134, 148
An Duanaire: An Irish Anthology, Poems of the Dispossessed, 1600–1900 (Kinsella), **Supp. V:** 266
An Giall (Behan), **Supp. II:** 71–73
Anacreontiques (Johnson), **II:** 198
"Anactoria" (Swinburne), **V:** 319–320, 321
"Anahorish" (Heaney), **Retro. Supp. I:** 125, 128
Anand, Mulk Raj, **Supp. IV:** 440
"Anarchist, An" (Conrad), **VI:** 148
Anathemata, The (Jones), **Supp. VII:** 167, 168, 169, 170, 175–178

Anatomy of Exchange–Alley, The (Defoe), **III:** 13
Anatomy of Frustration, The (Wells), **VI:** 228
Anatomy of Melancholy (Burton), **II:** 88, 106, 108; **IV:** 219
Anatomy of Oxford (eds. Day Lewis and Fenby), **Supp. III:** 118
Anatomy of Restlessness: Selected Writings, 1969–1989 (Chatwin), **Supp. IV:** 157, 160; **Supp. IX:** 52, 53, 61
"Ancestor" (Kinsella), **Supp. V:** 274
"Ancestor to Devotee" (Adcock), **Supp. XII:** 12–13
Ancestors (Brathwaite), **Supp. XII:** 33, 41–42, 45, 46
"Ancestors" (Cornford), **VIII:** 106
Ancestral Truths (Maitland), **Supp. XI:** 170–172
Anchises: Poems (Sisson), **Supp. XI:** 257
"Anchored Yachts on a Stormy Day" (Smith, I. C.), **Supp. IX:** 211
Ancient Allan, The (Haggard), **Supp. III:** 222
Ancient and English Versions of the Bible (Isaacs), **I:** 385
"Ancient Ballet, An" (Kinsella), **Supp. V:** 261
"Ancient Historian" (Wallace–Crabbe), **VIII:** 311
"Ancient Lights" (Clarke), **Supp. XV:** 27
Ancient Lights (Ford), **VI:** 319, 320
Ancient Lights: Poems and Satires, First Series (Clarke), **Supp. XV:** 26
"Ancient Mariner, The" (Coleridge), **III:** 330, 338; **IV:** viii, ix, 42, 44–48, 54, 55; **Retro. Supp. II:** 53–56
"Ancient Sage, The" (Tennyson), **IV:** 329
"Ancient to Ancients, An" (Hardy), **VI:** 13
"And country life I praise" (Bridges), **VI:** 75
"And death shall have no dominion" (Thomas), **Supp. I:** 174; **Retro. Supp. III:** 340, 344
And Our Faces, My Heart, Brief as Photos (Berger), **Supp. IV:** 94, 95
And the Girls in Their Sunday Dresses (Mda), **Supp. XV:** 198
And Then There Were None (Christie), *see* Ten Little Niggers
And What if the Pretender Should Come? (Defoe), **III:** 13
Anderson, Lindsay, **Supp. IV:** 78
Anderson, Sherwood, **VII:** 75
Anderton, Basil, **II:** 154, 157
André Gide: His Life and Work (tr. Richardson), **Supp. XIII:** 191
"Andrea del Sarto" (Browning), **IV:** 357, 361, 366; **Retro. Supp. II:** 27–28; **Retro. Supp. III:** 25
"Andrea del Sarto" (Symons), **Supp. XIV:** 271
Andrea of Hungary, and Giovanna of Naples (Landor), **IV:** 100
Andreas, **Retro. Supp. II:** 301
"Andrey Satchel and the Parson and Clerk" (Hardy), **VI:** 22
Androcles and the Lion (Shaw), **VI:** 116, 124, 129; **Retro. Supp. II:** 322

"Andromeda" (Hopkins), **V:** 370, 376
"Andromeda" (Kingsley), **Supp. XVI:** 204
Andromeda and Other Poems (Kingsley), **Supp. XVI:** 204
Andromeda Liberata (Chapman), **I:** 235, 254
Ane Prayer for the Pest (Henryson), **Supp. VII:** 146, 148
"Anecdote of 2 a.m." (Wain), **Supp. XVI:** 306
Anecdotes (Spence), **II:** 261
"Anecdotes, The" (Durrell), **Supp. I:** 124
Anecdotes of Johnson (Piozzi), **III:** 246
Anecdotes . . . of Mr. Pope . . . by the Rev. Joseph Spence (ed. Singer), **III:** 69, 78
Anecdotes of Sir W. Scott (Hogg), **Supp. X:** 111
Angel and Me: Short Stories for Holy Week (Maitland), **Supp. XI:** 177
"Angel and the Sweep, The" (Coppard), **VIII:** 92
Angel at the Gate, The (Harris), **Supp. V:** 137, 139
Angel Maker: The Short Stories of Sara Maitland (Maitland), **Supp. XI:** 165, 176
Angel Pavement (Priestley), **VII:** xviii, 211, 216–217
"Angel with Lute" (Conn), **Supp. XIII:** 81
"Angelica" (Blackwood), **Supp. IX:** 12
Angelina (Robinson), **Supp. XIII:** 208
Angels and Insects (Byatt), **Supp. IV:** 139, 151, 153–154
Angels and Insects (film), **Supp. IV:** 153
"Angels at the Ritz" (Trevor), **Supp. IV:** 503
Angels at the Ritz (Trevor), **Supp. IV:** 504
"Angle" (Dutton), **Supp. XII:** 90
"Angle–Land" (Jones), **Supp. VII:** 176
Anglican Essays (Sisson), **Supp. XI:** 255
Anglo–Italian Review (periodical) **VI:** 294
"Anglo–Saxon, The" (Golding), **Supp. I:** 78
Anglo–Saxon Attitudes (Wilson), **Supp. I:** 154, 155, 156, 159–160, 161, 162, 163
Anglo–Saxon Chronicle, **Retro. Supp. II:** 296, 297, 298, 307
Angrian chronicles (Brontë), **V:** 110–111, 120–121, 122, 124–125, 126, 135
Angry Letter in January, An (Aidoo), **Supp. XV:** 11–12
"Anima and Animus" (Jung), **Supp. IV:** 10–11
Anima Poetae: From the Unpublished Notebooks (Coleridge), **IV:** 56
Animadversions upon the Remonstrants Defense Against Smectymnuus (Milton), **II:** 175
Animal Farm (Orwell), **VII:** xx, 273, 278, 283–284; **Supp. I:** 28n, 29; **Supp. IV:** 31
Animal Lover's Book of Beastly Murder, The (Highsmith), **Supp. V:** 179

Animal Magnetism (Inchbald), **Supp. XV:** 148, 155
"Animals" (Burnside), **Supp. XIII:** 25
Animal's Arrival, The (Jennings), **Supp. V:** 208
Animated Nature (Goldsmith), *see* History of the Earth . . .
Animi Figura (Symonds), **Supp. XIV:** 252, 253
Ann Lee's (Bowen), **Supp. II:** 81
Ann Veronica: A Modern Love Story (Wells), **VI:** 227, 238
"Anna, Lady Braxby" (Hardy), **VI:** 22
Anna of the Five Towns (Bennett), **VI:** xiii, 248, 249, 252, 253, 266
Annals of a Publishing House (Oliphant), **Supp. X:** 221
Annals of Chile, The (Muldoon), **Supp. IV:** 428–432
Annals of the Five Senses (MacDiarmid), 302
Annan, Noel, **V:** 284, 290
Annan Water (Thompson), **Supp. XIV:** 286, 291, 293–294, 296
Anne Brontë (Gérin), **V:** 153
"Anne Killigrew" (Dryden), **II:** 303
Anne of Geierstein (Scott), **IV:** 39
Annie, Gwen, Lily, Pam, and Tulip (Kincaid), **Supp. VII:** 222
Annie John (Kincaid), **Supp. VII:** 217, 223–225, 229, 230
Anniversaries (Donne), **I:** 361–362, 364, 367; **Retro. Supp. II:** 88
Anniversary, The (Jewsbury), **Supp. XIV:** 157
"Anniversary" (Nye), **Supp. X:** 201
"Anniversary" (Wain), **Supp. XVI:** 306
"Anno Domini" (Raine), **Supp. XIII:** 164
Annotations of Scottish Songs by Burns (Cook), **III:** 322
Annual Register (periodical), **III:** 194, 205
Annunciation, The (Henryson), **Supp. VII:** 146, 148
"Annunciation, The" (Jennings), **Supp. V:** 212
"Annunciation, The" (Muir), **Supp. VI:** 207
Annunciation in a Welsh Hill Setting (Jones), **Supp. VII:** 180
"Annunciations" (Burnside), **Supp. XIII:** 15
Annus Domini: A Prayer for Each Day of the Year (Rossetti), **V:** 260; **Retro. Supp. III:** 263–264
"Annus Mirabilis" (Larkin), **Supp. I:** 284; **Retro. Supp. III:** 209
Annus Mirabilis: The Year of Wonder (Dryden), **II:** 292, 304; **Retro. Supp. III:** 61
"Anorexic" (Boland), **Supp. V:** 49
"Another All–Night Party" (Gunn), **Retro. Supp. III:** 125
Another Death in Venice (Hill, R.), **Supp. IX:** 111–112, 117
"Another Grace for a Child" (Herrick), **II:** 114
Another Mexico (Greene), *see* Lawless Roads, The

Another Part of the Wood (Bainbridge), **Supp. VI:** 17–19
Another September (Kinsella), **Supp. V:** 260
"Another September" (Kinsella), **Supp. V:** 260
Anowa (Aidoo), **Supp. XV:** 1, 3, 4–5
"Ansell" (Forster), **VI:** 398
Anstey, Christopher, **III:** 155
"Answer, The" (Thomas), **Supp. XII:** 287
"Answer, The" (Wycherley), **II:** 322
Answer from Limbo, An (Moore, B.), **Supp. IX:** 141, 142, 148, 150
"Answer to a Paper Called 'A Memorial of true Poor Inhabitants'" (Swift), **III:** 35
Answer to a Poisoned Book (More), **Supp. VII:** 245
Answer to a Question That No Body Thinks of, An (Defoe), **III:** 13
"Answer to Davenant" (Hobbes), **II:** 256n
"Answers" (Jennings), **Supp. V:** 206
"Answers to Correspondents: *Girls Own*, 1881" (Scupham), **Supp. XIII:** 220
"Ant, The" (Lovelace), **II:** 231
Ant and the Nightingale or Father Hubburd's Tales, The (Middleton), **II:** 3
"Ant–Lion, The" (Pritchett), **Supp. III:** 105–106
Antal, Frederick, **Supp. IV:** 80
"Antecedents of History, The" (Russell), **VIII:** 277
Antechinus: Poems 1975–1980 (Hope), **Supp. VII:** 159
"Antheap, The" (Lessing), **Supp. I:** 242
"Anthem for Doomed Youth" (Owen), **VI:** 443, 447, 448, 452; **Supp. IV:** 58
"Anthem of Earth, An" (Thompson), **V:** 448
"Anthologia Germanica" (Mangan), **Supp. XIII:** 116, 121, 123
Anthology of War Poetry, An (ed. Nichols), **VI:** 419
Anthony Trollope: A Critical Study (Cockshut), **V:** 98, 103
Antic Hay (Huxley), **VII:** 198, 201–202
"Anti–Christ; or, The Reunion of Christendom" (Chesterton), **VI:** 340–341
Anticipations of the Reaction of Mechanical and Scientific Progress upon Human Life and Thought (Wells), **VI:** 227, 240
Anti–Coningsby (Disraeli), **IV:** 308
Anti–Death League, The (Amis), **Supp. II:** 14–15
Antidotes (Sisson), **Supp. XI:** 262
Antigua, Penny, Puce (Graves), **VII:** 259
"Antigua Crossings" (Kincaid), **Supp. VII:** 220, 221
"Anti–Marriage League, The" (Oliphant), **Supp. X:** 221–222
Anti–Pamela; or, Feign'd Innocence Detected (Haywood), **Supp. XII:** 136
"Antipodes" (Carson), **Supp. XIII:** 63
Antipodes (Malouf), **Supp. XII:** 217–218
Antipodes, The (Brome), **Supp. X:** 49, 56, 58–61, 63

Antiquarian Prejudice (Betjeman), **VII:** 358, 359
Antiquary, The (Scott), **IV:** xvii 28, 32–33, 37, 39
"Antique Scene, The" (Gibbon), **Supp. XIV:** 102
Anti–Thelyphthora (Cowper), **III:** 220; **Retro. Supp. III:** 47
Antonina; or, The Fall of Rome (Collins), **Supp. VI:** 92, 95
Antonio: A Tragedy in Five Acts (Godwin), **Supp. XV:** 124
Antonio and Mellida (Marston), **II:** 27–28, 40
Antonioni, Michelangelo, **Supp. IV:** 434
Antonio's Revenge (Marston), **II:** 27–29, 36, 40
Antony and Cleopatra (Sedley), **II:** 263, 271
Antony and Cleopatra (Shakespeare), **I:** 318, 319–320; **II:** 70; **III:** 22; **Supp. IV:** 263
Antony and Octavus. Scenes for the Study (Landor), **IV:** 100
Ants, The (Churchill), **Supp. IV:** 180–181
"Antwerp" (Ford), **VI:** 323, 416
"Anxious in Dreamland" (Menand), **Supp. IV:** 305
Any Human Heart (Boyd), **Supp. XVI:** 40–41, 49
"Any Other Enemy" (Nye), **Supp. X:** 204–205
"Any Saint" (Thompson), **V: 444**
"Anybody's Alphabet" (Thomas), **Supp. XII:** 291
Anything for a Quiet Life (Middleton and Webster), **II:** 21, 69, 83, 85
Anzac Sonata, The (Stallworthy), **Supp. X:** 294, 298, 302
Apartheid and the Archbishop: The Life and Times of Geoffrey Clayton, Archbishop of Cape Town (Paton), **Supp. II:** 343, 356, 357–358
"Apartheid in Its Death Throes" (Paton), **Supp. II:** 342
"Apartment Cats" (Gunn), **Retro. Supp. III:** 122
"Ape, The" (Pritchett), **Supp. III:** 325
Apes of God, The (Lewis), **VII:** xv, 35, 71, 73, 74, 77, 79
"Aphasia in Childhood" (Burnside), **Supp. XIII:** 16–17
Aphorisms on Man (Lavater), **III:** 298
Aphrodite in Aulis (Moore), **VI:** 88, 95, 99
Apocalypse (Lawrence), **VII:** 91; **Retro. Supp. II:** 234
"Apollo and the Fates" (Browning), **IV:** 366
"Apollo in Picardy" (Pater), **V:** 355, 356
"Apollonius of Tyre" (Gower), **I:** 53
"Apologia pro Poemate Meo" (Owen), **VI:** 452
Apologia pro Vita Sua (Newman), **Supp. VII:** 289, 290, 291, 294, 295, 296, 298, 299–300
Apologie for Poetry (Sidney), *see Defence of Poesie, The Apologie for the Royal Party, An . . . By a Lover of Peace and of His Country* (Evelyn), **II:** 287
Apology Against a Pamphlet Call'd A Modest Confutation of the Animadversions upon the Remonstrant Against Smectymnuus, An (Milton), **II:** 175
"Apology for Plainspeaking, An" (Stephen), **V:** 284
Apology for Poetry, An (Sidney), **Retro. Supp. I:** 157
"Apology for Smectymnuus" (Milton), **Retro. Supp. II:** 269
Apology for the Bible (Watson), **III:** 301
Apology for the Life of Mrs. Shamela Andrews, An (Fielding), *see Shamela*
"Apology for the Revival of Christian Architecture in England, A" (Hill), **Supp. V:** 189, 191–192; **Retro. Supp. III:** 137
Apology for the Voyage to Guiana (Ralegh), **I:** 153
"Apology to Crickets" (Delanty), **Supp. XIV:** 75
Apophthegms (Bacon), **I:** 264, 273
"Apostasy, The" (Traherne), **II:** 191
Apostles, The (Moore), **VI:** 88, 96, 99
Apostes, The (Cambridge Society), **IV:** 331; **V:** 278; **VI:** 399
"Apotheosis of Tins, The" (Mahon), **Supp. VI:** 172
"Apparition of His Mistresse Calling Him to Elizium, The" (Herrick), **II:** 113
Appeal from the New to the Old Whigs, An (Burke), **III:** 205
Appeal to England, An (Swinburne), **V:** 332
Appeal to Honour and Justice, An (Defoe), **III:** 4, 13; **Retro. Supp. I:** 66, 67
Appeal to the Clergy of the Church of Scotland, An (Stevenson), **V:** 395
Appearance Is Against Them (Inchbald), **Supp. XV:** 153, 154
Appendix to John Bull Still in His Senses, An (Arbuthnot), **Supp. XVI:** 22
"Appius and Virginia" (Gower), **I:** 55
Appius and Virginia (R. B.), **I:** 216
Appius and Virginia (Webster), **II:** 68, 83, 85
Apple Broadcast, The (Redgrove), **Supp. VI:** 235
Apple Cart, The: A Political Extravaganza (Shaw), **VI:** 118, 120, 125–126, 127, 129
"Apple Picking" (Maitland), **Supp. XI:** 177
"Apple Tragedy" (Hughes), **Supp. I:** 351, 353
"Apple Tree, The" (du Maurier), **Supp. III:** 138
"Apple Tree, The" (Galsworthy), **VI:** 276
"Apple Tree, The" (Mansfield), **VII:** 173
Applebee, John, **III:** 7
Appley Dapply's Nursery Rhymes (Potter), **Supp. III:** 291
Apollonius of Tyre, **Retro. Supp. II:** 298
Apology for Poetry, An (Sidney), **Retro. Supp. II:** 332–334, 339
"Appraisal, An" (Compton–Burnett), **VII:** 59

Appreciations (Pater), **V:** 338, 339, 341, 351–352, 353–356
"Apprehension, The" (Traherne), **Supp. XI:** 270
"Apprentice" (Warner), **Supp. VII:** 380
"April" (Kavanagh), **Supp. VII:** 188
"April Epithalamium, An" (Stevenson), **Supp. VI:** 263
April Love (Hughes), **V:** 294
April Shroud, An (Hill, R.), **Supp. IX:** 113–114
"Apron of Flowers, The" (Herrick), **II:** 110
Apropos of Dolores (Wells), **VI:** 240
"Aquae Sulis" (Hardy), **Retro. Supp. I:** 121
"Aquarium" (Conn), **Supp. XIII:** 74
"Aquarius" (Armitage), **VIII:** 12
"Arab Love Song" (Thompson), **V:** 442, 445, 449
"Arabella" (Thackeray), **V:** 24
"Arabesque—The Mouse" (Coppard), **VIII:** 88
"Arabian" (Mangan), **Supp. XIII:** 125
Arabian Nights, The, **III:** 327, 335, 336; **Supp. IV:** 434
"Araby" (Joyce), **Retro. Supp. I:** 172
Aragon, Louis, **Supp. IV:** 466
"Aramantha" (Lovelace), **II:** 230, 231
Aran Islands, The (Synge), **VI:** 308–309; **Retro. Supp. I:** 291–294
Aran Trilogy (McDonagh), **Supp. XII:** 240, 242–243, 245
Ararat (Thomas), **Supp. IV:** 484
Aratra Pentelici (Ruskin), **V:** 184
Appendix to John Bull Still in His Senses, An (Arbuthnot), **Supp. XVI:** 22
Arbuthnot, John, **III:** 19, 34, 60; **Supp. XVI: 15–30**
"Arcades" (Milton), **II:** 159
Arcadia (Crace), **Supp. XIV:** 18, 19, 22, 24–25, 30
Arcadia (Sidney), **I:** 161, 163–169, 173, 317; **II:** 48, 53–54; **III:** 95; **Retro. Supp. II:** 330–332, 340
Arcadia (Stoppard), **Retro. Supp. II:** 355–356
Arcadian Rhetorike (Fraunce), **I:** 164
"Arch, The" (Soutar), **Supp. XVI:** 252–253
"Archdeacon Truggin" (Powys), **VIII:** 256
Archeology of Love, The (Murphy), **Supp. V:** 317
Archer, William, **II:** 79, 358, 363, 364; **V:** 103, 104, 113
"Archipelago, The" (tr. Constantine), **Supp. XV:** 70, 71, 72
Architectural Review (periodical), **VII:** 356, 358
Architecture in Britain: 1530–1830 (Reynolds), **II:** 336
Architecture, Industry and Wealth (Morris), **V:** 306
Archive Tennyson, The (Tennyson), **Retro. Supp. III:** 325
"Arctic Summer" (Forster), **VI:** 406
Arden of Feversham (Kyd), **I:** 212, 213, 218–219
Arden, John, **Supp. II: 21–42**

"Ardour and Memory" (Rossetti), **V:** 243
Ardours and Endurances (Nichols), **VI:** 423
"Are You Lonely in the Restaurant" (O'Nolan), **Supp. II:** 323
Area of Darkness, An (Naipaul), **Supp. I,** 383, 384, 387, 389, 390, 391–392, 394, 395, 399, 402
"Arena" (Scupham), **Supp. XIII:** 218
Arendt, Hannah, **Supp. IV:** 306
Areopagitica (Milton), **II:** 163, 164, 169, 174, 175; **IV:** 279; **Retro. Supp. II:** 277–279
Areté: The Arts Tri-Quarterly, **Supp. XIII:** 174, 175
Aretina (Mackenzie), **III:** 95
"Argentina 1978" (Butlin), **Supp. XVI:** 58
"Argonauts of the Air, The" (Wells), **VI:** 244
Argonauts of the Pacific (Malinowski), **Supp. III:** 186
Argufying (Empson), **Supp. II:** 180, 181
Argument . . . that the Abolishing of Christianity . . . . May . . . be Attended with some Inconveniences, An (Swift), **III:** 26, 35
"Argument for Divine Providence, Taken from the Constant Regularity Observed in the Births of Both Sexes, An" (Arbuthnot), **Supp. XVI:** 19–20
"Argument of His Book, The" (Herrick), **II:** 110
Argument Shewing that a Standing Army . . . Is Not Inconsistent with a Free Government, An (Defoe), **III,** 12
Ariadne Florentina (Ruskin), **V:** 184
Ariel Poems (Eliot), **VII:** 152
Arians of the Fourth Century, The (Newman), **Supp. VII:** 291
Arion and the Dolphin (Seth), **Supp. X:** 288
Aristocrats (Friel), **Supp. V:** 122
Aristomenes: or, The Royal Shepherd (Finch), **Supp. IX:** 74–76
Aristophanes, **V:** 227
Aristophanes' Apology (Browning), **IV:** 358, 367, 370, 374; **Retro. Supp. II:** 30; **Retro. Supp. III:** 30
Aristos, The: A Self-Portrait in Ideas (Fowles), **Supp. I:** 293–294, 295, 296
Ark, The (Scupham), **Supp. XIII:** 227–229
Arky Types (Maitland and Wandor), **Supp. XI:** 165, 170
"Armada, The" (Macaulay), **IV:** 283, 291
Armadale (Collins), **Supp. VI:** 91, 93–94, **98–100,** 101, 103
Armadillo (Boyd), **Supp. XVI:** 39–40
Armadillo (screenplay, Boyd), **Supp. XVI:** 46
Armah, Ayi Kwei, **Supp. X: 1–16**
Armitage, Simon, **VIII: 1–17**
Armourer's House, The (Sutcliff), **Supp. XVI:** 264
Arms and the Covenant (Churchill), **VI:** 356
Arms and the Man (Shaw), **VI:** 104, 110, 120; **Retro. Supp. II:** 313

Arms and the Women: An Elliad (Hill, R.), **Supp. IX:** 122
Armstrong, Isobel Mair, **V:** xi, xxvii, 339, 375
Armstrong, William, **V:** xviii, xxxvii
Armstrong's Last Goodnight (Arden), **Supp. II:** 29, 30
Arnold, Matthew, **IV:** 359; **V:** viii–xi, 14, 156–158, 160, **203–218,** 283, 285, 289, 342, 352–353; works, **III:** 23, 174, 277; **V:** 206–215; literary criticism, **I:** 423; **III:** 68, 277; **IV:** 220, 234, 323, 371; **V:** 160, 165–169, 352, 408; **Supp. II:** 44, 57; **Retro. Supp. I:** 59
Arnold, Thomas, **V:** 155–156, 157, 165, 207, 208, 277, 284, 349
Arnold Bennett (Lafourcade), **VI:** 268
Arnold Bennett (Pound), **VI:** 247, 268
Arnold Bennett (Swinnerton), **VI:** 268
Arnold Bennett: A Biography (Drabble), **VI:** 247, 253, 268; **Supp. IV:** 203
Arnold Bennett: A Last Word (Swinnerton), **VI:** 268
Arnold Bennett and H. G. Wells: A Record of a Personal and Literary Friendship (ed. Wilson), **VI:** 246, 267
Arnold Bennett in Love (ed. and tr. Beardmore and Beardmore), **VI:** 251, 268
Arnold Bennett: The AEvening Standard-"Years (ed. Mylett), **VI:** 265n, 266
Arouet, Françoise Marie, *see* Voltaire
Around Theatres (Beerbohm), **Supp. II:** 54, 55
"Aromatherapy" (Redgrove), **Supp. VI:** 236
Arragonian Queen, The (Haywood), **Supp. XII:** 135
"Arraheids" (Jamie), **Supp. XIV:** 138
Arraignment of London, The (Daborne and Tourneur), **II:** 37
Arraignment of Paris (Peele), **I:** 197–200
"Arrangements" (Dunn), **Supp. X:** 76
"Arrest of Oscar Wilde at the Cadogan Hotel, The" (Betjeman), **VII:** 356, 365–366
Arrival and Departure (Koestler), **Supp. I:** 27, 28, 30–31
"Arrivals" (Conn), **Supp. XIII:** 74
Arrivants, The: A New World Trilogy (Brathwaite), **Supp. XII:** 33, 34, 36–40, 41, 42, 44, 45
Arrow in the Blue (Koestler), **Supp. I:** 22, 25, 31, 34, 36
Arrow of Gold, A (Conrad), **VI:** 134, 144, 147
Ars Longa, Vita Brevis (Arden and D'Arcy), **Supp. II:** 29
Ars Poetica (Horace), **Retro. Supp. I:** 166
"Arsehole" (Raine), **Supp. XIII:** 168
"Arsonist" (Murphy), **Supp. V:** 326
Art and Action (Sisson), **Supp. XI:** 253
"Art and Criticism" (Harris), **Supp. V:** 140
"Art and Extinction" (Harrison), **Supp. V:** 156
Art & Lies: A Piece for Three Voices and a Bawd (Winterson), **Supp. IV:** 542, 547, 552–553, 554–555, 556, 557

"Art and Morality" (Stephen), **V:** 286
Art and Reality (Cary), **VII:** 186
Art and Revolution: Ernst Neizvestny and the Role of the Artist in the U.S.S.R. (Berger), **Supp. IV:** 79, 88
"Art and Science" (Richards), **Supp. II:** 408–409
"Art and the Class Struggle" (Cornford), **Supp. XIII:** 87
Art History and Class Consciousness (Hadjinicolaou), **Supp. IV:** 90
"Art McCooey" (Kavanagh), **Supp. VII:** 190
Art Objects: Essays on Ecstasy and Effrontery (Winterson), **Supp. IV:** 541, 542, 544, 557
Art of Angling, The (Barker), **II:** 131
Art of Being Ruled, The (Lewis), **VII:** 72, 75, 76
Art of Creation: Essays on the Self and Its Powers, The (Carpenter), **Supp. XIII:** 46–47
"Art of Dying, The" (Caudwell), **Supp. IX:** 35–38
Art of English Poetry, The (Puttenham), **I:** 94, 146, 214
Art of Fiction, The (James), **VI:** 46, 67
Art of Fiction, The (Kipling), **VI:** 204
Art of Fiction, The (Lodge), **Supp. IV:** 381
"Art of Fiction, The" (Woolf), **VII:** 21, 22
Art of Love, The (Ovid), **I:** 237–238
"Art of Malingering, The" (Cameron), **Supp. IX:** 18
"Art of Reading in Ignorance, The" (Pitter), **Supp. XIII:** 132
Art of Sinking in Poetry, The (Pope), **IV:** 187
Art of the Big Bass Drum, The (Kelman), **Supp. V:** 256
Art of the Novel, The (James), **VI:** 67
Art of Wordsworth, The (Abercrombie), **Supp. XVI:** 1
"Art Work" (Byatt), **Supp. IV:** 155
"Arthur Snatchfold" (Forster), **VI:** 411
Article of Charge Against Hastings (Burke), **III:** 205
"Articles of Inquiry Concerning Heavy and Light" (Bacon), **I:** 261
Articulate Energy (Davie), **Supp. VI:** 114
"Artifice of Versification, An" (Fuller), **Supp. VII:** 77
Artificial Princess, The (Firbank), **Supp. II:** 199, 205, 207–208
Artist Descending a Staircase (Stoppard), **Retro. Supp. II:** 349
Artist of the Floating World, An (Ishiguro), **Supp. IV:** 301, 304, 306, 309–311; **Retro. Supp. III:** 152–154, 155, 157, 161, 162
"Artist to His Blind Love, The" (Redgrove), **Supp. VI:** 234
"Artistic Career of Corky, The" (Wodehouse), **Supp. III:** 459
"Artistic Temperament of Stephen Carey, The" (Maugham), **VI:** 373
"Artists, The" (Thackeray), **V:** 22, 37
"Artists and Value" (Kelman), **Supp. V:** 257

Arts and Crafts Movement, The (Naylor), **VI:** 168
"Arundel Tomb, An" (Larkin), **Supp. I:** 280
"As a Woman of a Man" (Carpenter), **Supp. XIII:** 38
"As Always, a Painful Declaration of Independence—For Me" (Aidoo), **Supp. XV:** 11
As I Saw the USA (Morris), see *Coast to Coast*
As I Was Saying Yesterday: Selected Essays and Reviews (Beer), **Supp. XIV:** 12
As If By Magic (Wilson), **Supp. I:** 163–165, 166
"As It Should Be" (Mahon), **Supp. VI:** 170
"As kingfishers catch fire" (Hopkins), **V:** 371
"As Our Might Lessens" (Cornford), **Supp. XIII:** 88
"As So Often in Scotland" (Dutton), **Supp. XII:** 97
As the Crow Flies: A Lyric Play for the Air (Clarke), **Supp. XV:** 25
"As the Dust Begins to Settle" (Aidoo), **Supp. XV:** 10
"As the Greeks Dreamed" (Carpenter), **Supp. XIII:** 39
"As the Team's Head–Brass" (Thomas), **VI:** 425; **Supp. III:** 405
As You Like It (Shakespeare), **I:** 278, 312; **III:** 117; **Supp. IV:** 179
"Ascent into Hell" (Hope), **Supp. VII:** 153
Ascent of F6, The (Auden and Isherwood), **VII:** 312, 380, 383, 385; **Retro. Supp. I:** 7
Ascent to Omai (Harris), **Supp. V:** 135, 136, 138
"Ash Grove, The" (Thomas), **Supp. III:** 402
Ashenden (Maugham), **VI:** 371; **Supp. IV:** 9–10
Ashford, Daisy, **V:** 111, 262
Ashley, Lord, *see* Shaftesbury, seventh earl of
Ash–Wednesday (Eliot), **VII:** 144, 150, 151–152
Ashworth, Elizabeth, **Supp. IV:** 480
Asiatic Romance, An (Sisson), **Supp. XI:** 251
"Aside" (Thomas), **Supp. XII:** 290
Asimov, Isaac, **III:** 341
"Ask Me No More" (Tennyson), **IV:** 334
"Askam Unvisited" (Nicholson), **Supp. VI:** 214
"Askam Visited" (Nicholson), **Supp. VI:** 214
Asking Around (Hare), **Supp. IV:** 282, 298
Asking for the Moon (Hill, R.), **Supp. IX:** 118
"Asleep" (Owen), **VI:** 455
Asolando (Browning), **IV:** 359, 365, 374; **Retro. Supp. II:** 31; **Retro. Supp. III:** 31–32
"Aspects" (MacCaig), **Supp. VI:** 188

Aspects of E. M. Forster (Stallybrass), **VI:** 413
Aspects of Religion in the United States of America (Bird), **Supp. X:** 23
Aspects of the Novel (Forster), **V:** 229; **VI:** 397, 411, 412; **VII:** 21, 22; **Retro. Supp. II:** 149
"Aspens" (Thomas), **Supp. III:** 406
Aspern Papers, The (James), **VI:** 38, **46–48**
"Asphodel" (Malouf), **Supp. XII:** 219–220
Asquith, Herbert, **VI:** 417
Asquith, Raymond, **VI:** 417, 428
"Ass, The" (Vaughan), **II:** 186
"Assassination of John Fitzgerald Kennedy Considered as a Downhill Motor Race" (Ballard), **Supp. V:** 21
Assassins, The (Shelley), **Retro. Supp. I:** 247
"Assault, The" (Nichols), **VI:** 419
Assembling a Ghost (Redgrove), **Supp. VI:** 236
Assignation, The; or, Love in a Nunnery (Dryden), **II:** 305
"Assisi" (MacCaig), **Supp. VI:** 189–190, 194–195
"Assumption" (Beckett), **Retro. Supp. I:** 17
"Assunta 2" (Chatwin), **Supp. IV:** 173
"Astarte Syriaca" (Rossetti), **V:** 238, 240
Astonished Heart, The (Coward), **Supp. II:** 152
Astonishing the Gods (Okri), **Supp. V:** 347, 349, 353, 359, 360–361
Astraea Redux, "A Poem on the Happy Restoration and Return of His Sacred Majesty Charles the Second" (Dryden), **II:** 292, 304; **Retro. Supp. III:** 61
Astride the Two Cultures (Koestler), **Supp. I:** 36
"Astronomy" (Housman), **VI:** 161
Astronomy of Love, The (Stallworthy), **Supp. X:** 292, 298, 302
Astrophel (collection), **I:** 160
Astrophel. A Pastoral Elegy (Spenser), **I:** 126; **IV:** 205
Astrophel and Other Poems (Swinburne), **V:** 333
Astrophel and Stella (Sidney), **I:** 161, 169–173; **Retro. Supp. II:** 334–339, 340–341
Astrophil and Stella (Greville), **Supp. XI:** 111
Asylum Dance, The (Burnside), **Supp. XIII:** 24–25
"Asylum Dance, The" (Burnside), **Supp. XIII:** 24
Asylum Piece and Other Stories (Kavan), **Supp. VII:** 210–211, 212, 214
"At a Calvary near the Ancre" (Owen), **VI:** 450, 451
"At a Potato Digging" (Heaney), **Supp. II:** 270
"At a Warwickshire Mansion" (Fuller), **Supp. VII:** 73
"At an Intersection" (Gunn), **Retro. Supp. III:** 125

"At Bedtime" (Stallworthy), **Supp. X:** 294
"At Castle Boterel" (Hardy), **VI:** 18
"At Christ Church, Greyfriars" (Blunden), **Supp. XI:** 44
"At Coruisk" (Conn), **Supp. XIII:** 73
"At East Coker" (Day Lewis), **Supp. III:** 130
"At Endor" (Abercrombie), **Supp. XVI:** 9–10
"At Falkland Place" (Dunn), **Supp. X:** 77
"At First Sight" (Reid), **Supp. VII:** 328
At Freddie's (Fitzgerald), **Supp. V:** 96, 98, 101, 103–104
"At Grass" (Larkin), **Supp. I:** 277; **Retro. Supp. III:** 204–205, 206
"At Great Hampden" (Adcock), **Supp. XII:** 13
At Home: Memoirs (Plomer), **Supp. XI:** 223, 226
"At Isella" (James), **VI:** 69
"At Laban's Well" (Coppard), **VIII:** 95
At Lady Molly's (Powell), **VII:** 348
"At Last" (Kincaid), **Supp. VII:** 220–221
"At Last" (Nye), **Supp. X:** 204
"At Lehmann's" (Mansfield), **VII:** 172, 173
"At Rugmer" (Blunden), **Supp. XI:** 44
"At Senlis Once" (Blunden), **VI:** 428
At Swim-Two-Birds (O'Nolan), **Supp. II:** 323–326, 332, 336, 338
At the Aviary (Conn), **Supp. XIII:** 78–79
"At the Ball" (Fuller), **Supp. VII:** 80
"At the Barrier" (Gunn), **Retro. Supp. III:** 125
"At the Bay" (Mansfield), **VII:** 175, 177, 179, 180
At the Bottom of the River (Kincaid), **Supp. VII:** 217, 221, 222, 223, 224, 225
"At the British War Cemetery, Bayeux" (Causley), **VII:** 448
"At the Cavour" (Symons), **Supp. XIV:** 272
"At the Centre" (Gunn), **Supp. IV:** 267
"At the Crossroads" (Kinsella), **Supp. V:** 267
"At the Edge of a Birchwood" (Dunn), **Supp. X:** 76–77
"At the Edge of the Wood" (Redgrove), **Supp. VI:** 228
"At the End" (Cornford), **VIII:** 106
"At the End" (Thomas), **Supp. XII:** 292
"At the End of the Passage" (Kipling), **VI:** 173–175, 183, 184, 193
"At the Funeral of Robert Garioch" (Smith, I. C.), **Supp. IX:** 218–219
"At the Grave of Henry James" (Auden), **VII:** 380; **Retro. Supp. I:** 2
"At the Great Durbar" (Steel), **Supp. XII:** 268
"At the Great Wall of China" (Blunden), **VI:** 429
"At the 'Mermaid'" (Browning), **IV:** 35
"At the Head Table" (Kinsella), **Supp. V:** 273
"At the Musical Festival" (Nicholson), **Supp. VI:** 219

"At the Sale" (Smith, I. C.), **Supp. IX:** 220
"At the White Monument" (Redgrove), **Supp. VI:** 228–229, 237
Atalanta in Calydon (Swinburne), **IV:** 90; **V:** xxiii, 309, 313, 318, **321–324**, 331, 332; **VII:** 134
"Atheism" (Bacon), **III:** 39
"Atheist, The" (Powys), **VIII:** 249
Atheist's Tragedy, The (Tourneur), **II:** 29, 33, 36, 37, **38–40**, 41, 70
Athenaeum (periodical), **IV:** 252, 254, 262, 310, 315; **V:** 32, 134; **VI:** 167, 234, 374; **VII:** 32
"Athene's Song" (Boland), **Supp. V:** 39
Athenian Mercury (newspaper), **III:** 41
"Atlantic" (Russell), **VIII:** 291
"Atlantic" (Scupham), **Supp. XIII:** 220
Atlantic Monthly (periodical), **VI:** 29, 33
"Atlantis" (Auden), **Retro. Supp. I:** 10
Atlas (periodical), **V:** 144
Atrocity Exhibition, The (Ballard), **Supp. V:** 19, 21, 25
"Attack" (Sassoon), **VI:** 431
"Attempt at Jealousy, An" (Raine), **Supp. XIII:** 168
Attempt to Describe Hafod, An (Cumberland), **IV:** 47
Attenborough, Richard, **Supp. IV:** 455
Atterbury, Francis, **III:** 23
"Attic, The" (Mahon), **Supp. VI:** 175
Attlee, Clement, **VI:** 358
"Attracta" (Trevor), **Supp. IV:** 502
"Atumpan" (Brathwaite), **Supp. XII:** 38, 39
Atwood, Margaret, **Supp. IV:** 233
"Aubade" (Empson), **Supp. II:** 191
"Aubade" (Larkin), **Supp. I:** 284; **Retro. Supp. III:** 211
"Aubade" (Reed and Bliss), **Supp. XV:** 252–253
"Aubade" (Scupham), **Supp. XIII:** 228
"Aubade" (Sitwell), **VII:** 131
Aubreiad (O'Brian), **Supp. XII:** 253, 258, 259, 261–262
Aubrey, John, **I:** 260; **II:** 45, 46, 205–206, 226, 233
"Auction" (Murphy), **Supp. V:** 317
"Auction of the Ruby Slippers, The" (Rushdie), **Supp. IV:** 443
"Auction Sale, The" (Reed), **Supp. XV:** 244, 254, 255
Auction Sale and Other Poems (Reed), **Supp. XV:** 255
Auden, W. H., **I:** 92, **IV:** 106, 208; **V:** 46; **VI:** 160, 208; **VII:** xii, xviii, xix–xx, 153, **379–399**, 403, **407**; **Supp. II:** 143–144, 190, 200, 213, 267, 481–482, 485, 486, 493, 494; **Supp. III:** 60, 100, 117, 119, 123, 131; **Supp. IV:** 100, 256, 411, 422, 423; **Retro. Supp. I: 1–15**
"Audenesque for an Initiation" (Ewart), **Supp. VII:** 37
"Auditors In" (Kavanagh), **Supp. VII:** 195–196
"Audley Court" (Tennyson), **IV:** 326n
"Auguries of Innocence" (Blake), **III:** 300

"August for the People" (Auden), **Retro. Supp. I:** 7
August Is a Wicked Month (O'Brien), **Supp. V:** 339
"August Midnight, An" (Hardy), **Retro. Supp. I:** 119
"August 1914" (Rosenberg), **VI:** 434
Augusta Triumphans; or, The Way to Make London the Most Flourishing City . . . (Defoe), **III:** 14
Augustan Ages, The (Elton), **III:** 51n
Augustan Lyric (Davie), **Supp. VI:** 115
Augustans and Romantics (Butt and Dyson), **III:** 51n
Augustus Does His Bit (Shaw), **VI:** 120
"Auld Enemy, The" (Crawford), **Supp. XI:** 81
"Auld Lang Syne" (Burns), **III:** 321
Auld Licht Idylls, When a Man's Single (Barrie), **Supp. III:** 2, 3
"Auld Tree, The" (Soutar), **Supp. XVI:** 247–248, 251, 255, 256
Ault, Norman, **III:** 69, 78
"Aunt and the Sluggard, The" (Wodehouse), **Supp. III:** 447–448, 455, 457
"Aunt Janet's Armistice" (Jamie), **Supp. XIV:** 136
"Aunt Janet's Museum" (Jamie), **Supp. XIV:** 136
Aunt Judy's (periodical), **V:** 271
Aunt Julia and the Scriptwriter (screenplay, Boyd), **Supp. XVI:** 45–46
Aunts Aren't Gentlemen (Wodehouse), **Supp. III:** 455
Aunt's Story, The (White), **Supp. I:** 131, **134–136**, 148
Aureng-Zebe (Dryden), **II:** 295, 305
Aurora Floyd (Braddon), **VIII:** 35, 38, 42–44, 48
Aurora Leigh (Browning), **IV:** xxi, 311, 312, 314–315, 316–318, 321
Aus dem Zweiten Reich [From the Second Reich] (Bunting), **Supp. VII:** 4
Ausonius, **II:** 108, 185
"Auspicious Occasion" (Mistry), **Supp. X:** 138
Austen, Alfred, **V:** 439
Austen, Cassandra, **Retro. Supp. II:** 13–14
Austen, Jane, **III:** 90, 283, 335–336, 345; **IV:** xi, xiv, xvii, 30, **101–124**; **V:** 51; **Supp. II:** 384; **Supp. IV:** 154, 230, 233, 236, 237, 319; **Retro. Supp. II: 1–16**, 135
Austen-Leigh, J. E., **III:** 90
Austerlitz (Sebald), **VIII:** 295, 305–307
Austin, J. L., **Supp. IV:** 115
"Australia" (Hope), **Supp. VII:** 153
Australia and New Zealand (Trollope), **V:** 102
Australian Nationalists, The: Modern Critical Essays (Wallace-Crabbe), **VIII:** 3 **VIII:** 21, 320
Austri's effort (Þórðarson), **VIII:** 235
"Auteur Theory" (Hill, R.), **Supp. IX:** 118
"Author of 'Beltraffio,' The," (James), **VI:** 69

"Author to the Critical Peruser, The" (Traherne), **Supp. XI:** 274
"Author Upon Himself, The" (Swift), **III:** 19, 32
Authoress of the Odyssey, The (Butler), **Supp. II:** 114–116
Authorized Version of the Bible, see King James Version
Author's Apology, The (Bunyan), **II:** 246n
Author's Farce, The (Fielding), **III:** 105
"Author's Prologue" (Thomas), **Retro. Supp. III:** 336
"Autobiographical Essay" (Thomas), **Supp. XII:** 284
"Autobiographical Reflections on Politics" (Sisson), **Supp. XI:** 247
Autobiographical Writings (Newman), **Supp. VII:** 289, 290
Autobiographies (Symons), **Supp. XIV:** 268, 269
Autobiographies (Thomas), **Supp. XII:** 281, 286
Autobiographies (Yeats), **V:** 301, 304, 306, 404; **VI:** 317
"Autobiographies, The" (James), **VI:** 65
"Autobiography" (Gunn), **Supp. IV:** 270; **Retro. Supp. III:** 123, 124
"Autobiography" (MacNeice), **VII:** 401
Autobiography (Mangan), **Supp. XIII:** 114
"Autobiography" (Reid), **Supp. VII:** 325
Autobiography (Russell), **VII:** 90
"Autobiography" (Thomas), **Supp. XII:** 280–281
Autobiography, An (Muir), **Supp. VI:** 197, **198–200,** 201, 205
Autobiography, An (Trollope), **V:** 89, 90–93, 96, 101, 102
Autobiography and Letters of Mrs. M. O. W. Oliphant (Oliphant), **Supp. X:** 212–213, 223
Autobiography and Other Essays, An (Trevelyan), **VI:** 383, 386, 388
"Autobiography of a River, The" (Mitchell), **Supp. XIV:** 99
Autobiography of a Supertramp (Davies), **Supp. III:** 398; **Supp. XI:** 88, 90–91, 92
Autobiography of Alice B. Toklas, The (Stein), **Supp. IV:** 557
Autobiography of Edward Gibbon, The (ed. Smeaton), **III:** 229n
Autobiography of My Mother, The (Kincaid), **Supp. VII:** 217, 229–230
Autonomous Region, The: Poems and Photographs from Tibet (Jamie), **Supp. XIV:** 129, 139–142, 143
Autumn (Beer), **Supp. XIV:** 1, 5, 6
"Autumn" (Hulme), **Supp. VI:** 134, 136, 142
"Autumn" (tr. O'Connor), **Supp. XIV:** 221
Autumn (Thomson), **Supp. III:** 414–415, 416, 417, 420
"Autumn Chapter in a Novel" (Gunn), **Retro. Supp. III:** 120
"Autumn Evening" (Cornford), **VIII:** 102, 103, 112
Autumn Journal (MacNeice), **VII:** 412

Autumn Midnight (Cornford), **VIII:** 104, 105, 109
"Autumn Morning at Cambridge" (Cornford), **VIII:** 102, 103, 107
"Autumn 1939" (Fuller), **Supp. VII:** 69
"Autumn 1942" (Fuller), **VII:** 430–431
"Autumn on Nan-Yueh" (Empson), **Supp. II:** 191–192
Autumn Sequel (MacNeice), **VII:** 407, 412, 415
"Autumn Sunshine" (Trevor), **Supp. IV:** 504
"Autumn Walk" (Conn), **Supp. XIII:** 80
"Autumnall, The" (Donne), **II:** 118
Available for Dreams (Fuller), **Supp. VII:** 68, 79, 80, 81
Avatars, The (Russell), **VIII:** 277, 285, 290–291, 292
Ave (Moore), **VI:** 99
"Ave Atque Vale" (Swinburne), **V:** 314, 327
"Ave Imperatrix" (Kipling), **VI:** 201
Aveling, Edward, **VI:** 102
Avignon Quintet (Durrell), **Supp. I:** 100, 101, **118–121;** **Retro. Supp. III:** 86, 87, 92–94
"Avising the bright beams of those fair eyes" (Wyatt), **I:** 110
Avoidance of Literature, The: Collected Essays (Sisson), **Supp. XI:** 247,
"Avoirdupois" (Burnside), **Supp. XIII:** 19
Avowals (Moore), **VI:** 97–98, 99
"Awake, my heart, to be loved" (Bridges), **VI:** 74, 77
"Awake, thou that sleepest" (Rossetti), **Retro. Supp. III:** 253
Awakened Conscience, The (Dixon Hunt), **VI:** 167
"Awakening, The" (Brathwaite), **Supp. XII:** 39
Awakening Conscience, The (Holman Hunt), **VI:** 45, 51, 240
"Away with the Birds" (Healy), **Supp. IX:** 107
Awesome God: Creation, Commitment and Joy (Maitland), **Supp. XI:** 164, 165
Awfully Big Adventure, An (Bainbridge), **Supp. VI:** 18, **23–24**
Awkward Age, The (James), **VI:** 45, 56, 67
"Axeing Darkness / Here Below" (Dutton), **Supp. XII:** 94
"Axel's Castle" (Mahon), **Supp. VI:** 177
Ayala's Angel (Trollope), **V:** 100, 102
Ayckbourn, Alan, **Supp. V: 1–17**
Ayesha: The Return of She (Haggard), **Supp. III:** 214, 222
Aylott & Jones (publishers), **V:** 131
"Ayrshire Farm" (Conn), **Supp. XIII:** 71, 72

"Baa, Baa Black Sheep" (Kipling), **VI:** 166
"Babby" (Crawford), **Supp. XI:** 76
Babees Book, The (*Early English Poems and Treatises on Manners and Meals in Olden Time*) (ed. Furnival), **I:** 22, 26

Babel Tower (Byatt), **Supp. IV:** 139, 141, 149–151
"Babes" (Fallon), **Supp. XII:** 102
Babes in the Darkling Wood (Wells), **VI:** 228
"Baby Nurse, The" (Blackwood), **Supp. IX:** 5, 9
"Baby's cradle with no baby in it, A" (Rossetti), **V:** 255
Babylon Hotel (Bennett), see *Grand Babylon Hotel, The*
"Babysitting" (Galloway), **Supp. XII:** 126
Bachelors, The (Spark), **Supp. I:** 203, 204
Back (Green), **Supp. II:** 254, 258–260
"Back" (Scupham), **Supp. XIII:** 225
Back at the Spike (Constantine), **Supp. XV:** 66
"Back of Affluence" (Davie), **Supp. VI:** 110
"Back to Cambo" (Hartley), **Supp. VII:** 124
Back to Methuselah (Shaw), **VI: 121–122,** 124; **Retro. Supp. II:** 323
"Backfire" (Delanty), **Supp. XIV:** 68
"Background Material" (Harrison), **Supp. V:** 155
Background to Danger (Ambler), **Supp. IV:** 7–8
"Backlands" (Soutar), **Supp. XVI:** 256
Backward Look, The (O'Connor), **Supp. XIV:** 217
Backward Place, A (Jhabvala), **Supp. V:** 229
Backward Son, The (Spender), **Supp. II:** 484, 489
Backwater (Richardson), **Supp. XIII:** 182–183
Bacon, Francis, **I: 257–274; II:** 149, 196; **III:** 39; **IV:** 138, 278, 279; annotated list of works, **I:** 271–273; **Supp. III:** 361
Bad Boy (McEwan), **Supp. IV:** 400
"Bad Dreams in Vienna" (Malouf), **Supp. XII:** 220
"Bad Five Minutes in the Alps, A" (Stephen), **V:** 283
"Bad Girl, The" (Pitter), **Supp. XIII:** 141
Bad Land: An American Romance (Raban), **Supp. XI:** 236, 239, 241
"Bad Night, A" (Auden), **Retro. Supp. I:** 14
Bad Sister, The (Tennant), **Supp. IX:** 229, 230, 231–234, 235–236, 238, 239, 240
"Bad Thing, The" (Wain), **Supp. XVI:** 306
Bagehot, Walter, **IV:** 289, 291; **V:** xxiii, 156, 165, 170, 205, 212
"Baggot Street Deserta" (Kinsella), **Supp. V:** 259–260
Bagman, The; or, The Impromptu of Muswell Hill (Arden), **Supp. II:** 31, 32, 35
"Bagpipe Music" (MacNeice), **VII:** 413
Bailey, Benjamin, **IV:** 224, 229, 230, 232–233
Bailey, Paul, **Supp. IV:** 304
Baillie, Alexander, **V:** 368, 374, 375, 379
Bainbridge, Beryl, **Supp. VI: 17–27**

Baines, Jocelyn, **VI:** 133–134
Baird, Julian, **V:** 316, 317, 318, 335
"Bairns of Suzie: A Hex" (Jamie), **Supp. XIV:** 138
"Bairnsang" (Jamie), **Supp. XIV:** 141–142
"Baite, The" (Donne), **IV:** 327
Bajazet (tr. Hollinghurst), **Supp. X:** 132–134
Bakerman, Jane S., **Supp. IV:** 336
"Baker's Dozen, The" (Saki), **Supp. VI:** 243
Bakhtin, Mikhail, **Supp. IV:** 114
"Balakhana" (McGuckian), **Supp. V:** 284
"Balance, The" (Waugh), **Supp. VI:** 271
Balance of Terror (Shaffer), **Supp. I:** 314
Balaustion's Adventure (Browning), **IV:** 358, 374; **Retro. Supp. II:** 30; **Retro. Supp. III:** 30
"Balder Dead" (Arnold), **V:** 209, 216
Baldrs draumar, **VIII:** 231
Baldwin, Edwin, *see* Godwin, William
Baldwin, Stanley, **VI:** 353, 355
Bale, John, **I:** 1, 3
Balfour, Arthur, **VI:** 226, 241, 353
Balfour, Graham, **V:** 393, 397
"Balin and Balan" (Tennyson), **Retro. Supp. III:** 327
Balin; or, The Knight with Two Swords (Malory), **I:** 79
Ball and the Cross, The (Chesterton), **VI:** 338
"Ballad" (Soutar), **Supp. XVI:** 256
Ballad at Dead Men's Bay, The (Swinburne), **V:** 332
"Ballad of Bouillabaisse" (Thackeray), **V:** 19
"Ballad of Death, A" (Swinburne), **V:** 316, 317–318
Ballad of Jan Van Hunks, The (Rossetti), **V:** 238, 244, 245
"Ballad of Kynd Kittok, The" (Dunbar), **VIII:** 126
"Ballad of Life, A" (Swinburne), **V:** 317, 318
Ballad of Peckham Rye, The (Spark), **Supp. I:** 201, 203–204
Ballad of Reading Gaol, The (Wilde), **V:** xxvi, 417–418, 419; **Retro. Supp. II:** 372–373
Ballad of Sylvia and Ted, The (Tennant), **Supp. IX:** 239, 240
"Ballad of the Investiture 1969, A" (Betjeman), **VII:** 372
"Ballad of the Long-legged Bait" (Thomas), **Supp. I:** 177; **Retro. Supp. III:** 345
"Ballad of the Red-Headed Man" (Beer), **Supp. XIV:** 5
"Ballad of the Three Spectres" (Gurney), **VI:** 426
"Ballad of the Two Left Hands" (Dunn), **Supp. X:** 73
"Ballad of the Underpass" (Beer), **Supp. XIV:** 6
"Ballad of the White Horse, The" (Chesterton), **VI:** 338–339, 341
"Ballad of Villon and Fat Madge, The" (tr. Swinburne), **V:** 327

"Ballad on Mr. J.H. to Amoret, Asking Why I Was So Sad, A" (Behn), **Retro. Supp. III:** 6
Ballad Poetry of Ireland, The (ed. Duffy), **Supp. XIII:** 127
"Ballad upon a Wedding, A" (Suckling), **II:** 228–229
Ballade du temps jadis (Villon), **VI:** 254
"Ballade of Barnard Stewart, The" (Dunbar), **VIII:** 118
Ballade of Truthful Charles, The, and Other Poems (Swinburne), **V:** 333
Ballade on an Ale-Seller (Lydgate), **I:** 92
Ballads (Stevenson), **V:** 396
Ballads (Thackeray), **V:** 38
Ballads and Lyrical Pieces (Scott), **IV:** 38
Ballads and Other Poems (Tennyson), **IV:** 338
Ballads and Poems of Tragic Life (Meredith), **V:** 224, 234
Ballads and Sonnets (Rossetti), **V:** xxiv, 238, 244, 245
Ballads of the English Border (Swinburne), **V:** 333
Ballard, J. G., **III:** 341; **Supp. V:** 19–34
Ballast to the White Sea (Lowry), **Supp. III:** 273, 279
"Ane Ballat of Our Lady" (Dunbar). See "Hale, sterne superne"
Balliols, The (Waugh), **Supp. VI:** 273
Ballot (Smith), **Supp. VII:** 351
"Ballroom of Romance, The" (Trevor), **Supp. IV:** 503
"Bally *Power Play*" (Gunn), **Supp. IV:** 272
Ballygombeen Bequest, The (Arden and D'Arcy), **Supp. II:** 32, 35
Balthazar (Durrell), **Supp. I:** 104–105, 106, 107; **Retro. Supp. III:** 85, 88–89, 90
Balzac, Honoré de, **III:** 334, 339, 345; **IV:** 153n; **V:** xvi, xix–xxi, 17, 429; **Supp. IV:** 123, 136, 238, 459
Bamboo (Boyd), **Supp. XVI:** 31, 32–33, 36, 45, 46, 47
"Bamboo: A Ballad for Two Voices" (Plomer), **Supp. XI:** 226
Bamborough, J. B., **Retro. Supp. I:** 152
Bananas (ed. Tennant), **Supp. IX:** 228–229
Banco: The Further Adventures of Papillon (tr. O'Brian), **Supp. XII:** 252
Bancroft, John, **II:** 305
Bandamanna saga, **VIII:** 238, 241
"Bangor Requium" (Mahon), **Supp. VI:** 177
"Banim Creek" (Harris), **Supp. V:** 132
Banished Misfortune (Healy), **Supp. IX:** 96, 103–106
Banks, Iain, **Supp. XI:** 1–15
Banks, John, **II:** 305
"Bann Valley Eclogue" (Heaney), **Retro. Supp. I:** 134
Banned (Mda), **Supp. XV:** 197
Banshees of Inisheer, The (McDonagh), **Supp. XII:** 243
"Barbara of the House of Grebe" (Hardy), **VI:** 22; **Retro. Supp. I:** 117
Barbara, pseud. of Arnold Bennett

"Barbarian Catechism, A" (Wallace–Crabbe), **VIII:** 324
"Barbarian Pastorals" (Dunn), **Supp. X:** 72
Barbarians (Dunn), **Supp. X:** 71–73, 77
"Barbarians" (Dutton), **Supp. XII:** 90
Barbauld, Anna Laetitia, **III:** 88, 93
"Barber Cox and the Cutting of His Comb" (Thackeray), **V:** 21, 37
Barcellona; or, The Spanish Expedition under . . . Charles, Earl of Peterborough (Farquhar), **II:** 353, 355, 364
Barchester Towers (Trollope), **V:** xxii, 93, 101
"Bard, The" (Gray), **III:** 140–141
Bardic Tales (O'Grady), **Supp. V:** 36
"Bards of Passion . . ." (Keats), **IV:** 221
"Bare Abundance, The" (Dutton), **Supp. XII:** 89
Bare Abundance, The: Selected Poems, 1975–2001 (Dutton), **Supp. XII:** 83, 86, 88, 89–99
Barker, Granville, *see* Granville Barker, Harley
Barker, Sir Ernest, **III:** 196
Barker, Pat, **Supp. IV:** 45–63
Barker, Thomas, **II:** 131
Barker's Delight (Barker), *see Art of Angling, The*
Barksted, William, **II:** 31
"Barley" (Hughes), **Supp. I:** 358–359
"Barn, The" (Welch), **Supp. IX:** 268
Barnaby Rudge (Dickens), **V:** 42, 54, 55, 66, 71
Barnes, William, **VI:** 2
Barnes, Julian, **Supp. IV:** 65–76, 445, 542
"Barney Game, The" (Friel), **Supp. V:** 113
"Barnfloor and Winepress" (Hopkins), **V:** 381
"Barnsley Cricket Club" (Davie), **Supp. VI:** 109
Barrack-Room Ballads (Kipling), **VI:** 203, 204; **Retro. Supp. III:** 188
Barrel of a Pen: Resistance to Repression in Neo-Colonial Kenya (Ngũgĩ), **VIII:** 225
Barreca, Regina, **Supp. IV:** 531
Barren Fig Tree, The; or, The Doom . . . of the Fruitless Professor (Bunyan), **II:** 253
Barrett, Eaton Stannard, **III:** 335
Barrie, James M., **V:** 388, 392; **VI:** 265, 273, 280; **Supp. III:** 1–17, 138, 142
Barry Lyndon (Thackeray), **V:** 24, 28, 32, 38
Barrytown Trilogy, The (Doyle), **Supp. V:** 78, 80–87, 88, 89
Barsetshire novels (Trollope), **V:** 92–96, 98, 101
Bartas, Guillaume du, **II:** 138
Bartered Bride, The (Harrison), **Supp. V:** 150
Barth, John, **Supp. IV:** 116
Barthes, Roland, **Supp. IV:** 45, 115
Bartholomew Fair (Jonson), **I:** 228, 243, 324, 340, 342–343; **II:** 3; **Retro. Supp. I:** 164
Bartlett, Phyllis, **V:** x, xxvii

Barton, Bernard, **IV:** 341, 342, 343, 350
Barton, Eustace, **Supp. III:** 342
"Base Details" (Sassoon), **VI:** 430
Basement, The (Pinter), **Supp. I:** 371, 373, 374; **Retro. Supp. I:** 216
"Basement Room, The" (Greene), **Supp. I:** 2
Bashful Lover, The (Massinger), **Supp. XI:** 185
Basic Rules of Reason (Richards), **Supp. II:** 422
Basil: A Story of Modern Life (Collins), **Supp. VI:** 92, 95
Basil Seal Rides Again (Waugh), **VII:** 290
"Basking Shark" (MacCaig), **Supp. VI:** 192
Bate, Walter Jackson, **Retro. Supp. I:** 185
Bateman, Colin, **Supp. V:** 88
Bateson, F. W., **IV:** 217, 323n, 339
Bath (Sitwell), **VII:** 127
Bath Chronicle (periodical), **III:** 262
"Bath House, The" (Gunn), **Supp. IV:** 268–269
Bath–Intrigues: In Four Letters to a Friend in London (Haywood), **Supp. XII:** 135
Bathurst, Lord, **III:** 33
"Bats' Ultrasound" (Murray), **Supp. VII:** 281
Batsford Book of Light Verse for Children (Ewart), **Supp. VII:** 47
Batsford Book of Verse for Children (Ewart), **Supp. VII:** 47
"Battalion History, A" (Blunden), **Supp. XI:** 35
Battenhouse, Roy, **I:** 282
"Batter my heart, three person'd God" (Donne), **I:** 367–368; **II:** 122
"Batterer" (Adcock), **Supp. XII:** 4
Battiscombe, Georgina, **V:** xii, xxvii, 260
"Battle Hill Revisited" (Murphy), **Supp. V:** 323
Battle of Alcazar, The (Peele), **I:** 205, 206
Battle of Aughrim, The (Murphy), **Supp. V:** 321–324
"Battle of Aughrim, The" (Murphy), **Supp. V:** 317, 321–322
"Battle of Blenheim, The" (Southey), **IV:** 58, 67–68
Battle of Brunanburh, The, **Retro. Supp. II:** 307
Battle of Life, The (Dickens), **V:** 71
Battle of Maldon, The, **Retro. Supp. II:** 307
Battle of Marathon, The (Browning), **IV:** 310, 321
Battle of Shrivings, The (Shaffer), **Supp. I:** 323–324
Battle of the Books, The (Swift), **III:** 17, 23, 35; **Retro. Supp. I:** 276, 277
"Battle of the Goths and the Huns, The", *See Hlǫðskviða*
Baucis and Philemon (Swift), **III:** 35
Baudelaire, Charles **III:** 337, 338; **IV:** 153; **V:** xiii, xviii, xxii–xxiii, 310–318, 327, 329, 404, 405, 409, 411; **Supp. IV:** 163
Baum, L. Frank, **Supp. IV:** 450

Baumann, Paul, **Supp. IV:** 360
Baumgartner's Bombay (Desai), **Supp. V:** 53, 55, 66, 71–72
Bay (Lawrence), **VII:** 118
Bay at Nice, The (Hare), **Supp. IV:** 282, 293
Bayley, John, **Supp. I:** 222
Bayly, Lewis, **II:** 241
"Baymount" (Murphy), **Supp. V:** 328
"Bay-Tree, The" (Pitter), **Supp. XIII:** 143
"Be It Cosiness" (Beerbohm), **Supp. II:** 46
Be my Guest! (Ewart), **Supp. VII:** 41
"Be still, my soul" (Housman), **VI:** 162
Beach, J. W., **V:** 221n, 234
"Beach Head, The" (Gunn), **Retro. Supp. III:** 118
"Beach of Fales, The" (Stevenson), **V:** 396; **Retro. Supp. I:** 270
Beach of Falesá, The (screenplay, Thomas), **Retro. Supp. III:** 348
Beachcroft, T. O., **VII:** xxii
Beaconsfield, Lord, *see* Disraeli, Benjamin
"Bear in Mind" (Cameron), **Supp. IX:** 29
Beardsley, Aubrey, **V:** 318n, 412, 413
"Beast in the Jungle, The" (James), **VI:** 55, 64, 69
Beastly tales from Here and There (Seth), **Supp. X:** 287–288
Beasts and Super-Beasts (Saki), **Supp. VI:** 245, 251
Beasts' Confession to the Priest, The (Swift), **III:** 36
Beasts Royal (O'Brian), **Supp. XII:** 249
Beatrice (Haggard), **Supp. III:** 213
"Beatrice Signorini" (Browning), **Retro. Supp. III:** 31
Beattie, James, **IV:** 198
Beatty, David, **VI:** 351
Beau Austin (Stevenson), **V:** 396
Beauchamp's Career (Meredith), **V:** xxiv, 225, 228–230, 231, 234
Beaumont, Francis, **II:** 42–67, 79, 82, 87
Beaumont, Joseph, **II:** 180
Beaumont, Sir George, **IV:** 3, 12, 21, 22
Beauties and Furies, The (Stead), **Supp. IV:** 463–464
Beauties of English Poesy, The (ed. Goldsmith), **III:** 191
"Beautiful Lofty Things" (Yeats), **VI:** 216; **Retro. Supp. I:** 337
"Beautiful Sea, The" (Powys), **VIII:** 251
Beautiful Visit, The (Howard), **Supp. XI:** 137–138, 140–141, 148–149
"Beautiful Young Nymph Going to Bed, A" (Swift), **III:** 32, 36; **VI:** 256
"Beauty" (Thomas), **Supp. III:** 401–402
"Beauty and Duty" (Carpenter), **Supp. XIII:** 46
Beauty and the Beast (Hughes), **Supp. I:** 347
Beauty in a Trance, **II:** 100
Beauty Queen of Leenane, The (McDonagh), **Supp. XII:** 233, 234, 235–236, 238, 239, 241
Beautyful Ones Are Not Yet Born, The (Armah), **Supp. X:** 1–6, 12–13

Beauvoir, Simone de, **Supp. IV:** 232
Beaux' Stratagem, The (Farquhar), **II:** 334, 353, 359–360, 362, 364
"Beaver Ridge" (Fallon), **Supp. XII:** 113–114
"Because of the Dollars" (Conrad), **VI:** 148
"Because the pleasure-bird whistles" (Thomas), **Supp. I:** 176
Becket (Tennyson), **IV:** 328, 338; **Retro. Supp. III:** 329
Beckett, Samuel, **Supp. I:** 43–64; **Supp. IV:** 99, 106, 116, 180, 281, 284, 412, 429; **Retro. Supp. I:** 17–32
Beckford, William, **III:** 327–329, 345; **IV:** xv, 230
Bed Among the Lentils (Bennett), **VIII:** 27–28
"Bedbug, The" (Harrison), **Supp. V:** 151
Beddoes, Thomas, **V:** 330
Beddoes, Thomas Lovell, **Supp. XI:** 17–32
Bedford-Row Conspiracy, The (Thackeray), **V:** 21, 37
"Bedroom Eyes of Mrs. Vansittart, The" (Trevor), **Supp. IV:** 500
Bedroom Farce (Ayckbourn), **Supp. V:** 3, 12, 13, 14
Beds in the East (Burgess), **Supp. I:** 187
Bedtime Story (O'Casey), **VII:** 12
"Bedtime Story for my Son" (Redgrove), **Supp. VI:** 227–228, 236
Bee (periodical), **III:** 40, 179
Bee Hunter: Adventures of Beowulf (Nye), **Supp. X:** 193, 195
"Bee Orchd at Hodbarrow" (Nicholson), **Supp. VI:** 218
"Beechen Vigil" (Day Lewis), **Supp. III:** 121
Beechen Vigil and Other Poems (Day Lewis), **Supp. III:** 117, 120–121
"Beehive Cell" (Murphy), **Supp. V:** 329
Beekeepers, The (Redgrove), **Supp. VI:** 231
"Beeny Cliff" (Hardy), **Retro. Supp. I:** 118
Beer, Patricia, **Supp. XIV:** 1–15
Beerbohm, Max, **V:** 252, 390; **VI:** 365, 366; **Supp. II:** 43–59, 156
"Before Action" (Hodgson), **VI:** 422
"Before Dark" (Conn), **Supp. XIII:** 75
Before Dawn (Rattigan), **Supp. VII:** 315
"Before Her Portrait in Youth" (Thompson), **V:** 442
"Before I knocked" (Thomas), **Supp. I:** 175; **Retro. Supp. III:** 337–338
Before She Met Me (Barnes), **Supp. IV:** 65, 67–68
"Before Sleep" (Kinsella), **Supp. V:** 263
Before the Knowledge of Evil (Braddon), **VIII:** 36
"Before the Mirror" (Swinburne), **V:** 320
"Before the Party" (Maugham), **VI:** 370
"Before the Throne, and before the Lamb" (Rossetti), **Retro. Supp. III:** 258
Beggars (Davies), **Supp. XI:** 87, 88
Beggars Banquet (Rankin), **Supp. X:** 245–246, 253, 257
Beggar's Bush (Beaumont, Fletcher, Massinger), **II:** 66

Beggar's Opera, The (Gay), **III:** 54, 55, **61–64,** 65–67; **Supp. III:** 195; **Retro. Supp. I:** 80
"Beggar's Soliloquy, The" (Meredith), **V:** 220
Begin Here: A War–Time Essay (Sayers), **Supp. III:** 336
"Beginning, The" (Brooke), **Supp. III:** 52
Beginning of Spring, The (Fitzgerald), **Supp. V:** 98, 106
"Beginnings of Love, The" (Carpenter), **Supp. XIII:** 42
Beguilers, The (Thompson), **Supp. XIV:** 291, 292
Behan, Brendan, **Supp. II:** 61–76
"Behind the Façade" (Larkin), **Retro. Supp. III:** 212
Behind the Green Curtains (O'Casey), **VII:** 11
"Behind the Mirror" (Gunn), **Retro. Supp. III:** 124
"Behind the Scenes: Empire" (Symons), **Supp. XIV:** 272
Behn, Aphra, **Supp. III:** 19–33; **Retro. Supp. III:** 1–16
"Behold, Love, thy power how she despiseth" (Wyatt), **I:** 109
"Being Boring" (Cope), **VIII:** 80
"Being Born" (Gunn), **Retro. Supp. III:** 122
Being Dead (Crace), **Supp. XIV:** 18, 21, 23, 27–29
"Being Stolen From" (Trevor), **Supp. IV:** 504
"Being Treated, to Ellinda" (Lovelace), **II:** 231–232
"Beldonald Holbein, The" (James), **VI:** 69
"Beleaguered City, A" (Oliphant), **Supp. X:** 220
Belfast Confetti (Carson), **Supp. XIII:** 53, 54, 57–59
"Belfast vs. Dublin" (Boland), **Supp. V:** 36
"Belief" (Dutton), **Supp. XII:** 96
Belief and Creativity (Golding), **Supp. I:** 88
Belief in Immortality and Worship of the Dead, The (Frazer), **Supp. III:** 176
Believe As You List (Massinger), **Supp. XI:** 185
Believer, **Supp. XV:** 145
Belin, Mrs., **II:** 305
Belinda (Edgeworth), **Supp. III:** 157–158, 162
Belinda, An April Folly (Milne), **Supp. V:** 298–299
Bell, Acton, pseud. of Anne Brontë
Bell, Clive, **V:** 345
Bell, Currer, pseud. of Charlotte Brontë
Bell, Ellis, pseud. of Emily Brontë
Bell, Julian, **Supp. III:** 120
Bell, Quentin, **VII:** 35; **Retro. Supp. I:** 305
Bell, Robert, **I:** 98
Bell, Vanessa, **VI:** 118
Bell, The (Murdoch), **Supp. I:** 222, 223–224, 226, 228–229
"Bell of Aragon, The" (Collins), **III:** 163

"Bell Ringer, The" (Jennings), **Supp. V:** 218
"Belladonna" (Nye), **Supp. X:** 198
Bellamira; or, The Mistress (Sedley), **II:** 263
Belle Assemblée, La (tr. Haywood), **Supp. XII:** 135
"Belle Heaulmière" (tr. Swinburne), **V:** 327
"Belle of the Ball–Room" (Praed), **V:** 14
Belle's Stratagem, The (Cowley), **Supp. XVI:** 109, 110, 112, 114, 117–122, 123
Belloc, Hilaire, **VI:** 246, 320, 335, 337, 340, 447; **VII:** xiii; **Supp. IV:** 201
Belloc, Mrs. Lowndes, **Supp. II:** 135
Bellow, Saul, **Supp. IV:** 26, 27, 42, 234
Bells and Pomegranates (Browning), **IV:** 356, 373–374; **Retro. Supp. III:** 20–23, 24
Belmonte, Thomas, **Supp. IV:** 15
Belonging (Butlin), **Supp. XVI:** 52, 67–68
Below Loughrigg (Adcock), **Supp. XII:** 6
"Below The Devil's Punchbowl" (Delanty), **Supp. XIV:** 66
Belsey, Catherine, **Supp. IV:** 164
Belton Estate, The (Trollope), **V:** 100, 101
"Bench of Desolation, The" (James), **VI:** 69
Bend for Home, The (Healy), **Supp. IX:** 95, 96, 98–100, 101, 103, 106
Bend in the River, A (Naipaul), **Supp. I:** 393, **397–399,** 401
Bender, T. K., **V:** 364–365, 382
Bending of the Bough, The (Moore), **VI:** 87, 95–96, 98
Benedict, Ruth, **Supp. III:** 186
"Benediction" (Soutar), **Supp. XVI:** 254
Benjamin, Walter, **Supp. IV:** 82, 87, 88, 91
Benlowes, Edward, **II:** 123
Benn, Gotfried, **Supp. IV:** 411
"Bennelong" (Wallace-Crabbe), **VIII:** 319–320
Bennett, Alan, **VIII:** 19–34
Bennett, Arnold, **VI:** xi, xii, xiii, 226, 233n, **247–268,** 275; **VII:** xiv, xxi; **Supp. III:** 324, 325; **Supp. IV:** 229, 230–231, 233, 239, 241, 249, 252; **Retro. Supp. I:** 318
Bennett, Joan, **II:** 181, 187, 201, 202; **V:** 199, 201
Benson, A. C., **V:** 133, 151; **Supp. II:** 406, 418
Benstock, Bernard, **Supp. IV:** 320
"Bent Font, The" (Delanty), **Supp. XIV:** 70
Bentham, Jeremy, **IV:** xii, xv, 50, 130–133, 278, 295; **V:** viii
Bentley, Clerihew, **IV:** 101
Bentley, E. C., **VI:** 335
Bentley, G. E., Jr., **III:** 289n, 307
Bentley, Richard, **III:** 23
Bentley's Miscellany (periodical), **V:** 42
Benveniste, Émile, **Supp. IV:** 115
"Benvolio" (James), **VI:** 69
Beowulf, **I:** 69; **Supp. VI:** **29–44;** **Retro. Supp. II:** 298, 299, 305–306, 307

Beowulf (tr. Morgan), **Supp. IX:** 160–162
"Beowulf: The Monsters and the Critics" (Tolkien), **Supp. II:** 521
Beppo (Byron), **IV:** xvii, 172, 177, **182–184,** 186, 188, 192
Bequest to the Nation, A (Rattigan), **Supp. VII:** 320
Berdoe, Edward, **IV:** 371
Bérénice (Racine), **II:** 98
Bergerac, Cyrano de, *see* Cyrano de Bergerac
Bergonzi, Bernard, **VII:** xxi, xxxvii; **Supp. IV:** 233, 364
"Berkeley and 'Philosophic Words'" (Davie), **Supp. VI:** 107
Berkeley, George, **III:** 50
Berlin Noir (Kerr), **Supp. XII:** 186, 187–191, 192, 193, 194, 199
Berlin stories (Isherwood), **VII:** 309, 311–312
"Bermudas" (Marvell), **II:** 208, 210, 211, 217
Bernard, Charles de, **V:** 21
Bernard, Richard, **II:** 246
Bernard Shaw and Mrs. Patrick Campbell: Their Correspondence (ed. Dent), **VI:** 130
Bernard Shaw's Letters to Granville Barker (ed. Purdom), **VI:** 115n, 129
Bernard Shaw's Rhyming Picture Guide . . . (Shaw), **VI:** 130
"Bertie Changes His Mind" (Wodehouse), **Supp. III:** 458
Bertram; or, The Castle of St. Aldobrand; A Tragedy in Five Acts (Maturin), **VIII:** 201, 205–207
Bertrams, The (Trollope), **V:** 101
Besant, Annie, **VI:** 103, 249
Beside the Ocean of Time (Brown), **Supp. VI:** 64, **67–68**
"Beside the Seaside: A Holiday with Children" (Smith), **Retro. Supp. III:** 306
Bessie Smith (Kay), **Supp. XIII:** 101, 103–105
"Best Friend, The" (Davies), **Supp. XI:** 99
Best of Defoe's Review, The (ed. Payne), **III:** 41
Best of Enemies, The (Fry), **Supp. III:** 195
Best of Roald Dahl, The (Dahl), **Supp. IV:** 209
"Best of the Young British Novelists, The" (Granta special issue), **Supp. IV:** 304
Best Wine Last: An Autobiography through the Years 1932–1969, The (Waugh), **Supp. VI:** 268, **271–272,** 273, 275–276
"Bestre" (Lewis), **VII:** 77
Bethell, Augusta, **V:** 84
Betjeman, John, **VII:** xxi–xxii, **355–377**
Betrayal (Pinter), **Supp. I:** 377
Betrayal, The (Hartley), **Supp. VII:** 121, 131, 132
Betrayal of the Left, The (Orwell), **VII:** 284
"Betrayer, The" (Cornford), **VIII:** 112
Betrothed, The (Scott), **IV:** 39

324

Better Class of Person, A (Osborne), **Supp. I:** 329
Better Dead (Barrie), **Supp. III:** 2
"Better Resurrection, A" (Rossetti), **V:** 254
Between (Brooke–Rose), **Supp. IV:** 98, 99, 104, 105, 108–109, 112
Between Here and Now (Thomas), **Supp. XII:** 288–289
"Between Mouthfuls" (Ayckbourn), **Supp. V:** 11
Between the Acts (Woolf), **VII:** 18, 19, 22, 24, 26; **Retro. Supp. I:** 308, 321
"Between the Conceits" (Self), **Supp. V:** 402–403
Between the Iceberg and the Ship (Stevenson), **Supp. VI:** 257, 259, 264
Between the Lines: Yeats's Poetry in the Making (Stallworthy), **Supp. X:** 291
"Between the Lotus and the Robot" (Koestler), **Supp. I:** 34n
Between These Four Walls (Lodge and Bradbury), **Supp. IV:** 365
"Between Two Nowheres" (MacCaig), **Supp. VI:** 192
Between Us Girls (Orton), **Supp. V:** 363, 366–367, 372
"Bevel, The" (Kelman), **Supp. V:** 245
Bevis: The Story of a Boy (Jefferies), **Supp. XV:** 172–173
"Beware of Doubleness" (Lydgate), **I:** 64
"Beware of the Dog" (Dahl), **Supp. IV:** 209
Beyle, Marie Henri, *see* Stendhal
Beyond (Richards), **Supp. II:** 421, 426, **428–429**
Beyond Good and Evil (Nietzsche), **IV:** 121; **V:** xxv; **Supp. IV:** 50
"Beyond Howth Head" (Mahon), **Supp. VI:** 170, 175
Beyond Personality (Lewis), **Supp. III:** 248
Beyond Reductionism: New Perspectives in the Life Sciences (Koestler), **Supp. I:** 37, 38
Beyond the Bone (Hill), see *Urn Burial*
Beyond the Fringe (Bennett et al.), **VIII:** 19, 21, 22
Beyond the Mexique Bay (Huxley), **VII:** 201
"Beyond the Pale" (Kipling), **VI:** 178–180
"Beyond the Pale" (Trevor), **Supp. IV:** 502
"Beyond Words" (Okri), **Supp. V:** 360
BFG, The (Dahl), **Supp. IV:** 204, 207, 225
"Bhut–Baby, The" (Steel), **Supp. XII:** 269
Bhutto, Benazir, **Supp. IV:** 444, 455
Bhutto, Zulfikar Ali, **Supp. IV:** 444
Biala, Janice, **VI:** 324
"Bianca Among the Nightingales" (Browning), **IV:** 315
Biathanatos (Donne), **I:** 370; **Retro. Supp. II:** 96–97
Bible, *see* English Bible
Bible in Spain, The; or, The Journeys, Adventures, and Imprisonments of an Englishman in an Attempt to Circulate the Scriptures on the Peninsula (Borrow), **Supp. XII:** 17–18, 18–20, 31
Bible Stories: Memorable Acts of the Ancient Patriarchs, Judges, and Kings, Extracted from Their Original Historians: For the Use of Children (Godwin), **Supp. XV:** 125, 126
Bibliography of Henry James, A (Edel and Laurence), **VI:** 66
Bickerstaff, Isaac, pseud. of Sir Richard Steele and Joseph Addison
Bicycle and Other Poems (Malouf), **Supp. XII:** 219
Big Bazoohley, The (Carey), **Supp. XII:** 54
Big Day, The (Unsworth), **Supp. VII:** 354, 357
"Big Deaths, Little Deaths" (Thomas), **Supp. IV:** 492
Big Fellow, The (O'Connor), **Supp. XIV:** 216
Big H, The (Harrison), **Supp. V:** 150, 164
Big House, The (Behan), **Supp. II:** 70–71
"Big House in Ireland, A" (Blackwood), **Supp. IX:** 6
"Big Milk" (Kay), **Supp. XIII:** 102
Big Mouth Strikes Again: A Further Collection of Two-Fisted Journalism (Parsons), **Supp. XV:** 227, 237, 240
Big Toys (White), **Supp. I:** 131, 151
"Bigness on the Side of Good" (Scupham), **Supp. XIII:** 225
Bill for the Better Promotion of Oppression on the Sabbath Day, A (Peacock), **IV:** 170
"Billy" (Constantine), **Supp. XV:** 70
Billy Liar (Waterhouse), **Supp. XIII:** 266, 269–273, 274–275, 279
Billy Liar on the Moon (Waterhouse), **Supp. XIII:** 273
Bim, **Supp. XII:** 35, 43
"Bindi Mirror, The" (Delanty), **Supp. XIV:** 73
Bingo (Bond), **Supp. I:** 423, 433–434
"Binsey Poplars" (Hopkins), **V:** 370, 371
Binyon, Laurence, **VI:** 416, 439
Biographia Literaria (Coleridge), **IV:** xvii, 4, 6, 18, 25, 41, **44–45**, 50, 51, 52–53, 56; **Retro. Supp. II:** 62–64
"Biographical Notice of Ellis and Acton Bell" (Brontë), **V:** 131, 134, 152, 153
"Biography" (Thomas), **Supp. XII:** 279
Bird, Isabella, **Supp. X: 17–32**
"Bird and Beast" (Rossetti), **V:** 258
"Bird Auction, The" (McGuckian), **Supp. V:** 284
"Bird in the House" (Jennings), **Supp. V:** (Jennings), **Supp. V:** 218
"Bird in the Tree, The" (Pitter), **Supp. XIII:** 142
Bird of Night, The (Hill), **Supp. XIV:** 116, 117, 122–123
Bird of Paradise, The (Davies), **Supp. XI:** 99
Bird of Paradise (Drabble), **Supp. IV:** 230
"Bird Poised to Fly, The" (Highsmith), **Supp. V:** 180
"Bird Study" (Jennings), **Supp. V:** 218
"Birds" (Davies), **Supp. XI:** 100
"Birds, The" (du Maurier), **Supp. III:** 143, 147, 148
Birds, The (film), **III:** 343; **Supp. III:** 143
"Birds at Winter Nightfall" (Hardy), **Retro. Supp. I:** 119
Birds, Beasts and Flowers (Lawrence), **VII:** 90, 118, 119; **Retro. Supp. II:** 233–234
Birds Fall Down, The (West), **Supp. III:** 440, 444
Birds in Tiny Cages (Comyns), **VIII:** 56, 59–60
Birds of Heaven (Okri), **Supp. V:** 359, 360
"Birds of Paradise" (Rossetti), **V:** 255
Birds of Paradise, The (Scott), **Supp. I:** 259, **263–266,** 268
Birds of Passage (Kureishi), **Supp. XI:** 156, 157
Birds of Prey (Braddon), **VIII:** 47
Birds Without Wings (De Bernières), **Supp. XII:** 65–66, 68, 69, 77–78
"Birdsong" (Constantine), **Supp. XV:** 70
Birthday Letters (Hughes), **Retro. Supp. II:** 202, 216–218
Birkenhead, Lord (F. E. Smith), **VI:** 340–341
Birmingham Colony, **VI:** 167
Birney, Earle, **Supp. III:** 282
Birrell, A., **II:** 216
Birth by Drowning (Nicholson), **Supp. VI: 222–223**
Birth of Manly Virtue, The (Swift), **III:** 35
"Birth of the Squire, The" (Gay), **III:** 58
Birth of Tragedy, The (Nietsche), **Supp. IV:** 3, 9
"Birth Place" (Murphy), **Supp. V:** 328
"Birth–Bond, The" (Rossetti), **V:** 242
Birthday (Frayn), **Supp. VII:** 57
"Birthday, A" (Mansfield), **VII:** 172, 173
"Birthday, A" (Muir), **Supp. VI:** 207
"Birthday, A" (Rossetti), **V:** 252
Birthday Boys, The (Bainbridge), **Supp. VI: 24–25,** 26
Birthday Party (Milne), **Supp. V:** 309
Birthday Party, The (Pinter), **Supp. I:** 367, 369–370, 373, 380; **Retro. Supp. I:** 216–217, 224
"Birthdays" (MacCaig), **Supp. VI:** 192
"Birthing" (Delahunt), **Supp. XIV:** 50–51
"Birthplace, The" (James), **VI:** 69
"Birthright" (Nye), **Supp. X:** 205
Birthstone (Thomas), **Supp. IV:** 479, 480–481, 492
"Bishop Blougram's Apology" (Browning), **IV:** 357, 361, 363; **Retro. Supp. III:** 24, 26
"Bishop Burnet and Humphrey Hardcastle" (Landor), **IV:** 91
"Bishop Orders His Tomb at St. Praxed's Church, The" (Browning), **IV:** 356, 370, 372; **Retro. Supp. III:** 20, 22
Bishop's Bonfire, The (O'Casey), **VII:** xvii 10
"Bishop's Fool, The" (Lewis), **VII:** 80
Bishton, John, **Supp. IV:** 445
Bit o' Love, A (Galsworthy), **VI:** 280

"Bit of Honesty, A" (Nye), **Supp. X:** 202
Bit of Singing and Dancing, A (Hill), **Supp. XIV:** 118
"Bit of Young Life, A" (Gordimer), **Supp. II:** 232
Bit Off the Map, A (Wilson), **Supp. I:** 155
"Bit Off the Map, A" (Wilson), **Supp. I:** 155, 157, 161
"Bit Sonnet, A" (Butlin), **Supp. XVI:** 55
"Bitch" (Dahl), **Supp. IV:** 220
Bitter Fame (Stevenson), **Supp. VI: 263**
Bitter Lemons (Durrell), **Supp. I:** 104, 111–113; **Retro. Supp. III:** 85, 95
"Bitter Salvage" (Warner), **Supp. XI:** 298
Bitter Sweet (Coward), **Supp. II:** 142, 146, 147
Bjarnar saga Hítdœlakappa, **VIII:** 239
Black Album, The (Kureishi), **Supp. XI:** 153–155, 158–159
Black and Blue (Rankin), **Supp. X:** 243–245, 253–254
Black and Silver (Frayn), **Supp. VII:** 57
"Black and Tans,"**VII:** 2
Black and the Red, The (Smith, I. C.), **Supp. IX:** 210
Black and White (Collins), **Supp. VI:** 102
"Black and White Minstrel Show, The" (Jamie), **Supp. XIV:** 141
Black Arrow, The (Stevenson), **V:** 396
Black Bastard, The (Williams, C. W. S.), **Supp. IX:** 279
Black Book, The (Durrell), **Supp. I:** 93, 94, 96, **97–100**, 118, 122, 123; **Retro. Supp. III:** 83, 84, 86, 87–88, 95
Black Book, The (Middleton), **II:** 3
Black Book, The (Rankin), **Supp. X:** 244, 251–252
"Black Bottom" (Kay), **Supp. XIII:** 99, 103
Black Bryony (Powys), **VIII:** 250
Black Comedy (Shaffer), **Supp. I:** 317, 318, 321–322, 324
Black Daisies for the Bride (Harrison), **Supp. V:** 164
"Black Day" (Soutar), **Supp. XVI:** 242
Black Dog, The (Coppard), **VIII:** 94–95, 97
"Black Dog, The" (Coppard), **VIII:** 90, 94
Black Dogs (McEwan), **Supp. IV:** 389, 390, 398, 404–406
Black Dwarf, The (Scott), **IV:** 39
Black Fast: A Poetic Farce in One Act (Clarke), **Supp. XV:** 25
"Black Goddess, The" (Graves), **VII:** 261, 270
Black Goddess and the Sixth Sense, The (Redgrove), **Supp. VI:** 234–235
"Black Guillemot, The" (Nicholson), **Supp. VI: 218**
Black Hermit, The (Ngũgĩ), **VIII:** 214, 222–223
Black Hill, On the (Chatwin, B.), **Supp. IX:** 56–57, 59
Black House, The (Highsmith), **Supp. V:** 180
"Black Jackets" (Gunn), **Retro. Supp. III:** 121
Black Knight, The (Lydgate), see *Complaint of the Black Knight, The Black Lamb and Grey Falcon* (West), **Supp. III:** 434, 438–439, 445
"Black Lace Fan My Mother Gave Me, The" (Boland), **Supp. V:** 46–47
"Black Madonna, The" (Lessing), **Supp. I:** 242–243
"Black March" (Smith), **Supp. II:** 469
Black Marina (Tennant), **Supp. IX:** 239
Black Marsden (Harris), **Supp. V:** 138–139
Black Mass (Bond), **Supp. I:** 423, 429
"Black Mass, The" (Ewart), **Supp. VII:** 45
"Black Mate, The" (Conrad), **VI:** 135, 148
Black Mischief (Waugh), **VII:** 290, 294–295
"Black Mountain Poets: Charles Olson and Edward Dorn, The" (Davie), **Supp. VI:** 116
"Black Peril" (Plomer), **Supp. XI:** 218
Black Prince, The (Murdoch), **Supp. I:** 226, 228, 229–230
Black Robe (Moore, B.), **Supp. IX:** 144, 145, 151, 152–153
Black Robe, The (Collins), **Supp. VI:** 102–103
Black Ships Before Troy (Sutcliff), **Supp. XVI:** 273
Black Spiders (Jamie), **Supp. XIV:** 129–131, 133, 134, 143
"Black Spiders" (Jamie), **Supp. XIV:** 129, 130
Black Swan Green (Mitchell), **Supp. XIV:** 194, 206–208
"Black Takes White" (Cameron), **VII:** 426
Black Tower, The (James), **Supp. IV:** 319, 320, 325, 327–328
"Black Virgin" (McGuckian), **Supp. V:** 288
"Blackberry–Picking" (Heaney), **Retro. Supp. I:** 123
"Blackbird in a Sunset Bush" (MacCaig), **Supp. VI:** 192
Blackeyes (Potter, D.), **Supp. X:** 229
"Blackie the Electric Rembrandt" (Gunn), **Retro. Supp. III:** 121
"Blackness" (Kincaid), **Supp. VII:** 221, 223, 229
Black–out in Gretley (Priestley), **VII:** 212, 217
Blackstone, Bernard, **VII:** xiv, xxxvii
Blackstone, Sir William, **III:** 199
"Blackthorn Spray, The" (Stallworthy), **Supp. X:** 296–297
Blackwood, Caroline, **Supp. IX: 1–16**
Blackwood's (periodical), **IV:** xvii, 129, 145, 269–270, 274; **V:** 108–109, 111, 137, 142, 190, 191
"Blade, The" (Montague), **Supp. XV:** 219
Blair, Robert, **III:** 336
Blair, Tony, **Supp. IV:** 74
Blake (Ackroyd), **Supp. VI:** 10, **11**
Blake, Nicholas (pseud.), see Day Lewis, Cecil
Blake, Robert, **IV:** 296, 304, 306–308
Blake, William, **II:** 102, 115, 258; **III:** 174, **288–309**, 336; **IV:** 178; **V:** xiv–xvi, xviii, **244**, 316–317, 325, 329–330, 403; **V:** viii, 163; **VI:** viii; **VII:** 23–24; **Supp. II:** 523, 531; **Supp. IV:** 188, 410, 448; **Retro. Supp. I: 33–47**
Blake, William (neé Blech), **Supp. IV:** 459, 461
Blake's Chaucer: The Canterbury Pilgrims (Blake), **III:** 307
"Blake's Column" (Healy), **Supp. IX:** 105
"Blakesmoor in H—shire" (Lamb), **IV:** 76–77
Blandings Castle (Wodehouse), **Supp. III:** 453
"Blank" (Carson), **Supp. XIII:** 64
"Blank, A" (Gunn), **Supp. IV:** 278; **Retro. Supp. III:** 128
Blank Cheque, The (Carroll), **V:** 274
Blank Verse (Lloyd and Lamb), **IV:** 78, 85
Blasphemers' Banquet, The (Harrison), **Supp. V:** 164
Blast (periodical), **VII:** xiii, 72
Blasted (Kane), **VIII:** 147, 148, 149, 151–155, 156, 157, 158, 159
Blasting and Bombardiering (Lewis), **VII:** 72, 76, 77
Blather (periodical), **Supp. II:** 323, 338
Blatty, William Peter, **III:** 343, 345
Bleak House (Dickens), **IV:** 88; **V:** 4, 42, 47, 53, 54, 55, 59, 62–66, 68, 69, 70, 71; **Supp. IV:** 513
"Bleak Liturgies" (Thomas), **Supp. XII:** 290, 291
Bleeding Hearts (Rankin), **Supp. X:** 245
"Bleik" (Burnside), **Supp. XIII:** 26
Blenheim (Trevelyan), **VI:** 392–393
"Blessed Among Women" (Swinburne), **V:** 325
"Blessed Are Ye That Sow Beside All Waters: A Lay Sermon" (Coleridge), **IV:** 56
Blessed Body (More), **Supp. VII:** 245
"Blessed Damozel, The" (Rossetti), **V:** 236, 239, 315
Blessing, The (Mitford), **Supp. X:** 151, 158, 161, 163–165
"Blighters" (Sassoon), **VI:** 430
"Blind" (Abercrombie), **Supp. XVI:** 1–2
"Blind, The" (Burnside), **Supp. XIII:** 23
Blind Beggar of Alexandria, The (Chapman), **I:** 234, 243
Blind Date (film; Ambler), **Supp. IV:** 3
"Blind Elephant Man in the Underground, A" (Constantine), **Supp. XV:** 74
Blind Fireworks (MacNeice), **VII:** 411
Blind Love (Collins), **Supp. VI:** 103
"Blind Love" (Pritchett), **Supp. III: 325–327**
Blind Love and Other Stories (Pritchett), **Supp. III:** 313, 325
Blind Mice, The (Friel), **Supp. V:** 115
Blind Stitch, The (Delanty), **Supp. XIV:** 72, 74, 75
"Blinded Bird, The" (Hardy), **Retro. Supp. I:** 119
Blindness (Green), **Supp. II: 249–251**
Bliss (Carey), **Supp. XII:** 52–53, 55–56, 57, 58, 62
"Bliss" (Mansfield), **VII:** 174
"Blisse" (Traherne), **Supp. XI:** 270

"Blissful Land, The" (Reed), **Supp. XV:** 255

Blithe Spirit (Coward), **Supp. II:** 154–155, 156

"Blizzard Song" (Thomas), **Supp. IV:** 494

Bloch, Robert, **III:** 342

"Blodewedd" (Montague), **Supp. XV:** 217–218

Blomberg, Sven, **Supp. IV:** 88

"Blood" (Burnside), **Supp. XIII:** 27

Blood (Galloway), **Supp. XII:** 117, 120–123, 124

"Blood" (Galloway), **Supp. XII:** 122

"Blood" (Murray), **Supp. VII:** 273, 281, 282

Blood and Family (Kinsella), **Supp. V:** 270, 271

Blood and Sand (Sutcliff), **Supp. XVI:** 273

Blood Doctor, The (Rendell), **Supp. IX:** 200–201, 203

"Blood-feud of Toad-Water, The" (Saki), **Supp. VI:** 246

Blood Hunt (Rankin), **Supp. X:** 245

"Blood Is the Water" (Wallace-Crabbe), **VIII:** 316–317

Blood Knot, The (Fugard), **Supp. XV:** 102–103, 106

Blood of the Bambergs, The (Osborne), **Supp. I:** 335

Blood Red, Sister Rose (Keneally), **Supp. IV:** 346

Blood, Sweat and Tears (Churchill), **VI:** 349, 361

Blood Sympathy (Hill, R.), **Supp. IX:** 123

Blood Will Tell (Christie), *see Mrs. McGinty's Dead*

"Bloodlines" (Motion), **Supp. VII:** 263

"Bloody Chamber, The" (Carter), **Supp. III:** 88

Bloody Chamber and Other Stories, The (Carter), **Supp. III:** 79, 87, 88–89

"Bloody Cranesbill, The" (Nicholson), **Supp. VI:** 219

"Bloody Men" (Cope), **VIII:** 76

"Bloody Son, The" (Swinburne), **V:** 321

Bloom, Harold, **III:** 289n, 307; **V:** 309, 316, 329, 402

Bloomfield, Paul, **IV:** xii, xxiv, 306

Bloomsbury: A House of Lions (Edel), **VII:** 39

Bloomsbury Group, The (Johnstone), **VI:** 413

Blot in the Scutcheon, A (Browning), **IV:** 374; **Retro. Supp. III:** 20

"Blow, The" (Hardy), **VI:** 17

Blow Your House Down (retitled *Liza's England;* Barker), **Supp. IV:** 45, 46, 50–53, 57

"Bloweth Where it Listeth" (Pitter), **Supp. XIII:** 142

"Blucher and Sandt" (Landor), **IV:** 92

Bludy Serk, The (Henryson), **Supp. VII:** 146, 148

Blue Afternoon, The (Boyd), **Supp. XVI:** 38–39

"Blue Apron, The" (Malouf), **Supp. XII:** 220

Blue at the Mizzen (O'Brian), **Supp. XII:** 257, 259

"Blue bell is the sweetest Flower, The" (Brontë), **V:** 134

"Blue Boat, The" (Jamie), **Supp. XIV:** 143

"Blue Closet, The" (Morris), **IV:** 313

Blue Djinn of Babylon, The (Kerr), **Supp. XII:** 198

"Blue Dress, The" (Trevor), **Supp. IV:** 501

"Blue Eyes" (Warner), **Supp. VII:** 371

Blue Flower, The (Fitzgerald), **Supp. V:** 95, 96, 98, 99, 100, 107–108

"Blue Lenses, The" (du Maurier), **Supp. III:** 147

Blue Remembered Hills and Other Plays (Potter, D.), **Supp. X:** 229, 231–237

Blue Remembered Hills: A Recollection (Sutcliff), **Supp. XVI:** 263, 264–265, 273

"Bluebeard's Ghost" (Thackeray), **V:** 24, 38

Blunden, Edmund, **IV:** xi, xxiv, 86, 210, 254, 267, 316; **VI:** 416, **427–429,** 439, 454; **VII:** xvi; **Supp. XI:** 33–48

Blunderer, The (Highsmith), **Supp. V:** 170

Blyton, Enid, **Supp. IV:** 434

"Boarding House, The" (Joyce), **Retro. Supp. III:** 169

Boarding House, The (Trevor), **Supp. IV:** 501, 506–507, 511

"Boarding School Reminiscences" (Jewsbury), **Supp. XIV:** 150

Boas, F. S., **I:** 218, 275

Boat, The (Hartley), **Supp. VII:** 123, 127, 128

"Boat House, Bank Ground, Coniston, The" (Nicholson), **Supp. VI:** 216

Boat of Fate, The (Roberts, K.), **Supp. X:** 272–273

Boat That Mooed, The (Fry), **Supp. III:** 195

Boating for Beginners (Winterson), **Supp. IV:** 541, 542, 545–547, 555

"Bob Hope Classic Show (ITV) and 'Shelley Among the Ruins,' Lecture by Professor Timothy Webb—both Saturday evening, 26.9.81" (Ewart), **Supp. VII:** 45

"Bob Robinson's First Love" (Thackeray), **V:** 24, 38

"Bob's Lane" (Thomas), **Supp. III:** 394, 405

Boccaccio, Giovanni, **II:** 292, 304; **Supp. IV:** 461

Body, The (Kureishi), **Supp. XI:** 163

Body Below (film; Ambler), **Supp. IV:** 3

Body in the Library (Christie), **Supp. II:** 131, 132

Body Language (Ayckbourn), **Supp. V:** 3, 10, 11

Body Snatcher, The (Stevenson), **V:** 396

"Body's Beauty" (Rossetti), **V:** 237

Boehme, Jacob, **IV:** 45

"Boeotian Count, The" (Murray), **Supp. VII:** 275

Boesman and Lena (Fugard), **Supp. XV:** 103, 107–108

Boethius, **I:** 31, 32; **II:** 185

Bog Myrtle and Peat (Thompson), **Supp. XV:** 286, 288

Bog of Allen, The (Hall), **Supp. II:** 322

Bog People, The (Glob), **Retro. Supp. I:** 128

"Bogey Wife, The" (Jamie), **Supp. XIV:** 142

"Bogland" (Heaney), **Supp. II:** 271–272

"Bogy Man, The" (Coppard), **VIII:** 96

"Bohemians, The" (Gurney), **VI:** 427

Boiardo, Matteo, **IV:** 231

Boileau, Nicolas, **IV:** 92, 93

"Boisterous Poem about Poetry, A" (Wain), **Supp. XVI:** 306

Boke of Eneydos, The (Skelton), **I:** 82

Boklund, Gunnar, **II:** 73

Boland, Eavan, **Supp. V: 35–52**

Bold, Alan, **Supp. IV:** 256

Bold Stroke for a Husband, A (Inchbald), **Supp. XV:** 161

Böll, Heinrich, **Supp. IV:** 440

"Bombers" (Day Lewis), **Supp. III:** 127

"Bombing Practice" (Nicholson), **Supp. VI:** 214

Bonadventure, The: A Random Journal of an Atlantic Holiday (Blunden), **Supp. XI:** 36

"Bonaly" (Jamie), **Supp. XIV:** 141

Bond, Edward, **Supp. I: 421–436; Supp. IV:** 182

"Bond" (Dutton), **Supp. XII:** 92

Bond Honoured, A (Osborne), **Supp. I:** 335–336, 337–338

Bondman, The: And Antient Storie (Massinger), **Supp. XI:** 184, 185

Bonduca (Fletcher), **II:** 45, 58, 60, 65

"Bone Elephant, The" (Motion), **Supp. VII:** 262

"Bones of Contention" (O'Connor), **Supp. XIV:** 225

"Bonfire Under a Black Sun" (O'Casey), **VII:** 13

Bonnefon, Jean de, **II:** 108

"Bonny Broukit Bairn, The" (MacDiarmid), **Supp. XII:** 205–206

Boodle, Adelaide, **V:** 391, 393, 397

"Book, The" (Vaughan), **II:** 187

"Book Ends" (Harrison), **Supp. V:** 153–154

Book for Boys and Girls, A; or, Country Rhimes for Children (Bunyan), **II:** 253

Book of Ahania, The (Blake), **III:** 307; **Retro. Supp. I:** 44

Book of Answers, A (Hope), **Supp. VII:** 164

Book of Balaam's Ass, The (Jones), **Supp. VII:** 170

Book of Common Praise, The (Newman), **Supp. VII:** 291

Book of Ireland, A (O'Connor), **Supp. XIV:** 213

Book of Irish Verse (ed. Yeats), **Supp. XIII:** 114–115

Book of Los, The (Blake), **III:** 307

Book of Margery Kempe, The (Kempe), **Supp. XII:** 167–168, 169–171, 172, 173, 174, 175–181, 182

Book of Matches (Armitage), **VIII:** 1, 6–8

"Book of Matches" (Armitage), **VIII:** 8

Book of Mortals, A: Being a Record of the Good Deeds and Good Qualities of What Humanity Is Pleased to Call the Lower Animals (Steel), **Supp. XII:** 274

Book of Mrs. Noah, The (Roberts), **Supp. XV:** 266, 270

"Book of Nature" (Sisson), **Supp. XI:** 262

Book of Nonsense, A (Lear), **V:** xx, 76, 82–83, 87

Book of Prefaces, The (Gray, A.), **Supp. IX:** 92

"Book of Settlements, The", See *Landnámabók*

Book of Sir Lancelot and Queen Guinevere, The (Malory), **I:** 70–71, 77; **Retro. Supp. II:** 249–250

Book of Snobs, The (Thackeray), **V:** 24–25, 28, 38

Book of Spells, A (Maitland), **Supp. XI:** 170, 176, 177

Book of the Church, The (Southey), **IV:** 71

Book of the Duchess, The (Chaucer), **I:** 29, 31, 43, 54; **Retro. Supp. II:** 36–38

"Book of the Icelanders, The" (Ari), See *Íslendingabók*

Book of Thel, The (Blake), **III:** 302, 307; **Retro. Supp. I:** 35–36

Book of Tristram de Lyonesse (Malory), **Retro. Supp. II:** 248

Book of Urizen, The (Blake), see *First Book of Urizen, The*

Book of Victorian Narrative Verse, A (ed. Williams, C. W. S.), **Supp. IX:** 276

Book of Voyages, A (ed. O'Brian), **Supp. XII:** 249

Booke of Ayres, A (Campion), **Supp. XVI:** 93–94, 94–95, 96

Booke of Balettes, A (Wyatt), **I:** 97

Books and Persons: Being Comments on a Past Epoch (Bennett), **VI:** 265, 267

Books Do Furnish a Room (Powell), **VII:** 352

"Books for the Bairns" (Stead), **Supp. XIII:** 243

Books of Bale (Arden), **Supp. II:** 41

"Books of the Ocean's Love to Cynthia, The" (Ralegh), **I:** 147, 148, 149

Bookshop, The (Fitzgerald), **Supp. V:** 95, 97, 100, 101–102

Boon (Wells), **VI:** 227, 239–240, 333

Border Antiquities (Scott), **IV:** 38

Border Ballads (Swinburne), **V:** 333

"Border Campaign, The" (Heaney), **Retro. Supp. I:** 134

"Border Sick Call" (Montague), **Supp. XV:** 223

Borderers, The (Wordsworth), **III:** 338; **IV:** 3, 5–6, 25

"Borderland, A" (Scupham), **Supp. XIII:** 223

Borderline (Kureishi), **Supp. XI:** 156–157

Borderline Ballads (Plomer), **Supp. XI:** 226

Borges, Jorge Luis, **Supp. IV:** 558

Borges: A Reader (tr. Reid), **Supp. VII:** 332

"Borgia, thou once wert almost too august" (Landor), **IV:** 98

"Boris Is Buying Horses" (Berger), **Supp. IV:** 93

Born Guilty (Hill, R.), **Supp. IX:** 123

Born in Brooklyn: John Montague's America (Montague), **Supp. XV:** 215

Born in Exile (Gissing), **V:** 425, 428, 429–430, 437

"Born 1912" (Fuller), **Supp. VII:** 80

Born 1925: A Novel of Youth (Brittain), **Supp. X:** 46

"Born Yesterday" (Larkin), **Supp. I:** 278

Borough, The (Crabbe), **III:** 273–274, 275, 280, 281, 283–285, 286

Borrow, George, **Supp. XII:** 17–32

Borstal Boy (Behan), **Supp. II:** 61–63, 64, 69, 70, 72, 73

Bosch, Hieronymus, **Supp. IV:** 199, 249

"Boscombe Valley Mystery, The" (Doyle), **Supp. II:** 171

"Bosegran" (Jamie), **Supp. XIV:** 134–135

Boss Cupid (Gunn), **Retro. Supp. III:** 115, 116, 117, 122, 128–130

Bostock, Anya, **Supp. IV:** 87

Bostonians, The (James), **VI:** 39–41, 67

Boswell, James, **III:** 54, 107, 110–115, 117, 119–122, 234–251; **IV:** xv, xvi, 27, 88n, 280; **Retro. Supp. I:** 145–149

"Boswell and Rousseau" (Leigh), **III:** 246n

Boswell for the Defence 1769–1774 (ed. Pottle and Wimsatt), **III:** 249

Boswell in Extremis 1776–1778 (ed. Pottle and Weis), **III:** 249

Boswell in Holland 1763–1764 (ed. Pottle), **III:** 249

Boswell in Search of a Wife 1766–1769 (ed. Brady and Pottle), **III:** 249

Boswell: Lord of Auchinleck 1778–1782 (ed. Pottle and Reed), **III:** 249

Boswell on the Grand Tour: Germany and Switzerland 1764 (ed. Pottle), **III:** 249

Boswell on the Grand Tour: Italy . . . 1765–1766 (ed. Brady and Pottle), **III:** 249

Boswell: The Ominous Years 1774–1776 (ed. Pottle and Ryskamp), **III:** 249

Boswelliana . . . Memoir and Annotations by the Rev. Charles Rogers (Rogers), **III:** 249

Boswell's Book of Bad Verse (ed. Werner), **III:** 249

Boswell's London Journal 1762–1763 (ed. Pottle), **III:** 249

Boswell's Notebook, 1776–1777 (Boswell), **III:** 244, 249

Botanic Garden, a Poem, The. In Two Parts. Part I: Containing The Economy of Vegetation. Part II: The Loves of the Plants. With Philosophical Notes (Darwin), **Supp. XVI:** 127, 128–131, 135, 137, 138, 142

"Botany Bay Eclogues" (Southey), **IV:** 60

Bothie of Tober-na-Vuolich, The (Clough), **V:** 155, 156, 158, 159, 161–164, 166, 167, 169, 170

Bothie of Toper-na-Fuosich, The (Clough), **V:** 170

Bothwell (Swinburne), **V:** 314, 330, 331, 332

Botticelli, Sandro, **V:** 345

Bottle Factory Outing, The (Bainbridge), **Supp. VI:** 18–20, 24, 27

"Bottle Imp, The" (Stevenson), **V:** 396

Bottle in the Smoke, A (Wilson), **Supp. VI:** 304, 307

"Bottle of Ink, A" (Stallworthy), **Supp. X:** 296

Bottle's Path and Other Stories (Powys), **VIII:** 249, 255

Boucicault, Dion, **V:** 415; **VII:** 2

Bouge of Court, The (Skelton), **I:** 83, 84–85

Boughner, D. C., **I:** 186

"Bourgeois Psychology" (Caudwell), **Supp. IX:** 45

Boursault, Edme, **II:** 324, 332

Bow Down (Harrison), **Supp. V:** 164

"Bow in the Cloud, The" (Nicholson), **Supp. VI:** 215

Bowen, Elizabeth, **Supp. II:** 77–95; **Supp. IV:** 151, 500, 514

Bowen, Stella, **VI:** 324

Bowen's Court (Bowen), **Supp. II:** 78, 84, 91

"Bower, The" (Jamie), **Supp. XIV:** 143

Bowers, Fredson, **II:** 44

Bowles, Caroline, **IV:** 62, 63

"Bowling Alley and the Sun, or, How I Learned to Stop Worrying and Love America, The" (Lodge), **Supp. IV:** 373

Bowra, C. M., **VI:** 153

Bowra, Maurice, **V:** 252–256, 260

"Box of Ghosts, A" (Scupham), **Supp. XIII:** 224

Boy and the Magic, The (tr. Fry), **Supp. III:** 195

Boy book see (Galloway), **Supp. XII:** 117

Boy Comes Home, The (Milne), **Supp. V:** 299

"Boy from Birnam, The" (Dunn), **Supp. X:** 68

Boy Hairdresser, The (Orton), **Supp. V:** 363, 364, 367

Boy in the Bush, The (Lawrence), **VII:** 114; **Retro. Supp. II:** 230–231

"Boy Looked at Johnny, The": The Obituary of Rock and Roll (Parsons), **Supp. XV:** 227, 237, 240

Boy: Tales of Childhood (Dahl), **Supp. IV:** 204, 205, 206, 208, 225

Boy Who Followed Ripley, The (Highsmith), **Supp. V:** 171

"Boy Who Talked with Animals, The" (Dahl), **Supp. IV:** 223, 224

Boy Who Taught the Beekeeper to Read, The (Hill), **Supp. XIV:** 116, 126

Boy with a Cart, The; Cuthman, Saint of Sussex (Fry), **Supp. III:** 191, 194, 195, 196

Boyd, H. S., **IV:** 312

Boyd, William, **Supp. XVI:** 31–49

Boyer, Abel, **II:** 352

Boyfriends and Girlfriends (Dunn), **Supp. X:** 67–69

"Boyhood" (Nye), **Supp. X:** 204
Boyhood: Scenes from Provincial Life (Coetzee), **Supp. VI:** 77–78
Boyle, Robert, **III:** 23, 95
"Boys, The" (Nye), **Supp. X:** 201
Boys' Own Magazine, **Supp. XIII:** 234
"Boys' Weeklies" (Orwell), **Supp. III:** 107
Boys Who Stole the Funeral, The: A Novel Sequence (Murray), **Supp. VII:** 270, 284–286
"Boys with Coats" (Dunn), **Supp. X:** 71
Bradbrook, M. C., **I:** xi, 292, 329; **II:** 42, 78; **VII:** xiii–xiv, xxxvii, 234
Bradbury, Ray, **III:** 341
Bradbury, Malcolm, **Supp. IV:** 303, 365
Braddon, Mary Elizabeth, **V:** 327; **VIII:** **35–52**
Bradley, A. C., **IV:** 106, 123, 216, 235, 236
Bradley, F. H., **V:** xxi, 212, 217
Bradley, Henry, **VI:** 76
Brady, F., **III:** 249
Braine, John, **Supp. IV:** 238
Brand (Hill), **Supp. V:** 199, 200–201
Brander, Laurence, **IV:** xxiv; **VII:** xxii
Brantley, Ben, **Supp. IV:** 197–198
Branwell Brontë (Gerin), **V:** 153
Branwell's Blackwood's (periodical), **V:** 109, 123
Branwell's Young Men's (periodical), *see Branwell's Blackwood's*
Brass Butterfly, The (Golding), **Supp. I:** 65, 75
"Brassneck" (Armitage), **VIII:** 5
Brassneck (Hare and Brenton), **Supp. IV:** 281, 282, 283, 284–285, 289
Brathwaite, Kamau (Edward), **Supp. XII:** **33–48**
Brave and Cruel (Welch), **Supp. IX:** 267–269
Brave and Cruel (Welch), **Supp. IX:** 267, 269
"Brave Girl" (Davies), **Supp. XIV:** 41
Brave New World (Huxley), **III:** 341; **VII:** xviii, 200, 204
Brave New World Revisited (Huxley), **VII:** 207
"Brave Words for Brave Soldiers and Sailors" (Kingsley), **Supp. XVI:** 199
"Bravest Boat, The" (Lowry), **Supp. III:** 281
Brawne, Fanny, **IV:** 211, 216–220, 222, 226, 234
Bray, Charles, **V:** 188
Bray, William, **II:** 275, 276, 286
Brazzaville Beach (Boyd), **Supp. XVI:** 37–38, 39
Brazil (Gilliam), **Supp. IV:** 442, 455
"Breach, The" (Murray), **Supp. VII:** 276
"Bread and Wine" (tr. Constantine), **Supp. XV:** 70, 73–74
Bread of Truth, The (Thomas), **Supp. XII:** 284, 285
"Bréagh San Réilg, La" (Behan), **Supp. II:** 73
"Break, break, break" (Tennyson), **Retro. Supp. III:** 322
"Break My Heart" (Golding), **Supp. I:** 79

"Break of Day in the Trenches" (Rosenberg), **VI:** 433, 434
"Breake of day" (Donne), **Retro. Supp. II:** 88
Breakfast on Pluto (McCabe), **Supp. IX:** 127, 135–136, 138
"Breaking" (Carson), **Supp. XIII:** 66
"Breaking Ground" (Gunn), **Supp. IV:** 271; **Retro. Supp. III:** 123
Breaking News (Carson), **Supp. XIII:** 65–66
"Breaking the Blue" (McGuckian), **Supp. V:** 287
Breath (Beckett), **Supp. I:** 60; **Retro. Supp. I:** 26
Brecht, Bertolt, **II:** 359; **IV:** 183; **VI:** 109, 123; **Supp. II:** 23, 25, 28; **Supp. IV:** 82, 87, 180, 194, 198, 281, 298
"Bredon Hill" (Housman), **VI:** 158
Brendan (O'Connor), **Supp. II:** 63, 76
Brendan Behan's Island (Behan), **Supp. II:** 64, 66, 71, 73, 75
Brendan Behan's New York (Behan), **Supp. II:** 75
Brennoralt (Suckling), *see Discontented Colonel, The*
Brenton, Howard, **Supp. IV:** 281, 283, 284, 285
Brethren, The (Haggard), **Supp. III:** 214
"Breton Walks" (Mahon), **Supp. VI:** 168, 172
Brett, Raymond Laurence, **IV:** x, xi, xxiv, 57
"Brick" (Carson), **Supp. XIII:** 58
Brick Lane (Ali), **Supp. XIII:** 2–6, 7, 10, 11–12
"Brick Red" (Carson), **Supp. XIII:** 64
Brickfield, The (Hartley), **Supp. VII:** 131–132
Bricks to Babel (Koestler), **Supp. I:** 37
Bridal of Triermain, The (Scott), **IV:** 38
"Bride and Groom" (Hughes), **Supp. I:** 356
"Bride in the 30's, A" (Auden), **Retro. Supp. I:** 8
Bride of Abydos, The (Byron), **IV:** xvii, 172, 174–175, 192
Bride of Frankenstein (film), **III:** 342
Bride of Lammermoor, The (Scott), **IV:** xviii, 30, 36, 39
Brides of Reason (Davie), **Supp. VI:** 106–107
"Brides, The" (Hope), **Supp. VII:** 154
"Bride's Prelude, The" (Rossetti), **V:** 239, 240
Brides' Tragedy, The (Beddoes), **Supp. XI:** 17, 20–22, 29
Brideshead Revisited (Waugh), **VII:** xx–xxi, 290, 299–300; **Supp. IV:** 285
"Bridesmaid, The" (Tennyson), **Retro. Supp. III:** 322
Bridge, The (Banks), **Supp. XI:** 6–7
"Bridge, The" (Galloway), **Supp. XII:** 126–127
Bridge, The (Pitter), **Supp. XIII:** 135, 143
"Bridge, The" (Pitter), **Supp. XIII:** 143, 144
"Bridge, The" (Thomas), **Supp. III:** 401

"Bridge for the Living" (Larkin), **Supp. I:** 284; **Retro. Supp. III:** 211
"Bridge of Sighs, The" (Hood), **IV:** 252, 261, 264–265
Bridges, Robert, **II:** 160; **V:** xx, 205, 362–368, 370–372, 374, 376–381; **VI:** xv, **71–83**, 203
Brief Account of Mr. John Ginglicutt's Treatise Concerning the Altercation or Scolding of the Ancients, A (Arbuthnot), **Supp. XVI:** 27
Brief History of Moscovia . . . , A (Milton), **II:** 176
Brief Lives (Aubrey), **I:** 260
Brief Lives (Brookner), **Supp. IV:** 131–133
Brief Notes upon a Late Sermon . . . (Milton), **II:** 176
Brief Words: One Hundred Epigrams (Soutar), **Supp. XVI:** 251
Briefing for a Descent into Hell (Lessing), **Supp. I:** 248–249
Briggflatts (Bunting), **Supp. VII:** 1, 2, 5, 7, 9–13
Bright, A. H., **I:** 3
"Bright Building, The" (Graham), **Supp. VII:** 109, 110–111
"Bright–Cut Irish Silver" (Boland), **Supp. V:** 49–50
Bright Day (Priestley), **VII:** 209, 218–219
"Bright Star!" (Keats), **IV:** 221
Bright Temptation, The: A Romance (Clarke), **Supp. XV:** 23–24
Brightness to Cast Shadows, A (Constantine), **Supp. XV:** 66, 71, 73
Brighton Rock (Greene), **Supp. I:** 2, 3, 7–9, 11, 19; **Retro. Supp. II:** 153–155
"Brigid's Girdle, A" (Heaney), **Retro. Supp. I:** 132
"Brilliance" (Davie), **Supp. VI:** 113
"Brilliant Career, A" (Joyce), **Retro. Supp. I:** 170
Brimstone and Treacle (Potter, D.), **Supp. X:** 232, 234
"Bring Back the Cat!" (Hill, R.), **Supp. IX:** 118
Bring Larks and Heroes (Keneally), **Supp. IV:** 345, 347, 348–350
"Bringing to Light" (Gunn), **Supp. IV:** 269–270
Brink, Andre, **Supp. VI:** **45–59**
Brinkmanship of Galahad Threepwood, The (Wodehouse), *see Galahad at Blandings*
Brissenden, R. F., **III:** 86n
Bristow Merchant, The (Dekker and Ford), **II:** 89, 100
Britain and West Africa (Cary), **VII:** 186
Britannia (periodical), **V:** 144
Britannia (Thomson), **Supp. III:** 409, 411, 420
Britannia Rediviva: A Poem on the Birth of the Prince (Dryden), **II:** 304; **Retro. Supp. III:** 56
"Britannia Victrix" (Bridges), **VI:** 81
"British Church, The" (Herbert), **I:** 189
British Dramatists (Greene), **Supp. I:** 6, 11

"British Guiana" (Ewart), **Supp. VII:** 38
British History in the Nineteenth Century (Trevelyan), **VI:** 390
British Magazine (periodical), **III:** 149, 179, 188
British Museum Is Falling Down, The (Lodge), **Supp. IV:** 363, 365, 367, 369–370, 371
British Theatre, The (ed. Inchbald), **Supp. XV:** 149, 160
British Women Go to War (Priestley), **VII:** 212
Briton (Smollett), **III:** 149
Brittain, Vera, **II:** 246; **Supp. X: 33–48**
Britten, Benjamin, **Supp. IV:** 424
Brittle Joys (Maitland), **Supp. XI:** 165, 174–175
"Broad Bean Sermon, The" (Murray), **Supp. VII:** 275
"Broad Church, The" (Stephen), **V:** 283
Broadbent, J. B., **II:** 102, 116
Broadcast Talks (Lewis), **Supp. III:** 248
"Broagh" (Heaney), **Retro. Supp. I:** 128
"Brodgar Poems" (Brown), **Supp. VI:** 71
Broken Bridge, The (Pullman), **Supp. XIII:** 151, 153
Broken Chariot, The (Sillitoe), **Supp. V:** 411, 421
Broken Cistern, The (Dobrée), **V:** 221, 234
"Broken heart, The" (Donne), **Retro. Supp. II:** 90
Broken Heart, The (Ford), **II:** 89, 92, 93–98, 99, 100
"Broken Type, The" (Delanty), **Supp. XIV:** 70
"Broken Wings, The" (James), **VI:** 69
Brome, Richard, **II:** 87; **Supp. X: 49–64**
"Bronckhorst Divorce–Case, The" (Kipling), **Retro. Supp. III:** 185–186
Brontë, Anne, **IV:** 30; **V:** xviii, xx, xxi, 105, 106, 108, 110, 112–119, 122, 126, **128–130,** 131, 132, **134–135, 140–141, 145, 150, 153; Supp. III:** 195; **Supp. IV:** 239; **Retro. Supp. I:** 55–56
Brontë, Branwell, **V:** xvii, 13, 105, 106, 108–112, 117–119, 121–124, 126, 130, 131, 135, 141, 145, 150, 153
Brontë, Charlotte, **III:** 338, 344, 345; **IV:** 30, 106, 120; **V:** xvii, xx–xxii, 3, 13–14, 20, 68, 105–107, **108–112,** 113–118, **119–126,** 127, 129, 130–140, 144, 145–150, 152, 286; **Supp. III:** 144, 146; **Supp. IV:** 146, 471; **Retro. Supp. I:** 58–61
Brontë, Emily, **III:** 333, 338, 344, 345; **IV:** ix, xvii, xx–xxi, 13, 14, 105, 106, 108, 110, **112–117,** 118, 122, 130, 131, **132–135, 141–145,** 147, 150, 152–153, 254; **Supp. III:** 144; **Supp. IV:** 462, 513; **Retro. Supp. I:** 56–58
Brontë, Patrick, **V:** 105–108, 109, 122, 146, 151
Brontë Poems (ed. Benson), **V:** 133, 151
Brontë Sisters, **Retro. Supp. I: 49–62**
Brontë Story, The: A Reconsideration of Mrs. Gaskell's "Life of Charlotte Brontë" (Lane), **V:** 13n, 16
Brontës, The, Their Lives, Friendships and Correspondence (ed. Wise and Symington), **V:** 117, 118, 151
Brontës of Haworth, The (Fry), **Supp. III:** 195
Brontës' Web of Childhood, The (Ratchford), **V:** 151
"Bronze Head, The" (Yeats), **VI:** 217
Bronze Horseman: Selected Poems of Alexander Pushkin (tr. Thomas), **Supp. IV:** 495
Brooke, Arthur, **I:** 305
Brooke, Jocelyn, **VII:** xviii, xxxvii; **Supp. II:** 202, 203
Brooke, Rupert, **VI:** xvi, 416, **419–420,** 439; **VII:** 35; **Supp. II:** 310; **Supp. III: 45–61**
Brooke Kerith, The. A Syrian Story (Moore), **VI:** xii, 88, 89, **93–94,** 99
Brooke–Rose, Christine, **Supp. IV: 97–118**
"Brooklyn Heights" (Wain), **Supp. XVI:** 306
Brookner, Anita, **Supp. IV: 119–137**
Brooks, C., **IV:** 323n, 339
"Brooksmith" (James), **VI:** 48, 69
"Broom, The" (tr. Reed), **Supp. XV:** 254
"Broon's Bairn's Black, The" (Kay), **Supp. XIII:** 108
Brophy, Brigid, **IV:** 101
Brother Dusty–Feet (Sutcliff), **Supp. XVI:** 264
"Brother Fire" (MacNeice), **VII:** 414
Brotherly Love: A Sermon (Swift), III: 36
"Brothers" (Hopkins), **V:** 368–369
Brothers and Sisters (Compton–Burnett), **VII:** 61, 66, 67, 69
Brother's Keeper (Hill, R.), **Supp. IX:** 118
Brown, Charles, **IV:** 211, 221, 231–233
Brown, E. K., **V:** 211–212, 217
Brown, Ford Madox, **V:** 248
Brown, George Mackay, **Supp. VI: 61–73**
Brown, John, **II:** 245, 253, 254
Brown, Tom, **III:** 41
Brown Owl, The (Ford), **VI:** 320
Brownbread (Doyle), **Supp. V:** 77, 87–88
Browne, Moses, **II:** 142
Browne, Sir Thomas, **II: 145–157,** 185, 345n; **III:** 40
"Brownie" (Gissing), **V:** 437
"Brownie of Black Haggs, The" (Hogg), **Supp. X:** 110
Brownie of Bodsbeck and Other Tales, The (Hogg), **Supp. X:** 111–113, 117
Browning, Elizabeth Barrett, **IV:** xvi, xix–xxii, **310–322,** 356, 357; **Retro. Supp. II:** 23–24
Browning, Robert, **IV:** viii, xii, xiii, xix–xxiii, 240, 248, 252, 254, 311–312, 314, 318–319, 352, **354–375;** **V:** xxv, 209, 287, 315, 330; **VI:** 336; **Supp. IV:** 139; **Retro. Supp. II: 17–32;** **Retro. Supp. III: 17–33**
Browning Box, The; or, The Life and Works of Thomas Lovell Beddoes as Reflected in Letters by His Friends and Admirers (Beddoes)
Browning: "Men and Women" and Other Poems: A Casebook (ed. Watson), **IV:** 375
Browning Version, The (Rattigan), **Supp. VII:** 307, 315–316
Browning's Essay on Chatterton (ed. Smalley), **IV:** 374
Browning's Major Poetry (Jack), **IV:** 375
"Bruno" (Warner), **Supp. VII:** 381
"Bruno's Revenge" (Carroll), **V:** 270
"Brutal Sentimentalist, A" (Plomer), **Supp. XI:** 220
"Brute, The" (Conrad), **VI:** 148
Brutus (Pope), **III:** 71–72
Brutus's Orchard (Fuller), **Supp. VII:** 73–74
Bryan, Michael, see Moore, Brian
Bryce, James, **IV:** 289
Brydon, Diana, **Supp. IV:** 459, 462
Bryskett, Lodowick, **I:** 124
Bubble, The (Swift), **III:** 35
Bucer, Martin, **I:** 177
Buchan, John, **Supp. II:** 299, 306; **Supp. IV:** 7
Buchanan, Robert, **V:** 238, 245
"Bucket and the Rope, The" (Powys), **VIII:** 254–255
Buckhurst, Lord, see Dorset, earl of (Charles Sackville)
Buckingham, duke of (George Villiers), **II:** 206, 255, 294
Buckle, G. E., **IV:** 306–308
"Buckles of Superior Dosset, The" (Galsworthy), **VI:** 270
Bucolic Comedies (Sitwell), **VII:** 131, 132
"Bucolics" (Auden), **Retro. Supp. I:** 13
"Budapest: All Wars Are Civil Wars" (Butlin), **Supp. XVI:** 57
Buddha of Suburbia, The (Kureishi), **Supp. XI:** 157, 159
Budgell, Eustace, **III:** 48
Buffon, Georges–Louis, **Supp. II:** 106, 107, 108; **III:** 189
Buff (Fuller), **Supp. VII:** 74
"Bugle Call" (Thomas), **Supp. III:** 404
"Bugler's First Communion, The" (Hopkins), **V:** 368–369
Builder, The (Steel), **Supp. XII:** 275, 276
"Building, The" (Larkin), **Supp. I:** 280, 282, 283; **Retro. Supp. III:** 210
"Build–Up" (Ballard), **Supp. V:** 21
"Bujak and the Strong Force" (Amis), **Supp. IV:** 40
"Buladelah–Taree Song Cycle, The" (Murray), **Supp. VII:** 276–277
Bulgakov, Mikhail, **Supp. IV:** 445
"Bull" (MacCaig), **Supp. VI:** 188
"Bull: A Farce" (Self), **Supp. V:** 405–406
Bull from the Sea, The (Renault), **Supp. IX:** 180–181
Bull Ring, The (Hill, R.), **Supp. IX:** 118
"Bull That Thought, The" (Kipling), **VI:** 189, 190
"Bulldog"Drummond series (Sapper), **Supp. IV:** 500
"Bulletin" (Dutton), **Supp. XII:** 98
Bullett, Gerald, **V:** 196, 199, 200
Bulwer–Lytton, Edward, **III:** 340, 345; **IV:** 256, 295, 311; **V:** 22, 47
Bundle, The (Bond), **Supp. I:** 423
Bundle of Letters, A (James), **VI:** 67, 69

"Bungalows, The" (Plomer), **Supp. XI:** 226
Bunting, Basil, **Supp. VII: 1–15**
Bunyan, John, **I:** 16; **II: 240–254; III:** 82; **V:** 27
"Buoyancy" (Davies), **Supp. XIV:** 40
Buoyant Billions: A Comedy of No Manners in Prose (Shaw), **VI:** 127, 129
Burbidge, Thomas, **V:** 159
Burckhardt, Jakob, **V:** 342
"Burden of Itys, The" (Wilde), **V:** 401
"Burden of Ninevah, The" (Rossetti), **V:** 240, 241
"Burden of the Sea, The" (Jewsbury), **Supp. XIV:** 161
Bürger, Gottfried August, **IV: 44,** 48
Burger's Daughter (Gordimer), **Supp. II:** 225, 228, 230, 231, 232, **234–237,** 241, 242, 243
Burgess, Anthony, **Supp. I: 185–198; Supp. IV:** 4, 13, 234, 449
"Burghers, The" (Hardy), **Retro. Supp. I:** 120
"Burial Mound" (Conn), **Supp. XIII:** 77
"Burial of the Dead, The" (Eliot), **Retro. Supp. II:** 126
"Burial of the Rats, The" (Stoker), **Supp. III:** 382
Buried Alive (Bennett), **VI:** 250, 252, 257, 266
Buried Day, The (Day Lewis), **Supp. III:** 116, 128
Buried Harbour, The: Selected Poems of Giuseppe Ungaretti (ed. Hart), **Supp. XI:** 130
"Buried Life, The" (Arnold), **V:** 210
"Buried Treasure" (Pitter), **Supp. XIII:** 141
Burke, Edmund, **III:** 185, **193–206,** 274; **IV:** xii–xvi, 54, 127, 130, 133, 136–138, 271, 275; **VI:** 356; **Supp. III:** 371, 467, 468, 470
Burke, Kenneth, **Supp. IV:** 114
Burke and Bristol, 1774–1780 (Barker), **III:** 196
"Burleigh" (Macaulay), **IV:** 279
Burlington Magazine, **Supp. IV:** 121
"Burma Casualty" (Lewis), **VII:** 447
Burmann, Peter, **III:** 96
Burmese Days (Orwell), **VII:** 276, 278
Burn, The (Kelman), **Supp. V:** 243, 249, 250–251
Burne–Jones, Edward, **IV:** 346; **V:** 236, 293–296, 302, 318n, 355; **VI:** 166; **Supp. V:** 98, 99
Burney, Charles, Supp. **III:** 65–67
Burney, Frances, **Supp. III: 63–78**
Burning Cactus, The (Spender), **Supp. II:** 488
Burning Elvis (Burnside), **Supp. XIII:** 25, 28–29, 30
"Burning Elvis" (Burnside), **Supp. XIII:** 28
Burning of the Brothel, The (Hughes), **Supp. I:** 348
"Burning Times, The" (Maitland), **Supp. XI:** 176
"Burning Want" (Murray), **Supp. VII:** 283–284

Burning World, The (Ballard), **Supp. V:** 24
"Burns Ayont Auld Reekie/Burns Beyond Edinburgh" (Crawford), **Supp. XI:** 69
"Burns and His School" (Kingsley), **Supp. XVI:** 204
Burns, Robert, **III:** 310
Burnshaw, Stanley, **Supp. IV:** 460, 473
Burnside, John, **Supp. XIII: 13–33**
Burnt Diaries (Tennant), **Supp. IX:** 228, 229, 239
Burnt Flower–Bed, The (Reed), **Supp. XV:** 253
Burnt Ones, The (White), **Supp. I:** 131, 136, 143
Burnt–Out Case, A (Greene), **Supp. I:** 7, 13, 15, 16, 18; **Retro. Supp. II:** 162
"Burrington Combe" (Sisson), **Supp. XI:** 261
Burroughs, William S., **Supp. V:** 26
Busconductor Hines, The (Kelman), **Supp. V:** 242, 246–247
"Bush–Baby, The" (Pitter), **Supp. XIII:** 142
Business, The (Banks), **Supp. XI:** 13
Business of Good Government, The (Arden), **Supp. II:** 29
Busker, The (Kelman), **Supp. V:** 256
Busman's Honeymoon (Sayers), **Supp. III:** 335, 336, 347–348
"Busted Scotch" (Kelman), **Supp. V:** 249
"Busy" (Milne), **Supp. V:** 302
"But at the Stroke of Midnight" (Warner), **Supp. VII:** 381
"But For Lust" (Pitter), **Supp. XIII:** 134
...but the Clouds (Beckett), **Retro. Supp. I:** 29
But the Earth Abideth (Soutar), **Supp. XVI:** 253–254
"Butcher, The" (Raine), **Supp. XIII:** 164–165
Butcher Boy, The (McCabe), **Supp. IX:** 127, 128, 129–133, 135, 137, 138
Butcher's Dozen (Kinsella), **Supp. V:** 267
Butlin, Ron, **Supp. XVI: 51–70**
Butler, Samuel, **Supp. II: 97–119**
Butor, Michel, **Supp. IV:** 115
"Butterflies" (McEwan), **Supp. IV:** 391
Butterfly Tattoo, The (Pullman), **Supp. XIII:** 150, 151, 153
"Buzzard and Alder" (Stevenson), **Supp. VI:** 261
"By Achmelrich Bridge" (MacCaig), **Supp. VI:** 182
By and Large (Wallace–Crabbe), **VIII:** 324
"By Ferry to the Island" (Smith, I. C.), **Supp. IX:** 212
"By the burn" (Kelman), **Supp. V:** 250–251
By Jeeves (Ayckbourn and Webber), **Supp. V:** 3
"By Leave of Luck" (Cameron), **Supp. IX:** 24
By Night Unstarred (Kavanagh), **Supp. VII:** 189
By Still Waters (Russell), **VIII:** 286
"By the Fire–Side" (Browning), **Retro. Supp. II:** 23–24
By the Line (Keneally), **Supp. IV:** 345

"By the Sea" (Smith, I. C.), **Supp. IX:** 216
By Way of Introduction (Milne), **Supp. V:** 300
Byatt, A. S.(neé Antonia Drabble), **Supp. IV: 139–156,** 229
Bye–Bye, Blackbird (Desai), **Supp. V:** 55, 60–62
"Bylot Island" (Armitage), **VIII:** 4
"Byre" (MacCaig), **Supp. VI:** 188, 190, 194
"Byrnies, The" (Gunn), **Retro. Supp. III:** 121
Byrom, John, **Supp. XVI: 71–87**
Byron, George Gordon, Lord, **III:** 329; **IV:** x, xi, 46, 61, 91, 129, 132, 168, **171–194,** 198–199, 202, 206, 215, 281, 299; **V:** 111–112, 247, 324; **Supp. III:** 356, 365; and Coleridge, **IV:** 46, 48; and Hazlitt, **IV:** 129; and Shelley, **IV:** 159, 172, 176–177, 179, 181, 182, 198–199, 202, 206; **Retro. Supp. I:** 250–251; and Southey, **IV:** 61, 184–187; literary style, **III:** 336, 337–338; **IV:** viii, ix, xi, 129, 281; **V:** 17, 116; **VII:** xix
"Byron" (Durrell), **Supp. I:** 126
"Byron" (Macaulay), **IV:** 281
Byron, Robert, **Supp. IV:** 157
Byron and the Ruins of Paradise (Gleckner), **IV:** 173, 194
Byron in Italy (Quennell), **IV:** 194
Byron: The Years of Fame (Quennell), **IV:** 194
Byronic Hero, The Types and Prototypes (Thorslev), **IV:** 173, 194
Byron's Conspiracy (Chapman), **I:** 249–251
Byron's Tragedy (Chapman), *see Tragedy of Byron, The*
"Byzantium" (Yeats), **VI:** 215; **Retro. Supp. I:** 336–337
C (Reading), **VIII:** 265, 266–268, 269, 271, 273

"C. G. Jung's First Years" (Kinsella), **Supp. V:** 269
C. H. Sisson (Sisson), **Supp. XI:** 252
Cab at the Door, A (Pritchett), Supp. **III:** 311, 312
"Cabaco's Song" (Reed), **Supp. XV:** 254
Cabinet of Dr. Caligari, The (film), **III:** 342
Cadenus and Vanessa (Swift), **III:** 18, 31, 35; **Retro. Supp. I:** 283–284
"Caedmon" (Nicholson), **Supp. VI:** 216
Caesar and Cleopatra (Shaw), **VI:** 112; **Retro. Supp. II:** 316–317
Caesar and Pompey (Chapman), **I:** 252–253
Caesar Borgia (Lee), **II:** 305
Caesar: The Life Story of a Panda Leopard (O'Brian), **Supp. XII:** 249, 252
"Caesarean" (Fallon), **Supp. XII:** 109–110
Caesar's Fall (Drayton, Middleton, Munday, Webster, et al.), **II:** 68, 85
Caesars Vast Ghost (Durrell), **Retro. Supp. III:** 86
Caesar's Wife (Maugham), **VI:** 369

"Cage, The" (Montague), **Supp. XV:** 211, 214–215
"Cage at Cranford, The" (Gaskell), **Retro. Supp. III:** 104
"Cage of Sand" (Ballard), **Supp. V:** 24
Cage Without Grievance (Graham), **Supp. VII:** 105, 107–109, 112
"Caged Skylark, The" (Hopkins), **Retro. Supp. II:** 190
Cagliostro, Alessandro di, **III:** 332
Cahier d'un retour au pays natal (Césaire), **Supp. IV:** 77
Cain (Byron), **IV:** xviii, 173, 177, **178–182,** 193
Caitaani mūtharaba-in? (Ngũgĩ), **VIII:** 212, 215, 216, 221–222, 224
Cakes and Ale (Maugham), **VI:** 367, 371, 374, 377
"Cakes of Baby" (Davies), **Supp. XIV:** 45
Calderón de la Barca, Pedro, **II:** 312*n*, 313*n*; **IV:** 206, 342, 349
Caleb Field: A Tale of the Puritans (Oliphant), **Supp. X:** 219
Caleb Williams (Godwin), *see Adventures of Caleb Williams, The*
Caledonia (Defoe), **III:** 13
"Caledonian Antisyzygy, The" (MacDiarmid), **Supp. XII:** 214
"Calendar–Flush, A" (Cameron), **Supp. IX:** 24
Calendar of Love, A (Brown), **Supp. VI:** 64
Calendar of Modern Letters (periodical), **VII:** 233
"Calenture" (Reid), **Supp. VII:** 328
"Caliban upon Setebos" (Browning), **IV:** 358, 364, 370, 372; **Retro. Supp. II:** 26; **Retro. Supp. III:** 27
"Calidore" (Keats), **IV:** 214
Caliph's Design, The (Lewis), **VII:** 72, 75*n*
Call for the Dead (le Carré), **Supp. II:** 299, **305–307,** 308, 311; **Retro. Supp. III:** 216–217, 219, 220
Called to Be Saints (Rossetti), **V:** 260; **Retro. Supp. III:** 251, 263–264
Call-Girls, The (Koestler), **Supp. I:** 28*n*, 32
"Calling of Arthur, The" (Williams, C. W. S.), **Supp. IX:** 282
Callista: A Tale of the Third Century (Newman), **Supp. VII:** 299
"Calm, The" (Donne), **Retro. Supp. II:** 86
"Calmative, The" (Beckett), **Supp. I:** 50, 59; **Retro. Supp. I:** 21
Calvin, John, **I:** 241
Calvino, Italo, **Supp. IV:** 558
"Calypso" (Brathwaite), **Supp. XII:** 41
"Camberwell Beauty, The" (Pritchett), **Supp. III:** 312, **327–328,** 329
Camberwell Beauty and Other Stories, The (Pritchett), **Supp. III:** 313, 327
Cambises (Preston), **I:** 122, 213–214
"Cambridge" (Ewart), **Supp. VII:** 36
Cambridge (Phillips), **Supp. V:** 380, 386, 388–390
"Cambridge Autumn" (Cornford), **VIII:** 107

Cambridge Bibliography of English Literature, **III:** 51, 52
"Cambridgeshire" (Cornford), **VIII:** 106
"Cambridgeshire Childhood, A" (Scupham), **Supp. XIII:** 221
Cambyses (Preston), *see Cambises*
Camden, William, **Retro. Supp. I:** 152–153
Cameron, Norman, **VII:** 421, 422, 426; **Supp. IX:** 17–32
"Cameronian Preacher's Tale, The" (Hogg), **Supp. X:** 110
Camilla; or, A Picture of Youth (Burney), **Supp. III:** 64, 65, 68, 72, 73–75, 76
Cammaerts, Emile, **V:** 262, 274
"Camouflage" (Longley), **VIII:** 168
Camp, The (Sheridan), **III:** 253, 264
Camp One (Dutton), **Supp. XII:** 87–88, 95
Campaign, The (Addison), **III:** 46
Campaspe (Lyly), **I:** 198, 199–200
Campbell, Ian, **IV:** xii, xxiv, 250
Campbell, Joseph, **VII:** 53
Campbell, Roy, **IV:** 320; **VII:** 422, 428; **Supp. III:** 119
Campbell, Sue Ellen, **Supp. IV:** 336
Campbell's Kingdom (film, Ambler), **Supp. IV:** 3
Campensis, Joannes, **I:** 119
Campion, Thomas, **Supp. XVI: 89–107**
Campion's Works (Campion), **Supp. XVI:** 99
Camus, Albert, **Supp. IV:** 259
Can You Find Me: A Family History (Fry), **Supp. III:** 192, 193
Can You Forgive Her? (Trollope), **V:** 96, 101
"Can You Remember?" (Blunden), **Supp. XI:** 45
Canaan (Hill), **Supp. V:** 192–194; **Retro. Supp. III:** 138–139, 141, 143
"Canacee" (Gower), **I:** 53–54, 55
"Canal Bank Walk" (Kavanagh), **Supp. VII:** 197
Canal Dreams (Banks), **Supp. XI:** 8, 9
Canavans, The (Gregory), **VI:** 315
"Canberra Remnant" (Murray), **Supp. VII:** 273
"Cancer Hospital, The" (Fuller), **Supp. VII:** 80
Candida (Shaw), **III:** 263; **VI:** 108, 110–111, 113; **Retro. Supp. II:** 313–314
Candidate, The (Crabbe), **III:** 286
"Candidate, The" (Gray), **III:** 142
Candide (tr. Cameron, N.), **Supp. IX:** 28
Candide (Voltaire), **IV:** 295; **Supp. IV:** 221
"Candle Indoors, The" (Hopkins), **V:** 370
Candle of Vision, The (Russell), **VIII:** 277, 278–280, 288, 292
Candleford Green (Thompson), **Supp. XV:** 277, 279, 283, 290
"Candles, The" (Scupham), **Supp. XIII:** 222
Candy Floss Tree, The (Nicholson), **Supp. VI:** 218–219"Canoes, The" (Dunn), **Supp. X:** 67
Canning, George, **IV:** 132, 164
Canon of Thomas Middleton's Plays, The (Lake), **II:** 1, 21

Canopus in Argos, Archives (Lessing), **Supp. I:** 250–253
"Canterbury Cathedral" (Murphy), **Supp. V:** 328
Canterbury Tales, The (Chaucer), **I:** 1, 2, **20–47**; **Retro. Supp. I:** 45; **Retro. Supp. II:** 45–49, 125
Canticle of the Rose, The (Sitwell), **VII:** xvii, 130, 137
"Canto 45" (Pound), **Supp. IV:** 114, 115
"Canto Quinto" (Campion), **Supp. XVI:** 92–93
Cantos (Pound), **V:** 317*n*; **Supp. IV:** 100, 115
Cantos of Mutability (Spenser), **I:** 140
"Canzonet" (Reed), **Supp. XV:** 245
Cap, The, and, The Falcon (Tennyson), **IV:** 338
"Cap and Bells, The" (Keats), **IV:** 217
Cape of Storms: The First Life of Adamastor (Brink), **Supp. VI:** **54–55,** 57
Capell, Edward, **I:** 326
Caprice (Firbank), **Supp. II:** 201, 204, 205, **211–213**
Captain, The (Beaumont and Fletcher), **II:** 65
"Captain, The" (Reed), **Supp. XV:** 247
Captain Brassbound's Conversion (Shaw), **VI:** 110; **Retro. Supp. II:** 317
Captain Corelli's Mandolin (De Bernières), **Supp. XII:** 65, 68–69, 74–76, 78
Captain Fantom (Hill, R.), **Supp. IX:** 117
"Captain Henry Hastings" (Brontë), **V:** 122, 123–124, 135, 138, 151
"Captain in Time of Peace" (Gunn), **Retro. Supp. III:** 118
Captain Lavender (McGuckian), **Supp. V:** 280, 287–289
"Captain Lavender" (McGuckian), **Supp. V:** 289
"Captain Nemo" (Gunesekera), **Supp. X:** 86
"Captain Parry" (Hood), **IV:** 267
Captain Patch (Powys), **VIII:** 258
"Captain Rook and Mr. Pigeon" (Thackeray), **V:** 21, 37
Captain Singleton (Defoe), **III:** 8, 13; **Retro. Supp. I:** 72
Captains Courageous (Kipling), **VI:** 204; **Retro. Supp. III:** 194
"Captain's Doll, The" (Lawrence), **VII:** 90
Captive Lion and Other Poems, The (Davies), **Supp. XI:** 98
Captives, The (Gay), **III:** 60–61, 67
Captivity (Robinson), **Supp. XIII:** 200, 210
Car, Thomas, **II:** 181
Caravaggio, Michelangelo Merisi da, **Supp. IV:** 95, 262
"Carboniferous" (Morgan, E.), **Supp. IX:** 167
Carceri d'invenzione (Piranesi), **III:** 325
Card, The (Bennett), **VI:** 250, 258–259, 266; **Supp. III:** 324, 325
Card, The (film, Ambler), **Supp. IV:** 3
Card Castle (Waugh), **Supp. VI:** 270
Cardenio (Fletcher and Shakespeare), **II:** 43, 66, 87

"Cards" (Fallon), **Supp. XII:** 105
Cards on the Table (Christie), **Supp. II:** 131, 135
"Care" (Murphy), **Supp. V:** 327
"Careless Content" (Byrom), **Supp. XVI:** 80
"Careless Lover, The" (Suckling), **II:** 227
"Careless Talk" (Bowen), **Supp. II:** 93
Careless Widow and Other Stories, A (Pritchett), **Supp. III:** 328, 329
Caretaker, The (Pinter), **Supp. I:** 367, 368, 369, **372–374,** 379, 380, 381; **Retro. Supp. I:** 224–225
Carew, Thomas, **I:** 354; **II: 222–225,** 237
Carey, John, **V:** ix, xxvii, 39, 62, 73
Carey, Peter, **Supp. XII: 49–64**
Carlingford, Lord, *see* Fortescue, Chichester
"Carlow Village Schoolhouse" (Murphy), **Supp. V:** 328
Carlyle, A. J., **III:** 272*n*
Carlyle, Jane, **IV:** 239, 240
Carlyle, R. M., **III:** 272*n*
Carlyle, Thomas, **IV:** xii, 38, 41–42, 70, 231, **238–250,** 266*n*, 273, 289, 295, 301–302, 311, 324, 341–342; **V:** vii, ix, xii, 3, 5, 165, 182, 213*n*, 285, 319
"Carlyon Bay Hotel" (Murphy), **Supp. V:** 328
"Caramanian Exile, The" (tr. Mangan), **Supp. XIII:** 118, 125, 126
"Carmen Becceriense, Cum Prolegomenis et Commentario Critico, Edidit H. M. B."(Beerbohm), **Supp. II:** 44
Carmen Deo Nostro, Te Decet Hymnus, Sacred Poems, Collected (Crashaw), **II:** 180, 181, 184, 201
"Carmen Mortis" (Dutton), **Supp. XII:** 89
Carmen Triumphale, for the Commencement of the Year 1814 (Southey), **IV:** 71
"Carmilla" (Le Fanu), **III:** 340, 345; **Supp. III:** 385–836
Carmina V (Herrick), **II:** 108
Carn (McCabe), **Supp. IX:** 127, 128–129, 137, 138
Carnal Island, The (Fuller), **Supp. VII:** 77–78, 81
"Carnal Knowledge" (Gunn), **Supp. IV:** 258
Carnall, Geoffrey Douglas, **IV:** xxiv, 72, 156
Carnival Trilogy, The (Harris), **Supp. V:** 135, 136, 138, 140–141
"Carol" (Nicholson), **Supp. VI:** 214–215
"Carol on Corfu" (Durrell), **Supp. I:** 123–124, 126
Caroline (Maugham), **VI:** 369
"Caroline Vernon" (Brontë), **V:** 112, 122, 123, 124, 125, 138, 151
Carpenter, Edward, **VI:** 407, 408; **Supp. XIII: 35–52**
"Carpenter, The" (Hart), **Supp. XI:** 130, 131
"Carpenter's Shed" (Malouf), **Supp. XII:** 220
Carr, John Dickson, **Supp. IV:** 285
"Carrickfergus" (MacNeice), **VI:** 401
Carrington, Charles, **VI:** 166

"Carrion Comfort" (Hopkins), **V:** 374
Carroll, Lewis, **V:** xi, xix, xxii, xxvi, 86, 87, 8**7,** 113, 114, 179, **261–275; Supp. IV:** 199, 201
Carry On, Jeeves (Wodehouse), **Supp. III:** 455, 461, 462
Carson, Ciaran, **Supp. XIII: 53–67**
"Cart, The" (Scupham), **Supp. XIII:** 220
Carter, Angela, **III:** 341, 345; **Supp. III: 79–93; Supp. IV:** 46, 303, 459, 549, 558
Carter, Frederick, **VII:** 114
Cartoons: The Second Childhood of John Bull (Beerbohm), **Supp. II:** 51
Cartwright, John, **IV:** 103
Cartwright, William, **II:** 134, 185, 222, 237, 238
Cary, Joyce, **VII:** xvii, **185–196**
Caryl Churchill, A Casebook (King), **Supp. IV:** 194–195
"Casa d'Amunt" (Reid), **Supp. VII:** 329
Casa Guidi Windows (Browning), **IV:** 311, 314, 318, 321
"Casadh Súgaín Eile" (Behan), **Supp. II:** 68
Casanova (Miller), **Supp. XIV:** 179, 180, 182, 184–186, 188–189, 191
Casanova's Chinese Restaurant (Powell), **VII:** 348–349
Cascando (play, Beckett), **Supp. I:** 60
"Cascando" (poem, Beckett), **Supp. I:** 44
Case, A. E., **III:** 25, 36
Case for African Freedom, The (Cary), **VII:** 186
Case for Equality, The (Drabble), **Supp. IV:** 31, 233
Case is Alter'd, The (Jonson), **Retro. Supp. I:** 156–157
Case is Altered, The (Plomer), **Supp. XI:** 217–219
"Case of Bill Williams, The" (Kavan), **Supp. VII:** 210
Case of Conscience, A (Inchbald), **Supp. XV:** 159–160, 161
Case of Conscience Resolved, A (Bunyan), **II:** 253
Case of Elijah, The (Sterne), **III:** 135
Case of General Ople and Lady Camper, The (Meredith), **V:** 230–231, 234
"Case of Identity, A" (Doyle), **Supp. II:** 171
Case of Ireland . . . Stated, The (Molyneux), **III:** 27
Case of the Abominable Snowman, The (Day Lewis), **Supp. III:** 130
Case of the Midwife Toad, The (Koestler), **Supp. I:** 38
Case of Walter Bagehot, The (Sisson), **Supp. XI:** 250
Cashel Byron's Profession (Shaw), **VI:** 102, 103, 105–106, 109–110, 113, 129
Casino Royale (Fleming), **Supp. XIV:** 90–93, 95–96, 97
"Cask of Amontillado, The" (Poe), **III:** 339
Caspar Hauser (Constantine), **Supp. XV:** 66, 74–78
"Cassandra" (Maitland), **Supp. XI:** 174
Cassinus and Peter (Swift), **Retro. Supp. I:** 284

Cast in the Fire (Delanty), **Supp. XIV:** 65–67–71
"Castalian Spring" (Heaney), **Retro. Supp. I:** 134
"Castaway, The" (Cowper), **III:** 218–219; **Retro. Supp. III:** 42, 46
"Casting of the Bell, The" (Carson), **Supp. XIII:** 56
Casting Off (Howard), **Supp. XI:** 145, 147, 148
Castle, The (Kafka), **III:** 340, 345; **Supp. IV:** 439
Castle Corner (Cary), **VII:** 186
Castle Dangerous (Scott), **IV:** 39
Castle of Indolence, The (Thomson), **III:** 162, 163, 171, 172; **Supp. III:** 412, **425–428**
Castle of Otranto, The (Walpole), **III:** 324, **325–327,** 336, 345; **IV:** 30; **Supp. III:** 383–384
Castle of the Demon, The (Hill, R.), **Supp. IX:** 116
Castle Rackrent (Edgeworth), **Supp. III:** 154–155; **Supp. IV:** 502
Castle Richmond (Trollope), **V:** 101
Castle–Croquet (Carroll), **V:** 274
"Castles" (Conn), **Supp. XIII:** 78
Castles of Athlin and Dunbayne, The (Radcliffe), **IV:** 35; **Retro. Supp. III:** 234, 237–238
Casualties of Peace (O'Brien), **Supp. V:** 339
"Casualty" (Heaney), **Retro. Supp. I:** 130
Casuarina Tree, The (Maugham), **VI:** 370, 371
"Cat in the Tree, The" (Beer), **Supp. XIV:** 4
"Cat on a Turkey Plate" (Scupham), **Supp. XIII:** 229
"Cat–Faith" (Reid), **Supp. VII:** 328
Cat Nappers, The (Wodehouse), *see Aunts Aren't Gentlemen*
Cat on a Houseboat (Desai), **Supp. V:** 55, 62
Catalans, The (O'Brian), **Supp. XII:** 251
"Catarina to Camoens" (Browning), **IV:** 314
Catcher in the Rye, The (Salinger), **Supp. IV:** 28
Catepillar Stew (Ewart), **Supp. VII:** 47
Catharine and Petruchio, **I:** 327; *see also Taming of the Shrew, The*
Cather, Willa, **Supp. IV:** 151
Catherine (Thackeray), **V:** 22, 24, 28, 37
Cathleen ni Houlihan (Yeats and Gregory), **VI:** 218, 222, 309; **VII:** 4
Catholic Church, The (Newman), **Supp. VII:** 292
"Catholic Church and Cultural Life, The" (Lodge), **Supp. IV:** 376
Catholic Fireside, **Supp. XV:** 288, 289
"Catholic Homilies" (Ælfric of Eynsham), **Retro. Supp. II:** 297–298
"Catholic Novel in England from the Oxford Movement to the Present Day, The" (Lodge), **Supp. IV:** 364
Catholic Reaction, The (Symonds), **Supp. XIV:** 259

333

Catholics (Moore, B.), **Supp. IX:** 143, 151, 152
Cathures (Morgan, E.), **Supp. IX:** 160, 164, 170
Catiline (Jonson), **I:** 345–346; **Retro. Supp. I:** 161, 164
Cato (Addison), **III:** 46
Catriona (Stevenson), **V:** 387, 396; **Retro. Supp. I:** 267
Cat's Cradle Book, The (Warner), **Supp. VII:** 369, 381–382
"Cattledrive in Connaught, The" (Clarke), **Supp. XV:** 20
Cattledrive in Connaught and Other Poems, The (Clarke), **Supp. XV:** 19, 21
Catullus, **II:** 108; **IV:** 327; **Supp. IV:** 491
Caudwell, Christopher, **Supp. III:** 120; **Supp. IX: 33–48**
Caught (Green), **Supp. II: 254–256**
Cause Célèbre (Rattigan), **Supp. VII:** 318, 321
Cause For Alarm (Ambler), **Supp. IV:** 8–9
Causeries du lundi (Sainte-Beuve), **III:** 226
Causley, Charles, **VII:** 422, 434–435
"Caught in a Hurry" (Redgrove), **Supp. VI:** 231
Causeway (Longley ed.), **VIII:** 165–166
Caution to Stir up to Watch Against Sin (Bunyan), **II:** 253
Cavafy, C. P., **VI:** 408
Cavalcade (Coward), **VI:** 264; **Supp. II:** 147, 149, 150–151
Cave, Edward, **III:** 107
Cave and the Spring, The: Essays in Poetry (Hope), **Supp. VII:** 155, 163
Cave Birds (Hughes), **Supp. I:** 351, 356–357, 363
"Cave of Fancy, The" (Shelley), **Retro. Supp. III:** 289
Cavendish, George, **I:** 114
"Caverns of the Grave I've Seen, The" (Blake), **III:** 305
Caversham Entertainment (Campion), **Supp. XVI:** 98
Cawelti, John, **Supp. IV:** 7
Caxton, William, **I:** 67, 82; **Retro. Supp. II:** 242-2
Cayley, Charles Bagot, **V:** 250–251, 253, 259
Ceausescu, Nicolae, **Supp. IV:** 195, 196
Cecil Rhodes (Plomer), **Supp. XI:** 221
Cecilia; or, Memoirs of an Heiress (Burney), **Supp. III:** 63, 64, 67, 70, 71, 72
Cefalû (Durrell), **Supp. I:** 100, 101; **Retro. Supp. III:** 84
"Ceix and Alceone" (Gower), **I:** 53–54
"Celadon and Lydia" (Robinson), **Supp. XIII:** 200
Celan, Paul, **Supp. V:** 189–190, 199–200
Celebrations (Plomer), **Supp. XI:** 222
Celebrations and Elegies (Jennings), **Supp. V:** 217
"Celestial Omnibus" (Forster), **Supp I** 153
Celestial Omnibus, The (Forster), **VI:** 399
Celestials, **Supp. IV:** 344–345

"Celibacy" (Clarke), **Supp. XV:** 21
Celibate Lives (Moore), **VI:** 95
Celibates (Moore), **VI:** 87, 91, 95
Cellular Pathologie (Virchow), **V:** 348
Celt and Saxon (Meredith), **V:** 234
"Celtic Twilight" (MacCaig), **Supp. VI:** 187
Celtic Twilight, The, Men and Women, Ghouls and Faeries (Yeats), **VI:** 221
Cement Garden, The (McEwan), **Supp. IV:** 390, 392–393, 400, 407
Cenci, The (Shelley), **III:** 338; **IV:** xviii, 202, 208; **Supp. IV:** 468; **Retro. Supp. I:** 254
"Censored, Banned, Gagged" (Gordimer), **Supp. II:** 237
"Censors and Unconfessed History" (Gordimer), **Supp. II:** 237
"Centaur Within, The" (Wallace-Crabbe), **VIII:** 315
"Centaurs, The" (Longley), **VIII:** 168, 169, 171
"Centenary of Charles Dickens, The" (Joyce), **V:** 41
Centlivres, Susanna, **Supp. III:** 70
Centuries of Meditations (Traherne), **II:** 189n, 190, 192–193, 202; **Supp. XI:** 263, 264, 265–266, 269–273
Century of Roundels, A (Swinburne), **V:** 332
Century Was Young, The (Aragon), **Supp. IV:** 466
Century's Daughter, The (retitled *Liza's England,* Barker), **Supp. IV:** 45, 46, 53–56
"Ceremony after a fire raid" (Thomas), **Supp. I:** 178; **Retro. Supp. III:** 345
"Certain Mercies" (Graves), **VII:** 265
Certain Noble Plays of Japan (Yeats), **VI:** 218
Certain Satires (Marston), **II:** 25
Certaine Learned and Elegant Workes of the Right Honourable Fulke, Lord Brooke, Written in His Youth and Familiar Exercise with Sir Philip Sidney (Greville), **Supp. XI:** 106, 107–117
Cervantes, Miguel de, **IV:** 190
Césaire, Aimé, **Supp. IV:** 77
Cestus of Aglaia, The (Ruskin), **V:** 180–181, 184
Cetywayo and His White Neighbours (Haggard), **Supp. III:** 213, 214, 216–217
"Ceud Mile Failte" (Crawford), **Supp. XI:** 81
Chabot, Admiral of France (Chapman), **I:** 252–253
Chadourne, Marc, **III:** 329
"Chaffinch Map of Scotland, The" (Morgan, E.), **Supp. IX:** 166
"Chair that Will sat in, I sat in the best, The" (FitzGerald), **IV:** 341
Chain of Voices, A (Brink), **Supp. VI: 51–52,** 57
"Chalet" (Murphy), **Supp. V:** 329
Chalk Giants, The (Roberts, K.), **Supp. X:** 272–273
Chalkhill, John, **II:** 133
Chalmers, Alan, *see* Upward, Edward

Chamber Music (Joyce), **VII:** 41, 42; **Retro. Supp. I:** 171; **Retro. Supp. III:** 168
Chamberlain, Neville, **VI:** 353, 355–356
"Chambermaid's Second Song, The" (Yeats), **VI:** 215
Chambers, E. K., **I:** 299; **II:** 187; **IV:** 41, 57
Chambers, R. W., **I:** 3; **Retro. Supp. I:** 143
"Chamois, The" (du Maurier), **Supp. III:** 143, 147
Champion (periodical), **III:** 97–98, 105
"Champion of the World, The" (Dahl), **Supp. IV:** 214, 223
Chaplin (Boyd, Forbes and Goldman), **Supp. XVI:** 46
Chance (Conrad), **VI:** 144, 146; **Supp. IV:** 250; **Retro. Supp. II:** 82
"Chance, The" (Carey), **Supp. XII:** 54, 55
Chance Encounters (Hope), **Supp. VII:** 152
Chancer, A (Kelman), **Supp. V:** 242, 247–249
Chances, The (Fletcher), **II:** 65
Chandler, Edmund, **V:** 354, 359
Chandler, Raymond, **Supp. II:** 130, 135
"Chanel" (Durrell), **Supp. I:** 125
"Change" (Donne), **Retro. Supp. II:** 89
Change for the Better, A (Hill), **Supp. XIV:** 118
"Change of Policy, A" (Pritchett), **Supp. III:** 329
Change the Name (Kavan), **Supp. VII:** 212
"Changed Man, A" (Hardy), **VI:** 22
Changed Man, A, The Waiting Supper, and Other Tales (Hardy), **VI:** 20, 22
"Changeling, The" (Byatt), **Supp. IV:** 140
Changeling, The (Middleton and Rowley), **II:** 1, 3, 8, **14–18,** 21, 93
"Changeling, The" (Reed), **Supp. XV:** 255
Changes (Aidoo), **Supp. XV:** 1, 3–4
"Changing Face of Fiction, The" (Weldon), **Supp. IV:** 522, 533
Changing Places: A Tale of Two Campuses (Lodge), **Supp. IV:** 363, 365, 371, 372–375, 376, 377, 385
Changing Room, The (Storey), **Supp. I:** 408, 416–417
"Channel Passage, A" (Brooke), **Supp. III:** 53
Channel Passage, A, and Other Poems (Swinburne), **V:** 333
Chant of Jimmie Blacksmith, The (Keneally), **Supp. IV:** 345, 347–348, 350–352, 360
Chant of the Celestial Sailors, The (Pater), **V:** 357
"Chant-Pagan" (Kipling), **VI:** 203
Chants for Socialists (Morris), **V:** 306
Chaos and Night (Montherlant), **II:** 99n
"Chapel Organist, The" (Hardy), **Retro. Supp. I:** 120
"Chaperon, The" (James), **VI:** 69
Chapman, George, **I: 232–256,** 278, 288; **II:** 30, 37, 47, 55, 70, 71, 85; **IV:** 215,

255–256
Chapman, John, **V:** 189
Chapman, R. W., **III:** 249
Chappell, E., **II:** 288
"Chaps" (Crawford), **Supp. XI:** 74
Character and Opinions of Dr. Johnson, The (Swinburne), **V:** 333
Character of a Good Parson, The; Imitated from Chaucer, And Enlarged (tr. Dryden), **Retro. Supp. III:** 78, 80
Character of a Trimmer (Halifax), **III:** 40
"Character of a Virtuous Widow" (Webster), **II:** 77
Character of England, A, as It Was Lately Presented . . . (Evelyn), **II:** 287
"Character of Holland, The" (Marvell), **II:** 211, 219
"Character of Mr. Burke" (Hazlitt), **IV:** 136
Character of Robert Earl of Salisbury, The (Tourneur), **II:** 37, 41
Characterismes of Vertues and Vice (Hall), **II:** 81
Characteristicks (Shaftesbury), **III:** 44
"Characteristics" (Carlyle), **IV:** 241
Characteristics: In the Manner of Rochefoucault's Maxims (Hazlitt), **IV:** 132, 139
"Characters" (Dickens), **V:** 46
Characters (Theophrastus), **III:** 50
Characters (Webster), **II:** 68, 81
"Characters of Dramatic Writers Contemporary with Shakespeare" (Lamb), **IV:** 79, 80
Characters of Love, The: A Study in the Literature of Personality (Bayley), **Supp. I:** 222, 224
Characters of Shakespeare's Plays (Hazlitt), **I:** 329; **IV:** xvii, 129, 139
"Characters of the First Fifteen" (Ewart), **Supp. VII:** 36
"Chard Whitlow" (Reed), **Supp. XV:** 247, 256
Charge Delivered to the Grand Jury, A (Fielding), **III:** 105
"Charge of the Light Brigade, The" (Tennyson), **IV:** xxi, 325; **Retro. Supp. III:** 317, 327, 329
Charioteer, The (Renault), **Supp. IX:** 172, 176–178, 187
"Charity" (Cowper), **III:** 212
Charles, Amy, **Retro. Supp. II:** 174
"Charles Augustus Milverton" (Ewart), **Supp. VII:** 42
Charles Darwin, 1809–1882: A Centennial Commemoration (ed. Chapman), **Supp. XI:** 195
Charles Dickens (Swinburne), **V:** 333
Charles Dickens: A Critical Study (Gissing), **V:** 424, 435, 437
Charles I (Shelley), **IV:** 206
Charles Kingsley: His Letters and Memories of His Life (Kingsley), **Supp. XVI:** 194, 203
"Charles Lamb" (De Quincey), **IV:** 148
Charles Lamb and His Contemporaries (Blunden), **IV:** 86
"Charles Lamb, to those who know thee justly dear" (Southey), **IV:** 85
"Charles Maurras and the Idea of the Patriot King" (Sisson), **Supp. XI:** 246
Charley Is My Darling (Cary), **VII:** 186, 188, 189, 190–191
Charlie and the Chocolate Factory (Dahl), **Supp. IV:** 202–203, 207, 222–223
Charlie and the Great Glass Elevator (Dahl), **Supp. IV:** 207
"Charlotte Brontë as a Critic of *Wuthering Heights*" (Drew), **V:** 153
Charlotte Brontë, 1816–1916: A Centenary Memorial (ed. Wood), **V:** 152
"Charlotte Brontë in Brussels" (Spielman), **V:** 137n
Charlotte Brontë: The Evolution of Genius (Gérin), **V:** 111, 152
Charlotte Mew and Her Friends (Fitzgerald), **Supp. V:** 98–99
"Charm Against Amnesia, A" (Nye), **Supp. X:** 202
Charmed Circle, A (Kavan), **Supp. VII:** 203, 205, 206–207
"Charmed Sea, The" (Martineau), **Supp. XV:** 188
Charting the Journey (Kay), **Supp. XIII:** 108
Chartism (Carlyle), **IV:** xix, 240, 244–245, 249, 250; **V:** viii
Chase, The, and William and Helen (Scott), **IV:** 29, 38
Chaste Maid in Cheapside, A (Middleton), **II:** 1, 3, **6–8**, 10, 21
Chaste Wanton, The (Williams, C. W. S.), **Supp. IX:** 276–277
Chastelard (Swinburne), **V:** 313, 330, 331, 332
Chatterton (Ackroyd), **Supp. VI:** **7–8**
Chatterton, Thomas, **IV:** iv, 228; **V:** 405; **Supp. VI:** 344
Chatwin, Bruce, **Supp. IV:** **157–177**, **Supp. IX:** **49–63**
Chaucer, Geoffrey, **I:** 2, 15, 16, **19–47**, 49, 60, 67, 126; **II:** 70, 292, 302, 304; **IV:** 189; **V:** 298, 303; **Supp. IV:** 190; **Retro. Supp. II:** **33–50**, 125
Châtiments, Les (Hugo), **V:** 324
"Che cosa è Christo" (tr. Elizabeth I), **Supp. XVI:** 156
Cheap Clothes and Nasty (Kingsley), **Supp. XVI:** 203
"Cheap in August" (Greene), **Supp. I:** 16
"Chearfulness" (Vaughan), **II:** 186
"Cheat, The" (O'Connor), **Supp. XIV:** 226
"Cheek, The" (Hope), **Supp. VII:** 157–158
Cheery Soul, A (White), **Supp. I:** 131, 150
"Cheery Soul, A" (White), **Supp. I:** 143
Chekhov, Anton, **VI:** 372
"Chekhov and Zulu" (Rushdie), **Supp. IV:** 445
"Chemotherapy" (Delanty), **Supp. XIV:** 75
Cherry Orchard, The (tr. Frayn), **Supp. VII:** 61
"Cherry-ripe" (Herrick), **II:** 115
"Cherry Stones" (Milne), **Supp. V:** 302–303
"Cherry Tree, The" (Coppard), **VIII:** 94
"Cherry Tree, The" (Gunn), **Supp. IV:** 271; **Retro. Supp. III:** 124
"Cherry Tree, In December" (Conn), **Supp. XIII:** 75
"Chest" (Self), **Supp. V:** 403
Chest of Drawers, A (Raine), **Supp. XIII:** 173
Chester Nimmo trilogy (Cary), **VII:** 186, 191, 194–195; *see also Prisoner of Grace, Except the Lord, Not Honour More*
Chester, Robert, **I:** 313
Chesterton, G. K., **IV:** 107; **V:** xxiv, 60, 262, 296, 383, 391, 393, 397; **VI:** 200, 241, 248, **335–345**; **VII:** xiii
Chettle, Henry, **I:** 276, 296; **II:** 47, 68
"Chevalier" (Crawford), **Supp. XI:** 73
Chiaroscuro (Kay), **Supp. XIII:** 100
"Chief Characteristic of Metaphysical Poetry, The" (Beer), **Supp. XIV:** 8
Chief of Staff (Keneally), **Supp. IV:** 347
"Chief Petty Officer" (Causley), **VII:** 434
"Chiffonier, The" (Adcock), **Supp. XII:** 9
"Child, The" (Friel), **Supp. V:** 113
"Child and the Man, The" (Butlin), **Supp. XVI:** 59–60
"Child and the Shadow, The" (Jennings), **Supp. V:** 210
Child Christopher and Goldilind the Fair (Morris), **V:** 306
"Child and the Man, The" (Butlin), **Supp. XVI:** 59–60
"Child Dying, The" (Muir), **Supp. VI:** 207
"Child in the House, The" (Pater), **V:** 337, 357
Child in Time, The (McEwan), **Supp. IV:** 389, 390, 400–402, 404, 406, 407
"Child Lovers" (Davies), **Supp. XI:** 100
"Child of God" (Fallon), **Supp. XII:** 105
Child of Misfortune (Day Lewis), **Supp. III:** 118, 130–131
Child of Nature, The (Inchbald), **Supp. XV:** 155, 160
Child of Queen Victoria and Other Stories, The (Plomer), **Supp. XI:** 214–215
Child of Storm (Haggard), **Supp. III:** 214
Child of the Jago, The (Morrison), **VI:** 365–366
"Child with Pillar Box and Bin Bags" (Jamie), **Supp. XIV:** 137
Childe Harold's Pilgrimage (Byron), **III:** 337, 338; **IV:** x, xvii, 172, **175–178**, 180, 181, 188, 192; **V:** 329
"Childe Roland to the Dark Tower Came" (Browning), **IV:** 357; **VI:** 16; **Retro. Supp. III:** 26
"Childe–hood" (Vaughan), **II:** 188, 189, 190
Childermass (Lewis), **VII:** 71, 79, 80–81
"Childhood" (Clare), **Supp. XI:** 52–53
"Childhood" (Cornford), **VIII:** 112
"Childhood" (Muir), **Supp. VI:** 204–205
"Childhood Incident" (Nye), **Supp. X:** 203
Childhood of Edward Thomas, The (Thomas), **Supp. III:** 393

"Childish Prank, A" (Hughes), **Supp. I:** 353
"Children, The" (Soutar), **Supp. XVI:** 253, 254
"Children, Follow the Dwarfs" (Smith, I. C.), **Supp. IX:** 214
Children of Dynmouth, The (Trevor), **Supp. IV:** 501, 510–511
"Children of Freedom" (Carpenter), **Supp. XIII:** 38
Children of Men, The (James), **Supp. IV:** 320, 338–339, 340
"Children of Odin" (Scupham), **Supp. XIII:** 225
Children of the Chapel (Gordon), **V:** 313
"Children of the Zodiac, The" (Kipling), **VI:** 169, 189, 191–193
Children of Violence (Lessing), **Supp. I:** 238, 243–246
Children's Encyclopedia (Mee), **Supp. IV:** 256
"Child's Calendar, A" (Brown), **Supp. VI:** 71
"Child's Christmas in Wales, A" (Thomas), **Supp. I:** 183; **Retro. Supp. III:** 341, 343, 348
Child's Garden of Verses, A (Stevenson), **V:** 385, 387, 395; **Retro. Supp. I:** 264
Child's History of England, A (Dickens), **V:** 71
Child's Play: A Tragi-comedy in Three Acts of Violence With a Prologue and an Epilogue (Hill, R.), **Supp. IX:** 115–116
Chimeras, The (Mahon), **Supp. VI:** 173
Chimes, The (Dickens), **V:** 42, 64, 71
"Chimney Sweeper" (Blake), **III:** 297; **Retro. Supp. I:** 36, 42
China. A Revised Reprint of Articles from Titan . . . (DeQuincey), **IV:** 155
China Diary (Spender), **Supp. II:** 493
"China for Lovers" (Jamie), **Supp. XIV:** 138
Chinamen (Frayn), **Supp. VII:** 57–58
"Chinese Button, The" (Brooke-Rose), **Supp. IV:** 103
"Chinese Gordon on the Soudan" (Stead), **Supp. XIII:** 238–239
"Chinese Letters" (Goldsmith), *see Citizen of the World, The*
"Chinese Lobster, The" (Byatt), **Supp. IV:** 155
Chinese Love Pavilion, The (Scott), **Supp. I:** 259, 263
Chinese Pictures (Bird), **Supp. X:** 31
Chinese Tower, The (Conn), **Supp. XIII:** 71
"Chinoiserie" (Reading), **VIII:** 273
"Chip of Glass Ruby, A" (Gordimer), **Supp. II:** 232
"Chippenham" (Adcock), **Supp. XII:** 9
Chit-chat (periodical), **III:** 50
Chitty Chitty Bang Bang (film, Dahl), **Supp. IV:** 213
Chitty Chitty Bang Bang (Fleming), **Supp. IV:** 212–213
Chitty-Chitty-Bang-Bang (Fleming), **Supp. XIV:** 96
Chivers, Thomas Holley, **V:** 313
"Chloe" (Beer), **Supp. XIV:** 5

Chloe (Meredith), **V:** 231n, 234
Chloe Marr (Milne), **Supp. V:** 310
"Choice, The" (Symons), **Supp. XIV:** 274–275
Choice of Ballads, A (Plomer), **Supp. XI:** 222
Choice of George Herbert's Verse, A (ed. Thomas), **Supp. XII:** 282
Choice of Kipling's Prose, A (Maugham), **VI:** 200, 204
Choice of Wordsworth's Verse, A (ed. Thomas), **Supp. XII:** 282
"Choir School" (Murphy), **Supp. V:** 328
Chomei at Toyama (Bunting), **Supp. VII:** 4, 6–7
Chomsky, Noam, **Supp. IV:** 113–114
"Chorale" (Hope), **Supp. VII:** 158
Chorus of Disapproval, A (Ayckbourn), **Supp. V:** 3, 9–10, 14
"Chorus Sacerdotum" (Greville), **Supp. XI:** 108, 117–118
"Chorus Tartarorum" (Greville), **Supp. XI:** 117–118
Christ a Compleat Saviour in His Intercession (Bunyan), **II:** 253
Christ and Satan, **Retro. Supp. II:** 301
Christ in the Cupboard (Powys), **VIII:** 255
Christ Stopped at Eboli (Levi), **VI:** 299
"Christ Surprised" (Jennings), **Supp. V:** 217
"Christ upon the Waters" (Newman), **Supp. VII:** 298
Christabel (Coleridge), **II:** 179; **III:** 338; **IV:** ix, xvii, 29, 44, 48–49, 56, 218, 313; **Retro. Supp. II:** 58–59
Christe's Bloody Sweat (Ford), **II:** 88, 100
"Christening" (Murphy), **Supp. V:** 322
Christian Behaviour (Lewis), **Supp. III:** 248
Christian Behaviour . . . (Bunyan), **II:** 253
Christian Captives, The (Bridges), **VI:** 83
Christian Dialogue, A (Bunyan), **II:** 253
Christian Ethicks (Traherne), **II:** 190, 191, 201; **Supp. XI:** 263, 264, 265, 267, 277–279
Christian Hero, The (Steele), **III:** 43, 44, 53
Christian Morals (Browne), **II:** 149, 153, 154, 156; **III:** 40
Christian Prayers and Meditations in English, French, Italian, Spanish, Greek, and Latin (Elizabeth I), **Supp. XVI:** 154
Christie, Agatha, **III:** 341; **Supp. II:** 123–135; **Supp. III:** 334; **Supp. IV:** 500
Christina Alberta's Father (Wells), **VI:** 227
Christina Rossetti (Packer), **V:** 251, 252–253, 260
Christina Rossetti: A Divided Life (Battiscombe), **V:** 260
Christina Rossetti: The Complete Poems (Rossetti), **Retro. Supp. III:** 252, 253, 255, 256, 258, 260, 261, 262, 263
Christina Stead (Brydon), **Supp. IV:** 463
Christina Stead: A Biography (Rowley), **Supp. IV:** 459

"Christine's Letter" (Coppard), **VIII:** 96
"Christmas" (Constantine), **Supp. XV:** 73
"Christmas" (Smith, I. C.), **Supp. IX:** 221
"Christmas Antiphones" (Swinburne), **V:** 325
"Christmas at Sea" (Stevenson), **V:** 396
Christmas at Thompson Hall (Trollope), **V:** 102
Christmas Books (Dickens), **V:** 71
Christmas Carol, A (Dickens), **V:** xx, 42, 56–57, 71
"Christmas Carol, A" (Swinburne), **V:** 315
"Christmas Childhood, A" (Kavanagh), **Supp. VII:** 194
Christmas Comes But Once a Year (Chettle, Dekker, Heywood, Webster), **II:** 68, 85
"Christmas Day At Home" (Hollinghurst), **Supp. X:** 121
"Christmas Day in the Workhouse" (Wilson), **Supp. I:** 153, 157
"Christmas Eve" (Nye), **Supp. X:** 202, 205
Christmas Eve and Easter Day (Browning), **Retro. Supp. II:** 25–26; **Retro. Supp. III:** 23
"Christmas Garland Woven by Max Beerbohm, A" (Beerbohm), **Supp. II:** 45
Christmas Garland, A (Beerbohm), **Supp. II:** 45, 49
Christmas His Masque (Jonson), **Retro. Supp. I:** 165
Christmas Holiday (Maugham), **VI:** 377
"Christmas Life, The" (Cope), **VIII:** 80
"Christmas Midnight, The" (Scupham), **Supp. XIII:** 227
"Christmas 1987" (Scupham), **Supp. XIII:** 226
"Christmas Oratorio, A" (Auden), **Retro. Supp. I:** 10–11
Christmas Pudding (Mitford), **Supp. X:** 154–155
"Christmas Storms and Sunshine" (Gaskell), **V:** 15
Christmas-Eve and Easter-Day (Browning), **IV:** 357, 363, 370, 372, 374
Christopher, John, **Supp. V:** 22
Christopher and His Kind (Isherwood), **VII:** 318
"Christopher At Birth" (Longley), **VIII:** 167
Christopher Columbus (MacNeice), **VII:** 406
"Christopher Columbus and Queen Isabella of Spain Consummate Their Relationship" (Rushdie), **Supp. IV:** 452
Christopher Homm (Sisson), **Supp. XI:** 247–248, 249
"Christopher Marlowe" (Swinburne), **V:** 332
Christopher Marlowe in Relation to Greene, Peele and Lodge (Swinburne), **V:** 333
Christ's Hospital, A Retrospect (Blunden), **IV:** 86

CHRI–CLEA

"Christ's Hospital Five–and–Thirty Years Ago"(Lamb), **IV:** 42, 76
"Chronicle" (Constantine), **Supp. XV:** 73
"Chronicle, The" (Cowley), **II:** 198
Chronicle Historie of Perkin Warbeck, The (Ford), *see Perkin Warbeck*
chronicle history, **I:** 73
Chronicle of Carlingford series (ed. Fitzgerald), **Supp. V:** 98
Chronicle of Friendships, A, 1873–1900 (Low), **V:** 393, 397
Chronicle of Queen Fredegond, The (Swinburne), **V:** 333
Chronicle of the Cid (tr. Southey), **IV:** 71
"Chronicle of the Drum, The" (Thackeray), **V:** 17, 38
Chronicle of Youth: War Diary, 1913–1917 (Brittain), **Supp. X:** 47
Chronicles (Hall), **II:** 43
Chronicles of Barset (Trollope), **Supp. IV:** 231
Chronicles of Carlingford (Oliphant), **Supp. X:** 214, 219
Chronicles of Clovis, The (Saki), **Supp. VI:** 240–243, 245, 249
Chronicles of Narnia, The (Lewis), **Supp. III:** 247, 248, **259–261**
Chronicles of Robin Hood, The (Sutcliff), **Supp. XVI:** 264
Chronicles of the Canongate (Scott), **IV:** 39
Chroniques (Froissart), **I:** 21
"Chronopolis" (Ballard), **Supp. V:** 22
"Chrysalides" (Kinsella), **Supp. V:** 262
Chrysalids, The (Wyndham), **Supp. XIII:** 290–291, 292
Chrysaor (Landor), **IV:** 96
Church, Dean R. W., **I:** 186
Church and Queen. Five Speeches, 1860–1864 (Disraeli), **IV:** 308
"Church Going" (Larkin), **Supp. I:** 277, 279, 280, 285; **Retro. Supp. III:** 205
Church in Crisis, The (Wilson), **Supp. VI:** 305
"Church Service" (Vaughan), **II:** 187
"Church Windows, The" (Herbert), **II:** 127
"Churches of Northern France, The" (Morris), **V:** 293, 306
"Church–floore, The" (Herbert), **II:** 126; **Retro. Supp. II:** 178–179
"Church's Year Book" (Traherne), **Supp. XI:** 264, 274
Churchill, Caryl, **Supp. IV: 179–200**
Churchill, Lady Randolph, **VI:** 349
Churchill, Winston, **III:** 27; **VI:** xv, 261, 274, **347–362**, 369, 385, 392; **Supp. III:** 58–59; speeches, **VI:** 361
Churchill by His Contemporaries (ed. Eade), **VI:** 351n, 361
"Church–monuments" (Herbert), **II:** 127
"Church–warden and the Curate, The" (Tennyson), **IV:** 327
"Churl and the Bird, The" (Lydgate), **I:** 57
Chymist's Key, The (tr. Vaughan), **II:** 185, 201
Cibber, Colley, **I:** 327; **II:** 314, 324–326, 331, 334, 337
Cicadas, The (Huxley), **VII:** 199

"Cicero and His Brother" (Landor), **IV:** 90, 91
Ciceronianus (Harvey), **I:** 122
Ciceronis Amor: Tullies Love (Greene), **VIII:** 135, 143
"Cinders" (Hulme), **Supp. VI:** 133, 135–136, 140, **141,** 146
Cinkante balades (Gower), **I:** 56
"Cinnamon and Pearls" (Martineau), **Supp. XV:** 188
Cinque Ports, The (Ford), **VI:** 238, 332
Cinthio, Giraldi, **I:** 316; **II:** 71
Cion (Mda), **Supp. XV:** 201, 206–207
Circe (Davenant), **II:** 305
"Circe" (Longley), **VIII:** 167
"Circe Truggin" (Powys), **VIII:** 249
Circle, The (Maugham), **VI:** 369
"Circle of Deception" (Waugh), **Supp. VI:** 275
"Circled by Circe" (Gunesekera), **Supp. X:** 86
"Circuit of the World, The", *See Heimskringla*
Circular Billiards for Two Players (Carroll), **V:** 273
"Circulation, The" (Traherne), **Supp. XI:** 267
"Circus, A" (Delanty), **Supp. XIV:** 74–75
"Circus Animals' Desertion, The" (Yeats), **V:** 349; **VI:** 215; **Supp. III:** 102; **Retro. Supp. I:** 338
"Circus Wheel" (Redgrove), **Supp. VI:** 236
Citation and Examination of William Shakespeare . . . (Landor), **IV:** 100
Cities (Morris, J.), **Supp. X:** 172
"Cities, The" (Russell), **VIII:** 291
Cities (Symons), **Supp. XIV:** 279
Cities and Sea–Coasts and Islands (Symons), **Supp. XIV:** 276–277, 279, 281
Cities of Italy (Symons), **Supp. XIV:** 279
Cities, Plains and People (Durrell), **Supp. I:** 126; **Retro. Supp. III:** 84, 95
"Citizen" (Wallace-Crabbe), **VIII:** 311
Citizen of the World, The; or, Letters from a Chinese Philosopher . . . (Goldsmith), **III:** 177, 179, 185, 188–189, 191
City Madam, The (Massinger), **Supp. XI:** 183, 184, 185, 186, 190–192
"City of Brass, The" (Kipling), **VI:** 203
"City Sunset, A" (Hulme), **Supp. VI:** 136
"City Ways" (Amis), **Supp. II:** 2
City Witt: or, The Woman Wears the Breeches, The (Brome), **Supp. X:** 62
City Wives' Confederacy, The (Vanbrugh), *see Confederacy, The*
Civil and Military Gazette, **Retro. Supp. III:** 183, 184
Civilisation: Its Cause and Cure (Carpenter), **Supp. XIII:** 40–41
"Civilised, The," (Galsworthy), **VI:** 273, 274, 276
Civilization in the United States (Arnold), **V:** 216
Civilization of the Renaissance in Italy, The (Burckhardt), **V:** 342
Civitatis Amor (Middleton), **II:** 3

Cixous, Hélène, **Supp. IV:** 99, 117, 232, 547, 558
"Clachtoll" (MacCaig), **Supp. VI:** 186
"Claiming My Inheritance" (Butlin), **Supp. XVI:** 57
Clancy, Laurie, **Supp. IV:** 348
Clapp, Susannah, **Supp. IV:** 164
Clara (Galloway), **Supp. XII:** 117, 127–130
Clara Florise (Moore), **VI:** 96
Clare, John, **IV:** 260; **Supp. XI: 49–65**
Clare Drummer (Pritchett), **Supp. III:** 313
Clarel (Melville), **V:** 211
"Clarence Mangan" (Kinsella), **Supp. V:** 260
"Clare's Ghost" (Blunden), **Supp. XI:** 44
"Clarice of the Autumn Concerts" (Bennett), **VI:** 266
Clarissa (Richardson), **III:** 80–81, **85–89,** 91, 92, 95; **VI:** 266; **Supp. III:** 30–31; **Supp. IV:** 150; **Retro. Supp. I:** 81
"Clarissa": Preface, Hints of Prefaces and Postscripts (ed. Brissenden), **III:** 86n
"Clarissa Harlowe Poem, The" (Ewart), **Supp. VII:** 41
Clarissa Oakes (O'Brian), **Supp. XII:** 258–259
Clark, Kenneth, **III:** 325, 346
Clark, Sir George, **IV:** 290
Clarke, Austin, **Supp. XV: 15–31**
Clarke, Charles Cowden, **IV:** 214, 215
Clarke, Herbert E., **V:** 318n
Clarke, Samuel, **II:** 251
Clarke, Susanna, **Supp. XV: 33–47**
Clarkson, Catherine, **IV:** 49
"Class Front of Modern Art, The" (Cornford), **Supp. XIII:** 87
Classic Irish Drama (Armstrong), **VII:** 14
Classical Tradition, The: Greek and Roman Influence on Western Literature (Highet), **II:** 199n
Classics and Commercials (Wilson), **Supp. II:** 57
Claude Lorrain's House on the Tiber (Lear), **V:** 77
Claudius novels (Graves), **VII:** xviii, 259
Claudius the God and His Wife Messalina (Graves), **VII:** 259
"Claud's Dog" (Dahl), **Supp. IV:** 214
"Claus von Stauffenberg" (Gunn), **Retro. Supp. III:** 121
Claverings, The (Trollope), **V:** 99–100, 101
"Clay" (Gibbon), **Supp. XIV:** 104–105, 106
Clay. Whereabouts Unknown (Raine), **Supp. XIII:** 173
Clayhanger (Bennett), **VI:** 248, 250, 251, 257–258
Clayhanger series(Bennett), **VI:** xiii, 247, 248, 250, 251, 257–258
Clea (Durrell), **Supp. I:** 103, 104, 106, 107; **Retro. Supp. III:** 84, 85, 90
"Clean Bill, A" (Redgrove), **Supp. VI:** 234
"Cleaned Out" (Motion), **Supp. VII:** 263

"Cleaning Out the Workhouse" (McGuckian), **Supp. V:** 291
Cleanness (*Gawain*–Poet), **Supp. VII:** 83, 84, 98–99
Cleansed (Kane), **VIII:** 148, 151, 152, 156, 158–159, 160
Clear Horizon (Richardson), **Supp. XIII:** 186, 187, 191
Clear Light of Day (Desai), **Supp. V:** 53, 55, 62, 65–67, 68, 73
Clear State of the Case of Elizabeth Canning, A (Fielding), **III:** 105
"Clearances" (Heaney), **Supp. II:** 279–280; **Retro. Supp. I:** 131
"Clearances" (Jamie), **Supp. XIV:** 134
"Clearing" (Scupham), **Supp. XIII:** 227
"Cleator Moor" (Nicholson), **Supp. VI:** 214
"Cleggan Disaster, The" (Murphy), **Supp. V:** 313, 319–320
Cleomenes, The Spartan Hero (Dryden), **II:** 296, 305
"Cleon" (Browning), **IV:** 357, 360, 363; **Retro. Supp. III:** 26
Cleopatra (Daniel), **I:** 162
Cleopatra (Haggard), **Supp. III:** 213, 222
"Cleopatra" (Swinburne), **V:** 332
"Clergy, The" (Wilson), **Supp. VI:** 305
Clergyman's Daughter, A (Orwell), **VII:** 274, 278
"Clergyman's Doubts, A" (Butler), **Supp. II:** 117
Clergymen of the Church of England (Trollope), **V:** 101
"Cleric, The" (Heaney), **Supp. II:** 279
Clerk, N. W., *see* Lewis, C. S.
Clerk's Prologue, The (Chaucer), **I:** 29
Clerk's Tale, The (Chaucer), **I:** 34; **Supp. IV:** 190
Cleveland, John, **II:** 123
"Clicking of Cuthbert, The" (Wodehouse), **Supp. III:** 462
Clifford, J. L., **III:** 244n
Clifford, W. K., **V:** 409n
"Clifton and a Lad's Love" (Symonds), **Supp. XIV:** 262
"Climbing the Stork Pagoda" (Butlin), **Supp. XVI:** 55
"Clinical World of P. D. James, The" (Benstock), **Supp. IV:** 320
Clio: A Muse (Trevelyan), **VI:** 383–384
Clishbotham, Jedidiah, pseud. of Sir Walter Scott
"Clive" (Browning), **IV:** 367
"Clock (for Albert Ayler)" (Brathwaite), **Supp. XII:** 44
"Clock Ticks at Christmas, A" (Highsmith), **Supp. V:** 180
"Clocks, The" (Christie), **Supp. II:** 135
Clockwork; or, All Wound Up (Pullman), **Supp. XIII:** 151, 152
Clockwork Orange, A (Burgess), **Supp. I:** 190–191
Clockwork Testament, The; or, Enderby's End (Burgess), **Supp. I:** 189
Clodd, Edward, **V:** 429
Cloning of Joanna May, The (Weldon), **Supp. IV:** 535, 536
"Clopton Hall" (Gaskell), **V:** 3

"Clorinda and Damon" (Marvell), **II:** 210, 211
Clorinda Walks in Heaven (Coppard), **VIII:** 89, 93–94
"Clorinda Walks in Heaven" (Coppard), **VIII:** 88, 97
"Close of Play" (Dunn), **Supp. X:** 70
Close Quarters (Golding), **Retro. Supp. I:** 104
Close Up, **Supp. XIII:** 191
Closed Circle, The (Coe), **Supp. XV:** 49, 50, 51, 57, 58–59, 60
Closed Eye, A (Brookner), **Supp. IV:** 120, 133
Closing the Ring (Churchill), **VI:** 361
"Clothes Pit, The" (Dunn), **Supp. X:** 69
"Cloud, The" (Fowles), **Supp. I:** 304
"Cloud, The" (Shelley), **IV:** 196, 204
Cloud Atlas (Mitchell), **Supp. XIV:** 194, 195, 196, 197, 200–206, 207
Cloud Howe (Gibbon), **Supp. XIV:** 106, 110–111, 112
Cloud Nine (Churchill), **Supp. IV:** 179, 180, 188–189, 198
CloudCuckooLand (Armitage), **VIII:** 1, 11–14
Cloudesley, A Tale (Godwin), **Supp. XV:** 127–128
"Clouds" (Brooke), **VI:** 420
Clouds (Frayn), **Supp. VII:** 61
"Cloud–Sculptors of Coral–D, The" (Ballard), **Supp. V:** 26
Clouds of Witness (Sayers), **Supp. III:** 338, 339
"Cloud's Swan Song, The" (Thompson), **V:** 443
Clough, Arthur Hugh, **IV:** 371; **V:** ix, xi, xviii, xxii, 7, **155–171,** 207, 208n, 209, 211, 212
"Club in an Uproar, A" (Thackeray), **V:** 25
Clubbable Woman, A (Hill, R.), **Supp. IX:** 110, 112–113
Clune, Frank, **Supp. IV:** 350
Cnut, King, **Retro. Supp. II:** 293
Co-operation and Nationality (Russell), **VIII:** 286, 287
Coakley, Thomas P., **Supp. IV:** 350
"Coal, The" (Caudwell), **Supp. IX:** 38
Coal Face (Auden), **Retro. Supp. I:** 7
"Coast, The" (Fuller), **VII:** 431
Coast to Coast: An Account of a Visit to the United States (Morris, J.), **Supp. X:** 175, 181–182, 184
Coasting (Raban), **Supp. XI:** 227, 228–232
"Coat, A" (Yeats), **Retro. Supp. I:** 330
"Coat of Many Colors, A" (Desai), **Supp. V:** 53
Cobbett, William, **VI:** 337
Cobra Verde (film), **Supp. IV:** 168
Coburn, Kathleen, **IV:** 52, 55–57
Cocaine Nights (Ballard), **Supp. V:** 31–32, 34
"Cock: A Novelette" (Self), **Supp. V:** 404–405
Cock and Bull (Self), **Supp. V:** 404–406
Cock and the Fox, The (Henryson), **Supp. VII:** 136, 137–138, 147

Cock and the Jasp, The (Henryson), **Supp. VII:** 136, 137
"Cock Crows" (Hughes), **Retro. Supp. II:** 211
"Cock o' the North" (Crawford), **Supp. XI:** 68
Cock–a–Doodle Dandy (O'Casey), **VII:** xviii, 9–10
Cockatoos, The (White), **Supp. I:** 132, 147
Cockburn, Alexander, **Supp. IV:** 449
"Cockcrow" (Herrick), **II:** 114
"Cock–crowing" (Vaughan), **II:** 185
Cockrill, Maurice, **Supp. IV:** 231
"Cockroach" (Pitter), **Supp. XIII:** 140
Cockshut, A. O. J., **V:** 98, 100–101, 103
Cocktail Party, The (Eliot), **VII:** 158, 159, 160–161; **Retro. Supp. II:** 132
"Coda" (Hill), **Retro. Supp. III:** 145
"Coda" (Kinsella), **Supp. V:** 271
Coda (Raine), **Supp. XIII:** 173
Code of the Woosters, The (Wodehouse), **Supp. III:** 459–460
"Codham, Cockridden, and Childerditch" (Thomas), **Supp. III:** 401
Coe, Jonathan, **Supp. XV:** 49–63
Coelum Britannicum . . . (Carew), **II:** 222
Coetzee, J(ohn) M(ichael), **Supp. VI:** **75–90**
Coffin for Dimitrios, A (Ambler), **Supp. IV:** 9–11, 12
"Coffin on the Hill, The" (Welch), **Supp. IX:** 267–268
Coggan, Donald, archbishop of Canterbury, **I:** vi
Cohen, Francis, **IV:** 190
Cohn, Ruby, **Retro. Supp. I:** 215
Co–Incidence of Flesh (Fallon), **Supp. XII:** 102
Colasterion: A Reply to a Nameless Answer Against the Doctrine and Discipline of Divorce (Milton), **II:** 175
Colburn, Henry, **IV:** 254, 293; **V:** 135
"Cold, The" (Warner), **Supp. VII:** 380
"Cold, clear, and blue, The morning heaven" (Brontë), **V:** 115
Cold Coming, A (Harrison), **Supp. V:** 150
"Cold Coming, A" (Harrison), **Supp. V:** 161–163
Cold Heaven (Moore, B.), **Supp. IX:** 143, 144, 151–152
"Cold in the earth" (Brontë), **V:** 114, 133, 134
Cold Lazarus (Potter, D.), **Supp. X:** 228, 240–241
Colenso, Bishop John William, **V:** 283
Coleridge, Derwent, **IV:** 48–49, 52
Coleridge, Hartley, **IV:** 44; **V:** 105, 125
Coleridge, Samuel Taylor, **III:** 338; **IV:** viii–xii, **41–57,** 59, 75–78, 82, 84, 115, 204, 253, 257, 281; **V:** 244; **Retro. Supp. II:** 51–67; and De Quincey, **IV:** 143, 144, 150; and Hazlitt, **IV:** 125–130, 133–134, 137, 138; and Peacock, **IV:** 161–162, 167; and Wordsworth, **IV:** 3–4, 6, 15, 128; at Christ's Hospital, **IV:** 75–78, 82; critical works, **II:** 42, 119n, 155, 179, 249–250, 298; **III:** 174, 281, 286; **IV:** 4, 6, 18, 96, 253, 257; **Retro. Supp. II:** 172; literary

338

style, **II:** 154; **III:** 336, 338; **IV:** viii, xi, 18, 180; **V:** 62, 361, 447; Pater's essay in *"apppreciations*, **V:** 244, 340–341; **Supp. IV:** 425, 426–427
"Coleridge" (Mill), **IV:** 50, 56
"Coleridge" (Pater), **V:** 338, 340–341, 403
Coleridge on Imagination (Richards), **Supp. II:** 422–423, 429
Coleridge's Miscellaneous Criticism (ed. Raysor), **IV:** 46
Coleridge's Shakespearean Criticism (ed. Raysor), **IV:** 51, 52, 56
Colette, **Supp. III:** 86; **Supp. IV:** 136
"Coleum; or, The Origin of Things" (Bacon), **I:** 267
Colin Clout (Skelton), **I:** 84, 86, 87, 91–92
Colin Clout's Come Home Again (Spenser), **I:** 124, 127–128, 146–147
"Collaboration" (James), **VI:** 48, 69
Collaborators, The (Hill, R.), **Supp. IX:** 118
"Collar, The" (Herbert), **II:** 120–121, 216; **Retro. Supp. II:** 180
"Colleagues, The" (Upward), **Supp. XIII:** 252–253
Collected Critical Writings (Hill), **Retro. Supp. III:** 145
Collected Essays (Greene), **Supp. I:** 9
Collected Essays, Papers, etc. (Bridges), **VI:** 83
Collected Ewart 1933–1980, The (Ewart), **VII:** 423, **Supp. VII:** 35, 36, 37, 38, 41, 43
Collected Impressions (Bowen), **Supp. II:** 78, 82
Collected Later Poems, 1988–2000 (Thomas), **Supp. XII:** 282
Collected Letters (Cowen), **VI:** 448
Collected Novels and Memoirs of William Godwin (Godwin), **Supp. XV:** 116, 118, 119, 122
Collected Papers on Analytical Psychology (Jung), **Supp. IV:** 3, 4
Collected Plays (Maugham), **VI:** 367
Collected Plays (Rattigan), **Supp. VII:** 311, 312, 318
Collected Poems (Amis), **Supp. II:** 15
Collected Poems (Beer), **Supp. XIV:** 1–2, 4, 5
Collected Poems (Brooke), **Supp. III:** 55–56
Collected Poems (Bunting), **Supp. VII:** 6, 13–14
Collected Poems (Cameron), **Supp. IX:** 18, 24, 31
Collected Poems (Caudwell), **Supp. IX:** 33, 37
Collected Poems (Clarke), **Supp. XV:** 17–18, 26, 27, 28, 29
Collected Poems (Constantine), **Supp. XV:** 65, 69, 70, 71, 72, 73, 74, 76, 77, 78, 79, 80
Collected Poems (Cornford), **VIII:** 104, 112, 114
Collected Poems (Davies), **Supp. XI:** 89, 96
Collected Poems (Delanty), **Supp. XIV:** 78

Collected Poems (Durrell), **Supp. I: 124–126**; **Retro. Supp. III:** 85
Collected Poems (Empson), **Supp. II:** 179, 181, 192
Collected Poems (Ford), **VI:** 323, 332
Collected Poems (Gunn), **Retro. Supp. III:** 115, 129
Collected Poems (Jennings), **Supp. V:** 216
Collected Poems (Kingsley), **Supp. XVI:** 204
Collected Poems (Larkin), **Retro. Supp. III:** 211
Collected Poems (MacCaig), **Supp. VI:** 185, 187, 192
Collected Poems (MacDiarmid), **Supp. XII:** 203
Collected Poems (Mahon), **Supp. VI:** 165–167, 169–170, 172–177
Collected Poems (Montague), **Supp. XV:** 210, 211, 212, 213, 214, 215, 216, 217, 218, 219, 220, 221, 222–223
Collected Poems (Morgan **Supp. IX:** 157, 158, 160–161, 163
Collected Poems(Muir), **Supp. VI:** 201, 204–205, 208
Collected Poems (Murray), **Supp. VII:** 271, 273, 275, 277, 278, 279, 281, 283, 284
Collected Poems(Nicholson), **Supp. VI:** 213–214, 217–219
Collected Poems (Nye), **Supp. X:** 200, 202–205
Collected Stories (O'Connor), **Supp. XIV:** 214, 216, 224, 225, 226, 227, 228
Collected Poems (Pitter), **Supp. XIII:** 131, 136, 137, 142, 144, 145
Collected Poems (Plomer), **Supp. XI:** 213, 214, 216, 222
Collected Poems (Raine), **Supp. XIII:** 172
Collected Poems (Reed), **Supp. XV:** 244, 245, 247, 250, 251, 252, 253, 255–256
Collected Poems (Russell), **VIII:** 277, 2887
Collected Poems (Scupham), **Supp. XIII:** 217–231
Collected Poems, The (Seth), **Supp. X:** 279, 281, 284
Collected Poems (Sillitoe), **Supp. V:** 424
Collected Poems (Sisson), **Supp. XI:** 243, 245, 246, 248, 250, 251, 252, 253, 254, 255, 256, 257, 258, 259
Collected Poems (Smith), **Supp. II:** 464
Collected Poems (Smith, I. C.), **Supp. IX:** 209, 211, 214, 217, 219, 221
Collected Poems (Thomas), **Supp. I:** 169, 170, 171, 175, 179, 184; **Supp. III:** 393
Collected Poems (Warner), **Supp. VII:** 371, 372, 373
Collected Poems (Yeats), **Retro. Supp. I:** 330
Collected Poems 1909–1962 (Muir), **Supp. VI:** 205
Collected Poems 1928–1985 (Spender), **Supp. II:** 486, 493

Collected Poems 1930–1965 (Hope), **Supp. VII:** 153, 155, 156, 157, 159, 162, 164, 165
Collected Poems, 1931–1974 (Durrell), **Retro. Supp. III:** 86, 95
Collected Poems, 1934–1952, The (Thomas), **Retro. Supp. III:** 336–337, 347
Collected Poems, 1945–1990 (Thomas), **Supp. XII:** 279, 280, 282, 283, 284, 285, 286, 287, 288–289, 290, 292
Collected Poems 1950–1970 (Davie), **Supp. VI:** 105–106, 108, 110, 114
Collected Poems, 1953–1985 (Jennings), **Supp. V:** 211, 216, 218
Collected Poems 1955–1995 (Stevenson), **Supp. VI:** 254, 256–257, 260–262, 264–265
Collected Poems, 1956–1994 (Kinsella), **Supp. V:** 273, 274
Collected Poems 1980–1990 (Ewart), **Supp. VII:** 35, 43, 44, 46
Collected Poems of A. E. Coppard (Coppard), **VIII:** 91, 98
Collected Poems of Austin Clarke, The (Clarke), **Supp. XV:** 17, 19, 21, 22
Collected Poems of Robert Louis Stevenson (ed. Smith), **V:** 393
Collected Poems of Stevie Smith, The (Smith), **Retro. Supp. III:** 304, 305, 307, 308, 310, 311, 313, 314
Collected Poetry of Malcolm Lowry, The (ed. Scherf), **Supp. III:** 283
Collected Stories (Carey), **Supp. XII:** 54
Collected Stories (Maugham), **VI:** 370
Collected Stories (Thomas), **Supp. I:** 180, 181–182, 183
Collected Tales of A. E. Coppard, The (Coppard), **VIII:** 85, 89, 97
Collected Translations (Morgan, E.), **Supp. IX:** 169
Collected Translations (Sisson), **Supp. XI:** 252
Collected Verse, The (Carroll), **V:** 270, 273
Collected Works (Smith), **Supp. VII:** 340
Collected Works of Arthur Symons, The (Symons), **Supp. XIV:** 267, 270, 272, 273, 275, 276, 277, 279, 280
Collected Works of Izaak Walton (Keynes), **II:** 134
Collected Works of James Clarence Mangan: Poems (Mangan), **Supp. XIII:** 119–120, 122, 125
Collected Works of James Clarence Mangan: Prose (Mangan), **Supp. XIII:** 113–118, 120–127, 129
Collected Writings of T. E. Hulme (Hulme), **Supp. VI:** 134–136, 139–146
Collection, The (Pinter), **Supp. I:** 373, 374, 375
"Collection, The" (Pritchett), **Supp. III:** 315
Collection of Curious Papers, A (Byrom), **Supp. XVI:** 79
Collection of Farces and Other Afterpieces, A (ed. Inchbald), **Supp. XV:** 149, 160, 161

Collection of Meditations and Devotions in Three Parts, A (Traherne), **II:** 191, 201
Collection of Original Poems, A (Boswell), **III:** 247
Collection of Poems 1955–1988, A (Nye), **Supp. X:** 193–194, 197, 202–205
Collection Three (O'Connor), **Supp. XIV:** 219
Collection Two (O'Connor), **Supp. XIV:** 219
"Collective Invention, The" (Wallace-Crabbe), **VIII:** 317
Collector, The (Fowles), **Supp. I:** 291, 292, 293, 294–295, 297, 307, 310
Collector, The (Redgrove), **Supp. VI:** 227–228
"Collector Cleans His Picture, The" (Hardy), **Retro. Supp. I:** 120
"Collectors, The" (Mistry), **Supp. X:** 139
"College Garden, The" (Bridges), **VI:** 82
"College in the Reservoir, The" (Redgrove), **Supp. VI:** 235–236
"College Magazine, A" (Stevenson), **Retro. Supp. I:** 261
Collier, Jeremy, **II:** 303, 325, 331–332, 338, 340, 356; **III:** 44
Collier, John Payne, **I:** 285; **IV:** 52, 56
Collier's Friday Night, A (Lawrence), **VII:** 89, 121
Collingwood, R. G., **VI:** 203
Collingwood, S. D., **V:** 270, 273, 274
Collins, Michael, **VI:** 353
Collins, Phillip, **V:** 46, 73
Collins, Wilkie, **III:** 334, 338, 340, 345; **V:** xxii–xxiii, 42, 62; **Supp. III:** 341; **Supp. VI: 91–104**
Collins, William, **II:** 68, 323n; **III: 160–176**, 336; **IV:** 227
Collinson, James, **V:** 249
Colloquies on the Progress and Prospects of Society (Southey), *see* Sir Thomas More; or, Colloquies on the Progress . . .
Colman, George, **IV:** 271
Colombe's Birthday (Browning), **IV:** 374
"Colonel Fantock" (Sitwell), **VII:** 133
Colonel Jack (Defoe), **III:** 5, 6, 7, 8, 13
Colonel Quaritch, V. C. (Haggard), **Supp. III:** 213
Colonel Sun (Markham), **Supp. II:** 12
"Colonel's Lady, The" (Maugham), **VI:** 370
Color of Blood, The (Moore, B.), **Supp. IX:** 142, 144–145, 151, 152–153
"Color of Herring, The" (Reid), **Supp. VII:** 331
Color Studies in Paris (Symons), **Supp. XIV:** 281
"Colour Machine, The" (Gunn), **Supp. IV:** 267
Colour of Rain, The (Tennant), **Supp. IX:** 228, 229, 239
Coloured Countries, The (Waugh), **Supp. VI:** 272
"Colouring In" (Kay), **Supp. XIII:** 101, 107
"Colours of Good and Evil" (Bacon), *see* "Examples of the Colours of Good and Evil"

"Colubriad, The" (Cowper), **III:** 217–218
"Columban" (Crawford), **Supp. XI:** 76
"Columba's Song" (Morgan, E.), **Supp. IX:** 170
"Columbus in Chains" (Kincaid), **Supp. VII:** 223, 224
Colvin, Sidney, **V:** 386, **389–396**
"Coma Berenices" (Thomas), **Supp. IV:** 491
"Comála" (Macpherson), **VIII:** 188
"Combat, The" (Muir), **Supp. VI:** 200, 207
"Combat, The" (Thomas), **Supp. XII:** 292
Come and Go (Beckett), **Supp. I:** 60
Come and Welcome, to Jesus Christ (Bunyan), **II:** 253
Come Dance with Kitty Stobling and Other Poems (Kavanagh), **Supp. VII:** 193
"Come Death" (Smith), **Retro. Supp. III:** 313, 314
"Come, Fool" (Smith, I. C.), **Supp. IX:** 221
Comedians, The (Greene), **Supp. I:** 10, 13, 15–16; **Retro. Supp. II:** 162–164
Comedies (Wain), **Supp. XVI:** 301–302
"Comedy" (Fry), **Supp. III:** 201
"Comedy Of, The" (Scupham), **Supp. XIII:** 220–221, 223
Comedy of Dante Alighieri, The (tr. Sayers), **Supp. III:** 333, 336, 350
Comedy of Errors, The (Shakespeare), **I:** 302, 303, 312, 321; **Retro. Supp. III:** 273
"Come-on, The" (Dunn), **Supp. X:** 72
Comet, **Supp. XIII:** 116, 120
"Comet, The" (Pitter), **Supp. XIII:** 141
Comfort of Strangers, The (McEwan), **Supp. IV:** 390, 396–398, 400, 402
Comfortable Words to Christ's Lovers (Julian of Norwich), **Supp. XII:** 155
"Comforters, The" (Malouf), **Supp. XII:** 219
Comforters, The (Spark), **Supp. I:** 199, 200, 201–202, 213
Comic Annual, The (Hood), **IV:** 251, 252, 253–254, 258, 259, 266
"Comic Cuts" (Kelman), **Supp. V:** 256
Comic Romance of Monsieur Scarron, The (tr. Goldsmith), **III:** 191
Comical Revenge, The (Etherege), **II:** 266, 267–268, 271
Comicall Satyre of Every Man Out of His Humour, The (Jonson), **Retro. Supp. I:** 158, 159–160
"Coming" (Larkin), **Supp. I:** 285
"Coming, The" (Thomas), **Supp. XII:** 288
"Coming Day, The" (Upward), **Supp. XIII:** 262
Coming Day and Other Stories, The (Upward), **Supp. XIII:** 250, 262
"Coming Down Through Somerset" (Hughes), **Retro. Supp. II:** 211–212
"Coming Home" (Bowen), **Supp. II:** 81, 82
"Coming of Arthur" (Tennyson), **Retro. Supp. III:** 327

Coming of Gabrielle, The (Moore), **VI:** 96, 99
"Coming of the Anglo–Saxons, The" (Trevelyan), **VI:** 393
"Coming of the Cat, The" (Beer), **Supp. XIV:** 4
Coming of the Kings, The (Hughes), **Supp. I:** 347
"Coming Struggle for Power, The" (Cornford), **Supp. XIII:** 90
"Coming to Visit" (Motion), **Supp. VII:** 256
Coming Up for Air (Orwell), **VII:** 281–282
"Commemoration of King Charles the I, martyr'd on that day" (King), **Supp. VI:** 162
Commendatory Verses Prefixed to Heywood's Apology for Actors (Webster), **II:** 85
Commendatory Verses Prefixed to . . . Munday's Translation of Palmerin . . . (Webster), **II:** 85
"Comment on Christmas, A" (Arnold), **V:** 216
Commentaries of Caesar, The (Trollope), **V:** 102
Commentarius solutus (Bacon), **I:** 263, 272
"Commentary" (Auden), **Retro. Supp. I:** 9
"Commentary on Galatians, A" (Malouf), **Supp. XII:** 220
Commentary on Macaulay's History of England, A (Firth), **IV:** 290, 291
Coming on Strong (Butlin), **Supp. XVI:** 66
Commentary on the "Memoirs of Mr. Fox" (Landor), **IV:** 100
Commentary on the Collected Plays of W. B. Yeats (Jeffares and Knowland), **VI:** 224; **VI:** 224
Commentary on the Complete Poems of Gerard Manley Hopkins, A (Mariani), **V:** 373n, 378n 382
Comming of Good Luck, The (Herrick), **II:** 107
Commitments, The (Doyle), **Supp. V:** 77, 80–82, 93
"Committee Man of 'The Terror,' The" (Hardy), **VI:** 22
Commodore, The (O'Brian), **Supp. XII:** 259, 260–261
"Common and Peculiar" (Constantine), **Supp. XV:** 68
Common Asphodel, The (Graves), **VII:** 261
"Common Breath, The" (Stallworthy), **Supp. X:** 292
Common Chorus, The (Harrison), **Supp. V:** 164
"Common Entry" (Warner), **Supp. VII:** 371
Common Grace, A (MacCaig), **Supp. VI: 187**, 194
Common Knowledge (Burnside), **Supp. XIII:** 13, 14–16
Common Pursuit (Leavis), **VII:** 234, 246
Common Reader, The (Woolf), **VII:** 22, 28, 32–33

Common Sense of War and Peace, The: World Revolution or War Unending (Wells), **VI:** 245
Commonplace and Other Short Stories (Rossetti), **V:** 260
Commonplace Book of Robert Herrick, **II:** 103
"Commonsense About the War" (Shaw), **VI:** 119, 129
Commonweal (periodical), **V:** 302
Commonweal, The: A Song for Unionists (Swinburne), **V:** 332
"Commonwealth Literature Does Not Exist" (Rushdie), **Supp. IV:** 454–455
Communication Cord, The (Friel), **Supp. V:** 124–125
Communicating Doors (Ayckbourn), **Supp. V:** 3, 9, 11, 12
Communication to My Friends, A (Moore), **VI:** 89, 99
"Communion" (Coppard), **VIII:** 88, 93
"Communism in the Universities" (Cornford), **Supp. XIII:** 86–87
"Communist to Others, A" (Auden), **Retro. Supp. I:** 8
"Communitie" (Donne), **Retro. Supp. II:** 89
Companion to the Theatre, The (Haywood), **Supp. XII:** 135
Companions of the Day (Harris), **Supp. V:** 136, 138
Company (Beckett), **Supp. I:** 62; **Retro. Supp. I:** 29
"Company of Laughing Faces, A" (Gordimer), **Supp. II:** 232
"Company of Wolves, The" (Carter), **Supp. III:** 88
Compassion: An Ode (Hardy), **VI:** 20
"Compassionate Fool, The" (Cameron), **Supp. IX:** 24–25
Compendium of Authentic and Entertaining Voyages, A (Smollett), **IV:** 158
"Competition, The" (Dunn), **Supp. X:** 71
"Complaint of a Schoolmistress, The" (Jewsbury), **Supp. XIV:** 150
Complaint of Chaucer to His Purse (Chaucer), **I:** 31
Complaint of the Black Knight, The (Lydgate), **I:** 57, 60, 61, 65
Complaint of Venus, The (Chaucer), **I:** 31
Complaints (Spenser), **I:** 124
Compleat Angler, The (Walton), **II:** 131–136, **137–139**, 141–143
Compleat English Gentleman, The (Defoe), **III:** 5, 14
Compleat Gard'ner, The; or, Directions for . . . Fruit–Gardens and Kitchen–Gardens . . . (tr. Evelyn), **II:** 287
Complete Key to the Four Parts of Law is a Bottomless–Pit, A (Arbuthnot), **Supp. XVI:** 22
Compleat Tradesman, The (Defoe), **Retro. Supp. I:** 63
Compleat Vindication of the Licensers of the Stage, A (Johnson), **III:** 121; **Retro. Supp. I:** 141–142
"Complement, The" (Carew), **II:** 223–224
Complete Clerihews of Edward Clerihew Bentley (Ewart), **Supp. VII:** 43, 46

Complete Collected Essays (Pritchett), **Supp. III:** 313, 315
Complete Collected Stories (Pritchett), **Supp. III:** 312
Complete Collection of Genteel and Ingenious Conversation, A (Swift), **III:** 29, 36
Complete Doctor Stories, The (Dutton), **Supp. XII:** 82, 85
Complete English Tradesman, The (Defoe), **III:** 5, 14
Complete History of England . . . (Smollett), **III:** 148, 149, 158
Complete Indian Housekeeper & Cook, The: Giving the Duties of Mistress and Servants, the General Management of the House, and Practical Recipes for Cooking in All Its Branches (Steel), **Supp. XII:** 265, 267
Complete Little Ones (Ewart), **Supp. VII:** 45
Complete Plays, The (Behan), **Supp. II:** 67, 68, 69, 70, 73, 74
Complete Plays (Kane), **VIII:** 149
Complete Plays of Frances Burney, The (ed. Sabor), **Supp. III:** 64
Complete Poems (Muir), **Supp. VI:** 204
Complete Poems (Day Lewis), **Supp. III:** 130
Complete Poems and Fragments of Wilfred Owen, The (Stallworthy), **VI:** 458, 459; **Supp. X:** 292
Complete Poems of Emily Brontë, The (ed. Hatfield), **V:** 133, 152
Complete Poems of Hugh MacDiarmid, 1920–1976, The (MacDiarmid), **Supp. XII:** 201
Complete Poems of W. H. Davies, The (Davies), **Supp. XI:** 93, 95
"Complete Poetical Works of T.E. Hulme" (Hulme), **Supp. VI:** 136
Complete Saki, The (Saki), **Supp. VI:** 240
Complete Short Stories (Pritchett), **Supp. III:** 313
"Complete Stranger" (Dunn), **Supp. X:** 82
Complete Works of John Webster, The (ed. Lucas), **II:** 70n
"Complex Fate of Being American–Irish" (Montague), **Supp. XV:** 215
"Complicated Nature, A" (Trevor), **Supp. IV:** 500
Complicity (Banks), **Supp. XI:** 3–4, 5, 7, 12
"Composing Room, The" (Delanty), **Supp. XIV:** 69, 70
"Compound Fracture" (Kay), **Supp. XIII:** 99
Compton–Burnett, Ivy, **VII:** xvii, **59–70**; **Supp. IV:** 506
Comte, Auguste, **V:** 428–429
Comus (Milton), **II:** 50, 159–160, 166, 175; **Retro. Supp. II:** 273–275
Comyns, Barbara, **VIII: 53–66**
"Con Men, The" (Reading), **VIII:** 267
"Concealment, The" (Cowley), **II:** 196
"Conceit Begotten by the Eyes" (Ralegh), **I:** 148, 149
Concept of Nature in Nineteenth–Century Poetry, The (Beach), **V:** 221n

"Concentration City, The" (Ballard), **Supp. V:** 21
"Concerned Adolescent, The" (Cope), **VIII:** 77
"Concerning Geffray Teste Noir" (Morris), **V:** 293
Concerning Humour in Comedy (Congreve), **II:** 338, 341, 346, 350
"Concerning the Beautiful" (tr. Taylor), **III:** 291
Concerning the Eccentricities of Cardinal Pirelli (Firbank), **Supp. II:** 202, **220–222**
"Concerning the regal power" (King), **Supp. VI:** 158
Concerning the Relations of Great Britain, Spain, and Portugal . . . (Wordsworth), **IV:** 24
Concerning the Rule of Princes (tr. Trevisa), see *De Regimine Principum*
"Concert at Long Melford Church," (Beer), **Supp. XIV:** 3
"Concert Party: Busseboom" (Blunden), **VI:** 428
Conciones ad Populum (Coleridge), **IV:** 56
Concluding (Green), **Supp. II:** 260–263
Concordance to the Poems of Robert Browning, A (Broughton and Stelter), **IV:** 373
Concrete Garden, The (Dutton), **Supp. XII:** 83, 89, 97
Concrete Island (Ballard), **Supp. V:** 27, 28
Condemned Playground, The: Essays 1927–1944 (Connolly), **Supp. III:** **107–108**
"Condition of England, The" (Masterman), **VI:** viii, 273
Condition of the Working Class in England in 1844, The (Engels), **IV:** 249
"Condition of Women, The" (Oliphant), **Supp. X:** 222
"Condolence Visit" (Mistry), **Supp. X:** 140
Conduct of the Allies, The (Swift), **III:** 19, 26–27, 35; **Retro. Supp. I:** 274, 275
"Coney, The" (Muldoon), **Supp. IV:** 422
Confederacy, The (Vanbrugh), **II:** 325, 336
Confederates, The (Keneally), **Supp. IV:** 346, 348
Conference of Pleasure, A (Bacon), **I:** 265, 271
"Conference Presentation" (Aidoo), **Supp. XV:** 3, 12
Confessio amantis (Gower), **I:** 48, 49, 50–56, 58, 321
Confession of My Faith, A, . . . (Bunyan), **II:** 253
"Confession of Queen Gormlai" (Clarke), **Supp. XV:** 24
"Confessional" (Constantine), **Supp. XV:** 73
"Confessional Poetry" (Harrison), **Supp. V:** 153
Confessions (St. Augustine), **Supp. III:** 433

Confessions: A Study in Pathology (Symons), **Supp. XIV:** 279–281
Confessions of a Justified Sinner (Tennant), **Supp. IX:** 231–232
"Confessions of a Kept Ape" (McEwan), **Supp. IV:** 394
Confessions of a Young Man (Moore), **VI:** 85–86, 87, 89, 91, 96
"Confessions of an Airman" (Greig), **Supp. XVI:** 162
Confessions of an English Opium–Eater (De Quincey), **III:** 338; **IV:** xviii, 141, 143, 148–149, 150–153, 154, 155
Confessions of an Inquiring Spirit (Coleridge), **IV:** 53, 56
Confessions of an Irish Rebel (Behan), **Supp. II:** 63, 64–65, 71, 75, 76
"Confessions of an Only Child" (Malouf), **Supp. XII:** 220
"Confessor, a Sanctified Tale, The" (Robinson), **Supp. XIII:** 212
Confidence (James), **VI:** 67
Confidence Man, The (Melville), **Supp. IV:** 444
Confidential Agent, The (Greene), **Supp. I:** 3, 4, 7, 10; **Retro. Supp. II:** 155–156
Confidential Chats with Boys (Hollinghurst), **Supp. X:** 119, 121–122
Confidential Clerk, The (Eliot), **VII:** 161–162; **Retro. Supp. II:** 132
"Confined Love" (Donne), **Retro. Supp. II:** 89
Confines of Criticism, The (Housman), **VI:** 164
"Confirmation, The" (Muir), **Supp. VI:** 206
"Confirmation Suit, The" (Behan), **Supp. II:** 66–67
"Conflict, The" (Day Lewis), **Supp. III:** 120, 126
Conflict (Soutar), **Supp. XVI:** 244, 248–249
Confusion (Howard), **Supp. XI:** 145, 146, 147, 148
Confusions (Ayckbourn), **Supp. V:** 3, 11
Confutation of Tyndale's Answer (More), **Supp. VII:** 245
Congreve, William, **II:** 269, 289, 302, 304, 325, 336, **338–350,** 352; **III:** 45, 62
Coningsby (Disraeli), **IV:** xii, xx, 294, 300–303, 305, 307, 308; **V:** 4, 22
Conjugal Lewdness; or, Matrimonial Whoredom (Defoe), **III:** 14
"Conjugation" (Crawford), **Supp. XI:** 79–80
"Conjugial Angel, The" (Byatt), **Supp. IV:** 153
"Conjuror, The" (Beer), **Supp. XIV:** 5
Conn, Stewart, **Supp. XIII: 69–82**
Connell, John, **VI:** xv, xxxiii
"Connoisseur" (MacCaig), **Supp. VI:** 192–193
Connolly, Cyril, **VI:** 363, 371; **VII:** xvi, 37, 138, 310; **Supp. II:** 156, 199, 489, 493; **Supp. III: 95–113**
Connolly, T. L., **V:** 442n, 445, 447, 450, 451

"Connor Girls, The" (O'Brien), **Supp. V:** 339–340
Conny–Catching (Greene), **VIII:** 144
Conquest, Robert, **Supp. IV:** 256
Conquest of Granada by the Spaniards, The (Dryden), **II:** 294, 305
"Conquest of Syria, The: If Complete" (Lawrence), **Supp. II:** 287
Conquest of the Maya, The (Mitchell), **Supp. XIV:** 100
Conrad, Joseph, **VI:** xi, **133–150,** 170, 193, 242, 270, 279–280, 321; **VII:** 122; **Retro. Supp. II: 69–83**; list of short stories, **VI:** 149–150; **Supp. I:** 397–398; **Supp. II:** 290; **Supp. IV:** 5, 163, 233, 250, 251, 302, 403
Conrad in the Nineteenth Century (Watt), **VI:** 149
"Conrad's Darkness" (Naipaul), **Supp. I:** 397, 402, 403
Conrad's Prefaces to His Works (Garnett), **VI:** 149
"Conquistador" (Hope), **Supp. VII:** 158
Conscience of the Rich, The (Snow), **VII:** 324, 326–327
"Conscious" (Owen), **VI:** 451
Conscious and Verbal (Murray), **Supp. VII:** 271, 286–287
"Conscious Mind's Intelligible Structure, The: A Debate" (Hill), **Supp. V:** 183
"Conscript" (Larkin), **Supp. I:** 277
Conscription for Ireland: A Warning to England (Russell), **VIII:** 288
"Conscriptions: National Service 1952–1954" (Scupham), **Supp. XIII:** 222
Consequently I Rejoice (Jennings), **Supp. V:** 217
Conservationist, The (Gordimer), **Supp. II:** 230–231, 232, 239
"Consider" (Auden), **Retro. Supp. I:** 5
Consider (Rossetti), **V:** 260
Consider Phlebas (Banks), **Supp. XI:** 1, 10, 11–12
Consider the Lilies (Smith, I. C.), **Supp. IX:** 209–210
Considerations Touching the Likeliest Means to Remove Hirelings out of the Church (Milton), **II:** 176
"Considering the Snail" (Gunn), **Supp. IV:** 262–263; **Retro. Supp. III:** 120–121
"Consolation" (Stallworthy), **Supp. X:** 292
Consolation of Philosophy (Boethius), **I:** 31; **Retro. Supp. II:** 36, 296–297
Consolations (Fuller), **Supp. VII:** 79, 80, 81
Consolidator, The (Defoe), **III:** 4, 13
Constance (Durrell), **Supp. I:** 119, 120; **Retro. Supp. III:** 86, 93, 94
"Constant" (Cornford), **VIII:** 107
Constant, Benjamin, **Supp. IV:** 125, 126, 136
Constant Couple, The; or, A Trip to the Jubilee (Farquhar), **II:** 352, 356–357, 364
Constant Gardener, The (le Carré), **Retro. Supp. III:** 227, 228
Constant Wife, The (Maugham), **VI:** 369
Constantine, David, **Supp. XV: 65–81**

"Constantine and Silvester" (Gower), **I:** 53–54
Constantine the Great (Lee), **II:** 305
"Constellation" (Kelman), **Supp. V:** 255
"Constellation, The" (Vaughan), **II:** 186, 189
Constitutional (periodical), **V:** 19
Constitutional History of England, The (Hallam), **IV:** 283
Constructing Postmodernism (McHale), **Supp. IV:** 112
"Construction for I. K. Brunel" (Morgan, E.), **Supp. IX:** 158
Constructions (Frayn), **Supp. VII:** 51, 53, 58, 64
Contacts (Carey), **Supp. XII:** 51
"Contemplation" (Thompson), **V:** 442, 443
"Contemporaries" (Cornford), **VIII:** 105
Contemporaries of Shakespeare (Swinburne), **V:** 333
Contemporary Authors Autobiography Series (ed. Sarkissian), **Supp. XI:** 243, 244, 245, 249, 250, 251, 252
"Contemporary Film of Lancasters in Action, A" (Ewart), **Supp. VII:** 44
"Contemporary Sagas", *See Samtíðarsögur*
Continent (Crace), **Supp. XIV:** 18, 19, 20–23
Continual Dew (Betjeman), **VII:** 365
Continuation of the Complete History, A (Smollett), **III:** 148, 149, 158
Continuous: 50 Sonnets from "The School of Elegance" (Harrison), **Supp. V:** 150
Contractor, The (Storey), **Supp. I:** 408, 416–417, 418
Contrarini Fleming (Disraeli), **IV:** xix, 292–293, 294, 296–297, 299, 308
Contrary Experience, The (Read), **VI:** 416
"Contrast Between Two Executed Lords, The" (Byrom), **Supp. XVI:** 80
"Contrasts" (Smith, I. C.), **Supp. IX:** 216
Contre–Machiavel (Gentillet), **I:** 283
"Controversial Tree of Time, The" (Brathwaite), **Supp. XII:** 43
Conundrum (Morris, J.), **Supp. X:** 171–174, 179, 184
"Convenience" (Murphy), **Supp. V:** 328
"Convent Threshold, The" (Rossetti), **Retro. Supp. III:** 256–257
"Convergence of the Twain, The" (Hardy), **II:** 69; **VI:** 16; **Retro. Supp. I:** 119–120
"Conversation of prayer, The" (Thomas), **Supp. I:** 178
"Conversation, The" (Gunn), **Supp. IV:** 272; **Supp. IV:** 273
"Conversation with a Cupboard Man" (McEwan), **Supp. IV:** 392
"Conversation with Calliope" (Hope), **Supp. VII:** 162–163
Conversation with My Younger Self (Plomer), **Supp. XI:** 223
Conversations at Curlow Creek, The (Malouf), **Supp. XII:** 229–230
Conversations in Ebury Street (Moore), **V:** 129, 153; **VI:** 89, 98, 99

Conversations of James Northcote, Esq., R. A. (Hazlitt), **IV:** 134, 140
"Conversations with Goethe" (Lowry), **Supp. III:** 286
ConVERSations with Nathaniel Mackey (Brathwaite), **Supp. XII:** 46
"inline"Conversion" (Hulme), **Supp. VI:** 136
"Conversion" (Smith, I. C.), **Supp. IX:** 221
"Conversions" (Burnside), **Supp. XIII:** 21
"Convert, The" (Hart), **Supp. XI:** 123, 124
"Convict and the Fiddler, The" (Hardy), **Retro. Supp. I:** 121
Convivio (Dante), **I:** 27
Cook, D., **III:** 322
Cook, Eliza, **IV:** 259, 320
Cook, J. D., **V:** 279
Cooke, W., **III:** 184n
"Cool Web, The" (Graves), **VII:** 266
"Coole Park" (Yeats), **VI:** 212; **Retro. Supp. I:** 336
"Coole Park and Ballylee" (Yeats), **VI:** 215; **Retro. Supp. I:** 336
Cooper, Lettice Ulpha, **V:** x, xxvii, 397, 398
Cooper, William, **VII:** xxi, xxxvii
"Co-ordination" (Forster), **VI:** 399
"Coorie in the Corner" (Soutar), **Supp. XVI:** 245–246, 249–250
Coover, Robert, **Supp. IV:** 116
Cope, Wendy, **VIII: 67–84**
Copeland, T. W., **III:** 245n, 250
Copenhagen (Frayn), **Supp. VII:** 63–64
Coppard, A. E., **VIII: 85–99**
"Coppersmith" (Murphy), **Supp. V:** 325
Copy of a Letter Written to . . . Parliament, A (Suckling), **II:** 238
"Copy of Verses" (Byrom), **Supp. XVI:** 71–72, 73
Coral Island, The (Ballantyne), **Supp. I:** 68; **Retro. Supp. I:** 96
Corbett, Sir Julian, **I:** 146
Cordelia Gray novels (James) **Supp. IV:** 335–337
"Corinna's Going a–Maying" (Herrick), **II:** 109–110
"Coriolan" (Eliot), **VII:** 152–153, 158
Coriolanus (Shakespeare), **I:** 318; **II:** 70; **Retro. Supp. III:** 276
Coriolanus (Thomson), **Supp. III:** 411, 423
Corke, Helen, **VII:** 93
Corker's Freedom (Berger), **Supp. IV:** 79, 84, 85
Corkery, Daniel, **Supp. V:** 37, 41
"Cork's Gold Vessel" (Delanty), **Supp. XIV:** 67
"Cornac and His Wife, The" (Lewis), **VII:** 77, 78
Corneille, Pierre, **II:** 261, 270, 271
Cornelia (Kyd), **I:** 162, 220
Cornélie (Garaier), **I:** 220
Cornelius: A Business Affair in Three Transactions (Priestley), **VII:** 224
Corner That Held Them, The (Warner), **Supp. VII:** 376, 377–378

"Corner of the Eye, The" (Longley), **VIII:** 169
"Cornet Love" (McGuckian), **Supp. V:** 291
"Cornet Player Who Betrayed Ireland, The" (O'Connor), **Supp. XIV:** 214
Cornford, Frances, **VIII: 101–115**
Cornford, John, **Supp. XIII: 83–97**
Cornhill (periodical), **V:** xxii, 1, 20, 279; **VI:** 31
Cornhill Magazine, **Retro. Supp. III:** 100, 110
"Cornish April" (Cornford), **VIII:** 106
"Cornish Heroic Song for Valda Trevlyn" (MacDiarmid), **Supp. XII:** 214
Corno di Bassetto, pseud. of George Bernard Shaw
Cornwall, Barry, **IV:** 311
Cornwall, David John Moore, *see* le Carré, John
Cornwallis, Sir William, **III:** 39–40
Coronation Everest (Morris, J.), **Supp. X:** 175, 179
"Coronet, The" (Marvell), **II:** 113, 211, 216
Coronet for His Mistress Philosophy, A (Chapman), **I:** 234
"Corporal, The" (Gunn), **Retro. Supp. III:** 123
"Corposant" (Redgrove), **Supp. VI:** 228
"Corpse and the Flea, The" (Powys), **VIII:** 255
"Corregidor" (Nicholson), **Supp. VI:** 214
Correspondence (Flaubert), **V:** 353
Correspondence (Swift), **III:** 24
Correspondence of James Boswell and John Johnston . . . (ed. Walker), **III:** 249
Correspondence . . . of James Boswell Relating to the "Life of Johnson,"The (ed. Waingrow), **III:** 249
Correspondence of James Boswell with . . . the Club, The (ed. Fifer), **III:** 249
Correspondences (Stevenson), **Supp. VI:** 254, 256, **257–260**, 261
Corrida at San Feliu, The (Scott), **Supp. I:** 259, 263, 266
"Corridor, The" (Sisson), **Supp. XI:** 258
Corridors of Power (Snow), **VII:** xxvi, 324, 330–331
Corrigan (Blackwood), **Supp. IX:** 7–8, 13–14, 16
"Corruption" (Vaughan), **II:** 185, 186, 189
Corsair, The (Byron), **IV:** xvii, 172, 173, 175, 192; *see also* Turkish tales
Corson, James C., **IV:** 27, 38–40
"Corymbus for Autumn" (Thompson), **V:** 442
"Cosmologist" (Dunn), **Supp. X:** 70
Cosmopolitans (Maugham), **VI:** 370
"Cosmos" (Soutar), **Supp. XVI:** 253
"Cost of Life" (Motion), **Supp. VII:** 265, 266
"Costa Pool Bums" (Warner), **Supp. XI:** 294
"Cottage at Chigasaki, The" (Blunden), **Supp. XI:** 47
"Cottage Hospital, The" (Betjeman), **VII:** 375

Cotter's England (Stead), **Supp. IV:** 473–476
"Cotter's Saturday Night, The" (Burns), **III:** 311, 313, 315, 318
Cottle, Joseph, **IV:** 44, 45, 52, 56, 59
Cotton, Charles, **II:** 131 134, 137
Coué, Emile, **VI:** 264
"Could Be" (Thomas), **Supp. XII:** 290
"Council of the Seven Deadly Sins, The" (Nicholson), **Supp. VI:** 214–215
Count Belisarius (Graves), **VII:** xviii, 258
Count Julian (Landor), **IV:** 89, 96, 100
Count Karlstein (Pullman), **Supp. XIII:** 149–150
Count Robert of Paris (Scott), **IV:** 39
"Countdown" (Ayckbourn), **Supp. V:** 2, 4, 11
Counter–Attack (Sassoon), **VI:** 430, 431
"Counter Attack" (Stallworthy), **Supp. X:** 298
Counterblast (McLuhan), **VII:** 71n
Counterclock World (Dick), **Supp. IV:** 41
Counterparts (Fuller), **Supp. VII:** 72, 74
Counterpoint (Thomas), **Supp. XII:** 290, 291
"Counterpoint in Herbert" (Hayes), **Retro. Supp. II:** 181
Countess Cathleen, The (Yeats), **VI:** 87; **Retro. Supp. I:** 326
Countess Cathleen and Various Legends and Lyrics, The (Yeats), **VI:** 211, 309
Countess of Pembroke, **I:** 161, 163–169, 218
Countess of Pembroke's Arcadia, The (Sidney), *see Arcadia*
"Countess of Pembroke's Dream" (Hope), **Supp. VII:** 158
"Country Bedroom, The" (Cornford), **VIII:** 105
"Country Bedroom" (MacCaig), **Supp. VI:** 187
Country Calendar and Other Writings, A (Thompson), **Supp. XV:** 277
"Country Child Taking Notes, A" (Thompson), **Supp. XV:** 290
Country Comets (Day Lewis), **Supp. III:** 117, 120–121
"Country Dance" (Conn), **Supp. XIII:** 78
"Country Dance" (MacCaig), **Supp. VI:** 192
"Country for Old Men, A" (Smith, I. C.), **Supp. IX:** 224
Country Girls, The (O'Brien), **Supp. V:** 333–336
Country Girls Trilogy and Epilogue, The (O'Brien), **Supp. V:** 338
"Country House" (MacCaig), **Supp. VI:** 185–186, 194
Country House, The (Galsworthy), **VI:** 271, 272, 273, 275, 278, 282
Country House, The (Vanbrugh), **II:** 325, 333, 336
"Country Kitchen" (Dunn), **Supp. X:** 78
Country Life, (Ackroyd), **Supp. VI:** 3
"Country Measures" (Warner), **Supp. VII:** 371
"Country Music" (Fallon), **Supp. XII:** 110
"Country of the Blind, The" (Wells), **VI:** 234

Country of the Blind, The, and Other Stories (Wells), **VI:** 228, 244
"Country Sunday" (Coppard), **VIII:** 88
"Country Walk, A" (Kinsella), **Supp. V:** 262
Country-Wife, The (Wycherley), **I:** 243; **II:** 307, 308, **314–318**, 321, 360
"Coup: A Story, A" (Chatwin), **Supp. IV:** 167
"Coup de Poing" (Crawford), **Supp. XI:** 68–69
"Courage" (Gunn), **Retro. Supp. III:** 124
"Courage Means Running" (Empson), **Supp. II:** 191
Courier (periodical), **IV:** 50
Course of Lectures on the English Law, A: Delivered at the University of Oxford 1767–1773 (Johnson), **Retro. Supp. I:** 143
Court and the Castle, The (West), **Supp. III:** 438
"Court of Cupid, The" (Spenser), **I:** 123
"Court Revolt, The" (Gunn), **Supp. IV:** 257; **Retro. Supp. III:** 118
Courte of Venus, The (Wyatt), **I:** 97
"Courter, The" (Rushdie), **Supp. IV:** 438
"Courtesies of the Interregnum" (Gunn), **Supp. IV:** 277; **Retro. Supp. III:** 127
"Courtship of Ossian, The" (Macpherson), **VIII:** 186
Courtyards in Delft (Mahon), **Supp. VI:** 173
"Courtyards in Delft" (Mahon), **Supp. VI:** 174
Cousin Henry (Trollope), **V:** 102
"Cousin Kate" (Rossetti), **Retro. Supp. III:** 251
"Cousin Maria" (James), **VI:** 69
Cousin Phillis (Gaskell), **V:** 1, 2, 4, 8, 11, 15
Cousin Rosamund: A Saga of the Century (West), **Supp. III:** 443
Cousine Bette (Balzac), **V:** xx, 17
"Cousins, The" (Burne–Jones), **VI:** 167, 169
Cousins: A Memoir (Fugard), **Supp. XV:** 101
Covent Garden Drolery, The (Behn), **Supp. III:** 36
Covent Garden Journal, The (periodical), **III:** 103–104; **Retro. Supp. I:** 81
Covent Garden Tragedy, The (Fielding), **III:** 97, 105
"Coventry" (Davies), **Supp. XIV:** 39–40
Cover Her Face (James), **Supp. II:** 127; **Supp. IV:** 321–323
Coverdale, Myles, **I:** 377
"Covering End" (James), **VI:** 52, 69
Coward, Noël, **Supp. II:** 139–158
Cowasjee, S., **VII:** 4
Cowell, Edward, **IV:** 342–346
Cowley, Abraham, **II:** 123, 179, **194–200**, **202**, 236, 256, 259, 275, 347; **III:** 40, 118; **Retro. Supp. I:** 144
Cowley, Hannah, **Supp. XVI: 109–125**
Cowper, William, **II:** 119n, 196, 240; **III:** 173, **207–220**, 282; **IV:** xiv–xvi, 93, 184, 281; **Retro. Supp. III:** 35–52
"Cowper's Grave" (Browning), **IV:** 312, 313

"Cows on Killing Day, The" (Murray), **Supp. VII:** 282
"Cowyard Gates" (Murray), **Supp. VII:** 276
Cox, Charles Brian, **VI:** xi, xxxiii
"Cox's Diary" (Thackeray), *see* "Barber Cox and the Cutting of His Comb"
Coxcomb, The (Beaumont, Fletcher, Massinger), **II:** 66
Coxhead, Elizabeth, **VI:** xiv, xxxiii
"Coxon Fund, The" (James), **VI:** 69
Coyle, William, pseud. of Thomas Keneally
C. P. Snow (Karl), **VII:** 341
Crab Apple Jelly (O'Connor), **Supp. XIV:** 219
"Crab Feast, The" (Malouf), **Supp. XII:** 220
Crabbe, George, **III: 272–287**, 338; **IV:** xv, xvii, 103, 326; **V:** 6; **VI:** 378
Crace, Jim, **Supp. XIV: 17–33**
Crack, The (Tennant), *see* *Time of the Crack, The*
Cracking India (Sidhwa), **Supp. V:** 62
"Craggy Country" (Conn), **Supp. XIII:** 76–77
Craig, Hardin, **I:** 187, 326
Craig, W. J., **I:** 326
Craigie, Mrs., **VI:** 87
"Craigie Hill" (Conn), **Supp. XIII:** 71, 72
"Craigvara House" (Mahon), **Supp. VI:** 174
"Cramond Island" (Jamie), **Supp. XIV:** 130
Crampton Hodnet (Pym), **Supp. II: 364–366**, 370
Crane, Stephen, **VI:** 320; **Supp. IV:** 116
Cranford (Gaskell), **V:** xxi, 1–4, 8–10, 11, 14, 15; **Retro. Supp. III:** 99, 102, 104–105, 106, 112
Crank, **Supp. XIII:** 187
"Crankshaft" (Murray), **Supp. VII:** 283
"Crapy Cornelia" (James), **VI:** 69
Crash (Ballard), **Supp. V:** 19, 27, 28, 33–34
Crashaw, Richard, **II:** 90–91, 113, 122, 123, 126, **179–184, 200–201;** **V:** 325
Crave (Kane), **VIII:** 148, 150–151, 159–160
"Craven Arms" (Coppard), **VIII:** 90
Craven House (Hamilton), **Supp. XVI:** 179–181
"Craving for Spring" (Lawrence), **VII:** 118
Crawford, Robert, **Supp. XI: 67–84**
"Crawford's Consistency" (James), **VI:** 69
"Creation" (Carpenter), **Supp. XIII:** 46–47
Creative Element, The (Spender), **Supp. II:** 491
Creative Uses of Homosexuality in E. M. Forster, Ronald Firbank, and L. P. Hartley, The (Mistry), **Supp. X:** 120–121
"Creative Writer's Suicide, The" (Thomas), **Supp. XII:** 285
"Creative Writing: Can It/Should It Be Taught?" (Lodge), **Supp. IV:** 381

"Creator in Vienna" (Jennings), **Supp. V:** 218
Creators of Wonderland (Mespoulet), **V:** 266
Creatures Tamed by Cruelty (Butlin), **Supp. XVI:** 52, 53–55
Crediting Poetry (Heaney), **Retro. Supp. I:** 125
"Credits" (Stallworthy), **Supp. X:** 298
Creed or Chaos? and Other Essays in Popular Theology (Sayers), **Supp. III:** 336
Creighton, Joan, **Supp. IV:** 244
"Creosote" (Adcock), **Supp. XII:** 12
"Cricket Match, 1908" (Pitter), **Supp. XIII:** 145
Cripple of Inishmaan, The (McDonagh), **Supp. XII:** 233, 240–241, 242–243, 245
Cricket Country (Blunden), **Supp. XI:** 37
Cricket on the Hearth, The (Dickens), **V:** 71
Crime in Kensington (Caudwell), **Supp. IX:** 35
Crime of the Century, The (Amis), **Supp. II:** 12
Crime Omnibus (Fuller), **Supp. VII:** 70
Crime on Goat Island (Reed), **Supp. XV:** 253
Crime Times Three (James), **Supp. IV:** 323, 324, 325
Crimes (Churchill), **Supp. IV:** 181
"Criminal Ballad" (Hughes), **Supp. I:** 354
Criminal Case, A (Swinburne), **V:** 333
"Criminal Mastermind Is Confined, The" (Davies), **Supp. XIV:** 36
Criminal Minded (Rankin), **Supp. X:** 257
Crimson in the Tricolour, The (O'Casey), **VII:** 12
"Crinoline" (Thackeray), **V:** 22
"Crippled Aunt" (Conn), **Supp. XIII:** 73
"Crippled Bloom" (Coppard), **VIII:** 90
Crisis, The, a Sermon (Fielding), **III:** 105
Crisis Examined, The (Disraeli), **IV:** 308
Crisis in Physics, The (Caudwell), **Supp. IX:** 33, 43, 45–46
Crist, **Retro. Supp. II:** 303
Criterion (periodical), **VI:** 248; **VII:** xv 143, 165
Critic (periodical), **V:** 134
Critic, The (Sheridan), **III:** 253, **263–266**, 270
"Critic, The" (Wilde), **Retro. Supp. II:** 367
"Critic as Artist, The" (Wilde), **V:** 407, 408, 409
Critical and Historical Essays (Macaulay), **IV:** xx, 272, 277, **278–282**, 291
Critical Bibliography of Katherine Mansfield, The (Mantz), **VII:** 182
Critical Essays (Orwell), **VII:** 282
Critical Essays of the Seventeenth Century (Spingarn), **II:** 256n
Critical Essays on George Eliot (Hardy), **V:** 201
Critical Essays on the Poetry of Tennyson (ed. Killham), **IV:** 323n, 338, 339
Critical Observations on the Sixth Book of the Aeneid (Gibbon), **III:** 233

Critical Review (periodical), **III:** 147–148, 149, 179, 188
Critical Strictures on the New Tragedy of Elvira . . . (Boswell, Dempster, Erskine), **III:** 246
Critical Studies of the Works of Charles Dickens (Gissing), **V:** 437
"Criticism of Life, A" (Raine), **Supp. XIII:** 163
Criticism on Art: And Sketches of the Picture Galleries of England (Hazlitt), **IV:** 140
Crito (Plato), **Supp. IV:** 13
Croker, J. W., **IV:** 280
Crome Yellow (Huxley), **VII:** 197, 200
Cromwell (Carlyle), see *Oliver Cromwell's Letters and Speeches*
Cromwell (Storey), **Supp. I:** 418
Cromwell's Army (Firth), **II:** 241
Cronica tripertita (Gower), **I:** 50
Crook, Arthur, **Supp. IV:** 25
Crooked House (Christie), **Supp. II:** 125
Croquet Castles (Carroll), **V:** 274
Cross, John Walter, **V:** 13, 198, 200
Cross, Wilbur L, **III:** 125, 126, 135
Cross Channel (Barnes), **Supp. IV:** 65, 67, 75–76
"Crossing, The" (Kay), **Supp. XIII:** 101
"Crossing alone the nighted ferry" (Housman), **VI:** 161
"Crossing the Bar" (Tennyson), **Retro. Supp. III:** 317, 329
Crossing the Border: Essays on Scottish Literature (Morgan, E.), **Supp. IX:** 162
"Crossing the Loch" (Jamie), **Supp. XIV:** 140–141
"Crossing the Peak" (Scupham), **Supp. XIII:** 230
Crossing the River (Phillips), **Supp. V:** 380, 386, 390–391
Crotchet Castle (Peacock), **IV:** xix, 165–166, 169, 170
Crow (Hughes), **Supp. I:** 350–354, 363; **Retro. Supp. II:** 206–208
"Crow Alights" (Hughes), **Supp. I:** 352
"Crow Blacker than Ever" (Hughes), **Supp. I:** 353
"Crow Hears Fate Knock on the Door" (Hughes), **Supp. I:** 350
"Crow on the Beach" (Hughes), **Supp. I:** 352; **Retro. Supp. II:** 207
Crow Road, The (Banks), **Supp. XI:** 5
"Crow Tyrannosaurus" (Hughes), **Supp. I:** 352
"Crowdieknowe" (MacDiarmid), **Supp. XII:** 205
"Crown and Country" (Kay), **Supp. XIII:** 101
"Crow's Account of the Battle" (Hughes), **Supp. I:** 353
"Crow's Last Stand" (Hughes), **Retro. Supp. II:** 207–208
"Crow's Song of Himself" (Hughes), **Supp. I:** 353
"Crowd of Birds and Children, The" (Graham), **Supp. VII:** 110
Crowley, Aleister, **VI:** 374; **Supp. II:** 204
Crowley, Robert, **I:** 1, 3

Crown of All Homer's Works, The (Chapman), **I:** 236
Crown of Life, The (Gissing), **V:** 437
Crown of the Year (Fry), **Supp. III:** 195
Crown of Wild Olive, The (Ruskin), **V:** 184
"Crowning of Offa, The" (Hill), **Supp. V:** 195
Crowning Privilege, The (Graves), **VII:** 260, 268
"Crowson" (Nye), **Supp. X:** 201
"Croy. Ee. Gaw. Lonker. Pit." (Crawford), **Supp. XI:** 81
Cruel Sea, The (film, Ambler), **Supp. IV:** 3
"Cruelty and Love" (Lawrence), **VII:** 118
Cruelty of a Stepmother, The, **I:** 218
"Cruiskeen Lawn" (O'Nolan), **Supp. II:** 323, **329–333**, 336
Crusader Castles (Lawrence), **Supp. II:** 283, 284
Crux Ansata: An Indictment of the Roman Catholic Church (Wells), **VI:** 242, 244
"Cry Hope, Cry Fury!" (Ballard), **Supp. V:** 26
"Cry of the Children, The" (Browning), **IV:** xx 313
"Cry of the Human, The" (Browning), **IV:** 313
Cry of the Owl, The (Highsmith), **Supp. V:** 173
Cry, The Beloved Country (Paton), **Supp. II:** 341, 342, 343, 344, **345–350**, 351, 354
Cry, the Peacock (Desai), **Supp. V:** 54, 58–59, 75
"Cryptics, The" (Ewart), **Supp. VII:** 39
Crystal and Fox (Friel), **Supp. V:** 118–119
Crystal World, The (Ballard), **Supp. V:** 24, 25–26, 34
"Crystals Like Blood" (MacDiarmid), **Supp. XII:** 215
C. S. Lewis (Wilson), **Supp. VI:** 304, **305**
Cuala Press, **VI:** 221
"Cub" (Reading), **VIII:** 268
Cub, at Newmarket, The (Boswell), **III:** 247
Cuckold in Conceit, The (Vanbrugh), **II:** 337
"Cuckoo, The" (Thomas), **Supp. III:** 399–400
Cuckoo in the Nest, The (Oliphant), **Supp. X:** 220
Cuirassiers of the Frontier, The (Graves), **VII:** 267
"Culture" (Dutton), **Supp. XII:** 94
Culture and Anarchy (Arnold), **III:** 23; **V:** 203, 206, 213, 215, 216
Culture and Society (Williams), **Supp. IV:** 380
Cumberland, George, **IV:** 47
Cumberland, Richard, **II:** 363; **III:** 257
Cumberland and Westmoreland (Nicholson), **Supp. VI:** 223
Cunningham, William, **VI:** 385
Cup, The (Tennyson), **Retro. Supp. III:** 329

"Cup Too Low, A" (Ewart), **Supp. VII:** 39–40
"Cupid and Psyche" (tr. Pater), **V:** 351
"Cupid; or, The Atom" (Bacon), **I:** 267
Cupid's Revenge (Beaumont and Fletcher), **II:** 46, 65
Curate in Charge, The (Oliphant), **Supp. X:** 219–220
"Curate's Friend, The" (Forster), **VI:** 399
"Curate's Walk; The," (Thackeray), **V:** 25
"Cure, The" (Delanty), **Supp. XIV:** 70
Cure at Troy, The (Heaney), **Retro. Supp. I:** 131
Cure for a Cuckold, A (Rowley and Webster), **II:** 69, 83, 85
Curiosissima Curatoria (Carroll), **V:** 274
Curious Fragments (Lamb), **IV:** 79
"Curious if True" (Gaskell), **V:** 15
Curious Relations (ed. Plomer), **Supp. XI:** 221
"Curiosity" (Reid), **Supp. VII:** 330
"Curiosity and Scandal" (Jewsbury), **Supp. XIV:** 149
Curlew River: A Parable for Church Performance (Plomer), **Supp. XI:** 222
"Curse, The" (Healy), **Supp. IX:** 103–104
Curse of Eve, The (Steel), **Supp. XII:** 276
Curse of Kehama, The (Southey), **IV:** 65, 66, 71, 217
Curse of Minerva, The (Byron), **IV:** 192
Cursory Strictures on the Charge Delivered by Lord Chief Justice Eyre to the Grand Jury (Godwin), **Supp. XV:** 121
Curtain (Christie), **Supp. II:** 124, 125, 134
Curtis, Anthony, **VI:** xiii, xxxiii, 372
Curtis, L. P., **III:** 124*n*, 127*n*
Curtmantle (Fry), **Supp. III:** 195, **206–207**, 208
"Custom" (Carpenter), **Supp. XIII:** 41
Custom of the Country, The (Fletcher [and Massinger]), **II:** 66, 340
"Custom-House, The" (Hawthorne), **Supp. IV:** 116
"Customs" (Crawford), **Supp. XI:** 74
Cut by the County (Braddon), **VIII:** 49
"Cut Grass" (Larkin), **Supp. I:** 285
Cutlasses & Earrings: Feminist Poetry (ed. Wandor and Roberts), **Supp. XV:** 262
Cut-Rate Kingdom, The (Keneally), **Supp. IV:** 346
"Cutting Trail" (Dutton), **Supp. XII:** 93–94
Cyclopean Mistress, The (Redgrove), **Supp. VI:** 231
"Cygnet, The" (Pitter), **Supp. XIII:** 143
"Cygnus A." (Thomas), **Supp. IV:** 490, 491
Cymbeline (Shakespeare), **I:** 322; **Retro. Supp. III:** 270, 276, 277, 279, 281
Cymbeline Refinished (Shaw), **VI:** 129
"Cynddylan on a Tractor" (Thomas), **Supp. XII:** 283
"Cynic at Kilmainham Jail, A" (Boland), **Supp. V:** 36
Cynthia's Revels (Jonson), **I:** 346; **Retro. Supp. I:** 158, 160

"Cypress and Cedar" (Harrison), **Supp. V:** 161
Cyrano de Bergerac, **III:** 24
Cyrano de Bergerac (tr.. Fry), **Supp. III:** 195
Cyril Connolly: Journal and Memoirs (ed. Pryce–Jones), **Supp. III:** 96, 97, 112
"Cyril Tourneur" (Swinburne), **V:** 332

D. G. Rossetti: A Critical Essay (Ford), **VI:** 332
"D. G. Rossetti as a Translator" (Doughty), **V:** 246
D. H. Lawrence: A Calendar of His Works (Sugar), **VII:** 104, 115, 123
D. H. Lawrence: Novelist (Leavis), **VII:** 101, 234–235, 252–253
Da Silva da Silva's Cultivated Wilderness (Harris), **Supp. V:** 139, 140
Daborne, Robert, **II:** 37, 45
Dad's Tale (Ayckbourn), **Supp. V:** 2
"Daedalus" (Reid), **Supp. VII:** 331
"Daedalus; or, The Mechanic" (Bacon), **I:** 267
Daemon of the World, The (Shelley), **IV:** 209
Daffodil Murderer, The (Sassoon), **VI:** 429
"Daffodil Time" (Brown), **Supp. VI:** 72
Dahl, Roald, **Supp. IV: 201–227,** 449
Daiches, David, **V:** ix
Daily Graphic (periodical), **VI:** 350
Daily Life of the Aztecs (tr. O'Brian), **Supp. XII:** 252
Daily Mail, **Supp. XIII:** 265
Daily Mirror, **Supp. XIII:** 265; **Supp. XV:** 227, 228
Daily News (periodical), **VI:** 335
Daily Worker (periodical), **VI:** 242
Daisy Miller (James), **VI: 31–32,** 69
Dale, Colin (pseud., Lawrence), **Supp. II:** 295
Dali, Salvador, **Supp. IV:** 424
Dalinda; or, The Double Marriage (Haywood), **Supp. XII:** 144
Dalkey Archive, The (O'Nolan), **Supp. II:** 322, **337–338**
Dallas, Eneas Sweetland, **V:** 207
"Dalziel's Ghost" (Hill, R.), **Supp. IX:** 114
Damage (film, Hare), **Supp. IV:** 282, 292
Damage (play, Hare), **Supp. IV:** 282, 292
"Damnation of Byron, The" (Hope), **Supp. VII:** 159
Damon and Delia (Godwin), **Supp. XV:** 118–119
Dampier, William, **III:** 7, 24
"Danac" (Galsworthy), *see Country House, The*
Danae (Rembrandt), **Supp. IV:** 89
Dan Leno and the Limehouse Golem (Ackroyd), **Supp. VI:** 10–13
Danby, J. F., **II:** 46, 53, 64
"Dance, The" (Kinsella), **Supp. V:** 271
"Dance, The" (Larkin), **Retro. Supp. III:** 208, 211
Dance of Death, The, **I:** 15
"Dance of Death, The" (Beer), **Supp. XIV:** 5

Dance of Death, The (Strindberg), **Supp. I:** 57
"Dance the Putrefact" (Redgrove), **Supp. VI:** 234
Dance to the Music of Time, A (Powell), **VII:** xxi, 343, **347–353**; **Supp. II:** 4
Dancing Hippo, The (Motion), **Supp. VII:** 257
Dancing Mad (Davies), **Supp. XI:** 92
"Dancing Shoes" (Scupham), **Supp. XIII:** 226
Dancourt, Carton, **II:** 325, 336
"Dandies and Dandies" (Beerbohm), **Supp. II:** 46
Dangerous Corner (Priestley), **VII:** 223
Dangerous Love (Okri), **Supp. V:** 349, 359, 360
Dangerous Play: Poems 1974–1984 (Motion), **Supp. VII:** 251, 254, 255, 256–257, 264
Daniel, **Retro. Supp. II:** 301
Daniel, Samuel, **I:** 162
Daniel Deronda (Eliot), **V:** xxiv, 190, 197–198, 200; **Retro. Supp. II:** 115–116
Daniel Martin (Fowles), **Supp. I:** 291, 292, 293, **304–308,** 310
D'Annunzio, Gabriele, **V:** 310
"Danny Deever" (Kipling), **VI:** 203; **Retro. Supp. III:** 188
Danny, the Champion of the World (Dahl), **Supp. IV:** 214, 223
"Dans un Omnibus de Londre" (Fuller), **Supp. VII:** 80
Dante Alighieri, **II:** 75, 148; **III:** 306; **IV:** 93, 187; **Supp. IV:** 439, 493; **Retro. Supp. I:** 123–124
Dante and His Circle (Rossetti), **V:** 245
"Dante and the Lobster" (Beckett), **Retro. Supp. I:** 19
"Dante at Verona" (Rossetti), **V:** 239, 240
"Dante ... Bruno. Vico ... Joyce" (Beckett), **Retro. Supp. I:** 17
Dante's Drum Kit (Dunn), **Supp. X:** 78–80
"Dantesque and Platonic Ideals of Love, The" (Symonds), **Supp. XIV:** 262
"Dantis Tenebrae" (Rossetti), **V:** 243
Danvers, Charles, **IV:** 60
Daphnaida (Spenser), **I:** 124
"Daphne" (Sitwell), **VII:** 133
"'Daphne with Her Thighs in Bark' [Ezra Pound]" (Boland), **Supp. V:** 39
"Daphnis, an Elegiac Eclogue" (Vaughan), **II:** 185
"Daphnis and Chloe" (Marvell), **II:** 209, 211, 212
"Daphnis and Chloe" (tr. Moore), **VI:** 89
D'Arcy, Margaretta, **Supp. II:** 21, 29, 30, 31, 32–38, 39, 40–41
"Darcy in the Land of Youth" (O'Connor), **Supp. XIV:** 226
Darcy's Utopia (Weldon), **Supp. IV:** 528–529, 531
Dark–Adapted Eye, A (Rendell), **Supp. IX:** 201–203
"Dark Angel, The," (Johnson), **VI:** 211
Dark As the Grave Wherein My Friend Is Laid (Lowry), **Supp. III:** 274–275, 279, 280, **283–284**

"Dark Crossroads, The" (Dunn), **Supp. X:** 77
"Dark Dialogues, The" (Graham), **Supp. VII:** 114
Dark Flower, The (Galsworthy), **VI:** 274
Dark Frontier, The (Ambler), **Supp. IV:** 1, 3, 5–7
Dark Is Light Enough, The (Fry), **Supp. III:** 195, 203–204, 207
Dark Labyrinth, The (Durrell), **Retro. Supp. III:** 84
"Dark Lady, The" (Russell), **VIII:** 290
Dark Lady of the Sonnets, The (Shaw), **VI:** 115, 129
Dark Matter (Kerr), **Supp. XII:** 197–198
Dark Night's Work, A (Gaskell), **V:** 15
Dark Places of the Heart (Stead), *see Cotter's England*
"Dark Rapture" (Russell), **VIII:** 290
"Dark Rosaleen" (Mangan), **Supp. XIII:** 118, 128
Dark Side of the Moon, The (anon.), **Supp. IV:** 100
Dark Sisters, The (Kavan), **Supp. VII:** 205, 207
Dark Tide, The (Brittain), **Supp. X:** 37, 41
"Dark Times" (Harrison), **Supp. V:** 156–157
Dark Tower, The (MacNeice), **VII:** 407, 408
Dark Voices Ring (Mda), **Supp. XV:** 197
Darker Ends (Nye), **Supp. X:** 193, 200–202, 204
"Darkling Thrush, The" (Hardy), **VI:** 16; **Retro. Supp. I:** 119
Dark–Eyed Lady (Coppard), **VIII:** 89
Darkness at Noon (Koestler), **V:** 49; **Supp. I:** 22, 24, 27, 28, 29–30, 32, 33; **Supp. IV:** 74
Darkness Visible (Golding), **Supp. I: 83–86**; **Retro. Supp. I:** 101–102
Darling, You Shouldn't Have Gone to So Much Trouble (Blackwood), **Supp. IX:** 15
"Dartside" (Kingsley), **Supp. XVI:** 205
Darwin, Charles, **Supp. II:** 98, 100, 105–107, 119; **Supp. IV:** 6, 11, 460; **Supp. VII: 17–31**
Darwin, Erasmus, **Supp. II:** 106, 107; **Supp. III:** 360
Darwin, Erasmus, **Supp. XVI: 127–144**
"Darwin Among the Machines" (Butler), **Supp. II:** 98, 99
Darwin and Butler: Two Versions of Evolution (Willey), **Supp. II:** 103
"Darwin and Divinity" (Stephen), **V:** 284
Dashpers (Thompson), **Supp. XV:** 289, 290
Daughter of Jerusalem (Maitland), **Supp. XI:** 163, 165–166
Daughter of the East (Bhutto), **Supp. IV:** 455
"Daughter of the House" (Dutton), **Supp. XII:** 87
Daughter-in-Law, The (Lawrence), **VII:** 119, 121
Daughters and Sons (Compton–Burnett), **VII:** 60, 63, 64–65

Daughters of the House (Roberts), **Supp. XV:** 259, 261, 268, 269–270, 271, 273
"Daughters of the Late Colonel, The" (Mansfield), **VII:** 175, 177, 178
"Daughters of the Vicar" (Lawrence), **VII:** 114
"Daughters of War" (Rosenberg), **VI:** 434
Davenant, Charles, **II:** 305
Davenant, Sir William, **I:** 327; **II:** 87, 185, 196, 259
Davenport, Arnold, **IV:** 227
David, Jacques–Louis, **Supp. IV:** 122
David and Bethsabe (Peele), **I:** 198, 206–207
"David Balfour" (Stevenson), *see Catriona*
David Copperfield (Dickens), **V:** xxi, 7, 41, 42, 44, 59–62, 63, 67, 71
David Lodge (Bergonzi), **Supp. IV:** 364
Davideis (Cowley), **II:** 195, 198, 202
Davidson, John, **V:** 318n
Davie, Donald, **VI:** 220; **Supp. IV:** 256; **Supp. VI: 105–118**
Davies, Peter Ho, **Supp. XIV: 35–48**
Davies, W. H., **Supp. III:** 398
Davies, William H., **Supp. XI: 85–103**
Davies (Constantine), **Supp. XV:** 66
Davis, Clyde Brion, **V:** 394
Davis, H., **III:** 15n, 35
Davy, Sir Humphry, **IV:** 200; **Supp. III:** 359–360
Dawkins, R. M., **VI:** 295, 303–304
"Dawn" (Brooke), **Supp. III:** 53
"Dawn" Cornford), **VIII:** 102, 103
Dawn (Haggard), **Supp. III:** 213, 222
"Dawn at St. Patrick" (Mahon), **Supp. VI:** 174
"Dawn on the Somme" (Nichols), **VI:** 419
Dawn Wind (Sutcliff), **Supp. XVI:** 262, 268, 270–271
"Dawnings of Genius" (Clare), **Supp. XI:** 49
Dawn's Left Hand (Richardson), **Supp. XIII:** 186–187, 190–191
Dawson, Christopher, **III:** 227
Dawson, W. J., **IV:** 289, 291
"Day Dream, A" (Brontë), **V:** 142
"Day is Düne" (Soutar), **Supp. XVI:** 251
Day Lewis, Cecil, **V:** 220, 234; **VI:** x, xxxiii, 454, **VII:** 382, 410; **Supp. III: 115–132**
Day of Creation, The (Ballard), **Supp. V:** 29
"Day of Days, At" (James), **VI:** 69
"Day of Forever, The" (Ballard), **Supp. V:** 26
"Day of the Lord, The" (Kingsley), **Supp. XVI:** 204
"Day of the Ox" (Brown), **Supp. VI:** 69
"Day of the Rabblement, The" (Joyce), **Retro. Supp. I:** 170
Day of the Scorpion, The (Scott), **Supp. I:** 260, 267
Day of the Triffids, The (Wyndham), **Supp. XIII:** 281, 283–290, 292
Day Out, A (Bennett), **VIII:** 26–27
"Day They Burned the Books, The" (Rhys), **Supp. II:** 401

"Day We Got Drunk on Cake, The" (Trevor), **Supp. IV:** 500
Day Will Come, The (Braddon), **VIII:** 49
Day Will Dawn, The (Rattigan), **Supp. VII:** 311
Daydreamer, The (McEwan), **Supp. IV:** 390, 406–407
Daylight Moon and Other Poems, The (Murray), **Supp. VII:** 270, 271, 279–280, 281
Daylight on Saturday (Priestley), **VII:** 212, 217–218
Days and Nights (Symons), **Supp. XIV:** 267, 271–272
Days with Walt Whitman, with Some Notes on His Life and Work (Carpenter), **Supp. XIII:** 36
Day's Work, The (Kipling), **VI:** 204
De arte graphica (tr. Dryden), **II:** 305
De arte poetica (tr. Elizabeth I), **Supp. XVI:** 158
De augmentis scientiarum (Bacon), **I:** 260–261, 264; *see also Advancement of Learning, The*
"De Auro Potabili" (Campion), **Supp. XVI:** 100–101
de Beer, E. S., **II:** 276n, 287
De Bello Germanico: A Fragment of Trench History (Blunden), **Supp. XI:** 35, 38–39
De Bernières, Louis, **Supp. XII: 65–80**
De casibus virorum illustrium (Boccaccio), **I:** 57, 214
De consolatione philosophiae (tr. Elizabeth I), **Supp. XVI:** 158
De curiositate (tr. Elizabeth I), **Supp. XVI:** 158
De doctrina christiana (Milton), **II:** 176
De genealogia deorum (Boccaccio), **I:** 266
"De Grey: A Romance" (James), **VI:** 25–26, 69
De Guiana Carmen Epicum (Chapman), **I:** 234
"'De Gustibus—'" (Browning), **IV:** 356–357
De inventione (Cicero), **I:** 38–39
"De Jure Belli ac Pacis" (Hill), **Supp. V:** 192
de la Mare, Walter, **III:** 340, 345; **V:** 268, 274; **VII:** xiii; **Supp. III:** 398, 406
de Man, Paul, **Supp. IV:** 114, 115
De Profundis (Wilde), **V:** 416–417, 418, 419; **Retro. Supp. II:** 371–372
"De Profundis, or the Spirit of Despair" (Soutar), **Supp. XVI:** 244
De Proprietatibus Rerum (tr. Trevisa), **Supp. IX:** 243, 247, 251–252
"De Pulverea Coniuratione" (Campion), **Supp. XVI:** 99–100
De Quincey, Thomas, **III:** 338; **IV:** ix, xi–xii, xv, xviii, xxii, 49, 51, 137, **141–156,** 260, 261, 278; **V:** 353
De Quincey Memorials (ed. Japp), **IV:** 144, 155
"De Quincey on 'The Knocking at the Gate'" (Carnall), **IV:** 156
De re publica (Cicero), **Retro. Supp. II:** 36

De Regimine Principum (tr. Trevisa), **Supp. IX** 252, 255
De rerum natura (tr. Evelyn), **II:** 275, 287
De sapientia veterum (Bacon), **I:** 235, 266–267, 272
de Selincourt, E., **IV:** 25
De tranquillitate animi (tr. Wyatt), **I:** 99
De tristitia Christi (More), **Supp. VII:** 245, 248
"De Wets Come to Kloof Grange, The" (Lessing), **Supp. I:** 240–241
Deacon Brodie (Stevenson), **V:** 396; **Retro. Supp. I:** 260
"Dead, The" (Brooke), **VI:** 420; **Supp. III:** 57–58, 59; **Retro. Supp. I:** 19, 172
"Dead, The" (Joyce), **VII:** xiv, 44–45; **Supp. II:** 88; **Supp. IV:** 395, 396; **Retro. Supp. III:** 170
Dead Air (Banks), **Supp. XI:** 4–5, 13
"Dead and Alive" (Gissing), **V:** 437
Dead Babies (Amis), **Supp. IV:** 26, 29–31
"Dead Bride, The" (Hill), **Supp. V:** 189
"Dead Cat, On a" (Caudwell), **Supp. IX:** 38
"Dead City, The" (Rossetti), **Retro. Supp. III:** 254
Dead End (Mda), **Supp. XV:** 197, 198, 204
Dead Kingdom, The (Montague), **Supp. XV:** 221–222
"Dead Love" (Swinburne), **V:** 325, 331, 332
Dead Man Leading (Pritchett), **Supp. III:** 311, 312, 313, 314
"Dead Man's Dump" (Rosenberg), **VI:** 432, 434
Dead Meat (Kerr), **Supp. XII:** 187, 193–194, 196
"Dead on Arrival" (Kinsella), **Supp. V:** 261
"Dead One, The" (Cornford), **VIII:** 106
"Dead Painter, The" (Cornford), **VIII:** 106
Dead School, The (McCabe), **Supp. IX:** 133–135, 137, 138–139
Dead Sea Poems, The (Armitage), **VIII:** 1, 8–11, 15
Dead Secret, The (Collins), **Supp. VI:** 92, 95
Dead Souls (Rankin), **Supp. X:** 245, 255
"Dead–Beat, The" (Owen), **VI:** 451, 452
Deadheads (Hill, R.), **Supp. IX:** 115
Deadlock (Richardson), **Supp. XIII:** 184–185
"Deadlock in Darwinism, The" (Butler), **Supp. II:** 108
"Deadwater" (Butlin), **Supp. XVI:** 56
Dealings with the Firm of Dombey and Son . . . (Dickens), *see Dombey and Son*
Dean, L. F., **I:** 269
"Dean Swift Watches Some Cows" (Ewart), **Supp. VII:** 40
Deane, Seamus, **Supp. IV:** 424
Dear Brutus (Barrie), **Supp. III:** 5, 6, 8, 9, **11–14,** 138

"Dear Bryan Wynter" (Graham), **Supp. VII:** 115

Dear Deceit, The (Brooke-Rose), **Supp. IV:** 98, 99, 102–103

"Dear Karl" (Smith), **Retro. Supp. III:** 307

Dear Shadows (Wain), **Supp. XVI:** 305

Dearest Emmie (Hardy), **VI:** 20

"Death" (Macpherson), **VIII:** 181

"Death and Doctor Hornbook" (Burns), **III:** 319

"Death and Dying Words of Poor Mailie, The" (Burns), **IV:** 314, 315

Death and the Princess (Cornford), **VIII:** 103–104

"Death and the Professor" (Kinsella), **Supp. V:** 260

"Death Bed" (Kinsella), **Supp. V:** 267

"Death by Water" (Eliot), **VII:** 144–145; **Retro. Supp. II:** 128

Death Clock, The (Gissing), **V:** 437

Death Comes as the End (Christie), **Supp. II:** 132–133

"Death in Bangor" (Mahon), **Supp. VI:** 177

"Death in Ilium" (Kinsella), **Supp. V:** 263

Death in the Clouds (Christie; U.S. title, *Death in the Air*), **Supp. II:** 131

"Death in the Desert, A" (Browning), **IV:** 358, 364, 367, 372; **Retro. Supp. II:** 26

Death in Venice (Mann), **Supp. IV:** 397

"Death of a Chieftain" (Montague), **Supp. XV:** 222

Death of a Dormouse (Hill, R.), **Supp. IX:** 119

"Death of a Friar, The" (Abercrombie), **Supp. XVI:** 11

Death of a Naturalist (Heaney), **Supp. II:** 268, **269–270,** 271; **Supp. IV:** 412; **Retro. Supp. I:** 123, 124, **126–127**

Death of a Salesman (Miller), **VI:** 286

"Death of a Scientific Humanist, The" (Friel), **Supp. V:** 114

"Death of a Tsotsi" (Paton), **Supp. II:** 345

"Death of a Tyrant" (Kinsella), **Supp. V:** 261

"Death of Alexander the Great, The" (tr. Delanty), **Supp. XIV:** 76

Death of an Expert Witness (James), **Supp. IV:** 319, 328–330

"Death of an Old Lady" (MacNeice), **VII:** 401

"Death of an Old Old Man" (Dahl), **Supp. IV:** 210

"Death of Arthur, The" (Tennyson), **Retro. Supp. III:** 321

"Death of Bernard Barton" (FitzGerald), **IV:** 353

Death of Christopher Marlowe, The (Hotson), **I:** 275

Death of Cuchulain, The (Yeats), **VI:** 215, 222

"Death of General Uncebunke, The: A Biography in Little" (Durrell), **Retro. Supp. III:** 95

"Death of King George, The" (Betjeman), **VII:** 367

Death of Oenone, Akbar's Dream, and Other Poems, The (Tennyson), **IV:** 338; **Retro. Supp. III:** 329

"Death of Oscur, The" (Macpherson), **VIII:** 183

"Death of Simon Fuge, The" (Bennett), **VI:** 254

Death of Sir John Franklin, The (Swinburne), **V:** 333

"Death of the Duchess, The" (Eliot), **VII:** 150

Death of the Heart, The (Bowen), **Supp. II:** 77, 78, 79, 82, 84, **90–91**

Death of the King's Canary, The (Thomas), **Retro. Supp. III:** 347

"Death of the Lion, The" (James), **VI:** 69

"Death of Marilyn Monroe, The" (Morgan, E.), **Supp. IX:** 164–165

"Death of the Rev. George Crabbe" (FitzGerald), **IV:** 353

Death of Wallenstein, The (Coleridge), **IV:** 56

Death of William Posters, The (Sillitoe), **Supp. V:** 409, 410, 414, **421–422,** 423

"Death stands above me, whispering low" (Landor), **IV:** 98

Death Takes the Low Road (Hill, R.), **Supp. IX:** 116–117

"Death, the Cat" (Healy), **Supp. IX:** 106

"Death the Drummer" (Lewis), **VII:** 79

Death-Trap, The (Saki), **Supp. VI:** 250

Death Under Sail (Snow), **VII:** 323

"Deathbeds" (Ewart), **Supp. VII:** 45

"Death-Mask of John Clare, The" (Blunden), **Supp. XI:** 44

Deaths and Entrances (Thomas), **Supp. I:** 177–178

"Deaths and Entrances" (Thomas), **Retro. Supp. III:** 345

"Death's Chill Between" (Rossetti), **V:** 252

"Death's Door" (Gunn), **Retro. Supp. III:** 128

Death's Duel (Donne), **Retro. Supp. II:** 98

Death's Jest-Book (Hill, R.), **Supp. IX:** 122

Death's Jest-Book; or, The Fool's Tragedy (Beddoes), **Supp. XI:** 17, 18, 22, 24, 25–28, 29, 30–31

"Deathshead" (Hare), **Supp. IV:** 283

Debates in Parliament (Johnson), **III:** 108, 122

Debits and Credits (Kipling), **VI:** 173, 204

Deborah (Abercrombie), **Supp. XVI:** 3–4

"Deborah's Parrot, a Village Tale" (Robinson), **Supp. XIII:** 212

"Debt, The" (Kipling), **VI:** 201

Debut, The (Brookner; first published as *A Start in Life*), **Supp. IV:** 122, 123–124, 131

"Decadent Movement in Literature, The" (Symons), **Supp. XIV:** 267, 270, 271, 273

Decameron (Boccaccio), **I:** 313; **Supp. IV:** 461; **Retro. Supp. II:** 45–46

"Decapitation of Is" (Cameron), **Supp. IX:** 19

"Decay of Lying, The" (Wilde), **V:** 407–408; **Retro. Supp. II:** 366–367

"Deceased, The" (Douglas), **VII:** 440

"December" (Clare), **Supp. XI:** 59

"December's Door" (Dunn), **Supp. X:** 77

"Decency" (Burnside), **Supp. XIII:** 29

"Deception Bay" (Malouf), **Supp. XII:** 220

"Deceptions" (Larkin), **Supp. I:** 278

Deceptive Grin of the Gravel Porters, The (Ewart), **Supp. VII:** 39–40

Declaration (Maschler), **Supp. I:** 237, 238

Declaration of Rights (Shelley), **IV:** 208

Decline and Fall (Waugh), **VII:** 289–290, 291; **Supp. II:** 218

Decline and Fall of the Roman Empire, The (Gibbon), **III:** 109, 221, **225–233**

"Decline of the Novel, The" (Muir), **Supp. VI:** 202

Decline of the West, The (Spengler), **Supp. IV:** 12

Decolonizing the Mind: The Politics of Language in African Literature (Ngũgĩ), **Supp. V:** 56; **VIII:** 215, 223, 225

"Décor" (MacCaig), **Supp. VI:** 185

Decorative Art in America: A Lecture (Wilde), **V:** 419

"Dedicated Spirits, The" (Smith, I. C.), **Supp. IX:** 211

"Dedication" (Motion), **Supp. VII:** 260

"Dedicatory Letter" (Ford), **VI:** 331

Deep Blue Sea, The (Rattigan), **Supp. VII:** 309, 315, 317–318

Deep Water (Highsmith), **Supp. V:** 171–172

"Deepe Groane, fetch'd at the Funerall of that incomparable and Glorious Monarch, Charles the First, King of Great Britaine, France, and Ireland,&c., A" (King), **Supp. VI: 159–161**

"Deeply Morbid" (Smith), **Retro. Supp. III:** 310

"Deer" (Burnside), **Supp. XIII:** 25

Deer on the High Hills (Smith, I. C.), **Supp. IX:** 212

Deerbrook (Martineau), **Supp. XV:** 183, 188–189, 190, 191

Deerfield Series, The: Strength of Heart (Fallon), **Supp. XII:** 113–114

Defeat of Youth, The (Huxley), **VII:** 199

"Defence of an Essay of 'Dramatick Poesie'" (Dryden), **II:** 297, 305

"Defence of Criminals: A Criticism of Morality" (Carpenter), **Supp. XIII:** 41

Defence of English Commodities, A (Swift), **III:** 35

Defence of Guenevere, The (Morris), **V:** xxii, 293, 305–306, 312

Defence of Poesie, The (Sidney), **I:** 161–163, 169, 170, 173; **Retro. Supp. II:** 332–334, 339

"Defence of Poetry, A" (Shelley), **IV:** 168–169, 204, 208, 209; **Retro. Supp. I:** 250

Defence of the Doctrine of Justification, A, ... (Bunyan), **II:** 253

Defence of the Essay of Human Understanding, written by Mr. Lock (Trotter),

DEFE–DEVI

Supp. XVI: 287–288, 289
Defence of the Rockingham Party, in Their Late Coalition with the Right Honorable Frederic Lord North, A (Godwin), **Supp. XV:** 117
"Defense of Cosmetics, A" (Beerbohm), **Supp. II:** 45, 53
Defense of Curates (tr. Trevisa), see *Defensio Curatorum*
Defensio Curatorum (tr. Trevisa), **Supp. IX:** 252, 253–254
"Definition of Love, The" (Marvell), **II:** 208, 211, 215
Defoe, Daniel, **II:** 325; **III: 1–14,** 24, 39, 41–42, 50–53, 62, 82; **V:** 288; **Supp. III:** 22, 31; **Retro. Supp. I: 63–77**
"Deformed Mistress, The" (Suckling), **II:** 227
Deformed Transformed, The (Byron), **IV:** 193
"Degas's Laundresses" (Boland), **Supp. V:** 39–40
Degeneration (Nordau), **VI:** 107
Degrees of Freedom: The Novels of Iris Murdoch (Byatt), **Supp. IV:** 145
Deighton, Len, **Supp. IV:** 5, 13
"Deincarnation" (Crawford), **Supp. XI:** 78
Deirdre (Russell), **VIII:** 284, 287
Deirdre (Yeats), **VI:** 218
Deirdre of the Sorrows (Synge), **Retro. Supp. I:** 301–302
"Dejection" (Coleridge), **IV:** 41, 49, 50; **Retro. Supp. II:** 61
Déjuner sur l'herbe (Manet), **Supp. IV:** 480
Dekker, Thomas, **I:** 68, 69; **II:** 3, 21, 47, 71, 89, 100; **Retro. Supp. I:** 160
Delahunt, Meaghan, **Supp. XIV: 49–63**
Delanty, Greg, **Supp. XIV: 65–79**
"Delay" (Jennings), **Supp. V:** 208
"Delay Has Danger" (Crabbe), **III:** 285
Delight (Priestley), **VII:** 212
"Delight in Disorder" (Herrick), **II:** 104
Delillo, Don, **Supp. IV:** 487
Deloraine (Godwin), **Supp. XV:** 129
"Deluding of Gylfi, The", See *Gylfaginning*
"Demephon and Phillis" (Gower), **I:** 53–54
Demeter, and Other Poems (Tennyson), **IV:** 338; **Retro. Supp. III:** 329
"Demeter and Persephone" (Tennyson), **IV:** 328
"Demo" (Murray), **Supp. VII:** 284
"Democracy" (Lawrence), **VII:** 87–88
"Demolishers, The" (Morgan, E.), **Supp. IX:** 165
"Demon at the Walls of Time, The" (Morgan, E.), **Supp. IX:** 170
Demon in My View, A (Rendell), **Supp. IX:** 195
Demon Lover, The (Bowen; U.S. title, *Ivy Gripped the Steps*), **Supp. II:** 77, 92, 93
Demon of Progress in the Arts, The (Lewis), **VII:** 74
"Demonstration" (Adcock), **Supp. XII:** 9
"Demonstration, The" (Traherne), **Supp. XI:** 270

Demos (Gissing), **V:** 432–433, 437
Denham, Sir John, **II:** 236, 238
"Deniall" (Herbert), **II:** 127, 128; **Retro. Supp. II:** 180–181
Denis Duval (Thackeray), **V:** 27, 34, 36, 38
Dennis, John, **II:** 69, 310, 338, 340
Dennis, Nigel, **III:** 23, 37
"Dennis Haggarty's Wife" (Thackeray), **V:** 23–24
"Dennis Shand" (Rossetti), **V:** 239
Denry the Audacious (Bennett), see *Card, The*
Dent, Arthur, **II:** 241, 246
Dental Record, **Supp. XIII:** 188
Denzil Quarrier (Gissing), **V:** 437
Deor, **Retro. Supp. II:** 304
"Departing Ship" (Hart), **Supp. XI:** 122–123
Departmental Ditties (Kipling), **VI:** 168, 204; **Retro. Supp. III:** 183, 188
Departure, The (Hart), **Supp. XI:** 122–124
"Depression, A" (Jennings), **Supp. V:** 214
Der Rosenkavalier (Strauss), **Supp. IV:** 556
Derham, William, **III:** 49
Derrida, Jacques, **Supp. IV:** 115
Derry Down Derry, pseud. of Edward Lear
Dervorgilla (Gregory), **VI:** 315
Des Imagistes: An Anthology (ed. Pound), **Supp. III:** 397
Desai, Anita, **Supp. IV:** 440; **Supp. V: 53–76**
Desai, Kiran, **Supp. XV: 83–97**
Desani, G. V., **Supp. IV:** 443, 445
Descartes, René, **Supp. I:** 43–44
Descent into Hell (Williams, C. W. S.), **Supp. IX:** 281–282
"Descent into the Maelstrom, The" (Poe), **III:** 339
Descent of Man and Selection in Relation to Sex, On the (Darwin), **Supp. VII:** 17, 19, 25–28
"Descent of Odin, The" (Gray), **III:** 141
Descent of the Dove, The (Williams, C. W. S.), **Supp. IX:** 284
Descent of the Gods, The (Russell), **VIII:** 278–279, 288, 289
"Description of a City Shower, A" (Swift), **III:** 30
"Description of an Author's Bedchamber" (Goldsmith), **III:** 184
"Description of Antichrist and His Ruin, A" (Bunyan), **II:** 253
"Description of the Morning, A" (Swift), **III:** 30; **Retro. Supp. I:** 282–283
"Descriptions of the Falling Snow" (Butlin), **Supp. XVI:** 56
Description of the Scenery of the Lakes in the North of England, A (Wordsworth), **IV:** 25
Description of the Western Islands (Martin), **III:** 117
Descriptive Catalogue of Pictures . . . , A (Blake), **III:** 305, 307
Descriptive Sketches (Wordsworth), **IV:** xv, 1, 2, 4–5, 24
"Desecration" (Jhabvala), **Supp. V:** 236

"Desert, The" (Morgan, E.), **Supp. IX:** 167
Desert Highway (Priestley), **VII:** 227–228
"Deserted Garden, The" (Browning), **IV:** 312
Deserted Parks, The (Carroll), **V:** 274
Deserted Village, The (Goldsmith), **III:** 177, 180, 185, 186–187, 191, 277
Deserter, The (Abercrombie), **Supp. XVI:** 10
Design for Living (Coward), **Supp. II:** 151–152, 156
"Desirable Mansions" (Carpenter), **Supp. XIII:** 40
"Desire" (Hart), **Supp. XI:** 125
"Desire During Illness, A" (Soutar), **Supp. XVI:** 252
Desolation Island (O'Brian), **Supp. XII:** 256–257
Desperate Remedies (Hardy), **VI:** 2, 19–20; **Retro. Supp. I:** 111–112
"Despite and Still" (Graves), **VII:** 268
"Despondency, an Ode" (Burns), **III:** 315
Destinations (Morris, J.), **Supp. X:** 172, 183
"Destinie" (Cowley), **II:** 194, 195, 198
"Destiny and a Blue Cloak" (Hardy), **VI:** 20
Destiny of Nathalie 'X,' The (Boyd), **Supp. XVI:** 43–44
"Destroyers in the Arctic" (Ross), **VII:** 433
Destructive Element, The (Spender), **Supp. II:** 487–488, 489, 491
Detained: A Writer's Prison Diary (Ngũgĩ), **VIII:** 216, 221, 223, 224
"Deus Ex–Machina" (Kunzru), **Supp. XIV:** 176
"Developing Worlds" (Crawford), **Supp. XI:** 80
"Development" (Browning), **IV:** 365
Development of Christian Doctrine, The (Newman), **V:** 340
Development of Creole Society in Jamaica, 1770–1820, The (Brathwaite), **Supp. XII:** 35
"Development of Genius, The" (Browning), **IV:** 310
Devices and Desires (James), **Supp. IV:** 320, 331–333
"Devil, The" (Murray), **Supp. VII:** 284
"Devil and the Good Deed, The" (Powys), **VIII:** 251
Devil and the Lady, The (Tennyson), **IV:** 338
Devil Is an Ass, The: A Comedie (Jonson), **Retro. Supp. I:** 165
Devil of a State (Burgess), **Supp. I:** 187
Devil of Dowgate, The (Fletcher), **II:** 67
Devil on the Cross (Ngũgĩ). See *Caitaani mũtharaba–in?*
Devil, The World and the Flesh, The (Lodge), **Supp. IV:** 364
Devil to Pay, The (Sayers), **Supp. III:** 336, 349
"Devil–Dancers, The" (Plomer), **Supp. XI:** 214
"Devil's Advice to Story–tellers, The" (Graves), **VII:** 259, 263

349

"Devils and the Idols, The" (Carpenter), **Supp. XIII:** 46
Devil's Disciple, The (Shaw), **VI:** 104, 105, 110, 112; **Retro. Supp. II:** 316
"Devil's Due, The" (Swinburne), **V:** 332
Devil's Elixir, The (Hoffmann), **III:** 334, 345
Devil's Footprints, The (Burnside), **Supp. XIII:** 27
"Devil's Jig, The" (Nye), **Supp. X:** 204–205
Devil's Larder, The (Crace), **Supp. XIV:** 18, 29–30
Devil's Law–Case, The (Webster), **II:** 68, 82–83, 85
Devils of Loudon, The (Huxley), **VII:** 205–206
Devil's Walk, The (Coleridge and Southey), **IV:** 56, 208
Devil's Walk, The (Shelley), **IV:** 208
Devlin, Christopher, **V:** 372, 373, 381
Devolving English Literature (Crawford), **Supp. XI:** 71, 82, 83
"Devoted Friend, The" (Wilde), **Retro. Supp. II:** 365
Devotional Exercises: Consisting of Reflections and Prayers for the Use of Young Persons (Martineau), **Supp. XV:** 182, 185
Devotions upon Emergent Occasions and severall steps in my Sicknes (Donne), **Retro. Supp. II:** 97–98
Devout Trental for Old John Clarke (Skelton), **I:** 86
Dhomhnaill, Nuala Ní, **Supp. V:** 40–41
Diabolical Principle and the Dithyrambic Spectator (Lewis), **VII:** 72, 76, 83
"Dialect" (Burnside), **Supp. XIII:** 20–21
Dialectic of the Enlightenment (Adorno), **Supp. IV:** 29
Dialogue between a Lord and a Clerk on Translation (Trevisa), **Supp. IX:** 246, 248–249
Dialogue between a Soldier and a Clerk (tr. Trevisa), see *Dialogus inter Militem et Clericum*
Dialogue Between the Devil, The Pope, and the Pretender, The (Fielding), **III:** 105
"Dialogue Between the Resolved Soul and Created Pleasure, A" (Marvell), **II:** 208, 211, 216
"Dialogue Between the Soul and Body, A" (Marvell), **II:** 208, 211, 216
"Dialogue Between the Two Horses, The" (Marvell), **II:** 218
"Dialogue Between Thyrsis and Dorinda, A" (Marvell), **II:** 211
Dialogue Concerning Heresies, The (More), **Supp. VII:** 244
Dialogue of Comfort against Tribulation, A (More), **Supp. VII:** 245, 247–248
"Dialogue of Self and Soul" (Kavanagh), **Supp. VII:** 191
"Dialogue of Self and Soul, A" (Yeats), **Retro. Supp. I:** 336
"Dialogue on Dramatic Poetry" (Eliot), **VII:** 157; **Retro. Supp. II:** 131–132
Dialogue with Death (Koestler), **Supp. I:** 23–24

Dialogues Concerning Natural Religion (Hume), **Supp. III:** 240, 242–243
Dialogues of the Dead (Hill, R.), **Supp. IX:** 122
Dialogus inter Militem et Clericum (tr. Trevisa), **Supp. IX:** 252–253, 254
Diamond of Jannina, The (Plomer), **Supp. XI:** 221
Diamond Smugglers, The (Fleming), **Supp. XIV:** 95
Diamonds Are Forever (Fleming), **Supp. XIV:** 94, 97
Diana (Montemayor), **I:** 164, 302
Diana of the Crossways (Meredith), **V:** xxv, 227, 232–233, 234
Diana Trelawny (Oliphant), **Supp. X:** 217
"Diaphanéité" (Pater), **V:** 345, 348, 356
Diaries (Warner), **Supp. VII:** 382
Diaries of a Dying Man (Soutar), **Supp. XVI:** 241–242, 244, 247, 248, 250, 255, 256
Diaries of Jane Somers, The (Lessing), **Supp. I:** 253–255
Diaries of Lewis Carroll, The (ed. Green), **V:** 264, 274
Diaries, Prayers, and Annals (Johnson), **Retro. Supp. I:** 143
Diarmuid and Grania (Moore and Yeats), **VI:** 87, 96, 99
Diary (Evelyn), **II:** 274–280, 286–287
Diary (Pepys), **II:** 274, 280–286, 288, 310
Diary and Letters of Madame D'Arblay (ed. Barrett), **Supp. III:** 63
"Diary from the Trenches" (Hulme), **Supp. VI:** 139–141
"Diary Letter From Aragon" (Cornford), **Supp. XIII:** 90–91, 92
Diary of a Dead Officer (West), **VI:** 423
Diary of a Dying Man, The (Soutar), **Supp. XVI:** 241, 254
Diary of a Good Neighbour, The (Lessing), **Supp. I:** 253
[am.2]*Diary of a Journey into North Wales . . . , A* (Johnson), **III:** 122
Diary of a Madman, The (Gogol), **III:** 345
Diary of a Man of Fifty, The (James), **VI:** 67, 69
Diary of Fanny Burney (Burney), **III:** 243
Diary, Reminiscences and Correspondence of H. Crabb Robinson, The, **IV:** 52, 56, 81
Dibb, Michael, **Supp. IV:** 88
Dick, Philip K., **Supp. IV:** 41
"Dick King" (Kinsella), **Supp. V:** 261
Dick Willoughby (Day Lewis), **Supp. III:** 117
Dickens, Charles, **II:** 42; **III:** 151, 157, 340; **IV:** 27, 34, 38, 88, 240, 241, 247, 251, 252, 259, 295, 306; **V:** viii, ix, 3, 5, 6, 9, 14, 20, 22, 41–74, 148, 182, 191, 424, 435; **VI:** viii; **Supp. I:** 166–167; **Supp. IV:** 120, 202–203, 229, 379, 460, 505, 513, 514
Dickens (Ackroyd), **Supp. VI:** 8–9
Dickens and Daughter (Storey), **V:** 72
Dickens and the Twentieth Century (ed. Cross and Pearson), **V:** 63, 73

Dickens from Pickwick to Dombey (Marcus), **V:** 46
"Dickens in Memory" (Gissing), **V:** 437
Dickens: Interviews and Recollections (ed. Collins), **V:** 46
Dickens the Novelist (Leavis), **VII:** 250–251
Dickens Theatre, The (Garis), **V:** 70, 73
Dickinson, Goldsworthy Lowes, **VI:** 398, 399
Dickinson, Emily, **Supp. IV:** 139, 480
Dickson, Lovat, **VI:** 239
Dictionary of Madame de Sévigné (FitzGerald and Kerrich), **IV:** 349, 353
Dictionary of National Biography (ed. Stephen and Lee), **V:** xxv, 280–281, 290
Dictionary of the English Language, A (Johnson), **III:** 113–114, 115, 121; **Retro. Supp. I:** 137, 141, 142
Dictionary of the Khazars: A Lexicon Novel in 100,000 Words (Pavic), **Supp. IV:** 116
"Did any Punishment attend" (Sedley), **II:** 265
Did He Steal It? (Trollope), **V:** 102
Diderot, Denis, **Supp. IV:** 122, 136
Didion, Joan, **Supp. IV:** 163
"Didn't He Ramble" (Brathwaite), **Supp. XII:** 37, 44
Dido, Queen of Carthage (Marlowe), **I:** 278–279, 280–281, 292; **Retro. Supp. I:** 211
Die Ambassador (Brink), **Supp. VI:** 46–47
Die Another Day (Fleming), **Supp. XIV:** 95
Die Eerste lewe van Adamastor (Brink), **Supp. VI:** 54
Die muur van die pes (Brink), **Supp. VI:** 52
Die Räuber (Schiller), **IV:** xiv, 173
Die Spanier in Peru (Kotzebue), **III:** 254, 268
Dierdre of the Sorrows (Synge), **VI:** 310, 313
"Dies Irae" (Morgan, E.), **Supp. IX:** 160–162
"Dietary" (Lydgate), **I:** 58
"Differences, The" (Gunn), **Retro. Supp. III:** 128
Differences in Judgement about Water Baptism . . . (Bunyan), **II:** 253
Different Days (Cornford), **VIII:** 105–106
"Difficulties of a Bridegroom" (Hughes), **Supp. I:** 346
"Difficulties of a Statesman" (Eliot), **VII:** 152–153
Difficulties with Girls (Amis), **Supp. II:** 18
"Diffugere Nives" (Housman), **VI:** 155
"Digdog" (Pitter), **Supp. XIII:** 133, 140
"Digging" (Heaney), **Supp. II:** 270; **Retro. Supp. I:** 124, 126–127
"Digging for Pictures" (Golding), **Supp. I:** 65
"Digging Up Scotland" (Reid), **Supp. VII:** 336
Dilecta (Ruskin), **V:** 184

Dilemma of a Ghost, The (Aidoo), **Supp. XV:** 5–7
"Dilemma of Iphis, The" (Clarke), **Supp. XV:** 29
Dilke, Charles, **IV:** 254, 262, 306
"Dill Pickle, A" (Mansfield), **VII:** 174
Dimetos (Fugard), **Supp. XV:** 103, 110, 112
Dimple Hill (Richardson), **Supp. XIII:** 188
"Dingbat's Song, The" (Delanty), **Supp. XIV:** 70
"Dining" (Dunn), **Supp. X:** 76
Dining on Stones; or the Middle Ground (Sinclair), **Supp. XIV:** 232, 245–246
"Dining Room Tea" (Brooke), **Supp. III:** 49, 52
Dinner at Noon (documentary, Bennett), **VIII:** 25
"Dinner at Poplar, A" (Dickens), **V:** 41, 47n
"Dinner in the City, A" (Thackeray), **V:** 25
"Dinner with Dr. Azad" (Ali), **Supp. XIII:** 11
"Dinosaur, The" (Fallon), **Supp. XII:** 102
Diodorus Siculus (tr. Skelton), **I:** 82
"Diogenes and Plato" (Landor), **IV:** 91
"Dip in the Pool" (Dahl), **Supp. IV:** 217
Diplopic (Reading), **VIII:** 265, 266, 267, 271
Dipsychus (Clough), **V:** 156, 159, 161, 163–165, 167, 211
"Diptych" (Reading), **VIII:** 264
"Dirce" (Landor), **IV:** 96–97
"Directions" (Thomas), **Supp. XII:** 288
Directions to Servants (Swift), **III:** 36
"Dirge" (Eliot), **VII:** 150
"Dirge for the New Sunrise" (Sitwell), **VII:** 137
"Dirge of Jephthah's Daughter, The: Sung by the Virgins" (Herrick), **II:** 113
"Dirge of the Mad Priest" (Montague), **Supp. XV:** 214
Dirty Beasts (Dahl), **Supp. IV:** 226
Dirty Story (Ambler), **Supp. IV:** 16
"Dis aliter visum; or, Le Byron de nos jours" (Browning), **IV:** 366, 369
"Disabled" (Owen), **VI:** 447, 451, 452
"Disabused, The" (Day Lewis), **Supp. III:** 130
"Disappointmnt, The" (Behn), **Supp. III:** 39
Disappointment, The (Southern), **II:** 305
"Disc's Defects, A" (Fuller), **Supp. VII:** 80
Discarded Image, The: An Introduction to Medieval and Renaissance Literature (Lewis), **Supp. III:** 249, 264
Discarnation, The (Sisson), **Supp. XI:** 249, 256
"Discharge, The" (Herbert), **II:** 127
Discipulus, *see* Martineau, Harriet
Discontented Colonel, The (Suckling), **II:** 238
Discourse Concerning a Guide and Controversies (Trotter), **Supp. XVI:** 288–289
"Discourse Concerning the Original and Progress of Satire, A" (Dryden), **Retro. Supp. III:** 79
Discourse, Introductory to a Course of Lectures on Chemistry, A (Davy), **Supp. III:** 359–360
"Discourse from the Deck" (Gunn), **Supp. IV:** 269
"Discourse of a Lady Standing a Dinner to a Down–and–Out Friend" (Rhys), **Supp. II:** 390
Discourse of Civil Life (Bryskett), **I:** 124
Discourse of the Building of the House of God, A (Bunyan), **II:** 253
Discourse of the Contests and Dissensions between the Nobles and the Commons in Athens and Rome (Swift), **III:** 17, 35
Discourse on Pastoral Poetry, A (Pope), **III:** 56
Discourse on Satire (Dryden), **II:** 297
Discourse on the Love of Our Country (Price), **IV:** 126
Discourse on the Pindarique Ode, A (Congreve), **II:** 346–347
Discourse on 2 Corinthians, i, 9 . . . , A (Crabbe), **III:** 286
Discourse upon Comedy, A (Farquhar), **II:** 332, 355
Discourse upon the Pharisee and the Publicane, A (Bunyan), **II:** 253
Discourses Addressed to Mixed Congregations (Newman), **Supp. VII:** 297
Discourses by Way of Essays (Cowley), **III:** 40
Discourses in America (Arnold), **V:** 216
Discoveries (Jonson), **I:** 270; **Retro. Supp. I:** 166
Discovery of Guiana, The (Ralegh), **I:** 145, 146, 149, 151–153
Discovery of the Future, The (Wells), **VI:** 244
"Discretioun in Taking" (Dunbar), **VIII:** 122
"Disdaine Returned" (Carew), **II:** 225
"Disease of the Mind" (Cameron), **Supp. IX:** 18
Disenchantment (Montague), **VII:** 421
"Disenchantments" (Dunn), **Supp. X:** 78–79
Disgrace (Coetzee), **Supp. VI:** 76, **86–88**
"Disguises" (McEwan), **Supp. IV:** 391–392
"Disinheritance" (Jhabvala), **Supp. V:** 223–224, 228, 230, 232
"Disinherited, The" (Bowen), **Supp. II:** 77, 87–88
Disney, Walt, **Supp. IV:** 202, 211
"Disobedience" (Milne), **Supp. V:** 301
"Disorderly, The" (Murray), **Supp. VII:** 287
Dispatches from the Front Line of Popular Culture (Parsons), **Supp. XV:** 227, 229
"Displaced Person" (Murphy), **Supp. V:** 326
"Dispute at Sunrise" (Hart), **Supp. XI:** 129
Disraeli, Benjamin, **IV:** xii, xvi, xviii, xix, xx, xxiii, 271, 288, **292–309**; **V:** viii, x, xxiv, 2, 22; **VII:** xxi; **Supp. IV:** 379
Disraeli (Blake), **IV:** 307, 308
"Dissatisfaction" (Traherne), **II:** 192
"Dissection of a Beau's Head" (Byrom), **Supp. XVI:** 74
"Dissolution, The" (Donne), **Retro. Supp. II:** 92
Distances (Conn), **Supp. XIII:** 69
"Distant Fury of Battle, The" (Hill), **Supp. V:** 186
Disaffection, A (Kelman), **Supp. V:** 243, 249, 251–252
"Dissertation" (Macpherson), **VIII:** 188, 190
"Distant Past, The" (Trevor), **Supp. IV:** 504
"Distracted Preacher, The" (Hardy), **VI:** 22; **Retro. Supp. I:** 116
"Distraction" (Vaughan), **II:** 188
"Distress of Plenty" (Connolly), **Supp. III:** 108
Distress'd Wife, The (Gay), **III:** 67
"Disturber of the Traffic, The" (Kipling), **VI:** 169, **170–172**
"Disused Shed in County Wexford, A" (Mahon) **Supp. VI:** 169–170, 173
"Divali" (Seth), **Supp. X:** 279–280
"Dive" (Dutton), **Supp. XII:** 93
Diversions of Purley and Other Poems, The (Ackroyd), **Supp. VI:** 3Diversions of Purley and Other Poems, The (Ackroyd), Supp. VI: 3
"Diversity and Depth" (Wilson), **Supp. I:** 167
Diversity of Creatures, A (Kipling), **Retro. Supp. III:** 194
"Diverting History of John Gilpin, The" (Cowper), **Retro. Supp. III:** 36, 47
"Divided Life Re–Lived, The" (Fuller), **Supp. VII:** 72
Divine and Moral Songs for Children (Watts), **III:** 299
Divine Comedy, The (Dante), **II:** 148; **III:** 306; **IV:** 93, 187, 229; **Supp. I:** 76; Supp. IV: 439
"Divine Judgments" (Blake), **III:** 300
"Divine Meditations" (Donne), **Retro. Supp. II:** 98
"Divine Pastoral" (Byrom), **Supp. XVI:** 73
Divine Poems (Waller), **II:** 238
Divine Vision and Other Poems, The (Russell), **VIII:** 284–285
"Divine Wrath and Mercy" (Blake), **III:** 300
Diviner, The (Friel), **Supp. V:** 113
"Diviner, The" (Friel), **Supp. V:** 115
"Diviner, The" (Heaney), **Supp. II:** 269–270
"Diving into Dirt" (Sinclair), **Supp. XIV:** 243
"Division, The" (Hardy), **VI:** 17
"Division" (Montague), **Supp. XV:** 216
Division of the Spoils, A (Scott), **Supp. I:** 268, 271
Divisions on a Ground (Nye), **Supp. X:** 193, 200–202
Divorce (Williams, C. W. S.), **Supp. IX:** 272, 274
Dixon, Richard Watson, **V:** 362–365, 371, 372, 377, 379; **VI:** 76, 83, 167
Dixon Hunt, John, **VI:** 167

DIZZ–DOUG

"Dizzy" (Strachey), **IV:** 292
Do Me a Favour (Hill), **Supp. XIV:** 115, 118
"Do Not Disturb" (Montague), **Supp. XV:** 217
"Do not go gentle into that good night" (Thomas), **Supp. I:** 178; **Retro. Supp. III:** 340, 344–345, 347, 349
"Do Take Muriel Out" (Smith), **Supp. II:** 471, 472
Do What You Will (Huxley), **VII:** 201
"Do You Love Me?" (Carey), **Supp. XII:** 54, 55, 56, 57
"Do you remember me? or are you proud?" (Landor), **IV:** 99
Dobell, Sydney, **IV:** 310; **V:** 144–145
Dobrée, Bonamy, **II:** 362, 364; **III:** 33, 51, 53; **V:** 221, 234; **VI:** xi, 200–203; **V:** xxii
"Dockery and Son" (Larkin), **Supp. I:** 281, 285; **Retro. Supp. III:** 207, 211
Doctor, The (Southey), **IV:** 67n, 71
Doctor and the Devils, The (screenplay, Thomas), **Retro. Supp. III:** 348
Doctor Birch and His Young Friends (Thackeray), **V:** 38
Doctor Faustus (film), **III:** 344
Doctor Faustus (Marlowe), **I:** 212, 279–280, **287–290**; **Supp. IV:** 197
Doctor Fischer of Geneva; or, The Bomb Party (Greene), **Supp. I:** 1, 17–18
Doctor Is Sick, The (Burgess), **Supp. I:** 186, 189, 195
Doctor Therne (Haggard), **Supp. III:** 214
Doctor Thorne (Trollope), **V:** xxii, 93, 101
Doctors' Delusions, Crude Criminology, and Sham Education (Shaw), **VI:** 129
Doctor's Dilemma, The (Shaw), **VI:** xv 116, 129; **Retro. Supp. II:** 321–322
"Doctor's Family, The" (Oliphant), **Supp. X:** 214
"Doctor's Journal Entry for August 6, 1945, A" (Seth), **Supp. X:** 284
"Doctor's Legend, The" (Hardy), **VI:** 20
Doctors of Philosophy (Spark), **Supp. I:** 206
Doctor's Wife, The (Braddon), **VIII:** 44–46
Doctor's Wife, The (Moore, B.), **Supp. IX:** 144, 146, 147–148
Doctrine and Discipline of Divorce . . . , The (Milton), **II:** 175; **Retro. Supp. II:** 271
"Doctrine of Scattered Occasions, The" (Bacon), **I:** 261
Doctrine of the Law and Grace Unfolded, The (Bunyan), **II:** 253
Documents in the Case, The (Sayers and Eustace), **Supp. III:** 335, 342–343
Documents Relating to the Sentimental Agents in the Volyen Empire (Lessing), **Supp. I:** 252–253
Dodge, Mabel, **VII:** 109
Dodgson, Charles Lutwidge, *see* Carroll, Lewis
"Does It Matter?" (Sassoon), **VI:** 430
"Does It Pay?" (Carpenter), **Supp. XIII:** 40

"Does That Hurt?" (Motion), **Supp. VII:** 263–264
"Dog and the Lantern, The" (Powys), **VIII:** 255
"Dog and the Waterlily, The" (Cowper), **III:** 220
Dog Beneath the Skin, The (Auden and Isherwood), **VII:** 312, 380, 385; **Retro. Supp. I:** 7
Dog Fox Field (Murray), **Supp. VII:** 280–281, 282
"Dogged" (Saki), **Supp. VI:** 239
Dog's Ransom, A (Highsmith), **Supp. V:** 176–177
"Dogs" (Hughes), **Supp. I:** 346
"Doing Research for Historical Novels" (Keneally), **Supp. IV:** 344
Doktor Faustus (Mann), **III:** 344
Dolben, Digby Mackworth, **VI:** 72, 75
"Doldrums, The" (Kinsella), **Supp. V:** 261
"Doll, The" (O'Brien), **Supp. V:** 340
Doll's House, A (Ibsen), **IV:** xxiii, 118–119; **V:** xxiv; **VI:** ix, 111
"Doll's House, The" (Mansfield), **VII:** 175
"Doll's House on the Dal Lake, A" (Naipaul), **Supp. I:** 399
"Dollfuss Day, 1935" (Ewart), **Supp. VII:** 36
Dolly (Brookner), **Supp. IV:** 134–135, 136–137
Dolores (Compton-Burnett), **VII:** 59, 68
"Dolores" (Swinburne), **V:** 313, 320–321
"Dolorida" (Swinburne), **V:** 332
Dolphin, The (Lowell), **Supp. IV:** 423
Dombey and Son (Dickens), **IV:** 34; **V:** xxi, 42, 44, 47, 53, 57–59, 70, 71
"Domestic Interior" (Boland), **Supp. V:** 50
Domestic Relations (O'Connor), **Supp. XIV:** 223–224
"Domicilium" (Hardy), **VI:** 14
Don Fernando (Maugham), **VI:** 371
Don Juan (Byron), **I:** 291; **II:** 102n; **IV:** xvii, 171, 172, 173, 178, 183, 184, 185, **187–191**, 192
Don Quixote (Cervantes), **II:** 49; **IV:** 190; **V:** 46; **Retro. Supp. I:** 84
Don Quixote in England (Fielding), **III:** 105
Don Sebastian, King of Portugal (Dryden), **II:** 305
"Donahue's Sister" (Gunn), **Retro. Supp. III:** 125
"Donald MacDonald" (Hogg), **Supp. X:** 106
"Dong with a Luminous Nose, The" (Lear), **V:** 85
"Donkey, The" (Smith), **Supp. II:** 468
"Donkey's Ears: Politovsky's Letters Home, The" (Dunn), **Supp. X:** 80–82
Donkeys' Years (Frayn), **Supp. VII:** 60–61
Donne, John, **I: 352–369**; **II:** 102, 113, 114, 118, 121–124, 126–128, 132, 134–138, 140–143, 147, 185, 196, 197, 209, 215, 221, 222, 226; **IV:** 327; **Supp. II:** 181, 182; **Supp. III:** 51, 57; **Retro. Supp. II: 85–99**, 173, 175, 259, 260

Donne, William Bodham, **IV:** 340, 344, 351
Donnelly, M. C., **V:** 427, 438
Donohue, J. W., **III:** 268
Don't Look Now (du Maurier), **Supp. III:** 148
Don't Tell Alfred (Mitford), **Supp. X:** 152, 158, 164–167
"Doodle Bugs" (Harrison), **Supp. V:** 151
"Doom of the Griffiths, The" (Gaskell), **V:** 15
Doom of Youth, The (Lewis), **VII:** 72
"Door in the Wall, The" (Wells), **VI:** 235, 244
Door Into the Dark (Heaney), **Supp. II:** 268, **271–272**; **Retro. Supp. I:** 127
Dorando, A Spanish Tale (Boswell), **III:** 247
Dorian Gray (Wilde), *see Picture of Dorian Gray, The*
"Dorinda's sparkling Wit, and Eyes" (Dorset), **II:** 262
Dorking Thigh and Other Satires, The (Plomer), **Supp. XI:** 222
Dorothy Wordsworth (Selincourt), **IV:** 143
Dorset, earl of (Charles Sackville), **II:** 255, **261–263**, 266, 268, 270–271
Dorset Farm Laborer Past and Present, The, (Hardy), **VI:** 20
Dostoyevsky, Fyodor, **Supp. IV:** 1, 139
Dostoevsky: The Making of a Novelist (Simmons), **V:** 46
Doting (Green), **Supp. II:** 263, 264
Double Falsehood, The (Theobald), **II:** 66, 87
"Double Life" (MacCaig), **Supp. VI:** 186
Double Lives: An Autobiography (Plomer), **Supp. XI:** 210, 214, 215, 223
"Double Looking Glass, The" (Hope), **Supp. VII:** 159
Double Man, The (Auden), **Retro. Supp. I:** 10
Double Marriage, The (Fletcher and Massinger), **II:** 66
"Double Rock, The" (King), **Supp. VI:** 151
Double Tongue, The (Golding), **Retro. Supp. I:** 106–107
"Double Vision of Michael Robartes, The" (Yeats), **VI:** 217
Double-Dealer, The (Congreve), **II:** 338, 341–342, 350
Doublets: A Word-Puzzle (Carroll), **V:** 273
"Doubt of Future Foes, The" (Elizabeth I), **Supp. XVI:** 152
Doubtfire (Nye), **Supp. X:** 193–196, 203, 206
Doubtful Paradise (Friel), **Supp. V:** 115
Doughty, Charles, **Supp. II:** 294–295
Doughty, Oswald, **V:** xi, xxvii, 246, 297n, 307
Douglas, Gavin, **I:** 116–118; **III:** 311
Douglas, Keith, **VII:** xxii, 422, **440–444**
Douglas, Lord Alfred, **V:** 411, 416–417, 420
Douglas, Norman, **VI: 293–305**

Douglas Cause, The (Boswell), **III:** 247
Douglas Jerrold's Weekly (periodical), **V:** 144
"Dovecote" (McGuckian), **Supp. V:** 280
"Dover" (Auden), **VII:** 379
Dover Road, The (Milne), **Supp. V:** 299
"Down" (Graves), **VII:** 264
Down Among the Gods (Thompson), **Supp. XIV:** 286, 287
Down Among the Women (Weldon), **Supp. IV:** 524–525
Down and Out in Paris and London (Orwell), **VII:** xx, 275, 277; **Supp. IV:** 17
"Down at the Dump" (White), **Supp. I:** 143
Down by the River (O'Brien), **Supp. V:** 344–345
"Down by the Sally-Garden" (Yeats), **VII:** 368
"Down Darkening" (Nye), **Supp. X:** 205
Down from the Hill (Sillitoe), **Supp. V:** 411
"Down Kaunda Street" (Fuller), **Supp. VII:** 80
"Down on the Farm" (Plomer), **Supp. XI:** 214
Down There on a Visit (Isherwood), **VII:** 315–316
Downfall and Death of King Oedipus, The (FitzGerald), **IV:** 353
Downriver (Sinclair), **Supp. XIV:** 235, 238, 242
Downs, Brian, **III:** 84, 93
"Downs, The" (Bridges), **VI:** 78
Downstairs (Churchill), **Supp. IV:** 180
Downstream (Kinsella), **Supp. V:** 259, 260, 261–262
"Downstream" (Kinsella), **Supp. V:** 262
"Downward Pulse, The" (Cameron), **Supp. IX:** 27
Dowson, Ernest, **V:** 441; **VI:** 210
Doyle, Arthur Conan, **III:** 341, 345; **Supp. II:** 126, 127, **159–176**
Doyle, Roddy, **Supp. V: 77–93**
Dr. Faust's Sea-Spiral Spirit (Redgrove), **Supp. VI:** 231, 233–234
Dr. Goldsmith's Roman History Abridged by Himself . . . (Goldsmith), **III:** 191
Dr. Jekyll and Mr. Hyde (Stevenson), *see Strange Case of Dr. Jekyll and Mr. Hyde, The*
Dr. No (Fleming), **Supp. XIV:** 91, 95, 96, 97
"Dr. Woolacott" (Forster), **VI:** 406
Dr. Wortle's School (Trollope), **V:** 100, 102
Drabble, Antonia, *see* Byatt, A. S.
Drabble, Margaret, **VI:** 247, 253, 268; **Supp. IV:** 141, **229–254**
Dracula (Stoker), **III:** 334, 342, 345; **Supp. III: 375–377**, 381, 382, 383, **386–390**
Dracula (films), **III:** 342; **Supp. III:** 375–377
"Dracula's Guest" (Stoker), **Supp. III:** 383, 385
"Draff" (Beckett), **Retro. Supp. I:** 19
Drafts and Fragments of Verse (Collins), **II:** 323n

"Dragon Class" (Dutton), **Supp. XII:** 88–89
"Dragon Dreams" (Maitland), **Supp. XI:** 170
Dragon of the Apocalypse (Carter), **VII:** 114
"Dragonfly" (Fallon), **Supp. XII:** 103
"Dragon's Blood" (Carson), **Supp. XIII:** 64
Drake, Nathan, **III:** 51
"Drama and Life" (Joyce), **Retro. Supp. I:** 170
Drama in Muslin, A (Moore), **VI:** 86, 89, **90–91,** 98
"Drama of Exile, A" (Browning), **IV:** 313
Drama of Love and Death, The (Carpenter), **Supp. XIII:** 42
Dramatic Character in the English Romantic Age (Donohue), **III:** 268n
Dramatic Historiographer, The; or, The British Theatre Delineated (Haywood), **Supp. XII:** 135
Dramatic Idyls (Browning), **IV:** xxiii, 358, 374; **V:** xxiv; **Retro. Supp. III:** 31
Dramatic Lyrics (Browning), **IV:** xx, 374; **Retro. Supp. III:** 20–21
Dramatic Romances and Lyrics (Browning), **IV:** 374; **Retro. Supp. III:** 20, 22
Dramatic Works of Richard Brinsley Sheridan, The (ed. Price), **III:** 258
Dramatis Personae (Browning), **IV:** xxii, 358, 364, 374; **Retro. Supp. II:** 26–27; **Retro. Supp. III:** 26–27, 32
Dramatis Personae (Symons), **Supp. XIV:** 274
Dramatis Personae (Yeats), **VI:** 317
Drapier's Letters, The (Swift), **III:** 20n 28, 31, 35; **Retro. Supp. I:** 274
"Drawing Room, Annerley, 1996" (Hart), **Supp. XI:** 131
"Drawing you, heavy with sleep" (Warner), **Supp. VII:** 373
Drayton, Michael, **I:** 196, 278; **II:** 68 134, 138
"Dread of Height, The" (Thompson), **V:** **444**
Dreadful Pleasures (Twitchell), **Supp. III:** 383
"Dream" (Heaney), **Supp. II:** 271
"Dream" (Kinsella), **Supp. V:** 273
"Dream, A" (Healy), **Supp. IX:** 106
"Dream, A" (Pitter), **Supp. XIII:** 145
"Dream, The" (Galsworthy), **VI:** 280
"Dream, The" (MacCaig), **Supp. VI:** 185
"Dream, The. A Song" (Behn), **Supp. III:** 37–38
Dream and Thing (Muir), **Supp. VI:** 208
Dream Children (Wilson), **Supp. VI:** **308–309**
"Dream in Three Colours, A" (McGuckian), **Supp. V:** 285
Dream Lover, The (Boyd), **Supp. XVI:** 32, 43
Dream of Darkness (Hill, R.), **Supp. IX:** 119
Dream of Destiny, A (Bennett), **VI:** 262
"Dream of Eugene Aram, The Murderer, The" (Hood), **IV:** 256, 261–262, 264,

267; **Supp. III:** 378
Dream of Fair to Middling Women, A (Beckett), **Retro. Supp. I:** 17
"Dream of France, A" (Hart), **Supp. XI:** 123
Dream of Gerontius, The (Newman), **Supp. VII:** 293, 300, 301
"Dream of Heaven, A" (Fallon), **Supp. XII:** 105
Dream of John Ball, A (Morris), **V:** 301, 302–303, 305, 306
"Dream of Nourishment" (Smith), **Supp. II:** 466
"Dream of Private Clitus, The" (Jones), **Supp. VII:** 175
Dream of Scipio, The (Cicero), **IV:** 189
Dream of the Rood, The, **I:** 11; **Retro. Supp. II:** 302, 307
"Dream Play" (Mahon), **Supp. VI:** 178
Dream State: The New Scottish Poets (Crawford), **Supp. XI:** 67
Dream Stuff (Malouf), **Supp. XII:** 218
"Dream Work" (Hope), **Supp. VII:** 155
Dreamchild (Potter, D.), **Supp. X:** 236
"Dream-Fugue" (De Quincey), **IV:** 153–154
"Dream-Language of Fergus, The" (McGuckian), **Supp. V:** 285–286
"Dream-Pedlary" (Beddoes), **Supp. XI:** 30
Dreaming in Bronze (Thomas), **Supp. IV:** 490
"Dreaming Spires" (Campbell), **VII:** 430
"Dreams" (Spenser), **I:** 123
Dreams of Leaving (Hare), **Supp. IV:** 282, 289
"Dreams Old and Nascent" (Lawrence), **VII:** 118
"Dream-Tryst" (Thompson), **V:** 444
Drebbel, Cornelius, **I:** 268
"Dresden" (Carson), **Supp. XIII:** 58
Dressed as for a Tarot Pack (Redgrove), **Supp. V:** 236
"Dressing" (Vaughan), **II:** 186
Dressing Up—Transvestism and Drag: The History of an Obsession (Ackroyd), **Supp. VI:** 3–4, 12
Dressmaker, The (Bainbridge), **Supp. VI:** 19–20, 24
"Dressmaker, The" (Hart), **Supp. XI:** 130–131
Drew, Philip, **IV:** xiii, xxiv, 375
"Drink to Me Only with Thine Eyes" (Jonson), **I:** 346; **VI:** 16
Drinkers of Infinity (Koestler), **Supp. I:** 34, 34n
"Drinking" (Cowley), **II:** 198
Driver's Seat, The (Spark), **Supp. I:** 200, 209–210, 218n
"Driving Through Sawmill Towns" (Murray), **Supp. VII:** 271
Driving West (Beer), **Supp. XIV:** 1, 4
Droe wit seisoen, 'n (Brink), **Supp. VI:** **50–51**
"Droit de Seigneur: 1820" (Murphy), **Supp. V:** 321
Drought, The (Ballard), **Supp. V:** 24–25, 34
"Drowned Field, The" (Hollinghurst), **Supp. X:** 121

"Drowned Giant, The" (Ballard), **Supp. V:** 23
Drowned World, The (Ballard), **Supp. V:** 22–23, 24, 34
"Drowning" (Adcock), **Supp. XII:** 9
Drumlin (ed. Healy), **Supp. IX:** 95
"Drummer Hodge" (Housman), **VI:** 161; **Retro. Supp. I:** 120
Drummond of Hawthornden, William, **I:** 328, 349
Drums of Father Ned, The (O'Casey), **VII:** 10–11
Drums under the Windows (O'Casey), **VII:** 9, 12
Drunk Man Looks at the Thistle, A (MacDiarmid), **Supp. XII:** 202, 203, 207–210, 211, 213, 215
Drunken Sailor, The (Cary), **VII:** 186, 191
Drunken Sailor (Montague), **Supp. XV:** 217
"Dry Point" (Larkin), **Supp. I:** 277
Dry Salvages, The (Eliot), **V:** 241; **VII:** 143, 144, 152, 154, 155
Dry, White Season, A (Brink), **Supp. VI:** 50–51
Dryden, John, **I:** 176, 327, 328, 341, 349; **II:** 166–167, 195, 198, 200, **289–306**, 325, 338, 340, 348, 350, 352, 354–355; **III:** 40, 47, 68, 73–74, 118; **IV:** 93, 196, 287; **V:** 376; **Supp. III:** 19, 24, 27, 36, 37, 40; **Supp. V:** 201–202; **Retro. Supp. III:** 53–81
Dryden, John, The younger, **II:** 305
"Dryden's Prize-Song" (Hill), **Supp. V:** 201–202
Du Bellay, Joachim, **I:** 126; **V:** 345
Du Bois, W. E. B., **Supp. IV:** 86
du Maurier, Daphne, **III:** 343; **Supp. III:** 133–149
du Maurier, George, **V:** 403; **Supp. III:** 133–137, 141
du Maurier, Guy, **Supp. III:** 147, 148
Du Mauriers, The (du Maurier), **Supp. III:** 135–136, 137, 139
Dual Tradition: An Essay on Poetry and Politics in Ireland (Kinsella), **Supp. V:** 272, 273–274
Dublin Penny Journal, **Supp. XIII:** 116
Dublin Satirist, **Supp. XIII:** 116
Dublin University Magazine, **Supp. XIII:** 116, 117, 118, 119, 121, 124
Dubliners (Joyce), **VII:** xiv, 41, 43–45, 47–52; critical studies, **VII:** 57; **Supp. I:** 45; **Supp. IV:** 395; **Retro. Supp. I:** 171–173; **Retro. Supp. III:** 167, 168–170, 174
"Dubious" (Seth), **Supp. X:** 279
"Duchess of Hamptonshire, The" (Hardy), **VI:** 22
Duchess of Malfi, The (Webster), **II:** 68, 70–73, **76–78,** 79, 81, 82, 84, 85
Duchess of Padua, The (Wilde), **V:** 419; **Retro. Supp. II:** 362–363
"Duddon Estuary, The" (Nicholson), **Supp. VI:** 214
Due Preparations for the Plague (Defoe), **III:** 13
"Duel, The" (Conrad), **VI:** 148
Duel of Angels (Fry), **Supp. III:** 195

"Duel of the Crabs, The" (Dorset), **II:** 271
Duenna, The (Sheridan), **III:** 253, 257, 259–261, 270
"Duffy's Circus" (Muldoon), **Supp. IV:** 415
Dufy, Raoul, **Supp. IV:** 81
Dugdale, Florence Emily, **VI:** 17n
Dugdale, Sir William, **II:** 274
Dugmore, C. W., **I:** 177n
Dujardin, Edouard, **VI:** 87
Duke of Gandia, The (Swinburne), **V:** 333
Duke of Guise, The (Dryden), **II:** 305
Duke of Millaine, The (Massinger), **Supp. XI:** 183
Duke's Children, The (Trollope), **V:** 96, 99, 101, 102
"Duke's Reappearance, The" (Hardy), **VI:** 22
"Dulce et Decorum Est" (Owen), **VI:** 448, 451
"Dull London" (Lawrence), **VII:** 94, 116, 121
"Dulwich Gallery, The" (Hazlitt), **IV:** 135–136
Dumas père, Alexandre, **III:** 332, 334, 339
Dumb House, The (Burnside), **Supp. XIII:** 16–17, 19, 27–28, 30
Dumb Instrument (Welch), **Supp. IX:** 269–270
Dumb Virgin, The; or, The Force of Imagination (Behn), **Supp. III:** 31
Dumb Waiter, The (Pinter), **Supp. I:** 369, 370–371, 381; **Retro. Supp. I:** 222
"Dumnesse" (Traherne), **II:** 189; **Supp. XI:** 270
Dun Cow, The (Landor), **IV:** 100
Dun Emer Press, **VI:** 221
"Dunbar and the Language of Poetry" (Morgan, E.), **Supp. IX:** 160
Dunbar, William, **I:** 23; **VIII:** 117–130
"Dunbar at Oxinfurde" (Dunbar), **VIII:** 122–123
Duncan, Robert, **Supp. IV:** 269
"Duncan" (Gunn), **Retro. Supp. III:** 129
Dunciad, The (Pope), **II:** 259, 311; **III:** 73, 77, 95; **IV:** 187; **Supp. III:** 421–422; **Retro. Supp. I:** 76, 231, 235, 238–240
"Dunciad Minimus" (Hope), **Supp. VII:** 161
Dunciad Minor: A Heroick Poem (Hope), **Supp. VII:** 161–163
Dunciad of Today, The; and, The Modern Aesop (Disraeli), **IV:** 308
Dunciad Variorum, The (Pope), **Retro. Supp. I:** 238
Dunn, Douglas **Supp. X:** 65–84
Dunn, Nell, **VI:** 271
Dunne, John William, **VII:** 209, 210
Duns Scotus, John, **V:** 363, 370, 371; **Retro. Supp. II:** 187–188
"Duns Scotus's Oxford" (Hopkins), **V:** 363, 367, 370
Dunsany, Lord Edward, **III:** 340
Dunton, John, **III:** 41
Dupee, F. W., **VI:** 31, 45
"Dura Mater" (Kinsella), **Supp. V:** 272
Dürer, Albrecht, **Supp. IV:** 125

"Duriesdyke" (Swinburne), **V:** 333
"During Wind and Rain" (Cornford), **VIII:** 114
"During Wind and Rain" (Hardy), **VI:** 17
Durrell, Lawrence, **Supp. I:** 93–128; **Retro. Supp. III:** 83–98
Dusklands (Coetzee), **Supp. VI:** 78–80, 81
"Dusky Ruth" (Coppard), **VIII:** 88, 90, 93
Dusky Ruth and Other Stories (Coppard), **VIII:** 90
"Dust" (Brooke), **Supp. III:** 52
"Dust, The" (Brathwaite), **Supp. XII:** 37–38, 40, 45
"Dust, The" (Redgrove), **Supp. VI:** 228
"Dust As We Are" (Hughes), **Retro. Supp. II:** 214
"Dustmen, The" (Mayhew), **Supp. XVI:** 218–220
Dutch Courtesan, The (Marston), **II:** 30, 40
Dutch Girls (Boyd), **Supp. XVI:** 45
Dutch Interior (O'Connor), **Supp. XIV:** 213, 218, 221–222, 226
Dutch Love, The (Behn), **Supp. III:** 26–27, 40; **Retro. Supp. III:** 3
Duties of Clerks of Petty Sessions in Ireland, The (Stoker), **Supp. III:** 379
Dutiful Daughter, A (Keneally), **Supp. IV:** 345
Dutton, G. F., **Supp. XII:** 81–99
"Duty—that's to say complying" (Clough), **V:** 160
Dwarfs, The (play, Pinter), **Supp. I:** 373
"Dwarfs, The" (unpublished novel, Pinter), **Supp. I:** 367
Dwarves of Death, The (Coe), **Supp. XV:** 49, 50, 53, 54–55, 60
Dyer, John, **IV:** 199
Dyer, Sir Edward, **I:** 123
Dyer's Hand, The, and Other Essays (Auden), **V:** 46; **VII:** 394, 395
Dyet of Poland, The (Defoe), **III:** 13
"Dying" (Scupham), **Supp. XIII:** 226, 227
"Dying Agnostic, The" (Soutar), **Supp. XVI:** 244
Dying Gaul and Other Writings, The (Jones), **Supp. VII:** 171, 180
"Dying Is Not Setting Out" (Smith, I. C.), **Supp. IX:** 211
Dying Paralytic (Greuze), **Supp. IV:** 122
"Dying Race, A" (Motion), **Supp. VII:** 254
"Dying Swan, The" (Tennyson), **IV:** 329
"Dykes, The" (Kipling), **VI:** 203
Dylan Thomas: The Collected Stories (Thomas), **Retro. Supp. III:** 347, 348
Dymer (Lewis), **Supp. III:** 250
Dynamics of a Particle, The (Carroll), **V:** 274
Dynasts, The: A Drama of the Napoleonic Wars (Hardy), **VI:** 6–7, **10–12**; **Retro. Supp. I:** 121
Dyson, A. E., **III:** 51
"Dyvers thy death doo dyverslye bemone" (Surrey), **I:** 115
Eagle of the Ninth, The (play, Sutcliff and Rensten), **Supp. XVI:** 273

Eagle of the Ninth, The (Sutcliff), **Supp. XVI:** 261, 262, 266–267, 268

E. M. Forster: A Study (Trilling), **VI:** 413
E. M. Forster: A Tribute, with Selections from His Writings on India (Natwar-Singh), **VI:** 413
E. M. Forster: The Critical Heritage (ed. Gardner), **VI:** 413
"Each Time There's an Injustice on Earth" (tr. Delanty), **Supp. XIV:** 76
"Eagle Pair" (Murray), **Supp. VII:** 283
Eagles' Nest (Kavan), **Supp. VII:** 213–214
Eagle's Nest, The (Ruskin), **V:** 184
Eagleton, Terry, **Supp. IV:** 164, 365, 380
Eames, Hugh, **Supp. IV:** 3
Ear to the Ground, An (Conn), **Supp. XIII:** 70, 72–73
"Earl Robert" (Swinburne), **V:** 333
Earle, John, **IV:** 286
"Earlswood" (Adcock), **Supp. XII:** 9
"Early Days" (Conn), **Supp. XIII:** 78
Early Days (Storey), **Supp. I:** 419
Early Diary of Frances Burney, The (eds. Troide et al.), **Supp. III:** 64
Early Essays (Eliot), **V:** 200
Early Greek Travellers and the Hellenic Ideal (Constantine), **Supp. XV:** 66
Early Italian Poets, The (Rossetti), **V:** 245
Early Kings of Norway, The (Carlyle), **IV:** 250
Early Lessons (Edgeworth), **Supp. III:** 152
"Early Life and Works of Thomas Hardy, 1840–1878" (Reed), **Supp. XV:** 247
"Early Life of Ben Jonson, The" (Bamborough), **Retro. Supp. I:** 152
Early Morning (Bond), **Supp. I:** 422, 423, 426–428, 430
"Early One Morning" (Warner), **Supp. VII:** 379
Early Plays, The (Hare), **Supp. IV:** 283
Early Poems and Juvenilia (Larkin), **Retro. Supp. III:** 212
Early Poems of John Clare, The (Clare), **Supp. XI:** 51
"Early Spring" (Smith, I. C.), **Supp. IX:** 221
"Early Stuff" (Reading), **VIII:** 263
"Early Summer" (Scupham), **Supp. XIII:** 218
"Early Verses of Compliment to Miss Rose Baring" (Tennyson), **Retro. Supp. III:** 321–322
Early Years of Alec Waugh, The (Waugh), **Supp. VI:** 267–270, 272, 274
Earnest Atheist, The (Muggeridge), **Supp. II:** 118, 119
"Ears in the turrets hear" (Thomas), **Supp. I:** 174; **Retro. Supp. III:** 339
Earth Breath and Other Poems, The (Russell), **VIII:** 282
Earth Owl, The (Hughes), **Supp. I:** 348
Earthly Paradise, The (Morris), **V:** xxiii, **296–299**, 302, 304, 306
Earthly Paradise (Stallworthy), **Supp. X:** 291, 301–302

Earthly Powers (Burgess), **Supp. I:** 193
Earths in Our Solar System (Swedenborg), **III:** 297
Earthworks (Harrison), **Supp. V:** 149, 150
"East Anglian Church-yard" (Cornford), **VIII:** 113
"East Coker" (Eliot), **II:** 173; **VII:** 154, 155
East into Upper East: Plain Tales from New York and Delhi (Jhabvala), **Supp. V:** 235
"East London" (Arnold), **V:** 209
"East of Cairo" (Carson), **Supp. XIII:** 57
East of Suez (Maugham), **VI:** 369
"East Riding" (Dunn), **Supp. X:** 81–82
East, West: Stories (Rushdie), **Supp. IV:** 438, 443, 452
"East Window" (Dutton), **Supp. XII:** 90–91
Eastaway, Edward (pseud.), *see* Thomas, Edward
"Easter 1916" (O'Connor), **Supp. XIV:** 224
"Easter 1916" (Yeats), **VI:** 219, 220; **Retro. Supp. I:** 332
"Easter Day" (Crashaw), **II:** 183
"Easter Day, Naples, 1849" (Clough), **V:** 165
"Easter Day II" (Clough), **V:** 159
Easter Greeting for Every Child Who Loves AAlice,"An (Carroll), **V:** 273
"Easter Hymn" (Housman), **VI:** 161
"Easter 1916" (Yeats), **VI:** 219, 220
"Easter Prayer" (Fallon), **Supp. XII:** 114
Easter Rebellion of 1916, **VI:** 212; **VII:** 3
"Easter Wings" (Herbert), **II:** 128; **Retro. Supp. II:** 178
Eastern Front, The (Churchill), **VI:** 359
Eastern Life, Present and Past (Martineau), **Supp. XV:** 185–186, 187
Eastern Tales (Voltaire), **III:** 327
Eastlake, Lady Elizabeth, **Retro. Supp. I:** 59
Eastward Ho! (Chapman, Jonson, Marston), **I:** 234, 254 **II:** 30, 40; **Retro. Supp. I:** 162
Easy Death (Churchill), **Supp. IV:** 180
Easy Virtue (Coward), **Supp. II:** 145, 146, 148
Eating Pavlova (Thomas), **Supp. IV:** 488–489
Eaton, H. A., **IV:** 142*n*, 155, 156
"Eaves, The" (Nye), **Supp. X:** 200
Ebb-Tide, The (Stevenson), **V:** 384, 387, 390, 396
Ebony Tower, The (Fowles), **Supp. I:** **303–304**
"Ebony Tower, The" (Fowles), **Supp. I:** 303
Ecce Ancilla Domini! (Rossetti), **V:** 236, 248
"Ecchoing Green, The" (Blake), **Retro. Supp. I:** 37, 42
Ecclesiastical History of the English People (Bede), **Retro. Supp. II:** 296
Ecclesiastical Polity (Hooker), **II:** 147
Ecclesiastical Sonnets (Wordsworth), **IV:** **22, 25**

"Echo from Willowwood, An" (Rossetti), **V:** 259
Echo Gate, The (Longley), **VIII:** 166, 172, 173–174
"Echo Pit Road" (Burnside), **Supp. XIII:** 23
"Echoes of Foreign Song" (Mangan), **Supp. XIII:** 118
Echoes Return Slow, The (Thomas), **Supp. XII:** 280, 281, 283, 284, 288, 289, 290
Echo's Bones (Beckett), **Supp. I:** 44, 60–61
"Eclipse" (Armitage), **VIII:** 11, 12–14
"Eclogue for Christmas, An" (MacNeice), **VII:** 416
Eclogues (Vergil), **III:** 222*n*
Eclogues of Virgil, The (tr. Day Lewis), **Supp. III:** 118
Eco, Umberto, **Supp. IV:** 116
Economics of Ireland, and the Policy of the British Government, The (Russell), **VIII:** 289
"Economies or Dispensations of the Eternal" (Newman), **Supp. VII:** 291
Eagle of the Ninth, The (play, Sutcliff and Rensten), **Supp. XVI:** 273
Eagle of the Ninth, The (Sutcliff), **Supp. XVI:** 261, 262, 266–267, 268
Ecstasy, The (Donne), **I:** 238, 355, 358
Edel, Leon, **VI:** 49, 55
"Eden" (Traherne), **II:** 189; **Supp. XI:** 266
Eden End (Priestley), **VII:** 224
"Eden of the Sea, The" (Jewsbury), **Supp. XIV:** 162
Edge of Being, The (Spender), **Supp. II:** 486, 491
Edge of the Orison: In the Traces of John Clare's "Journey Out of Essex" (Sinclair), **Supp. XIV:** 232, 244–245
Edge of the Unknown (Doyle), **Supp. II:** 163–164
Edgeworth, Maria, **Supp. III:** **151–168**; **Supp. IV:** 502
Edgeworth, Richard Lovell, **Supp. III:** 151–153, 163
"Edinburgh Court" (MacCaig), **Supp. VI:** 194
"Edinburgh: A Place of My Own" (Butlin), **Supp. XVI:** 57
Edinburgh: Picturesque Notes (Stevenson), **V:** 395; **Retro. Supp. I:** 261
Edinburgh Review (periodical), **III:** 276, 285; **IV:** xvi, 129, 145, 269–270, 272, 278; **Supp. XII:** 119
"Edinburgh Spring" (MacCaig), **Supp. VI:** 194
Edith Sitwell (Bowra), **VII:** 141
Edith's Diary (Highsmith), **Supp. V:** 177–178, 180
Editor's Tales, An (Trollope), **V:** 102
Edmonds, Helen, *see* Kavan, Anna
Edmund Blunden: Poems of Many Years (Blunden), **Supp. XI:** 33, 34, 35, 36, 37
Education, An (screenplay, Hornby), **Supp. XV:** 145

Education and the University (Leavis), **VII:** 238, 241

"Education of Otis Yeere, The" (Kipling), **VI:** 183, 184

Edward I (Peele), **I:** 205–206, 208

Edward II (Marlowe), **I:** 278, **286–287**; **Retro. Supp. I:** 201–202, 209–211

Edward III (anon.), **V:** 328

Edward and Eleonora (Thomson), **Supp. III:** 411, 424

Edward Burne-Jones (Fitzgerald), **Supp. V:** 98

"Edward Cracroft Lefroy" (Symonds), **Supp. XIV:** 262

Edward Carpenter: In Appreciation (ed. Beith), **Supp. XIII:** 48–50

"Edward Dorn and the Treasures of Comedy" (Davie), **Supp. VI:** 116

Edward Lear in Greece (Lear), **V:** 87

Edward Lear's Indian Journal (ed. Murphy), **V:** 78, 79, 87

"Edward the Conqueror" (Dahl), **Supp. IV:** 215

Edwards, H. L. R., **I:** 87

"Edwin and Angelina: A Ballad" (Goldsmith), **III:** 185, 191

Edwin Drood (Dickens), **V:** xxiii, 42, 69, 72

"Edwin Morris" (Tennyson), **IV:** 326n

Edwy and Elgiva (Burney), **Supp. III:** 67, 71

"Eemis Stane, The" (MacDiarmid), **Supp. XII:** 206

"Eftir Geving I Speik of Taking" (Dunbar), **VIII:** 122

Egan, Pierce, **IV:** 260n

"Egg-Head" (Hughes), **Supp. I:** 348–349

Egils saga Skalla-Grímssonar, **VIII:** 238, 239

Egoist, The (Meredith), **V:** x, xxiv, 227, 230–232, 234

"Egremont" (Nicholson), **Supp. VI:** 214

"Egypt" (Fraser), **VII:** 425

"Egypt from My Inside" (Golding), **Supp. I:** 65, 83, 84, 89

"Egypt from My Outside" (Golding), **Supp. I:** 84, 89

Egyptian Journal, An (Golding), **Supp. I:** 89–90; **Retro. Supp. I:** 103

"Egyptian Nights" (Pushkin), **Supp. IV:** 484

Eh Joe (Beckett), **Supp. I:** 59–60

Eichmann in Jerusalem (Arendt), **Supp. IV:** 306

"Eight Arms to Hold You" (Kureishi), **Supp. XI:** 161

"Eight Awful Animals" (Ewart), **Supp. VII:** 39

Eight Dramas of Calderón (tr. FitzGerald), **IV:** 353

"Eight o'clock" (Housman), **VI:** 160

Eight or Nine Wise Words about Letter-Writing (Carroll), **V:** 273

Eight Short Stories (Waugh), **Supp. VI:** 273

"Eight Stanzas" (Mangan), **Supp. XIII:** 119

"Eight Suits, The" (Ewart), **Supp. VII:** 39

18 Poems (Thomas), **Supp. I:** 170, 171, 172; **Retro. Supp. III:** 335, 337

Eighteen-Eighties, The (ed. de la Mare), **V:** 268, 274

"Eighth Planet, The" (Maitland), **Supp. XI:** 174

85 Poems (Ewart), **Supp. VII:** 34–35, 46

ΕΙΚΟΝΟΚΛΑΣΤΗΣ: . . . (Milton), **II:** 175

Einstein's Monsters (Amis), **Supp. IV:** 40, 42

Eiríks saga rauða, **VIII:** 240

Ekblad, Inga Stina, **II:** 77, 86

"El Dorado" (Fallon), **Supp. XII:** 105

El maestro de danzar (Calderón), **II:** 313n

"Elaine" (Tennyson), **Retro. Supp. III:** 327

Elder Brother, The (Fletcher and Massinger), **II:** 66

Elder Statesman, The (Eliot), **VII:** 161, 162; **Retro. Supp. II:** 132

Elders and Betters (Compton-Burnett), **VII:** 63, 66

Eldest Son, The (Galsworthy), **VI:** 269, 287

"Eldon Hole" (Constantine), **Supp. XV:** 73

"Eldorado" (Lessing), **Supp. I:** 240

Eleanora, A Panegyric Poem Dedicated to the Memory of the Late Countess of Abingdon (Dryden), **Retro. Supp. III:** 56

Eleanor's Victory (Braddon), **VIII:** 36, 44

Election, An (Swinburne), **V:** 332

"Election in Ajmer, The" (Naipaul), **Supp. I:** 395

Elections to the Hebdomadal Council, The (Carroll), **V:** 274

Elective Affinities (tr. Constantine), **Supp. XV:** 66

Electric Brae (Greig), **Supp. XVI:** 165–167, 168

Electric Light (Heaney), **Retro. Supp. I:** 133–135

"Electric Orchard, The" (Muldoon), **Supp. IV:** 413

"Electricity" (Crace), **Supp. XIV:** 22

Electrification of the Soviet Union, The (Raine), **Supp. XIII:** 168–170, 171

"Elegiac Stanzas, Suggested by a Picture of Peele Castle . . . . A (Wordsworth), **IV:** 21–22

Elegiarum Liber (Campion), **Supp. XVI:** 99

"Elegie. Princesse Katherine, An" (Lovelace), **II:** 230

"Elegie upon the Death of . . . Dr. John Donne" (Carew), **II:** 223

Elegies (Donne), **I:** 360–361; **Retro. Supp. II:** 89–90

Elegies (Dunn), **Supp. X:** 75–77

Elegies (Johannes Secundus), **II:** 108

Elegies for the Dead in Cyrenaica (Henderson), **VII:** 425

"Elegy" (Gunn), **Supp. IV:** 271–272, 274; **Retro. Supp. III:** 125

"Elegy" (Thomas), **Retro. Supp. III:** 347

"Elegy, An" (Wallace-Crabbe), **VIII:** 322

"Elegy: The Absences" (Malouf), **Supp. XII:** 220

Elegy and Other Poems, An (Blunden), **Supp. XI:** 45

"Elegy Before Death" (Day Lewis), **Supp. III:** 129

"Elegy for an Irish Speaker" (McGuckian), **Supp. V:** 285, 290

"Elegy for Margaret" (Spender), **Supp. II:** 490

"Elegy for W. H. Auden" (Jennings), **Supp. V:** 217

"Elegy in April and September" (Owen), **VI:** 453

"Elegy on Dead Fashion" (Sitwell), **VII:** 133

Elegy on Dicky and Dolly, An (Swift), **III:** 36

Elegy on Dr. Donne, An (Walton), **II:** 136

"Elegy on Marlowe's Untimely Death" (Nashe), **I:** 278

"Elegy on the Death of a Mad Dog" (Goldsmith), **III:** 184

Elegy on the Death of an Amiable Young Lady . . ., An (Boswell), **III:** 247

"Elegy on the Dust" (Gunn), **Supp. IV:** 264

"Elegy on the Tironian and Tirconellian Princes Buried at Rome, An" (Mangan), **Supp. XIII:** 127

Elegy on the Usurper O. C., An (Dryden), **II:** 304

"Elegy to the Memory of an Unfortunate Lady" (Pope), **III:** 70, 288

Elegy upon the Death of My Lord Francis Villiers, An (Marvell), **II:** 219

"Elegy upon the most Incomparable King Charls the First, An" (King), **Supp. VI:** 159

"Elegy Written in a Country Churchyard" (Gray), **III:** 119, 137, **138–139**, 144–145; **Retro. Supp. I:** 144

"Elementary Sketches of Moral Philosophy" (Smith), **Supp. VII:** 342

Elementary, The (Mulcaster), **I:** 122

Elements of Drawing, The (Ruskin), **V:** 184

"Elements of Geometry, The" (Malouf), **Supp. XII:** 220

Elements of Perspective, The (Ruskin), **V:** 184

Elene, **Retro. Supp. II:** 302–303

Eleonora: A Panegyrical Poem (Dryden), **II:** 304

"Elephant and Colosseum" (Lowry), **Supp. III:** 281

"Elephant and the Tragopan, The" (Seth), **Supp. X:** 287

Elephants Can Remember (Christie), **Supp. II:** 135

"Elgin Marbles, The" (Crawford), **Supp. XI:** 75

Elia, pseud. of Charles Lamb

"Eliduc" (Fowles), **Supp. I:** 303

Elinor and Marianne: A Sequel to Jane Austen's Sense and Sensibility (Tennant), **Supp. IX:** 237–238, 239–240

"Elinor Barley" (Warner), **Supp. VII:** 379

"Elinor and Marianne" (Austen), *see Sense and Sensibility*

Eliot, George, **III:** 157; **IV:** 238, 323; **V:** ix–x, xviii, xxii–xxiv, 2, 6, 7, 14, 45, 52, 56, 57, 63, 66, 67, **187–201,** 212, **VI:** 23; **Supp. IV:** 146, 169, 230, 233, 239–240, 243, 379, 471, 513; **Retro. Supp. II: 101–117**

Eliot T. S., **II:** 148; **IV:** 271; **V:** xxv, 241 309 402; **VII:** xii–xiii, xv, 34, **143–170;** **Retro. Supp. II: 119–133;** and Matthew Arnold, **V:** 204, 205–206, 210, 215; and Yeats, **VI:** 207, 208; influence on modern literature, **I:** 98; **VII:** xii–xiii, xv, 34 143–144, 153–154, 165–166; **Retro. Supp. I:** 3; list of collected essays, **VII:** 169–170; literary criticism, **I:** 232, 275, 280; **II:** 16, 42, 83, 179, 196, 204, 208, 219; **III:** 51, 305; **IV:** 195, 234; **V:** 204–206, 210, 215, 310, 367; **VI:** 207, 226; **VII:** 162–165; **Retro. Supp. I:** 166; **Retro. Supp. II:** 173–174; style, **II:** 173; **IV:** 323, 329; in drama, **VII:** 157–162; in poetry, **VII:** 144–157; **Supp. I:** 122–123; **Supp. II:** 151, 181, 420, 428, 487; **Supp. III:** 122; **Supp. IV:** 58, 100, 139, 142, 180, 249, 260, 330, 377, 558

"Elixir" (Murphy), **Supp. V:** 326

"Ella of Garveloch" (Martineau), **Supp. XV:** 188

"Ella Wheeler Wilcox Woo, The" (Ewart), **Supp. VII:** 41

"Elvers, The" (Nicholson), **Supp. VI:** 214

"Ely Place" (Kinsella), **Supp. V:** 267

Elizabeth Alone (Trevor), **Supp. IV:** 509–510

Elizabeth and Essex (Strachey), **Supp. II: 514–517**

Elizabeth and Her German Garden (Forster), **VI:** 406

Elizabeth Cooper (Moore), **VI:** 96, 99

Elizabeth I: Collected Works (Elizabeth I), **Supp. XVI:** 147, 149, 152, 154, 156

Elizabeth I, Queen of England, **Supp. IV:** 146

Elizabeth I, Queen of England, **Supp. XVI: 145–159**

Elizabeth I: Translations, 1544–1589 (Elizabeth I), **Supp. XVI:** 157

Elizabethan Drama and Shakespeare's Early Plays (Talbert), **I:** 224

"Elizas, The" (Gurney), **VI:** 425

"Ellen Orford" (Crabbe), **III:** 281

Ellen Terry and Bernard Shaw, a Correspondence (ed. St. John), **VI:** 130

Ellis, Annie Raine, **Supp. III:** 63, 65

Ellis, Havelock, **I:** 281

Ellis–Fermor, U. M., **I:** 284, 292

"Elm Tree, The" (Hood), **IV:** 261–262, 264

"Eloisa to Abelard" (Pope), **III:** 70, 75–76, 77; **V:** 319, 321

Elopement into Exile (Pritchett), *see Shirley Sanz*

Eloquence of the British Senate, The (Hazlitt), **IV:** 130, 139

Elton, Oliver, **III:** 51

"Elvis Presley" (Gunn), **Retro. Supp. III:** 119–120

Emancipated, The (Gissing), **V:** 437

"Embankment, The" (Hulme), **Supp. VI:** 134, 136

Embarrassments (James), **VI:** 49, 67

Embers (Beckett), **Supp. I:** 58

Emblem Hurlstone (Hall), **Supp. VI:** 129–130

Emblems of Love (Abercrombie), **Supp. XVI:** 2–3

"Emerald Dove, The" (Murray), **Supp. VII:** 281

Emerald Germs of Ireland (McCabe), **Supp. IX:** 135, 137–138

"Emerald Isle, Sri Lanka, The" (Delanty), **Supp. XIV:** 73

"Emerging" (Thomas), **Supp. XII:** 286–287

Emerson, Ralph Waldo, **IV:** xx, 54, 81, 240; **V:** xxv

Emigrant Ship, The (Stevenson), **Retro. Supp. I:** 262

Emigrant Train, The (Stevenson), **Retro. Supp. I:** 262

Emigrants, The (Lamming), **Supp. IV:** 445

Emigrants, The (Sebald), **VIII:** 295, 300–303, 308

Emilia in England (Meredith), *see Sandra Belloni*

Emilie de Coulanges (Edgeworth), **Supp. III:** 158

"Emily and Oswin" (Upward), **Supp. XIII:** 262

Emily Brontë: *A Biography* (Gérin), **V:** 153

Emily Butter: An Occasion Recalled (Reed and Swann), **Supp. XV:** 253

"Emily Dickinson" (Cope), **VIII:** 73

"Emily Dickinson" (Longley), **VIII:** 167

Eminent Victorians (Wilson), **Supp. VI:** 305

Eminent Victorians (Strachey), **V:** 13, 157, 170; **Supp. II:** 498, 499, **503–511**

Emma (Austen), **IV:** xvii, 108, 109, 111, 112, 113, 114, 115, 117, 119, 120, 122; **VI:** 106; **Supp. IV:** 154, 236; **Retro. Supp. II:** 11–12

Emma in Love: Jane Austen's Emma Continued (Tennant), **Supp. IX:** 238, 239–240

Emotions Are Not Skilled Workers, The (Wallace–Crabbe), **VIII:** 318

Empedocles on Etna (Arnold), **IV:** 231; **V:** xxi, 206, 207, 209, 210, 211, 216

"Emperor Alexander and Capo d'Istria" (Landor), **IV:** 92

"Emperor and the Little Girl, The" (Shaw), **VI:** 120

Emperor Constantine, The (Sayers), **Supp. III:** 336, 350

"Emperor's Tomb Found in China" (Fuller), **Supp. VII:** 80

Emperor of Ice-Cream (Moore, B.), **Supp. IX:** 141, 142–143, 144, 146, 147

Emperour of the East, The (Massinger), **Supp. XI:** 184

"Empire" (Carpenter), **Supp. XIII:** 39

Empire of the Sun (Ballard), **Supp. V:** 19, 29–30, 31, 35

Empire State (Bateman), **Supp. V:** 88

"Empires" (Dunn), **Supp. X:** 72–73

"Employment (I)" (Herbert), **Retro. Supp. II:** 180

Empson, William, **I:** 282; **II:** 124, 130; **V:** 367, 381; **Supp. II: 179–197**

"Empty Birdhouse, The" (Highsmith), **Supp. V:** 180

"Empty Church, The" (Thomas), **Supp. XII:** 284, 287

"Empty Heart, The" (Nye), **Supp. X:** 204

Empty Purse, The (Meredith), **V:** 223, 234

"Empty Vessel" (MacDiarmid), **Supp. XII:** 206–207

"Enallos and Cymodameia" (Landor), **IV:** 96

Enchafèd Flood, The (Auden), **VII:** 380, 394

Enchanted Isle, The (Dryden), **I:** 327

"Enchanted Thicket, The" (Carpenter), **Supp. XIII:** 40

Enchantment and Other Poems (Russell), **VIII:** 290

"Enchantment of Islands" (Brown), **Supp. VI:** 61

Enchantress, The, and Other Poems (Browning), **IV:** 321

Enclosure, The (Hill), **Supp. XIV:** 115, 117, 118

Encounter, **Supp. II:** 491

Encounters (Bowen), **Supp. II:** 79, 81

Encyclopaedia Britannica, **Supp. III:** 171

"End, An" (Nye), **Supp. X:** 204

"End, The" (Beckett), **Supp. I:** 50; **Retro. Supp. I:** 21

"End, The" (Cornford), **VIII:** 107

"End, The" (Milne), **Supp. V:** 303

"End, The" (Owen), **VI:** 449

"End of a Journey" (Hope), **Supp. VII:** 156–157

End of a War, The (Read), **VI:** 436, 437

"End of an Impulse, The" (Reed), **Supp. XV:** 248

End of Drought (Pitter), **Supp. XIII:** 136, 145

End of the Affair, The (Greene), **Supp. I:** 2, 8, 12–13, 14; **Retro. Supp. II:** 159–160

End of the Beginning, The (O'Casey), **VII:** 12

End of the Chapter (Galsworthy), **VI:** 275, 282

"End of the City" (Fuller), **Supp. VII:** 69

"End of the Relationship, The" (Self), **Supp. V:** 403

"End of the Tether, The" (Conrad), **VI:** 148

End of the World, The (Abercrombie), **Supp. XVI:** 7–8

Enderby Outside (Burgess), **Supp. I:** 189, 194–195

Enderby's Dark Lady; or, No End to Enderby (Burgess), **Supp. I:** 189

Endgame (Beckett), **Supp. I:** 49, 51, 52, 53, 56–57, 62; **Retro. Supp. I:** 24–25
"Ending, An" (Cope), **VIII:** 81
Ending in Earnest (West), **Supp. III:** 438
Ending Up (Amis), **Supp. II:** 18
Endiomion (Lyly), **I:** 202
Endless Night (Christie), **Supp. II:** 125, 130, 132, 135
Ends and Beginnings (Smith, I. C.), **Supp. IX:** 221–222
Ends and Means (Huxley), **VII:** xvii 205
Endymion (Disraeli), **IV:** xxiii, 294, 295, 296, 306, 307, 308; **V:** xxiv
"Endymion" (Keats), **III:** 174, 338; **IV:** x, xvii, 205, 211, 214, 216–217, 218, 222–224, 227, 229, 230, 233, 235; **Retro. Supp. I:** 184, 189–192
"Enemies, The" (Jennings), **Supp. V:** 211
Enemies of Promise (Connolly), **VI:** 363; **Supp. III:** 95, 96, 97, 98, **100–102**
"Enemy, The" (Naipaul), **Supp. I:** 386n
"Enemy Dead, The" (Gutteridge), **VII:** 433
Enemy in the Blanket, The (Burgess), **Supp. I:** 187–188
"Enemy Interlude" (Lewis), **VII:** 71
Enemy of the People, An (Ibsen), **VI:** ix
Enemy of the Stars, The (Lewis), **VII:** 72, 73, 74–75
Enemy Within, The (Friel), **Supp. V:** 115–116
Enemy's Country, The: Word, Contexture, and Other Circumstances of Language (Hill), **Supp. V:** 196, 201; **Retro. Supp. III:** 145
"Engineer's Corner" (Cope), **VIII:** 71
England (Davie), **Supp. VI:** 111–112
"England" (Stevenson), **Supp. VI:** 255–256, 264
"England" (Thomas), **Supp. III:** 404
England and the Italian Question (Arnold), **V:** 216
England in the Age of Wycliffe (Trevelyan), **VI:** 385–386
England Made Me (Greene; U.S. title, *The Shipwrecked*), **Supp. I:** 6, 7
"England, My England" (Lawrence) **VII:** xv, 114; **Retro. Supp. II:** 153
England, My England, and Other Stories (Lawrence), **VII:** 114
England Under Queen Anne (Trevelyan), **VI: 391–393**
England Under the Stuarts (Trevelyan), **VI:** 386
England Your England (Orwell), **VII:** 282
"England's Answer" (Kipling), **VI:** 192
England's Helicon, **I:** 291
England's Hour (Brittain), **Supp. X:** 45
"England's Ideal" (Carpenter), **Supp. XIII:** 40
England's Ideal, and Other Papers on Social Subjects (Carpenter), **Supp. XIII:** 40
"England's Ireland" (Hare), **Supp. IV:** 281
England's Pleasant Land (Forster), **VI:** 411
"English and the Afrikaans Writer" (Brink), **Supp. VI:** 48–49
English, David, **Supp. IV:** 348

English Bards and Scotch Reviewers (Byron), **IV:** x, xvi, 129, 171, 192
English Bible, **I: 370–388;** list of versions, **I:** 387
"English Climate" (Warner), **Supp. VII:** 380
English Comic Characters, The (Priestley), **VII:** 211
English Eccentrics, The (Sitwell), **VII:** 127
English Folk–Songs (ed. Barrett), **V:** 263n
English Grammar (Jonson), **Retro. Supp. I:** 166
English Historical Review, **VI:** 387
English Hours (James), **VI:** 46, 67
English Humour (Priestley), **VII:** 213
English Humourists of the Eighteenth Century, The (Thackeray), **III:** 124, 146n; **V:** 20, 31, 38
English Journey (Bainbridge), **Supp. VI:** 22–23
English Journey (Priestley), **VII:** 212, 213–214
English Literature: A Survey for Students (Burgess), **Supp. I:** 189
English Literature and Society in the Eighteenth Century (Stephen), **III:** 41; **V:** 290
"English Literature and the Small Coterie" (Kelman), **Supp. V:** 257
English Literature, 1815–1832 (ed. Jack), **IV: 40, 140**
English Literature in Our Time and the University (Leavis), **VII:** 169, 235, 236–237, 253
English Literature in the Sixteenth Century, Excluding Drama (Lewis), **Supp. III:** 249, 264
"English Mail–Coach, The" (De Quincey), **IV:** 149, 153, 155
English Mirror, The (Whetstone), **I:** 282
English Moor, The (Brome), **Supp. X:** 62
English Music (Ackroyd), **Supp. VI:** 9–10, 11, 12
English Novel, The (Ford), **VI:** 322, 332
English Novel, The: A Short Critical History (Allen), **V:** 219
English Novelists (Bowen), **Supp. II:** 91–92
English Pastoral Poetry (Empson), *see Some Versions of Pastoral*
English People, The (Orwell), **VII:** 282
English Poems (Blunden), **VI:** 429
"English Poet, An" (Pater), **V:** 356, 357
English Poetry (Bateson), **IV:** 217, 323n, 339
English Poetry and the English Language (Leavis), **VII:** 234
English Poetry 1900–1950: An Assessment (Sisson), **Supp. XI:** 249–250, 257
English Poetry of the First World War (Owen), **VI:** 453
English Poets (Browning), **IV:** 321
English Prisons under Local Government (Webb), **VI:** 129
English Protestant's Plea, The (King), **Supp. VI:** 152
"English Renaissance of Art, The" (Wilde), **V:** 403–404

English Renaissance Poetry (ed. Williams), **Supp. XI:** 116, 117
English Review (periodical), **VI:** xi–xii, 294, 323–324; **VII:** 89
English Revolution, 1688–1689 (Trevelyan), **VI:** 391
"English School, An" (Kipling), **VI:** 201
English Seamen (Southey and Bell), **IV:** 71
English Sermon, 1750–1850, The (ed. Nye), **Supp. X:** 205
English Social History: A Survey of Six Centuries (Trevelyan), **VI:** xv, 393–394
English Songs of Italian Freedom (Trevelyan), **V:** 227
English South African's View of the Situation, An (Schreiner), **Supp. II:** 453
English Through Pictures (Richards), **Supp. II:** 425, 430
English Town in the Last Hundred Years (Betjeman), **VII:** 360
English Traits (Emerson), **IV:** 54
English Utilitarians, The (Stephen), **V:** 279, 288–289
"English Wife, The" (Ewart), **Supp. VII:** 36
English Without Tears (Rattigan), **Supp. VII:** 311
English Works of George Herbert (Palmer), **Retro. Supp. II:** 173
Englishman (periodical), **III:** 7, 50, 53
Englishman Abroad, An (Bennett), **VIII:** 30, 31
"Englishman in Italy, The" (Browning), **IV:** 368; **Retro. Supp. III:** 22
Englishman in Patagonia, An (Pilkington), **Supp. IV:** 164
Englishman Looks at the World, An (Wells), **VI:** 244
Englishman's Home, An (du Maurier), **Supp. III:** 147, 148
"Englishmen and Italians" (Trevelyan), **V:** 227; **VI:** 388n
Englishness of English Literature, The (Ackroyd), **Supp. VI:** 12
Englishwoman in America, The (Bird) **Supp. X:** 19–22, 24, 29
"Engraving from a Child's Encyclopaedia" (Carson), **Supp. XIII:** 56
"Enid" (Tennyson), **Retro. Supp. III:** 327
"Enigma, The" (Fowles), **Supp. I:** 303–304
Enjoy (Bennett), **VIII:** 28–29
Ennui (Edgeworth), **Supp. III:** 154, 156, **158–160**
Enoch Arden (Tennyson), **IV:** xxii, 388; **V:** 6; **Retro. Supp. III:** 328, 330
"Enoch Soames" (Beerbohm), **Supp. II:** 56
Enormous Crocodile, The (Dahl), **Supp. IV:** 207
"Enormous Space, The" (Ballard), **Supp. V:** 33
"Enough" (Nye), **Supp. X:** 205
Enough Is as Good as a Feast (Wager), **I:** 213
Enough of Green, (Stevenson), **Supp. VI:** 260

Enquirer: Reflections on Education, Manners, and Literature, in a Series of Essays (Godwin), **Supp. XV:** 122–123, 128
"Enquirie, The" (Traherne), **Supp. XI:** 268
Enquiry Concerning Human Understanding, An (Hume), **Supp. III:** 231, 238, 243–244
Enquiry Concerning Political Justice, An (Godwin), **IV:** xv, 181; **Supp. III:** 370; **Retro. Supp. I:** 245
Enquiry Concerning Political Justice, and Its Influence on General Virtue and Happiness, An (Godwin), **Supp. XV:** 119, 120–121, 122, 124, 126, 127, 128
Enquiry Concerning the Principles of Morals, An (Hume), **Supp. III:** 231, 238, 244
Enquiry into the Causes of the Late Increase of Robbers (Fielding), **III:** 104; **Retro. Supp. I:** 81
Enquiry into the Occasional Conformity of Dissenters . . . . An (Defoe), **III:** 12
Enquiry into the Present State of Polite Learning in Europe, An (Goldsmith), **III:** 179, 191
"Enquiry into Two Inches of Ivory, An" (Raine), **Supp. XIII:** 165
Enright, D. J., **Supp. IV:** 256, 354
"Enter a Cloud" (Graham), **Supp. VII:** 103
"Enter a Dragoon" (Hardy), **VI:** 22
Enter a Free Man (Stoppard), **Supp. I:** 437, 439–440, 445
"Enter One in Sumptuous Armour" (Lowry), **Supp. III:** 285
Entertainer, The (Osborne), **Supp. I:** 332–333, 336–337, 339
Entertaining Mr. Sloane (Orton), **Supp. V:** 364, 367, 370–371, 372, 373–374
Entertainment (Middleton), **II:** 3
"Entertainment for David Wright on His Being Sixty, An" (Graham), **Supp. VII:** 116
"Entertainment of the Queen and Prince at Althorpe (Jonson), **Retro. Supp. I:** 161
Enthusiasm (Byrom), **Supp. XVI:** 75, 76–79
"Entire Fabric, The" (Kinsella), **Supp. V:** 268
"Entrance" (Kinsella), **Supp. V:** 271
"Entreating of Sorrow" (Ralegh), **I:** 147–148
"Envoi" (Stallworthy), **Supp. X:** 297
"Envoy" (Carson), **Supp. XIII:** 65
Envoy Extraordinary: A Study of Vijaya Lakshmi Pandit and Her Contribution to Modern India (Brittain), **Supp. X:** 47
"Envoy Extraordinary" (Golding), **Supp. I:** 75, 82, 83
"Eolian Harp, The" (Coleridge), **IV:** 46; **Retro. Supp. II:** 52
Epicoene (Johnson), **I:** 339, 341; **Retro. Supp. I:** 163
"Epicure, The" (Cowley), **II:** 198
"Epicurus, Leontion and Ternissa" (Landor), **IV:** 94, 96–97

Epigram CXX (Jonson), **I:** 347
"Epigram to My Muse, the Lady Digby, on Her Husband, Sir Kenelm Digby" (Jonson), **Retro. Supp. I:** 151
Epigrammata (More), **Supp. VII:** 234, 236–237
Epigrammatum sacrorum liber (Crashaw), **II:** 179, 201
Epigrams (Jonson), **Retro. Supp. I:** 164
Epilogue (Graves), **VII:** 261
"Epilogue: Seven Decades" (Morgan, E.), **Supp. IX:** 164
"Epilogue to an Empire" (Stallworthy), **Supp. X:** 295
Epilogue to the Satires (Pope), **III:** 74, 78
"Epipsychidion" (Shelley), **IV:** xviii, 204, 208; **VI:** 401; **Retro. Supp. I:** 254–255
Epistle (Trevisa), **Supp. IX:** 248, 249
"Epistle, An: Edward Sackville to Venetia Digby" (Hope), **Supp. VII:** 159
"Epistle Containing the Strange Medical Experience of Karshish, the Arab Physician, An" (Browning), **Retro. Supp. III:** 26
"Epistle from Holofernes, An" (Hope), **Supp. VII:** 157
Epistle to a Canary (Browning), **IV:** 321
Epistle to a Friend; Occasioned by a Sermon Intituled The False Claims to Martyrdom Consider'd (Byrom), **Supp. XVI:** 81
"Epistle to a Friend on the Art of English Poetry, An" (Byrom), **Supp. XVI:** 73
Epistle to a Gentleman of the Temple, An (Byrom), **Supp. XVI:** 75–76
Epistle to a Lady . . . , An (Swift), **III:** 36
Epistle to Augustus (Pope), **II:** 196
Epistle to Cobham, An (Pope), see *Moral Essays*
"Epistle to Davie" (Burns), **III:** 316
"Epistle to Dr. Arbuthnot" (Pope), **III:** 71, 74–75, 78; **Retro. Supp. I:** 229
"Epistle to Henry Reynolds" (Drayton), **I:** 196
Epistle to Her Grace Henrietta . . . , An (Gay), **III:** 67
"Epistle to John Hamilton Reynolds" (Keats), **IV:** 221
Epistle to . . . Lord Carteret, An (Swift), **III:** 35
"Epistle to Mr. Dryden, An, . . ." (Wycherley), **II:** 322
Epistle to the . . . Earl of Burlington, An (Pope), see *Moral Essays*
"Epistle to the Rev. William Bull, An" (Cowper), **Retro. Supp. III:** 47
Epistle upon an Epistle, An (Swift), **III:** 35
Epistles to the King and Duke (Wycherley), **II:** 321
Epistola adversus Jovinianum (St. Jerome), **I:** 35
"Epitaph" (Sisson), **Supp. XI:** 243
"Epitaph for a Reviewer" (Cornford), **VIII:** 113
Epitaph For A Spy (Ambler), **Supp. IV:** 8

"Epitaph for Anton Schmidt" (Gunn), **Supp. IV:** 264
Epitaph for George Dillon (Osborne), **Supp. I:** 329–330, 333
"Epitaph on a Fir–Tree" (Murphy), **Supp. V:** 317–318
"Epitaph on a Hare" (Cowper), **Retro. Supp. III:** 36
"Epitaph on a Jacobite" (Macaulay), **IV:** 283
"Epitaph on a Potential Poet who learned the meaning of every word in the English Dictionary" (Soutar), **Supp. XVI:** 249
"Epitaph on an Army of Mercenaries" (Housman), **VI:** 161, 415–416
"Epitaph on Francis Charteris" (Arbuthnot), **Supp. XVI:** 27–28
Epitaph on George Moore (Morgan), **VI:** 86
"Epitaph on the Admirable Dramaticke Poet, W. Shakespeare, An" (Milton), **II:** 175
"Epitaph on the Lady Mary Villers" (Carew), **II:** 224
"Epitaphs" (Warner), **Supp. VII:** 371
Epitaphs and Occasions (Fuller), **Supp. VII:** 72
"Epitaphs for Soldiers" (Fuller), **Supp. VII:** 72
Epitaphium Damonis (Milton), **II:** 175
"Epithalamion" (Hopkins), **V:** 376, 377
"Epithalamion" (Scupham), **Supp. XIII:** 229
Epithalamion (Spenser), **I:** 130–131; see also *Amoretti and Epithalamion*
"Epithalamion for Gloucester" (Lydgate), **I:** 58
"Epithalamion Thamesis" (Spenser), **I:** 123
"Epithalamium" (Burnside), **Supp. XIII:** 23
"Epithalamium" (Motion), **Supp. VII:** 266
Epoch and Artist (Jones), **Supp. VII:** 168, 170, 171
Epping Hunt, The (Hood), **IV:** 256, 257, 267
Equal Love (Davies), **Supp. XIV:** 35, 36, 40–45
"Equal Love" (Davies), **Supp. XIV:** 42–43
Equal Music, An (Seth), **Supp. X:** 277, 288–290
Equal Skies, The (MacCaig), **Supp. VI:** 193
Equus (Shaffer), **Supp. I:** 318, 323, **324–326,** 327
Erdman, D. V., **III:** 289n, 307
Erechtheus (Swinburne), **V:** 314, 331, 332
Erewhon (Butler), **Supp. II:** 99–101
Erewhon Revisited (Butler), **Supp. II:** 99, 111, 116–117
Eric Ambler (Lewis), **Supp. IV:** 13
Eric Brighteyes (Haggard), **Supp. III:** 214
Eridanus (Lowry), **Supp. III:** 280
Ermine, The (Pitter), **Supp. XIII:** 135, 144

"Ermine, The" (Pitter), **Supp. XIII:** 144
Ernie's Incredible Illucinations (Ayckbourn), **Supp. V:** 2
"Eros and Anteros" (Symonds), **Supp. XIV:** 252
Eros and Psyche (Bridges), **VI:** 83
"Erotion" (Swinburne), **V:** 320
Erpingham Camp, The (Orton), **Supp. V:** 367, 371, 375–376
"Errata" (Rushdie), **Supp. IV:** 442
Erskine, Andrew, **III:** 247
"Erstwhile" (Wallace–Crabbe), **VIII:** 323
Esau (Kerr), **Supp. XII:** 186–187, 194, 195
Escape (Galsworthy), **VI:** 275, 287
"Escaped Cock, The" (Lawrence), **VII:** 91, 115
"Escaped From The Massacre?" (Carson), **Supp. XIII:** 54
"Escapement" (Ballard), **Supp. V:** 21
"Escapist, The" (Day Lewis), **Supp. III:** 127–128
"Eschatology" (Thomas), **Supp. XII:** 290
"Escorial, The" (Hopkins), **V:** 361
Esio Trot (Dahl), **Supp. IV:** 225
Esmond in India (Jhabvala), **Supp. V:** 226–227
Espalier, The (Warner), **Supp. VII:** 370, 371
"Especially when the October Wind" (Thomas), **Supp. I:** 173
Espedair Street (Banks), **Supp. XI:** 5–6
Esprit de Corps (Durrell), **Supp. I:** 113; **Retro. Supp. III:** 85
Essai sur l'étude de la littérature (Gibbon), **III:** 222, 223
Essais (Montaigne), **III:** 39
Essay Concerning Human Understanding (Locke), **III:** 22; **Supp. III:** 233
"Essay Concerning Humour in Comedy, An" (Congreve), *see Concerning Humour in Comedy*
Essay Concerning the Effects of Air on Human Bodies, An (Arbuthnot), **Supp. XVI:** 28
Essay Concerning the Nature of Aliments, and the Choice of Them, According to the Different Constitution of Human Bodies, An (Arbuthnot), **Supp. XVI:** 27
Essay Concerning the Nature of Aliments, and the Choice of Them, According to the Different Constitution of Human Bodies, An (Arbuthnot): *To Which Is Added, Practical Rules of Diet in the Various Consitutions and Diseases of Human Bodies* (Arbuthnot), **Supp. XVI:** 27
Essay of Dramatic Poesy (Dryden), **Retro. Supp. III:** 79
Essay of Dramatick Poesy (Dryden), **I:** 328, 349; **II:** 301, 302, 305; **III:** 40
"Essay on Burmese Days" (Orwell), **VII:** 276
"Essay on Christianity, An" (Shelley), **IV:** 199, 209
Essay on Comedy and the Uses of the Comic Spirit, An (Meredith), **V:** 224–225, 234

Essay on Criticism, An (Pope), **II:** 197; **III:** 68, 72, 77; **Retro. Supp. I:** 230, 231, 233
Essay on Irish Bulls (Edgeworth), **Supp. III:** 155–156
Essay on Man, An (Pope), **III:** 72, 76, 77–78, 280; **Retro. Supp. I:** 229–231, 235
Essay on Mind, An (Browning), **IV:** 310, 316, 321
"Essay on Percy Bysshe Shelley, An" (Browning), **IV:** 357, 366, 374
Essay on Sepulchres: or, A Proposal for Erecting Some Memorial of the Illustrious Dead in All Ages on the Spot Where Their Remains Have Been Interred (Godwin), **Supp. XV:** 126
Essay on the Development of Christian Doctrine, An (Newman), **Supp. VII:** 296–297, 301
Essay on the Dramatic Poetry of the Last Age (Dryden), **I:** 328
Essay on the External use of Water . . ., An (Smollett), **III:** 158
Essay on the First Book of T. Lucretius Carus de Rerum Natura, An (Evelyn), *see De rerum natura*
"Essay on Freewill" (Caudwell), **Supp. IX:** 38
Essay on the Genius and Writings of Pope (Warton), **III:** 170*n*
Essay on the Genius of George Cruikshank, An (Thackeray), **V:** 37
Essay on the History and Reality of Apparitions, An (Defoe), **III:** 14
Essay on the Idea of Comedy (Meredith), **I:** 201–202
Essay on the Lives and Works of Our Uneducated Poets (Southey), **IV:** 71
Essay on the Principle of Population (Malthus), **IV:** xvi, 127
Essay on the Principles of Human Action, An (Hazlitt), **IV:** 128, 139
Essay on the Theatre; Or, A Comparison Between the Laughing and Sentimental Comedy (Goldsmith), **III:** 187, 256
Essay on the Theory of the Earth (Cuvier), **IV:** 181
Essay on the Usefulness of Mathematical Learning, An (Arbuthnot), **Supp. XVI:** 17–18
Essay Towards a Theory of Art, An (Abercrombie), **Supp. XVI:** 12
Essay to Revive the Antient Education of Gentlewomen, An (Makin), **Supp. III:** 21
Essay Towards an Abridgement of the English History, An (Burke), **III:** 205
Essay upon Projects, An (Defoe), **III:** 12; **Retro. Supp. I:** 64, 75
Essayes (Cornwallis), **III:** 39
Essays (Bacon), **I:** 258, 259, 260, 271; **III:** 39
Essays (Goldsmith), **III:** 180
Essays and Leaves from a Note–book (Eliot), **V:** 200
Essays and Reviews (Newman), **V:** 340
Essays and Studies (Swinburne), **V:** 298, 332

Essays and Treatises on Several Subjects (Hume), **Supp. III:** 238
Essays from "The Guardian" (Pater), **V:** 357
Essays Illustrative of the Tatler (Drake), **III:** 51
Essays in Criticism (Arnold), **III:** 277; **V:** xxiii, 203, 204–205, 212, 213, 214, 215, 216
Essays in Divinity (Donne), **I:** 353, 360, 363; **Retro. Supp. II:** 95
Essays in London and Elsewhere (James), **VI:** 49, 67
Essays in Verse and Prose (Cowley), **II:** 195
Essays, Moral and Political (Hume), **Supp. III:** 231, 237
Essays, Moral and Political (Southey), **IV:** 71
Essays of Elia (Lamb), **IV:** xviii, 73, 74, 75, 76, 82–83, 85
Essays of Five Decades (Priestley), **VII:** 212
Essays on Freethinking and Plainspeaking (Stephen), **V:** 283, 289
Essays on His Own Times (Coleridge), **IV:** 56
Essays on Literature and Society (Muir), **Supp. VI:** 202
Essays on Shakespeare (Empson), **Supp. II:** 180, 193
Essays, Speculative and Suggestive (Ellis and Symonds), **Supp. XIV:** 262
Essays, Theological and Literary (Hutton), **V:** 157, 170
Essence of Christianity, The (tr. Eliot), **V:** 200
Essence of the Douglas Cause, The (Boswell), **III:** 247
"Essential Beauty" (Larkin), **Supp. I:** 279; **Retro. Supp. III:** 206
Essential Gesture (Gordimer), **Supp. II:** 226, 237, 239, 242, 243
"Essential Gesture, The" (Gordimer), **Supp. II:** 225
Essential Reading (Reading), **VIII:** 270–271
Essex Poems (Davie), **Supp. VI:** 109–111
Esslin, Martin, **Supp. IV:** 181; **Retro. Supp. I:** 218–219
Estate of Poetry, The (Muir), **Supp. VI:** 197–198, 202, **203,** 209
Esther Waters (Moore), **VI:** ix, xii, 87, 89, 91–92, 96, 98
Estuary, The (Beer), **Supp. XIV:** 4
"Et Cetera" (Carson), **Supp. XIII:** 60
"Et Dona Ferentes" (Wilson), **Supp. I:** 157
Et Nobis Puer Natus Est (Dunbar), **VIII:** 128
"Et Tu, Healy" (Joyce), **Retro. Supp. I:** 169; **Retro. Supp. III:** 165
"Eternal City" (Malouf), **Supp. XII:** 220
"Eternal Contemporaries" (Durrell), **Supp. I:** 124
Eternal Moment, The (Forster), **VI:** 399, 400
"Eternal Wedding, The" (Abercrombie), **Supp. XVI:** 2

Eternity to Season: Poems of Separation and Reunion (Harris), **Supp. V:** 132, 136

"Ether" (Burnside), **Supp. XIII:** 25

Etherege, Sir George, **II:** 255, 256, **266–269, 271,** 305

Etherege and the Seventeenth-Century Comedy of Manners (Underwood), **II:** 256*n*

Ethical Characters (Theophrastus), **II:** 68

Ethics of the Dust, The (Ruskin), **V:** 180, 184

Ethnic Radio (Murray), **Supp. VII:** 270, 276–277

Etruscan Places (Lawrence), **VII:** 116, 117

Euclid and His Modern Rivals (Carroll), **V:** 264, 274

Eugene Aram (Bulwer-Lytton), **IV:** 256; **V:** 22, 46

"Eugene Aram" (Hood), *see* "Dream of Eugene Aram, The Murderer, The"

Eugene Onegin (Pushkin), **Supp. IV:** 485

"Eugene Pickering" (James), **VI:** 69

Eugenia (Chapman), **I:** 236, 240

Eugénie Grandet (Balzac), **Supp. IV:** 124

Eugenius Philalethes, pseud. of Thomas Vaughan

"Eulenspiegelei" (Smith), **Retro. Supp. III:** 307

Euphranor: A Dialogue on Youth (FitzGerald), **IV:** 344, 353

Euphues and His England (Lyly), **I:** 194, 195–196

Euphues, The Anatomy of Wit (Lyly), **I:** 165, 193–196

Euripides, **IV:** 358; **V:** 321–324

Europa's Lover (Dunn), **Supp. X:** 75

"Europe" (James), **VI:** 69

Europe. A Prophecy (Blake), **III:** 302, 307; **Retro. Supp. I:** 39, 41–42

European Tribe, The (Phillips), **Supp. V:** 380, 384–385

European Witness (Spender), **Supp. II:** 489–490

Europeans, The (James), **VI:** 29–31

"Eurydice" (Sitwell), **VII:** 136–137

Eurydice, a Farce (Fielding), **III:** 105

"Eurydice to Orpheus" (Browning), **Retro. Supp. II:** 28; **Retro. Supp. III:** 27

"Eurynome" (Nye), **Supp. X:** 203

Eustace and Hilda: A Trilogy (Hartley), **Supp. VII:** 119, 120, 122, 123–124, 127, 131, 132

Eustace Diamonds, The (Fuller), **Supp. VII:** 72

Eustace Diamonds, The (Trollope), **V:** xxiv, 96, 98, 101, 102

Eustace, Robert, *see* Barton, Eustace

Eva Trout (Bowen), **Supp. II:** 82, 94

"Evacuees, The" (Nicholson), **Supp. VI:** 214

Evagatory (Reading), **VIII:** 272–273

Evan Harrington (Meredith), **V:** xxii, 227, 234

Evangelium Nicodemi (tr. Trevisa), **Supp. IX:** 252, 254–255

Evans, Abel, **II:** 335

Evans, G. Blakemore, **I:** 326

Evans, Marian, *see* Eliot, George

"Eve" (Rossetti), **V:** 258

"Eve of St. Agnes, The" (Keats), **III:** 338; **IV:** viii, xviii, 212, **216–219,** 231, 235; **V:** 352; **Retro. Supp. I:** 193

Eve of Saint John, The (Scott), **IV:** 38

"Eve of St. Mark, The" (Hill), **Supp. V:** 191

"Eve of St. Mark, The" (Keats), **IV:** 212, 216, 218, 220, 226

"Eveline" (Joyce), **Retro. Supp. I:** 172

"Even the Trees" (Kay), **Supp. XIII:** 104

"Evening Alone at Bunyah" (Murray), **Supp. VII:** 272

Eve's Ransom (Gissing), **V:** 437

Evelina (Burney), **III:** 90, 91; **IV:** 279; **Supp. III:** 64, 67, 68, 69, 70, 71–72, 75–76

"Eveline" (Joyce), **VII: 44**

Evelyn, John, **II:** 194, 196, **273–280, 286–287**

Evelyn Innes (Moore), **VI:** 87, 92

Evelyn Waugh (Lodge), **Supp. IV:** 365

"Even So" (Rossetti), **V:** 242

"Even Such Is Time" (Ralegh), **I:** 148–149

Evening (Macaulay), **IV:** 290

Evening Colonnade, The (Connolly), **Supp. III:** 98, 110, 111

Evening Standard (periodical), **VI:** 247, 252, 265

Evening Walk, An (Wordsworth), **IV:** xv 2, 4–5, 24

Evening's Love, An; or, The Mock Astrologer (Dryden), **II:** 305

Events and Wisdom (Davie), **Supp. VI:** 109

"Events at Drimaghleen" (Trevor), **Supp. IV:** 505

"Events in your life" (Kelman), **Supp. V:** 251

Ever After (Swift), **Supp. V:** 438–440

"Ever drifting down the stream" (Carroll), **V:** 270

"Ever Fixed Mark, An" (Amis), **Supp. II:** 3

"Ever mine hap is slack and slow in coming" (Wyatt), **I:** 110

"Everlasting Gospel" (Blake), **III:** 304

Everlasting Man, The (Chesterton), **VI:** 341–342

Everlasting Spell, The: A Study of Keats and His Friends (Richardson), **IV:** 236

"Evermore" (Barnes), **Supp. IV:** 75–76

Every Changing Shape (Jennings), **Supp. V:** 207, 213, 215

Every Day of the Week (Sillitoe), **Supp. V:** 423

Every Good Boy Deserves Favour (Stoppard), **Supp. I:** 450, 451, 453; **Retro. Supp. II:** 351

Every Man for Himself (Bainbridge), **Supp. VI: 25–26,** 27

Every Man His Own Priest (Radcliffe), **Retro. Supp. III:** 239

Every Man out of His Humor (Jonson), **I:** 336–337, 338–340; **II:** 24, 27

Every-Body's Business, Is No-Body's Business (Defoe), **III:** 13–14

Everybody's Political What's What? (Shaw), **VI:** 125, 129

Everyman, **II:** 70

Everyman in His Humor (Jonson), **I:** 336–337; **Retro. Supp. I:** 154, 157–159, 166

Everyone Has His Fault (Inchbald), **Supp. XV:** 157–158

"Everything Counts" (Aidoo), **Supp. XV:** 2, 7–8

"Everything that is born must die" (Rossetti), **V:** 254

"Everything You Can Remember in Thirty Seconds Is Yours to Keep" (Davies), **Supp. XIV:** 43–44

Evidence for the Resurrection of Jesus Christ as Given by the Four Evangelists, Critically Examined (Butler), **Supp. II:** 99, 102

Evidences of Christianity (Paley), **IV:** 144

Evil Genius: A Domestic Story, The (Collins), **Supp. VI:** 103

Evolution and Poetic Belief (Roppen), **V:** 221*n*

"Evolution of Tears, The" (Wallace-Crabbe), **VIII:** 322–323

Evolution Old and New (Butler), **Supp. II:** 106, 107

Ewart, Gavin, **VII:** 422, 423–424, **Supp. VII: 33–49**

Ewart Quarto, The (Ewart), **Supp. VII:** 44

"Ewes" (Fallon), **Supp. XII:** 108

"Ex Lab" (Reading), **VIII:** 265

Ex Voto (Butler), **Supp. II:** 114

"Exact Fare Please" (Dutton), **Supp. XII:** 91

Examen Poeticum (ed. Dryden), **II:** 290, 291, 301, 305; **Retro. Supp. III:** 63

Examination, The (Pinter), **Supp. I:** 371

"Examination at the Womb Door" (Hughes), **Supp. I:** 352; **Retro. Supp. II:** 207

Examination of Certain Abuses, An (Swift), **III:** 36

Examination of Dr. Woodward's Account of the Deluge (Arbuthnot), **Supp. XVI:** 17

Examiner (periodical), **III:** 19, 26, 35, 39; **IV:** 129

"Example of a Treatise on Universal Justice; or, The Fountains of Equity" (Bacon), **I:** 261

"Examples of Antitheses" (Bacon), **I:** 261

"Examples of the Colours of Good and Evil" (Bacon), **I:** 261, 264

Examples of the Interposition of Providence in . . . Murder (Fielding), **III:** 105

"Excavations" (Scupham), **Supp. XIII:** 219

"Excellent New Ballad, An" (Montrose), **II:** 236–237

Excellent Women (Pym), **Supp. II: 367–370**

Except the Lord (Cary), **VII:** 186, 194–195

"Exercise in the Pathetic Fallacy" (Pitter), **Supp. XIII:** 145

Excession (Banks), **Supp. XI:** 12

"Exchange of Letters" (Cope), **VIII:** 78–79
"Excursion" (Richardson), **Supp. XIII:** 192
Excursion, The (Wordsworth), **IV:** xvii, 5, 22–24, 95, 129, 214, 230, 233
Excursions in the Real World (Trevor), **Supp. IV:** 499
"Excuse, The" (Davies), **Supp. XI:** 98
"Execration Upon Vulcan, An" (Jonson), **Retro. Supp. I:** 165
"Execution of Cornelius Vane, The" (Read), **VI:** 436
"Exequy To his Matchlesse never to be forgotten Friend, An" (King), **Supp. VI:** 153
"Exequy, The" (King), **Supp. VI: 153–155,** 159, 161
"Exercisers" (Mistry), **Supp. X:** 139–140
Exeter Book, The, **Retro. Supp. II:** 303–305
"Exeunt Omnes" (Cornford), **VIII:** 114
"Exfoliation" (Carpenter), **Supp. XIII:** 41
"Exhortation" (Shelley), **IV:** 196
Exiles (Joyce), **VII:** 42–43; **Supp. II:** 74; **Retro. Supp. I:** 175–176; **Retro. Supp. III:** 170, 173–174
Exiles, The (Smith, I. C.), **Supp. IX:** 218–219
"Existentialists and Mystics" (Murdoch), **Supp. I:** 216–217, 219, 220
"Exit" (Kinsella), **Supp. V:** 271
Exit Lines (Hill, R.), **Supp. IX:** 115
Exits and Entrances (Fugard), **Supp. XV:** 104
Exorcist, The (film), **III:** 343, 345
Exodus, **Retro. Supp. II:** 301
"Exotic Pleasures" (Carey), **Supp. XII:** 55
"Expanding Universe, The" (Nicholson), **Supp. VI:** 217
Expectant Silence, The (Soutar), **Supp. XVI:** 254
"Expected, The" (Delanty), **Supp. XIV:** 74
Expedition of Humphrey Clinker, The (Smollett), *see Humphrey Clinker*
Expedition of Orsua and the Crimes of Aquirre, The (Southey), **IV:** 71
"Expelled, The" (Beckett), **Supp. I:** 49–50; **Retro. Supp. I:** 21
"Experience of a Scotsman, The" (Mayhew), **Supp. XVI:** 211–214
Experience of India, An (Jhabvala), **Supp. V:** 235
"Experience with Images" (MacNeice), **VII:** 401, 414, 419
Experiment, The (Defoe), **III:** 13
Experiment in Autobiography (Wells), **V:** 426–427, 429, 438; **VI:** xi, 225, 320, 333
Experiment in Criticism, An (Lewis), **Supp. III:** 249, 264
Experimental Drama (Armstrong), **VII:** 14
Experimenting with an Amen (Thomas), **Supp. XII:** 289
Experiments (Douglas), **VI:** 296, 305
"Expiation" (Jhabvala), **Supp. V:** 236

"Explained" (Milne), **Supp. V:** 303
"Explaining France" (Motion), **Supp. VII:** 256
Exploded View, An (Longley), **VIII:** 166, 169–172
Explorations (Knights), **II:** 123
"Explorer, The" (Plomer), **Supp. XI:** 213
"Explorers, The" (Hope), **Supp. VII:** 154
"Explosion, The" (Larkin), **Supp. I:** 285–286; **Retro. Supp. III:** 211
Exposition of the First Ten Chapters of Genesis, An (Bunyan), **II:** 253
Expostulation (Jonson), **I:** 243
"Expostulation and Inadequate Reply" (Fuller), **Supp. VII:** 73
"Expostulation and Reply" (Wordsworth), **IV:** 7
"Exposure" (Heaney), **Supp. II:** 275
"Exposure" (Owen), **VI:** 446, 450, 452, 455, 457
Exposure of Luxury, The: Radical Themes in Thackeray (Hardy), **V:** 39
Expression of the Emotions in Man and Animals, The (Darwin), **Supp. VII:** 26–28
"Expurgations" (Nye), **Supp. X:** 200
"Ex-Queen Among the Astronomers, The" (Adcock), **Supp. XII:** 7
"Exstasie, The" (Donne), **II:** 197; **Retro. Supp. II:** 88
"Extempore Effusion on the Death of the Ettrick Shepherd" (Wordsworth), **IV:** 73
Extending the Territory (Jennings), **Supp. V:** 216
"Extracts from a Lady's Log-Book" (Jewsbury), **Supp. XIV:** 161
Extravagant Strangers: A Literature of Belonging (ed. Phillips), **Supp. V:** 380
Extravagaria (tr. Reid), **Supp. VII:** 332
Exquisite Instrument, The (Butlin), **Supp. XVI:** 52, 55–56
Exultations (Pound), **Supp. III:** 398
Eye for an Eye, An (Trollope), **V:** 102
Eye in the Door, The (Barker), **Supp. IV:** 45, 46, 57, 59–61
"Eye of Allah, The" (Kipling), **VI:** 169, 190–191
Eye of the Hurricane, The (Adcock), **Supp. XII:** 1, 4
Eye of the Scarecrow, The (Harris), **Supp. V:** 136–137, 139, 140
Eye of the Storm, The (White), **Supp. I:** 132, 146–147
Eye to Eye (Fallon), **Supp. XII:** 105, 110–112, 114
Eyeless in Gaza (Huxley), **II:** 173; **VII:** 204–205
"Eyes and Tears" (Marvell), **II:** 209, 211
Eyes of Asia, The (Kipling), **VI:** 204
"Eyewitness" (Armitage), **VIII:** 4
Eyrbyggja saga, **VIII:** 235, 239, 240
Ezra Pound and His Work (Ackroyd), **Supp. VI:** 4
"Ezra Pound in Pisa" (Davie), **Supp. VI:** 110, 113
Ezra Pound: Poet as Sculptor (Davie), **Supp. VI:** 115

*F*aber Book of Contemporary Irish Poetry, The (ed. Muldoon), **Supp. IV:** 409, 410–411, 422, 424
Faber Book of Pop, The (ed. Kureishi and Savage), **Supp. XI:** 159
Faber Book of Sonnets (ed. Nye), **Supp. X:** 193
Faber Book of Twentieth-Century Women's Poetry, The (ed. Adcock), **Supp. XII:** 2
"Faber Melancholy, A" (Dunn), **Supp. X:** 70
Fabian Essays in Socialism (Shaw), **VI:** 129
Fabian Freeway (Martin), **VI:** 242
Fabian Society, **Supp. IV:** 233
"Fable" (Golding), **Supp. I:** 67, 83
"Fable of the Widow and Her Cat, A" (Swift), **III:** 27, 31
Fables (Dryden), **II:** 293, 301, 304; **III:** 40; **IV:** 287; **Retro. Supp. III:** 78, 81
Fables (Gay), **III:** 59, 67
Fables (Powys). *See No Painted Plumage*
Fables (Stevenson), **V:** 396
"Fables, The" (Malouf), **Supp. XII:** 220
Fables, Ancient and Modern: Adapted for the Use of Children (Godwin), **Supp. XV:** 126
Façade (Sitwell and Walton), **VII:** xv, xvii, 128, 130, 131n, 132
"Face of an Old Highland Woman" (Smith, I. C.), **Supp. IX:** 213
Face of the Deep, The (Rossetti), **V:** 260; **Retro. Supp. III:** 251, 252–253, 254, 256, 260, 263–264
Face to Face: Short Stories (Gordimer), **Supp. II:** 226
"Faces" (Conn), **Supp. XIII:** 79
"Faces, The" (James), **VI:** 69
"Faces Come Thicker at Night" (Scupham), **Supp. XIII:** 228
Facial Justice (Hartley), **Supp. VII:** 131
Facilitators, The (Redgrove), **Supp. VI:** 231
"Facing the Pacific at Night" (Hart), **Supp. XI:** 129
Facsimile of the First Folio, A (Shakespeare), **Retro. Supp. III:** 282–283
"Factory-Owner, The" (Plomer), **Supp. XI:** 213
Fadiman, Clifton, **Supp. IV:** 460
Faerie Queene, The (Spenser), **I:** 121, 123, 124, **131–141,** 266; **II:** 50; **IV:** 59, 198, 213; **V:** 142
"Faery Song, A" (Yeats), **VI:** 211
"Faeth Fiadha: The Breastplate of Saint Patrick" (Kinsella), **Supp. V:** 264
"Fafaia" (Brooke), **Supp. III:** 55–56
"Fag Hags" (Maitland), **Supp. XI:** 174
Fagrskinna, **VIII:** 242
"Failed Mystic" (MacCaig), **Supp. VI:** 188, 194
"Failure, A" (Thackeray), **V:** 18
Fair Exchange (Roberts), **Supp. XV:** 271, 272
Fair Haven, The (Butler), **Supp. II:** 99, **101–103,** 104, 117
"Fair in the Woods, The" (Gunn), **Retro. Supp. III:** 122, 129

"Fair Ines" (Hood), **IV:** 255
Fair Jilt, The; or, The Amours of Prince Tarquin and Miranda (Behn), **Supp. III:** 29, 31–32; **Retro. Supp. III:** 5
Fair Maid of the Inn, The (Ford, Massinger, Webster), **II:** 66, 69, 83, 85
Fair Margaret (Haggard), **Supp. III:** 214
Fair Quarrel, A (Middleton and Rowley), **II:** 1, 3, 21
"Fair Singer, The" (Marvell), **II:** 211
Fairfield, Cicely, *see* West, Rebecca
Fairly Dangerous Thing, A (Hill, R.), **Supp. IX:** 111, 114
Fairly Honourable Defeat, A (Murdoch), **Supp. I:** 226, 227, 228, 232–233
Fairy and Folk Tales of the Irish Peasantry (ed. Yeats), **VI:** 222
Fairy Caravan, The (Potter), **Supp. III:** 291, 303–304, 305, 306, 307
Fairy Knight, The (Dekker and Ford), **II:** 89, 100
"Fairy Poems" (Robinson), **Supp. XIII:** 206
"Faith" (Burnside), **Supp. XIII:** 21
"Faith" (Herbert), **II:** 127
Faith Healer (Friel), **Supp. V:** 123
"Faith Healing" (Larkin), **Supp. I:** 280–281, 282, 285
"Faith in a God of Love" (Tennyson), **Retro. Supp. III:** 325
"Faith on Trial, A" (Meredith), **V:** 222
Faithful Fictions: The Catholic Novel in British Literature (Woodman), **Supp. IV:** 364
Faithful Friends, The, **II:** 67
Faithful Narrative of . . . Habbakkuk Hilding, A (Smollett), **III:** 158
Faithful Shepherdess, The (Fletcher), **II:** 45, 46, 49–52, 53, 62, 65, 82
"Faithful Wife, The" (Beer), **Supp. XIV:** 4–5
"Faithfull Bird, The" (Cowper), **Retro. Supp. III:** 47
"Faithfulness of GOD in the Promises, The" (Blake), **III:** 300
"Faithless Nelly Gray" (Hood), **IV:** 257
"Faithless Sally Brown" (Hood), **IV:** 257
Faiz, Faiz Ahmad, **Supp. IV:** 434
Falcon, The (Tennyson), **Retro. Supp. III:** 329
"Falk" (Conrad), **VI:** 148
Falkner (Shelley), **Supp. III:** 371; **Retro. Supp. III:** 290
"Fall in Ghosts" (Blunden), **Supp. XI:** 45
"Fall of a Sparrow" (Stallworthy), **Supp. X:** 294
Fall of Hyperion, The (Keats), **IV:** xi, 211–213, 220, **227–231**, 234, 235
Fall of Kelvin Walker, The (Gray, A.), **Supp. IX:** 80, 85, 89
Fall of Princes, The (Lydgate), **I:** 57, 58, 59, 64
Fall of Robespierre, The (Coleridge and Southey), **IV:** 55
"Fall of Rome, The" (Auden), **Retro. Supp. I:** 11
"Fall of the House of Usher, The" (Poe), **III:** 339

"Fall of the West, The" (Wallace–Crabbe), **VIII:** 321
Fallen Angels (Coward), **Supp. II:** 141, 145
Fallen Leaves, The (Collins), **Supp. VI:** 93, 102
"Fallen Majesty" (Yeats), **VI:** 216
"Fallen Rake, The" (Gunn), **Retro. Supp. III:** 121
"Fallen Yew, A" (Thompson), **V:** 442
Falling (Howard), **Supp. XI:** 142, 144–145
Falling into Language (Wallace–Crabbe), **VIII:** 323
Falling Out of Love and Other Poems, A (Sillitoe), **Supp. V:** 424
Fallon, Peter, **Supp. XII: 101–116**
"Fallow Deer at the Lonely House, The" (Hardy), **Retro. Supp. I:** 119
Fallowell, Duncan, **Supp. IV:** 173
"Falls" (Ewart), **Supp. VII:** 39
Falls, The (Rankin), **Supp. X:** 245
False Alarm, The (Johnson), **III:** 121
False Friend, The (Robinson), **Supp. XIII:** 204, 211
False Friend, The (Vanbrugh), **II:** 325, 333, 336
"False Morality of the Lady Novelists, The" (Greg), **V:** 7
False One, The (Fletcher and Massinger), **II:** 43, 66
"False though she be to me and love" (Congreve), **II:** 269
Falstaff (Nye), **Supp. X:** 193, 195
Fame's Memoriall; or, The Earle of Devonshire Deceased (Ford), **II:** 100
Familiar and Courtly Letters Written by Monsieur Voiture (ed. Boyer), **II:** 352, 364
"Familiar Endeavours" (Wallace–Crabbe), **VIII:** 317
"Familiar Epistles to a Friend" (Byrom), **Supp. XVI:** 78
Familiar Letters (Richardson), **III:** 81, 83, 92
Familiar Letters (Rochester), **II:** 270
Familiar Studies of Men and Books (Stevenson), **V:** 395; **Retro. Supp. I:** 262–263
Familiar Tree, A (Stallworthy), **Supp. X:** 294, 297–298, 302
Families of Plants, The (tr. Darwin), **Supp. XVI:** 128
Family (Doyle), **Supp. V:** 78, 91
Family (Hill), **Supp. XIV:** 116, 117, 118, 123–124
Family Album (Coward), **Supp. II:** 153
Family and a Fortune, A (Compton-Burnett), **VII:** 60, 61, 62, 63, 66
Family and Friends (Brookner), **Supp. IV:** 127–129
Family Instructor, The (Defoe), **III:** 13, 82; **Retro. Supp. I:** 68
Family Madness, A (Keneally), **Supp. IV:** 346
"Family Man and the Rake, The" (Delanty), **Supp. XIV:** 73
Family Matters (Mistry), **Supp. X:** 144, 147–148

Family Memories (West), **Supp. III:** 431, 432, 433, 434
Family of Love, The (Dekker and Middleton), **II:** 3, 21
Family of Swift, The (Swift), **Retro. Supp. I:** 274
Family Prayers (Butler), **Supp. II:** 103
"Family Reunion" (Scupham), **Supp. XIII:** 229–230
Family Reunion, The (Eliot), **VII:** 146, 151, 154, 158, 160; **Retro. Supp. II:** 132
Family Romance, A (Brookner), *see* Dolly
"Family Sagas", *See Íslendinga sögur*
"Family Seat" (Murphy), **Supp. V:** 328
Family Sins (Trevor), **Supp. IV:** 505
"Family Supper, A" (Ishiguro), **Supp. IV:** 304; Retro. Supp. III: 161
"Family Tree" (Conn), **Supp. XIII:** 76
Family Tree, The (Plomer), **Supp. XI:** 216
"Family Visit" (Conn), **Supp. XIII:** 73
Family Voices (Pinter), **Supp. I:** 378
Family Way, The (Parsons), **Supp. XV:** 232–233, 234–235, 236, 240
"Famine, The" (Mangan), **Supp. XIII:** 126
Famished Road, The (Okri), **Supp. V:** 347, 348, 349, 350, 351, 352–353, 357–359
Famous for the Creatures (Motion), **Supp. VII:** 252
"Famous Ghost of St. Ives, The" (Redgrove), **Supp. VI:** 235–237
Famous History of Sir Thomas Wyat, The (Webster), **II:** 85
Famous Tragedy of the Queen of Cornwall . . . , The (Hardy), **VI:** 20
Famous Victoria of Henry V, The, **I:** 308–309
Fan, The: A Poem (Gay), **III:** 67
Fanatic Heart, A (O'Brien), **Supp. V:** 339
Fancies, Chaste and Noble, The (Ford), **II:** 89, 91–92, 99, 100
"Fancy" (Keats), **IV:** 221
"Fancy, A" (Greville), **Supp. XI:** 109
Fancy and Imagination (Brett), **IV:** 57
Fanfare for Elizabeth (Sitwell), **VII:** 127
"Fanny and Annie" (Lawrence), **VII:** 90, 114, 115
Fanny Brawne: A Biography (Richardson), **IV:** 236
Fanny's First Play (Shaw), **VI:** 115, 116, 117, 129
Fanon, Frantz, **Supp. IV:** 105
"Fanon the Awakener" (Armah), **Supp. X:** 2
Fanshawe, Sir Richard, **II:** 49, 222, 237
Fanshen (Hare), **Supp. IV:** 282, 284
Fanshen (Hinton), **Supp. IV:** 284
"Fantasia" (Redgrove), **Supp. VI:** 231
Fantasia of the Unconscious (Lawrence), **VII:** 122; **Retro. Supp. II:** 234
"Fantasia on 'Horbury'" (Hill), **Supp. V:** 187
Fantastic Beasts and Where to Find Them (Rowling), **Supp. XVI:** 239
Fantastic Mr. Fox (Dahl), **Supp. IV:** 203, 223
fantasy fiction, **VI:** 228–235, 338, 399

Fantasy and Fugue (Fuller), **Supp. VII:** 71–72
Fantomina (Haywood), **Supp. XII:** 135
Far Cry (MacCaig), **Supp. VI:** 184–185
"Far—Far—Away" (Tennyson), **IV:** 330
Far from the Madding Crowd (Hardy), **VI:** 1, 5–6; **Retro. Supp. I:** 113–114
Far Journey of Oudin, The (Harris), **Supp. V:** 132, 134, 135
Far Journeys (Chatwin), **Supp. IV:** 157
Far Side of the World, The (O'Brian), **Supp. XII:** 256
"Fare Thee Well" (Byron), **IV:** 192
Fares Please! An Omnibus (Coppard), **VIII:** 89
"Farewell, A" (Arnold), **V:** 216
"Farewell, fair Armida" (Dryden), **Retro. Supp. III:** 75–76
Farewell the Trumpets: An Imperial Retreat (Morris, J.), **Supp. X:** 179, 181
"Farewell to Angria" (Brontë), **V:** 125
"Farewell to Essay-Writing, A" (Hazlitt), **IV:** 135
Farewell to Military Profession (Rich), **I:** 312
Farewell to Poesy (Davies), **Supp. XI:** 96
"Farewell to Tobacco" (Lamb), **IV:** 81
Farfetched Fables (Shaw), **VI:** 125, 126
Farina (Meredith), **V:** 225, 234
Farm, The (Storey), **Supp. I:** 408, 411, 412, 414
"Farm Funeral" (Conn), **Supp. XIII:** 72
Farmer Giles of Ham (Tolkien), **Supp. II:** 521
"Farmer's Ingle, The" (Fergusson), **III:** 318
Farmer's Year, A (Haggard), **Supp. III:** 214
"Farmhouse Time" (Beer), **Supp. XIV:** 5
Farnham, William, **I:** 214
Farquhar, George, **II:** 334–335, 351–365
Farrell, Barry, **Supp. IV:** 223
"Farrers of Budge Row, The" (Martineau), **Supp. XV:** 188
Farther Adventures of Robinson Crusoe, The (Defoe), **III:** 13; **Retro. Supp. I:** 71
Farthing Hall (Walpole and Priestley), **VII:** 211
Fascination (Boyd), **Supp. XVI:** 44
Fascinating Foundling, The (Shaw), **VI:** 129
"Fashionable Authoress, The" (Thackeray), **V:** 22, 37
Fashionable Lover, The (Cumberland), **III:** 257
"Fasternis Eve in Hell" (Dunbar), **VIII:** 126
Fasti (Ovid), **II:** 110n
"Fat Contributor Papers, The" (Thackeray), **V:** 25, 38
"Fat Man in History, The" (Carey), **Supp. XII:** 54
Fat Man in History, The: Short Stories (Carey), **Supp. XII:** 52, 54
Fat Man in History and Other Stories, The (Carey), **Supp. XII:** 52, 55
Fat Woman's Joke, The (Weldon), **Supp. IV:** 521, 522–524, 525

"Fat Yank's Lament, The" (Delanty), **Supp. XIV:** 68
"Fatal Boots, The" (Thackeray), **V:** 21, 37
Fatal Dowry, The (Massinger and Field), **Supp. XI:** 182, 184
Fatal Friendship, The (Trotter), **Supp. XVI:** 277, 281–283, 284
Fatal Gift, The (Waugh), **Supp. VI:** 276
Fatal Inversion, A (Rendell), **Supp. IX:** 201
Fatal Revenge, The; or, The Family of Montorio (Maturin), **VIII:** 200, 207
Fatal Secret, The (Haywood), **Supp. XII:** 135
"Fatal Sisters, The" (Gray), **III:** 141
Fatality in Fleet Street (Caudwell), **Supp. IX:** 35
Fate of Homo Sapiens, The (Wells), **VI:** 228
Fate of Mary Rose, The (Blackwood), **Supp. IX:** 11–12
"Fate Playing" (Hughes), **Retro. Supp. II:** 217
"Fates, The" (Owen), **VI:** 449
Fates of the Apostles, **Retro. Supp. II:** 301
Father and His Fate, A (Compton-Burnett), **VII:** 61, 63
"Father and Lover" (Rossetti), **V:** 260
"Father and Son" (Butler), **Supp. II:** 97
Father Brown stories (Chesterton), **VI:** 338
Father Damien (Stevenson), **V:** 383, 390, 396
"Father Mat" (Kavanagh), **Supp. VII:** 194
Fathers and Sons (tr. Friel), **Supp. V:** 124
Father's Comedy, The (Fuller), **Supp. VII:** 74, 75–76, 77, 81
"Fathers, Sons and Lovers" (Thomas), **Supp. IV:** 493
Fathers, The; or, The Good-Natur'd Man (Fielding), **III:** 98, 105
"Fatigue, The" (Jones), **Supp. VII:** 175
Faulkener: A Tragedy (Godwin), **Supp. XV:** 126
Faulkner, Charles, **VI:** 167
"Fault" (Dutton), **Supp. XII:** 95–96
"Faunal" (Reading), **VIII:** 273
Faust (tr. Constantine), **Supp. XV:** 67
Faust (Goethe), **III:** 344; **IV:** xvi, xix, 179
Faust (Nye), **Supp. X:** 195
"Faustine" (Swinburne), **V:** 320
Faustine (Tennant), **Supp. IX:** 231, 238
Faustus and the Censor (Empson), **Supp. II:** 180, **196–197**
Faustus Kelly (O'Nolan), **Supp. II:** 323, **335–337**
Fawkes, F., **III:** 170n
Fawn, The (Marston), **II:** 30, 40
Fay Weldon's Wicked Fictions (Weldon), **Supp. IV:** 522, 531
"Fear" (Collins), **III:** 166, 171, 336
"Fear, A" (Jennings), **Supp. V:** 214
Fear, The (Keneally), **Supp. IV:** 345
Fearful Pleasures (Coppard), **VIII:** 91, 97

"Fearless" (Galloway), **Supp. XII:** 121–122
Fears in Solitude . . . (Coleridge), **IV:** 55
Feast Days (Burnside), **Supp. XIII:** 13, 16–18
Feast of Bacchus, The (Bridges), **VI:** 83
"Feast of Famine, The" (Stevenson), **V:** 396
Feast of Lupercal, The (Moore, B.), **Supp. IX:** 142, 143, 146–147
"Feastday of Peace, The" (McGuckian), **Supp. V:** 291
"February" (Hughes), **Supp. I:** 342
"February" (Jamie), **Supp. XIV:** 141
Feed My Swine (Powys), **VIII:** 249, 255
"Feeding Ducks" (MacCaig), **Supp. VI:** 187
Feeding the Mind (Carroll), **V:** 274
"Feel of Hands, The" (Gunn), **Retro. Supp. III:** 121
"Feeling into Words" (Heaney), **Supp. II:** 272, 273
Feersum Endjinn (Banks), **Supp. XI:** 12, 13
Felicia's Journey (Trevor), **Supp. IV:** 505, 517
"Félise" (Swinburne), **V:** 321
Felix Holt, The Radical (Eliot), **V:** xxiii, 195–196, 199, 200; **Retro. Supp. II:** 111–112
"Felix Randal" (Hopkins), **V:** 368–369, 371; **Retro. Supp. II:** 196
Fell of Dark (Hill, R.), **Supp. IX:** 110–111
"Fellow-Townsmen" (Hardy), **VI:** 22
Fellowship of the Ring (Tolkien), **Supp. II:** 519
Felony: The Private History of the Aspern Papers (Tennant), **Supp. IX:** 239
Female Friends (Weldon), **Supp. IV:** 534–535
"Female God, The" (Rosenberg), **VI:** 432
Female Spectator (Haywood), **Supp. XII:** 136, 142–144
"Female Vagrant, The" (Wordsworth), **IV:** 5
"Female Writers on Practical Divinity" (Martineau), **Supp. XV:** 182
"Feminine Christs, The" (McGuckian), **Supp. V:** 290
Feminine Mystique, The (Freidan), **Supp. IV:** 232
"Feminist Writer's Progress, A" (Maitland), **Supp. XI:** 163, 164, 168
Fen (Churchill), **Supp. IV:** 179, 188, 191–192, 198
Fénelon, François, **III:** 95, 99
Feng: A Poem (Wain), **Supp. XVI:** 307
Fenton, James, **Supp. IV:** 450
Fenwick, Isabella, **IV:** 2
Ferdinand Count Fathom (Smollett), **III:** 153, 158
Fergus (Moore, B.), **Supp. IX:** 143, 148, 150, 154
Ferguson, Helen, *see* Kavan, Anna
Fergusson, Robert, **III:** 312–313, 316, 317, 318
Ferishtah's Fancies (Browning), **IV:** 359, 374
Fermor, Patrick Leigh, **Supp. IV:** 160

"Fern Hill" (Thomas), **Supp. I:** 177, 178, 179; **Retro. Supp. III:** 341, 343, 345–346, 349
Fernandez, Ramon, **V:** 225–226
"Ferret" (Conn), **Supp. XIII:** 71
Ferrex and Porrex (Norton and Sackville), *see Gorboduc*
Festival at Farbridge (Priestley), **VII:** 219–210
"Festubert: The Old German Line" (Blunden), **VI:** 428
"Fetching Cows" (MacCaig), **Supp. VI:** 188
"Fetish" (Harris), **Supp. V:** 138
Feuerbach, Ludwig, **IV:** 364
"Feuille d'Album" (Mansfield), **VII:** 364
Fever Pitch (Hornby), **Supp. XV:** 133, 134, 135–136, 137–139, 140, 144, 145
Fever Pitch (screenplay, Hornby), **Supp. XV:** 144
"Few Crusted Characters, A" (Hardy), **VI:** 20, 22
Few Green Leaves, A (Pym), **Supp. II:** 370, **382–384**
Few Late Chrysanthemums, A (Betjeman), **VII:** 369–371
Few Sighs from Hell, A (Bunyan), **II:** 253
Fichte, Johann Gottlieb, **V:** 348
Ficino (philosopher), **I:** 237
"Ficino Notebook" (Traherne), **Supp. XI:** 264
Fiction (Reading), **VIII:** 264, 273
"Fiction" (Reading), **VIII:** 264
Fiction and the Reading Public (Leavis), **VII:** 233, 234
Fiction-Makers, The (Stevenson), **Supp. VI: 262–263**
"Fiction: The House Party" (Ewart), **Supp. VII:** 42
"Fictions" (Reid), **Supp. VII:** 334
"Fiddler of the Reels, The" (Hardy), **VI:** 22
Field, Isobel, **V:** 393, 397
Field, Nathaniel, **II:** 45, 66, 67
Field of Mustard, The (Coppard), **VIII:** 95–96
"Field of Mustard, The" (Coppard), **VIII:** 90, 96
"Field of Vision" (Heaney), **Retro. Supp. I:** 132
Field of Waterloo, The (Scott), **IV:** 38
Field Work (Heaney), **Supp. II:** 268, **275–277**; **Retro. Supp. I:** 124, 130
Fielding, Henry, **II:** 273; **III:** 62, 84, **94–106**, 148, 150; **IV:** 106, 189; **V:** 52, 287; **Supp. II:** 57, 194, 195; **Supp. IV:** 244; **Retro. Supp. I: 79–92**
Fielding, K. J., **V:** 43, 72
"Fields" (Burnside), **Supp. XIII:** 24
Fifer, C. N., **III:** 249
Fifine at the Fair (Browning), **IV:** 358, 367, 374; **Retro. Supp. II:**25; **Retro. Supp. III:** 31
Fifteen Dead (Kinsella), **Supp. V:** 267
"Fifth Philosopher's Song" (Huxley), **VII:** 199
"Fifth Province, The" (Delanty), **Supp. XIV:** 71–72
Fifth, Queen, The (Ford), **VI:** 324

Fifth Queen Crowned, The (Ford), **VI:** 325, 326
"Fifties, The" (Fuller), **Supp. VII:** 73
"Fifty Faggots" (Thomas), **Supp. III:** 403
"Fifty Pounds" (Coppard), **VIII:** 96
Fifty Years of English Literature, 1900–1950 (Scott–James), **VI:** 21
Fifty Years of Europe: An Album (Morris, J.), **Supp. X:** 185–186
"Fig Tree, The" (Ngũgĩ). *See* "Mugumo"
"Fight, The" (Thomas), **Supp. I:** 181
Fight for Barbara, The (Lawrence), **VII:** 120
"Fight to a Finish" (Sassoon), **VI:** 430
"Fight with a Water Spirit" (Cameron), **Supp. IX:** 19, 20, 22
Fighting Terms (Gunn), **Supp. IV:** 256, 257–259; **Retro. Supp. III:** 115, 116, 117–119, 122
"Figure in the Carpet, The" (James), **VI:** 69
Figure in the Cave and Other Essays, The (Montague), **Supp. XV:** 210, 211, 213, 217, 221, 223
Figure of Beatrice: A Study of Dante, The (Williams, C. W. S.), **Supp. IX:** 279, 284–285
"Figures on the Freize" (Reid), **Supp. VII:** 330
File on a Diplomat (Brink), **Supp. VI:** 46
Filibusters in Barbary (Lewis), **VII:** 83
Fille du Policeman (Swinburne), **V:** 325, 333
Film (Beckett), **Supp. I:** 51, 59, 60
Filostrato (Boccaccio), **I:** 30
Filthy Lucre (Bainbridge), **Supp. VI:** 23
Final Demands (Reading), **VIII:** 271, 273
Final Passage, The (Phillips), **Supp. V:** 380–383
"Final Problem, The" (Doyle), **Supp. II:** 160, 172–173
Final Unfinished Voyage of Jack Aubrey, The (O'Brian), **Supp. XII:** 259
"Finale" (Dutton), **Supp. XII:** 99
Finch, Anne, **Supp. IX: 65–78**
Finden's Byron Beauties (Finden), **V:** 111
Finding the Dead (Fallon), **Supp. XII:** 104
Findings (Jamie), **Supp. XIV:** 129, 139, 144–145
"Findings" (Jamie), **Supp. XIV:** 145
Findlater, Richard, **VII:** 8
Fine Arts, The (Symonds), **Supp. XIV:** 256–257, 257–259
Fine Balance, A (Mistry), **Supp. X:** 142, 145–149
Finer Grain, The (James), **VI:** 67
Fingal (Macpherson), **VIII:** 181–182, 186–189, 190, 191, 192, 193, 194
"Fingal's Visit to Norway" (Macpherson), **VIII:** 186
Finished (Haggard), **Supp. III:** 214
"Finistére" (Kinsella), **Supp. V:** 268
Finnegans Wake (Joyce), **VII:** 42, 46, 52–54; critical studies, **VII:** 58; **Supp. III:** 108; **Retro. Supp. I:** 169, 179–181; **Retro. Supp. III:** 168, 177–179
Firbank, Ronald, **VII:** 132, 200; **Supp. II: 199–223**

"Fire and Ice" (Kinsella), **Supp. V:** 261
Fire and the Sun, The: Why Plato Banished the Artists (Murdoch), **Supp. I:** 230, 232
"Fire and the Tide" (Stevenson), **Supp. VI:** 260
Fire Down Below (Golding), **Retro. Supp. I:** 104–105
"Fire, Famine and Slaughter" (Coleridge), **Retro. Supp. II:** 53
Fire from Heaven (Renault), **Supp. IX:** 184–185
"Fire in the Wood, The" (Welch), **Supp. IX:** 267
Fire of the Lord, The (Nicholson), **Supp. VI:** 219
Fire on the Mountain (Desai), **Supp. V:** 53, 55, 64–65, 73
"Fire Sermon, The" (Eliot), **Retro. Supp. II:** 127–128
Fires of Baäl, The (Clarke), **Supp. XV:** 18
Firework-Maker's Daughter, The (Pullman), **Supp. XIII:** 152
"Fireworks Poems" (Cope), **VIII:** 81
"Firing Practice" (Motion), **Supp. VII:** 251, 254, 257, 260
"Firm of Happiness, Ltd., The" (Cameron), **Supp. IX:** 25–26
"Firm Views" (Hart), **Supp. XI:** 129
First Affair, The (Fallon), **Supp. XII:** 101, 102–103
First and Last Loves (Betjeman), **VII:** 357, 358, 359
First & Last Things (Wells), **VI:** 244
First and Second Poems (Pitter), **Supp. XIII:** 133, 137–139
First Anniversary, The (Donne), **I:** 188, 356; **Retro. Supp. II:** 94
"First Anniversary of the Government under O. C., The" (Marvell), **II:** 210, 211; **Retro. Supp. II:** 262–263
First Book of Odes (Bunting), **Supp. VII:** 5, 13
First Book of Urizen, The (Blake), **III:** 299, 300, 306, 307; **Retro. Supp. I:** 43–44
"First Countess of Wessex, The" (Hardy), **VI:** 22
First Earthquake, The (Redgrove), **Supp. VI:** 236
First Eleven, The (Ewart), **Supp. VII:** 41
First Episode (Rattigan), **Supp. VII:** 308
First Flight, The (Heaney), **Supp. II:** 278
First Folio (Shakespeare), **I:** 299, 324, 325
First Grammatical Treatise, **VIII:** 236
First Gun, The (Jefferies), **Supp. XV:** 166
First Hundred Years of Thomas Hardy, The (Weber), **VI:** 19
"First Hymn to Lenin" (MacDiarmid), **Supp. III:** 119; **Supp. XII:** 211
"'First Impression' (Tokyo), A" (Blunden), **Supp. XI:** 35
"First Impressions" (Austen), *see Pride and Prejudice*
"First Journey, The" (Graham), **Supp. VII:** 109
First Lady Chatterley, The (Lawrence), **VII:** 111–112

First Language (Carson), **Supp. XIII:** 54, 59–60
First Light (Ackroyd), **Supp. VI:** 1, 8
"First Light" (Kinsella), **Supp. V:** 263
First Life of Adamastor, The (Brink), **Supp. VI: 54–55,** 57
"First Love" (Beckett), **Retro. Supp. I:** 21
"First Love" (Beer), **Supp. XIV:** 5
First Love, Last Rites (McEwan), **Supp. IV:** 390–392
"First Man, The" (Gunn), **Supp. IV:** 264–265
First Men in the Moon, The, (Wells), **VI:** 229, 234, 244
"First Men on Mercury, The" (Morgan, E.), **Supp. IX:** 169
First Ode of the Second Book of Horace Paraphras'd, The (Swift), **III:** 35
"First Place, A: The Mapping of a World" (Malouf), Supp. XII: 218
First Poems (Muir), **Supp. VI:** 198, **204–205**
First Poems (Pitter), **Supp. XIII:** 132, 134
First Satire (Wyatt), **I:** 111
First Satire of the Second Book of Horace, Imitated, The (Pope), **III:** 234
First Steps in Reading English (Richards), **Supp. II:** 425
First Things Last (Malouf), **Supp. XII:** 220
"First Things Last" (Malouf), **Supp. XII:** 220
"First Things, Last Things" (Scupham), **Supp. XIII:** 228
"First Winter of War" (Fuller), **Supp. VII:** 69
First World War, see World War I
First Year in Canterbury Settlement, A (Butler), **Supp. II:** 98, 112
Firstborn, The (Fry), **Supp. III:** 195, 196, 198–199, 207
Firth, Sir Charles Harding, **II:** 241; **III:** 25, 36; **IV:** 289, 290, 291
Fischer, Ernst, **Supp. II:** 228
"Fish" (Lawrence), **VII:** 119
"Fish, The" (Brooke), **Supp. III:** 53, 56, 60
Fish Preferred (Wodehouse), **Supp. III:** 460
"Fishermen, The" (Mangan), **Supp. XIII:** 122
"Fisherman, The" (Yeats), **VI:** 214; **Retro. Supp. I:** 331
"Fishermen with Ploughs: A Poem Cycle" (Brown), **Supp. VI:** 63
"Fishes in a Chinese Restaurant" (Carson), **Supp. XIII:** 56
"Fishing" (Thomas), **Supp. XII:** 287
Fishing for Amber (Carson), **Supp. XIII:** 54, 56, 63–65
Fishmonger's Fiddle (Coppard), **VIII:** 89, 95
"Fishmonger's Fiddle" (Coppard), **VIII:** 95
"Fishy Waters" (Rhys), **Supp. II:** 401
Fit for the Future: The Guide for Women Who Want to Live Well (Winterson), **Supp. IV:** 542

"Fitz–Boodle Papers, The" (Thackeray), **V:** 38
FitzGerald, Edward, **IV:** xvii, xxii, xxiii, 310, **340–353; V:** xxv
Fitzgerald, Penelope, **Supp. V: 95–109**
Fitzgerald, Percy, **III:** 125, 135
Five (Lessing), **Supp. I:** 239, 240, 241, 242
Five Autumn Songs for Children's Voices (Hughes), **Supp. I:** 357
"Five Dreams" (Nye), **Supp. X:** 205
"Five Dreams and a Vision" (Pitter), **Supp. XIII:** 144
"Five Eleven Ninety Nine" (Armitage), **VIII:** 9–11, 15
Five Finger Exercise (Shaffer), **Supp. I:** 313, **314–317,** 319, 322, 323, 327
Five Looks at Elizabeth Bishop (Stevenson), **Supp. VI:** 264–265
"Five Minutes" (Nicholson), **Supp. VI:** 216
Five Metaphysical Poets (Bennett), **II:** 181, 202
Five Nations, The (Kipling), **VI:** 204; **Retro. Supp. III:** 194
Five Novelettes by Charlotte Brontë (ed. Gérin), **V:** 151
"Five Orange Pips, The" (Doyle), **Supp. II:** 174
"Five Poems on Film Directors" (Morgan, E.), **Supp. IX:** 163
Five Red Herrings, The (Sayers), **Supp. III:** 334, 343–344
Five Rivers (Nicholson), **Supp. VI: 213–215,** 216
Five Sermons on the Errors of the Roman Catholic Church (Maturin), **VIII:** 197, 208
"Five Songs" (Auden), **Retro. Supp. I:** 11–12
"Five Students, The" (Hardy), **VI:** 17
Five Tales (Galsworthy), **VI:** 276
Five Uncollected Essays of Matthew Arnold (ed. Allott), **V:** 216
Five Years of Youth (Martineau), **Supp. XV:** 185
Fivefold Screen, The (Plomer), **Supp. XI:** 213
Five–Year Plan, A (Kerr), **Supp. XII:** 194, 195
Fixed Period, The (Trollope), **V:** 102
Flag on the Island, A (Naipaul), **Supp. I:** 394
Flame, The: A Play in One Act (Clarke), **Supp. XV:** 24
Flame in Your Heart, A (Greig), **Supp. XVI:** 161, 162, 170
Flame in Your Heart, A (Jamie), **Supp. XIV:** 129, 131–134, 143
Flame of Life, The (Sillitoe), **Supp. V:** 410, 421, 424
Flame Tree (Hart), **Supp. XI:** 126–127
"Flaming Heart Upon the Book and Picture of the Seraphicall Saint Teresa, The" (Crashaw), **II:** 182
"Flaming sighs that boil within my breast, The" (Wyatt), **I:** 109–110
Flare Path (Rattigan), **Supp. VII:** 311–312, 313, 314
Flatman, Thomas, **II:** 133

"Flatting Mill, The" (Cowper), **Retro. Supp. III:** 48
Flaubert, Gustave, **V:** xviii–xxiv, 340, 353, 429; **Supp. IV:** 68, 69, 136, 157, 163, 167
Flaubert's Parrot (Barnes), **Supp. IV:** 65, 67, 68–70, 72, 73
Flaws in the Glass: A Self–Portrait (White), **Supp. I:** 129, 130, 132, 149
Flea, The (Donne), **I:** 355; **Retro. Supp. II:** 88
"Fleckno, an English Priest at Rome" (Marvell), **II:** 211
"Fleet" (Coppard), **VIII:** 88
Fleetwood; or, The New Man of Feeling (Godwin), **Supp. XV:** 125–126
Fleming, Ian, **Supp. IV:** 212
Fleming, Ian, **Supp. XIV: 81–98**
Flesh & Blood (Roberts), **Supp. XV:** 270–271, 273
Fletcher, Ian, **V:** xii, xiii, xxvii, 359
Fletcher, Ifan Kyrle, **Supp. II:** 201, 202, 203
Fletcher, John, **II: 42–67,** 79, 82, 87–88, 90, 91, 93, 185, 305, 340, 357, 359
Fletcher, Phineas, **II:** 138
Fletcher, Thomas, **II:** 21
Fleurs du Mal (Baudelaire), **V:** xxii, 316, 329, 411
Fleurs du Mal (Swinburne), **V:** 329, 331, 333
"Flickerbridge" (James), **VI:** 69
"Flight" (Conn), **Supp. XIII:** 72
Flight from the Enchanter, The (Murdoch), **Supp. I: 220–222**
Flight into Camden (Storey), **Supp. I:** 408, 410–411, 414, 415, 419
"Flight of the Duchess, The" (Browning), **IV:** 356, 361, 368; **Retro. Supp. II:** 24; **Retro. Supp. III:** 22, 23
"Flight of the Earls, The" (Boland), **Supp. V:** 36
Flight of the Falcon, The (du Maurier), **Supp. III:** 139, 141
Flight to Africa and Other Poems (Clarke), **Supp. XV:** 27–28
Flint Anchor, The (Warner), **Supp. VII:** 376, 378–379
"Flitting, The" (McGuckian), **Supp. V:** 281
Flood, A (Moore), **VI:** 99
Flood, The (Rankin), **Supp. X:** 244, 246–247, 250
"Flooded Meadows" (Gunn), **Supp. IV:** 267; **Retro. Supp. III:** 122
Floor Games (Wells), **VI:** 227
"Flora" (Dutton), **Supp. XII:** 88
Flora Selbornesis (White), **Supp. VI:** 282–283
"Florent" (Gower), **I:** 55
Florentine Painting and Its Social Background (Antal), **Supp. IV:** 80
Flores Solitudinis (Vaughan), **II:** 185, 201
Floud, Peter, **V:** 296, 307
"Flower, The" (Herbert), **II:** 119n 125; **Retro. Supp. II:** 177–178
Flower Beneath the Foot, The (Firbank), **Supp. II:** 202, 205, **216–218**

Flower Master, The (McGuckian), **Supp. V:** 277, 278, 281–282
"Flower Master, The" (McGuckian), **Supp. V:** 281
Flower Master and Other Poems, The (McGuckian), **Supp. V:** 281
"Flower Poem" (Hope), **Supp. VII:** 154
Flowers and Shadows (Okri), **Supp. V:** 347–348, 350, 352, 354–355
Flower of Courtesy (Lydgate), **I:** 57, 60, 62
"Flowering Absence, A" (Montague), **Supp. XV:** 210, 217
Flowering Death of a Salesman (Stoppard), **Supp. I:** 439
Flowering Rifle (Campbell), **VII:** 428
Flowering Wilderness (Galsworthy), **VI:** 275, 282
Flowers and Insects (Hughes), **Retro. Supp. II:** 214
"Flowers of Empire, The" (Kincaid), **Supp. VII:** 229
"Flowers of Evil" (Kincaid), **Supp. VII:** 219
Flowers of Passion (Moore), **VI:** 85, 98
Flurried Years, The (Hunt), **VI:** 333
Flush: A Biography (Woolf), **Retro. Supp. I:** 308, 320–321
Flute–Player, The (Thomas), **Supp. IV:** 479–480, 481
"Fly, The" (Blake), **III:** 295–296
"Fly, The" (Chatwin), **Supp. IV:** 158
"Fly, The" (Mansfield), **VII:** 176
Fly Away Peter (Malouf), **Supp. XII:** 217, 224–225
"Flying Above California" (Gunn), **Supp. IV:** 263
"Flying Ace, The" (Redgrove), **Supp. VI:** 236
"Flying Bum, The" (Plomer), **Supp. XI:** 222
Flying Hero Class (Keneally), **Supp. IV:** 347
Flying in to Love (Thomas), **Supp. IV:** 486–487
Flying Inn, The (Chesterton), **VI:** 340
"Flying to Belfast, 1977" (Raine), **Supp. XIII:** 167
"Flyting of Crawford and Herbert, The" (Crawford and Herbert), **Supp. XI:** 68
"Flyting of Dunbar and Kennedie, The" (Dunbar), **VIII:** 117, 118, 126–127
"Focherty" (MacDiarmid), **Supp. XII:** 205
Foe (Coetzee), **Supp. VI:** 75–76, **83–84**
Foe–Farrell (Quiller–Couch), **V:** 384
"Foetal Monitor Day, The" (Delanty), **Supp. XIV:** 74
Folding Star, The (Hollinghurst), **Supp. X:** 120–122, 128–134
"Folie à Deux" (Burnside), **Supp. XIII:** 29
"Folk Wisdom" (Kinsella), **Supp. V:** 263
"Folklore" (Murray), **Supp. VII:** 276
Folk–Lore in the Old Testament (Frazer), **Supp. III:** 176
Follow My Leader (Rattigan), **Supp. VII:** 310
"Follower" (Heaney), **Supp. IV:** 410
"Followers, The" (Thomas), **Supp. I:** 183

Following a Lark (Brown), **Supp. VI:** 72
"Folly" (Murphy), **Supp. V:** 327
Folly of Industry, The (Wycherley), **II:** 322
"Fond Memory" (Boland), **Supp. V:** 35
Fontaine amoureuse, **I:** 33
"Food of the Dead" (Graves), **VII:** 269
Food, Sex, and God: On Inspiration and Writing (Roberts), **Supp. XV:** 259, 270, 273
Fool, The (Bond), **Supp. I:** 423, 434, 435
Fool of the World and Other Poems, The (Symons), **Supp. XIV:** 279
"Fool's Song" (Cornford), **VIII:** 107
Fools of Fortune (Trevor), **Supp. IV:** 502, 503, 512–514, 517
Foot of Clive, The (Berger), **Supp. IV:** 79, 84–85
"Football at Slack" (Hughes), **Retro. Supp. II:** 210–211
Foote, Samuel, **III:** 253; **V:** 261
Footfalls (Beckett), **Retro. Supp. I:** 28
Footnote to History, A: Eight Years of Trouble in Samoa (Stevenson), **V:** 396
"Footsteps of Death, The" (Steel), **Supp. XII:** 269
"For a Five–Year–Old" (Adcock), **Supp. XII:** 5
"For a Greeting" (MacCaig), **Supp. VI:** 185
"For a Sundial" (Soutar), **Supp. XVI:** 251
"For a Young Matron" (McGuckian), **Supp. V:** 284–285
For All That I Found There (Blackwood), **Supp. IX:** 3–6, 8–9, 11
"For All We Have and Are" (Kipling), **VI:** 415
"For Andrew" (Adcock), **Supp. XII:** 5
"For Ann Scott–Moncrieff" (Muir), **Supp. VI:** 207
For Children: The Gates of Paradise (Blake), **III:** 307
"For Conscience' Sake" (Hardy), **VI:** 22
For Crying Out Loud (Wallace–Crabbe), **VIII:** 322–323
"For Des Esseintes" (Symons), **Supp. XIV:** 281
"For Each and For All" (Martineau), **Supp. XV:** 185
"For Heidi with Blue Hair" (Adcock), **Supp. XII:** 9
"For John Heath–Stubbs" (Graham), **Supp. VII:** 116
For Love Alone (Stead), **Supp. IV:** 470–473
For Love and Life (Oliphant), **Supp. X:** 220
For Love & Money: Writing, Reading, Traveling, 1967–1987 (Raban), **Supp. XI:** 228
"For M. S. Singing *Frühlingsglaube* in 1945" (Cornford), **VIII:** 111
For Queen and Country: Britain in the Victorian Age (ed. Drabble), **Supp. IV:** 230
"For Ring–Givers" (Reid), **Supp. VII:** 329
For Services Rendered (Maugham), **VI:** 368

"For St. James" (Nicholson), **Supp. VI:** 214
"For the Fallen" (Binyon), **VI:** 416; **VII:** 448
For the Islands I sing (Brown), **Supp. VI:** 61–66, 68–69
For the Municipality's Elderly (Reading), **VIII:** 262–263
"For the Previous Owner" (McGuckian), **Supp. V:** 283
For the Sexes: The Gates of Paradise (Blake), **III:** 307
For the Time Being (Auden), **VII:** 379; **Retro. Supp. I:** 10–11
For the Unfallen: Poems (Hill), **Supp. V:** 184–186
For the Unfallen: Poems 1952–1958 (Hill), **Retro. Supp. III:** 133, 134, 135
"For to Admire" (Kipling), **VI:** 203
"For Us All" (Pitter), **Supp. XIII:** 143
"For Whom Things Did Not Change" (Aidoo), **Supp. XV:** 8
"For Years Now" (Constantine), **Supp. XV:** 71
For Your Eyes Only (Fleming), **Supp. XIV:** 96, 97
"Forbidden Love of Noreen Tiernan, The" (McCabe), **Supp. IX:** 136–137
"Force, The" (Redgrove), **Supp. VI:** 231
Force, The (Redgrove), **Supp. VI:** 231
Force of Nature, The (Haywood), **Supp. XII:** 135
"Force that through the green fuse drives the flower, The" (Thomas), **II:** 156; **Supp. I: 171–173,** 177; **Retro. Supp. III:** 337
Forc'd Marriage, The; or, The Jealous Bridegroom (Behn), **Supp. III:** 22, 24, 25–26
Forced Marriage, The; or, The Jealous Bridegroom (Behn), **Retro. Supp. III:** 3, 10
Ford, Charles, **III:** 33, 34
Ford, Ford Madox, **VI:** 145–146, 238, **319–333,** 416, 439; **VII:** xi, xv, xxi, 89
Ford, John, **II:** 57, 69, 83, 85, **87–101**
Ford Madox Ford (Rhys), **Supp. II:** 388, 390, 391
Ford Madox Ford: Letters (ed. Ludwig), **VI:** 332
"Fordham Castle" (James), **VI:** 69
"Forebears" (Conn), **Supp. XIII:** 72
"Forefathers" (Blunden), **Supp. XI:** 42–43, 45
Foreign Parts (Galloway), **Supp. XII:** 117, 123–126, 129, 130
Foreigners, The (Tutchin), **III:** 3
"Foregone Conclusion, The" (Warner), **Supp. VII:** 380
"Foreplay" (Maitland), **Supp. XI:** 175
"Forerunners, The" (Herbert), **Retro. Supp. II:** 180
"Forest, The" (Constantine), **Supp. XV:** 74
Forest, The (Galsworthy), **VI:** 276, 287
Forest, The (Jonson), **Retro. Supp. I:** 164
Forest and Game–Law Tales (Martineau), **Supp. XV:** 184

Forest Minstrel, The (Hogg), **Supp. X:** 106

"Forest of Beguilement, The" (Burnside), **Supp. XIII:** 16

"Forest Path to the Spring, The" (Lowry), **Supp. III:** 270, 282

Forester, C. S., **Supp. IV:** 207, 208

"Foresterhill" (Brown), **Supp. VI:** 59

Foresters, The (Tennyson), **IV:** 328, 338; **Retro. Supp. III:** 329

Forests of Lithuania, The (Davie), **Supp. VI:** 108, 115

Forewords and Afterwords (Auden), **VII:** 394; **Retro. Supp. I:** 1, 6

"Forge, The" (Carson), **Supp. XIII:** 56

Forge, The (Hall), **Supp. VI:** 120–121, 124–125

"Forge, The" (Heaney), **Supp. II:** 271; **Retro. Supp. I:** 128

"Forge, The" (Russell), **VIII:** 291

"Forget about me" (tr. Reid), **Supp. VII:** 332

Forget-Me-Not (Jewsbury), **Supp. XIV:** 157

"Forget not yet" (Wyatt), **I:** 106

Forging of Fantom, The (Hill, R.), **Supp. IX:** 117

Forgive Me, Sire (Cameron), **Supp. IX:** 17, 29

"Forgive Me, Sire" (Cameron), **Supp. IX:** 25–27

"Forgiveness" (Jennings), **Supp. V:** 217–218

"Forgiveness, A" (Browning), **IV:** 360

Forgiveness of Sins, The (Williams, C. W. S.), **Supp. IX:** 284

"Forgotten" (Milne), **Supp. V:** 303

"Forgotten of the Foot" (Stevenson), **Supp. VI:** 262

"Form and Realism in the West Indian Artist" (Harris), **Supp. V:** 145

"Former House, A" (Nye), **Supp. X:** 205

"Former Paths" (Thomas), **Supp. XII:** 281

Forms of Exile (Montague), **Supp. XV:** 213–214

Fornaldarsögur, **VIII:** 236

Forrest, James F., **II:** 245n

Fors Clavigera (Ruskin), **V:** 174, 181, 184

"Forsaken" (Gibbon), **Supp. XIV:** 104, 106, 112

"Forsaken Garden, A" (Swinburne), **V:** 314, 327

Forster, E. M., **IV:** 302, 306; **V:** xxiv, 208, 229, 230; **VI:** xii, 365, **397–413**; **VII:** xi, xv, 18, 21, 34, 35, 122, 144; **Supp. I:** 260; **Supp. II:** 199, 205, 210, 223, 227, 289, 293; **Supp. III:** 49; **Supp. IV:** 440, 489; **Retro. Supp. II: 135–150**

Forster, John, **IV:** 87, 89, 95, 99, 100, 240; **V:** 47, 72

Forsyte Saga, The (Galsworthy), **VI:** xiii, 269, 272, 274; see also *Man of Property, The*; "Indian Summer of a Forsyte"; *In Chancery; To Let*

Fortescue, Chichester, **V:** 76–83, 85

Fortnightly Review (periodical), **V:** 279, 338; **Supp. XIII:** 191

Fortunate Isles, and Their Union, The (Jonson), **Retro. Supp. I:** 165

Fortunate Mistress, The: or, A History of . . . Mademoiselle de Beleau . . . (Defoe), **III:** 13

"Fortune, A" (Fallon), **Supp. XII:** 112–113

Fortune of War, The (O'Brian), **Supp. XII:** 256

Fortunes and Misfortunes of the Famous Moll Flanders, The (Defoe), see *Moll Flanders*

Fortunes of Falstaff, The (Wilson), **III:** 116n

Fortunes of Nigel, The (Scott), **IV:** 30, 35, 37, 39

Fortunes of Perkin Warbeck, The: A Romance (Shelley), **Retro. Supp. III:** 287, 290, 293–297

"Fortune-Teller, a Gypsy Tale, The" (Robinson), **Supp. XIII:** 212

Forty New Poems (Davies), **Supp. XI:** 97

Forty Years On (Bennett), **VIII:** 20–21, 22–23

"Forty-seventh Saturday, The" (Trevor), **Supp. IV:** 501

Forward from Liberalism (Spender), **Supp. II:** 488

Fóstbrœðra saga, **VIII:** 239, 241

Foster, A. D., **III:** 345

"Fostering" (Fallon), **Supp. XII:** 107–108, 109

Foucault, Michel, **Supp. IV:** 442

Foucault's Pendulum (Eco), **Supp. IV:** 116

"Found" (Rossetti), **V:** 240

Found in the Street (Highsmith), **Supp. V:** 171, 178–179

"Foundation of the Kingdom of Angria" (Brontë), **V:** 110–111

Foundations of Aesthetics, The (Richards and Ogden), **Supp. II:** 408, **409–410**

Foundations of Joy, The (Wallace-Crabbe), **VIII:** 318

"Fountain" (Jamie), **Supp. XIV:** 137

"Fountain" (Jennings), **Supp. V:** 210, 212

Fountain of Magic, The (tr. O'Connor), **Supp. XIV:** 222

Fountain of Self-love, The (Jonson), **Retro. Supp. I:** 158, 160

Fountain Overflows, The (West), **Supp. III:** 431–432, 443

Fountains in the Sand (Douglas), **VI:** 294, 297, 299, 300, 305

Four Ages of Poetry, The (Peacock), **IV:** 168–169, 170

Four and a Half Dancing Men (Stevenson), **Supp. VI: 264**

Four Banks of the River of Space, The (Harris), **Supp. V:** 137, 140, 142–144

Four Countries (Plomer), **Supp. XI:** 216, 222

Four Day's Wonder (Milne), **Supp. V:** 310

Four-Dimensional Nightmare, The (Ballard), **Supp. V:** 23

Four Dissertations (Hume), **Supp. III:** 231, 238

4.50 from Paddington (Christie; U.S. title, *What Mrs. McGillicuddy Saw*), **Supp. II:** 132

Four Georges, The (Thackeray), **V:** 20, 34–35, 38

Fourth Horseman, The (Thompson), **Supp. XIV:** 295–296

Four Hymns (Spenser), **I:** 124

Four Last Things (More), **Supp. VII:** 234, 246–247

Four Lectures (Trollope), **V:** 102

"Four Letter Word, A" (Sisson), **Supp. XI:** 253

Four Loves, The (Lewis), **Supp. III:** 249, 264–265

"Four Meetings" (James), **VI:** 69

Four Plays (Stevenson and Henley), **V:** 396

Four Plays (White), **Supp. I:** 131

Four Plays for Dancers (Yeats), **VI:** 218

4.48 Psychosis (Kane), **VIII:** 148, 149, 150–151, 155, 159–160

Four Prentices of London with the Conquest of Jerusalem (Heywood), **II:** 48

Four Quartets (Eliot), **VII:** 143, 148, 153–157; **Retro. Supp. II:** 121, 130–131; see also "The Dry Salvages,""East Coker,""Little Gidding"

"Four Sonnets" (Carson), **Supp. XIII:** 59

"Four Walks in the Country near Saint Brieuc" (Mahon) **Supp. VI:** 168

Four Zoas, The (Blake), **III:** 300, 302–303, 307; **Retro. Supp. I:** 44

Four-Gated City, The (Lessing), **Supp. I:** 245, 248, 250, 251, 255

Foure-footed Beastes (Topsel), **II:** 137

"14 November 1973" (Betjeman), **VII:** 372

Fourteenth Century Verse and Prose (Sisam), **I:** 20, 21

Fourth Book of Ayres (Campion), **Supp. XVI:** 96–97

"Fourth of May, The" (Ewart), **Supp. VII:** 36

Fowler, Alastair, **I:** 237

Fowler, H. W., **VI:** 76

Fowles, John, **Supp. I: 291–311**

"Fowls Celestial and Terrestrial" (Pitter), **Supp. XIII:** 140

Foxe, The (Jonson), **Retro. Supp. I:** 163, 164

Fox and the Wolf, The (Henryson), **Supp. VII:** 136, 138, 140

Fox, Caroline, **IV:** 54

Fox, Chris, **Supp. IV:** 88

Fox, George, **IV:** 45

Fox, Ralph, **Supp. IV:** 464, 466

"Fox, The" (Lawrence), **VII:** 90, 91

Fox, the Wolf, and the Cadger, The (Henryson), **Supp. VII:** 136, 140

Fox, the Wolf, and the Husbandman, The (Henryson), **Supp. VII:** 136, 140

"Fox Trot" (Sitwell), **VII:** 131

Foxe, that begylit the Wolf, in the Schadow of the Mone, The (Henryson), see *Fox, the Wolf, and the Husbandman, The*

"Fra Lippo Lippi" (Browning), **IV:** 357, 361, 369; **Retro. Supp. II:** 27; **Retro. Supp. III:** 25

Fra Rupert: The Last Part of a Trilogy (Landor), **IV:** 100
"Fracture" (Dutton), **Supp. XII:** 97–98
"Fragment" (Brooke), **VI:** 421
"Fragment" (Robinson), **Supp. XIII:** 202
"Fragment of a Greek Tragedy" (Housman), **VI:** 156
Fragmenta Aurea (Suckling), **II:** 238
Fragments (Armah), **Supp. X:** 1–6, 12
"Fragments" (Hulme), **Supp. VI:** 137–138
Fragments of Ancient Poetry (Macpherson), **VIII:** 183–185, 187, 189, 194
"Fragoletta" (Swinburne), **V:** 320
"Frail as thy love, The flowers were dead" (Peacock), **IV:** 157
"Frame for Poetry, A" (Thomas), **Supp. XII:** 279
Framley Parsonage (Trollope), **V:** xxii, 93, 101
"France" (Dunn), **Supp. X:** 76
"France, an Ode" (Coleridge), **IV:** 55
"France, December 1870" (Meredith), **V:** 223
"Frances" (Adcock), **Supp. XII:** 13
"Frances" (Brontë), **V:** 132
Francophile, The (Friel), **Supp. V:** 115
Francillon, R. E., **V:** 83
Francis, Dick, **Supp. IV:** 285
Francis, G. H., **IV:** 270
Francis, P., **III:** 249
"Francis Beaumont" (Swinburne), **V:** 332
Franck, Richard, **II:** 131–132
"Frank Fane: A Ballad" (Swinburne), **V:** 332
Frankenstein (Pullman), **Supp. XIII:** 151
Frankenstein; or, The Modern Prometheus (Shelley), **III: 329–331,** 341, 342, 345; **Supp. III:** 355, **356–363,** 369, 372, 385; **Retro. Supp. I:** 247; **Retro. Supp. III:** 287, 288, 289, 290–293, 297
Frankenstein Un-bound (Aldiss), **III:** 341, 345
Franklin's Tale, The (Chaucer), **I:** 23
Fraser, Antonia, **Supp. V:** 20
Fraser, G. S., **VI:** xiv, xxxiii; **VII:** xviii, 422, 425, 443
Fraser's (periodical), **IV:** 259; **V:** 19, 22, 111, 142
"Frater Ave atque Vale" (Tennyson), **IV:** 327, 336
Fraternity (Galsworthy), **VI:** 274, 278, 279–280, 285
"Frau Brechenmacher Attends a Wedding" (Mansfield), **VII:** 172
"Frau Fischer" (Mansfield), **VII:** 172
Fraud (Brookner), **Supp. IV:** 134
Fraunce, Abraham, **I:** 122, 164
Frayn, Michael, **Supp. VII: 51–65**
Frazer, Sir James George, **V:** 204; **Supp. III: 169–190; Supp. IV:** 11, 19
Fred and Madge (Orton), **Supp. V:** 363, 366–367, 372
Frederick the Great (Mitford), **Supp. X:** 167
Fredy Neptune (Murray), **Supp. VII:** 271, 284–286
"Freddy" (Smith), **Supp. II:** 462

Fredolfo (Maturin), **VIII:** 207, 208, 209
Free and Offenceless Justification of a Lately Published and Most Maliciously Misinterpreted Poem Entitled "Andromeda Liberata, A" (Chapman), **I:** 254
Free Fall (Golding), **Supp. I: 75–78,** 81, 83, 85; **Retro. Supp. I:** 98
Free Inquiry into the Nature and Origin of Evil (Jenyns), **Retro. Supp. I:** 148
"Free Radio, The" (Rushdie), **Supp. IV:** 438
Free Thoughts on Public Affairs (Hazlitt), **IV:** 139
"Free Verse: A Post Mortem" (Hope), **Supp. VII:** 155
"Free Women" (Lessing), **Supp. I:** 246–247
Freedom of the City, The (Friel), **Supp. V:** 111, 112, 120–121
Free–Holder (periodical), **III:** 51, 53
Free–Holders Plea against . . . Elections of Parliament–Men, The (Defoe), **III:** 12
Freelands, The (Galsworthy), **VI:** 279
Freeman, Rosemary, **Retro. Supp. II:** 178
Freidan, Betty, **Supp. IV:** 232
French, Sean, **Supp. IV:** 173
French Eton, A (Arnold), **V:** 206, 216
"French Flu, The" (Koestler), **Supp. I:** 35
French Gardiner, The: Instructing How to Cultivate All Sorts of Fruit–Trees . . . (tr. Evelyn), **II:** 287
French Lieutenant's Woman, The (Fowles), **Supp. I:** 291, **300–303**
French Lyrics (Swinburne), **V:** 333
French Poets and Novelists (James), **VI:** 67
French Revolution, The (Blake), **III:** 307; **Retro. Supp. I:** 37
French Revolution, The (Carlyle), **IV:** xii, xix, 240, 243, 245, 249, 250
French Without Tears (Rattigan), **Supp. VII:** 308–310, 311
Frenchman's Creek (du Maurier), **Supp. III:** 144
"Frenzy of Suibhne, The" (Clarke), **Supp. XV:** 19–20
Frequencies (Thomas), **Supp. XII:** 286, 287–288
Frere, John Hookham, **IV:** 182–183
"Fresh Water" (Motion), **Supp. VII:** 259, 262, 263, 264
Freud, Sigmund, **Supp. IV:** 6, 87, 331, 481, 482, 488, 489, 493
"Freya of the Seven Isles" (Conrad), **VI:** 148
Friar Bacon and Friar Bungay (Greene), **II:** 3; **VIII:** 139, 140–142
Friar's Tale, The (Chaucer), **I:** 30
"Friary" (Murphy), **Supp. V:** 329
"Friday; or, The Dirge" (Gay), **III:** 56
Friedman, A., **III:** 178, 190
Friel, Brian, **Supp. V: 111–129**
Friend (periodical), **IV:** 50, 55, 56
"Friend, The" (Milne), **Supp. V:** 303
Friend from England, A (Brookner), **Supp. IV:** 129–130

Friend of Heraclitus (Beer), **Supp. XIV:** 1, 5
"Friendly Epistle to Mrs. Fry, A" (Hood), **IV:** 257, 267
Friendly Tree, The (Day Lewis), **Supp. III:** 118, 130–131
Friendly Young Ladies, The (Renault), **Supp. IX:** 174–175
Friends and Relations (Bowen), **Supp. II:** 84, **86–87**
"Friends of the Friends, The" (James), **VI:** 69
"Friendship–Customs in the Pagan and Early World" (Carpenter), **Supp. XIII:** 44
"Friendship in Early Christian and Mediaeval Times" (Carpenter), **Supp. XIII:** 44
Friendship's Garland (Arnold), **V:** 206, 213n, 215, 216
Friendships Offering (Jewsbury), **Supp. XIV:** 157
Fringe of Leaves, A (White), **Supp. I:** 132, 147–148
"Frog" (Burnside), **Supp. XIII:** 18
"Frog and the Nightingale, The" (Seth), **Supp. X:** 287
Frog He Would A–Fishing Go, A (Potter), **Supp. III:** 298
Frog Prince and Other Poems (Smith), **Supp. II:** 463; **Retro. Supp. III:** 313
"Frogmen" (Davies), **Supp. XIV:** 35, 42
"Frogs, The" (Nye), **Supp. X:** 203
Froissart, Jean, **I:** 21
Frolic and the Gentle, The (Ward), **IV:** 86
"From a Brother's Standpoint" (Beerbohm), **Supp. II:** 53–54
"From a Notebook" (Soutar), **Supp. XVI:** 254
From a View to a Death (Powell), **VII:** 345, 353
From Adam's Peak to Elephanta: Sketches in Ceylon and India (Carpenter), **Supp. XIII:** 45–46
"From an Unfinished Poem" (Stevenson), **Supp. VI:** 262–263
From Bourgeois Land (Smith, I. C.), **Supp. IX:** 213–214, 216, 220–221
From Centre City (Kinsella), **Supp. V:** 272
From Doon with Death (Rendell), **Supp. IX:** 190–191, 197
From Every Chink of the Ark (Redgrove), **Supp. VI:** 234, 236
From Feathers to Iron (Day Lewis), **Supp. III:** 118, 122, 123–124
"From Friend to Friend" (Symonds), **Supp. XIV:** 252
From Glasgow to Saturn (Morgan, E.), **Supp. IX:** 157–159, 162, 163, 167–170
From Heaven Lake: Travels Through Sinkiang and Tibet (Seth), **Supp. X:** 277, 280–281, 290
From Man to Man (Schreiner), **Supp. II:** 439, 440, 441, 442, **450–452**
"From My Diary. July 1914" (Owen), **VI:** 446

From My Guy to Sci-Fi: Genre and Women's Writing in the Postmodern World (ed. Carr), **Supp. XI:** 164
"From my sad Retirement" (King), **Supp. VI:** 159
"From My Study" (Stevenson), **Supp. VI:** 264
From Russia with Love (Fleming), **Supp. XIV:** 91, 94–95, 96, 97
From Sea to Sea (Kipling), **Retro. Supp. III:** 187
"From Sorrow Sorrow Yet Is Born" (Tennyson), **IV:** 329
"From the Answers to Job" (Redgrove), **Supp. VI:** 235
"From the Cliff" (Beer), **Supp. XIV:** 5–6
From the Five Rivers (Steel), **Supp. XII:** 269
From the Four Winds (Galsworthy), **VI:** 276
"From the Frontier of Writing" (Heaney), **Supp. II:** 280
"From the Greek" (Landor), **IV:** 98
From the Joke Shop (Fuller), **Supp. VII:** 79
"From the Life of a Dowser" (Redgrove), **Supp. VI:** 235, 237
"From the Middle Distance" (Armitage), **VIII:** 9
"From the New World" (Davie), **Supp. VI:** 110
"From the Night of Forebeing" (Thompson), **V:** 443, 448
"From the Painting *Back from Market* by Chardin" (Boland), **Supp. V:** 40
"From the Royal College of Surgeons of Edinburgh" (Greig), **Supp. XVI:** 163
From "The School of Eloquence" (Harrison), **Supp. V:** 150
"From the Top" (Crawford), **Supp. XI:** 80
"From the Wave" (Gunn), **Supp. IV:** 267; **Retro. Supp. III:** 120, 123
"From the Wilderness" (Soutar), **Supp. XVI:** 251
"From Tuscan cam my ladies worthi race" (Surrey), **I:** 114
Frontier Wolf (Sutcliff), **Supp. XVI:** 268
"Frontliners" (Gunesekera), **Supp. X:** 87
Frost, Robert, **VI:** 424; **Supp. III:** 394–395; **Supp. IV:** 413, 420, 423, 480, 487
"Frost at Midnight" (Coleridge), **IV:** 41, 44, 55; **Retro. Supp. II:** 60
Frost in the Flower, The (O'Casey), **VII:** 12
Froude, James Anthony, **IV:** 238, 240, 250, 324; **V:** 278, 287
"Frozen" (tr. Delanty), **Supp. XIV:** 77
Frozen Deep, The (Collins), **V:** 42; **Supp. VI:** 92, 95
Frozen Flame, The (O'Brian), **Supp. XII:** 251
"Fruit" (Betjeman), **VII:** 373
Fry, Christopher, **IV:** 318; **Supp. III:** 191–210
Fry, Roger, **VII:** xii, 34
"Frying-Pan, The" (O'Connor), **Supp. XIV:** 227–228

"Fuchsia Blaze, The" (Delanty), **Supp. XIV:** 66
Fuel for the Flame (Waugh), **Supp. VI:** 276
Fuentes, Carlos, **Supp. IV:** 116, 440
Fugard, Athol, **Supp. XV: 99–114**
Fugitive, The (Galsworthy), **VI:** 283
"Fugitive" (Russell), **VIII:** 291
Fugitive Pieces (Byron), **IV:** 192
Fulbecke, William, **I:** 218
"Fulbright Scholars" (Hughes), **Retro. Supp. II:** 217
Fulford, William, **VI:** 167
"Full Measures" (Redgrove), **Supp. VI:** 235
Full Moon (Wodehouse), **Supp. III:** 459
"Full Moon and Little Frieda" (Hughes), **Supp. I:** 349–350
"Full Moon at Tierz: Before the Storming of Huesca" (Cornford), **Supp. XIII:** 90–91
Full Moon in March, A (Yeats), **VI:** 222
Fuller, Roy, **VII:** 422, 428–431, **Supp. VII: 67–82**
Fuller, Thomas, **I:** 178; **II:** 45; **Retro. Supp. I:** 152
Fully Empowered (tr. Reid), **Supp. VII:** 332
"Fulmars" (Constantine), **Supp. XV:** 80
Fumed Oak (Coward), **Supp. II:** 153
Fumifugium; or, The Inconvenience of Aer and Smoak . . . (Evelyn), **II:** 287
"Function of Criticism at the Present Time, The" (Arnold), **V:** 204–205, 212, 213
Function of Poetry in the Drama, The (Abercrombie), **Supp. XVI:** 2
"Function of Poetry in the Drama, The" (Abercrombie), **Supp. XVI:** 4–5
"Funeral, The" (Redgrove), **Supp. VI:** 235
Funeral, The (Steele), **II:** 359
"Funeral Blues" (Auden), **Retro. Supp. I:** 6
Funeral Games (Orton), **Supp. V:** 367, 372, 376–377
Funeral Games (Renault), **Supp. IX:** 186–187
"Funeral Music" (Hill), **Supp. V:** 187–188; **Retro. Supp. III:** 135
"Funeral of Youth, The: Threnody" (Brooke), **Supp. III:** 55
"Funeral Poem Upon the Death of . . . Sir Francis Vere, A,"**II:** 37, 41
"Funerall, The" (Donne), **Retro. Supp. II:** 89–90
"Fungi" (Stevenson), **Supp. VI:** 256
"Funnel, The" (Coppard), **VIII:** 96
Furbank, P. N., **VI:** 397; **Supp. II:** 109, 119
Furetière, Antoine, **II:** 354
"Furies, The" (Nye), **Supp. X:** 200
Furies, The (Roberts, K.), **Supp. X:** 261, 263–264
"Furnace, The" (Kinsella), **Supp. V:** 271
Furness, H. H., **I:** 326
Furnivall, F. J., **VI:** 102
Further Requirements: Interviews, Broadcasts, Statements, and Reviews (Larkin), **Retro. Supp. III:** 201, 205, 206, 211
Further Studies in a Dying Culture (Caudwell), **Supp. IX:** 33, 43–47
Fussell, Paul, **Supp. IV:** 22, 57
"Fust and His Friends" (Browning), **IV:** 366
"Futility" (Owen), **VI:** 453, 455
Futility Machine, The (Carey), **Supp. XII:** 51–52
"Future, The" (Arnold), **V:** 210
"Future, The" (Murray), **Supp. VII:** 277
Future in America, The: A Search After Reality (Wells), **VI:** 244
Future of Ireland and the Awakening of the Fires, The (Russell), **VIII:** 282
"Future of Irish Literature, The" (O'Connor), **Supp. XIV:** 218, 227
"Future Work" (Adcock), **Supp. XII:** 6
"Futures in Feminist Fiction" (Maitland), **Supp. XI:** 164
"Futurity" (Browning), **IV:** 313
Fyvel, T. R., **VII:** 284

G. (Berger), **Supp. IV:** 79, 85–88, 94
G. B. Shaw (Chesterton), **VI:** 130
G. M. Trevelyan (Moorman), **VI:** 396
"Gabor" (Swift), **Supp. V:** 432
"Gabriel-Ernest" (Saki), **Supp. VI:** 244
Gabriel's Gift (Kureishi), **Supp. XI:** 158–159
"Gabrielle de Bergerac" (James), **VI:** 67, 69
Gadfly, The (Voynich), **VI:** 107
"Gaelic Proverb, The" (Smith, I. C.), **Supp. IX:** 222
"Gaelic Songs" (Smith, I. C.), **Supp. IX:** 215–216
"Gaels in Glasgow/Bangladeshis in Bradford" (Crawford), **Supp. XI:** 73
Gager, William, **I:** 193
"Gala Programme: An Unrecorded Episode in Roman History, The" (Saki), **Supp. VI:** 242
Galahad at Blandings (Wodehouse), **Supp. III:** 460
Galatea (Pullman), **Supp. XIII:** 149
Galile (Brecht), **IV:** 182
Galland, Antoine, **III:** 327
Gallathea (Lyly), **I:** 200–202
"Gallery, The" (Hart), **Supp. XI:** 123
"Gallery, The" (Marvell), **II:** 211
Galloway, Janice, **Supp. XII: 117–132**
Galsworthy, Ada, **VI:** 271, 272, 273, 274, 282
Galsworthy, John, **V:** xxii, 270n; **VI:** ix, xiii, 133, 260, **269–291; VII:** xii, xiv; **Supp. I:** 163; **Supp. IV:** 229
Galsworthy the Man (Sauter), **VI:** 284
Galt, John, **IV:** 35
"Game, The" (Boland), **Supp. V:** 35
Game, The (Byatt), **Supp. IV:** 139, 141, 143–145, 154
"Game, The" (Motion), **Supp. VII:** 265
Game at Chess, A (Middleton), **II:** 1, 2, 3, **18–21**
Game for the Living, A (Highsmith), **Supp. V:** 172
"Game of Chess, A" (Eliot), **Retro. Supp. II:** 127

GAME–GENE

Game of Cricket, A (Ayckbourn), **Supp. V:** 3
"Game of Glass, A" (Reid), **Supp. VII:** 327
Game of Logic, The (Carroll), **V:** 273
"Games at Twilight" (Desai), **Supp. V:** 65
Games at Twilight and Other Stories (Desai), **Supp. V:** 55, 65
"Gamester, The" (Robinson), **Supp. XIII:** 205
Gandhi (film), **Supp. IV:** 455
Gandhi, Indira, **Supp. IV:** 165, 231
"Ganymede" (du Maurier), **Supp. III:** 135, 148
Gaol Gate, The (Gregory), **VI:** 315
"Gap, The" (Thomas), **Supp. XII:** 287
"Garbh mac Stairn" (Macpherson), **VIII:** 186
García Márquez, Gabriel, **Supp. IV:** 93, 116, 440, 441, 454, 558
Garden Kalendar (White), **Supp. VI:** 279, 282
"Garden, The" (Cowley), **II:** 194
"Garden, The" (Marvell), **II:** 208, 210, 211, 212, 213–214; **Supp. IV:** 271; **Retro. Supp. II:** 261, 263
"Garden in September, The" (Bridges), **VI:** 78
"Garden Lantern" (Scupham), **Supp. XIII:** 220
Garden of Cyrus, The (Browne), **II:** 148, **150–153,** 154, 155, 156
"Garden of Eros, The" (Wilde), **V:** 401, 402
Garden of Fidelity, The: Being the Autobiography of Flora Annie Steel, 1847–1929 (Steel), **Supp. XII:** 265, 266, 267, 273, 275, 276, 277
"Garden of Love, The" (Blake), **Retro. Supp. I:** 42
"Garden of Proserpine, The" (Swinburne), **V:** 320, 321
"Garden of Remembrance" (Kinsella), **Supp. V:** 261
"Garden of the Innocent" (Nicholson), **Supp. VI:** 215
"Garden of Time, The" (Ballard), **Supp. V:** 22
"Garden on the Point, A" (Kinsella), **Supp. V:** 261
Garden Party, A (Behan), **Supp. II:** 67, 68
"Garden Party, The" (Davie), **Supp. VI:** 106
Garden Party, The (Mansfield), **VII:** xv, 171, 177
"Gardener, The" (Kipling), **VI:** 197; **Retro. Supp. III:** 194
"Gardeners" (Dunn), **Supp. X:** 72
Gardeners and Astronomers (Sitwell), **VII:** 138
"Gardener's Daughter, The" (Tennyson), **IV:** 326; **Retro. Supp. III:** 322
Gardener's Year, A (Haggard), **Supp. III:** 214
"Gardens, The" (Scupham), **Supp. XIII:** 223
"Gardens go on forever" (Kelman), **Supp. V:** 256

Gardiner, S. R., **I:** 146
Gardiner, Judith Kegan, **Supp. IV:** 459
Gardner, Helen, **II:** 121, 129
Gardner, Philip, **VI:** xii, xxxiii
Gareth and Lynette (Tennyson), **IV:** 338; **Retro. Supp. III:** 327
Gargantua and Pantagruel (Rabelais), **Supp. IV:** 464
Garibaldi and the Making of Italy (Trevelyan), **VI:** 388–389
Garibaldi and the Thousand (Trevelyan), **VI:** 388–389
Garibaldi, Giuseppe, **Supp. IV:** 86
Garibaldi's Defence of the Roman Republic (Trevelyan), **VI:** xv, **387–389,** 394
Garis, Robert, **V:** 49–50, 70, 73
Garland of Laurel, The (Skelton), **I:** 81, 82, 90, 93–94
Garmont of Gud Ladeis, The (Henryson), **Supp. VII:** 146, 148
Garner, Ross, **II:** 186
Garnered Sheaves: Essays, Addresses, and Reviews (Frazer), **Supp. III:** 172
Garnett, Edward, **VI:** 135, 149, 273, 277, 278, 283, 366, 373; **VII:** xiv, 89
Garnett, Robert, **I:** 218
"Garret" (Cornford), **Supp. XIII:** 85
Garrett, John, **Supp. IV:** 256
Garrick, David, **I:** 327
Garrick Year, The (Drabble), **Supp. IV:** 230, 236–237
"Garrison, The" (Auden), **Retro. Supp. I:** 13
Garrod, H. W., **III:** 170n, 176
Gascoigne, George, **I:** 215–216, 298
Gas-fitters' Ball, The (Pullman), **Supp. XIII:** 152
Gaskell, Elizabeth, **IV:** 241, 248; **V:** viii, x, xvi, xxi–xxiii, **1–16,** 108, 116, 122, 137, 147–150; **VI:** viii; **Supp. IV:** 119, 379; **Retro. Supp. III:** 99–113
Gaskill, William, **II:** 6
Gaslight (Hamilton), **Supp. XVI:** 177, 179
"Gaspar Ruiz" (Conrad), **VI:** 148
"Gas-Poker, The" (Gunn), **Retro. Supp. III:** 129
Gaston de Blondeville; or, The Court of King Henry III, Keeping Festival in Ardenne (Radcliffe), **Retro. Supp. III:** 234, 247–249
Gaston de Latour (Pater), **V:** 318n, 357
"Gate" (Fallon), **Supp. XII:** 114–115
Gate, The (Day Lewis), **Supp. III:** 118, 129–130
Gate of Angels, The (Fitzgerald), **Supp. V:** 96, 98, 106–107
"Gate of the Hundred Sorrows, The" (Kipling), **Retro. Supp. III:** 185
"Gatehouse, The" (Scupham), **Supp. XIII:** 221–222
Gates of Eden, The (Thompson), **Supp. XV:** 288
Gates of Ivory, The (Drabble), **Supp. IV:** 231, 250–252
Gates of Paradise, The (Blake), *see For Children: The Gates of Paradise; For the Sexes: The Gates of Paradise*
Gates of Pearl, The (Steel), **Supp. XII:** 277

Gates of Wrath, The (Bennett), **VI:** 249
"Gathered Church, A" (Davie), **Supp. VI:** 107
Gathered Church, The (Davie), **Supp. VI:** 105, 115
"Gathering Mushrooms" (Muldoon), **Supp. IV:** 420
"Gathering Sticks on Sunday" (Nicholson), **Supp. VI:** 217
Gathering Storm, The (Churchill), **VI:** 361
Gathering Storm, The (Empson), **Supp. II:** 179, 184, 190
Gatty, Margaret, **V:** 270
"Gaudeamus igitur" (tr. Symonds), **Supp. XIV:** 253
Gaudete (Hughes), **Supp. I: 359–363;** **Retro. Supp. II:** 209–210
Gaudy Night (Sayers), **Supp. III:** 334, 341, 343, 346–347
"Gauguin" (Raine), **Supp. XIII:** 168
Gaunt, William, **VI:** 169
Gautier, Théophile, **IV:** 153n; **V:** 320n, 346, 404, 410–411; **Supp. IV:** 490
Gavin Ewart Show, The (Ewart), **Supp. VII:** 40
Gawain–Poet, The, **Supp. VII:** 83–101
Gay Hunter (Mitchell), **Supp. XIV:** 100
Gay, John, **II:** 348; **III:** 19, 24, 44, **54–67,** 74
Gayton, Edward, **I:** 279
Gaze of the Gorgon, The (Harrison), **Supp. V:** 160, 164
Gebir (Landor), **IV:** xvi, 88, 95, 99, 100, 217
Gebirus, poema (Landor), **IV:** 99–100
"Gecko and Vasco da Gama, The" (Delanty), **Supp. XIV:** 73
"Geese, The" (Sisson), **Supp. XI:** 258
Gem (periodical), **IV:** 252
"Gemini" (Kipling), **VI:** 184
"General, The" (Sassoon), **VI:** 430
General, The (Sillitoe), **Supp. V:** 410, 415
"General Election, A" (Rushdie), **Supp. IV:** 456
General Grant: An Estimate (Arnold), **V:** 216
General History of Discoveries . . . in Useful Arts, A (Defoe), **III:** 14
General History of Music (Burney), **Supp. III:** 66
General History of the Robberies and Murders of . . . Pyrates, A (Defoe), **III:** 13
General History of the Turkes (Knolles), **III:** 108
General Inventorie of the History of France (Brimeston), **I:** 249
General Prologue, The (Chaucer), **I:** 23, 26, 27–28, 38–40
"General Satyre, A" (Dunbar), **VIII:** 122, 126
"Generations" (Stevenson), **Supp. VI:** 257
Generous Days, The (Spender), **Supp. II:** 493
Genesis (Crace), **Supp. XIV:** 19, 23, 30
Genesis, **Retro. Supp. II:** 301
"Genesis" (Hill), **Supp. V:** 184–185

"Genesis" (Swinburne), **V:** 325
"Genesis and Catastrophe" (Dahl), **Supp. IV:** 221
Genesis B, **Retro. Supp. II:** 301
Geneva (Shaw), **VI:** 125, 127–128, 129; **Retro. Supp. II:** 324
Genius of the Future: Studies in French Art Criticism, The (Brookner), **Supp. IV:** 122–123
Genius of the Thames, The (Peacock), **IV:** 169
Genius of Thomas Hardy, The (ed. Drabble), **Supp. IV:** 230
"Gentians" (McGuckian), **Supp. V:** 281
"Gentle Demolition, A" (Butlin), **Supp. XVI:** 56
Gentle Island, The (Friel), **Supp. V:** 119–120
"Gentle Joy" (Pitter), **Supp. XIII:** 141
"Gentle Sex, The" (Ewart), **Supp. VII:** 42
Gentlemen and Ladies (Hill), **Supp. XIV:** 118
Gentleman Dancing–Master, The (Wycherley), **II:** 308, 309, **313–314,** 321
Gentleman in the Parlour, The (Maugham), **VI:** 371
Gentleman Usher, The (Chapman), **I:** 244–245
Gentleman's Magazine (periodical), **III:** 107
Gentlemen in England (Wilson), **Supp. VI:** 302–303, 305
Gentler Birth, A (Fallon), **Supp. XII:** 104
Gentlewomen's Companion, The (Woolley), **Supp. III:** 21
Genuine Dialogue Between a Gentlewoman at Derby and Her Maid Jenny, A (Byrom), **Supp. XVI:** 81
Geoffrey de Vinsauf, **I:** 23 39–40, 59
Geography and History of England, The (Goldsmith), **III:** 191
George, Henry, **VI:** 102
"George and the Seraph" (Brooke-Rose), **Supp. IV:** 103
George Bernard Shaw (Chesterton), **VI:** 344
George Crabbe and His Times (Huchon), **III:** 273n
George Eliot (Stephen), **V:** 289
George Eliot: Her Life and Books (Bullet), **V:** 196, 200–201
George Eliot, Selected Essays, Poems and Other Writings (Byatt), **Supp. IV:** 151
George Eliot's Life as Related in Her Letters and Journals (ed. Cross), **V:** 13, 200
George Gissing: Grave Comedian (Donnelly), **V:** 427n, 438
"George Herbert: The Art of Plainness" (Stein), **Retro. Supp. II:** 181
George Moore: L'homme et l'oeuvre (Noel), **VI:** 98, 99
George Orwell (Fyvel), **VII:** 287
George Passant (Snow), **VII:** 324, 325–326
George Silverman's Explanation (Dickens), **V:** 72

George's Ghosts (Maddox), **Retro. Supp. I:** 327, 328
George's Marvellous Medicine (Dahl), **Supp. IV:** 204–205
"Georgian Boyhood, A" (Connolly), **Supp. III:** 1–2
Georgian Poetry 1911–1912 (ed. Marsh), **VI:** 416, 419, 420, 453; **VII:** xvi; **Supp. III:** 45, 53–54, 397
"Georgina's Reasons" (James), **VI:** 69
Gerard; or, The World, the Flesh, and the Devil (Braddon), **VIII:** 49
Gerald: A Portrait (du Maurier), **Supp. III:** 134–135, 138–139
Gerard Manley Hopkins: A Critical Symposium (Kenyon Critics), **V:** 382
Gerard Manley Hopkins: The Classical Background . . . (Bender), **V:** 364–365, 382
"Geriatric" (Thomas), **Supp. XII:** 291
Géricault, Théodore, **Supp. IV:** 71–72, 73
Gérin, Winifred, **V:** x, xxvii, 111, 151, 152, 153
Germ (periodical), **V:** xxi, 235–236, 249
German Anthology: A Series of Translations from the Most Popular of the German Poets (tr. Mangan), **Supp. XIII:** 118
"German Chronicle" (Hulme), **Supp. VI:** 139
German Requiem, A (Kerr), **Supp. XII:** 187, 188, 191
"Germinal" (Russell), **VIII:** 290
"Gerontion" (Eliot), **VII:** 144, 146, 147, 152; **Retro. Supp. II:** 123–124
Gerugte van Reen (Brink), **Supp. VI:** 49
Gesta Romanorum, **I:** 52 53
"Gethsemane" (Nicholson), **Supp. VI:** 214
Get Ready for Battle (Jhabvala), **Supp. V:** 228–229
"Getting at Stars" (Armitage), **VIII:** 4
Getting It Right (Howard), **Supp. XI:** 135, 141, 143–144, 148
Getting Married (Shaw), **VI:** 115, 117–118
"Getting Off the Altitude" (Lessing), **Supp. I:** 240
Getting On (Bennett), **VIII:** 20, 21, 25–26
"Getting Poisoned" (Ishiguro), **Supp. IV:** 303; **Retro. Supp. III:** 161
"Getting there" (Kelman), **Supp. V:** 249
Getting to Know the General (Greene), **Supp. I:** 1, 13, 14, 17
Geulincx, Arnold, **Supp. I: 44**
"Geve place ye lovers" (Surrey), **I:** 120
"Geysers, The" (Gunn), **Supp. IV:** 268, 269, 276; **Retro. Supp. III:** 117, 123, 124
"Ghana: To Be a Woman" (Aidoo), **Supp. XV:** 1–2, 3, 4
Ghastly Good Taste (Betjeman), **VII:** 357, 361
"Ghazel and Song" (Mangan), **Supp. XIII:** 125

"Ghetto–Blastir" (Crawford), **Supp. XI:** 68
Ghost Child, The (Tennant), **Supp. IX:** 239
Ghost in the Machine, The (Koestler), **Supp. I:** 37, 38
"Ghost of Ferozsha Baag, The" (Mistry), **Supp. X:** 138–139
Ghost of Lucrece, The (Middleton), **II:** 3
Ghost Orchid, The (Longley), **VIII:** 175–177
"Ghost Orchid, The" (Longley), **VIII:** 175–176
Ghost Road, The (Barker), **Supp. IV:** 45, 46, 57, 61–63
Ghost Trio (Beckett), **Retro. Supp. I:** 29
"Ghost–Crabs" (Hughes), **Supp. I:** 349, 350; **Retro. Supp. II:** 206
"Ghostkeeper" (Lowry), **Supp. III:** 285
"Ghostly Father, The" (Redgrove), **Supp. VI:** 228
"Ghosts" (Redgrove), **Supp. VI:** 228, 236
"Ghosts" (Reid), **Supp. VII:** 327
Ghosts at Cockcrow (Conn), **Supp. XIII:** 71, 79–81
"Ghosts at Cockcrow" (Conn), **Supp. XIII:** 80
"Ghost's Moonshine, The" (Beddoes), **Supp. XI:** 29
Ghostwritten (Mitchell), **Supp. XIV:** 193–196, 197, 198, 202, 206, 207
Giants' Bread (Christie), **Supp. II:** 133
Giaour, The (Byron), **III:** 338; **IV:** xvii, 172, 173–174, 180, 192
Gibbon, Edward, **III:** 109, **221–233; IV:** xiv, xvi, 93, 284; **V:** 425; **VI:** 347, 353, 383, 390n
Gibbon, Lewis Grassic, **Supp. XIV: 99–113**
Gibbons, Brian, **I:** 281
Gibson, W. W., **VI:** 416
Gide, André, **V:** xxiii, 402
Gidez, Richard B., **Supp. IV:** 326, 339–340
Gifford, William, **II:** 96; **IV:** 133
Gift, The (Scupham), **Supp. XIII:** 220
"Gift of Boxes, A" (Longley), **VIII:** 176
Gift of Stones, The (Crace), **Supp. XIV:** 18, 19, 22–23, 24
Gift Songs (Burnside), **Supp. XIII:** 27
"Gifts" (Thomas), **Supp. XII:** 285
"Giggling" (Adcock), **Supp. XII:** 13
"Gigolo and Gigolette" (Maugham), **VI:** 370
Gil Blas (tr. Smollett), **III:** 150
Gil Perez, The Gallician (tr. FitzGerald), **IV:** 344
Gilbert, Elliott, **VI:** 194
"Gilbert" (Brontë), **V:** 131–132
Gilbert, Peter, **Supp. IV:** 354
Gilbert, Sandra, **Retro. Supp. I:** 59–60
"Gilbert's Mother" (Trevor), **Supp. IV:** 505
Gilchrist, Andrew, **Retro. Supp. I:** 46
Gilfillan, George, **I:** 98
"Gilles de Retz" (Keyes), **VII:** 437
Gilliam, Terry, **Supp. IV:** 455
Gillman, James, **IV:** 48–49, 50, 56
Gilman, Charlotte Perkins, **Supp. III:** 147

Gilpin, William, **IV:** 36, 37
Gilson, Étienne, **VI:** 341
"Gin and Goldenrod" (Lowry), **Supp. III:** 282
"Gin ye had come last nicht" (Soutar), **Supp. XVI:** 248
"Ginger Hero" (Friel), **Supp. V:** 113
Ginger, You're Barmy (Lodge), **Supp. IV:** 364–365, 368–369, 371
Giorgione da Castelfranco, **V:** 345, 348
"Giorgione" (Pater), **V:** 345, 348, 353
"Gipsy Vans" (Kipling), **VI:** 193, 196
"Giraffes, The" (Fuller), **VII:** 430, **Supp. VII:** 70
"Girl" (Kincaid), **Supp. VII:** 220, 221, 223
"Girl at the Seaside" (Murphy), **Supp. V:** 313, 318
"Girl From Zlot, The" (Stallworthy), **Supp. X:** 299–300
Girl, 20 (Amis), **Supp. II:** 15–16; **Supp. IV:** 29
"Girl from Quesbrada, The" (Delahunt), **Supp. XIV:** 53
Girl in Winter, A (Larkin), **Supp. I:** 286, 287; **Retro. Supp. III:** 200, 202–203
Girl Weeping for the Death of Her Canary (Greuze), **Supp. IV:** 122
Girl Who Can and Other Stories, The (Aidoo), **Supp. XV:** 9–10
"Girl Who Loved Graveyards, The" (James), **Supp. IV:** 340
Girlhood of Mary Virgin, The (Rossetti), **V:** 236, 248, 249
Girlitude: A Memoir of the 50s and 60s (Tennant), **Supp. IX:** 239
Girls in Their Married Bliss (O'Brien), **Supp. V:** 334, 337–338
"Girls in Their Season" (Mahon), **Supp. VI:** 167
"Girls Next Door, The" (Gunn), **Retro. Supp. III:** 125
Girls of Slender Means, The (Spark), **Supp. I:** 200, 204, 206
"Girls on a Bridge" (Mahon), **Supp. VI:** 174
Gisborne, John, **IV:** 206
Gísla saga Súrssonar, **VIII:** 241
Gismond of Salerne (Wilmot), **I:** 216
Gissing, George, **V:** xiii, xxii, xxv–xxvi, 69, **423–438; VI:** 365; **Supp. IV:** 7–8
Gittings, Robert, **Supp. III:** 194
"Give Her A Pattern" (Lawrence), **II:** 330n
Give Me Your Answer, Do! (Friel), **Supp. V:** 127–128
"Given Heart, The" (Cowley), **II:** 197
Giving Alms No Charity . . . (Defoe), **III:** 13
Gladiators, The (Koestler), **Supp. I:** 27, 28, 29n
"Glanmore Revisited" (Heaney), **Retro. Supp. I:** 132
"Glanmore Sonnets" (Heaney), **Supp. II:** 276
Glanvill, Joseph, **II:** 275
"Glasgow" (Gibbon), **Supp. XIV:** 102–103
"Glasgow 5 March 1971" (Morgan, E.), **Supp. IX:** 162

"Glasgow Green" (Morgan, E.), **Supp. IX:** 158
Glasgow Herald, **Supp. XII:** 207
"Glasgow October 1971" (Morgan, E.), **Supp. IX:** 162
Glass-Blowers, The (du Maurier), **Supp. III:** 136, 138
Glass Cell, The (Highsmith), **Supp. V:** 174
Glass Cottage, A Nautical Romance, The (Redgrove), **Supp. VI:** 230–231
Glass of Blessings, A (Pym), **Supp. II:** **377–378**
"Glass of the Sinful Soul, A" (tr. Elizabeth I), **Supp. XVI:** 155–156
Glass Town chronicles (Brontës), **V:** 110–111
Glaucus: or, The Wonders of the Shore (Kingsley), **Supp. XVI:** 203–204
Gleanings by an Undergraduate (Soutar), **Supp. XVI:** 243–244
Gleanings from the Menagerie and Aviary at Knowsley Hall (Lear), **V:** 76, 87
Gleanings from the Work of George Fox (ed. Richardson), **Supp. XIII:** 187
Gleckner, R. F., **IV:** 173, 194
Glen, Heather, **III:** 297
"Glen Strathfarrar" (Kay), **Supp. XIII:** 107
Glendinning, Victoria, **Supp. II:** 78, 80, 90, 95
"Glimpse, The" (Cornford), **VIII:** 106
Glimpse of America, A (Stoker), **Supp. III:** 380
Glimpse of Reality, The (Shaw), **VI:** 129
Gloag, Julian, **Supp. IV:** 390
"Globe in North Carolina, The" (Mahon), **Supp. VI:** 174
"Gloire de Dijon" (Lawrence), **Retro. Supp. II:** 233
Gloriana: Opera in Three Acts (Plomer), **Supp. XI:** 222
Glorious First of June, The, **III:** 266
"Glory" (Scupham), **Supp. XIII:** 225
"Glory, A" (Armitage), **VIII:** 11
"Glory of Women" (Sassoon), **VI:** 430
"Glossaire, Une/A Glossary" (Roberts), **Supp. XV:** 262–263
"Gnomes" (Ewart), **Supp. VII:** 39
gnomic moralizing poem, **I:** 57
"Go for" (Thomas), **Supp. III:** 399
"Go, Lovely Rose!" (Waller), **II:** 234
Go, Piteous Heart (Skelton), **I:** 83
Go When You See the Green Man Walking (Brooke-Rose), **Supp. IV:** 103–104
"Goal" (Dutton), **Supp. XII:** 96–97
"Goal of Valerius" (Bacon), **I:** 263
Go-Between, The (Hartley), **Supp. VII:** 119, 120, 121, 127–129, 131, 132; **Retro. Supp. I:** 227
Goat Green; or, The Better Gift (Powys), **VIII:** 255
Goat's Song, A (Healy), **Supp. IX:** 96–98, 101–103
"Goblin Market" (Rossetti), **V:** 250, 256–258; **Retro. Supp. III:** 255
Goblin Market and Other Poems (Rossetti), **V:** xxii, 250, 260; **Retro. Supp. III:** 251, 255, 256
Goblins, The (Suckling), **II:** 226
"God" (Powys), **VIII:** 248
"God, The" (Pitter), **Supp. XIII:** 134
"God Almighty the First Garden Made" (Jamie), **Supp. XIV:** 135
God and His Gifts, A (Compton-Burnett), **VII:** 60, 64, 65
God and the Bible (Arnold), **V:** 216
"God and the Jolly Bored Bog-Mouse" (Cope), **VIII:** 74
God Bless Karl Marx! (Sisson), **Supp. XI:** 251
"God! How I Hate You, You Young Cheerful Men" (West), **VI:** 423
"God Moves in a Mysterious Way" (Cowper), **III:** 210
God of Glass, The (Redgrove), **Supp. VI:** 231
God of Small Things (Roy), **Supp. V:** 67, 75
God that Failed, The (Crossman), **Supp. I:** 25
"God the Drinker" (Smith), **Retro. Supp. III:** 310–311
"God the Eater" (Smith), **Supp. II:** 468
God the Invisible King (Wells), **VI:** 227
"God Who Eats Corn, The" (Murphy), **Supp. V:** 313, 323–324
"Godfather Dottery" (Powys), **VIII:** 258
"Gods as Dwelling in the Physiological Centres, The" (Carpenter), **Supp. XIII:** 46
"God's Eternity" (Blake), **III:** 300
"God's Funeral" (Hardy), **Retro. Supp. I:** 121
God's Funeral (Wilson), **Supp. VI:** 298, 306, 308, **309**
"God's Grandeur" (Hopkins), **V:** 366; **Retro. Supp. II:** 195
"God's Judgement on a Wicked Bishop" (Southey), **IV:** 67
"Gods of the Copybook Heading, The" (Ewart), **Supp. VII:** 41
Gods of War, with Other Poems (Russell), **VIII:** 287
God's Revenge Against Murder (Reynolds), **II:** 14
Godber, Joyce, **II:** 243, 254
"Goddess, The" (Gunn), **Supp. IV:** 266, 271
Godman, Stanley, **V:** 271, 274
Godolphin, Sidney, **II:** 237, 238, 271
Godwin, E. W., **V:** 404
Godwin, Mary Wollstonecraft, *see* Shelley, Mary Wollstonecraft
Godwin, William, **III:** 329, 330, 332, 340, 345; **IV:** xv, 3, 43, 127, 173, 181, 195–197; **Supp. III:** 355, 363, 370, 474, 476, 480; **Supp. XV:** **115–131**
Goethe, Johann Wolfgang von, **III:** 344; **IV:** xiv–xix, 179, 240, 245, 249; **V:** 214, 343, 344, 402; **Supp. IV:** 28, 479
Goethe's Faust (MacNeice), **VII:** 408–410
Gogh, Vincent van, **Supp. IV:** 148, 154
Gogol, Nikolai, **III:** 340, 345; **Supp. III:** 17
"Going, The" (Hardy), **VI:** 18; **Retro. Supp. I:** 118

"Going Back" (Adcock), **Supp. XII:** 8
"Going Back" (Stevenson), **Supp. VI:** 265
"Going, Going" (Larkin), **Supp. I:** 283; **Retro. Supp. III:** 209
Going Home (Lessing), **Supp. I:** 237
"Going Home" (Mahon), **Supp. VI:** 172
"Going Home (A Letter to Colombo)" (Gunesekera), **Supp. X: 86**
Going On (Reading), **VIII:** 207, 268, 269
"Going Out: Lancasters, 1944" (Scupham), **Supp. XIII:** 224–225
Going Solo (Dahl), **Supp. IV:** 206, 208, 210, 211, 222, 225
Going Their Own Ways (Waugh), **Supp. VI:** 273
"Going to Italy" (Davie), **Supp. VI:** 107
"Going to See a Man Hanged" (Thackeray), **V:** 23, 37
Gold, Mike, **Supp. IV:** 464
Gold: A Poem (Brooke–Rose)), **Supp. IV:** 99, 100
Gold Coast Customs (Sitwell), **VII:** xvii, 132, 133–134
Gold in the Sea, The (Friel), **Supp. V:** 113
"Gold in the Sea, The" (Friel), **Supp. V:** 114
"Golden Age, The" (Behn), **Supp. III:** 39–40; **Retro. Supp. III:** 5–6, 7, 10, 12
Golden Ass (Apulius), **Supp. IV:** 414
Golden Bird, The (Brown), **Supp. VI:** 64
Golden Book of St. John Chrysostom, The, Concerning the Education of Children (tr. Evelyn), **II:** 275, 287
Golden Bough, The (Frazer), **V:** 204; **Supp. III:** 170, 172, 173, 174, 175, 176–182, 184, 185, 186, 187; **Supp. IV:** 12
Golden Bowl, The (James), **VI:** 53, 55, 60–62, 67; **Supp. IV:** 243
Golden Calf, The (Braddon), **VIII:** 49
"Golden Calf" (MacCaig), **Supp. VI:** 186
Golden Chersonese, The (Bird), **Supp. X:** 19, 30–31
Golden Child, The (Fitzgerald), **Supp. V:** 98, 100–101
Golden Compass, The (Pullman), **Supp. XIII:** 153, 155–156
Golden Echo, The (Garnett), **VI:** 333
Golden Gate: A Novel in Verse, The (Seth), **Supp. X:** 277–279, 281–283, 285–290
"Golden Hair" (Owen), **VI:** 449
Golden Labyrinth, The (Knight), **IV:** 328n, 339
Golden Lads: Sir Francis Bacon, Anthony Bacon, and Their Friends (du Maurier), **Supp. III:** 139
Golden Lion of Granpère, The (Trollope), **V:** 102
"Golden Lyric, The" (Smith, I. C.), **Supp. IX:** 222
Golden Mean, The (Ford), **II:** 88, 100
Golden Notebook, The (Lessing), **Supp. I:** 238, **246–248**, 254, 256; **Supp. IV:** 473
Golden Ocean, The (O'Brian), **Supp. XII:** 248, 251, 252

Golden Peak, The: Travels in North Pakistan (Jamie), **Supp. XIV:** 129, 144
"Golden Speech" (Elizabeth I), **Supp. XVI:** 153
"Golden Stool, The" (Brathwaite), **Supp. XII:** 39
Golden Targe, The (Dunbar), **I:** 23
Golden Treasury, The (Palgrave), **II:** 208; **IV:** xxii, 196, 337
Golden Treasury of Irish Poetry, A: A.D. 600 to 1200 (tr. O'Connor), **Supp. XIV:** 219
"Golden Years, The" (Behn), **Retro. Supp. III:** 13
Goldeneye (Fleming), **Supp. XIV:** 95
Goldfinger (Fleming), **Supp. XIV:** 91, 96, 97
"Goldfish Nation" (Cope), **VIII:** 77
Golding, Arthur, **I:** 161
Golding, William, **Supp. I: 65–91; Supp. IV:** 392–393; **Retro. Supp. I: 93–107**
Goldring, Douglas, **VI:** 324, 419
Goldsmith, Oliver, **II:** 362, 363; **III:** 40, 110, 149, 165, 173, **177–192**, 256, 277, 278; **Retro. Supp. I:** 149
Goldsworthy Lowes Dickinson (Forster), **VI:** 411
Goldyn Targe, The (Dunbar), **VIII:** 120, 123–124
"Goldyn Targe, The" (Dunbar), **VIII:** 118
Gollancz, Victor, **VII:** xix, 279, 381
Gondal literature (Brontë), **V:** 113–117, 133, 142
Gondal Poems (Brontë), **V:** 152
Gondal's Queen (Ratchford), **V:** 133, 152
Gondibert (Davenant), **II:** 196, 259
"Gone" (Montague), **Supp. XV:** 221
Gonne, Maud, **VI:** 207, 210, 211, 212
Good and Bad at Games (Boyd), **Supp. XVI:** 32, 45
Good and Faithful Servant, The (Orton), **Supp. V:** 364, 367, 370, 371, 372, 374–375
Good Apprentice, The (Murdoch), **Supp. I:** 231, 232, 233
Good Angel, Bad Angel (Butlin), **Supp. XVI:** 52
"Good Aunt, The" (Edgeworth), **Supp. III:** 162
"Good Climate, Friendly Inhabitants" (Gordimer), **Supp. II:** 232
Good Companions, The (Priestley), **VII:** xviii, 209, 211, 215–216
"Good Counsel to a Young Maid" (Carew), **II:** 224
"Good Fences" (Burnside), **Supp. XIII:** 27
Good Fight, The (Kinsella), **Supp. V:** 267
"Good Flying Days" (Scupham), **Supp. XIII:** 224
Good Hanging and Other Stories, A (Rankin), **Supp. X:** 244, 246, 250
"Good Friday" (Herbert), **II:** 128
"Good Friday: Rex Tragicus; or, Christ Going to His Crosse" (Herrick), **II:** 114
"Good Friday, 1613" (Donne), **I:** 368
Good Grief (Waterhouse), **Supp. XIII:** 273–274
Good Kipling, The (Gilbert), **VI:** 194

"Good ladies ye that have" (Sumy), **I:** 120
Good Man in Africa, A (Boyd), **Supp. XVI:** 31, 32, 33–34, 40
Good Man in Africa, A (screenplay, Boyd), **Supp. XVI:** 46
"Good Morning" (Scupham), **Supp. XIII:** 218
Good Morning. Midnight (Rhys), **Supp. II:** 388, **396–398**
"Good Morrow, The" (MacCaig), **Supp. VI:** 185
Good Natur'd Man, The (Goldsmith), **III:** 111, 180, 187, 191
"Good Neighbor, The" (Burnside), **Supp. XIII:** 26–27
"Good Neighbors" (Burnside), **Supp. XIII:** 26–27
Good News for the Vilest of Men; or, A Help for Despairing Souls (Bunyan), **II:** 253
"Good Night" (Kinsella), **Supp. V:** 267
Good Night Sweet Ladies (Blackwood), **Supp. IX:** 8, 12–13
Good Soldier, The (Ford), **VI:** 49; **VI:** 319, 323, **327–328**, 329
Good Son, The (film), **Supp. IV:** 390, 400
Good Terrorist, The (Lessing), **Supp. I:** 255–256
Good Time Was Had by All, A (Smith), **Supp. II:** 462; **Retro. Supp. III:** 302, 304–305
Good Times, The (Kelman), **Supp. V:** 243, 254–256
"Good Town, The" (Muir), **Supp. VI:** 207
Goodbye (Adcock), **Supp. XII:** 14–15
Goodbye Earth and Other Poems (Richards), **Supp. II:** 427, 428
"Good-bye in fear, good-bye in sorrow" (Rossetti), **V:** 255
"Goodbye Marcus, Goodbye Rose" (Rhys), **Supp. II:** 401
Goodbye to All That (Graves), **VI:** xvi; **VII:** xviii, 257, 258
Goodbye to Berlin (Isherwood), **VII:** xx
Goodbye to Berlin (Wilson), **Supp. I:** 156
"Good–Bye to the Mezzogiorno" (Auden), **Retro. Supp. I:** 13
"Goodbye to the USA" (Davie), **Supp. VI:** 113
"Good–Morrow, The" (Donne), **II:** 197
"Goodness—the American Neurosis" (Rushdie), **Supp. IV:** 455–456
"Good–night" (Thomas), **Supp. III:** 400
Goopy Gyne Bagha Byne (film), **Supp. IV:** 450
"Goose, The" (Longley), **VIII:** 172–173
Goose Cross (Kavan), **Supp. VII:** 208
"Goose Fair" (Lawrence), **VII:** 114
"Goose to Donkey" (Murray), **Supp. VII:** 282
"Gooseberry Season" (Armitage), **VIII:** 5
Gorboduc (Norton and Sackville), **I:** 161–162, 214–216
Gordimer, Nadine, **Supp. II: 225–243**
Gordon, D. J., **I:** 237, 239
Gordon, Ian Alistair, **VII:** xvii, xxxvii
Gorgon's Head and Other Literary Pieces, The (Frazer), **Supp. III:** 176

Gorse Fires (Longley), **VIII:** 166, 169, 174–175
Gorse Trilogy, The (Hamilton), **Supp. XVI:** 188–190
Gorton, Mary, **V:** 312, 313, 315–316, 330
Gospel of Nicodemus (tr. Trevisa), see *Evangelium Nicodemi*
Gosse, Edmund, **II:** 354, 361, 363, 364; **V:** 311, 313, 334, 392, 395
Gossip from the Forest (Keneally), **Supp. IV:** 346
Gosson, Stephen, **I:** 161
Gothic Architecture (Morris), **V:** 306
Gothic fiction, **III: 324–346; IV:** 110, 111; **V:** 142–143
Gothic Revival, The (Clark), **III:** 325, 346
"Gourmet, The" (Ishiguro), **Supp. IV:** 304, 306; **Retro. Supp. III:** 162
Government of the Tongue: The 1986 T. S. Eliot Memorial Lectures and Other Critical Writings (Heaney), **Supp. II:** 268, 269; **Retro. Supp. I:** 131
Gower, John, **I:** 20, 41, **48–56,** 57, 321
"Gowk, The" (Soutar), **Supp. XVI:** 246, 247, 250
Goya, Francisco de, **Supp. IV:** 125
Grace Abounding to the Chief of Sinners (Bunyan), **II:** 240, 241, 243–245, 250, 253; **Supp. IV:** 242
Grace Darling (Swinburne), **V:** 333
"Grace of the Way" (Thompson), **V:** 442
"Graceland" (Burnside), **Supp. XIII:** 28
Graffigny, Mme de, **Supp. III:** 75
Graham Greene (Lodge), **Supp. IV:** 365
Graham, James, see Montrose, marquess of
Graham, W. S., **Supp. VII: 103–117**
Grain Kings, The (Roberts, K.), **Supp. X:** 270–271
"Grain Kings, The" (Roberts, K.), **Supp. X:** 271
Grain of Wheat, A (Ngũgĩ), **VIII:** 212, 219–220
"Graínne" (Roberts, K.), **Supp. X:** 273–274
Grammar of Assent, An Essay in Aid of a (Newman), **V:** 340, **Supp. VII:** 301–302
Grammar of Metaphor, A (Brooke-Rose)), **Supp. IV:** 98, 113
"Grammarian's Funeral, A" (Browning), **IV:** 357, 361, 366
Grand Alliance, The (Churchill), **VI:** 361
Grand Babylon Hotel, The (Bennett), **VI:** 249, 253, 262, 266
"Grand Ballet" (Cornford), **VIII:** 113
Grand Meaulnes, Le (Alain-Fournier), **Supp. I:** 299
"Grandfather" (Burnside), **Supp. XIII:** 19
"Grandmother's Story, The" (Murray), **Supp. VII:** 280
"Grandparent's" (Spender), **Supp. II:** 494
Grania (Gregory), **VI:** 316
Granny Scarecrow (Stevenson), **Supp. VI: 265**
Grant, Duncan, **VI:** 118
Granta (periodical), **Supp. IV:** 304; **Supp. XII:** 66; **Supp. XIII:** 11

"Grantchester" (Brooke), **Supp. III:** 52, 60
Granville Barker, Harley, **I:** 329; **VI:** ix, 104, 113, 273
Grass, Günter, **Supp. IV:** 440
Grass Is Singing, The (Lessing), **Supp. I:** 237, 239, 243, 248
"Grass Widows, The" (Trevor), **Supp. IV:** 503
Grasshopper (Rendell), **Supp. IX:** 189, 203
"Gratiana Dancing and Singing" (Lovelace), **II:** 230
Grave, The (Blair), **Retro. Supp. I:** 45
"Grave, The" (tr. Morgan), **Supp. IX:** 161
"Grave by the Handpost, The" (Hardy), **VI:** 22
"Grave Song" (Montague), **Supp. XV:** 216–217
"Gravel Walks, The" (Heaney), **Retro. Supp. I:** 133
Graves, Robert, **II:** 94; **VI:** xvi, 207, 211, 219, 419; **VII:** xvi, xviii–xx, **257–272; Supp. II:** 185; **Supp. III:** 60; **Supp. IV:** 558; **Retro. Supp. I:** 144
"Graveyard in Queens, A" (Montague), **Supp. XV:** 215–216
"Gravities: West" (Fallon), **Supp. XII:** 111
Gravity's Rainbow (Pynchon), **Supp. IV:** 116
Gray, Alasdair, **Supp. IX: 79–93**
Gray, Thomas, **II:** 200; **III:** 118, 119, **136–145,** 173, 294, 325
"Gray's Anatomy" (Malouf), **Supp. XII:** 220
Great Adventure, The (Bennett), **VI:** 250, 266; see also *Buried Alive*
Great Apes (Self), **Supp. V:** 398–400
"Great Automatic Grammatisator, The" (Dahl), **Supp. IV:** 216–217
Great Boer War, The (Doyle), **Supp. II:** 160
Great Broxopp, The (Milne), **Supp. V:** 299
Great Catherine (Shaw), **VI:** 119
Great Cloak, The (Montague), **Supp. XV:** 212, 220–221, 222
Great Contemporaries (Churchill), **VI:** 354, 356
Great Depression, **VII:** xix
Great Desire I Had, The (Reed), **Supp. XV:** 252
Great Divorce, The (Lewis), **Supp. III:** 56
Great Duke of Florence, The (Massinger), **Supp. XI:** 184
Great Exhibition, The (Hare), **Supp. IV:** 281
Great Expectations (Dickens), **V:** xxii, 42, 60, 63, 66–68, 72
Great Favourite, The; or, The Duke of Lerma (Howard), **II:** 100
Great Fire of London, The (Ackroyd), **Supp. VI:** 4–5, 10
"Great Good Place, The" (James), **VI:** 69
Great Granny Webster (Blackwood), **Supp. IX:** 2, 6, 10–11, 16
Great Hoggarty Diamond, The (Thackeray), **V:** 21, 38

Great Hunger, The (Kavanagh), **Supp. VII:** 187, 190–192, 193, 194, 199
Great Instauration, The (Bacon), **I:** 259, 272
Great Law of Subordination Consider'd, The (Defoe), **III:** 13
"Great Lover, The" (Brooke), **Supp. III:** 556
"Great Man, The" (Caudwell), **Supp. IX:** 35, 37
"Great Man, The" (Motion), **Supp. VII:** 256
"Great McEwen, Scottish Hypnotist, The" (Crawford), **Supp. XI:** 71
"Great men have been among us" (Wordsworth), **II:** 208
Great Moments in Aviation (film), **Supp. IV:** 542
Great Port: A Passage through New York, The (Morris, J.), **Supp. X:** 182
"Great Ship, The" (Delanty), **Supp. XIV:** 75
Great Short Stories of Detection, Mystery and Horror (ed. Sayers), **III:** 341; **Supp. III:** 340, 341
"Great Spirits Now on Earth Are Sojourning . . . A" (Keats), **IV:** 214
"Great Spunky Unflincher: Laurence Sterne, B. S. Johnson, and Me: The 2004 Laurence Sterne Memorial Lecture" (Coe), **Supp. XV:** 52
Great Trade Route (Ford), **VI:** 324
Great Tradition, The (Leavis), **VI:** 68, 149; **VII:** 234, **248–251; Retro. Supp. I:** 90
"Great Unknown, The" (Hood), **IV:** 267
Great Victorian Collection, The (Moore, B.), **Supp. IX:** 143–144, 154
Great War and Modern Memory, The (Fussell), **Supp. IV:** 57
Great World, The (Malouf), **Supp. XII:** 218, 226–227
Greater Lakeland (Nicholson), **Supp. VI:** 223
"Greater Love" (Owen), **VI:** 450
Greater Trumps, The (Williams, C. W. S.), **Supp. IX:** 281
Greatest Plague of Life, The (Mayhew and Mayhew), **Supp. XVI:** 211–214
"Greatest TV Show on Earth, The" (Ballard), **Supp. V:** 28
Greatness of the Soul, A, . . . (Bunyan), **II:** 253
Greber, Giacomo, **II:** 325
Grecian History, The (Goldsmith), **III:** 181, 191
Greek Christian Poets, The, and the English Poets (Browning), **IV:** 321
"Greek Interpreter, The" (Doyle), **Supp. II:** l67
Greek Islands, The (Durrell), **Supp. I:** 102; **Retro. Supp. III:** 84
Greek Studies (Pater), **V:** 355, 357
Greeks have a word for it, The (Unsworth), **Supp. VII:** 354, 355–356, 357, 359
Green Fool, The (Kavanagh), **Supp. VII:** 183, 186, 187, 188, 194, 199
Green, Henry, **Supp. II: 247–264**

"Green Hills of Africa, The" (Fuller), **Supp. VII:** 69
"Greenhouse Effect, The" (Adcock), **Supp. XII:** 12
Green, Joseph Henry, **IV:** 57
Green, Roger Lancelyn, **V:** 265n, 273, 274
Green Crow, The (O'Casey), **VII:** 13
"Green Geese" (Sitwell), **VII:** 131
"Green, Green Is Aghir" (Cameron), **VII:** 426; **Supp. IX:** 27
Green Helmet, The (Yeats), **VI:** 222
"Green Hills of Africa" (Fuller), **VII:** 429, 432
"Green Leaf, The" (Smith, I. C.), **Supp. IX:** 223
Green Man, The (Amis), **Supp. II:** 13–14
"Green Mountain, Black Mountain" (Stevenson), **Supp. VI:** 256–257, 261–262, 266
"Green Room, The" (Delanty), **Supp. XIV:** 75
Green Shore, The (Nicholson), **Supp. VI: 219–220**
Green Song (Sitwell), **VII:** 132, 135, 136
"Green Tea" (Le Fanu), **III:** 340, 345
"Greenden" (Gibbon), **Supp. XIV:** 104, 105
Greene, Graham, **VI:** 329, 370; **VII:** xii; **Supp. I: 1–20; Supp. II:** 311, 324; **Supp. IV:** 4, 10, 13, 17, 21, 157, 365, 369, 373–374, 505; **Supp. V:** 26; **Retro. Supp. II: 151–167**
Greene, Robert, **I:** 165, 220, 275, 286, 296, 322; **II:** 3; **VIII: 131–146**
Greene's Arcadia (Greene). See *Menaphon*
Greenlees, Ian Gordon, **VI:** xxxiii
"Greenshank" (MacCaig), **Supp. VI:** 192
Greenvoe (Brown), **Supp. VI:** 64, **65–66**
"Greenwich—Whitebait" (Thackeray), **V:** 38
Greenwood, Edward Baker, **VII:** xix, xxxvii
Greenwood, Frederick, **V:** 1
Greer, Germaine, **Supp. IV:** 436
Greg, W. R., **V:** 5, 7, 15
Greg, W. W., **I:** 279
Gregory, Lady Augusta, **VI:** 210, 218, **307–312, 314–316,** 317–318; **VII:** 1, 3, 42
Gregory, Sir Richard, **VI:** 233
Greiffenhagen, Maurice, **VI:** 91
Greig, Andrew, **Supp. XVI: 161–175**
Gremlins, The (Dahl), **Supp. IV:** 202, 211–212
"Grenadier" (Housman), **VI:** 160
Grenfell, Julian, **VI:** xvi, 417–418, 420
"Greta Garbo's Feet" (Delanty), **Supp. XIV:** 52–53
"Gretchen" (Gissing), **V:** 437
"Gretna Green" (Behan), **Supp. II:** 64
Grettis saga, **VIII:** 234–235, 238, 241
Greuze, Jean–Baptiste, **Supp. IV:** 122
Greuze: The Rise and Fall of an Eighteenth Century Phenomenon (Brookner), **Supp. IV:** 122
Greville, Fulke, **VI:** 160, 164; **Supp. IV:** 256; **Supp. XI: 105–119**
Grey Area (Self), **Supp. V:** 402–404

Grey Eminence (Huxley), **VII:** 205
"Grey Eye Weeping, A" (tr. O'Connor), **Supp. XIV:** 221
Grey of Fallodon (Trevelyan), **VI:** 383, 391
Grey Granite (Gibbon), **Supp. XIV:** 102, 106, 111–113
"Grey Woman, The" (Gaskell), **V:** 15
Greybeards at Play (Chesterton), **VI:** 336
Greyhound for Breakfast (Kelman), **Supp. V:** 242, 249–250
"Greyhound for Breakfast" (Kelman), **Supp. V:** 250
Grid, The (Kerr), **Supp. XII:** 194, 195
Gridiron, The (Kerr), **Supp. XII:** 194, 195
"Grief" (Browning), **IV:** 313, 318
Grief Observed, A (Lewis), **Supp. III:** 249
"Grief on the Death of Prince Henry, A" (Tourneur), **II:** 37, 41
Grierson, Herbert J. C., **II:** 121, 130, 196, 200, 202, 258; **Retro. Supp. II:** 173
Grigson, Geoffrey, **IV:** 47; **VII:** xvi
Grim Smile of the Five Towns, The (Bennett), **VI:** 250, 253–254
Grímnismál, **VIII:** 230
Grimus (Rushdie), **Supp. IV:** 435, 438–439, 443, 450
"Grip, The" (Delahunt), **Supp. XIV:** 59
Gris, Juan, **Supp. IV:** 81
"Grisly Folk, The" (Wells), **Retro. Supp. I:** 96
Groatsworth of Wit, A (Greene), **I:** 275, 276; **VIII:** 131, 132
Grænlendinga saga, **VIII:** 240
Grosskurth, Phyllis, **V:** xxvii
Grote, George, **IV:** 289
Group of Noble Dames, A (Hardy), **VI:** 20, 22
"Grove, The" (Muir), **Supp. VI:** 206
"Growing, Flying, Happening" (Reid), **Supp. VII:** 328
"Growing Old" (Arnold), **V:** 203
Growing Pains: The Shaping of a Writer (du Maurier), **Supp. III:** 135, 142, 144
Growing Points (Jennings), **Supp. V:** 217
Growing Rich (Weldon), **Supp. IV:** 531, 533
Growth of Love, The (Bridges), **VI:** 81, 83
Growth of Plato's Ideal Theory, The (Frazer), **Supp. III:** 170–171
"Grub First, Then Ethics" (Auden), **Retro. Supp. I:** 7, 13
Grünewald, Mathias, **Supp. IV:** 85
Gryffydh, Jane, **IV:** 159
Gryll Grange (Peacock), **IV:** xxii, 166–167, 170
Grylls, R. Glynn, **V:** 247, 260; **VII:** xvii, xxxviii
Guardian (periodical), **III:** 46, 49, 50; **Supp. XIII:** 1
Guardian, The (Cowley), **II:** 194, 202
Guardian, The (Massinger), **Supp. XI:** 184
Guarini, Guarino, **II:** 49–50
Gubar, Susan, **Retro. Supp. I:** 59–60
"Gude Grey Katt, The" (Hogg), **Supp. X:** 110

"Guerrillas" (Dunn), **Supp. X:** 70–71
Guerrillas (Naipaul), **Supp. I:** 396–397
Guest from the Future, The (Stallworthy), **Supp. X:** 298–302
"Guest from the Future, The" (Stallworthy), **Supp. X:** 298
Guest of Honour, A (Gordimer), **Supp. II:** 229–230, 231
Guests of the Nation (O'Connor), **Supp. XIV:** 215, 224
"Guid Scots Death, A" (Kay), **Supp. XIII:** 108
Guide Through the District of the Lakes in the North of England, A (Wordsworth), **IV:** 25
Guide to Kulchur (Pound), **VI:** 333
Guide to Liphook, A, **Supp. XV:** 288
"Guide to the Perplexed" (Malouf), **Supp. XII:** 220
Guido della Colonna, **I:** 57
Guild of St. George, The, **V:** 182
Guillaume de Deguilleville, **I:** 57
Guillaume de Lorris, **I:** 71
"Guilt and Sorrow" (Wordsworth), **IV:** 5, 45
"Guinevere" (Tennyson), **IV:** 336–337, 338; **Retro. Supp. III:** 327
Guise, The (Marlowe), see *Massacre at Paris, The*
Guise, The (Webster), **II:** 68, 85
"Guisers, The" (Jamie), **Supp. XIV:** 129, 130
"Guitarist Tunes Up, The" (Cornford), **VIII:** 114
Gulliver's Travels (Swift), **II:** 261; **III:** 11, 20, **23–26,** 28, 35; **VI:** 121–122; **Supp. IV:** 502; **Retro. Supp. I:** 274, 275, 276–277, 279–282
Gun for Sale, A (Greene; U.S. title, *This Gun for Hire*), **Supp. I:** 3, 6–7, 10; **Retro. Supp. II:** 153
Gunesekera, Romesh, **Supp. X: 85–102**
"Gunesh Chund" (Steel), **Supp. XII:** 269
"Gunga Din" (Kipling), **Retro. Supp. III:** 188
Gunn, Ander, **Supp. IV:** 265
Gunn, Thom, **Supp. IV: 255–279; Retro. Supp. III: 115–131**
Gunnlaugs saga ormstunga, **VIII:** 239
Guns of Navarone, The (film, Ambler), **Supp. IV:** 3
Gurdjieff, Georges I., **Supp. IV:** 1, 5
Gurney, Ivor, **VI:** 416, **425–427**
Gussow, Mel, **Retro. Supp. I:** 217–218
Gutch, J. M., **IV:** 78, 81
Guthlac, **Retro. Supp. II:** 303
Gutteridge, Bernard, **VII:** 422, 432–433
Guy Domville (James), **VI:** 39
Guy Mannering (Scott), **IV:** xvii, 31–32, 38
Guy of Warwick (Lydgate), **I:** 58
Guy Renton (Waugh), **Supp. VI:** 274–275
Guyana Quartet (Harris), **Supp. V:** 132, 133, 135
Guzman Go Home and Other Stories (Sillitoe), **Supp. V:** 410
Gyðinga saga, **VIII:** 237
Gylfaginning, **VIII:** 243
"Gym(Murphy), **Supp. V:** 328

Gypsies Metamorphos'd (Jonson), **II:** 111n
"Gypsonhilia" (Hart), **Supp. XI:** 128–129
"Gyrtt in my giltetesse gowne" (Surrey), **I:** 115

H. G. Wells and His Critics (Raknem), **VI:** 228, 245, 246
H. G. Wells: His Turbulent Life and Times (Dickson), **VI:** 246
H. G. Wells: The Critical Heritage (ed. Parrinder), **VI:** 246
"H. J. B." (Scupham), **Supp. XIII:** 221
Ha! Ha! Among the Trumpets (Lewis), **VII:** 447, 448
Habeas Corpus (Bennett), **VIII:** 25
Habermas, Jürgen, **Supp. IV:** 112
Habington, William, **II:** 222, 237, 238
Habit of Loving, The (Lessing), **Supp. I:** 244
"Habit of Perfection, The" (Hopkins), **V:** 362, 381
"Habitat" (Burnside), **Supp. XIII:** 25
"Habitat, A" (Scupham), **Supp. XIII:** 228
"Hackit" (Jamie), **Supp. XIV:** 141
Hadjinicolaou, Nicos, **Supp. IV:** 90
"Hag, The" (Herrick), **II:** 111
Haggard, H. Rider, **Supp. III:** 211–228; **Supp. IV:** 201, 484
Haight, Gordon, **V:** 199, 200, 201
Hail and Farewell (Moore), **VI:** xii, 85, 88, 97, 99
"Hail to Thee, Bard!" (Mangan), **Supp. XIII:** 119–120
"Hailstones" (Heaney), **Supp. II:** 280
"Hair, The" (Caudwell), **Supp. IX:** 37
Hakluyt, Richard, **I:** 150, 267; **III:** 7
Halcyon; or, The Future of Monogamy (Brittain), **Supp. X:** 39
Hale, Kathleen, **Supp. IV:** 231
"Hale, sterne superne" (Dunbar), **VIII:** 128–129
"Half-a-Crown's Worth of Cheap Knowledge" (Thackeray), **V:** 22, 37
Half-Mother, The (Tennant), see *Woman Beware Woman*
Halfway House (Blunden), **Supp. XI:** 46
Halidon Hill (Scott), **IV:** 39
Halifax, marquess of, **III:** 38, 39, 40, 46
Hall, Donald, **Supp. IV:** 256
Hall, Edward, **II:** 43
Hall, Joseph, **II:** 25–26, 81; **IV:** 286
Hall, Radclyffe, **VI:** 411; **Supp. VI:** 119–132
Hall, Samuel (pseud., O'Nolan), **Supp. II:** 322
"Hall, The" (Hart), **Supp. XI:** 124
Hall of Healing (O'Casey), **VII:** 11–12
Hall of the Saurians (Redgrove), **Supp. VI:** 236
Hallam, Arthur, **IV:** 234, 235, 328–336, 338
Hallam, Henry, **IV:** 283
Haller, Albrecht von, **III:** 88
Hallfreðar saga vandræðaskálds, **VIII:** 239
Halloran's Little Boat (Keneally), **Supp. IV:** 348
"Hallowe'en" (Burns), **III:** 315

"Halloween" (Burnside), **Supp. XIII:** 18
Hallowe'en Party (Christie), **Supp. II:** 125, 134
"Hallucination" (Symons), **Supp. XIV:** 273–274
"Hallway, The" (Healy), **Supp. IX:** 107
"Ham and Eggs" (Abercrombie), **Supp. XVI:** 10
Ham Funeral, The (White), **Supp. I:** 131, 134, 149, 150
"Hamadryad, The" (Landor), **IV:** 96
Hamburger, Michael, **Supp. V:** 199
Hamilton, Patrick, **Supp. XVI:** 177–191
Hamilton, Sir George Rostrevor, **IV:** xxiv
Hamlet (early version), **I:** 212, 221, 315
Hamlet (Shakespeare), **I:** 188, 280, 313, 315–316; **II:** 29, 36, 71, 75, 84; **III:** 170, 234; **V:** 328; **Supp. IV:** 63, 149, 283, 295; **Retro. Supp. III:** 270, 272–273, 275
Hamlet in Autumn (Smith, I. C.), **Supp. IX:** 215
"Hamlet, Princess of Denmark" (Beerbohm), **Supp. II:** 55
"Hammer, The" (Hart), **Supp. XI:** 127
Hammerton, Sir John, **V:** 393, 397
Hammett, Dashiell, **Supp. II:** 130, 132
Hampden, John, **V:** 393, 395
"Hampstead: the Horse Chestnut Trees" (Gunn), **Supp. IV:** 270–271
Hampton, Christopher, **Supp. IV:** 281
"Hand, The" (Highsmith), **Supp. V:** 179–180
"Hand and Soul" (Rossetti), **V:** 236, 320
Hand in Hand (Stallworthy), **Supp. X:** 294, 296
Hand of Ethelberta, The: A Comedy in Chapters (Hardy), **VI:** 4, 6, 20; **Retro. Supp. I:** 114
"Hand of Solo, A" (Kinsella), **Supp. V:** 267, 274
"Hand that signed the paper, The" (Thomas), **Supp. I:** 174; **Retro. Supp. III:** 339–340
"Handful of Air, A" (Fallon), **Supp. XII:** 111
Handful of Dust, A (Waugh), **VII:** xx, 294, 295–297
Handful of Earth, A (Soutar), **Supp. XVI:** 252–253
"Handful of People, A" (Ewart), **Supp. VII:** 39
"Hands" (Ewart), **Supp. VII:** 39
"Hands" (Hughes), **Retro. Supp. II:** 212
Hands Across the Sea (Coward), **Supp. II:** 153
"Handsome Heart, The" (Hopkins), **V:** 368–369
Handsworth Songs (film), **Supp. IV:** 445
Hanged by the Neck (Koestler), **Supp. I:** 36
"Hanging, A" (Powell), **VII:** 276
Hanging Garden, The (Rankin), **Supp. X:**
Hanging Judge, The (Stevenson), **V:** 396
"Hangover Square" (Mahon), **Supp. VI:** 177
"Hangzhou Garden, A" (Seth), **Supp. X:** 281
Hanno (Mitchell), **Supp. XIV:** 100

Hapgood (Stoppard), **Retro. Supp. II:** 354–355
Happier Life, The (Dunn), **Supp. X:** 70–71
"Happily Ever After" (Huxley), **VII:** 199–200
Happiness of Getting It Down Right, The: Letters of Frank O'Connor and William Maxwell (O'Connor), **Supp. XIV:** 216, 219, 224
"Happiness" (Owen), **VI:** 449, 458
"Happinesse to Hospitalitie; or, A Hearty Wish to Good House-keeping" (Herrick), **II:** 111
Happy Days (Beckett), **Supp. I:** 46, 52, 54, 56, 57, 60; **Retro. Supp. I:** 26–27
"Happy Family, A" (Trevor), **Supp. IV:** 503
"Happy Few" (Beer), **Supp. XIV:** 14
Happy Haven, The (Arden), **Supp. II:** 29
"Happy Hunting Grounds, The" (Hamilton), **Supp. XVI:** 177
Happy Hypocrite: A Fairy Tale for Tired Men, The (Beerbohm), **Supp. II:** 45, 46
"Happy Man, The" (Thomson), **Supp. III:** 417
"Happy New Year, A" (Cornford), **Supp. XIII:** 89
"Happy old man, whose worth all mankind knows" (Flatman), **II:** 133
Happy Pair, The (Sedley), **II:** 266, 271
"Happy Prince, The" (Wilde), **V:** 406, 419; **Retro. Supp. II:** 365; **Retro. Supp. II:** 365
Happy Valley (White), **Supp. I:** 130, 132–133, 136
Haq, Zia ul–, **Supp. IV:** 444
Hárbarðsljóð, **VIII:** 230
Hard Life, The (O'Nolan), **Supp. II:** 336–337
Hard Times (Dickens), **IV:** 247; **V:** viii, xxi, 4, 42, 47, 59, 63–64, 68, 70, 71
Hardie and Baird: The Last Days (Kelman), **Supp. V:** 256–257
Hardie and Baird and Other Plays (Kelman), **Supp. V:** 256–257
"Hardness of Light, The" (Davie), **Supp. VI:** 109
Hardy, Barbara, **V:** ix, xxviii, 39, 73, 201
Hardy, G. H., **VII:** 239–240
Hardy, Thomas, **II:** 69; **III:** 278; **V:** xx–xxvi, 144, 279, 429; **VI:** x, 1–22, 253, 377; **VII:** xvi; list of short stories, **VI:** 22; **Supp. IV:** 94, 116, 146, 471, 493; **Retro. Supp. I:** 109–122
"Hardy and the Hag" (Fowles), **Supp. I:** 302, 305
Hardy of Wessex (Weber), **VI:** 21
Hare, J. C., **IV:** 54
Hare, David, **Supp. IV:** 182, **281–300**
"Harelaw" (Conn), **Supp. XIII:** 71, 72
"Harem Trousers" (McGuckian), **Supp. V:** 286
Harington, Sir John, **I:** 131
"Hark, My Soul! It Is the Lord" (Cowper), **III:** 210
"Hark! the Dog's Howl" (Tennyson), **IV:** 332

Harland's Half Acre (Malouf), **Supp. XII:** 225–226
Harlequinade (Rattigan), **Supp. VII:** 315–316
Harlot's House, The (Wilde), **V:** 410, 418, 419
Harm Done (Rendell), **Supp. IX:** 189, 196, 198, 199, 201
"Harmonies" (Kinsella), **Supp. V:** 271
"Harmony" (Pitter), **Supp. XIII:** 138
"Harmony, The" (Redgrove), **Supp. VI:** 236
"Harmony of the Spheres, The" (Rushdie), **Supp. IV:** 445
Harness Room, The (Hartley), **Supp. VII:** 132
Harold (Tennyson), **IV:** 328, 338; **Retro. Supp. III:** 329
Harold Muggins Is a Martyr (Arden and D'Arcy), **Supp. II:** 31
Harold the Dauntless (Scott), **IV:** 39
Harold's Leap (Smith), **Supp. II:** 462; **Retro. Supp. III:** 309–310
Haroun and the Sea of Stories (Rushdie), **Supp. IV:** 433, 438, 450–451
Harriet Hume: A London Fantasy (West), **Supp. III:** 441–442
Harriet Martineau's Autobiography, with Memorials by Maria Weston Chapman (Martineau), **Supp. XV:** 181, 182, 183, 184, 185, 187–188, 190, 191, 192
Harriet Said? (Bainbridge), **Supp. VI:** 17, **19**
Harrington (Edgeworth), **Supp. III: 161–163**
Harriot, Thomas, **I:** 277, 278
Harris, Frank, **VI:** 102
Harris, John Beynon, *see* Wyndham, John
Harris, Joseph, **II:** 305
Harris, Wilson, **Supp. V: 131–147**
"Harris East End" (MacCaig), **Supp. VI:** 182
Harrison, Frederic, **V:** 428–429
Harrison, Tony, **Supp. V: 149–165**
Harry Heathcote of Gangoil (Trollope), **V:** 102
"Harry Ploughman" (Hopkins), **V:** 376–377
Harry Potter and the Chamber of Secrets (Rowling), **Supp. XVI:** 229, 237
Harry Potter and the Deathly Hallows (Rowling), **Supp. XVI:** 237
Harry Potter and the Goblet of Fire (Rowling), **Supp. XVI:** 237
Harry Potter and the Philosopher's Stone (Rowling), **Supp. XVI:** 230–231, 232, 233, 234–237
Harry Potter and the Prisoner of Azkaban (Rowling), **Supp. XVI:** 237
Harry Potter and the Sorcerer's Stone (Rowling), **Supp. XVI:** 233
Harsh Voice, The (West), **Supp. III:** 442
Hart, Kevin, **Supp. XI: 121–133**
Hartley, David, **IV:** 43, 45, 50, 165
Hartley, L. P., **Supp. VII: 119–133**
Hartmann, Edward von, **Supp. II:** 108
"Harunobu: 'Catching Fireflies'" (Burnside), **Supp. XIII:** 25
"Harvest Bow, The" (Heaney), **Supp. II:** 276–277

Harvest Festival, The (O'Casey), **VII:** 12
"Harvest Home" (Robinson), **Supp. XIII:** 213
"Harvesting, The" (Hughes), **Supp. II:** 348
Harvesting the Edge: Some Personal Explorations from a Marginal Garden (Dutton), **Supp. XII:** 84–85
Harvey, Christopher, **II:** 138; **Retro. Supp. II:** 172
Harvey, Gabriel, **I:** 122–123, 125; **II:** 25
Harvey, T. W. J., **V:** 63, 199, 201
Harvey, William, **I:** 264
"Has Your Soul Slipped" (Owen), **VI:** 446
Hashemite Kings, The (Morris, J.), **Supp. X:** 175
"Hassock and the Psalter, The" (Powys), **VIII:** 255
Hastings, Warren, **IV:** xv–xvi, 271, 278
Hatfield, C. W., **V:** 133, 151, 152, 153
"Hatred and Vengeance, My Eternal Portion" (Cowper), **Retro. Supp. III:** 36, 46
Háttatal, VIII: 243
Haunch of Venison, The (Goldsmith), **III:** 191
Haunted and the Haunters, The (Bulwer–Lytton), **III:** 340, 345
"Haunted House, The" (Graves), **VII:** 263
"Haunted House, The" (Hood), **IV:** 261, 262
Haunted Man and the Ghost's Bargain, The (Dickens), **V:** 71
Haunted Storm, The (Pullman), **Supp. XIII:** 149
"Haunter, The" (Hardy), **VI:** 18; **Retro. Supp. I:** 117
Haunter of the Dark, The . . . (Lovecraft), **III:** 345
Hávamál, VIII: 230, 232
Have His Carcase (Sayers), **Supp. III:** 345–346
"Haven Gained, The" (Jewsbury), **Supp. XIV:** 162
Having a Wonderful Time (Churchill), **Supp. IV:** 180, 181
Haw Lantern, The (Heaney), **Supp. II:** 268, **279–281**; **Retro. Supp. I:** 131–132
Hawaiian Archipelago, The (Bird), **Supp. X:** 19, 24–26, 28
Hawes, Stephen, **I:** 49, 81
"Hawk, The" (Brown), **Supp. VI: 71**
Hawk in the Rain, The (Hughes), **Supp. I:** 343, 345, 363
"Hawk in the Rain, The" (Hughes), **Supp. I:** 345; **Retro. Supp. II:** 200, 202–204
"Hawk Roosting" (Hughes), **Retro. Supp. II:** 204
Hawkfall (Brown), **Supp. VI:** 69
Hawkins, Lewis Weldon, **VI:** 85
Hawkins, Sir John, **II:** 143
Hawksmoor (Ackroyd), **Supp. VI:** 6–7, 10–11
Hawthorne, Nathaniel, **III:** 339, 345; **VI:** 27, 33–34; **Supp. IV:** 116
Hawthorne (James), **VI:** 33–34, 67

Haxton, Gerald, **VI:** 369
"Hay Devil, The" (Burnside), **Supp. XIII:** 24–25
Hay Fever (Coward), **Supp. II:** 139, 141, **143–145**, 148, 156
Haydn and the Valve Trumpet (Raine), **Supp. XIII:** 175
Haydon, Benjamin, **IV:** 214, 227, 312
Hayes, Albert McHarg, **Retro. Supp. II:** 181
"Haymaking" (Thomas), **Supp. III:** 399, 405
"Haystack in the Floods, The" (Morris), **V:** 293
Hayter, Alethea, **III:** 338, 346; **IV:** xxiv–xxv, 57, 322
Haywood, Eliza, **Supp. XII: 133–148**
Hazard, Paul, **III:** 72
"Hazards of the House" (Dunn), **Supp. X:** 68
Hazlitt, William, **I:** 121, 164; **II:** 153, 332, 333, 337, 343, 346, 349, 354, 361, 363, 364; **III:** 68, 70, 76, 78, 165, 276–277; **IV:** ix, xi, xiv, xvii–xix, 38, 39, 41, 50, **125–140**, 217; **Retro. Supp. I:** 147; **Retro. Supp. II:** 51, 52
"He" (Lessing), **Supp. I:** 244
He Came Down from Heaven (Williams, C. W. S.), **Supp. IX:** 284
He Knew He Was Right (Trollope), **V:** 98, 99, 102
"He Revisits His First School" (Hardy), **VI:** 17
"He saw my heart's woe" (Brontë), **V:** 132
"He Says Goodbye in November" (Cornford), **VIII:** 114
He That Will Not When He May (Oliphant), **Supp. X:** 220
"He Thinks of His Past Greatness . . . When a Part of the Constellations of Heaven" (Yeats), **VI:** 211
"He thought he saw a Banker's Clerk" (Carroll), **V:** 270
"He Wonders Whether to Praise or to Blame Her" (Brooke), **Supp. III:** 55
Head to Toe (Orton), **Supp. V:** 363, 365–366
"Head Spider, The" (Murray), **Supp. VII:** 283, 284
Heading Home (Hare), **Supp. IV:** 288, 290–291
Headlong (Frayn), **Supp. VII:** 64, 65
Headlong Hall (Peacock), **IV:** xvii, **160–163**, 164, 165, 168, 169
"Healer, The" (Beer), **Supp. XIV:** 4
Healers, The (Armah), **Supp. X:** 1–3, 6–11, 13
Healing Art, The (Wilson), **Supp. VI:** **299–300,** 301, 303, 308
"Healing of Mis, The" (Clarke), **Supp. XV:** 29
Health and Holiness (Thompson), **V:** 450, 451
"Healthy Landscape with Dormouse" (Warner), **Supp. VII:** 380
Healy, Dermot, **Supp. IX: 95–108**
Heaney, Seamus, **Supp. II: 267–281**; **Supp. IV:** 410, 412, 416, 420–421, 427, 428; **Retro. Supp. I: 123–135**

Hear Us O Lord from Heaven Thy Dwelling Place (Lowry), **Supp. III: 281–282**
Hearing Secret Harmonies (Powell), **VII:** 352, 353
"Hears not my Phillis, how the Birds" (Sedley), **II:** 264
Heart and Science (Collins), **Supp. VI:** 102–103
"Heart, II, The" (Thompson), **V:** 443
Heart Clock (Hill, R.), **Supp. IX:** 111
"Heart Knoweth Its Own Bitterness, The" (Rossetti), **V:** 253–254
"Heart of a King, The" (Plomer), **Supp. XI:** 222
Heart of Darkness (Conrad), **VI:** 135, **136–139,** 172; **Supp. IV:** 189, 250, 403; **Retro. Supp. II:** 73–75
"Heart of John Middleton, The" (Gaskell), **V:** 15
Heart of Mid–Lothian, The (Scott), **IV:** xvii, 30, 31, 33–34, 35, 36, 39; **V:** 5
Heart of Redness, The (Mda), **Supp. XV:** 203–204, 205, 207
Heart of the Country, The (Weldon), **Supp. IV:** 526–528
Heart of the Matter, The (Greene), **Supp. I:** 2, 8, 11–12, 13; **Retro. Supp. II:** 157–159
Heart to Heart (Rattigan), **Supp. VII:** 320
Heartbreak (Maitland), **Supp. XI:** 163
"Heartbreak Hotel" (Brathwaite), **Supp. XII:** 42
Heartbreak House (Shaw), **V:** 423; **VI:** viii, xv, 118, **120–121,** 127, 129; **Retro. Supp. II:** 322–323
Heartland (Harris), **Supp. V:** 135, 136
"Heartland, The" (Fallon), **Supp. XII:** 109
Hearts and Lives of Men, The (Weldon), **Supp. IV:** 536
"Heart's Chill Between" (Rossetti), **V:** 249, 252
"Heart's Desire is Full of Sleep, The" (Pitter), **Supp. XIII:** 145
"Heat" (Hart), **Supp. XI:** 131
Heat and Dust (Jhabvala), **Supp. V:** 224, 230, 231–232, 238
Heat of the Day, The (Bowen), **Supp. II:** 77, 78, 79, 93, 95
"Heather Ale" (Stevenson), **V:** 396
Heather Field, The (Martyn), **IV:** 87, 95
Heatherley (Thompson), **Supp. XV:** 277, 284, 290
"Heaven" (Brooke), **Supp. III:** 56, 60
Heaven and Earth (Byron), **IV:** 178, 193
Heaven and Its Wonders, and Hell (Swedenborg), **Retro. Supp. I:** 38
Heaven to Find, A (Pitter), **Supp. XIII:** 136, 145
Heavenly Foot–man, The (Bunyan), **II:** 246, 253
Heaven's Command: An Imperial Progress (Morris, J.), **Supp. X:** 173, 179–180
Heaven's Edge (Gunesekera), **Supp. X:** 85–86, 96–100
"Heber" (Smith), **Supp. II:** 466
Hebert, Ann Marie, **Supp. IV:** 523

Hebrew Melodies, Ancient and Modern . . . (Byron), **IV:** 192
"Hebrides, The" (Longley), **VIII:** 168–169
Hecatommitthi (Cinthio), **I:** 316
Hedda Gabler (Ibsen), **Supp. IV:** 163, 286
Hedge, Backwards, A (Reed), **Supp. XV:** 253
"Hedgehog" (Muldoon), **Supp. IV:** 414
"Hee–Haw" (Warner), **Supp. VII:** 380
Heel of Achilles, The (Koestler), **Supp. I:** 36
"Heepocondry" (Crawford), **Supp. XI:** 75
"Heera Nund" (Steel), **Supp. XII:** 268–269
Hegel, Georg Wilhelm Friedrich, **Supp. II:** 22
Heiðreks saga, **VIII:** 231
"Height–ho on a Winter Afternoon" (Davie), **Supp. VI:** 107–108
"Heil Baldwin" (Caudwell), **Supp. IX:** 38
Heilbrun, Carolyn G., **Supp. IV:** 336
Heimskringla, **VIII:** 235, 242
Heine, Heinrich, **IV:** xviii, 296
Heinemann, William, **VII:** 91
"Heiress, The" (McGuckian), **Supp. V:** 282
"Heirloom" (Conn), **Supp. XIII:** 80
Heit, S. Mark, **Supp. IV:** 339
"Hélas" (Wilde), **V:** 401
Helen (Scott), **Supp. III:** 151, **165–166**
Helena (Waugh), **VII:** 292, 293–294, 301
Hélène Fourment in a Fur Coat (Rubens), **Supp. IV:** 89
"Helen's Rape" (Gunn), **Retro. Supp. III:** 118
"Helicon" (Carson), **Supp. XIII:** 63
Hellas (Shelley), **IV:** xviii, 206, 208; **Retro. Supp. I:** 255
Hellbox, The (Delanty), **Supp. XIV:** 69–72, 74, 75
"Hellbox, The" (Delanty), **Supp. XIV:** 69, 71, 72
Hellenics, The (Landor), **IV:** 96, 100
"Helmet, The" (Longley), **VIII:** 176
Héloise and Abélard (Moore), **VI:** xii, 88, 89, **94–95,** 99
"Helplessly" (Smith, I. C.), **Supp. IX:** 217
Hemans, Felicia, **IV:** 311
Hemingway, Ernest, **Supp. III:** 105; **Supp. IV:** 163, 209, 500
Hemlock and After (Wilson), **Supp. I:** 155–156, 157, 158–159, 160, 161, 164
Hello, America (Ballard), **Supp. V:** 29
Hello and Goodbye (Fugard), **Supp. XV:** 103, 106–107
"Help, Good Shepherd" (Pitter), **Supp. XIII:** 141
"Hen Under Bay Tree" (Pitter), **Supp. XIII:** 144
"Hen Woman" (Kinsella), **Supp. V:** 266–267
Henceforward (Ayckbourn), **Supp. V:** 3, 10, 11, 13
"Hendecasyllabics" (Swinburne), **V:** 321

"Hendecasyllabics" (Tennyson), **IV:** 327–328
Henderson, Hamish, **VII:** 422, 425–426
Henderson, Hubert, **VII:** 35
Henderson, Philip, **V:** xii, xviii, 335
Henderson, T. F., **IV:** 290n
Hengist, King of Kent; or, The Mayor of Quinborough (Middleton), **II:** 3, 21
Henley, William Ernest, **V:** 386, 389, 391–392; **VI:** 159; **Retro. Supp. I:** 260, 264
Henn, T. R., **VI:** 220
"Henrietta Marr" (Moore), **VI:** 87
Henrietta Temple (Disraeli), **IV:** xix, 293, 298–299, 307, 308
"Henrik Ibsen" (James), **VI:** 49
Henry Esmond (Thackeray), *see History of Henry Esmond, Esq. . . ., The*
Henry for Hugh (Ford), **VI:** 331
"Henry James" (Nye), **Supp. X:** 201
Henry James (ed. Tanner), **VI:** 68
Henry James (West), **Supp. III:** 437
"Henry James: The Religious Aspect" (Greene), **Supp. I:** 8
Henry Mayhew: London Labour and the London Poor (Mayhew), **Supp. XVI:** 209–218
"Henry Petroski, The Pencil. A History. Faber and Faber, £14.95" (Dunn), **Supp. X:** 79
"Henry Purcell" (Hopkins), **V:** 370–371; **Retro. Supp. II:** 196
Henry Reed: Collected Poems (Stallworthy), **Supp. X:** 292
Henry II (Bancroft), **II:** 305
Henry IV (Shakespeare), **I:** 308–309, 320
Henry V (Shakespeare), **I:** 309; **V:** 383; **Supp. IV:** 258; **Retro. Supp. III:** 274–275
Henry VI (Shakespeare), **Retro. Supp. III:** 270, 273
Henry VI, Part 3 (Shakespeare), **Retro. Supp. III:** 270
Henry VI trilogy (Shakespeare), **I:** 286, 299–300, 309
Henry VI's Triumphal Entry into London (Lydgate), **I:** 58
Henry VIII (Shakespeare), **I:** 324; **II:** 43, 66, 87; **V:** 328; **Retro. Supp. III:** 281
"Henry VIII and Ann Boleyn" (Landor), **IV:** 92
Henry Vaughan: Experience and the Tradition (Garner), **II:** 186n
Henry's Past (Churchill), **Supp. IV:** 181
Henryson, Robert, **Supp. VII: 135–149**
Henslowe, Philip, **I:** 228, 235, 284; **II:** 3, 25, 68
Henty, G. A., **Supp. IV:** 201
"Her Day" (Upward), **Supp. XIII:** 260
"Her Second Husband Hears Her Story" (Hardy), **Retro. Supp. I:** 120
Her Triumph (Johnson), **I:** 347
Her Vertical Smile (Kinsella), **Supp. V:** 270–271
Her Victory (Sillitoe), **Supp. V:** 411, 415, 422, 425
Herakles (Euripides), **IV:** 358
Herald of Literature: or, A Review of the Most Considerable Publications That Will Be Made in the Course of the

Ensuing Winter (Godwin), **Supp. XV:** 117–118
Herbert, Edward, pseud. of John Hamilton Reynolds
Herbert, Edward, *see* Herbert of Cherbury, Lord
Herbert, George, **II:** 113, **117–130**, 133, 134, 137, 138, 140–142, 184, 187, 216, 221; **Retro. Supp. II: 169–184**
Herbert of Cherbury, Lord, **II:** 117–118, 222, 237, 238
Herbert's Remains (Oley), **Retro. Supp. II:** 170–171
Hercule Poirot's Last Case (Christie), **Supp. II:** 125
"Hercules" (Armitage), **VIII:** 12
"Hercules and Antaeus" (Heaney), **Supp. II:** 274–275
Hercules Oetaeus (Seneca), **I:** 248
"Hercules Oetaeus" (tr. Elizabeth I), **Supp. XVI:** 158
"Here" (Burnside), **Supp. XIII:** 26
"Here" (Larkin), **Supp. I:** 279, 285; **Retro. Supp. III:** 206
"Here and There" (Dunn), **Supp. X:** 77–78
"Here Be Dragons" (Dunn), **Supp. X:** 72
Here Comes Everybody: An Introduction to James Joyce for the Ordinary Reader (Burgess), **Supp. I:** 194, 196–197
Here Lies: An Autobiography (Ambler), **Supp. IV:** 1, 2, 3, 4
"Heredity" (Harrison), **Supp. V:** 152
Heretics (Chesterton), **VI:** 204, 336–337
Hereward the Wake: Last of the English (Kingsley), **Supp. XVI:** 199–201, 205
Hering, Carl Ewald, **Supp. II:** 107–108
Heritage and Its History, A (Compton-Burnett), **VII:** 60, 61, 65
"Heritage Center, Cobh 1993, The" (Delanty), **Supp. XIV:** 68
Hermaphrodite Album, The (Redgrove), **Supp. VI:** 230
"Hermaphroditus" (Swinburne), **V:** 320
Hermetical Physick . . . Englished (tr. Vaughan), **II:** 185, 201
Hermit of Marlow, The, pseud. of Percy Bysshe Shelley
"Hero" (Rossetti), **V:** 260
"Hero and Leander" (Hood), **IV:** 255–256, 267
Hero and Leander (Marlowe), **I:** 234, 237–240, 276, 278, 280, 288, **290–291**, 292; **Retro. Supp. I:** 211
Hero and Leander, in Burlesque (Wycherley), **II:** 321
"Hero as King, The" (Carlyle), **IV:** 245, 246
Hero Rises Up, The (Arden and D'Arcy), **Supp. II:** 31
"Heroine, The" (Highsmith), **Supp. V:** 180
Herodotus, **Supp. IV:** 110
Heroes and Hero-Worship (Carlyle), **IV:** xx, 240, 244–246, 249, 250, 341
Heroes and Villains (Carter), **Supp. III:** 81, 84

Heroic Idylls, with Additional Poems (Landor), **IV:** 100
Heroic Stanzas (Dryden), **Retro. Supp. III:** 60
"Heroic Stanzas" (Dryden), **II:** 292
Heroine, The; or, The Adventures of Cherubina (Barrett), **III:** 335
"Heroism" (Cowper), **Retro. Supp. III:** 48
"Heron, The" (Nye), **Supp. X:** 205
"Heron and Li Po on the Blackwater" (Delanty), **Supp. XIV:** 73
Heron Caught in Weeds, A (Roberts, K.), **Supp. X:** 273–275
Herrick, Robert, **II: 102–116**, 121
"Herriots, The" (Smith), **Retro. Supp. III:** 305
Herself Surprised (Cary), **VII:** 186, 188, 191–192
"Hertha" (Swinburne), **V:** 325
Hervarar saga, *See Heiðreks saga*
"Hervé Riel" (Browning), **IV:** 367
Herzog, Werner, **IV:** 180
"Hesperia" (Swinburne), **V:** 320, 321
Hesperides, The (Herrick), **II:** 102, 103, 104, 106, 110, 112, 115, 116
"Hespirides, The" (Tennyson), **Retro. Supp. III:** 320
Hester (Oliphant), **Supp. X:** 217–218
"Hester Dominy" (Powys), **VIII:** 250
"Hestia–or the Spirit of Peace" (Soutar), **Supp. XVI:** 243
"Heu quam Remotuss Vescor ab Ominus" (Cowper), **Retro. Supp. III:** 46
Hexameron; or, Meditations on the Six Days of Creation, and Meditations and Devotions on the Life of Christ (Traherne), **Supp. XI:** 264, 265, 273–274
Heyday of Sir Walter Scott, The (Davie), **Supp. VI:** 114–115
Heylyn, Peter, **I:** 169
Heywood, Jasper, **I:** 215
Heywood, Thomas, **II:** 19, 47, 48, 68, 83
"Hexagon" (Murphy), **Supp. V:** 328
Hibberd, Dominic, **VI:** xvi, xxxiii
"Hidden History, A" (Okri), **Supp. V:** 352
Hidden Ireland, The (Corkery), **Supp. V:** 41
"Hidden Law" (MacCaig), **Supp. VI:** 186
Hide, The (Unsworth), **Supp. VII:** 354, 356
"Hide and Seek" (Gunn), **Supp. IV:** 272
Hide and Seek (Collins), **Supp. VI:** 92, 95
Hide and Seek (Rankin), **Supp. X:** 244, 246, 248–250
Hide and Seek (Swinburne), **V:** 334
"Hiding Beneath the Furze: Autumn 1939" (Reed), **Supp. XV:** 249
Higden, Ranulf, **I:** 22
Higgins, F. R., **Supp. IV:** 411, 413
"Higgler, The" (Coppard), **VIII:** 85, 90, 95
Higgler and Other Tales, The (Coppard), **VIII:** 90
High Fidelity (Hornby), **Supp. XV:** 133, 139–140, 141, 144, 145
High Fidelity (screenplay, Hornby), **Supp. XV:** 144

High Fidelity: The Musical, **Supp. XV:** 145
"High Flats at Craigston, The" (Dutton), **Supp. XII:** 91
High Island: New and Selected Poems (Murphy), **Supp. V:** 313, 315, 316, 324–325
"High Land" (Kay), **Supp. XIII:** 107
"High Life in Verdopolis" (Brontë), **V:** 135
High Tide in the Garden (Adcock), **Supp. XII:** 5
"High wavering heather . . . " (Brontë), **V:** 113
High Windows (Larkin), **Supp. I:** 277, 280, **281–284**, 285, 286; **Retro. Supp. III:** 204
"High Windows" (Larkin), **Retro. Supp. III:** 209
Higher Ground (Phillips), **Supp. V:** 380, 386–388
Higher Schools and Universities in Germany (Arnold), **V:** 216
"Higher Standards" (Wilson), **Supp. I:** 155
Highet, Gilbert, **II:** 199
Highland Fling (Mitford), **Supp. X:** 152–154
"Highland Funeral" (MacCaig), **Supp. VI:** 193
Highland Widow, The (Scott), **IV:** 39
Highlander, The (Macpherson), **VIII:** 181–182, 190
Highly Dangerous (Ambler), **Supp. IV:** 3
High-Rise (Ballard), **Supp. V:** 27
High Summer (Rattigan), **Supp. VII:** 315
Highsmith, Patricia, **Supp. IV:** 285; **Supp. V: 167–182**
"Highwayman and the Saint, The" (Friel), **Supp. V:** 118
Hilaire Belloc (Wilson), **Supp. VI:** 301–302
Hilda Lessways (Bennett), **VI:** 258; **Supp. IV:** 238
Hilda Tablet and Others: Four Pieces for Radio (Reed), **Supp. XV:** 255
Hill, G. B., **III:** 233, 234n
Hill, Geoffrey, **Supp. V: 183–203**; **Retro. Supp. III: 133–147**
Hill, Susan, **Supp. XIV: 115–128**
"Hill, The" (Brooke), **Supp. III:** 51
Hill, The (Mda), **Supp. XV:** 197
Hill of Devi, The (Forster), **VI:** 397, 408, 411
"Hill of Venus, The" (Morris), **V:** 298
Hill, Reginald, **Supp. IX: 109–126**
Hilton, Walter, **Supp. I:** 74
Hind and the Panther, The (Dryden), **II:** 291, 292, 299–300, 304; **Retro. Supp. III:** 54
Hinge of Faith, The (Churchill), **VI:** 361
Hinman, Charlton, **I:** 326–327
Hinterland, The (Scupham), **Supp. XIII:** 219–220, 223
"Hinterland, The" (Scupham), **Supp. XIII:** 224, 227
Hinton, William, **Supp. IV:** 284
"Hint to a Young Person ..., A" (Byrom), **Supp. XVI:** 85
"Hints" (Reading), **VIII:** 265–266

Hints Towards the Formation of a More Comprehensive Theory of Life (Coleridge), **IV:** 56

Hippolytus (Euripides), **V:** 322, 324

"Hippy Wordsworth" (Beer), **Supp. XIV:** 14

Hips and Haws (Coppard), **VIII:** 89, 98

Hireling, The (Hartley), **Supp. VII:** 129–131

"His Age, Dedicated to his Peculiar Friend, M. John Wickes" (Herrick), **II:** 112

His Arraignment (Jonson), **Retro. Supp. I:** 158

"His Chosen Calling" (Naipaul), **Supp. I:** 385

"His Country" (Hardy), **Retro. Supp. I:** 120–121

His Dark Materials (Pullman), **Supp. XIII:** 149, 150, 151, 153–160

His Darling Sin (Braddon), **VIII:** 49

"His Fare-well to Sack" (Herrick), **II:** 111

"His Father's Hands" (Kinsella), **Supp. V:** 268

"His Last Bow" (Doyle), **Supp. II:** 175

"His Letanie, to the Holy Spirit" (Herrick), **II:** 114

His Majesties Declaration Defended (Dryden), **II:** 305

His Majesty Preserved . . . Dictated to Samuel Pepys by the King . . . (ed. Rees-Mogg), **II:** 288

His Noble Numbers (Herrick), **II:** 102, 103, 112, 114, 115, 116

"His Returne to London" (Herrick), **II:** 103

His Second War (Waugh), **Supp. VI:** 274

Historia naturalis et experimentalis (Bacon), **I:** 259, 273

Historia regis Henrici Septimi (André), **I:** 270

Historiae adversum paganos (Orosius), **Retro. Supp. II:** 296

"Historian, The" (Fuller), **Supp. VII:** 74

"Historian of Silence, The" (Hart), **Supp. XI:** 130

Historical Account of the Theatre in Europe, An (Riccoboni), **II:** 348

Historical Register, The (Fielding), **III:** 97, 98, 105; **Retro. Supp. I:** 82

Historical Relation of the Island of Ceylon, An (Knox), **III:** 7

"Historical Sketches of the Reign of George Second" (Oliphant), **Supp. X:** 222

"Historical Society" (Murphy), **Supp. V:** 322

Histories of Desire (Butlin), **Supp. XVI:** 57–58

"History" (Burnside), **Supp. XIII:** 26

"History" (Macaulay), **IV:** 284

History: The Home Movie (Raine), **Supp. XIII:** 171–173

History and Adventures of an Atom, The (Smollett), **III:** 149–150, 158

History and Adventures of Joseph Andrews and of His Friend Mr. Abraham Adams (Fielding), **Retro. Supp. I:** 80, 83–86

History and Management of the East India Company (Macpherson), **VIII:** 193

History and Remarkable Life of . . . Col. Jack (Defoe), see *Colonel Jack*

History Maker, A (Gray, A.), **Supp. IX:** 80, 87–88

History of a Good Warm Watch-Coat, The (Sterne), see *Political Romance, A*

"History of a Nonchalant, The" (Jewsbury), **Supp. XIV:** 159

"History of a Piece of Paper" (Sisson), **Supp. XI:** 244

"History of a Realist, The" (Jewsbury), **Supp. XIV:** 159

History of a Six Weeks' Tour Through a Part of France . . . (Shelley and Shelley), **IV:** 208; **Supp. III:** 355; **Retro. Supp. III:** 288

"History of an Enthusiast, The" (Jewsbury), **Supp. XIV:** 158–159

"History of Angria" (Brontë), **V:** 110–111, 118

History of Antonio and Mellida, The (Marston), see *Antonio and Mellida*

History of Brazil (Southey), **IV:** 68, 71

History of Britain . . . , The (Milton), **II:** 176

History of British India, The, (Mill), **V:** 288

History of Dorastus and Fawni, The (Greene). See *Pandosto: or, The Triumph of Time*

History of England (Hume), **II:** 148; **IV:** 273; **Supp. III:** 229, 238–239

History of England, An (Goldsmith), **III:** 180, 181, 189, 191

History of England, The (Trevelyan), **VI:** xv, 390–391, 393

History of England During the Thirty Years' Peace: 1816–1846 (Martineau), **Supp. XV:** 184

History of England from the Accession of James II, The (Macaulay), **II:** 255; **IV:** xx, 272, 273, 280, 282, **283–290,** 291

History of England in the Eighteenth Century (Lecky), **Supp. V:** 41

History of English Thought in the Eighteenth Century (Stephen), **V:** 280, 288, 289

History of Frederick the Great, The (Carlyle), **IV:** xxi, 240, 246, 249, 250

History of Friar Francis, The, **I:** 218

History of Great Britain from the Restoration to the Accession of the House of Hanover (Macpherson), **VIII:** 192, 193

History of Henry Esmond, Esq. . . . , The (Thackeray), **V:** xxi, 20, **31–33,** 38

History of Jemmy and Jenny Jessamy, The (Haywood), **Supp. XII:** 144

History of John Bull, The (Arbuthnot), **Supp. XVI:** 20–22

History of King Richard III, The (More), **Supp. VII:** 234, 237–238, 246

History of Leonora Meadowson, The (Haywood), **Supp. XII:** 144

History of Madan, The (Beaumont), **II:** 67

History of Miss Betsy Thoughtless, The (Haywood), **Supp. XII:** 135, 136, 144–146

History of Mr. Polly, The (Wells), **VI:** xii, 225, 238–239

History of My Own Times (Burnet), **III:** 39

History of Orlando Furioso, The (Greene), **VIII:** 140

History of Pendennis, The (Thackeray), **V:** xxi, **28–31,** 33, 35, 38; **VI:** 354

History of Rasselas Prince of Abyssina, The (Johnson), **III:** 112–113, 121; **IV:** 47; **Retro. Supp. I:** 139–140, 148

History of Samuel Titmarsh and the Great Hoggarty Diamond, The (Thackeray), see *Great Hoggarty Diamond, The*

History of Shikasta (Lessing), **Supp. I:** 251

History of Sir Charles Grandison, The (Richardson), see *Sir Charles Grandison*

History of the Adventures of Joseph Andrews . . . , The (Fielding), see *Joseph Andrews*

"History of the Boswell Papers" (Pottle), **III:** 240n

History of the Church of Scotland (Spottiswoode), **II:** 142

History of the Commonwealth of England: From Its Commencement, to the Restoration of Charles the Second (Godwin), **Supp. XV:** 127

History of the Earth, and Animated Nature, An (Goldsmith), **III:** 180, 181, 189–190, 191

History of the English-Speaking Peoples, A (Churchill), **VI:** 356

History of the Four Last Years of Queen Anne, The (Swift), **III:** 27, 36

"History of the Hardcomes, The" (Hardy), **VI:** 22

History of the Italian Renaissance (Symonds), **V:** 83

History of the Kentish Petition, The (Defoe), **III:** 12

History of the League, The (tr. Dryden), **II:** 305

History of the Life of William Pitt, Earl of Chatham, The (Godwin), **Supp. XV:** 117

"History of the Next French Revolution, The" (Thackeray), **V:** 38

History of the Nun, The; or, The Fair Vow-Breaker (Behn), **Supp. III:** 32

History of the Peninsular War (Southey), **IV:** 58, 63, 71; **V:** 109

History of the Plague Year, A (Defoe), **Retro. Supp. I:** 68

History of the Pyrates, The (Defoe), **III:** 13

History of the Reign of Henry the Seventh, The (Bacon), **I:** 259, 269, 270, 272

History of the Royal Society of London (Sprat), **II:** 196; **III:** 29

"History of the Scuphams" (Scupham), **Supp. XIII:** 227

History of the Union of Great Britain, The (Defoe), **III:** 4, 13; **Retro. Supp. I:** 65

"History of the Voice" (Brathwaite), **Supp. XII:** 44–45
History of the Wars of . . . Charles XII . . ., The (Defoe), **III:** 13
"History of the Winds" (Bacon), **I:** 263
History of the World in 10 Chapters, A (Barnes), **Supp. IV:** 65, 67, 71–72, 73
History of the World, The (Ralegh), **I:** 145, 146, 149, 153–157
History of Titus Andronicus, The, **I:** 305
History of Tom Jones, a Foundling, The (Fielding), *see Tom Jones*
History of Van's House, The, **II:** 335
History Plays, The (Hare), **Supp. IV:** 283
Histriomastix (Prynne), **II:** 339; **Supp. III:** 23
Histriomastix; or, The Player Whipt (Marston), **II:** 27, 28, 40
Hitchcock, Alfred, **III:** 342–343; **Supp. III:** 147, 148, 149
"Hitcher" (Armitage), **VIII:** 8
"Hitchhiker, The" (Dahl), **Supp. IV:** 201
Hitherto unpublished Poems and Stories . . . (Browning), **IV:** 321
Hjálmarr's Death-Song, **VIII:** 232
Hlǫðskviða, **VIII:** 231
H'm (Thomas), **Supp. XII:** 286
"H'm" (Thomas), **Supp. XII:** 288
H.M.S. Surprise (O'Brian), **Supp. XII:** 255, 256
Hoare, D.M., **V:** 299, 306
Hobbes, John Oliver, pseud. of Mrs. Craigie
Hobbes, Thomas, **II:** 190, 196, 256, 294; **III:** 22; **IV:** 121, 138
Hobbit, The (Tolkien), **Supp. II:** 520, 521, 525, 527–528, 529, 530, 531–532
Hobsbaum, Philip, **Retro. Supp. I:** 126; **Retro. Supp. II:** 200
Hoccleve, Thomas, **I:** 49
"Hock-Cart; or, Harvest Home, The" (Herrick), **II:** 110–111
Hockney's Alphabet (McEwan), **Supp. IV:** 389
Ho Davies, Peter, *see* Davies, Peter Ho
Hodder, E., **IV:** 62n
Hodge and His Masters (Jefferies), **Supp. XV:** 166, 168–171
Hodgkins, Howard, **Supp. IV:** 170
Hodgson, W. N., **VI:** 422, 423
Hoff, Benjamin, **Supp. V:** 311
Hoffman, Calvin, **I:** 277
Hoffman, Heinrich, **I:** 25; **Supp. III:** 296
Hoffmann, E. T. A., **III:** 333, 334, 345
"Hoffmeier's Antelope" (Swift), **Supp. V:** 432
Hofmeyr (Paton; U.S. title, *South African Tragedy: The Life and Times of Jan Hofmeyr*), **Supp. II:** 356–357, 358
Hogarth Press, **VII:** xv, 17, 34
Hogg, James, **IV:** xvii, 73; **Supp. X:** 103–118
Hogg, Thomas Jefferson, **IV:** 196, 198, 209
Hoggart, Richard, **VII:** xx, xxxviii; **Supp. IV:** 473
Hold Your Hour and Have Another (Behan), **Supp. II:** 65–66, 70
Hölderlin (Constantine), **Supp. XV:** 66, 67–68

Hölderlin's Sophocles (tr. Constantine), **Supp. XV:** 66, 69
Holiday, The (Smith), **Supp. II:** 462, 474, **476–478**; **Retro. Supp. III:** 308
Holiday Romance (Dickens), **V:** 72
Holiday Round, The (Milne), **Supp. V:** 298
"Holidays" (Kincaid), **Supp. VII:** 220
Hollinghurst, Alan, **Supp. X: 119–135**
Hollington, Michael, **Supp. IV:** 357
Hollis, Maurice Christopher, **VI:** xxxiii
Hollis, Richard, **Supp. IV:** 88
"Hollow Men, The" (Eliot), **VII:** 150–151, 158; **Retro. Supp. II:** 129–130
"Hollow Note, A" (Montague), **Supp. XV:** 214
Hollow's Mill (Brontë), *see Shirley*
Holloway, John, **VII:** 82
Holroyd, Michael, **Supp. IV:** 231
"Holy Baptisme I" (Herbert), **II:** 128
Holy City, The; or, The New Jerusalem (Bunyan), **II:** 253
"Holy Fair, The" (Burns), **III:** 311, 315, 317
Holy Grail, The (Tennyson), **Retro. Supp. III:** 327
"Holy Grail, The" (Tennyson), **Retro. Supp. III:** 327
Holy Grail, The, and Other Poems (Tennyson), **IV:** 338
"Holy Experiment, The" (Nye), **Supp. X:** 203
Holy Life, The Beauty of Christianity, A (Bunyan), **II:** 253
"Holy Mountain, The" (Nicholson), **Supp. VI:** 215
"Holy Scriptures" (Vaughan), **II:** 187
"Holy Scriptures II, The" (Herbert), **Retro. Supp. II:** 174
Holy Sinner, The (Mann), **II:** 97n
Holy Sonnets (Donne), **I:** 362, 366, 367; **Retro. Supp. II:** 96
Holy War, The: Made by Shaddai . . . (Bunyan), **II:** 246, 250, 251–252, 253
"Holy Willie's Prayer" (Burns), **III:** 311, 313, 319
"Holy-Cross Day" (Browning), **IV:** 367; **Retro. Supp. III:** 25
"Holyhead, September 25, 1717" (Swift), **III:** 32
"Homage to a Government" (Larkin), **Supp. I:** 284; **Retro. Supp. III:** 209
Homage to Catalonia (Orwell), **VII:** 275, 280–281
Homage to Clio (Auden), **VII:** 392
"Homage to Burns" (Brown), **Supp. VI:** 72
"Homage to George Orwell" (Smith, I. C.), **Supp. IX:** 215
"Homage to the British Museum" (Empson), **Supp. II:** 182
"Homage to William Cowper" (Davie), **Supp. VI:** 106
"Homages" (Hart), **Supp. XI:** 123
Homans, Margaret, **Retro. Supp. I:** 189
"Home" (Beer), **Supp. XIV:** 4
"Home" (Burnside), **Supp. XIII:** 14–15
"Home" (Carson), **Supp. XIII:** 66
"Home" (Ewart), **Supp. VII:** 37
"Home" (Fallon), **Supp. XII:** 106

Home (Storey), **Supp. I:** 408, 413, 417
"Home Again" (Montague), **Supp. XV:** 214
Home and Beauty (Maugham), **VI:** 368–369
Home and Dry (Fuller), **Supp. VII:** 70, 81
"Home at Grasmere" (Wordsworth), **IV:** 3, 23–24
Home Chat (Coward), **Supp. II:** 146
"Home Conveyancing Kit, The" (Wallace-Crabbe), **VIII:** 320
"Home for a couple of days" (Kelman), **Supp. V:** 250
"Home for the Highland Cattle, A" (Lessing), **Supp. I:** 241–242
"Home from Home" (Delanty), **Supp. XIV:** 65, 67
Home Front (Bishton and Reardon), **Supp. V:** 445
Home Letters (Disraeli) **IV:** 296, 308
Home Letters of T. E. Lawrence and His Brothers, The (Lawrence), **Supp. II:** 286
"Home Thoughts from Abroad" (Browning), **IV:** 356
"Home Thoughts Abroad" (Newman), **Supp. VII:** 293
Home Truths (Maitland), **Supp. XI:** 163, 170–172, 175
"Home [2]" (Thomas), **Supp. III:** 405
"Home [3]" (Thomas), **Supp. III:** 404
Home University Library, **VI:** 337, 391
Homebush Boy (Keneally), **Supp. IV:** 344, 347
Homecoming, The (Pinter), **Supp. I:** 375, 380, 381; **Retro. Supp. I:** 225–226
Homecoming: Essays on African and Caribbean Literature, Culture, and Politics (Ngũgĩ), **VIII:** 214, 224
Homecomings (Snow), **VII:** xxi, 324, 329, 335
"Homemade" (McEwan), **Supp. IV:** 389, 391, 395
"Homemaking" (Kincaid), **Supp. VII:** 229
Homer, **I:** 236; **II:** 304, 347; **III:** 217, 220; **IV:** 204, 215
Homeric Hymns (tr. Chapman), **I:** 236
"Homesick in Old Age" (Kinsella), **Supp. V:** 263
"Home-Thoughts, from Abroad" (Browning), **Retro. Supp. III:** 17
"Homeward Prospect, The" (Day Lewis), **Supp. III:** 129
Homeward: Songs by the Way (Russell), **VIII:** 280, 282
Homiletic Fragment I, **Retro. Supp. II:** 301–302
"Homogenic Attachment, The" (Carpenter), **Supp. XIII:** 43
"Homogenic Love: And Its Place in a Free Society" (Carpenter), **Supp. XIII:** 41, 42–43
Hone, Joseph, **VI:** 88
Hone, William, **IV:** 255
Honest Man's Fortune, The (Field, Fletcher, Massinger), **II:** 66
Honest Whore, The (Dekker and Middleton), **II:** 3, 21, 89

Honey for the Bears (Burgess), **Supp. I:** 191
"Honey from Palaiochora" (Constantine), **Supp. XV:** 78
Honeybuzzard (Carter), *see Shadow Dance*
Honeycomb (Richardson), **Supp. XIII:** 182, 183, 189
Honeymoon Voyage, The (Thomas), **Supp. IV:** 490
Hong Kong House, A: Poems 1951–1961 (Blunden), **Supp. XI:** 34, 38
"Hong Kong Story" (Nye), **Supp. X:** 201–202
Honorary Consul, The (Greene), **Supp. I:** 7, 10, 13, 16; **Retro. Supp. II:** 164–165
Honour of the Garter, The (Peele), **I:** 205
Honour Triumphant; or, The Peeres Challenge (Ford), **II:** 88, 100
Honourable Deceivers, The; or, All Right at the Last (Trotter), **Supp. XVI:** 287
"Honourable Estate, An" (Gunesekera), **Supp. X:** 86
Honourable Estate: A Novel of Transition (Brittain), **Supp. X:** 41–43, 46–47
"Honourable Laura, The" (Hardy), **VI:** 22
Honourable Schoolboy, The (le Carré), **Supp. II:** 301, **313–314**, 315; **Retro. Supp. III:** 2 to **Retro. Supp. III:** 221, 219
Hood, Thomas, **IV:** xvi, xx, **251–267**, 311
Hood's (periodical), **IV:** 252, 261, 263, 264
"Hood's Literary Reminiscences" (Blunden), **IV:** 267
Hood's Own (Hood), **IV:** 251–252, 253, 254, 266
Hook, Theodore, **IV:** 254
Hooker, Richard, **I: 176–190**, 362; **II:** 133, 137, 140–142, 147
Hoop, The (Burnside), **Supp. XIII:** 13, 14
"Hope" (Cornford), **VIII:** 105, 112
"Hope" (Cowper), **III:** 212
Hope, A. D., **Supp. VII: 151–166**
"Hope Abandoned" (Davies), **Supp. XI:** 97
Hope for Poetry, A (Day Lewis), **Supp. III:** 117, 119
Hopes and Fears for Art (Morris), **V:** 301, 306
Hopkins, Gerard Manley, **II:** 123, 181; **IV:** xx; **V:** ix, xi, xxv, 53, 205, 210, 261, 309–310, 338, **361–382**; **VI:** 75, 83; **Supp. II:** 269; **Supp. IV:** 344, 345; **Retro. Supp. II:** 173, **185–198**
Hopkins (MacKenzie), **V:** 375n 382
Hopkinson, Sir Tom, **V:** xx, xxxviii
Horace, **II:** 108, 112, 199, 200, 265, 292, 300, 309, 347; **IV:** 327
"Horae Canonicae" (Auden), **Retro. Supp. I:** 12–13
Horae Solitariae (Thomas), **Supp. III:** 394
"Horatian Ode . . . , An" (Marvell), **II:** 204, 208, 209, 210, 211, 216–217; **Retro. Supp. II:** 263–264
"Horatius" (Macaulay), **IV:** 282

Horestes (Pickering), **I:** 213, 216–218
Horizon (periodical), **Supp. II:** 489; **Supp. III: 102–103**, 105, 106–107, 108–109
Hornby, Nick, **Supp. XV: 133–146**
Horne, Richard Hengist, **IV:** 312, 321, 322
Hornet (periodical), **VI:** 102
Horniman, Annie, **VI:** 309; **VII:** 1
"Horns Away" (Lydgate), **I:** 64
Horse and His Boy, The (Lewis), **Supp. III:** 248, 260
"Horse at Balaklava, 1854" (Carson), **Supp. XIII:** 66
"Horse Dealer's Daughter, The" (Lawrence), **VII:** 114
"Horse–Drawn Caravan" (Murphy), **Supp. V:** 329
Horse-Eaters, The: Poems and Satires, Third Series (Clarke), **Supp. XV:** 26
"Horse, Goose and Sheep, The" (Lydgate), **I:** 57
Horseman's Word, The (Morgan, E.), **Supp. IX:** 166
"Horses" (Muir), **Supp. VI:** 204–205 "Horses" (Muir), Supp. VI: 204–205
Horse's Mouth, The (Cary), **VII:** 186, 188, 191, 192, 193–194
Hoskins, John, **II:** 165–166, 167
"Hospital Barge" (Owen), **VI:** 454
Hostage, The (Behan), **Supp. II:** 70, **72–73**, 74
Hostages to Fortune (Braddon), **VIII:** 49
Hosts of the Lord, The (Steel), **Supp. XII:** 274
Hot Anger Soon Cold (Jonson), **Retro. Supp. I:** 157
Hot Countries, The (Waugh), **Supp. VI:** 272, 274
Hot Gates, The (Golding), **Supp. I:** 81; **Retro. Supp. I:** 93
Hotel, The (Bowen), **Supp. II: 82–83**
Hotel de Dream (Tennant), **Supp. IX:** 230
Hotel du Lac (Brookner), **Supp. IV:** 120, 121, 126–127, 136
Hotel in Amsterdam, The (Osborne), **Supp. I:** 338–339
"Hotel of the Idle Moon, The" (Trevor), **Supp. IV:** 501
"Hotel Room in Chartres" (Lowry), **Supp. III:** 272
Hothouse, The (Pinter), **Supp. I:** 377–378
Hothouse by the East River, The (Spark), **Supp. I:** 210
Hotson, Leslie, **I:** 275, 276
Hotspur: A Ballad for Music (Adcock and Whitehead), **Supp. XII:** 9
"Hottentot Venus" (Kay), **Supp. XIII:** 101
Houd–den–bek (Brink), **Supp. VI:** 51
Hough, Graham, **IV:** 323n, 339; **V:** 355, 359
Houghton, Lord, *see* Monckton Milnes, Richard
Hound of Death, The (Christie), **III:** 341
"Hound of Heaven, The" (Thompson), **V:** 445–447, 449, 450

Hound of the Baskervilles, The (Doyle), **III:** 341, 342, 345; **Supp. II:** 161, 163, 164, 170, 171, 172
"Hour and the Ghost, The" (Rossetti), **V:** 256
Hour and the Man, The: A Historical Romance (Martineau), **Supp. XV:** 189–190
Hour of Magic and Other Poems, The (Davies), **Supp. XI:** 99
Hours in a Library (Stephen), **V:** 279, 285, 286, 287, 289
Hours of Idleness (Byron), **IV:** xvi 192
House, Humphry, **IV:** 167
"House" (Browning), **IV:** 359; **Retro. Supp. II:** 29
"House, The" (Constantine), **Supp. XV:** 80
House and Its Head, A (Compton-Burnett), **VII:** 61
"House and Man" (Thomas), **Supp. III:** 403, 404
House at Pooh Corner, The (Milne), **Supp. V:** 295, 305, 306, 307, 308–309
"House Building" (Gunesekera), **Supp. X:** 86
House by the Churchyard, The (Le Fanu), **III:** 340, 345
House for Mr Biswas, A (Naipaul), **Supp. I:** 383, 386, **387–389**
House for the Truth, A (Wain), **Supp. XVI:** 303, 307
"House Grown Silent, The" (Warner), **Supp. VII:** 371
"House Guest" (Conn), **Supp. XIII:** 79
House in Corfu: A Family's Sojourn in Greece, A (Tennant), **Supp. IX:** 239
House in Paris, The (Bowen), **Supp. II:** 77, 82, 84, 89–90
"House in the Acorn, The" (Redgrove), **Supp. VI:** 236
"House–martins" (Adcock), **Supp. XII:** 12
House of All Nations (Stead), **Supp. IV:** 464–467
"House of Aries, The" (Hughes), **Supp. I:** 346
"House of Beauty, The" (Christie), **Supp. II:** 124
House of Children, A (Cary), **VII:** 186, 187, 189
"House of Christmas, The" (Chesterton), **VI:** 344
House of Cobwebs, The (Gissing), **V:** 437
House of Doctor Dee (Ackroyd), **Supp. VI:** 4, 10
House of Dolls, The (Comyns), **VIII:** 53, 65
"House of Dreams, The" (Thomas), **Supp. IV:** 493
House of Fame, The (Chaucer), **I:** 23, 30; **Retro. Supp. II:** 38–39
"House of Geraniums, A" (Scupham), **Supp. XIII:** 224
House of Hospitalities, The (Tennant), **Supp. IX:** 239
House of Life, The (Rossetti), **V:** 237, 238, 241, 242, 243, 244, 245
"House of Over-Dew, The" (Smith), **Retro. Supp. III:** 314

House of Pomegranates, A (Wilde), **V:** 419; **Retro. Supp. II:** 365
House of Seven Gables, The (Hawthorne), **III:** 339, 345
House of Sleep, The (Coe), **Supp. XV:** 50, 51, 52, 53, 57, 60–61, 63
House of Sleep, The (Kavan), **Supp. VII:** 212–213
House of Splendid Isolation (O'Brien), **Supp. V:** 341–344
House on the Beach, The (Meredith), **V:** 230–231, 234
House on the Strand, The (du Maurier), **Supp. III:** 138, 139, 140, 141, 147
House of Titans and Other Poems, The (Russell), **VIII:** 277, 290, 292
"House of Titans, The" (Russell), **VIII:** 290
"House We Lived In, The" (Smith, I. C.), **Supp. IX:** 214
House with the Echo, The (Powys), **VIII:** 248, 249, 254
Household Education (Martineau), **Supp. XV:** 184
"Household Spirits" (Kinsella), **Supp. V:** 272
Household Words (periodical), **V:** xxi, 3, 42; **Retro. Supp. III:** 99–100, 104, 105
Householder, The (Jhabvala), **Supp. V:** 227–228, 237
Housekeeping vs. the Dirt (Hornby), **Supp. XV:** 145
Housman, A. E., **III:** 68, 70; **V:** xxii, xxvi, 311; **VI:** ix, xv–xvi, **151–164**, 415
Housman, Laurence, **V:** 402, 420
Housman: 1897–1936 (Richards), **VI:** 164
How About Europe? (Douglas), **VI:** 295, 305
"How Are the Children Robin" (Graham), **Supp. VII:** 115
How Brophy Made Good (Hare), **Supp. IV:** 281
How Can We Know? (Wilson), **Supp. VI:** 305
"How Distant" (Larkin), **Supp. I:** 284
"How Do You See"(Smith), **Supp. II:** 467; **Retro. Supp. III:** 314
How Far Can You Go? (Lodge; U.S. title, *Souls and Bodies*), **Supp. IV:** 366, 368, 371, 372, 375–376, 381, 408
How He Lied to Her Husband (Shaw), **VI:** 129
How I Became a Holy Mother and Other Stories (Jhabvala), **Supp. V:** 235
"How I Became a Socialist" (Orwell), **VII:** 276–277
How It Is (Beckett), **Supp. I:** 43, 50, 52, 54–55, 58
"How It Strikes a Contemporary" (Browning), **IV:** 354, 367, 373; **Retro. Supp. III:** 25
How Late It Was, How Late (Kelman), **Supp. V:** 243, 252–254
How Lisa Loved the King (Eliot), **V:** 200
"How Many Bards" (Keats), **IV:** 215
"How Pillingshot Scored" (Wodehouse), **Supp. III:** 449–450

How Right You Are, Jeeves (Wodehouse), **Supp. III:** 460, 461, 462
"How Seagulls Move" (Butlin), **Supp. XVI:** 55
"How shall my animal" (Thomas), **Retro. Supp. III:** 342
"How Sleep the Brave" (Collins), **III:** 166
"How soon the servant sun" (Thomas), **Supp. I:** 174
"How Sweet the Name of Jesus Sounds" (Newton), **III:** 210
"How the Angels Fly In" (Butlin), **Supp. XVI:** 66
How the "Mastiffs" Went to Iceland (Trollope), **V:** 102
How the Other Half Lives (Ayckbourn), **Supp. V:** 2, 4, 9, 11, 12
How the Whale Became (Hughes), **Supp. I:** 346
"How They Brought the Good News from Ghent to Aix (16—)" (Browning), **IV:** 356, 361
How this foirsaid Tod maid his Confession to Freir Wolf Waitskaith (Henryson), see *Fox and the Wolf, The*
"How to Accomplish It" (Newman), **Supp. VII:** 293
"How to Be an Expatriate" (Davies), **Supp. XIV:** 42
How to Be Good (Hornby), **Supp. XV:** 133–134, 142–143
How to Become an Author (Bennett), **VI:** 264
"How to get away with Suicide" (Kay), **Supp. XIII:** 107
"How to Kill" (Douglas), **VII: 443**
How to Live on 24 Hours a Day (Bennett), **VI:** 264
How to Observe Morals and Manners (Martineau), **Supp. XV:** 186
How to Read (Pound), **VII:** 235
How to Read a Page (Richards), **Supp. II:** 426
How to Settle the Irish Question (Shaw), **VI:** 119, 129
"How to Teach Reading" (Leavis), **VII:** 235, 248
"How would the ogling sparks despise" (Etherege), **II:** 268
"How You Love Our Lady" (Blackwood), **Supp. IX:** 9
Howard, Elizabeth Jane, **Supp. XI: 135–149**
Howard, Henry, earl of Surrey, see Surrey, Henry Howard, earl of
Howard, R., **V:** 418
Howard, Sir Robert, **II:** 100
Howards End (Forster), **VI:** viii, xii, 397, 398, 401, **404–406**, 407; **Supp. I:** 161; **Retro. Supp. II:** 143–145
Howarth, R. G., **II:** 69
Howe, Irving, **VI:** 41
Howells, William Dean, **VI:** 23, 29, 33
Howitt, William, **IV:** 212
Hrafnkels saga, **VIII:** 242
Hubert de Sevrac: A Romance of the Eighteenth Century (Robinson), **Supp. XIII:** 209
Hubert De Vere (Burney), **Supp. III:** 71

Huchon, René, **III:** 273n
Hudibras (Butler), **II:** 145
Hudson, Derek, **V:** xi, xxviii, 263, 274
Hudson, W. H., **V:** 429
Hudson Letter, The (Mahon), **Supp. VI:** 175–176
Hue and Cry, The (Inchbald), **Supp. XV:** 156
Hueffer, Ford Madox, see Ford, Ford Madox
"Hug, The" (Gunn), **Supp. IV:** 274–275, 276, 277; **Retro. Supp. III:** 128
Huggan, Graham, **Supp. IV:** 170
Hugh Primas and the Archpoet (tr. Adcock), **Supp. XII:** 10
Hugh Selwyn Mauberley (Pound), **VI:** 417; **VII:** xvi
Hughes, Arthur, **V:** 294
Hughes, John, **I:** 121, 122; **III:** 40
Hughes, Ted, **Supp. I: 341–366**; **Supp. IV:** 257; **Supp. V:** xxx; **Retro. Supp. I:** 126; **Retro. Supp. II: 199–219**
Hughes, Thomas, **I:** 218; **V:** xxii, 170; **Supp. IV:** 506
Hughes, Willie, **V:** 405
Hugo, Victor, **III:** 334; **V:** xxii, xxv, 22, 320; **Supp. IV:** 86
Hugo (Bennett), **VI:** 249
Huis clos (Sartre), **Supp. IV:** 39
"Hull Case, The" (Davies), **Supp. XIV:** 40–41
Hullabaloo in the Guava Orchard (Desai), **Supp. XV:** 83, 84–88, 90
Hulme, T. E., **VI:** 416; **Supp. VI: 133–147**
Hulse, Michael, **Supp. IV:** 354
"Human Abstract, The" (Blake), **III:** 296
Human Age, The (Lewis), **VII:** 80
Human Face, The (Smith, I. C.), **Supp. IX:** 221–223
Human Factor, The (Greene), **Supp. I:** 2, 11, 16–17; **Retro. Supp. II:** 165–166
"Human Harvest, A" (Fallon), **Supp. XII:** 112–113
"Human Life, on the Denial of Immortality" (Coleridge), **Retro. Supp. II:** 65
Human Machine, The (Bennett), **VI:** 250
Human Odds and Ends (Gissing), **V:** 437
"Human Seasons, The" (Keats), **IV:** 232
Human Shows, Far Phantasies, Songs and Trifles (Hardy), **VI:** 20
Human Voices (Fitzgerald), **Supp. V:** 95, 100, 103
"Humanism and the Religious Attitude" (Hulme), **Supp. VI:** 135, 140
"Humanitad" (Wilde), **V:** 401–402
Humble Administrator's Garden, The (Seth), **Supp. X:** 281
"Humble Petition of Frances Harris" (Swift), **III:** 30–31
Humboldt's Gift (Bellow), **Supp. IV:** 27, 33, 42
Hume, David, **III:** 148; **IV:** xiv, 138, 145, 273, 288; **V:** 288, 343; **Supp. III: 220–245**
Humiliation with Honour (Brittain), **Supp. X:** 45
"Humility" (Brome), **Supp. X:** 55
Humorous Day's Mirth, A (Chapman), **I:** 243, 244

Humorous Lieutenant, The (Fletcher), **II:** 45, 60–61, 65, 359
Humours of the Court (Bridges), **VI:** 83
Humphrey Bogart: Take It and Like It (Coe), **Supp. XV:** 49
Humphrey Clinker (Smollett), **III:** 147, 150, **155–157**, 158
"Hunchback in the Park, The" (Thomas), **Supp. I:** 177, 178; **Retro. Supp. III:** 343
Hundred Days, The (O'Brian), **Supp. XII:** 259
"Hundred Years, A" (Motion), **Supp. VII:** 266
Hundredth Story, The (Coppard), **VIII:** 89
Hungarian Lift-Jet, The (Banks), **Supp. XI:** 1
"Hunger" (Lessing), **Supp. I:** 240
Hunger Demon, The (Clarke), **Supp. XV:** 23
"Hungry" (Scupham), **Supp. XIII:** 218
"Hungry Eye, A" (Fallon), **Supp. XII:** 103
Hungry Generations (Wain), **Supp. XVI:** 301–302
Hungry Hill (du Maurier), **Supp. III:** 144
Hunt, John, **IV:** 129, 132
Hunt, Leigh, **II:** 332, 355, 357, 359, 363; **IV:** ix, 80, 104, 129, 132, 163, 172, 198, 202, 205–206, 209, 212–217, 230, 306; **Retro. Supp. I:** 183, 248
Hunt, Violet, **VI:** 324
Hunt, William Holman, **V:** 45, 77–78, 235, 236, 240
Hunt by Night, The (Mahon), **Supp. VI:** 173–174, 177
"Hunt by Night, The" (Mahon), **Supp. VI:** 174
"Hunt of Eildon, The" (Hogg), **Supp. X:** 111
"Hunted Beast, The" (Powys), **VIII:** 247–248
Hunted Down (Dickens), **VI:** 66, 72
"Hunter, The" (Macpherson), **VIII:** 181
Hunter, G. K., **I:** 165; **II:** 29, 41
Hunting of Cupid, The (Peele), **I:** 205
Hunting of the Snark, The (Carroll), **V:** 270, 272, 273
Hunting Sketches (Trollope), **V:** 101
Huntley, F. L, **II:** 152, 157
"Huntsman, The" (Lowbury), **VII:** 431–432
"Huntsmen" (Nye), **Supp. X:** 198
Hurd, Michael, **VI:** 427
Hurd, Richard, **I:** 122
Hurly Burly (Coppard), **VIII:** 93–94
"Hurrahing in Harvest" (Hopkins), **V:** 366, 367, 368
Hurry on Down (Wain), **Supp. XVI:** 295, 297–298, 299
"Husband and Wife" (Rossetti), **V:** 259
Husband His Own Cuckold, The (Dryden the younger), **II:** 305
"Husband's Aubade, The" (Delanty), **Supp. XIV:** 73
Husband's Message, The, **Retro. Supp. II:** 305
Hussein: An Entertainment (O'Brian), **Supp. XII:** 249

Hussey, Maurice, **II:** 250, 254
"Hut, The" (Pitter), **Supp. XIII:** 142
Hutcheon, Linda, **Supp. IV:** 162
Hutchinson, F. E., **II:** 121, 123, 126, 129
Hutchinson, Sara, **IV:** 15, 49, 50, 54
Hutton, James, **IV:** 200
Hutton, R. H., **V:** 157–158, 168, 170
Huxley, Aldous, **II:** 105, 173; **III:** 341; **IV:** 303; **V:** xxii, 53; **VII:** xii, xvii–xviii, 79, **197–208**; **Retro. Supp. II:** 182
Huxley, Thomas, **V:** xxii, 182, 284
Hyacinth Halvey (Gregory), **VI:** 315, 316
Hyde, Douglas, **VI:** 307; **VII:** 1
Hyde–Lees, George, **VI:** 213
Hydriotaphia (Browne), **II:** **150–153**, 154, 155, 156
Hygiasticon (Lessius), **II:** 181n
Hymenaei (Jonson), **I:** 239
"Hymn to Love" (Abercrombie), **Supp. XVI:** 2
Hymiskviða, **VIII:** 230
"Hymn before Sun–rise, in the Vale of Chamouni" (Coleridge), **Retro. Supp. II:** 59–60
"Hymn of Apollo" (Shelley), **II:** 200; **IV:** 203
Hymn of Nature, A (Bridges), **VI:** 81
"Hymn to Adversity" (Gray), **III:** 137
Hymn to Christ on the Cross (Chapman), **I:** 241–242
"Hymn to Colour" (Meredith), **V:** 222
Hymn to Diana (Jonson), **I:** 346; **Retro. Supp. I:** 162
Hymn to Harmony, A (Congreve), **II:** 350
"Hymn to Intellectual Beauty" (Shelley), **IV:** 198
"Hymn. To Light" (Cowley), **II:** 198, 200, 259
"Hymn to Love" (Abercrombie), **Supp. XVI:** 2
"Hymn to Mercury" (Shelley), **IV:** 196, 204
"Hymn to Pan" (Keats), **IV:** 216, 217, 222
"Hymn to Proust" (Ewart), **Supp. VII:** 38
"Hymn to the Name and Honor of the Admirable Sainte Teresa, A" (Crashaw), **II:** 179, 182
Hymn to the Pillory, A (Defoe), **III:** 13; **Retro. Supp. I:** 65, 67–68
"Hymn to the Sun" (Hood), **IV:** 255
"Hymn to the Virgin" (Burnside), **Supp. XIII:** 21
"Hymn to the Winds" (du Bellay), **V:** 345
"Hymn to Venus" (Shelley), **IV:** 209
"Hymne of the Nativity, A" (Crashaw), **II:** 180, 183
"Hymne to God the Father, A" (Donne), **Retro. Supp. II:** 98
Hymns (Spenser), **I:** 131
Hymns Ancient and Modern (Betjeman), **VII:** 363–364
"Hymns to Lenin" (MacDiarmid), **Supp. XII:** 211
Hymnus in Cynthiam (Chapman), **I:** 240

Hyperion (Keats), **IV:** 95, 204, 211, 212, 213, **227–231**, 235; **VI:** 455; **Retro. Supp. I:** 194
Hypnerstomachia (Colonna), **I:** 134
Hypochondriack, The (Boswell), **III:** 237, 240, 243, 248
"Hypogram and Inscription" (de Man), **Supp. IV:** 115
Hysterical Disorders of Warfare (Yealland), **Supp. IV:** 58

"I" (Thomas), **Supp. XII:** 290
I abide and abide and better abide" (Wyatt), **I:** 108, 109
"I Am": The Selected Poetry of John Clare (Clare), **Supp. XI:** 51, 62
I Am a Camera (Isherwood), **VII:** 311
I Am Lazarus: Short Stories (Kavan), **Supp. VII:** 210–211
I Am Mary Dunne (Moore, B.), **Supp. IX:** 143, 148, 149–150, 153
"I am Raftery" (Mahon), **Supp. VI:** 170
"I Bring Her a Flower" (Warner), **Supp. VII:** 371
I Can Remember Robert Louis Stevenson (ed. Masson), **V:** 393, 397
"I care not if I live" (Bridges), **VI:** 81
I, Claudius (Graves), **VII:** 259
I Crossed the Minch (MacNeice), **VII:** 403, 411
"I dined with a Jew" (Macaulay), **IV:** 283
"I Don't Know, What Do You Think" (Davies), **Supp. XIV:** 37, 39
"I Do, You Do" (Motion), **Supp. VII:** 260
"I Dreamt Gallipoli Beach" (Hart), **Supp. XI:** 123
"I find no peace and all my war is done" (Wyatt), **I:** 110
"I go night–shopping like Frank O'Hara I go bopping" (Mahon), **Supp. VI:** 175
"I Have Been Taught" (Muir), **Supp. VI:** 208
"I have longed to move away" (Thomas), **Supp. I:** 174
"I have loved and so doth she" (Wyatt), **I:** 102
"I Hear Thy Call" (Carpenter), **Supp. XIII:** 38
"I heard an Angel singing" (Blake), **III:** 296
"I, in my intricate image" (Thomas), **Supp. I:** 174
I Knock at the Door (O'Casey), **VII:** 12
"I know a Bank Whereon the Wild Thyme Grows" (Shakespeare), **IV:** 222
"I lead a life unpleasant"(Wyatt), **I:** 104
I Like It Here (Amis), **Supp. II:** **8–10**, 12
I Live under a Black Sun (Sitwell), **VII:** 127, 135, 139
"I Look into My Glass" (Hardy), **VI:** 16
I Lost My Memory, The Case As the Patient Saw It (Anon.), **Supp. IV:** 5
"I love all beauteous things" (Bridges), **VI:** 72
"I.M. G.MacB." (Reading), **VIII:** 273
"I make this in a warring absence" (Thomas), **Retro. Supp. III:** 341, 344

"I never shall love the snow again" (Bridges), **VI:** 77
"I Ordained the Devil" (McCabe), **Supp. IX:** 136
I promessi sposi (Manzoni), **III:** 334
"I Remember" (Hood), **IV:** 255
"I Remember, I Remember" (Larkin), **Supp. I:** 275, 277; **Retro. Supp. III:** 199, 212
"I Say I Say I Say" (Armitage), **VIII:** 9
"I Say No" (Collins), **Supp. VI:** 93, 103
"I see the boys of summer" (Thomas), **Supp. I:** 173
I Speak of Africa (Plomer), **Supp. XI:** 213, 214, 216
"I Stood Tip-toe" (Keats), **IV:** 214, 216
"I strove with none" (Landor), **IV:** 98
"I Suppose You Know This Isn't a Merry-go-round" (Constantine), **Supp. XV:** 71–72
"I that in heill wes" (Dunbar), **VIII:** 121
"I took my heart in my hand" (Rossetti), **V:** 252
"I wake and feel the fell of dark" (Hopkins), **V:** 374n, 375
"I Wandered Lonely as a Cloud" (Wordsworth), **IV:** 22
I Want It Now (Amis), **Supp. II:** 15
I Was a Rat! or, The Scarlet Slippers (Pullman), **Supp. XIII:** 152
"I Will Lend You Malcolm" (Graham), **Supp. VII:** 116
I Will Marry When I Want (Ngũgĩ). See *Ngaahika ndeenda*
"I will not let thee go" (Bridges), **VI:** 74, 77
I Will Pray with the Spirit (Bunyan), **II:** 253
"I will write" (Graves), **VII:** 269
"I would be a bird" (Bridges), **VI:** 81–82
Ian Hamilton's March (Churchill), **VI:** 351
"Ianthe"poems (Landor), **IV:** 88, 89, 92, 99
Ibrahim (Scudéry), **III:** 95
"Ibrahim Pacha and Wellington" (Mangan), **Supp. XIII:** 127
Ibsen, Henrik, **IV:** 118; **V:** xxiii–xxvi, 414; **VI:** viii–ix, 104, 110, 269; **Supp. III:** 4, 12; **Supp. IV:** 1, 286; **Retro. Supp. I:** 170; **Retro. Supp. II:** 309
Ibsen's Ghost; or, Toole Up to Date (Barrie), **Supp. III:** 4, 9
Ice (Kavan), **Supp. VII:** 201, 208, 214–215
Ice Age, The (Drabble), **Supp. IV:** 230, 245–246, 247
Ice Cream War, An (Boyd), **Supp. XVI:** 33, 34–35
Ice in the Bedroom (Wodehouse), **Supp. III:** 460
"Ice Queen of Ararat, The" (Jamie), **Supp. XIV:** 139
Icelandic journals (Morris), **V:** 299, 300–301, 307
"Icy Road" (MacCaig), **Supp. VI:** 188–189
Idea of a University, The (Newman), **Supp. VII:** 294, 296, 298–299

Idea of Christian Society, The (Eliot), **VII:** 153
Idea of Comedy, The, and the Uses of the Comic Spirit (Meredith), see *Essay on Comedy and the Uses of the Comic Spirit*
"Idea of Entropy at Maenporth Beach, The" (Redgrove), **Supp. VI:** 233–234, 237
Idea of Great Poetry, The (Abercrombie), **Supp. XVI:** 11, 12
"Idea of Perfection, The" (Murdoch), **Supp. I:** 217, 220
Idea of the Perfection of Painting, An (tr. Evelyn), **II:** 287
Ideal Husband, An (Wilde), **V:** 414–415, 419
Ideals in Ireland (ed. Lady Gregory), **VI:** 98
Ideals in Ireland: Priest or Hero? (Russell), **VIII:** 282, 284
Ideas and Places (Connolly), **Supp. III:** 110
Ideas of Good and Evil (Yeats), **V:** 301, 306
"Idenborough" (Warner), **Supp. VII:** 380
Identical Twins (Churchill), **Supp. IV:** 181
Identifying Poets: Self and Territory in Twentieth-Century Poetry (Crawford), **Supp. XI:** 71
"Identities" (Muldoon), **Supp. IV:** 414, 424
"Ides of March, The" (Fuller), **Supp. VII:** 73
Idiocy of Idealism, The (Levy), **VI:** 303
"Idiot Boy, The" (Wordsworth), **IV:** 7, 11
"Idiots, The" (Conrad), **VI:** 148
"Idle Reverie, An" (Russell), **VIII:** 290
Idleness of Business, The, A Satyr . . . (Wycherley), see *Folly of Industry, The*
Idler (periodical), **III:** 111–112, 121; **Retro. Supp. I:** 145
Idol Hunter, The (Unsworth) see *Pascali's Island*
"Idyll" (Cope), **VIII:** 80
Idyllia heroica decem (Landor), **IV:** 100
"Idylls of the King" (Hill), **Supp. V:** 191
Idylls of the King (Tennyson), **IV:** xxii, 328, 336–337, 338; **Retro. Supp. III:** 317, 318, 321, 322, 327, 329, 330
"If" (Kipling), **Retro. Supp. III:** 194
"If by Dull Rhymes Our English Must be Chained . . .." (Keats), **IV:** 221
If Christ Came to Chicago! A Plea for the Union of All Who Love in the Service of All Who Suffer (Stead), **Supp. XIII:** 242–243
"If I Could Tell You" (Auden), **Retro. Supp. I:** 10
If I Don't Know (Cope), **VIII:** 67, 70, 79–84
"If I Lie Down" (Smith), **Retro. Supp. III:** 308
If I Were Four and Twenty: Swedenborg, Mediums and Desolate Places (Yeats), **VI:** 222
"If I were tickled by the rub of lover" (Thomas), **Supp. I:** 172

"If in the world there be more woes"(Wyatt), **I:** 104
"If, My Darling" (Larkin), **Supp. I:** 277, 285; **Retro. Supp. III:** 205
"If my head hurt a hair's foot" (Thomas), **Supp. I:** 176–177
"If Only" (Dunn), **Supp. X:** 82
"If She's Your Lover Now" (Fallon), **Supp. XII:** 103
If the Old Could . . . (Lessing), **Supp. I:** 253, 254
"If This Were Faith" (Stevenson), **V:** 385
"If You Came" (Pitter), **Supp. XIII:** 142, 143
If You're Glad I'll Be Frank (Stoppard), **Supp. I:** 439, 445
Ignatius His Conclave (Donne), **Retro. Supp. II:** 95
"Ignorance" (Larkin), **Retro. Supp. III:** 207
"Ikey" (Brown), **Supp. VI:** 68
Ikons, The (Durrell), **Supp. I:** 121
Ikons and Other Poems (Durrell), **Retro. Supp. III:** 85, 95
"Il Conde" (Conrad), **VI: 148**
Il cortegiano (Castiglione), **I:** 265
Il Filostrato (Boccaccio), **Retro. Supp. II:** 40–42
Il pastor fido (Guarini), **II:** 49–50
Il pecorone (Fiorentino), **I:** 310
"Il Penseroso" (Milton), **II:** 158–159; **III:** 211n; **IV:** 14–15
Ilex Tree, The (Murray), **Supp. VII:** 270, 271–272
Iliad, The (tr. Cowper), **III:** 220
Iliad, The (tr. Macpherson), **VIII:** 192
Iliad, The (tr. Pope), **III:** 77
Ill Beginning Has a Good End, An, and a Bad Beginning May Have a Good End (Ford), **II:** 89, 100
"I'll come when thou art saddest" (Brontë), **V:** 127
I'll Leave It To You (Coward), **Supp. II:** 141
I'll Never Be Young Again (du Maurier), **Supp. III:** 139–140, 144
Ill Seen Ill Said (Beckett), **Retro. Supp. I:** 29
I'll Stand by You (Warner), **Supp. VII:** 370, 382
I'll Tell You What (Inchbald), **Supp. XV:** 148, 153–154, 155, 156, 160
"Illiterations" (Brooke-Rose)), **Supp. IV:** 97
"Illuminated Man, The" (Ballard), **Supp. V:** 24
Illusion (Carey and Mullins), **Supp. XII:** 53
Illusion and Reality: A Study of the Sources of Poetry (Caudwell), **Supp. III:** 120, **Supp. IX:** 33–36, 40–44, 46
"Illusions" (Blunden), **Supp. XI:** 45
"Illusions of Anti-Realism" (Brooke-Rose), **Supp. IV:** 116
Illustrated Excursions in Italy (Lear), **V:** 77, 79, 87
Illustrated London News (periodical), **VI:** 337
Illustrations of Latin Lyrical Metres (Clough), **V:** 170

Illustrations of Political Economy (Martineau), **Supp. XV:** 183, 184, 185, 188, 189, 190, 191–192
Illustrations of the Family of Psittacidae, or Parrots (Lear), **V:** 76, 79, 87
Illywhacker (Carey), **Supp. XII:** 49, 50, 51, 53, 55, 56–57, 57–58, 62
I'm Deadly Serious (Wallace-Crabbe), **VIII:** 321–322
I'm Dying Laughing (Stead), **Supp. IV:** 473, 476
"I'm happiest when most away" (Brontë), **V:** 116
I'm the King of the Castle (Hill), **Supp. XIV:** 115, 117, 119–120, 127
"Image, The" (Day Lewis), **Supp. III:** 115–116
"Image, The" (Fuller), **Supp. VII:** 73
"Image, The" (Warner), **Supp. VII:** 371
Image and Superscription (Mitchell), **Supp. XIV:** 100
"Image from Beckett, An" (Mahon), **Supp. VI:** 169, 172
Image Men, The (Priestley), **VII:** 209, 210, 218, 221–223
Image of a Society (Fuller), **Supp. VII:** 68, 74–75
"Images" (Fuller), **Supp. VII:** 80
"Images of Africa at Century's End" (Aidoo), **Supp. XV:** 11, 12
Imaginary Conversations (Landor), **IV:** xviii, 87, 88, 89, **90–94,** 96–97, 99, 100
Imaginary Conversations of Greeks and Romans (Landor), **IV:** 100
Imaginary Homelands: Essays and Criticism (Rushdie), **Supp. IV:** 171, 434
Imaginary Life, An (Malouf), **Supp. XII:** 217, 222–224, 228
Imaginary Love Affair, An (Ewart), **Supp. VII:** 41
Imaginary Portraits (Pater), **V:** 339, 340, 348–349, 355, 356
Imagination Dead Imagine (Beckett), **Supp. I:** 53, 61; **Retro. Supp. I:** 29
Imagination in the Modern World, The (Spender), **Supp. II:** 492
Imaginations and Reveries (Russell), **VIII:** 277, 281, 284, 287, 292
"Imaginative Woman, An" (Hardy), **VI:** 22
Imaginings of Sand (Brink), **Supp. VI:** 57
"Imagist" (Joyce), **Retro. Supp. III:** 170
Imitation Game, The (McEwan), **Supp. IV:** 390, 398–399
"Imitation of Spenser" (Keats), **IV:** 213; **Retro. Supp. I:** 187
Imitations of English Poets (Pope), **Retro. Supp. I:** 231–232
Imitation of the Sixth Satire of the Second Book of Horace, An (Swift), **III:** 36
Imitations of Horace (Pope), **II:** 298; **III:** 77; **Retro. Supp. I:** 230, 235–238
Immaturity (Shaw), **VI:** 105
"Immigrant" (Adcock), **Supp. XII:** 8
Immorality and Profaneness of the English Stage, A (Collier), *see Short View of the Immorality . . . , A*

Immorality, Debauchery and Prophaneness (Meriton), **II:** 340
Immortal Dickens, The (Gissing), **V:** 437
"Immortals, The" (Amis), **Supp. IV:** 40
"Immram" (Muldoon), **Supp. IV:** 415–418, 420, 421, 425
Imogen: A Pastoral Romance (Godwin), **Supp. XV:** 119
Impartial Reflections on the Present Situation of the Queen of France (Robinson), **Supp. XIII:** 202
"Impercipient, The" (Hardy), **Retro. Supp. I:** 121
"Imperial Adam" (Hope), **Supp. VII:** 158
"Imperial Elegy, An" (Owen), **VI:** 448
Imperial Palace (Bennett), **VI:** xiii, 247, 250, 251, 262–263
Implements in Their Places (Graham), **Supp. VII:** 103, 115–116
Importance of Being Earnest, The (Wilde), **V:** xxvi, 415, 416, 419; **Supp. II:** 50, 143, 148; **Retro. Supp. II:** 350, 370, 314–315
"Importance of Elsewhere, The" (Larkin), **Retro. Supp. III:** 206
"Importance of Glasgow in My Work, The" (Kelman), **Supp. V:** 257
Importance of the Guardian Considered, The (Swift), **III:** 35
"Impossibility" (Crawford), **Supp. XI:** 77
Impossible Saints (Roberts), **Supp. XV:** 267, 270, 273
Impossible Thing, An: A Tale (Congreve), **II:** 350
"Impression" (Symons), **Supp. XIV:** 275
Impressions and Opinions (Moore), **VI:** 87
Impressions of America (Wilde), **V:** 419
Impressions of Theophrastus Such (Eliot), **V:** 198, 200
Impressionist, The (Kunzru), **Supp. XIV:** 165, 166–169, 172, 175, 176
Imprisonment (Shaw), **VI:** 129
Impromptu in Moribundia (Hamilton), **Supp. XVI:** 177
"Improvement, The" (Traherne), **Supp. XI:** 267
"Improvisation" (Gunn), **Supp. IV:** 276
"Improvisation on 'Warum istuns das Licht gegeben' " (Hill), **Retro. Supp. III:** 144
"Improvisations for Jimi Hendrix" (Hill), **Retro. Supp. III:** 142–144
Improvisatore, in Three Fyttes, with Other Poems by Thomas Lovell Beddoes, The (Beddoes), **Supp. XI:** 17, 19–20, 21, 28
"Improviso" (Soutar), **Supp. XVI:** 251
"In a Balcony" (Browning), **Retro. Supp. III:** 23
"In a Blue Time" (Kureishi), **Supp. XI:** 158
In a Bombed House, 1941: An Elegy in Memory of Anthony Butts (Plomer), **Supp. XI:** 222
"In a Country Church" (Thomas), **Supp. XII:** 283–284, 286, 287
"In a Dark Wood" (Sisson), **Supp. XI:** 248

In a Free State (Naipaul), **VII:** xx; **Supp. I:** 383, 390, 393, **394–396,** 397
"In a Free State"(Naipaul), **Supp. I:** 395, 396
In a German Pension (Mansfield), **VII:** 171, 172–173
In a Glass Darkly (Le Fanu), **III:** 345
"In an Illuminated Missal" (Kingsley), **Supp. XVI:** 204
"In a Shaken House" (Warner), **Supp. VII:** 380
"In a Strange City" (Russell), **VIII:** 291
In a Time of Violence (Boland), **Supp. V:** 43
"In a Valley of Cauterez" (Tennyson), **Retro. Supp. III:** 320
"In an Artist's Studio" (Rossetti), **V:** 249; **Retro. Supp. III:** 262–263
"In an Illuminated Missal" (Kingsley), **Supp. XVI:** 204
"In an Omnibus" (Symons), **Supp. XIV:** 279
"In Another Country" (Ewart), **Supp. VII:** 45
In Another Light (Greig), **Supp. XVI:** 161, 172–174
"In Barnum" (Campion), **Supp. XVI:** 90
"In Between Talking About the Elephant" (Kay), **Supp. XIII:** 109, 110
In Between the Sheets (McEwan), **Supp. IV:** 390, 394–396
In Black and White (Kipling), **Retro. Supp. III:** 186
"In Broken Images"(Graves), **VII:** 267
"In California" (Davie), **Supp. VI:** 109
"In Carrowdore Churchyard" (Mahon), **Supp. VI:** 167–168
In Celebration (Storey), **Supp. I:** 408, 411, 412, 413–414
In Chancery (Galsworthy), **VI:** 274
"In Church" (Thomas), **Supp. XII:** 285–286, 287
In country sleep (Thomas), **Retro. Supp. III:** 346
"In country sleep" (Thomas), **Retro. Supp. III:** 346
In Custody (Desai), **Supp. V:** 53, 55, 65, 68, 69–71
"In Deep and Solemn Dreams"(Tennyson), **IV:** 329
"In Defence of Milton" (Leavis), **VII:** 246
In Defence of T.S. Eliot (Raine), **Supp. XIII:** 163, 170–171, 175
"In Defense of Astigmatism" (Wodehouse), **Supp. III:** 454
"In Defense of the Novel, Yet Again" (Rushdie), **Supp. IV:** 455
"In dungeons dark I cannot sing"(Brontë), **V:** 115–116
"In Eosdem" (Campion), **Supp. XVI:** 94
In Excited Reverie: A Centenary Tribute to William Butler Yeats, 1865–1939 (ed. Jeffares and Cross), **VI:** 224
"In Flanders Fields" (McCrae), **VI:** 434
"In from Spain" (Powys), **VIII:** 251
"In Fuscinum" (Campion), **Supp. XVI:** 101
"In God We Trust" (Rushdie), **Supp. IV:** 434, 456

"In Good Faith" (Rushdie), **Supp. IV:** 437, 450

In Good King Charles's Golden Days (Shaw), **VI:** 125, 127, 129

"In Heat" (Crace), **Supp. XIV:** 21

In Her Own Image (Boland), **Supp. V:** 48

"In Her Own Image" (Boland), **Supp. V:** 48, 49

"In His Own Image" (Boland), **Supp. V:** 48–49

"In Insula Avalonia" (Sisson), **Supp. XI:** 258

"In Lambeth Palace Road" (Fuller), **Supp. VII:** 76

"In Lausum" (Campion), **Supp. XVI:** 100

In Light and Darkness (Wallace–Crabbe), **VIII:** 311

"In Love for Long" (Muir), **Supp. VI:** 206–207

"In Lycium et Clytham" (Campion), **Supp. XVI:** 94

"In Me Two Worlds" (Day Lewis), **Supp. III:** 126

"In Memoriam" (Longley), **VIII:** 169

In Memoriam (Tennyson), **IV:** xxi, 234, 248, 292, 310, 313, 323, 325–328, 330, 333–338, 371; **V:** 285, 455

In Memoriam A.H.H. (Tennyson), **Retro. Supp. III:** 317, 321, 324–326, 330, 331

"In Memoriam, Amada" (Reid), **Supp. VII:** 333

"In Memoriam (Easter, 1915)" (Thomas), **VI:** 424–425; **Supp. III:** 403, 404

"In Memoriam 8571 Private J. W. Gleave" (Constantine), **Supp. XV:** 71

"In Memoriam George Forrest" (Dutton), **Supp. XII:** 98–99

"In Memoriam: Gillian Rose" (Hill), **Retro. Supp. III:** 145

"In Memoriam Jimi Hendrix" (Butlin), **Supp. XVI:** 54

In Memoriam James Joyce (MacDiarmid), **Supp. XII:** 203

"In Memoriam James Joyce" (MacDiarmid), **Supp. XII:** 214

"In Memoriam W. H. Auden" (Hart), **Supp. XI:** 123

"In Memory of Ernst Toller" (Auden), **Retro. Supp. I:** 9

"In Memory of Eva Gore–Booth and Con Markiewicz" (Yeats), **VI:** 217

"In Memory of Major Robert Gregory" (Yeats), **Retro. Supp. I:** 331

"In Memory of my Cat, Domino" (Fuller), **Supp. VII:** 77

"In Memory of My Mother" (Kavanagh), **Supp. VII:** 198

"In Memory of Sigmund Freud" (Auden), **VII:** 379; **Retro. Supp. I:** 1

"In Memory of Stevie Smith" (Beer), **Supp. XIV:** 4

"In Memory of W. B. Yeats" (Auden), **VI:** 208; **Retro. Supp. I:** 1, 9

"In Memory of Zoe Yalland" (Motion), **Supp. VII:** 264

"In More's Hotel" (Nye), **Supp. X:** 202

"In My Country" (Kay), **Supp. XIII:** 108

"In my craft or sullen art"(Thomas), **Supp. I:** 178

"In My Dreams" (Smith), **Supp. II:** 466

In My Good Books (Pritchett), **Supp. III:** 313

"In My Own Album" (Lamb), **IV:** 83

In Our Infancy (Corke), **VII:** 93

"In Our Midst": The Letters of Callicrates to Dione, Queen of the Xanthians, Concerning England and the English (Stead), **Supp. XIII:** 242

In Our Time (Hemingway), **Supp. IV:** 163

In Parenthesis (Jones), **VI:** xvi, 437–438, **Supp. VII:** 167, 168, 169, 170, 171–175, 177

In Parenthesis (radio adaptation, Thomas), **Retro. Supp. III:** 348

In Patagonia (Chatwin), **Supp. IV:** 157, 159, 161, 163–165, 173; **Supp. IX:** 53–55, 56, 59

"In Praise of Cities" (Gunn), **Retro. Supp. III:** 120

"In Praise of Lessius His Rule of Health" (Crashaw), **II:** 181n

"In Praise of Limestone"(Auden), **VII:** 390, 391; **Retro. Supp. I:** 12

In Praise of Love (Rattigan), **Supp. VII:** 320–321

"In Procession" (Graves), **VII:** 264

In Pursuit of the English (Lessing), **Supp. I:** 237–238

"In Santa Maria del Popolo" (Gunn), **Supp. IV:** 262

"In Se" (Campion), **Supp. XVI:** 101

In Search of Love and Beauty (Jhabvala), **Supp. V:** 223, 233

"In Sickness and in Health" (Auden), **Retro. Supp. I:** 10

In Single Strictness (Moore), **VI:** 87, 95, 99

"In Sobieski's Shield" (Morgan, E.), **Supp. IX:** 158, 164

"In Such a Poise Is Love" (Reid), **Supp. VII:** 328–329

"In Summer" (Wallace–Crabbe), **VIII:** 311

"In Tabaccam" (Campion), **Supp. XVI:** 100

"In Tenebris II" (Hardy), **VI:** 14

In the Blood (Conn), **Supp. XIII:** 77–78

"In the Cutting of a Drink" (Aidoo), **Supp. XV:** 8–9

"In the Dark" (Raine), **Supp. XIII:** 167

In the Middle (Smith, I. C.), **Supp. IX:** 217–218

In the Middle of the Wood (Smith, I. C.), **Supp. IX:** 209

In the Beginning (Douglas), **VI:** 303, 304, 305

In the Blue House (Delahunt), **Supp. XIV:** 53–59, 62, 63

In the Cage (James), **VI:** 67, 69

"In the City of Red Dust" (Okri), **Supp. V:** 352

"In the Classics Room" (Smith, I. C.), **Supp. IX:** 214–215

In the Country of the Skin (Redgrove), **Supp. VI:** 230

In the Days of the Comet (Wells), **VI:** 227, 237, 244

"In the Garden" (Richardson), **Supp. XIII:** 190

"In the Garden at Swainston" (Tennyson), **IV:** 336

"In the Great Metropolis" (Clough), **V:** 164

In the Green Tree (Lewis), **VII:** 447

"In the Grip of Light" (Larkin), **Retro. Supp. III:** 203, 204

In the Heart of the Country (Coetzee), **Supp. VI:** 76, **80–81**

"In the House of Suddhoo" (Kipling), **VI:** 170

In the Key of Blue and Other Prose Essays (Ellis and Symonds), **Supp. XIV:** 262

"In the Kibble Palace" (Conn), **Supp. XIII:** 74, 75

In the Kibble Palace: New and Selected Poems (Conn), **Supp. XIII:** 71, 75

In the Labyrinth (Robbe–Grillet), **Supp. IV:** 116

In the Meantime (Jennings), **Supp. V:** 219

In the Night (Kelman), **Supp. V:** 256

"In the Night" (Jennings), **Supp. V:** 211–212

"In the Night" (Kincaid), **Supp. VII:** 220

"In the Nursery" (Stevenson), **Supp. VI:** 264

In the Permanent Way (Steel), **Supp. XII:** 269

In the Pink (Blackwood), **Supp. IX:** 14–15

"In the Pullman" (Kay), **Supp. XIII:** 104

In the Red Kitchen (Roberts), **Supp. XV:** 259, 268, 269, 271

"In the Ringwood" (Kinsella), **Supp. V:** 260

"In the rude age when science was not so rife" (Surrey), **I:** 115–116

"In the Same Boat" (Kipling), **VI:** 193

In the Scales of Fate (Pietrkiewicz), **Supp. IV:** 98

In the Seven Woods (Yeats), **VI:** 213, 222

In the Shadow of the Glen (Synge), **Retro. Supp. I:** 295–296

"In the Snack–bar" (Morgan, E.), **Supp. IX:**158

In the South Seas (Stevenson), **V:** 396

In the Springtime of the Year (Hill), **Supp. XIV:** 117, 123–124

In the Stopping Train (Davie), **Supp. VI:** 112

"In the Stopping Train" (Davie), **Supp. VI:** 112

In the Thirties (Upward), **Supp. XIII:** 250, 255–257

"In the thistledown fall" (Thomas), **Retro. Supp. III:** 347

In the Time of Tyrants (Soutar), **Supp. XVI:** 253, 254

"In the Time of Tyrants" (Soutar), **Supp. XVI:** 254

"In the Tool Shed" (Greig), **Supp. XVI:** 162

"In the Train" (O'Connor), **Supp. XIV:** 225, 226

In the Trojan Ditch: Collected Poems and Selected Translations (Sisson), **Supp. XI:** 243, 248, 250, 252, 253, 256–257
In the Twilight (Swinburne), **V:** 333
"In the Vermilion Cathedral" (Redgrove), **Supp. VI:** 234
"In the White Giants Thigh" (Thomas), **Retro. Supp. III:** 347
In the Year of Jubilee (Gissing), **V:** 437
"In This Time" (Jennings), **Supp. V:** 214
"In Time of Absence" (Graves), **VII:** 270
"In Time of 'The Breaking of Nations'" (Hardy), **Retro. Supp. I:** 120
"In Time of Tumult" (Soutar), **Supp. XVI:** 254
"In Time of War" (Auden), **Retro. Supp. I:** 9
"In Times of War" (Delanty), **Supp. XIV:** 77
"In to thir dirk and drublie days" (Dunbar), **VIII:** 121
In Touch with the Infinite (Betjeman), **VII:** 365
In Trouble Again: A Journey Between the Orinoco and the Amazon (O'Hanlon), **Supp. XI:** 196, 199–202, 207
"In Trust" (Gunn), **Retro. Supp. III:** 129
In Which We Serve (Coward), **Supp. II:** 154
In Wicklow, West Kerry, and Connemara (Synge), **VI:** 309, 317
"In Youth" (Smith, I. C.), **Supp. IX:** 214
In Youth is Pleasure (Welch), **Supp. IX:** 261, 263, 264–266
Inadmissible Evidence (Osborne), **Supp. I:** 330, 333, 336–337
"Inarticulates" (MacCaig), **Supp. VI:** 191
Inca of Perusalem, The (Shaw), **VI:** 120
"Incandescence" (Boyd), **Supp. XVI:** 44
"Incantation in Time of Peace" (Montague), **Supp. XV:** 214
"Incarnate One, The" (Muir), **Supp. VI:** 208
"Incantata" (Muldoon), **Supp. IV:** 428–429, 430, 431–432
"Incendiary Method, The" (Murray), **Supp. VII:** 273
Inchbald, Elizabeth, **Supp. XV: 147–163**
"Inchcape Rock, The" (Southey), **IV:** 58
"Incident" (Smith, I. C.), **Supp. IX:** 217
Incident Book, The (Adcock), **Supp. XII:** 3, 8–9
"Incident in Hyde Park, 1803" (Blunden), **Supp. XI:** 46
"Incident in the Life of Mr. George Crookhill" (Hardy), **VI:** 22
"Incident on a Journey" (Gunn), **Supp. IV:** 256, 258–259; **Retro. Supp. III:** 118
"Incident Room" (Scupham), **Supp. XIII:** 222
Incidents at the Shrine (Okri), **Supp. V:** 347, 348, 352, 355–356
"Incidents at the Shrine" (Okri), **Supp. V:** 356–357
Incidents in the Rue Laugier (Brookner), **Supp. IV:** 135–136
Inclinations (Firbank), **Supp. II:** 201, 202, 209–211
Inclinations (Sackville-West), **VII:** 70

Incline Our Hearts (Wilson), **Supp. VI:** 307
Incognita; or, Love and Duty Reconcil'd (Congreve), **II:** 338, 346
Inconstant, The; or, The Way to Win Him (Farquhar), **II:** 352–353, 357, 362, 364
Incredulity of Father Brown, The (Chesterton), **VI:** 338
"Incubus, or the Impossibility of Self-Determination as to Desire (Self), **Supp. V:** 402
"Indaba Without Fear" (Paton), **Supp. II:** 360
"Indefinite Exposure" (Gunesekera), **Supp. X:** 86
"Independence" (Motion), **Supp. VII:** 255
Independent Labour Party, **VII:** 280
Independent Review (periodical), **VI:** 399
Independent Theatre Society, **VI:** 104
Index to AIn Memoriam,"An (ed. Carroll), **V:** 274
Index to the Private Papers of James Boswell . . . (ed. Pottle et al.), **III:** 249
India (Steel), **Supp. XII:** 274
India: A Wounded Civilization (Naipaul), **Supp. I:** 385, 399, 401
"India, the Wisdom–Land" (Carpenter), **Supp. XIII:** 39
India Through the Ages: A Popular and Picturesque History of Hindustan (Steel), **Supp. XII:** 274
Indian Education Minutes . . . , The (Macaulay), **IV:** 291
Indian Emperor, The (Dryden), **Retro. Supp. III:** 60
Indian Emperour, The; or, The Conquest of Mexico . . . , Being the Sequel to the Indian Queen (Dryden), **II:** 290, 294, 305
"Indian Fiction Today" (Desai), **Supp. V:** 67
Indian Ink (Stoppard), **Retro. Supp. II:** 356–357
Indian Journal (Lear), see *Edward Lear's Indian Journal*
Indian Queen, The (Dryden), **II:** 305; **Retro. Supp. III:** 60
"Indian Serenade, The" (Shelley), **IV:** 195, 203
"Indian Summer of a Forsyte" (Galsworthy), **VI:** 274, 276, 283
"Indian Summer, Vermont" (Stevenson), **Supp. VI:** 255
"Indian Tree" (Gunesekera), **Supp. X:** 87
"Indifferent, The" (Donne), **Retro. Supp. II:** 89
Indiscretion in the Life of an Heiress, An (Hardy), **VI:** 20
"Induction" (Clarke), **Supp. XV:** 19
Induction, The (Field), **II:** 66
"Induction" (Sackville), **I:** 169
Inebriety (Crabbe), **III:** 274, 278–279, 286
"Inequity of the Fathers upon the Children, The" (Rossetti), **Retro. Supp. III:** 251
"Infancy" (Crabbe), **III:** 273, 281
"Infant-Ey, An" (Traherne), **Supp. XI:** 266, 267

"Inferior Religions" (Lewis), **VII:** 77
Infernal Desire Machine of Dr. Hoffman, The (Carter), **III:** 345; **Supp. III:** 84–85, 89
Infernal Marriage, The (Disraeli), **IV:** 297, 299, 308
Infernal World of Branwell Brontë, The (Carter), **Supp. III:** 139
Inferno (Dante), **Retro. Supp. II:** 36
Inferno (tr. Carson), **Supp. XIII:** 66
Infidel, The (Braddon), **VIII:** 49
Infinite Rehearsal, The (Harris), **Supp. V:** 140, 141–142, 144
Information, The (Amis), **Supp. IV:** 26, 37–39, 42
"Informer, The" (Conrad), **VI:** 148
Infuence of the Roman Censorship on the Morals of the People, The (Swinburne), **V:** 333
Ingannati: The Deceived . . . and Aelia Laelia Crispis (Peacock), **IV:** 170
Inge, William Ralph, **VI:** 344
Ingelow, Jean, **Supp. IV:** 256
Ingenious Pain (Miller), **Supp. XIV:** 179, 180, 181–184, 185, 186, 189, 190, 191
"Ingram Lake, or, Five Acts on the House" (Morgan, E.), **Supp. IX:** 161, 163
Ingrowing Thoughts (Thomas), **Supp. XII:** 288
"Inheritance" (Butlin), **Supp. XVI:** 57
"Inheritance" (Conn), **Supp. XIII:** 78
"Inheritance" (Murphy), **Supp. V:** 322
Inheritance of Loss, The (Desai), **Supp. XV:** 83–84, 85, 88–96
"Inherited Estate, The" (Gunn), **Retro. Supp. III:** 120
"Inheritors, The" (Conn), **Supp. XIII:** 80
Inheritors, The (Golding), **Supp. I:** 67, **70–72**, 75, 84; **Retro. Supp. I:** 96–97
Inheritors, The: An Extravagant Story (Conrad and Ford), **VI:** 146, 148, 321, 332
Inishfallen, Fare Thee Well (O'Casey), **VII:** 4, 12
Injur'd Husband, The; or, The Mistaken Resentment, **Supp. XII:** 140
Injur'd Husband, The; or, The Mistaken Resentment, and Lasselia; or, The Self-Abandoned (Haywood), **Supp. XII:** 137
Injury Time (Bainbridge), **Supp. VI:** 21
"Inland" (Motion), **Supp. VII:** 254, 255
Inland Voyage, An (Stevenson), **V:** 386, 395; **Retro. Supp. I:** 261
Inn Album, The (Browning), **IV:** 358, 367, 369–370, 374; **Retro. Supp. II:** 30; **Retro. Supp. III:** 31
"Inn of the Two Witches, The" (Conrad), **VI:** 148
Inner and Outer Ireland, The (Russell), **VIII:** 289
Inner Harbour, The (Adcock), **Supp. XII:** 6–8
"Inniskeen Road: July Evening" (Kavanagh), **Supp. VII:** 188
Innocence (Fitzgerald), **Supp. V:** 100, 104–106
"Innocence" (Gunn), **Supp. IV:** 262; **Retro. Supp. III:** 121, 126, 127

"Innocence" (Traherne), **Supp. XI:** 266
Innocence of Father Brown, The (Chesterton), **VI:** 338
Innocent, The (McEwan), **Supp. IV:** 390, 399, 402–404, 405, 406
Innocent and the Guilty, The (Warner), **Supp. VII:** 381
Innocent Birds (Powys), **VIII:** 251, 256, 258
Innocent Blood (James), **Supp. IV:** 337–338, 340
"Innocents, The" (Abercrombie), **Supp. XVI:** 9
"Innumerable Christ, The" (MacDiarmid), **Supp. XII:** 205
Inquiry into the Nature & Causes of the Wealth of Nations (Smith), **IV:** xiv, 145
Insatiate Countess, The (Barsted and Marston), **II:** 31, 40
"Inscribed to Maria, My Beloved Daughter" (Robinson), **Supp. XIII:** 199
"Insect World, The" (Rhys), **Supp. II:** 402
"Insensibility" (Owen), **VI:** 453, 455
"Inside" (Burnside), **Supp. XIII:** 14
Inside a Pyramid (Golding), **Supp. I:** 82
Inside Mr Enderby (Burgess), **Supp. I:** 185, 186, 189, 194
Inside the Whale (Orwell), **VII:** 282
"Inside the Whale" (Orwell), **Supp. IV:** 110, 455
Insight and Outlook: An Enquiry into the Common Foundations of Science, Art and Social Ethics (Koestler), **Supp. I:** 37
"Insight at Flame Lake" (Amis), **Supp. IV:** 40
"Insomnia" (Hart), **Supp. XI:** 125
"Installation Ode" (Gray), **III:** 142
Instamatic Poems (Morgan, E.), **Supp. IX:** 162–163
"Instance, An" (Reid), **Supp. VII:** 328
"Instant, The" (Redgrove), **Supp. VI:** 231
Instant in the Wind, An (Brink), **Supp. VI:** 49
"Instead of an Interview" (Adcock), **Supp. XII:** 8
Instead of Trees (Priestley), **VII:** 209–210
Institution de la religion chrestienne (tr. Elizabeth I), **Supp. XVI:** 156
"Instruction, The" (Traherne), **Supp. XI:** 268
Instructions Concerning Erecting of a Liberty (tr. Evelyn), **II:** 287
Instructions for the Ignorant (Bunyan), **II:** 253
"Instructions to a Painter . . . A (Waller), **II:** 233
"Instructions to an Actor" (Morgan, E.), **Supp. IX:** 164
Instrument of Thy Peace (Paton), **Supp. II:** 358–359
Insular Celts, The (Carson), **Supp. XIII:** 55
Inteendeel (Brink), **Supp. VI:** 56
"Intellectual Felicity" (Boswell), **III:** 237
Intelligence (journal), **III:** 35

Intelligent Woman's Guide to Socialism and Capitalism, The (Shaw), **VI:** 116, 125
"Intensive Care Unit, The" (Ballard), **Supp. V:** 28
Intentions (Wilde), **V:** 407, 419; **Retro. Supp. II:** 367–368
Intercom Conspiracy, The (Ambler), **Supp. IV:** 4, 16, 18, 20–21
"Intercom Quartet, The" (Brooke–Rose)), **Supp. IV:** 110–113
"Interference" (Barnes), **Supp. IV:** 75
Interim (Richardson), **Supp. XIII:** 184, 189–190
"Interior Mountaineer" (Redgrove), **Supp. VI:** 236
"Interior with Weaver" (Carson), **Supp. XIII:** 56
"Interloper, The" (Hardy), **VI:** 17
"Interlopers at the Knapp" (Hardy), **VI:** 22
"Interlude, An" (Swinburne), **V:** 321
Interludes and Poems (Abercrombie), **Supp. XVI:** 1–2
"Intermediate as Warrior, The" (Carpenter), **Supp. XIII:** 44
"Intermediate in the Service of Religion, The" (Carpenter), **Supp. XIII:** 44
Intermediate Sex, The (Carpenter), **Supp. XIII:** 41, 43–44
"Intermediate Sex, The" (Carpenter), **VI:** 407; **Supp. XIII:** 41, 43
Intermediate Types Among Primitive Folk (Carpenter), **Supp. XIII:** 41, 44
"Intermezzo" (Kinsella), **Supp. V:** 271
"International Episode, An" (James), **VI:** 69
International Guerrillas (film), **Supp. IV:** 438
internationalism, **VI:** 241n; **VII:** 229
Interpretation in Teaching (Richards), **Supp. II:** 423, 430
Interpretation of Genesis, An (Powys), **VIII:** 246–247
Interpreters, The (Russell), **VIII:** 289, 290, 292
"Interrogator, The" (Jennings), **Supp. V:** 215
"Interruption" (Gunn), **Supp. IV:** 273, 274
"Interval, The" (Reed), **Supp. XV:** 255
"Interview" (Dutton), **Supp. XII:** 87, 95
"Interview, The" (Blackwood), **Supp. IX:** 9
"Interview" (Nye), **Supp. X:** 201
Interview, The (Sillitoe), **Supp. V:** 411
"Interview with a Woman Doing the Worst Paid Convict Work" (Mayhew), **Supp. XVI:** 216
Intimacy (Kureishi), **Supp. XI:** 157, 158
"Intimacy" (Montague), **Supp. XV:** 218
Intimate Exchanges (Ayckbourn), **Supp. V:** 3, 6, 12, 14
"Intimate Supper" (Redgrove), **Supp. VI:** 234
"Intimate World of Ivy Compton–Burnett, The" (Karl), **VII:** 70
"Intimations of Immortality . . . A (Wordsworth), *see* AOde. Intimations of Immortality from Recollections of Early Childhood"
Into a Room: Poems of William Soutar (Soutar), **Supp. XVI:** 256–257
"Into Arcadia" (Heaney), **Retro. Supp. I:** 134
Into Battle (Churchill), **VI:** 356
"Into Battle" (Grenfell), **VI:** 418
"Into her Lying Down Head" (Thomas), **Supp. I:** 178
Into the Heart of Borneo: An Account of a Journey Made in 1983 to the Mountains of Batu Tiban with James Fenton (O'Hanlon), **Supp. XI:** 196–199, 202, 206, 207–208
Into Their Labours (Berger), **Supp. IV:** 80, 90–95
Intriguing Chambermaid, The (Fielding), **III:** 105
"Introduction" (Blake), **Retro. Supp. I:** 37
Introduction 7: Stories by New Writers (Faber & Faber), **Supp. IV:** 303
Introduction to the History of Great Britain and Ireland, An (Macpherson), **VIII:** 192
Introduction to the Metaphysical Poets, An (Beer), **Supp. XIV:** 8, 9
Introduction to the Study of Browning, An (Symons), **Supp. XIV:** 267
Introduction to the Study of Dante, An (Symonds), **Supp. XIV:** 251
Introductory Lecture (Housman), **VI:** 164
"Introductory Rhymes" (Yeats), **Retro. Supp. I:** 330
Intruder, The (Hardy), **VI:** 20
"Invader, The" (Cameron), **Supp. IX:** 26, 27
Invaders, The (Plomer), **Supp. XI:** 219–221
Invasion of the Space Invaders (Amis), **Supp. V:** 42
Invective against Jonson, The (Chapman), **I:** 243
Invention of Love, The (Stoppard), **Retro. Supp. II:** 357–358
"Inversion Layer: Oxfordshire" (Wallace–Crabbe), **VIII:** 323
Inversions (Banks), **Supp. XI:** 5, 10, 13
"Inversnaid" (Hopkins), **V:** 368, 372
"Investigation After Midnight" (Upward), **Supp. XIII:** 262
Invincibles, The (O'Connor), **Supp. XIV:** 223
Invisible Friends (Ayckbourn), **Supp. V:** 3, 12, 14–15
Invisible Man, The: A Grotesque Romance (Wells), **VI:** 226, 232–233, 244
Invisible Writing, The (Koestler), **Supp. I:** 22, 23, 24, 32, 37
"Invitation, An" (Mangan), **Supp. XIII:** 127
"Invitation, The" (Shelley), **IV:** 196
"Invocation" (Hope), **Supp. VII:** 154
"Invocation" (Sitwell), **VII:** 136
"Inward Bound" (MacCaig), **Supp. VI:** 192
Inward Eye, The (MacCaig), **Supp. VI:** 184–185
"Io" (Carson), **Supp. XIII:** 63
"Iolaire" (Smith, I. C.), **Supp. IX:** 219

Ioläus: An Anthology of Friendship (Carpenter), **Supp. XIII:** 37, 44–45
Ion (Plato), **IV:** 48
Ionian Mission, The (O'Brian), **Supp. XII:** 256, 259–260
"Iowa" (Davie), **Supp. VI:** 110
Iphigenia (Peele), **I:** 198
"Iphis and Araxarathen" (Gower), **I:** 53–54
Iqbal, Muhammad, **Supp. IV:** 448
"Ireland" (Swift), **III:** 31
Ireland and the Empire at the Court of Conscience (Russell), **VIII:** 289, 292
Ireland, Past and Future (Russell), **VIII:** 289
Ireland Since the Rising (Coogan), **VII:** 9
Ireland, Your Only Place (Morris, J.), **Supp. X:** 177
Ireland's Abbey Theatre (Robinson), **VI:** 317
Ireland's Literary Renaissance (Boyd), **VI:** 316
Irene: A Tragedy (Fielding), **III:** 109, 121
Irene: A Tragedy (Johnson), **Retro. Supp. I:** 138–139
Irigaray, Luce, **Supp. IV:** 232
"Irish Airman Foresees His Death, An" (Yeats), **Retro. Supp. I:** 331
"Irish Channel" (O'Connor), **Supp. XIV:** 222
"Irish Child in England" (Boland), **Supp. V:** 35
Irish Drama, The (Malone), **VI:** 316
Irish Dramatic Movement, The (Ellis-Fermor), **VI:** 317
Irish dramatic revival, **VI:** xiv, 207, 218, 307–310; **VII:** 3
Irish Essays and Others (Arnold), **V:** 216
Irish Faust, An (Durrell), **Supp. I:** 126, 127
Irish Faustus, An (Durrell), **Retro. Supp. III:** 85
Irish for No, The (Carson), **Supp. XIII:** 53, 54, 55, 57–59
Irish Homestead, **Retro. Supp. III:** 167–168
Irish Impressions (Chesterton), **VI:** 345
Irish Miles (O'Connor), **Supp. XIV:** 218
Irish Penny Journal, **Supp. XIII:** 126
"Irish Revel" (O'Brien), **Supp. V:** 340
Irish Sketch Book, The (Thackeray), **V:** 25, 38
Irishman, **Supp. XIII:** 114, 119
Iron, Ralph (pseud., Schreiner), **Supp. II:** 448–449
"Iron Landscapes" (Gunn), **Retro. Supp. III:** 124
Iron Man, The (Hughes), **Supp. I:** 346
Ironhand (Arden), **Supp. II:** 29
Irrational Knot, The (Shaw), **VI:** 102, 103, 105, 129
Irving, Washington, **III:** 54
Is He Popenjoy? (Trollope), **V:** 100, 102
"Is Nothing Sacred?" (Rushdie), **Supp. IV:** 437, 442–443
Is That All There Is? (Boyd), **Supp. XVI:** 32
Is There a Church of England? (Sisson), **Supp. XI:** 251

Isabel Clarendon (Gissing), **V:** 437
"Isabella" (Keats), **IV:** xviii, 216, 217–218, 235; **Retro. Supp. I:** 193–194
"Isba Song" (McGuckian), **Supp. V:** 283
"Ischia" (Auden), **Retro. Supp. I:** 12
Isenheim Altar (Grünewald), **Supp. IV:** 85
"Iseult Blaunchesmains" (Reed), **Supp. XV:** 248
Isherwood, Christopher, **VII:** xx, **309–320; Supp. II:** 408, 485, 486; **Retro. Supp. I:** 3, 7, 9
Ishiguro, Kazuo, **Supp. IV:** 75, **301–317; Retro. Supp. III:** 149–163
Ishmael (Braddon), **VIII:** 49
"Ishmael" (Reed), **Supp. XV:** 254
Island, The (Byron), **IV:** xviii 173, 193
"Island, The" (Caudwell), **Supp. IX:** 37
Island, The (Fugard), **Supp. XV:** 100, 103, 109
Island (Huxley), **VII:** xviii, 206
"Island, The" (Jennings), **Supp. V:** 209
"Island, The" (Thomas), **Supp. XII:** 288
Island in the Moon, An (Blake), **III:** 290, 292; **Retro. Supp. I:** 34
Island in the Sun (Waugh), **Supp. VI:** 267, 274, **275**
Island Nights' Entertainments (Stevenson), **V:** 387, 396
Island of Dr. Moreau, The (Wells), **VI:** 230–231
Island of Goats (Reed), **Supp. XV:** 253
Island of Statues, The (Yeats), **Retro. Supp. I:** 325
Island of Terrible Friends (Strutton), **Supp. IV:** 346
Island of the Mighty, The (Arden and D'Arcy), **Supp. II:** 30, **32–35,** 39
Island Pharisees, The (Galsworthy), **VI:** 271, 273, 274, 277, 281
Island Princess, The (Fletcher), **II:** 45, 60, 65
"Islanders, The" (Kipling), **VI:** 169, 203
Islands (Brathwaite), **Supp. XII:** 33, 38, 39–40, 45
Isle of Dogs, The (Jonson/Nashe), **Retro. Supp. I:** 156
Isle of Man, The (Bernard), **II:** 246
"Isle of Voices, The" (Stevenson), **V:** 396
Íslendinga sögur (Ari), **VIII:** 235, 236
"Isobel" (Golding), **Supp. I:** 66
"Isobel's Child" (Browning), **IV:** 313
"Isopes Fabules" (Lydgate), **I:** 57
Israel: Poems on a Hebrew Theme (Sillitoe), **Supp. V:** 411
Israel's Hope Encouraged (Bunyan), **II:** 253
"It Happened in 1936" (Waugh), **Supp. VI:** 273
"It is a beauteous evening, calm and free" (Wordsworth), **IV:** 22
"It May Never Happen" (Pritchett), **Supp. III:** 315
It May Never Happen and Other Stories (Pritchett), **Supp. III: 318–319**
It Was a Lover and His Lass (Oliphant), **Supp. X:** 220
"It Was Upon a Lammas Night" (Burns), **III:** 315

It's a Battlefield (Greene), **Supp. I:** 2, 5–6; **Retro. Supp. II:** 152–153
"It's a Long, Long Way" (Thomas), **Supp. III:** 404
"It's a Woman's World" (Boland), **Supp. V:** 41
It's an Old Country (Priestley), **VII:** 211
"It's Hopeless" (MacCaig), **Supp. VI:** 191
It's Me O Lord! (Coppard), **VIII:** 85, 86, 88, 90
"It's No Pain" (Redgrove), **Supp. VI:** 234
Italian, The (Radcliffe), **III:** 331–332, 335, 337, 345; **IV:** 173; **Supp. III:** 384; **Retro. Supp. III:** 234, 245–247
Italian Byways (Symonds), **Supp. XIV:** 251
Italian Hours (James), **VI:** 43, 67
"Italian in England, The" (Browning), **Retro. Supp. III:** 22
Italian Letters; or, The History of the Count de St. Julien (Godwin), **Supp. XV:** 119
Italian Mother, The, and Other Poems (Swinburne), **V:** 333
Italian Visit, An (Day Lewis), **Supp. III:** 118, 122, 129
"Italian Whirligig" (Coppard), **VIII:** 95
Italics of Walter Savage Landor, The (Landor), **IV:** 100
"Italio, Io Ti Saluto" (Rossetti), **V:** 250
"Italy and the World" (Browning), **IV:** 318
"Itinerary of Ua Clerigh, The" (Clarke), **Supp. XV:** 19
"It's Done This!" (Adcock), **Supp. XII:** 13
"Itylus" (Swinburne), **V:** 319
Ivanhoe (Scott), **IV:** xviii, 31, 34, 39
"I've Thirty Months" (Synge), **VI:** 314
Ivory Door, The (Milne), **Supp. V:** 300–301
Ivory Gate, The (Beddoes), **Supp. XI:** 29
Ivory Tower, The (James), **VI:** 64, 65
"Ivry: A Song of the Huguenots" (Macaulay), **IV:** 283, 291
Ivy Compton-Burnett (Iprigg), **VII:** 70
"Ivy Day in the Committee Room" (Joyce), **VII:** 44, 45; **Retro. Supp. III:** 169
Ivy Gripped the Steps (Bowen), *see Demon Lover, The*
Ixion in Heaven (Disraeli), **IV:** 297, 299, 308

J. *B. Priestley, The Dramatist* (Lloyd-Evans), **VII:** 223, 231
"J Car, The" (Gunn), **Retro. Supp. III:** 127
J. M. Synge and the Irish Dramatic Movement (Bickley), **VI:** 317
"J. W. 51B A Convoy" (Ross), **VII:** 434
"Jabberwocky" (Carroll), **V:** 265
"Jacinth" (Carson), **Supp. XIII:** 63
Jack, Ian Robert James, **II:** 298; **III:** 125n; **IV:** xi, xxv, 40, 140, 236, 373, 375
Jack Drum's Entertainment (Marston), **II:** 27, 40

JACK–JOHA

Jack Flea's Birthday Celebration (McEwan), **Supp. IV:** 390, 398
Jack Maggs (Carey), **Supp. XII:** 49, 54, 60–61
Jack Straw (Maugham), **VI:** 368
Jack Straw's Castle (Gunn), **Supp. IV:** 257, 268–271; **Retro. Supp. III:** 116, 119, 123–124, 125
"Jack Straw's Castle" (Gunn), **Supp. IV:** 270; **Retro. Supp. III:** 123, 124, 125
Jackdaw, The (Gregory), **VI:** 315
Jacko: The Great Intruder (Keneally), **Supp. IV:** 347
Jackson, T. A., **V:** 51
Jacob, Giles, **II:** 348
Jacob's Room (Woolf), **VII:** 18, 20, 26–27, 38; **Retro. Supp. I:** 307, 316
Jacobite's Journal, The (Fielding), **III:** 105; **Retro. Supp. I:** 81
Jacques–Louis David: A Personal Interpretation (Brookner), **Supp. IV:** 122
Jacta Alea Est (Wilde), **V:** 400
"Jacta est alea" (Carson), **Supp. XIII:** 60
Jaggard, William, **I:** 307
"Jaguar, The" (Hughes), **Retro. Supp. II:** 203
Jaguar Smile: A Nicaraguan Journey, The (Rushdie), **Supp. IV:** 436, 454
Jake's Thing (Amis), **Supp. II:** 16–17; **Supp. IV:** 29
Jakobson, Roman, **Supp. IV:** 115
"Jam Tart" (Auden), **Retro. Supp. I:** 6
Jamaica Inn (du Maurier), **Supp. III:** 139, 144, 145, 147
James, Henry, **II:** 42; **III:** 334, 340, 345; **IV:** 35, 107, 319, 323, 369, 371, 372; **V:** x, xx, xiv–xxvi, 2, 48, 51, 70, 95, 97, 98, 102, 191, 199, 205, 210, 295, 384, 390–392; **VI:** x–xi, 5, 23–69, 227, 236, 239, 266, 320, 322; list of short stories and novellas, **VI:** 69; **Supp. II:** 80–81, 89, 487–488, 492; **Supp. III:** 47–48, 60, 217, 437; **Supp. IV:** 97, 116, 133, 153, 233, 243, 371, 503, 511
James, M. R., **III:** 340
James, P. D., **Supp. II:** 127; **Supp. IV:** **319–341**
James, Richard, **II:** 102
James, William, **V:** xxv, 272; **VI:** 24
James IV (Greene), **VIII:** 142
James and the Giant Peach (Dahl), **Supp. IV:** 202, 213, 222
James and the Giant Peach (film), **Supp. IV:** 203
James Hogg: Selected Poems (ed. Mack), **Supp. X:** 108–109
James Hogg: Selected Poems and Songs (ed. Groves), **Supp. X:** 110
James Hogg: Selected Stories and Sketches (ed. Mack), **Supp. X:** 110–111
"James Honeyman" (Auden), **Retro. Supp. I:** 8
James Joyce and the Making of AUlysses" (Budgen) **VII:** 56
"James Lee's Wife" (Browning), **IV:** 367, 369; **Retro. Supp. III:** 26
James Rigg, Still Further Extract from The Recluse, A Poem (Hogg), **Supp. X:** 109–110
James Russell Lowell: His Message and How It Helped Me (Stead), **Supp. XIII:** 234
Jamie, Kathleen, **Supp. XIV: 129–147**
Jamie on a Flying Visit (Frayn), **Supp. VII:** 56–57
Jane and Prudence (Pym), **Supp. II:** **370–372**
"Jane Austen at the Window" (Beer), **Supp. XIV:** 4
Jane Austen: The Critical Heritage (ed. Southam), **IV:** 122, 124
Jane Austen's Literary Manuscripts (ed. Southam), **IV:** 124
Jane Eyre (Brontë), **III:** 338, 344, 345; **V:** xx, 106, 108, 112, 124, 135, **137–140**, 145, 147, 148, 152; **VII:** 101; **Supp. III:** 146; **Supp. IV:** 236, 452, 471; **Retro. Supp. I:** 50, 52, 53–55, 56, 58–60
"Janeites, The" (Kipling), **IV:** 106
"Jane's Marriage" (Kipling), **IV:** 106, 109
Janet (Oliphant), **Supp. X:** 219
"Janet's Repentance" (Eliot), **V:** 190–191; **Retro. Supp. II:** 104
Janowitz, Haas, **III:** 342
"January 1795" (Robinson), **Supp. XIII:** 208
"January 10th, 1990" (Scupham), **Supp. XIII:** 227
"January 12, 1996" (Longley), **VIII:** 177
Janus: A Summing Up (Koestler), **Supp. I:** 35, 37, 38–39
Japp, A. H., **IV:** 144*n*, 155
Jarrell, Randall, **VI:** 165, 194, 200; **Supp. IV:** 460
"Jars, The" (Brown), **Supp. VI:** 71–72
"Jasmine" (Naipaul), **Supp. I:** 383
"Jason and Medea" (Gower), **I:** 54, 56
Jasper (Robinson), **Supp. XIII:** 213
"Jasper" (Robinson), **Supp. XIII:** 210
"Jawbone Walk" (Conn), **Supp. XIII:** 78
"Jazz and the West Indian Novel" (Brathwaite), **Supp. XII:** 43–44
"Je est un autre" (Durrell), **Supp. I:** 126
"Je ne parle pas Français" (Mansfield), **VII:** 174, 177
"Je ne regrettais rien" (Morgan, E.), **Supp. IX:** 165
"Je t'adore" (Kinsella), **Supp. V:** 263
"Jealousy" (Brooke), **Supp. III:** 52
Jeames's Diary; or, Sudden Wealth (Thackeray), **V:** 38
Jean de Meung, **I:** 49
Jeeves (Ayckbourn and Webber), **Supp. V:** 3
"Jeeves and the Hard–Boiled Egg" (Wodehouse), **Supp. III:** 455, 458
Jeeves and the Tie That Binds (Wodehouse), *see Much Obliged*
"Jeeves Takes Charge" (Wodehouse), **Supp. III:** 456, 457–458
Jeffares, Alexander Norman, **VI:** xxxiii–xxxiv, 98, 221
Jefferies, Richard, **Supp. XV: 165–179**
Jefferson, D. W., **III:** 182, 183
Jeffrey, Francis, **III:** 276, 285; **IV:** 31, 39, 60, 72, 129, 269
Jeffrey, Sara, **IV:** 225

Jeffrey Bernard is Unwell (Waterhouse), **Supp. XIII:** 275, 276–278
Jenkin, Fleeming, **V:** 386
Jenkyn, D., **Supp. IV:** 346
Jennings, Elizabeth, **Supp. IV:** 256; **Supp. V: 205–221**
"Jenny" (Rossetti), **V:** 240
Jenyns, Soame, **Retro. Supp. I:** 148
Jerrold, Douglas, **V:** 19
Jerrold, W. C., **IV:** 252, 254, 267
"Jersey Villas" (James), **III:** 69
Jerusalem (Blake), **III:** 303, 304–305, 307; **V:** xvi, 330; **Retro. Supp. I:** 45–46
Jerusalem: Its History and Hope (Oliphant), **Supp. X:** 222
Jerusalem Sinner Saved (Bunyan), see *Good News for the Vilest of Men*
Jerusalem the Golden (Drabble), **Supp. IV:** 230, 231, 238–239, 241, 243, 248, 251
Jesus (Wilson), **Supp. VI:** 306
Jess (Haggard), **Supp. III:** 213
Jesting Pilate (Huxley), **VII:** 201
Jew of Malta, The (Marlowe), **I:** 212, 280, **282–285**, 310; **Retro. Supp. I:** 208–209
Jew Süss (Feuchtwanger), **VI:** 265
Jewel in the Crown, The (Scott), **Supp. I:** 266–267, 269–270
Jeweller of Amsterdam, The (Field, Fletcher, Massinger), **II:** 67
Jewels of Song (Davies), **Supp. XI:** 93
"Jews, The" (Vaughan), **II:** 189
Jews in Germany (tr. Richardson), **Supp. XIII:** 191
Jewsbury, Maria Jane, **Supp. XIV: 149–164**
Jezebel Mort and Other Poems (Symons), **Supp. XIV:** 281
Jhabvala, Ruth Prawer, **Supp. V: 223–239**
Jill (Larkin), **Supp. I:** 276, 286–287; **Retro. Supp. III:** 201, 203, 210
Jill Somerset (Waugh), **Supp. VI:** 273
"Jimmy" (Constantine), **Supp. XV:** 70
Jimmy Governor (Clune), **Supp. IV:** 350
Jitta's Atonement (Shaw), **VI:** 129
Jizzen (Jamie), **Supp. XIV:** 129, 140–142
"Joachim du Bellay" (Pater), **V:** 344
Joan and Peter (Wells), **VI:** 240
Joan of Arc (Southey), **IV:** 59, 60, 63–64, 71
Joannis Miltonii Pro se defensio . . . (Milton), **II:** 176
Job (biblical book), **III:** 307
Jocasta (Gascoigne), **I:** 215–216
Jocelyn (Galsworthy), **VI:** 277
"Jochanan Hakkadosh" (Browning), **IV:** 365
Jocoseria (Browning), **IV:** 359, 374; **Retro. Supp. III:** 30
"Joe Soap" (Motion), **Supp. VII:** 260–261, 262
Joe's Ark (Potter, D.), **Supp. X:** 229, 237–240
"Johann Joachim Quantz's Five Lessons" (Graham), **Supp. VII:** 116
"Johannes Agricola in Meditation" (Browning), **IV:** 360; **Retro. Supp.**

III: 20, 21, 22
Johannes Secundus, II: 108
John Austen and the Inseparables (Richardson), **Supp. XIII:** 191
"John Betjeman's Brighton" (Ewart), **Supp. VII:** 37
John Bull in His Senses (Arbuthnot), **Supp. XVI:** 21
John Bull's Other Island (Shaw), **VI:** 112, **113–115**; **Retro. Supp. II:** 320–321
John Bull Still in His Senses (Arbuthnot), **Supp. XVI:** 21–22
John Caldigate (Trollope), **V:** 102
"John Clare" (Cope), **VIII:** 82
John Clare: Poems, Chiefly from Manuscript (Clare), **Supp. XI:** 36, 63
John Clare by Himself (Clare), **Supp. XI:** 51
"John Fletcher" (Swinburne), **V:** 332
John Gabriel Borkman (Ibsen), **VI:** 110
"John Galsworthy" (Lawrence), **VI:** 275–276, 290
John Galsworthy (Mottram), **VI:** 271, 275, 290
"John Galsworthy, An Appreciation" (Conrad), **VI:** 290
"John Gilpin" (Cowper), **III:** 212, 220; **Retro. Supp. III:** 41
John Keats: A Reassessment (ed. Muir), **IV:** 219, 227, 236
John Keats: His Like and Writings (Bush), **IV:** 224, 236
John Knox (Muir), **Supp. VI:** 198
"John Knox" (Smith, I. C.), **Supp. IX:** 211–212
"John Logie Baird" (Crawford), **Supp. XI:** 71
John M. Synge (Masefield), **VI:** 317
John Marchmont's Legacy (Braddon), **VIII:** 44, 46
"John Milton and My Father" (Beer), **Supp. XIV:** 4
"John Norton" (Moore), **VI:** 98
"John of the Cross" (Jennings), **Supp. V:** 207
"John Ruskin" (Proust), **V:** 183
John Ruskin: The Portrait of a Prophet (Quennell), **V:** 185
John Sherman and Dhoya (Yeats), **VI:** 221
John Thomas and Lady Jane (Lawrence), **VII:** 111–112
"John Uskglass and the Cumbrian Charcoal Burner" (Clarke), **Supp. XV:** 45
John Woodvil (Lamb), **IV:** 78–79, 85
Johnnie Sahib (Scott), **Supp. I:** 259, 261
Johnno (Malouf), **Supp. XII:** 221–222
Johnny I Hardly Knew You (O'Brien), **Supp. V:** 338, 339
Johnny in the Clouds (Rattigan), *seeWay to the Stars, The*
Johnson, Edgar, **IV:** 27, 40; **V:** 60, 72
Johnson Is Leaving (Wain), **Supp. XVI:** 305
Johnson, James, **III:** 320, 322
Johnson, Joseph, **Retro. Supp. I:** 37
Johnson, Lionel, **VI:** 3, 210, 211
Johnson, Samuel, **III:** 54, 96, **107–123**, 127, 151, 275; **IV:** xiv, xv, 27, 31, 34, 88n, 101, 138, 268, 299; **V:** 9, 281, 287; **VI:** 363; **Retro. Supp. I: 137–150**; and Boswell, **III:** 234, 235, 238, 239, 243–249; and Collins, **III:** 160, 163, 164, 171, 173; and Crabbe, **III:** 280–282; and Goldsmith, **III:** 177, 180, 181, 189; dictionary, **III:** 113–116; **V:** 281, 434; literary criticism, **I:** 326; **II:** 123, 173, 197, 200, 259, 263, 293, 301, 347; **III:** 11, 88, 94, 139, 257, 275; **IV:** 101; on Addison and Steele, **III:** 39, 42, 44, 49, 51; **Supp. IV:** 271
Johnson, W. E., **Supp. II:** 406
Johnson over Jordan (Priestley), **VII:** 226–227
"Joker, The" (Wallace–Crabbe), **VIII:** 315–316
"Joker as Told" (Murray), **Supp. VII:** 279
Joking Apart (Ayckbourn), **Supp. V:** 3, 9, 13, 14
Jolly Beggars, The (Burns), **III:** 319–320
"Jolly Corner, The" (James), **Retro. Supp. I:** 2
Jonah Who Will Be 25 in the Year 2000 (film), **Supp. IV:** 79
Jonathan Strange & Mr Norrell (Clarke), **Supp. XV:** 37–47
Jonathan Swift (Stephen), **V:** 289
Jonathan Wild (Fielding), **III:** 99, 103, 105, 150; **Retro. Supp. I:** 80–81, 90
Jones, David, **VI:** xvi, 436, 437–439, **Supp. VII: 167–182**
Jones, Henry Arthur, **VI:** 367, 376
Jones, Henry Festing, **Supp. II:** 103–104, 112, 114, 117, 118
Jonestown (Harris), **Supp. V:** 144–145
Jonson, Ben, **I:** 228, 234–235, 270, **335–351**; **II:** 3, 4, 24, 25, 27, 28, 30, 45, 47, 48, 55, 65, 79, 87, 104, 108, 110, 111n, 115, 118, 141, 199, 221–223; **IV:** 35, 327; **V:** 46, 56; **Supp. IV:** 256; **Retro. Supp. I: 151–167**
Jonsonus Virbius (Digby), **Retro. Supp. I:** 166
Jonsonus Virbius (King), **Supp. VI:** 157
Joseph Andrews (Fielding), **III:** 94, 95, 96, 99–100, 101, 105; **Retro. Supp. I:** 80, 83–86
Joseph Banks: A Life (O'Brian), **Supp. XII:** 257–258
Joseph Conrad (Baines), **VI:** 133–134
Joseph Conrad (Ford), **VI:** 321, 322
Joseph Conrad (Walpole), **VI:** 149
Joseph Conrad: A Personal Reminiscence (Ford), **VI:** 149
Joseph Conrad: The Modern Imagination (Cox), **VI:** 149
Joseph Conrad and Charles Darwin: The Influence of Scientific Thought on Conrad's Fiction (O'Hanlon), **Supp. XI:** 195
"Joseph Grimaldi" (Hood), **IV:** 267
"Joseph Yates' Temptation" (Gissing), **V:** 437
Journal (Mansfield), **VII:** 181, 182
Journal, 1825–32 (Scott), **IV:** 39
Journal and Letters of Fanny Burney, The (eds. Hemlow et al.), **Supp. III:** 63
Journal of Bridget Hitler, The (Bainbridge), **Supp. VI:** 22
"Journal of a Dead Man" (Butlin), **Supp. XVI:** 60
Journal of a Dublin Lady, The (Swift), **III:** 35
Journal of a Landscape Painter in Corsica (Lear), **V:** 87
Journal of a Tour in Scotland in 1819 (Southey), **IV:** 71
Journal of a Tour in the Netherlands in the Autumn of 1815 (Southey), **IV:** 71
Journal of a Tour to the Hebrides, The (Boswell), **III:** 117, 234n, 235, 243, 245, 248, 249
Journal of a Voyage to Lisbon, The (Fielding), **III:** 104, 105
Journal of Beatrix Potter from 1881 to 1897, The (ed. Linder), **Supp. III: 292–295**
"Journal of My Jaunt, Harvest 1762" (Boswell), **III:** 241–242
Journal of Researches into the Geology and Natural History of the various countries visited by HMS Beagle (Darwin), **Supp. VII:** 18–19
Journal of the Plague Year, A (Defoe), **III:** 5–6, 8, 13; **Retro. Supp. I:** 63, 73–74
Journal to Eliza, The (Sterne), **III:** 125, 126, 132, 135
Journal to Stella (Swift), **II:** 335; **III:** 32–33, 34; **Retro. Supp. I:** 274
Journalism (Mahon), **Supp. VI:** 166
Journalism for Women: A Practical Guide (Bennett), **VI:** 264, 266
Journals (Shelley), **Retro. Supp. III:** 290, 298
Journals and Papers of Gerard Manley Hopkins, The (ed. House and Storey), **V:** 362, 363, 371, 378–379, 381
Journals 1939–1983 (Spender), **Supp. II:** 481, 487, 490, 493
Journals of a Landscape Painter in Albania etc. (Lear), **V:** 77, 79–80, 87
Journals of a Landscape Painter in Southern Calabria . . . (Lear), **V:** 77, 79, 87
Journals of a Residence in Portugal, 1800–1801, and a Visit to France, 1838 (Southey), **IV:** 71
Journals of Arnold Bennett (Bennett), **VI:** 265, 267
"Journals of Progress" (Durrell), **Supp. I:** 124
"Journey, The" (Boland), **Supp. V:** 41
"Journey, The" (Constantine), **Supp. XV:** 73
"Journey Back, The" (Muir), **Supp. VI:** 207
Journey Continued (Paton), **Supp. II:** 356, 359
Journey from Cornhill to Grand Cairo, A (Thackeray), *see Notes of a Journey from Cornhill to Grand Cairo*
Journey from This World to the Next (Fielding), **Retro. Supp. I:** 80
Journey into Fear (Ambler), **Supp. IV:** 11–12
Journey Made in the Summer of 1794, A: Through Holland and the Western Frontier of Germany, with a Return

down the Rhine; to Which Are Added, Observations During a Tour to the Lakes of Lancashire, Westmoreland, and Cumberland (Radcliffe), **Retro. Supp. III:** 234, 244–245
"Journey of John Gilpin, The" (Cowper), *see* AJohn Gilpin"
"Journey of the Magi, The" (Eliot), **VII:** 152
Journey Through France (Piozzi), **III:** 134
Journey to a War (Auden and Isherwood), **VII:** 312; **Retro. Supp. I:** 9
Journey to Armenia (Mandelstam), **Supp. IV:** 163, 170
"Journey to Bruges, The" (Mansfield), **VII:** 172
Journey to Ithaca (Desai), **Supp. V:** 56, 66, 73–74
Journey to London, A (Vanbrugh), **II:** 326, 333–334, 336
Journey to Oxiana (Byron), **Supp. IV:** 157, 170
Journey to Paradise (Richardson), **Supp. XIII:** 180, 181
"Journey to Paradise" (Richardson), **Supp. XIII:** 180, 191
Journey to the Border (Upward), **Supp. XIII:** 250, 251, 253–254, 259, 260
Journey to the Hebrides (Johnson), **IV:** 281
Journey to the Western Islands of Scotland, A (Johnson), **III:** 117, 121; **Retro. Supp. I:** 143
Journey Without Maps (Greene), **Supp. I:** 9; **Retro. Supp. II:** 153
"Journeying North" (Conn), **Supp. XIII:** 72–73
Journeys (Morris, J.), **Supp. X:** 172, 183
Journeys and Places (Muir), **Supp. VI:** 204, **205–206**
Journeys in Persia and Kurdistan (Bird), **Supp. X:** 31
"Journeywoman, The" (Roberts), **Supp. XV:** 261
Jovial Crew, A (Brome **Supp. X:** 49, 55–59, 62–63
Jowett, Benjamin, **V:** 278, 284, 285, 312, 338, 400
"Joy" (Dutton), **Supp. XII:** 94
Joy (Galsworthy), **VI:** 269, 285
"Joy Gordon" (Redgrove), **Supp. VI:** 236
Joyce (Oliphant), **Supp. X:** 218
Joyce, James, **IV:** 189; **V:** xxv, 41; **VII:** xii, xiv, 18, **41–58; VII:** 54–58; **Supp. I:** 43, 196–197; **Supp. II:** 74, 88, 327, 332, 338, 420, 525; **Supp. III:** 108; **Supp. IV:** 27, 233, 234, 363, 364, 365, 371, 390, 395, 396, 407, 411, 424, 426, 427, 500, 514; **Retro. Supp. I:** 18, 19, **169–182**; **Retro. Supp. III:** **165–180**
Joyce, Jeremiah, **V:** 174n
Joys of War (Mda), **Supp. XV:** 197–198
"Jubilate Matteo" (Ewart), **Supp. VII:** 44
"Judas Tree, The" (Welch), **Supp. IX:** 269
Jude the Obscure (Hardy), **VI:** 4, 5, 7, 8, 9; **Supp. IV:** 116; **Retro. Supp. I:** 110, 116

"Judge, The" (Crawford), **Supp. XI:** 75–76
Judge, The (West), **Supp. III:** 441, 442
"Judge's House, The" (Stoker), **Supp. III:** 382
"Judge Chutney's Final Summary" (Armitage), **VIII:** 6
Judgement of Martin Bucer . . . , The (Milton), **II:** 175
Judgement of Paris, The (Congreve), **II:** 347, 350
Judgement in Stone, A (Rendell), **Supp. IX:** 192, 194–195
Judge's Wife, The (Churchill), **Supp. IV:** 181
"Judging Distances" (Reed), **VII:** 422; **Supp. XV:** 248, 250, 256
Judgment on Deltchev (Ambler), **Supp. IV:** 4, 12–13, 21
Judith, **Supp. VI:** 29; **Retro. Supp. II:** 305, 306
Judith (Bennett), **VI:** 267
"Judith" (Coppard), **VIII:** 96
Judith (Giraudoux), **Supp. III:** 195
"Judkin of the Parcels" (Saki), **Supp. VI:** 245
Jugement du roi de Behaingne, **I:** 32
"Juggling Jerry" (Meredith), **V:** 220
"Julia" (Brontë), **V:** 122, 151
Julia and the Bazooka and Other Stories (Kavan), **Supp. VII:** 202, 205, 214
"Julia Bride" (James), **VI:** 67, 69
"Julia's Churching; or, Purification" (Herrick), **II:** 112
"Julian and Maddalo" (Shelley), **IV:** 182, 201–202; **Retro. Supp. I:** 251
"Julian M. & A. G. Rochelle" (Brontë), **V:** 133
Julian of Norwich, **I:** 20; **Retro. Supp. II:** 303; **Supp. XII: 149–166**
Julius Caesar (Shakespeare), **I:** 313, 314–315
"July Evening" (MacCaig), **Supp. VI:** 187, 194
"July Storm" (Healy), **Supp. IX:** 106
July's People (Gordimer), **Supp. II:** 231, 238–239, 241
Jumpers (Stoppard), **Supp. I:** 438, 444, 445–447, 451; **Retro. Supp. II:** 347–349
"Jumping Boy, The" (Hill), **Retro. Supp. III:** 144
Jumping Off Shadows (ed. Delanty), **Supp. XIV:** 65, 75
Jump-to-Glory Jane (Meredith), **V:** 234
"June Bracken and Heather" (Tennyson), **IV:** 336
"June the 30th, 1934" (Lowry), **Supp. III:** 285
"June to December" (Cope), **VIII:** 72
Jung, Carl, **Supp. IV:** 1, 4–5, 6, 10–11,
"Jungle, The" (Lewis), **VII:** 447
Jungle Book, The (Kipling), **Retro. Supp. III:** 189–191, 196, 197
"Jungle Book" (Scupham), **Supp. XIII:** 225
Jungle Books, The (Kipling), **VI:** 188, 199
Juniper Tree, The (Comyns), **VIII:** 53, 63–64, 65

Junius Manuscript, **Retro. Supp. II:** 298–299, 301
Junk Mail (Self), **Supp. V:** 406–407
"Junkie" (Morgan, E.), **Supp. IX:** 164
Juno and the Paycock (O'Casey), **VII:** xviii, 4–5, 6, 11
Juno in Arcadia (Brome), **Supp. X:** 52
Jure Divino (Defoe), **III:** 4, 13
"Jury, The" (Hart), **Supp. XI:** 125
Jusserand, Jean, **I:** 98
Just Between Ourselves (Ayckbourn), **Supp. V:** 3, 13
"Just Lie Back and Think of the Empire" (Roberts), **Supp. XV:** 262, 273
Just Like the Resurrection (Beer), **Supp. XIV:** 2–3
Just So Stories (Kipling), **Retro. Supp. III:** 194, 196
Just So Stories for Little Children (Kipling), **VI:** 188, 204
Just Vengeance, The (Sayers), **Supp. III:** 336, 350
Justice (Galsworthy), **VI:** xiii, 269, 273–274, 286–287
Justine (Durrell), **Supp. I:** 104, 105, 106; **Retro. Supp. III:** 83, 84, 85, 89, 90
Juvenal, **II:** 30, 292, 347, 348; **III:** 42; **IV:** 188
Juvenilia 1 (Nye), **Supp. X:** 192, 194, 196–200, 202–203, 205
Juvenilia 2 (Nye), **Supp. X:** 192–194, 197–200, 204–205

"Kaa's Hunting" (Kipling), **Retro. Supp. III:** 192
Kabla–Khun" (Dunn), **Supp. X:** 79
Kaeti and Company (Roberts, K.), **Supp. X:** 273
Kaeti on Tour (Roberts, K.), **Supp. X:** 273
Kafka, Franz, **III:** 340, 345; **Supp. IV:** 1, 199, 407, 439
Kafka's Dick (Bennett), **VIII:** 29–30
"Kail and Callaloo" (Kay), **Supp. XIII:** 108
Kain, Saul, pseud. of Siegfried Sassoon
Kaisers of Carnuntum, The (Harrison), **Supp. V:** 164
Kakutani, Michiko, **Supp. IV:** 304
Kalendarium Hortense (Evelyn), **II:** 287
Kallman, Chester, **VII:** 422, 424; **Retro. Supp. I:** 9–10, 13
Kama Sutra, **Supp. IV:** 493
Kane, Sarah, **VIII: 147–161**
Kangaroo (Lawrence), **VII:** 90, **107–109,** 119
Kant, Immanuel, **IV:** xiv, 50, 52, 145
Kanthapura (Rao), **Supp. V:** 56
"Karain: A Memory" (Conrad), **VI:** 148
"Karakoram Highway" (Jamie), **Supp. XIV:** 134, 135–136
Karaoke (Potter, D.), **Supp. X:** 228, 240–241
Karl, Frederick R., **VI:** 135, 149
Karl–Ludwig's Window, (Saki), **Supp. VI:** 250
"Karshish" (Browning), **IV:** 357, 360, 363
Katchen's Caprices (Trollope), **V:** 101

"Kate's Garden" (Burnside), **Supp. XIII:** 29
"Kathe Kollwitz" (Rukeyser), **Supp. V:** 261
Katherine Mansfield (Alpers), **VII:** 183
Kathleen and Frank (Isherwood), **VII:** 316–317
Kathleen Listens In (O'Casey), **VII:** 12
"Kathleen ny Houlahan" (Mangan), **Supp. XIII:** 127
"Katina" (Dahl), **Supp. IV:** 210
Kavan, Anna, **Supp. VII: 201–215**
Kavanagh, Julia, **IV:** 108, 122
Kavanagh, Dan, pseud. of Julian Barnes
Kavanagh, Patrick, **Supp. IV:** 409, 410, 412, 428, 542; **Supp. VII: 183–199**; **Retro. Supp. I:** 126
Kay, Jackie, **Supp. XIII: 99–111**
Kazin, Alfred, **Supp. IV:** 460
Keats, John, **II:** 102, 122, 192, 200; **III:** 174, 337, 338; **IV:** viii–xii, 81, 95, 129, 178, 196, 198, 204–205, **211–237**, 255, 284, 316, 323, 332, 349, 355; **V:** 173, 361, 401, 403; **Supp. I:** 218; **Supp. V:** 38; **Retro. Supp. I: 183–197**
Keats and the Mirror of Art (Jack), **IV:** 236
"Keats at Highgate" (Gunn), **Retro. Supp. III:** 125
Keats Circle, The: Letters and Papers . . . (Rollins), **IV:** 231, 232, 235
Keats: The Critical Heritage (ed. Matthews), **IV:** 237
Keats's Publisher: A Memoir of John Taylor (Blunden), **IV:** 236; **Supp. XI:** 37
Keble, John, **V:** xix, 252
"Keel, Ram, Stauros" (Jones), **Supp. VII:** 177
"Keen, Fitful Gusts" (Keats), **IV:** 215
"Keep Culture Out of Cambridge" (Cornford), **Supp. XIII:** 87–88
Keep the Aspidistra Flying (Orwell), **VII:** 275, 278–279
"Keep the Home Fires Burning" (Novello), **VI:** 435
"Keeper of the Rothenstein Tomb, The" (Sinclair), **Supp. XIV:** 232–233, 237–238, 242, 245
"Keepsake, The" (Adcock), **Supp. XII:** 9
Keeton, G. W., **IV:** 286
Kell, Joseph, *see* Burgess, Anthony
Kellys and the O'Kellys, The (Trollope), **V:** 101
Kelman, James, **Supp. V: 241–258**
Kelmscott Press, publishers, **V:** xxv, 302
Kelsall, Malcolm Miles, **IV:** x, xxv
Kelvin, Norman, **V:** 221, 234
Kemble, Fanny, **IV:** 340, 350–351
Kemp, Harry, **Supp. III:** 120
Kempe, Margery, **Supp. XII: 167–183**
Keneally, Thomas, **Supp. IV: 343–362**
Kenilworth (Scott), **IV:** xviii, 39
Kennedy, John F., **Supp. IV:** 486
Kenner, Hugh, **VI:** 323
Kennis van die aand (Brink), **Supp. VI: 47–48**, 49
"Kensington Gardens" (Adcock), **Supp. XII:** 13, 14–15
Kenyon, Frederic, **IV:** 312, 321

Kenyon, John, **IV:** 311, 356
Kept (Waugh), **Supp. VI:** 270
Kept in the Dark (Trollope), **V:** 102
Kermode, Frank, **I:** 237; **V:** 344, 355, 359, 412, 420; **VI:** 147, 208
Kerr, Philip, **Supp. XII: 185–200**
Kettle, Thomas, **VI:** 336
Key of the Field, The (Powys), **VIII:** 255
Key to Modern British Poetry (Durrell), **Retro. Supp. III:** 86, 96
Key to Modern Poetry, A (Durrell), **Supp. I:** 100, **121–123**, 125, 126, 127
Key to My Heart, The (Pritchett), **Supp. III: 324–325**
"Key to My Heart, The" (Pritchett), **Supp. III:** 324
Key to the Door (Sillitoe), **Supp. V:** 410, 415
Keyes, Sidney, **VII:** xxii, 422, **433–440**
Keynes, G. L., **II:** 134; **III:** 289n, 307, 308, 309
Kickleburys on the Rhine, The (Thackeray), **V:** 38
Kid (Armitage), **VIII:** 1, 4–6
"Kid" (Armitage), **VIII:** 5
Kidnapped (Stevenson), **V:** 383, 384, 387, 395; **Retro. Supp. I:** 266–267
Kids, The (Parsons), **Supp. XV:** 227, 228, 229, 237–238, 239
Kierkegaard, Sören, **Supp. I:** 79
"Kierkegaard" (Thomas), **Supp. XII:** 285
"Kilchrenan" (Conn), **Supp. XIII:** 72
"Kill, A" (Hughes), **Supp. I:** 352
"Killary Hostel" (Murphy), **Supp. V:** 328
Killham, John, **IV:** 323n, 338, 339; **VII: 248–249**
Killing Bottle, The (Hartley), **Supp. VII:** 123
Killing Kindness, A (Hill, R.), **Supp. IX:** 114–115, 117, 122
Killing the Lawyers (Hill, R.), **Supp. IX:** 123
Killing Time (Armitage), **VIII:** 1, 15–16
"Killing Time" (Harrison), **Supp. V:** 156
"Kilmarnock Edition" (Conn), **Supp. XIII:** 77–78
"Kilmeny" (Hogg), **Supp. X:** 107–110
Kiltartan History Book, The (Gregory), **VI:** 318
Kiltartan Molière, The (Gregory), **VI:** 316, 318
Kiltartan Poetry Book, The (Gregory), **VI:** 318
Kilvert, Francis, **V:** 269; **Supp. IV:** 169
Kim (Kipling), **VI:** 166, 168, 169, **185–189; Supp. IV:** 443; **Retro. Supp. III:** 192, 193–194, 195, 196, 197
Kincaid, Jamaica, **Supp. VII: 217–232**
Kind Are Her Answers (Renault), **Supp. IX:** 173–174
"Kind Ghosts, The" (Owen), **VI:** 447, 455, 457
Kind Keeper, The; or, Mr Limberham (Dryden), **II:** 294305
Kind of Alaska, A (Pinter), **Supp. I:** 378
Kind of Anger, A (Ambler), **Supp. IV:** 16, 18–20
"Kind of Business: The Academic Critic in America, A" (Lodge), **Supp. IV:** 374

Kind of Poetry I Want, The (MacDiarmid), **Supp. XII:** 203
Kind of Scar, A (Boland), **Supp. V:** 35
"Kindertotenlieder" (Longley), **VIII:** 169–170
Kindness in a Corner (Powys), **VIII:** 248, 249, 256
Kindness of Women, The (Ballard), **Supp. V:** 24, 28, 31, 33
Kindly Light (Wilson), **Supp. VI:** 299, 308
Kindly Ones, The (Powell), **VII:** 344, 347, 348, 349, 350
King, Francis Henry, **VII:** xx, xxxviii; **Supp. IV:** 302
King, Bishop Henry, **II:** 121, 221; **Supp. VI: 149–163**
King, Kimball, **Supp. IV:** 194–195
King, S., **III:** 345
King, T., **II:** 336
King and Me, The (Kureishi), **Supp. XI:** 153–154
King and No King, A (Beaumont and Fletcher), **II:** 43, 45, 52, 54, 57–58, 65
King Arthur; or, The British Worthy (Dryden), **II:** 294, 296, 305
"King Arthur's Tomb" (Morris), **V:** 293
"King Billy" (Morgan, E.), **Supp. IX:** 158
"King Duffus" (Warner), **Supp. VII:** 373
"King James I and Isaac Casaubon" (Landor), **IV:** 92
King James Version of the Bible, **I:** 370, 377–380
King John (Shakespeare), **I:** 286, 301; **Retro. Supp. III:** 277
"King John's Castle" (Kinsella), **Supp. V:** 260
King Lear (Shakespeare), **I:** 316–317; **II:** 69, 295; **III:** 116, 295; **IV:** 232; **Supp. II:** 194; **Supp. IV:** 149, 171, 282, 283, 294, 335; **Retro. Supp. I:** 34–35; **Retro. Supp. III:** 270, 276–277
King Log (Hill), **Supp. V:** 186–189; **Retro. Supp. III:** 135–136
King Must Die, The (Renault), **Supp. IX:** 178–180, 187
"King of Beasts" (MacCaig), **Supp. VI:** 189
King of Hearts, The (Golding), **Supp. I:** 82
King of Pirates, The . . . (Defoe), **III:** 13
King of the Golden River, The; or, The Black Brothers (Ruskin), **V:** 184
"King of the World, The" (Coppard), **VIII:** 92
"King Pim" (Powys), **VIII:** 248, 249
King Solomon's Mines (Haggard), **Supp. III:** 211, 213, **215–217, 218–219**, 227; **Supp. VI:** 484
King Stephen (Keats), **IV:** 231
King Victor and King Charles (Browning), **IV:** 373
"Kingdom of God, The" (Thompson), **V:** 449–450
"Kingdom of Heaven, The" (Powys), **VIII:** 256

Kingdom of the Wicked, The (Burgess), **Supp. I:** 186, 193
Kingdoms of Elfin (Warner), **Supp. VII:** 369, 371, 381
King–Errant (Steel), **Supp. XII:** 275
"Kingfisher" (Nye), **Supp. X:** 192, 205
"Kingfisher, The" (Davies), **Supp. XI:** 96–97
"Kingfisher, The" (Powys), **VIII:** 251
King's General, The (du Maurier), **Supp. III:** 146
Kings, Lords and Commons: An Anthology from the Irish (tr. O'Connor), **Supp. XIV:** 221, 222
"King's Tragedy, The" (Rossetti), **V:** 238, 244
"Kings" (Jennings), **Supp. V:** 211, 218
"Kings' Sagas", See Konunga sögur
Kingsland, W. G., **IV:** 371
Kingsley, Charles, **IV:** 195; **V:** viii, xxi, 2, 4, 283; **VI:** 266; **Supp. IV:** 256
Kingsley, Charles, **Supp. XVI: 193–207**
Kinsayder, W., pseud. of John Marston
Kinsella, Thomas, **VI:** 220; **Supp. V: 259–275**
Kinsley, James, **III:** 310n 322
Kipling, Rudyard, **IV:** 106, 109; **V:** xxiii–xxvi; **VI:** ix, xi, xv, **165–206,** 415; **VII:** 33; poetry, **VI:** 200–203; list of short stories, **VI:** 205–206; **Supp. I:** 167, 261; **Supp. IV:** 17, 201, 394, 440, 506; **Retro. Supp. III: 181–198**
Kipling and the Critics (Gilbert), **VI:** 195n
Kipling: Realist and Fabulist (Dobrée), **VI:** xi, 200–203, 205
"Kipper" (Carson), **Supp. XIII:** 63
Kipps: The Story of a Simple Soul (Wells), **VI:** xii, 225, 236–237
Kirk, Russell, **IV:** 276
Kirkpatrick, T. P. C. **III:** 180n
Kirsteen: The Story of a Scotch Family Seventy Years Ago (Oliphant), **Supp. X:** 217–219
Kiss, The (Clarke), **Supp. XV:** 25
"Kiss, The" (Sassoon), **VI:** 429
Kiss for Cinderalla, A (Barrie), **Supp. III:** 8, 9
Kiss Kiss (Dahl), **Supp. IV:** 214, 215, 218
"Kiss Me Again, Stranger" (du Maurier), **Supp. III:** 134
Kissing the Gunner's Daughter (Rendell), **Supp. IX:** 195, 196, 198
Kitaj, R. B., **Supp. IV:** 119
Kitay, Mike, **Supp. IV:** 256, 257
"Kitchen Maid" (Conn), **Supp. XIII:** 74
"Kitchen Sonnets" (Fuller), **Supp. VII:** 80
"Kitchen Window" (Nye), **Supp. X:** 198
Kitchener, Field Marshall Lord, **VI:** 351
Kiteworld (Roberts, K.), **Supp. X:** 261, 264, 271–273
Kittredge, G. L., **I:** 326
Klee, Paul, **Supp. IV:** 80
Klosterheim (De Quincey), **IV:** 149, 155
KMT: In the House of Life (Armah), **Supp. X:** 14
Knave of Hearts (Symons), **Supp. XIV:** 281

"Kneeling" (Thomas), **Supp. XII:** 286
"Kneeshaw Goes to War" (Read), **VI:** 437
Knife, The (Hare), **Supp. IV:** 282
"Knife–Play" (Adcock), **Supp. XII:** 4–5
Knight, G. W., **IV:** 328n, 339
"Knight, The" (Hughes), **Supp. I:** 356
Knight of the Burning Pestle, The (Beaumont), **II:** 45, 46, 48–49, 65, 66
"Knight of the Cart, The" (Malory), **I:** 70
Knight with the Two Swords, The (Malory), **I:** 73
Knights, The (tr. Delanty), **Supp. XIV:** 76
Knights, L. C., **II:** 123, 126, 130
Knights of Malta, The (Field, Fletcher, Massinger), **II:** 66
Knight's Fee (Sutcliff), **Supp. XVI:** 262, 269, 270
Knight's Tale, The (Chaucer), **I:** 21, 23, 30, 31, 40
Knoblock, Edward, **VI:** 263, 267; **VII:** 223
"Knockbrack" (Murphy), **Supp. V:** 327
"Knole" (Fuller), **Supp. VII:** 72
Knolles, Richard, **III:** 108
Knots and Crosses (Rankin), **Supp. X:** 244–249
Know Yourself (Arbuthnot), **Supp. XVI:** 28
"Knowledge" (Crawford), **Supp. XI:** 76
Knowles, Sheridan, **IV:** 311
Knox, Robert, **III:** 7
Knox, Ronald, **Supp. II:** 124, 126
Knox Brothers, The (Fitzgerald), **Supp. V:** 95, 96, 98
Knuckle (Hare), **Supp. IV:** 282, 285–286
Kodak Mantra Diaries, The (Sinclair), **Supp. XIV:** 234
Koestler, Arthur, **V:** 49; **Supp. I: 21–41;** **Supp. III:** 107; **Supp. IV:** 68
"Koi" (Burnside), **Supp. XIII:** 25
Kokoschka, Oskar, **Supp. IV:** 81
Kontakian for You Departed (Paton), **Supp. II:** 343, 359
Konträre Geschlechtsgefühl, Das (Ellis and Symonds), **Supp. XIV:** 261
Konunga sögur, **VIII:** 236
Korea and Her Neighbors (Bird), **Supp. X:** 31
Kormaks saga
"Kosciusko and Poniatowski" (Landor), **IV:** 92
"Kosovo" (Conn), **Supp. XIII:** 80
Kostakis, George, **Supp. IV:** 174
Kotzebue, August von, **III:** 254, 268
"Kraken, The" (Tennyson), **IV:** 329; **VI:** 16
Krapp's Last Tape (Beckett), **Supp. I:** 46, 55, 58, 61; **Retro. Supp. I:** 25–26
Krause, Ernest, **Supp. II:** 107
"Kristbjorg's Story: In the Black Hills" (Lowry), **Supp. III:** 285
Kristeva, Julia, **Supp. IV:** 115, 232
Krutch, J. W., **III:** 246
"Kubla Khan" (Coleridge), **IV:** ix, xvii, 44, 46–48, 56; **V:** 272, 447; **Supp. IV:** 425; **Retro. Supp. II:** 56–58
Kullus (Pinter), **Supp. I:** 368, 371
Kumar, Gobind, **Supp. IV:** 449

"Kumquat for John Keats, A" (Harrison), **Supp. V:** 160
Kundera, Milan, **Supp. IV:** 440
Kunzru, Hari, **Supp. XIV: 165–177**
Kureishi, Hanif, **Supp. XI: 151–162**
Kurosawa, Akira, **Supp. IV:** 434
Kyd, Thomas, **I:** 162, **212–231,** 277, 278, 291; **II:** 25, 28, 74
"Kyogle Line, The" (Malouf), **Supp. XII:** 218

"La Belle Dame Sans Merci" (Keats), **IV:** 216, 219, 235, 313
La Bete Humaine (Zola), **Supp. IV:** 249
La Chapelle, Jean de, **II:** 358
La Die de Fénelon (Ramsay), **III:** 99
La Fayette, Madame de, **Supp. IV:** 136
"La Fontaine and La Rochefoucault" (Landor), **IV:** 91
"La Grosse Fifi" (Rhys), **Supp. II:** 390
La maison de campagne (Dancourt), **II:** 325
La Mordida (Lowry), **Supp. III:** 280
"La Nuit Blanche" (Kipling), **VI:** 193
La parisienne (Becque), **VI:** 369
La Princesse de Clèves (La Fayette), **Supp. IV:** 136
"La Rochefoucauld" (Durrell), **Supp. I:** 126
La Saisiaz (Browning), **IV:** 359, 364–365, 374
La Soeur de la Reine (Swinburne), **V:** 325, 333
La strage degli innocenti (Marino), **II:** 183
La traicion busca el castigo (Roias Zorilla), **II:** 325
La Vendée: An Historical Romance (Trollope), **V:** 101
La vida de la Santa Madre Teresa de Jesus, **II:** 182
La vida es sueño (Calderón), **IV:** 349
La vie de Fénelon (Ramsay), **III:** 99
Labels (De Bernières), **Supp. XII:** 66
Labels (Waugh), **VII:** 292–293
Laboratories of the Spirit (Thomas), **Supp. XII:** 286
Laborators, The (Redgrove), **Supp. VI:** 236
Labours of Hercules, The (Christie), **Supp. II:** 135
Laburnum Grove (Priestley), **VII:** 224
Labyrinth, The (Muir), **Supp. VI:** 204, **207**
Labyrinthine Ways, The (Greene), see *Power and the Glory, The*
Lacan, Jacques, **Supp. IV:** 99, 115
"Lachrimae, or Seven Tears Figured in Seven Passionate Pavanas" (Hill), **Supp. V:** 189, 190; **Retro. Supp. III:** 137
"Lachrimae Amantis" (Hill), **Supp. V:** 191; **Retro. Supp. III:** 137
"Lachrimae Verae" (Hill), **Supp. V:** 190
"Laconics: The Forty Acres" (Murray), **Supp. VII:** 276
"Ladder and the Tree, The" (Golding), **Supp. I:** 65
Ladder of Perfection (Hilton), **Supp. I:** 74

"Ladders, The" (Malouf), **Supp. XII:** 220
Ladies from the Sea (Hope), **Supp. VII:** 160
Ladies of Alderley, The (ed. Mitford), **Supp. X:** 156
"Ladies of Grace Adieu, The" (Clarke), **Supp. XV:** 36, 43, 47
Ladies of Grace Adieu and Other Stories, The (Clarke), **Supp. XV:** 43
Ladies Triall, The (Ford), *see Lady's Trial, The*
Ladies Whose Bright Eyes (Ford), **VI:** 327
"Ladle" (Berger), **Supp. IV:** 93
Lady Anna (Trollope), **V:** 102
"Lady Appledore's Mesalliance" (Firbank), **Supp. II:** 207
"Lady Artemis, The" (Maitland), **Supp. XI:** 175
Lady Athlyne (Stoker), **Supp. III:** 381
Lady Audley's Secret (Braddon), **VIII:** 35, 41–42, 43, 48, 50
"Lady Barbarina" (James), **VI:** 69
Lady Chatterley's Lover (Lawrence), **VII:** 87, 88, 91, **110–113; Supp. IV:** 149, 234, 369; **Retro. Supp. II:** 226, 231–232
"Lady Delavoy" (James), **VI:** 69
Lady Frederick (Maugham), **VI:** 367–368
"Lady Geraldine's Courtship" (Browning), **IV:** 311; **Retro. Supp. III:** 23
Lady Gregory, **VI:** xiv
Lady Gregory: A Literary Portrait (Coxhead), **VI:** 318
Lady Hamilton and the Elephant Man (Constantine), **Supp. XV:** 78
"Lady Icenway, The" (Hardy), **VI:** 22
Lady in the Van, The (Bennett), **VIII:** 33
Lady into Woman: A History of Women from Victoria to Elizabeth II (Brittain), **Supp. X:** 46
Lady Jane (Chettle, Dekker, Heywood, Webster), **II:** 68
Lady Lisa Lyon (Mapplethorpe photography collection), **Supp. IV:** 170
"Lady Louisa and the Wallflowers" (Powys), **VIII:** 249
Lady Maisie's Bairn and Other Poems (Swinburne), **V:** 333
"Lady Mottisfont" (Hardy), **VI:** 22
Lady of Launay, The (Trollope), **V:** 102
Lady of May, The (Sidney), **I:** 161; **Retro. Supp. II:** 330
"Lady of Quality, A" (Kinsella), **Supp. V:** 260
"Lady of Shalott, The" (Tennyson), **IV:** xix, 231, 313, 329, 331–332; **Retro. Supp. III:** 317, 320–321, 327
Lady of the Lake, The (Scott), **IV:** xvii, 29, 38
"Lady of the Pool, The" (Jones), **Supp. VII:** 176, 177, 178
"Lady of the Sagas, The" (O'Connor), **Supp. XIV:** 226
Lady of the Shroud, The (Stoker), **Supp. III:** 381
"Lady Penelope, The" (Hardy), **VI:** 22
"Lady Rogue Singleton" (Smith), **Supp. II:** 466–467, 470

Lady Susan (Austen), **IV:** 108, 109, 122; **Supp. IV:** 230
Lady Windermere's Fan (Wilde), **V:** xxvi, 412, 413–414, 419; **Retro. Supp. II:** 369
Lady with a Laptop (Thomas), **Supp. IV:** 489–490
"Lady with the Dog, The" (Chekhov), **V:** 241
"Lady with Unicorn" (Maitland), **Supp. XI:** 170
"Ladybird, The" (Lawrence), **VII:** 115
"Lady's Dream, The" (Hood), **IV:** 261, 264
"Lady's Dressing Room, The" (Swift), **III:** 32
Lady's Life in the Rocky Mountains, A (Bird), **Supp. X:** 17, 19, 22, 24, 26–28, 30
Lady's Magazine (periodical), **III:** 179
"Lady's Maid, The" (Mansfield), **VII:** 174–175
Lady's Not for Burning (Fry), **Supp. III:** 195, 202
Lady's Pictorial (periodical), **VI:** 87, 91
Lady's Trial, The (Ford), **II:** 89, 91, 99, 100
Lady's World, The (periodical), **Retro. Supp. II:** 364
Lafourcade, Georges, **VI:** 247, 256, 259, 260, 262, 263, 268
"Lagoon, The" (Conrad), **VI:** 136, 148
Lair of the White Worm, The (Stoker), **Supp. III:** 381–382
Laird of Abbotsford: A View of Sirt Walter Scott, The (Wilson), **Supp. VI:** 301
Lake, David J., **II:** 1, 2, 21
Lake, The (Moore), **VI:** xii, 88, 89, 92–93, 98
"Lake Isle of Innisfree, The" (Yeats), **VI:** 207, 211; **Retro. Supp. I:** 329
Lake of Darkness, The (Rendell), **Supp. IX:** 196
"Lake of Tuonela, The" (Roberts, K.), **Supp. X:** 270–271
Lakers, The (Nicholson), **Supp. VI:** 223
"Lal" (Steel), **Supp. XII:** 266, 268
"L'Allegro" (Milton), **II:** 158–159; **IV:** 199
Lamarck, Jean-Baptiste, **Supp. II:** 105–106, 107, 118, 119
Lamb, Charles, **II:** 80, 86, 119n, 143, 153, 256, 340, 361, 363, 364; **IV:** xi, xiv, xvi xviii, xix, 41, 42, **73–86,** 128, 135, 137, 148, 252–253, 255, 257, 259, 260, 320, 341, 349; **V:** 328
Lamb, John, **IV:** 74, 77, 84
Lamb, Mary, **IV:** xvi, 77–78, 80, 83–84, 128, 135
"Lamb to the Slaughter" (Dahl), **Supp. IV:** 215, 219
Lambert, Gavin, **Supp. IV:** 3, 8
"Lament" (Gunn), **Supp. IV:** 277–278; **Retro. Supp. III:** 127
"Lament" (Montague), **Supp. XV:** 216
Lament for a Lover (Highsmith), **Supp. V:** 170
"Lament for One's Self" (Pitter), **Supp. XIII:** 134

"Lament for the Great Music" (MacDiarmid), **Supp. XII:** 203
"Lament for the Makaris, The" (Dunbar), **VIII:** 118, 121, 127–128
Lament of Tasso, The (Byron), **IV:** 192
"Lament of the Duke of Medina Sidonia" (Beer), **Supp. XIV:** 5
"Lament of the Images" (Okri), **Supp. V:** 359
"Lament over the Ruins of the Abbey of Teach Molaga" (Mangan), **Supp. XIII:** 128
Lamia (Keats), **III:** 338; **IV:** xviii, 216, 217, 219–220, 231, 235; **Retro. Supp. I:** 192–193
Lamia, Isabella, The Eve of St. Agnes, and Other Poems (Keats), **IV:** xviii, 211, 235; **Retro. Supp. I:** 184, 192–196
Lamming, George, **Supp. IV:** 445
"Lamp and the Jar, The" (Hope), **Supp. VII:** 158
Lamp and the Lute, The (Dobrée), **VI:** 204
Lampitt Papers, The (Wilson), **Supp. VI:** 297, 304, **306–307**
Lanark: A Life in Four Books (Gray, A.), **Supp. IX:** 79–83, 84–86, 88–89
Lancelot and Guinevere (Malory), **I:** 70–71, 77
Lancelot du Laik, **I:** 73
Lancelot, The Death of Rudel, and Other Poems (Swinburne), **V:** 333
"Lancer" (Housman), **VI:** 160
"Land, The" (Gibbon), **Supp. XIV:** 99, 103
"Land Girl at the Boss's Grave, The" (Beer), **Supp. XIV:** 4
"Land of Counterpane, The" (Stevenson), **Retro. Supp. I:** 260
Land of Heart's Desire, The (Yeats), **VI:** 221; **Retro. Supp. I:** 326
"Land of Loss, The" (Kinsella), **Supp. V:** 271
Land of Promise, The (Maugham), **VI:** 369
"Land under the Ice, The" (Nicholson), **Supp. VI:** 216
Landfall, **Supp. XII:** 3
"Landing" (Montague), **Supp. XV:** 219
Landing on the Sun, A (Frayn), **Supp. VII:** 62–63
"Landlady, The" (Behan), **Supp. II:** 63–64
"Landlady, The" (Dahl), **Supp. IV:** 215–216, 217
Landleaguers, The (Trollope), **V:** 102
Landlocked (Lessing), **Supp. I:** 245, 248
Landmarks in French Literature (Strachey), **Supp. II: 502–503**
Landnámabók, **VIII:** 235, 238
Landon, Letitia, **IV:** 311
Landor, Walter Savage, **II:** 293; **III:** 139; **IV:** xiv, xvi, xviii, xix, xxii, **87–100,** 252, 254, 356; **V:** 320
Landor's Tower; or, The Imaginary Conversations (Sinclair), **Supp. XIV:** 232
Landscape (Pinter), **Supp. I:** 375–376
"Landscape Painter, A" (James), **VI:** 69

"Landscape with One Figure" (Dunn), **Supp. X:** 70
Landscapes Within, The (Okri), **Supp. V:** 347, 348, 350, 352, 353–354, 360
Landseer, Edwin, **V:** 175
Lane, Margaret, **V:** 13*n*, 16
Lang, Andrew, **V:** 392–393, 395; **VI:** 158; **Supp. II:** 115
Lang, C. Y., **V:** 334, 335
Langland, William, **I:** vii, **1–18**
"Language Ah Now You Have Me" (Graham), **Supp. VII:** 115
Language Made Plain (Burgess), **Supp. I:** 197
"Language of Crying, The" (Delanty), **Supp. XIV:** 75
Language of Fiction: Essays in Criticism and Verbal Analysis of the English Novel (Lodge), **Supp. II:** 9; **Supp. IV:** 365, 366
Language, Truth and Logic (Ayer), **VII:** 240
Languages of Love, The (Brooke–Rose), **Supp. IV:** 99, 100–101
Lannering, Jan, **III:** 52
"Lantern Bearers, The" (Stevenson), **V:** 385
Lantern Bearers, The (Sutcliff), **Supp. XVI:** 261, 262, 263, 266, 268, 270, 271
"Lantern out of Doors, The," (Hopkins), **V:** 380
Lantern Slides (O'Brien), **Supp. V:** 341
Laodicean, A; or, The Castle of the De Stancys (Hardy), **VI:** 4–5, 20
Laon and Cynthia (Shelley), **IV:** 195, 196, 198, 208; **Retro. Supp. I:** 249–250; *see also* Revolt of Islam, The
"Lapis Lazuli" (Yeats), **Retro. Supp. I:** 337
Lara (Byron), **IV:** xvii, 172, 173, 175, 192; *see also* Turkish tales
"Large Cool Store, The" (Larkin), **Supp. I:** 279
Lark, The (Fry), **Supp. III:** 195
"Lark Ascending, The" (Meredith), **V:** 221, 223
Lark Rise (Thompson), **Supp. XV:** 277, 279, 280, 282, 289
Lark Rise to Candleford: A Trilogy by Flora Thompson (Thompson), **Supp. XV:** 277, 278, 279, 280, 284, 286–287, 290, 291
Larkin, Philip, **Supp. I:** 275–290; **Supp. II:** 2, 3, 375; **Supp. IV:** 256, 431; **Retro. Supp. III: 198–213**
"Larkin Automatic Car Wash, The" (Ewart), **Supp. VII:** 41
"Lars Porsena of Clusium" (Macaulay), **IV:** 282
Lars Porsena; or, The Future of Swearing and Improper Language (Graves), **VII:** 259–260
"Lascar, The" (Robinson), **Supp. XIII:** 212
Lasselia; or, The Self–Abandoned (Haywood), **Supp. XII:** 137, 140
"Last Address, The" (Lowry), **Supp. III:** 272

Last and the First, The (Compton–Burnett), **VII:** 59, 61, 67
"Last Ark, The" (Tolkien), **Supp. II:** 522
Last Battle, The (Lewis), **Supp. III:** 248, 261
"Last Christmas" (Conn), **Supp. XIII:** 74
Last Chronicle of Barset, The (Trollope), **II:** 173; **V:** xxiii, 93–95, 101
"Last Coiffeur, The" (Delanty), **Supp. XIV:** 77
"Last Confession, A" (Rossetti), **V:** 240–241
"Last Day of Summer, The" (McEwan), **Supp. IV:** 390
Last Days of Lord Byron, The (Parry), **IV:** 191, 193
Last Days of Sodom, The (Orton), **Supp. V:** 364
"Last Duchess" (Hardy), **Retro. Supp. I:** 120
Last Essay (Conrad), **VI:** 148
Last Essays of Elia, The (Lamb), **IV:** xix, 76–77, 82–83, 85
Last Essays on Church and Religion (Arnold), **V:** 212, 216
Last Fight of the Revenge at Sea, The (Ralegh), **I:** 145, 149–150
Last Fruit off the Old Tree, The (Landor), **IV:** 100
"Last Galway Hooker, The" (Murphy), **Supp. V:** 313, 316, 319
Last Generation in England, The (Gaskell), **Retro. Supp. III:** 104
"Last Hellos, The" (Murray), **Supp. VII:** 283
"Last Instructions to a Painter, The" (Marvell), **II:** 217–218
Last Letters from Hav (Morris, J.), **Supp. X:** 171, 185–186
Last Loves (Sillitoe), **Supp. V:** 411, 414, 415–416, 425
"Last Man, The" (Gunn), **Supp. IV:** 264; **Retro. Supp. III:** 121
Last Man, The (Shelley), **Supp. III: 364–371**; **Retro. Supp. III:** 287, 290, 297–299
"Last Moa, The" (Adcock), **Supp. XII:** 12
Last Night's Fun (Carson), **Supp. XIII:** 53, 55, 61–63
"Last of March (Written at Lolham Brigs), The" (Clare), **Supp. XI:** 57
Last of the Country House Murders, The (Tennant), **Supp. IX:** 230
Last of the Duchess, The (Blackwood), **Supp. IX:** 8, 13–14
"Last of the Fire Kings" (Mahon), **Supp. VI:** 172
Last of the High Kings, The (Thompson), **Supp. XIV:** 296–297
Last of the Wine, The (Renault), **Supp. IX:** 182–183, 187
Last Orders (Swift), **Supp. V:** 440–441
Last Poems (Browning), **IV:** 312, 315, 357
Last Poems (Fuller), **Supp. VII:** 79
Last Poems (Housman), **VI:** 157, 158, 160, 161, 162, 164
Last Poems (Meredith), **V:** 234
Last Poems (Reading), **VIII:** 273

Last Poems (Yeats), **VI:** 214
Last Poems and Two Plays (Yeats), **VI:** 213
Last Pool and Other Stories, The (O'Brian), **Supp. XII:** 251
Last Post (Ford), **VI:** 319, 330–331
Last Pre–Raphaelite, The: A Record of the Life and Writings of Ford Madox Ford (Goldring), **VI:** 333
"Last Requests" (Longley), **VIII:** 173
Last September, The (Bowen), **Supp. II:** 77, 78, 79, 83–86, 89
Last Sheaf, A (Welch), **Supp. IX:** 267
Last Summer, The (Smith, I. C.), **Supp. IX:** 209
Last Testament of Oscar Wilde, The (Ackroyd), **Supp. VI:** 5
Last Thing (Snow), **VII:** xxi, 324, 332–333
"Last Things, The" (Ewart), **Supp. VII:** 40
"Last to Go" (Pinter), **Retro. Supp. I:** 217
"Last Tournament, The" (Tennyson), **V:** 327; **Retro. Supp. III:** 327
"Last Will and Testament" (Auden), **Retro. Supp. I:** 7
Last Words of Thomas Carlyle, The (Carlyle), **IV:** 250
Late Augustans, The (Davie), **Supp. VI:** 115
Late Bourgeois World, The (Gordimer), **Supp. II:** 228, 229, 231, 233, 234, 236, 238
Late Call (Wilson), **Supp. I:** 156, 161–162, 163
Late Harvest (Douglas), **VI:** 300, 302–303, 305, 333
Late Mr. Shakespeare, The (Nye), **Supp. X:** 194, 196, 200, 202–203, 206
Late Murder in Whitechapel, The; or, Keep the Widow Waking, see Late Murder of the Son . . .
Late Murder of the Son Upon the Mother, A; or, Keep the Widow Waking (Dekker, Ford, Rowley, Webster), **II:** 85–86, 89, 100
"Late Period" (Fuller), **Supp. VII:** 78
Late Picking, A: Poems 1965–1974 (Hope), **Supp. VII:** 157, 158
Late Pickings (Ewart), **Supp. VII:** 45
Latecomers (Brookner), **Supp. IV:** 130–131, 136
Later and Italian Poems of Milton (tr. Cowper), **III:** 220
Later Days (Davies), **Supp. XI:** 91, 92
"Later Decalogue, The," (Clough), **V:** 155
"Later Life" (Rossetti), **Retro. Supp. III:** 251
"Later Poems" (Bridges), **VI:** 78, 83
Later Poems (Clarke), **Supp. XV:** 26
Later Poems, 1972–1982 (Thomas), **Supp. XII:** 288
Latter–Day Pamphlets (Carlyle), **IV:** xxi, 240, 247–248, 249, 250
"Laud and Praise made for our Sovereign Lord The King" (Skelton), **I:** 88–89
Laugh and Lie Down (Swinburne), **V:** 312, 332

Laugh and Lie Down; or, The World's Folly (Tourneur), **II:** 37
Laughable Lyrics (Lear), **V:** 78, 85, 87
Laughing Anne (Conrad), **VI:** 148
"Laughter" (Beerbohm), **Supp. II:** 47–48
"Laughter Beneath the Bridge" (Okri), **Supp. V:** 355
Laughter in the Next Room (Sitwell), **VII:** 130, 135
Launch–Site for English Studies: Three Centuries of Literary Studies at the University of St. Andrews (ed. Crawford), **Supp. XI:** 76, 82
"Laundon, City of the Moon" (Redgrove), **Supp. VI:** 234
"Laundress, The" (Kinsella), **Supp. V:** 261
"Laurel Axe, The" (Hill), **Retro. Supp. III:** 137
"Laus Veneris" (Swinburne), **IV:** 346; **V:** 316, 318, 320, 327, 346
L'Autre monde ou les états et empires de la lune (Cyrano de Bergerac), **III:** 24
Lavater, J. C., **III:** 298
"Lavatory Attendant, The" (Cope), **VIII:** 74
Lavengro: The Scholar, the Gipsy, the Priest (Borrow), **Supp. XII:** 17, 20–27, 31
Law, William, **IV:** 45
Law Against Lovers, The (Davenant), **I:** 327
Law and the Grace, The (Smith, I. C.), **Supp. IX:** 212–213
Law and the Lady, The (Collins), **Supp. VI:** 102
Law Hill poems (Brontë), **V:** 126–128
Law Is a Bottomless–Pit (Arbuthnot), **Supp. XVI:** 20–**Supp. XVI:** 21
Law of the Threshold, The (Steel), **Supp. XII:** 275–276
Lawless Roads, The (Greene; U.S. title, *nother Mexico*), **Supp. I:** 9, 10
Lawrence, D. H., **II:** 330; **IV:** 106, 119, 120, 195; **V:** xxv, 6, 47; **VI:** 235, 243, 248, 259, 275–276, 283, 363, 409, 416; **VI:** xii, xiv–xvi, 18, 75, **87–126,** 201, 203–204, 215; **Supp. II:** 492; **Supp. III:** 86, 91, 397–398; **Supp. IV:** 5, 94, 139, 233, 241, 369; **Retro. Supp. II:** 221–235
Lawrence, Frieda, **VII:** 90, 111
Lawrence, T. E., **VI:** 207, 408; **Supp. II:** 147, **283–297; Supp. IV:** 160
"Lawrence, of virtuous father virtuous son" (Milton), **II:** 163
Laws of Candy, The, **II:** 67
Lawson, Henry, **Supp. IV:** 460
Laxdæla saga, **VIII:** 238, 239, 240
"Lay By" (Hare), **Supp. IV:** 281, 283
Lay Down Your Arms (Potter, D.), **Supp. X:** 231
"Lay for New Lovers" (Reid), **Supp. VII:** 325
Lay Morals and Other Papers (Stevenson), **V:** 396
Lay of Lilies, A, and Other Poems (Swinburne), **V:** 333
"Lay of the Bell, The" (Mangan), **Supp. XIII:** 121–122

"Lay of the Brown Rosary, The" (Browning), **IV:** 313
"Lay of the Labourer, The" (Hood), **IV:** 252, 261, 265–266
Lay of The Last Minstrel, The (Scott), **IV:** xvi, 29, 38, 48, 218
"Lay of the Laureate" (Southey), **IV:** 61, 71
Lays of Leisure Hours (Jewsbury), **Supp. XIV:** 149, 156–157
Layamon, **I:** 72
"Laying a Lawn" (Raine), **Supp. XIII:** 167
Laying on of Hands, The: Stories (Bennett), **VIII:** 20
Lays of Ancient Rome (Macaulay), **IV:** xx, 272, 282–283, 290–291
"Lays of Many Lands" (Mangan), **Supp. XIII:** 118
"Lazarus and the Sea" (Redgrove), **Supp. VI: 225–227,** 231
"Lazarus Not Raised" (Gunn), **Supp. IV:** 259; **Retro. Supp. III:** 118
Lazy Tour of Two Idle Apprentices, The (Collins), **Supp. VI:** 92
Lazy Tour of Two Idle Apprentices, The (Dickens), **V:** 72
Le Carré, John, **Supp. II: 299–319; Supp. IV:** 4, 5, 9, 13, 14, 15, 17, 22, 445, 449; **Retro. Supp. III: 215–231**
"Le christianisme" (Owen), **VI:** 445, 450
Le dépit amoureux (Molière), **II:** 325, 336
Le Fanu, Sheridan, **III:** 333, 340, 342, 343, 345; **Supp. II:** 78–79, 81; **Supp. III:** 385–386
Le Gallienne, Richard, **V:** 412, 413
Le Jugement du Roy de Behaingne (Machaut), **Retro. Supp. II:** 37
Le misanthrope (Molière), **II:** 318
Le roman bourgeois (Furetière), **II:** 354
Le Roman de la Rose (Guillaurne), **Retro. Supp. II:** 36
Le Sage, Alain René, **II:** 325; **III:** 150
"Lea, The" (Soutar), **Supp. XVI:** 250
"Lead" (Kinsella), **Supp. V:** 260
"Lead, Kindly Light" (Newman), **Supp. VII:** 291
"Leaden Echo and the Golden Echo, The" (Hopkins), **V:** 371
Leader (periodical), **V:** 189
Leaf and the Marble, The (Smith, I. C.), **Supp. IX:** 209, 223
"Leaf Blown Upstream, A" (Nye), **Supp. X:** 201
"Leaf by Niggle" (Tolkien), **Supp. II:** 521
"Leaf Used as a Bookmark, A" (Nye), **Supp. X:** 203
Leak in the Universe, A (Richards), **Supp. II:** 426–427
Lean Tales (Kelman, Owens, and Gray), **Supp. V:** 249; **Supp. IX:** 80, 82, 90
"Leaning Tower, The" (Woolf), **VII:** 26; **Retro. Supp. I:** 310
Lear (Bond), **Supp. I:** 423, 427, **430–432,** 433, 435
Lear, Edward, **V:** xi, xvii, xv, xxv, **75–87,** 262; **Supp. IV:** 201
Lear Coloured Bird Book for Children, The (Lear), **V:** 86, 87

Lear in Sicily (ed. Proby), **V:** 87
Lear in the Original (ed. Liebert), **V:** 87
Learned Comment upon Dr. Hare's Excellent Sermon, A (Swift), **III,** 35
Learned Hippopotamus, The (Ewart), **Supp. VII:** 47
"Learning Gaelic" (Burnside), **Supp. XIII:** 20
Learning Human: Selected Prose (Murray), **Supp. VII:** 271
Learning Laughter (Spender), **Supp. II:** 491
"Learning to Swim" (Swift), **Supp. V:** 431–432
Learning to Swim and Other Stories (Swift), **Supp. V:** 431–434
"Learning's Little Tribute" (Wilson), **Supp. I:** 157
Lease of Life (film, Ambler), **Supp. IV:** 3
"Leather Goods" (Redgrove), **Supp. VI:** 236
"Leave the Door Open" (Scupham), **Supp. XIII:** 224
"Leaves from a Young Person's Notebook" (Welch), **Supp. IX:** 267, 268
"Leave–Taking, A" (Swinburne), **V:** 319
"Leaving Barra" (MacNeice), **VI:** 411–412
"Leaving Belfast" (Motion), **Supp. VII:** 254, 262
"Leaving Dundee" (Dunn), **Supp. X:** 77
Leavis, F. R., **II:** 254, 258, 271; **III:** 68, 78; **IV:** 227, 323, 338, 339; **V:** 195, 199, 201, 237, 309, 355, 375, 381, 382; **VI:** 13; **V:** xvi, xix, 72–73, 88, 101, 102, **233–256; Supp. II:** 2, 179, 429; **Supp. III:** 60; **Supp. IV:** 142, 229–230, 233, 256; **Retro. Supp. I:** 90
Leavis, Q. D., **II:** 250; **V:** 286, 290; **VI:** 377; **VII:** 233, 238, 250
Leben des Galilei (Brecht), **Supp. IV:** 298
Leben Jesu, Das (tr. Eliot), **V:** 189, 200
"Lecknavarna" (Murphy), **Supp. V:** 328
Lecky, William, **IV:** 289
Lecky, William E. H., **Supp. V:** 41
L'école des femmes (Molière), **II:** 314
L'école des maris (Molière), **II:** 314
"Lecture on Modern Poetry, A" (Hulme), **Supp. VI:** 135–136, 138, 142–144
Lectures Chiefly on the Dramatic Literature of the Age of Elizabeth (Hazlitt), **IV:** xviii, 125, 129–130, 139
Lectures on Architecture and Paintings (Ruskin), **V:** 184
Lectures on Art (Ruskin), **V:** 184
Lectures on Certain Difficulties Felt by Anglicans in Submitting to the Catholic Church (Newman), **Supp. VII:** 297–298
Lectures on Justifiation (Newman), **II:** 243n; **Supp. VII:** 294, 301
Lectures on Shakespeare (Coleridge), **IV:** xvii, 52, 56
Lectures on the Early History of the Kingship (Frazer), **Supp. III:** 175
Lectures on the English Comic Writers (Hazlitt), **IV:** xviii, 129–130, 131, 136, 139

Lectures on the English Poets (Hazlitt), **IV:** xvii, 41, 129–130, 139; **Retro. Supp. II:** 51
Lectures on the Present Position of Catholics in England (Newman), **Supp. VII:** 298
Lectures on the Prophetical Office of the Church Viewed Relatively to Romanism and Popular Protestantism (Newman), **Supp. VII:** 293–294, 301, 302
"Leda and the Swan" (Yeats), **V:** 345
Lee, George John Vandeleur, **VI:** 101
Lee, Gypsy Rose, **Supp. IV:** 422, 423, 424
Lee, Hermione, **Retro. Supp. I:** 305
Lee, J., **II:** 336
Lee, Nathaniel, **II:** 305
Lee, Sidney, **V:** 280
Leech, Clifford, **II:** 44, 49, 52, 60, 62, 64, 70, 86, 90*n*, 100
Leech, John, **IV:** 258
Leenane Trilogy, The (McDonagh), **Supp. XII:** 233, 234–237, 238, 239, 240, 241
Left Bank and Other Stories, The (Rhys), **Supp. II:** 388, **389–390**
Left–Handed Liberty (Arden), **Supp. II:** 29, 30
Left Heresy in Literature and Art, The (Kemp and Riding), **Supp. III:** 120
Left Leg, The (Powys), **VIII:** 249, 250
"Left, Right, Left, Right: The Arrival of Tony Blair" (Barnes), **Supp. IV:** 74
"Legacie, The" (Donne), **Retro. Supp. II:** 88, 91–92
"Legacy, The" (King), **Supp. VI:** 152–153
"Legacy, The" (Motion), **Supp. VII:** 261
Legacy of Cain, The (Collins), **Supp. VI:** 103
"Legend" (Fallon), **Supp. XII:** 103
Legend of Good Women, The (Chaucer), **I:** 24–31, 38; **Retro. Supp. II:** 40
Legend of Juba;, The, and Other Poems (Eliot), **V:** 200
Legend of Montrose, A (Scott), **IV:** xviii, 35, 39
Legend of the Rhine, A (Thackeray), **V:** 38
"Legacy on My Fiftieth Birthday, A" (Stevenson), **Supp. VI:** 262
Legendre's Elements of Geometry (Carlyle), **IV:** 250
"Legends of Ancient Eire, The" (Russell), **VIII:** 282
Legends of Angria (ed. Ratchford), **V:** 112
Léger, Fernand, **Supp. IV:** 81
"Legion Club, The" (Swift), **III:** 21, 31
Legion Hall Bombing, The (Churchill), **Supp. IV:** 181
Legion's Memorial to the House of Commons (Defoe), **III:** 12; **Retro. Supp. I:** 67
Legislation (Ruskin), **V:** 178
Legouis, Pierre, **II:** 207, 209, 218, 219, 220
Lehmann, John Frederick, **VII:** xvii, xxx-viii
Leigh, R. A., **III:** 246*n*

Leigh Hunt's Examiner Examined (Blunden), **IV:** 236
Leila, A Tale (Browning), **IV:** 321
"Leisure" (Blunden), **Supp. XI:** 42
"Leisure" (Lamb), **IV:** 83
"Leith Races" (Fergusson), **III:** 317
"L.E.L." (Rossetti), **Retro. Supp. III:** 263
Leland, John, **I:** 113
Lemady (Roberts, K.), **Supp. X:** 261
Lemon, Mark, **IV:** 263
"Lend Me Your Light" (Mistry), **Supp. X:** 141–142
"Lenin" (Smith, I. C.), **Supp. IX:** 212–213, 216
"Lenten Offering, The" (Warner), **Supp. VII:** 371
Leonard's War: A Love Story (Sillitoe), **Supp. V:** 411
"Leonardo Da Vinci" (Pater), **V:** 345–347, 348
Leonora (Edgeworth), **Supp. III:** 158
"'Leopard' George" (Lessing), **Supp. I:** 242
"Lepanto" (Chesterton), **VI:** 340
"Leper, The" (Swinburne), **V:** 315
"Leper, The" (Thompson), **Supp. XV:** 286
"Leper's Walk" (Delanty), **Supp. XIV:** 74
LeQueux, William, **Supp. II:** 299
"Lerici" (Gunn), **Supp. IV:** 259
Les aventures de Télémaque (Fénelon), **III:** 95, 99
Les bourgeoises à la mode (Dancourt), **II:** 325, 336
Les carrosses d'Orleans (La Chapelle), **II:** 358
"Les Chats" (Baudelaire), **Supp. IV:** 115
Les Damnés de la terre (Fanon), **Supp. IV:** 105
Les fables d'Ésope (Boursault), **II:** 324
Les Heures de silence (tr. Richardson), **Supp. XIII:** 191
Les Misérables (Hugo), **Supp. IV:** 86
"Les Noyades" (Swinburne), **V:** 319, 320
"Les Vaches" (Clough), **V:** 168
Lesbia Brandon (Swinburne), **V:** 313, 325, 326–327, 332
Leslie Stephen (MacCarthy), **V:** 284, 290
Leslie Stephen and Matthew Arnold as Critics of Wordsworth (Wilson), **V:** 287, 290
Leslie Stephen: Cambridge Critic (Leavis), **VII:** 238
Leslie Stephen: His Thought and Character in Relation to His Time (Annan), **V:** 284–285, 290
Less Deceived, The (Larkin), **Supp. I:** 275, 277, 278, 279, 285; **Retro. Supp. III:** 204–205, 208–211, 210
Less Than Angels (Pym), **Supp. II: 372–374**
"Lesser Arts, The" (Morris), **V:** 291, 301
Lessing, Doris, **Supp. I: 237–257; Supp. IV:** 78, 233, 234, 473
Lessing, Gotthold Ephraim, **IV:** 53
Lessius, **II:** 181*n*
Lessness (Beckett), **Supp. I:** 52, 61

Lesson from Aloes, A (Fugard), **Supp. XV:** 103, 110
"Lesson in Music, A" (Reid), **Supp. VII:** 324–325
"Lesson of the Master, The" (James), **VI:** 48, 67, 69
"Lessons in Survival" (Scupham), **Supp. XIII:** 218, 219
"Lessons of the Summer" (Fuller), **Supp. VII:** 80
Lessons of the War (Reed), **VII:** 422; **Supp. XV:** 243, 244, 245, 247, 249–251, 254, 255
L'Estrange, Sir Robert, **III:** 41
"Let Him Loose" (Cameron), **Supp. IX:** 24
Let It Bleed (Rankin), **Supp. X:** 244, 251, 253
"Let It Go" (Empson), **Supp. II:** 180, 194
Let Me Alone (Kavan), **Supp. VII:** 202–204, 205, 206, 207, 214
"Let that be a Lesson" (Kelman), **Supp. V:** 249
"Let the Brothels of Paris be opened" (Blake), **III:** 299
Let the People Sing (Priestley), **VII:** 217
"Let Them Call It Jazz" (Rhys), **Supp. II:** 402
"Let them rejoice in their beds" (Rossetti), **Retro. Supp. III:** 258–259
"Let Us Now Praise Unknown Women and Our Mothers Who Begat Us" (Maitland), **Supp. XI:** 175
Let's Have Some Poetry! (Jennings), **Supp. V:** 206, 214
Lethaby, W. R., **V:** 291, 296, 306
"Letter, The" (Beer), **Supp. XIV:** 5
"Letter, The" (Brontë), **V:** 132
"Letter, The" (Hart), **Supp. XI:** 130
Letter, The (Maugham), **VI:** 369
"Letter, The" (Smith, I. C.), **Supp. IX:** 215
"Letter, The" (Thomas), **Supp. XII:** 290
Letter Addressed to His Grace the Duke of Norfolk (Newman), **Supp. VII:** 302
Letter and Spirit: Notes on the Commandments (Rossetti), **V:** 260; **Retro. Supp. III:** 252, 263–264
Letter . . . Concerning the Sacramental Test, A (Swift), **III:** 35
Letter from a Member . . . in Ireland to a Member in England, A (Defoe), **III:** 18
Letter from Amsterdam to a Friend in England, A, **II:** 206
"Letter from Armenia, A" (Hill), **Supp. V:** 189
"Letter from Artemiza . . . to Chloë, A" (Rochester), **II;** 260, 270; **Supp. III:** 70
"Letter from Hamnovoe" (Brown), **Supp. VI:** 64
"Letter from Home, The" (Kincaid), **Supp. VII:** 221
Letter . . . in Vindication of His Conduct with Regard to the Affairs of Ireland, A (Burke), **III:** 205
Letter of Advice to a Young Poet, A (Swift), **III:** 35

Letter of Marque (O'Brian), **Supp. XII:** 257

Letter of Thanks . . . to the . . . Bishop of S. Asaph, A (Swift), **III:** 35

Letter of Travell, A (Greville), **Supp. XI:** 108

Letter . . . on the Conduct of the Minority in Parliament, A (Burke), **III:** 205

"Letter to —, April 4, 1802, A" (Coleridge), **Retro. Supp. II:** 61

"Letter to a Brother of the Pen in Tribulation, A" (Behn), **Supp. III:** 40

Letter . . . to a Country Gentleman . . . , A (Swift), **III:** 35

Letter to a Friend, A (Browne), **II:** 153, 156

"Letter to a Friend" (Stallworthy), **Supp. X:** 295

"Letter to a Friend on Leaving Town" (Robinson), **Supp. XIII:** 199

Letter . . . to a Gentleman Designing for Holy Orders, A (Swift), **III:** 35

Letter to a Member of the National Assembly, A (Burke), **III:** 205

Letter to a Monk (More), **Supp. VII:** 240, 241–242

Letter to a Noble Lord (Burke), **IV:** 127

Letter to a Peer of Ireland on the Penal Laws (Burke), **III:** 205

"Letter to an Exile" (Motion), **Supp. VII:** 254, 257

Letter to an Honourable Lady, A (Greville), **Supp. XI:** 108

Letter to Brixius (More), **Supp. VII:** 241

"Letter to Curtis Bradford, A" (Davie), **Supp. VI:** 109

Letter to Dorp (More), **Supp. VII:** 240–241

Letter To Dr. Holdsworth, Occasioned By His Sermon Preached before the University of Oxford, A: On Easter Monday Concerning the Resurrection of the Same Body (Trotter), **Supp. XVI:** 289–290

Letter to Edward Lee (More), **Supp. VII:** 240

"Letter to John Donne, A" (Sisson), **Supp. XI:** 256

Letter to John Murray, Esq., "Touching" Lord Nugent (Southey), **IV:** 71

"Letter to Lord Byron" (Auden), **IV:** 106; **Supp. II:** 200; **Retro. Supp. I:** 7

Letter to Lord Ellenborough, A (Shelley), **IV:** 208

"Letter to Maria Gisborne" (Shelley), **IV:** 204

"Letter to Mr. Creech at Oxford, A" (Behn), **Supp. III:** 41

Letter to Mr. Harding the Printer, A (Swift), **III:** 35

Letter to Oxford (More), **Supp. VII:** 240–241

Letter to Peace–Lovers (Brittain), **Supp. X:** 45

"Letter to R.L., Esq., on his Departure from London, A" (Byrom), **Supp. XVI:** 73–74

Letter to Robert MacQueen Lord Braxfield . . . , A (Boswell), **III:** 248

Letter to Samuel Whitbread (Malthus), **IV:** 127

"Letter to Sara Hutchinson" (Coleridge), **IV:** 15

Letter to Sir Hercules Langrishe on . . . the Roman Catholics .. . . , A (Burke), **III:** 205

"Letter to Sylvia Plath" (Stevenson), **Supp. VI:** 263–264

"Letter to the Bishop of Llandaff" (Wordsworth), **IV:** 2

Letter to the Noble Lord on the Attacks Made upon Him . . . in the House of Lords, A (Burke), **III:** 205

Letter to the People of Scotland, on . . . the Articles of the Union, A (Boswell), **III:** 248

Letter to the People of Scotland, on the Present State of the Nation, A (Boswell), **III:** 248

Letter to the Shop–Keepers . . . of Ireland, A (Swift), **III:** 28, 35

Letter to the Whole People of Ireland, A (Swift), **III:** 35

Letter to the Women of England, A (Robinson), **Supp. XIII:** 195, 196, 211

Letter to Viscount Cobham, A (Congreve), **II:** 350

Letter to . . . Viscount Molesworth, A (Swift), **III:** 35

"Letter to William Coldstream" (Auden), **Retro. Supp. I:** 7

Letter to William Gifford, Esq., A (Hazlitt), **IV:** 139

Letter to William Smith, Esq., MP, A (Southey), **IV:** 71

Letter Writers, The (Fielding), **III:** 97, 105

Letter Written to a Gentleman in the Country, A . . . (Milton), **II:** 176

Letterbook of Sir George Etherege, The (ed. Rosenfeld), **II:** 271

"Letterfrack Industrial School" (Murphy), **Supp. V:** 316

Letters (Coleridge), **II:** 119n

Letters (Warner), **Supp. VII:** 377, 382

Letters Addressed to Lord Liverpool, and the Parliament . . . (Landor), **IV:** 100

Letters and Diaries (Newman), **Supp. VII:** 293, 297

Letters and Journals (Byron), **IV:** 185, 193

Letters and Journals of Lord Byron, with Notices of His Life, by T. Moore (Moore), **IV:** 193, 281; **V:** 116

Letters and Papers of John Addington Symonds (Symonds), **Supp. XIV:** 263–264

Letters and Passages from . . . Clarissa (Richardson), **III:** 92

Letters and Private Papers of W. M. Thackeray (ed. Ray), **V:** 37, 140

Letters and Prose Writings (Cowper), **Retro. Supp. III:** 35, 37, 38, 39, 40, 41, 42, 43, 46, 48

Letters and Works of Lady Mary Wortley Montagu, **II:** 326n

Letters for Literary Ladies (Edgeworth), **Supp. III:** 153

Letters from a Citizen of the World (Goldsmith), *see Citizen of the World, The*

Letters from a Lost Generation: The First World War Letters of Vera Brittain and Four Friends, Roland Leighton, Edward Brittain, Victor Richardson, Geoffrey Thurlow (Brittain), **Supp. X:** 47

Letters from America (Brooke), **Supp. III:** 47, 50, 54–55, 59–60

Letters from Darkness (tr. Adcock), **Supp. XII:** 11

Letters from England: By Don Manuel Alvarez Espriella (Southey), **IV:** 60, 68–69, 71

Letters from Iceland (Auden and MacNeice), **VII:** 403; **Retro. Supp. I:** 7

Letters from Ireland (Martineau), **Supp. XV:** 186

Letters from John Galsworthy (ed. Garnett), **VI:** 290

Letters from Julia; or, Light from the Borderland (Stead), **Supp. XIII:** 243

Letters from London (Barnes), **Supp. IV:** 65, 74–75

"Letters From The Alphabet" (Carson), **Supp. XIII:** 60–61

Letters from the Lake Poets to D. Stuart (ed. Coleridge), **IV:** 144

"Letters from the Rocky Mountains" (Bird), **Supp. X:** 28

Letters from W. S. Landor to R. W. Emerson (Landor), **IV:** 100

Letters of a Conservative, The (Landor), **IV:** 100

Letters of Alfred Lord Tennyson, The (Tennyson), **Retro. Supp. III:** 328

"Letters of an Englishman" (Brontë), **V:** lll

Letters of an Old Playgoer (Arnold), **V:** 216

Letters of Charles Lamb . . . , The (ed. Lucas), **II:** 119n, **IV:** 84, 86

Letters of Christina Rossetti, The (Rossetti), **Retro. Supp. III:** 254, 260

Letters of Elizabeth Barrett Browning (ed. Kenyon), **IV:** 312, 321

Letters of G. M. Hopkins to Robert Bridges (ed. Abbott), **VI:** 83

Letters of Hugh MacDiarmid, The (MacDiarmid), **Supp. XII:** 209

Letters of James Boswell . . . (ed. Francis), **III:** 249

Letters of James Boswell (ed. Tinker), **III:** 234n, 249

Letters of John Clare, The (Clare), **Supp. XI:** 55, 56, 57, 62

Letters of John Keats to Fanny Browne, **Retro. Supp. I:** 185

Letters of Laurence Sterne (ed. Curtis), **III:** 124n

Letters of Matthew Arnold, 1848–1888 (ed. Russell), **V:** 205, 206, 208, 211, 216

Letters of Mrs. Gaskell, The (ed. Chapell and Pollard), **V:** 108, 137, 151; **Retro. Supp. III:** 103, 109, 112

Letters of Robert Browning (Browning), **Retro. Supp. III:** 26
Letters of Robert Browning and Elizabeth Barrett, 1845–46, **IV:** 318–319, 320, 321
Letters of Runnymede (Disraeli), **IV:** 298, 308
Letters of State, Written by Mr. John Milton . . . (Milton), **II:** 176
Letters of T. E. Lawrence, The (Lawrence), **Supp. II:** 287, 290
Letters of Travel (Kipling), **Retro. Supp. III:** 187
Letters of W. B. Yeats (ed. Wade), **VII:** 134
Letters of Walter Savage Landor, Private and Public (ed. Wheeler), **IV:** 89, 98, 100
Letters of William and Dorothy Wordsworth (ed. Selincourt), **IV:** 11, 25
Letters of Wit, Politicks and Morality, **II:** 352, 364
Letters on Several Occasions (Dennis), **II:** 338
Letters on the Laws of Man's Nature and Development (Martineau), **Supp. XV:** 187, 191
Letters on the Subject of the Catholics, to my brother Abraham, who lives in the Country (Smith), **Supp. VII:** 343
Letters to a Young Gentleman . . . (Swift), **III:** 29
"Letters to a Young Man" (De Quincey), **IV:** 146
Letters to Alice on First Reading Jane Austen (Weldon), **Supp. IV:** 521–522, 536
Letters to Archdeacon Singleton (Smith), **Supp. VII:** 349–350
Letters to Five Artists (Wain), **Supp. XVI:** 306–307
Letters to Henrietta (Bird), **Supp. X:** 23–27,
Letters to Malcolm: Chiefly on Prayer (Lewis), **Supp. III:** 249, 264, 265
Letters to T. E. Lawrence (Lawrence), **Supp. II:** 293
Letters to the Sheriffs of Bristol . . . (Burke), **III:** 205
"Letters to the Winner" (Murray), **Supp. VII:** 279
Letters to the Young (Jewsbury), **Supp. XIV:** 149, 154–156
Letters with a Chapter of Biography, The (Sorley), **VI:** 421
Letters Written During a Short Residence in Spain and Portugal (Southey), **IV:** 71
Letters Written During a Short Residence in Sweden, Norway, and Denmark (Wollstonecraft), **Supp. III:** 473–475, 479
Letters Written to and for Particular Friends (Richardson), *see Familiar Letters*
"Letting in the Jungle" (Kipling), **Retro. Supp. III:** 191–192
"Letting the Demons Speak" (Butlin), **Supp. XVI:** 57–58

Lettres d'une péruvienne (Graffigny), **Supp. III:** 75
Letty Fox: Her Luck (Stead), **Supp. IV:** 473
Levanter, The (Ambler), **Supp. IV:** 16
"Level–Crossing, The" (Warner), **Supp. VII:** 380
Levi, Peter, **Supp. IV:** 159
Leviathan (Hobbes), **II:** 190; **III:** 22; **IV:** 138
Levin, Harry, **I:** 288, 292
Levin, Ira, **III:** 343
Levin, Richard, **II:** 4, 23
Lévi–Strauss, Claude, **Supp. IV:** 115
Levitt, Morton, **Supp. IV:** 233
Levy, Paul, **Supp. IV:** 145
Lewes, George Henry, **IV:** 101, 122; **V:** 137, 189–190, 192, 198; **Retro. Supp. II:** 102–103
Lewis, Alun, **VII:** xxii, 422, **444–448**
Lewis Baboon Turned Honest, and John Bull Politician (Arbuthnot), **Supp. XVI:** 22
Lewis, C. Day, *see* Day Lewis, Cecil
Lewis, C. S., **I:** 81, 95, 117; **III:** 51; **V:** 301, 306; **VII:** 356; **Supp. I:** 71, 72; **Supp. III: 247–268**
Lewis, Matthew, **III:** 331, 332–333, 336, 340, 343, 345; **Supp. III:** 384
Lewis, Peter, **Supp. IV:** 13
Lewis, Wyndham, **VI:** 118, 216, 247, 322; **VII:** xii, xv, 35, 41, 45, 49, 50, **71–85; Supp. IV:** 5
"Lewis Carroll" (de la Mare), **V:** 268, 274
Lewis Carroll (Hudson), **V:** 262–263, 274
Lewis Eliot stories (Snow), **VII:** 322; *see Strangers and Brothers* cycle
Lewis Seymour and Some Women (Moore), **VI:** 86, 89–90, 98, 99
"Lexicography" (Ewart), **Supp. VII:** 45
"Liar, The" (James), **VI:** 69
"Libbie Marsh's Three Eras" (Gaskell), **V:** 15
Libel on D[octor] Delany, A (Swift), **III:** 35
Liber Amoris (Hazlitt), **IV:** 128, 131–132, 133, 139
Liber niger (Edward IV), **I:** 25, 44
Liberal (periodical), **IV:** 132, 172
"Liberty" (Collins), **III:** 166, 172
Liberty (Thomson), **Supp. III:** 411–412, **419–422**
Libra (Delillo), **Supp. IV:** 487
"Libraries. A Celebration" (Dunn), **Supp. X:** 79
Library, The (Crabbe), **III:** 274, 280, 286
"Library Window, The" (Oliphant), **Supp. X:** 220
Licking Hitler (Hare), **Supp. IV:** 282, 287–288
"Licorice Fields at Pontefract, The" (Betjeman), **VII:** 368
Lidoff, Joan, **Supp. IV:** 459
"Lie, The" (Ralegh), **I:** 148
Lie About My Father, A (Burnside), **Supp. XIII:** 28, 30–31
Lie of the Land, The (Beer), **Supp. XIV:** 11
Lies of Silence (Moore, B.), **Supp. IX:** 146, 148–149

"Lieutenant Bligh and Two Midshipmen" (Brown), **Supp. VI:** 70
Lieutenant of Inishmore, The (McDonagh), **Supp. XII:** 233, 238, 241–243, 245
Life, A (Smith, I. C.), **Supp. IX:** 219–220
"Life, A" (Thomas), **Supp. XII:** 280
"Life, The" (Ewart), **Supp. VII:** 39
Life, Adventures, and Pyracies of . . . Captain Singleton, The (Defoe), *see Captain Singleton*
Life After Death (Toynbee), **Supp. I:** 40
Life and Adventures of Martin Chuzzlewit, The (Dickens), *see Martin Chuzzlewit*
Life and Adventures of Nicholas Nickleby, The (Dickens), *see Nicholas Nickleby*
Life and Art (Hardy), **VI:** 20
"Life and Character of Dean Swift, The" (Swift), **III:** 23, 32, 36
Life and Correspondence of Robert Southey, The (Southey), **IV:** 62, 72
Life and Correspondence of Thomas Arnold, The (Stanley), **V:** 13
"Life and Death of God, The" (Ballard), **Supp. V:** 28
Life and Death of Jason, The (Morris), **V:** 296, 297, 298, 304, 306
Life and Death of Mr. Badman, The (Bunyan), **II:** 242, 248, 250–251, 253
Life and Death of My Lord Gilles de Rais, The (Nye), **Supp. X:** 195, 199
Life and Death of Robert Greene (Greene), **VIII:** 133
Life and Death of Tom Thumb, the Great, The (Fielding), **Retro. Supp. I:** 82
"Life and Fame" (Cowley), **II:** 196
Life and Habit (Butler), **Supp. II,** 102, 104–105, 106, 107, 111
Life and Labours of Blessed John Baptist De La Salle, The (Thompson), **V:** 450, 451
Life and Letters of John Galsworthy, The (Marrot), **V:** 270; **VI:** 287
Life and Letters of Leslie Stephen, The (Maitland), **V:** 277, 290
Life and Letters, The (Macaulay), **IV:** 270–271, 284, 291
Life and Loves of a She–Devil, The (Weldon), **Supp. IV:** 537–538
Life and Opinions of Tristram Shandy, Gentleman, The (Sterne), *see Tristram Shandy*
"Life and Poetry of Keats, The" (Masson), **IV:** 212, 235
Life and Strange Surprizing Adventures of Robinson Crusoe . . . , The (Defoe), *see Robinson Crusoe*
Life and the Poet (Spender), **Supp. II:** 489
Life and Times of Laurence Sterne, The (Cross), **III:** 125
Life and Times of Michael K (Coetzee), **Supp. VI:** 76, **82–83**
Life and Work of Harold Pinter, The (Billington), **Retro. Supp. I:** 216
Life as We Have Known It (Woolf), **Retro. Supp. I:** 314

"Life and Writings of Addison" (Macaulay), **IV:** 282
Life Goes On (Sillitoe), **Supp. V:** 411
"Life in a Love" (Browning), **IV:** 365
Life in Greece from Homer to Menander (Mahafty), **V:** 400
"Life in London" (Egan), **IV:** 260
Life in Manchester (Gaskell), **V:** 15
Life in the Sick-Room (Martineau), **Supp. XV:** 184
"Life in the Wild" (Martineau), **Supp. XV:** 188
"Life Is the Desert and the Solitude" (Mangan), **Supp. XIII:** 120
Life, Letters, and Literary Remains of John Keats (Milnes), **IV:** 211, 235, 351; **Retro. Supp. I:** 185–186
Life Mask (Kay), **Supp. XIII:** 102, 107, 108
Life of Addison (Johnson), **III:** 42
Life of Alexander Pope (Ruffhead), **III:** 69n, 71
Life of Algernon Charles Swinburne, The (Gosse), **V:** 311, 334
Life of Benjamin Disraeli, Earl of Beaconsfield, The (Monypenny and Buckle), **IV:** 292, 295, 300, 307, 308
Life of . . . Bolingbroke, The (Goldsmith), **III:** 189, 191
Life of Charlotte Brontë, The (Gaskell), **V:** xii, 1–2, 3, 13–14, 15, 108, 122; **Retro. Supp. III:** 100, 109
Life of Christina Rossetti, The (Sanders), **V:** 250, 260
Life of Cicero, The (Trollope), **V:** 102
Life of Collins (Johnson), **III:** 164, 171
Life of Crabbe (Crabbe), **III:** 272
Life of Dr. Donne, The (Walton), **II:** 132, 136, 140, 141, 142
Life of Dr. Robert Sanderson, The (Walton), **II:** 133, 135, 136–137, 140, 142
Life of Dryden, The (Scott), **IV:** 38
Life of Geoffrey Chaucer the Early English Poet, Including Memoirs of His Near Friend and Kinsman, John of Gaunt, Duke of Lancaster: With Sketches of the Manners, Opinions, Arts, and Literature of England in the Fourteenth Century (Godwin), **Supp. XV:** 124–125
Life of George Moore, The (Horne), **VI:** 87, 96, 99
Life of Henry Fawcett, The (Stephen), **V:** 289
Life of John Bright, The (Trevelyan), **VI:** 389
Life of John Hales, The (Walton), **II:** 136
Life of John Milton, The (Wilson), **Supp. VI:** 301–302
Life of John Sterling (Carlyle), **IV:** 41–42, 240, 249, 250
Life of Johnson, The (Boswell), **I:** 30; **III:** 58, 114n, 115, 120, 234, 238, 239, 243–248; **IV:** xv, 280; **Retro. Supp. I:** 145–148
Life of Katherine Mansfield, The (Mantz and Murry), **VII:** 183
Life of Lady Jane Grey, and of Lord Guildford Dudley Her Husband, The (Godwin), **Supp. XV:** 126
"Life of Ma Parker"(Mansfield), **VII:** 175, 177
Life of Man, The (Arden), **Supp. II:** 28
Life of Mr. George Herbert, The (Walton), **II:** 119–120, 133, 140, 142, 143; **Retro. Supp. II:** 171–172
Life of Mr. Jonathan Wild the Great, The (Fielding), *see Jonathan Wild*
Life of Mr. Richard Hooker, The (Walton), **II:** 133, 134, 135, 140–143
Life of Mr. Richard Savage (Johnson), **III:** 108, 121
Life of Mrs. Godolphin, The (Evelyn), **II:** 275, 287
"Life of Mrs. Radcliffe" (Scott), **IV:** 35
Life of Mrs. Robert Louis Stevenson, The (Sanchez), **V:** 393, 397
Life of Napoleon, The (Scott), **IV:** 38
Life of Napoleon Bonaparte, The (Hazlitt), **IV:** 135, 140
Life of Nelson, The (Southey), **IV:** xvii, 58, 69, 71, 280
Life of Our Lady, The (Lydgate), **I:** 22, 57, 65–66
Life of Pico (More), **Supp. VII:** 233, 234, 238
Life of Pope (Johnson), **Retro. Supp. I:** 144–145
Life of Richard Nash, The (Goldsmith), **III:** 189, 191
Life of Robert Louis Stevenson, The (Balfour), **V:** 393, 397
Life of Robert Louis Stevenson, The (Masson), **V:** 393, 397
Life of Rudyard Kipling, The (Carrington), **VI:** 166
Life of Saint Albion, The (Lydgate), **I:** 57
Life of Saint Cecilia, The (Chaucer), **I:** 31
Life of Saint Edmund, The (Lydgate), **I:** 57
Life of Saint Francis Xavier, The (tr. Dryden), **II:** 305
Life of Samuel Johnson, The (Boswell), *see Life of Johnson, The*
Life of Schiller (Carlyle), **IV:** 241, 249, 250
Life of Sir Henry Wotton, The (Walton), **II:** 133, 141, 142, 143
Life of Sir James Fitzjames Stephen, The (Stephen), **V:** 289
Life of Sterling (Carlyle), *see Life of John Sterling*
"Life of the Emperor Julius" (Brontë), **V:** 113
"Life of the Imagination, The" (Gordimer), **Supp. II:** 233–234
Life of the Renowned Sir Philip Sidney, The (Greville), **Supp. XI:** 106, 107–108, 117, 118
Life of the Rev. Andrew Bell, The (Southey and Southey), **IV:** 71
Life of the Seventh Earl of Shaftesbury (Hodder), **IV:** 62
Life of Thomas Hardy (Hardy), **VI:** 14–15
Life of Thomas More, The (Ackroyd), **Supp. VI:** 12, 13
"Life of Thomas Parnell" (Goldsmith), **III:** 189

Life of Wesley, The (Southey), **IV:** 68, 71
Life of William Blake (Gilchrist), **Retro. Supp. I:** 46
Life of William Morris, The (Mackail), **V:** 294, 297, 306
"Life Sentence" (West), **Supp. III:** 442
"Life to Come, The" (Forster), **VI:** 411
"Life with a Hole in It, The" (Larkin), **Supp. I:** 284
"Life–Exam, A" (Crawford), **Supp. XI:** 76
Life's Handicap (Kipling), **VI:** 204
Life's Little Ironies (Hardy), **VI:** 20, 22
Life's Morning, A (Gissing), **V:** 437
"Liffey Hill, The" (Kinsella), **Supp. V:** 267
"Lifted Veil, The" (Eliot), **V:** 198
Light and the Dark, The (Snow), **VII:** 324, 327
Light Beyond the Forest, The (Sutcliff), **Supp. XVI:** 271–273
"Light breaks where no sun shines" (Thomas), **Supp. I:** 172; **Retro. Supp. III:** 337
Light for Them That Sit in Darkness . . . (Bunyan), **II:** 253
"Light Frozen on the Oaks" (Scupham), **Supp. XIII:** 229
Light Garden of the Angel King: Journeys in Afghanistan, The (Levi), **Supp. IV:** 159
Light Heart, The (Jonson), **Retro. Supp. I:** 165
"Light Man, A" (James), **VI:** 25, 69
Light Music, (Mahon), **Supp. VI:** 173
Light of Day, The (Ambler), **Supp. IV:** 4, 16–17
Light Shining in Buckinghamshire (Churchill), **Supp. IV:** 180, 186–188
"Light Shining Out of Darkness" (Cowper), **III:** 211; **Retro. Supp. III:** 44
Light That Failed, The (Kipling), **VI:** 166, 169, 189–190, 204; **Retro. Supp. III:** 183, 189, 196
Light Trap, The (Burnside), **Supp. XIII:** 25–26
"Light Trap, The" (Burnside), **Supp. XIII:** 25–26
"Light Woman, A" (Browning), **IV:** 369
Light Years, The (Howard), **Supp. XI:** 135, 145, 147, 148, 149
"Lightening Hours, The" (Fallon), **Supp. XII:** 103
Lighthouse, The (Collins), **Supp. VI:** 95
"Lighthouse Invites the Storm, The" (Lowry), **Supp. III:** 282
Lighthouse Invites the Storm, The (Lowry), **Supp. III:** 282
"Lighting Rehearsal" (Scupham), **Supp. XIII:** 220
"Lights Among Redwood" (Gunn), **Supp. IV:** 263
"Lights of the English Lake District" (Martineau), **Supp. XV:** 186
"Lights Out" (Thomas), **Supp. III:** 401
Lights Out for the Territory: Nine Excursions in the Secret History of London (Sinclair), **Supp. XIV:** 232, 233, 236–237, 238, 239–241, 242–243, 244, 246

"Liglag" (Crawford), **Supp. XI:** 78
Like a Fiery Elephant: The Story of B. S. Johnson (Coe), **Supp. XV:** 51, 52, 59–60, 62
"Like a Vocation" (Auden), **Retro. Supp. I:** 9
Like Birds, Like Fishes and Other Stories (Jhabvala), **Supp. V:** 235
"Like Dolmens Round My Childhood" (Montague), **Supp. XV:** 215
Like It Or Not (Ewart), **Supp. VII:** 47
Lilac and Flag: An Old Wives' Tale of a City (Berger), **Supp. IV:** 93–95
Lilian (Bennett), **VI:** 250, 259–260
Lilliesleaf (Oliphant), **Supp. X:** 214
"Lilly in a Christal, The" (Herrick), **II:** 104
"Lily Adair" (Chivers), **V:** 313
Limbo (Huxley), **VII:** 199, 200
Limbo (Raine), **Supp. XIII:** 173
"Limbs" (Scupham), **Supp. XIII:** 218
Limelight Blues (Parsons), **Supp. XV:** 228–229
Lincoln: A Foreigner's Quest (Morris, J.), **Supp. X:** 173, 182–183
Lincolnshire poems (Tennyson), **IV:** 327, 336
Linda Tressel (Trollope), **V:** 102
Linden Tree, The (Priestley), **VII:** 209, 228–229
Line of Life, A (Ford), **II:** 88, 100
"Lines: I Am" (Clare), **Supp. XI:** 49, 62
"Lines Composed a Few Miles Above Tintern Abbey" (Wordsworth), **IV:** ix, 3, 7, 8, 9–10, 11, 44, 198, 215, 233
"Lines Composed in a Wood on a Windy Day" (Brontë), **V:** 132
"Lines Composed While Climbing the Left Ascent of Brockley Combe" (Coleridge), **IV: 43–44**
"Lines for a Book" (Gunn), **Supp. IV:** 260, 261
"Lines for Cuscuscaraway . . ." (Elliot), **VII:** 163
"Lines for Thanksgiving" (McGuckian), **Supp. V:** 289
"Lines of Desire" (Motion), **Supp. VII:** 254, 260–261
Lines of the Hand, The (Hart), **Supp. XI:** 122, 123–125
"Lines on a Young Lady's Photograph Album" (Larkin), **Supp. I:** 285; **Retro. Supp. III:** 204
"Lines on the Loss of the *Titanic*" (Hardy), **VI:** 16
"Lines to Him Who Will Understand Them" (Robinson), **Supp. XIII:** 204, 205
"Lines Written Among the Euganean Hills" (Shelley), **IV:** 199; **Retro. Supp. I:** 250–251
"Lines Written in the Bay of Lerici" (Shelley), **IV:** 206
"Lines Written on a Seat" (Kavanagh), **Supp. VII:** 198
"Lingam and the Yoni, The" (Hope), **Supp. VII:** 154
"Linnet in the rocky dells, The" (Brontë), **V:** 115

"Linnet's Petition, The" (Robinson), **Supp. XIII:** 199
Lion and the Fox, The (Lewis), **VII:** 72, 74, 82
Lion and the Mouse, The (Henryson), **Supp. VII:** 136, 139
Lion and the Ostrich, The (Koestler), **Supp. I:** 35
Lion and the Unicorn, The (Orwell), **VII:** 282
"Lion Hunts" (Beer), **Supp. XIV:** 3
Lion, The Witch, and the Wardrobe, The (Lewis), **Supp. III:** 248, 260
Lions and Shadows (Isherwood), **VII:** 310, 312
Lions and Shadows (Upward), **Supp. XIII:** 251
Lipstick on Your Collar (Potter, D.), **Supp. X:** 231
Lipton Story: A Centennial Biography, A (Waugh), **Supp. VI:** 275
Liquid City (Sinclair), **Supp. XIV:** 238, 240
"Lisbeth" (Kipling), **Retro. Supp. III:** 184–185
Listen to the Voice: Selected Stories (Smith, I. C.), **Supp. IX:** 210
Listener, **Supp. XV:** 244, 245, 247, 248, 251, 254, 255
"Listeners, The" (Nye), **Supp. X:** 192, 198, 202
Listening to the Orchestra (Hill), **Supp. XIV:** 116, 126
"Litanie, The" (Donne), **Retro. Supp. II:** 96
Litanies de Satan (Baudelaire), **V:** 310
"Litany, A" (Swinburne), **V:** 320
"Literae Orientales" (Mangan), **Supp. XIII:** 116, 124–126
Literary and General Lectures and Essays (Kingsley), **Supp. XVI:** 204
"Literary Criticism and Philosophy: A Reply" (Leavis), **VII:** 241–242
Literary Criticisms by Francis Thompson (ed. Connolly), **V:** 450, 451
Literary History of England in the End of the Eighteenth and Beginning of the Nineteenth Century (Oliphant), **Supp. X:** 222
"Literary Lights" (Gibbon), **Supp. XIV:** 103, 104
Literary Reminiscences (Hood), **IV:** 252, 253, 254, 259–260, 266
Literary Souvenir, The (Jewsbury), **Supp. XIV:** 157
Literary Studies (Bagehot), **V:** 156, 170
Literary Taste: How to Form It (Bennett), **VI:** 266
Literature and Dogma (Arnold), **V:** xxiv, 203, 212, 216
"Literature and Offence" (Brink), **Supp. VI:** 47
"Literature and the Irish Language" (Moore), **VI:** 98
Literature and Western Man (Priestley), **VII:** 209, 214–215
Literature at Nurse; or, Circulating Morals (Moore), **VI:** 90, 98
"Literature, Feminism, and the African Woman Today" (Aidoo), **Supp. XV:** 6, 11–12
Literature in Ireland (Clarke), **Supp. XV:** 16
Lithuania (Brooke), **Supp. III:** 47, 54
"Little Aeneid, The" (Malouf), **Supp. XII:** 220
"Little and a lone green lane" (Brontë), **V:** 112–113
"Little Black Boy, The" (Blake), **Supp. IV:** 188; **Retro. Supp. I:** 36
"Little Boy Lost, The" (Blake), **III:** 292
"Little Cloud, A" (Joyce), **Retro. Supp. III:** 169
Little Dinner at Timmins's, A (Thackeray), **V:** 24, 38
Little Dorrit (Dickens), **V:** xxii, 41, 42, 47, 55, 63, 64–66, 68, 69, 70, 72
Little Dream, The (Galsworthy), **VI:** 274
Little Drummer Girl, The (le Carré), **Supp. II:** 305, 306, 307, 311, 313, **315–318**; **Retro. Supp. III:** 215, 221–222, 224
Little French Lawyer, The (Fletcher and Massinger), **II:** 66
"Little Ghost Who Died for Love, The" (Sitwell), **VII:** 133
"Little Gidding" (Eliot), **VII:** 154, 155, 156
Little Girl, The (Mansfield), **VII:** 171
Little Girls, The (Bowen), **Supp. II:** 77, 82, 84, 94
Little Gray Home in the West (Arden and D'Arcy), **Supp. II:** 32, 35
Little Green Man (Armitage), **VIII:** 1
Little Hotel, The (Stead), **Supp. IV:** 473, 476
"Little India" (Delanty), **Supp. XIV:** 72–73
Little Learning, A (Waugh), **Supp. VI:** 271
Little Men (Alcott), **Supp. IV:** 255
Little Minister, The (Barrie), **Supp. III:** 1, 3, 8
Little Monasteries, The (tr. O'Connor), **Supp. XIV:** 223
"Little Mother, The" (O'Connor), **Supp. XIV:** 226
"Little Paul and the Sea" (Stevenson), **Supp. VI:** 264
"Little Photographer, The" (du Maurier), **Supp. III:** 135
"Little Puppy That Could, The" (Amis), **Supp. IV:** 40
"Little Red Twin" (Hughes), **Supp. I:** 359
Little Review, **Supp. XIII:** 189
Little Tales of Misogyny (Highsmith), **Supp. V:** 177, 180
Little Tea, a Little Chat, A (Stead), **Supp. IV:** 462, 473
"Little Tembi" (Lessing), **Supp. I:** 241
Little Tour in France, A (James), **VI:** 45–46, 67
"Little Travels and Roadside Sketches" (Thackeray), **V:** 38
Little Wars: A Game for Boys (Wells), **VI:** 227, 244
"Little While, A" (Rossetti), **V:** 242
"Little while, a little while, A," (Brontë), **V:** 127–128

Littlewood, Joan, **Supp. II:** 68, 70, 73, 74
Live and Let Die (Fleming), **Supp. XIV:** 91, 93–94
Live Like Pigs (Arden), **Supp. II:** 24–25, 29
Lively, Penelope, **Supp. IV:** 304
"Lively sparks that issue from those eyes, The" (Wyatt), **I:** 109
"Liverpool Address, A" (Arnold), **V:** 213, 216
Lives, (Mahon), **Supp. VI: 168–171,** 172
"Lives" (Mahon), **Supp. VI:** 169
Lives, The (Walton), **II:** 131, 134–137, 139, **140–143;** *see also* individual works: *Life of Dr. Donne; Life of Dr. Robert Sanderson; Life of Mr. George Herbert; Life of Mr. Richard Hooker; Life of Sir Henry Wotton*
Lives of the British Admirals (Southey and Bell), **IV:** 71
Lives of the English Poets, The (Johnson), **II:** 259; **III:** 118–119, 122, 160, 173, 189; **Retro. Supp. I:** 143–145, 274
Lives of the Hunted (Seton), **Supp. IV:** 158
Lives of the 'Lustrious: A Dictionary of Irrational Biography (Stephen and Lee), **V:** 290
Lives of the Necromancers: or, An Account of the Most Eminent Persons in Successive Ages, Who Have Claimed for Themselves, or to Whom Has Been Imputed by Others, the Exercise of Magical Power (Godwin), **Supp. XV:** 129–130
Lives of the Novelists (Scott), **III:** 146n; **IV:** 38, 39
Lives of the Poets, The (Johnson), *see Lives of the English Poets, The*
Lives of the English Saints (Newman), **Supp. VII:** 296
Livia (Durrell), **Supp. I:** 118, 119; **Retro. Supp. III:** 86, 93
Living (Green), **Supp. II:** 251–253
Living and the Dead, The (White), **Supp. I:** 129, 130, 134
Living Daylights, The (Fleming), **Supp. XIV:** 96
Living in America (Stevenson), **Supp. VI: 254–256**
"Living in Time" (Reid), **Supp. VII:** 329
Living Language, A (Constantine), **Supp. XV:** 65, 70, 71
Living Novel, The (Pritchett), **IV:** 306
Living Nowhere (Burnside), **Supp. XIII:** 23, 25, 30
Living Principle, The (Leaves), **VII:** 237
Living Quarters (Friel), **Supp. V:** 122
Living Room, The (Greene), **Supp. I:** 13; **Retro. Supp. II:** 161–162
Living Together (Ayckbourn), **Supp. V:** 2, 5
Living Torch, The (Russell), **VIII:** 277, 286, 290, 292
"Livings" (Larkin), **Supp. I:** 277, 282; **Retro. Supp. III:** 210
Livingstone's Companions (Gordimer), **Supp. II:** 229, 233

Liza of Lambeth (Maugham), **VI:** 364–365
Liza's England (Barker), *see Century's Daughter, The*
"Lizbie Brown" (Hardy), **Retro. Supp. I:** 110
"Lizzie Leigh" (Gaskell), **V:** 3, 15; **Retro. Supp. III:** 100
Ljósvetninga saga, **VIII:** 242
"Llanrhaeadr ym Mochnant" (Thomas), **Supp. XII:** 285
Lloyd, Charles, **IV:** 78
Lloyd George, David, **VI:** 264, 340, 352, 353; **VII:** 2
Loaves and Fishes (Brown), **Supp. VI:** 65, 71
"Lob"(Thomas), **Supp. III:** 394, 405
Lobo, Jeronimo, **III:** 107, 112
Local Habitation (Nicholson), **Supp. VI:** 213, **217–218**
"Local Habitation" (Soutar), **Supp. XVI:** 254, 256
Locations (Morris, J.), **Supp. X:** 172, 183
"Loch Ness Monster's Song, The" (Morgan, E.), **Supp. IX:** 162–163, 169
"Loch Roe" (MacCaig), **Supp. VI:** 182
"Loch Sionascaig" (MacCaig), **Supp. VI:** 195
"Lock, The" (Coppard), **VIII:** 88
"Lock the Door, Lariston" (Hogg), **Supp. X:** 110
"Lock up, fair lids, The treasure of my heart" (Sidney), **I:** 169
Locke, John, **III:** 22; **IV:** 169; **Supp. III:** 33, 233
"Locket, The" (Montague), **Supp. XV:** 210, 221
Lockhart, J. G., **IV:** 27, 30, 34, 36, 38, 39, 294; **V:** 140
"Locksley Hall" (Tennyson), **IV:** 325, 333, 334–335; **Retro. Supp. III:** 322, 323, 324, 326
Locksley Hall Sixty Years After (Tennyson), **Retro. Supp. III:** 328
"Locksley Hall Sixty Years After" (Tennyson), **IV:** 328, 338; **Retro. Supp. III:** 328
Locust Room, The (Burnside), **Supp. XIII:** 23, 29–30
"Locust Songs" (Hill), **Supp. V:** 187
Lodge, David, **Supp. II:** 9, 10; **Supp. IV:** 102, 139, **363–387,** 546; **Retro. Supp. I:** 217
Lodge, Thomas, **I:** 306, 312
"Lodging for the Night, A" (Stevenson), **V:** 384, 395
"Lodging House Fire, The" (Davies), **Supp. XI:** 94–95
"Lodgings for the Night" (Caudwell), **Supp. IX:** 35, 37
Lodore (Shelley), **Supp. III:** 371, 372; **Retro. Supp. III:** 290
Loftis, John, **III:** 255, 271
"Lofty in the Palais de Danse" (Gunn), **Supp. IV:** 258
"Lofty Sky, The" (Thomas), **Supp. III:** 401
Logan, Annie R. M., **VI:** 23
Logan Stone (Thomas), **Supp. IV:** 490

"Logan Stone" (Thomas), **Supp. IV:** 491, 492
"Loganair" (Crawford), **Supp. XI:** 75
"Logic of Dreams" (Fuller), **Supp. VII:** 74
Logic of Political Economy, The (De Quincey), **IV:** 155
"Logical Ballad of Home Rule, A" (Swinburne), **V:** 332
"Logos" (Hughes), **Supp. I:** 350
Loiners, The (Harrison), **Supp. V:** 149, 150–151
"Lois the Witch" (Gaskell), **V:** 15
Loitering with Intent (Spark), **Supp. I:** 204, 212, 213
Lokasenna, **VIII:** 230, 241
Lolita (Nabokov), **Supp. IV:** 26, 30
Lolly Willowes (Warner), **Supp. VII:** 370, 373–374, 375, 381
Lombroso, Cesare, **V:** 272
Londinium Redivivum (Evelyn), **II:** 287
"London" (Blake), **III:** 294, 295
"London" (Johnson), **III:** 57, 108, 114, 121; **Retro. Supp. I:** 137
London (Russell), **Supp. IV:** 126
"London" (Symons), **Supp. XIV:** 279
London: A Book of Aspects (Symons), **Supp. XIV:** 279
London Assurance (Boucicault), **V:** 415
"London by Lamplight" (Meredith), **V:** 219
London: City of Disappearances (ed. Sinclair), **Supp. XIV:** 243–244
London Fields (Amis), **Supp. IV:** 26, 27, 35–37
"London hast thou accusèd me" (Surrey), **I:** 113, 116
London Journal 1762–1763 (Boswell), **III:** 239, 240, 242
London Kills Me: Three Screenplays and Four Essays (Kureishi), **Supp. XI:** 156–157, 159, 161
London Labour and the London Poor (Mayhew), **Supp. XVI:** 209–210, 214, 218–220, 223
London Lickpenny (Ackroyd), **Supp. VI:** 3
London Life, A (James), **VI:** 67, 69
London Magazine (periodical), **III:** 263; **IV:** xviii, 252, 253, 257, 260; **V:** 386
London Mercury (periodical), **VII:** 211
London Nights (Symons), **Supp. XIV:** 267, 270, 272, 276, 277, 278
London Orbital: A Walk Around the M25 (Sinclair), **Supp. XIV:** 232, 236, 244, 245
London Pride (Braddon), **VIII:** 49
London Review of Books, **Supp. IV:** 121
"London Revisited" (Beerbohm), **Supp. II:** 52
"London Snow" (Bridges), **VI:** 78
London Spy (periodical), **III:** 41
London Street Games (Douglas), **VI:** 304, 305
"London Suburb, A" (Smith), **Retro. Supp. III:** 306
London: The Biography (Ackroyd), **Supp. VI:** 13
London to Ladysmith via Pretoria (Churchill), **VI:** 351

London Tradesmen (Trollope), **V:** 102
London Zoo (Sisson), **Supp. XI:** 249
"Londoner" (Adcock), **Supp. XII:** 8
Londoners (Ewart), **Supp. VII:** 38
"Lone Voices" (Amis), **Supp. II:** 11
"Loneliest Mountain, The" (Davies), **Supp. XI:** 100
"Loneliness" (Auden), **Retro. Supp. I:** 13
"Loneliness" (Behan), **Supp. II:** 64
"Loneliness of the Long-Distance Runner, The" (Sillitoe), **Supp. V:** 409, 410, 413, 419–421
Lonely Girl, The (O'Brien), **Supp. V:** 334, 336–337
"Lonely Lady, The" (Powys), **VIII:** 254, 258
Lonely Londoners, The (Selvon), **Supp. IV:** 445
"Lonely Love" (Blunden), **Supp. XI:** 46–47
Lonely Passion of Judith Hearne, The (Moore, B.), **Supp. IX:** 141, 142, 143, 144, 146
Lonely Unicorn, The (Waugh), **Supp. VI:** 270
Lonely Voice, The: A Study of the Short Story (O'Connor), **Supp. XIV:** 211–212, 219
Lonesome West, The (McDonagh), **Supp. XII:** 233, 235, 236–237, 238, 239, 245
"Long ages past" (Owen), **VI:** 448
"Long Ago" (Dunn), **Supp. X:** 80
Long Day Wanes, The (Burgess), *see Malayan trilogy*
Long Kill, The (Hill, R.), **Supp. IX:** 119
Long River, The (Smith, I. C.), **Supp. IX:** 211
"Long Story, A" (Gray), **III:** 140
Long View, The (Howard), **Supp. XI:** 135, 138–139
Long Way Down, A (Hornby), **Supp. XV:** 134, 143
"Longbeards' Saga, The" (Kingsley), **Supp. XVI:** 204
"Longes MACnUSNIG: The Exile of the Sons of Usnech and The Exile of Fergus and The Death of the Sons of Usnech and of Deidre" (Kinsella), **Supp. V:** 264
Longest Day, The (Clough), **V:** 170
Longest Journey, The (Forster), **VI:** 398, **401–403,** 407; **Retro. Supp. II:** 136, 139–141
"Long-Legged Fly" (Yeats), **Retro. Supp. I:** 337
Longley, Michael, **VIII: 163–178; Supp. IV:** 412
"Longstaff's Marriage" (James), **VI:** 69
Lonsdale, R., **III:** 142n, 144
"Look" (Motion), **Supp. VII:** 259
Look After Lulu (Coward), **Supp. II:** 155
Look at All Those Roses (Bowen), **Supp. II:** 92–93
Look at Me (Brookner), **Supp. IV:** 125–126
"Look at the Children" (Graham), **Supp. VII:** 116
"Look at the Cloud His Evening Playing Cards" (Graham), **Supp. VII:** 116

Look Back in Anger (Osborne), **Supp. I:** 329, **330–332,** 338; **Supp. II:** 4, 70, 155; **Supp. III:** 191; **Supp. IV:** 282, 283
Look Look (Frayn), **Supp. VII:** 61
Look, Stranger! (Auden), **VII:** xix, 384
Look to Windward (Banks), **Supp. XI:** 9–10, 12
Look! We Have Come Through! (Lawrence), **VII:** 127; **Retro. Supp. II:** 233
"Looking and Finding" (Scupham), **Supp. XIII:** 223
Looking Back (Adcock), **Supp. XII:** 11, 12–13
Looking Back (Douglas), **VI:** 304, 305
Looking Back (Maugham), **VI:** 365
"Looking Back" (Vaughan), **II:** 185, 188
Looking for a Language (Fry), **Supp. III:** 191
"Looking for Weldon Kees" (Armitage), **VIII:** 6
"Looking Glass, The" (Nye), **Supp. X:** 205
Looking Glass, The (Roberts), **Supp. XV:** 271–272
Looking Glass, The: A True History of the Early Years of an Artist: Calculated to Awaken the Emulation of Young Persons of Both Sexes, in the Pursuit of Every Laudable Attainment: Particularly in the Cultivation of the Fine Arts (Godwin), **Supp. XV:** 126
Looking Glass War, The (le Carré), **II:** 308, 309–310; **Supp. IV:** 22
Looking on Darkness (Brink), **Supp. VI:** 48
Looking-Glass War, The (le Carré), **Retro. Supp. III:** 218, 219, 220, 226
Loom of Youth, The (Waugh), **Supp. VI:** 267, **268–269**
"Loose Saraband, A" (Lovelace), **II:** 232
"Loosestrife" (Delanty), **Supp. XIV:** 77–78
Loot (Orton), **Supp. V:** 363, 367, 371, 375
Lopez, Bernard, **VI:** 85
Loquituri (Bunting), **Supp. VII:** 5
"Lorca" (Thomas), **Supp. IV:** 493
"Lord Arthur Savile's Crime" (Wilde), **V:** 405, 419; **Retro. Supp. II:** 365
"Lord Beaupre" (James), **VI:** 69
"Lord Carlisle on Pope" (De Quincey), **IV:** 146
Lord Chancellor Jeffreys and the Stuart Cause (Keeton), **IV:** 286
Lord Cucumber (Orton), **Supp. V:** 363
Lord George Bentinck (Disraeli), **IV:** 303, 308
Lord Gregory (Carson), **Supp. XIII:** 65
Lord Grey of the Reform Bill (Trevelyan), **VI:** 389–390
Lord Hay's Masque (Campion), **Supp. XVI:** 92, 97–98
Lord Jim (Conrad), **VII:** 34, **139–140,** 148; **Supp. II:** 290; **Retro. Supp. II:** 69, 75–77
Lord Malquist and Mr Moon (Stoppard), **Supp. I:** 438
"Lord of Ennerdale, The" (Scott), **IV:** 31

Lords of Limit, The: Essays on Literature and Ideas (Hill), **Supp. V:** 201
"Lord of the Dynamos" (Wells), **VI:** 235
Lord of the Flies (Golding), **Supp. I:** 67, 68–70, 71, 72, 75, 83; **Supp. IV:** 393; **Retro. Supp. I:** 94–97
Lord of the Isles, The (Scott), **IV:** 39
Lord of the Rings, The (Tolkien), **Supp. II:** 519, 520, 521, 524, 525, 527, 528, 529–530, 531, 532–534; **Supp. IV:** 116
Lord Ormont and His Aminta (Meredith), **V:** 226, 232, 233, 234
Lord Palmerston (Trollope), **V:** 102
Lord Peter Views the Body (Sayers), **Supp. III:** 340
Lord Raingo (Bennett), **VI:** 250, 252, 261–262
Lord Randolph Churchill (Churchill), **VI:** 352
Lord Soulis (Swinburne), **V:** 333
Lords and Commons (tr. O'Connor), **Supp. XIV:** 222
"Lords of Hell and the Word, The" (Brown), **Supp. VI:** 72
Lords of Limit, The: Essays on Literature and Ideas (Hill), **Retro. Supp. III:** 139, 142, 145
Lord's Masque, The (Campion), **Supp. XVI:** 92, 98
Lorenz, Konrad, **Supp. IV:** 162
Losing Nelson (Unsworth), **Supp. VII:** 365, 366–367
"Losing Touch" (Conn), **Supp. XIII:** 78
Loss and Gain (Newman), **Supp. VII:** 293, 297, 299
Loss of El Dorado, The (Naipaul), **Supp. I:** 390, 392–393
"Loss of the Eurydice, The" (Hopkins), **V:** 369–370, 379
Loss of the Magyar and Other Poems (Beer), **Supp. XIV:** 1, 2
Lost Childhood, and Other Essays, The (Greene), **VI:** 333; **Supp. I:** 2
"Lost Days" (Rossetti), **V:** 243
Lost Eden, A (Braddon), **VIII:** 37
Lost Empires (Priestley), **VII:** 220–221
Lost Explorer, The (Carson), **Supp. XIII:** 55, 57
Lost Field, The (Fallon), **Supp. XII:** 106–107, 114, 115
Lost Flying Boat, The (Sillitoe), **Supp. V:** 411
Lost Girl, The (Lawrence), **VII:** 90, 104–106; **Retro. Supp. II:** 229
"Lost Heifer, The" (Clarke), **Supp. XV:** 20, 30
"Lost Leader, The" (Browning), **IV:** 356; **Retro. Supp. III:** 22
"Lost Legion, The" (Kipling), **VI:** 193
"Lost Mistress, The" (Browning), **IV:** 369
Lost Ones, The (Beckett), **Supp. I:** 47, 55, 61–62
"Lost Proofs, The" (Powys), **VIII:** 248, 249
Lost Season, A (Fuller), **Supp. VII:** 69–70
"Lost Selves" (Blunden), **Supp. XI:** 46
"Lost Tribe, The" (Pitter), **Supp. XIII:** 143

LOST–LOVE

Lost Trumpet, The (Mitchell), **Supp. XIV:** 100

"Lost Way, The" (Delanty), **Supp. XIV:** 70–71

"Lost Woman, The" (Beer), **Supp. XIV:** 5

Lost World, The (Doyle), **Supp. II:** 159

"Lot and His Daughters" (Hope), **Supp. VII:** 158

Lothair (Disraeli), **IV:** xxiii, 294, 296, 304, 306, 307, 308

Loti, Pierre, **Retro. Supp. I:** 291

"Lotos–Eaters, The" (Tennyson), **Retro. Supp. III:** 320, 321

"Lotos–Garland of Antinous, The" (Symonds), **Supp. XIV:** 252

Lotta Schmidt (Trollope), **V:** 101

Lottery, The (Fielding), **III:** 105

"Lotus, The" (Rhys), **Supp. II:** 402

Lotus and the Robot, The (Koestler), **Supp. I:** 34n

"Lotus–Eaters, The" (Tennyson), **IV:** xix; **V:** ix

"Loud without the wind was roaring" (Brontë), **V:** 127

"Loudest Lay, The" (Warner), **Supp. VII:** 371–372

Lough Derg (Kavanagh), **Supp. VII:** 192–193, 199

"Loughcrew" (Fallon), **Supp. XII:** 106, 107

Louis Percy (Brookner), **Supp. IV:** 131

"Louisa in the Lane" (Hardy), **Retro. Supp. I:** 110

"Louisa Pallant" (James), **VI:** 69

"Lourd on my Hert" (MacDiarmid), **Supp. XII:** 210–211

"Love" (Brooke), **Supp. III:** 55

"Love" (Carpenter), **Supp. XIII:** 46

Love (Carter), **Supp. III:** 79, 81, 82, 83

"Love, A Greeting" (Montague), **Supp. XV:** 219

Love After All (Ayckbourn), **Supp. V:** 2

"Love Again" (Larkin), **Retro. Supp. III:** 211

Love All (Sayers), **Supp. III:** 348

Love Among the Artists (Shaw), **VI:** 103, 105, 106, 129

Love Among the Chickens (Wodehouse), **Supp. III:** 450

"Love Among the Haystacks" (Lawrence), **VII:** 115

"Love Among the Ruins" (Browning), **IV:** 357, 369; **Retro. Supp. III:** 24

Love Among the Ruins (Waugh), **VII:** 302

Love and a Bottle (Farquhar), **II:** 352, 356, 364

Love and Business (Farquhar), **II:** 352, 355, 364

"Love and Debt Alike Troublesome" (Suckling), **II:** 227

Love and Fashion (Burney), **Supp. III:** 64

Love and Freindship [sic] and Other Early Works (Austen), **IV:** 122

"Love and Life" (Cowley), **II:** 197, 198

"Love and Life" (Rochester), **II:** 258

Love and Mr. Lewisham (Wells), **VI:** 235–236, 244

Love and Napalm: Export U.S.A (Ballard), **Supp. V:** 26

Love and other Deaths (Thomas), **Supp. IV:** 490

Love and Truth (Walton), **II:** 134, 143

"Love Arm'd" (Behn), **Supp. III:** 36, 37

"Love Armed" (Behn), **Retro. Supp. III:** 6

"Love Axe/l, The: Developing a Caribbean Aesthetic 1962–1974" (Brathwaite), **Supp. XII:** 35

Love At A Loss; or, Most Votes Carry (Trotter), **Supp. XVI:** 286–287

"Love Declared" (Thompson), **V:** 442

Love Department, The (Trevor), **Supp. IV:** 501, 507–508

Love for Love (Congreve), **II:** 324, 338, 342–343, 350

Love for Love: An Anthology of Love Poems (ed. Burnside and Finlay), **Supp. XIII:** 31

"Love from the North" (Rossetti), **V:** 259

"Love, Hate, and Kicking Ass" (Crace), **Supp. XIV:** 31

Love in a Blue Time (Kureishi), **Supp. XI:** 157–158

Love in a Cold Climate (Mitford), **Supp. X:** 151–152, 161–163

"Love in a Colder Climate" (Ballard), **Supp. V:** 33

Love in a Life (Motion), **Supp. VII:** 253, 254, 257, 258–260, 261, 263

"Love in a Valley" (Betjeman), **VII:** 366

Love in a Wood; or, St. James's Park (Wycherley), **II:** 308, 309, **311–313**, 321

"Love in Dian's Lap" (Thompson), **V:** 441

Love in Excess; or, The Fatal Enquiry (Haywood); **Supp. XII:** 133, 137–140, 144, 145

Love in Idleness (Nicholls), **IV:** 98n

Love in Idleness (Rattigan), **Supp. VII:** 313

Love in Several Masques (Fielding), **III:** 96, 105; **Retro. Supp. I:** 79–80, 81–82

"Love in the Environs of Voronezh" (Sillitoe), **Supp. V:** 424

Love in the Environs of Voronezh and Other Poems (Sillitoe), **Supp. V:** 424

"Love in the Valley" (Meredith), **V:** 219–220

"Love Is Dead" (Betjeman), **VII:** 359–360

Love Is Enough (Morris), **V:** 299n, 306

"Love Is Like a Dizziness" (Hogg), **Supp. X:** 106

"Love Letters to a Gentleman" (Behn), **Retro. Supp. III:** 4

"Love Making by Candlelight" (Dunn), **Supp. X:** 77

"Love Match, A" (Warner), **Supp. VII:** 380

Love Object, The (O'Brien), **Supp. V:** 339

Love or Nothing (Dunn), **Supp. X:** 71

"Love Poem" (Burnside), **Supp. XIII:** 20

"Love Poem" (Dunn), **Supp. X:** 70

"Love Poem" (Longley), **VIII:** 170–171

Love Poems (Davies), **Supp. XI:** 100

"Love Song of Har Dyal, The" (Swift), **VI:** 202

"Love Song of J. Alfred Prufrock, The" (Eliot), **V:** 163; **VII:** 144; **Supp. IV:** 260; **Retro. Supp. II:** 121, 122–123

"Love Songs in Age" (Larkin), **Supp. I:** 281; **Retro. Supp. III:** 207

Love Songs of Connacht (Clarke), **Supp. XV:** 16

"Love still has something of the Sea" (Sedley); **II:** 264

"Love Tale" (Robinson), **Supp. XIII:** 212

"Love that doth raine and live within my thought" (Surrey), **I:** 115

"Love, thou art best of Human Joys" (Finch), **Supp. IX:** 76

"Love III" (Herbert), **II:** 129; **Retro. Supp. II:** 183

Love Triumphant; or, Nature Will Prevail (Dryden), **II:** 305

Love Unknown (Wilson) **Supp. VI:** 302, **303–304**

Lovecraft, H. P., **II:** 340, 343, 345

Loved One, The (Waugh), **VII:** 301

Love–Hate Relations (Spender), **Supp. II:** 492

Lovel the Widower (Thackeray), **V:** 35, 37, 38

Lovelace, Richard, **II:** 222, **229–232**

Love–Letters Between a Nobleman and His Sister (Behn), **Supp. III:** 30–31, 37, 39; **Retro. Supp. III:** 4, 5, 7–8, 10, 13

"Lovely Land, The" (Mangan), **Supp. XIII:** 127

Lover (periodical), **III:** 50, 53

Lover, The (Pinter), **Supp. I:** 373, 374, 375; **Retro. Supp. I:** 223–224

"Lover of Things, The" (Hall), **Supp. VI:** 121

Lover's Assistant, The (Fielding), see *Ovid's Art of Love Paraphrased*

"Lover's Complaint, A, "**I:** 307

Lovers (Friel), **Supp. V:** 118

"Lovers' Epitaph" (Soutar), **Supp. XVI:** 251

"Lovers How They Come and Part" (Herrick), **II:** 107

"Lovers in Pairs" (Ewart), **Supp. VII:** 46

"Lover's Journey, The" (Crabbe), **III:** 282–283

Lover's Melancholy, The (Ford), **II:** 88–91, 100

Lovers in London (Milne), **Supp. V:** 297, 298

Lovers No Conjurers (Inchbald), **Supp. XV:** 156–157

"Lovers of Orelay, The" (Moore), **VI:** 96

"Lovers of Their Time" (Trevor), **Supp. IV:** 504

Lover's Progress, The (Fletcher and Massinger), **II:** 66

"Lover's Quarrel, A" (Browning), **Retro. Supp. II:** 25; **Retro. Supp. III:** 24

Lovers' Quarrels . . . (King), **II:** 336

"Lovers' Rock, The" (Southey), **IV:** 66

Lover's Tale, The (Tennyson), **IV:** 338

"Lover's Tale, The" (Tennyson), **Retro. Supp. III:** 327

Lovers' Vows (Inchbald), **Supp. XV:** 147, 159, 160–161
Love's Catechism Compiled by the Author of The Recruiting Officer (Farquhar), **II:** 364
Love's Coming-of-Age (Carpenter), **Supp. XIII:** 41–43
Love's Cross Currents (Swinburne), **V:** 313, 323, 325–326, 330, 333
Love's Cruelty (Symons), **Supp. XIV:** 281
Love's Cure (Beaumont, Fletcher, Massinger), **II:** 66
"Loves Deitie" (Donne), **Retro. Supp. II:** 93
"Love's Journeys" (Redgrove), **Supp. VI:** 234
Love's Labour's Lost (Shakespeare), **I:** 303–304; **Retro. Supp. II:** 330; **Retro. Supp. III:** 268, 269, 277, 280
Love's Last Shift (Cibber), **II:** 324, 326
Love's Martyr (Chester), **I:** 313
Love's Metamorphosis (Lyly), **I:** 202
"Love's Nocturn" (Rossetti), **V:** 241
Loves of Amos and Laura, The (S.P.), **II:** 132
Loves of Cass McGuire, The (Friel), **Supp. V:** 118
Loves of Ergasto, The (Greber), **II:** 325
Loves of the Plants, The (Darwin), **Supp. XVI:** 128–129, 133–134, 138
"Love's Payment" (Davies), **Supp. XI:** 100
"Love's Philosophy" (Shelley), **IV:** 203
Love's Pilgrimage (Beaumont and Fletcher), **II:** 65
Love Poems and Elegies (Smith, I. C.), **Supp. IX:** 216
Love's Riddle (Cowley), **II:** 194, 202
Love's Sacrifice (Ford), **II:** 88, 89, 92, 96, 97, 99, 100
"Love's Siege" (Suckling), **II:** 226–227
"Love's Ultimate Meaning" (Carpenter), **Supp. XIII:** 42
"Loves Usury" (Donne), **Retro. Supp. II:** 89
Lovesick (Churchill), **Supp. IV:** 181
Lovesick Maid, The (Brome), **Supp. X:** 52
"Love-silly and Jubilant" (Fallon), **Supp. XII:** 102–103
Loving (Green), **Supp. II:** 247, 254, **256–258**
"Loving Hitler" (Adcock), **Supp. XII:** 3, 9
Loving Memory (Harrison), **Supp. V:** 164
"Loving Reflections" (Montague), **Supp. XV:** 218
Loving Spirit, The (du Maurier), **Supp. III:** 133, 141, 144–145
Low Road, The (Hill), see *Death Takes the Low Road*
Low, Will, **V:** 393, 397
"Low Barometer" (Bridges), **VI:** 80
Lowbury, Edward, **VII:** 422, 431–432
Lowell, Amy, **Supp. III:** 397
Lowell, James Russell, **I:** 121
Lowell, Robert, **Supp. II:** 276; **Supp. IV:** 423; **Retro. Supp. I:** 129, 130
Lowes, J. L., **IV:** 47, 57

Lowry, Malcolm, **Supp. III: 269–286**
Loyal Brother, The (Southern), **II:** 305
Loyal General, The (Tate), **II:** 305
"Loyal Mother, The" (Hughes), **Supp. I:** 356
Loyal Subject, The (Fletcher), **II:** 45, 65
Loyalties (Galsworthy), **VI:** xiii, 275, 287
Lucas, E. V., **IV:** 74, 76n, 84, 85, 86
Lucas, F. L., **II:** 69, 70n, 80, 83, 85
Lucasta (Lovelace), **II:** 238
"Luceys, The " (O'Connor), **Supp. XIV:** 227
Lucian, **III:** 24
Lucie-Smith, Edward, **IV:** 372, 373
"Lucifer" (Cameron), **Supp. IX:** 29
Luck of Barry Lyndon, The (Thackeray), see *Barry Lyndon*
Luck of Ginger Coffey, The (Moore, B.), **Supp. IX:** 142, 148–149, 153
Luck, or Cunning (Butler), **Supp. II:** 106, 107, 108, 113
"Lucky" (Greig), **Supp. XVI:** 163
"Lucky Bag" (Jamie), **Supp. XIV:** 142
"Lucky Break—How I Became a Writer" (Dahl), **Supp. IV:** 209, 211
Lucky Chance, The; or, An Alderman's Bargain (Behn), **Supp. III:** 26, 29; **Retro. Supp. III:** 8
Lucky Jim (Amis), **Supp. II:** 2, 3, 4, 5–6, 7; **Supp. IV:** 25, 27, 28, 377
"Lucky Jim's Politics" (Amis), **Supp. II:** 11–12
Lucky Poet: A Self-Study in Literature and Political Ideas (MacDiarmid), **Supp. XII:** 203, 204–205
"Lucrece" (Gower), **I:** 54
Lucretia Borgia: The Chronicle of Tebaldeo Tebaldei (Swinburne), **V:** 325, 333
Lucretius, **II:** 275, 292, 300, 301; **IV:** 316
"Lucubratio Ebria" (Butler), **Supp. II:** 98, 99
Lucubrationes (More), **Supp. VII:** 240
Lucy (Kincaid), **Supp. VII:** 217, 219, 227–229
"Lucy Grange" (Lessing), **Supp. I:** 240
Lucy In Her Pink Jacket (Coppard), **VIII:** 90, 97
"Lucy"poems (Wordsworth), **IV:** 3, 18; **V:** 11
Lud Heat: A Book of the Dead Hamlets (Sinclair), **Supp. XIV:** 233, 234
"Lui et Elles" (Moore), **VI:** 87
Lukács, György, **Supp. IV:** 81, 82, 87
"Lullaby" (Auden), **VII:** 383, 398; **Retro. Supp. I:** 6
"Lullaby" (Nye), **Supp. X:** 205
"Lullaby" (Sitwell), **VII:** 135
"Lullaby for Jumbo" (Sitwell), **VII:** 132
"Lumber Room, The" (Saki), **Supp. VI:** 245
Lunar Caustic (Lowry), **Supp. III:** 269, 270, **271–273,** 280, 283
"Lunch" (Boyd), **Supp. XVI:** 44
Lunch and Counter Lunch (Murray), **Supp. VII:** 270, 275–276
"Lunch with Pancho Villa" (Muldoon), **Supp. IV:** 414–415
Luncheon of the Boating Party, The (Conn), **Supp. XIII:** 75–77, 79

"Luncheon of the Boating Party, The" (Conn), **Supp. XIII:** 75–76, 80
Lupercal (Hughes), **Supp. I:** 343, 345, 363; **Retro. Supp. I:** 126; **Retro. Supp. II:** 204–205
Luria: and a Soul's Tragedy (Browning), **IV:** 374
"Lust" (Brooke), **Supp. III:** 53
Luther (Osborne), **Supp. I:** 334–335, 338
"Lux Perpetua" (Brown), **Supp. VI:** 72
"Luxury" (Coppard), **VIII:** 94
"Lycidas" (Milton), **II:** 160–161, 164, 165, 168, 169, 175; **III:** 118–119, 120; **IV:** 205; **VI:** 73; **Retro. Supp. II:** 275–277
Lycidus; or, The Lover in Fashion (Behn), **Supp. III:** 37
"Lycus, The Centaur" (Hood), **IV:** 256, 267
Lydgate, John, **I:** 22, 49, **57–66**
Lydia Livingstone (Chatwin, B.), **Supp. IX:** 61
Lyell, Sir Charles, **IV:** 325
Lyfe of Johan Picus Erle of Myrandula (More), **Supp. VII:** 246
Lying Days, The (Gordimer), **Supp. II:** 226–227
Lying in the Sun (O'Brian), **Supp. XII:** 251
Lying Together (Thomas), **Supp. IV:** 485–486
Lyly, John, **I: 191–211,** 303
Lynch & Boyle (Seth), **Supp. X:** 283, 290
Lyra and the Birds (Pullman), **Supp. XIII:** 153, 159–160
Lyra's Oxford (Pullman), **Supp. XIII:** 153, 159–160
Lyric Impulse, The (Day Lewis), **Supp. III:** 118, 131
"Lyrical Ballad, A" (Motion), **Supp. VII:** 256–257
Lyrical Ballads (Cowper), **Retro. Supp. III:** 35
Lyrical Ballads (Wordsworth and Coleridge), **III:** 174, 336; **IV:** ix, viii, x, xvi, 3, 4, 5, **6–11,** 18, 24, **44–45,** 55, 77, 111, 138–139, 142; **Retro. Supp. II:** 53–54
Lyrical Tales (Robinson), **Supp. XIII:** 195, 196, 211–213
Lyttelton, George, **III:** 118
Lyttleton, Dame Edith, **VII:** 32

*M*abinogion, **I:** 73
"Mabinog's Liturgy" (Jones), **Supp. VII:** 177
Mac (Pinter), **Supp. I:** 367
Mac Flecknoe; or, A Satyre Upon the . . . Poet, T. S. (Dryden), **II:** 299, 304; **Retro. Supp. III:** 58, 62, 63–66, 77
"McAndrew's Hymn" (Kipling), **VI:** 202
Macaulay, Rose, **VII:** 37
Macaulay, Thomas Babington, **II:** 240, 241, 254, 255, 307; **III:** 51, 53, 72; **IV:** xii, xvi, xx, xxii, 101, 122, **268–291,** 295; **V:** viii; **VI:** 347, 353, 383, 392
Macbeth (Shakespeare), **I:** 317–318, 327; **II:** 97, 281; **IV:** 79–80, 188; **V:** 375;

Supp. IV: 283 **Retro. Supp. III:** 270, 276
MacCaig, Norman, **Supp. VI: 181–195**
MacCarthy, Desmond, **V:** 284, 286, 290; **VI:** 363, 385; **VII:** 32; **Supp. III:** 98
McCabe, Patrick, **Supp. IX: 127–139**
McCarthy, Mary, **Supp. IV:** 234
McCartney, Colum, **Retro. Supp. I:** 131
McClintock, Anne, **Supp. IV:** 167
McClure, John, **Supp. IV:** 163
McCullers, Carson, **Supp. IV:** 422, 424
McCullough, Colleen, **Supp. IV:** 343
MacDermots of Ballycloran, The (Trollope), **V:** 101
MacDiarmid, Hugh, **III:** 310; **Supp. III:** 119; **Supp. XII: 201–216**
McDonagh, Martin, **Supp. XII: 233–246**
Macdonald, George, **V:** 266; **Supp. IV:** 201
Macdonald, Mary, **V:** 266, 272
McElroy, Joseph, **Supp. IV:** 116
McEwan, Ian, **Supp. IV:** 65, 75, **389–408**; **Supp. V:** xxx
McGann, Jerome J., **V:** 314, 335
McGrotty and Ludmilla (Gray, A.), **Supp. IX:** 80, 89
McGuckian, Medbh, **Supp. V: 277–293**
McHale, Brian, **Supp. IV:** 112
Machiavelli, Niccolò, **II:** 71, 72; **IV:** 279; **Retro. Supp. I:** 204
"Machine" (Cornford), **Supp. XIII:** 84–85
"Machine Stops, The" (Forster), **VI:** 399
Machynlleth Triad, A (Morris, J.), **Supp. X:** 185–186
McInherny, Frances, **Supp. IV:** 347, 353
Mack, Maynard, **Retro. Supp. I:** 229
Mackail, J. W., **V:** 294, 296, 297, 306
McKane, Richard, **Supp. IV:** 494–495
Mackay, M. E., **V:** 223, 234
Mackenzie, Compton, **VII:** 278
Mackenzie, Henry, **III:** 87; **IV:** 79
MacKenzie, Jean, **VI:** 227, 243
MacKenzie, Norman, **V:** 374n, 375n, 381, 382; **VI:** 227, 243
McKenney, Ruth, **Supp. IV:** 476
Mackenzie, Sir George, **III:** 95
"Mackery End, in Hertfordshire" (Lamb), **IV:** 83
MacLaren, Moray, **V:** 393, 398
McLeehan, Marshall, **IV:** 323n, 338, 339
Maclure, Millar, **I:** 291
Macmillan's (periodical), **VI:** 351; **Supp. XII:** 266, 268, 269, 270
MacNeice, Louis, **VII:** 153, 382, 385, **401–418**; **Supp. III:** 119; **Supp. IV:** 423, 424
Macpherson, James, **III:** 336; **VIII: 179–195**; **Supp. II:** 523
Macready, William Charles, **I:** 327
McTaggart, J. M. E., **Supp. II:** 406
Mad British Pervert Has a Sexual Fantasy About the 10th Street Bridge in Calgary, A (De Bernières), **Supp. XII:** 66
Mad Forest: A Play from Romania (Churchill), **Supp. IV:** 179, 188, 195–196, 198, 199
Mad Islands, The (MacNeice), **VII:** 405, 407
Mad Lady's Garland, A (Pitter), **Supp. XIII:** 133–134, 135, 139–140
Mad Lover, The (Fletcher), **II:** 45, 55, 65
"Mad Maids Song, The" (Herrick), **II:** 112
"Mad Mullinix and Timothy" (Swift), **III:** 31
Mad Soldier's Song (Hardy), **VI:** 11
Mad World, My Masters, A (Middleton), **II:** 3, 4, 21
Madagascar; or, Robert Drury's Journal (Defoe), **III:** 14
Madame Bovary (Flaubert), **V:** xxii, 429; **Supp. IV:** 68, 69
"Madame de Mauves" (James), **VI:** 69; **Supp. IV:** 133
Madame de Pompadour (Mitford), **Supp. X:** 163
"Madame Rosette" (Dahl), **Supp. IV:** 209–210
Madan, Falconer, **V:** 264, 274
Madder (Constantine), **Supp. XV:** 66, 72, 73
Maddox, Brenda, **Retro. Supp. I:** 327, 328
"Mademoiselle" (Stevenson), **Supp. VI:** 255
Mademoiselle de Maupin (Gautier), **V:** 320n
Madge, Charles, **VII:** xix
"Madhouse Cells" (Browning), **Retro. Supp. III:** 21
"Madman and the Child, The" (Cornford), **VIII:** 107
Madness of George III, The (Bennett), **VIII:** 31–33
Madoc (Muldoon), **Supp. IV:** 420, 424–427, 428
"Madoc" (Muldoon), **Supp. IV:** 422, 425–427, 430
Madoc (Southey), **IV:** 63, 64–65, 71
"Madoc" (Southey), **Supp. IV:** 425
"Madonna" (Kinsella), **Supp. V:** 273
Madonna and Other Poems (Kinsella), **Supp. V:** 272–273
Madonna of Excelsior, The (Mda), **Supp. XV:** 204–205, 206
Madonna of the Future and Other Tales, The (James), **VI:** 67, 69
"Madonna of the Trenches, A" (Kipling), **VI:** 193, **194–196**
Madras House, The (Shaw), **VI:** 118
Madwoman in the Attic, The (Gilbert/Gubar), **Retro. Supp. I:** 59–60
Maggot, A (Fowles), **Supp. I:** 309–310
"Magi" (Brown), **Supp. VI:** 71
Magic (Chesterton), **VI:** 340
Magic Apple Tree, The (Hill), **Supp. XIV:** 118
Magic Box, The (Ambler), **Supp. IV:** 3
Magic Drum, The (Tennant), **Supp. IX:** 239
Magic Finger, The (Dahl), **Supp. IV:** 201
"Magic Finger, The" (Dahl), **Supp. IV:** 223–224
Magic Toyshop, The (Carter), **III:** 345; **Supp. III:** 80, 81, 82
Magic Wheel, The (eds. Swift and Profumo), **Supp. V:** 427
Magician, The (Maugham), **VI:** 374

Magician's Nephew, The (Lewis), **Supp. III:** 248
Magician's Wife, The (Moore, B.), **Supp. IX:** 141, 145–146
Maginn, William, **V:** 19
"Magna Est Veritas" (Smith), **Supp. II:** 471, 472
"Magnanimity" (Kinsella), **Supp. V:** 263
Magnetic Mountain, The (Day Lewis), **Supp. III:** 117, 122, 124–126
Magnetick Lady, The (Jonson), **Retro. Supp. I:** 165
"Magnificat" (Roberts), **Supp. XV:** 262
Magnificence (Skelton), **I:** 90
"Magnolia" (Fuller), **Supp. VII:** 78
Magnus (Brown), **Supp. VI: 66–67**
"Magnus" (Macpherson), **VIII:** 186
Magnusson, Erika, **V:** 299, 300, 306
Magus, The (Fowles), **Supp. I:** 291, 292, 293, **295–299**, 310
Mahafty, John Pentland, **V:** 400, 401
Mahon, Derek, **Supp. IV:** 412; **Supp. VI: 165–180**
"Mahratta Ghats, The" (Lewis), **VII:** 446–447
Maid in the Mill, The (Fletcher and Rowley), **II:** 66
Maid in Waiting (Galsworthy), **VI:** 275
Maid Marian (Peacock), **IV:** xviii, 167–168, 170
Maid of Arragon, The (Cowley), **Supp. XVI:** 109
Maid of Bath, The (Foote), **III:** 253
"Maid of Craca, The" (Macpherson), **VIII:** 186, 187
Maid of Honour, The (Massinger), **Supp. XI:** 184
"Maiden Name" (Larkin), **Supp. I:** 277; **Retro. Supp. III:** 204
"Maiden Tribute of Modern Babylon, The" (Stead), **Supp. XIII:** 239–240
Maiden Voyage (Welch), **Supp. IX:** 261, 263–264
Maiden's Dream, A (Greene), **VIII:** 142
"Maid's Burial, The" (Pitter), **Supp. XIII:** 138, 139
Maid's Tragedy, The (Beaumont and Fletcher), **II:** 44, 45, **54–57**, 58, 60, 65
Maid's Tragedy, Alter'd, The (Waller), **II:** 238
Mailer, Norman, **Supp. IV:** 17–18
"Maim'd Debauchee, The" (Rochester), **II:** 259–260
"Main Road" (Pritchett), **Supp. III:** 316–317
Mainly on the Air (Beerbohm), **Supp. II:** 52
Maitland, F. W., **V:** 277, 290; **VI:** 385
Maitland, Sara, **Supp. XI: 163–178**
Maitland, Thomas, pseud. of Algernon Charles Swinburne
Maitū njugīra (Ngũgĩ wa Thiong'o/Ngũgĩ wa Mĩriĩ), **VIII:** 216, 224, 225
Maiwa's Revenge (Haggard), **Supp. III:** 213
Majeske, Penelope, **Supp. IV:** 330
"Majesty of the Law, The" (O'Connor), **Supp. XIV:** 224, 225
Major, John, **Supp. IV:** 437–438

Major Barbara (Shaw), **VII:** xv, 102, 108, **113–115,** 124; **Retro. Supp. II:** 321
Major Political Essays (Shaw), **VI:** 129
Major Victorian Poets, The: Reconsiderations (Armstrong), **IV:** 339
"Makar, The" (Soutar), **Supp. XVI:** 258
Make Death Love Me (Rendell), **Supp. IX:** 192–194
Make Thyself Many (Powys), **VIII:** 255
"Maker on High, The" (tr. Morgan, E.), see *Altus Prosator*
Makers of Florence, The (Oliphant), **Supp. X:** 222
Makers of Modern Rome, The (Oliphant), **Supp. X:** 222
Makers of Venice, The (Oliphant), **Supp. X:** 222
Makin, Bathsua, **Supp. III:** 21
"Making a Movie" (Kay), **Supp. XIII:** 110
"Making a Rat" (Hart), **Supp. XI:** 130
Making Cocoa for Kingsley Amis (Cope), **VIII:** 67, 69, 70–74, 81
Making History (Friel), **Supp. V:** 125
Making of a Poem, The (Spender), **Supp. II:** 481, 492
Making of an Immortal, The (Moore), **VI:** 96, 99
"Making of an Irish Goddess, The" (Boland), **Supp. V:** 44–45
"Making of the Drum" (Brathwaite), **Supp. XII:** 38
Making of the English Working Class, The (Thompson), **Supp. IV:** 473
Making of the Representative for Planet 8, The (Lessing), **Supp. I:** 252, 254
"Making Poetry" (Stevenson), **Supp. VI:** 262
Mal vu, mal dit (Beckett), **Supp. I:** 62
"Malayalam Box, The" (Delanty), **Supp. XIV:** 74
Malayan trilogy (Burgess), **Supp. I:** 187
Malcolm Lowry: Psalms and Songs (Lowry), **Supp. III:** 285
Malcolm Mooney's Land (Graham), **Supp. VII:** 104, 106, 109, 113–115, 116
Malcontent, The (Marston), **II:** 27, 30, **31–33,** 36, 40, 68
Malcontents, The (Snow), **VII:** 336–337
Male Child, A (Scott), **Supp. I:** 263
"Male-ing Names in the Sun" (Aidoo), **Supp. XV:** 2
Malign Fiesta (Lewis), **VII:** 72, 80
Malinowski, Bronislaw, **Supp. III:** 186
Mallet, David, **Supp. III:** 412, 424–425
Malone, Edmond, **I:** 326
Malone Dies (Beckett), **Supp. I:** 50, 51, 52–53, 63; **Supp. IV:** 106; **Retro. Supp. I:** 18, 22–23
Malory, Sir Thomas, **I: 67–80; IV:** 336, 337; **Retro. Supp. II: 237–252**
Malouf, David, **Supp. XII: 217–232**
Malraux, André, **VI:** 240
"Maltese Cat, The" (Kipling), **VI:** 200
Malthus, Thomas, **IV:** xvi, 127, 133
Mamillia: A Mirror, or Looking-Glasse for the Ladies of England (Greene), **VIII:** 135, 140

"Man"(Herbert), **Retro. Supp. II:** 176–177
"Man"(Vaughan), **II:** 186, 188
Man, The (Stoker), **Supp. III:** 381
Man Above Men (Hare), **Supp. IV:** 282, 289
"Man and Bird" (Mahon), **Supp. VI:** 168
"Man and Boy" (Heaney), **Retro. Supp. I:** 132
Man and Boy (Parsons), **Supp. XV:** 227, 228, 229, 230, 231, 232, 234–235, 236, 238, 239, 240
Man and Boy (Rattigan), **Supp. VII:** 318, 320
"Man and Dog" (Thomas), **Supp. III:** 394, 403, 405
Man and Literature (Nicholson), **Supp. VI:** 213, 223
Man and Superman: A Comedy and a Philosophy (Shaw), **IV:** 161; **VI: 112–113,** 114, 127, 129; **Retro. Supp. II:** 309, 317–320
Man and Time (Priestley), **VII:** 213
Man and Two Women, A (Lessing), **Supp. I:** 244, 248
Man and Wife (Collins), **Supp. VI:** 102
"Man and Wife" (Constantine), **Supp. XV:** 79
Man and Wife (Parsons), **Supp. XV:** 229, 230–231, 232, 234–235, 236, 238, 239, 240
Man Born to Be King, The (Sayers), **Supp. III:** 336, 349–350
"Man Called East, The" (Redgrove), **Supp. VI:** 236
Man Could Stand Up, A (Ford), **VI:** 319, 329
Man Does, Woman Is (Graves), **VII:** 268
"Man Friday" (Hope), **Supp. VII:** 164–165
"Man From the Caravan, The" (Coppard), **VIII:** 96
Man from the North, A (Bennett), **VI:** 248, 253
"Man from the South" (Dahl), **Supp. IV:** 215, 217–218
"Man I Killed, The" (Hardy), **Retro. Supp. I:** 120
"Man in Assynt, A" (MacCaig), **Supp. VI:** 191
Man in My Position, A (MacCaig), **Supp. VI: 191–192**
"Man in the Cloak, The" (Mangan), **Supp. XIII:** 117
Man in the Picture, The: A Ghost Story (Hill), **Supp. XIV:** 118, 126
Man Lying On A Wall (Longley), **VIII:** 166, 172–173
"Man Lying On A Wall" (Longley), **VIII:** 172
Man Named East, The (Redgrove), **Supp. VI:** 235–236
Man of Destiny, The (Shaw), **VI:** 112
Man of Devon, A (Galsworthy), **VI:** 277
Man of Honour, A (Maugham), **VI:** 367, 368
Man of Law's Tale, The (Chaucer), **I:** 24, 34, 43, 51, 57
Man of Mode, The; or, Sir Fopling Flutter (Etherege), **II:** 256, 266, 271, 305

Man of Nazareth, The (Burgess), **Supp. I:** 193
Man of Property, A (Galsworthy), **VI:** 271, 272, 273, 274, 275, 276, 278, 282–283
Man of Quality, A (Lee), **II:** 336
Man of the Moment (Ayckbourn), **Supp. V:** 3, 7–8, 10
"Man of Vision" (Crawford), **Supp. XI:** 71
"Man on the Edge" (Scupham), **Supp. XIII:** 218
Man to Man (Boyd), **Supp. XVI:** 46
"Man Was Made to Mourn, a Dirge" (Burns), **III:** 315
"Man Who Changes His Mind, The" (Ambler), **Supp. IV:** 5
"Man Who Could Work Miracles, The" (Wells), **VI:** 235
"Man Who Died, The" (Lawrence), **VII:** 115; **Retro. Supp. II:** 233
Man Who Loved Children, The (Stead), **Supp. IV:** 460, 467–470, 473
"Man Who Loved Islands, The" (Lawrence), **VII:** 115
"Man Who Walked on the Moon, The" (Ballard), **Supp. V:** 33
Man Who Walks, The (Warner), **Supp. XI:** 282, 287, 290–293
"Man Who Was Answered by His Own Self, The" (Burnside), **Supp. XIII:** 23
Man Who Was Thursday, The (Chesterton), **VI:** 338
Man Who Wasn't There, The (Barker), **Supp. IV:** 45, 46, 56–57
"Man Who Would Be King, The" (Kipling), **Retro. Supp. III:** 186–187
"Man with a Past, The" (Hardy), **VI:** 17
"Man with Night Sweats, The" (Gunn), **Supp. IV:** 276–277; **Retro. Supp. III:** 126–128
Man with Night Sweats, The (Gunn), **Supp. IV:** 255, 257, 274–278; **Retro. Supp. III:** 124, 126–128, 129
"Man with the Dog, The" (Jhabvala), **Supp. V:** 236
Man with the Golden Gun, The (Fleming), **Supp. XIV:** 96
"Man with the Twisted Lip, The" (Doyle), **Supp. II:** 171
Man Within, The (Greene), **Supp. I:** 2; **Retro. Supp. II:** 152
"Man Without a Temperament, The" (Mansfield), **VII:** 174, 177
"Mana Aboda" (Hulme), **Supp. VI:** 136
Manalive (Chesterton), **VI:** 340
Mañanas de abril y mayo (Calderón), **II:** 312n
Manchester Enthusiasts, The (Arden and D'Arcy), **Supp. II:** 39
"Manchester Marriage, The" (Gaskell), **V:** 6n, 14, 15
"Manchester Strike, A" (Martineau), **Supp. XV:** 188, 189
Manciple's Prologue, The (Chaucer), **I:** 24
Manciple's Tale, The (Chaucer), **I:** 55
"Mandalay" (Kipling), **Retro. Supp. III:** 188
"Mandela" (Motion), **Supp. VII:** 266

Mandelbaum Gate, The (Spark), **Supp. I:** **206–208,** 213
Mandelstam, Osip, **Supp. IV:** 163, 493
Mandeville: A Tale of the Seventeenth Century in England (Godwin), **Supp. XV:** 127
"Mandrake" (Burnside), **Supp. XIII:** 23
Manet, Edouard, **Supp. IV:** 480
Manfred (Byron), **III:** 338; **IV:** xvii, 172, 173, 177, **178–182,** 192
Mangan, James Clarence, **Supp. XIII:** **113–130**
Mangan Inheritance, The (Moore), **Supp. IX** 144, 148, 150–151, 153
Manhatten '45 (Morris, J.), **Supp. X:** 182
"Manhole 69" (Ballard), **Supp. V:** 21
"Maniac, The" (Robinson), **Supp. XIII:** 206, 210
"Manifesto" (Morgan, E.), **Supp. IX:** 163
"Mani, The" (Delahunt), **Supp. XIV:** 59
Manifold, John, **VII:** 422, 426–427
Manin and the Venetian Revolution of 1848 (Trevelyan), **VI:** 389
Mankind in the Making (Wells), **VI:** 227, 236
Manly, J. M., **I:** 1
"Man–Man" (Naipaul), **Supp. I:** 385
Mann, Thomas, **II:** 97; **III:** 344; **Supp. IV:** 397
Manner of the World Nowadays, The (Skelton), **I:** 89
Mannerly Margery Milk and Ale (Skelton), **I:** 83
Manners, Mrs. Horace, pseud. of Algernon Charles Swinburne
"Manners, The" (Collins), **III:** 161, 162, 166, 171
Manning, Cardinal, **V:** 181
Manoeuvring (Edgeworth), **Supp. III:** 158
"Manor Farm, The" (Thomas), **Supp. III:** 399, 405
"Mans medley" (Herbert), **Retro. Supp. II:** 181–182
Manservant and Maidservant (Compton-Burnett), **VII:** 62, 63, 67
Mansfield, Katherine, **IV:** 106; **VI:** 375; **VII:** xv, xvii, **171–184,** 314; list of short stories, **VII:** 183–184
Mansfield Park (Austen), **IV:** xvii, 102–103, 108, 109, 111, 112, 115–119, 122; **Retro. Supp. II:** 9–11
Mantissa (Fowles), **Supp. I:** 308–309, 310
Manto, Saadat Hasan, **Supp. IV:** 440
Mantz, Ruth, **VII:** 176
Manuel (Maturin), **VIII:** 207, 208
"Manus Animam Pinxit" (Thompson), **V:** 442
Many Dimensions (Williams, C. W. S.), **Supp. IX:** 281
Many Moods: A Volume of Verse (Symonds), **Supp. XIV:** 252
Manzoni, Alessandro, **III:** 334
"Map, The" (Hart), **Supp. XI:** 130
Map, Walter, **I:** 35
Map of Love, The (Thomas), **Supp. I:** 176–177, 180; **Retro. Supp. III:** 335, 341–343

"Map of the City, A" (Gunn), **Supp. IV:** 262, 274
Map of the World, A (Hare), **Supp. IV:** 282, 288–289, 293
Map of Verona, A (Reed), **VII:** 423
"Map of Verona, A" (Reed), **Supp. XV:** 249, 250, 255
Map of Verona, A: Poems (Reed), **Supp. XV:** 243, 245, 248–249, 251, 254, 255
Map of Verona and Other Poems, A (Reed), **Supp. XV:** 248
Mapp Showing . . . Salvation and Damnation, A (Bunyan), **II:** 253
"Mappa Mundi" (Constantine), **Supp. XV:** 73
Mappings (Seth), **Supp. X:** 279–280
Mapplethorpe, Robert, **Supp. IV:** 170, 273
Mara, Bernard, *see* Moore, Brian
Marble Faun, The (Hawthorne), **VI:** 27
March of Literature, The (Ford), **VI:** 321, 322, 324
March Violets (Kerr), **Supp. XII:** 187, 188–189
"Marchese Pallavicini and Walter Landor" (Landor), **IV:** 90
March Moonlight (Richardson), **Supp. XIII:** 181, 188, 192
Marching Soldier (Cary), **VII:** 186
"Marching to Zion" (Coppard), **VIII:** 91–92
"Marchioness of Stonehenge, The" (Hardy), **VI:** 22
Marcliffe, Theophilous, *see* Godwin, William
Marconi's Cottage (McGuckian), **Supp. V:** 284, 286–287
Marcus, Jane, **Retro. Supp. I:** 306
Marcus, S., **V:** 46, 73
Marfan (Reading), **VIII:** 262, 274–275
Margaret Drabble: Puritanism and Permissiveness (Myer), **Supp. IV:** 233
Margaret Ogilvy (Barrie), **Supp. III:** 3
Margin Released (Priestley), **VII:** 209, 210, 211
"Margins" (Conn), **Supp. XIII:** 72
Margoliouth, H. M., **II:** 214n, 219
Mari Magno (Clough), **V:** 159, 168
Maria; or, The Wrongs of Woman (Wollstonecraft), **Supp. III:** 466, **476–480**
"Mariana" (Tennyson), **IV:** 329, 331; **Retro. Supp. III:** 317
"Mariana in the South" (Tennyson), **IV:** 329, 331
Mariani, Paul L., **V:** 373n, 378, 382
Marianne Thornton (Forster), **VI:** 397, 411
Marie (Haggard), **Supp. III:** 214
"Marie Antoinette's Lamentation, in her Prison of the Temple" (Robinson), **Supp. XIII:** 202
Marinetti, Filippo T., **Supp. III:** 396
"Marina" (Eliot), **Retro. Supp. II:** 130
"Marine Lament" (Cameron), **Supp. IX:** 19
"Mariner's Compass, The" (Armitage), **VIII:** 11
Marino, Giambattista, **II:** 180, 183
Marino Faliero (Swinburne), **V:** 332

Marino Faliero, Doge of Venice (Byron), **IV:** xviii, 178–179, 193
Marion Fay (Trollope), **V:** 102
Marionette, The (Muir), **Supp. VI:** 198, **203–204**
Marius the Epicurean (Pater), **V:** xxv, 339, 348, **349–351,** 354, 355, 356, 411
Marjorie, **VI:** 249; pseud. of Arnold Bennett
"Mark of the Beast, The" (Kipling), **VI:** 183, 193
Mark of the Warrior, The (Scott), **Supp. I:** 263
Mark Only (Powys), **VIII:** 250–251
Markandaya, Kamala, **Supp. IV:** 440
"Markers" (Thomas), **Supp. XII:** 290
"Market at Turk" (Gunn), **Supp. IV:** 260–261
Market Bell, The (Powys), **VIII:** 251, 258
Market of Seleukia, The (Morris, J.), **Supp. X:** 175
"Market Square" (Milne), **Supp. V:** 302
Markey, Constance, **Supp. IV:** 347, 360
Markham, Robert, **Supp. II:** 12; pseud. of Kingsley Amis
"Markheim" (Stevenson), **V:** 395; **Retro. Supp. I:** 267
Marking Time (Howard), **Supp. XI:** 145, 146, 147, 148
"Mark–2 Wife, The" (Trevor), **Supp. IV:** 503
Marlborough: His Life and Times (Churchill), **VI:** 354–355
Marlowe, Christopher, **I:** 212, 228–229, **275–294,** 336; **II:** 69, 138; **III:** 344; **IV:** 255, 327; **Supp. IV:** 197; **Retro. Supp. I:** **199–213**
Marlowe and His Circle (Boas), **I:** 275, 293
Marlowe and the Early Shakespeare (Wilson), **I:** 286
Marmion (Scott), **IV:** xvi, 29, 30, 38, 129
Marmor Norfolciense (Johnson), **III:** 121; **Retro. Supp. I:** 141
Marquise, The (Coward), **Supp. II:** 146
"Marriage, A" (Thomas), **Supp. XII:** 290
Marriage A-la-Mode (Dryden), **II:** 293, 296, 305
"Marriage in a Free Society" (Carpenter), **Supp. XIII:** 41, 42
Marriage of Heaven and Hell, The (Blake), **III:** 289, 297–298, 304, 307; **V:** xv, 329–330, 331; **Supp. IV:** 448; **Retro. Supp. I:** 38–39
Marriage of Mona Lisa, The (Swinburne), **V:** 333
"Marriage of Tirzah and Ahirad, The" (Macaulay), **IV:** 283
Marriages Between Zones Three, Four and Five, The (Lessing), **Supp. I:** 251
Married Life (Bennett), *see Plain Man and His Wife, The*
Married Man, The (Inchbald), **Supp. XV:** 147, 155–156
Married Man, The (Lawrence), **VII:** 120
"Married Man's Story, A" (Mansfield), **VII:** 174
Married to a Spy (Waugh), **Supp. VI:** 276

411

"Married to Death" (Smith), **Retro. Supp. III:** 306–307
"Married Woman" (Kay), **Supp. XIII:** 110
Marryat, Captain Frederick, **Supp. IV:** 201
Marsh, Charles, **Supp. IV:** 214, 218
Marsh, Edward, **VI:** 416, 419, 420, 425, 430, 432, 452; **VII:** xvi; **Supp. III:** 47, 48, 53, 54, 60, 397
"Marsh of Ages, The" (Cameron), **Supp. IX:** 19
Marshall, William, **II:** 141
Marston, John, **I:** 234, 238, 340; **II:** 4, 24–33, 34–37, 40–41, 47, 68, 72; **Retro. Supp. I:** 160
Marston, Philip, **V:** 245
Marston, R. B., **II:** 131
"Martha and Mary Raise Consciousness from the Dead" (Roberts), **Supp. XV:** 262, 263
"Martha Blake" (Clarke), **Supp. XV:** 28
"Martha Blake at Fifty-One" (Clarke), **Supp. XV:** 28, 30
Martha Quest (Lessing), **Supp. I:** 237, 239, 243–244; **Supp. IV:** 238
Martial, **II:** 104, 265
Martian, The (du Maurier), **Supp. III:** 134, 151
"Martian Sends a Postcard Home, A" (Cope), **VIII:** 74
Martian Sends a Postcard Home, A (Raine), **Supp. XIII:** 166–167
"Martian Sends a Postcard Home, A" (Raine), **Supp. XIII:** 166–167
Martin, John, **V:** 110
Martin, L. C., **II:** 183, 184n, 200
Martin, Martin, **III:** 117
Martin Chuzzlewit (Dickens), **V:** xx, 42, 47, 54–56, 58, 59, 68, 71; **Supp. IV:** 366, 381
Martin Chuzzlewit (teleplay, Lodge), **Supp. IV:** 366, 381
Martin Luther (Lopez and Moore), **VI:** 85, 95, 98
Martineau, Harriet, **IV:** 311; **V:** 125–126, 146; **Supp. XV: 181–194**
Martyn, Edward, **VI:** 309
Martyrdom of Man (Reade), **Supp. IV:** 2
"Martyrs' Song" (Rossetti), **V:** 256
Martz, Louis, **V:** 366, 382
"Maruti" (Delanty), **Supp. XIV:** 73
Marvell, Andrew, **II:** 113, 121, 123, 166, 195–199, **204–220**, 255, 261; **Supp. III:** 51, 56; **Supp. IV:** 271; **Retro. Supp. II: 253–268**
Marvell and the Civic Crown (Patterson), **Retro. Supp. II:** 265
"Marvellous Bell, The" (Mangan), **Supp. XIII:** 122
Marwick, A., **IV:** 290, 291
Marwood, Arthur, **VI:** 323, 331
Marxism, **Supp. I:** 24–25, 26, 30, 31, 238
"Marxist Interpretation of Literature, A" (Upward), **Supp. XIII:** 254
Mary, A Fiction (Wollstonecraft), **Supp. III:** 466, 476
"Mary: A Legend of the '45" (Abercrombie), **Supp. XVI:** 2

"Mary and Gabriel" (Brooke), **Supp. III:** 55
Mary and the Bramble (Abercrombie), **Supp. XVI:** 9
Mary Anne (du Maurier), **Supp. III:** 137
Mary Barton (Gaskell), **V:** viii, x, xxi, 1, 2, 4–5, 6, 15; **Retro. Supp. III:** 99, 100, 101, 102–103, 104, 105, 106, 108, 110, 112
"Mary Burnet" (Hogg), **Supp. X:** 110
"'Mary Gloster', The," (Kipling), **VI:** 202
Mary Gresley (Trollope), **V:** 101
"Mary Magdalene and the Sun" (Constantine), **Supp. XV:** 72
"Mary Postgate" (Kipling), **VI:** 197, 206; **Retro. Supp. III:** 194
"Mary Queen of Scots" (Swinburne), **V:** 332
Mary Rose (Barrie), **Supp. III:** 8, 9
"Mary Shelley on Broughty Ferry Beach" (Crawford), **Supp. XI:** 74
Mary Stuart (Swinburne), **V:** 330, 332
"Mary the Cook-Maid's Letter . . . " (Swift), **III:** 31
"Mary's Magnificat" (Jennings), **Supp. V:** 217
mas v. Mastermind (Ayckbourn), **Supp. V:** 2
"Masculine Birth of Time, The" (Bacon), **I:** 263
"Masculine Protest, The " (O'Connor), **Supp. XIV:** 227
Masculinity (Crawford), **Supp. XI:** 67, 74–76
Masefield, John, **VI:** 429; **VII:** xii, xiii
Mask of Apollo (Renault), **Supp. IX:** 183–184, 187
Mask of Apollo and Other Stories, The (Russell), **VIII:** 285
Mask of Dimitrios, The (Ambler), **Supp. IV:** 21
"Mask of Love" (Kinsella), **Supp. V:** 262
Masks (Brathwaite), **Supp. XII:** 33, 38–39
Mason, William, **III:** 141, 142, 145
"Masque, The" (Auden), **Retro. Supp. I:** 11
"Masque of Anarchy, The" (Shelley), **IV:** xviii, 202–203, 206, 208; **Retro. Supp. I:** 253–254
Masque of Blackness, The (Jonson), **Retro. Supp. I:** 161–162
Masque of Queenes (Jonson), **II:** 111n; **Retro. Supp. I:** 162
Masque of the Manuscript, The (Williams, C. W. S.), **Supp. IX:** 276
Masqueraders, The (Haywood), **Supp. XII:** 135
Mass and the English Reformers, The (Dugmore), **I:** 177n
Mass for Hard Times (Thomas), **Supp. XII:** 285, 290–291
"Mass for Hard Times" (Thomas), **Supp. XII:** 290, 291
Massacre, The (Inchbald), **Supp. XV:** 147–148, 149, 157
Massacre at Paris, The (Marlowe), **I:** 249, 276, 279–280, **285–286**; **Retro. Supp. I:** 211

Massinger, Philip, **II:** 44, 45, 50, 66–67, 69, 83, 87; **Supp. XI: 179–194**
Masson, David, **IV:** 212, 235
Masson, Rosaline, **V:** 393, 397
"Mastectomy" (Boland), **Supp. V:** (Boland), **Supp. V:** 49
Master, The (Brontë), *see Professor, The*
"Master, The" (Wilde), **Retro. Supp. II:** 371
Master and Commander (O'Brian), **Supp. XII:** 252–254, 256, 257
Master and Margarita, The (Bulgakov), **Supp. IV:** 448
Master Georgie (Bainbridge), **Supp. VI: 26–27**
"*Master Harold*" ... *and the Boys* (Fugard), **Supp. XV:** 101, 104, 110–111
"Master Hugues of Saxe-Gotha" (Browning), **Retro. Supp. III:** 25
Master Humphrey's Clock (Dickens), **V:** 42, 53–54, 71
"Master John Horseleigh, Knight" (Hardy), **VI:** 22
Master of Ballantrae, The (Stevenson), **V:** 383–384, 387, 396; **Retro. Supp. I:** 268–269
Master of Petersburg, The (Coetzee), **Supp. VI:** 75–76, **85–86**, 88
Master of the House, The (Hall), **Supp. VI:** 120, 122, 128
"Master Printer, The" (Delanty), **Supp. XIV:** 66
Masterman, C. F. G., **VI:** viii, 320
Masters, John, **Supp. IV:** 440
Masters, The (Snow), **VII:** xxi, 327–328, 330
"Match, The" (Marvell), **II:** 211
Match for the Devil, A (Nicholson), **Supp. VI: 222**
"Match-Maker, The" (Saki), **Supp. VI:** 240
"Mater Dolorosa" (Swinburne), **V:** 325
"Mater Triumphalis" (Swinburne), **V:** 325
Materials for a Description of Capri (Douglas), **VI:** 305
Mathilda (Shelley), **Supp. III: 363–364**
"Mathilda's England" (Trevor), **Supp. IV:** 504
Matigari (Ngũgĩ), **VIII:** 215, 216, 221–222
Matilda (Dahl), **Supp. IV:** 203, 207, 226
Matilda (film), **Supp. IV:** 203
Matilda (Shelley), **Retro. Supp. III:** 289
"Matins" (Montague), **Supp. XV:** 217
Matisse, Henri, **Supp. IV:** 81, 154
Matisse Stories, The (Byatt), **Supp. IV:** 151, 154–155
Matlock's System (Hill), *see Heart Clock*
"Matres Dolorosae" (Bridges), **VI:** 81
"Matron" (Blackwood), **Supp. IX:** 12
"Mattens" (Herbert), **II:** 127; **Retro. Supp. II:** 179
"Matter and Consciousness" (Carpenter), **Supp. XIII:** 46
"Matter of Fact, A" (Kipling), **VI:** 193
Matter of Wales: Epic Views of a Small Country, The (Morris), *see Wales: Epic Views of a Small Country*

Matthew Arnold: A Study in Conflict (Brown), **V:** 211–212, 217
Matthew Arnold: A Symposium (ed. Allott), **V:** 218
Matthews, Geoffrey Maurice, **IV:** x, xxv, 207, 208, 209, 237
"Matthew's War" (Jamie), **Supp. XIV:** 136
Matthews, William, **I:** 68
Matthiessen, F. O., **V:** 204
Matthieu de Vendôme, **I:** 23, 39–40
"Mature Art" (MacDiarmid), **Supp. XII:** 214
Maturin, Charles, **III:** 327, 331, 333–334, 336, 345; **VIII: 197–210; Supp. III:** 384
Maud (Tennyson), **IV:** xxi, 325, 328, 330–331, 333–336, 337, 338; **VI:** 420
"Maud" (Tennyson), **Retro. Supp. III:** 321, 322
Maud, and Other Poems (Tennyson), **Retro. Supp. III:** 317, 322, 324, 326–327, 330
Maude: A Story for Girls (Rossetti), **V:** 260; **Retro. Supp. III:** 256, 257
"Maude Clare" (Rossetti), **Retro. Supp. III:** 251
"Maud-Evelyn" (James), **VI:** 69
Maugham, Syrie, **VI:** 369
Maugham, W. Somerset, **VI:** xi, xiii, 200, **363–381; VII:** 318–319; list of short stories and sketches, **VI:** 379–381; **Supp. II:** 7, 141, 156–157; **Supp. IV:** 9–10, 21, 500
Maumbury Ring (Hardy), **VI:** 20
Maupassant, Guy de, **III:** 340, **Supp. IV:** 500
Maurice (Forster), **VI:** xii, 397, **407–408,** 412; **Retro. Supp. II:** 145–146
Maurice, Frederick D., **IV:** 54; **V:** xxi, 284, 285
Mauritius Command, The (O'Brian), **Supp. XII:** 256, 258
Mavis Belfrage (Gray, A.), **Supp. IX:** 80, 91
Max in Verse (Beerbohm), **Supp. II:** 44
Maxfield, James F., **Supp. IV:** 336
"May and Death" (Browning), **Retro. Supp. III:** 26
May Day (Chapman), **I:** 244
"May Day in the Eighties" (Thompson), **Supp. XV:** 289
"May Day, 1937" (Nicholson), **Supp. VI:** 214
"May Day Song for North Oxford" (Betjeman), **VII:** 356
"May 23" (Thomas), **Supp. III:** 405
Maybe Day in Kazakhstan, A (Harrison), **Supp. V:** 164
"Mayday in Holderness" (Hughes), **Supp. I:** 344
Mayer, Carl, **III:** 342
"Mayfly" (MacNeice), **VII:** 411
Mayhew, Henry, **Supp. XVI: 209–224**
Mayo, Robert, **IV:** ix
"Mayo Monologues" (Longley), **VIII:** 174
Mayor of Casterbridge: The Life and Death of a Man of Character, The (Hardy), **VI:** 3, 5, 7, 8, 9–10, 20

Maze Plays (Ayckbourn), **Supp. V:** 12
Mazeppa (Byron), **IV:** xvii, 173, 192
Mazzini, Giuseppi, **V:** 313, 314, 324, 325
Mda, Zakes, **Supp. XV: 195–208**
Me Again: Uncollected Writings of Stevie Smith (Smith), **Retro. Supp. III:** 306, 311, 312, 313, 314
Me, I'm Afraid of Virginia Woolf (Bennett), **VIII:** 27
Me, Myself, and I (Ayckbourn), **Supp. V:** 13
"Meadowsweet" (Jamie), **Supp. XIV:** 142
Meaning of Meaning, The (Richards and Ogden), **Supp. II:** 405, 408, **410–411,** 414
"Meaning of the Wild Body, The" (Lewis), **VII:** 77
Meaning of Treason, The (West), **Supp. III:** 440, 445
Measure for Measure (Shakespeare), **I:** 313–314, 327; **II:** 30, 70, 168; **V:** 341, 351; **Retro. Supp. III:** 275, 276, 277
Measures, (MacCaig), **Supp. VI: 188–189,** 194
"Meat, The" (Galloway), **Supp. XII:** 121
"Mechanical Genius, The" (Naipaul), **Supp. I:** 385
Mechanical Womb, The (Orton), **Supp. V:** 364
Medal: A Satyre Against Sedition, The (Dryden), **II:** 299, 304; **Retro. Supp. III:** 62
Medea (Seneca), **II:** 71
Medea: A Sex-War Opera (Harrison), **Supp. V:** 164
"Medico's Song" (Wallace–Crabbe), **VIII:** 324
Medieval Heritage of Elizabethan Tragedy (Farnham), **I:** 214
"Meditation of Mordred, The" (Williams, C. W. S.), **Supp. IX:** 283
Meditation upon a Broom-Stick, A (Swift), **III:** 35
"Meditation with Mountains" (Wallace–Crabbe), **VIII:** 317–318
Meditations Collected from the Sacred Books . . . (Richardson), **III:** 92
"Meditations in Time of Civil War" (Yeats), **V:** 317; **VII:** 24; **Retro. Supp. I:** 334–335
Meditations of Daniel Defoe, The (Defoe), **III:** 12
"Meditations with Memories" (Wallace–Crabbe), **VIII:** 317
"Mediterranean" (Redgrove), **Supp. VI:** 231
Mediterranean Scenes (Bennett), **VI:** 264, 267
"Medussa's Ankles" (Byatt), **Supp. IV:** 154–155
Medwin, Thomas, **IV:** 196, 209
Mee, Arthur, **Supp. IV:** 256
Meet My Father (Ayckbourn), **Supp. V:** 2
"Meet Nurse!" (Hope), **Supp. VII:** 151
Meeting by the River, A (Isherwood), **VII:** 317
"Meeting My Former Self" (Cameron), **Supp. IX:** 24

"Meeting of David and Jonathan, The" (Symonds), **Supp. XIV:** 252
"Meeting of Minds, The" (Coe), **Supp. XV:** 54
Meeting Place (Kay), **Supp. XIII:** 100
Meeting the British (Muldoon), **Supp. IV:** 421–424
Meeting the Comet (Adcock), **Supp. XII:** 8
"Megaliths and Water" (Scupham), **Supp. XIII:** 221
"Melancholia" (Bridges), **VI:** 80
"Melancholy" (Bridges), **VI:** 80
"Melancholy Hussar of the German Legion, The" (Hardy), **VI:** 20, 22; **Retro. Supp. I:** 116
"Melbourne" (Wallace–Crabbe), **VIII:** 313
"Melbourne in 1963" (Wallace–Crabbe), **VIII:** 313–314
Melbourne or the Bush (Wallace–Crabbe), **VIII:** 313–314, 319, 320
Melchiori, Giorgio, **VI:** 208
Meleager (Euripides), **V:** 322, 323
Melincourt (Peacock), **IV:** xvii, 162, 163–164, 165, 168, 170
Melly, Diana, **Supp. IV:** 168
Melmoth Reconciled (Balzac), **III:** 334, 339
Melmoth the Wanderer (Maturin), **III:** 327, 333–334, 335, 345; **VIII:** 197–200, 201–205, 208–209; **Supp. III:** 384–385
Melnikov, Konstantin, **Supp. IV:** 174
"Melon" (Barnes), **Supp. IV:** 75
Melville, Herman, **IV:** 97; **V:** xvii, xx–xxi, xxv, 211; **VI:** 363; **Supp. IV:** 160
Memento Mori (Spark), **Supp. I:** 203
"Memoir" (Scott), **IV:** 28, 30, 35–36, 39
"Memoir of Bernard Barton" (FitzGerald), **IV:** 353
"Memoir of Cowper: An Autobiography" (ed. Quinlan), **III:** 220
"Memoir" of Fleeming Jenkin (Stevenson), **V:** 386, 395
Memoir of Jane Austen (Austen-Leigh), **III:** 90
"Memoir of My Father, A" (Amis), **Supp. II:** 1
Memoir of the Author's Life and Familiar Anecdotes of Sir Walter Scott (Hogg), **Supp. X:** 105
Memoir of the Bobotes (Cary), **VII:** 185
Mémoire justificatif etc. (Gibbon), **III:** 233
Mémoires littéraires de la Grande Bretagne (periodical), **III:** 233
Memoirs (Amis), **Supp. IV:** 27
Memoirs (Robinson), **Supp. XIII:** 196–197, 198, 199, 200, 201, 203, 204, 207, 213
Memoirs (Temple), **III:** 19
Memoirs of a Cavalier, The (Defoe), **III:** 6, 13; **VI:** 353, 359; **Retro. Supp. I:** 66, 68, 71–72
Memoirs of a Certain Island Adjacent to the Kingdom of Utopia (Haywood), **Supp. XII:** 135, 141
"Memoirs of a Heavy Drinking Man, The" (Hamilton), **Supp. XVI:** 177,

178
Memoirs of a Midget (de la Mare), **III:** 340, 345
Memoirs of a Physician, The (Dumas père), **III:** 332
Memoirs of a Protestant, The (tr. Goldsmith), **III:** 191
Memoirs of a Survivor, The (Lessing), **Supp. I:** 249–250, 254
Memoirs of Barry Lyndon, Esq., The (Thackeray), see *Barry Lyndon*
Memoirs of Doctor Burney (Burney), **Supp. III:** 68
Memoirs of Himself (Stevenson), **V:** 396
"Memoirs of James Boswell, Esq." (Boswell), **III:** 248
Memoirs of John Addington Symonds, The: The Secret Homosexual Life of a Leading Nineteenth-Century Man of the Letters (Symonds), **Supp. XIV:** 250, 251, 252, 253, 262–263
Memoirs of Jonathan Swift (Scott), **IV:** 38
Memoirs of Lord Byron, The (Nye), **Supp. X:** 195–196
Memoirs of Martinus Scriblerus, The (Arbuthnot), **Supp. XVI:** 24–25
Memoirs of Martin Scriblerus, (Pope), **III:** 24, 77; **Retro. Supp. I:** 234
"Memoirs of M. de Voltaire" (Goldsmith), **III:** 189
Memoirs of My Dead Life (Moore), **VI:** 87, 88, 95, 96, 97, 98–99
"Memoirs of Percy Bysshe Shelley" (Peacock), **IV:** 158, 169, 170
Memoirs of the Author of "A Vindication of the Rights of Woman" (Godwin), **Supp. III:** 465; **Supp. XV:** 123
Memoirs of the Baron de Brosse (Haywood), **Supp. XII:** 135
Memoirs of the Late Thomas Holcroft . . . (Hazlitt), **IV:** 128, 139
Memoirs of the Life of Edward Gibbon, The (ed. Hill), **III:** 221n, 233
Memoirs of the Life of Sir Walter Scott, Bart. (Lockhart), **IV:** 27, 30, 34, 35–36, 39
Memoirs of the Life of William Collins, Esp., R.A. (1848) (Collins), **Supp. VI:** 92, 95
Memoirs of the Navy (Pepys), **II:** 281, 288
"Memoirs of the World" (Gunn), **Supp. IV:** 264
Memoirs Relating to . . . Queen Anne's Ministry (Swift), **III:** 27
"Memorabilia" (Browning), **IV:** 354–355
Memorable Masque of the Middle Temple and Lincoln's Inn, The (Chapman), **I:** 235
Memorial, The (Isherwood), **VII:** 205, 310–311
"Memorial for the City" (Auden), **VII:** 388, 393; **Retro. Supp. I:** 8
Memorials of a Tour on the Continent (Wordsworth), **IV:** 24–25
Memorials of Edward Burne-Jones (Burne-Jones), **V:** 295–296, 306
"Memorials of Gormandising" (Thackeray), **V:** 23, 24, 38

Memorials of Thomas Hood (Hood and Broderip), **IV:** 251, 261, 267
Memorials of Two Sisters, Susanna and Catherine Winkworth (ed. Shaen), **V:** 149
Memories and Adventures (Doyle), **Supp. II:** 159
Memories and Hallucinations (Thomas), **Supp. IV:** 479, 480, 482, 483, 484, 486
Memories and Portraits (Stevenson), **V:** 390, 395
"Memories of a Catholic Childhood" (Lodge), **Supp. IV:** 363–364
"Memories of a Working Women's Guild" (Woolf), **Retro. Supp. I:** 311
Memories of the Space Age (Ballard), **Supp. V:** 24
"Memories of the Space Age" (Ballard), **Supp. V:** 33
Memories of Vailiona (Osborne and Strong), **V:** 393, 397
"Memories of Youghal" (Trevor), **Supp. IV:** 501
"Memory, A" (Brooke), **Supp. III:** 55
"Memory and Imagination" (Dunn), **Supp. X:** 77
"Memory Man" (Ewart), **Supp. VII:** 41
Memory of Ben Jonson Revived by the Friends of the Muses, The (Digby), **Retro. Supp. I:** 166
"Memory Unsettled" (Gunn), **Supp. IV:** 277; **Retro. Supp. III:** 127, 128
"Men and Their Boring Arguments" (Cope), **VIII:** 78
Men and Wives (Compton-Burnett), **VII:** 64, 65, 66–67
Men and Women (Browning), **IV:** xiii, xxi, 357, 363, 374; **Retro. Supp. II:** 26, 27–28; **Retro. Supp. III:** 23, 24–26, 27
Men at Arms (Waugh), **VII:** 304; see also *Sword of Honour* trilogy
Men Like Gods (Wells), **VI:** 226 240 244; **VII:** 204
Men on Ice (Greig), **Supp. XVI:** 161–162
Men on Women on Men (Ayckbourn), **Supp. V:** 3
"Men Sign the Sea" (Graham), **Supp. VII:** 110
"Men Who March Away" (Hardy), **VI:** 415, 421; **Retro. Supp. I:** 120
"Men With Coats Thrashing" (Lowry), **Supp. III:** 283
Men Without Art (Lewis), **VII:** 72, 76
"Menace, The" (du Maurier), **Supp. III:** 139
"Menace, The" (Gunn), **Supp. IV:** 261
Menand, Louis, **Supp. IV:** 305
Mendelson, Edward, **Retro. Supp. I:** 12
"Menelaus and Helen" (Brooke), **Supp. III:** 52
Menaphon (Greene), **I:** 165; **VIII:** 135, 138–139, 143
Mencius on the Mind (Richards), **Supp. II:** 421
Men-of-War: Life in Nelson's Navy (O'Brian), **Supp. XII:** 255
Men's Wives (Thackeray), **V:** 23, 35, 38

"Mental Cases" (Owen), **VI:** 456, 457
Mental Efficiency (Bennett), **VI:** 250, 266
Merchant of Venice, The (Shakespeare), **I:** 310
Merchant's Tale, The (Chaucer), **I:** 36, 41–42
Mercian Hymns (Hill), **Supp. V:** 187, 189, 194–196; **Retro. Supp. III:** 133, 135, 136–137, 146
Mercier and Camier (Beckett), **Supp. I:** 50–51; **Retro. Supp. I:** 21
"Mercury and the Elephant" (Finch), **Supp. IX:** 71–72
"Mercy" (Collins), **III:** 166
Mercy Boys, The (Burnside), **Supp. XIII:** 28
Mer de Glace (Meale and Malouf), **Supp. XII:** 218
Mere Accident, A (Moore), **VI:** 86, 91
Mere Christianity (Lewis), **Supp. III:** 248
"Mere Interlude, A" (Hardy), **VI:** 22
Meredith (Sassoon), **V:** 219, 234
Meredith, George, **II:** 104, 342, 345; **IV:** 160; **V:** x, xviii, xxii–xxvi, **219–234**, 244, 432; **VI:** 2
Meredith, H. O., **VI:** 399
Meredith et la France (Mackay), **V:** 223, 234
"Meredithian Sonnets" (Fuller), **Supp. VII:** 74
Meres, Francis, **I:** 212, 234, 296, 307
Merie Tales, The, **I:** 83, 93
Meriton, George, **II:** 340
Merkin, Daphne, **Supp. IV:** 145–146
Merleau-Ponty, Maurice, **Supp. IV:** 79, 88
Merlin (Nye), **Supp. X:** 195
"Merlin and the Gleam" (Tennyson), **IV:** 329
"Merlin and Vivien" (Tennyson), **Retro. Supp. III:** 327
Mermaid, Dragon, Fiend (Graves), **VII:** 264
Merope (Arnold), **V:** 209, 216
"Merry Beggars, The" (Brome), **Supp. X:** 55
Merry England (periodical), **V:** 440
Merry Jests of George Peele, The, **I:** 194
Merry Men, and Other Tales and Fables, The (Stevenson), **V:** 395; **Retro. Supp. I:** 267
Merry Wives of Windsor, The (Shakespeare), **I:** 295, 311; **III:** 117; **Retro. Supp. III:** 268–269
Merry-Go-Round, The (Lawrence), **VII:** 120
Merry-Go-Round, The (Maugham), **VI:** 372
Mescellanies (Fielding), **Retro. Supp. I:** 80
Meschonnic, Henri, **Supp. IV:** 115
"Mesmerism" (Browning), **Retro. Supp. III:** 24
Mespoulet, M., **V:** 266
"Message, The" (Donne), **Retro. Supp. II:** 90
"Message, The" (Russell), **VIII:** 280–281
"Message Clear" (Morgan, E.), **Supp. IX:** 165

"Message from Mars, The" (Ballard), **Supp. V:** 33
Messages (Fernandez), **V:** 225–226
"Messdick" (Ross), **VII:** 433
Messenger, The (Kinsella), **Supp. V:** 269–270
"M. E. T." (Thomas), **Supp. III:** 401
"Metamorphoses" (Malouf), **Supp. XII:** 220
Metamorphoses (Ovid), **III:** 54; **V:** 321; **Retro. Supp. II:** 36, 215
Metamorphoses (Sisson), **Supp. XI:** 249
Metamorphosis (Kafka), **III:** 340, 345
Metamorphosis of Pygmalion's Image (Marston), **I:** 238; **II:** 25, 40
"Metaphor Now Standing at Platform 8, The" (Armitage), **VIII:** 5–6
"Metaphorical Gymnasia" (Dutton), **Supp. XII:** 97
Metaphysical Lyrics and Poems of the Seventeenth Century (Grierson), **Retro. Supp. II:** 173
"Metaphysical Poets and the Twentieth Century, The" (Beer), **Supp. XIV:** 8
Metempsycosis: Poêma Satyricon (Donne), **Retro. Supp. II:** 94
"Methinks the poor Town has been troubled too long" (Dorset), **II:** 262
"Method. For Rongald Gaskell" (Davie), **Supp. VI:** 106
Metrical Tales and Other Poems (Southey), **IV:** 71
Metroland (Barnes), **Supp. IV:** 65, 66–67, 71, 76
Mew, Charlotte, **Supp. V:** 97, 98–99
Meynell, Wilfred, **V:** 440, 451
MF (Burgess), **Supp. I:** 197
"Mianserin Sonnets" (Fuller), **Supp. VII:** 79
Micah Clark (Doyle), **Supp. II:** 159, 163
"Michael" (Wordsworth), **IV:** 8, 18–19
Michael and Mary (Milne), **Supp. V:** 299
Michael Robartes and the Dancer (Yeats), **VI:** 217; **Retro. Supp. I:** 331–333
"Michael X and the Black Power Killings in Trinidad" (Naipaul), **Supp. I:** 396
Michaelmas Term (Middleton), **II:** 3, 4, 21
Michaelmas Term at St. Bride's (Larkin), **Retro. Supp. III:** 200, 201
Michelet, Jules, **V:** 346
Microcosmography (Earle), **IV:** 286
Micro-Cynicon, Six Snarling Satires (Middleton), **II:** 2–3
Midas (Lyly), **I:** 198, 202, 203
"Middle Age" (Dunn), **Supp. X:** 80
Middle Age of Mrs Eliot, The (Wilson), **Supp. I:** 160–161
Middle Ground, The (Drabble), **Supp. IV:** 230, 231, 234, 246–247, 248
Middle Mist, The (Renault), see *Friendly Young Ladies, The*
"Middle of a War" (Fuller), **VII:** 429; **Supp. VII:** 69
Middle Passage, The (Naipaul), **Supp. I:** 386, 390–391, 393, 403
"Middle-Sea and Lear-Sea" (Jones), **Supp. VII:** 176
Middle Years, The (James), **VI:** 65, 69

"Middle Years, The" (Ewart), **Supp. VII:** 39
"Middle Years, The" (James), **VI:** 69
Middlemarch (Eliot), **III:** 157; **V:** ix–x, xxiv, 196–197, 200; **Supp. IV:** 243; **Retro. Supp. II:** 113–114
Middlemen: A Satire, The (Brooke-Rose)), **Supp. IV:** 99, 103
Middleton, D., **V:** 253
Middleton, Thomas, **II:** 1–23, 30, 33, 68–70, 72, 83, 85, 93, 100; **IV:** 79
Midnight All Day (Kureishi), **Supp. XI:** 158
Midnight Bell, The (Hamilton), **Supp. XVI:** 178, 182, 183–184, 185
"Midnight Court, The" (tr. O'Connor), **Supp. XIV:** 221
Midnight Hour, The (Inchbald), **Supp. XV:** 155, 160
"Midnight Hour, The" (Powys), **VIII:** 256
Midnight Oil (Pritchett), **Supp. III:** 312, 313
Midnight on the Desert (Priestley), **VII:** 209, 212
"Midnight Skaters, The" (Blunden), **VI:** 429; **Supp. XI:** 45
Midnight's Children (Rushdie), **Supp. IV:** 162, 433, 435, 436, 438, 439–444, 445, 448, 449, 456; **Supp. V:** 67, 68
"Midnight's Choice" (Thompson), **Supp. XIV:** 286, 287–288
"Midsummer Cushion, The" (Clare), **Supp. XI:** 60
"Midsummer Holiday, A, and Other Poems" (Swinburne), **V:** 332
"Midsummer Ice" (Murray), **Supp. VII:** 278
"Midsummer Night's Dream, A" (Scupham), **Supp. XIII:** 223
Midsummer Night's Dream, A (Shakespeare), **I:** 304–305, 311–312; **II:** 51, 281; **Supp. IV:** 198; **Retro. Supp. I:** 125
Mid-Victorian Memories (Francillon), **V:** 83
"Midwich Cuckoos, The" (Wyndham), **Supp. XIII:** 291–292
"Mightier than Mammon, A" (Carpenter), **Supp. XIII:** 39
Mightier Than the Sword (Ford), **VI:** 320–321
Mighty and Their Full, The (Compton-Burnett), **VII:** 61, 62
Mighty Magician, The (FitzGerald), **IV:** 353
"Migrants" (Thomas), **Supp. XII:** 290
Miguel Street (Naipaul), **Supp. I:** 383, 385–386
"Mike: A Public School Story" (Wodehouse), **Supp. III:** 449
Mike Fletcher (Moore), **VI:** 87, 91
"Mildred Lawson" (Moore), **VI:** 98
Milesian Chief, The (Maturin), **VIII:** 201, 207
Milestones (Bennett), **VI:** 250, 263, 264
Milford, H., **III:** 208n

"Milford: East Wing" (Murphy), **Supp. V:** 328
Military Memoirs of Capt. George Carleton, The (Defoe), **III:** 14
Military Philosophers, The (Powell), **VII:** 349
"Milk–cart, The" (Morgan, E.), **Supp. IX:** 168
"Milk–Wort and Bog–Cotton" (MacDiarmid), **Supp. XII:** 212
Mill, James, **IV:** 159; **V:** 288
Mill, John Stuart, **IV:** 50, 56, 246, 355; **V:** xxi–xxii, xxiv, 182, 279, 288, 343
Mill on the Floss, The (Eliot), **V:** xxii, 14, 192–194, 200; **Supp. IV:** 240, 471; **Retro. Supp. II:** 106–108
Millais, John Everett, **V:** 235, 236, 379
Miller, Andrew, **Supp. XIV:** 179–192
Miller, Arthur, **VI:** 286
Miller, Henry, **Supp. IV:** 110–111
Miller, J. Hillis, **VI:** 147
Miller, Karl, **Supp. IV:** 169
"Miller's Daughter, The" (tr. Mangan), **Supp. XIII:** 127
"Miller's Daughter, The" (Tennyson), **IV:** 326
Miller's Tale, The (Chaucer), **I:** 37
Millet, Jean François, **Supp. IV:** 90
Millett, Kate, **Supp. IV:** 188
Millionairess, The (Shaw), **VI:** 102, 127
"Millom Cricket Field" (Nicholson), **Supp. VI:** 216
"Millom Old Quarry" (Nicholson), **Supp. VI:** 216
Mills, C. M., pseud. of Elizabeth Gaskell
Millstone, The (Drabble), **Supp. IV:** 230, 237–238
Milne, A. A., **Supp. V:** 295–312
"Milnes, Richard Monckton" (Lord Houghton), *see* Monckton Milnes, Richard
Milton, Edith, **Supp. IV:** 305–306
Milton (Blake), **III:** 303–304, 307; **V:** xvi 330; **Retro. Supp. I:** 45
Milton (Meredith), **V:** 234
"Milton" (Macaulay), **IV:** 278, 279
"Milton as Muse" (Hill), **Retro. Supp. III:** 142
Milton in America (Ackroyd), **Supp. VI:** 11–12, 13
Milton, John, **II:** 50–52, 113, **158–178,** 195, 196, 198, 199, 205, 206, 236, 302; **III:** 43, 118–119, 167n, 211n, 220, 302; **IV:** 9, 11–12, 14, 22, 23, 93, 95, 185, 186, 200, 205, 229, 269, 278, 279, 352; **V:** 365–366; **Supp. III:** 169; **Retro. Supp. II:** 269–289
Milton's God (Empson), **Supp. II:** 180, 195–196
Milton's Prosody (Bridges), **VI:** 83
Mimic Men, The (Naipaul), **Supp. I:** 383, 386, 390, 392, 393–394, 395, 399
"Mina Laury" (Brontë), **V:** 122, 123, 149, 151
Mind at the End of Its Tether (Wells), **VI:** xiii; **VI:** 228, 242
Mind Has Mountains, The (Jennings), **Supp. V:** 213, 215–216
Mind in Chains, The (ed. Day Lewis), **Supp. III:** 118

"Mind Is Its Own Place, The" (Wallace-Crabbe), **VIII:** 316
Mind of the Maker, The (Sayers), **Supp. III:** 345, 347
Mind to Murder, A (James), **Supp. IV:** 319, 321, 323–324
Mind's Eye, The (Blunden), **Supp. XI:** 35
"Mine old dear enemy, my froward master" (Wyatt), **I:** 105
"Miner's Hut" (Murphy), **Supp. V:** 328
"Miners" (Owen), **VI:** 452, 454
"Minerva's Bird, Athene Noctua" (Thomas), **Supp. XII:** 289
"Minimal" (Dutton), **Supp. XII:** 90, 91
Minister, The (Thomas), **Supp. XII:** 283, 284
"Ministrations" (Conn), **Supp. XIII:** 80
Ministry of Fear, The (Greene), **Supp. I:** 10–11, 12; **Retro. Supp. II:** 157
Minor Poems of Robert Southey, The (Southey), **IV:** 71
Minpins, The (Dahl), **Supp. IV:** 204, 224
Minstrel, The (Beattie), **IV:** 198
Minstrelsy of the Scottish Border (ed. Scott), **IV:** 29, 39
"Mint" (Heaney), **Retro. Supp. I:** 133
Mint, The (Lawrence), **Supp. II:** 283, **291–294**
Minute by Glass Minute (Stevenson), **Supp. VI:** 261
Minute for Murder (Day Lewis), **Supp. III:** 130
"Minutes of Glory" (Ngũgĩ), **VIII:** 220
Minutes of the Negotiations of Monsr. Mesnager, . . . (Defoe), **III:** 13
"Mirabeau" (Macaulay), **IV:** 278
"Miracle, The" (Gunn), **Retro. Supp. III:** 125, 129
"Miracle Cure" (Lowbury), **VII:** 432
"Miracle of Purun Bhagat, The" (Kipling), **Retro. Supp. III:** 192, 194
Miracles (Lewis), **Supp. III:** 248, 255, 258–259
"Miraculous Issue, The" (Dutton), **Supp. XII:** 89
Mirèio (Mistral), **V:** 219
Miroir de l'âme pecheresse, Le (tr. Elizabeth I), **Supp. XVI:** 155
Mirour de l'omme (Gower), **I:** 48, 49
"Mirror, The" (Delanty), **Supp. XIV:** 70
Mirror for Magistrates, The, **I:** 162, 214
"Mirror for Poets, A" (Gunn), **Retro. Supp. III:** 118
"Mirror in February" (Kinsella), **Supp. V:** 262
Mirror in the Roadway, The: A Study of the Modern Novel (O'Connor), **Supp. XIV:** 211, 219
Mirror of the Mother, The: Selected Poems, 1975–1985 (Roberts), **Supp. XV:** 261, 262
"Mirror of the Sinful Soul, The" (tr. Elizabeth I), **Supp. XVI:** 152, 157
Mirror of the Sea: Memories and Impressions, The (Conrad), **VI:** 138, 148
Mirror Wall, The (Murphy), **Supp. V:** 313, 329–330
Mirrour; or, Looking-Glasse Both for Saints and Sinners, A (Clarke), **II:** 251

Misadventures of John Nicholson, The (Stevenson), **V:** 396
Misalliance (Shaw), **VI:** xv, 115, 117, 118, 120, 129; **Retro. Supp. II:** 321
Misalliance, The (Brookner), **Supp. IV:** 129
Misanthrope, The (tr. Harrison), **Supp. V:** 149–150, 163
"Misanthropos" (Gunn), **Supp. IV:** 264–265, 268, 270; **Retro. Supp. III:** 121
"Misapprehension" (Traherne), **Supp. XI:** 266
Miscellanea (Temple), **III:** 40
Miscellaneous Essays (St. Évremond), **III:** 47
Miscellaneous Observations on the Tragedy of Macbeth (Johnson), **III:** 108, 116, 121
Miscellaneous Poems (Byrom), **Supp. XVI:** 71, 73, 76, 81
Miscellaneous Poems (Marvell), **II:** 207
Miscellaneous Studies (Pater), **V:** 348, 357
Miscellaneous Works of the Duke of Buckingham, **II:** 268
Miscellaneous Works of the Late Dr. Arbuthnot, The (Arbuthnot), **Supp. XVI:** 3
Miscellaneous Works . . . with Memoirs of His Life (Gibbon), **III:** 233
Miscellanies (Cowley), **II:** 198
Miscellanies (Martineau), **Supp. XV:** 186
Miscellanies (Pope and Swift), **II:** 335
Miscellanies (Swinburne), **V:** 332
Miscellanies; A Serious Address to the People of Great Britain (Fielding), **III:** 105
Miscellanies, Aesthetic and Literary . . . (Coleridge), **IV:** 56
Miscellany (Tonson), **III:** 69
Miscellany of New Poems, A (Behn), **Supp. III:** 36
Miscellany Poems (Wycherley), **II:** 321
Miscellany Poems, on Several Occasions (Finch), **Supp. IX:** 65, 67, 74, 77
Miscellany Tracts (Browne), **II:** 156
Mischmasch (Carroll), **V:** 274
"Mise Eire" (Boland), **Supp. V:** 45–46
Miser, The (Fielding), **III:** 105
"Miser and the Poet, The" (Finch), **Supp. IX:** 72–74
"Miserie" (Herbert), **II:** 128–129
Miseries of War, The (Ralegh), **I:** 158
Misfortunes of Arthur, The (Hughes), **I:** 218
Misfortunes of Elphin, The (Peacock), **IV:** xviii, 163, 167–168, 170
Mishan, E. J., **VI:** 240
"Misplaced Attachment of Mr. John Dounce, The" (Dickens), **V:** 46
"Miss Brill" (Mansfield), **VII:** 175
Miss Gomez and the Brethren (Trevor), **Supp. IV:** 507, 508–509
"Miss Gunton of Poughkeepsie" (James), **VI:** 69
Miss Herbert (The Suburban Wife) (Stead), **Supp. IV:** 473, 476
"Miss Kilmansegg and Her Precious Leg" (Hood), **IV:** 258–259
Miss Lucy in Town (Fielding), **III:** 105

Miss Mackenzie (Trollope), **V:** 101
Miss Marjoribanks (Oliphant), **Supp. X:** 214, 216–217, 219–220
Miss Marple's Last Case (Christie), **Supp. II:** 125
Miss Ogilvy Finds Herself (Hall), **Supp. VI:** 120–121, 128
"Miss Ogilvy Finds Herself" (Hall), **Supp. VI:** 121
"Miss Pulkinhorn" (Golding), **Supp. I:** 78–79, 80
"Miss Smith" (Trevor), **Supp. IV:** 502, 510
Miss Stuart's Legacy (Steel), **Supp. XII:** 269–270, 271
"Miss Tickletoby's Lectures on English History" (Thackeray), **V:** 38
"Miss Twye" (Ewart), **Supp. VII:** 36
"Missing" (Cornford), **VIII:** 1141
"Missing, The" (Gunn), **Supp. IV:** 276; **Retro. Supp. III:** 128
"Missing Dates" (Empson), **Supp. II:** 184, 190
Missing Link, The (Thompson), **Supp. XIV:** 289–290
Mission Song, The (le Carré), **Retro. Supp. III:** 228–229
Mist in the Mirror, The (Hill), **Supp. XIV:** 125, 127
Mistake, The (Vanbrugh), **II:** 325, 333, 336
Mistakes, The (Harris), **II:** 305
Mistakes of a Night, The (Hogg), **Supp. X:** 105–106
Mr. A's Amazing Mr. Pim Passes By (Milne), **Supp. V:** 299
"Mr. and Mrs. Dove" (Mansfield), **VII:** 180
"Mr. and Mrs. Frank Berry" (Thackeray), **V:** 23
Mr. and Mrs. Nobody (Waterhouse), **Supp. XIII:** 275–276
Mr. and Mrs. Scotland Are Dead: Poems (Jamie), **Supp. XIV:** 129, 143
"Mr. and Mrs. Scotland Are Dead" (Jamie), **Supp. XIV:** 138
"Mr. Apollinax" (Eliot), **VII:** 144
Mr. Beluncle (Pritchett), **Supp. III:** 311, 313, 314–315
Mr. Bennett and Mrs. Brown (Woolf), **VI:** 247, 267, 275, 290; **VII:** xiv, xv
"Mr. Bennett and Mrs. Brown" (Woolf), **Supp. II:** 341; **Retro. Supp. I:** 309
"Mr. Bleaney" (Larkin), **Supp. I:** 281; **Retro. Supp. III:** 207
"Mr. Bodkin" (Hood), **IV:** 267
Mr. Britling Sees It Through (Wells), **VI:** 227, 240
"Mr. Brown's Letters to a Young Man About Town" (Thackeray), **V:** 38
Mr. Bunyan's Last Sermon (Bunyan), **II:** 253
Mr. C[olli]n's Discourse of Free-Thinking (Swift), **III:** 35
"Mr. Crabbe—Mr. Campbell" (Hazlitt), **III:** 276
"Mr. Dottery's Trousers" (Powys), **VIII:** 248, 249
"Mr. Eliot's Sunday Morning Service" (Eliot), **VII:** 145

"Mr. Feasey" (Dahl), **Supp. IV:** 214
Mr. Foot (Frayn), **Supp. VII:** 57
Mr. Fortune's Maggot (Warner), **Supp. VII:** 370, 374–375, 379
Mr Fox (Comyns), **VIII:** 53, 56, 64–65
"Mr. Gilfil's Love Story" (Eliot), **V:** 190; **Retro. Supp. II:** 103–104
"Mr. Gladstone Goes to Heaven" (Beerbohm), **Supp. II:** 51
"Mr. Graham" (Hood), **IV:** 267
Mr. H (Lamb), **IV:** 80–81, 85
"Mr. Harrison's Confessions" (Gaskell), **V:** 14, 15; **Retro. Supp. III:** 104
Mister Heracles (Armitage), **VIII:** 1
Mr. John Milton's Character of the Long Parliament and Assembly of Divines . . . (Milton), **II:** 176
Mister Johnson (Cary), **VII:** 186, 187, 189, 190–191
"Mr. Know–All" (Maugham), **VI:** 370
Mr. Macaulay's Character of the Clergy in the Latter Part of the Seventeenth Century Considered (Babington), **IV:** 291
"Mr. McNamara" (Trevor), **Supp. IV:** 501
Mr. Meeson's Will (Haggard), **Supp. III:** 213
Mr. Noon (Lawrence), **Retro. Supp. II:** 229–230
"Mr. Norris and I" (Isherwood), **VII:** 311–312
Mr. Norris Changes Trains (Isherwood), **VII:** xx, 311–312
"Mr. Pim and the Holy Crumb" (Powys), **VIII:** 255, 257
Mr. Polly (Wells), *see History of Mr. Polly, The*
Mr. Pope's Welcome from Greece (Gay), **II:** 348
Mr. Prohack (Bennett), **VI:** 260, 267
"Mr. Reginald Peacock's Day" (Mansfield), **VII:** 174
"Mr. Robert Herricke His Farewell unto Poetrie" (Herrick), **II:** 112
"Mr. Robert Montgomery's Poems" (Macaulay), **IV:** 280
Mr Sampath (Naipaul), **Supp. I:** 400
Mr. Scarborough's Family (Trollope), **V:** 98, 102
"Mr Simonelli; or, The Fairy Widower" (Clarke), **Supp. XV:** 36–37
"Mr. Sludge 'the Medium' " (Browning), **IV:** 358, 368; **Retro. Supp. II:** 26–27; **Retro. Supp. III:** 27
Mr. Smirke; or, The Divine in Mode (Marvell), **II:** 219
Mr. Stone and the Knights Companion (Naipaul), **Supp. I:** 383, 389
"Mr. Strugnell" (Cope), **VIII:** 73
Mr Tasker's Gods (Powys), **VIII:** 2 **VIII:** 51, 249–250
"Mr. Tennyson" (Trevor), **Supp. IV:** 502
Mr. Waller's Speech in the Painted Chamber (Waller), **II:** 238
"Mr. Waterman" (Redgrove), **Supp. VI:** 228–229, 231, 235, 237
Mr. Weston's Good Wine (Powys), **VII:** 21; **VIII:** 245, 248, 252–254, 255, 256

Mr Whatnot (Ayckbourn), **Supp. V:** 2, 13
"Mr. Whistler's Ten O'Clock" (Wilde), **V:** 407
Mr. Wrong (Howard), **Supp. XI:** 141, 142
"Mistletoe, a Christmas Tale, The" (Robinson), **Supp. XIII:** 212
Mistral, Frederic, **V:** 219
Mistras, The (Cowley), **II:** 194, 198, 202, 236
"Mrs. Acland's Ghosts" (Trevor), **Supp. IV:** 503
"Mrs. Bathurst" (Kipling), **VI:** 193–194
Mrs. Beer's House: An Autobiography of Childhood (Beer), **Supp. XIV:** 1, 4, 7–8, 14
Mrs. Browning: A Poet's Work and Its Setting (Hayter), **IV:** 322
"Mrs. Cibber" (Roberts, K.), **Supp. X:** 273
Mrs. Craddock (Maugham), **VI:** 367
Mrs. Dalloway (Woolf), **VI:** 275, 279; **VII:** xv, 18, 21, 24, 28–29; **Supp. IV:** 234, 246; **Retro. Supp. I:** 316–317
Mrs. de Winter (Hill), **Supp. XIV:** 116, 125–126
Mrs. Dot (Maugham), **VI:** 368
Mrs. Eckdorf in O'Neill's Hotel (Trevor), **Supp. IV:** 501, 508
Mrs. Fisher; or, The Future of Humour (Graves), **VII:** 259–260
Mrs. Harris's Petition (Swift), **Retro. Supp. I:** 283
"Mrs. Jaypher found a wafer" (Lear), **V:** 86
Mrs. Leicester's School (Lamb and Lamb), **IV:** 80, 85
Mrs. McGinty's Dead (Christie; U.S. title, *Blood Will Tell*), **Supp. II:** 135
"Mrs. Medwin" (James), **VI:** 69
"Mrs. Nelly's Complaint," **II:** 268
Mistress of Men (Steel), **Supp. XII:** 275
"Mistress of Vision, The" (Thompson), **V:** 447–448
"Mrs. Packletide's Tiger" (Saki), **Supp. VI:** 242
Mrs. Perkins's Ball (Thackeray), **V:** 24, 38
Mrs. Shakespeare: The Complete Works (Nye), **Supp. X:** 196
"Mrs. Silly" (Trevor), **Supp. IV:** 502
"Mrs. Simpkins" (Smith), **Supp. II:** 470
"Mrs. Temperley" (James), **VI:** 69
Mrs. Warren's Profession (Shaw), **V:** 413; **VI:** 108, 109; **Retro. Supp. II:** 312–313
Mistressclass, The (Roberts), **Supp. XV:** 271, 272–273
Mistry, Rohinton, **Supp. X: 137–149**
"Mists" (Redgrove), **Supp. VI:** 228
Mist's Weekly Journal (newspaper), **III:** 4
Mitchell, David, **Supp. XIV: 193–209**
Mitchell, James Leslie, *see* Gibbon, Lewis Grassic
Mitford, Mary Russell, **IV:** 311, 312
Mitford, Nancy, **VII:** 290; **Supp. X: 151–163**
Mithridates (Lee), **II:** 305
Mixed Essays (Arnold), **V:** 213n, 216

Mixed Feelings: Nineteen Poems (Wain), **Supp. XVI:** 306
"Mixed Marriage" (Muldoon), **Supp. IV:** 415
Mnemosyne Lay in Dust (Clarke), **Supp. XV:** 28–29
Mo, Timothy, **Supp. IV:** 390
"Moa Point" (Adcock), **Supp. XII:** 6
Mob, The (Galsworthy), **VI:** 280, 288
Moby–Dick (Melville), **VI:** 363
Moby Dick: A Play for Radio from Herman Melville's Novel (Reed), **Supp. XV:** 245, 248, 251, 252, 254, 255
Mock Doctor, The (Fielding), **III** 105
Mock Speech from the Throne (Marvell), **II:** 207
Mock–Mourners, The: . . . Elegy on King William (Defoe), **III:** 12
Mockery Gap (Powys), **VIII:** 251, 256
"Model Prisons" (Carlyle), **IV:** 247
Mock's Curse: Nineteen Stories (Powys), **VIII:** 251, 252, 256
Modern Comedy, A (Galsworthy), **VI:** 270, 275
Modern Fiction (Woolf), **VII:** xiv; **Retro. Supp. I:** 308–309
Modern Husband, The (Fielding), **III:** 105
Modern Irish Short Stories (ed. O'Connor), **Supp. XIV:** 226
"Modern Love" (Meredith), **V:** 220, 234, 244
Modern Love, and Poems of the English Roadside . . . (Meredith), **V:** xxii, 220, 234
Modern Lover, A (Moore), **VI:** 86, 89, 98
Modern Manners (Robinson), **Supp. XIII:** 207
"Modern Money–Lending, and the Meaning of Dividends: A Tract for the Wealthy" (Carpenter), **Supp. XIII:** 40
Modern Movement: 100 Key Books from England, France, and America, 1880–1950, The (Connolly), **VI:** 371
Modern Painters (Ruskin), **V:** xx, 175–176, 180, 184, 282
Modern Painting (Moore), **VI:** 87
Modern Poet, The: Poetry, Academia, and Knowledge Since the 1750s (Crawford), **Supp. XI:** 82–83
Modern Poetry: A Personal Essay (MacNeice), **VII:** 403, 404, 410
Modern Poetry in Translation, **Supp. XV:** 67
"Modern Science: A Criticism" (Carpenter), **Supp. XIII:** 41
Modern Theatre, The (ed. Inchbald), **Supp. XV:** 149, 160, 161
"Modern Times" (Delanty), **Supp. XIV:** 70
"Modern Times" (Wallace–Crabbe), **VIII:** 324
Modern Utopia, A (Wells), **VI:** 227, 234, 241, 244
"Modern Warning, The" (James), **VI:** 48, 69
Modernism and Romance (Scott–James), **VI:** 21
Modes of Modern Writing: Metaphor, Metonymy, and the Typology of Mod-

ern Literature, The (Lodge), **Supp. IV:** 365, 377

"Modest Proposal" (Ewart), **Supp. VII:** 46

Modest Proposal, A (Swift), **III:** 21, 28, 29, 35; **Supp. IV:** 482

"Moestitiae Encomium" (Thompson), **V:** 450

Moffatt, James, **I:** 382–383

Mogul Tale, The (Inchbald), **Supp. XV:** 148, 153, 154, 156

Mohocks, The (Gay), **III:** 60, 67

Mohr, Jean, **Supp. IV:** 79

Moi, Toril, **Retro. Supp. I:** 312

"Moisture–Number, The" (Redgrove), **Supp. VI:** 235

Molière (Jean Baptiste Poquelin), **II:** 314, 318, 325, 336, 337, 350; **V:** 224

Moll Flanders (Defoe), **III:** 5, 6, 7, 8, 9, 13, 95; **Retro. Supp. I:** 72–73

Molloy (Beckett), **Supp. I:** 51–52; **Supp. IV:** 106; **Retro. Supp. I:** 18, 21–22

Molly Sweeney (Friel), **Supp. V:** 127

"Molly Gone" (Hardy), **Retro. Supp. I:** 118

Moly (Gunn), **Supp. IV:** 257, 266–268; **Retro. Supp. III:** 116, 117, 120, 122–123, 125, 129, 130

"Moly" (Gunn), **Supp. IV:** 267; **Retro. Supp. III:** 116, 117, 122, 123

Molyneux, William, **III:** 27

"Moment, The: Summer's Night" (Woolf), **Retro. Supp. I:** 309

"Moment in Eternity, A" (MacDiarmid), **Supp. XII:** 204

Moment Next to Nothing, The: A Play in Three Acts (Clarke), **Supp. XV:** 25

"Moment of Cubism, The" (Berger), **Supp. IV:** 79

Moment of Love, A (Moore), see *Feast of Lupercal, The*

Moments of Being (Woolf), **VII:** 33; **Retro. Supp. I:** 305, 315

Moments of Grace (Jennings), **Supp. V:** 217–218

Moments of Vision, and Miscellaneous Verses (Hardy), **VI:** 20

Monastery, The (Scott), **IV:** xviii, 39

Monckton Milnes, Richard (Lord Houghton), **IV:** 211, 234, 235, 251, 252, 254, 302, 351; **V:** 312, 313, 334; **Retro. Supp. I:** 185–186

Monday Morning (Hamilton), **Supp. XVI:** 179

"Monday; or, The Squabble" (Gay), **III:** 56

Monday or Tuesday (Woolf), **VII:** 20, 21, 38; **Retro. Supp. I:** 307

Mondo Desperado (McCabe), **Supp. IX:** 127, 136–137

Money: A Suicide Note (Amis), **Supp. IV:** 26, 32–35, 37, 40

Money in the Bank (Wodehouse), **Supp. III:** 459

"Money–Man Only" (Smith, I. C.), **Supp. IX:** 213–214

"Money Singing" (Motion), **Supp. VII:** 261

Monk, The (Lewis), **III:** 332–333, 335, 345; **Supp. III:** 384

Monkfish Moon (Gunesekera), **Supp. X:** 85–88, 95, 100

Monks and the Giants, The (Frere), see *Whistlecraft*

Monks of St. Mark, The (Peacock), **IV:** 158, 169

Monk's Prologue, The (Chaucer), **II:** 70

Monk's Tale, The (Chaucer), **I:** 31

Monk's Tale, The (Lydgate), **I:** 57

"Monna Innominata" (Rossetti), **V:** 251; **Retro. Supp. III:** 251, 260

"Mono–Cellular" (Self), **Supp. V:** 402

Monody on the Death of the Right Hon. R. B. Sheridan . . . (Byron), **IV:** 192

"Monody to the Memory of Chatterton" (Robinson), **Supp. XIII:** 206

"Monody to the Memory of Sir Joshua Reynolds" (Robinson), **Supp. XIII:** 202

"Monody to the Memory of the Late Queen of France" (Robinson), **Supp. XIII:** 202

"Monologue, or The Five Lost Géricaults" (Constantine), **Supp. XV:** 79

Monro, Harold, **VI:** 448

"Mons Meg" (Crawford), **Supp. XI:** 81–82

Monsieur (Durrell), **Supp. I:** 118, 119; **Retro. Supp. III:** 86, 87, 92–93, 94

Monsieur de Pourceaugnac (Molière), **II:** 325, 337, 339, 347, 350

Monsieur d'Olive (Chapman), **I:** 244–245

"M. Prudhomme at the International Exhibition" (Swinburne), **V:** 333

Monsieur Thomas (Fletcher), **II:** 45, 61, 65

Monsignor Quixote (Greene), **Supp. I:** 18–19; **Retro. Supp. II:** 166

Monster (Beamish and Galloway), **Supp. XII:** 117

Monstre Gai (Lewis), **VII:** 72, 80

"Mont Blanc" (Shelley), **IV:** 198; **Retro. Supp. I:** 248

Montagu, Lady Mary Wortley, **II:** 326

Montague, John, **VI:** 220; **Supp. XV:** **209–225**

Montaigne, Michel Eyquem de, **II:** 25, 30, 80, 104, 108, 146; **III:** 39

Monte Verité (du Maurier), **Supp. III:** 143–144, 147, 148

Montemayor, Jorge de, **I:** 164, 302

Montezuma's Daughter (Haggard), **Supp. III:** 214

Montgomery, Robert, **IV:** 280

Month (periodical), **V:** 365, 379

Month in the Country, A (tr. Friel), **Supp. V:** 124

Montherlant, Henry de, **II:** 99n

Monthly Repository, **Supp. XV:** 182

Monthly Review (periodical), **III:** 147, 188

Montrose, marquess of, **II:** 222, 236–237, 238

Monument, The: A Study of the Last Years of the Italian Poet Giacomo Leopardi (Reed), **Supp. XV:** 252

"Monument Maker, The" (Hardy), **Retro. Supp. I:** 117

Monumental Column, A. Erected to . . . Prince of Wales (Webster), **II:** 68, 85

"Monuments of Honour" (Webster), **II:** 68, 85

Monye, A. A., **Supp. II:** 350

Monypenny, W. F., **IV:** 292, 295, 300, 307, 308

"Moon and a Cloud, The" (Davies), **Supp. XI:** 91

Moon and Sixpence, The (Maugham), **VI:** xiii, 365, 374, **375–376**

Moon Country: Further Reports from Iceland (Armitage), **VIII:** 2

"Moon Fever" (Nye), **Supp. X:** 205

"Moon Tunes" (Coe), **Supp. XV:** 50

Mooncranker's Gift (Unsworth), **Supp. VII:** 354, 356–357

Moonlight (Pinter), **Retro. Supp. I:** 226

"Moonlight Night on the Port" (Keyes), **VII:** 439

Moonlight on the Highway (Potter, D.), **Supp. X:** 231

Moonraker (Fleming), **Supp. XIV:** 94

Moon's Ottery (Beer), **Supp. XIV:** 1, 5, 11–12

"Moonshine" (Murphy), **Supp. V:** 326

Moonstone, The (Collins), **III:** 340, 345; **Supp. VI:** 91, 93, **100–102**

"Moor, The" (Thomas), **Supp. XII:** 285

Moorcock, Michael, **Supp. V:** 24, 25, 32

Moore, Brian, **Supp. IX:** **141–155**

Moore, G. E., **Supp. I:** 217; **Supp. II:** 406–407; **Supp. III:** 46, 49

Moore, George, **IV:** 102; **V:** xxi, xxvi, 129, 153; **VI:** xii **85–99**, 207, 239, 270, 365

Moore, John Robert, **III:** 1, 12

Moore, Marianne, **IV:** 6; **Supp. IV:** = 262–263

Moore, Thomas, **IV:** xvi, 193, 205; **V:** 116

"Moore's Life of Lord Byron" (Macaulay), **IV:** 281–282

"Moorings" (MacCaig), **Supp. VI:** 187

Moorland Cottage, The (Gaskell), **V:** 14, 15; **Retro. Supp. III:** 100, 103

Moorman, Mary, **IV:** 4, 25

Moor's Last Sigh, The (Rushdie), **Supp. IV:** 433, 438, 444, 446, 448, 451–454, 456

Moortown (Hughes), **Supp. I:** 354, 357; **Retro. Supp. II:** 211–212

"Mora Montravers" (James), **VI:** 69

Moral and Political Lecture, A (Coleridge), **IV:** 56

Moral Epistle, Respectfully Dedicated to Earl Stanhope (Landor), **IV:** 99

Moral Ending and Other Stories, A (Warner), **Supp. VII:** 379

Moral Essays (Pope), **III:** 74–75, 77, 78; **Retro. Supp. I:** 145; **Retro. Supp. I:** 235

Moralities (Kinsella), **Supp. V:** 260, 261

"Morality and the Novel" (Lawrence), **VII:** 87

Morality Play (Unsworth), **Supp. VII:** 362, 364–365

Morall Fabillis of Esope the Phrygian, The (Henryson), **Supp. VII:** 136–142, 145

"Morals of Pruning, The" (Pitter), **Supp. XIII:** 143
Morando, the Tritameron of Love (Greene), **VIII:** 142–143
"Morbidezza" (Symons), **Supp. XIV:** 275
"Mordecai and Cocking" (Coppard), **VIII:** 95
More, Hannah, **IV:** 269
More, Paul Elmer, **II:** 152
More, Sir Thomas, **I:** 325; **II:** 24; **IV:** 69, **Supp. VII: 233–250**
"More a Man Has the More a Man Wants, The" (Muldoon), **Supp. IV:** 420–421, 425
More Dissemblers Besides Women (Middleton), **II:** 3, 21
"More Essex Poems" (Davie), **Supp. VI:** 110–111
More New Arabian Nights: The Dynamiter (Stevenson), **V:** 395
More Nonsense, Pictures, Rhymes, Botany (Lear), **V:** 78, 87
More Poems (Housman), **VI:** 152, 157, 161–162
More Pricks than Kicks (Beckett), **Supp. I:** 45–46; **Retro. Supp. I:** 19
More Reformation: A Satyr upon Himself . . . (Defoe), **III:** 13
More Short-Ways with the Dissenters (Defoe), **III:** 13
More Stories (O'Connor), **Supp. XIV:** 219
More Tales I Tell My Mother (ed. Fairbairns et al.), **Supp. XI:** 163; **Supp. XV:** 262–263
More Trivia (Connolly), **Supp. III:** 98
More Women than Men (Compton-Burnett), **VII:** 61–62
Morgan, Edwin, **Supp. IX: 157–170**
Morgan, Margery M., **VI:** xiii, xiv–xv, xxxiv
Morgann, Maurice, **IV:** xiv, 168
Morgante Maggiore (Pulci), **IV:** 182
Morison, James Augustus Cotter, **IV:** 289, 291
Morkinskinna, **VIII:** 242
Morland, Dick *see* Hill, Reginald
Morley, Frank, **IV:** 79, 86
Morley, John, **VI:** 2, 157, 336
Morley, Lord John, **III:** 201, 205; **IV:** 289, 291; **V:** 279, 280, 284, 290, 313, 334
Mormons, or Latterday Saints, The: With Memoirs of the Life and Death of Joseph Smith, the "American Mahomet" (Mayhew), **Supp. XVI:** 221–223
"Morning" (Davie), **Supp. VI:** 112
"Morning Call" (Murphy), **Supp. V:** 326
Morning Chronicle, The (periodical), **IV:** 43, 128, 129; **V:** 41
Morning Chronicle, The (periodical), **Supp. XVI:** 210, 214–216, 217, 221
"Morning Coffee" (Kinsella), **Supp. V:** 273
"Morning Glory" (Pitter), **Supp. XIII:** 145
"Morning, Midday, and Evening Sacrifice" (Hopkins), **V:** 370
Morning Post (periodical), **III:** 269; **VI:** 351; **Supp. XIII:** 207, 210, 211, 213

"Morning Prayer" (Elizabeth I), **Supp. XVI:** 154
Morning Star (Haggard), **Supp. III:** 214
"Morning Sun" (MacNeice), **III:** 411
Mornings in Mexico (Lawrence), **VII:** 116, 117
"Morning-watch, The" (Vaughan), **II:** 187
Moronic Inferno, The (AAnd Other Visits to America") (Amis), **Supp. IV:** 42, 43
"Morpho Eugenia" (Byatt), **Supp. IV:** 140, 153–154
Morrell, Ottoline, **VII:** 103
Morrell, Sir Charles, **V:** 111
Morris, Jan, **Supp. X: 171–189**
Morris, Margaret, **VI:** 274
Morris, May, **V:** 298, 301, 305
Morris, William, **IV:** 218; **V:** ix, xi, xii, xix, xxii–xxvi, 236–238, **291–307,** 312, 365, 401, 409; **VI:** 103, 167–168, 283
Morris & Co., **V:** 295, 296, 302
"Morris's Life and Death of Jason" (Swinburne), **V:** 298
Morrison, Arthur, **VI:** 365–366
Mortal Causes (Rankin), **Supp. X:** 244, 251–252
Mortal Coils (Huxley), **VII:** 200
Mortal Consequences (Symons), **Supp. IV:** 3
Morte Arthur, Le, **I:** 72, 73
Morte Darthur, Le (Malory), **I:** 67, 68–79; **V:** 294; **Retro. Supp. II:** 237–239, 240–251
"Morte d'Arthur" (Tennyson), **IV:** xx, 332–334, 336; **Retro. Supp. III:** 322, 327
"Mortier Water-Organ Called Oscar, The" (Redgrove), **Supp. VI:** 236
"Mortification" (Herbert), **II:** 127
Mortimer His Fall (Jonson), **Retro. Supp. I:** 166
Mortmere Stories, The (Upward), **Supp. XIII:** 251–252
Morvern Callar (Warner), **Supp. XI:** 281, 282–286, 287, 288, 289, 290, 293
Mosada, a Dramatic Poem (Yeats), **VI:** 221
"Mosaics in the Imperial Palace" (Constantine), **Supp. XV:** 80
Moseley, Humphrey, **II:** 89
Moses (Carpenter), **Supp. XIII:** 36
Moses (Rosenberg), **VI:** 433
Moses' Rock (O'Connor), **Supp. XIV:** 223
Moses the Lawgiver (Keneally), **Supp. IV:** 346
"Mosquito" (Lawrence), **VII:** 119
Mossycoat (Pullman), **Supp. XIII:** 152
"Most Extraordinary Case, A" (James), **VI:** 69
Most Piteous Tale of the Morte Arthur Saunz Guerdon, The (Malory), **I:** 72, 77
Most Wanted Man, A (le Carré), **Retro. Supp. III:** 229
"Moth" (Thomas), **Supp. XII:** 290
"Mother, The" (Stevenson), **Supp. VI:** 256

Mother and Son (Compton-Burnett), **VII:** 64, 65, 68–69
"Mother and Son" (Stallworthy), **Supp. X:** 297
Mother Bombie (Lyly), **I:** 203–204
"Mother Country" (Rossetti), **V:** 255
Mother Country, The (Kureishi), **Supp. XI:** 154
Mother Courage (Brecht), **VI:** 123
"Mother Dressmaking" (Raine), **Supp. XIII:** 167
Mother Hubberd's Tale (Spenser), **I:** 124, 131
Mother Ireland (O'Brien), **Supp. V:** 338
"Mother-May-I" (Jamie), **Supp. XIV:** 137
"Mother Kamchatka; or, Mr. Mainchance in Search of the Truth" (Plomer), **Supp. XI:** 216
"Mother of the Muses, The" (Harrison), **Supp. V:** 161
"Mother of the World, The" (Powys), **VIII:** 251, 252
Mother Poem (Brathwaite), **Supp. XII:** 33, 41, 42, 46
Mother, Sing for Me (Ngũgĩ). *See Maitũ njugĩra*
"Mother Speaks, The" (Day Lewis), **Supp. III:** 125
"Mother to Child Asleep" (Cornford), **VIII:** 107
"Mother Tongue" (Stallworthy), **Supp. X:** 298
Mother, What Is Man? (Smith), **Supp. II:** 462; **Retro. Supp. III:** 307–308
Mother's Day (Storey), **Supp. I:** 420
"Mother's Sense of Fun" (Wilson), **Supp. I:** 153, 157–158
"Moths and Mercury-Vapor Lamp" (Pitter), **Supp. XIII:** 145
Motion, Andrew, **Supp. VII: 251–267**
"Motions of the Earth, The" (Nicholson), **Supp. VI:** 217
Motteux, Pierre, **II:** 352, 353
"Mount Badon" (Williams, C. W. S.), **Supp. IX:** 282–283
Mount of Olives, The; or, Solitary Devotions . . . (Vaughan), **II:** 185, 201
Mount Zion (Betjeman), **VII:** 364
"Mount Zion" (Hughes), **Supp. I:** 341
Mountain Bard, The (Hogg), **Supp. X:** 106
"Mountain Path" (Cornford), **VIII:** 107
"Mountain Shadow" (Gunesekera), **Supp. X:** 87
Mountain Town in France, A (Stevenson), **V:** 396
"Mountaineering Poetry: The Metaphorical Imperative" (Dutton), **Supp. XII:** 86
Mountains and Molehills (Cornford), **VIII:** 106, 107–108, 109
Mountolive (Durrell), **Supp. I:** 104, 106, 108, 109; **Retro. Supp. III:** 85, 89–90
"Mourning" (Marvell), **II:** 209, 212
Mourning Bride, The (Congreve), **II:** 338, 347, 350
Mourning Muse of Alexis, The: A Pastoral (Congreve), **II:** 350

"Mouse and the Woman, The" (Thomas), **Retro. Supp. III:** 347–348
Mousetrap, The (Christie), **Supp. II:** 125, 134
"Move, The" (Crawford), **Supp. XI:** 74–75
"Movement of Bodies, The" (Reed), **Supp. XV:** 250–251
Movevent, The, **Supp. IV:** 256
Moving Finger, The (Christie), **Supp. II:** 132
"Moving In" (Carson), **Supp. XIII:** 56
"Moving In" (Conn), **Supp. XIII:** 75
Moving Out (Behan), **Supp. II:** 67, 68, 70
"Moving Round the House" (Scupham), **Supp. XIII:** 226
Moving Target, A (Golding), **Supp. I:** 88
Moving the Center: The Struggle for Cultural Freedoms (Ngũgĩ), **VIII:** 217, 225
"Mower to the Glo–Worms, The" (Marvell), **II:** 209; **Retro. Supp. III:** 190, 191
"Mowgli's Brothers" (Kipling), **VI:** 199
Moxon, Edward, **IV:** 83, 86, 252
Mr. Johnson (screenplay, Boyd), **Supp. XVI:** 45
Mr. Stimson and Mr. Gorse (Hamilton), **Supp. XVI:** 188–189
Much Ado About Nothing (Shakespeare), **I:** 310–311, 327; **Retro. Supp. III:** 277
Much Obliged (Wodehouse), **Supp. III:** 460
"Mucheleney Abbey" (Sisson), **Supp. XI:** 258
"Mud Vision, The" (Heaney), **Supp. II:** 281
Mudlark Poems & Grand Buveur, The (Redgrove), **Supp. VI:** 236
"Mud–Larks, The" (Mayhew), **Supp. XVI:** 220–**Supp. XVI:** 221
Mudtower, The (Stevenson), **Supp. VI:** 253
Muggeridge, Malcolm, **VI:** 356; **VII:** 276; **Supp. II:** 118, 119
"Mugumo" (Ngũgĩ), **VIII:** 220
Muiopotmos (Spenser), **I:** 124
Muir, Edwin, **I:** 247; **IV:** 27, 40; **Supp. V:** 208; **Supp. VI: 197–209**
Muir, K., **IV:** 219, 236
Mulberry Bush, The (Wilson), **Supp. I:** 154–155
Mulberry Garden, The (Sedley), **II:** 263–264, 271
"Mulberry Tree, The" (Bowen), **Supp. II:** 78, 92
Mulberry Tree, The (Bowen), **Supp. II:** 80
Mulcaster, Richard, **I:** 122
Muldoon, Paul, **Supp. IV: 409–432**
Mule on the Minaret, The (Waugh), **Supp. VI:** 274
Mules (Muldoon), **Supp. IV:** 414–415
Mullan, John, **Retro. Supp. I:** 69–70
Müller, Max, **V:** 203
"Mulwhevin" (Dunn), **Supp. X:** 68
"Mum" (Crawford), **Supp. XI:** 70–71

Mum and Mr. Armitage (Bainbridge), **Supp. VI:** 23
Mummer's Wife, A (Moore), **VI:** xii, 86, 90, 98
"Mummia" (Brooke), **Supp. III:** 52, 60
"Mummy, The" (Morgan, E.), **Supp. IX:** 163
"Mummy to the Rescue" (Wilson), **Supp. I:** 153
"Mundus and Paulina" (Gower), **I:** 53–54
Mundus Muliebris; or, The Ladies–Dressing Room Unlock'd (Evelyn), **II:** 287
Mundy Scheme, The (Friel), **Supp. V:** 119
Munera Pulveris (Ruskin), **V:** 184
"Municipal Gallery Revisited, The" (Yeats), **VI:** 216; **Retro. Supp. I:** 337–338
Munnings, Sir Alfred, **VI:** 210
"Murad the Unlucky" (Brooke), **Supp. III:** 55
"Murder" (Nye), **Supp. X:** 198
Murder at the Vicarage (Christie), **Supp. II:** 130, 131
"Murder Considered as One of the Fine Arts" (De Quincey), **IV:** 149–150
Murder in the Calais Coach (Christie), see *Murder on the Orient Express*
Murder in the Cathedral (Eliot), **VII:** 153, 157, 159; **Retro. Supp. II:** 132
Murder in Triplicate (James), **Supp. IV:** 320, 327
"Murder, 1986" (James), **Supp. IV:** 340
Murder of John Brewer, The (Kyd), **I:** 218
Murder of Quality, A (le Carré), **Supp. II:** 300, **302–303**; **Retro. Supp. III:** 216, 217
Murder of Roger Ackroyd, The (Christie), **Supp. II:** 124, 128, 135
"Murder of Santa Claus, The" (James), **Supp. IV:** 340
Murder of the Man Who Was Shakespeare, The (Hoffman), **I:** 277
Murder on the Orient Express (Christie; U.S. title, *Murder in the Calais Coach*), **Supp. II:** 128, 130, 134, 135
Murderous Michael, **I:** 218
"Murdered Drinker, The" (Graham), **Supp. VII:** 115
"Murders in the Rue Morgue, The" (Poe), **III:** 339
Murdoch, Iris, **III:** 341, 345; **VI:** 372; **Supp. I: 215–235; Supp. IV:** 100, 139, 145, 234
Murmuring Judges (Hare), **Supp. IV:** 282, 294, 296–297, 298
Murnau, F. W., **III:** 342
Murphy (Beckett), **Supp. I:** 46–47, 48, 51, 62, 220; **Retro. Supp. I:** 19–20
Murphy, Richard, **VI:** 220; **Supp. V: 313–331**
Murray, Gilbert, **VI:** 153, 273, 274
Murray, John, **IV:** 182, 188, 190, 193, 294
Murray, Les, **Supp. VII: 269–288**
Murray, Nicholas, **Supp. IV:** 171
Murray, Sir James, **III:** 113
Murry, John Middleton, **III:** 68; **VI:** 207, 375, 446; **VII:** 37, 106, 173–174, 181–182

"Muse, The" (Cowley), **II:** 195, 200
"Muse Among the Motors, A" (Kipling), **VI:** 202
"Musée des Beaux Arts" (Auden), **VII:** 379, 385–386; **Retro. Supp. I:** 8
"Muses Dirge, The" (James), **II:** 102
"Museum" (MacNeice), **VII:** 412
Museum of Cheats, The (Warner), **Supp. VII:** 380
Museum Pieces (Plomer), **Supp. XI:** 221
"Music" (Owen), **VI:** 449
Music: An Ode (Swinburne), **V:** 333
Music at Night (Priestley), **VII:** 225–226
Music Cure, The (Shaw), **VI:** 129
"Music for Octopi" (Redgrove), **Supp. VI:** 234
Music of Division, The (Wallace–Crabbe), **VIII:** 311
Music of Time novel cycle (Powell), see *Dance to the Music of Time, A*
Music on Clinton Street (McCabe), **Supp. IX:** 127
"Music on the Hill, The" (Saki), **Supp. VI:** 243–244
"Musical Instrument, A" (Browning), **IV:** 315
"Musician, The" (Dunn), **Supp. X:** 73
Musicks Duell (Crashaw), **II:** 90–91
Musil, Robert, **Supp. IV:** 70
Musique Discrète: A Request Programme of Music by Dame Hilda Tablet (Reed), **Supp. XV:** 253
Muslin (Moore), **VI:** 98; see *Drama in Muslin, A*
Mustapha (Greville), **Supp. XI:** 108, 117
"Mute Phenomena, The" (Mahon), **Supp. VI:** 173
"Mutual Life" (MacCaig), **Supp. VI:** 188
"My Aged Uncle Arly" (Lear), **V:** 85–86
My Beautiful Laundrette (Kureishi), **Supp. XI:** 155–156
My Birds (Davies), **Supp. XI:** 92
My Brother (Kincaid), **Supp. VII:** 217, 230–231
My Brother Evelyn and Other Profiles (Waugh), **Supp. VI:** 269, 276
"My Canadian Uncle" (Smith, I. C.), **Supp. IX:** 224
"My Care" (Fallon), **Supp. XII:** 108, 109
My Child, My Sister (Fuller), **Supp. VII:** 74, 76, 77, 81
My Children! My Africa! and Selected Shorter Plays (Fugard), **Supp. XV:** 100, 104, 112
"My Christ Is No Statue" (Fallon), **Supp. XII:** 102
"My Company" (Read), **VI:** 437
My Cousin Rachel (du Maurier), **Supp. III:** 134, 139, 140, 141, 147
"My Darling Dear, My Daisy Flower" (Skelton), **I:** 83
"My Daughter the Fox" (Kay), **Supp. XIII:** 109
My Days and Dreams (Carpenter), **Supp. XIII:** 35–36, 40, 45
My Dear Dorothea: A Practical System of Moral Education for Females (Shaw), **VI:** 109, 130
"My Death" (Hart), **Supp. XI:** 125

"My delight and thy delight" (Bridges), **VI:** 77
"My Diary": The Early Years of My Daughter Marianne (Gaskell), **V:** 15
"My Doves" (Browning), **IV:** 313
"My Dream" (Rossetti), **V:** 256
"My Dyet" (Cowley), **II:** 197, 198
My Early Life (Churchill), **VI:** 354
"My Father" (Adcock), **Supp. XII:** 12
"My Father, William Blake, and a Buddhist Monk United in Songs of Experience" (Delahunt), **Supp. XIV:** 59
My Father's Son (O'Connor), **Supp. XIV:** 212, 216–217, 220
My Father's Trapdoors (Redgrove), **Supp. VI:** 236
My Favourite Wife (Parsons), **Supp. XV:** 229, 233–234, 234–235, 236–237, 238–239, 240
"My First Acquaintance with Poets" (Hazlitt), **IV:** 126, 132
"My First Book" (Stevenson), **Retro. Supp. I:** 260
"My First Marriage" (Jhabvala), **Supp. V:** 236
"My Friend Bingham" (James), **VI:** 69
My Fellow Devils (Hartley), **Supp. VII:** 127–128, 132
"My Friend Bruce Lee" (McCabe), **Supp. IX:** 136
"My galley charged with forgetfulness" (Wyatt), **I:** 110
My Garden (Davies), **Supp. XI:** 92
My Garden Book (Kincaid), **Supp. VII:** 217, 229, 230, 231
"My Ghost" (Wallace-Crabbe), **VIII:** 324
"My Grandparents" (Burnside), **Supp. XIII:** 19
My Guru and His Disciple (Isherwood), **VII:** 318
My House in Umbria (Trevor), **Supp. IV:** 516–517
"My House Is Tiny" (Healy), **Supp. IX:** 106–107
"My Hundredth Tale" (Coppard), **VIII:** 97
My Idea of Fun: A Cautionary Tale (Self), **Supp. V:** 396–398
"My Inheritance" (Butlin), **Supp. XVI:** 57
"My Joyce" (Lodge), **Supp. IV:** 364
"My Lady" (Conn), **Supp. XIII:** 81
"My Lady Love, My Dove" (Dahl), **Supp. IV:** 217
My Lady Ludlow (Gaskell), **V:** 15
"My Last Duchess" (Browning), **IV:** 356, 360, 372; **Retro. Supp. II:** 22–23; **Retro. Supp. III:** 20–21, 31
"My Last Duchess" (Symons), **Supp. XIV:** 271
"My Last Mistress" (Stallworthy), **Supp. X:** 300–301
My Life as a Fake (Carey), **Supp. XII:** 54, 60, 61, 62
"My Life up to Now" (Gunn), **Supp. IV:** 255, 265, 266, 268, 269, 273; **Retro. Supp. III:** 117
"My Literary Love Affair" (Coe), **Supp. XV:** 52

"My love whose heart is tender said to me" (Rossetti), **V:** 251
"My Lover" (Cope), **VIII:** 72–73
"My Luncheon Hour" (Coppard), **VIII:** 87
"My lute awake!" (Wyatt), **I:** 105–106
My Man Jeeves (Wodehouse), **Supp. III:** 455
"My Man of Flesh and Straw" (Stallworthy), **Supp. X:** 292
"My Mother" (Kincaid), **Supp. VII:** 221
"My Mother's Pride" (Gunn), **Retro. Supp. III:** 129
"My own heart let me more have pity on" (Hopkins), **V:** 375–376
"My Own Life" (Hume), **Supp. III:** 229
"My pen take pain a little space" (Wyatt), **I:** 106
"My Picture Left in Scotland" (Jonson), **Retro. Supp. I:** 152
My Revolutions (Kunzru), **Supp. XIV:** 172–175
My Sad Captains (Gunn), **Supp. IV:** 257, 262–264; **Retro. Supp. III:** 117, 120–122
"My Sad Captains" (Gunn), **Supp. IV:** 263–264; **Retro. Supp. III:** 117, 121–122, 130
"My Sailor Father" (Smith, I. C.), **Supp. IX:** 216
My Sister Eileen (McKenney), **Supp. IV:** 476
"My Sister's Sleep" (Rossetti), **V:** 239, 240, 242
"My Sister's War" (Thomas), **Supp. IV:** 492
"My Son the Fanatic" (Kureishi), **Supp. XI:** 157–158
My Son's Story (Gordimer), **Supp. II:** 233, 240–242
"My Spectre" (Blake), **V:** 244
"My spirit kisseth thine" (Bridges), **VI:** 77
"My true love hath my heart, and I have his" (Sidney), **I:** 169
"My Uncle" (Nye), **Supp. X:** 202
My Uncle Oswald (Dahl), **Supp. IV:** 213, 219, 220
My Very Own Story (Ayckbourn), **Supp. V:** 3, 11, 13
My World as in My Time (Newbolt), **VI:** 75
My Year (Dahl), **Supp. IV:** 225
Myer, Valerie Grosvenor, **Supp. IV:** 230
Myers, William Francis, **VII:** xx, xxxviii
Myles Before Myles, A Selection of the Earlier Writings of Brian O'Nolan (O'Nolan), **Supp. II:** 322, 323, 324
Myrick, K. O., **I:** 160, 167
"Myself in India" (Jhabvala), **Supp. V:** 227, 229–230
Myself When Young: Confessions (Waugh), **Supp. VI:** 270
Mysteries, The (Harrison), **Supp. V:** 150, 163
Mysteries of Udolpho, The (Radcliffe), **III:** 331–332, 335, 345; **IV:** xvi, 111; **Supp. III:** 384; **Retro. Supp. III:** 234, 236, 242–244, 246, 249

Mysterious Affair at Styles, The (Christie), **Supp. II:** 124, 129–130
"Mysterious Kôr" (Bowen), **Supp. II:** 77, 82, 93
"Mystery, The" (Soutar), **Supp. XVI:** 254
Mystery of Charles Dickens, The (Ackroyd), **Supp. VI:** 13
Mystery of Edwin Drood, The (Dickens), see *Edwin Drood*
"Mystery of Sasaesa Valley" (Doyle), **Supp. II:** 159
Mystery of the Blue Train (Christie), **Supp. II:** 125
Mystery of the Charity of Charles Péguy, The (Hill), **Supp. V:** 189, 196–198; **Retro. Supp. III:** 137–138
Mystery of the Fall (Clough), **V:** 159, 161
Mystery of the Sea, The (Stoker), **Supp. III:** 381
Mystery Revealed: . . . Containing . . . Testimonials Respecting the . . . Cock Lane Ghost, The (Goldsmith), **III:** 191
Mystic Masseur, The (Naipaul), **Supp. I:** 383, 386, 387, 393
"Mystique of Ingmar Bergman, The" (Blackwood), **Supp. IX:** 6
"Mysticism and Democracy" (Hill), **Supp. V:** 192–193; **Retro. Supp. III:** 138–139
Myth of Modernism (Bergonzi), **Supp. IV:** 364
Myth of Shakespeare, A (Williams, C. W. S.), **Supp. IX:** 276
Myth of the Twin, The (Burnside), **Supp. XIII:** 19–21
"Myth of the Twin, The" (Burnside), **Supp. XIII:** 19
"Mythical Journey, The" (Muir), **Supp. VI:** 206
Mythologiae sive explicationis fabularum (Conti), **I:** 266
"Mythological Sonnets" (Fuller), **Supp. VII:** 73
"Mythology" (Motion), **Supp. VII:** 266
"Myths" (Delanty), **Supp. XIV:** 67

'N Droë wit seisoen (Brink), **Supp. VI:** 50
'n Oomblik in die wind (Brink), **Supp. VI:** 49
"Naaman" (Nicholson), **Supp. VI:** 216
"Nabara, The" (Day Lewis), **Supp. III:** 127
Nabokov, Vladimir, **Supp. IV:** 26–27, 43, 153, 302
Nacht and Träume (Beckett), **Retro. Supp. I:** 29
Nada the Lily (Haggard), **Supp. III:** 214
Nadel, G. H., **I:** 269
"Nadia Boulanger Has the Last Word" (Butlin), **Supp. XVI:** 66
Naipaul, V. S., **VII:** xx; **Supp. I:** 383–405; **Supp. IV:** 302
Naive and Sentimental Lover, The (le Carré), **Supp. II:** 300, 310–311, 317; **Retro. Supp. III:** 219
"Nakamura" (Plomer), **Supp. XI:** 216
Naked Warriors (Read), **VI:** 436
"Namaqualand After Rain" (Plomer), **Supp. XI:** 213

Name and Nature of Poetry, The (Housman), **VI:** 157, 162–164
Name of Action, The (Greene), **Supp. I:** 3
Name of the Rose, The (Eco), **Supp. IV:** 116
"Nameless One, The" (Mangan), **Supp. XIII:** 129
"Names" (Cope), **VIII:** 79
"Names" (Kay), **Supp. XIII:** 99
"Naming of Offa, The" (Hill), **Supp. V:** 195
"Naming of Parts" (Reed), **VII:** 422 **Supp. XV:** 243, 244–245, 248, 249, 250, 256
Nannie's Night Out (O'Casey), **VII:** 11–12
Napier, Macvey, **IV:** 272
"Napier's Bones" (Crawford), **Supp. XI:** 74
Napoleon of Notting Hill, The (Chesterton), **VI:** 335, 338, 343–344
Napoleon III in Italy and Other Poems (Browning), see *Poems Before Congress*
Narayan, R. K., **Supp. IV:** 440
Narcissus (Carpenter), **Supp. XIII:** 36
"Narcissus" (Gower), **I:** 53–54
"Narcissus Bay" (Welch), **Supp. IX:** 267, 268
Nares, Edward, **IV:** 280
Narrative of All the Robberies, . . . of John Sheppard, A (Defoe), **III:** 13
"Narrative of Jacobus Coetzee, The" (Coetzee), **Supp. VI:** 76, **79–80**
Narrow Corner, The (Maugham), **VI:** 375
Narrow Place, The (Muir), **Supp. VI:** 204, **206**
"Narrow Place, The" (Muir), **Supp. VI:** 206
Narrow Road to the Deep North (Bond), **Supp. I:** 423, 427, 428–429, 430, 435
"Narrow Sea, The" (Graves), **VII:** 270
"Narrow Vessel, A" (Thompson), **V:** 441
Nashe, Thomas, **I:** 114, 123, 171, 199, 221, 278, 279, 281, 288; **II:** 25; **Supp. II:** 188; **Retro. Supp. I:** 156
Nat Tate: An American Artist, 1928–1960 (Boyd), **Supp. XVI:** 33, 44–**Supp. XVI:** 45
"Nathair" (Delanty), **Supp. XIV:** 67
Nation (periodical), **VI:** 455; **Supp. XIII:** 117, 118, 127
Nation Review (publication), **Supp. IV:** 346
National Being, The: Some Thoughts on Irish Polity (Russell), **VIII:** 277, 287, 288, 292
National Observer (periodical), **VI:** 350
National Standard (periodical), **V:** 19
National Tales (Hood), **IV:** 255, 259, 267
"National Trust" (Harrison), **Supp. V:** 153
Native Companions: Essays and Comments on Australian Literature 1936–1966 (Hope), **Supp. VII:** 151, 153, 159, 164
"Native Health" (Dunn), **Supp. X:** 68
"Nativity" (Thomas), **Supp. XII:** 290
"Natura" (Scupham), **Supp. XIII:** 221
"Natura Naturans" (Clough), **V:** 159–160

Natural Causes (Motion), **Supp. VII:** 254, 257–258, 263
Natural Curiosity, A (Drabble), **Supp. IV:** 231, 249–250
Natural Daughter, The (Robinson), **Supp. XIII:** 211
"Natural History" (Sisson), **Supp. XI:** 243
Natural History and Antiquities of Selborne, The, (White), **Supp. VI:** 279–284, **285–293**
Natural History of Religion, The (Hume), **Supp. III:** 240–241
"natural man,"**VII:** 94
"Natural Son" (Murphy), **Supp. V:** 327, 329
"Natural Sorrow, A" (Pitter), **Supp. XIII:** 142
Naturalist's Calendar, with Observations in Various Branches of Natural History, A (White), **Supp. VI:** 283
Naturalist's Journal (White), **Supp. VI:** 283, 292
"Naturally the Foundation Will Bear Your Expenses" (Larkin), **Supp. I:** 285
Nature (Davies), **Supp. XI:** 91
Nature and Art (Inchbald), **Supp. XV:** 147, 149, 150, 151–152, 160
Nature in English Literature (Blunden), **Supp. XI:** 42, 43
"Nature, Language, the Sea: An Essay" (Wallace–Crabbe), **VIII:** 315
Nature of a Crime, The (Conrad), **VI:** 148
Nature of Blood, The (Phillips), **Supp. V:** 380, 391–394
Nature of Cold Weather, The (Redgrove), **Supp. VI: 227–229,** 236
"Nature of Cold Weather, The" (Redgrove), **Supp. VI:** 228,237
"Nature of Gothic, The" (Ruskin), **V:** 176
Nature of History, The (Marwick), **IV:** 290, 291
"Nature of Man, The" (Sisson), **Supp. XI:** 251
Nature of Passion, The (Jhabvala), **Supp. V:** 226
"Nature of the Scholar, The" (Fichte), **V:** 348
Nature Poems (Davies), **Supp. III:** 398
"Nature That Washt Her Hands in Milk" (Ralegh), **I:** 149
Natwar–Singh, K., **VI:** 408
Naufragium Joculare (Cowley), **II:** 194, 202
Naulahka (Kipling and Balestier), **VI:** 204; **Retro. Supp. III:** 189
"Naval History" (Kelman), **Supp. V:** 250
"Naval Treaty, The" (Doyle), **Supp. II:** 169, 175
Navigation and Commerce (Evelyn), **II:** 287
"Navy's Here, The" (Redgrove), **Supp. VI:** 234
Naylor, Gillian, **VI:** 168
Nazarene Gospel Restored, The (Graves and Podro), **VII:** 262
Nazism, **VI:** 242
"NB" (Reading), **VIII:** 266
Neal, Patricia, **Supp. IV:** 214, 218, 223
Near and Far (Blunden), **VI:** 428

"Near Lanivet" (Hardy), **VI:** 17
"Near Perigord" (Pound), **V:** 304
Neb (Thomas), **Supp. XII:** 280, 289
"Necessary Blindness, A" (Nye), **Supp. X:** 204
Necessity of Art, The (Fischer), **Supp. II:** 228
Necessity of Atheism, The (Shelley and Hogg), **IV:** xvii, 196, 208; **Retro. Supp. I:** 244
"Necessity of Not Believing, The" (Smith), **Supp. II:** 467
Necessity of Poetry, The (Bridges), **VI:** 75–76, 82, 83
"Necessity's Child" (Wilson), **Supp. I:** 153–154
"Neck" (Dahl), **Supp. IV:** 217
"Ned Bratts" (Browning), **IV:** 370; **Retro. Supp. II:** 29–30
Ned Kelly and the City of the Bees (Keneally), **Supp. IV:** 346
"Ned Skinner" (Muldoon), **Supp. IV:** 415
"Need to Be Versed in Country Things, The" (Frost), **Supp. IV:** 423
Needham, Gwendolyn, **V:** 60
Needle's Eye, The (Drabble), **Supp. IV:** 230, 234, 241, 242–243, 245, 251
"Needlework" (Dunn), **Supp. X:** 68
"Negative Love" (Donne), **Retro. Supp. II:** 93
"Neglected Graveyard, Luskentyre" (MacCaig), **Supp. VI:** 182, 189, 194
"Negro Girl, The" (Robinson), **Supp. XIII:** 204, 212
"Negro's Complaint, The" (Cowper), **Retro. Supp. III:** 36
"Negus" (Brathwaite), **Supp. XII:** 44
"Neighbours" (Cornford), **VIII:** 107
Neighbours in a Thicket (Malouf), **Supp. XII:** 217, 219–220
Neizvestny, Ernst, **Supp. IV:** 88
"Nell Barnes" (Davies), **Supp. XI:** 97–98
"Nelly Trim" (Warner), **Supp. VII:** 371
Nelson, W., **I:** 86
"Nemesis" (Carson), **Supp. XIII:** 63–64
"Neolithic" (Dutton), **Supp. XII:** 90
Nerinda (Douglas), **VI:** 300, 305
Nero Part I (Bridges), **VI:** 83
Nero Part II (Bridges), **VI:** 83
Nesbit, E., **Supp. II:** 140, 144, 149
"Nest in a Wall, A" (Murphy), **Supp. V:** 326
Nest of Tigers, A: Edith, Osbert and Sacheverell in Their Times (Lehmann), **VII:** 141
Nether World, The (Gissing), **V:** 424, 437
Netherwood (White), **Supp. I:** 131, 151
"Netting, The" (Murphy), **Supp. V:** 318
Nettles (Lawrence), **VII:** 118
"Netty Sargent's Copyhold" (Hardy), **VI:** 22
"Neurotic, The" (Day Lewis), **Supp. III:** 129
Neutral Ground (Corke), **VII:** 93
"Neutral Tones" (Hardy), **Retro. Supp. I:** 110, 117
Never Let Me Go (Ishiguro), **Retro. Supp. III:** 160–161, 162
Never Say Never Again (Fleming), **Supp. XIV:** 95

New Age (periodical), **VI:** 247, 265; **VII:** 172; **Supp. XIII:** 131–132
New and Collected Poems 1934–84 (Fuller), **Supp. VII:** 68, 72, 73, 74, 79
New and Collected Poems, 1952–1992 (Hill), **Supp. V:** 184; **Retro. Supp. III:** 139
New and Improved Grammar of the English Tongue, A (Hazlitt), **IV:** 139
New and Old: A Volume of Verse (Symonds), **Supp. XIV:** 252
New and Selected Poems (Davie), **Supp. VI:** 108
New and Selected Poems (Hart), **Supp. XI:** 122
New and Selected Poems of Patrick Galvin (ed. Delanty), **Supp. XIV:** 75
New and Useful Concordance, A (Bunyan), **II:** 253
New Apocalypse, The (MacCaig), **Supp. VI:** 184
New Arabian Nights (Stevenson), **V:** 384n, 386, 395; **Retro. Supp. I:** 263
New Arcadia (Sidney), **Retro. Supp. II:** 332
New Atlantis (Bacon), **I:** 259, 265, 267–269, 273
"New Ballad of Tannhäuser, A" (Davidson), **V:** 318n
New Bath Guide (Anstey), **III:** 155
New Bats in Old Belfries (Betjeman), **VII:** 368–369
New Bearings in English Poetry (Leavis), **V:** 375, 381; **VI:** 21; **VII:** 234, 244–246
"New Beginning, A" (Kinsella), **Supp. V:** 270
New Belfry of Christ Church, The (Carroll), **V:** 274
"New Cemetery, The" (Nicholson), **Supp. VI:** 219
New Characters . . . of Severall Persons . . . (Webster), **II:** 85
New Chatto Poets 2 (ed. Ehrhardt et al.), **Supp. XI:** 71
New Confessions, The (Boyd), **Supp. XVI:** 36–37
New Country, **Supp. XIII:** 252–253
New Country (ed. Roberts), **VII:** xix, 411
New Cratylus, The: Notes on the Craft of Poetry (Hope), **Supp. VII:** 151, 155
"New Delhi Romance, A" (Jhabvala), **Supp. V:** 236–237
New Discovery of an Old Intreague, An (Defoe), **III:** 12; **Retro. Supp. I:** 67
New Divan, The (Morgan, E.), **Supp. IX:** 159, 161, 163
New Dominion, A (Jhabvala), **Supp. V:** 230–231
"New Drama" (Joyce), **Retro. Supp. I:** 170
New Dunciad, The (Pope), **III:** 73, 78; **Retro. Supp. I:** 238
"New Empire Within Britain, The" (Rushdie), **Supp. IV:** 436, 445
"New England Winter, A" (James), **VI:** 69
New Essays by De Quincey (ed. Tave); **IV:** 155

New Estate, The (Carson), **Supp. XIII:** 55–57, 58
New Ewart, The: Poems 1980–82 (Ewart), **Supp. VII:** 34, 44, 45
New Family Instructor, A (Defoe), **III:** 14
"New Forge" (Murphy), **Supp. V:** 328
New Form of Intermittent Light for Lighthouses, A (Stevenson), **V:** 395
"New God, The: A Miracle" (Abercrombie), **Supp. XVI:** 2
New Grub Street (Gissing), **V:** xxv, 426, 427, 429, 430, 434–435, 437; **VI:** 377; **Supp. IV:** 7
"New Hampshire" (Reid), **Supp. VII:** 326
New Inn; The Noble Gentlemen (Jonson), **II:** 65; **Retro. Supp. I:** 165
New Journey to Paris, A (Swift), **III:** 35
"New King for the Congo: Mobutu and the Nihilism of Africa" (Naipaul), **Supp. I:** 398
New Light on Piers Plowman (Bright), **I:** 3
New Lines (Conquest), **Supp. IV:** 256
New Lives for Old (Snow), **VII:** 323
New Love-Poems (Scott), **IV:** 39
New Machiavelli, The (Wells), **VI:** 226, 239, 244
New Magdalen, The (Collins), **Supp. VI:** 102
New Meaning of Treason, The (West), **Supp. III:** 440, 444
New Men, The (Snow), **VII:** xxi, 324, 328–329, 330
New Method of Evaluation as Applied to ð, The (Carroll), **V:** 274
New Monthly (periodical), **IV:** 252, 254, 258
"New Morality, The" (Carpenter), **Supp. XIII:** 41
New Musical Express, **Supp. XV:** 227, 229
"New Novel, The" (James), **VI:** xii
New Numbers (periodical), **VI:** 420; **Supp. III:** 47
New Oxford Book of Irish Verse, The (Kinsella), **Supp. V:** 274
New Oxford Book of Sixteenth Century Verse, The (ed. Jones), **Supp. XI:** 116
New Poems (Adcock), **Supp. XII:** 11, 13
New Poems (Arnold), **V:** xxiii, 204, 209, 216
"New Poems" (Bridges), **VI:** 77
New Poems (Constantine), **Supp. XV:** 72, 74
New Poems (Davies), **Supp. III:** 398
New Poems (Davies), **Supp. XI:** 85, 88, 96, 97
New Poems (Fuller), **Supp. VII:** 76–77
New Poems (Kinsella), **Supp. V:** 266, 274
New Poems (Thompson), **V:** 444, 446, 451
New Poems by Robert Browning and Elizabeth Barrett Browning (ed. Kenyon), **IV:** 321
New Poems Hitherto Unpublished or Uncollected . . . (Rossetti), **V:** 260
New Policemen, The (Thompson), **Supp. XIV:** 286, 291, 294–295, 296
"New Women" (Beer), **Supp. XIV:** 13

New Quixote, The (Frayn), **Supp. VII:** 57
New Review (periodical), **VI:** 136
New Rhythm and Other Pieces, The (Firbank), **Supp. II:** 202, 205, 207, 222
New Satyr on the Parliament, A (Defoe), **Retro. Supp. I:** 67
New Selected Poems (Heaney), **Retro. Supp. I:** 131
New Selected Poems 1964–2000 (Dunn), **Supp. X:** 67, 70–71, 76, 81
New Selected Poems of Stevie Smith (Smith), **Retro. Supp. III:** 311
New Signatures (Day Lewis), **Supp. III:** 125
New Signatures (ed. Roberts), **VII:** 411; **Supp. II:** 486
"New Song, A" (Heaney), **Supp. II:** 273
New Statesman (periodical), **VI:** 119, 250, 371; **VII:** 32; **Supp. IV:** 26, 66, 78, 80, 81; **Supp. XII:** 2, 186, 199; **Supp. XIII:** 167
New Statesman and Nation, **Supp. XV:** 244, 247
New Stories I (ed. Drabble), **Supp. IV:** 230
New Territory (Boland), **Supp. V:** 35, 36
New Testament in Modern English (Phillips), **I:** 383
New Testament in Modern Speech (Weymouth), **I:** 382
New Voyage Round the World, A (Dampier), **III:** 7, 24
New Voyage Round the World, A (Defoe), **III:** 5, 13
New Way of Making Fowre Parts in Counter-point, A (Campion), **Supp. XVI:** 92, 102
New Way to Pay Old Debts, A (Massinger), **Supp. XI:** 180, 184, 185, 186–190, 191
New Weather (Muldoon), **Supp. IV:** 412–414, 416
"New Weather" (Muldoon), **Supp. IV:** 413
New Witness (periodical), **VI:** 340, 341
"New World A'Comin'" (Brathwaite), **Supp. XII:** 36–37
New World Symphony, A (Larkin), **Retro. Supp. III:** 203, 212
New Worlds for Old (Wells), **VI:** 242
New Writing IV, **Supp. XIII:** 91–92
New Writings of William Hazlitt (ed. Howe), **IV:** 140
"New Year Behind the Asylum" (Constantine), **Supp. XV:** 79
New Year Letter (Auden), **VII:** 379, 382, 388, 390, 393; **Retro. Supp. I:** 10
"New Year Wishes for the English" (Davie), **Supp. VI:** 110
"New Year's Burden, A" (Rossetti), **V:** 242
"New Year's Gift to the King" (Dunbar), **VIII:** 118
"New York" (Russell), **VIII:** 291
New Yorker, **Supp. XV:** 144–145
Newbolt, Henry, **VI:** 75, 417
Newby, T. C., **V:** 140

Newcomes, The (Thackeray), **V:** xxii, 18, 19, **28–31**, 35, 38, 69
Newell, K. B., **VI:** 235, 237
"Newgate" novels, **V:** 22, 47
Newman, F. W., **V:** 208n
Newman, John Henry, **II:** 243; **III:** 46; **IV:** 63, 64; **V:** xi, xxv, 156, 214, 283, 340; **Supp. VII: 289–305**
"News" (Carson), **Supp. XIII:** 66
"News" (Traherne), **II:** 191, 194
News and Weather, The (Fallon), **Supp. XII:** 108–110, 114
"News for the Church" (O'Connor), **Supp. XIV:** 219
"News from Ireland, The" (Trevor), **Supp. IV:** 504–505
News from Nowhere (Morris), **V:** xxv, 291, 301–304, 306, 409
"News from the Sun" (Ballard), **Supp. V:** 22
"News in Flight" (Delanty), **Supp. XIV:** 77, 78
"News of the World" (Fallon), **Supp. XII:** 114
News of the World: Selected and New Poems (Fallon), **Supp. XII:** 114–115
News of the World: Selected Poems (Fallon), **Supp. XII:** 105–106, 112
Newspaper, The (Crabbe), **III:** 275, 286
Newspoems (Morgan, E.), **Supp. IX:** 163
"Newsreel" (Day Lewis), **Supp. III:** 127
"Newstead Abbey" (Fuller), **Supp. VII:** 73
Newton, Isaac, **Supp. III:** 418–419
Newton, J. F., **IV:** 158
Newton, John, **III:** 210
"Newts" (Thomas), **Supp. XII:** 290
"Next Boat to Douala" (Boyd), **Supp. XVI:** 32
Next Door Neighbours (Inchbald), **Supp. XV:** 156, 157, 160
"Next Life, The" (Davies), **Supp. XIV:** 36, 41
"Next of Kin" (Beer), **Supp. XIV:** 2
"Next, Please" (Larkin), **Supp. I:** 278
"Next Time, The" (James), **VI:** 69
Ngaahika ndeenda (Ngũgĩ wa Thiong'o/Ngũgĩ wa Mĩriĩ), **VIII:** 215–216, 223–224
Ngũgĩ wa Thiong'o, **Supp. V:** 56; **VIII: 211–226**
Nibelungenlied, **VIII:** 231
Nice and the Good, The (Murdoch), **Supp. I:** 226, 227
"Nice Day at School" (Trevor), **Supp. IV:** 504
"Nice to Be Nice" (Kelman), **Supp. V:** 245–246
Nice Valour, The (Fletcher and Middleton), **II:** 21, 66
Nice Work (Lodge), **Supp. IV:** 363, 366, 372, 378–380, 383, 385
Nice Work (television adaptation), **Supp. IV:** 381
Nicholas Nickleby (Dickens), **IV:** 69; **V:** xix, 42, 50–53, 54, 71
Nicholls, Bowyer, **IV:** 98
Nichols, Robert, **VI:** 419
Nicholson, Norman, **Supp. VI: 211–224**

Nichomachean Ethics (Johnson), **Retro. Supp. I:** 149
"Nicht Flittin" (Crawford), **Supp. XI:** 70–71
Nicoll, Allardyce, **II:** 363
Nietzsche, Friedrich Wilhelm, **IV:** 121, 179; **Supp. IV:** 3, 6, 9, 10, 12, 17, 50, 108
Nigger of the "Narcissus," The (Conrad), **VI:** 136, 137, 148; **Retro. Supp. II:** 71–73
Nigger Question, The (Carlyle), **IV:** 247, 250
Night (Pinter), **Supp. I:** 376
Night (Harris), **Supp. V:** 138, 139
Night (O'Brien), **Supp. V:** 338
"Night, The" (Vaughan), **II:** 186, 188
Night and Day (Rosenberg), **VI:** 432
Night and Day (Stoppard), **Supp. I:** 451; **Retro. Supp. II:** 352–353
Night and Day (Woolf), **VII:** 20, 27; **Retro. Supp. I:** 307, 316
Night and Morning: Poems (Clarke), **Supp. XV:** 22–23, 26, 28
"Night and the Merry Man" (Browning), **IV:** 313
"Night Before the War, The" (Plomer), **Supp. XI:** 222
Night Fears and Other Stories (Hartley), **Supp. VII:** 121–122
Night Feed (Boland), **Supp. V:** 50
"Night Feed" (Boland), **Supp. V:** 50
"Night Kitchen" (Scupham), **Supp. XIII:** 230
Night Mail (Auden), **Retro. Supp. I:** 7
Night Manager, The (le Carré), **Retro. Supp. III:** 224–225
"Night of Frost in May" (Meredith), **V:** 223
Night on Bald Mountain (White), **Supp. I:** 131, 136, **149–151**
"Night Out" (Rhys), **Supp. II:** 402
Night Out, A (Pinter), **Supp. I:** 371–372, 375; **Retro. Supp. I:** 223
"Night Patrol" (West), **VI:** 423
"Night School" (Pinter), **Supp. I:** 373, 375
"Night Sister" (Jennings), **Supp. V:** 215
"Night Songs" (Kinsella), **Supp. V:** 261
"Night Taxi" (Gunn), **Supp. IV:** 272–273, 274
Night the Prowler, The (White), **Supp. I:** 131, 132
Night Thoughts (Young), **III:** 302, 307; **Retro. Supp. I:** 43
Night to Remember, A (Ambler), **Supp. IV:** 3
Night to Remember, A (film), **Supp. IV:** 2
Night Visits (Butlin), **Supp. XVI:** 52, 63–64, 68
Night Walk and Other Stories, The (Upward), **Supp. XIII:** 250, 259, 260
Night Walker, The (Fletcher and Shirley), **II:** 66
Night Watch (Scupham), **Supp. XIII:** 229–230
"Night Wind, The" (Brontë), **V:** 133, 142
"Nightclub" (MacNeice), **VII:** 414
Night-Comers, The (Ambler), see *State of Siege*
Night-Comers, The (film), **Supp. IV:** 3

Night-Crossing (Mahon), **Supp. VI: 167–168**, 169
"Nightfall (For an Athlete Dying Young)" (Hollinghurst), **Supp. X:** 121
Nightfishing, The (Graham), **Supp. VII:** 105, 106, 111–113, 114, 116
"Nightingale and the Rose, The" (Wilde), **Retro. Supp. II:** 365
"Nightingale's Nest, The" (Clare), **Supp. XI:** 50, 60
"Nightmare" (Soutar), **Supp. XVI:** 254
"Nightmare, A" (Rossetti), **V:** 256
Nightmare Abbey (Peacock), **III:** 336, 345; **IV:** xvii, 158, 162, 164–165, 170, 177
"Nightpiece to Julia, The" (Herrick), **II:** 111
Nightrunners of Bengal (film, Ambler), **Supp. IV:** 3
Nights at the Alexandra (Trevor), **Supp. IV:** 514–515
Nights at the Circus (Carter), **Supp. III:** 79, 87, 89–90, 91–92
"Night's Fall Unlocks the Dirge of the Sea" (Graham), **Supp. VII:** 110
"Nightwalker" (Kinsella), **Supp. V:** 263
Nightwalker and Other Poems (Kinsella), **Supp. V:** 262, 263–264
Nin, Anaïs, **Supp. IV:** 110, 111
Nina Balatka (Trollope), **V:** 101
Nine Essays (Housman), **VI:** 164
Nine Experiments (Spender), **Supp. II:** 481, 486
Nine Tailors, The (Sayers), **Supp. III:** 343, 344–345
"Ninemaidens" (Thomas), **Supp. IV:** 494
"1938" (Kinsella), **Supp. V:** 271
1985 (Burgess), **Supp. I:** 193
Nineteen Eighty-four (Orwell), **III:** 341; **VII:** xx, 204, 274, 279–280, 284–285
1982 Janine (Gray, A.), **Supp. IX:** 80, 83–85, 86
1914 (Brooke), **Supp. III:** 48, 52, 56–58
"1914" (Owen), **VI:** 444
1914 and Other Poems (Brooke), **VI:** 420; **Supp. III:** 48, 55
1914. Five Sonnets (Brooke), **VI:** 420
1900 (West), **Supp. III:** 432, 445
"Nineteen Hundred and Nineteen" (Yeats), **VI:** 217; **Retro. Supp. I:** 335
"1953," A Version of Racine's Andromaque (Raine), **Supp. XIII:** 170–171
"1916 Seen from 1922" (Blunden), **Supp. XI:** 45
"Nineteen Songs" (Hart), **Supp. XI:** 132
"1938" (Kinsella), **Supp. V:** 271
"Nineteenth Century, The" (Thompson), **V:** 442
Nineteenth Century: A Dialogue in Utopia, The (Ellis), **VI:** 241n
Nip in the Air, A (Betjeman), **VII:** 357
Niven, Alastair, **VII:** xiv, xxxviii
Njáls saga, **VIII:** 238, 240
"Njamba Nene" stories (Ngũgĩ), **VIII:** 222
No (Ackroyd), **Supp. VI:** 2
No Abolition of Slavery . . . (Boswell), **III:** 248
No Continuing City (Longley), **VIII:** 163, 165, 167–169, 170, 171, 175

"No Easy Thing" (Hart), **Supp. XI:** 132
No Enemy (Ford), **VI:** 324
No Exit (Sartre), **III:** 329, 345
"No Flowers by Request" (Ewart), **Supp. VII:** 36
No Fond Return of Love (Pym), **Supp. II: 374–375,** 381
No Fool Like an Old Fool (Ewart), **Supp. VII:** 41
No for an Answer (Larkin), **Retro. Supp. III:** 203, 212
"No Ghosts" (Plomer), **Supp. XI:** 222
No Home but the Struggle (Upward), **Supp. XIII:** 250, 255, 257, 258–259
"No Immortality?" (Cornford), **VIII:** 105, 109
No Laughing Matter (Wilson), **Supp. I:** 162–163
No Man's Land (Hill, R.), **Supp. IX:** 117–118, 121
No Man's Land (Pinter), **Supp. I:** 377
No Mercy: A Journey to the Heart of the Congo (O'Hanlon), **Supp. XI:** 196, 202–206, *207*, 208
No More Angels (Butlin), **Supp. XVI:** 54, 66–67, 68
No More Parades (Ford), **VI:** 319, 329
No Name (Collins), **Supp. VI:** 91, 93–94, **97–98,** 102
No Other Life (Moore, B.), **Supp. IX:** 151, 152–153
No Painted Plumage (Powys), **VIII:** 245, 254–255, 256, 257, 258
No Quarter (Waugh), **Supp. VI:** 275
"No Rest for the Wicked" (Mahon), **Supp. VI:** 167
"No Return" (Smith, I. C.), **Supp. IX:** 218
"No Road" (Larkin), **Supp. I:** 285
"No Room" (Powys), **VIII:** 249, 254, 258
"No Saviours" (Aidoo), **Supp. XV:** 8
"No Smoking" (Ewart), **Supp. VII:** 47
No Star on the Way Back (Nicholson), **Supp. VI:** 217
No Sweetness Here (Aidoo), **Supp. XV:** 2, 7–9
"No Sweetness Here" (Aidoo), **Supp. XV:** 1
"No, Thank You John" (Rossetti), **V:** 256
No Truce with the Furies (Thomas), **Supp. XII:** 282, 285, 286, 290, 291–292
No Truce with Time (Waugh), **Supp. VI:** 274
No Wit, No Help Like a Woman's (Middleton), **II:** 3, 21
"No Muses" (Smith, I. C.), **Supp. IX:** 222
"No Witchcraft for Sale" (Lessing), **Supp. I:** 241, 242
"No worst, There is none" (Hopkins), **V:** 374
Noah and the Waters (Day Lewis), **Supp. III:** 118, 126, 127
"Noble Child is Born, The" (Dunbar). *See Et Nobis Puer Natus Est*
Noble Jilt, The (Trollope), **V:** 102
Noble Numbers (Herrick), see *His Noble Numbers*
Nobleman, The (Tourneur), **II:** 37

Noblesse Oblige (Mitford), **Supp. X:** 163
"Nocturnal Reverie" (Finch), **Supp. IX:** 76
Nocturnal upon S. Lucy's Day, A (Donne), **I:** 358, 359–360; **II:** 128; **Retro. Supp. II:** 91
"Nocturne" (Coppard), **VIII:** 88
"Nocturne" (Murphy), **Supp. V:** 325
Nocturnes: Five Stories of Music and Nightfall (Ishiguro), **Retro. Supp. III:** 161
No–Good Friday (Fugard), **Supp. XV:** 102, 105
Noh theater, **VI:** 218
Noise (Kunzru), **Supp. XIV:** 165, 176
Noises Off (Frayn), **Supp. VII:** 61
"Noisy Flushes the Birds" (Pritchett), **Supp. III:** 324–325
"Noisy in the Doghouse" (Pritchett), **Supp. III:** 324, 325
"Noli emulari" (Wyatt), **I:** 102
"Noli Me Tangere Incident" (Burnside), **Supp. XIII:** 17
Nollius, **II:** 185, 201
Nomadic Alternative, The (Chatwin, B.), **Supp. IX:** 52, 58
"Nona Vincent" (James), **VI:** 69
"Nones" (Auden), **Retro. Supp. I:** 2
Nongogo (Fugard), **Supp. XV:** 102, 105
Nonsense Songs, Stories, Botany and Alphabets (Lear), **V:** 78, 84, 87
Non–Stop Connolly Show, The (Arden and D'Arcy), **Supp. II:** 28, 30, **35–38,** 39
Nooks and Byways of Italy, The (Ramage), **VI:** 298
"Noon at St. Michael's" (Mahon), **Supp. VI:** 174
"Noonday Axeman" (Murray), **Supp. VII:** 272
"No–One" (Thomas), **Supp. XII:** 281, 286
"Nora on the Pavement" (Symons), **Supp. XIV:** 276
Normal Skin, A (Burnside), **Supp. XIII:** 23–24
"Normal Skin, A" (Burnside), **Supp. XIII:** 23
Norman Douglas (Dawkins), **VI:** 303–304
Norman Conquests, The (Ayckbourn), **Supp. V:** 2, 5, 9, 10, 11, 14
Normyx, pseud. of Norman Douglas
North, Thomas, **I:** 314
North (Heaney), **Supp. II:** 268, **273–275;** **Supp. IV:** 412, 420–421, 427; **Retro. Supp. I:** 124, 125, 129–130
"North, The" (Burnside), **Supp. XIII:** 20, 21
"North Africa" (Morgan, E.), **Supp. IX:** 167
North America (Trollope), **V:** 101
North and South (Gaskell), **V:** xxii, **1–6,** 8, 15; **Retro. Supp. III:** 99, 100, 101, 102, 105–109, 110, 112
"North and South, The" (Browning), **IV:** 315
North Face (Renault), **Supp. IX:** 175–176

"North London Book of the Dead, The" (Self), **Supp. V:** 400
"North Sea" (Keyes), **VII:** 437
"North Sea off Carnoustie" (Stevenson), **Supp. VI:** 260
North Ship, The (Larkin), **Supp. I:** 276–277; **Retro. Supp. III:** 203, 212
North Wiltshire Herald, **Supp. XV:** 165, 166
"North Wind, The" (Bridges), **VI:** 80
Northanger Abbey (Austen), **III:** 335–336, 345; **IV:** xvii, 103, 104, 107–110, 112–114, 122; **Retro. Supp. II:** 4–6
Northanger Novels, The (Sadleir), **III:** 335, 346
Northern Echo, **Supp. XIII:** 235, 236–237
"Northern Farmer, New Style" (Tennyson), **IV:** 327; **Retro. Supp. III:** 322
"Northern Farmer, Old Style" (Tennyson), **IV:** 327
Northern Lasse, The (Brome), **Supp. X:** 52, 55, 61
"Northern Lights" (Montague), **Supp. XV:** 222
Northern Lights (Pullman), **Supp. XIII:** 150, 153, 155–156
Northern Lights: A Poet's Sources (Brown), **Supp. VI:** 61, 64
"Northern Line, The: End of Leave, 1950s" (Scupham), **Supp. XIII:** 230
Northern Memoirs (Franck), **II:** 131
Northward Ho! (Dekker, Marston, Webster), **I:** 234–235, 236, 244; **II:** 68, 85
Norton, Charles Eliot, **IV:** 346; **V:** 3, 9, 299; **VI:** 41
Norton, Thomas, **I:** 214
"Nose, The" (Gogol), **III:** 340, 345
Nosferatu (film), **III:** 342; **IV:** 180
"Nostalgia in the Afternoon" (Heaney), **Retro. Supp. I:** 126
Nostromo (Conrad), **VI:** 140–143; **Retro. Supp. II:** 77–80
Not a Drum Was Heard (Reed), **Supp. XV:** 253
"Not Abstract" (Jennings), **Supp. V:** 217
"Not After Midnight" (du Maurier), **Supp. III:** 135
"Not Celia, that I juster am" (Sedley), **II:** 265
"Not Dead Yet Lily?" (Butlin), **Supp. XVI:** 66–67
Not for Publication (Gordimer), **Supp. II:** 232
Not Honour More (Cary), **VII:** 186, 194–195
Not I (Beckett), **Supp. I:** 61; **Retro. Supp. I:** 27–28
"Not Ideas, But Obsessions" (Naipaul), **Supp. I:** 399
"Not Looking" (Nye), **Supp. X:** 201
Not . . . not . . . not . . . not enough oxygen (Churchill), **Supp. IV:** 181
"Not Not While the Giro" (Kelman), **Supp. V:** 246
Not Not While the Giro and Other Stories (Kelman), **Supp. V:** 242, 244–246

"Not Now for My Sins' Sake" (Reid), **Supp. VII:** 325–326
"Not on Sad Stygian Shore" (Butler), **Supp. II:** 111
"Not Only But Also" (Constantine), **Supp. XV:** 80
"Not Palaces" (Spender), **Supp. II:** 494
"Not Proven" (Day Lewis), **Supp. III:** 130
Not–So–Stories (Saki), **Supp. VI:** 240
Not That He Brought Flowers (Thomas), **Supp. XII:** 284
"Not the Place's Fault" (Larkin), **Retro. Supp. III:** 201
Not to Disturb (Spark), **Supp. I:** 200, 201, 210
Not Waving But Drowning (Smith), **Supp. II:** 463; **Retro. Supp. III:** 309, 310–311
"Not Waving But Drowning" (Smith), **Supp. II:** 467; **Retro. Supp. III:** 309, 310
Not Without Glory (Scannell), **VII:** 424, 426
Not Without Honor (Brittain), **Supp. X:** 33, 38
"Not yet Afterwards" (MacCaig), **Supp. VI:** 185
"Notable Discovery of Cosenage, A" (Greene), **VIII:** 144
"Note for American Readers" (Byatt), **Supp. IV:** 149
"Notes from a Spanish Village" (Reid), **Supp. VII:** 334,335–336
Note on Charlotte Brontë, A (Swinburne), **V:** 332
"Note on F. W. Bussell" (Pater), **V:** 356–357
"Note on 'To Autumn,' A" (Davenport), **IV:** 227
"Note on Zulfikar Ghose's 'Nature Strategies'" (Harris), **Supp. V:** 145
"Note to the Difficult One, A" (Graham), **Supp. VII:** 115
Notebook (Maugham), **VI:** 370
"Notebook, A" (Hulme), **Supp. VI:** 135, 140, 145
Note–Book of Edmund Burke (ed. Somerset), **III:** 205
Notebook on William Shakespeare, A (Sitwell), **VII:** 127, 139, 140
Note–Books (Butler), **Supp. II:** 100, 102, 105, **108–111,** 115, 117, 118, 119
Notebooks (Thomas), **Supp. I:** 170
Notebooks, 1960–1977 (Fugard), **Supp. XV:** 100–101, 106, 107
Notebooks of Henry James, The (ed. Matthiessen and Murdock), **VI:** 38
Notebooks of Robinson Crusoe, and Other Poems, The (Smith, I. C.), **Supp. IX:** 216, 217
Notebooks of Samuel Taylor Coleridge, The (ed. Coburn), **IV:** 48, 53, 56
Notes and Index to . . . the Letters of Sir Walter Scott (Corson), **IV:** 27, 39
Notes and Observations on the Empress of Morocco (Dryden), **II:** 297, 305
Notes and Reviews (James), **V:** 199
Notes by an Oxford Chiel (Carroll), **V:** 274

Notes for a New Culture: An Essay on Modernism (Ackroyd), **Supp. VI:** 2, 12–13
Notes for Poems (Plomer), **Supp. XI:** 213
"Notes from a Book of Hours" (Jennings), **Supp. V:** 211
"Notes from a War Diary" (Scupham), **Supp. XIII:** 221
Notes from the Land of the Dead and Other Poems (Kinsella), **Supp. V:** 266, 274
Notes of a Journey from Cornhill to Grand Cairo (Thackeray), **V:** 25, 37, 38
Notes of a Journey Through France and Italy (Hazlitt), **IV:** 134, 140
Notes of a Son and Brother (James), **VI:** 59, 65–66
Notes of an English Republican on the Muscovite Crusade (Swinburne), **V:** 332
"Notes on Being a Foreigner" (Reid), **Supp. VII:** 323
"Notes on Designs of the Old Masters at Florence" (Swinburne), **V:** 329
Notes on English Divines (Coleridge), **IV:** 56
"Notes on Joseph Conrad" (Symons), **VI:** 149
"Notes on Language and Style" (Hulme), **Supp. VI:** 135–136, 141–143, 146
Notes on Life and Letters (Conrad), **VI:** 67, 148
"Notes on Novelists" (James), **V:** 384, 392; **VI:** 149
Notes on Old Edinburgh (Bird), **Supp. X:** 23
Notes on . . . Pictures Exhibited in the Rooms of the Royal Academy (Ruskin), **V:** 184
Notes on Poems and Reviews (Swinburne), **V:** 316, 329, 332
Notes on Sculptures in Rome and Florence . . . (Shelley), **IV:** 209
"Notes on Technical Matters" (Sitwell), **VII:** 139
Notes on the Construction of Sheep–Folds (Ruskin), **V:** 184
Notes on the Royal Academy Exhibition, 1868 (Swinburne), **V:** 329, 332
Notes on "The Testament of Beauty" (Smith), **VI:** 83
Notes on the Turner Gallery at Marlborough House (Ruskin), **V:** 184
"Notes on Writing a Novel" (Bowen), **Supp. II:** 90
Notes Theological, Political, and Miscellaneous (Coleridge), **IV:** 56
Nothing (Green), **Supp. II: 263–264**
Nothing for Anyone (Reading), **VIII:** 264, 267, 274
Nothing Like Leather (Pritchett), **Supp. III:** 313–314
Nothing Like the Sun (Burgess), **Supp. I:** 194, 196
Nothing Sacred (Carter), **Supp. III:** 80, 86–87
Nothing So Simple as Climbing (Dutton), **Supp. XII:** 85

"Nothing Will Die" (Tennyson), **Retro. Supp. III:** 321
"Notice in Heaven" (Morgan, E.), **Supp. IX:** 163
"Notice in Hell" (Morgan, E.), **Supp. IX:** 163
Nott, John, **II:** 102
"Nottingham and the Mining Country" (Lawrence), **VII:** 88, 89, 91, 121; **Retro. Supp. II:** 221
Nouvelles (Beckett), **Supp. I:** 49–50
Novak, Maximillian, **Retro. Supp. I:** 66–67, 68–69
Novel and the People, The (Fox), **Supp. IV:** 466
Novel Now, The (Burgess), **Supp. I:** 194
Novel on Yellow Paper (Smith), **Supp. II:** 460, 462, 469, 473, 474–476; **Retro. Supp. III:** 302, 303–304, 306, 308
Novel Since 1939, The (Reed), **Supp. XV:** 248
Novelist, The (portrait; Kitaj), **Supp. IV:** 119
Novelist at the Crossroads, and Other Essays on Fiction, The (Lodge), **Supp. IV:** 365
"Novelist at Work, The" (Cary), **VII:** 187
"Novelist Today: Still at the Crossroads?, The" (Lodge), **Supp. IV:** 367
"Novelist's Poison, The" (Keneally), **Supp. IV:** 343
Novels of E. M. Forster, The (Woolf), **VI:** 413
Novels of George Eliot: A Study in Form, The (Hardy), **V:** 201
Novels of George Meredith, and Some Notes on the English Novel, The (Sitwell), **V:** 230, 234
Novels Up to Now (radio series), **VI:** 372
"November" (Armitage), **VIII:** 3–4
"November" (Bridges), **VI:** 79–80
"November 1, 1931" (Blunden), **Supp. XI:** 33
"November 24th, 1989" (Scupham), **Supp. XIII:** 226
Novum organum (Bacon), **I:** 259, 260, 263–264, 272; **IV:** 279
"Now"(Thomas), **Supp. I:** 174
Now and in Time to Be (Keneally), **Supp. IV:** 347
"Now I know what love may be" (Cameron), see "Nunc Scio Quid Sit Amor"
"Now in the Time of This Mortal Living" (Nicholson), **Supp. VI:** 214
"Now Sleeps the Crimson Petal" (Tennyson), **IV:** 334
"Now sleeps the crimson petal now the white" (Tennyson), **Retro. Supp. III:** 317, 323
Now We Are Six (Milne), **Supp. V:** 295, 302–303
"Now Let Me Roll" (Cameron), **Supp. IX:** 27
"Now, Zero" (Ballard), **Supp. V:** 21
"Nuance" (Thomas), **Supp. XII:** 286
"Nude" (Constantine), **Supp. XV:** 80
Nude with Violin (Coward), **Supp. II:** 155

Number9Dream (Mitchell), **Supp. XIV:** 193, 195, 196–200, 206
Numbers (Sisson), **Supp. XI:** 249
"Numina at the Street Parties, The" (Redgrove), **Supp. VI:** 235
Numismata: A Discourse of Medals . . . (Evelyn), **II:** 287
"Nunc Dimittis" (Dahl), **Supp. IV:** 215, 217
"Nunc Scio Quid Sit Amor" (Cameron, N.), **Supp. IX:** 19–20, 22
Nunquam (Durrell), **Supp. I: 94,** 103, **113–118,** 120; **Retro. Supp. III:** 85, 91
Nuns and Soldiers (Murdoch), **Supp. I:** 231, 233
Nun's Priest's Tale, The (Chaucer), **I:** 21
"Nuptial Fish, The" (Delanty), **Supp. XIV:** 73
"Nuptiall Song, A; or, Epithalamie, on Sir Clipseby Crew and his Lady" (Herrick), **II:** 105, 106
"Nuptials of Attila, The" (Meredith), **V:** 221
"Nurse" (Cornford), **VIII:** 107
Nursery Alice, The (Carroll), **V:** 273
Nursery Rhymes (Sitwell), **VII:** 138
"Nursery Songs" (Reid), **Supp. VII:** 326
"Nurse's Song" (Blake), **III:** 292; **Retro. Supp. I:** 42
Nussey, Ellen, **V:** 108, 109, 113, 117, 118, 126, 152
Nutmeg of Consolation, The (O'Brian), **Supp. XII:** 258–259
Nuts of Knowledge, The (Russell), **VIII:** 284
"Nutty" (Aidoo), **Supp. XV:** 10
Nye, Robert, **Supp. X: 191–207**
"Nymph Complaining for the Death of Her Faun, The" (Marvell), **II:** 211, 215–216
"Nympholept, A" (Swinburne), **V:** 328

"O Dreams, O Destinations" (Day Lewis), **Supp. III:** 122
"O! for a Closer Walk with God" (Cowper), **III:** 210
"O happy dames, that may embrace" (Surrey), **I:** 115, 120
"O land of Empire, art and love!" (Clough), **V:** 158
O Mistress Mine (Rattigan), see *Love in Idleness*
O Rathaille, Aogan, **Supp. IV:** 418–419
"O Tell Me the Truth About Love" (Auden), **Retro. Supp. I:** 6
Ó Tuama, Seán, **Supp. V:** 266
"O World of many Worlds" (Owen), **VI:** 445
"O Youth whose hope is high" (Bridges), **VI:** 159
Oak Leaves and Lavender (O'Casey), **VII:** 7, 8
Oases (Reid), **Supp. VII:** 333–337
Ob. (Reading), **VIII:** 273
"Oban" (Smith, I. C.), **Supp. IX:** 220
"Obedience" (Herbert), **II:** 126
"Obelisk, The" (Forster), **VI:** 411
Oberland (Richardson), **Supp. XIII:** 186, 191

"Obermann Once More" (Arnold), **V:** 210
Oberon (Jonson), **I:** 344–345
"Object Lessons" (Boland), **Supp. V:** 38–39
Object Lessons: The Life of the Woman and the Poet in Our Time (Boland), **Supp. V:** 35, 36, 37, 42, 43, 46
"Object of the Attack, The" (Ballard), **Supp. V:** 33
Objections to Sex and Violence (Churchill), **Supp. IV:** 182–183, 184, 198
"Objects, Odours" (Wallace-Crabbe), **VIII:** 321
O'Brian, Patrick, **Supp. XII: 247–264**
O'Brien, Conor Cruise, **Supp. IV:** 449
O'Brien, E. J., **VII:** 176
O'Brien, Edna, **Supp. V: 333–346**
O'Brien, Flann, see O'Nolan, Brian
Obsequies to the Memory of Mr. Edward King (Milton), **II:** 175
"Observation Car" (Hope), **Supp. VII:** 154
"Observations" (Beer), **Supp. XIV:** 5
"Observations in the Art of English Poesie" (Campion), **Supp. XVI:** 91, 96, 101–102, 102
Observations on a Late State of the Nation (Burke), **III:** 205
Observations on Macbeth (Johnson), see *Miscellaneous Observations on the Tragedy of Macbeth*
Observations . . . on Squire Foote's Dramatic Entertainment . . . (Boswell), **III:** 247
Observations Relative . . . to Picturesque Beauty . . . [in] the High-Lands of Scotland (Gilpin), **IV:** 36
Observations upon the Articles of Peace with the Irish Rebels . . . . (Milton), **II:** 176
Observator (periodical), **III:** 41; **Supp. IV:** 121
O'Casey, Sean, **VI:** xiv, 214, 218, 314–315; **VII:** xviii, **1–15;** list of articles, **VII:** 14–15; **Supp. II:** 335–336
Occasion for Loving (Gordimer), **Supp. II:** 227, 228, 231, 232, 233
Occasion of Sin, The: Stories by John Montague (Montague), **Supp. XV:** 222
Occasional Verses (FitzGerald), **IV:** 353
Occasions of Poetry, The (Gunn), **Retro. Supp. III:** 116, 117–118, 123
Occasions of Poetry, The (ed. Wilmer), **Supp. IV:** 255, 263
Ocean of Story (Stead), **Supp. IV:** 476
Oceanides, The (Jewsbury), **Supp. XIV:** 149, 152, 161–162
O'Connor, Frank, **Supp. IV:** 514; **Supp. XIV: 211–230**
O'Connor, Monsignor John, **VI:** 338
O'Connor, Ulick, **Supp. II:** 63, 70, 76
October and Other Poems (Bridges), **VI:** 81, 83
"October Dawn" (Hughes), **Supp. I: 344**
October Ferry to Gabriola (Lowry), **Supp. III:** 284–285
October Man, The (film, Ambler), **Supp. IV:** 3

"October Dawn" (Hughes), **Retro. Supp. II:** 203
"October Salmon" (Hughes), **Supp. I:** 363; **Retro. Supp. II:** 213–214
Odd Girl Out, The (Howard), **Supp. XI:** 141, 142–143, 145
Odd Women, The (Gissing), **V:** 428, 433–434, 437
Oddments Inklings Omens Moments (Reid), **Supp. VII:** 327–329
Ode (Dryden), **Retro. Supp. III:** 76
Ode ad Gustavem regem. Ode ad Gustavem exulem (Landor), **IV:** 100
"Ode: Autumn" (Hood), **IV:** 255
"Ode for Music" (Gray), see "Installation Ode"
"Ode. Intimations of Immortality from Recollections of Early Childhood" (Wordsworth), **II:** 189, 200; **IV:** xvi, 21, 22
"Ode on a Distant Prospect of Eton College" (Gray), **III:** 137, 144
"Ode on a Grecian Urn" (Keats), **III:** 174, 337; **IV:** 222–223, 225, 226; **Supp. V:** 38; **Retro. Supp. I:** 195–196
"Ode on Indolence" (Keats), **IV:** 221, 225–226
"Ode on Melancholy" (Keats), **III:** 337; **IV:** 224–225
"Ode on Mrs. Arabella Hunt Singing" (Congreve), **II:** 348
Ode, on the Death of Mr. Henry Purcell, An (Dryden), **II:** 304
"Ode on the Death of Mr. Thomson" (Collins), **III:** 163, 175
"Ode on the Death of Sir H. Morison" (Jonson), **II:** 199
Ode on the Death of the Duke of Wellington (Tennyson), **II:** 200; **IV:** 338
Ode on the Departing Year (Coleridge), **IV:** 55
Ode on the Installation of . . . Prince Albert as Chancellor of . . . Cambridge (Wordsworth), **IV:** 25
"Ode on the Insurrection at Candia" (Swinburne), **V:** 313
"Ode on the Morning of Christ's Nativity" (Milton), **Retro. Supp. II:** 272
"Ode on the Pleasure Arising from Vicissitude" (Gray), **III:** 141, 144
"Ode on the Popular Superstitions of the Highlands of Scotland" (Collins), **III:** 163, 171–173, 175
Ode on the Proclamation of the French Republic (Swinburne), **V:** 332
"Ode on the Spring" (Gray), **III:** 137, 295
"Ode on Wellington" (Tennyson), **Retro. Supp. III:** 329
"Ode Performed in the Senate House at Cambridge" (Gray), **III:** 145
Ode Prefixed to S. Harrison's Arches of Triumph . . . (Webster), **II:** 85
"Ode to a Lady on the Death of Colonel Ross" (Collins), **III:** 162
"Ode to a Nightingale" (Keats), **II:** 122; **IV:** 212, 221, 222–223, 224, 226; **Retro. Supp. I:** 195–196
"Ode to Apollo" (Keats), **IV:** 221, 227

"Ode to Delia Crusca" (Robinson), **Supp. XIII:** 206
"Ode to Duty" (Wordsworth), **II:** 303
"Ode to Evening" (Blunden), **Supp. XI:** 43
"Ode to Evening" (Collins), **III:** 166, 173; **IV:** 227
"Ode to Fear" (Collins), see "Fear"
Ode to Himself (Jonson), **I:** 336
Ode to Independence (Smollett), **III:** 158
"Ode to John Warner" (Auden), **Retro. Supp. I:** 8
"Ode to Liberty" (Shelley), **IV:** 203
"Ode to Master Endymion Porter, Upon his Brothers Death, An" (Herrick), **II:** 112
"Ode to May" (Keats), **IV:** 221, 222
Ode to Mazzini (Swinburne), **V:** 333
"Ode to Memory" (Tennyson), **IV:** 329
"Ode to Mr. Congreve" (Swift), **III:** 30
"Ode to Naples" (Shelley), **II:** 200; **IV:** 195
Ode to Napoleon Buonaparte (Byron), **IV:** 192
"Ode to Pity" (Collins), **III:** 164
"Ode to Psyche" (Keats), **IV:** 221–222
"Ode to Rae Wilson" (Hood), **IV:** 261, 262–263
"Ode to Rapture" (Robinson), **Supp. XIII:** 206
"Ode to Sir William Temple" (Swift), **III:** 30
"Ode to Sorrow" (Keats), **IV:** 216, 224
"Ode to the Harp of...Louisa" (Robinson), **Supp. XIII:** 206
"Ode to the Moon" (Hood), **IV:** 255
"Ode to the Nightingale" (Robinson), **Supp. XIII:** 206
"Ode to the Setting Sun" (Thompson), **V:** 448, 449
"Ode to the Snowdrop" (Robinson), **Supp. XIII:** 210
"Ode to the West Wind" (Shelley), **II:** 200; **IV:** xviii, 198, 203
Ode to Tragedy, An (Boswell), **III:** 247
"Ode upon Dr. Harvey" (Cowley), **II:** 196, 198
"Ode: Written at the Beginning of the Year 1746" (Collins), **III:** 169
Odes (Gray), **III:** 145
Odes and Addresses to Great People (Hood and Reynolds), **IV:** 253, 257, 267
Odes in Contribution to the Song of French History (Meredith), **V:** 223, 234
Odes on Several Descriptive and Allegorical Subjects (Collins), **III:** 162, 163, 165–166, 175
Odes on the Comic Spirit (Meredith), **V:** 234
"Odes III, 29" (tr. Dryden), **Retro. Supp. III:** 78
Odes to . . . the Emperor of Russia, and . . . the King of Prussia (Southey), **IV:** 71
Odette d'Antrevernes (Firbank), **Supp. II:** 199, 201, 205–206
"Odour, The" (Traherne), **Supp. XI:** 269

"Odour of Chrysanthemums" (Lawrence), **VII:** 114; **Retro. Supp. II:** 232–233
"Odysseus of Hermes" (Gunn), **Supp. IV:** 275
Odyssey (Homer), **Supp. IV:** 234, 267, 428
Odyssey (tr. Cowper), **III:** 220
"Odyssey" (Longley), **VIII:** 167
Odyssey (tr. Pope), **III:** 70, 77
Odyssey, The (Butler translation), **Supp. II:** 114, 115
Odyssey of Homer, The (Lawrence translation), **Supp. II:** 283, 294
Odyssey of Homer, done into English Verse, The (Morris), **V:** 306
Oedipus Tyrannus; or, Swellfoot the Tyrant (Shelley), **IV:** 208
Of Ancient and Modern Learning (Temple), **III:** 23
"Of Commerce and Society: The Death of Shelley" (Hill), **Supp. V:** 186
"Of Democritus and Heraclitus" (Montaigne), **III:** 39
"Of Discourse" (Cornwallis), **III:** 39–40
"Of Divine Love" (Waller), **II:** 235
Of Dramatic Poesy (Dryden), **Retro. Supp. III:** 61
Of Dramatick Poesie, An Essay (Dryden), see *Essay of Dramatick Poesy*
Of Education (Milton), **II:** 162–163, 175
"Of Eloquence" (Goldsmith), **III:** 186
"Of English Verse" (Waller), **II:** 233–234
"Of Essay Writing" (Hume), **Supp. III:** 231–232
"Of Greatness" (Cowley), **III:** 40
"Of Himself" (Cowper), **Retro. Supp. III:** 44
Of Human Bondage (Maugham), **VI:** xiii, 365, 373–374
Of Hypatia: or, New Foes with an Old Face (Kingsley), **Supp. XVI:** 197–198, 204
Of Justification by Imputed Righteousness (Bunyan), **II:** 253
"Of Liberty" (Cowley), **II:** 198
Of Liberty and Loyalty (Swinburne), **V:** 333
Of Liberty and Servitude (tr. Evelyn), **II:** 287
Of Magnanimity and Chastity (Traherne), **II:** 202
"Of Masques" (Bacon), **I:** 268
"Of My Self" (Cowley), **II:** 195
"Of Nature: Laud and Plaint" (Thompson), **V:** 443
"Of Only a Single Poem" (Dutton), **Supp. XII:** 95, 96
"Of Pacchiarotto" (Browning), **IV:** 366
"Of Pachiarotto, and How He Worked in Distemper" (Browning), **Retro. Supp. III:** 30
"Of Plants" (Cowley), **Supp. III:** 36
"Of Pleasing" (Congreve), **II:** 349
"Of Poetry" (Temple), **III:** 23, 190
Of Prelatical Episcopacy . . . (Milton), **II:** 175
Of Reformation Touching Church Discipline in England (Milton), **II:** 162, 175

"Of Silence and the Air" (Pitter), **Supp. XIII:** 141–142
Of Style (Hughes), **III:** 40
Of the Characters of Women (Pope), see *Moral Essays*
Of the Friendship of Amis and Amile, Done into English (Morris), **V:** 306
Of the House of the Forest of Lebanon (Bunyan), **II:** 253
Of the Knowledge of Ourselves and of God (Julian of Norwich), **Supp. XII:** 155
Of the Lady Mary (Waller), **II:** 238
Of the Law and a Christian (Bunyan), **II:** 253
Of the Laws of Chance (Arbuthnot), **Supp. XVI:** 16
Of the Laws of Ecclesiastical Polity (Hooker), **I:** 176, 179–190
Of the Trinity and a Christian (Bunyan), **II:** 253
"Of the Uncomplicated Dairy Girl" (Smith, I. C.), **Supp. IX:** 216
Of the Use of Riches, an Epistle to . . . Bathurst (Pope), see *Moral Essays*
Of True Greatness (Fielding), **III:** 105
Of True Religion, Haeresie, Schism, Toleration, . . . (Milton), **II:** 176
"Of White Hairs and Cricket" (Mistry), **Supp. X:** 140–141
Off Colour (Kay), **Supp. XIII:** 101, 108
"Off the Map" (Malouf), **Supp. XII:** 220
"Offa's Leechdom" (Hill), **Supp. V:** 194
"Offa's Second Defence of the English People" (Hill), **Supp. V:** 195
Offer of the Clarendon Trustees, The (Carroll), **V:** 274
"Office for the Dead" (Kinsella), **Supp. V:** 263
"Office Friendships" (Ewart), **Supp. VII:** 39
"Office Girl" (Hart), **Supp. XI:** 123
Office Suite (Bennett), **VIII:** 27
Officers and Gentlemen (Waugh), **VII:** 302, 304; see also *Sword of Honour* trilogy
"Officers Mess" (Ewarts), **VII:** 423; **Supp. VII:** 37
Offshore (Fitzgerald), **Supp. V:** 96, 97, 98, 102
"Oflag Night Piece: Colditz" (Riviere), **VII:** 424
Ogden, C. K., **Supp. II:** 405, 406, 407–408, 409, 410, 411, 422, 424
Ogg, David, **II:** 243
O'Grady, Standish James, **Supp. V:** 36
"Oh, dreadful is the check—intense the agony" (Brontë), **V:** 116
"Oh, Madam" (Bowen), **Supp. II:** 92–93
"Oh! That 'Twere Possible" (Tennyson), **IV:** 330, 332; **Retro. Supp. III:** 321, 326, 327
Oh What a Lovely War (musical), **VI:** 436
O'Hanlon, Redmond, **Supp. XI: 195–208**
Ohio Impromptu (Beckett), **Supp. I:** 61
"O'Hussey's Ode to the Maguire" (Mangan), **Supp. XIII:** 118
"Ointment" (Soutar), **Supp. XVI:** 244
"Oklahoma Kid, The" (Montague), **Supp. XV:** 215

Okri, Ben, **Supp. V: 347–362**
Óláfs saga helga, VIII: 242
"Olalla" (Stevenson), V: 395
"Old, The" (Hart), **Supp. XI:** 123
"Old Aberdeen" (Kay), **Supp. XIII:** 108
Old Adam, The (Bennett), *see Regent, The*
"Old Andrey's Experience as a Musician" (Hardy), VI: 22
"Old Atheist Pauses by the Sea, An" (Kinsella), **Supp. V:** 261
Old Batchelour, The (Congreve), II: 338, 340–341, 349
"Old Benchers of the Inner Temple, The" (Lamb), IV: 74
Old Boys, The (Trevor), **Supp. IV:** 505–506, 507, 517
Old Calabria (Douglas), VI: 294, 295–296, 297, 298, 299, 305
"Old Chartist, The" (Meredith), V: 220
"Old Chief Mshlanga, The" (Lessing), **Supp. I:** 242
"Old China" (Lamb), IV: 82
"Old Church Tower and the Garden Wall, The" (Brontë), V: 134
"Old Colonial Boy, The" (Carson), **Supp. XIII:** 54
"Old Crofter" (MacCaig), **Supp. VI:** 192
Old Country, The (Bennett), VIII: 30
Old Curiosity Shop, The (Dickens), V: xx, 42, 53, 71
Old Debauchees, The (Fielding), III: 105
Old Devils, The (Amis), **Supp. II:** 3, 18–19; **Supp. IV:** 37
"Old Dispensary" (Murphy), **Supp. V:** 329
Old English (Galsworthy), VI: 275, 284
Old English Baron, The (Reeve), III: 345
"Old Familiar Faces, The" (Lamb), IV: 78
"Old Folks at Home" (Highsmith), **Supp. V:** 180
"Old Fools, The" (Larkin), **Supp. I:** 282–283, 285; **Retro. Supp. III:** 210
Old Fortunatus (Dekker), II: 71, 89
"Old Francis" (Kelman), **Supp. V:** 249
Old French Romances, Done into English (Morris), V: 306
"Old Friend, The" (Cornford), VIII: 106
Old Gang and the New Gang, The (Lewis), VII: 83
"Old Garbo" (Thomas), **Supp. I:** 181
Old Glory: An American Voyage (Raban), **Supp. XI:** 227, 232–235
"Old Hands" (Scupham), **Supp. XIII:** 226
"Old Harry" (Kinsella), **Supp. V:** 261
"Old Holborn" (Kelman), **Supp. V:** 256
"Old Homes" (Blunden), **Supp. XI:** 34, 44
"Old House" (Redgrove), **Supp. VI:** 228
Old Huntsman, The (Sassoon), VI: 423, 430, 453
"Old John's Place" (Lessing), **Supp. I:** 240
Old Joiner of Aldgate, The (Chapman), I: 234, 244
"Old Lady" (Smith, I. C.), **Supp. IX:** 221
Old Lady Shows Her Medals, The (Barrie), **Supp. III:** 6, 9, 16

Old Law, The (Massinger, Middleton, Rowley), II: 21;**Supp. XI:** 182
Old Lights for New Chancels (Betjeman), VII: 361, 367, 368
"Old Main Street, Holborn Hill, Millom" (Nicholson), **Supp. VI:** 216–217
"Old Man" (Jennings), **Supp. V:** 210
"Old Man" (Thomas), **Supp. III:** 402
"Old Man, The" (du Maurier), **Supp. III:** 142–143
"Old Man and the Sea, The" (Morgan, E.), **Supp. IX:** 164
Old Man of the Mountains, The (Nicholson), **Supp. VI: 220–221,** 222
Old Man Taught Wisdom, An (Fielding), III: 105
Old Man's Love, An (Trollope), V: 102
"Old Meg" (Gunn), **Supp. IV:** 276
Old Men at the Zoo, The (Wilson), **Supp. I:** 154, 161
Old Mrs. Chundle (Hardy), VI: 20
Old Mortality (Scott), IV: 33, 39
"Old Negatives" (Gray, A.), **Supp. IX:** 91–92
Old Norse Literature, **VIII: 227–244**
"Old Nurse's Story, The" (Gaskell), V: 14, 15
"Old Poet, The" (tr. O'Connor), **Supp. XIV:** 223
Old Possum's Book of Practical Cats (Eliot), VII: 167
Old Pub Near the Angel, An (Kelman), **Supp. V:** 242, 244, 245
"Old Pub Near the Angel, An" (Kelman), **Supp. V:** 245
"Old Queenie" (Thompson), **Supp. XV:** 289
Old Reliable, The (Wodehouse), **Supp. III:** 451
Old Times (Pinter), **Supp. I:** 376–377
"Old Tongue" (Kay), **Supp. XIII:** 108
"Old Toy, The" (Fuller), **Supp. VII:** 79
"Old Vicarage, Grantchester, The" (Brooke), **Supp. III:** 47, 50, 54
Old Whig (periodical), III: 51, 53
Old Wife's Tale, The (Peele), I: 206–208
Old Wives' Tale, The (Bennett), VI: xiii, 247, 249, 250, 251, **254–257**
"Old Woman" (Smith, I. C.), **Supp. IX:** 211, 213
"Old Woman, An" (Sitwell), VII: 135–136
"Old Woman and Her Cat, An" (Lessing), **Supp. I:** 253–254
"Old Woman in Spring, The" (Cornford), VIII: 112
"Old Woman of Berkeley, The" (Southey), IV: 67
"Old Woman Speaks of the Moon, An" (Pitter), **Supp. XIII:** 142
"Old Women, The" (Brown), **Supp. VI:** 71
"Old Women without Gardens" (Dunn), **Supp. X:** 67
"Oldest Place, The" (Kinsella), **Supp. V:** 268
Oldham, John, II: 259
Oley, Barnabas, II: 141; **Retro. Supp. II:** 170–171
"Olga" (Blackwood), **Supp. IX:** 12

Olinda's Adventures (Trotter), **Supp. XVI:** 279–280, 281
Oliphant, Margaret, **Supp. X: 209–225**
"Olive and Camilla" (Coppard), VIII: 96
Oliver, H. J., I: 281
"Oliver Cromwell and Walter Noble" (Landor), IV: 92
Oliver Cromwell's Letters and Speeches (Carlyle), IV: 240, 244, 246, 249, 250, 342
Oliver Newman (Southey), IV: 71
"Oliver Plunkett" (Longley), VIII: 173
Oliver Twist (Dickens), V: xix, 42, 47–50, 51, 55, 56, 66, 71
Olney Hymns (Cowper), III: 210, 211, 220; **Retro. Supp. III:** 40, 43–44
Olor Iscanus . . . (Vaughan), II: 185, 201
Olympia (Manet), **Supp. IV:** 480
"Olympians, The" (Abercrombie), **Supp. XVI:** 4–5
O'Malley, Mary, **Supp. IV:** 181
Oman, Sir Charles, VI: 387
Omega Workshop, VI: 118
Omen, The (film), III: 343, 345
Omniana; or, Horae otiosiores (Southey and Coleridge), IV: 71
"On a Brede of Divers Colours Woven by Four Ladies" (Waller), II: 233
On a Calm Shore (Cornford), VIII: 113–114
"On a Chalk Mark on the Door" (Thackeray), V: 34
On a Chinese Screen (Maugham), VI: 371
"On a Cold, Dead Beauty" (Soutar), **Supp. XVI:** 249
"On a Croft by the Kirkaig" (MacCaig), **Supp. VI:** 194
"On a Dead Child" (Bridges), VI: 77–78
"On a Drop of Dew" (Marvell), II: 211
"On a Girdle" (Waller), II: 235
"On a Joke I Once Heard from the Late Thomas Hood" (Thackeray), IV: 251–252
"On a Midsummer Eve" (Hardy), **Retro. Supp. I:** 119
"On a Mourner" (Tennyson), IV: 332
"On a Prayer Booke Sent to Mrs. M. R."Crashaw), II: 181
"On a Raised Beach" (MacDiarmid), **Supp. XII:** 201, 212–214
"On a Return from Egypt" (Douglas), VII: 444
"On a Train" (Cope), VIII: 80
"On a Troopship" (Sisson), **Supp. XI:** 247, 248, 254
"On a Wedding Anniversary" (Thomas), **Retro. Supp. III:** 344, 345
"On Actors and Acting" (Hazlitt), IV: 137
"On Adventure" (Rushdie), **Supp. IV:** 455
On Alterations in the Liturgy (Newman), **Supp. VII:** 292
"On an Atlantic Steamship" (Carpenter), **Supp. XIII:** 38
"On an Insignificant" (Coleridge), **Retro. Supp. II:** 65
On Baile's Strand (Yeats), VI: 218, 309
On Ballycastle Beach (McGuckian), **Supp. V:** 282, 284–286

"On Ballycastle Beach" (McGuckian), **Supp. V:** 285
On Becoming a Fairy Godmother (Maitland), **Supp. XI:** 174–175
"On Becoming a Non–Stammering Stammerer" (Mitchell), **Supp. XIV:** 208
On Becoming a Writer (Brittain), **Supp. X:** 45
"On Being English but Not British" (Fowles), **Supp. I:** 292
On Beulah Height (Hill, R.), **Supp. IX:** 121–122, 123
"On Board the *West Hardaway*" (Lowry), **Supp. III:** 285
"On Byron and Byronism" (Williams, C. W. S.), **Supp. IX:** 278
On Christian Doctrine (Milton), **Retro. Supp. II:** 271
"On Classical Themes" (Symonds), **Supp. XIV:** 252
"On Craigie Hill" (Conn), **Supp. XIII:** 72
"On Dryden and Pope" (Hazlitt), **IV:** 217
On English Poetry (Graves), **VII:** 260
"On Fairy–Stories" (Tolkien), **Supp. II:** 521, 535
"On Familiar Style" (Hazlitt), **IV:** 138
"On Finding an Old Photograph" (Cope), **VIII:** 73
"On First Looking into Chapman's Homer" (Keats), **IV:** 214, 215–216; **Retro. Supp. I:** 188
"On First Looking into Loeb's Horace" (Durrell), **Supp. I:** 126
On Forsyte 'Change (Galsworthy), **VI:** 270, 275
On Gender and Writing (ed. Wandor), **Supp. XI:** 163, 174, 176
"On 'God' and 'Good' " (Murdoch), **Supp. I:** 217–218, 224–225
"On Greenhow Hill" (Kipling), **VI:** 191
"On Hearing Bartok's Concerto for Orchestra" (Fuller), **Supp. VII:** 72
"On Heaven" (Ford), **VI:** 323
"On Her Endeavouring to Conceal Her Grief at Parting" (Cowper), **Retro. Supp. III:** 45
"On Her Leaving Town After the Coronation" (Pope), **III:** 76
"On Her Loving Two Equally" (Behn), **Supp. III:** 38
On Her Majesty's Secret Service (Fleming), **Supp. XIV:** 96
"On Himself" (Herrick), **II:** 113
On His Grace the Duke of Marlborough (Wycherley), **II:** 322
"On his Grace the Duke of Marlborough, after his victory at Ramellies" (Trotter), **Supp. XVI:** 279
"On his Grace the Duke of Marlborough's Return from his Expedition into Germany, after the battle of Blenheim" (Trotter), **Supp. XVI:** 279
"On His Heid–Ake" (Dunbar), **VIII:** 123
"On Home Beaches" (Murray), **Supp. VII:** 283
"On Installing an American Kitchen in Lower Austria" (Auden), **Retro. Supp. I:** 13

"On Jupiter" (Morgan, E.), **Supp. IX:** 167
"On Keats" (Rossetti), **Retro. Supp. III:** 257–258, 259
"On Leaving the Cottage of My Birth" (Clare), **Supp. XI:** 59–60
"On Leaving the Party" (Delahunt), **Supp. XIV:** 49
"On Living for Others" (Warner), **Supp. VII:** 380
"On Living to One's–Self" (Hazlitt), **IV:** 137
"On Marriage" (Crashaw), **II:** 180
"On Men and Pictures" (Thackeray), **V:** 37
"On Milton" (De Quincey), **IV:** 146
"On Monsieur's Departure" (Elizabeth I), **Supp. XVI:** 152
"On Mr. Milton's 'Paradise Lost'" (Marvell), **II:** 206
"On My First Daughter" (Jonson), **Retro. Supp. I:** 155
"On My First Son" (Jonson), **Retro. Supp. I:** 155
"On My Thirty-fifth Birthday" (Nicholson), **Supp. VI:** 217
"On Not Being Milton" (Harrison), **Supp. V:** 152–153
"On Not Knowing Greek" (Woolf), **VII:** 35
"On Not Remembering Some Lines Of A Song" (Carson), **Supp. XIII:** 59
"On Not Saying Anything" (Day Lewis), **Supp. III:** 130
"On One Who Affected an Effeminate Manner" (Tennyson), **Retro. Supp. III:** 325; **Retro. Supp. III:** 325
"On Palestinian Identity: A Conversation with Edward Said" (Rushdie), **Supp. IV:** 456
"On Passing" (Dutton), **Supp. XII:** 95
"On Personal Character" (Hazlitt), **IV:** 136
"On Peter Scupham" (Scupham), **Supp. XIII:** 218, 219
"On Poetry: A Rhapsody" (Swift), **III:** 30, 36
"On Poetry in General" (Hazlitt), **IV:** 130, 138
"On Preaching the Gospel" (Newman), **Supp. VII:** 294
"On Preparing to Read Kipling" (Hardy), **VI:** 195
"On Reading *Crowds and Power*" (Hill), **Retro. Supp. III:** 145
"On Reading That the Rebuilding of Ypres Approached Completion" (Blunden), **Supp. XI:** 40
"On Receiving News of the War" (Rosenberg), **VI:** 432
"On Renoir's *The Grape–Pickers*" (Boland), **Supp. V:** 40
"On Ribbons" (Thackeray), **V:** 34
"On Seeing England for the First Time" (Kincaid), **Supp. VII:** 218, 225, 228
"On Seeing the Elgin Marbles" (Keats), **IV:** 212–213, 214
On Seeming to Presume (Durrell), **Supp. I:** 124; **Retro. Supp. III:** 95

"On Sentimental Comedy" (Goldsmith), *see Essay on the Theatre* . . .
"On Silence" (Pope), **Retro. Supp. I:** 233
"On Sitting Back and Thinking of Porter's Boeotia" (Murray), **Supp. VII:** 274
"On Some Characteristics of Modern Poetry" (Hallam), **IV:** 234, 235
"On Some Obscure Poetry" (Lander), **IV:** 98
"On Spies" (Jonson), **Retro. Supp. I:** 156
"On Stella's Birthday, . . . A.D. 1718–" (Swift), **III:** 31
"On Style" (De Quincey), **IV:** 148
"On the Application of Thought to Textual Criticism" (Housman), **VI:** 154, 164
On the Black Hill (Chatwin), **Supp. IV:** 158, 168–170, 173
On the Boiler (Yeats), **Retro. Supp. I:** 337
On the Choice of a Profession (Stevenson), **V:** 396
On the Choice of Books (Carlyle), **IV:** 250
"On the City Wall" (Kipling), **VI:** 184
"On the Cliffs" (Swinburne), **V:** 327
"On the Closing of Millom Iron Works" (Nicholson), **Supp. VI:** 218
"On the Conduct of the Understanding" (Smith), **Supp. VII:** 342
"On the Connection Between Homosexuality and Divination" (Carpenter), **Supp. XIII:** 44
On the Constitution of the Church and State (Coleridge), **IV:** 54, 55, 56; **Retro. Supp. II:** 64
On the Contrary (Brink), **Supp. VI:** 56–57
"On the Death of a Certain Journal" (Kingsley), **Supp. XVI:** 194
"On the Death of Dr. Robert Levet" (Johnson), **III:** 120
"On the Death of General Schomberg . . . " (Farquhar), **II:** 351
"On the Death of Marshal Keith" (Macpherson), **VIII:** 181
"On the Death of Mr. Crashaw" (Cowley), **II:** 198
"On the Death of Mr. William Hervey" (Cowley), **II:** 198
"On the Death of Sir Henry Wootton" (Cowley), **II:** 198
"On the Death of Sir W. Russell" (Cowper), **Retro. Supp. III:** 45–46
"On the Departure" (Sisson), **Supp. XI:** 258
On the Dignity of Man (Mirandola), **I:** 253
"On the Discovery of a Lady's Painting" (Waller), **II:** 233
"On the Dismantling of Millom Ironworks" (Nicholson), **Supp. VI:** 218–219
"On the Dunes" (Cornford), **VIII:** 105
On the Edge of the Cliff and Other Stories (Pritchett), **Supp. III:** 328
"On the English Novelists" (Hazlitt), **IV:** 136–137
On the Face of the Waters (Steel), **Supp. XII:** 271–273, 274

"On the Feeling of Immortality in Youth" (Hazlitt), **IV:** 126
On the Frontier (Auden and Isherwood), **VII:** 312; **Retro. Supp. I:** 7
"On the Genius and Character of Hogarth" (Lamb), **IV:** 80
"On the Head of a Stag" (Waller), **II:** 233
"On the Heath" (Symons), **Supp. XIV:** 275, 279
On the Herpetology of the Grand Duchy of Baden (Douglas), **VI:** 300, 305
"On the Influence of the Audience" (Bridges), **VI:** 83
"On the Knocking at the Gate in 'Macbeth'" (De Quincey), **IV:** 146, 149
"On the Lancashire Coast" (Nicholson), **Supp. VI:** 216
"On the Living Poets" (Hazlitt), **IV:** 130
On the Look-out: A Partial Autobiography (Sisson), **Supp. XI:** 243, 244, 245, 246, 247, 248, 254
On the Margin (Bennett), **VIII:** 19, 22
On the Margin (Huxley), **VII:** 201
"On the means of improving people" (Southey), **IV:** 102
"On the Medusa of Leonardo da Vinci in the Florentine Gallery" (Shelley), **III:** 337
"On the Morning of Christ's Nativity" (Milton), **II:** 199; **IV:** 222
"On the Move" (Gunn), **Supp. IV:** 259–260, 261; **Retro. Supp. III:** 115, 119, 120
"On the Origin of Beauty: A Platonic Dialogue" (Hopkins), **V:** 362; **Retro. Supp. II:** 187
On the Origin of Species by Means of Natural Selection (Darwin), **V:** xxii, 279, 287; **Supp. II:** 98
"On the Periodical Essayists" (Hazlitt), **IV:** 136
On the Place of Gilbert Chesterton in English Letters (Belloc), **VI:** 345
"On the Pleasure of Painting" (Hazlitt), **IV:** 137–138
"On the Profession of a Player" (Boswell), **III:** 248
"On the Receipt of My Mother's Picture" (Cowper), **III:** 208, 220
"On the Receipt of My Mother's Picture out of Norfolk" (Cowper), **Retro. Supp. III:** 37
"On the Renovation of Ellis Island" (Delanty), **Supp. XIV:** 68
"On the Road with Mrs. G." (Chatwin), **Supp. IV:** 165
On the Rocks (Shaw), **VI:** 125, 126, 127; **Retro. Supp. II:** 324
"On Roofs of Terry Street" (Dunn), **Supp. X:** 69
"On the School Bus" (Adcock), **Supp. XII:** 9
"On the Scotch Character" (Hazlitt), **IV:** 132
"On the Sea" (Keats), **IV:** 216
"On the Second Story" (Steel), **Supp. XII:** 269
"On the Spirit of Monarchy" (Hazlitt), **IV:** 132

On the Study of Celtic Literature (Arnold), **V:** 203, 212, 216
On the Sublime and Beautiful (Burke), **III:** 195, 198, 205
"On the Supernatural in Poetry" (Radcliffe), **Retro. Supp. III:** 246
"On the Table " (Motion), **Supp. VII:** 262–263, 264
On the Thermal Influence of Forests (Stevenson), **V:** 395
"On the Terraces" (Davies), **Supp. XIV:** 44–45
"On the Toilet Table of Queen Marie-Antoinette" (Nicholls), **IV:** 98
"On the Tragedies of Shakespeare . . . with Reference to . . . . Stage Representation" (Lamb), **IV:** 80
"On the Victory Obtained by Blake" (Marvell), **II:** 211
"On the Way to the Castle" (Adcock), **Supp. XII:** 10–11
"On the Western Circuit" (Hardy), **VI:** 22
"On the Wounds of Our Crucified Lord" (Crashaw), **II:** 182
On the Yankee Station (Boyd), **Supp. XVI:** 32, 43–44
"On the Zattere" (Trevor), **Supp. IV:** 502
"On This Island" (Auden), **Retro. Supp. I:** 7
"On Toleration" (Smith), **Supp. VII:** 347
On Translating Homer (Arnold), **V:** xxii, 212, 215, 216
On Translating Homer: Last Words (Arnold), **V:** 214, 215, 216
"On Whether Loneliness Ever Has a Beginning" (Dunn), **Supp. X: 82**
"On Wit and Humour" (Hazlitt), **II:** 332
"On Wordsworth's Poetry" (De Quincey), **IV:** 146, 148
"On Writing a Novel" (Fowles), **Supp. I:** 293
"On Yeti Tracks" (Chatwin), **Supp. IV:** 157
Once a Week (Milne), **Supp. V:** 298
"Once as me thought Fortune me kissed" (Wyatt), **I:** 102
"Once at Piertarvit" (Reid), **Supp. VII:** 327–328
"Once I Did Think" (Caudwell), **Supp. IX:** 35
"Once in a Lifetime, Snow" (Murray), **Supp. VII:** 273
Once in Europa (Berger), **Supp. IV:** 93, 94
Once on a Time (Milne), **Supp. V:** 298
"Once Upon a Time" (Gordimer), **Supp. II:** 233
"One" (Fallon), **Supp. XII:** 104
"One, The" (Kavanagh), **Supp. VII:** 198
One and Other Poems (Kinsella), **Supp. V:** 267–268
"One at a Time" (Carpenter), **Supp. XIII:** 39
"One Before the Last, The" (Brooke), **Supp. III:** 51
"One by One" (Davies), **Supp. XI:** 101
"1 Crich Circle, Littleover, Derby" (Scupham), **Supp. XIII:** 224
One Day (Douglas), **VI:** 299, 300, 305
"One Day" (Stallworthy), **Supp. X:** 298

"One Day" (Thomas), **Supp. XII:** 290
"One Eye on India" (Sisson), **Supp. XI:** 247
One Fat Englishman (Amis), **Supp. II:** 10, 11, 15
One Fond Embrace (Kinsella), **Supp. V:** 272
One Foot in Eden (Muir), **Supp. VI:** 204, 206, **207–208**
One for My Baby (Parsons), **Supp. XV:** 229, 231–232, 234–235, 235–236, 237, 239–240
One for the Grave (MacNeice), **VII:** 405, 406, 408
One for the Road (Pinter), **Supp. I:** 378, 381
One Hand Clapping (Burgess), **Supp. I:** 186
One Hundred Years of Solitude (García Márquez), **Supp. IV:** 116
One Morning Like a Bird (Miller), **Supp. XIV:** 179, 180, 181, 185, 186, 189, 190, 191–192
"One Mystery, The" (Mangan), **Supp. XIII:** 120
One of Our Conquerors (Meredith), **V:** 232, 233, 234
"One Off the Short List" (Lessing), **Supp. I:** 244
"One Out of Many" (Naipaul), **Supp. I:** 395
"One Sea-side Grave" (Rossetti), **V:** 255
One Small Step (Hill, R.), **Supp. IX:** 123
"One Sunday" (Mistry), **Supp. X:** 138, 140
"One Thing and Another" (Dunn), **Supp. X:** 80
One Thing Is Needful (Bunyan), **II:** 253
One Thing More; or, Caedmon Construed (Fry), **Supp. III:** 191, 196–197
"One Thousand Days in a Balloon" (Rushdie), **Supp. IV:** 437
"One Token" (Davies), **Supp. XI:** 94
"One Viceroy Resigns" (Kipling), **VI:** 202
"One We Knew" (Hardy), **Retro. Supp. I:** 118
"One Who Disappeared" (Motion), **Supp. VII:** 258
One Who Set Out to Study Fear, The (Redgrove), **Supp. VI:** 231
"One Word More" (Browning), **IV:** 357
"One Writer's Education" (Armah), **Supp. X:** 1
One-Way Song (Lewis), **VII:** 72, 76
O'Neill, Eugene, **Supp. III:** 12
Onion, Memory, The (Raine), **Supp. XIII:** 163, 164–166, 168
Only Child, An (O'Connor), **Supp. XIV:** 212, 213, 214, 216, 217, 221, 222, 225
Only Game, The (Hill, R.), **Supp. IX:** 119–120
Only Human (Thompson), **Supp. XIV:** 289, 290–291
"Only our love hath no decay" (Donne), **II:** 221
Only Penitent, The (Powys), **VIII:** 255–256
Only Problem, The (Spark), **Supp. I:** 212–213

"Only the Devil" (Powys), **VIII:** 248–249
"Only This" (Dahl), **Supp. IV:** 211
O'Nolan, Brian, **Supp. II: 321–338; Supp. IV:** 412
Open Conspiracy, The, Blueprints for a World Revolution (Wells), **VI:** 240, 242
Open Court (Kinsella), **Supp. V:** 272, 273
"Open Court" (Kinsella), **Supp. V:** 273
Open Door (Fry), **Supp. III:** 194
"Open Door, The" (Oliphant), **Supp. X:** 220
Open Door, The (Sillitoe), **Supp. V:** 411, 415
Open Letter to the Revd. Dr. Hyde in Defence of Father Damien, An (Stevenson), *see* Father Damien
"Open Secrets" (Motion), **Supp. VII:** 255–256
Opened Ground (Heaney), **Retro. Supp. I:** 124
"Opening, The" (Crawford), **Supp. XI:** 80
"Opening a Place of Social Prayer" (Cowper), **III:** 211
"Opera" (Carson), **Supp. XIII:** 60–61
Opera Et Cetera (Carson), **Supp. XIII:** 59–61, 63, 65
Opera of Operas, The (Haywood and Hatchett), **Supp. XII:** 141
Operette (Coward), **Supp. II:** 152
"Opinions of the Press" (Reading), **VIII:** 264
Opium and the Romantic Imagination (Hayter), **III:** 338, 346; **IV:** 57
"Opium Smoker, The" (Symons), **Supp. XIV:** 271–272
Oppenheim, E. Phillips, **VI:** 249
Optimists, The (Miller), **Supp. XIV:** 179, 181, 182, 189–191
Opus 7 (Warner), **Supp. VII:** 372
Or Shall We Die? (McEwan), **Supp. IV:** 390
"Or, Solitude" (Davie), **Supp. VI:** 110
Or Where a Young Penguin Lies Screaming (Ewart), **Supp. VII:** 41
Oracle, **Supp. XIII:** 202
"Oracle, The" (Coppard), **VIII:** 88
"Oracles, The" (Housman), **VI:** 161
Orage, A. R., **VI:** 247, 265, **VII:** 172
"Oral" (Crawford), **Supp. XI:** 79
"Orange March" (Murphy), **Supp. V:** 322
"Oranges" (Constantine), **Supp. XV:** 73
Oranges Are Not the Only Fruit (Winterson), **Supp. IV:** 541, 542, 543–545, 546, 547–548, 552, 553, 555, 557
Oratio Anniversaria Harvaeana (Arbuthnot), **Supp. XVI:** 26
Orators, The (Auden), **VII:** 345, 380, 382; **Retro. Supp. I:** 5
"Orchard, The" (Conn), **Supp. XIII:** 71
Orchard End (Redgrove), **Supp. VI:** 236
"Orchards half the way, The" (Housman), **VI:** 159
Orchards of Syon, The (Hill), **Retro. Supp. III:** 41–142, 143
"Ordeal" (Richardson), **Supp. XIII:** 191

Ordeal by Innocence (Christie), **Supp. II:** 125
Ordeal of George Meredith, The, A Biography (Stevenson), **V:** 230, 234
Ordeal of Gilbert Pinfold, The (Waugh), **VII:** 291, 293, 302–303
Ordeal of Richard Feverel, The (Meredith), **V:** xxii, 225, 226–227, 234
Ordeal of Sigbjorn Wilderness, The (Lowry), **Supp. III:** 280
Orestes (tr. Delanty), **Supp. XIV:** 76
Order of the Day, The (Greig), **Supp. XVI:** 162
"Ordered South" (Stevenson), **Retro. Supp. I:** 261
"Ordered World, An" (Burnside), **Supp. XIII:** 22
"Ordination, The" (Burns), **III:** 311, 319
Oresteia, The (tr. Harrison), **Supp. V:** 163
Orestes (Caudwell), **Supp. IX:** 37–39
Orestes (Fugard), **Supp. XV:** 108
"Orf" (Hughes), **Supp. I:** 359
"Orford" (Davie), **Supp. VI:** 110
Orford, fourth earl of, *see* Walpole, Horace
Orgel, Stephen, **I:** 237, 239
Orghast (Hughes), **Supp. I:** 354
Orient Express (Greene), **Supp. I:** *see* Stamboul Train
Orient Express (tr. Adcock), **Supp. XII:** 11
"Orient Ode" (Thompson), **V:** 448
"Oriental Eclogues" (Collins), *see* "Persian Eclogues"
Orientations (Maugham), **VI:** 367
Origin, Nature, and Object of the New System of Education, The (Southey), **IV:** 71
Origin of Species by Means of Natural Selection, or the Preservation of Favoured Races in the Struggle for Life (Darwin), **Supp. VII:** 17, 19, 23–25
Origin of the Family, Private Property, and the State, The (Engels), **Supp. II:** 454
Original and Progress of Satire, The (Dryden), **II:** 301
Original Letters &c of Sir John Falstaff (White and Lamb), **IV:** 79, 85
Original Michael Frayn, The (Frayn), **Supp. VII:** 51
Original Papers, containing the Secret of Great Britain from the Restoration to the Accession of the House of Hanover (Macpherson), **VIII:** 192, 193
"Original Place, The" (Muir), **Supp. VI:** 206
Original Poetry by Victor and Cazire (Shelley and Shelley), **IV:** 208
Original Power of the Collective Body of the People of England, Examined and Asserted, The (Defoe), **Retro. Supp. I:** 68
"Original Simplicitie" (Traherne), **Supp. XI:** 266
Original Sin (James), **Supp. IV:** 333–335
"Original Sins of Edward Tripp, The" (Trevor), **Supp. IV:** 503

Origine of Sciences, The (Pope), **Retro. Supp. I:** 234
Origins (Thompson), **Supp. XIV:** 289, 291, 292, 296
Origins of the English Imagination, The (Ackroyd), **Supp. VI:** 13
"Orkney Haiku" (Jamie), **Supp. XIV:** 136
Orkney Tapestry, An (Brown), **Supp. VI:** 64–65
"Orkney: The Whale Islands" (Brown), **Supp. VI:** 72
Orkneyinga saga, **VIII:** 236
Orlando (Woolf), **VII:** 21, 28, 35, 38; **Supp. V:** 557; **Retro. Supp. I:** 314, 318–319
Orlando furioso (Ariosto), **I:** 131, 138
Orley Farm (Trollope), **V:** xxii, 100, 101
Ormond (Edgeworth), **Supp. III:** 154, 156, **163–165**
"Ornithological Section, The" (Longley), **VIII:** 168, 172
Oroonoko (Behn), **Retro. Supp. III:** 2, 4, 5, 13–15
Oroonoko: A Tragedy (Southerne), **Supp. III:** 34–35
Oroonoko, and Other Writings (Behn), **Retro. Supp. III:** 4, 5, 6, 8–9, 13, 14
Oroonoko; or, The Royal Slave (Behn), **Supp. III:** 21, 22–23, 32–36, 39
Oroonoko, The Rover and Other Works (Behn), **Retro. Supp. III:** 11
Orpheus (Hope), **Supp. VII:** 165
Orpheus (Hughes), **Supp. I:** 347
Orpheus and Eurydice (Henryson), **Supp. VII:** 136, 145–146
"Orpheus in Hell" (Thomas), **Supp. IV:** 493
"Orpheus; or, Philosophy" (Bacon), **I:** 267
Orphide and Other Poems (Clarke), **Supp. XV:** 29
"Orr Mount" (Dunn), **Supp. X:** 68
Ortelius, Abraham, **I:** 282
Orthodoxy (Chesterton), **VI:** 336
Orton, Joe, **Supp. V: 363–378**
Orton Diaries, The (Orton), **Supp. V:** 363, 367–369
Orwell, George, **III:** 341; **V:** 24, 31; **VI:** 240, 242; **VII:** xii, xx, **273–287; Supp. I:** 28n; **Supp. III:** 96, 107; **Supp. IV:** 17, 81, 110–111, 440, 445
Osborne, John, **VI:** 101; **Supp. I: 329–340; Supp. II:** 4, 70, 139, 155; **Supp. III:** 191; **Supp. IV:** 180, 281, 283
Osbourne, Lloyd, **V:** 384, 387, 393, 395, 396, 397
Oscar and Lucinda (Carey), **Supp. XII:** 49, 50, 53, 57, 58–59
Oscar Wilde. Art and Egoism (Shewan), **V:** 409, 421
O'Shaughnessy, Arthur, **VI:** 158
Osiris Rising (Armah), **Supp. X:** 1–2, 11–12, 14
Othello (Shakespeare), **I:** 316; **II:** 71, 79; **III:** 116; **Supp. IV:** 285; **Retro. Supp. III:** 276
"Other, The" (Thomas), **Supp. III:** 403
"Other Boat, The" (Forster), **VI:** 406, 411–412

Other House, The (James), **VI:** 48, 49, 67
Other House, The (Stevenson), **Supp. VI:** 263–265
"Other Kingdom" (Forster), **VI:** 399, 402
Other Lovers (Kay), **Supp. XIII:** 100–101, 104, 107–108
Other People: A Mystery Story (Amis), **Supp. IV:** 26, 39–40
Other People's Clerihews (Ewart), **Supp. VII:** 46
"Other People's Houses" (Reid), **Supp. VII:** 336
Other People's Worlds (Trevor), **Supp. IV:** 501, 506, 511–512, 517
Other Places (Pinter), **Supp. I:** 378
"Other Tiger, The" (tr. Reid), **Supp. VII:** 332–333
"Other Times" (Nye), **Supp. X:** 198–199
Other Tongues: Young Scottish Poets in English, Scots, and Gaelic (ed. Crawford), **Supp. XI:** 67
Other Voices (Maitland), **Supp. XI:** 163
"Others, The" (Ewart), **Supp. VII:** 39, 40
Otho the Great (Keats and Brown), **IV:** 231, 235
Otranto (Walpole), *see Castle of Otranto, The*
"Otter, An" (Hughes), **Retro. Supp. II:** 204–205
"Otters" (Longley), **VIII:** 174
Ouch (Ackroyd), **Supp. VI:** 3–4
Ounce, Dice, Trice (Reid), **Supp. VII:** 326
Our Betters (Maugham), **VI:** 368, 369
"Our Bias" (Auden), **VII:** 387
"Our Cabal" (Behn), **Retro. Supp. III:** 4
Our Corner (periodical), **VI:** 103
Our Country's Good (Keneally), **Supp. IV:** 346
Our Exagmination Round His Factification for Incamination of Work in Progress (Beckett et al.), **Supp. I:** 43n
Our Exploits at West Poley (Hardy), **VI:** 20
"Our Father" (Davie), **Supp. VI:** 113
"Our Father's Works" (Blunden), **Supp. XI:** 42
Our Family (Hood), **IV:** 254, 259
Our First Leader (Morris, J.), **Supp. X:** 186
Our Friend the Charlatan (Gissing), **V:** 437
Our Game (le Carré), **Retro. Supp. III:** 225
"Our Hunting Fathers" (Auden), **VII:** 108
"Our Lives Now" (Fallon), **Supp. XII:** 114
Our Man in Havana (Greene), **Supp. I:** 7, 11, 13, 14–15; **Retro. Supp. II:** 161
"Our Mother" (Kinsella), **Supp. V:** 263
Our Mother's House (Gloag), **Supp. IV:** 390
Our Mutual Friend (Dickens), **V:** xxiii, 42, 44, 55, 68–69, 72; **Supp. IV:** 247
Our Old Home (Hawthorne), **VI:** 34
"Our Parish" (Dickens), **V:** 43, 46
Our Republic (Keneally), **Supp. IV:** 347
Our Sister Killjoy: or, Reflections from a Black-Eyed Squint (Aidoo), **Supp. XV:** 2–3
"Our Society at Cranford" (Gaskell), **Retro. Supp. III:** 104
Our Song (Waterhouse), **Supp. XIII:** 273
Our Spoons Came From Woolworths (Comyns), **VIII:** 56–58
"Our Thrones Decay" (Russell), **VIII:** 285
"Our Village—by a Villager" (Hood), **IV:** 257
Our Women: Chapters on the Sex-Discord (Bennett), **VI:** 267
Out (Brooke-Rose)), **Supp. IV:** 99, 104, 105–106
"Out and Away" (Kavan), **Supp. VII:** 202
Out Late (Scupham), **Supp. XIII:** 217, 223–224
Out of Bounds (Stallworthy), **Supp. X:** 292–293
"Out of Doors" (Thompson), **Supp. XV:** 286
Out of India (Jhabvala), **Supp. V:** 235–236
Out of India (Kipling), **VI:** 204
Out of Ireland (Kinsella), **Supp. V:** 271
"Out of Ireland" (Kinsella), **Supp. V:** 271
"Out of the Ordinary" (Delanty), **Supp. XIV:** 65–66, 77
Out of the Picture (MacNeice), **VII:** 405
Out of the Red, into the Blue (Comyns), **VIII:** 63
Out of the Shelter (Lodge), **Supp. IV:** 364, 365, 370–371, 372
"Out of the signs" (Thomas), **Supp. I:** 174
Out of the Silent Planet (Lewis), **Supp. III:** 249, 252–253
Out of the Whirlpool (Sillitoe), **Supp. V:** 411
Out of This World (Swift), **Supp. V:** 437–438
Outback (Keneally), **Supp. IV:** 346
Outcast, The (Sutcliff), **Supp. XVI:** 261–262
"Outcast, The" (Tennyson), **IV:** 329
Outcast of the Islands, An (Conrad), **VI:** 136, 137, 148; **Retro. Supp. II:** 71
Outcasts, The (Sitwell), **VII:** 138
Outcry, The (Julia), **VI:** 67
"Outdoor Concert, The" (Gunn), **Supp. IV:** 269
"Outer Planet, The" (Nicholson), **Supp. VI:** 217
Outidana, or Effusions, Amorous, Pathetic and Fantastical (Beddoes), **Supp. XI:** 28–29
Outline of History: Being a Plain History of Life and Mankind, The (Wells), **VI:** 245
Outlines of Romantic Theology (Williams, C. W. S.), **Supp. IX:** 275, 284
Outlook (Richardson), **Supp. XIII:** 191
"Outlook, Uncertain" (Reid), **Supp. VII:** 330
Outlying Stations, The (Warner), **Supp. XI:** 294
"Outpost of Progress, An" (Conrad), **VI:** 136, 148
Outriders: A Liberal View of Britain, The (Morris, J.), **Supp. X:** 175
"Outside the Whale" (Rushdie), **Supp. IV:** 455
Outskirts (Kureishi), **Supp. XI:** 154
"Outstation, The" (Maugham), **VI:** 370, 371, 380
"Outward Bound" (Morgan, E.), **Supp. IX:** 167
"Outward-Bound Ship, The" (Jewsbury), **Supp. XIV:** 161
"Ovando" (Kincaid), **Supp. VII:** 225
"Over Mother, The" (McGuckian), **Supp. V:** 288
"Over Sir John's Hill" (Thomas), **Supp. I:** 179; **Retro. Supp. III:** 343, 346–347
Over the Frontier (Smith), **Supp. II:** 462, 474; **Retro. Supp. III:** 306, 308
"Over the Hill" (Warner), **Supp. VII:** 380
"Over the Hills" (Thomas), **Supp. III:** 400
"Over the Rainbow" (Rushdie), **Supp. IV:** 434
Over the River (Galsworthy), **VI:** 272, 275
Over the River (Gregory), **VI:** 318
Over to Candleford (Thompson), **Supp. XV:** 277, 279, 280–281, 282, 289
Over to You: Ten Stories of Flyers and Flying (Dahl), **Supp. IV:** 208–211, 213
Overbury, Sir Thomas, **IV:** 286
"Overcoat, The" (Gogol), **III:** 340, 345
Overcrowded Barracoon, The (Naipaul), **Supp. I:** 384
"Overcrowded Barracoon, The" (Naipaul), **Supp. I:** 402
"Overloaded Man, The" (Ballard), **Supp. V:** 33
Overruled (Shaw), **VI:** 129
"Overture" (Kinsella), **Supp. V:** 270–271
"Overtures to Death" (Day Lewis), **Supp. III:** 122
Overtures to Death (Day Lewis), **Supp. III:** 118, 127–128
Ovid, **II:** 110n, 185, 292, 304, 347; **III:** 54; **V:** 319, 321
"Ovid in the Third Reich" (Hill), **Supp. V:** 187; **Retro. Supp. III:** 135
"Ovid on West 4th" (Mahon), **Supp. VI:** 176
Ovid's Art of Love Paraphrased (Fielding), **III:** 105
Ovid's Banquet of Sense (Chapman), **I:** 237–238
Ovid's Epistles, Translated by Several Hands (Dryden), **Supp. III:** 36; **Retro. Supp. III:** 62, 63, 80
Ovid's Fasti (tr. Frazer), **Supp. III:** 176
Owen, Wilfred, **VI:** xvi, 329, 416, 417, 419, 423, **443–460**; **VII:** xvi, 421; list of poems, **VI:** 458–459; **Supp. IV:** 57, 58
"Owen Wingrave," (James), **VI:** 69
"Owl, The" (Thomas), **VI:** 424; **Supp. III:** 403–404
"Owl and Mouse" (Smith, I. C.), **Supp. IX:** 218
"Owl and the Pussy-cat, The" (Lear), **V:** 83–84, 87

433

Owls and Artificers (Fuller), **Supp. VII:** 77

Owners (Churchill), **Supp. IV:** 179, 180, 181–182, 198

"Oxen, The" (Hardy), **VI:** 16

Oxford (Morris, J.), **Supp. X:** 176, 178

Oxford Book of English Verse, The (ed. Quiller–Couch), **II:** 102, 121

Oxford Book of Oxford, The (ed. Morris), **Supp. X:** 178

Oxford Book of Modern Verse, The, **VI:** 219

Oxford Book of Regency Verse, The (ed. Williams, C. W. S.), **Supp. IX:** 276

Oxford Book of Mystical Verse, The (ed. Williams, C. W. S.), **Supp. IX:** 274

Oxford Book of Twentieth–Century English Verse, The (ed. Larkin), **Supp. I:** 286; **Retro. Supp. III:** 200

Oxford Book of War Poetry, The (ed. Stallworthy), **Supp. X:** 292

Oxford Companion to English Literature, **Supp. IV:** 229, 231, 247, 252; **Supp. IX:** 276

Oxford Dictionary of Quotations, The (ed. Williams, C. W. S.), **Supp. IX:** 276

Oxford Lectures on Poetry (Bradley), **IV:** 216, 236

"Oxford Leave" (Ewart), **Supp. VII:** 37

"Oxford" papers (De Quincey), **IV:** 148

Oxford Poetry (eds. Day Lewis and Auden), **Supp. III:** 117; **Retro. Supp. I:** 3; **Supp. IX:** 17

"Oxford Staircase" (Murphy), **Supp. V:** 315

Oxford University and the Co-operative Movement (Russell), **VIII:** 287

Oxford University Chest (Betjeman), **VII:** 356

"Oxfordshire Hamlet in the Eighties, An" (Thompson), **Supp. XV:** 289

Oxygen (Miller), **Supp. XIV:** 179, 180, 181, 185, 186–190, 191

"P. & O.," (Maugham), **VI:** 370–371

"P. D. James' Dark Interiors" (Majeske), **Supp. IV:** 330

P. R. B.: An Essay on the Pre'Raphaelite Brotherhood, 1847–1854 (Waugh), **VII:** 291

"P.S." (Reading), **VIII:** 265–266

Pablo Ruiz Picasso: A Biography (O'Brian), **Supp. XII:** 255–256

Pacchiarotto and How He Worked in Distemper (Browning), **IV:** 359, 374; *see also* "Of Pacchiarotton"

Pacific 1860 (Coward), **Supp. II:** 155

Pacificator, The (Defoe), **III:** 12; **Retro. Supp. I:** 67

"Pack Horse and the Carrier, The" (Gay), **III:** 59–60

Pack My Bag: A Self Portrait (Green), **Supp. II: 247–248,** 251, 255

Packer, Lona Mosk, **V:** 251, 252–253, 260

"Pad, Pad" (Smith), **Supp. II:** 470

"Paddiad, The" (Kavanagh), **Supp. VII:** 193–194

Paddock and the Mouse, The (Henryson), **Supp. VII:** 136, 141–142, 147

Paddy Clarke Ha Ha Ha (Doyle), **Supp. V:** 78, 89–91, 92

Pagan and Christian Creeds (Carpenter), **Supp. XIII:** 47–48

Pagan Mysteries in the Renaissance (Wind), **V:** 317*n*

Pagan Place, A (O'Brien), **Supp. V:** 338–339

Pagan Poems (Moore), **VI:** 98

Page of Plymouth, The (Jonson/Dekker), **Retro. Supp. I:** 157

Pageant and Other Poems, A (Rossetti), **V:** 251, 260; **Retro. Supp. III:** 251, 260

"Pageant of Knowledge" (Lydgate), **I:** 58

"Pageants" (Spenser), **I:** 123

Paid on Both Sides (Auden), **Retro. Supp. I:** 4–5

Painful Adventures of Pericles, Prince of Tyre (Wilkins), **I:** 321

"Painful Case, A" (Joyce), **Retro. Supp. I:** 172

"Painful Pleasure of Suspense, The" (Dahl), **Supp. IV:** 222

"Pains of Sleep, The" (Coleridge), **IV:** xvii, 48, 56

Painter, William, **I:** 297; **II:** 76

Painter of His Own Dishonour, The (tr. FitzGerald), **IV: 344–345**

Painter of Our Time (Berger), **Supp. IV:** 79, 81–84, 88

Painter's Eye, The (James), **VI:** 67

Painting and the Fine Arts (Haydon and Hazlitt), **IV:** 140

"Painting It In" (Stevenson), **Supp. VI:** 264

Pair of Blue Eyes, A: A Novel (Hardy), **VI:** 3, 4, 20; **Retro. Supp. I:** 110, 111–112

"Palace of Art, The" (Tennyson), **IV:** 331; **Retro. Supp. III:** 320, 321

"Palace of Pan, The" (Swinburne), **V:** 328

Palace of Pleasure (Painter), **I:** 297, 313; **II:** 76

Palace of the Peacock (Harris), **Supp. V:** 132–136

Palace Pier (Waterhouse), **Supp. XIII:** 279

"Pale Butterwort" (Longley), **VIII:** 177

Pale Companion, The (Motion), **Supp. VII:** 252

Pale Criminal, The (Kerr), **Supp. XII:** 187, 190–191

Pale Fire (Nabokov), **Supp. IV:** 26, 27

Pale Horse, The (Christie), **Supp. II:** 125, 135

Pale View of the Hills, A (Ishiguro), **Supp. IV:** 301, 303, 304, 305–306, 307–309, 310; **Retro. Supp. III:** 149, 150–152, 157, 162

Paleface (Lewis), **VII:** 72, 75

Paley, William, **IV:** 144

Paley, Grace, **Supp. IV:** 151

Palgrave, Francis Turner, **II:** 208; **IV:** xxii, 196

Palicio (Bridges), **VI:** 83

"Palindrome Stitch, The" (Delanty), **Supp. XIV:** 73–74

Pall Mall Gazette, **Supp. XIII:** 237–241; **Supp. XV:** 166

Palladas: Poems (Harrison), **Supp. V:** 163

Palladis Tamia (Meres), **I:** 296

"Palladium" (Arnold), **V:** 209

Palmer, George Herbert, **Retro. Supp. II:** 173

Palmer, John, **II:** 267, 271

Palmerin of England, **II:** 49; tr. Southey, **IV:** 71

"Palmer's 'Heroides' of Ovid" (Housman), **VI:** 156

Palmyra (Peacock), **IV:** 158, 169

"Pambo" (Browning), **Retro. Supp. III:** 30–31

Pamela (Richardson), **III:** 80, **82–85,** 92, 94, 95, 98; **Retro. Supp. I:** 80, 83, 85–86

Pamphlet Against Anthologies, A (Graves), **VI:** 207; **VII:** 260–261

"Pan and Pitys" (Landor), **IV:** 96

"Pan and Thalassius" (Swinburne), **V:** 328

"Pan; or, Nature" (Bacon), **I:** 267

"Pandora" (James), **VI:** 69

Pandosto (Greene), **I:** 165, 322; **VIII:** 131, 135–138, 139

"Panegerick to Sir Lewis Pemberton, A" (Herrick), **II:** 110

Panegyric to Charles the Second, Presented . . . the Day of His Coronation . . . (Evelyn), **II:** 287

Panegyrick to My Lord Protector, A (Waller), **II:** 238

Panic Spring (Durrell), **Supp. I:** 95, 96; **Retro. Supp. III:** 87

Panofsky, Erwin, **I:** 237

"Panoptics" (Wallace–Crabbe), **VIII:** 321

"Pantarkes, The" (Symonds), **Supp. XIV:** 252

"Panthea" (Wilde), **V:** 401

Pantheon, The; or, Ancient History of the Gods of Greece and Rome: Intended to Facilitate the Understanding of Classical Authors, and of the Poets in General (Godwin), **Supp. XV:** 126

"Paperback Writer: Dream of the Perfect Novel" (Warner), **Supp. XI:** 281

Paoli, Pasquale di, **III:** 235, 236, 243

"Paolo to Francesca" (Wallace–Crabbe), **VIII:** 311

Paper Houses (Plomer), **Supp. XI:** 216

Paper Houses: A Memoir of the '70s and Beyond (Roberts), **Supp. XV:** 260, 261, 273

Paper Men, The (Golding), **Supp. I:** 88–89; **Retro. Supp. I:** 102–103

Paper Money Lyrics, and Other Poems (Peacock), **IV:** 170

Paperbark Tree, The: Selected Prose (Murray), **Supp. VII:** 270, 271, 273, 274, 277

"Papered Parlour, A" (Powys), **VIII:** 251

"Papers, The" (James), **VI:** 69

Papers by Mr. Yellowplush (Thackeray), *see Yellowplush Correspondence, The*

Papillon (tr. O'Brian), **Supp. XII:** 252

"Parable Island" (Heaney), **Supp. II:** 280

Paracelsus (Browning), **IV:** xix, 355, 365, 368, 373; **Retro. Supp. II:** 20; **Retro. Supp. III:** 18, 19
Parade's End (Ford), **VI:** 321, 324, 328, 329–330; **VII:** xv
Paradise (Raine), **Supp. XIII:** 173
Paradise Lost (Milton), **I:** 188–189; **II:** 158, 161, **165–171**, 174, 176, 198, 294, 302; **III:** 118, 302; **IV:** 11–12, 15, 47, 88, 93, 95, 186, 200, 204, 229; ed. Bentley, **VI:** 153; **Retro. Supp. I:** 184; **Retro. Supp. II:** 279–284
Paradise News (Lodge), **Supp. IV:** 366, 374, 381–383, 384, 385
Paradise Regained (Milton), **II:** 171–172, 174, 176; **Retro. Supp. II:** 284–285
"Paradox, The" (Donne), **Retro. Supp. II:** 91
"Paradox, The" (Pitter), **Supp. XIII:** 141
Paradoxes and Problems (Donne), **Retro. Supp. II:** 97
"Paraffin Lamp, The" (Brown), **Supp. VI:** 69–70
Parallel of the Antient Architecture with the Modern, A (tr. Evelyn), **II:** 287
"Paraphrase on Oenone to Paris" (Behn), **Supp. III:** 36
Parasitaster (Marston), see *Fawn, The*
Parasites, The (du Maurier), **Supp. III:** 139, 143
Pardoner's Tale, The (Chaucer), **I:** 21, 42
Pardoner's Tale, The (Wain), **Supp. XVI:** 297, 300–301, 306
"Parents" (Spender), **Supp. II:** 483
Parents and Children (Compton-Burnett), **VII:** 62, 65, 66, 67
Parent's Assistant, The (Edgeworth), **Supp. III:** 152
Pargiters, The (Woolf), **Retro. Supp. I:** 308, 320
Paridiso (Dante), **Supp. IV:** 439
Paris by Night (film), **Supp. IV:** 282, 292
Paris Nights (Bennett), **VI:** 259, 264
Paris Sketch Book, The (Thackeray), **V:** 22, 37
Parish Register, The (Crabbe), **III:** 275, 279, 283
Parisian Sketches (James), **VI:** 67
Parisina (Byron), **IV:** 173, 192
Parker, Brian, **II:** 6
Parker, W. R., **II:** 165*n*
Parkinson, T., **VI:** 220
Parlement of Foules (Chaucer), see *Parliament of Fowls, The*
Parleyings with Certain People of Importance in Their Day . . . .. (Browning), **IV:** 359, 374
"Parliament, The" (Dunn), **Supp. X:** 73–74
Parliament of Birds (tr. FitzGerald), **IV:** 348–349, 353
Parliament of Fowls, The (Chaucer), **I:** 31, 38, 60; **Retro. Supp. II:** 39–40
Parliament of Love, The (Massinger), **Supp. XI:** 182, 183
Parliamentary Speeches of Lord Byron, The (Byron), **IV:** 193
Parnell, Thomas, **III:** 19
Parnell and His Island (Moore), **VI:** 86

Parochial and Plain Sermons (Newman), **Supp. VII:** 292
"Parousia" (Burnside), **Supp. XIII:** 22
Parr, Samuel, **IV:** 88
Parrot (Haywood), **Supp. XII:** 142
Parry, William, **IV:** 191, 193
"Parson Hawker's Farewell" (Beer), **Supp. XIV:** 5
Parsons, Tony, **Supp. XV: 227–241**
Parson's Daughter, The (Trollope), **V:** 101
"Parson's Pleasure" (Dahl), **Supp. IV:** 217
Parson's Tale, The (Chaucer), **I:** 34–35
"Part of Ourselves, A" (Fallon), **Supp. XII:** 111–112, 112–113
Part of the Seventh Epistle of the First Book of Horace Imitated (Swift), **III:** 35
"Parthenogenesis" (Dhomhnaill), **Supp. V:** 40–41
Partial Portraits (James), **V:** 95, 97, 102; **VI:** x, 46
"Particles of a Wave" (Maitland), **Supp. XI:** 168
"Partie Fine, The" (Thackeray), **V:** 24, 38
"Parting" (Thomas), **Supp. III:** 305
"Parting in War-Time" (Cornford), **VIII:** 112
"Partition" (Auden), **Retro. Supp. I:** 14
"Partner, The" (Conrad), **VI:** 148
Partnership, The (Unsworth), **Supp. VII:** 354–355, 356
"Party" (Smith, I. C.), **Supp. IX:** 215
Party Going (Green), **Supp. II: 253–254**
Pascal, Blaise, **II:** 146, 244; **V:** 339; **Supp. IV:** 160
Pascali's Island (Unsworth), **Supp. VII:** 355, 356, 357–359, 360
Pascoe's Ghost (Hill, R.), **Supp. IX:** 114, 118
Pasiphaë: A Poem (Swinburne), **V:** 333
Pasmore (Storey), **Supp. I:** 408, 410, 411–412, 413, 414–415
Pasquin (Fielding), **III:** 97, 98, 104, 105; **Retro. Supp. I:** 82
"Passage" (Dutton), **Supp. XII:** 97
Passage of Arms (Ambler), **Supp. IV:** 16
"Passage to Africa, A" (Plomer), **Supp. XI:** 213
Passage to India, A (Forster), **VI:** 183, 397, 401, 401, **408–410**; **VII:** xv; **Retro. Supp. II:** 146–149
Passage to Juneau: A Sea and Its Meanings (Raban), **Supp. XI:** 228, 232, 237–238
Passages in the Life of an Individual (Brontë), see *Agnes Grey*
Passages in the Life of Mrs. Margaret Maitland of Sunnyside (Oliphant), **Supp. X:** 210–211, 214
Passages of Joy, The (Gunn), **Supp. IV:** 257, 271–274; **Retro. Supp. III:** 115–116, 124–126
Passenger (Keneally), **Supp. IV:** 346
Passenger to Frankfurt (Christie), **Supp. II:** 123, 125, 130, 132
"Passer'by, A" (Bridges), **VI:** 78
"Passing Events" (Brontë), **V:** 122, 123, 151

"Passing of Arthur, The" (Tennyson), **Retro. Supp. III:** 327
"Passing of the Dragons, The" (Roberts, K.), **Supp. X:** 270–271
Passing of the Essenes, The (Moore), **VI:** 96, 99
"Passing of the Shee, The" (Synge), **VI:** 314
"Passing Stranger, The" (Symonds), **Supp. XIV:** 252
Passion (Bond), **Supp. I:** 423, 429–430
"Passion, The" (Collins), **III:** 166, 168, 174
"Passion, The" (Vaughan), **II:** 187
Passion, The (Winterson), **Supp. IV:** 542, 548, 553–554, 555–556
Passion Fruit: Romantic Fiction with a Twist (Winterson), **Supp. IV:** 542
Passion of New Eve, The (Carter), **Supp. III:** 84, 85–86, 91
Passion Play, A (Shaw), **VI:** 107
Passion, Poison, and Petrification; or, The Fatal Gazogene (Shaw), **VI:** 129
Passionate Century of Love (Watson), **I:** 193
Passionate Friends, The (Ambler), **Supp. IV:** 3
"Passionate Man's Pilgrimage, The" (Ralegh), **I:** 148, 149
"Passionate Pilgrim, A" (James), **VI:** 69
Passionate Pilgrim, The, **I:** 291, 307
Passionate Pilgrim and Other Tales, A (James), **VI:** 67
Passionate Shepherd to His Love, The (Marlowe), **I:** 149, 284, 291; **IV:** 327; **Retro. Supp. I:** 203–204
"Passionate Woman, A" (Ewart), **Supp. VII:** 42
"Passions: An Ode. Set to Music, The" (Collins), **III:** 163, 175
Passions of the Mind (Byatt), **Supp. IV:** 139, 140, 141, 146, 151
"Passport to Eternity" (Ballard), **Supp. V:** 20
Passwords: Places, Poems, Preoccupations (Reid), **Supp. VII:** 324, 330, 336
Past and Present (Carlyle), **IV:** xx, 240, 244, 249, 250, 266*n*, 301
"Past ruin'd Ilion Helen lives" (Landor), **IV:** 99
"Past Ever Present, The" (Murray), **Supp. VII:** 280–281
"Paste" (James), **VI:** 69
"Pastels: Masks and Faces" (Symons), **Supp. XIV:** 273, 275
"Pastoral, A" (Byrom), **Supp. XVI:** 71–72, 73
Pastoral Care (Pope Gregory), **Retro. Supp. II:** 295
Pastoral Lives of Daphnis and Chloë. Done into English (Moore), **VI:** 99
"Pastoral Stanzas. Written at Fifteen Years of Age" (Robinson), **Supp. XIII:** 199–200
Pastorals (Blunden), **VI:** 427
Pastorals (Pope), **III:** 69
Pastorals of Virgil (tr. Thornton), **III:** 307
Pastors and Masters (Compton-Burnett), **VII:** 59, 65, 68
Pat and Roald (Farrell), **Supp. IV:** 223

PAT C–PENW

"Pat Cloherty's Version of *The Maisie*" (Murphy), **Supp. V:** 325
"Patagonia, The," (James), **VI:** 49
"Patchwork Quilt, The" (Carson), **Supp. XIII:** 57
Pater, Walter Horatio, **V:** xiii, xix, xxiv–xxvi, 286–287, 314, 323, 324, 329, **337–360**, 362, 400–401, 403, 408, 410, 411; **VI:** ix, 4 365
"Pater on Style" (Chandler), **V:** 359
Paterson, Banjo, **Supp. IV:** 460
"Path of Duty, The" (James), **VI:** 69
"Pathetic Fallacy" (Delanty), **Supp. XIV:** 73
Patience (Gawain–Poet), **Supp. VII:** 83, 84, 96–98
"Patience, hard thing!" (Hopkins), **V:** 375
Patmore, Coventry, **V:** 372, 379, 441
"Patmos" (Durrell), **Supp. I:** 125
Paton, Alan, **Supp. II: 341–359**
"Patricia, Edith, and Arnold," (Thomas), **Supp. I:** 181
Patrician, The (Galsworthy), **VI:** 273, 278
"Patricians" (Dunn), **Supp. X:** 69
"Patrick Sarsfield's Portrait" (Murphy), **Supp. V:** 323
Patriot (Johnson), **III:** 121
"Patriot, The" (O'Connor), **Supp. XIV:** 223
Patriot for Me, A (Osborne), **Supp. I:** 335, 337
"Patrol: Buonomary" (Gutteridge), **VII:** 432–433
Patronage (Edgeworth), **Supp. III:** 151, 158
Pattern of Maugham, The (Curtis), **VI:** 379
Pattern of Painful Adventures, The (Twine), **I:** 321
Patterns of Culture (Benedict), **Supp. III:** 186
Paul (Wilson), **Supp. VI:** 306
Pauli, Charles Paine, **Supp. II:** 98, 116
Pauline: A Fragment of a Confession (Browning), **IV:** xix, 354, 355, 373; **Retro. Supp. II:** 19; **Retro. Supp. III:** 18–19
Paul's Departure and Crown (Bunyan), **II:** 253
Paul's Letters to His Kinsfolk (Scott), **IV:** 38
Pausanias' Description of Greece (Frazer), Supp.**III:** 172, 173
"Pause en Route" (Kinsella), **Supp. V:** 261
"Pavana Dolorosa" (Hill), **Supp. V:** 190–191
Pavane (Roberts, K.), **Supp. X:** 261, 264–270, 275
Pavic, Milorad, **Supp. IV:** 116
"Pavilion on the Links, The" (Stevenson), **V:** 395; **Retro. Supp. I:** 263
"Pawnbroker's Shop, The" (Dickens), **V:** 45, 47, 48
Pax Britannica: The Climax of an Empire (Morris, J.), **Supp. X:** 179–181, 183
Paying Guest, The (Gissing), **V:** 437
Payne, W. L., **III:** 41n

"Peace" (Brooke), **VI:** 420; **Supp. III:** 56, 57
"Peace" (Collins), **III:** 166, 168
"Peace" (Hopkins), **V:** 370
"Peace" (Vaughan), **II:** 186, 187
Peace and the Protestant Succession, The (Trevelyan), **VI:** 392–393
Peace Conference Hints (Shaw), **VI:** 119, 129
"Peace from Ghosts" (Cameron), **Supp. IX:** 19
Peace in Our Time (Coward), **Supp. II:** 151, 154
Peace of the World, The (Wells), **VI:** 244
Peaceable Principles and True (Bunyan), **II:** 253
"Peaches, The" (Thomas), **Supp. I:** 181; **Retro. Supp. III:** 348
Peacock, Thomas Love, **III:** 336, 345; **IV:** xv, xvii–xix, xxii, **157–170**, 177, 198, 204, 306; **V:** 220; **VII:** 200, 211
Peacock Garden, The (Desai), **Supp. V:** 55, 62–63
Pear Is Ripe, The: A Memoir (Montague), **Supp. XV:** 212
Pearl (Arden), **Supp. II:** 39–40
Pearl (Gawain–Poet), **Supp. VII:** 83, 84, 91–96, 98
"Pearl, Matth.13. 45., The" (Herbert), **Retro. Supp. II:** 175
"Pearl Necklace, A" (Hall), **Supp. VI:** 119
Pearl'Maiden (Haggard), **Supp. III:** 214
Pearsall Smith, Logan, **VI:** 76
"Peasant, A" (Thomas), **Supp. XII:** 284
Peasant Mandarin, The: Prose Pieces (Murray), **Supp. VII:** 270, 271
"Peasants, The" (Lewis), **VII:** 447
Pecket, Thomas, **Supp. III:** 385
Peckham, Morse, **V:** 316, 335
Pedlar, The (Wordsworth), **IV:** 24
Peele, George, **I: 191–211**, 278, 286, 305
"Peele Castle" (Wordsworth), see AElegiac Stanzas, Suggested by a Picture of Peele Castle . . . A
"Peep into a Picture Book, A" (Brontë), **V:** 109
Peer Gynt (Ibsen), **Supp. III:** 195
Pegasus (Day Lewis), **Supp. III:** 118, 129–130
"Pegasus" (Kavanagh), **Supp. VII:** 193
Pelagea and Other Poems (Coppard), **VIII:** 89, 98
Pelican History of English Literature, The, **I:** 102
Pell, J. P., **V:** 161
"Pelleas and Ettarre" (Tennyson), **Retro. Supp. III:** 327
Pelles, George, **VI:** 23
Pelt of Wasps, The (Constantine), **Supp. XV:** 66, 78, 79
Pemberly; or, Pride and Prejudice Continued (Tennant), see *Pemberly: The Sequel to Pride and Prejudice*
Pemberly: The Sequel to Pride and Prejudice (Tennant), **Supp. IX:** 237–238, 239–240
"Pen Llŷn" (Thomas), **Supp. XII:** 290
"Pen, Pencil and Poison" (Wilde), **V:** 405, 407; **Retro. Supp. II:** 367–368

Pen Portraits and Reviews (Shaw), **VI:** 129
Pen Shop, The (Kinsella), **Supp. V:** 272, 273, 274
Pendennis (Tackeray), see *History of Pendennis, The*
"Penelope" (Burnside), **Supp. XIII:** 17
"Penelope" (Maitland), **Supp. XI:** 175
Penelope (Maugham), **VI:** 369
Penfriends from Portlock (Wilson), **Sup. VI:** 298, 304
Penguin Book of Contemporary British Poetry, The (ed. Motion), **Supp. VII:** 252, 254, 255, 257
Penguin Book of Contemporary Irish Poetry, The (ed. Fallon and Mahon), **Supp. XII:** 101
Penguin Book of Lesbian Short Stories, The (ed. Winterson), **Supp. IV:** 542
Penguin Book of Light Verse (ed. Ewart), **Supp. VII:** 43, 47
Penguin Book of Love Poetry, The (ed. Stallworthy), **Supp. X:** 292
Penguin Book of Modern British Short Stories (ed. Bradbury), **Supp. IV:** 304
Penguin Book of Religious Verse, The (ed. Thomas), **Supp. XII:** 282
Penguin Modern Poets II (Thomas), **Supp. IV:** 490
Penguin Modern Poets 9 (ed. Burnside, Crawford and Jamie), **Supp. XI:** 67
Peniel (Hart), **Supp. XI:** 122, 128–130, 132
Penitential Psalms (Wyatt), **I:** 101–102, 108, 111
Pennies from Heaven (Potter, D.), **Supp. X:** 229, 231
"Pennines in April" (Hughes), **Supp. I:** 344
Penny in the Clouds, A: More Memories of Ireland and England (Clarke), **Supp. XV:** 16, 27
"Penny Plain and Twopence Coloured, A" (Stevenson), **V:** 385
Penny Wheep (MacDiarmid), **Supp. XII:** 202, 205
Penny Whistles (Stevenson), see *Child's Garden of Verses, A*
Penpoints, Gunpoints, and Dreams: Towards a Critical Theory of the Arts and the State in Africa (Ngũgĩ), **VIII:** 216, 225
Pensées (Pascal), **Supp. IV:** 160
"Penshurst, To" (Jonson), **II:** 223
Pension Beaurepas, The (James), **VI:** 69
Pentameron and Pentalogia, The (Landor), **IV:** 89, 90–91, 93, 100
"Pentecost Castle, The" (Hill), **Supp. V:** 189, 190, 199
"Pentecostal" (Malouf), **Supp. XII:** 220–221
"Penthouse Apartment, The" (Trevor), **Supp. IV:** 502
Pentland Rising, The (Stevenson), **V:** 395; **Retro. Supp. I:** 260
Penultimate Poems (Ewart), **Supp. VII:** 45–46
"Penwith" (Thomas), **Supp. IV:** 492

People Are Living There (Fugard), **Supp. XV:** 103, 106, 107
People Who Knock on the Door (Highsmith), **Supp. V:** 178
People with the Dogs, The (Stead), **Supp. IV:** 473
People's Otherworld, The (Murray), **Supp. VII:** 270, 277–279
"People's Park and the Battle of Berkeley, The" (Lodge), **Supp. IV:** 374
Pepys, Samuel, **II:** 145, 195, 273, 274, 275, 278, **280–288,** 310
Per Amica Silentia Lunae (Yeats), **VI:** 209
"Perchance a Jealous Foe" (Ewart), **Supp. VII:** 42
Percy, Thomas, **III:** 336; **IV:** 28–29
Percy Bysshe Shelley (Swinburne), **V:** 333
"Perdita" (Warner), **Supp. VII:** 379
Perduta Gente (Reading), **VIII:** 265, 271–272, 273
Père Goriot (Balzac), **Supp. IV:** 238
Peregrine Pickle (Smollett), **III:** 149, 150, 152–153, 158
Perelandra (Lewis), **Supp. I:** 74; **Supp. III:** 249, 252, 253–254
Perennial Philosophy, The (Huxley), **VII:** xviii, 206
"Perfect" (MacDiarmid), **Supp. XII:** 215
Perfect Alibi, The (Milne), **Supp. V:** 310
"Perfect Critic, The" (Eliot), **VII:** 163
"Perfect Day" (Jamie), **Supp. XIV:** 138
Perfect Fool, The (Fuller), **Supp. VII:** 74, 75
Perfect Happiness (Churchill), **Supp. IV:** 181
Perfect Spy, A (le Carré), **Supp. II: 300–302,** 304, 305; **Retro. Supp. III:** 222–223
Perfect Wagnerite, The (Shaw), **VI:** 129
Perfect Woman, The (Butlin), **Supp. XVI:** 52–53
"Perfect World, A" (Motion), **Supp. VII:** 265, 266
Performing Flea (Wodehouse), **Supp. III:** 460
"Perhaps" (Thomas), **Supp. XII:** 287
Pericles (Shakespeare), **I:** 321–322; **II:** 48
Pericles and Aspasia (Landor), **IV:** xix, 89, 92, 94–95, 100
Pericles and Other Studies (Swinburne), **V:** 333
Perimeter: Caroline Blackwood at Greenham Common, On the (Blackwood), **Supp. IX:** 14–15
Peripatetic, The (Thelwall), **IV:** 103
Perkin Warbeck (Ford), **II:** 89, 92, 96, 97, 100
Perkin Warbeck (Shelley), **Supp. III:** 371
Perkins, Richard, **II:** 68
"Permanence of the Young Men, The" (Soutar), **Supp. XVI:** 254
"Permanent Cabaret" (Jamie), **Supp. XIV:** 131
Permanent Red: Essays in Seeing (Berger), **Supp. IV:** 79, 81
Permanent Way, The (Warner), **Supp. XI:** 294

Pernicious Consequences of the New Heresie of the Jesuites . . . . , The (tr. Evelyn), **II:** 287
Peronnik the Fool (Moore), **VI:** 99
Perpetual Curate, The (Oliphant), **Supp. X:** 213–216
Perry, Thomas Sergeant, **VI:** 24
Persephone in Hades (Pitter), **Supp. XIII:** 133, 139, 141, 142
Persian Boy, The (Renault), **Supp. IX:** 185–186
"Persian Eclogues" (Collins), **III:** 160, 164–165, 175
"Persian Passion Play, A" (Arnold), **V:** 216
"Person, The" (Traherne), **Supp. XI:** 268, 270
Personae (Pound), **Supp. III:** 398
Personal and Possessive (Thomas), **Supp. IV:** 490
Personal Heresy, The: A Controversy (Lewis), **Supp. III:** 249
Personal History, Adventures, Experience, and Observation of David Copperfield, The (Dickens), *see David Copperfield*
Personal Landscape (periodical), **VII:** 425, 443
Personal Places (Kinsella), **Supp. V:** 272
"Personal Problem" (Kavanagh), **Supp. VII:** 198
Personal Record, A (Conrad), **VI:** 134, 148; **Retro. Supp. II:** 69
Personal Reminiscences of Henry Irving (Stoker), **Supp. III:** 381
Persons from Porlock (MacNeice), **VII:** 408
Persse, Jocelyn, **VI:** 55
Persuasion (Austen), **IV:** xvii, 106–109, 111, 113, 115–120, 122; **Retro. Supp. II:** 12–13
"Perturbations of Uranus, The" (Fuller), **Supp. VII:** 73
"Pervasion of Rouge, The" (Beerbohm), **Supp. II:** 45
"Peshawar Vale Hunt, The" (Stallworthy), **Supp. X:** 295–296
"Pessimism in Literature" (Forster), **VI:** 410
Pesthouse, The (Crace), **Supp. XIV:** 17, 18, 19, 23–24, 30–31
Petals of Blood (Ngũgĩ), **VIII:** 212, 215, 220–221
Peter Bell (Wordsworth), **IV:** xviii 2
Peter Bell the Third (Shelley), **IV:** 203, 207
"Peter Grimes" (Crabbe), **III:** 283, 284–285
Peter Ibbetson (du Maurier), **Supp. III:** 134, 135, 136, 137, 138, 139
Peter Pan; or, The Boy Who Would Not Grow Up (Barrie), **Supp. III:** 2, **6–8**
"Peter Wentworth in Heaven" (Adcock), **Supp. XII:** 13
Petrarch's Seven Penitential Psalms (Chapman), **I:** 241–242
Peverel Papers, The: Nature Notes 1921–1927 (Thompson), **Supp. XV:** 286, 287, 288, 289, 290, 291

Peveril of the Peak (Scott), **IV:** xviii, 36, 37, 39
Pfeil, Fred, **Supp. IV:** 94
Phaedra (tr. Morgan), **Supp. IX:** 157
Phaedra (Seneca), **II:** 97
Phaedra's Love (Kane), **VIII:** 148, 149, 156
"Phaèthôn" (Meredith), **V:** 224
"Phallus in Wonderland" (Ewart), **Supp. VII:** 36
Phantasmagoria (Carroll), **V:** 270, 273
Phantasmagoria; or, Sketches of Life and Literature (Jewsbury), **Supp. XIV:** 149, 150–153, 156
Phantom Rickshaw, The (Kipling), **Retro. Supp. III:** 186
"Phantom Rickshaw, The" (Kipling), **Retro. Supp. III:** 186
"Phantom–Wooer, The" (Beddoes), **Supp. XI:** 30
Pharos, pseud. of E. M. Forster
Pharos and Pharillon (Forster), **VI:** 408
Pharsalia (tr. Marlowe), **I:** 276, 291
Phases of Faith (Newman), **V:** 208n
"Pheasant in a Cemetery" (Smith, I. C.), **Supp. IX:** 224
"Phebus and Cornide" (Gower), **I:** 55
Philadelphia, Here I Come! (Friel), **Supp. V:** 111, 116–118
Philanderer, The (Shaw), **VI:** 107, 109; **Retro. Supp. II:** 312
Philaster (Beaumont and Fletcher), **II:** 45, 46, **52–54,** 55, 65
Philby Conspiracy, The (Page, Leitch, and Knightley), **Supp. II:** 302, 303, 311–312
"Philemon and Baucis" (Gunn), **Retro. Supp. III:** 128
Philip (Thackeray), *see Adventures of Philip on His Way Through the World, The*
Philip Larkin (Motion), **Supp. VII:** 253
Philip Sparrow (Skelton), **I:** 84, 86–88
Philip Webb and His Work (Lethaby), **V:** 291, 292, 296, 306
Philips, Ambrose, **III:** 56
Philips, Katherine, **II:** 185
Phillips, Caryl, **Supp. V: 379–394**
Phillipps, Sir Thomas, **II:** 103
Phillips, Edward, **II:** 347
"Phillis is my only Joy" (Sedley), **II:** 265
"Phillis, let's shun the common Fate" (Sedley), **II:** 263
Phillpotts, Eden, **VI:** 266
"Philosopher, The" (Brontë), **V:** 134
"Philosopher and the Birds, The" (Murphy), **Supp. V:** 318
Philosopher's Pupil, The (Murdoch), **Supp. I:** 231, 232–233
Philosophical Discourse of Earth, An, Relating to . . . . Plants, &c. (Evelyn), **II:** 287
Philosophical Enquiry into the Origin of Our Ideas of the Sublime and Beautiful, A (Burke), *see On the Sublime and Beautiful*
Philosophical Essays Concerning Human Understanding (Hume), **Supp. III:** 238

Philosophical Investigation, A (Kerr), **Supp. XII:** 186, 187, 191–193, 195, 196
Philosophical Lectures of S. T. Coleridge, The (ed. Coburn), **IV:** 52, 56
"Philosophical View of Reform, A" (Shelley), **IV:** 199, 209; **Retro. Supp. I:** 254
"Philosophy of Furniture, The" (Hart), **Supp. XI:** 130
"Philosophy of Herodotus" (De Quincey), **IV:** 147–148
Philosophy of Melancholy, The (Peacock), **IV:** 158, 169
Philosophy of Nesessity, The (Bray), **V:** 188
Philosophy of Rhetoric (Richards), **Supp. II:** 416, 423
Philosophy of the Unconscious (Hartmann), **Supp. II:** 108
Phineas Finn (Trollope), **V:** 96, 98, 101, 102
Phineas Redux (Trollope), **V:** 96, 98, 101, 102
Phoebe Junior (Oliphant), **Supp. X:** 214, 217, 219
Phoenix (Abercrombie), **Supp. XVI:** 10–11
Phoenix (Storey), **Supp. I:** 408, 420
Phoenix, The, **Retro. Supp. II:** 303
Phoenix, The (Middleton), **II:** 21, 30
Phoenix and the Turtle, The (Shakespeare), **I:** 34, 313
"Phoenix Park" (Kinsella), **Supp. V:** 264
"Phoenix Rose Again, The" (Golding), **Supp. I:** 66
Phoenix Too Frequent, A (Fry), **Supp. III:** 194–195, 201–202
Phytologia: or, The Philosophy of Agriculture and Gardening (Darwin), **Supp. XVI:** 128
"Pioneers" (Jamie), **Supp. XIV:** 141
"Photograph, The" (Smith), **Retro. Supp. III:** 307
"Photograph of My Grandfather, A" (Burnside), **Supp. XIII:** 19
Photographs and Notebooks (Chatwin, B.), **Supp. IX:** 61–62
"Photograph of Emigrants" (Smith, I. C.), **Supp. IX:** 221
Physicists, The (Snow), **VII:** 339–340
Physico'Theology (Derham), **III:** 49
"Pibroch" (Hughes), **Supp. I:** 350
Picasso, Pablo, **Supp. IV:** 81, 87, 88
Piccolomini; or, The First Part of Wallenstein, The (Coleridge), **IV:** 55–56
Pickering, John, **I:** 213, 216–218
Pickwick Papers (Dickens), **V:** xix, 9, 42, 46–47, 48, 52, 59, 62, 71
Pico della Mirandola, **II:** 146; **V:** 344
"Pictor Ignotus" (Browning), **Retro. Supp. III:** 20
"Pictor Ignotus, Florence 15" A (Browning), **IV:** 356, 361; **Retro. Supp. II:** 27
"Pictorial Rhapsody, A" (Thackeray), **V:** 37
Picture, The (Massinger), **Supp. XI:** 184
Picture and Text (James), **VI:** 46, 67

"Picture of a Nativity" (Hill), **Supp. V:** 186
Picture of Dorian Gray, The (Wilde), **III:** 334, 345; **V:** xxv, 339, 399, 410–411, 417, 419; **Retro. Supp. II:** 368
"Picture of Little T. C. in a Prospect of Flowers, The" (Marvell), **II:** 211, 215
Picture of Palermo (tr. Robinson), **Supp. XIII:** 213
"Picture This" (Motion), **Supp. VII:** 266
Picturegoers, The (Lodge), **Supp. IV:** 364, 367–368, 369, 371, 372, 381, 382
"Pictures" (Kelman), **Supp. V:** 250
Pictures at an Exhibition (Thomas), **Supp. IV:** 487–488
"Pictures from a Japanese Printmaker" (Redgrove), **Supp. VI:** 234
"Pictures from an Ecclesiastical Furnisher's" (Redgrove), **Supp. VI:** 234
Pictures from Italy (Dickens), **V:** 71
Pictures in the Hallway (O'Casey), **VII:** 9, 12
Pictures of Perfection (Hill, R.), **Supp. IX:** 121, 122–123
Picturesque Landscape and English Romantic Poetry (Watson), **IV:** 26
"Piece of Cake, A" (Dahl), **Supp. IV:** 208, 209
Piece of the Night, A (Roberts), **Supp. XV:** 259, 260, 263–264, 265, 266
"Pied Beauty" (Hopkins), **V:** 367; **Retro. Supp. II:** 196
"Pied Piper of Hamelin, The" (Browning), **IV:** 356, 367; **Retro. Supp. III:** 25
Pied Piper of Lovers (Durrell), **Supp. I:** 95; **Retro. Supp. III:** 83, 87
"Pipistrelles" (Jamie), **Supp. XIV:** 143
"Pier Bar" (Murphy), **Supp. V:** 328
Pier Glass, The (Graves), **VII:** 263–264
Pierrot mon ami (Queneau), **Supp. I:** 220
Piers Plowman (Langland), **I:** 1–18
Pietà (Thomas), **Supp. XII:** 284, 285
"Pietà" (Thomas), **Supp. XII:** 285
Pietrkiewicz, Jerzy, **Supp. IV:** 98
"Piffingcap" (Coppard), **VIII:** 88, 92
"Pig"(Dahl), **Supp. IV:** 221
Pig, The (Lessing), **Supp. I:** 240
Pig Earth (Berger), **Supp. IV:** 90, 92, 93
Pigeon, The (Galsworthy), **VI:** 271, 274, 287–288
Pigeon Pie (Mitford), **Supp. X:** 156–157
"Pigeons" (Reid), **Supp. VII:** 329
"Pigs" (Gunesekera), **Supp. X:** 87
"Pigs" (Murray), **Supp. VII:** 282
Pigs Have Wings (Wodehouse), **Supp. III:** 453–454, 458–459, 462
"Pike, The" (Blunden), **Supp. XI:** 42, 43
Pilgrim, The (Fletcher), **II:** 65
Pilgrim, The (Vanbrugh), **II:** 289, 305, 325, 336
"Pilgrim Fathers" (Adcock), **Supp. XII:** 13
Pilgrim to Compostella, The (Southey), **IV:** 71
"Pilgrimage" (Clarke), **Supp. XV:** 21–22
Pilgrimage (Richardson), **Supp. XIII:** 179, 180, 181–188, 190–191, 192

Pilgrimage and Other Poems (Clarke), **Supp. XV:** 20–22, 23, 26
"Pilgrimage of Pleasure, The" (Swinburne), **V:** 332
Pilgrimage of the Life of Man (Lydgate), **I:** 57
"Pilgrimages" (Thomas), **Supp. XII:** 288
Pilgrims of Hope (Morris), **V:** 301, 306
Pilgrim's Progress, The (Bunyan), **I:** 16, 57; **II:** 240, 241, 243, 244, **245–250,** 253; **III:** 82; **V:** 27; **Supp. IV:** 242
Pilgrim's Progress (Hill, R.), **Supp. IX:** 121–122
Pilgrim's Regress, The (Lewis), **Supp. III:** 249, **250–252,** 264
Pilkington, John, **Supp. IV:** 164
"Pillar of the Cloud" (Newman), see "Lead, Kindly Light"
"Pillar of the Community, A" (Kinsella), **Supp. V:** 261
Pillars of Society, The (Ibsen), **V:** xxiv, 414
"Pillow hot . . . , The" (tr. McKane), **Supp. IV:** 494
"Pillow hot . . . , The" (tr. Thomas), **Supp. IV:** 494
Pillowman, The (McDonagh), **Supp. XII:** 233–234, 238, 241, 243–246
Pinch of Snuff, A (Hill, R.), **Supp. IX:** 114
Pincher Martin (Golding), **Supp. I:** 67, 72–75, 76, 77, 83, 218n; **Retro. Supp. I:** 97
Pindar, **II:** 198–199; **IV:** 95, 316
Pindaric Ode, Humbly Offer'd to the King . . . , A (Congreve), **II:** 350
"Pindaric Poem to the Reverend Doctor Burnet, A" (Behn), **Supp. III:** 41; **Retro. Supp. III:** 4
Pindarique Ode on the victorious Progress of Her Majesties Arms, A (Congreve), **II:** 350
Pindarique Odes (Cowley), **II:** 197, 199, 202
"Pineapple and the Bee, The" (Cowper), **Retro. Supp. III:** 47
Pinero, Arthur Wing, **V:** 413; **VI:** 269, 368
Pink Furniture (Coppard), **VIII:** 91, 97
Pinter, Harold, **Supp. I: 367–382; Supp. IV:** 180, 290, 390, 437, 456; **Retro. Supp. I: 215–228**
Pinter Problem, The (Quigley), **Retro. Supp. I:** 227
Pioneer, **Retro. Supp. III:** 186, 187
"Pioneers, The" (Plomer), **Supp. XI:** 213
Piozzi, Hester Lynch, **III:** 134, 246
Pipelines (Bevan and Galloway), **Supp. XII:** 117
Pippa Passes (Browning), **IV:** 356, 362–363, 370, 373; **Retro. Supp. II:** 20–21; **Retro. Supp. III:** 20, 22
Piranesi Giovanni Battista, **III:** 325, 338
Pirate, The (Scott), **IV:** 36, 39
"Pirate and the Apothecary, The" (Stevenson), **V:** 391
"Pisgah" (Nicholson), **Supp. VI: 219**
"Pit and the Pendulum, The" (Poe), **III:** 339
Pit Strike (Sillitoe), **Supp. V:** 411

Pithy, Pleasant, and Profitable Works of John Skelton, The (ed. Stow), **I:** 94
Pitter, Ruth, **Supp. XIII: 131–147**
Pitter on Cats (Pitter), **Supp. XIII:** 135, 144
"Pity" (Collins), **III:** 166
"Pity of It, The" (Hardy), **Retro. Supp. I:** 120
"Pixie" (Brathwaite), **Supp. XII:** 42
Pizarro (Sheridan), **III: 267–270**
Place at Whitton, A (Keneally), **Supp. IV:** 345
"Place in Tuscany, A" (Malouf), **Supp. XII:** 220
"Place of Friendship in Greek Life and Thought, The" (Carpenter), **Supp. XIII:** 44
Place of the Lion, The (Williams, C. W. S.), **Supp. IX:** 281, 284
"Place of the Uranian in Society, The" (Carpenter), **Supp. XIII:** 43, 44
Place Where Souls Are Born: A Journey to the Southwest, The (Keneally), **Supp. IV:** 343, 347, 357–358
Place with the Pigs, A (Fugard), **Supp. XV:** 104
"Placeless Heaven, The" (Heaney), **Supp. II:** 280; **Retro. Supp. I:** 131
Places (Morris, J.), **Supp. X:** 172, 183
"Places, Loved Ones" (Larkin), **Supp. I:** 278
Plain Man and His Plain Wife, The (Bennett), **VI:** 264, 267
Plain Speaker, The (Hazlitt), **IV:** 131, 134, 136, 140
Plain Tales from the Hills (Kipling), **VI:** 168, 204; **Retro. Supp. III:** 183, 184–186, 197
Plain' Dealer, The (Wycherley), **II:** 308, **318–320**, 321, 322, 343
Plaine Mans Path' Way to Heaven, The (Dent), **II:** 241, 246
"Plains, The" (Fuller), **VII:** 430; **Supp. VII:** 69
Plains of Cement, The (Hamilton), **Supp. XVI:** 182, 185–186
"Plan, The" (O'Brien), **Supp. V:** 340
Plan for the Conduct of Female Education, in Boarding Schools (Darwin), **Supp. XVI:** 128, 131–132
Plan of a Dictionary of the English Language, The (Johnson), **III:** 113, 121; see also *Dictionary of the English Language, A*
Plan of a Novel . . . With Opinions on A Mansfield Park"and AEmma" . . . (Austen), **IV:** 112, 122
Plan of the English Commerce, A (Defoe), **III:** 14
Planes of Bedford Square, The (Plomer), **Supp. XI:** 222
"Planetist" (Crawford), **Supp. XI:** 79
"Plantations, The" (Scupham), **Supp. XIII:** 224
"Planter of Malata, The" (Conrad), **VI:** 148
"Plas–yn–Rhiw" (Thomas), **Supp. XII:** 290
Plath, Sylvia, **Supp. I:** 346, 350; **Supp. IV:** 252, 430; **Retro. Supp. II:** 199, 200–201, 216–218

Platinum Logic (Parsons), **Supp. XV:** 227, 228, 229, 234, 238
Plato, **IV:** 47–48, 54; **V:** 339; **Supp. III:** 125; **Supp. IV:** 13
Plato and Platonism (Pater), **V:** 339, 355, 356
Plato Papers: A Novel, The (Ackroyd), **Supp. VI:** 4, 11, 13
Plato Papers: A Prophesy, The (Ackroyd), **Supp. VI:** 13
"Platonic Blow, by Miss Oral" (Auden), **Retro. Supp. I:** 12
"Platonic Ideas and Heredity" (Carpenter), **Supp. XIII:** 46
"Platonic Love" (Cowley), **II:** 197
Play (Beckett), **Supp. I:** 46, 58; **Retro. Supp. I:** 27
Play from Romania, A, see Mad Forest
Playboy of the Western World, The (Synge), **VI:** xiv, 308, 309–310, 312–313, 316; **Retro. Supp. I:** 291, 298–300
Player of Games, The (Banks), **Supp. XI:** 1, 9, 10
"Players, The" (Davies), **Supp. XI:** 100–101
Playfellow, The (Martineau), **Supp. XV:** 185
Playground of Europe, The (Stephen), **V:** 282, 289
Playing Away (Phillips), **Supp. V:** 380
"Playing with Terror" (Ricks), **Supp. IV:** 398
Playland, and Other Words (Fugard), **Supp. XV:** 104, 111, 112–113
Playmaker, The (Keneally), **Supp. IV:** 346
"Plays" (Landor), **IV:** 98
Plays and Poems of Thomas Lovell Beddoes (Beddoes), **Supp. XI:** 18, 21, 22, 23, 24, 26, 28–29, 30
Plays for England (Osborne), **Supp. I:** 335
Plays for Puritans (Shaw), **VI:** 109
Plays of Hannah Cowley, The (Cowley), **Supp. XVI:** 109, 123
Plays of William Shakespeare, The (ed. Johnson), **III:** 115–117, 121; **Retro. Supp. I:** 138, 144
Plays: One (Arden), **Supp. II:** 30
Plays: Pleasant and Unpleasant (Shaw), **VI:** ix, 104, **107–112**; **Retro. Supp. II:** 313–315
Plaza de Toros, The (Scott), **Supp. I:** 266
Plea for Justice, A (Russell), **VIII:** 289
"Poem" (Armitage), **VIII:** 5
Plea of the Midsummer Fairies, The (Hood), **IV:** 253, 255, 261, 267
Pleasant Notes upon Don Quixote (Gayton), **I:** 279
"Pleasaunce" (Dutton), **Supp. XII:** 95
"Please Baby Don't Cry" (Blackwood), **Supp. IX:** 9
"Please Identify Yourself" (Adcock), **Supp. XII:** 6
Pleasure (Waugh), **Supp. VI:** 270
Pleasure Dome, The (Greene), **Supp. I:** 3, 9

"Pleasure Island" (Auden), **Retro. Supp. I:** 12
Pleasure of Poetry, The (Sitwell), **VII:** 129–130
Pleasure of Reading, The (Fraser), **Supp. V:** 20
"Pleasure Principle, The" (Larkin), **Retro. Supp. III:** 200
Pleasure Steamers, The (Motion), **Supp. VII:** 253–255, 257
Pleasures of a Tangled Life (Morris, J.), **Supp. X:** 183
"Pleasures of a Technological University, The" (Morgan, E.), **Supp. IX:** 158–159
Pleasures of the Flesh (Ewart), **Supp. VII:** 38–39
Pleasures of War, The (Maitland), **Supp. XI:** 163
Plebeian (periodical), **III:** 51, 53
Pléiade, **I:** 170
Plenty (Hare), **Supp. IV:** 282, 286–287, 293
Plomer, William, **Supp. XI: 209–225**
Plot Discovered, The (Coleridge), **IV:** 56
Plot Succeeds, The: A Poetic Pantomime (Clarke), **Supp. XV:** 25
Plotinus, **III:** 291
Plotting and Writing Suspense Fiction (Highsmith), **Supp. V:** 167, 171, 174, 177
Plough, The (Walker), **V:** 377
Plough and the Stars, The (O'Casey), **VI:** 214; **VII:** xviii, 5–6
"Ploughland" (Scupham), **Supp. XIII:** 219
Ploughman and Other Poems (Kavanagh), **Supp. VII:** 187–188
Ploughman, and Other Poems, A (White), **Supp. I:** 130
Ploughman's Lunch, The (McEwan), **Supp. IV:** 389, 390, 399–400
Plumb, Sir John Harold, **IV:** 290; **VI:** xv, xxxiv, 391n
Plumed Serpent, The (Lawrence), **VII:** 87–88, 91, **109–110**, 123; **Retro. Supp. II:** 231
Plutarch, **II:** 185
Plutarch's Lives (tr. Goldsmith), **III:** 191
Plutarch's Lives. The translation called Dryden's . . . (ed. Clough), **V:** 157, 170
Plutus, The God of Riches (tr. Fielding), **III:** 105
Plymley, Peter, see Smith, Sydney
PN Review (periodical), **Supp. IV:** 256; **Supp. XIII:** 223
Pocket Guide to Traditional Irish Music (Carson), **Supp. XIII:** 61
Podro, Joshua, **VII:** 262
Poe, Edgar Allan, **III:** 329, 333, 334, 338–339, 340, 343, 345; **IV:** 311, 319; **V:** xvi, xx–xxi; **VI:** 371
"Poem" (Cornford), **Supp. XIII:** 91–92
"Poem" (Welch), **Supp. IX:** 269–270
"Poem About a Ball in the Nineteenth Century" (Empson), **Supp. II:** 180–181, 183
"Poem about Poems About Vietnam, A" (Stallworthy), **Supp. X:** 294–295, 302

Poem Address'd to the Quidnunc's, at St. James's Coffee-House London, A. Occasion'd by the Death of the Duke of Orleans (Arbuthnot), **Supp. XVI:** 26
"Poem as Abstract" (Davie), **Supp. VI:** 106
"Poem by the Boy Outside the Fire Station" (Armitage), **VIII:** 4
"Poem Composed in Santa Barbara" (Cope), **VIII:** 78
"Poem Feigned to Have Been Written by an Electronic Brain" (Wain), **Supp. XVI:** 306
"Poem from the North," (Keyes), **VII:** 439
"Poem for My Father" (Reid), **Supp. VII:** 325
"Poem in October" (Thomas), **Supp. I:** 177, 178–179; **Retro. Supp. III:** 343, 34
Poem in St. James's Park, A (Waller), **II:** 238
"Poem in Seven Books, A" (Blake), **Retro. Supp. I:** 37
"Poem in Winter" (Jennings), **Supp. V:** 213–214
"Poem of Lewis" (Smith, I. C.), **Supp. IX:** 211
"Poem of the Midway" (Thomas), **Supp. IV:** 493
"Poem on His Birthday" (Thomas), **Supp. I:** 179; **Retro. Supp. III:** 346, 347, 349
Poem on the Late Civil War, A (Cowley), **II:** 202
"Poem on the Theme of Humour, A" (Cope), **VIII:** 81
Poem Sacred to the Memory of Sir Isaac Newton, A (Thomson), **Supp. III:** 411, 418–419
"Poem Upon the Death of O. C., A" (Marvell), **II:** 205, 211
"Poem with the Answer, A" (Suckling), **II:** 228
"Poem Without a Main Verb" (Wain), **Supp. XVI:** 306
Poemata et Epigrammata, . . . (Crashaw), **II:** 201
Poemata et inscriptiones (Landor), **IV:** 100
Poems [1853] (Arnold), **V:** xxi, 165, 209, 216
Poems [1854] (Arnold), **V:** 216
Poems [1855] (Arnold), **V:** 216
Poems [1857] (Arnold), **V:** 216
Poems (Bridges), **VI:** 83
Poems (Brooke), **Supp. III:** 51–53
Poems [1844] (Browning), **IV:** xx, 311, 313–314, 321, 356
Poems [1850] (Browning), **IV:** 311, 321
Poems (Byron), **IV:** 192
Poems (Carew), **II:** 238
Poems (Caudwell), **Supp. IX:** 33, 35
Poems (Clough), **V:** 170
Poems (Cornford), **VIII:** 102, 103
Poems (Cowley), **II:** 194, 198, 199, 202
Poems (Cowper), **Retro. Supp. III:** 35, 36, 37, 38, 39, 41, 42, 43, 44, 45, 46, 47, 48

Poems (Crabbe), **III:** 286
Poems (Eliot), **VII:** 146, 150
Poems (Empson), **Supp. II:** 180
Poems (Gay), **III:** 55
Poems (Golding), **Supp. I:** 66
"Poems, 1912–13" (Hardy), **Retro. Supp. I:** 117
Poems (Hood), **IV:** 252, 261, 266
Poems (Jennings), **Supp. V:** 208
Poems (Keats), **IV:** xvii, 211, 213–214, 216, 235; **Retro. Supp. I:** 183, 187–188
Poems (Kinsella), **Supp. V:** 260
Poems (Lovell and Southey), **IV:** 71
Poems (Meredith), **V:** xxi, 219, 234
Poems (Robinson), **Supp. XIII:** 199, 202, 205, 206, 207
Poems (C. Rossetti), **V:** 260
Poems [1870] (D. G. Rossetti), **V:** xxiii, 237, 238, 245
Poems [1873] (D. G. Rossetti), **V:** 245
Poems [1881] (D. G. Rossetti), **V:** 238, 245
Poems (Ruskin), **V:** 184
Poems (Sassoon), **VI:** 429
Poems (Southey), **IV:** 71
Poems (Spender), **Supp. II:** 483, 486–487
Poems [1833] (Tennyson), **IV:** 326, 329, 338; **Retro. Supp. III:** 321, 322–323
Poems [1842] (Tennyson), **IV:** xx, 326, 333–334, 335, 338; **Retro. Supp. III:** 320, 327
Poems (Thompson), **V:** 439, 451
Poems (Waller), **II:** 238
Poems (Wilde), **V:** 401–402, 419; **Retro. Supp. II:** 361–362
Poems, The (Landor), **IV:** xvi, 99
Poems, The (Swift), **III:** 15n, 35
Poems, The (Thomas), **Supp. I:** 170
Poems Against Economics (Murray), **Supp. VII:** 270, 273–275
Poems and Ballads (Swinburne), **V:** xxiii, 309, 310, 313, **314–321**, 327, 330, 332
"Poems and Ballads of Goethe" (Clough), **V:** 170
Poems and Ballads: Second Series (Swinburne), **V:** xxiv, 314, 327, 332
Poems and Ballads: Third Series (Swinburne), **V:** 332
Poems and Letters of Bernard Barton (ed. FitzGerald), **IV:** 343–344, 353
Poems and Lyrics of the Joy of Earth (Meredith), **V:** 221, 224, 234
Poems and Melodramas (Davie), **Supp. VI:** 113
Poems and Metrical Tales (Southey), **IV:** 71
Poems and Prose Remains of A. H. Clough, The (ed. Clough and Symonds), **V:** 159, 170
Poems and Songs, The (Burns), **III:** 310n, 322
Poems and Songs (Ewart), **Supp. VII:** 34, 36–37
Poems and Translations (Kinsella), **Supp. V:** 264
Poems Before Congress (Browning), **IV:** 312, 315, 321

Poems by Alfred, Lord Tennyson (Lear), **V:** 78, 87
Poems by Charles Kingsley (Kingsley), **Supp. XVI:** 194, 204
Poems by Currer, Ellis and Acton Bell (Brontës), **V:** xx, 131–134, 151
Poems by John Clare (Clare), **Supp. XI:** 63
Poems by the Author of the Growth of Love (Bridges), **VI:** 83
Poems by the Way (Morris), **V:** 306
Poems by Two Brothers (Tennyson and Tennyson), **IV:** 337–338; **Retro. Supp. III:** 319
Poems, Centuries, and Three Thanksgivings (Traherne), **Supp. XI:** 263–264, 265, 266, 267, 268, 269, 270, 271, 272, 273, 274, 275, 276, 278
Poems Chiefly in the Scottish Dialect (Burns), **III:** 315
Poems, Chiefly Lyrical (Tennyson), **IV:** xix, 326, 329, 331, 338; **Retro. Supp. III:** 320, 321, 322, 327, 331
Poems Chiefly of Early and Late Years (Wordsworth), **IV:** xx, 25
Poems, Descriptive of Rural Life and Scenery (Clare), **Supp. XI:** 49, 54–55
Poems, Elegies, Paradoxes, and Sonnets (King), **Supp. VI:** 162
"Poems for Angus" (MacCaig), **Supp. VI:** 193
Poems for Donalda (Smith, I. C.), **Supp. IX:** 217
Poems for Young Ladies (Goldsmith), **III:** 191
Poems from Centre City (Kinsella), **Supp. V:** 272
Poems from the Arabic and Persian (Landor), **IV:** 99
"Poems from the Diaries" (Soutar), **Supp. XVI:** 255
Poems from the Russian (Cornford), **VIII:** 110–111
Poems from Villon, and Other Fragments (Swinburne), **V:** 333
Poems in Prose (Wilde), **Retro. Supp. II:** 371
Poems in Scots (Soutar), **Supp. XVI:** 251–252, 256, 258
Poems in Scots and English (Soutar), **Supp. XVI:** 256
Poems, in Two Volumes (Wordsworth), **IV:** 22, 24
Poems 1926–1966 (Pitter), **Supp. XIII:** 136, 145–146
Poems, 1930 (Auden), **VII:** xix
Poems 1938–1945 (Graves), **VII:** 267–268
Poems, 1943–1947 (Day Lewis), **Supp. III:** 118, 128
Poems 1950 (Bunting), **Supp. VII:** 5, 13
Poems 1960–2000 (Adcock), **Supp. XII:** 2, 11, 13, 14–15
Poems 1962–1978 (Mahon), **Supp. VI:** 173–174
Poems of Conformity (Williams, C. W. S.), **Supp. IX:** 274
Poems of Dedication (Spender), **Supp. II:** 489, 490

POEM–POET

Poems of Edmund Blunden, The (Blunden), **Supp. XI:** 36, 37, 44
Poems of Felicity (Traherne), **II:** 191, 202; **Supp. XI:** 266
Poems of Henry Vaughan, Silurist, The (ed. Chambers), **II:** 187
Poems of John Keats, The (ed. Allott), **IV:** 223n 224, 234–235
Poems of Lascelles Abercrombie, The (Abercrombie), **Supp. XVI:** 2, 3, 5, 7, 8, 9, 10, 11
"Poems of 1912–13" (Hardy), **VI:** 14
Poems of Ossian, The (Macpherson), **III:** 336; **VIII:** 180, 181, 182, 183, 184, 185, 187, 188, 190, 191, 192, 193, 194
Poems of Tennyson, The (Tennyson), **Retro. Supp. III:** 320, 321, 322, 323, 324, 325, 326, 327, 328, 329
Poems of the War and After (Brittain), **Supp. X:** 41
Poems of William Cowper, The (Cowper), **Retro. Supp. III:** 35
Poems of William Dunbar, The (Dunbar), **VIII:** 118–119
Poems of William Soutar (Soutar), **Supp. XVI:** 242, 245, 246, 248, 250, 251, 252, 253, 254–255, 257, 258
Poems of William Soutar: A New Selection (Soutar), **Supp. XVI:** 256
Poems of Wit and Humour (Hood), **IV:** 257, 266
Poems on His Domestic Circumstances (Byron), **IV:** 192
Poems on Several Occasions (Haywood), **Supp. XII:** 135
Poems on the Death of Priscilla Farmer (Lloyd and Lamb), **IV:** 78, 85
Poems on the Theatre (Brecht), **Supp. IV:** 87
Poems on Various Occasions (Byron), **IV:** 192
Poems on Various Subjects (Coleridge), **IV:** 43, 55, 78, 85
Poems Original and Translated (Byron), **IV:** 192
Poems Translated from the French of Madame de la Mothe Guion (tr. Cowper), **III:** 220
Poems upon Several Occasions: With a Voyage to the Island of Love (Behn), **Supp. III:** 36; **Retro. Supp. III:** 5–6, 8
Poems, with the Tenth Satyre of Juvenal Englished (Vaughan), **II:** 184–185, 201
"Poet, The" (Hulme), **Supp. VI:** 135
"Poet, The" (Sillitoe), **Supp. V:** 425
Poet and Dancer (Jhabvala), **Supp. V:** 223, 234, 235
"Poet Hood, The" (Blunden), **IV:** 267
Poet in the Imaginary Museum, The (Davie), **Supp. VI:** 115, 117
"Poet in the Imaginary Museum, The" (Davie), **Supp. VI:** 115
poet laureateship, **IV:** 61, 310, 311, 324
"Poet on the Island, The" (Murphy), **Supp. V:** 318
"Poet O'Rahilly, The" (Kinsella), **Supp. V:** 263

"Poet, The Reader and The Citizen, The" (Constantine), **Supp. XV:** 72
"Poet with Sea Horse" (Reid), **Supp. VII:** 328
Poetaster (Jonson), **I:** 339, 340; **Retro. Supp. I:** 158
"Poetic Diction in English" (Bridges), **VI:** 73
Poetic Image, The (Day Lewis), **Supp. III:** 118
"Poetic Imagination, The" (Muir), **Supp. VI:** 202–203
Poetic Mirror, The (Hogg), **Supp. X:** 109–110
Poetic Unreason (Graves), **VII:** 257, 260
Poetical Blossomes (Cowley), **II:** 194, 202
Poetical Calendar (Fawkes and Woty), **III:** 170n
"Poetical Character, The" (Collins), **III:** 166, 168
"Poetical Epistle to Lady Austen, A" (Cowper), **Retro. Supp. III:** 41
Poetical Fragments (Swinburne), **V:** 333
Poetical Pieces (Lamb), **IV:** 74
Poetical Register (Jacob), **II:** 348
Poetical Sketches (Blake), **III:** 289, 290; **Retro. Supp. I:** 33–34
"Poetical Version of a Letter, from Jacob Behmen, to a Friend, A" (Byrom), **Supp. XVI:** 76
Poetical Works, The, . . . (Traherne), **II:** 201–202
Poetical Works, The (Southey), **IV:** 71
Poetical Works (Bridges), **VI:** 83
Poetical Works of George Crabbe, The (ed. Carlyle and Carlyle), **III:** 272n
Poetical Works of George Meredith, The (ed. Trevelyan), **V:** 223, 234
Poetical Works of Gray and Collins, The (ed. Poole and Stone), **III:** 161n
Poetical Works of John Gay, The (ed. Faber), **III:** 66, 67
Poetical Works of the Late Mrs. Mary Robinson, The (Robinson), **Supp. XIII:** 199, 202, 204, 206, 207, 213
"Poetics of Sex, The" (Winterson), **Supp. IV:** 547, 551–552, 553
Poetria nova (Geoffroy of Vinsauf), **I:** 59
"Poetry"[broadcast] (Bridges), **VI:** 83
"Poetry" (Moore), **IV:** 6
Poetry and Belief (Wallace-Crabbe), **VIII:** 316, 319
Poetry and Contemporary Speech (Abercrombie), **Supp. XVI:** 5, 13
"Poetry and the Other Modern Arts" (Davie), **Supp. VI:** 115–116
Poetry and Philosophy of George Meredith, The (Trevelyan), **VI:** 383
Poetry and Prose (ed. Sparrow), **VI:** 83
"Poetry and Striptease" (Thomas), **Supp. IV:** 491
"Poetry as 'Menace' and 'Atonement' " (Hill), **Retro. Supp. III:** 142
Poetry at Present (Williams, C. W. S.), **Supp. IX:** 277
Poetry by the Author of Gebir (Landor), **IV:** 99
Poetry for Children (Lamb and Lamb), **IV:** 85

Poetry for Supper (Thomas), **Supp. XII:** 284
"Poetry in Public" (Motion), **Supp. VII:** 265
Poetry in the Making (Hughes), **Supp. I:** 347
Poetry Northwest, **Supp. XIII:** 136
"Poetry of a Root-Crop, The" (Kingsley), **Supp. XVI:** 205
Poetry of Anna Matilda, The: Containing "A Tale for Jealousy," "The Funeral," Her Correspondence with Delia Crusca, and Several Other Poetical Pieces (Cowley), **Supp. XVI:** 122–123
Poetry of Browning, The (Drew), **IV:** 375
"Poetry of Departures" (Larkin), **Supp. I:** 277, 278–279
Poetry of Edward Thomas, The (Motion), **Supp. VII:** 252, 253, 258, 263
Poetry of Ezra Pound, The (Kenner), **VI:** 333
"Poetry of Friendship Among Greeks and Romans" (Carpenter), **Supp. XIII:** 44
Poetry of Meditation, The (Martz), **V:** 366, 382
Poetry of Nonsense, The (Cammaerts), **V:** 262, 274
"Poetry of Pope, The" (De Quincey), **IV:** 146
"Poetry of Protest, A" (Davie), **Supp. VI:** 116
Poetry of the First World War (Hibberd), **VI:** 460
"Poetry of the Present" (Constantine), **Supp. XV:** 71
Poetry of Thomas Hardy, The (Day Lewis), **VI:** 21
"Poetry of W. B. Yeats, The" (Eliot), **VI:** 207n, 223
Poetry of W. B. Yeats, The (MacNeice), **VII:** 404
"Poetry of Wordsworth, The" (De Quincey), **IV:** 146, 148
"Poetry Perpetuates the Poet" (Herrick), **II:** 115
Poetry Primer, A (Constantine), **Supp. XV:** 80
Poets and Poetry of Munster, The (tr. Mangan), **Supp. XIII:** 119, 129
Poet's Calendar, A (Davies), **Supp. XI:** 101
"Poets Call on the Goddess Echo, The" (Scupham), **Supp. XIII:** 224
"Poet's Epitaph, A" (Davies), **Supp. XI:** 95–96
"Poet'Scholar, The" (Davie), **Supp. VI:** 105
"Poets Lie where they Fell, The" (Mahon), **Supp. VI:** 167
"Poet's Mind, A" (Tennyson), **Retro. Supp. III:** 321
Poet's Notebook, A (Sitwell), **VII:** 127, 139
Poets of the First World War (Stallworthy), **VI:** 441
Poet's Pilgrimage, A (Davies), **Supp. XI:** 89–91
"Poet's Pilgrimage to Waterloo, The" (Southey), **IV:** 66, 71

441

Poet's Polemic, A: Otro Mundo Es Posible: Poetry, Dissidence and Reality TV (Burnside), **Supp. XIII:** 31
Poet's Tongue, The (Auden and Garrett), **Supp. IV:** 256; **Retro. Supp. I:** 6–7
"Poet's Vow, The" (Browning), **IV:** 313
"Poggio" (Durrell), **Supp. I:** 126
Point Counter Point (Huxley), **VII:** xviii, 201, 202–204
"Point of It, The" (Forster), **V:** 208
Point Valaine (Coward), **Supp. II:** 152
Pointed Roofs (Richardson), **Supp. XIII:** 179, 181–182, 187–188, 189, 190
Points of View (Maugham), **VI:** 374, 377
Pointz Hall (Woolf), **Retro. Supp. I:** 308
"Poison" (Dahl), **Supp. IV:** 206, 215
Poisoned Lands, and Other Poems (Montague), **Supp. XV:** 213
Pol Pot, **Supp. IV:** 247
Polanski, Roman, **III:** 343
Polaris (Weldon), **Supp. IV:** 521
"Police, The: Seven Voices" (Murray), **Supp. VII:** 276
Polidori, John, **III:** 329, 334, 338; **Supp. III:** 385
Polite Conversations (Swift), **III:** 36
Political Economy of Art, The (Ruskin), **V:** 184
Political Essays (Hazlitt), **IV:** 129, 139
Political History of the Devil, The (Defoe), **III:** 5, 14
Political Justice (Godwin), **IV:** 43
"Political Kiss, A" (Adcock), **Supp. XII:** 13
"Political Poem" (Ewart), **Supp. VII:** 36
Political Romance, A (Sterne), **III:** 127, 135
Political Situation, The (Schreiner), **Supp. I:** 453
Political Thought in England, 1848–1914 (Walker), **IV:** 304
Politicks of Laurence Sterne, The (Curtis), **III:** 127n
"Politics" (Durrell), **Supp. I:** 124
"Politics and the English Language" (Orwell), **Supp. III:** 107; **Supp. IV:** 455
Politics for the People, **Supp. XVI:** 203
"Politics of King Lear, The" (Muir), **Supp. VI:** 202
"Politics of Mecca, The" (Lawrence), **Supp. II:** 286–287
"Politics vs. Literature" (Orwell), **VII:** 273, 282
Poliziano, Angelo, **I:** 240
Poll Degree from a Third Point of View, The (Stephen), **V:** 289
Pollock, Jackson, **Supp. IV:** 80
Polly (Gay), **III:** 55, 65–67
"Polonius" (FitzGerald), **IV:** 353
Polonius: A Collection of Wise Saws and Modern Instances (FitzGerald), **IV:** 344, 353
Polychronicon (Higden), **I:** 22
Polychronicon (tr. Trevisa), **Supp. IX:** 243–252, 256–259
Polysyllabic Spree, The (Hornby), **Supp. XV:** 145
"Pomegranates of Patmos, The" (Harrison), **Supp. V:** 160

Pomes Penyeach (Joyce), **VII:** 42; **Retro. Supp. III:** 168
Pomona (Evelyn), **II:** 287
Pompeii (Macaulay), **IV:** 290
"Pompeii" (Mangan), **Supp. XIII:** 122
Pompey the Great (tr. Dorset et al.), **II:** 270, 271
"Pond, The" (Byrom), **Supp. XVI:** 76
"Ponte di Paradiso, The" (Symonds), **Supp. XIV:** 252
Pooh Perplex: A Freshman Casebook (Crews), **Supp. V:** 311
Poole, A. L., **III:** 161n
Poole, Thomas, **IV:** 42, 43, 51
"Poor" (Raine), **Supp. XIII:** 168
Poor Clare (Hartley), **Supp. VII:** 132
"Poor Ghost" (Beer), **Supp. XIV:** 6
"Poor Koko" (Fowles), **Supp. I:** 303
"Poor Man, The" (Coppard), **VIII:** 94
"Poor Man and the Lady, The" (Hardy), **VI:** 2, 20; **Retro. Supp. I:** 112
"Poor Man Escapes, A" (Fleming), **Supp. XIV:** 85
"Poor Man's Guide to Southern Tuscany, A" (Malouf), **Supp. XII:** 220
Poor Man's Plea, The (Defoe), **III:** 2, 12; **Retro. Supp. I:** 74–75
"Poor Marguerite" (Robinson), **Supp. XIII:** 212
"Poor Mary" (Warner), **Supp. VII:** 380
"Poor Mathias" (Arnold), **V:** 207
Poor Miss Finch (Collins), **Supp. VI:** 102–103
Poor Mouth, The (O'Nolan), **Supp. II:** 333–335
"Poor Richard" (James), **VI:** 69
Poor Things (Gray, A.), **Supp. IX:** 80, 85–87
Poor Tom (Muir), **Supp. VI:** 198
Pope, Alexander, **I:** 326, 328; **II:** 195–197, 236, 259, 261, 263, 298, 308–309, 311, 321, 332, 335, 344; **III:** 1, 19, 20, 33, 46, 50, 54, 56, 60, 62, 68–79, 95, 118, 167n, 234, 278, 280–282, 288; **IV:** 104, 182, 187, 189–190, 280; **V:** 319; **Supp. III:** 421–422; **Retro. Supp. I:** 76, 229–242
Pope's Wedding, The (Bond), **Supp. I:** 422, 423–425, 426, 427, 435
Popery: British and Foreign (Landor), **IV:** 100
"Poplar Field, The" (Cowper), **III:** 218; **Retro. Supp. III:** 50
Popper, Karl, **Supp. IV:** 115
"Poppies" (Nye), **Supp. X:** 204–205
"Poppy grows upon the shore, A" (Bridges), **VI:** 78
Popular Education of France with Notices of that of Holland and Switzerland, The (Arnold), **V:** 216
"Popular Fallacies" (Lamb), **IV:** 82
Porcupine, The (Barnes), **Supp. IV:** 65, 67, 68, 73, 74
"Pornography" (Raine), **Supp. XIII:** 168
"Pornography and Obscenity" (Lawrence), **VII:** 91, 101, 122
"Pornography" (McEwan), **Supp. IV:** 394–395
"Porphyria's Lover" (Browning), **IV:** 360; **V:** 315; **Retro. Supp. II:** 22; **Retro. Supp. III:** 20, 21–22

Porson, Richard, **IV:** 63
"Portico" (Murphy), **Supp. V:** 327
"Portobello Beach" (Greig), **Supp. XVI:** 162
"Portobello Road, The" (Spark), **Supp. I:** 200
"Portrait, The" (Gogol), **III:** 340, 345
"Portrait, The" (Oliphant), **Supp. X:** 220
"Portrait, The" (Rossetti), **V:** 239
Portrait, The (Swinburne), **V:** 333
Portrait of a Gentleman in Slippers (Milne), **Supp. V:** 300
"Portrait of a Grandfather, The" (Bridges), **VI:** 78
"Portrait of a Lady" (Eliot), **VII:** 144
Portrait of a Lady, The (James), **V:** xxiv, 51; **VI:** 25, 26, 35–38; **Supp. IV:** 243
"Portrait of an Emperor, The" (Plomer), **Supp. XI:** 216
"Portrait of Mr. W. H., The" (Wilde), **V:** 405–406, 419; **Retro. Supp. II:** 365–366
Portrait of Rossetti (Grylls), **V:** 247, 249, 260
"Portrait of the Artist, A" (Joyce), **Retro. Supp. III:** 167
"Portrait of the Artist, A" (Kinsella), **Supp. V:** 272
"Portrait of the Artist, A" (Mahon), **Supp. VI:** 168
Portrait of the Artist as a Young Dog (Thomas), **Supp. I:** 176, 180, 181, 182; **Retro. Supp. III:** 335, 343, 346, 347, 348
Portrait of the Artist as a Young Man, A (Joyce), **VII:** xiv, 45–47; critical studies, **VII:** 57; **Supp. IV:** 364, 371; **Retro. Supp. I:** 169, 170, 173–175; **Retro. Supp. III:** 166, 167, 168, 170–173, 174, 175
"Portrait of the Artist as Émigré" (Berger), *see Painter of Our Time, A*
"Portrait of the Beatnik: Letter from California" (Blackwood), **Supp. IX:** 5–6, 9
"Portrait of the Engineer, A" (Kinsella), **Supp. V:** 261
Portrait of the Lakes (Nicholson), **Supp. VI:** 223
Portrait of Orkney (Brown), **Supp. VI:** 65
"Portraits" (Thomas), **Supp. IV:** 494
Portraits Contemporains (Sainte'Beuve), **V:** 212
Portraits from Memory (Russell), **VI:** 170
"Portraits in the Nude" (Plomer), **Supp. XI:** 214
Portraits of Places (James), **VI:** 67
"Ports" (Burnside), **Supp. XIII:** 24
Portugal History, The; or, A Relation of the Troubles . . . in the Court of Portugal . . . (Pepys), **II:** 288
Pose (After the Painting Mrs. Badham by Ingres) (Boland), **Supp. V:** 40
Positions (Mulcaster), **I:** 122
Positive Philosophy of Auguste Comte, Freely Translated and Condensed by Harriet Martineau, The (tr. Martineau), **Supp. XV:** 187

"Positive Season, The" (Fallon), **Supp. XII:** 104–105
Positives (Gunn), **Supp. IV:** 257, 264, 265, 266
Possession: A Romance (Byatt), **Supp. IV:** 139, 149, 151–153
Post Captain (O'Brian), **Supp. XII:** 254–255
"Post Office" (Adcock), **Supp. XII:** 9
Postal Problem, A (Carroll), **V:** 274
"Posterity" (Larkin), **Supp. I:** 282; **Retro. Supp. III:** 210
Posthumous Fragments of Margaret Nicholson . . . (ed. Shelley), **IV:** 208
Posthumous Papers of the Pickwick Club, The (Dickens), see *Pickwick Papers*
Posthumous Poems (Day Lewis), **Supp. III:** 130
Posthumous Poems (Shelley), **IV:** 208
Posthumous Poems, The (Swinburne), **V:** 333
Posthumous Tales (Crabbe), **III:** 278, 286
Posthumous Works of the Author of "A Vindication of the Rights of Woman" (ed. Godwin), *Supp. XV:* 123
"Postmodern Blues" (Wallace–Crabbe), **VIII:** 324
Post'Mortem (Coward), **Supp. II:** 149–150, 151
"Postponing the Bungalow" (Dunn), **Supp. X:** 68
"Postscript" (Fuller), **Supp. VII:** 81
"Postscript: for Gweno" (Lewis), **VII:** 444, 446
"Postscripts" (radio broadcasts), **VII:** 212
Poet Geranium, The (Nicholson), **Supp. VI:** 213, 216–217
Pot of Broth, The (Yeats), **VI:** 218
"Potato Gatherers, The" (Friel), **Supp. V:** 114
Potter, Beatrix, **Supp. III:** 287–309
Potter, Cherry, **Supp. IV:** 181
Potter, Dennis, **Supp. X:** 227–242
Potter's Thumb, The (Steel), **Supp. XII:** 270–271
Potting Shed, The (Greene), **Supp. I:** 13; **Retro. Supp. II:** 162
"Potting Shed Tutti—Frutti" (Pitter), **Supp. XIII:** 145
Pottle, F. A., **III:** 234n, 239, 240, 247, 249
Pound, Ezra, **I:** 98; **IV:** 323, 327, 329, 372; **V:** xxv, 304, 317n; **VI:** 207, 216, 247, 323, 417; **VII:** xiii, xvi, 89, 148, 149; **Supp. III:** 53–54, 397, 398; **Supp. IV:** 99, 100, 114–115, 116, 411, 559
Pound on Demand, A (O'Casey), **VII:** 12
"Pour Commencer" (Stallworthy), **Supp. X:** 297
"Poussin" (MacNeice), **VII:** 411
Powell, Anthony, **VI:** 235; **VII:** xxi, **343–359**; **Supp. II:** 4; **Supp. IV:** 505
Powell, Edgar, **VI:** 385
Powell, L F., **III:** 234n
Power and the Glory, The (Greene; U.S. title, *The Labyrinthine Ways*), **Supp. I:** 5, 8, 9–10, 13, 14, 18; **Retro. Supp. II:** 156–157
Power in Men (Cary), **VII:** 186, 187

Power of Grace Illustrated (tr. Cowper), **III:** 220
Powers, Mary, **Supp. IV:** 423, 428
Powys, T. F., **VII:** 21, 234; **VIII: 245–259**
Practical Criticism (Richards), **Supp. II:** 185, 405, **418–421,** 423, 430
Practical Education (Edgeworth), **Supp. III:** 152
Practice of Piety, The (Bayly), **II:** 241
Practice of Writing, The (Lodge), **Supp. IV:** 366, 381
Praed, Winthrop Mackworth, **IV:** 269, 283; **V:** 14
Praeterita (Ruskin), **V:** 174, 175, 182, 184
"Prague Milk Bottle, The" (Motion), **Supp. VII:** 262
"Praise for Mercies, Spiritual and Temporal" (Blake), **III:** 294
"Praise for the Fountain Opened" (Cowper), **III:** 211
Praise of Age, The (Henryson), **Supp. VII:** 146, 148
"Praise of My Lady" (Morris), **V:** 295
"Praise of Pindar, The" (Cowley), **II:** 200
Praise Singer, The (Renault), **Supp. IX:** 181–182, 187
"Praise II" (Herbert), **II:** 129; **Retro. Supp. II:** 177
Praises (Jennings), **Supp. V:** 219
Prancing Nigger (Firbank; British title, *Sorrow in Sunlight*), **Supp. II:** 200, 202, 204, 205, 211, 213, **218–220, 222, 223**
Prater Violet (Isherwood), **VII:** 313–314
Pravda (Hare and Brenton), **Supp. IV:** 282, 283, 284, 285, 286, 293
Praxis (Weldon), **Supp. IV:** 522, 525–526, 528, 533
"Prayer" (Jamie), **Supp. XIV:** 141, 142
"Prayer, A" (Joyce), **Retro. Supp. I:** 179
"Prayer Before Birth" (MacNeice), **VII:** 415
"Prayer Book, 1579–1582" (Elizabeth I), **Supp. XVI:** 154–**Supp. XVI:** 155
"Prayer for My Daughter, A" (Yeats), **VI:** 217, 220; **Supp. V:** 39; **Retro. Supp. I:** 333
"Prayer 1" (Herbert), **II:** 122; **Retro. Supp. II:** 179
"Prayer to St. Blaise" (Delanty), **Supp. XIV:** 73
"Prayers of the Pope, The" (Williams, C. W. S.), **Supp. IX:** 283
Prayers or Meditations (tr. Elizabeth I), **Supp. XVI:** 156
Prayers Written at Vailima (Stevenson), **V:** 396
Praz, Mario, **I:** 146, 292, 354; **II:** 123; **III:** 329, 337, 344–345, 346; **V:** 412, 420; **VII:** 60, 62, 70
"Preamble" (Nye), **Supp. X:** 198
"Precautions in Free Thought" (Butler), **Supp. II:** 99
"Predators, The" (Conn), **Supp. XIII:** 73
Predictions for the Year 1708 (Swift), **III:** 35
Pre'eminent Victorian: A Study of Tennyson, The (Richardson), **IV:** 339

"Preface" (Arnold), **Supp. II:** 57
"Preface: Mainly About Myself" (Shaw), **VI:** 129
Preface to Paradise Lost, " (Lewis), **Supp. III:** 240, 265
Preface to the Dramatic Works of Dryden (ed. Congreve), **II:** 348, 350
Prefaces (Dryden), **IV:** 349
"Prefaces" (Housman), **VI:** 156
"Prefatory Letter on Reading the Bible for the First Time" (Moore), **VI:** 96
"Prefatory Poem to My Brother's Sonnets" (Tennyson), **IV:** 327, 336; **Retro. Supp. III:** 319
"Preference" (Thomas), **Supp. XII:** 290
Preferred Lies: A Journey to the Heart of Scottish Golf (Greig), **Supp. XVI:** 161, 174–175
Prehistories (Scupham), **Supp. XIII:** 219, 220, 223
Preiching of the Swallow, The (Henryson), **Supp. VII:** 136, 139–140
Preliminary Essays (Wain), **Supp. XVI:** 293, 302–303
"Prelude" (Brathwaite), **Supp. XII:** 36
"Prelude" (Mansfield), **VII:** 177, 179, 180
"Prelude, A" (Lawrence), **VII:** 114
Prelude, The (Wordsworth) **IV:** ix–x, xxi, 1, 2, 3, **11–17,** 24, 25, 43, 151, 315; **V:** 310
"Prelude and History" (Redgrove), **Supp. VI:** 236
"Prelude to Life, A" (Symons), **Supp. XIV:** 267
"Preludes" (Eliot), **Retro. Supp. II:** 121
"Preludes" (Malouf), **Supp. XII:** 220
"Premature Rejoicing" (Blunden), **Supp. XI:** 43
Premonition to Princes, A (Ralegh), **I:** 154
Preoccupations: Selected Prose 1968–1978 (Heaney), **Supp. II:** 268–269, 272, 273
Pre'Raphaelite Imagination, The (Dixon Hunt), **VI:** 167
"Pre–Raphaelite Paintings" (Raine), **Supp. XIII:** 164
Pre'Raphaelitism (Ruskin), **V:** 184
Prerogative of Parliaments, The (Ralegh), **I:** 157–158
"Preparation for a Sea Voyage" (Butlin), **Supp. XVI:** 56
"Presage of the Ruin of the Turkish Empire, A" (Waller), **II:** 233
Presbyterians' Plea of Merit, The (Swift), **III:** 36
Prescott, William H., **VI:** 394
"Presence" (Conn), **Supp. XIII:** 78
"Presence, The" (Thomas), **Supp. XII:** 288–289
Presence of Spain, The (Morris), see *Spain*
"Present" (Cope), **VIII:** 80–81
Present and the Past, The (Compton'Burnett), **VII:** 61, 62
"Present and the Past: Eliot's Demonstration, The" (Leavis), **VII:** 237
"Present Estate of Pompeii" (Lowry), **Supp. III:** 281–282

"Present King of France Is Bald, The" (Hart), **Supp. XI:** 130
Present Laughter (Coward), **Supp. II:** 153–154, 156
Present Position of History, The (Trevelyan), **VI:** 383
Present State of All Nations, The (Smollet), **III:** 158
"Present State of the Manners, Society, Etc., Etc., of the Metropolis of England, The" (Robinson), **Supp. XIII:** 213
Present State of the Parties in Great Britain, The (Defoe), **III:** 13
Present State of Wit, The (Gay), **III:** 44, 67
"Present Time, The" (Carlyle), **IV:** 247–248
Present Times (Storey), **Supp. I:** 408, 419–420
"Preserve and Renovate" (Dunn), **Supp. X:** 80
"Preserved" (Ewart), **Supp. VII:** 44
President's Child, The (Weldon), **Supp. IV:** 530–531
Press Cuttings: A Topical Sketch (Shaw), **VI:** 115, 117, 118–119, 129
Press, John, **VI:** xvi, xxxiv; **VII:** xxii, xxxviii
"Presser, The" (Coppard), **VIII:** 86, 96–97
Preston, Thomas, **I:** 122, 213
Pretty Lady, The (Bennett), **VI:** 250, 251, 259
"Pretty Maids All in a Row" (Cameron), **Supp. IX:** 19
Previous Convictions (Connolly), **Supp. III:** 110
Prévost, Antoine, **III:** 333
Price, Alan, **VI:** 314
Price, Cecil, **III:** 258n, 261, 264, 268, 271
Price, Cormell, **VI:** 166, 167
Price, Richard, **IV:** 126
"Price, The" (Stevenson), **Supp. VI:** 260
Price of Everything, The (Motion), **Supp. VII:** 253, 254, 260–262
Price of Salt, The (Highsmith), **Supp. V:** 167, 169–170
"Price of Sixpense, The" (Nicholson), **Supp. VI:** 219
Price of Stone, The (Murphy), **Supp. V:** 313, 315, 316, 326–329
"Price of Stone, The" (Murphy), **Supp. V:** 327
"Price of Things, The" (Ewart), **Supp. VII:** 42
"Pride" (Kay), **Supp. XIII:** 108–109
Pride and Prejudice (Austen), **III:** 91, 336; **IV:** xvii, 103–104, 108–120, 122; **Supp. IV:** 235, 521; **Retro. Supp. II:** 7–9
Pride and Prejudice (television adaptation, Weldon), **Supp. IV:** 521
"Pride of the Village" (Blunden), **Supp. XI:** 44
Pride's Cure (Lamb), see *John Woodvie*
Priest to the Temple, A; or, The Country Parson His Character etc. (Herbert), **II:** 120, 141; **Retro. Supp. II:** 176

Priestley, J. B., **IV:** 160, 170; **V:** xxvi, 96; **VII:** xii, xviii, 60, **209–231**
Priestley, Joseph, **III:** 290
"Prima Belladonna" (Ballard), **Supp. V:** 21
Primal Scene, As It Were, The: Nine Studies in Disloyalty (Reed), **Supp. XV:** 253
"Prime Minister" (Churchill), **VI:** 349
Prime Minister, The (Trollope), **V:** xxiv, 96, 97, 98–99, 101, 102
Prime of Miss Jean Brodie, The (Spark), **Supp. I:** 200, 201, 204–206
Primer, The; or, Office of the B. Virgin Mary (Dryden), **II:** 304
Prince, F. T., **VII:** xxii 422, 427
Prince Caspian (Lewis), **Supp. III:** 248, 260
Prince Hohenstiel'Schwangau, Saviour of Society (Browning), **IV:** 358, 369, 374
Prince of Dreamers, A (Steel), **Supp. XII:** 275
Prince Otto (Stevenson), **V:** 386, 395
Prince Prolétaire (Swinburne), **V:** 333
"Prince Roman" (Conrad), **VI:** 148
"Prince's Progress, The" (Rossetti), **V:** 250, 258, 259
Prince's Progress and Other Poems, The (Rossetti), **V:** 250, 260; **Retro. Supp. III:** 251, 263
Princess, The (Tennyson), **IV:** xx, 323, 325, 328, 333–334, 336, 338; **Retro. Supp. III:** 317, 323, 330
Princess Casamassima, The (James), **VI:** 27, 39, **41–43**, 67
Princess Cinderella and Her Wicked Sisters (Tennant), **Supp. IX:** 239
"Princess of Kingdom Gone, The" (Coppard), **VIII:** 92
Princess Zoubaroff, The (Firbank), **Supp. II:** 202, 204, 205, **215–216**
Principia Ethica (Moore), **Supp. III:** 49
Principle and Practice (Martineau), **Supp. XV:** 185
Principles and Persuasions (West), **VI:** 241
Principles of Literary Criticism (Richards), **Supp. II:** 405, **411–417**
Principles of Literary Criticism (Abercrombie), **Supp. XVI:** 12
Pringle, David, **Supp. V:** 32
"Printers Devil, The" (Delanty), **Supp. XIV:** 70
Prior, Matthew, **II:** 265
Prioress's Prologue, The (Chaucer), **I:** 37
Prioress's Tale, The (Chaucer), **I:** 22, 34
"Prison" (Murphy), **Supp. V:** 329
Prison Cell and Barrel Mystery, The (Reading), **VIII:** 263
"Prisoner, The" (Brontë), **V:** 142, 143, 254
"Prisoner, The" (Browning), **IV:** 313–314
Prisoner of Chillon, The (Byron), **IV:** 180, 192
Prisoner of Grace (Cary), **VII:** 186, 194–195
Prisoners (Stevenson), **Supp. VI:** 265
Prisoners of Mainz, The (Waugh), **Supp. VI:** 269

"Prisoner's Progress" (MacNeice), **VII:** 406
Prisons We Choose to Live Inside (Lessing), **Supp. I:** 239, 254–255
Pritchett, V. S., **IV:** 120, 298, 306; **Supp. III:** 99, 102, 211, **311–331**
"Private, A" (Thomas), **Supp. III:** 403, 404, 406
Private Country, A (Durrell), **Retro. Supp. III:** 84, 95
Private Ear, The (Shaffer), **Supp. I:** 317–318, 322, 323, 327
Private Journal and Literary Remains of John Byrom, The (Byrom), **Supp. XVI:** 72, 74, 75, 77, 78, 82–85
"Private Life, The" (James), **VI:** 48, 67, 69; **Retro. Supp. I:** 2
Private Life of Henry Maitland, The (Roberts), **V:** 425, 427, 438
Private Life of Hilda Tablet, The: A Parenthesis for Radio (Reed), **Supp. XV:** 253
Private Lives (Coward), **Supp. II:** 139, **147–149**, 155–156
Private Memoirs and Confessions of a Justified Sinner, The (Hogg), **Supp. X:** 103, 114–118
Private Papers of Henry Ryecroft, The (Gissing), **V:** 424, 425, 427, **430–432**, 436, 437
Private Papers of James Boswell . . . , The (ed. Pottle and Scott), **III:** 234n, 247, 249
"Private Place, The" (Muir), **Supp. VI:** 206
"Private Prayers of Elizabeth I at Court, 1563, The" (Elizabeth I), **Supp. XVI:** 154
"Private Property" (Carpenter), **Supp. XIII:** 40
"Private Tuition by Mr. Bose" (Desai), **Supp. V:** 65
Private View, A (Brookner), **Supp. IV:** 135
Privy Seal (Ford), **VI:** 324, 326
"Prize, The" (Nye), **Supp. X:** 205
"Prize–Winning Poem, The" (Adcock), **Supp. XII:** 8
"Pro and Con on Aragon" (Stead), **Supp. IV:** 466
"Pro Marcello" (tr. Elizabeth I), **Supp. XVI:** 158
Pro populo anglicano defensio . . . (Milton), **II:** 176
Pro populo anglicano definsio secunda (Milton), **II:** 176
"Probable Future of Metaphysics, The" (Hopkins), **V:** 362
"Problem, The" (Swift), **III:** 32
Problem in Greek Ethics, Being an Inquiry into the Phenomenon of Sexual Inversion, Addressed Especially to Medical Psychologists and Jurists, A (Symonds), **Supp. XIV:** 253–254, 261
Problem in Modern Ethics, Being an Inquiry into the Phenomenon of Sexual Inversion, Addressed Especially to Medical Psychologists and Jurists, A (Symonds), **Supp. XIV:** 259–260

Problem of Pain, The (Lewis), **Supp. I:** 71; **Supp. III:** 248, 255–256
"Problem of Prose, The" (Leavis), **VII:** 248
"Problem of Thor Bridge, The" (Doyle), **Supp. II:** 172, 174
Process of Real Freedom, The (Cary), **VII:** 186
"Process of Separation, A" (Burnside), **Supp. XIII:** 23
"Procession, The" (Upward), **Supp. XIII:** 259–260
"Procrastination" (Crabbe), **III:** 281, 285
Prodigal Child, A (Storey), **Supp. I:** 408, 419
Prodigal Son, The: Third Parable for Church Performance (Plomer), **Supp. XI:** 222
"Prodigy, The" (Soutar), **Supp. XVI:** 256
"Proferred Love Rejected" (Suckling), **II:** 227
Professing Poetry (Wain), **Supp. XVI:** 303
Professional Foul (Stoppard), **Supp. I:** 451, 453; **Retro. Supp. II:** 351–352
"Professions for Women" (Woolf), **Retro. Supp. I:** 310
Professor, The (Brontë), **V:** xxii, 112, 122, 123, 125, 132, **134–137**, 148, 150, 151, 152; **Retro. Supp. I:** 52
"Professor, The" (Thackeray), **V:** 21, 37
"Professor Fargo" (James), **VI:** 69
Professors and Gods (Fuller), **Supp. VII:** 77
Professor's Love Story, The (Barrie), **Supp. III:** 4
Profile of Arthur J. Mason, A (Ishiguro), **Retro. Supp. III:** 154, 161
"Profile of Arthur J. Mason, A" (Ishiguro), **Supp. IV:** 304
Profitable Meditations . . . (Bunyan), **II:** 253
"Programme Note" (Fuller), **Supp. VII:** 80
Progress and Poverty (George), **VI:** viii
Progress of Julius, The (du Maurier), **Supp. III:** 139, 140, 144
Progress of Liberty, The (Robinson), **Supp. XIII:** 204, 211, 213
"Progress of Poesy" (Gray), **II:** 200; **III:** 140
"Progress of Poesy, The" (Arnold), **V:** 209
"Progress of the Soul, The" (Donne), **II:** 209
Progymnasmata (More), **Supp. VII:** 236
"Project for a New Novel" (Ballard), **Supp. V:** 21
Project for the Advancement of Religion . . . , A (Swift), **III:** 26, 35, 46
"Proletariat and Poetry, The" (Day Lewis), **Supp. III:** 120
Prolific and the Devourer, The (Auden), **Retro. Supp. I:** 10
Prologue (Henryson), **Supp. VII:** 136
"Prologue to an Autobiography" (Naipaul), **Supp. I:** 385
Prometheus Bound (Aeschylus), **IV:** 199
Prometheus Bound, Translated from the Greek of Aeschylus (Browning), **IV:** 310, 321
Prometheus on His Crag (Hughes), **Supp. I:** 354–355, 363
Prometheus the Firegiver (Bridges), **VI:** 83
Prometheus Unbound (Shelley), **III:** 331; **IV:** xviii, 176, 179, 196, 198, **199–201**, 202, 207, 208; **VI:** 449–450; **Supp. III:** 370; **Retro. Supp. I:** 250, 251–253
"Promise, The" (James), **VI:** 49
Promise and Fulfillment (Koestler), **Supp. I:** 33
Promise of Love (Renault), see *Purposes of Love*
Promise of May, The (Tennyson), **Retro. Supp. III:** 329
Promised Land, The (Carpenter), **Supp. XIII:** 36
Promos and Cassandra (Whetstone), **I:** 313
Promus of Formularies and Elegancies, A (Bacon), **I:** 264, 271
"Propagation of Knowledge" (Kipling), **VI:** 200
Proper Marriage, A (Lessing), **Supp. I:** 238, 244
Proper Studies (Huxley), **VII:** 198, 201
Properties of Things, On the (tr. Trevisa), see *De Proprietatibus Rerum*
"Property of Colette Nervi, The" (Trevor), **Supp. IV:** 500
Prophecy (Seltzer), **III:** 345
Prophecy of Dante, The (Byron), **IV:** 193
Prophesy to the Wind (Nicholson), **Supp. VI: 221–222**
Prophetess, The (Fletcher and Massinger), **II:** 55, 66
Prophetic Book, The (Raine), **Supp. XIII:** 173
"Prophetic Book, The" (Raine), **Supp. XIII:** 173
"Prophets, The" (Auden), **Retro. Supp. I:** 9
"Prophet's Hair, The" (Rushdie), **Supp. IV:** 438
Proposal for Correcting . . . the English Tongue, A (Swift), **III:** 29, 35
Proposal for Giving Badges to the Beggars . . . of Dublin, A (Swift), **III:** 36
Proposal for Making an Effectual Provision for the Poor, A (Fielding), **III:** 105; **Retro. Supp. I:** 81
Proposal for Putting Reform to the Vote, A (Shelley), **IV:** 208
Proposals for an Association of . . . Philanthropists . . . (Shelley), **IV:** 208
Proposals for Printing a Very Curious Discourse, in Two Volumes in Quarto, Intitled ΩΕΥΔΟΛΟΥΙΑ ΠΟΛΙΤΙΚΗ; *or, A Treatise of the Art of Political Lying, with an Abstract of the First Volume of the Said Treatise* (Arbuthnot), **Supp. XVI:** 22–23
Proposals for Publishing Monthly . . . (Smollett), **III:** 148
Proposals for the Universal Use of Irish Manufacture . . . (Swift), **III:** 27–28, 35

Propositions for the Advancement of Experimental Philosophy, A (Cowley), **II:** 196, 202
Prose of John Clare, The (Clare), **Supp. XI:** 53, 58
Prose Works, The (Swift), **III:** 15n 35
Proserpine, The (Rossetti), **V:** 295
Prosody of "Paradise Lost" and "Samson Agonistes," The (Bridges), **VI:** 83
"Prospect from the Silver Hill, The" (Crace), **Supp. XIV:** 22
Prospero's Cell (Durrell), **Supp. I:** 96, 100, 110–111; **Retro. Supp. III:** 95
"Prospice" (Browning), **Retro. Supp. III:** 27
Protestant Monastery, The; or, A Complaint against the Brutality of the Present Age (Defoe), **III:** 14
"Proteus; or, Matter" (Bacon), **I:** 267
Prothalamion (Spenser), **I:** 124, 131
"Proud word you never spoke, but you will speak" (Landor), **IV:** 99
Proust, Marcel, **V:** xxiv, 45, 174, 183; **Supp. I:** 44–45; **Supp. IV:** 126, 136, 139
Proust Screenplay, The (Pinter), **Supp. I:** 378
Provence (Ford), **VI:** 324
"Proverbs of Hell" (Blake), **III:** 298; **Retro. Supp. I:** 38
Providence (Brookner), **Supp. IV:** 124–125, 131
"Providence" (Herbert), **Retro. Supp. II:** 177
"Providence and the Guitar" (Stevenson), **V:** 395
Provincial Pleasures (Nicholson), **Supp. VI:** 223
Provok'd Husband, The (Cibber), **II:** 326, 337
Provok'd Wife, The (Vanbrugh), **II:** 325, **329–332**, 334, 336, 360
Provost, The (Galt), **IV:** 35
Prussian Officer, The, and Other Stories (Lawrence), **VII:** 114
Pryce'Jones, Alan, **VII:** 70
Prynne, William, **II:** 339; **Supp. III:** 23
"Psalm of Montreal, A" (Butler), **Supp. II:** 105
"Psalms of Assize" (Hill), **Supp. V:** 193
Pseudodoxia Epidemica (Browne), **II:** 149–150, 151, 155, 156, 345n
Pseudo-Martyr (Donne), **I:** 352–353, 362; **Retro. Supp. II:** 97
Psmith Journalist (Wodehouse), **Supp. III:** 450
Psyche's Task (Frazer), **Supp. III:** 185
Psycho (film), **III:** 342–343
Psycho Apocalypté, a Lyrical Drama (Browning and Horne), **IV:** 321
Psychoanalysis and the Unconscious (Lawrence), **VII:** 122; **Retro. Supp. II:** 234
"Psychological Warfare" (Reed), **Supp. XV:** 245, 250, 251
"Psychology of Advertising, The" (Sayers), **Supp. III:** 345
Psychology of the Poet Shelley (Carpenter), **Supp. XIII:** 45

Psychology of the Unconscious (Jung), **Supp. IV:** 3
"Psychopolis" (McEwan), **Supp. IV:** 395–396
Puberty Tree, The (Thomas), **Supp. IV:** 490
"Puberty Tree, The" (Thomas), **Supp. IV:** 492–493
Public Address (Blake), **III:** 305
Public Burning, The (Coover), **Supp. IV:** 116
Public Eye, The (Shaffer), **Supp. I:** 317, 318–319, 327
"Public Footpath To" (Scupham), **Supp. XIII:** 219
Public Image, The (Spark), **Supp. I:** 200, 208–209, 218n
Public Ledger (periodical), **III:** 179, 188
Public School Life: Boys, Parents, Masters (Waugh), **Supp. VI:** 267, 270
Public School Verse (Cameron), **Supp. IX:** 17
"Public Son of a Public Man, The" (Spender), **Supp. II:** 483
"Public–House Confidence" (Cameron), **Supp. IX:** 22–23
Publick Employment and an Active Life Prefer'd to Solitude (Evelyn), **II:** 287
Publick Spirit of the Whigs, The (Swift), **III:** 35
"Puck and Saturn" (Wallace–Crabbe), **VIII:** 323
"Puck Is Not Sure About Apollo" (Wallace–Crabbe), **VIII:** 321
Puck of Pook's Hill (Kipling), **VI:** viii, 169, 204; **Retro. Supp. III:** 190, 194–195, 197
Puffball (Weldon), **Supp. IV:** 531, 533–534
Pulci, Luigi, **IV:** 182, 188
Pullman, Philip, **Supp. XIII: 149–161**
Pumpkin Eater, The (Pinter), **Supp. I:** 374
Punch (periodical), **IV:** 263; **V:** xx, 19, 23, 24–25; **VI:** 367, 368; **Supp. II:** 47, 49
Punch (periodical), **Supp. XVI:** 209, 210–211
Punch's Prize Novelists (Thackeray), **V:** 22, 38
"Punishment Enough" (Cameron), **Supp. IX:** 29
"Pupil, The" (James), **VI:** 49, 69
Purcell, Henry, **Retro. Supp. II:** 196
Purcell Commemoration Ode (Bridges), **VI:** 81
Purchas's Pilgrimage, **IV:** 46
Pure in Heart, The (Hill), **Supp. XIV:** 116, 126
Pure Poetry. An Anthology (Moore), **VI:** 99
Purgatorio (Dante), **Supp. IV:** 439
Purgatorio (Heaney), **Retro. Supp. I:** 124
Purgatorio II (Eliot), **VII:** 151
Purgatory (Yeats), **VI:** 219
Puritan, The (anonymous), **I:** 194; **II:** 21
Puritan and the Papist, The (Cowley), **II:** 202

Purity of Diction in English Verse (Davie), **Supp. VI:** 107, **114**
"Purl and Plain" (Coppard), **VIII:** 96
"Purple" (Owen), **VI:** 449
Purple Dust (O'Casey), **VII:** 7, 8
"Purple Jar, The" (Edgeworth), **Supp. III:** 153
Purple Plain, The (Ambler), **Supp. IV:** 3
Purposes of Love (Renault), **Supp. IX:** 172–173
Pursuit of Love, The (Mitford), **Supp. X:** 151–152, 156, 158–161, 163
Pushkin, Aleksander, **III:** 339, 345; **Supp. IV:** 484, 495
Puss in Boots: The Adventures of That Most Enterprising Feline (Pullman), **Supp. XIII:** 152
Put Out More Flags (Waugh), **VII:** 290, 297–298, 300, 313
Puttenham, George, **I:** 94, 114, 119, 146, 214
Puzzleheaded Girl, The (Stead), **Supp. IV:** 476
"Puzzling Nature of Blue, The" (Carey), **Supp. XII:** 55
"Pygmalion" (Beddoes), **Supp. XI:** 28–29
"Pygmalion" (Gower), **I:** 53–54
Pygmalion (Shaw), **VI:** xv, 108, 115, 116–117, 120; **Retro. Supp. II:** 322
"Pylons, The" (Spender), **Supp. II:** 48
Pym, Barbara, **Supp. II: 363–384**
Pynchon, Thomas, **Supp. IV:** 116, 163
Pynson, Richard, **I:** 99
Pyramid, The (Golding), **Supp. I:** 81–82; **Retro. Supp. I:** 100–101
"Pyramis or The House of Ascent" (Hope), **Supp. VII:** 154
"Pyramus and Thisbe" (Gower), **I:** 53–54, 55

"Qua cursum ventus" (Clough), **V:** 160
Quadrille (Coward), **Supp. II:** 155
"Quaint Mazes" (Hill), **Supp. V:** 191
Quakers Past and Present, The (Richardson), **Supp. XIII:** 187
"Quality of Arnold Bennett, The" (Wain), **Supp. XVI:** 302–303
"Quality of Sprawl, The" (Murray), **Supp. VII:** 278–279
Quality Street (Barrie), **Supp. III:** 6, 8
"Quantity Theory of Insanity, The" (Self), **Supp. V:** 402
Quantity Theory of Insanity, The: Together with Five Supporting Propositions (Self), **Supp. V:** 395, 400–402
Quantum of Solace (Fleming), **Supp. XIV:** 95
Quarantine (Crace), **Supp. XIV:** 17–18, 26–27, 28
Quare Fellow, The (Behan), **Supp. II:** 65, **68–70**, 73
Quaritch, Bernard, **IV:** 343, 346, 348, 349
Quarles, Francis, **II:** 139, 246
"Quarrel, The" (Cornford), **VIII:** 113
Quarterly Review (periodical), **IV:** xvi, 60–61, 69, 133, 204–205, 269–270; **V:** 140
Quartermaine, Peter, **Supp. IV:** 348

Quartet (Rhys), **Supp. II:** 388, **390–392**, 403
Quartet in Autumn (Pym), **Supp. II: 380–382**
Queen, The; or, The Excellency of Her Sex (Ford), **II:** 88, 89, 91, 96, 100
Queen and the Rebels, The (Reed), **Supp. XV:** 253
"Queen Annelida and False Arcite" (Browning), **IV:** 321
"Queen Elizabeth I Prayers and Verses, 1569" (Elizabeth I), **Supp. XVI:** 154
Queen Elizabeth Story, The (Sutcliff), **Supp. XVI:** 264
Queen Is Crowned, A (Fry), **Supp. III:** 195
Queen Mab (Shelley), **IV:** xvii, 197, 201, 207, 208; **Retro. Supp. I:** 245–246
Queen Mary (Tennyson), **IV:** 328, 338; **Retro. Supp. III:** 329
Queen of Corinth, The (Field, Fletcher, Massinger), **II:** 66
Queen of Hearts, The (Collins), **Supp. VI:** 95
Queen of Sheba, The (Jamie), **Supp. XIV:** 129, 136–139, 143
"Queen of Sheba, The" (Jamie), **Supp. XIV:** 137, 138, 142
"Queen of Sheba, The" (Montague), **Supp. XV:** 218
"Queen of Spades, The" (Pushkin), **III:** 339–340, 345
Queen of Stones (Tennant), **Supp. IX:** 231, 233–235
Queen of the Air, The (Ruskin), **V:** 174, 180, 181, 184
Queen of the Dawn (Haggard), **Supp. III:** 222
Queen Sheba's Ring (Haggard), **Supp. III:** 214
Queen Victoria (Strachey), **Supp. II: 512–514**
Queen Was in the Parlor, The (Coward), **Supp. II:** 141, 146
Queen Yseult (Swinburne), **V:** 333
Queenhoo' Hall (Strutt), **IV:** 31
"Queenie Fat and Thin" (Brooke'Rose), **Supp. IV:** 103
Queen' Mother, The (Swinburne), **V:** 312, 313, 314, 330, 331, 332
Queen's Tragedy, The (Swinburne), **V:** 333
Queen's Wake, The (Hogg), **Supp. X:** 106–107, 110
Queery Leary Nonsense (Lear), **V:** 87
Quennell, Peter, **V:** xii, xviii, 192, 193, 194; **VI:** 237; **Supp. III:** 107
Quentin Durward (Scott), **IV:** xviii, 37, 39
"Quest, The" (Saki), **Supp. VI:** 249
Quest sonnets (Auden), **VII:** 380–381; **Retro. Supp. I:** 2, 10
"Question" (Thomas), **Supp. XII:** 290, 291
"Question, A" (Synge), **VI:** 314
"Question, The" (Shelley), **IV:** 203
"Question for Walter, A" (Longley), **VIII:** 163–164
"Question in the Cobweb, The" (Reid), **Supp. VII:** 326

Question of Attribution, A (Bennett), **VIII:** 30, 31
Question of Blood, A (Rankin), **Supp. X:** 245, 257
"Question of Form and Content, A" (Stallworthy), **Supp. X:** 297–298
"Question of Place, A" (Berger), **Supp. IV:** 92
Question of Proof, A (Day Lewis), **Supp. III:** 117, 131
Question of Upbringing, A (Powell), **VII:** 343, 347, 350, 351
"Question Time" (Carson), **Supp. XIII:** 54
Questions about the . . . Seventh'Day Sabbath (Bunyan), **II:** 253
"Questions and Answers" (Roberts), **Supp. XV:** 264
"Questions in a Wood" (Graves), **VII:** 268
"Qui laborat orat" (Clough), **V:** 160
Quidditch Through the Ages (Rowling), **Supp. XVI:** 239
"Quidditie, The" (Herbert), **Retro. Supp. II:** 179
Quidnunckis, The (Arbuthnot), **Supp. XVI:** 26
Quiet American, The (Greene), **Supp. I:** 7, 13, 14; **Supp. IV:** 369; **Retro. Supp. II:** 160–161
Quiet Life, A (Bainbridge), **Supp. VI:** 17, 21–22, 26–27
Quiet Memorandum, The (Pinter), **Supp. I:** 374
"Quiet Neighbours" (Warner), **Supp. VII:** 371
Quiet Wedding (Rattigan), **Supp. VII:** 311
"Quiet Woman, The" (Coppard), **VIII:** 93
"Quiet Woman of Chancery Lane, The" (Redgrove), **Supp. VI:** 235, 237
Quigley, Austin E., **Retro. Supp. I:** 227
Quiller'Couch, Sir Arthur, **II:** 121, 191; **V:** 384
Quillinan, Edward, **IV:** 143n
Quinlan, M. J., **III:** 220
Quinn Manuscript, **VII:** 148
Quintessence of Ibsenism, The (Shaw), **VI:** 104, 106, 129
"Quintets for Robert Morley" (Murray), **Supp. VII:** 278, 283
Quinx (Durrell), **Supp. I:** 119, 120; **Retro. Supp. III:** 86, 87, 94
"Quip, The" (Herbert), **II:** 126
"Quis Optimus Reipvb. Status (What Is The Best Form of the Commonwealth?)" (More), **Supp. VII:** 238
Quite Early One Morning (Thomas), **Retro. Supp. III:** 348
"Quite Early One Morning" (Thomas), **Supp. I:** 183; **Retro. Supp. III:** 343, 348
"Quitting Bulleen" (Wallace-Crabbe), **VIII:** 316
Quoof (Muldoon), **Supp. IV:** 418–421, 422, 423, 425
"Quorum Poram" (Pitter), **Supp. XIII:** 137

"R. E." (Burnside), **Supp. XIII:** 21
"R. B." (Abercrombie), **Supp. XVI:** 9
"R. I. P." (Gissing), **V:** 43
"R. I. P." (Thomas), **Supp. XII:** 285
R.L.S. and His Sine Qua Non (Boodle), **V:** 391, 393, 397
R. S. Thomas: Selected Prose (Thomas), **Supp. XII:** 279, 282
Raban, Jonathan, **Supp. XI: 227–241**
"Rabbit" (Rowling), **Supp. XVI:** 225–226, 230
"Rabbit Catcher, The" (Hughes), **Retro. Supp. II:** 217–218
Rabelais, François, **III:** 24; **Supp. IV:** 464
"Race, Racist, Racism" (Kay), **Supp. XIII:** 101
Rachel Papers, The (Amis), **Supp. IV:** 26, 27, 28–29, 30
Rachel Ray (Trollope), **V:** 101
Racine, Jean Baptiste, **II:** 98; **V:** 22
Racing Demon (Hare), **Supp. IV:** 282, 294–296, 298
Radcliffe, Ann, **III:** 327, 331–332, 333, 335–338, 345; **IV:** xvi, 30, 35, 36, 111, 173, 218; **Supp. III:** 384; **Retro. Supp. III: 233–250**
Radcliffe (Storey), **Supp. I:** 408, 410, 414, 415–416, 418–419
Radclyffe Hall: A Case of Obscenity? (Brittain), **Supp. X:** 47
Radiant Way, The (Drabble), **Supp. IV:** 231, 234, 247–249, 250
Radical Imagination, The (Harris), **Supp. V:** 140, 145
Radon Daughters (Sinclair), **Supp. XIV:** 233, 235, 237, 238
Rafferty, Terrence, **Supp. IV:** 357, 360
Raffety, F. W., **III:** l99n
Raft of the Medusa, The (Géricault), **Supp. IV:** 71–72
"Rage for Order" (Mahon), **Supp. VI:** 170
Rage of the Vulture, The (Unsworth), **Supp. VII:** 356, 357, 359–360
Ragtime in Unfamiliar Bars (Butlin), **Supp. XVI:** 52, 56–57
"Ragtime in Unfamiliar Bars" (Butlin), **Supp. XVI:** 56
Raiders' Dawn (Lewis), **VII:** 445, 448
Railway Accident, The (Upward), **Supp. XIII:** 249–250, 251–252, 253, 260
"Railway Library, The" (Crawford), **Supp. XI:** 71
Railway Man and His Children, The (Oliphant), **Supp. X:** 219
Rain (Maugham), **VI:** 369
"Rain" (Thomas), **VI:** 424; **Supp. III:** 400, 401
Rain and the Glass: New and Selected Poems, The (Nye), **Supp. X:** 199
Rain Before It Falls, The (Coe), **Supp. XV:** 49, 50, 51, 58, 60, 61–62, 63
"Rain Charm for the Duchy" (Hughes), **Supp. I:** 365; **Retro. Supp. II:** 214
"Rain Horse, The" (Hughes), **Supp. I:** 348
"Rain in Spain, The" (Reid), **Supp. VII:** 328

"Rain in the Eaves, The" (Nye), **Supp. X:** 200
"Rain Stick, The" (Heaney), **Retro. Supp. I:** 132–133
Rain upon Godshill (Priestley), **VII:** 209, 210
"Rain Upon the Roof, The" (Nye), **Supp. X:** 202
Rainbow, The (Lawrence), **VI:** 232, 276, 283; **VII:** 88, 90, 93, **98–101**; **Retro. Supp. II:** 227–228
"Rainbow Sign, The" (Kureishi), **Supp. XI:** 159–161
Raine, Craig, **Supp. XIII: 163–178**
Raine, Kathleen, **III:** 297, 308
"Rainy Night, A" (Lowry), **Supp. III:** 270
Raj Quartet (Scott), **Supp. I:** 259, 260, 261–262, **266–272**
"Rajah's Diamond, The" (Stevenson), **V:** 395
Rajan, B., **VI:** 219
Rake's Progress, The (Auden/Kallman), **Retro. Supp. I:** 10
Raknem, Ingwald, **VI:** 228
Ralegh, Sir Walter, **I: 145–159**, 277, 278, 291; **II:** 138; **III:** 120, 122, 245; **VI:** 76, 157; **Retro. Supp. I:** 203–204
Raleigh, Sir Walter, *see* Ralegh, Sir Walter
Ralph the Heir (Trollope), **V:** 100, 102
"Ram, The" (Armitage), **VIII:** 12
Rambler (Newman), **Supp. VII:** 299
Rambler (periodical), **II:** 142; **III:** 94, 110–111, 112, 119, 121; **Retro. Supp. I:** 137, 140–141, 149
Rambles Among the Oases of Tunisia (Douglas), **VI:** 305
Rambles in Germany and Italy in 1840, 1842, and 1843 (Shelley), **Retro. Supp. III:** 290
"Ramification" (Carson), **Supp. XIII:** 63
Ramillies and the Union with Scotland (Trevelyan), **VI:** 392–393
Ramsay, Allan, **III:** 312, 313; **IV:** 28
Ramsay, Andrew, **III:** 99, 100
Randall, Anne Frances, *see* Robinson, Mary Darby
Randall, H. S., **IV:** 275
Randolph, Thomas, **II:** 222, 237, 238
"Range" (Scupham), **Supp. XIII:** 222
Rank and Riches (Collins), **Supp. VI:** 93
Ranke, Leopold von, **IV:** 288
Rankin, Ian, **Supp. X: 243–260**
Rao, Raja, **Supp. IV:** 440; **Supp. V:** 56
"Rapallo" (Gunn), **Retro. Supp. III:** 129
Rape of Lucrece, The (Shakespeare), **I:** 306–307, 325; **II:** 3; **Retro. Supp. III:** 278
Rape of the Lock, The (Pope), **III:** 70–71, 75, 77; **Retro. Supp. I:** 231, 233
"Rape of the Sherlock, The" (Milne), **Supp. V:** 297
Rape upon Rape (Fielding), **III:** 105
"Rapparees" (Murphy), **Supp. V:** 323
"Raptor" (Thomas), **Supp. XII:** 291–292
"Rapture, A" (Carew), **II:** 223
"Rapture, The" (Traherne), **Supp. XI:** 266

"Rapunzel Revisited" (Maitland), **Supp. XI:** 170
Rash Act, The (Ford), **VI:** 319, 331
Rash Resolve, The; or, The Untimely Discovery (Haywood), **Supp. XII:** 140
"Raising a Glass" (Delanty), **Supp. XIV:** 73
"Raspberry Jam" (Wilson), **Supp. I:** 154, 157
"Raspberrying" (Reading), **VIII:** 263
"Rastignac at 45" (Gunn), **Retro. Supp. III:** 121
Rat Trap, The (Coward), **Supp. II:** 146
"Ratatouille" (Dunn), **Supp. X:** 74
"Ratcatcher, The" (Dahl), **Supp. IV:** 214
Ratchford, Fannie, **V:** 133, 151, 152
"Rational and Humane Society, A" (Carpenter), **Supp. XIII:** 41
"Rats, The" (Sillitoe), **Supp. V:** 424
Rats and Other Poems, The (Sillitoe), **Supp. V:** 409, 424
Rattigan, Terence, **Supp. VII: 307–322**
Raven, The (Poe), **V:** xx, 409
"Ravenna" (Wilde), **V:** 401, 409
"Ravenswing, The" (Thackeray), **V:** 23, 35, 36
Raw Material (Sillitoe), **Supp. V:** 411, 414–415, 422, 423
Raw Spirit: In Search of the Perfect Dram (Banks), **Supp. XI:** 1, 13, 14
"Rawdon's Roof" (Lawrence), **VII:** 91
Rawley, William, **I:** 257
Ray, G. N., **V:** 37, 39
Ray, Satyajit, **Supp. IV:** 434, 450
Raymond Asquith: Life and Letters (Jolliffe), **VI:** 428
Raysor, T. M., **IV:** 46, 51, 52, 56, 57
Razor's Edge, The (Maugham), **VI:** 374, 377–378
Read, Herbert, **III:** 134; **VI:** 416, 436–437; **VII:** 437
Reade, Winwood, **Supp. IV:** 2
Reader (periodical), **III:** 50, 53
Reader, The, **Supp. XV:** 67, 68
Reader, I Married Him (Beer), **Supp. XIV:** 9, 11
Reader, I Married Him (Roberts), **Supp. XV:** 273
Reader's Guide to G. M. Hopkins, A (MacKenzie), **V:** 374, 382
Reader's Guide to Joseph Conrad, A (Karl), **VI:** 135
Readie & Easie Way to Establish a Free Commonwealth . . . (Milton), **II:** 176; **Retro. Supp. II:** 271
Reading, Peter, **VIII: 261–275**
"Reading, A" (Cope), **VIII:** 81–82
"Reading and Writhing in a Double Bind" (Lodge), **Supp. IV:** 385
"Reading Berryman's Dream Songs at the Writer's Retreat" (Cope), **VIII:** 79
"Reading Lesson, The" (Murphy), **Supp. V:** 316, 325
Reading of Earth, A (Meredith), **V:** 221, 234
Reading of George Herbert, A (Tuve), **II:** 124, 130; **Retro. Supp. II:** 174
Reading of Life, A, and Other Poems (Meredith), **V:** 234

"Reading Robert Southey to My Daughter" (Nye), **Supp. X:** 201
"Reading Scheme" (Cope), **VIII:** 71
"Reading the Banns" (Armitage), **VIII:** 8
"Reading the Elephant" (Motion), **Supp. VII:** 260, 263
Reading Turgenev (Trevor), **Supp. IV:** 516
Readings in Crabbe's ATales of the Hall" (Fitzgerald), **IV:** 349, 353
Reagan, Ronald, **Supp. IV:** 485
"Real and Made–Up People" (Amis), **Supp. II:** 10
"Real Estate" (Wallace–Crabbe), **VIII:** 318
Real Inspector Hound, The (Stoppard), **Supp. I:** 443–444; **Retro. Supp. II:** 345–346
Real Robert Louis Stevenson, The, and Other Critical Essays (Thompson), **V:** 450, 451
"Real Thing, The" (James), **VI:** 48, 69
Real Thing, The (Stoppard), **Supp. I:** 451–452; **Retro. Supp. II:** 353–354
"Real World, The" (Hart), **Supp. XI:** 127
Realists, The (Snow), **VII:** 338–339
"Realm of Possibility" (Conn), **Supp. XIII:** 80
Realms of Gold, The (Drabble), **Supp. IV:** 230, 232, 243–245, 246, 248, 251
"Realpolitik" (Wilson), **Supp. I:** 154, 157
Reardon, Derek, **Supp. IV:** 445
"Rear-Guard, The" (Sassoon), **VI:** 431; **Supp. III:** 59
"Reason, The" (Thomas), **Supp. XII:** 290
Reason and Sensuality (Lydgate), **I:** 57, 64
Reason of Church Government Urg'd Against Prelaty, The (Milton), **II:** 162, 175; **Retro. Supp. II:** 269, 276
"Reason our Foe, let us destroy" (Wycherley), **II:** 321
Reason Why, The (Rendell), **Supp. IX:** 196
Reasonable Life, The: Being Hints for Men and Women (Bennett), *see Mental Efficiency*
Reasons Against the Succession of the House of Hanover (Defoe), **III:** 13
"Reasons for Attendance" (Larkin), **Retro. Supp. III:** 205
Reasons Humbly Offer'd by the Company Exercising the Trade and Mystery of Upholders, Against Part of the Bill for the Better Viewing, Searching, and Examing Drugs, Medicines, &c. (Arbuthnot), **Supp. XVI:** 26
"Reassurance, The" (Gunn), **Retro. Supp. III:** 127, 128
"Reawakening" (Conn), **Supp. XIII:** 74
Rebecca (du Maurier), **Supp. III:** 134, 135, 137–138, 139, 141, 142, 143, 144, 145–146, 147
Rebecca and Rowena: A Romance upon Romance (Thackeray), **V:** 38
Rebecca's Daughters (Thomas), **Retro. Supp. III:** 347
Rebel General, The (Wallace–Crabbe), **VIII:** 314, 318

Rebel General, The (Wallace–Crabbe), **VIII:** 315
Rebels, The (Ngũgĩ), **VIII:** 222
Rebus: The St. Leonard's Years (Rankin), **Supp. X:** 251, 253
"Recall" (Crawford), **Supp. XI:** 75
Recalled to Life (Hill, R.), **Supp. IX:** 120–121
"Recantation, A" (Kipling), **VI:** 192–193
"Receipt to Restore Stella's Youth . . . , A" (Swift), **III:** 32
"Recessional" (Kipling), **VI:** 203; **Retro. Supp. III:** 196
Recklings (Hughes), **Supp. I:** 346, 348
"Reckoning of Meter", *See Háttatal*
"Recollection, A" (Cornford), **VIII:** 103, 112
"Recollections" (Pearsall Smith), **VI:** 76
Recollections of Christ's Hospital (Lamb), **IV:** 85
"Recollections of Journey from Essex" (Clare), **Supp. XI:** 62
"Recollections of Solitude" (Bridges), **VI:** 74
Recollections of the Lake Poets (De Quincey), **IV:** 146n, 155
"Reconcilement between Jacob Tonson and Mr. Congreve, The" (Rowe), **II:** 324
"Record, The" (Warner), **Supp. VII:** 371
"Record of Badalia Herodsfoot, The" (Kipling), **VI:** 167, 168
Record of Friendship, A (Swinburne), **V:** 333
Record of Friendship and Criticism, A (Smith), **V:** 391, 396, 398
Records of a Family of Engineers (Stevenson), **V:** 387, 396
Recoveries (Jennings), **Supp. V:** 211
"Recovery" (Conn), **Supp. XIII:** 75
"Recovery, The" (Vaughan), **II:** 185
Recruiting Officer, The (Farquhar), **II:** 353, 358–359, 360, 361, 362, 364
"Rector, The" (Oliphant), **Supp. X:** 214
Rector and the Doctor's Family, The (Oliphant), **Supp. X:** 214–215
Rectory Umbrella and Mischmasch, The (Carroll), **V:** 264, 273
"Recycling" (Dutton), **Supp. XII:** 89
"Red"(Hughes), **Retro. Supp. II:** 218
Red Badge of Courage, The (Crane), **Supp. IV:** 116
Red Book, The (Delahunt), **Supp. XIV:** 59–63
Red Christmas (Hill, R.), **Supp. IX:** 116–117
Red Cotton Night–Cap Country (Browning), **IV:** 358, 369, 371, 374; **Retro. Supp. III:** 30, 31
Red Days and White Nights (Koestler), **Supp. I:** 23
Red Dog (De Bernières), **Supp. XII:** 65, 69, 77
"Red Front" (Warner), **Supp. VII:** 372
"Red Graveyard, The" (Kay), **Supp. XIII:** 104
Red Harvest (Hammett), **Supp. II:** 130
Red House Mystery, The (Milne), **Supp. V:** 310
Red Peppers (Coward), **Supp. II:** 153

"Red, Red Rose, A" (Burns), **III:** 321
Red Roses for Me (O'Casey), **VII:** 9
"Red Rubber Gloves" (Brooke–Rose)), **Supp. IV:** 104
"Redeeming the Time" (Hill), **Supp. V:** 186
"Redemption" (Herbert), **II:** 126–127
Redgauntlet (Scott), **IV:** xviii, 31, 35, 39
Redgrove, Peter, **Supp. VI: 225–238**
"Red–Headed League, The" (Doyle), **Supp. II:** 170
Redimiculum Matellarum [A Necklace of Chamberpots] (Bunting), **Supp. VII:** 4
"Redriff" (Jones), **Supp. VII:** 176
Reed, Henry, **VII:** 422–423, 449; Supp. XV: 243–257
Reed, J. W., **III:** 249
"Reed, A" (Browning), **IV:** 313
Reed Bed, The (Healy), **Supp. IX:** 96, 106, 107
Reef (Gunesekera), **Supp. X:** 85–100
Rees–Mogg, W., **II:** 288
Reeve, C., **III:** 345
Reeve, Clara, **III:** 80
Reeve's Tale, The (Chaucer), **I:** 37, 41
"Reflection from Anita Loos" (Empson), **Supp. II:** 183–184
Reflections (Greene), **Retro. Supp. II:** 166–167
"Reflections" (Thomas), **Supp. XII:** 291
"Reflections of a Kept Ape" (McEwan), **Supp. IV:** 394
Reflections on a Marine Venus (Durrell), **Retro. Supp. III:** 95
"Reflections on a Peninsula" (Koestler), **Supp. I:** 34
Reflections on Hanging (Koestler), **Supp. I:** 36
"Reflections on Leaving a Place of Retirement" (Coleridge), **IV:** 44
"Reflections on the Death of a Porcupine" (Lawrence), **VII:** 103–104, 110, 119
Reflections on the French Revolution (Burke), **III:** 195, 197, 201–205; **IV:** xv, 127; **Supp. III:** 371, 467, 468, 470
Reflections on the Late Alarming Bankruptcies in Scotland (Boswell), **III:** 248
Reflections on the Psalms (Lewis), **Supp. III:** 249, 264
Reflections on Violence (Hulme), **Supp. VI:** 145
Reflections upon Ancient and Modern Learning (Wotton), **III:** 23
Reflections upon the Late Great Revolution (Defoe), **Retro. Supp. I:** 64
Reflector (periodical), **IV:** 80
Reformation of Manners (Defoe), **III:** 12
"Refusal to mourn, A" (Thomas), **Supp. I:** 178
"Refusal to Mourn the Death, by Fire, of a Child in London, A" (Thomas), **Retro. Supp. III:** 345
Refutation of Deism, in a Dialogue, A (Shelley), **IV:** 208
"Refutation of Philosophies" (Bacon), **I:** 263
"Regency Houses" (Day Lewis), **Supp. III:** 127–128

Regeneration (Barker), **Supp. IV:** 45, 46, 57–59
Regeneration (Haggard), **Supp. III:** 214
"Regeneration" (Vaughan), **II:** 185, 187
Regent, The (Bennett), **VI:** 259, 267
Regicide, The (Smollett), **III:** 158
"Regina Cara" (Bridges), **VI:** 81
Reginald (Saki), **Supp. VI:** 240–242
"Reginald at the Theatre" (Saki), **Supp. VI:** 241–242
Reginald in Russia and Other Sketches (Saki), **Supp. VI:** 243–246
"Reginald on the Academy" (Saki), **Supp. VI:** 240
"Reginald's Choir Treat" (Saki), **Supp. VI:** 241, 249
Region of the Summer Stars, The (Williams, C. W. S.), **Supp. IX:** 283
"Regret" (Swinburne), **V:** 332
"Regrets" (Aidoo), **Supp. XV:** 10
Rehabilitations (Lewis), **Supp. III:** 249
Rehearsal, The (Buckingham), **II:** 206, 294
Rehearsal Transpros'd, The (Marvell), **II:** 205, 206–207, 209, 218, 219; **Retro. Supp. II:** 257–258, 264–266
Reid, Alastair, **Supp. VII: 323–337**
Reid, J. C., **IV:** 254, 267
Reign of Sparrows, The (Fuller), **Supp. VII:** 79
"Reiteration" (Conn), **Supp. XIII:** 73
"Reiterative" (Reading), **VIII:** 274
Rejected Address (Smith), **IV:** 253
"Relapse, The" (Vaughan), **II:** 187
Relapse, The; or, Virtue in Danger (Vanbrugh), **II:** 324, 326–329, 332, 334, 335, 336; **III:** 253, 261
Relation Between Michael Angelo and Tintoret, The (Ruskin), **V:** 184
Relationship of the Imprisonment of Mr. John Bunyan, A (Bunyan), **II:** 253
Relative Values (Coward), **Supp. II:** 155
Relatively Speaking (Ayckbourn), **Supp. V:** 2, 4, 13
"Relativity" (Empson), **Supp. II:** 182
"Release, The" (Gunn), **Retro. Supp. III:** 123, 124
"Release from Fever" (Cameron), **Supp. IX:** 23
"Relief" (Davies), **Supp. XIV:** 36, 37–38
Religio Laici; or, A Layman's Faith (Dryden), **I:** 176, 189; **II:** 291, 299, 304; **Retro. Supp. III:** 54
Religio Medici (Browne), **II:** 146–148, 150, 152, 156, 185; **III:** 40; **VII:** 29
"Religion" (Gibbon), **Supp. XIV:** 100, 103–104
"Religion" (Vaughan), **II:** 189
Religious Courtship: . . . Historical Discourses on . . . Marrying . . . (Defoe), **III:** 13
"Religious Musings" (Coleridge), **IV:** 43; **Retro. Supp. II:** 52
Reliques of Ancient English Poetry (Percy), **III:** 336; **IV:** 28–29
Reliquiae Wottonianae, **II:** 142
"Remain, ah not in youth alone" (Landor), **IV:** 99
Remains (Newman), **Supp. VII:** 295

Remains of Elmet (Hughes), **Supp. I:** 342; **Retro. Supp. II:** 210–211
Remains of Sir Fulke Grevill, Lord Brooke, The: Being Poems of Monarchy and Religion (Greville), **Supp. XI:** 108
Remains of Sir Walter Ralegh, The, **I:** 146, 157
Remains of the Day, The (Ishiguro), **Supp. IV:** 301–302, 304, 305, 306, 307, 311–314; **Retro. Supp. III:** 150, 154–157, 158, 161
Remake (Brooke–Rose), **Supp. IV:** 98, 99, 102
"Remarkable Rocket, The" (Wilde), **Retro. Supp. II:** 365
Remarks on Certain Passages of the 39 Articles (Newman), **Supp. VII:** 295–296
Remarks on the British Theatre (Inchbald), **Supp. XV:** 160–161
Remarks Upon a Late Disingenuous Discourse (Marvell), **II:** 219; **Retro. Supp. II:** 266
"Rembrandt's Late Self–Portraits" (Jennings), **Supp. V:** 211
Remede de Fortune (Machaut), **Retro. Supp. II:** 37
"Remember" (Rossetti), **VII:** 64
Remember Me (Weldon), **Supp. IV:** 535–536
"Remember Me When I Am Gone Away" (Rossetti), **V:** 249
"Remember Young Cecil" (Kelman), **Supp. V:** 245
Remembering Babylon (Malouf), **Supp. XII:** 218, 227–229
"Remembering Carrigskeewaun" (Longley), **VIII:** 174
"Remembering Lunch" (Dunn), **Supp. X:** 74
"Remembering Old Wars" (Kinsella), **Supp. V:** 263
Remembering Sion (Ryan), **VII:** 2
"Remembering the 90s" (Mahon), **Supp. VI:** 177
"Remembering the Thirties" (Davie), **Supp. VI:** 106
"Remembrances" (Clare), **Supp. XI:** 52
Remembrances of Words and Matter Against Richard Cholmeley, **I:** 277
Reminiscences (Carlyle), **IV:** 70n, 239, 240, 245, 250
"Reminiscences of Charlotte Brontë" (Nussey), **V:** 108, 109, 152
Reminiscences of the Impressionistic Painters (Moore), **VI:** 99
Remorse (Coleridge), **IV:** 56
Remorse: A Study in Saffron (Wilde), **V:** 419
"Removal" (Conn), **Supp. XIII:** 74, 75
"Removal from Terry Street, A" (Dunn), **Supp. X** 69–70
"Renaissance, The" (Symonds), **Supp. XIV:** 250
"Renaissance and Modern Times, The" (Carpenter), **Supp. XIII:** 44
Renaissance in Italy, The (Symonds), **Supp. XIV:** 249, 255–259

Renaissance: Studies in Art and Poetry, The (Pater), *see Studies in the History of the Renaissance*
Renan, Joseph Ernest, **II:** 244
Renault, Mary, **Supp. IX: 171–188**
Rendell, Ruth, **Supp. IX: 189–206**
Renegade Poet, And Other Essays, A (Thompson), **V:** 451
Renegado, The (Massinger), **Supp. XI:** 182, 184, 193
"Renounce thy God" (Dunbar), **VIII:** 122
"Renunciation" (Symonds), **Supp. XIV:** 251
"Repeated Rediscovery of America, The" (Wallace–Crabbe), **VIII:** 319
"Repentance" (Herbert), **II:** 128
Repentance of Robert Greene, The (Greene), **VIII:** 132, 134
"Rephan" (Browning), **IV:** 365
Replication (Skelton), **I:** 93
Reply to the Essay on Population, by the Rev. T. R. Malthus, A (Hazlitt), **IV:** 127, 139
"Report from Below, A" (Hood), **IV:** 258
"Report of an Adjudged Case" (Cowper), **Retro. Supp. III:** 47
"Report on a Threatened City" (Lessing), **Supp. I:** 250n
"Report on an Unidentified Space Station" (Ballard), **Supp. V:** 33
"Report on Experience" (Blunden), **VI:** 428;**Supp. XI:** 39
Report on the Salvation Army Colonies (Haggard), **Supp. III:** 214
"Report to the Trustees of the Bellahouston Travelling Scholarship, A" (Gray, A.), **Supp. IX:** 79–80, 82, 90
"Reported Missing" (Scannell), **VII:** 424
Reports on Elementary Schools, 1852–1882 (Arnold), **V:** 216
Reprinted Pieces (Dickens), **V:** 72
Reprisal, The (Smollett), **III:** 149, 158
Reproof: A Satire (Smollett), **III:** 158
Reptonian, The, **Supp. XIII:** 250
"Republic of Fife, The" (Jamie), **Supp. XIV:** 138–139
"Requiem" (Maitland), **Supp. XI:** 175
"Requiem" (Stevenson), **V:** 383; **Retro. Supp. I:** 268
"Requiem" (tr. Thomas), **Supp. IV:** 494–495
"Requiem for the Croppies" (Heaney), **Retro. Supp. I:** 127–128
"Requiescat" (Arnold), **V:** 211
"Requiescat" (Wilde), **V:** 400
Required Writing (Larkin), **Supp. I:** 286, 288; **Retro. Supp. III:** 199, 200, 204
"Re-Reading Jane" (Stevenson), **Supp. VI:** 262
Rescue, The (Conrad), **VI:** 136, 147
Resentment (Waugh), **Supp. VI:** 270
"Reservoirs" (Thomas), **Supp. XII:** 279
Residues (Thomas), **Supp. XII:** 282
"Resignation" (Arnold), **V:** 210
"Resolution and Independence" (Wordsworth), **IV:** 19–20, 22; **V:** 352
"Resound my voice, ye woods that hear me plain" (Wyatt), **I:** 110
Responsibilities (Yeats), **VI:** 213; **Retro. Supp. I:** 330

"Responsibility" (MacCaig), **Supp. VI:** 189
Responsio ad Lutherum (More), **Supp. VII:** 242–243
Ressoning betuix Aige and Yowth, The (Henryson), **Supp. VII:** 146, 147
Ressoning betuix Deth and Man, The (Henryson), **Supp. VII:** 146, 147
Restless (Boyd), **Supp. XVI:** 42–43
Restoration (Bond), **Supp. I:** 423, 434, 435
Restoration of Arnold Middleton, The (Storey), **Supp. I:** 408, 411, 412–413, 414, 415, 417
"Resurgam" (Pitter), **Supp. XIII:** 139–140
"Resurrection, The" (Cowley), **II:** 200
Resurrection, The (Yeats), **VI:** xiv, 222
"Resurrection and Immortality" (Vaughan), **II:** 185, 186
Resurrection at Sorrow Hill (Harris), **Supp. V:** 144
Resurrection Men (Rankin), **Supp. X:** 245, 256–257
Resurrection of the Dead, The, . . . (Bunyan), **II:** 253
"Retaliation" (Goldsmith), **III:** 181, 185, 191
"Reticence of Lady Anne, The" (Saki), **Supp. VI:** 245
"Retired" (Thomas), **Supp. XII:** 291
"Retired Cat, The" (Cowper), **III:** 217; **Retro. Supp. III:** 36
"Retirement" (Vaughan), **II:** 187, 188, 189
"Retreat, The" (King), **Supp. VI:** 153
"Retreate, The" (Vaughan), **II:** 186, 188–189
"Retrospect" (Brooke), **Supp. III:** 56
"Retrospect: From a Street in Chelsea" (Day Lewis), **Supp. III:** 121
Retrospect of Western Travel (Martineau), **Supp. XV:** 186
"Retrospective Review" (Hood), **IV:** 255
"Return, The" (Conrad), **VI:** 148
"Return, The" (Muir), **Supp. VI:** 207
"Return, A" (Russell), **VIII:** 284
"Return" (Soutar), **Supp. XVI:** 250
"Return, The" (Stallworthy), **Supp. X:** 298
"Return in Harvest" (O'Connor), **Supp. XIV:** 222
Return from Parnassus, The, part 2, **II:** 27
"Return from the Freudian Islands, The" (Hope), **Supp. VII:** 155–156, 157
"Return from the Islands" (Redgrove), **Supp. VI:** 235
Return of Eva Peron, The (Naipaul), **Supp. I:** 396, 397, 398, 399
"Return of the Druses, The" (Browning), **IV:** 374
"Return of the Iron Man, The" (Hughes), **Supp. I:** 346
Return of John Macnab, The (Greig), **Supp. XVI:** 167–168, 174
Return of the King, The (Tolkien), **Supp. II:** 519
Return of the Native, The (Hardy), **V:** xxiv, 279; **VI:** 1–2, 5, 6, 7, 8; **Retro.**

Supp. I: 114
Return of the Soldier, The (West), **Supp. III:** 440, 441
"Return of the Swallow, The" (Soutar), **Supp. XVI:** 252
Return of Ulysses, The (Bridges), **VI:** 83
Return to Abyssinia (White), **Supp. I:** 131
Return to My Native Land (tr. Berger), **Supp. IV:** 77
Return to Naples (Reed), **Supp. XV:** 247, 252
Return to Night (Renault), **Supp. IX:** 175
Return to Oasis (Durrell), **VII:** 425
"Return to the Council House" (Smith, I. C.), **Supp. IX:** 214
Return to Yesterday (Ford), **VI:** 149
Returning (O'Brien), **Supp. V:** 339
"Returning of Issue" (Reed), **Supp. XV:** 250, 251
"Returning, We Hear the Larks" (Rosenberg), **VI:** 434–435
Revaluation (Leavis), **III:** 68; **VII:** 234, 236, 244–245
"Reveille" (Hughes), **Supp. I:** 350
Revelation of Love, A (Julian of Norwich), **Supp. XII:** 149, 150, 153–162, 163–165
Revelations of Divine Love (Julian of Norwich), **I:** 20–21; **Supp. XII:** 155
"Revenge, A" (Symons), **Supp. XIV:** 271
Revenge for Love, The (Lewis), **VII:** 72, 74, 81
Revenge Is Sweet: Two Short Stories (Hardy), **VI:** 20
Revenge of Bussy D'Ambois, The (Chapman), **I:** 251–252, 253; **II:** 37
Revenger's Tragedy, The, **II:** 1–2, 21, 29, **33–36**, 37, 39, 40, 41, 70, 97
Revengers' Comedies, The (Ayckbourn), **Supp. V:** 3, 10
Reverberator, The (James), **VI:** 67
"Reverie" (Browning), **IV:** 365
Reveries over Childhood and Youth (Yeats), **VI:** 222
Reversals (Stevenson), **Supp. VI:** 255–256
"Reversals" (Stevenson), **Supp. VI:** 256
Reverse of the Medal, The (O'Brian), **Supp. XII:** 256, 257, 258, 260
Review (periodical), **II:** 325; **III:** 4, 13, 39, 41, 42, 51, 53
"Review, The" (Traherne), **Supp. XI:** 269
Review Christmas Annuals, **Supp. XIII:** 242
Review of Reviews, **Supp. XIII:** 241–243
Review of some poems by Alexander Smith and Matthew Arnold (Clough), **V:** 158
Review of the Affairs of France, A . . . (Defoe), **III:** 13; **Retro. Supp. I:** 65
Review of the Proceedings Against Dr. Bentley, A (Byrom), **Supp. XVI:** 79
Review of the State of the British Nation, A (Defoe), **Retro. Supp. I:** 65
"Reviewer's ABC, A" (Aiken), **VII:** 149
Revised Version of the Bible, **I:** 381–382
"Revision" (Adcock), **Supp. XII:** 8
Revival of Learning, The (Symonds), **Supp. XIV:** 256

Revolt in the Desert (Lawrence), **Supp. II:** 288, 289–290, 293
Revolt of Aphrodite, The (Durrell), **Retro. Supp. III:** 85, 86, 87, 90–92
Revolt of Islam, The (Shelley), **IV:** xvii, 198, 203, 208; **VI:** 455; **Retro. Supp. I:** 249–250
"Revolt of the Tartars" (De Quincey), **IV:** 149
Revolt of the Triffids, The (Wyndham), **Supp. XIII:** 281
Revolving Lights (Richardson), **Supp. XIII:** 184–185, 190
"Revolution" (Housman), **VI:** 160
Revolution in Tanner's Lane, The (Rutherford), **VI:** 240
Revolution of Sweden, The (Trotter), **Supp. XVI:** 279, 284–286
Revolution Script, The (Moore, B.), **Supp. IX:** 141, 143
Revolutionary Epick, The (Disraeli), **IV:** 306, 308
Revolving Lights (Richardson), **Retro. Supp. I:** 313–314
Revue des Deux Mondes (Montégut), **V:** 102
Revue d'ethnographie et de sociologie, **Supp. XIII:** 44
"Revulsion" (Davie), **Supp. VI:** 110, 112
Rewards and Fairies (Kipling), **Retro. Supp. III:** 190, 195
"Rex Imperator" (Wilson), **Supp. I:** 155, 156
"Reynard the Fox" (Masefield), **VI:** 338
Reynolds, G. W. M., **III:** 335
Reynolds, Henry, **Supp. IV:** 350
Reynolds, John, **II:** 14
Reynolds, John Hamilton, **IV:** 215, 221, 226, 228, 229, 232, 233, 253, 257, 259, 281
Reynolds, Sir Joshua, **II:** 336; **III:** 305
"Rhapsody of Life's Progress, A" (Browning), **IV:** 313
"Rhapsody on a Windy Night" (Eliot), **Retro. Supp. II:** 121–122
Rhetor (Harvey), **I:** 122
"Rhetoric" (De Quincey), **IV:** 147
"Rhetoric" (Jennings), **Supp. V:** 218
"Rhetoric and Poetic Drama" (Eliot), **VII:** 157
"Rhetoric of a Journey" (Fuller), **Supp. VII:** 72
Rhetoric of the Unreal: Studies in Narrative and Structure, Especially of the Fantastic, A (Brooke–Rose)), **Supp. IV:** 97, 99, 115, 116
"Rhetorical Meditations in Time of Peace" (Montague), **Supp. XV:** 213
"Rhineland Journal" (Spender), **Supp. II:** 489
Rhoda Fleming (Meredith), **V:** xxiii, 227n, 234
"Rhodian Captain" (Durrell), **Supp. I:** 124
Rhododaphne (Peacock), **IV:** 158, 170
Rhyme? and Reason? (Carroll), **V:** 270, 273
Rhyme Stew (Dahl), **Supp. IV:** 226
"Rhyming Cufflinks" (Raine), **Supp. XIII:** 164

Rhys, Jean, **Supp. II: 387–403; Supp. V:** 40; **Retro. Supp. I:** 60
"Rhythm and Imagery in British Poetry" (Empson), **Supp. II:** 195
"Ribblesdale" (Hopkins), **V:** 367, 372; **Retro. Supp. II:** 191
Ribner, Irving, **I:** 287
Riccoboni, Luigi, **II:** 348
Riceyman Steps (Bennett), **VI:** 250, 252, 260–261
Rich, Barnaby, **I:** 312
Rich (Raine), **Supp. XIII:** 167–168
"Rich" (Raine), **Supp. XIII:** 168
Rich Get Rich (Kavan), **Supp. VII:** 208–209
Richard II (Shakespeare), **I:** 286, 308; **Retro. Supp. III:** 273–274, 278
Richard III (Shakespeare), **I:** 285, 299–301
"Richard Martin" (Hood), **IV:** 267
Richard Rolle of Hampole, **I:** 20
Richard Temple (O'Brian), **Supp. XII:** 251, 252
Richards, I. A., **III:** 324; **V:** 367, 381; **VI:** 207, 208; **VII:** xiii, 233, 239; **Supp. II:** 185, 193, **405–431**
Richard's Cork Leg (Behan), **Supp. II:** 65, 74
Richards, Grant, **VI:** 158
Richardson, Betty, **Supp. IV:** 330
Richardson, Dorothy, **VI:** 372; **VII:** 20; **Supp. IV:** 233; **Retro. Supp. I:** 313–314; **Supp. XIII: 179–193**
Richardson, Elaine Cynthia Potter, *see* Kincaid, Jamaica
Richardson, Joanna, **IV:** xxv, 236; **V:** xi, xviii
Richardson, Samuel, **III: 80–93,** 94, 98, 333; **VI:** 266 **Supp. II:** 10; **Supp. III:** 26, 30–31; **Supp. IV:** 150; **Retro. Supp. I:** 80
"Richey" (Adcock), **Supp. XII:** 6
"Richt Respeck for Cuddies, A" (tr. Morgan, E.), **Supp. IX:** 168
Ricks, Christopher, **Supp. IV:** 394, 398
Riddarasögur, **VIII:** 236
"Riddle of Houdini, The" (Doyle), **Supp. II:** 163–164
Riddle of Midnight, The (film, Rushdie), **Supp. IV:** 436, 441
Riddles in Scots (Soutar), **Supp. XVI:** 253
"Ride from Milan, The" (Swinburne), **V:** 325, 333
"Ride Round the Parapet, The" (Mangan), **Supp. XIII:** 122
Riders in the Chariot (White), **Supp. I:** 131, 132, 133, 136, **141–143,** 152
Riders to the Sea (Synge), **VI:** xvi, 308, 309, 310–311; **Retro. Supp. I:** 296
Ridiculous Mountains, The (Dutton), **Supp. XII:** 85
Riding, Laura, **VI:** 207; **VII:** 258, 260, 261, 263, 269; **Supp. II:** 185; **Supp. III:** 120
Riding Lights (MacCaig), **Supp. VI:** 181, **185–186,** 190, 194
Riffaterre, Michael, **Supp. IV:** 115
Rigby, Elizabeth, **V:** 138

"Right Apprehension" (Traherne), **Supp. XI:** 266
Right at Last and Other Tales (Gaskell), **V:** 15
Right Ho, Jeeves (Wodehouse), **Supp. III:** 458, 461
"Right Possessor, The" (Gunn), **Retro. Supp. III:** 118
"Right Season, The" (Kay), **Supp. XIII:** 104
Right to an Answer, The (Burgess), **Supp. I:** 187, 188–189, 190, 195, 196
Righter, Anne, **I:** 224, 269, 329
Rights of Great Britain asserted against the Claims of America (Macpherson), **VIII:** 193
Rights of Passage (Brathwaite), **Supp. XII:** 33, 34, 36–38, 39, 40, 41, 45
Rígsþula, **VIII:** 231
Rilke, Rainer Maria, **VI:** 215; **Supp. IV:** 480
Rimbaud, Jean Nicolas, **Supp. IV:** 163
"Rime of the Ancient Mariner, The" (Coleridge), *see* "Ancient Mariner, The"
Riming Poem, The, **Retro. Supp. II:** 304
Ring, The (Wagner), **V:** 300
Ring and the Book, The (Browning), **IV:** xxiii, 358, 362, 369, 373, 374; **Retro. Supp. II:** 28–29; **Retro. Supp. III:** 17, 27–30, 31
Ring Round the Moon (Fry), **Supp. III:** 195, 207
"Ringed Plover by a Water's Edge" (MacCaig), **Supp. VI:** 192
Rings of Saturn, The (Sebald), **VIII:** 295, 303–305, 308
Rings on a Tree (MacCaig), **Supp. VI:** 190
Ripley Under Ground (Highsmith), **Supp. V:** 171
Ripley Under Water (Highsmith), **Supp. V:** 171
Ripley's Game (Highsmith), **Supp. V:** 171
Ripple from the Storm, A (Lessing), **Supp. I:** 244–245
Rise and Fall of the House of Windsor, The (Wilson), **Sup. VI:** 308
"Rise of Historical Criticism, The" (Wilde), **V:** 401, 419
Rise of Iskander, The (Disraeli), **IV:** 308
Rise of the Russian Empire, The (Saki), **Supp. VI:** 239
"Rising, The" (Delanty), **Supp. XIV:** 66–67
"Rising Five" (Nicholson), **Supp. VI: 216**
Rising of the Moon, The (Gregory), **VI:** 315, 316
Risk of Darkness, The (Hill), **Supp. XIV:** 116, 126
Ritchie, Lady Anne, **V:** 10
"Rite and Fore–Time" (Jones), **Supp. VII:** 176
Rite of the Passion, The (Williams, C. W. S.), **Supp. IX:** 276–277
"Rites" (Brathwaite), **Supp. XII:** 40, 45
Rites of Passage (Golding), **Supp. I:** 86–87; **Retro. Supp. I:** 103–104
"Rites of Passage" (Gunn), **Supp. IV:** 266; **Retro. Supp. III:** 122

"Ritual of Departure" (Kinsella), **Supp. V:** 264
"Rival, The" (Warner), **Supp. VII:** 371
Rival Ladies, The (Dryden), **II:** 293, 297, 305
Rivals, The (Sheridan), **III:** 253, **257–259**, 270
Rive, Richard, **Supp. II:** 342–343, 350
River (Hughes), **Supp. I:** 363; **Retro. Supp. II:** 212–214
"River, The" (Muir), **Supp. VI:** 206
"River" (Wallace–Crabbe), **VIII:** 320
River Between, The (Ngũgĩ), **VIII:** 218–219
River Dudden, The, a Series of Sonnets (Wordsworth), **IV:** 24
River Girl, The (Cope), **VIII:** 69, 74–75
"River God, The" (Smith), **Supp. II:** 472
River Town, A (Keneally), **Supp. IV:** 347, 348
River War, The (Churchill), **VI:** 351
Rivers, W. H. R., **Supp. IV:** 46, 57, 58
Riverside Chaucer, The (ed. Benson), **Retro. Supp. II:** 49
Riverside Villas Murder, The (Amis), **Supp. II:** 12
Riviere, Michael, **VII:** 422, 424
Road, The (Mda), **Supp. XV:** 197, 198
"Road from Colonus, The" (Forster), **VI:** 399
"Road Hazard, The" (Delanty), **Supp. XIV:** 75
Road Rage (Rendell), **Supp. IX:** 196, 198
"Road These Times Must Take, The" (Day Lewis), **Supp. III:** 126–127
Road to Camlann (Sutcliff), **Supp. XVI:** 262, 271–272, 273
"Road to Emmaus, The" (Brown), **Supp. VI:** 70
Road to Huddersifield: A Journey to Five Continents, The (Morris), see *World Bank: A Prospect, The*
Road to Mecca, The (Fugard), **Supp. XV:** 101, 104, 111–112
Road to Samarcand, The (O'Brian), **Supp. XII:** 251
"Road to the Big City, A" (Lessing), **Supp. I:** 240
Road to Volgograd (Sillitoe), **Supp. V:** 409
Road to Wigan Pier, The (Orwell), **VII:** 274, 279–280
Road to Xanadu, The (Lowes), **IV:** 47, 57
"Road Uphill, The," (Maugham), **VI:** 377
"Roads" (Burnside), **Supp. XIII:** 24
"Roads" (Stevenson), **V:** 386
"Roads" (Thomas), **Supp. III:** 404, 406
Roald Dahl's Revolting Rhymes (Dahl), **Supp. IV:** 226
Roaring Girl, The (Dekker and Middleton), **II:** 3, 21
Roaring Queen, The (Lewis), **VII:** 82
Rob Roy (Scott), **IV:** xvii, 33, 34, 39
Robbe–Grillet, Alain, **Supp. IV:** 99, 104, 115, 116
Robbery Under Law (Waugh), **VII:** 292, 294
Robbins, Bruce, **Supp. IV:** 95

Robe of Rosheen, The (O'Casey), **VII:** 12
Robene and Makyne (Henryson), **Supp. VII:** 146, 147
Robert Bridges and Gerard Manley Hopkins (Ritz), **VI:** 83
Robert Bridges 1844–1930 (Thompson), **VI:** 83
"Robert Bridges: His Work on the English Language" (Daryush), **VI:** 76
Robert Browning (ed. Armstrong), **IV:** 375
Robert Browning (Chesterton), **VI:** 344
Robert Browning (Jack), **IV:** 375
Robert Browning: A Collection of Critical Essays (Drew), **IV:** 375
Robert Burns (Swinburne), **V:** 333
Robert Graves: His Life and Work (Seymour–Smith), **VII:** 272
Robert Louis Stevenson (Chesterton), **V:** 391, 393, 397; **VI:** 345
Robert Louis Stevenson (Cooper), **V:** 397, 398
Robert Louis Stevenson. An Essay (Stephen), **V:** 290
Robert Louis Stevenson: Man and Writer (Stewart), **V:** 393, 397
Robert Macaire (Stevenson), **V:** 396
Robert of Sicily: Opera for Children (Fry and Tippett), **Supp. III:** 194
Robert Southey and His Age (Carnall), **IV:** 72
Robert the Second, King of Scots (Jonson/Chettle/Dekker), **Retro. Supp. I:** 157
Roberts, Keith, **Supp. X:** **261–276**
Roberts, Michael, **VII:** xix, 411
Roberts, Michèle, **Supp. XV:** **259–275**
Roberts, Morley, **V:** 425, 427, 428, 438
Robertson, Thomas, **V:** 330; **VI:** 269
Robin Hood: A Fragment, by the Late Robert Southey, and Caroline Southey, **IV:** 71
Robinson, Henry Crabb, **IV:** 11, 52, 56, 81
Robinson, Henry Morton, **VII:** 53
Robinson, Lennox, **VI:** 96
Robinson, Mary Darby, **Supp. XIII:** **195–216**
Robinson (Spark), **Supp. I:** 201, 202–203
Robinson Crusoe (Defoe), **III:** 1, 5, 6, 7, 8, 10–12, 13, 24, 42, 50, 95; **Supp. I:** 73; **Retro. Supp. I:** 65–66, 68, 70–71
"Robinson Tradition, The" (Milne), **Supp. V:** 304
"Robinson's Life Sentence" (Armitage), **VIII:** 6
"Robinson's Resignation" (Armitage), **VIII:** 6
Roche, Denis, **Supp. IV:** 115
Roche, Maurice, **Supp. IV:** 116
Rochester, earl of, **II:** 208n, 255, 256, **257–261**, 269–270; **Supp. III:** 39, 40, 70
Rock, The (Eliot), **VII:** 153
"Rock, The" (Hughes), **Supp. I:** 341, 342; **Retro. Supp. II:** 199
Rock Face (Nicholson), **Supp. VI:** 213, **216–217**
Rock Pool, The (Connolly), **Supp. III:** **98–100**

Rockaby (Beckett), **Supp. I:** 61; **Retro. Supp. I:** 28–29
"Rocking–Horse Winner, The" (Lawrence), **Supp. IV:** 511
Roderick Hudson (James), **VI:** 24, **26–28**, 42, 67
Roderick Random (Smollett), **III:** 150–152, 158
Roderick, The Last of the Goths (Southey), **IV:** 65–66, 68, 71
Rodinsky's Room (Sinclair), **Supp. XIV:** 241, 242, 244
Rodker, John, **VI:** 327
Roe Head journals (Brontë), **V:** 119–122
"Roger Ascham and Lady Jane Grey" (Landor), **IV:** 92
"Roger Bear's Philosophical Pantoum" (Cope), **VIII:** 76–77
Roger Fry (Woolf), **Retro. Supp. I:** 308
Rogers, Charles, **III:** 249
Rogers, Woodes, **III:** 7
"Rois Fainéants" (Auden), **Retro. Supp. I:** 14
"Roísín Dubh" (Mangan), **Supp. XIII:** 129
Rojas Zorilla, Francisco de, **II:** 325
Rokeby (Scott), **IV:** 38
Roland Whately (Waugh), **Supp. VI:** 270
"Roll for Joe, A" (Kelman), **Supp. V:** 244–245
"Rolling English Road, The" (Chesterton), **I:** 16
Rollins, Hyder, **IV:** 231, 232, 235
Rollo, Duke of Normandy (Chapman, Fletcher, Jonson, Massinger), **II:** 45, 66
Roman Actor, The (Massinger), **Supp. XI:** 180–181, 183
Roman de la rose, **I:** 28, 49; tr. Chaucer, **I:** 28, 31
Roman de Troie (Benoît de Sainte-Maure), **I:** 53
Roman expérimental (Zola), **V:** 286
Roman Forgeries; or, A True Account of False Records Discovering the Impostures and Counterfeit Antiquities of the Church of Rome (Traherne), **II:** 190, 191, 201; **Supp. XI:** 264, 265, 276–277
Roman History, The (Goldsmith), **III:** 180, 181, 191
Roman Poems (Sisson), **Supp. XI:** 249
Roman Quarry and Other Sequences, The (Jones), **Supp. VII:** 167, 171
"Roman Thoughts in Autumn" (Wallace-Crabbe), **VIII:** 317
Romance (Conrad and Ford), **VI:** 146, 148, 321
"Romance" (Sitwell), **VII:** 132–133
Romance and Realism (Caudwell), **Supp. IX:** 33, 43, 45–46
"Romance in Ireland" (Yeats), **Retro. Supp. I:** 330
"Romance of Certain Old Clothes, The" (James), **VI:** 69
Romance of the Forest, The (Radcliffe), **Retro. Supp. III:** 234, 240–242, 246
"Romance of the Lily, The" (Beddoes), **Supp. XI:** 28
"Romania" (Adcock), **Supp. XII:** 11

Romanno Bridge (Greig), **Supp. XVI:** 174

Romantic Adventures of A Milkmaid, The (Hardy), **VI:** 20, 22

Romantic Agony, The (Praz), **III:** 337, 346; **V:** 412, 420

Romantic Image (Kermode), **V:** 344, 359, 412

Romantic Poetry and the Fine Arts (Blunden), **IV:** 236

"Romanticism and Classicism" (Hulme), **Supp. VI:** 135, 138, 142–145

Romany Rye, The; A Sequel to "Lavengro" (Borrow), **Supp. XII:** 17, 27–28

"Romaunt of Margaret, The" (Browning), **IV:** 313

Romeo and Juliet (Shakespeare), **I:** 229, 305–306, 320; **II:** 281; **IV:** 218; **Retro. Supp. III:** 268, 273, 277–278, 282

Romola (Eliot), **V:** xxii, 66, 194–195, 200; **Retro. Supp. II:** 110–111

Romulus and Hersilia; or, The Sabine War (Behn), **Supp. III:** 29

"Rondeau Redoublé" (Cope), **VIII:** 71

Rondeaux Parisiens (Swinburne), **V:** 333

"Rooftop, The" (Gunn), **Retro. Supp. III:** 122

"Roof-Tree" (Murphy), **Supp. V:** 329

Rookwood (Ainsworth), **V:** 47

Room, The (Day Lewis), **Supp. III:** 118, 129–130

"Room, The" (Day Lewis), **Supp. III:** 130

Room, The (Pinter), **Supp. I:** 367, 369; **Retro. Supp. I:** 216, 218, 221–222

"Room Above the Square" (Spender), **Supp. II:** 494

Room at the Top (Braine), **Supp. IV:** 238

Room of One's Own, A (Woolf), **VII:** 22–23, 25–26, 27, 38; **Supp. III:** 19, 41–42; **Supp. V:** 36; **Retro. Supp. I:** 310–314

Room with a View, A (Forster), **VI:** 398, 399, **403–404**; **Retro. Supp. II:** 141–143

"Rooms, The" (Stallworthy), **Supp. X:** 298

"Rooms of Other Women Poets, The" (Boland), **Supp. V:** 37

Rope (Hamilton), **Supp. XVI:** 177, 179

Root and Branch (Stallworthy), **Supp. X:** 293–296

Rootham, Helen, **VII:** 129

Roots (Brathwaite), **Supp. XII:** 43, 44, 45

"Roots" (Brathwaite), **Supp. XII:** 43

Roots of Coincidence (Koestler), **Supp. I:** 39

"Roots of Honour, The" (Ruskin), **V:** 179–180

Roots of the Mountains, The (Morris), **V:** 302, 306

Roppen, G., **V:** 221*n*

Rosalind and Helen (Shelley), **IV:** 208

Rosalynde (Lodge), **I:** 312

Rosamond, Queen of the Lombards (Swinburne), **V:** 312–314, 330, 331, 332, 333

Rose, Ellen Cronan, **Supp. IV:** 232

"Rose, The" (Southey), **IV:** 64

Rose, The (Yeats), **Retro. Supp. I:** 330

Rose and Crown (O'Casey), **VII:** 13

Rose and the Ring, The (Thackeray), **V:** 38, 261

Rose Blanche (McEwan), **Supp. IV:** 390

Rose in the Heart, A (O'Brien), **Supp. V:** 339

"Rose in the Heart of New York, A" (O'Brien), **Supp. V:** 340–341

"Rose Mary" (Rossetti), **V:** 238, 244

Rose of Life, The (Braddon), **VIII:** 49

"Rosebud, The" (Tennyson), **Retro. Supp. III:** 322

Rosemary's Baby (film), **III:** 343

Rosenberg, Bruce, **Supp. IV:** 7

Rosenberg, Eleanor, **I:** 233

Rosenberg, Isaac, **VI:** xvi, 417, 420, **432–435**; **VII:** xvi; **Supp. III:** 59

Rosenberg, John, **V:** 316, 334

Rosencrantz and Guildenstern Are Dead (Stoppard), **Supp. I:** **440–443**, 444, 451; **Retro. Supp. II:** 343–345

Rosenfeld, S., **II:** 271

Rosengarten (Bevan and Galloway), **Supp. XII:** 117

"Roses on the Terrace, The" (Tennyson), **IV:** 329, 336

"Rosie Plum" (Powys), **VIII:** 251

Rosie Plum and Other Stories (Powys), **VIII:** 251, 252

"Rosiphelee" (Gower), **I:** 53–54

Ross (Rattigan), **Supp. VII:** 320, 321

Ross, Alan, **VII:** xxii, 422, 433–434

Ross, John Hume (pseud., Lawrence), **Supp. II:** 286, 295

Rossetti, Christina, **V:** xi–xii, xix, xxii, xxvi, **247–260**; **Supp. IV:** 139; **Retro. Supp. III:** **251–265**

Rossetti, Dante Gabriel, **IV:** 346; **V:** ix, xi, xii, xviii, xxiii–xxv, **235–246**, 247–253, 259, 293–296, 298, 299, 312–315, 320, 329, 355, 401; **VI:** 167

Rossetti, Maria **V:** 251, 253

Rossetti, William, **V:** 235, 236, 245, 246, 248–249, 251–253, 260

Rossetti (Waugh), **VII:** 291

Rossetti and His Circle (Beerbohm), **Supp. II:** 51

"Rossetti's Conception of the 'Poetic' " (Doughty), **V:** 246

Røstvig, Maren-Sofie, **I:** 237

"Rosyfingered, The" (MacCaig), **Supp. VI:** 186

"Rot, The" (Lewis), **VII:** 73

Rotten Elements, The (Upward), **Supp. XIII:** 250, 255, 257

"Rotter, The" (Nye), **Supp. X:** 204

Rotters Club, The (Coe), **Supp. XV:** 49–50, 51, 52, 57–58, 59, 62

Rotting Hill (Lewis), **VII:** 72

Rough Field, The (Montague), **Supp. XV:** 209, 212, 215, 216, 219–220, 222

Rough Justice (Braddon), **VIII:** 37, 49

Rough Shoot (film, Ambler), **Supp. IV:** 3

"Roull of Corstorphin" (Conn), **Supp. XIII:** 80–81

Round and Round the Garden (Ayckbourn), **Supp. V:** 2, 5

"Round Another Point" (Larkin), **Retro. Supp. III:** 203

Round of Applause, A (MacCaig), **Supp. VI:** **187–188**, 190, 194–195

Round Table, The (Hazlitt), **IV:** xvii, 129, 137, 139

Round Table, The; or, King Arthur's Feast (Peacock), **IV:** 170

"Round Table Manners" (Nye), **Supp. X:** 202–203

Round Sofa, The (Gaskell), **V:** 3, 15

Roundabout Papers (Thackeray), **V:** 34, 35, 38

Roundheads, The; or, The Good Old Cause (Behn), **Supp. III:** 25; **Retro. Supp. III:** 13

Rounding the Horn: Collected Poems (Stallworthy), **Supp. X:** 292–294, 298, 302

Rousseau, Jean Jacques, **III:** 235, 236; **IV:** xiv, 207; **Supp. III:** 239–240

"ROUTINE DRUGS I—for Eldred" (Aidoo), **Supp. XV:** 10–11

"ROUTINE DRUGS II—" (Aidoo), **Supp. XV:** 11

Rover, The (Conrad), **VI:** 144, 147, 148

Rover, The; or, The Banish'd Cavaliers (Behn), **Supp. III:** 26, 27–29, 31

Rover Part 1, The (Behn), **Retro. Supp. III:** 2, 4, 10–12

Rover Part 2, The (Behn), **Retro. Supp. III:** 12, 13

Royal Edinburgh (Oliphant), **Supp. X:** 222

"Royal Princess, A" (Rossetti), **Retro. Supp. III:** 251, 261, 262

Rowe, Nicholas, **I:** 326

Rowley, Hazel, **Supp. IV:** 459, 460

Rowley, William, **II:** 1, 3, 14, 15, 18, 21, 66, 69, 83, 89, 100

Rowling, J. K., **Supp. XVI:** **225–240**

Roxana (Defoe), **III:** 8–9, 14; **Retro. Supp. I:** 69, 74

Roy, Arundhati, **Supp. V:** xxx, 67, 75

Royal Academy, The (Moore), **VI:** 98

Royal Beasts, The (Empson), **Supp. II:** 180, 184

Royal Combat, The (Ford), **II:** 100

Royal Court Theatre, **VI:** 101

Royal Hunt of the Sun, The (Shaffer), **Supp. I:** 314, **319–322**, 323, 324, 327

"Royal Jelly" (Dahl), **Supp. IV:** 221

"Royal Man" (Muir), **I:** 247

"Royal Naval Air Station" (Fuller), **Supp. VII:** 69

Royal Pardon, The (Arden and D'Arcy), **Supp. II:** 30

"Royal Visit, A" (Montague), **Supp. XV:** 214

Rubáiyát of Omar Khayyám, The (FitzGerald), **IV:** xxii, 342–343, **345–348**, 349, 352, 353; **V:** 318

Rubin, Merle, **Supp. IV:** 360

Ruby in the Smoke, The (Pullman), **Supp. XIII:** 150, 151

Rudd, Margaret, **VI:** 209

Rudd, Steele, **Supp. IV:** 460

Rude Assignment (Lewis), **VI:** 333; **VII:** xv, 72, 74, 76

Rude Potato, The (Pitter), **Supp. XIII:** 134, 135, 142–143

Rudolf II, Emperor of Holy Roman Empire, **Supp. IV:** 174
Rudyard Kipling (Sutcliff), **Supp. XVI:** 262
Rudyard Kipling, Realist and Fabulist (Dobrée), **VI:** 200–203
Rudyard Kipling to Rider Haggard (ed. Cohen), **VI:** 204
Ruell, Patrick, *see* Hill, Reginald
Ruffhead, O., **III:** 69*n*, 71
Ruffian on the Stair, The (Orton), **Supp. V:** 367, 370, 372, 373
"Rugby Chapel" (Arnold), **V:** 203
"Ruin, The" (tr. Morgan), **Supp. IX:** 160
Ruin, The, **Retro. Supp. II:** 305
Ruined Boys, The (Fuller), **Supp. VII:** 74, 75
"Ruined Cottage, The," (Wordsworth), **IV:** 23, 24
"Ruined Farm, The" (Plomer), **Supp. XI:** 213
"Ruined Maid, The" (Hardy), **Retro. Supp. I:** 120
Ruins and Visions (Spender), **Supp. II:** 486, 489
Ruins of Time, The (Spenser), **I:** 124
Rukeyser, Muriel, **Supp. V:** 261
Rule a Wife and Have a Wife (Fletcher), **II:** 45, 65
Rule Britannia (du Maurier), **Supp. III:** 133, 147
"Rule, Britannia" (Thomson), **Supp. III:** 412, 425
"Rules and Lessons" (Vaughan), **II:** 187
Rules for Court Circular (Carroll), **V:** 274
"Rummy Affair of Old Biffy, The" (Wodehouse), **Supp. III:** 455, 457
Ruling Passion (Hill, R.), **Supp. IX:** 113–114
Rumors of Rain (Brink), **Supp. VI: 49–50**
Rumour at Nightfall (Greene), **Supp. I:** 3
"Run"(Motion), **Supp. V:** 259
Runaway, The (Cowley), **Supp. XVI:** 110–111, 114, 122
Rungs of Time (Wallace–Crabbe), **VIII:** 323–324, 325
"Running Stream, The" (Blunden), **Supp. XI:** 43–44
Running Wild (Ballard), **Supp. V:** 30–31
Rural Denmark (Haggard), **Supp. III:** 214
Rural England (Haggard), **Supp. III:** 214
Rural Minstrel, The (Brontë), **V:** 107, 151
Rural Muse, The: Poems (Clare), **Supp. XI:** 59, 60, 63
Rural Sports: A Poem (Gay), **III:** 67
Rushdie, Salman, **Supp. IV:** 65, 75, 116, 157, 160, 161, 162, 170–171, 174, 302, **433–456; Supp. V:** 67, 68, 74
Rushing to Paradise (Ballard), **Supp. V:** 31
Ruskin, John, **IV:** 320, 346; **V:** xii, xviii, xx–xxii, xxvi, 3, 9, 17, 20, 85–86, **173–185,** 235, 236, 291–292, 345, 362, 400; **VI:** 167
Ruskin's Politics (Shaw), **VI:** 129
Russ, R. P. *see* O'Brian, Patrick
Russell, Bertrand, **VI:** xi, 170, 385; **VII:** 90
Russell, G. W. E., **IV:** 292, 304

Russell, George William, **VIII: 277–293**
Russell, John, **Supp. IV:** 126
Russia House, The (le Carré), **Supp. II:** 300, 310, 311, 313, **318–319**; **Retro. Supp. III:** 223
Russian Interpreter, The (Frayn), **Supp. VII:** 52–53, 54
Russian Nights (Thomas), **Supp. IV:** 483–486
Rusticus (Poliziano), **I:** 240
"Ruth" (Crabbe), **V:** 6
Ruth (Gaskell), **V:** xxi, 1, 6–7, 15; **Retro. Supp. III:** 100, 101, 103–104, 110
"Ruth" (Hood), **IV:** 255
Ryan, Desmond, **VII:** 2
"Ryecroft" (Butlin), **Supp. XVI:** 58
Rymer, James Malcolm, **Supp. III:** 385
Rymer, Thomas, **I:** 328
Ryskamp, C., **III:** 249
"Ryton Firs" (Abercrombie), **Supp. XVI:** 10

"**S.** K." (Thomas), **Supp. XII:** 285
S. T. Coleridge (ed. Brett), **IV:** 57
"Sabbath" (Fallon), **Supp. XII:** 108
"Sabbath" (Jamie), **Supp. XIV:** 145
"Sabbath Morning at Sea, A" (Browning), **IV:** 313
"Sabbath Park" (McGuckian), **Supp. V:** 283–284
Sackville, Charles, *see* Dorset, earl of
Sackville, Thomas, **I:** 169, 214
Sackville–West, Edward, **VII:** 35, 59
Sacred and Profane Love Machine, The (Murdoch), **Supp. I:** 224
"Sacred Chow" (Desai), **Supp. XV:** 92
Sacred Flame, The (Maugham), **VI:** 369
Sacred Fount, The (James), **VI:** 56–57, 67
Sacred Hunger (Unsworth), **Supp. VII:** 353, 357, 361, 363–364
"Sacred Ridges above Diamond Creek" (Wallace–Crabbe), **VIII:** 320
Sacred Wood, The (Eliot), **I:** 293; **V:** 310, 334; **VII:** 149, 164; **Retro. Supp. I:** 166
"Sacrifice" (Kinsella), **Supp. V:** 267
"Sacrifice, The" (Herbert), **II:** 124, 128
"Sad Poem" (Cornford), **Supp. XIII:** 89
"Sad Fortunes of the Reverend Amos Barton, The" (Eliot), **Retro. Supp. II:** 103
Sad One, The (Suckling), **II:** 226
Sad Shepherd, The (Jonson), **Retro. Supp. I:** 166
"Sad Steps" (Larkin), **Supp. I:** 284
"Sadak the Wanderer" (Shelley), **IV:** 20
Saddest Music in the World, The (Ishiguro), **Retro. Supp. III:** 161–162
Sade, marquis de, **V:** 316–317
Sadeian Woman, The: An Exercise in Cultural History (Carter), **Supp. III:** 87–88
Sadleir, Michael, **III:** 335, 346; **V:** 100, 101, 102
"Sadness of Cricket, The" (Ewart), **Supp. VII:** 45–46
Sado (Plomer), **Supp. XI:** 215–216
"Safe" (Davies), **Supp. XIV:** 38–39

"Safe as Houses" (Drabble), **Supp. IV:** 231
"Safety" (Brooke), **Supp. III:** 57
"Saga of Bjǫrn Champion of the Folk of Hít–Dale, The", *See Bjarnar saga Hítdœlakappa*
"Saga of Egill Skalla–Grimr's Son, The", *See Egils saga Skalla–Grímssonar*
"Saga of Eiríkr the Red, The", *See Eiríks saga rauða*
"Saga of Gísli Súrr's Son, The", *See Gísla saga Súrssonar*
"Saga of Glúmr of the Slayings, The", *See Víga–Glúms saga*
"Saga of Gunnlaugr Serpent–Tongue, The", *See Gunnlaugs saga ormstunga*
"Saga of Hallfreðr the Awkward Poet, The", *See Hallfreðar saga vandræðaskálds,* 239
"Saga of Ljótr from Vellir, The", *See Valla–Ljóts saga*
"Saga of Njáll of the Burning, The", *See Njáls saga*
"Saga of St Óláfr, The", *See Óláfs saga helga*
"Saga of the Confederates, The", *See Bandamanna saga*
"Saga of the Descendants of Sturla, The", *See Sturlunga saga*
"Saga of the Folk of Bright–Water, The", *See Ljósvetninga saga*
"Saga of the Folk of Laxdale, The", *Laxdœla saga*
"Saga of the Foster Brothers, The", *See Fóstbrœðra saga*
"Saga of the Greenlanders, The", *See Grœnlendinga saga*
"Saga of the Shingle–Dwellers, The", *See Eyrbyggja saga*
Saga Library, The (Morris, Magnusson), **V:** 306
Sagar, Keith, **VII:** 104
"Sagas of Ancient Times", *See Fornaldarsögur*
"Sagas of Icelanders", *See Íslendinga sögur*
"Sagas of Knights", *See Riddarasögur*
Sage, Lorna, **Supp. IV:** 346
"Sage to the Young Man, The" (Housman), **VI:** 159
Said, Edward, **Supp. IV:** 164, 449
Saigon: Year of the Cat (Hare), **Supp. IV:** 282, 289
Sail Away (Coward), **Supp. II:** 155
Sailing Alone Around the World (Slocum), **Supp. II:** 158
"Sailing the High Seas" (Maitland), **Supp. XI:** 175–176
Sailing to an Island (Murphy), **Supp. V:** 317–320
"Sailing to an Island" (Murphy), **Supp. V:** 319
"Sailing to Byzantium" (Yeats), **Retro. Supp. I:** 333–334
"Sailor, What of the Isles?" (Sitwell), **VII:** 138
"Sailor's Harbour" (Reed), **Supp. XV:** 244
"Sailor's Mother, The" (Wordsworth), **IV:** 21

"Saint, The" (Maugham), **VI:** 377
"Saint, The" (Pritchett), **Supp. III:** 315, 318–319
"Saint about to fall, A" (Thomas), **Retro. Supp. III:** 342, 344
"St. Alphonsus Rodriquez" (Hopkins), **V:** 376, 378
Saint and Mary Kate, The (O'Connor), **Supp. XIV:** 217
"St. Anthony's Shirt" (Day Lewis), **Supp. III:** 115
St. Augustine (West), **Supp. III:** 433
St Bartholomew's Eve: A Tale of the Sixteenth Century in Two Cantos (Newman), **Supp. VII:** 289
Sainte–Beuve, Charles, **III:** 226, 230; **V:** 212
"St. Botolph's" (Hughes), **Retro. Supp. II:** 217
"St. Bride's" (Jamie), **Supp. XIV:** 141, 142
St. Catherine's Clock (Kinsella), **Supp. V:** 271
St. Évremond, Charles de, **III:** 47
St. Francis of Assisi (Chesterton), **VI:** 341
Saint Ignatius Loyola (Thompson), **V:** 450, 451
St. Irvine (Shelley), **III:** 338
St. Irvyne; or, The Rosicrucian (Shelley), **IV:** 208
St. Ives (Stevenson and Quiller–Couch), **V:** 384, 387, 396
"St James" (Reading), **VIII:** 263
Saint Joan (Shaw), **VI:** xv, 120, **123–125**; **Retro. Supp. II:** 323–324
St. Joan of the Stockyards (Brecht), **VI:** 123
St. Kilda's Parliament (Dunn), **Supp. X:** 66, 73–75, 77
St. Leon: A Tale of the Sixteenth Century (Godwin), **III:** 332; **Supp. XV:** 123–124, 125
"St. Martin's Summer" (Browning), **IV:** 369
"Sainte Mary Magdalene; or, The Weeper" (Crashaw), *see* AWeeper, The"
"St. Mawr" (Lawrence), **VII:** 115; **Retro. Supp. II:** 232
"St. Patrick's Day" (Mahon), **Supp. VI:** 178
St. Patrick's Day (Sheridan), **III:** 253, 259, 270
St. Paul and Protestantism (Arnold), **V:** 216
St. Paul's boys' theater, **I:** 197
St. Ronan's Well (Scott), **IV:** 36, 37, 39
"St. Simeon Stylites" (Tennyson), **IV:** xx, 332
St. Thomas Aquinas (Chesterton), **VI:** 341
St. Valentine's Day (Scott), **IV:** 39
"St. Winefred's Well" (Hopkins), **V:** 371
"Saints and Lodgers" (Davies), **Supp. XI:** 94
Saint's Knowledge of Christ's Love, The (Bunyan), **II:** 253
Saint's Privilege and Profit, The (Bunyan), **II:** 253

Saint's Progress (Galsworthy), **VI:** 272, 279, 280–281
Saint's Tragedy, The: or, The True Story of Elizabeth of Hungary, Landgravine of Thuringia, Saint of the Roman Calendar (Kingsley), **Supp. XVI:** 202
Saintsbury, George, **II:** 211; **IV:** 271, 282, 306; **V:** 31, 38; **VI:** 266
Saki (H. H. Munro), **Supp. II:** 140–141, 144, 149; **Supp. VI: 239–252**
Sale of Saint Thomas, The (Abercrombie), **Supp. XVI:** 5–6, 7, 11
Salem Chapel (Oliphant), **Supp. X:** 214–215, 221
"Sales" (Davies), **Supp. XIV:** 43
Salámón and Absál . . . Translated from . . . Jámí (FitzGerald), **IV:** 342, 345, 353
Salih, Tayeb, **Supp. IV:** 449
Salinger, J. D., **Supp. IV:** 28
"Salisbury Plain"poems (Wordsworth), **IV:** 2, 3, 4, 5–6, 23, 24
Sally Bowles (Isherwood), **VII:** 311
"Salmon Eggs" (Hughes), **Supp. I:** 363, 364; **Retro. Supp. II:** 213
Salomé (Wilde), **V:** xxvi, 412–413, 419; **Retro. Supp. II:** 370–371
Salsette and Elephanta (Ruskin), **V:** 184
Salt Lands, The (Shaffer), **Supp. I:** 314
"Salt of the Earth, The" (West), **Supp. III:** 442
"Salt Stream, The" (Redgrove), **Supp. VI:** 231–232
Salt Water (Motion), **Supp. VII:** 259, 262–264
Salter, F. M., **I:** 82
Salutation (Russell), **VIII:** 288
"Salutation, The" (Traherne), **II:** 191; **Supp. XI:** 268
Salutation, The (Warner), **Supp. VII:** 379–380
"Salvation of Swithin Forsyte, The" (Galsworthy), **VI:** 274, 277
"Salvatore" (Maugham), **VI:** 370
Salve (Moore), **VI:** 99
Salzburg Tales, The (Stead), **Supp. IV:** 461
"Same Day" (MacCaig), **Supp. VI:** 186
"Same Fault, The" (Montague), **Supp. XV:** 219–220
Sammy and Rosie Get Laid (Kureishi), **Supp. XI:** 156, 161
Samson Agonistes (Milton), **II:** 165, 172–174, 176; **Retro. Supp. II:** 285–288
Samtíðarsögur, **VIII:** 236
Samuel Johnson (Krutch), **III:** 246
Samuel Johnson (Stephen), **V:** 281, 289
Samuel Johnson (Wain), **Supp. XVI:** 293, 303–304
"Samuel Johnson and John Horne (Tooke)" (Landor), **IV:** 92
Samuel Pepys's Naval Minutes (ed. Tanner), **II:** 288
Samuel Pepys's APenny Merriments". . . Together with Comments . . . (ed. Thompson), **II:** 288
Samuel Taylor Coleridge: A Biographical Study (Chambers), **IV:** 41, 57
Samuel Titmarsh and the Great Hoggarty Diamond (Thackeray), *see* Great Hoggarty Diamond, The

"San Francisco Streets" (Gunn), **Retro. Supp. III:** 125
Sanchez, Nellie, **V:** 393, 397
Sand, George, **V:** 22, 141, 207
"Sand–Between–the–Toes" (Milne), **Supp. V:** 302
"Sand Coast Sonnets, The" (Murray), **Supp. VII:** 283
Sandboy, The (Frayn), **Supp. VII:** 58
Sandcastle, The (Murdoch), **VII:** 66; **Supp. I:** 222–223, 225
Sanders, M. F., **V:** 250, 260
Sanderson, Robert, **II:** 136–137, 140, 142
Sandglass, The (Gunesekera), **Supp. X:** 85–86, 92–96, 98–100
Sandison, Alan G., **VI:** xi, xxxiv
Sanditon (Austen), **IV:** 108, 110, 122
Sandkastele (Brink), **Supp. VI:** 57
Sandra Belloni (Meredith), **V:** 226, 227, 234
"Sandro Botticelli" (Pater), **V:** 345, 348
"Sands of Dee, The" (Kingsley), **Supp. XVI:** 205
"Sandstone Keepsake" (Heaney), **Supp. II:** 277
Sangschaw (MacDiarmid), **Supp. XII:** 202, 204, 205, 206
Sanity of Art, The (Shaw), **VI:** 106–107, 129
Sans (Beckett), **Supp. I:** *see* Lessness
"Santa Maria del Popolo" (Gunn), **Retro. Supp. III:** 121
Santal (Firbank), **Supp. II:** 202, 204, **214–215**, 223
Sapho and Phao (Lyly), **I:** 198, 201–202
"Sapho to Philænis" (Donne), **Retro. Supp. II:** 92–93
Sapper, **Supp. IV:** 500
"Sapphics" (Swinburne), **V:** 321
Sappho (Durrell), **Supp. I:** 126–127; bRetro. Supp. III:** 85
Sappho and Phaon, a Series of Legitimate Sonnets, with Thoughts on Poetical Subjects & Anecdotes of the Grecian Poetess (Robinson), **Supp. XIII:** 204, 208–209
"Sappho to Phaon" (Ovid), **V:** 319
Saramago, Jose, **Supp. V:** xxx
Sardanapalus (Byron), **IV:** xviii, 178–179, 193
Sarraute, Nathalie, **Supp. IV:** 99
Sarton, May, **Supp. II:** 82
Sartor Resartus (Carlyle), **IV:** xii, xix, 231, 239–240, 242–243, 249, 250
Sartre, Jean-Paul, **III:** 329, 345; **Supp. I:** 216, 217, 221, 222, 452–453; **Supp. III:** 109; **Supp. IV:** 39, 79, 105, 259
Sartre: Romantic Rationalist (Murdoch), **Supp. I:** 219–220, 222
Sassoon, Siegfried, **V:** 219, 234; **VI:** xvi, 416, **429–431**, 451, 454, 456–457; **VII:** xvi; **Supp. III:** 59; **Supp. IV:** 57–58
"Satan in a Barrel" (Lowry), **Supp. III:** 270
Satan in Search of a Wife (Lamb), **IV:** 84, 85
Satanic Verses, The (Rushdie), **Supp. IV:** 116, 433, 434, 436, 437, 438, 445–

450, 451, 452, 456
Satan's Invisible World Displayed; or, Despairing Democracy: A Study of Greater New York (Stead), **Supp. XIII:** 242–243
"Satiety" (Symons), **Supp. XIV:** 271
Satire and Fiction (Lewis), **VII:** 72, 77
"Satire and Sympathy: Some Consequences of the Intrusive Narration in *Tom Jones* and Other Comic Novels" (Coe), **Supp. XV:** 52–53
Satire on Satirists, A, and Admonition to Detractors (Landor), **IV:** 100
Satires (Donne), **I:** 361; **Retro. Supp. II:** 86
Satires (Wyatt), **I:** 100, 101–102, 111
Satires of Circumstance (Hardy), **VI:** 14, 20; **Retro. Supp. I:** 117
Satires of Circumstance (Sorley), **VI:** 421
"Satiric Muse, The " (Hope), **Supp. VII:** 163
"Satisfactory, The" (Pritchett), **Supp. III: 319–320**
"Saturday; or, The Flights" (Gay), **III:** 56
Saturday Life, A (Hall), **Supp. VI:** 120–122
"Saturday Night" (Gunn), **Supp. IV:** 269
Saturday Night and Sunday Morning (Sillitoe), **Supp. V:** 409, 410, 413, 416–419
Saturday Review (periodical), **V:** 279; **VI:** 103, 106, 366; **Supp. II:** 45, 48, 53, 54, 55; **Supp. XIII:** 187
"Saturnalia" (Gunn), **Supp. IV:** 269
"Saturnalia" (Wilson), **Supp. I:** 158
"Satyr Against Mankind, A" (Rochester), **II:** 208*n*, 256, 260–261, 270
"Satyrical Elegy on the Death of a Late Famous General, A" (Swift), **III:** 31
Saucer of Larks, The (Friel), **Supp. V:** 113
"Saul" (Browning), **IV:** 363
Saunders, Charles, **II:** 305
Sauter, Rudolf, **VI:** 284
Sauve Qui Peut (Durrell), **Supp. I:** 113; **Retro. Supp. III:** 85
Savage, Eliza Mary Ann, **Supp. II:** 99, 104, 111
Savage, Richard, **III:** 108
Savage and the City in the Work of T. S. Eliot, The (Crawford), **Supp. XI:** 67, 71, 82
Savage Gold (Fuller), **Supp. VII:** 70
Savage Pilgrimage, The (Carswell), **VII:** 123
Save It for the Minister (Churchill, Potter, O'Malley), **Supp. IV:** 181
Save the Beloved Country (Paton), **Supp. II:** 359, 360
Saved (Bond), **Supp. I:** 421, 422–423, 425–426, 427, 435
Saved By Grace (Bunyan), **II:** 253
Savile, George, *see* Halifax, marquess of
Saville (Storey), **Supp. I:** 419
Saviour of Society, The (Swinburne), **V:** 333
"Savonarola Brown" (Beerbohm), **Supp. II:** 5l, 56
Savonarola e il priore di San Marco (Landor), **IV:** 100

Savrola (Churchill), **VI:** 351
Say Hi to the Rivers and the Mountains (Coe), **Supp. XV:** 50
"Say not of me that weakly I declined" (Stevenson), **V:** 390
"Say not the struggle nought availeth" (Clough), **V:** 158–159, 165, 166, 167
Sayers, Dorothy L., **III:** 341; **VI:** 345; **Supp. II:** 124, 126, 127, 135; **Supp. III: 333–353; Supp. IV:** 2, 3, 500
"Scale" (Self), **Supp. V:** 403–404
"Scales, The" (Longley), **VIII:** 176
"Scalding, The" (Delanty), **Supp. XIV:** 73
Scandal (Wilson), **Supp. VI:** 302–303, 308
"Scandal in Bohemia, A" (Doyle), **Supp. I:** 173
Scandal of Father Brown, The (Chesterton), **VI:** 338
Scandalous Woman, A (O'Brien), **Supp. V:** 339
Scannell, Vernon, **VII:** 422, 423–424
"Scapegoat" (Scupham), **Supp. XIII:** 222
Scapegoat, The (du Maurier), **Supp. III:** 136, 139, 140–141
"Scapegoat, The" (Pritchett), **Supp. III:** 312, 317–318
Scapegoats and Rabies (Hughes), **Supp. I:** 348
Scarcity of Love, A (Kavan), **Supp. VII:** 213, 214
Scarecrow and His Servant, The (Pullman), **Supp. XIII:** 152–153
"Scarecrow in the Schoolmaster's Oats, The" (Brown), **Supp. VI:** 71
Scarlet Tree, The (Sitwell), **VII:** 128–129
Scarperer, The (Behan), **Supp. II:** 67
Scarron, Paul, **II:** 354
"Scenes" (Dickens), **V:** 44–46
Scenes and Actions (Caudwell), **Supp. IX:** 33, 37
"Scènes de la Vie Bohème: *Episode of a Night of May*" (Symons), **Supp. XIV:** 272
Scenes from Comus (Hill), **Retro. Supp. III:** 142–143, 144
Scenes from Italy's War (Trevelyan), **VI:** 389
"Scenes from the Fall of Troy" (Morris), **V:** 297
Scenes of Clerical Life (Eliot), **V:** xxii, 2, 190–191, 200; **Retro. Supp. II:** 103–104
Scenic Railway, The (Upward), **Supp. XIII:** 250, 260, 261–262
"Scenic Railway, The" (Upward), **Supp. XIII:** 261–262
Scenic Route, The (Adcock), **Supp. XII:** 6
Sceptick (Ralegh), **I:** 157
Schelling, Friedrich Wilhelm, **V:** 347
Scheme and Estimates for a National Theatre, A (Archer and Barker), **VI:** 104, 113
Schepisi, Fred, **Supp. IV:** 345
Schiller, Friedrich von, **IV:** xiv, xvi 173, 241
Schindler's Ark (Keneally), *see Schindler's List*

Schindler's List (Keneally), **Supp. IV:** 343, 346, 348, 354–357, 358
"Schir, I complayne off iniuris" (Dunbar), **VIII:** 119, 121
"Schir, Ye have mony Servitouris" (Dunbar), **VIII:** 122
Schirmer Inheritance, The (Ambler), **Supp. IV:** 4, 13–16, 21
Schlegel, A. W., **I:** 329; **IV:** vii, xvii; **V:** 62
Schneider, Elizabeth, **V:** 366, 382
"Scholar, The" (Cornford), **VIII:** 113
"Scholar and Gypsy" (Desai), **Supp. V:** 65
"Scholar Gipsy, The" (Arnold), **V:** xxi, 209, 210, 211, 216
School for Husbands (Mahon), **Supp. VI:** 175
School for Wives (Mahon), **Supp. VI:** 175
School for Scandal, The (Sheridan), **III:** 97, 100, 253, **261–264**, 270
School of Abuse (Gosson), **I:** 161
School of Athens, The (Renault), **Supp. IX:** 185
School of Donne, The (Alvarez), **II:** 125*n*
"School of Eloquence, The" (Harrison), **Supp. V:** 150, 151–157
"School Stories" (Wodehouse), **Supp. III:** 449
"School Story, A" (Trevor), **Supp. IV:** 502
"School Teacher" (Smith, I. C.), **Supp. IX:** 211
School Ties (Boyd), **Supp. XVI:** 32
Schoolboy Lyrics (Kipling), **Retro. Supp. III:** 183
Schoolboy Verses (Kipling), **VI:** 200
"Schoolboys" (McEwan), **Supp. IV:** 393
Schools and Universities on the Continent (Arnold), **V:** 216
Schopenhauer, Arthur, **Supp. IV:** 6
Schreber's Nervous Illness (Churchill), **Supp. IV:** 181
Schreiner, Olive, **Supp. II: 435–457**
Schwindel. Gefühle (Sebald). *See Vertigo*
Science and Poetry (Richards), **VI:** 207, 208; **Supp. II:** 405, 412, 413, 414, **417–418,** 419
Science of Ethics, The (Stephen), **V:** 284–285, 289
"Science of History, The" (Froude), **IV:** 324
Science of Life, The (Wells), **VI:** 225
"Science of the Future, The: A Forecast" (Carpenter), **Supp. XIII:** 41
Scilla's Metamorphosis (Lodge), **I:** 306
"Scipio, Polybius, and Panaetius" (Landor), **IV:** 94
Scoop (screenplay, Boyd), **Supp. XVI:** 45
Scoop (Waugh), **VII:** 297
Scornful Lady, The (Beaumont and Fletcher), **II:** 65
"Scorpion, The" (Plomer), **Supp. XI:** 213–214
Scorpion and Other Poems (Smith), **Supp. II:** 463; **Retro. Supp. III:** 313, 314
Scorpion God, The (Golding), **Supp. I:** 82–83

Scot, William, **Supp. III:** 20, 22, 23
"Scotch Drink" (Burns), **III:** 315
"Scotland" (Crawford), **Supp. XI:** 72
"Scotland" (Greig), **Supp. XVI:** 163
"Scotland" (Reid), **Supp. VII:** 331
"Scotland in the 1890s" (Crawford), **Supp. XI:** 71
Scotland, the Place of Visions (Morris, J.), **Supp. X:** 177
"Scots and Off–Scots Words" (Crawford), **Supp. XI:** 80–81
"Scots Gamelan" (Crawford), **Supp. XI:** 69–70
Scots Hairst, A (Gibbon), **Supp. XIV:** 99
Scots Musical Museum (Johnson), **III:** 320, 322
Scots Quair, A (Gibbon), **Supp. XIV:** 99, 100, 101, 104, 106–113
Scott, Geoffrey, **III:** 234n, 238, 249
Scott, John, **IV:** 252, 253
Scott, Paul, **Supp. I: 259–274; Supp. IV:** 440
Scott, Robert Falcon, **II:** 273
Scott, Sir Walter **II:** 276; **III:** 146, 157, 326, 335, 336, 338; **IV:** viii, xi, xiv, **27–40,** 45, 48, 102, 111, 122, 129, 133–136, 167, 168, 173, 254, 270, 281; **V:** 392; **VI:** 412; **Supp. III:** 151, 154, 167
Scott Moncrieff, Charles, **VI:** 454, 455
Scottish Assembly, A (Crawford), **Supp. XI:** 67, 70, 71–72, 73, 75, 78
Scottish Chapbook, **Supp. XII:** 204
Scottish Invention of English Literature, The (ed. Crawford), **Supp. XI:** 76, 82, 83
Scottish Journey (Muir), **Supp. VI:** 198, 201
Scottish Scene; or, The Intelligent Man's Guide to Albyn (Gibbon), **Supp. XIV:** 99–100, 102–106
Scott-James, Rolfe Arnold, **VI:** x, xxxiv, 1
Scott-Kilvert, Ian Stanley, **VI:** xvi, xxxiv; **VII:** xxii
Scott–King's Modern Europe (Waugh), **VII:** 301
"Scott's Arks" (Dunn), **Supp. X:** 82
Scotus, Duns, *see* Duns Scotus, John
Scourge of Villainy, The (Marston), **II:** 25, 26, 40
Scrapbook (Mansfield), **VII:** 181
Screams and Other Poems, The (Richards), **Supp. II:** 407, 427
Screwtape Letters, The (Lewis), **Supp. III:** 248, 255, 256–257
"Scribe in the Woods, The" (Carson), **Supp. XIII:** 56
"Script for an Unchanging Voice" (McGuckian), **Supp. V:** 292
Scriptorum illustrium maioris Britanniae catalogus (Bale), **I:** 1
Scrutiny (periodical), **VII:** 233, 238, 243, 251–252, 256; **Supp. III:** 107
Scudéry, Georges de, **III:** 95
Sculptura; or, The History . . . of Chalcography and Engraving in Copper (Evelyn), **II:** 287

Scum of the Earth (Koestler), **Supp. I:** 26
Scupham, Peter, **Supp. XIII: 218–232**
"Scylla and Charybdis" (Kinsella), **Supp. V:** 261
Sea, The (Bond), **Supp. I:** 423, 427, 432–433, 435
Sea, The Sea, The (Murdoch), **Supp. I:** 231, 232
Sea and Sardinia (Lawrence), **VII:** 116–117
Sea and the Mirror, The (Auden), **VII:** 379, 380, 388, 389; **Retro. Supp. I:** 11
"Sea and the Skylark, The" (Hopkins), **V:** 367
Sea Change, The (Howard), **Supp. XI:** 135, 137, 139–140, 146
"Sea in Winter, The" (Mahon), **Supp. VI:** 173, 175
"Sea Limits" (Rossetti), **V:** 241
Sea Gull, The (tr. Frayn), **Supp. VII:** 61
"Sea Horse Family, The" (Delanty), **Supp. XIV:** 74
"Sea–Sand" (Healy), **Supp. IX:** 106
Sea to the West (Nicholson), **Supp. VI:** 213, **218–219**
"Sea to the West" (Nicholson), **Supp. VI:** 219
"Sea Urchin" (Jamie), **Supp. XIV:** 141
Sea Voyage, The (Fletcher and Massinger), **II:** 43, 66
"Sea Voyage, The" (Hart), **Supp. XI:** 123
Seafarer, The, **Retro. Supp. II:** 303–304
"Seafarer, The" (tr. Morgan), **Supp. IX:** 160
"Seafarer, The" (Pound), **Supp. IV:** 100, 115
Sea–King's Daughter and Eureka!, The (Brown), **Supp. VI:** 71–73
"Seals at High Island" (Murphy), **Supp. V:** 324
"Sea-Mists of the Winter, The" (Lewis), **VII:** 84
"Seamless Garment, The" (MacDiarmid), **Supp. XII:** 211–212, 213
Sean O'Casey: The Man Behind the Plays (Cowasjee), **VII:** 4
Search, The (Snow), **VII:** 321–322, 323–324
"Search, The" (Vaughan), **VII:** 187
"Search After Happiness, The" (Brontë), **V:** 110
Search After Sunrise: A Traveller's Story (Brittain), **Supp. X:** 46
"Searching for a Gift" (Delanty), **Supp. XIV:** 68
"Seaside Walk, A" (Browning), **IV:** 313
Season at Sarsaparilla, The (White), **Supp. I:** 131, 149
Season in Purgatory (Keneally), **Supp. IV:** 346
Season Songs (Hughes), **Supp. I:** 357–359; **Retro. Supp. II:** 208–209
Seasonable Counsel; or, Advice to Sufferers (Bunyan), **II:** 253
Season's Greetings (Ayckbourn), **Supp. V:** 3, 10, 13, 14
"Seasons, The" (Thomas), **Supp. XII:** 290

Seasons, The (Thomson), **Supp. III:** 409, 410, 411, **412–419,** 420, 428; **Retro. Supp. I:** 241
"Seated Woman" (Hart), **Supp. XI:** 123
"Sea–watching" (Thomas), **Supp. XII:** 288
Sebald, W. G., **VIII: 295–309**
Sebastian (Durrell), **Supp. I:** 120; **Retro. Supp. III:** 86, 93–94
Seccombe, Thomas, **V:** 425, 437
Second Angel, The (Kerr), **Supp. XII:** 187, 194, 195–197
"Second Best, The" (Arnold), **V:** 209
"Second Best" (Brooke), **Supp. III:** 49
Second Book of Ayres (Campion), **Supp. XVI:** 94, 101
Second Book of Odes (Bunting), **Supp. VII:** 13–14
Second Brother, The (Beddoes), **Supp. XI:** 22, 23
"Second Coming, The" (Yeats), **VI:** xiv; **Retro. Supp. I:** 332–333
Second Curtain, The (Fuller), **Supp. VII:** 71, 72, 81
Second Defence of the People of England, The (Milton), **II:** 164; **Retro. Supp. II:** 270
Second Epistle of the Second Book (Pope), **Retro. Supp. I:** 230
Second Funeral of Napoleon, The (Thackeray), **V:** 22, 38
"Second Hand Clothes" (Dunn), **Supp. X:** 74
"Second Hut, The" (Lessing), **Supp. I:** 240–241
Second Journal to Eliza, The, **III:** 135
Second Jungle Book, The (Kipling), **VI:** 204; **Retro. Supp. III:** 189–190, 191–192, 194, 196, 197
Second Kiss, The: A Light Comedy (Clarke), **Supp. XV:** 25
"Second Language" (Carson), **Supp. XIII:** 60
Second Life, The (Morgan, E.), **Supp. IX:** 158, 159, 163–168
"Second Life, The" (Morgan, E.), **Supp. IX:** 165
Second Maiden's Tragedy, The (Middleton), **II:** 2, 3, **8–10,** 21
Second Mrs. Tanqueray, The (Pinero), **V:** 413
Second Nun's Tale, The (Chaucer), **I:** 31, 34, 43
"Second Opinion" (Dunn), **Supp. X:** 76
Second Part of Conny–Catching, The (Greene), **VIII:** 144–145
Second Part of Mr. Waller's Poems, The (Waller), **II:** 238
Second Part of Pilgrim's Progress, The (T. S.), **II:** 248
Second Part of the Bloody Conquests of Mighty Tamburlaine, The (Marlowe), *see Tamburlaine, Part 2*
Second Part of The Rover, The (Behn), **Supp. III:** 27
2nd Poems (Graham), **Supp. VII:** 109–110
Second Satire (Wyatt), **I:** 111
Second Sex, The (Beauvoir), **Supp. IV:** 232

"Second Sight" (Longley), **VIII:** 173
Second Treatise on Government (Locke), **Supp. III:** 33
"Second Visit, A" (Warner), **Supp. VII:** 380
Second World War (Churchill), **VI:** 359–360
Secord, Arthur Wellesley, **III:** 41
"Secret Agent, The" (Auden), **Retro. Supp. I:** 3
Secret Agent (Conrad), **Supp. IV:** 1
Secret Agent, The (Conrad), **VI: 143–144,** 148; **Retro. Supp. II:** 80–81
Secret Brother, The (Jennings), **Supp. V:** 216
Secret Dispatches from Arabia (Lawrence), **Supp. II:** 295
"Secret Garden, The" (Kinsella), **Supp. V:** 263
Secret Glass, The (Bainbridge), **Supp. VI:** 20
Secret History of the Present Intrigues of the Court of Caramania, The (Haywood), **Supp. XII:** 141
Secret History of the White Staff, The, . . . (Defoe), **III:** 13
"Secret History of World War 3, The" (Ballard), **Supp. V:** 33
Secret Ladder, The (Harris), **Supp. V:** 132, 135, 139
Secret Lives (Ngũgĩ), **VIII:** 220
Secret Love; or, The Maiden Queen (Dryden), **II:** 305; **Retro. Supp. III:** 61
Secret Narratives (Motion), **Supp. VII:** 255–256, 257, 263
Secret of Father Brown, The (Chesterton), **VI:** 338
Secret Pilgrim, The (le Carré), **Supp. II:** 319; **Retro. Supp. III:** 224, 228
Secret Rapture, The (Hare), **Supp. IV:** 282, 292, 293–294, 296
Secret Rose (Yeats), **VI:** 222
"Secret Sharer, The" (Conrad), **VI: 145–147**
"Secret Sharer, The" (Gunn), **Supp. IV:** 256, 259
Secret Villages (Dunn), **Supp. X:** 67–68
Secret Water (Ransome), **Supp. I:** 68
Secrets (Davies), **Supp. XI:** 100
"Section 28" (Morgan, E.), **Supp. IX:** 160
"Secular, The" (Wallace–Crabbe), **VIII:** 315
Secular Lyrics of the XIVth and XVth Centuries (Robbins), **I:** 40
"Secular Masque, The" (Dryden), **II:** 289, 290, 305, 325
"Sedge–Warblers" (Thomas), **Supp. III:** 406
Sedley, Sir Charles, **II:** 255, 261, **263–266,** 271
"Seductio ad Absurdam" (Lowry), **Supp. III:** 285
"See where the Thames" (Cowper), **Retro. Supp. III:** 45
"Seed Growing Secretly, The" (Vaughan), **II:** 189
Seed of Chaos: What Mass Bombing Really Means (Brittain), **Supp. X:** 45

"Seed Picture, The" (McGuckian), **Supp. V:** 281, 285
Seeds in the Wind: Poems in Scots for Children (Soutar), **Supp. XVI:** 249–250, 254, 255, 256, 257
Seeds of Time, The (Wyndham), **Supp. XIII:** 290
Seeing Things (Heaney), **Retro. Supp. I:** 124, 131–132
Seek and Find (Rossetti), **V:** 260; **Retro. Supp. III:** 263–264
"Seers" (Blunden), **Supp. XI:** 34
"Seesaw" (Gunn), **Supp. IV:** 275–276
Seicentismo e Marinismo in Inghilterra (Praz), **II:** 123
Sejanus (Jonson), **I:** 235, 242, 249, 345–346; **Retro. Supp. I:** 161, 164
Select British Poets; or, New Elegant Extracts from Chaucer to the Present Time (Hazlitt), **IV:** 139
Select Collection of Original Scottish Airs (Thomson), **III:** 322
"Select Meditations" (Traherne), **Supp. XI:** 264, 265, 266
Select Poets of Great Britain (Hazlitt), **IV:** 139
Selected Essays of Cyril Connolly, The (ed. Quennell), **Supp. III:** 107
Selected Letters of Edwin Muir (Muir), **Supp. VI:** 203
Selected Letters of Philip Larkin, 1940–1985 (Larkin), **Retro. Supp. III:** 202, 203, 212
Selected Life, A (Kinsella), **Supp. V:** 267
Selected Plays [of Lady Gregory] (ed. Coxhead), **VI:** 317
Selected Poems (Adcock), **Supp. XII:** 8
Selected Poems (Armitage), **VIII:** 1–2
Selected Poems (Beer), **Supp. XIV:** 1, 2, 5
Selected Poems (Burnside), **Supp. XIII:** 27
Selected Poems (Clarke), **Supp. XV:** 29
Selected Poems (Conn), **Supp. XIII:** 73, 76, 78, 79
Selected Poems (Constantine), **Supp. XV:** 65, 66
Selected Poems (Gunn and Hughes), **Supp. IV:** 257
Selected Poems (Harrison), **Supp. V:** 150, 157, 160
Selected Poems (Hölderlin, tr. Constantine), **Supp. XV:** 66, 68–69, 70, 71, 73–74
Selected Poems (Hope), **Supp. VII:** 156, 159
Selected Poems (Hughes), **Supp. I: 364–365**
Selected Poems (Mahon), **Supp. VI:** 166–167, 169–174*Selected Poems* (Mahon), **Supp. VI:** 166–167, 169–174
Selected Poems (Mangan), **Supp. XIII:** 119, 120–121, 122, 123, 124, 125, 126, 127, 128, 129
Selected Poems (Muldoon), **Supp. IV:** 413
Selected Poems (Murray), **Supp. VII:** 270
Selected Poems (Plomer), **Supp. XI:** 223

Selected Poems (Smith), **Supp. II:** 463; **Retro. Supp. III:** 313
Selected Poems (Robinson), **Supp. XIII:** 199, 203, 204, 206, 207, 208, 209, 210, 212, 213
Selected Poems (Russell), **VIII:** 292
Selected Poems (Spender), **Supp. II:** 486, 489
Selected Poems (Stevenson), **Supp. VI:** 256, 261–263
Selected Poems (D.M. Thomas), **Supp. IV:** 490, 494
Selected Poems (R.S. Thomas), **Supp. XII:** 282
Selected Poems of Boris Pasternak (tr. Stallworthy), **Supp. X:** 292
Selected Poems of Edward Thomas (ed. Thomas), **Supp. XII:** 282
Selected Poems of Fulke Greville (Greville), **Supp. XI:** 105, 109, 114, 116
Selected Poems of Kyriakos Charalambides (tr. Delanty), **Supp. XIV:** 76
Selected Poems of Malcolm Lowry (tr. Birney), **Supp. III:** 282
Selected Poems of Séan ó Ríordáin (tr. Delanty), **Supp. XIV:** 77
Selected Poems 1954–1992 (Brown), **Supp. VI:** 70–72
Selected Poems 1956–1994 (Wallace–Crabbe), **VIII:** 311, 312, 313, 314, 315, 317, 318, 319, 320
Selected Poems, 1959–1989 (Malouf), **Supp. XII:** 220
Selected Poems 1964–1983 (Dunn), **Supp. X:** 69
Selected Poems 1976–1997 (Motion), **Supp. VII:** 252, 257
Selected Prose (Housman), **VI:** 154
Selected Prose of Christina Rossetti (Rossetti), **Retro. Supp. III:** 260
Selected Speeches (Disraeli), **IV:** 308
Selected Stories (Friel), **Supp. V:** 113
Selected Stories (Gordimer), **Supp. II:** 231, 232, 234, 242
Selected Stories (Plomer), **Supp. XI:** 223
"Selected Translations" (Sisson), **Supp. XI:** 248
Selected Works (Tennyson), **Retro. Supp. III:** 327
Selected Writings (Symons), **Supp. XIV:** 269, 273
Selected Writings of Fulke Greville (Greville), **Supp. XI:** 105, 117
Selection of Kipling's Verse (Eliot), **VI:** 202
Self, Will, **Supp. IV:** 26; **Supp. V: 395–408**
"Self and its Affiliations, The" (Carpenter), **Supp. XIII:** 46
Self and Self–Management (Bennett), **VI:** 264
"Self Justification" (Harrison), **Supp. V:** 155–156
Self Portrait (Kavanagh), **Supp. VII:** 197–198
"Self Portrait" (O'Connor), **Supp. XIV:** 222
"Self Portrait: Nearing Sixty" (Waugh), **Supp. VI:** 276

"Selfish Giant, The" (Wilde), **Retro. Supp. II:** 365
"Self-Release" (Kinsella), **Supp. V:** 270
"Self-Renewal" (Kinsella), **Supp. V:** 270
"Self's the Man" (Larkin), **Supp. I:** 281; **Retro. Supp. III:** 207
"Self-Scrutiny" (Kinsella), **Supp. V:** 270
"Self-Unseeing, The" (Hardy), **VI:** 13; **Retro. Supp. I:** 118
Selimus, **I:** 220
Seltzer, David, **III:** 343, 345
"Selves" (Gunn), **Supp. IV:** 272
Selvon, Samuel, **Supp. IV:** 445
"Semi-Monde," (Coward), **Supp. II:** 146
"Semiology and Rhetoric" (de Man), **Supp. IV:** 114
Señor Vivo and the Coca Lord (De Bernières), **Supp. XII:** 65, 70, 72–73
"Send-Off, The" (Owen), **VI:** 447, 452
Seneca, **I:** 214–215; **II:** 25, 28, 71, 97
"Sensation Novels" (Oliphant), **Supp. X:** 221
Sense and Sensibility (Austen), **III:** 91, 336; **IV:** xvii, 108, 109, 111, 112, **114–122**; **Retro. Supp. II:** 6–7
Sense of Detachment, A (Osborne), **Supp. I:** 339
Sense of Movement, The (Gunn), **Supp. IV:** 257, 259–262; **Retro. Supp. III:** 115, 116, 119–120, 121, 122
Sense of the Past, The (James), **VI:** 64–65
Sense of the World, A (Jennings), **Supp. V:** 210, 212, 214
"Sensitive Plant, The" (Shelley), **IV:** 203
"Sentence, The" (tr. McKane), **Supp. IV:** 494–495
"Sentence, The" (tr. Thomas), **Supp. IV:** 494–495
"Sentimental Blues" (Ewart), **Supp. VII:** 36
"Sentimental Education, The" (Ewart), **Supp. VII:** 40
Sentimental Journey, A (Sterne), **III:** 124, 127, 132–134, 135
Sentimental Tommy (Barrie), **Supp. III:** 3
Sententia (Elizabeth I), **Supp. XVI:** 157
Sentiments of a Church-of-England Man, The (Swift), **III:** 26
"Sentry, The" (Owen), **VI:** 448, 451
Separate Saga of St Óláfr, The, **VIII:** 235
Separate Tables: Table by the Window and Table Number Seven (Rattigan), **Supp. VII:** 313, 318–319
"Sephestia's Song to Her Child" (Greene), **VIII:** 143
"September 1, 1939" (Auden), **Retro. Supp. I:** 10, **Retro. Supp. I:** 14
"September Dawn" (O'Connor), **Supp. XIV:** 224, 226
"September Soliloquy" (Cornford), **VIII:** 114
"September Song" (Hill), **Supp. V:** 187
September Tide (du Maurier), **Supp. III:** 143
"Septuagesima" (Burnside), **Supp. XIII:** 16
"Sepulchre" (Herbert), **II:** 128
"Sequence" (Beer), **Supp. XIV:** 6
Sequence for Francis Parkman, A (Davie), **Supp. VI:** 108–109, 115

"Sequence in Hospital" (Jennings), **Supp. V:** 214
Sequence of Sonnets on the Death of Robert Browning, A (Swinburne), **V:** 333
Serafino Aquilano, **I:** 103, 105, 110
"Seraph and the Zambesi, The," (Spark), **Supp. I:** 199
"Seraphim, The" (Browning), **IV:** 312, 313
Seraphim, The, and Other Poems (Browning), **IV:** xix, 311, 312–313, 321
"Serenade" (Sitwell), **VII:** 135
Sergeant Lamb (Graves), **VII:** 258
"Serial Dreamer, The" (Upward), **Supp. XIII:** 262
Serious and Pathetical Contemplation of the Mercies of God, in Several Most Devout and Sublime Thanksgivings for the Same, A (Traherne), **II:** 201; **Supp. XI:** 274–276
Serious Call to a Devout and Holy Life, A (Byrom), **Supp. XVI:** 75
Serious Concerns (Cope), **VIII:** 67, 69, 75–79
Serious Money (Churchill), **Supp. IV:** 179, 180, 184, 192–195, 198
Serious Reflections During . . . ARobinson Crusoe" (Defoe), **III:** 12, 13; **Retro. Supp. I:** 71
Serjeant Musgrave's Dance (Arden), **Supp. II:** **25–28**, 29, 30, 35, 38
"Sermon, The" (Redgrove), **Supp. VI:** 228–229, 232, 235, 237
"Sermon in the Guava Tree, The" (Desai), **Supp. XV:** 84
Sermon Preached at Pauls Crosse, the 25. Of November. 1621, A (King), **Supp. VI:** 152
Sermon Preach'd to the People at the Mercat Cross of Edinburgh, A; on the Subject of the Union (Arbuthnot), **Supp. XVI:** 19
"Sermon to Our Later Prodigal Son" (Meredith), **V:** 223
Sermons (Donne), **I:** 364–366; **II:** 142; **Retro. Supp. II:** 96
Sermons: An Exposition upon the Lord's Prayer (King), **Supp. VI:** 152, 155, 158, 161
Sermons and Devotional Writings of Gerard Manley Hopkins, The (ed. Devlin), **V:** 372, 381
Sermons, Chiefly on the Theory of Religious Belief, Preached Before the University of Oxford (Newman), **Supp. VII:** 296
"Serpent-Charm, The" (Gissing), **V:** 437
Servant, The (Pinter), **Supp. I:** 374; **Retro. Supp. I:** 226
"Servant Boy" (Heaney), **Retro. Supp. I:** 128
"Servant Girl Speaks, A" (Lawrence), **VII:** 118
"Servants' Quarters, The" (Hardy), **Retro. Supp. I:** 121
Service of Clouds, The (Hill), **Supp. XIV:** 116, 126

"Serving Maid, The" (Kinsella), **Supp. V:** 263
Sesame and Lilies (Ruskin), **V:** 180, 184
"Session of the Poets, A" (Suckling), **II:** 229
"Sestina of the Tramp Royal" (Kipling), **VI:** 202, 203
Set in Darkness (Rankin), **Supp. X:** 245, 255–256
Set of Six, A (Conrad), **VI:** 148
Seth, Vikram, **Supp. X:** **277–290**
Seton, Ernest Thompson, **Supp. IV:** 158
"Setteragic On" (Warner), **Supp. VII:** 380
Setting the World on Fire (Wilson), **Supp. I:** 165–166
"Settlements" (Burnside), **Supp. XIII:** 24
"Settlers" (Adcock), **Supp. XII:** 8
"Seven Ages, The" (Auden), **Retro. Supp. I:** 11
Seven at a Stroke (Fry), **Supp. III:** 194
Seven Cardinal Virtues, The (ed. Fell), **Supp. XI:** 163
"Seven Conjectural Readings" (Warner), **Supp. VII:** 373
Seven Days in the New Crete (Graves), **VII:** 259
Seven Deadly Sins, The (ed. Fell), **Supp. XI:** 163
"Seven Deadly Sins: A Mask, The" (Nye), **Supp. X:** 202
"Seven Good Germans" (Henderson), **VII:** 426
Seven Journeys, The (Graham), **Supp. VII:** 111
Seven Lamps of Architecture, The (Ruskin), **V:** xxi, 176, 184
Seven Lectures on Shakespeare and Milton (Coleridge), **IV:** 56
"Seven Letters" (Graham), **Supp. VII:** 111
Seven Men (Beerbohm), **Supp. II:** 55–56
Seven Men and Two Others (Beerbohm), **Supp. II:** 55
Seven Men of Vision: An Appreciation (Jennings), **Supp. V:** 217
"7, Middagh Street" (Muldoon), **Supp. IV:** 411, 422, 424
"7 Newton Road, Harston, Cambridge" (Scupham), **Supp. XIII:** 224
Seven Pillars of Wisdom (Lawrence), **VI:** 408; **Supp. II:** 283, 284, 285, 286, **287–291**
"Seven Poets, The" (Brown), **Supp. VI:** 69
Seven Poor Men of Sydney (Stead), **Supp. IV:** 461–464
"Seven Rocks, The" (Nicholson), **Supp. VI:** **216–217**
"Seven Sages, The" (Yeats), **Supp. II:** 84–85
Seven Seas, The (Kipling), **VI:** 204
Seven Short Plays (Gregory), **VI:** 315
Seven Types of Ambiguity (Empson), **I:** 282; **II:** 124, 130; **VII:** 260; **Supp. II:** 179, 180, 183, **185–189**, 190, 197
Seven Winters (Bowen), **Supp. II:** 77–78, 91
Seven Women (Barrie), **Supp. III:** 5

SEVE–SHEL

Sevenoaks Essays (Sisson), **Supp. XI:** 249, 256
"1740" (Kinsella), **Supp. V:** 271
"1738" (Stallworthy), **Supp. X:** 297
Seventh Man: Migrant Workers in Europe, A (Berger), **Supp. IV:** 79
Several Perceptions (Carter), **Supp. III:** 80, 81, 82–83
"Several Questions Answered" (Blake), **III:** 293
"Severe Gale 8" (Kay), **Supp. XIII:** 99
Severed Head, A (Murdoch), **Supp. I:** 215, 224, 225, 228
Severn and Somme (Gurney), **VI:** 425
"Sewage Pipe Pool, The" (Nye), **Supp. X:** 203
"Sex That Doesn't Shop, The" (Saki), **Supp. VI:** 246
Sexing the Cherry (Winterson), **Supp. IV:** 541, 542, 545, 547, 549, 552, 554, 556, 557
"Sex–Love: And Its Place in Free Society" (Carpenter), **Supp. XIII:** 41
"Sexton's Hero, The" (Gaskell), **V:** 15
Sexual Inversion (Ellis and Symonds), **Supp. XIV:** 261–262
Sexual Politics (Millett), **Supp. IV:** 188
Seymour-Smith, Martin, **VII:** xviii, xxxviii
Shabby Genteel Story, A (Thackeray), **V:** 21, 35, 37
"Shack, The" (Cameron), **Supp. IX:** 27
Shade Those Laurels (Connolly), **Supp. III:** 111–112
Shadow Dance (Carter), **III:** 345; **Supp. III:** 79, 80, 81, 89
Shadow in the North, The (Pullman), **Supp. XIII:** 151
Shadow in the Plate, The (Pullman), **Supp. XIII:** 151
Shadow of a Gunman, The (O'Casey), **VI:** 316; **VII:** xviii, 3–4, 6, 12
"Shadow of Black Combe, The" (Nicholson), **Supp. VI:** 218
Shadow of Cain, The (Sitwell), **VII:** xvii, 137
Shadow of Dante, A (Rossetti), **V:** 253n
Shadow of Hiroshima, The (Harrison), **Supp. V:** 164
Shadow of Night (Chapman), **I:** 234, 237
Shadow of the Glen, The (Synge), **VI:** 308, 309, 310, 316
Shadow of the Sun, The (Byatt), **Supp. IV:** 140, 141, 142–143, 147, 148, 149, 155
Shadow Play (Coward), **Supp. II:** 152–153
"Shadow Suite" (Brathwaite), **Supp. XII:** 35
Shadow-Line, The: A Confession (Conrad), **VI:** 135, 146–147, 148
"Shadows" (Lawrence), **VII:** 119
"Shadows in the Water" (Traherne), **II:** 192; **Supp. XI:** 269
Shadows of Ecstasy (Williams, C. W. S.), **Supp. IX:** 279–280
Shadows of the Evening (Coward), **Supp. II:** 156
Shadowy Waters, The (Yeats), **VI:** 218, 222

Shadwell, Thomas, **I:** 327; **II:** 305, 359
"Shadwell Stair" (Owen), **VI:** 451
Shaffer, Anthony, **Supp. I:** 313
Shaffer, Peter, **Supp. I: 313–328**
Shaftesbury, earl of, **Supp. III:** 424
Shaftesbury, seventh earl of, **IV:** 62
Shaftesbury, third earl of, **III:** 44, 46, 198
Shahnameh (Persian epic), **Supp. IV:** 439
Shakes Versus Shav (Shaw), **VI:** 130
Shakespear, Olivia, **VI:** 210, 212, 214
Shakespeare, William, **I:** 188, **295–334; II:** 87, 221, 281, 302; **III:** 115–117; **IV:** 149, 232, 352; **V:** 41, 328; and Collins, **IV:** 165, 165n, 170; and Jonson, **I:** 335–337, **II:** 281; **Retro. Supp. I:** 158, 165; and Kyd, **I:** 228–229; and Marlowe, **I:** 275–279, 286; and Middleton, **IV:** 79–80; and Webster, **II:** 71–72, 74–75, 79; influence on English literature, **II:** 29, 42–43, 47, 48, 54–55, 79, 82, 84; **III:** 115–116, 167n; **IV:** 35, 51–52; **V:** 405; **Supp. I:** 196, 227; **Supp. II:** 193, 194; **Supp. IV:** 158, 171, 283, 558; **Retro. Supp. III: 267–285**
Shakespeare (Swinburne), **V:** 333
"Shakespeare and Stage Costume" (Wilde), **V:** 407
Shakespeare and the Allegory of Evil (Spivack), **I:** 214
Shakespeare and the Goddess of Complete Being (Hughes), **Retro. Supp. II:** 202
Shakespeare and the Idea of the Play (Righter), **I:** 224
"Shakespeare and the Stoicism of Seneca" (Eliot), **I:** 275
"Shakespeare as a Man" (Stephen), **V:** 287
Shakespeare Wallah (Jhabvala), **Supp. V:** 237–238
Shakespeare Wrote for Money (Hornby), **Supp. XV:** 145
Shakespeare's Predecessors in the English Drama (Ellis and Symonds), **Supp. XIV:** 262
Shakespeare's Sonnets Reconsidered (Butler), **Supp. II:** 116
Shall I Call Thee Bard: A Portrait of Jason Strugnell (Cope), **VIII:** 69
Shall We Join the Ladies? (Barrie), **Supp. III:** 6, 9, 16–17
Shaman (Raine), **Supp. XIII:** 173
"Shamdev; The Wolf–Boy" (Chatwin), **Supp. IV:** 157
Shame (Rushdie), **Supp. IV:** 116, 433, 436, 440, 443, 444–445, 448, 449
Shamela (Fielding), **III:** 84, 98, 105; **Retro. Supp. I:** 80; **Retro. Supp. I:** 82–83
Shamrock Tea (Carson), **Supp. XIII:** 63–65
Shape of Things to Come, The (Wells), **VI:** 228, 241
"Shape–Changer, The" (Wallace–Crabbe), **VIII:** 318–319
"Shapes and Shadows" (Mahon), **Supp. VI:** 178
SHAR: Hurricane Poem (Brathwaite), **Supp. XII:** 35–36

Sharawaggi: Poems in Scots (Crawford and Herbert), **Supp. XI:** 67–71, 72
Shards of Memory (Jhabvala), **Supp. V:** 233, 234–235
"Shark! Shark!" (Kay), **Supp. XIII:** 109
"Sharp Trajectories" (Davie), **Supp. VI:** 116
Sharp, William, **IV:** 370
Sharpeville Sequence (Bond), **Supp. I:** 429
Sharrock, Roger, **II:** 246, 254
Shaving of Shagpat, The (Meredith), **V:** 225, 234
Shaw, George Bernard, **III:** 263; **V:** xxii, xxv, xxvi, 284, 301, 305–306, 423, 433; **VI:** viii, ix, xiv–xv, **101–132,** 147, 343; **Supp. II:** 24, 45, 51, 54, 55, 117–118, 288, 296–297; **Supp. III:** 6; **Supp. IV:** 233, 288, 292; **Retro. Supp. II: 309–325**
Shaw Gives Himself Away: An Autobiographical Miscellany (Shaw), **VI:** 129
Shaw-Stewart, Patrick, **VI:** 418–419, 420
She (Haggard), **Supp. III:** 211, 212, 213, 219–222, 223–227
"She Cries" (Montague), **Supp. XV:** 219
She Plays with the Darkness (Mda), **Supp. XV:** 199, 202–203
She Stoops to Conquer (Goldsmith), **II:** 362; **III:** 177, 181, 183, 188, 191, 256
She Wou'd if She Cou'd (Etherege), **II:** 266, 268, 271
Sheaf of Verses, A (Hall), **Supp. VI:** 119
"Sheep" (Hughes), **Retro. Supp. II:** 209
Sheep and the Dog, The (Henryson), **Supp. VII:** 136, 138–139, 141
"Sheepdog Trials in Hyde Park" (Day Lewis), **Supp. III:** 130
"Sheer Edge" (Malouf), **Supp. XII:** 219
"She's all my fancy painted him" (Carroll), **V:** 264
Shelf Life (Powell), **Supp. IV:** 258
"Shell" (Kay), **Supp. XIII:** 102, 109
Shelley, Mary Wollstonecraft, **III: 329–331,** 336, 341, 342, 345; **IV:** xv, xvi, xvii, 118, 197, 201, 202, 203; **Supp. III: 355–373,** 385; **Supp. IV:** 546; **Retro. Supp. I:** 246; **Retro. Supp. III: 287–300**
Shelley, Percy Bysshe, **II:** 102, 200; **III:** 329, 330, 333, 336–338; **IV:** vii–xii, 63, 132, 158–159, 161, 163, 164, 168–169, 172, 176–179, 182, **195–210,** 217, 234, 281, 299, 349, 354, 357, 366, 372; **V:** 214, 330, 401, 403; **VI:** 453; **Supp. III:** 355, 357–358, 364–365, 370; **Supp. IV:** 468; **Retro. Supp. I: 243–257**
Shelley (Swinburne), **V:** 333
Shelley (Thompson), **V:** 450, 451
Shelley: A Life Story (Blunden), **IV:** 210
Shelley and Keats as They Struck Their Contemporaries (Blunden), **IV:** 210
Shelley's Idols of the Cave (Butler), **IV:** 210
"Shelley's Skylark" (Hardy), **Retro. Supp. I:** 119
Shells by a Stream (Blunden), **Supp. XI:** 37

Shelmalier (McGuckian), **Supp. V:** 280, 290–292
"Shelmalier" (McGuckian), **Supp. V:** 291
Shelter, The (Phillips), **Supp. V:** 380
Sheol (Raine), **Supp. XIII:** 173
Shepheardes Calendar (Spenser), *see Shepherd's Calendar, The*
Shepheard's Oracles, The (Quarles), **II:** 139
Shepherd, Ettrick, *see* Hogg, James
Shepherd, and Other Poems of Peace and War, The (Blunden), **Supp. XI:** 36, 42
"Shepherd and the Nymph, The" (Landor), **IV:** 96
Shepherd of the Giant Mountains, The (tr. Smedley), **V:** 265
"Shepherd's Brow, The" (Hopkins), **V:** 376, 378n
Shepherd's Calendar, The (Spenser), **I:** 97, 121, 123, 124–128, 162
Shepherd's Calendar, The; with Village Stories, and Other Poems (Clare), **Supp. XI:** 59
"Shepherd's Carol" (Nicholson), **Supp. VI:** 214–215
Shepherd's Life, A (Hudson), **V:** 429
Shepherd's Week, The (Gay), **III:** 55, 56, 67
Sheppey (Maugham), **VI:** 377
Sherburn, George, **III:** 73, 78
Sheridan, Richard Brinsley, **II:** 334, 336; **III:** 32, 97, 101, **252–271**
Sheridan, Susan, **Supp. IV:** 459
Sherlock Holmes and the Limehouse Horror (Pullman), **Supp. XIII:** 151
"Sherthursdaye and Venus Day" (Jones), **Supp. VII:** 177
Shewan, R., **V:** 409n, 421
"She-Who-Would-Be-King" (Aidoo), **Supp. XV:** 9
Shewing of a Vision, The (Julian of Norwich), **Supp. XII:** 155
Shewings of the Lady Julian, The (Julian of Norwich), **Supp. XII:** 155
Shewing-Up of Blanco Posnet, The: A Sermon in Crude Melodrama (Shaw), **VI:** 115, 117, 124, 129
"Shian Bay" (Graham), **Supp. VII:** 110–111
"Shield of Achilles, The" (Auden), **VII:** 388, 390–391, 397–398; **Retro. Supp. I:** 10
Shield Ring, The (Sutcliff), **Supp. XVI:** 269, 273
Shikasta (Lessing), **Supp. I:** 250, 251, 252, 253
Shining, The (King), **III:** 345
"Shining Gift, The" (Wallace-Crabbe), **VIII:** 323
Ship of Birth, The (Delanty), **Supp. XIV:** 74–75
"Ship of The Wind, The" (Longley), **VIII:** 175
"Ship That Found Herself, The" (Kipling), **VI:** 170
Shipman's Tale, The (Chaucer), **I:** 36
"Ships" (Dunn), **Supp. X:** 70
Shipwreck (Fowles), **Supp. I:** 292
Shipwrecked, The (Greene), *see England Made Me*

Shires, The (Davie), **Supp. VI:** 111–112
Shirley, James, **II:** 44, 66, 87
Shirley (Brontë), **V:** xxi, 12, 106, 112, **145–147,** 152; **Retro. Supp. I:** 53, 54, 60
Shirley Sanz (Pritchett), **Supp. III:** 313
"Shit" (Gunn), **Retro. Supp. III:** 129
Shrimp and the Anemone, The (Hartley), **Supp. VII:** 119, 124–125
"Shoals Returning, The" (Kinsella), **Supp. V:** 263
Shoemaker of Merano, The (Hall), **Supp. VI:** 130
Shoemaker's Holiday, The (Dekker), **II:** 89
"Shooting an Elephant" (Orwell), **VII:** 273, 276, 282
Shooting Niagara—"nd After? (Carlyle), **IV:** xxii, 240, 247, 250
"Shore Road, The" (MacCaig), **Supp. VI:** 187, 195
Short Account of a Late Short Administration, A (Burke), **III:** 205
Short Character of . . . [the Earl of Wharton], A (Swift), **III:** 35
Short Historical Essay . . . , A (Marvell), **II:** 219
"Short History of British India, A" (Hill), **Supp. V:** 191
"Short History of the English Novel, A" (Self), **Supp. V:** 403
Short History of the English People (Green), **VI:** 390
Short Stories, Scraps, and Shavings (Shaw), **VI:** 129
short story, **VI:** 369–370; **VII:** xvii, 178–181
"Short Story, The" (Bowen), **Supp. II:** 86
Short Story, The (O'Connor), **Supp. XIV:** 224
Short View of the Immorality and Profaneness of the English Stage, A (Collier), **II:** 303, 325, 338, 340, 356; **III:** 44
Short View of the State of Ireland, A (Swift), **III:** 28, 35; **Retro. Supp. I:** 276
*Short Vindication of A*The Relapse*"and A*The Provok'd Wife,"A, . . . by the Author* (Vanbrugh), **II:** 332, 336
Shortened History of England, A (Trevelyan), **VI:** 395
Shorter, Clement, **V:** 150, 151–153
Shorter Finnegans Wake, A (Burgess), **Supp. I:** 197
Shorter Poems (Bridges), **VI:** 72, 73, 81
Shortest Way to Peace and Union, The (Defoe), **III:** 13
Shortest Way with the Dissenters, The (Defoe), **III:** 2, 3, 12–13; **Retro. Supp. I:** 64–65, 67
"Shot, The" (Jennings), **Supp. V:** 210
Shot, The (Kerr), **Supp. XII:** 194–195
"Shot Down over Libya" (Dahl), **Supp. IV:** 202, 207–208, 209
Shot in the Park, A (Plomer), **Supp. XI:** 222
"Should lanterns shine" (Thomas), **Supp. I:** 174

Shoulder of Shasta, The (Stoker), **Supp. III:** 381
Shout, The (Graves), **VII:** 259
"Show me, dear Christ, thy spouse" (Donne), **I:** 367, 368
"Show Saturday" (Larkin), **Supp. I:** 283, 285; **Retro. Supp. III:** 209
Shrapnel Academy, The (Weldon), **Supp. IV:** 529–530, 531
Shropshire Lad, A (Housman), **VI:** ix, xv, 157, 158–160, 164
Shroud for a Nightingale (James), **Supp. IV:** 319, 320, 323, 326–327
"Shrove Tuesday in Paris" (Thackeray), **V:** 22, 38
"Shutterbug, The" (Delanty), **Supp. XIV:** 74
Shuttlecock (Swift), **Supp. V:** 429–431
"Siberia" (Mangan), **Supp. XIII:** 126
"Sibylla Palmifera" (Rossetti), **V:** 237
Sibylline Leaves (Coleridge), **IV:** 56
"Sibyl's Prophecy, The", *See Vǫluspá*
"Sic Tydingis Hard I at the Sessioun" (Dunbar), **VIII:** 122
"Sic Vita" (King), **Supp. VI:** 162
Sicilian Carousel (Durrell), **Supp. I:** 102; **Retro. Supp. III:** 95
Sicilian Lover, The (Robinson), **Supp. XIII:** 209
Sicilian Romance, A (Radcliffe), **III:** 338; **Retro. Supp. III:** 238–239–249
"Sick King in Bokhara, The" (Arnold), **V:** 210
Sidgwick, Henry, **V:** 284, 285
Sidhwa, Bapsi, **Supp. V:** 62
Sidley, Sir Charles, *see* Sedley, Sir Charles
Sidney, Sir Philip, **I:** 123, **160–175; II:** 46, 48, 53, 80, 158, 221, 339; **III:** 95; **Retro. Supp. I:** 157; **Retro. Supp. II: 327–342**
Siege (Fry), **Supp. III:** 194
Siege of Corinth, The (Byron), **IV:** 172, 192; *see also* Turkish tales
Siege of London, The (James), **VI:** 67
Siege of Pevensey, The (Burney), **Supp. III:** 71
Siege of Pleasure, The (Hamilton), **Supp. XVI:** 182, 184–185
Siege of Thebes, The (Lydgate), **I:** 57, 61, 65
"Siena" (Swinburne), **V:** 325, 332
"Sierra Nevada" (Stevenson), **Supp. VI:** 254–255
"Siesta of a Hungarian Snake" (Morgan, E.), **Supp. IX:** 166
"Sigh, A" (Finch), **Supp. IX:** 67–68
"Sighs and Grones" (Herbert), **II:** 128
"Sight" (Robinson), **Supp. XIII:** 207
Sight for Sore Eyes, A (Rendell), **Supp. IX:** 195, 200–201
Sight, The Cavern of Woe, and Solitude (Robinson), **Supp. XIII:** 207
Sign of Four, The (Doyle), **Supp. II:** 160, 162–163, 164–165, 167, 171, 173, 176
Sign of the Cross, The (Barrett), **VI:** 124
Signal Driver (White), **Supp. I:** 131, 151
Signals of Distress (Crace), **Supp. XIV:** 18, 19, 23, 25–26

Significance of Locality in the Poetry of Friedrich Hölderlin, The (Constantine), **Supp. XV:** 66
"Significance of Nothing, The" (Raine), **Supp. XIII:** 164
"Signpost, The" (Thomas), **Supp. III:** 403, 404
"Signs" (Stevenson), **Supp. VI:** 263
Signs of Change (Morris), **V:** 306
"Signs of the Times" (Carlyle), **IV:** 241–242, 243, 249, 324; **V:** viii
Sigurd the Volsung (Morris), *see Story of Sigurd the Volsung and the Fall of the Niblungs, The*
Silas Marner (Eliot), **V:** xxii, 194, 200; **Retro. Supp. II:** 108–110
"Silecroft Shore" (Nicholson), **Supp. VI:** 216
Silence (Pinter), **Supp. I:** 376
"Silence" (Traherne), **Supp. XI:** 270
Silence Among the Weapons (Arden), **Supp. II:** 41
Silence in the Garden, The (Trevor), **Supp. IV:** 505, 506, 515–516, 517
"Silence Is Possible" (Burnside), **Supp. XIII:** 14
"Silent One, The" (Gurney), **VI:** 427
Silent Passenger, The (Sayers), **Supp. III:** 335
"Silent Voices, The" (Tennyson), **IV:** 329
Silent Voices: An Anthology of Romanian Women Poets (tr. Deletant and Walker), **Supp. XII:** 11
Silent Woman, The (Jonson), **Retro. Supp. I:** 163
Silex Scintillans: . . . (Vaughan), **II:** 184, 185, 186, 201
Silhouettes (Symons), **Supp. XIV:** 267, 272, 276, 278
Sillitoe, Alan, **Supp. V: 409–426**
Silmarillion, The (Tolkien), **Supp. II:** 519, 520, 521, 525, 527
Silver, Brenda, **Retro. Supp. I:** 305
"Silver Age, The" (Gunn), **Retro. Supp. III:** 120
"Silver Blaze" (Doyle), **Supp. II:** 167
Silver Box, The (Galsworthy), **VI:** 273, 284–285
Silver Branch, The (Sutcliff), **Supp. XVI:** 261, 266, 267–268
Silver Bucket, The (Orton), **Supp. V:** 364
Silver Chair, The (Lewis), **Supp. III:** 248
Silver Circus (Coppard), **VIII:** 96–97
"Silver Crucifix on My Desk, A" (Hart), **Supp. XI:** 127–128
"Silver Flask, The" (Montague), **Supp. XV:** 209, 221–222
"Silver Plate, A" (Raine), **Supp. XIII:** 168
"Silver Screen, The" (Davies), **Supp. XIV:** 36, 40
Silver Spoon, The (Galsworthy), **VI:** 275
Silver Stair, The (Williams, C. W. S.), **Supp. IX:** 273, 274
Silver Tassie, The (O'Casey), **VII:** 6–7
Silverado Squatters, The (Stevenson), **V:** 386, 395; **Retro. Supp. I:** 262
"Silvia" (Etherege), **II:** 267
"Sim" (Gibbon), **Supp. XIV:** 104, 105–106

Simenon, Georges, **III:** 341
"Simile" (Constantine), **Supp. XV:** 80
Simisola (Rendell), **Supp. IX:** 196, 198–199
Simmons, Ernest, **V:** 46
Simmons, James, **Supp. IV:** 412
Simon (Sutcliff), **Supp. XVI:** 262, 265–266, 268
"Simon Lee" (Wordsworth), **IV:** 7, 8–9, 10
Simonetta Perkins (Hartley), **Supp. VII:** 122–123, 126
Simonidea (Landor), **IV:** 100
Simple and Religious Consultation (Bucer), **I:** 177
"Simple Simon" (Coppard), **VIII:** 97
Simple Story, A (Inchbald), **Supp. XV:** 147, 148–149, 150–151, 152, 153
"Simple Susan" (Edgeworth), **Supp. III:** 153
Simpleton of the Unexpected Isles, The (Shaw), **VI:** 125, 126, 127, 129
"Simplicities" (Wallace-Crabbe), **VIII:** 324–325
Simplicity (Collins), **III:** 166
"Simplification of Life" (Carpenter), **Supp. XIII:** 40
"Simplify Me When I'm Dead" (Douglas), **VII:** 440
Simpson, Alan, **Supp. II:** 68, 70, 74
Simpson, Percy, **I:** 279
Simpson, Richard, **IV:** 107, 122
"Simultaneous Translation" (Crawford), **Supp. XI:** 73
Sinai Sort, The (MacCaig), **Supp. VI: 186–187**
"Since thou, O fondest and truest" (Bridges), **VI:** 74, 77
"Sincerest Critick of My Prose, or Rhime" (Congreve), **II:** 349
Sinclair, Iain, **Supp. XIV: 231–248**
"Sindhi Woman" (Stallworthy), **Supp. X:** 293
Singer, S. W., **III:** 69
"Singing, 1977" (Fuller), **Supp. VII:** 79
"Singing Bush, The" (Soutar), **Supp. XVI:** 256
Singing Detective, The (Potter, D.), **Supp. X:** 229
Singing Men at Cashel, The (Clarke), **Supp. XV:** 24
Singing School: The Making of a Poet (Stallworthy), **Supp. X:** 291–292, 301–303
Singing the Sadness (Hill, R.), **Supp. IX:** 123
Single and Single (le Carré), **Retro. Supp. III:** 226–227
Single Man, A (Isherwood), **VII:** 309, 316–317
Singleton's Law (Hill), see *Albion! Albion!*
Sing-Song (Rossetti), **V:** 251, 255, 260
Singular Preference, The (Quennell), **VI:** 237, 245
Sinjohn, John, pseud. of John Galsworthy
"Sinking" (Pitter), **Supp. XIII:** 135
"Sins and Virtues" (Crace), **Supp. XIV:** 21–22

Sins of the Fathers and Other Tales (Gissing), **V:** 437
Sir Charles Grandison (Richardson), **III:** 80, 90–91, 92; **IV:** 124
"Sir David Brewster Invents the Kaleidoscope" (Crawford), **Supp. XI:** 71
"Sir Dominick Ferrand" (James), **VI:** 69
"Sir Edmund Orme" (James), **VI:** 69
"Sir Eustace Grey" (Crabbe), **III:** 282
"Sir Galahad and the Islands" (Brathwaite), **Supp. XII:** 43
Sir Gawain and the Carl of Carlisle, **I:** 71
Sir Gawain and the Green Knight, (*Gawain*–Poet), **I:** 2, 28, 69, 71; **Supp. VII:** 83, 84–91, 94, 98
Sir George Otto Trevelyan: A Memoir (Trevelyan), **VI:** 383, 391
Sir Harry Hotspur of Humblethwaite (Trollope), **V:** 100, 102
Sir Harry Wildair, Being the Sequel of A"The Trip to the Jubilee" (Farquhar), **II:** 352, 357, 364
Sir Hornbook; or, Childe Launcelot's Expedition (Peacock), **IV:** 169
Sir John Vanbrugh's Justificahon of . . . the Duke of Marlborough's Late Tryal (Vanbrugh), **II:** 336
Sir Launcelot Greaves (Smollett), **III:** 149, 153, 158
Sir Martin Mar–All; or, The Feign'd Innocence (Dryden), **II:** 305
Sir Nigel (Doyle), **Supp. II:** 159
Sir Patient Fancy (Behn), **Retro. Supp. III:** 4
Sir Proteus, a Satirical Ballad (Peacock), **IV:** 169
Sir Thomas More; or, Colloquies on the Progress and Prospects of Society (Southey), **IV:** 69, 70, 71, 280
Sir Thomas Wyatt (Dekker and Webster), **II:** 68
Sir Tom (Oliphant), **Supp. X:** 219
Sir Tristrem (Thomas the Rhymer), **IV:** 29
"Sir Walter Scott" (Carlyle), **IV:** 38
Sir Walter Scott: The Great Unknown (Johnson), **IV:** 40
"Sir William Herschel's Long Year" (Hope), **Supp. VII:** 164–165
"Sire de Maletroit's Door, The" (Stevenson), **V:** 395
Siren Land (Douglas), **VI:** 293, 294, 295, 297, 305
"Sirens, The" (Manifold), **VII:** 426
Sirian Experiments, The: The Report by Ambien II, of the Five (Lessing), **Supp. I:** 250, 252
Sirocco (Coward), **Supp. II:** 141, 146, 148
"Siskin" (Stevenson), **Supp. VI:** 256
Sisson, C. H., **Supp. XI: 243–262**
Sisson, C. J., **I:** 178n, 326
Sister Anne (Potter), **Supp. III:** 304
Sister Eucharia: A Play in Three Scenes (Clarke), **Supp. XV:** 24
"Sister Helen" (Rossetti), **IV:** 313; **V:** 239, 245
"Sister Imelda" (O'Brien), **Supp. V:** 340
"Sister Maude" (Rossetti), **V:** 259

Sister Songs (Thompson), **V:** 443, 449, 450, 451
Sister Teresa (Moore), **VI:** 87, 92, 98
Sisterly Feelings (Ayckbourn), **Supp. V:** 3, 6, 10, 11–12, 13, 14
"Sisters" (Kinsella), **Supp. V:** 261
Sisters, The (Conrad), **VI:** 148
"Sisters, The" (Joyce), **Retro. Supp. I:** 171–172; **Retro. Supp. III:** 167, 169, 170
Sisters, The (Swinburne), **V:** 330, 333
Sisters and Strangers: A Moral Tale (Tennant), **Supp. IX:** 235, 236
Sisters by a River (Comyns), **VIII:** 54, 55, 56
"Sitting, The" (Day Lewis), **Supp. III:** 128–129
"Situation in Catalonia, The" (Cornford), **Supp. XIII:** 90–93
Situation of the Novel, The (Bergonzi), **Supp. IV:** 233
Sitwell, Edith, **I:** 83; **III:** 73, 78; **VI:** 454; **VII:** xv–xvii, **127–141**
Sitwell, Osbert, **V:** 230, 234; **VII:** xvi, 128, 130, 135; **Supp. II:** 199, 201–202, 203
Sitwell, Sacheverell, **VII:** xvi, 128
Six (Crace), **Supp. XIV:** 18, 30
Six Distinguishing Characters of a Parliament–Man, The (Defoe), **III:** 12
Six Dramas of Calderón. Freely Translated (FitzGerald), **IV:** 342, 344–345, 353
Six Epistles to Eva Hesse (Davie), **Supp. VI:** 111
"Six o'clock in Princes Street" (Owen), **VI:** 451
Six of Calais, The (Shaw), **VI:** 129
Six Poems (Thomas), **Supp. III:** 399
Six Queer Things, The (Caudwell), **Supp. IX:** 35
Six Stories Written in the First Person Singular (Maugham), **VI:** 374
Six Voices: Contemporary Australian Poets (Wallace–Crabb)e ed.), **VIII:** 314–315
"Six Weeks at Heppenheim" (Gaskell), **V:** 14, 15
"Six Years After" (Mansfield), **VII:** 176
"Six Young Men" (Hughes), **Supp. I:** 344; **Retro. Supp. II:** 203–204
"Sixpence" (Mansfield), **VII:** 175, 177
Sixteen Occasional Poems 1990–2000 (Gray, A.), **Supp. IX:** 88, 91–92
Sixteen Self Sketches (Shaw), **VI:** 102, 129
Sixth Beatitude, The (Hall), **Supp. VI:** 120, 122, **130**
Sixth Heaven, The (Hartley), **Supp. VII:** 124, 125, 127
"Sixth Journey, The" (Graham), **Supp. VII:** 109
"Sixty Drops of Laudanum" (Mangan), **Supp. XIII:** 117
Sizemore, Christine Wick, **Supp. IV:** 336
Sizwe Bansi Is Dead (Fugard), **Supp. XV:** 100, 103, 109
"Skating" (Motion), **Supp. VII:** 251, 256
Skeat, W. W., **I:** 17

"Skeins o Geese" (Jamie), **Supp. XIV:** 139
"Skeleton, The" (Pritchett), **Supp. III:** 325
"Skeleton of the Future (at Lenin's Tomb), The" (MacDiarmid), **Supp. XII:** 211
Skelton, John, **I: 81–96**
"Sketch, A" (Rossetti), **V:** 250
Sketch Book (Irving), **III:** 54
"Sketch from Private Life, A" (Byron), **IV:** 192
"Sketch of the Great Dejection, A" (Gunn), **Supp. IV:** 274; **Retro. Supp. III:** 116
"Sketch of the Past, A" (Woolf), **Retro. Supp. I:** 314–315
Sketches and Essays (Hazlitt), **IV:** 140
"Sketches and Reminiscences of Irish Writers" (Mangan), **Supp. XIII:** 114
Sketches and Reviews (Pater), **V:** 357
Sketches and Studies in Italy (Symonds), **Supp. XIV:** 251
Sketches and Travels in London (Thackeray), **V:** 38
Sketches by Boz (Dickens), **V:** xix, 42, 43–46, 47, 52, 71
"Sketches for a Self–Portrait" (Day Lewis), **Supp. III:** 128
Sketches from Cambridge, by a Don (Stephen), **V:** 289
Sketches in Italy and Greece (Symonds), **Supp. XIV:** 251–252
Sketches in the Life of John Clare, Written by Himself (Clare), **Supp. XI:** 50, 53
"Sketches of Irish Writers" (Mangan), **Supp. XIII:** 119, 124
Sketches of the Principal Picture–Galleries in England (Hazlitt), **IV:** 132, 139
"Skin" (Dahl), **Supp. IV:** 216
Skin (Kane), **VIII:** 148, 149, 157–158
Skin Chairs, The (Comyns), **VIII:** 53, 55, 62–63
Skin Game, The (Galsworthy), **VI:** 275, 280, 288
Skírnismál, **VIII:** 230
Skotlands rímur, **VIII:** 243
Skriker, The (Churchill), **Supp. IV:** 179, 180, 197–198
Skull Beneath the Skin, The (James), **Supp. II:** 127; **Supp. IV:** 335–336, 337
Skull in Connemara, A (McDonagh), **Supp. XII:** 233, 235, 236, 237, 238, 245
"Sky Burning Up Above the Man, The" (Keneally), **Supp. IV:** 345
"Sky like a Slaughterhouse" (Constantine), **Supp. XV:** 78
Skyhorse (Stallworthy), **Supp. X:** 301
"Skylarks" (Hughes), **Retro. Supp. II:** 206
Skylight (Hare), **Supp. IV:** 282, 298–299
"Skylight, The" (Heaney), **Retro. Supp. I:** 132
Slag (Hare), **Supp. IV:** 281, 283
Slam (Hornby), **Supp. XV:** 134, 145
"Slate" (Morgan, E.), **Supp. IX:** 167
"Slaves in Love" (Beer), **Supp. XIV:** 13

Slaves of Solitude, The (Hamilton), **Supp. XVI:** 179–181, 181–182
"Sleep" (Cowley), **II:** 196
"Sleep, The" (Browning), **IV:** 312
"Sleep and Poetry" (Keats), **IV:** 214–215, 217, 228, 231; **Retro. Supp. I:** 184, 188
Sleep Has His House (Kavan), see *House of Sleep, The*
Sleep It Off, Lady (Rhys), **Supp. II:** 389, 401, 402
Sleep of Prisoners, A (Fry), **Supp. III:** 194, 195, 199–200
Sleep of Reason, The (Snow), **VII:** 324, 331–332
Sleep with Me (Kureishi), **Supp. XI:** 155
Sleeper (Constantine), **Supp. XV:** 78
Sleepers of Mars (Wyndham), **Supp. XIII:** 282
Sleepers of Roraima (Harris), **Supp. V:** 132
Sleep of the Great Hypnotist, The (Redgrove), **Supp. VI:** 231
"Sleeping at Last" (Rossetti), **V:** 251–252, 259
Sleeping Beauty, The (Sitwell), **VII:** 132
Sleeping Fires (Gissing), **V:** 437
Sleeping Lord and Other Fragments, The (Jones), **Supp. VII:** 167, 170, 178–180
Sleeping Murder (Christie), **Supp. II:** 125, 134
Sleeping Prince, The (Rattigan), **Supp. VII:** 318–319
Sleepwalkers, The: A History of Man's Changing Vision of the Universe (Koestler), **Supp. I:** 37–38
Sleuths, Inc. (Eames), **Supp. IV:** 3
"Slice of Cake, A" (Scupham), **Supp. XIII:** 230
Slight Ache, A (Pinter), **Supp. I:** 369, 371; **Retro. Supp. I:** 222–223
"Slips" (McGuckian), **Supp. V:** 281–282
Slipstream: A Memoir (Howard), **Supp. XI:** 135, 136, 141, 143, 144, 145–146
Slocum, Joshua, **Supp. IV:** 158
Slot Machine, The (Sillitoe), **Supp. V:** 411
"Slough" (Betjeman), **VII:** 366
Slow Chocolate Autopsy: Incidents from the Notorious Career of Norton, Prisoner of London (Sinclair), **Supp. XIV:** 233–234, 237, 245
Slow Dance, A (Montague), **Supp. XV:** 222
Slow Digestions of the Night, The (Crace), **Supp. XIV:** 29
"Slow Walker" (Gunn), **Retro. Supp. III:** 125
"Slumber Did My Spirit Seal, A" (Wordsworth), **IV:** 18
"Small Boy" (MacCaig), **Supp. VI:** 194
Small Boy and Others, A (James), **VI:** 65
Small Containers, The (Scupham), **Supp. XIII:** 218
Small Family Business, A (Ayckbourn), **Supp. V:** 3, 12, 14
Small g: A Summer Idyll (Highsmith), **Supp. V:** 179

Small House at Allington, The (Trollope), **V:** xxiii, 101
"Small Personal Voice, The" (Lessing), **Supp. I:** 238
Small Place, A (Kincaid), **Supp. VII:** 217, 225–226, 230, 231
"Small Plant, The" (Pitter), **Supp. XIII:** 144
Small Town in Germany, A (le Carré), **Supp. II:** 300, **303–305,** 307; **Retro. Supp. III:** 218–219
"Small World" (Davies), **Supp. XIV:** 41–42
Small World: An Academic Romance (Lodge), **Supp. IV:** 363, 366, 371, 372, 374, 376–378, 384, 385
"*Small World:* An Introduction" (Lodge), **Supp. IV:** 377
Smashing the Piano (Montague), **Supp. XV:** 210, 211, 219
Smeaton, O., **III:** 229*n*
Smeddum: A Lewis Grassic Gibbon Anthology (Gibbon), **Supp. XIV:** 99, 100, 102, 103, 104, 105
"Smeddum" (Gibbon), **Supp. XIV:** 105
"Smile" (Thomas), **Supp. IV:** 491–492
"Smile of Fortune, A" (Conrad), **VI:** 148
Smile Please (Rhys), **Supp. II:** 387, 388, 389, 394, 395, 396
Smiles, Samuel, **VI:** 264
Smiley's People (le Carré), **Supp. II:** 305, 311, **314–315; Retro. Supp. III:** 219, 221
Smith, Adam, **IV:** xiv, 144–145; **V:** viii
Smith, Alexander, **IV:** 320; **V:** 158
Smith, Edmund, **III:** 118
Smith, George, **V:** 13, 131, 132, 147, 149, 150, 279–280
Smith, Henry Nash, **VI:** 24
Smith, Iain Chrichton, **Supp. IX:** **207–225**
Smith, James, **IV:** 253
Smith, Janet Adam, **V:** 391, 393, 395–398
Smith, Logan Pearsall, **Supp. III:** 98, 111
Smith, Nichol, **III:** 21
Smith, Stevie, **Supp. II:** **459–478; Retro. Supp. III:** **301–316**
Smith, Sydney, **IV:** 268, 272; **Supp. VII:** **339–352**
Smith, William Robertson, **Supp. III:** 171
Smith (Maugham), **VI:** 368
Smith and the Pharaohs and Other Tales (Haggard), **Supp. III:** 214, 222
Smith, Elder & Co. (publishers), **V:** 131, 140, 145, 150; *see also* Smith, George
Smith of Wootton Major (Tolkien), **Supp. II:** 521
Smithers, Peter, **III:** 42, 53
"Smithfield Market" (Carson), **Supp. XIII:** 57
"Smoke" (Mahon), **Supp. VI:** 177
"Smokers for Celibacy" (Adcock), **Supp. XII:** 12
Smollett, Tobias, **III:** **146–159; V:** xiv 52
Smyer, Richard I., **Supp. IV:** 338
"Snail Watcher, The" (Highsmith), **Supp. V:** 180

Snail Watcher and Other Stories, The (Highsmith), **Supp. V:** 180
"Snake" (Lawrence), **VII:** 119; **Retro. Supp. II:** 233–234
Snake's Pass, The (Stoker), **Supp. III:** 381
"Snap–dragon" (Lawrence), **VII:** 118
Snapper, The (Doyle), **Supp. V:** 77, 82–85, 88
"Snayl, The" (Lovelace), **II:** 231
"Sneaker's A" (Mahon), **Supp. VI:** 175–176
"Sniff, The" (Pritchett), **Supp. III:** 319, **320–321**
"Sniper, The" (Sillitoe), **Supp. V:** 414
Snobs of England, The (Thackeray), *see Book of Snobs, The*
Snodgrass, Chris, **V:** 314
Snooty Baronet (Lewis), **VII:** 77
Snorra Edda, **VIII:** 243
Snow, C. P., **VI:** 235; **VII:** xii, xxi, 235, **321–341**
"Snow" (Hughes), **Supp. I:** 348
"Snow" (MacNeice), **VII:** 412
"Snow and Wind Canticle to an Unborn Child" (Delanty), **Supp. XIV:** 74
"Snow Joke" (Armitage), **VIII:** 3
Snow on the North Side of Lucifer (Sillitoe), **Supp. V:** 424, 425
Snow Party, The (Mahon), **Supp. VI:** 169, **172–173**
"Snow Party, The" (Mahon), **Supp. VI:** 172
"Snow White's Journey to the City" (Fallon), **Supp. XII:** 102
Snowing Globe, The (Scupham), **Supp. XIII:** 218, 219
"Snowmanshit" (Redgrove), **Supp. VI:** 234
Snowstop (Sillitoe), **Supp. V:** 411
"Snow–White and the Seven Dwarfs" (Dahl), **Supp. IV:** 226
"So crewell prison howe could betyde, alas" (Surrey), **I:** 113
"So Good of Their Kind" (Pitter), **Supp. XIII:** 145
"So I Thought She Must Have Been Forgiven" (Pitter), **Supp. XIII:** 145
So Lovers Dream (Waugh), **Supp. VI:** 272
"So Much Depends" (Cope), **VIII:** 78
"So On He Fares" (Moore), **VI:** 93
"So sweet love seemed that April morn" (Bridges), **VI:** 77
"So to Fatness Come" (Smith), **Supp. II:** 472
"So you think I Am a Mule?" (Kay), **Supp. XIII:** 108
Soaking The Heat (Kureishi), **Supp. XI:** 153
"Soap-Pig, The" (Muldoon), **Supp. IV:** 423
"Sobieski's Shield" (Hill), **Retro. Supp. III:** 139
"Social Life in Roman Britain" (Trevelyan), **VI:** 393
"Social Progress and Individual Effort" (Carpenter), **Supp. XIII:** 40
Social Rights and Duties (Stephen), **V:** 289

Socialism and the Family (Wells), **VI:** 244
Socialism and the New Life (Carpenter), **Supp. XIII:** 36
Socialism: Its Growth and Outcome (Morris and Box), **V:** 306
"Socialism: Principles and Outlook" (Shaw), **VI:** 129
Society for Pure English Tracts, **VI:** 83
Society in America (Martineau), **Supp. XV:** 186
"Sociological Cure for Shellshock, A" (Hibberd), **VI:** 460
"Sofa in the Forties, A" (Heaney), **Retro. Supp. I:** 133
Soft Side, The (James), **VI:** 67
Soft Voice of the Serpent and Other Stories, The (Gordimer), **Supp. II:** 226
"Soho Hospital for Women, The" (Adcock), **Supp. XII:** 7
"Sohrab and Rustum" (Arnold), **V:** xxi, 208, 209, 210, 216
Soil Map, The (McGuckian), **Supp. V:** 282
"Solar" (Larkin), **Retro. Supp. III:** 208
Soldier (Scupham), **Supp. XIII:** 218
"Soldier, The" (Brooke), **VI:** 420, 421; **Supp. I:** 57, 58
"Soldier, The" (Hopkins), **V:** 372
Soldier and a Scholar, A (Swift), **III:** 36
Soldier of Humour (ed. Rosenthal), **VII:** 73
Soldier, Soldier (Arden), **Supp. II:** 28
Soldier's Art, The (Powell), **VII:** 349
"Soldiers Bathing" (Prince), **VII:** xxii 427
Soldier's Declaration, A (Sassoon), **Supp. IV:** 57
Soldier's Embrace, A (Gordimer), **Supp. II:** 232
"Soldiers of the Queen" (Kipling), **VI:** 417
"Soldiers on the Platform" (Cornford), **VIII:** 111
Soldiers Three (Kipling), **VI:** 204; **Retro. Supp. III:** 186
"Sole of a Foot, The" (Hughes), **Supp. I:** 357
"Solemn Meditation, A" (Pitter), **Supp. XIII:** 135, 141
Solid Geometry (McEwan), **Supp. IV:** 390, 398
"Solid House, A" (Rhys), **Supp. II:** 402
Solid Mandala, The (White), **Supp. I:** 131, **143–145,** 148, 152
"Solid Objects" (Woolf), **VII:** 31
"Soliloquies" (Hill), **Supp. V:** 187
Soliloquies (St. Augustine), **Retro. Supp. II:** 297
Soliloquies of a Hermit (Powys), **VIII:** 246, 247, 249
"Soliloquy by the Well" (Redgrove), **Supp. V:** 230
"Soliloquy of the Spanish Cloister" (Browning), **IV:** 356, 360, 367; **Retro. Supp. III:** 20, 22
Soliman and Perseda, **I:** 220
"Solitariness" (Soutar), **Supp. XVI:** 250
"Solitary Confinement" (Koestler), **Supp. I:** 36

"Solitary Reaper, The" (Wordsworth), **IV:** 22
"Solitary Shapers, The" (Wallace-Crabbe), **VIII:** 320
Solitary Way, The (Soutar), **Supp. XVI:** 250–251
"Solitude" (Carroll), **V:** 263
"Solitude" (Milne), **Supp. V:** 303
"Solitude" (Traherne), **II:** 192
Sollers, Philippe, **Supp. IV:** 115, 116
Solomon, Simeon, **V:** 312, 314, 320
Solomon's Temple Spiritualized (Bunyan), **II:** 253
Solon, **II:** 70
"Sols" (Constantine), **Supp. XV:** 73
"Solstice" (Jamie), **Supp. XIV:** 141
Solstices (MacNeice), **VII:** 416
"Solution, The" (James), **VI:** 69
Some Advice . . . to the Members of the October Club (Swift), **III:** 35
Some Arguments Against Enlarging the Power of the Bishop (Swift), **III:** 35
Some Branch Against the Sky (Dutton), **Supp. XII:** 83
Some Branch Against the Sky: Gardening in the Wild (Dutton), **Supp. XII:** 84
"Some Days Were Running Legs" (Smith, I. C.), **Supp. IX:** 211
Some Do Not (Ford), **VI:** 319
Some Early Impressions (Stephen), **V:** 278, 281, 290
Some Free Thoughts upon the Present State of Affairs (Swift), **III:** 27, 36
Some Friends of Walt Whitman: A Study in Sex–Psychology (Carpenter), **Supp. XIII:** 45
Some Gospel–Truths Opened According to the Scriptures (Bunyan), **II:** 253
Some Imagist Poets (ed. Lowell), **Supp. III:** 397
Some Irish Essays (Russell), **VIII:** 286
"Some More Light Verse" (Cope), **VIII:** 77
Some Lie and Some Die (Rendell), **Supp. IX:** 191–192, 197–198
Some Observations upon a Paper (Swift), **III:** 35
Some Papers Proper to Be Read Before the Royal Society (Fielding), **III:** 105
Some Passages in the Life of Major Gahagan (Thackeray), see *Tremendous Adventures of Major Gahagan, The*
Some Popular Fallacies About Vivisection (Carroll), **V:** 273
Some Reasons Against the . . . Tyth of Hemp . . . (Swift), **III:** 36
Some Reasons to Prove That No Person Is Obliged . . . as a Whig, etc. (Swift), **III:** 35
Some Recent Attacks: Essays Cultural and Political (Kelman), **Supp. V:** 257
Some Remarks on the Barrier Treaty (Swift), **III:** 35
Some Remarks upon a Pamphlet (Swift), **III:** 35
Some Reminiscences (Conrad), **VI:** 148
Some Tame Gazelle (Pym), **Supp. II: 366–367,** 380
Some Time Never: A Fable for Supermen (Dahl), **Supp. IV:** 211, 213, 214

"Some Time with Stephen: A Diary" (Kureishi), **Supp. XI:** 161
Some Versions of Pastoral (Empson; US. title, *English Pastoral Poetry*), **Supp. II:** 179, 184, 188, **189–190,** 197
"Someone Had To" (Galloway), **Supp. XII:** 126
Someone Like You (Dahl), **Supp. IV:** 206, 214, 215
Someone Talking to Sometime (Aidoo), **Supp. XV:** 10–11
Somers, Jane, see *Diaries of Jane Somers, The*
Somerset Masque, The (Campion), **Supp. XVI:** 92, 98–99
Somerset Maugham (Brander), **VI:** 379
Somerset Maugham (Curtis), **VI:** 379
Somervell, Robert, **VI:** 385
Something Childish, and Other Stories (Mansfield), **VII:** 171
"Something Else" (Priestley), **VII:** 212–213
Something for the Ghosts (Constantine), **Supp. XV:** 66–67, 79
Something Fresh (Wodehouse), see *Something New*
Something in Disguise (Howard), **Supp. XI:** 135, 141, 142
Something Leather (Gray, A.), **Supp. IX:** 80, 82, 83–86, 91
Something New (Wodehouse), **Supp. III:** 452, 453
Something of Myself: For My Friends, Known and Unknown (Kipling), **Retro. Supp. III:** 181, 182, 183, 184, 186, 187, 188, 189, 190, 193, 195
"Something the Cat Dragged In" (Highsmith), **Supp. V:** 180
"Sometime I fled the fire that me brent" (Wyatt), **I:** 103–104
Somewhere Is Such a Kingdom: Poems, 1952–1971 (Hill), **Supp. V:** 184; **Retro. Supp. III:** 134, 136
Somnium Scipionis (Cicero), **IV:** 189
"Son, The" (Swift), **Supp. V:** 432–433
Son of Man (Potter, D.), **Supp. X:** 229, 236–237, 239
Son of the Soil, A (Oliphant), **Supp. X:** 219
Son of Frankenstein (film), **III:** 342
Son of Learning, The: A Poetic Comedy in Three Acts (Clarke), **Supp. XV:** 23
"Sonata Form" (Galloway), **Supp. XII:** 127
"Sonata in X" (Thomas), **Supp. XII:** 290–291
"Sonatas in Silence" (Owen), **VI:** 449, 451, 454
Sone and Air of the Foirsaid Foxe, called Father wer, The: Alswa the Parliament of fourfuttit Beistis, halden be the Lyoun (Henryson), see *Trial of the Fox, The*
"Song" (Blake), **III:** 290
"Song" (Collins), **III:** 170
"Song" (Congreve, two poems), **II:** 347–348
"Song" (Ewart), **Supp. VII:** 36
"Song" (Goldsmith), **III:** 184–185
"Song" (Lewis), **VII:** 446

"Song" (Nicholson), **Supp. VI:** 216
"Song" (Soutar), **Supp. XVI:** 252
"Song" (Tennyson), **IV:** 329
"Song, A" (Rochester), **II:** 258
"Song [3]" (Thomas), **Supp. III:** 401
"Song, The" (Muir), **Supp. VI:** 208
"Song About Major Eatherly, A" (Wain), **Supp. XVI:** 306
Song and Its Fountains (Russell), **VIII:** 290, 292
"Song at the Beginning of Autumn" (Jennings), **Supp. V:** 214
Song at the Year's Turning: Poems, 1942–1954 (Thomas), **Supp. XII:** 283
Song at Twilight, A (Coward), **Supp. II:** 156–157
Song for a Birth or a Death (Jennings), **Supp. V:** 213, 215
"Song for a Birth or a Death" (Jennings), **Supp. V:** 215
"Song for a Corncrake" (Murphy), **Supp. V:** 324
"Song for a Phallus" (Hughes), **Supp. I:** 351
"Song for Coffee–Drinkers" (Mangan), **Supp. XIII:** 125
"Song for the Four Seasons" (Reid), **Supp. VII:** 326
"Song for the Swifts" (Jennings), **Supp. V:** 218
Song for St. Cecilia's Day, A (Dryden), **II:** 304
Song for St. Cecilia's Day 1687, A (Dryden), **Retro. Supp. III:** 76–77
"Song for Simeon, A" (Eliot), **VII:** 152
"Song for Sophie: A Granddaughter, born 1998" (Scupham), **Supp. XIII:** 229
"Song from Armenia, A" (Hill), **Supp. V:** 189
"Song from Cymbeline, A" (Collins), **III:** 163, 169–170
"Song from the Waters" (Beddoes), **Supp. XI:** 30
"Song in Storm, A" (Kipling), **VI:** 201
"Song in the Songless" (Meredith), **V:** 223
"Song of a Camera" (Gunn), **Supp. IV:** 273; **Retro. Supp. III:** 125
Song of Hylas (Morris), **VII:** 164
Song of Italy, A (Swinburne), **V:** 313, 332
Song of Liberty, A (Blake), **III:** 307
"Song of Life, The" (Davies), **Supp. XI:** 98
Song of Life and Other Poems, The (Davies), **Supp. XI:** 98
Song of Los, The (Blake), **III:** 307; **Retro. Supp. I:** 44
"Song of Poplars" (Huxley), **VII:** 199
"Song of Rahero, The" (Stevenson), **V:** 396
Song of Roland, **I:** 69
Song of Songs (Redgrove), **Supp. VI:** 233
Song of Stone, A (Banks), **Supp. XI:** 8–9
"Song of Sunday" (Jamie), **Supp. XIV:** 141
"Song of the Albanian" (Mangan), **Supp. XIII:** 126
"Song of the Amateur Psychologist" (Empson), **Supp. II:** 181
"Song of the Bower" (Rossetti), **V:** 243

Song of the Cold, The (Sitwell), **VII:** 132, 136, 137
Song of the Dark Queen (Sutcliff), **Supp. XVI:** 263
"Song of the Fourth Magus" (Nye), **Supp. X:** 202
"Song of the Heads, The" (tr. O'Connor), **Supp. XIV:** 222
"Song of the Militant Romance, The" (Lewis), **VII:** 79
"Song of the Night" (Kinsella), **Supp. V:** 269
Song of the Night and Other Poems (Kinsella), **Supp. V:** 269
"Song of the Old Mother, The" (O'Connor), **Supp. XIV:** 224
"Song of the Petrel, A" (Morgan, E.), **Supp. IX:** 161
"Song of the Rat" (Hughes), **Supp. I:** 348
"Song of the Shirt, The" (Hood), **IV:** 252, 261, 263–264
"Song of the Wandering Aengus" (O'Connor), **Supp. XIV:** 224
"Songs of Women" (Beer), **Supp. XIV:** 13
"Song Talk" (Nye), **Supp. X:** 206
"Song. To Celia" (Jonson), **Retro. Supp. I:** 164
"Song Written at Sea . . ." (Dorset), **II:** 261–262, 270
"Songbook of Sebastian Arrurruz, The" (Hill), **Supp. V:** 187, 188–189
Songlines, The (Chatwin), **Supp. IV:** 157, 158, 160, 161, 162, 163, 170–173, 174; **Supp. IX:** 49, 52, 57–59, 60, 61
Songs, The (Burns), **III:** 322
Songs and Sonnets (Donne), **I:** 357, 358, 360, 368
Songs Before Sunrise (Swinburne), **V:** xxiii, 313, 314, 324–325, 331, 332
"Songs for Strangers and Pilgrims" (Rossetti), **V:** 251, 254n, 260
"Songs in a Cornfield" (Rossetti), **V:** 258
Songs of Chaos (Read), **VI:** 436
Songs of Enchantment (Okri), **Supp. V:** 348–349, 350, 353, 358–359
Songes and Sonnettes . . . (pub. Tottel), see *Tottel's Miscellany*
Songs of Experience (Blake), **III:** 292, 293, 294, 297; **Retro. Supp. I:** 34, 36–37
Songs of Innocence (Blake), **III:** 292, 297, 307
Songs of Innocence and of Experience (Blake), **III:** 290, 299, 307; **V:** xv, 330; **Retro. Supp. I:** 36, 42–43
Songs of Mourning: Bewailing the Untimely Death of Prince Henry (Campion), **Supp. XVI:** 92
Songs of the Psyche (Kinsella), **Supp. V:** 270
"Songs of the PWD Man, The" (Harrison), **Supp. V:** 151
Songs of the Springtides (Swinburne), **V:** 332
Songs of Travel (Stevenson), **V:** 385, 396
Songs of Two Nations (Swinburne), **V:** 332
Songs Wing to Wing (Thompson), see *Sister Songs*

"Songster, The" (Smith), **Supp. II:** 465
"Sonnet" (Beddoes), **Supp. XI:** 29
"Sonnet, A" (Jennings), **Supp. V:** 207
"Sonnet, 1940" (Ewart), **VII:** 423
"Sonnet on the Death of Richard West" (Gray), **III:** 137
"Sonnet to Henry Lawes" (Milton), **II:** 175
"Sonnet to Liberty" (Wilde), **V:** 401
"Sonnet to Mr. Cyriack Skinner Upon His Blindness" (Milton), **II:** 164
"Sonnet to Mrs. Charlotte Smith, on Hearing that Her Son Was Wounded at the Siege of Dunkirk" (Robinson), **Supp. XIII:** 208
"Sonnet to My Beloved Daughter" (Robinson), **Supp. XIII:** 199
"Sonnet to my Friend with an identity disc" (Owen), **VI:** 449
sonnets (Bridges), **VI:** 81
Sonnets (Shakespeare), **I:** 307–308; **Retro. Supp. III:** 277, 279–280
"Sonnets are full of love" (Rossetti), **Retro. Supp. III:** 252
"Sonnets for August 1945" (Harrison), **Supp. V:** 161–162
"Sonnets for August 1945" (Harrison), **Supp. V:** 161–162
"Sonnets for Five Seasons" (Stevenson), **Supp. VI:** 262
"Sonnets from Hellas" (Heaney), **Retro. Supp. I:** 133–134
Sonnets from Scotland (Morgan, E.), **Supp. IX:** 167
"Sonnets from the Portuguese" (Browning), **IV:** xxi, 311, 314, 320, 321
Sonnets of Michael Angelo Buonarroti and Tommaso Campanella, The (tr. Symonds), **Supp. XIV:** 260–261
Sonnets of William Wordsworth, The, **IV:** 25
Sonnets to Fanny Kelly (Lamb), **IV:** 81, 83
"Sonnets to the Left" (Wallace-Crabbe), **VIII:** 322
"Sonogram" (Delanty), **Supp. XIV:** 74
Sons and Lovers (Lawrence), **VII:** 88, 89, 91, 92, **95–98**; **Retro. Supp. II:** 227
"Sons of the Brave" (Kinsella), **Supp. V:** 261
Sons of Thunder, The (Chatwin, B.), **Supp. IX:** 61
Sorceress (Oliphant), **Supp. X:** 219
"Sorescu's Circles" (Longley), **VIII:** 176–177
"Sorrow" (Muir), **Supp. VI:** 207
Sort of Freedom, A (Friel), **Supp. V:** 115
"Son's Veto, The" (Hardy), **VI:** 22
Sophonisba (Marston), see *Wonder of Women, The*
Sopranos, The (Warner), **Supp. XI:** 282, 283, 287, 289–290, 294
Sordello (Browning), **IV:** xix, 355, 371, 373; **Retro. Supp. III:** 18, 19, 22
Sorel, Georges, **VI:** 170
Sorley, Charles Hamilton, **VI:** xvi, 415, 417, 420, **421–422**

Sorrow in Sunlight (Firbank), see *Prancing Nigger*
"Sorrow of Socks, The" (Cope), **VIII:** 82
"Sorrow of true love is a great sorrow, The" (Thomas), **Supp. III:** 396
"Sorrows of Innisfail, The" (Mangan), **Supp. XIII:** 118
"Sorrows of Memory, The" (Robinson), **Supp. XIII:** 204–205
Sorrows of Young Werther, The (Goethe), **IV:** xiv, 59; **Supp. IV:** 28
Sorry Meniscus: Excursions to the Millennium Dome (Sinclair), **Supp. XIV:** 243, 244
"Sort of" (Fuller), **Supp. VII:** 80
"Sort of Exile in Lyme Regis, A" (Fowles), **Supp. I:** 292
"Sospetto d'Herode" (Crashaw), **II:** 180, 183–184
Sotheby, William, **IV:** 50
Sot-Weed Factor, The (Barth), **Supp. IV:** 116
"Souillac: Le Sacrifice d'Abraham" (Thomas), **Supp. XII:** 285
"Soul and Body" (Abercrombie), **Supp. XVI:** 2
Soul and Body I, **Retro. Supp. II:** 301
Soul for Sale, A: Poems (Kavanagh), **Supp. VII:** 193, 199
"Solfb6c266e64]ash;Je|fb6e205061]rterre" (Morgan, E.), **Supp. IX:** 161
Soul of Man Under Socialism, The (Wilde), **V:** 409, 413, 415, 419
"Soul of Man Under Socialism, The" (Wilde), **Supp. IV:** 288; **Retro. Supp. II:** 367
Songs of Mourning: Bewailing the Untimely Death of Prince Henry (Campion), **Supp. XVI:** 92
"Soul Says" (Hart), **Supp. XI:** 131
Souls and Bodies (Lodge), see *How Far Can You Go?*
"Soul's Beauty," (Rossetti), **V:** 237
Soul's Destroyer and Other Poems, The (Davies), **Supp. XI:** 86, 93–96, 100
"Soul's Expression, The" (Browning), **IV:** 313
Souls of Black Folk, The (Du Bois), **Supp. IV:** 86
"Soul's Travelling, The" (Browning), **IV:** 313
Sound Barrier, The (Rattigan), **Supp. VII:** 318
"Sound Machine, The" (Dahl), **Supp. IV:** 214–215
Sound of My Voice, The (Butlin), **Supp. XVI:** 51, 52, 53, 61–63, 64, 65
"Sound of the River, The" (Rhys), **Supp. II:** 402
"Sounds of a Devon Village" (Davie), **Supp. VI:** 113
"Sounds of the Day" (MacCaig), **Supp. VI:** 189
Soursweet (film), **Supp. IV:** 390, 399
Soursweet (Mo), **Supp. IV:** 390, 400
Soutar, William, **Supp. XVI:** **241–259**
South Africa (Trollope), **V:** 102
South African Autobiography, The (Plomer), **Supp. XI:** 223

South African Winter (Morris, J.), **Supp. X:** 175
"South African Writers and English Readers" (Plomer), **Supp. XI:** 209
South Sea Bubble (Coward), **Supp. II:** 155
South Seas, The (Stevenson), **V:** 396
South Wind (Douglas), **VI:** 293, 294, 300–302, 304, 305; **VII:** 200
Southam, Brian Charles, **IV:** xi, xiii, xxv, 122, 124, 337
Southern, Thomas, **II:** 305
"Southern Night, A" (Arnold), **V:** 210
Southerne, Thomas, **Supp. III:** 34–35
Southey, Cuthbert, **IV:** 62, 72
Southey, Robert, **III:** 276, 335; **IV:** viii–ix, xiv, xvii, 43, 45, 52, **58–72**, 85, 88, 89, 92, 102, 128, 129, 162, 168, 184–187, 270, 276, 280; **V:** xx, 105, 121; **Supp. IV:** 425, 426–427
"Southey and Landor" (Landor), **IV:** 93
"Southey and Porson" (Landor), **IV:** 93, 97
"Southey's *Colloquies*" (Macaulay), **IV:** 280
Southey's Common-place Book (ed. Warter), **IV:** 71
"South-Sea House, The" (Lamb), **IV:** 81–82
Southward (Delanty), **Supp. XIV:** 66, 67, 71
"South-Wester The" (Meredith), **V:** 223
Souvenirs (Fuller), **Supp. VII:** 67, 81
Sovereign Remedy, A (Steel), **Supp. XII:** 274–275
Sovereignty of Good, The (Murdoch), **Supp. I:** 217–218, 225
"Soviet Myth and Reality" (Koestler), **Supp. I:** 27
"Sow's Ear, The" (Sisson), **Supp. XI:** 258
Space Vampires (Wilson), **III:** 341
"Space-ship, The" (Smith, I. C.), **Supp. IX:** 216
Spain (Morris, J.), **Supp. X:** 176, 178–179
"Spain 1937" (Auden), **VII:** 384; **Retro. Supp. I:** 8
Spanbroekmolen (Roberts, K.), **Supp. X:** 274–275
Spanish Curate, The (Fletcher and Massinger), **II:** 66
Spanish Fryar, The; or, The Double Discovery (Dryden), **II:** 305
Spanish Gipsy, The (Middleton and Rowley), **II:** 100
Spanish Gypsy, The (Eliot), **V:** 198, 200
"Spanish Maids in England, The" (Cornford), **VIII:** 112–113
"Spanish Military Nun, The" (De Quincey), **IV:** 149
"Spanish Oranges" (Dunn), **Supp. X:** 80
Spanish Tragedy, The (Kyd), **I:** 212, 213, 218, 220, **221–229**; **II:** 25, 28–29, 69
"Spanish Train, The" (Scupham), **Supp. XIII:** 225
Spanish Virgin and Other Stories, The (Pritchett), **Supp. III:** 316, 317
Spanner and Pen (Fuller), **Supp. VII:** 67, 68, 74, 81

Sparagus Garden, The (Brome), **Supp. X:** 52, 61–62
"Spared" (Cope), **VIII:** 84
Spark, Muriel, **Supp. I: 199–214; Supp. IV:** 100, 234
"Sparrow" (MacCaig), **Supp. VI:** 192
Sparrow, John, **VI:** xv, xxxiv; **VII:** 355, 363
Sparrow, The (Ayckbourn), **Supp. V:** 2
Spartacus (Mitchell), **Supp. XIV:** 99, 100–102
"Spate in Winter Midnight" (MacCaig), **Supp. VI:** 187
"Spätlese, The" (Hope), **Supp. VII:** 157
Speak, Parrot (Skelton), **I:** 83, 90–91
Speak for England, Arthur (Bennett), **VIII:** 22–25
Speak of the Mearns, The (Gibbon), **Supp. XIV:** 113
"Speak to Me" (Tennyson), **IV:** 332
"Speakeasy Oath, The" (Delanty), **Supp. XIV:** 74
Speaker (periodical), **VI:** 87, 335
Speaker of Mandarin (Rendell), **Supp. IX:** 192, 198
"Speaking a Foreign Language" (Reid), **Supp. VII:** 330
Speaking Likeness (Rossetti), **V:** 260; **Retro. Supp. III:** 251
"Speaking of Hurricanes" (Aidoo), **Supp. XV:** 12
Speaking Stones, The (Fallon), **Supp. XII:** 104–105, 114
"Speaking Stones, The" (Fallon), **Supp. XII:** 104
Speaking with the Angel (Hornby), **Supp. XV:** 142
"Special Type, The" (James), **VI:** 69
"Specimen of an Induction to a Poem" (Keats), **IV:** 214
Specimens of English Dramatic Poets (Lamb), **IV:** xvi 79, 85
Specimens of German Romance (Carlyle), **IV:** 250
Specimens of Modern Poets: The Heptalogia . . . (Swinburne), **V:** 332
Speckled Bird, The (Yeats), **VI:** 222; **Retro. Supp. I:** 326
Spectator (periodical), **III:** 39, 41, 44, **46–50**, 52, 53; **V:** 86, 238; **VI:** 87; **Supp. IV:** 121
Spectatorial Essays (Strachey), **Supp. II:** 497, 502
"Spectre of the Real, The" (Hardy), **VI:** 20
Speculations (Hulme), **Supp. VI:** 134, 140
Speculative Dialogues (Abercrombie), **Supp. XVI:** 2
Speculative Instruments (Richards), **Supp. I:** 426
Speculum hominis (Gower), **I:** 48
Speculum meditantis (Gower), **I:** 48
Speculum Principis (Skelton), **I:** 84
Spedding, James, **I:** 257n, 259, 264, 324
Speech Against Prelates Innovations (Waller), **II:** 238
Speech . . . Against Warren Hastings (Sheridan), **III:** 270

Speech . . . for the Better Security of the Independence of Parliament (Burke), **III:** 205
Speech, 4 July 1643 (Waller), **II:** 238
Speech . . . in Bristol upon . . . His Parliamentary Conduct, A (Burke), **III:** 205
Speech on American Taxation (Burke), **III:** 205
Speech . . . on Mr. Fox's East India Bill (Burke), **III:** 205
Speech on Moving His Resolutions for Conciliation with the Colonies (Burke), **III:** 205
Speech on Parliamentary Reform (Macaulay), **IV:** 274
Speech on the Anatomy Bill (Macaulay), **IV:** 277
Speech on the Army Estimates (Burke), **III:** 205
Speech on the Edinburgh Election (Macaulay), **IV:** 274
Speech on the People's Charter (Macaulay), **IV:** 274
Speech on the Ten Hours Bill (Macaulay), **IV:** 276–277
Speech Relative to the Nabob of Arcot's Debts (Burke), **III:** 205
Speech! Speech! (Hill), **Retro. Supp. III:** 140–141, 143, 146
Speech to the Electors of Bristol (Burke), **III:** 205
"Speech to the Troops at Tilbury" (Elizabeth I), **Supp. XVI:** 153
Speeches on Parliamentary Reform (Disraeli), **IV:** 308
Speeches on the Conservative Policy of the Last Thirty Years (Disraeli), **IV:** 308
Speeches, Parliamentary and Miscellaneous (Macaulay), **IV:** 291
Speedy Post, A (Webster), **II:** 69, 85
Spell, The (Hollinghurst), **Supp. X:** 120, 132–134
Spell, The: An Extravaganza (Brontë), **V:** 151
Spell for Green Corn, A (Brown), **Supp. VI: 72–73**
Spell of Words, A (Jennings), **Supp. V:** 219
"Spelt from Sybil's Leaves" (Hopkins), **V:** 372–373
Spence, Joseph, **II:** 261; **III:** 69, 86n
Spencer, Baldwin, **Supp. III:** 187–188
Spencer, Herbert, **V:** 182, 189, 284
Spender, Stephen, **VII:** 153, 382, 410; **Supp. II: 481–495; Supp. III:** 103, 117, 119; **Supp. IV:** 95
Spengler, Osvald, **Supp. IV:** 1, 3, 10, 11, 12, 17
Spenser, Edmund, **I: 121–144**, 146; **II:** 50, 302; **III:** 167n; **IV:** 59, 61, 93, 205; **V:** 318
Sphinx (Thomas), **Supp. IV:** 485
"Sphinx, The" (Rossetti), **V:** 241
Sphinx, The (Wilde), **V:** 409–410, 415, 419; **Retro. Supp. II:** 371
"Sphinx; or, Science" (Bacon), **I:** 267
"Spider, The" (Nye), **Supp. X:** 205
Spider (Weldon), **Supp. IV:** 521

Spielmann, M. H., **V:** 137, 152
Spiess, Johann, **III:** 344
Spingarn, J. E., **II:** 256n
"Spinoza" (Hart), **Supp. XI:** 123
"Spinster Sweet-Arts, The" (Tennyson), **IV:** 327
"Spiral, The" (Reid), **Supp. VII:** 330
Spiral Ascent, The (Upward), **Supp. XIII:** 250, 251, 254–259, 260
Spire, The (Golding), **Supp. I:** 67, **79–81**, 83; **Retro. Supp. I:** 99–100
"Spirit, The" (Traherne), **Supp. XI:** 267
"Spirit Dolls, The" (McGuckian), **Supp. V:** 292
"Spirit is Too Blunt an Instrument, The" (Stevenson), **Supp. VI:** 256
Spirit Level, The (Heaney), **Retro. Supp. I:** 132–133
Spirit Machines (Crawford), **Supp. XI:** 67, 76–79
Spirit of British Administration and Some European Comparisons, The (Sisson), **Supp. XI:** 249, 258
Spirit of England (Sutcliff), **Supp. XVI:** 264
Spirit of Man, The (ed. Bridges), **II:** 160; **VI:** 76, 83
Spirit of the Age, The (Hazlitt), **III:** 276; **IV:** xi, 39, 129, 131, 132–134, 137, 139
Spirit of Whiggism, The (Disraeli), **IV:** 308
Spirit Rise, A (Warner), **Supp. VII:** 380
Spirit Watches, The (Pitter), **Supp. XIII:** 134, 135, 142
Spirits in Bondage (Lewis), **Supp. III:** 250
Spiritual Adventures (Symons), **Supp. XIV:** 279
Spiritual Exercises (Loyola), **V:** 362, 367, 371, 373n; **Retro. Supp. II:** 188
Spiritual Exercises (Spender), **Supp. II:** 489
"Spiritual Explorations" (Spender), **Supp. II:** 489, 490
"Spite of thy hap hap hath well happed" (Wyatt), **I:** 103
Spitzer, L., **IV:** 323n, 339
Spivack, Bernard, **I:** 214
Spivak, Gayatri, **Retro. Supp. I:** 60
"Spleen, The" (Finch), **Supp. IX:** 69–70, 76
"Splinters, The" (Delanty), **Supp. XIV:** 68–69
Splitting (Weldon), **Supp. IV:** 535
Spoils, The (Bunting), **Supp. VII:** 5, 7–9
Spoils of Poynton, The (James), **VI: 49–50**
"Spoilt Child, The" (Motion), **Supp. VII:** 251
"Spoons" (Kay), **Supp. XIII:** 108
Sport of Nature, A (Gordimer), **Supp. II:** 232, 239–240, 241, 242
"Spot of Night Fishing (for Kenny Crichton), A" (Warner), **Supp. XI:** 294
Spottiswoode, John, **II:** 142
Sprat, Thomas, **II:** 195, 196, 198, 200, 202, 294; **III:** 29

"Spraying the Potatoes" (Kavanagh), **Supp. VII:** 190
Spreading the News (Gregory), **VI:** 309, 315, 316
Sprigg, Christopher St. John, *see* Caudwell, Christopher
"Sprig of Lime, The" (Nichols), **VI:** 419
Sprightly Running (Wain), **Supp. XVI:** 293, 294, 295
"Spring, The" (Carew), **II:** 225
"Spring, The" (Cowley), **II:** 197
"Spring" (Crawford), **Supp. XI:** 70–71
"Spring" (Hopkins), **V:** 368
"Spring, The" (Pitter), **Supp. XIII:** 142
Spring (Thomson), **Supp. III:** 413–414, 415, 416,
"Spring and Fall" (Hopkins), **V:** 371–372, 381; **Retro. Supp. II:** 196–197
Spring Days (Moore), **VI:** 87, 91
Spring Fever (Wodehouse), **Supp. III:** 451
"Spring Hail" (Murray), **Supp. VII:** 272, 279, 281
Spring Morning (Cornford), **VIII:** 102, 103, 104, 112
"Spring Morning" (Milne), **Supp. V:** 302
"Spring Nature Notes" (Hughes), **Supp. I:** 358
"Spring 1942" (Fuller), **VII:** 429
"Spring Offensive" (Owen), **VI:** 455, 456, 458
"Spring Song" (Fallon), **Supp. XII:** 110
"Spring Song" (Milne), **Supp. V:** 309–310
Spring, Summer, Autumn, Winter (Hughes), **Supp. I:** 357
Spring-Heeled Jack (Pullman), **Supp. XIII:** 152
sprung rhythm, **V:** 363, 365, 367, 374, 376, 379, 380
Spy in the Family, A (Waugh), **Supp. VI:** 276
Spy on the Conjurer, A (Haywood), **Supp. XII:** 135
Spy Story, The (Cawelti and Rosenberg), **Supp. IV:** 7
Spy Who Came In from the Cold, The (le Carré), **Supp. II:** 299, 301, 305, **307–309**, 313, 315, 316, 317; **Retro. Supp. III:** 216, 217–218, 220
Spy Who Loved Me, The (Fleming), **Supp. XIV:** 96
Spy's Wife, The (Hill, R.), **Supp. IX:** 117, 119
Square Cat, The (Ayckbourn), **Supp. V:** 2
Square Egg and Other Sketches, The (Saki), **Supp. VI:** 242, 250–251
Square Rounds (Harrison), **Supp. V:** 164
Squaring the Circle (Stoppard), **Supp. I:** 449–450, 451
Squaring the Waves (Dutton), **Supp. XII:** 88–89
"Squarings" (Heaney), **Retro. Supp. I:** 132
"Squatter" (Mistry), **Supp. X:** 140–142
"Squaw, The" (Stoker), **Supp. III:** 382–383
Squire, J. C., **VII:** xvi
Squire Arden (Oliphant), **Supp. X:** 220

"Squire Hooper" (Hardy), **Retro. Supp. I:** 121, 418, 420
"Squire Petrick's Lady" (Hardy), **VI:** 22
Squire Trelooby (Congreve, Vanbrugh, Walsh), **II:** 325, 336, 339, 347, 350
Squire's Masque, The (Campion), **Supp. xvi:** 92, 98–99
"Squire's 'Round Robin,' The" (Jefferies), **Supp. XV:** 169, 170
Squire's Tale, The (Chaucer), **I:** 23, 24
"Squirrel and the Crow, The" (Cope), **VIII:** 81
"Sredni Vashtar" (Saki), **Supp. VI: 245–246**
"Stabilities" (Stevenson), **Supp. VI:** 256
Stade, George, **Supp. IV:** 402
"Staff and Scrip, The" (Rossetti), **V:** 240
Staffordshire Sentinel (periodical), **VI:** 248
"Stag in a Neglected Hayfield" (MacCraig), **Supp. VI:** 192
Stage Coach, The, **II:** 353, 358, 364
Stained Radiance (Mitchell), **Supp. XIV:** 100
Staircase, The (Abercrombie), **Supp. XVI:** 8
Stalin, Joseph, **Supp. IV:** 82
Stalky & Co. (Kipling), **VI:** 204; **Supp. IV:** 506; **Retro. Supp. III:** 183, 193
Stallworthy, Jon, **VI:** 220, 438; **Supp. X: 291–304**
Stallybrass, Oliver, **VI:** 397
Stamboul Train (Greene; US. title, *Orient Express*), **Supp. I:** 3, 4–5; **Retro. Supp. II:** 152
Stand Up, Nigel Barton (Potter, D.), **Supp. X:** 228, 230–233
Standard of Behavior, A (Trevor), **Supp. IV:** 505
Standing Room Only (Ayckbourn), **Supp. V:** 2, 11
Stanley, Arthur, **V:** 13, 349
Stanley and Iris (film), **Supp. IV:** 45
Stanley and The Women (Amis), **Supp. II:** 17–18
Stanleys of Alderley, The (ed. Mitford), **Supp. X:** 156
Stans puer ad mensam (Lydgate), **I:** 58
"Stanzas" (Hood), **IV:** 263
"Stanzas" (Tennyson), **Retro. Supp. III:** 321
"Stanzas from the Grande Chartreuse" (Arnold), **V:** 210
"Stanzas in Memory of the Author of 'Obermann' " (Arnold), **V:** 206
"Stanzas Inscribed to a Once Dear Friend, When Confined by Severe Indisposition, in March 1793" (Robinson), **Supp. XIII:** 204
"Stanzas, Written Between Dover and Calais, July 20, 1792" (Robinson), **Supp. XIII:** 203–204
"Stanzas Written in Dejection" (Shelley), **IV:** 201
"Stanzas, written on the 14th of February to my once dear Valentine" (Robinson), **Supp. XIII:** 204
Staple of News, The (Jonson), **Retro. Supp. I:** 165
Star (periodical), **VI:** 103

Star Factory, The (Carson), **Supp. XIII:** 53, 55, 56, 61–63
Star over Bethlehem (Fry), **Supp. III:** 195
Star Turns Red, The (O'Casey), **VII:** 7–8
"Starcross Ferry, The" (Beer), **Supp. XIV:** 8
Stares (Fuller), **Supp. VII:** 81
"Stare's Nest by My Window, The" (Yeats), **VI:** 212
Staring at the Sun (Barnes), **Supp. IV:** 65, 67, 70–71
"Starlight Night, The" (Hopkins), **V:** 366, 367; **Retro. Supp. II:** 190
"Stars" (Brontë), **V:** 133, 142
Stars and Bars (Boyd), **Supp. XVI:** 35–36, 40, 47
Stars and Bars (screenplay, Boyd), **Supp. XVI:** 46
Stars of the New Curfew (Okri), **Supp. V:** 347, 348, 352, 355, 356–357
Start in Life, A (Brookner), *see Debut, The*
Start in Life, A (Sillitoe), **Supp. V:** 410, 413
Starting Point (Day Lewis), **Supp. III:** 118, 130–131
State of France, . . . in the IXth Year of . . . , Lewis XIII, The (Evelyn), **II:** 287
State of Independence, A (Phillips), **Supp. V:** 380, 383–384
State of Innocence, The (Dryden), **II:** 290, 294, 305
"State of Poetry, The" (Jennings), **Supp. V:** 215
"State of Religious Parties, The" (Newman), **Supp. VII:** 294
State of Siege (Ambler; formerly *The Night-Comers*), **Supp. IV:** 4, 16
State of the Art, The (Banks), **Supp. XI:** 10–11
"State of the Country, The" (Mangan), **Supp. XIII:** 118
"State of the Nation, The" (Fallon), **Supp. XII:** 111
"Stately Palace, The" (Soutar), **Supp. XVI:** 249
States of Emergency (Brink), **Supp. VI:** 53–54
Statesman's Manual, The (Coleridge), **IV:** 56; **Retro. Supp. II:** 64
Statement, The (Moore, B.), **Supp. IX:** 152
"Statements, The" (Ewart), **Supp. VII:** 39
Statements After an Arrest Under the Immorality Act (Fugard), **Supp. XV:** 100, 103, 108–109
Statements. Three Plays (Fugard), **Supp. XV:** 108, 110
Station Island (Heaney), **Supp. II:** 268, **277–279**
"Station Island" (Heaney), **Supp. II:** 277–278; **Retro. Supp. I:** 124, 130–131
Stations (Heaney), **Retro. Supp. I:** 129
"Statue and the Bust, The" (Browning), **IV:** 366
"Statue in Stocks-Market, The" (Marvell), **II:** 218

"Statue of life, A" (O'Connor), **Supp. XIV:** 214
"Statues, The" (Yeats), **VI:** 215
Staying On (Scott), **Supp. I:** 259, 272–274
Stead, Christina, **Supp. IV: 459–477**
Stead, William Thomas, **Supp. XIII: 233–247**
"Steam Washing Co., The" (Hood), **IV:** 267
Steel, Flora Annie, **Supp. XII: 265–278**
"Steel, The" (Murray), **Supp. VII:** 278
Steel Glass, The (Gascoigne), **I:** 149
Steele, Richard, **II:** 359; **III:** 7, 18, 19, **38–53**
"Steep and her own world" (Thomas), **Supp. III:** 401
Steep Holm (Fowles), **Supp. I:** 292
"Steep Stone Steps" (Cameron), **Supp. IX:** 27
Steevens, G. W., **VI:** 351
Steevens, George, **I:** 326
Steffan, Truman Guy, **IV:** 179, 193
Stein, Arnold, **Retro. Supp. II:** 181
Stein, Gertrude, **VI:** 252; **VII:** 83; **Supp. IV:** 416, 542, 556, 557–558
Steiner, George, **Supp. IV:** 455
"Stella at Wood-Park" (Swift), **III:** 32
"Stella Maris" (Symons), **Supp. XIV:** 270, 277–278
"Stella's Birth Day, 1725" (Swift), **III:** 32
"Stella's Birthday . . . A.D. 1720–21" (Swift), **III:** 32
"Stella's Birthday, March 13, 1727" (Swift), **III:** 32
Stella's Birth-Days: A Poem (Swift), **III:** 36
Stendhal, **Supp. IV:** 136, 459
Step by Step (Churchill), **VI:** 356
Stepdaughter, The (Blackwood), **Supp. IX:** 3, 10, 16
Stephen, Janus K., **IV:** 10–11, 268
Stephen, Leslie, **II:** 156, 157; **III:** 42; **IV:** 301, 304–306; **V:** xix, xxv, xxvi, **277–290**, 386; **VII:** xxii, 17, 238
Stephen Hero (Joyce), **VII:** 45–46, 48
"Stephen Hero" (Joyce), **Retro. Supp. III:** 167, 171
Stephens, Frederick, **V:** 235, 236
Stephens, James, **VI:** 88
Steps to the Temple. Sacred Poems, with Other Delights of the Muses (Crashaw), **II:** 179, 180, 184, 201
Sterling, John, **IV:** 54
Stern, Gladys Bronwen, **IV:** 123; **V:** xiii, xxviii, 395
Stern, J. B., **I:** 291
Stern, Laurence, **III: 124–135,** 150, 153, 155, 157; **IV:** 79, 183; **VII:** 20; **Supp. II:** 204; **Supp. III:** 108
Sterts and Stobies (Crawford), **Supp. XI:** 67
Stet (Reading), **VIII:** 261, 269–271, 273
Steuart, J. A., **V:** 392, 397
Stevens, Wallace, **V:** 412; **Supp. IV:** 257, 414; **Supp. V:** 183
Stevenson, Anne, **Supp. VI: 253–268**
Stevenson, L., **V:** 230, 234

Stevenson, Robert Louis, **I:** 1; **II:** 153; **III:** 330, 334, 345; **V:** xiii, xxi, xxv, vxvi, 219, 233, **383–398**; **Supp. IV:** 61; **Retro. Supp. I: 259–272**
Stevenson and Edinburgh: A Centenary Study (MacLaren), **V:** 393, 398
Stevenson Companion, The (ed. Hampden), **V:** 393, 395
Stevensoniana (ed. Hammerton), **V:** 393, 397
Stewart, J. I. M., **I:** 329; **IV:** xxv; **VII:** xiv, xxxviii
Stiff Upper Lip (Durrell), **Supp. I:** 113; **Retro. Supp. III:** 85
Still by Choice (Pitter), **Supp. XIII:** 136, 145
Still Centre, The (Spender), **Supp. II:** 488, 489
"Still Falls the Rain" (Sitwell), **VII:** xvii, 135, 137
Still Glides the Stream (Thompson), **Supp. XV:** 290, 291
Still Life (Byatt), **Supp. IV:** 139, 145, 147–149, 151, 154
Still Life (Coward), **Supp. II:** 153
Still Life (Soutar), **Supp. XVI:** 249
"Still Life" (Gunn), **Retro. Supp. III:** 127, 128
"Still Life, with Aunt Brigid" (Montague), **Supp. XV:** 210
Stirling, William Alexander, earl of, *see* Alexander, William
Stoats in the Sunlight (Conn), **Supp. XIII:** 70, 71–72
"Stoic, A" (Galsworthy), **VI:** 275, 284
"Stoke or Basingstoke" (Reed), **Supp. XV:** 247
Stoker, Bram, **III:** 334, 342, 343, 344, 345; **Supp. III: 375–391**
Stokes, John, **V:** xiii, xxviii
Stolen Bacillus, The, and Other Incidents (Wells), **VI:** 226, 243
"Stolen Child, The" (Yeats), **Retro. Supp. I:** 329
Stolen Light: Selected Poems (Conn), **Supp. XIII:** 79
Stone, C., **III:** 161n
"Stone" (Dutton), **Supp. XII:** 92
"Stone Age Decadent, A" (Wallace-Crabbe), **VIII:** 321
"Stone and Mr. Thomas, The" (Powys), **VIII:** 258
"Stone Mania" (Murphy), **Supp. V:** 326
Stone Virgin (Unsworth), **Supp. VII:** 355, 356, 357, 360–361, 362, 365
"Stone-In-Oxney" (Longley), **VIII:** 169, 175
Stones of the Field, The (Thomas), **Supp. XII:** 282, 283, 284
Stones of Venice, The (Ruskin), **V:** xxi, 173, 176–177, 180, 184, 292
"Stony Grey Soil "(Kavanagh), **Supp. VII:** 189–190
Stony Limits and Other Poems (MacDiarmid), **Supp. XII:** 202, 212–216
"Stooping to Drink" (Malouf), **Supp. XII:** 220
Stoppard, Tom, **Supp. I: 437–454**; **Retro. Supp. II: 343–358**

Storey, David, **Supp. I: 407–420**
Storey, Graham, **V:** xi, xxviii, 381
Stories, Dreams, and Allegories (Schreiner), **Supp. II:** 450
Stories from ABlack and White" (Hardy), **VI:** 20
Stories of Frank O'Connor, The (O'Connor), **Supp. XIV:** 219
Stories of Red Hanrahan (Yeats), **VI:** 222
Stories of the Seen and Unseen (Oliphant), **Supp. X:** 220
Stories, Theories and Things (Brooke-Rose)), **Supp. IV:** 99, 110
"Stories, Theories and Things" (Brooke-Rose)), **Supp. IV:** 116
Stories We Could Tell (Parsons), **Supp. XV:** 229, 237, 240
"Storm" (Nye), **Supp. X:** 204-205
"Storm" (Owen), **VI:** 449
"Storm, The" (Brown), **Supp. VI:** 70–71
"Storm, The" (Donne), **Retro. Supp. II:** 86
"Storm, The" (Hart), **Supp. XI:** 126–127
"Storm, The" (Hill), **Retro. Supp. III:** 144
Storm, The; or, A Collection of . . . Casualties and Disasters . . . (Defoe), **III:** 13; **Retro. Supp. I:** 68
Storm and Other Poems (Sillitoe), **Supp. V:** 424
"Storm Bird, Storm Dreamer" (Ballard), **Supp. V:** 26
"Storm in Istanbul" (Jamie), **Supp. XIV:** 130
"Storm is over, The land hushes to rest, The" (Bridges), **VI:** 79
"Stormpetrel" (Murphy), **Supp. V:** 315
"Stormscape" (Davies), **Supp. XI:** 87
"Storm–Wind" (Ballard), **Supp. V:** 22
"Story, A" (Smitch, I. C.), **Supp. IX:** 222
"Story, A" (Thomas), **Supp. I:** 183
Story and the Fable, The (Muir), **Supp. VI:** 198
"Story by Maupassant, A" (O'Connor), **Supp. XIV:** 226
"Story in It, The" (James), **VI:** 69
"Story of a Masterpiece, The" (James), **VI:** 69
Story of a Non–Marrying Man, The (Lessing), **Supp. I:** 253–254
"Story of a Panic, The" (Forster), **VI:** 399
"Story of a Story, The" (Smith), **Retro. Supp. III:** 306
"Story of a Year, The" (James), **VI:** 69
Story of an African Farm, The (Schreiner), **Supp. II:** 435, 438, 439, 440, 441, **445–447**, 449, 451, 453, 456
Story of Fabian Socialism, The (Cole), **VI:** 131
Story of Grettir the strong, The (Morris and Magnusson), **V:** 306
Story of My Heart, The: My Autobiography (Jefferies), **Supp. XV:** 165, 171–172
Story of Rimini, The (Hunt), **IV:** 214
Story of San Michele, The (Munthe), **VI:** 265
Story of Sigurd the Volsung and the Fall of the Niblungs, The (Morris), **V:** xxiv, 299–300, 304, 306

Story of the Gadsbys, The (Kipling), **Retro. Supp. III:** 186
Story of the Glittering Plain, The (Morris), **V:** 306
Story of the Injured Lady, The (Swift), **III:** 27
Story of the Malakand Field Force (Churchill), **VI:** 351
Story of the Peasant–Boy Philosopher, The (Mayhew), **Supp. XVI:** 210
Story of the Sundering Flood, The (Morris), **V:** 306
"Story of the Three Bears, The" (Southey), **IV:** 58, 67
"Story of the Unknown Church, The" (Morris), **V:** 293, 303
Story of the Volsungs and . . . Songs from the Elder Edda, The (Morris and Magnusson), **V:** 299, 306
Story So Far, The (Ayckbourn), **Supp. V:** 2
"Storyteller, The" (Berger), **Supp. IV:** 90, 91
Story–Teller, The (Highsmith), **Supp. V:** 174–175
Storyteller, The (Sillitoe), **Supp. V:** 410
Story–Teller's Holiday, A (Moore), **VI:** 88, 95, 99
Stout, Mira, **Supp. IV:** 75
Stovel, Nora Foster, **Supp. IV:** 245, 249
Stowe, Harriet Beecher, **V:** xxi, 3
Strachey, J. St. Loe, **V:** 75, 86, 87
Strachey, Lytton, **III:** 21, 28; **IV:** 292; **V:** 13, 157, 170, 277; **VI:** 155, 247, 372, 407; **VII:** 34, 35; **Supp. II:** **497–517**
Strado, Famiano, **II:** 90
Strafford: An Historical Tragedy (Browning), **IV:** 373; **Retro. Supp. III:** 19–20
Strait Gate, The . . . (Bunyan), **II:** 253
"Strand at Lough Beg, The" (Heaney), **Supp. II:** 278
Strange and the Good, The (Fuller), **Supp. VII:** 81
"Strange and Sometimes Sadness, A" (Ishiguro), **Supp. IV:** 303, 304; **Retro. Supp. III:** 161
Strange Case of Dr. Jekyll and Mr. Hyde, The (Stevenson), **III:** 330, 342, 345; **V:** xxv, 383, 387, 388, 395; **VI:** 106; **Supp. IV:** 61; **Retro. Supp. I:** 263, 264–266
"Strange Comfort Afforded by the Profession" (Lowry), **Supp. III:** 281
Strange Fruit (Phillips), **Supp. V:** 380
"Strange Happenings in the Guava Orchard" (Desai), **Supp. XV:** 84
Strange Meeting (Hill), **Supp. XIV:** 116, 120–121, 122, 127
"Strange Meeting" (Owen), **VI:** 444, 445, 449, 454, 457–458
Strange Necessity, The (West), **Supp. III:** 438
"Strange Ride of Morrowbie Jukes, The" (Kipling), **VI: 175–178**
Strange Ride of Rudyard Kipling, The (Wilson), **VI:** 165; **Supp. I:** 167
Strange World, A (Braddon), **VIII:** 37
Stranger, The (Kotzebue), **III:** 268

Stranger Still, A (Kavan), **Supp. VII:** 207–208, 209
Stranger With a Bag, A (Warner), **Supp. VII:** 380
Strangers: A Family Romance (Tennant), **Supp. IX:** 239
Strangers and Brothers cycle (Snow), **VII:** xxi, 322, **324–336**
Strangers on a Train (Highsmith), **Supp. V:** 167, 168–169
Strapless (film), **Supp. IV:** 282, 291–292
"Strategist, The" (Saki), **Supp. VI:** 243
"Stratton Water" (Rossetti), **V:** 239
Strauss, Richard, **Supp. IV:** 556
"Strawberry Hill" (Hughes), **Supp. I:** 342
Strawgirl (Kay), **Supp. XIII:** 99
Strayed Reveller, The (Arnold), **V:** xxi, 209, 216
"Straying Student, The" (Clarke), **Supp. XV:** 23, 30
"Streams" (Constantine), **Supp. XV:** 71
"Street in Cumberland, A" (Nicholson), **Supp. VI:** 216
"Street, November 11th, The" (Soutar), **Supp. XVI:** 244
"Street Song" (Gunn), **Retro. Supp. III:** 122
Street Songs (Sitwell), **VII:** 135
Streets of Pompeii, The (Reed), **Supp. XV:** 252
Streets of Pompeii and Other Plays for Radio, The (Reed), **Supp. XV:** 249, 252, 254, 255
"Streets of the Spirits" (Redgrove), **Supp. VI:** 235
"Strength of Heart" (Fallon), **Supp. XII:** 114
"Strephon and Chloe" (Swift), **III:** 32; **Retro. Supp. I:** 284, 285
Stretto (Butlin), **Supp. XVI:** 52, 54
Strickland, Agnes, **I:** 84
Strictures on AConingsby" (Disraeli), **IV:** 308
"Strictures on Pictures" (Thackeray), **V:** 37
Striding Folly (Sayers), **Supp. III:** 335
Strife (Galsworthy), **VI:** xiii, 269, 285–286
Strike at Arlingford, The (Moore), **VI:** 95
Strike the Father Dead (Wain), **Supp. XVI:** 294, 297, 298–299
Still Life (Soutar), **Supp. XVI:** 249
Strindberg, August, **Supp. III:** 12
Stringham, Charles, **IV:** 372
Strings Are False, The (MacNeice), **VII:** 406
Strip Jack (Rankin), **Supp. X:** 244, 250–251, 253
Strode, Ralph, **I:** 49
Strong, Roy, **I:** 237
Strong Poison (Sayers), **Supp. III:** 339, 342, 343, 345
Strong Words: Modern Poets on Modern Poetry (ed. Herbert and Hollis), **Supp. XIII:** 31
Stronger Climate, A: Nine Stories (Jhabvala), **Supp. V:** 235
Structure and Distribution of Coral Reefs, On the (Darwin), **Supp. VII:** 19

Structural Analysis of Pound's Usura Canto: Jakobsonand Applied to Free Verse, A (Brooke–Rose)), **Supp. IV:** 99, 114
Structural Transformation of the Public Sphere, The (Habermas), **Supp. IV:** 112
Structure in Four Novels by H. G. Wells (Newell), **VI:** 245, 246
Structure of Complex Words, The (Empson), **Supp. II:** 180, **192–195,** 197
"Studies in a Dying Culture" (Caudwell), **Supp. IX:** 36
Struggle of the Modern, The (Spender), **Supp. II:** 492
Struggles of Brown, Jones and Robinson, The (Trollope), **V:** 102
"Strugnell's Christian Songs" (Cope), **VIII:** 78
"Strugnell's Sonnets" (Cope), **VIII:** 73–74
Strutt, Joseph, **IV:** 31
Strutton, Bill, **Supp. IV:** 346
Struwwelpeter (Hoffman), **I:** 25; **Supp. III:** 296
Stuart, D. M., **V:** 247, 256, 260
"Stubb's Calendar" (Thackeray), *see A Fatal Boots, The"*
Studies in a Dying Culture (Caudwell), **Supp. IX:** 33, 43–47
Studies in Classic American Literature (Lawrence), **VII:** 90; **Retro. Supp. II:** 234
Studies in Ezra Pound (Davie), **Supp. VI:** 115
Studies in Prose and Poetry (Swinburne), **II:** 102; **V:** 333
Studies in Prose and Verse (Symons), **Supp. XIV:** 274
Studies in Song (Swinburne), **V:** 332
"Studies in Strange Sins" (Symons), **Supp. XIV:** 281
Studies in the History of the Renaissance (Pater), **V:** xxiv, 286–287, 323, 338–339, **341–348,** 351, 355–356, 400, 411
Studies in the Prose Style of Joseph Addison (Lannering), **III:** 52
Studies in Words (Lewis), **Supp. III:** 249, 264
Studies of a Biographer (Stephen), **V:** 280, 285, 287, 289
Studies of the Greek Poets (Symonds), **Supp. XIV:** 254–255
Studies on Modern Painters (Symons), **Supp. XIV:** 274
"Studio 5, the Stars" (Ballard), **Supp. V:** 26
Study in Scarlet, A (Doyle), **Supp. II:** 159, 160, 162, 163, 164, 167, 169, 170, 171, 172, 173, 174, 176
Study in Temperament, A (Firbank), **Supp. II:** 201, 206–207
Study of Ben Jonson, A (Swinburne), **V:** 332
"Study of Reading Habits, A" (Larkin), **Retro. Supp. III:** 206
Study of Shakespeare, A (Swinburne), **V:** 328, 332

Study of the Women Characters of Jane Austen, Charlotte Brontë, Elizabeth Gaskell and George Eliot, A (Beer), **Supp. XIV:** 9
"Study of Thomas Hardy" (Lawrence), **VI:** 20; **Retro. Supp. II:** 234
Study of Victor Hugo, A (Swinburne), **V:** 332
"Stuff Your Classical Heritage" (Wallace–Crabbe), **VIII:** 321–322
Sturlunga saga, **VIII:** 242
"Style" (Pater), **V:** 339, 347, 353–355
Style and Faith (Hill), **Retro. Supp. III:** 145, 146
Stylistic Development of Keats, The (Bate), **Retro. Supp. I:** 185
Subhuman Redneck Poems (Murray), **Supp. VII:** 271, 283–284
Subject of Scandal and Concern, A (Osborne), **Supp. I:** 334
"Sublime and the Beautiful Revisited, The" (Murdoch), **Supp. I:** 216–217, 223
"Sublime and the Good, The" (Murdoch), **Supp. I:** 216–217, 218, 220
Subsequent to Summer (Fuller), **Supp. VII:** 79
Substance of the Speech . . . in Answer to . . . the Report of the Committee of Managers (Burke), **III:** 205
Substance of the Speeches for the Retrenchment of Public Expenses (Burke), **III:** 205
Subtle Knife, The (Pullman), **Supp. XIII:** 150, 153, 156–157
"Suburban Dream" (Muir), **Supp. VI:** 207
Success (Amis), **Supp. IV:** 26, 27, 31–32, 37
"Success" (Empson), **Supp. II:** 180, 189
Success and Failure of Picasso, The (Berger), **Supp. IV:** 79, 88
"Successor, The" (Cameron), **Supp. IX:** 23, 27
Such (Brooke–Rose)), **Supp. IV:** 99, 104, 105, 106–108
Such a Long Journey (Mistry), **Supp. X:** 142–146
"Such Darling Dodos" (Wilson), **Supp. I:** 154
"Such nights as these in England . . . A (Swinburne), **V:** 310
Such Stuff as Dreams Are Made On (tr. FitzGerald), **IV:** 349, 353
Such, Such Were the Joys (Orwell), **VII:** 275, 282
Such Things Are (Inchbald), **Supp. XV:** 147, 149, 154–155, 156, 157, 160
Such Was My Singing (Nichols), **VI:** 419
Suckling, Sir John, **I:** 337; **II:** 222, 223, **226–229**
"Sudden Heaven" (Pitter), **Supp. XIII:** 141
"Sudden Light" (Rossetti), **V:** 241, 242
Sudden Times (Healy), **Supp. IX:** 96, 100–103
"Suddenly" (Thomas), **Supp. XII:** 289
Sue, Eugène, **VI:** 228
"Suet Pudding, A" (Powys), **VIII:** 255

Suffrage of Elvira, The (Naipaul), **Supp. I:** 386–387, 388
"Sufism" (Jennings), **Supp. V:** 217
Sugar and Other Stories (Byatt), **Supp. IV:** 140, 151
Sugar and Rum (Unsworth), **Supp. VII:** 357, 361–363, 366
"Suicide" (Blackwood), **Supp. IX:** 7
Suicide Bridge: A Book of the Furies: A Mythology of the South and East (Sinclair), **Supp. XIV:** 233, 234, 237, 245
"Suicide Club, The" (Stevenson), **V:** 395; **Retro. Supp. I:** 263
Suitable Boy, A (Seth), **Supp. X:** 277, 279, 281–288, 290
"Suitcases" (Jamie), **Supp. XIV:** 141
Suite in Three Keys (Coward), **Supp. II:** 156–157
Suits, The (tr. Delanty), **Supp. XIV:** 76
"Sullens Sisters, The" (Coppard), **VIII:** 90
Sultan in Oman (Morris, J.), **Supp. X:** 175
Sultry Month, A: Scenes of London Literary Life in 1846 (Hayter), **IV:** 322
Sum Practysis of Medecyn (Henryson), **Supp. VII:** 146, 147
Summer (Bond), **Supp. I:** 423, 434–435
Summer (Thomson), **Supp. III:** 411, 414, 416, 417, 418, 419
"Summer after the War, The" (Ishiguro), **Retro. Supp. III:** 161
"Summer Afternoon" (Conn), **Supp. XIII:** 73
Summer Before the Dark, The (Lessing), **Supp. I:** 249, 253
Summer Bird–Cage, A (Drabble), **Supp. IV:** 230, 234–236, 241
Summer Day's Dream (Priestley), **VII:** 229
Summer Islands (Douglas), **VI:** 295, 305
"Summer Lightning" (Davie), **Supp. VI:** 112–113
Summer Lightning (Wodehouse), *see Fish Preferred*
"Summer Night, A" (Auden), **Retro. Supp. I:** 6
Summer Palaces (Scupham), **Supp. XIII:** 220–222, 223
Summer Rites (Rankin), **Supp. X:** 246
"Summer Waterfall, Glendale" (MacCaig), **Supp. VI:** 182
Summer Will Show (Warner), **Supp. VII:** 376
"Summerhouse on the Mound, The" (Bridges), **VI:** 74
Summers, M., **III:** 345
"Summer's Breath" (Wallace–Crabbe), **VIII:** 324
"Summer's Day, On a" (Smith, I. C.), **Supp. IX:** 215
Summertime (Reed), **Supp. XV:** 253
Summing Up, The (Maugham), **VI:** 364, 374
Summit (Thomas), **Supp. IV:** 485, 489
Summit Fever (Greig), **Supp. XVI:** 163–165, 167
Summoned by Bells (Betjeman), **VII:** 355, 356, 361, 373–374

Sumner, Rosemary, **Retro. Supp. I:** 115
"Sun & Moon" (Longley), **VIII:** 176
"Sun and the Fish, The" (Woolf), **Retro. Supp. I:** 308
Sun Before Departure (Sillitoe), **Supp. V:** 424, 425
Sun Dances at Easter, The: A Romance (Clarke), **Supp. XV:** 24, 25
Sun King, The (Mitford), **Supp. X:** 167
Sun Poem (Brathwaite), **Supp. XII:** 33, 41, 46
"Sun used to shine, The" (Thomas), **Supp. III:** 395
"Sun Valley" (Thomas), **Supp. IV:** 493
"Sunburst" (Davie), **Supp. VI:** 110
"Sunday" (Hughes), **Supp. I:** 341–342, 348
"Sunday" (Upward), **Supp. XIII:** 252
"Sunday Afternoon" (Bowen), **Supp. II:** 77
"Sunday at Home" (Smith), **Retro. Supp. III:** 306
Sunday Morning at the Centre of the World (De Bernières), **Supp. XII:** 66
"Sundew, The" (Swinburne), **V:** 315, 332
"Sunken Rock, The" (Jewsbury), **Supp. XIV:** 162
"Sunlight" (Gunn), **Supp. IV:** 268
"Sunlight in a Room" (Hart), **Supp. XI:** 127
"Sunlight on the Garden" (MacNeice), **VII:** 413
"Sunne Rising, The" (Donne), **II:** 127; **Retro. Supp. II:** 88–89, 90–91
"Sunny Jim" (Montague), **Supp. XV:** 211
"Sunny Prestatyn" (Larkin), **Supp. I:** 285; **Retro. Supp. III:** 206
Sunny Side, The (Milne), **Supp. V:** 298
"Sunrise, A" (Owen), **VI:** 449
Sun's Darling, The (Dekker and Ford), **II:** 89, 100
Sun's Net, The (Brown), **Supp. VI:** 69
Sunset Across the Bay (Bennett), **VIII:** 27
Sunset and Evening Star (O'Casey), **VII:** 13
Sunset at Blandings (Wodehouse), **Supp. III:** 452–453
"Sunset on Mount Blanc" (Stephen), **V:** 282
Sunset Song (Gibbon), **Supp. XIV:** 106, 107–109, 113
"Sunsets" (Aldington), **VI:** 416
"Sunsum" (Brathwaite), **Supp. XII:** 39
"Sunt Leones" (Smith), **Retro. Supp. III:** 304, 305
"Suntrap" (Murphy), **Supp. V:** 328
"Sunup" (Murphy), **Supp. V:** 325
"Super Flumina Babylonis" (Swinburne), **V:** 325
"Superannuated Man, The" (Lamb), **IV:** 83
Supernatural Horror in Literature (Lovecraft), **III:** 340
Supernatural Omnibus, The (Summers), **III:** 345
"Superstition" (Bacon), **III:** 39
"Superstition" (Hogg), **Supp. X:** 104, 110
"Superstitious Man's Story, The" (Hardy), **VI:** 22

Supper at Emmaus (Caravaggio), **Supp. IV:** 95
Supplication of Souls (More), **Supp. VII:** 244–245
"Supports, The" (Kipling), **VI:** 189
"Supposed Confessions of a Second-rate Sensitive Mind in Dejection" (Owen), **VI:** 445
"Supposed Confessions of a Second-Rate Sensitive Mind Not in Unity with Itself" (Tennyson), **Retro. Supp. III:** 321
Supposes (Gascoigne), **I:** 298, 303
"Sure" (Thomas), **Supp. XII:** 291
"Sure Proof" (MacCaig), **Supp. VI:** 191
"Surface Textures" (Desai), **Supp. V:** 65
Surgeon's Daughter, The (Scott), **IV:** 34–35, 39
Surgeon's Mate, The (O'Brian), **Supp. XII:** 256
Surprise, The (Haywood), **Supp. XII:** 135
Surprised by Joy: The Shape of My Early Life (Lewis), **Supp. III:** 247, 248
"Surrender, The" (King), **Supp. VI:** 151, 153
Surrey, Henry Howard, earl of, **I:** 97, 98, 113
Surroundings (MacCaig), **Supp. VI: 189–190,** 195
Survey of Experimental Philosophy, A (Goldsmith), **III:** 189, 191
Survey of Modernist Poetry, A (Riding and Graves), **VII:** 260; **Supp. II:** 185
"Surview" (Hardy), **VI:** 13
"Survival" (Wyndham), **Supp. XIII:** 290
Surviving Passages (Greig), **Supp. XVI:** 162, 163
"Survivor" (Kinsella), **Supp. V:** 267
Survivor, The (Keneally), **Supp. IV:** 345
Survivors, The (Beer), **Supp. XIV:** 2
"Survivors" (Ross), **VII:** 433
Suspense (Conrad), **VI:** 147
Suspension of Mercy, A (Highsmith), **Supp. V:** 174–175
"Suspiria de Profundis" (De Quincey), **IV:** 148, 153, 154
"Sussex Auction, A" (Richardson), **Supp. XIII:** 187
Sutcliff, Rosemary, **Supp. XVI: 261–275**
Sverris saga, **VIII:** 242
"Swallow, The" (Cowley), **II:** 198
Swallow (Thomas), **Supp. IV:** 483, 484–485
"Swallows" (Jamie), **Supp. XIV:** 143
"Swallows' Nest, The" (Jamie), **Supp. XIV:** 143
"Swan, The" (Dahl), **Supp. IV:** 207, 223, 224
"Swan, The" (Pitter), **Supp. XIII:** 138
"Swan, A Man, A" (Blunden), **Supp. XI:** 47
"Swan Bathing, The" (Pitter), **Supp. XIII:** 143
"Swan-Neck, The" (Kingsley), **Supp. XVI:** 204
Swan Song (Galsworthy), **VI:** 275
"Swans Mating" (Longley), **VIII:** 171–172, 173

"Swans on an Autumn River" (Warner), **Supp. VII:** 380
"Swatting Flies" (Beer), **Supp. XIV:** 4
Swearer's Bank, The (Swift), **III:** 35
Swedenborg, Emanuel, **III:** 292, 297; **Retro. Supp. I:** 39
Sweeney Agonistes (Eliot), **VII:** 157–158
"Sweeney Among the Nightingales" (Eliot), **VII:** xiii, 145
Sweeney Astray (Heaney), **Supp. II:** 268, 277, 278; **Retro. Supp. I:** 129
"Sweeney Erect" (Eliot), **VII:** 145
Sweeney poems (Eliot), **VII:** 145–146; see also "Sweeney Among the Nightingales"; "Sweeney Erect"
"Sweeney Redivivus" (Heaney), **Supp. II:** 277, 278
Sweet Dove Died, The (Pym), **Supp. II: 378–380**
Sweet Dreams (Frayn), **Supp. VII:** 56, 58–60, 61, 65
"Sweet Other Flesh" (Pitter), **Supp. XIII:** 145
Sweet Smell of Psychosis (Self), **Supp. V:** 406
"Sweet Things" (Gunn), **Supp. IV:** 272; **Retro. Supp. III:** 125
Sweet William (Bainbridge), **Supp. VI:** 18, 20–22, 24
"Sweet William's Farewell to Black-ey'd Susan" (Gay), **III:** 58
"Sweetheart of M. Brisieux, The" (James), **VI:** 69
Sweets of Pimlico, The (Wilson), **Supp. VI:** 297, **298–299,** 301
Sweet-Shop Owner, The (Swift), **Supp. V:** 427–429
Swift, Graham, **Supp. IV:** 65; **Supp. V: 427–442**
Swift, Jonathan, **II:** 240, 259, 261, 269, 273, 335; **III: 15–37,** 39, 44, 53, 55, 76; **IV:** 160, 257, 258; **VII:** 127; **Retro. Supp. I: 273–287**
"Swift has sailed into his rest" (Yeats), **III:** 21
"Swifts" (Hughes), **Retro. Supp. II:** 208–209
"Swifts" (Stevenson), **Supp. VI:** 265
"Swigs" (Dunn), **Supp. X:** 79
Swimming Free: On and Below the Surface of Lake, River, and Sea (Dutton), **Supp. XII:** 83, 84, 92
Swimming in the Flood (Burnside), **Supp. XIII:** 21–22, 23
"Swimming in the Flood" (Burnside), **Supp. XIII:** 22
"Swimming Lesson, A" (Burnside), **Supp. XIII:** 22
"Swimming Lessons" (Mistry), **Supp. X:** 141–142
Swimming Lessons and Other Stories from Ferozsha Baag (Mistry), **Supp. X:** 138–142
Swimming Pool Library, The (Hollinghurst), **Supp. X:** 119–120, 122–129, 132, 134
"Swim in Co. Wicklow, A" (Mahon), **Supp. VI:** 178
Swinburne, Algernon Charles, **II:** 102; **III:** 174; **IV:** 90, 337, 346, 370; **V:** xi,

xii, 236, 284, 286, 298–299, **309–335,** 346, 355, 365, 401

Swinburne: The Portrait of a Poet (Henderson), **V:** 335

"Swing, The" (Heaney), **Retro. Supp. I:** 133

"Swing, The" (Wallace-Crabbe), **VIII:** 311

"Swing of the Pendulum, The" (Mansfield), **VII:** 172

Swinging the Maelstrom (Lowry), **Supp. III:** 272

Swinnerton, Frank, **VI:** 247, 268; **VII:** 223

"Switch, The" (Malouf), **Supp. XII:** 220

Switch Bitch (Dahl), **Supp. IV:** 219

Switchers (Thompson), **Supp. XIV:** 286, 287, 290

Sword and the Circle, The (Sutcliff), **Supp. XVI:** 271–272

Sword at Sunset (Sutcliff), **Supp. XVI:** 262, 268

"Sword Music" (Stallworthy), **Supp. X:** 296

Sword of Honor (screenplay, Boyd), **Supp. XVI:** 46

Sword of Honour trilogy (Waugh), **VII:** xx–xxi, 303–306; see also *Men at Arms; Officers and Gentlemen; Unconditional Surrender*

Sword of the West, The (Clarke), **Supp. XV:** 18

Sword Song (Sutcliff), **Supp. XVI:** 264, 268, 273

Sybil (Disraeli), **IV:** xii, xx, 296, 300, 301–302, 305, 307, 308; **V:** viii, x, 2, 4

Sycamore Tree, The (Brooke-Rose)), **Supp. IV:** 99, 101–102

"Sydney and the Bush" (Murray), **Supp. VII:** 276

Sykes Davies, Hugh, **IV:** xii, xxv; **V:** x, xxviii, 103

Sylphid, The (Robinson), **Supp. XIII:** 211

Sylva (Cowley), **II:** 202

Sylva; or, A Discourse of Forest-Trees (Evelyn), **II:** 275, 287

Sylva sylvarum (Bacon), **I:** 259, 263, 273

Sylvae (ed. Dryden), **II:** 301, 304; **Retro. Supp. III:** 62, 63

Sylvia and Ted: A Novel (Tennant), see *Ballad of Sylvia and Ted, The*

Sylvia's Lovers (Gaskell), **V:** 1, 4, 6, 7–8, 12, 15; **Retro. Supp. III:** 100, 109–110

Sylvie and Bruno (Carroll), **V:** 270–271, 273

Sylvie and Bruno Concluded (Carroll), **V:** 271, 273

Symbolic Logic (Carroll), **V:** 271, 274

Symbolist Movement in Literature, The (Symons), **VI:** ix; **Supp. XIV:** 267, 268–269, 270, 274, 281

Symonds, John Addington, **V:** 83; **Supp. XIV: 249–266**

Symons, Arthur, **VI:** ix; **Supp. XIV: 267–283**

Symons, Julian, **Supp. IV:** 3, 339

"Sympathy in White Major" (Larkin), **Supp. I:** 282; **Retro. Supp. III:** 210

Synge, John Millington, **II:** 258; **VI:** xiv, **307–314,** 317; **VII:** 3, 42; **Retro. Supp. I: 289–303**

Synge and Anglo-Irish Drama (Price), **VI:** 317

Synge and the Ireland of His Time (Yeats), **VI:** 222, 317

Syntactic Structures (Chomsky), **Supp. IV:** 113–114

"Syntax of Seasons, The" (Reid), **Supp. VII:** 330

"Synth" (Roberts, K.), **Supp. X:** 262–263

Syrie Maugham (Fisher), **VI:** 379

System of Logic (Mill), **V:** 279

System of Magick, A; or, A History of the Black Art (Defoe), **III:** 14

System of Vegetables, The (Darwin), **Supp. XVI:** 128

Systema medicinae hermeticae generale (Nollius), **II:** 201

Syzygies and Lanrick (Carroll), **V:** 273–274

T. E. Hulme: The Selected Writings (Hulme), **Supp. VI:** 135–136, 138, 140, 142, 143

T. E. Lawrence: The Selected Letters (Lawrence), **Supp. II:** 283, 286, 289, 290, 293, 295, 296, 297

T. Fisher Unwin (publisher), **VI:** 373

T. S. Eliot (Ackroyd), **Supp. VI:** 5–6, 8

T. S. Eliot (Bergonzi), **VII:** 169

T.S. Eliot (Raine), **Supp. XIII:** 175

"T. S. Eliot" (Forster), **VII:** 144

"T. S. Eliot and Ezra Pound" (Ewart), **Supp. VII:** 45

"T. S. Eliot as Critic" (Leavis), **VII:** 233

"Tabill of Confessioun, The" (Dunbar), **VIII:** 119

"Table, The" (Trevor), **Supp. IV:** 500

Table Book (Hone), **IV:** 255

Table Manners (Ayckbourn), **Supp. V:** 2, 5

Table Near the Band, A (Milne), **Supp. V:** 309

"Table Talk" (Cowper), **Retro. Supp. III:** 41, 47, 48

Table Talk (Hazlitt), **IV:** xviii, 131, 137, 139

Table Talk, and Other Poems (Cowper), **III:** 220

Table Talk 1941–1944 (Cameron), **Supp. IX:** 28

Tables of Ancient Coins, Weights, and Measures (Arbuthnot), **Supp. XVI:** 18, 26

Tables of the Grecian, Roman, and Jewish Measures, Weights, and Coins, Reduc'd to the English Standard (Arbuthnot), **Supp. XVI:** 18

Tables Turned, The (Morris), **V:** 306

"Tables Turned, The" (Wordsworth), **IV:** 7, 225

Taburlaine the Great, Part I (Marlowe), **Retro. Supp. I:** 204–206

Taburlaine the Great, Part II (Marlowe), **Retro. Supp. I:** 206–207

"Tadnol" (Powys), **VIII:** 248

"Taft's Wife" (Blackwood), **Supp. IX:** 12

"Tagging the Stealer" (Delanty), **Supp. XIV:** 74

Tagore, Rabindranath, **Supp. IV:** 440, 454

Tailor of Gloucester, The (Potter), **Supp. III:** 290, 301–302

Tailor of Panama, The (le Carré), **Retro. Supp. III:** 225–226

Taill of Schir Chantecleir and the Foxe, The (Henryson), see *Cock and the Fox, The*

Taill of the Uponlondis Mous and the Burges Mous, The (Henryson), see *Two Mice, The*

"Tail-less Fox, The" (Thompson), **Supp. XV:** 289

Táin, The (Kinsella), **Supp. V:** 264–266

Take a Girl Like You (Amis), **Supp. II:** 10–11, 18

Taken Care of (Sitwell), **VII:** 128, 132

Takeover, The (Spark), **Supp. I:** 211–212

"Taking Down the Christmas Tree" (Stevenson), **Supp. VI:** 262

Taking Steps (Ayckbourn), **Supp. V:** 3, 12, 13

Talbert, E. W., **I:** 224

"Talbot Road" (Gunn), **Supp. IV:** 272, 273–274; **Retro. Supp. III:** 125–126

"Tale, The" (Conrad), **VI:** 148

"Tale of a Scholar" (Upward), **Supp. XIII:** 251

Tale of a Town, The (Martyn), **VI:** 95

"Tale of a Trumpet, A" (Hood), **IV:** 258

Tale of a Tub, A (Swift), **II:** 259, 269; **III:** 17, 19, **21–23,** 35; **Retro. Supp. I:** 273, 276, 277–278

Tale of Balen, The (Swinburne), **V:** 333

Tale of Benjamin Bunny, The (Potter), **Supp. III:** 290, 299

Tale of Beowulf, Done out of the Old English Tongue, The (Morris, Wyatt), **V:** 306

Tale of Ginger and Pickles, The (Potter), **Supp. III:** 290, 299

Tale of Jemima Puddle-Duck, The (Potter), **Supp. III:** 290, 303

Tale of Johnny Town-Mouse, The (Potter), **Supp. III:** 297, 304, 307

Tale of King Arthur, The (Malory), **I:** 68

Tale of Little Pig Robinson, The (Potter), **Supp. III:** 288, 289, 297, 304–305

Tale of Mr. Jeremy Fisher, The (Potter), **Supp. III:** 298, 303

Tale of Mr. Tod, The (Potter), **Supp. III:** 290, 299

Tale of Mrs. Tiggy-Winkle, The (Potter), **Supp. III:** 290, 301–302

Tale of Mrs. Tittlemouse, The (Potter), **Supp. III:** 298, 301

Tale of Paraguay, A (Southey), **IV:** 66–67, 68, 71

Tale of Peter Rabbit, The (Potter), **Supp. III:** 287, 288, 290, 293, **295–296,** 299

Tale of Pigling Bland, The (Potter), **Supp. III:** 288–289, 290, 291, 304

Tale of Rosamund Gray and Old Blind Margaret, A (Lamb), **IV:** 79, 85

Tale of Samuel Whiskers, The (Potter), **Supp. III:** 290, 297, 301, 305

Tale of Sir Gareth of Orkeney that was called Bewmaynes, The (Malory), **I:** 72, 73; **Retro. Supp. II:** 243, 247
Tale of Sir Lancelot and Queen Guinevere (Malory), **Retro. Supp. II:** 243, 244
Tale of Sir Thopas, The (Chaucer), **I:** 67, 71
"Tale of Society As It Is, A" (Shelley), **Retro. Supp. I:** 245
Tale of Squirrel Nutkin, The (Potter), **Supp. III:** 288, 290, 301
Tale of the House of the Wolflings, A (Morris), **V:** 302, 306
Tale of the Noble King Arthur that was Emperor himself through Dignity of his Hands (Malory), **I:** 69, 72, 77–79
Tale of the Pie and the Patty-Pan, The (Potter), **Supp. III:** 290, 299
Tale of the Sankgreal, The (Malory), **I:** 69; **Retro. Supp. II:** 248–249
Tale of the Sea, A (Conrad), **VI:** 148
Tale of Timmy Tiptoes, The (Potter), **Supp. III:** 290
"Tale of Tod Lapraik, The" (Stevenson), **Retro. Supp. I:** 267
Tale of Tom Kitten, The (Potter), **Supp. III:** 290, 299, 300, 302, 303
Tale of Two Bad Mice, The (Potter), **Supp. III:** 290, 300–301
Tale of Two Cities, A (Dickens), **V:** xxii, 41, 42, 57, 63, 66, 72
"Talent and Friendship" (Kinsella), **Supp. V:** 270
Talent to Annoy, A (Mitford), **Supp. X:** 163
Talented Mr. Ripley, The (Highsmith), **Supp. V:** 170
Tales (Crabbe), **III:** 278, 285, 286; *see also Tales in Verse; Tales of the Hall; Posthumous Tales*
"Tales" (Dickens), **V:** 46
Tales and Sketches (Disraeli), **IV:** 308
Tales from a Troubled Land (Paton), **Supp. II: 344–345,** 348, 354
Tales from Angria (Brontë), **V:** 151
Tales from Ovid (Hughes), **Retro. Supp. II:** 202, 214–216
Tales from Shakespeare (Lamb and Lamb), **IV:** xvi, 80, 85
Tales I Tell My Mother: A Collection of Feminist Short Stories (ed. Fairbairns et al.), **Supp. XI:** 163, 164, 175; **Supp. XV:** 261–262, 263
Tales I Told My Mother (Nye), **Supp. X:** 195
Tales in Verse (Crabbe), **III:** 275, 278, 279, 281, 286
Tales of a Grandfather (Scott), **IV:** 38
Tales of All Countries (Trollope), **V:** 101
Tales of Beedle the Bard, The (Rowling), **Supp. XVI:** 239
Tales of Good and Evil (Gogol), **III:** 345
Tales of Hearsay (Conrad), **VI:** 148
Tales of Hoffmann (Hoffmann), **III:** 334, 345
Tales of Mean Streets (Morrison), **VI:** 365
Tales of My Landlord (Scott), **IV:** 39
Tales of Natural and Unnatural Catastrophes (Highsmith), **Supp. V:** 179

Tales of St. Austin's (Wodehouse), **Supp. III:** 449–450
Tales of Sir Gareth (Malory), **I:** 68
Tales of the Crusaders (Scott), **IV:** 39
Tales of the Five Towns (Bennett), **VI:** 253
Tales of the Hall (Crabbe), **III:** 278, 285, 286; **V:** xvii, 6
"Tales of the Islanders" (Brontë), **V:** 107, 114, 135
Tales of the Punjab (Steel), **Supp. XII:** 266
Tales of the Tides, and Other Stories (Steel), **Supp. XII:** 275
Tales of Three Cities (James), **VI:** 67
Tales of Unrest (Conrad), **VI:** 148
Talfourd, Field, **IV:** 311
Taliesin (Nye), **Supp. X:** 193
"Taliessin on the Death of Virgil" (Williams, C. W. S.), **Supp. IX:** 283
"Taliessin Returns to Logres" (Williams, C. W. S.), **Supp. IX:** 282
Taliessin Through Logres (Williams, C. W. S.), **Supp. IX:** 282–283
Talisman, The (Scott), **IV:** 39
"Tall Story, A" (Burnside), **Supp. XIII:** 18
Talk Magazine, **Supp. XIII:** 174
Talk Stories (Kincaid), **Supp. VII:** 217, 231
Talkies (Crawford), **Supp. XI:** 67, 72–74
Talking Bronco (Campbell), **Supp. III:** 119
Talking Heads (Bennett), **VIII:** 27–28
Talking It Over (Barnes), **Supp. IV:** 65, 67, 68, 72–74
Talking of Jane Austen (Kaye–Smith and Stern), **IV:** 123
"Talking Skull" (Crace), **Supp. XIV:** 21
"Talking to Myself" (Auden), **Retro. Supp. I:** 13
"Tam o' Shanter" (Burns), **III:** 320
Tamburlaine the Great (Marlowe), **I:** 212, 243, 276, 278, 279–280, **281–282; II:** 69, 305
Tamburlaine, Part 2 (Marlowe), **I:** 281–282, 283
"Tamer and Hawk" (Gunn), **Supp. IV:** 258; **Retro. Supp. III:** 118
Taming of the Shrew, The (Shakespeare), **I:** 298, 302, 303, 327; **II:** 68; **Retro. Supp. III:** 268, 271–272, 273
Tamworth Reading Room, The (Newman), **Supp. VII:** 294
Tancred (Disraeli), **IV:** 294, 297, 300, 302–303, 307, 308
Tancred and Gismund (Wilmot), **I:** 216
Tancred and Sigismunda (Thomson), **Supp. III:** 411, 423, 424
Tangier Papers of Samuel Pepys, The (ed. Chappell), **II:** 288
Tangled Tale, A (Carroll), **V:** 273
"Tannahill" (Dunn), **Supp. X:** 74–75
Tanner, Alain, **Supp. IV:** 79, 95
Tanner, J. R., **II:** 288
Tanner, Tony, **VI:** xxxiv
Tannhäuser and Other Poems (Clarke), **V:** 318n
"Tano" (Brathwaite), **Supp. XII:** 39
Tao of Pooh, The (Hoff), **Supp. V:** 311

"Tapestry Moths" (Redgrove), **Supp. VI:** 235–236
"Tapestry Trees" (Morris), **V:** 304–305
"Tardy Spring" (Meredith), **V:** 223
Tares (Thomas), **Supp. XII:** 284
Tarr (Lewis), **VII:** xv, 72
"Tarry delight, so seldom met" (Housman), **VI:** 161
Tarry Flynn (Kavanagh), **Supp. VII:** 186, 194–195, 199
Task, The (Cowper), **III:** 208, **212–217,** 220; **IV:** xv, 184; **Retro. Supp. III:** 35, 36, 37, 39, 41, 42–43, 46, 48–50
"Task, The" (Nye), **Supp. X:** 205
Tasso, Torquato, **II:** 49; **III:** 171
"Taste" (Dahl), **Supp. IV:** 215, 217
Taste and Remember (Plomer), **Supp. XI:** 214, 222
Taste for Death, A (James), **Supp. IV:** 320, 330–331
Taste of Honey, A (Rattigan), **Supp. VII:** 320
"Taste of the Fruit, The" (Plomer), **Supp. XI:** 214
Tate, Nahum, **I:** 327; **II:** 305
Tatler (periodical), **II:** 339; **III:** 18, 29, 30, 35, 39, **41–45,** 46, 51, 52, 53
Tausk, Victor, **Supp. IV:** 493
Tawney, R. H., **I:** 253
Tax Inspector, The (Carey), **Supp. XII:** 51, 54, 59–60, 62
Taxation No Tyranny (Johnson), **III:** 121; **Retro. Supp. I:** 142–143
"Taxonomy" (Burnside), **Supp. XIII:** 25
"Tay Moses, The" (Jamie), **Supp. XIV:** 141
Taylor, A. L., **V:** 270, 272, 274
Taylor, A. J. P., **IV:** 290, 303
Taylor, Henry, **IV:** 62n
Taylor, Jeremy, **Supp. IV:** 163
Taylor, John, **IV:** 231, 233, 253
Taylor, Mary, **V:** 117
Taylor, Thomas, **III:** 291
Taylor, Tom, **V:** 330
"Tchaikovsky Decides Which World He Belongs To" (Butlin), **Supp. XVI:** 65–66
Te of Piglet, The (Hoff), **Supp. V:** 311
"Tea"(Saki), **Supp. VI:** 244
Tea Party (Pinter), **Supp. I:** 375
"Tea with an Artist" (Rhys), **Supp. II:** 390
"Tea with Mrs. Bittell" (Pritchett), **Supp. III:** 328–329
"Teachers" (Dunn), **Supp. X:** 82
"Teacher's Tale, The" (Cope), **VIII:** 83
Teapots and Quails (Lear), **V:** 87
"Tear" (Kinsella), **Supp. V:** 274
"Teare, The" (Crashaw), **II:** 183
"Tearing" (Montague), **Supp. XV:** 220
"Tears" (Thomas), **VI:** 424
"Tears" (Vaughan), **II:** 187
"Tears are Salt" (Smith, I. C.), **Supp. IX:** 217–218
"Tears, Idle Tears" (Hough), **IV:** 323n, 339
"Tears, Idle Tears" (Tennyson), **IV:** 329–330, 334; **Retro. Supp. III:** 323
"'Tears, Idle Tears' Again" (Spitzer), **IV:** 323n, 339

Tears of Amaryllis for Amyntas, The: A Pastoral. (Congreve), **II:** 350
Tears of Peace, The (Chapman), **I:** 240–241
"Teasers, The" (Empson), **Supp. II:** 190
Tea–Table (periodical), **III:** 50
Tea–Table Miscellany, The (Ramsay), **III:** 312; **IV:** 28–29
Tebbit, Norman, **Supp. IV:** 449
"Technical Manifesto of Futurist Literature" (Marinetti), **Supp. III:** 396
Technical Supplement, A (Kinsella), **Supp. V:** 268–269
"Technological Crisis, The" (Richards), **Supp. II:** 426
"'Teem'" (Kipling), **VI:** 169, 189
"Teeth" (Kay), **Supp. XIII:** 101
Teeth 'n' Smiles (Hare), **Supp. IV:** 282, 283–284
Tel Quel circle, **Supp. IV:** 115
"Telephone" (Seth), **Supp. X:** 284
"Tell me, Dorinda, why so gay" (Dorset), **II:** 262–263
"Tell me no more how fair she is" (King), **Supp. VI:** 151
"Tell me not here, it needs not saying" (Housman), **VI:** 160
"Tell me what means that sigh" (Landor), **IV:** 98
"Tell Me Who to Kill" (Naipaul), **Supp. I:** 395, 396
"Tell Us" (Thomas), **Supp. XII:** 290
Tellers and Listeners: The Narrative of Imagination (Hardy), **V:** 73
Tellers of Tales (Maugham), **VI:** 372
"Telling Myself" (Motion), **Supp. VII:** 256
"Telling Part, The" (Kay), **Supp. XIII:** 103
Temora, an Ancient Epic Poem (Macpherson), **VIII:** 189–191, 193, 194
"Temper, The" (Herbert), **II:** 125
Tempest, The (Shakespeare), **I:** 323–324; **II:** 55; **III:** 117; bRetro. Supp. III: 281–282
Tempest, The; or, The Enchanted Island (Dryden), **II:** 305
Temple, Sir William, **III:** 16, 19, 23, 40, 190
Temple, The (Herbert), **II:** 119, 121–125, 128, 129, 184; **Retro. Supp. II:** 172, 173, 174–182
"Temple, The" (Herrick), **II:** 113
Temple, The (Spender), **Supp. II:** 485, 493
Temple Bar (Forster), **VI:** 399
Temple Beau, The (Fielding), **III:** 96, 98, 105
Temple of Fame, The (Pope), **III:** 71, 77; **Retro. Supp. I:** 233
Temple of Glass, The (Lydgate), **I:** 57, 62, 65
Temple of Nature, The; or, The Origin of Society (Darwin), **Supp. XVI:** 127, 128, 134–137, 138, 139, 140
Temporary Kings (Powell), **VII:** 352
Temporary Life, A (Storey), **Supp. I:** 408, 410, 411, 412, 413, 414–415, 416, 417–418, 419

"Temporis Partus Masculus" (Bacon), **Supp. III:** 361
Temptation of Eileen Hughes, The (Moore, B.), **Supp. IX:** 144, 151
ten Brink, Bernard, **I:** 98
Ten Burnt Offerings (MacNeice), **VII:** 415
"Ten Ghazals" (Hart), **Supp. XI:** 124–125
"Ten Lines a Day" (Boswell), **III:** 237
Ten Little Indians, see *Ten Little Niggers*
Ten Little Niggers (Christie; US. title, *"nd Then There Were None*), **Supp. II:** 131, 132, 134
"Ten Memorial Poems" (Fuller), **Supp. VII:** 72
Ten Novels and Their Authors (Maugham), **VI:** 363–364
"Ten O'Clock Lecture" (Whistler), **V:** 407; **VI:** 103
"Ten Pence Story" (Armitage), **VIII:** 4
Ten Tales Tall & True (Gray, A.), **Supp. IX:** 79, 80, 90–91
Ten Times Table (Ayckbourn), **Supp. V:** 3, 10, 14
"Tenant, The" (Healy), **Supp. IX:** 96, 104–105
Tenant of Wildfell Hall, The (Brontë), **V:** xxi, 130, 153; **Supp. III:** 195; **Retro. Supp. I:** 50, 52, 53, 54, 55–56
Tender Only to One (Smith), **Supp. II:** 462; **Retro. Supp. III:** 307
"Tender Only to One" (Smith), **Retro. Supp. III:** 307
"Tenebrae" (Clarke), **Supp. XV:** 22–23
Tenebrae (Hill), **Supp. V:** 189–192, 199; **Retro. Supp. III:** 135, 137, 141, 143, 146
Tennant, Emma, **Supp. IX: 227–241**
Tenniel, John, **V:** 266, 267
"Tennis Court, The" (Trevor), **Supp. IV:** 504
Tennyson, Alfred, **II:** 200, 208; **IV:** viii, xii–xiii, 196, 240, 292, 310, 313, **323–339**, 341, 344, 351, 352, 371; **V:** ix, 77–79, 85, 182, 285, 299, 311, 327, 330, 365, 401; **VI:** 455–456; **Retro. Supp. III: 317–333**
Tennyson, Emily, **V:** 81
Tennyson, Frederic, **IV:** 350, 351
Tennyson, Hallam, **IV:** 324, 329, 332, 338
"Tennyson and Picturesque Poetry" (McLuhan), **IV:** 323n, 338, 339
"Tennyson and the Romantic Epic" (McLuhan), **IV:** 323n, 339
Tennyson Archive, The (Tennyson), **Retro. Supp. III:** 317
Tennyson: Poet and Prophet (Henderson), **IV:** 339
Tenth Man, The (Greene), **Supp. I:** 1, 11
Tenth Satire (Juvenal), **Retro. Supp. I:** 139
"Tents, The" (Scupham), **Supp. XIII:** 222
Tenure of Kings and Magistrates, The (Milton), **II:** 176
Teresa of Watling Street (Bennett), **VI:** 249
"Teresa's Wedding" (Trevor), **Supp. IV:** 503

"Tereus" (Gower), **I:** 54
"Terminal" (Gunn), **Retro. Supp. III:** 127
"Terminal Beach, The" (Ballard), **Supp. V:** 23, 25, 34
Terminal Beach, The (Ballard), **Supp. V:** 23
Terminations (James), **VI:** 49, 67
"Terminus" (Emerson), **IV:** 81
"Terra Australis" (Wallace–Crabbe), **VIII:** 314
"Terra Firma" (Conn), **Supp. XIII:** 78
"Terra Incognita" (Lawrence), **VII:** 119
Terra Nostra (Fuentes), **Supp. IV:** 116
"Terrapin, The" (Highsmith), **Supp. V:** 180
Terrible Sonnets (Hopkins), **Retro. Supp. II:** 197–198
"Territorial" (Motion), **Supp. VII:** 260
Territorial Rights (Spark), **Supp. I:** 211, 212
"Terrors of Basket Weaving, The" (Highsmith), **Supp. V:** 180
Terrors of Dr. Trevils, The (Redgrove), **Supp. VI:** 230
Terry, Ellen, **VI:** 104
Terry Hogan, an Eclogue (Landor), **IV:** 100
Terry Street (Dunn), **Supp. X:** 66, 69–70, 73
Teseide (Boccaccio), **I:** 30
Tess (Tennant), **Supp. IX:** 231, 236–238
Tess of the d'Urbervilles: A Pure Woman Faithfully Presented (Hardy), **VI:** 5, 9, 20; **Supp. IV:** 243, 471; **Retro. Supp. I:** 115–116
"Test Case" (Kinsella), **Supp. V:** 261
"Test of Manhood, The" (Meredith), **V:** 222
Testament (Lydgate), **I:** 65
Testament of Beauty, The (Bridges), **VI:** 72, 73, 74, 75, 82
Testament of Cresseid, The (Henryson), **Supp. VII:** 135, 136, 142–145, 146
Testament of Experience: An Autobiographical Story of the Years 1925–1960 (Brittain), **Supp. X:** 39–40, 44, 46
Testament of Friendship: The Story of Winifred Holtby (Brittain), **Supp. X:** 42, 44
Testament of Love, The (Usk), **I:** 2
Testament of Youth: An Autobiographical Study of the Years 1900–1925 (Brittain), **Supp. X:** 33–36, 38, 40–41, 43–44, 46–47
Testimonies (O'Brian), **Supp. XII:** 251
"Tête à Tête (Kinsella), **Supp. V:** 260
Tetrachordon: . . . (Milton), **II:** 175
Textermination (Brooke–Rose)), **Supp. IV:** 97, 100, 112
Texts and Pretexts (Huxley), **VII:** 204; **Retro. Supp. II:** 182
Texts for Nothing (Beckett), **Supp. I:** 51, 53, 60
Thackeray, Anne Isabella, **VI:** 4
Thackeray, Bal, **Supp. IV:** 438
Thackeray, William Makepeace, **II:** 363; **III:** 124, 125, 146; **IV:** 240, 251, 254, 257, 266, 272, 301, 306, 340; **V:** ix,

THAC–THIR

17–39, 56, 62, 68, 69, 139, 140, 147, 179, 191, 279; **Supp. IV:** 238, 244
Thackeray (Trollope), **V:** 102
Thackeray: Prodigal Genius (Carey), **V:** 39
Thalaba the Destroyer (Southey), **III:** 335; **IV:** 64, 65, 71, 197, 217
"Thalassius" (Swinburne), **V:** 327
Thalia Rediviva (Vaughan), **II:** 185, 201
"Than on this fals warld I cry fy" (Dunbar), **VIII:** 122
"Thank You, Fog" (Auden), **Retro. Supp. I:** 14
Thank You, Jeeves (Wodehouse), **Supp. III:** 455, 460
"Thanksgiving for a Habitat" (Auden), **Retro. Supp. I:** 13
Thanksgiving Ode, 18 January 1816 (Wordsworth), **IV:** 24
Thanksgivings (Traherne), **II:** 190–191;**Supp. XI:** 264, 265, 274
"Thanksgivings for the Body" (Traherne), **Supp. XI:** 274
That American Woman (Waugh), **Supp. VI:** 272
That Hideous Strength (Lewis), **Supp. III:** 249, 252, 254–255
"That Hollywood Movie with the Big Shark" (Warner), **Supp. XI:** 294
"That Island Formed You" (Smith, I. C.), **Supp. IX:** 216
"That Morning" (Hughes), **Supp. I:** 364
"That Nature Is a Heraclitean Fire" (Hopkins), **V:** 376, 377
"That Now Is Hay Some-tyme Was Grase" (Lydgate), **I:** 57
"That Raven" (Nye), **Supp. X:** 198, 202
"That Room" (Montague), **Supp. XV:** 218
That Summer (Greig), **Supp. XVI:** 161, 163, 170–171, 173
"That the Science of Cartography Is Limited" (Boland), **Supp. V:** 43–44, 46
That Time (Beckett), **Supp. I:** 61; **Retro. Supp. I:** 28
That Uncertain Feeling (Amis), **Supp. II:** 7–8
"That Weird Sall Never Daunton Me" (Cameron), **Supp. IX:** 29–31
Thatcher, Margaret, **Supp. IV:** 74–75, 437
"Thaw" (Jamie), **Supp. XIV:** 141
"Thaw, A" (Redgrove), **Supp. VI:** 234
Thealma and Clearchus (Chalkhill), **II:** 133
Theatre (periodical), **III:** 50, 53
"Theatre of God's Judgements" (Beard), **Retro. Supp. I:** 204
Theatrical Companion to Maugham (Mander and Mitchenson), **VI:** 379
Theatrum Orbis Terrarum (Ortelius), **I:** 282
Theatrum Poetarum (Phillips), **II:** 347
"Their Finest Hour" (Churchill), **VI:** 358
"Their Lonely Betters" (Auden), **VII:** 387
"Their Quiet Lives" (Warner), **Supp. VII:** 380
"Their Very Memory" (Blunden), **VI:** 428; **Supp. XI:** 41

"Thieving Boy, A" (Hollinghurst), **Supp. X:** 122–123
Thelwall, John, **IV:** 103
"Them! Not Us!" (Butlin), **Supp. XVI:** 52
Themes and Conventions of Elizabethan Tragedy (Bradbrook), **I:** 293; **II:** 78
Themes on a Variation (Morgan, E.), **Supp. IX:** 160, 166, 170
"Then dawns the Invisible . . ." (Brontë), **V:** 143; *see also* "Prisoner, The"
Theobald, Lewis, **I:** 324, 326; **II:** 66, 87; **III:** 51
"Theodolinde" (James), **VI:** 69
Theodore (Boyle), **III:** 95
"Theology" (Hughes), **Supp. I:** 350
"Theology of Fitness, The" (Sisson), **Supp. XI:** 256
Théophile (Swinburne), **V:** 333
Theophrastus, **II:** 68, 81; **III:** 50
"Theory of Everything, A" (Burnside), **Supp. XIII:** 25
Theory of Permanent Adolescence, The (Connolly), **Supp. III:** 97
Theory of Poetry, The (Abercrombie), **Supp. XVI:** 11, 12–13
"Theory of the Earth" (Morgan, E.), **Supp. IX:** 167
Theory of the Leisure Class, The (Veblen), **VI:** 283
Therapy (Lodge), **Supp. IV:** 366, 381, 383–385
"There" (Wallace-Crabbe), **VIII:** 321
"There Are Nights That Are so Still" (Thomas), **Supp. XII:** 289–290
There Are No Ghosts in the Soviet Union (Hill, R.), **Supp. IX:** 118
There is a Happy Land (Waterhouse), **Supp. XIII:** 266–269, 270, 272
"There is a hill beside the silver Thames" (Bridges), **VI:** 78
"There Is a House Not Made with Hands" (Watts), **III:** 288
"There Is No Conversation" (West), **Supp. III:** 442
There Is No Natural Religion (Blake), **III:** 292, 307; **Retro. Supp. I:** 35
"There Is No Sorrow" (Smith, I. C.), **Supp. IX:** 218
"There Is Nothing" (Gurney), **VI:** 426–427
"There was a Saviour" (Thomas), **Supp. I:** 177, 178
"There was a time" (Thomas), **Supp. III:** 404
"There was an old Derry down Derry" (Lear), **V:** 82
"There Was an Old Man in a Barge" (Lear), **V:** 83
"There Was an Old Man of Blackheath" (Lear), **V:** 86
"There Was an Old Man of Three Bridges" (Lear), **V:** 86
"There was never nothing more me pained" (Wyatt), **I:** 103
"There Will Be No Peace" (Auden), **Retro. Supp. I:** 13
"There's Nothing Here" (Muir), **Supp. VI:** 208

"Thermal Stair, The" (Graham), **Supp. VII:** 114
These Demented Lands (Warner), **Supp. XI:** 282, 285, 286–289, 294
"These Summer-Birds did with thy Master stay" (Herrick), **II:** 103
These the Companions (Davie), **Supp. VI:** 105, 109, 111, 113, 117
These Twain (Bennett), **VI:** 258
Theses Medicae de Secretione Animali (Arbuthnot), **Supp. XVI:** 16–17
"Theses on the Philosophy of History" (Benjamin), **Supp. IV:** 87
Thespian Magazine (periodical), **III:** 263
"Thespians at Thermopylae, The" (Cameron), **Supp. IX:** 19
"They" (Kipling), **VI:** 199
"They" (Sassoon), **VI:** 430
"They" (Wallace-Crabbe), **VIII:** 322
"They All Go to the Mountains Now" (Brooke-Rose)), **Supp. IV:** 103
"They Are All Gone into the World of Light!" (Vaughan), **II:** 188
They Came to a City (Priestley), **VII:** 210, 227
"They flee from me" (Wyatt), **I:** 102
"They Shall Not Grow Old" (Dahl), **Supp. IV:** 210, 224
They Walk in the City (Priestley), **VII:** 217
They Went (Douglas), **VI:** 303, 304, 305
"Thief" (Graves), **VII:** 267
Thierry and Theodoret (Beaumont, Fletcher, Massinger), **II:** 66
Thieves in the Night (Koestler), **Supp. I:** 27–28, 32–33
"Thin Air" (Armitage), **VIII:** 11
Thin Air (Thompson), **Supp. XIV:** 291
"Thing Itself, The" (Wallace-Crabbe), **VIII:** 321
"Things" (Adcock), **Supp. XII:** 6
Things as They Are; or, The Adventures of Caleb Williams (Godwin), **Supp. XV:** 121–122, 123, 124, 128
Things That Have Interested Me (Bennett), **VI:** 267
Things That Interested Me (Bennett), **VI:** 267
Things We Do for Love (Ayckbourn), **Supp. V:** 3–4, 12–13
Things Which Have Interested Me (Bennett), **VI:** 267
"Think of England" (Davies), **Supp. XIV:** 36
"Thinking as a Hobby" (Golding), **Supp. I:** 75
"Thinking of Mr. D." (Kinsella), **Supp. V:** 260
Thinking Reed, The (West), **Supp. III:** 442
"Thir Lady is Fair" (Dunbar), **VIII:** 122
Third and Fourth Booke of Ayres (Campion), **Supp. XVI:** 92, 94, 95–96, 96
Third Booke of Ayres (Campion), **Supp. XVI:** 96
"Third Eyelid, The" (Beer), **Supp. XIV:** 5
"Third Journey, The" (Graham), **Supp. VII:** 109

Third Kiss, The: A Comedy in One Act (Clarke), **Supp. XV:** 25
Third Man, The (Greene), **Supp. I:** 11; **Retro. Supp. II:** 159
"Third Person, The" (James), **VI:** 69
Third Policeman, The (O'Nolan), **Supp. II:** 322, **326–329**, 337, 338
"Third Prize, The" (Coppard), **VIII:** 96
Third Satire (Wyatt), **I:** 111
"Third Ypres" (Blunden), **Supp. XI:** 46
"Thirteen Steps and the Thirteenth of March" (Dunn), **Supp. X:** 76
Thirteen Such Years (Waugh), **Supp. VI:** 272–273
Thirteen–Gun Salute, The (O'Brian), **Supp. XII:** 258–259
Thirteenth Disciple, The (Mitchell), **Supp. XIV:** 100
Thirteenth Tribe, The (Koestler), **Supp. I:** 33
30 Days in Sydney: A Wildly Distorted Account (Carey), **Supp. XII:** 50, 52, 54, 60, 62
"30 December" (Cope), **VIII:** 80
"38 Phoenix Street" (Kinsella), **Supp. V:** 268
Thirty–Nine Steps, The (Buchan), **Supp. II:** 299, 306; **Supp. IV:** 7
31 Poems (Dutton), **Supp. XII:** 87
36 Hours (film), **Supp. IV:** 209
"Thirty–Three Triads" (Kinsella), **Supp. V:** 264
"This Be the Verse" (Larkin), **Supp. I:** 284; **Retro. Supp. III:** 209–210, 211–212
"This bread I break" (Thomas), **Supp. I:** 174
"This Day, Under My Hand" (Malouf), **Supp. XII:** 219
"This Embroidery" (Butlin), **Supp. XVI:** 55
This Life, This Life (Greig), **Supp. XVI:** 161, 162, 163
"This England" (Thomas), **Supp. III:** 404
This England: An Anthology from Her Writers (ed. Thomas), **Supp. III: 404–405**
"This evening, Delia, you and I" (Cowper), **Retro. Supp. III:** 45
This Gun for Hire (Greene), *see Gun for Sale, A*
This Happy Breed (Coward), **Supp. II:** 151, 154
"This Hinder Nicht in Dunfermeling" (Dunbar), **VIII:** 122
"This Is No Case of Petty Right or Wrong" (Thomas), **VI:** 424; **Supp. III:** 395
"This Is Thyself" (Powys), **VIII:** 247
This Is Where I Came In (Ayckbourn), **Supp. V:** 3, 11, 13
"This Is Your Subject Speaking" (Motion), **Supp. VII:** 257
"This Last Pain" (Empson), **Supp. II:** 184–185
This Life I've Loved (Field), **V:** 393, 397
"This Lime Tree Bower My Prison" (Coleridge), **IV:** 41, 44; **Retro. Supp. II:** 52
This Misery of Boots (Wells), **VI:** 244

This My Hand (Caudwell), **Supp. IX:** 33, 35, 37, 39–40, 46
This Real Night (West), **Supp. III:** 443
"This Side of the Truth" (Thomas), **Retro. Supp. III:** 344
This Sporting Life (Storey), **Supp. I:** 407, **408–410**, 414, 415, 416
"This Stone Is Thinking of Vienna" (Hart), **Supp. XI:** 130
This Sweet Sickness (Highsmith), **Supp. V:** 172–173
This Time Tomorrow (Ngũgĩ), **VIII:** 213, 222
This Was a Man (Coward), **Supp. II:** 146
"This was for youth, Strength, Mirth and wit that Time" (Walton), **II:** 141
This Was the Old Chief's Country (Lessing), **Supp. I:** 239
This Year of Grace! (Coward), **Supp. II:** 146
Thistle Rises, The (MacDiarmid), **Supp. XII:** 208
"Thistles" (Hughes), **Retro. Supp. II:** 205–206
Thistles and Roses (Smith, I. C.), **Supp. IX:** 211–212
Thom Gunn and Ted Hughes (Bold), **Supp. IV:** 256, 257
"Thom Gunn at 60" (Hall), **Supp. IV:** 256
Thomae Campiani Epigrammatum Liber Secundus (Campion), **Supp. XVI:** 92, 94, 99
Thomae Campiani Poemata (Campion), **Supp. XVI:** 90, 99
Thomas, D. M., **Supp. IV: 479–497**
Thomas, Dylan, **II:** 156; **Supp. I: 169–184**; **Supp. III:** 107; **Supp. V:** 252, 263; **Retro. Supp. III: 335–350**
Thomas, Edward, **IV:** 218; **V:** 313, 334, 355, 358; **VI:** 420–421, **423–425**; **VII:** xvi, 382; **Supp. III: 393–408**
Thomas, R. S., **Supp. XII: 279–294**
"Thomas Bewick" (Gunn), **Supp. IV:** 269
"Thomas Campey and the Copernican System" (Harrison), **Supp. V:** 151
Thomas Campion and the Art of English Poetry (Clarke), **Supp. XV:** 16
Thomas Carlyle (Campbell), **IV:** 250
Thomas Carlyle (Froude), **IV:** 238–239, 250
Thomas Cranmer of Canterbury (Williams, C. W. S.), **Supp. IX:** 284
Thomas De Quincey: A Biography (Eaton), **IV:** 142, 156
Thomas De Quincey: His Life and Writings (Page), **IV:** 152, 155
"Thomas Gray" (Arnold), **III:** 277
Thomas Hardy (Blunden), **Supp. XI:** 37
Thomas Hardy: A Bibliographical Study (Purdy), **VI:** 19
Thomas Hardy and British Poetry (Davie), **Supp. VI:** 115
Thomas Hardy: A Critical Study (Abercrombie), **Supp. XVI:** 4
Thomas Hobbes (Stephen), **V:** 289
Thomas Hood (Reid), **IV:** 267
Thomas Hood and Charles Lamb (ed. Jerrold), **IV:** 252, 253, 267

Thomas Hood: His Life and Times (Jerrold), **IV:** 267
Thomas Love Peacock (Priestley), **IV:** 159–160, 170
Thomas Nabbes (Swinburne), **V:** 333
Thomas Stevenson, Civil Engineer (Stevenson), **V:** 395
Thomas the Rhymer, **IV:** 29, 219
Thomas Traherne: Centuries, Poems, and Thanksgivings (Traherne), **Supp. XI:** 266
Thompson, E. P., **Supp. IV:** 95, 473
Thompson, Flora, **Supp. XV: 277–292**
Thompson, Francis, **III:** 338; **V:** xxii, xxvi, 439–452
Thompson, Kate, **Supp. XIV: 285–298**
Thompson, R., **II:** 288
Thomson, George, **III:** 322
Thomson, James, **III:** 162, 171, 312; **Supp. III:** 409–429; **Retro. Supp. I:** 241
Thor, with Angels (Fry), **Supp. III:** 195, 197–198
"Thorn, The" (Wordsworth), **IV:** 6, 7
Thornton, R. K. R., **V:** 377, 382
Thornton, Robert, **III:** 307
Thorsler, Jr., P. L., **IV:** 173, 194
Those Barren Leaves (Huxley), **VII:** 79, 199, 202
Those Were the Days (Milne), **Supp. V:** 298
Those Were the Days: The Holocaust through the Eyes of the Perpetrators and Bystanders, **Supp. IV:** 488
"Those White, Ancient Birds" (Hart), **Supp. XI:** 131–132
Those Who Walk Away (Highsmith), **Supp. V:** 175
"Thou art an Atheist, *Quintus,* and a Wit" (Sedley), **II:** 265–266
"Thou art fair and few are fairer" (Shelley), **IV:** 203
"Thou art indeed just, Lord" (Hopkins), **V:** 376, 378
"Thou damn'd Antipodes to Common sense" (Dorset), **II:** 263
"Thou that know'st for whom I mourne" (Vaughan), **II:** 187
"Though this the port and I thy servant true" (Wyatt), **I:** 106
"Though, Phillis, your prevailing charms," **II:** 257
"Thought" (Lawrence), **VII:** 119
"Thought Against Drought" (Pitter), **Supp. XIII:** 141
Thought Power (Besant), **VI:** 249
"Thought–Fox, The" (Hughes), **Supp. I:** 347
Thoughts (Beddoes), **Supp. XI:** 20
"Thoughts" (Traherne), **Supp. XI:** 269
"Thoughts about the Person from Porlock" (Smith), **Retro. Supp. III:** 311–312
Thoughts and Details on Scarcity . . . (Burke), **III:** 205
Thoughts for a Convention (Russell), **VIII:** 288
Thoughts in the Wilderness (Priestley), **VII:** 212

"Thoughts of a Suicide" (Tennyson), *see* "Two Voices, The"
"Thoughts of God, The" (Soutar), **Supp. XVI:** 249
Thoughts of Murdo (Smith, I. C.), **Supp. IX:** 210–211
"Thoughts of the Commandant of the Fortress of St Vaast-la-Hougue" (Constantine), **Supp. XV:** 73
"Thoughts on Criticism, by a Critic" (Stephen), **V:** 286
Thoughts on Man, His Nature, Productions, and Discoveries: Interspersed with Some Particulars Respecting the Author (Godwin), **Supp. XV:** 128
"Thoughts on Shelley and Byron" (Kingsley), **Supp. XVI:** 204
Thoughts on South Africa (Schreiner), **Supp. II:** 453, 454, 457
Thoughts on the Cause of the Present Discontents (Burke), **III:** 197
Thoughts on the Education of Daughters; . . . (Wollstonecraft), **Supp. III:** 466
Thoughts on the . . . Falkland's Islands (Johnson), **III:** 121; **Retro. Supp. I:** 142
Thoughts on the Ministerial Commission (Newman), **Supp. VII:** 291
"Thoughts on the Shape of the Human Body" (Brooke), **Supp. III:** 52–53
"Thoughts on Unpacking" (Gunn), **Supp. IV:** 262; **Retro. Supp. III:** 120
Thrale, Hester, *see* Piozzi, Hester Lynch
"Thrawn Janet" (Stevenson), **V:** 395; **Retro. Supp. I:** 267
Thre Deid Pollis, The (Henryson), **Supp. VII:** 146, 148
"Thread of Life, The" (Rossetti), **Retro. Supp. III:** 260–261
"Three Against One" (Beer), **Supp. XIV:** 7
"Three Aquarium Portraits" (Redgrove), **Supp. VI:** 234, 236
"Three Baroque Meditations" (Hill), **Supp. V:** 187, 188
Three Bear Witness (O'Brian), **Supp. XII:** 251
"Three Black Crows, The" (Byrom), **Supp. XVI:** 77
"Three Blind Mice" (Christie), **Supp. II:** 134
Three Brothers, The (Muir), **Supp. VI:** 198
Three Brothers, The (Oliphant), **Supp. X:** 217
Three Cheers for the Paraclete (Keneally), **Supp. IV:** 345
Three Chinese Poets: Translations of Poems by Wang Wei, Li Bai and Du Fu (tr. Seth), **Supp. X:** 277, 284
Three Clerks, The (Trollope), **V:** 101
Three Continents (Jhabvala), **Supp. V:** 233–234, 235
Three Dialogues (Beckett), **Retro. Supp. I:** 18–19, 22
Three Essays, Moral and Political (Hume), **Supp. III:** 239
"Three Fishers, The" (Kingsley), **Supp. XVI:** 204

"Three Folk Poems" (Plomer), **Supp. XI:** 210
Three Friends (Bridges), **VI:** 72, 83
Three Glasgow Writers (Kelman), **Supp. V:** 241
Three Go Back (Mitchell), **Supp. XIV:** 100
Three Guineas (Woolf), **VII:** 22, 25, 27, 29, 38; **Supp. IV:** 399; **Retro. Supp. I:** 308, 311
Three Histories, The (Jewsbury), **Supp. XIV:** 149, 154, 158–159
Three Hours After Marriage (Gay, Pope, and Arbuthnot), **III:** 60, 67
Three Hours after Marriage (Gay, Pope, and Arbuthnot), **Supp. XVI:** 25
3 in 1 (Reading), **VIII:** 271
Three Letters, Written in Spain, to D. Francisco Riguelme (Landor), **IV:** 100
"Three Little Pigs, The" (Dahl), **Supp. IV:** 226
"Three Lives of Lucie Cabrol, The" (Berger), **Supp. IV:** 92–93, 94
Three Memorials on French Affairs . . . (Burke), **III:** 205
Three Men in New Suits (Priestley), **VII:** 218
Three Northern Love Stories (Morris and Magnusson), **V:** 306
Three of Them (Douglas), **VI:** 300, 305
Three Old Brothers (O'Connor), **Supp. XIV:** 222
Three Perils of Man, The (Hogg), **Supp. X:** 113–114
Three Perils of Woman, The (Hogg), **Supp. X:** 113–114
Three Plays (Betti, tr. Reed), **Supp. XV:** 243, 253, 254
Three Plays (Williams, C. W. S.), **Supp. IX:** 276–277
Three Plays for Puritans (Shaw), **VI:** 104, 112, 129; **Retro. Supp. II:** 315–317
"Three Poems about Children" (Clarke), **Supp. XV:** 26
"Three Poems in Memory of My Mother, Miriam Murray neé Arnall" (Murray), **Supp. VII:** 278
"Three Poems of Drowning" (Graham), **Supp. VII:** 110
"Three Poets" (Dunn), **Supp. X:** 82–83
Three Port Elizabeth Plays (Fugard), **Supp. XV:** 107
Three proper, and witty, familiar Letters (Spenser), **I:** 123
Three Regional Voices: Iain Crichton Smith, Barry Tebb, Michael Longley (Smith, I. C.), **Supp. IX:** 213
Three Sermons (Swift), **III:** 36
Three Short Stories (Powys), **VIII:** 249, 256
Three Sisters, The (tr. Frayn), **Supp. VII:** 61
Three Sisters, The (tr. Friel), **Supp. V:** 124
"Three Songs for Monaro Pubs" (Hope), **Supp. VII:** 158
"Three Sonnets to a Coquette" (Tennyson), **Retro. Supp. III:** 322

"Three Stages of Consciousness, The" (Carpenter), **Supp. XIII:** 46
"Three Strangers, The" (Hardy), **VI:** 20, 22
Three Sunsets and Other Poems (Carroll), **V:** 274
Three Times Table (Maitland), **Supp. XI:** 163, 168–170, 174
Three Voices of Poetry, The (Eliot), **VII:** 161, 162
Three Wayfarers, The: A Pastoral Play in One Act (Hardy), **VI:** 20
"Three Weeks to Argentina" (Ewart), **Supp. VII:** 45
"Three Women's Texts and a Critique of Imperialism" (Spivak), **Retro. Supp. I:** 60
"Three Words" (Reed), **Supp. XV:** 255
Three Years in a Curatorship (Carroll), **V:** 274
Threnodia Augustalis (Goldsmith), **III:** 191
Threnodia Augustalis: A Funeral . . . Poem to . . . King Charles II (Dryden), **II:** 304; **Retro. Supp. III:** 56
"Threshold" (Thomas), **Supp. XII:** 288
Thrice a Stranger (Brittain), **Supp. X:** 44
Thrilling Cities (Fleming), **Supp. XIV:** 96
"Thrissil and the Rois, The" (Dunbar), **VIII:** 118
Thrissill and the Rois, The (Dunbar), **VIII:** 121
"Through the Looking Glass" (Auden), **VII:** 381
Through the Looking-Glass and What Alice Found There (Carroll), **V:** xxiii, 261, 262, 264, 265, 267–269, 270–273
Through the Panama (Lowry), **Supp. III:** 269, 280, 282, 283
"Through These Pale Gold Days" (Rosenberg), **VI:** 435
"Thrown Away" (Kipling), **Retro. Supp. III:** 185
Thru (Brooke-Rose)), **Supp. IV:** 98, 99, 105, 109–110, 112
"Thrush in February, The" (Meredith), **V:** 222
"Thrushes" (Hughes), **Supp. I:** 345
"Thrust & Parry" (Delanty), **Supp. XIV:** 66
"Thunder and a Boy" (Jennings), **Supp. V:** 218
Thunder in the Air (Conn), **Supp. XIII:** 71
Thunderball (Fleming), **Supp. XIV:** 91, 96
Thunderbolt's Waxwork (Pullman), **Supp. XIII:** 152
Thurley, Geoffrey, **Supp. II:** 494
"Thursday; or, The Spell" (Gay), **III:** 56
Thursday's Child: A Pageant (Fry), **Supp. III:** 194
Thus to Revisit (Ford), **VI:** 321, 323
"Thy Beautiful Flock" (Powys), **VIII:** 254
Thyestes (Seneca), **I:** 215; **II:** 71
"Thyrsis" (Arnold), **V:** 157–158, 159, 165, 209, 210, 211; **VI:** 73
Thyrza (Gissing), **V:** 437

"Tiare Tahiti" (Brooke), **Supp. III:** 56
"Tibby Hyslop's Dream" (Hogg), **Supp. X:** 110
Tib's Eve (Carson), **Supp. XIII:** 65
"Tich Miller" (Cope), **VIII:** 73
Tickell, Thomas, **III:** 50
Ticonderoga (Stevenson), **V:** 395
Tide and Stone Walls (Sillitoe), **Supp. V:** 424
"Tidings from the Sissioun" (Dunbar), **VIII:** 126
"Tie" (Delanty), **Supp. XIV:** 66
"Tierra del Fuego" (Caudwell), **Supp. IX:** 38
Tietjens tetralogy (Ford), **VI:** xii, 319, **328–331; VII:** xxi; *see also Last Post; Man Could Stand Up, A; No More Parades; Some Do Not*
"Tiger, The" (Coppard), **VIII:** 94, 97
Tiger at the Gates (Fry), **Supp. III:** 195
Tiger in the Well, The (Pullman), **Supp. XIII:** 151
"Time of Barmecides, The" (Mangan), **Supp. XIII:** 125
"Tiger! Tiger!" (Kipling), **VI:** 199; **Retro. Supp. III:** 190–191, 192
Tigers (Adcock), **Supp. XII:** 4–5
Tigers Are Better-Looking (Rhys), **Supp. II:** 389, 390, 401, 402
Tiger's Bones, The (Hughes), **Supp. I:** 346–347
"Till September Petronella" (Rhys), **Supp. II:** 401–402
Till We Have Faces (Lewis), **Supp. III:** 248, **262–264,** 265
Tillotson, Kathleen, **IV:** 34; **V:** 73
Tilting Room, The (Butlin), **Supp. XVI:** 52, 58–59, 65, 66, 67, 68
"Tilting Room, The" (Butlin), **Supp. XVI:** 59–60, 62
Timber (Jonson), **Retro. Supp. I:** 166
Timbuctoo (Tennyson), **IV:** 338
"Timbuctoo" (Tennyson), **Retro. Supp. III:** 319, 321
"Time" (Dutton), **Supp. XII:** 97
Time and the Conways (Priestley), **VII:** 212, 224–225
Time and Tide (O'Brien), **Supp. V:** 341
Time and Tide by Weare and Tyne (Ruskin), **V:** 184
Time and Time Again (Ayckbourn), **Supp. V:** 2, 4–5, 9, 10, 13–14
Time and Western Man (Lewis), **VII:** 72, 74, 75, 83, 262
"Time Disease, The" (Amis), **Supp. IV:** 40
Time Flies: A Reading Diary (Rossetti), **V:** 260; **Retro. Supp. III:** 251, 257, 263–264
Time for a Tiger (Burgess), **Supp. I:** 187
Time Importuned (Warner), **Supp. VII:** 370, 371–372
Time in a Red Coat (Brown), **Supp. VI:** 66, 69–70
Time in Rome, A (Bowen), **Supp. II:** 80, 94
Time Machine, The: An Invention (Wells), **VI:** ix, xii, 226, 229–230
Time Must Have a Stop (Huxley), **VII:** 205

Time of Hope (Snow), **VII:** xxi, 321, 324–325
Time of the Crack, The (Tennant), **Supp. IX:** 229–230
Time of My Life (Ayckbourn), **Supp. V:** 3, 8, 10, 11, 13, 14
"Time of Plague, The" (Gunn), **Supp. IV:** 277
Time of the Angels, The (Murdoch), **III:** 341, 345; **Supp. I:** 225–226, 227, 228
"Time of the Roses" (Mangan), **Supp. XIII:** 124–125
"Time of Waiting, A" (Graves), **VII:** 269
Time Present (Osborne), **Supp. I:** 338
"Time the Tiger" (Lewis), **VII:** 74
Time to Dance, A (Day Lewis), **Supp. III:** 118, 126
Time to Go, A (O'Casey), **VII:** 12
Time to Keep, A (Brown), **Supp. VI:** 64, 70
Time Traveller, The: The Life of H. G. Wells (MacKenzie and MacKenzie), **VI:** 228, 246
"Timehri" (Brathwaite), **Supp. XII:** 34, 46
"Timekeeping" (Cope), **VIII:** 81
"Timer" (Harrison), **Supp. V:** 150
Time's Arrow; or The Nature of the Offence (Amis), **Supp. IV:** 40–42
"Time's Fool" (Pitter), **Supp. XIII:** 142
Time's Laughingstocks and other Verses (Hardy), **VI:** 20
Times (periodical), **IV:** xv, 272, 278; **V:** 93, 279; **Supp. XII:** 2
Times Literary Supplement, **Supp. IV:** 25, 66, 121
Time's Pocket (O'Connor), **Supp. XIV:** 223
"Time-Tombs, The" (Ballard), **Supp. V:** 21
Time-Zones (Adcock), **Supp. XII:** 10–11, 11–12
"Timing" (Kay), **Supp. XIII:** 109
Timon of Athens (Shakespeare), **I:** 318–319, 321; **II:** 70
Tin Drum, The (Grass), **Supp. IV:** 440
Tin Men, The (Frayn), **Supp. VII:** 51–52, 64
Tin Princess, The (Pullman), **Supp. XIII:** 151–152
Tinker, C. B., **III:** 234n, 249, 250
"Tinker, The" (Wordsworth), **IV:** 21
Tinker, Tailor, Soldier, Spy (le Carré), **Supp. II:** 306, **311–313,** 314; **Retro. Supp. III:** 216, 219–220, 221
Tinker's Wedding, The (Synge), **VI:** 311, 313–314; **Retro. Supp. I:** 296–297
"Tintagel" (Reed), **Supp. XV:** 249
"Tintern Abbey" (Wordsworth), *see* "Lines Composed a Few Miles Above Tintern Abbey"
Tiny Tears (Fuller), **Supp. VII:** 78
Tip of my Tongue, The (Crawford), **Supp. XI:** 67, 79–82
"Tipperary" (Thomas), **Supp. III:** 404
"Tirade for the Mimic Muse" (Boland), **Supp. V:** 49
Tireless Traveller, The (Trollope), **V:** 102
"Tiresias" (Tennyson), **IV:** 328, 332–334, 338; **Retro. Supp. III:** 327

Tiresias: A Poem (Clarke), **Supp. XV:** 29
Tiresias and Other Poems (Tennyson), **Retro. Supp. III:** 327
"Tiriel" (Blake), **III:** 298, 302; **Retro. Supp. I:** 34–35
"Tirocinium; or, A Review of Schools" (Cowper), **III:** 208; **Retro. Supp. III:** 38
'Tis Pity She's a Whore (Ford), **II:** 57, 88, 89, 90, 92–93, 99, 100
Tit-Bits (periodical), **VI:** 135, 248
"Tithe Barn, The" (Powys), **VIII:** 248, 249
Tithe Barn, The and The Dove and the Eage (Powys), **VIII:** 248
"Tithon" (Tennyson), **IV:** 332–334; *see also* "Tithonus"
"Tithonus" (Tennyson), **IV:** 328, 333
Title, The (Bennett), **VI:** 250, 264
Title and Pedigree of Henry VI (Lydgate), **I:** 58
Titmarsh, Michael Angelo, pseud. of William Makepeace Thackeray
Titus Andronicus (Shakespeare), **I:** 279, 305; **II:** 69; **Retro. Supp. III:** 270, 273, 279, 280
"Titus Hoyt, I A" (Naipaul), **Supp. I:** 385
"To a Black Greyhound" (Grenfell), **VI:** 418
"To a Brother in the Mystery" (Davie), **Supp. VI:** 113–114
"To a Butterfly" (Wordsworth), **IV:** 21
"To a Cretan Monk in Thanks for a Flask of Wine" (Murphy), **Supp. V:** 318
"To a Cold Beauty" (Hood), **IV:** 255
"To a Comrade in Flanders" (Owen), **VI:** 452
"To a Devout Young Gentlewoman" (Sedley), **II:** 264
"To a Dictionary Maker" (Nye), **Supp. X:** 201
"To a False Friend. In Imitation of Sappho" (Robinson), **Supp. XIII:** 204–205
"To a Fat Lady Seen from the Train" (Cornford), **VIII:** 102
"To a *Fine Singer,* who had gotten a *Cold;* . . . " (Wycherley), **II:** 320
"To a Fine Young *Woman* . . . " (Wycherley), **II:** 320
"To a Friend in Time of Trouble" (Gunn), **Supp. IV:** 274, 275
"To a Friend mourning the Death of Miss—" (Macpherson), **VIII:** 181
"To A. L." (Carew), **II:** 224–225
"To a Lady in a Letter" (Rochester), **II:** 258
To a Lady More Cruel Than Fair (Vanbrugh), **II:** 336
"To a Lady on Her Passion for Old China" (Gay), **III:** 58, 67
"To a Lady on the Death of Colonel Ross . . . " (Collins), **III:** 166, 169
"To a Louse" (Burns), **III:** 315, 317–318
"To a Mountain Daisy" (Burns), **III:** 313, 315, 317, 318
"To a Mouse" (Burns), **III:** 315, 317, 318
"To a Nightingale" (Coleridge), **IV:** 222
"To a Skylark" (Shelley), **III:** 337

"To a Snail" (Moore), **Supp. IV:** 262–263

"To a Very Young Lady" (Etherege), **II:** 267

"To Alastair Campbell" (Adcock), **Supp. XII:** 4

"To Althea from Prison" (Lovelace), **II:** 231, 232

"To Amarantha, That She Would Dishevell Her Haire" (Lovelace), **II:** 230

"To Amoret Gone from Him" (Vaughan), **II:** 185

"To Amoret, of the Difference 'twixt Him, . . . " (Vaughan), **II:** 185

"To an English Friend in Africa" (Okri), **Supp. V:** 359

"To an Infant Daughter" (Clare), **Supp. XI:** 55

"To an Old Lady" (Empson), **Supp. II:** 182–183

"To an Unborn Pauper Child" (Hardy), **Retro. Supp. I:** 121

"To an Unknown Reader" (Fuller), **Supp. VII:** 78

"To and Fro" (McEwan), **Supp. IV:** 395

"To Anthea" (Herrick), **II:** 105–106, 108

"To Any Dead Officer" (Sassoon), **VI:** 431

To Asmara (Keneally), **Supp. IV:** 346

"To Augustus" (Pope), **Retro. Supp. I:** 230–231

"To Autumn" (Keats), **IV:** 221, 226–227, 228, 232

To Be a Pilgrim (Cary), **VII:** 186, 187, 191, 192–194

"To Be a Poet" (Stevenson), **Supp. VI:** 260

"To Be Less Philosophical" (Graves), **VII:** 266

"To Blossoms" (Herrick), **II:** 112

"To Call Paula Paul" (McGuckian), **Supp. V:** 286

"To Carry the Child" (Smith), **Retro. Supp. III:** 313

To Catch a Spy (Ambler), **Supp. IV:** 4, 17

"To cause accord or to agree" (Wyatt), **I:** 109

"To Celia" (Johnson), **IV:** 327

"To Cesario" (Robinson), **Supp. XIII:** 206

"To Charles Cowden Clarke" (Keats), **IV:** 214, 215

"To Certain English Poets" (Davie), **Supp. VI:** 110

"To Charles Cowden Clarke" (Keats), **Retro. Supp. I:** 188

"To Christopher North" (Tennyson), **Retro. Supp. III:** 320

To Circumjack Cencrastus; or, The Curly Snake (MacDiarmid), **Supp. XII:** 201, 210–211, 216

"To Constantia Singing" (Shelley), **IV:** 209

"To Daffodills" (Herrick), **II:** 112

"To Deanbourn" (Herrick), **II:** 103

"To Dianeme" (Herrick), **II:** 107, 112

"To E. Fitzgerald" (Tennyson), **IV:** 336

"To Edward Thomas" (Lewis), **VII:** 445

"To E. L., on his Travels in Greece" (Tennyson), **V:** 79

"To Electra" (Herrick), **II:** 105

"To Everlasting Oblivion" (Marston), **II:** 25

"To Fanny" (Keats), **IV:** 220–221

"To George Felton Mathew" (Keats), **IV:** 214

"To Germany" (Sorley), **VI:** 421

"To God" (Gurney), **VI:** 426

"To Helen" (Thomas), **Supp. III:** 401

"To Henry Wright, of Mobberley, Esq." (Byrom), **Supp. XVI:** 73

"To Him Who Said No to the Glare of the Open Day" (Aidoo), **Supp. XV:** 11

"To His Coy Mistress" (Marvell), **II:** 197, 198, 208–209, 211, 214–215; **Retro. Supp. II:** 259–261

"To his inconstant Friend" (King), **Supp. VI:** 151

"To His Lost Lover" (Armitage), **VIII:** 8

"To His Love" (Gurney), **VI:** 426

"To His Lovely Mistresses" (Herrick), **II:** 113

To His Sacred Majesty, a Panegyrick on His Coronation (Dryden), **II:** 304; **Retro. Supp. III:** 61

"To His Sweet Savior" (Herrick), **II:** 114

"To His Wife" (Hill), **Supp. V:** 189

"To Hope" (Keats), **Retro. Supp. I:** 188

"To Ireland in the Coming Times" (Yeats), **Retro. Supp. I:** 330

"To J. F. H. (1897–1934)" (Muir), **Supp. VI:** 206

"To Joan Eardley" (Morgan, E.), **Supp. IX:** 165

"To Julia, The Flaminica Dialis, or Queen–

To Keep the Ball Rolling (Powell), **VII:** 351

"To King Henry IV, in Praise of Peace" (Gower), **I:** 56

"To Leonard Clark" (Graham), **Supp. VII:** 116

To Let (Galsworthy), **VI:** 272, 274, 275, 282

To Lighten My House (Reid), **Supp. VII:** 325–327

"To Live Merrily, and to Trust to Good Verses" (Herrick), **II:** 115

To Live with Little (Chapman), **I:** 254

"To Lizbie Browne" (Hardy), **VI:** 16

"To Lord Stanhope" (Coleridge), **IV:** 43

"To Louisa in the Lane" (Thomas), **Supp. IV:** 493

"To Lucasta, Going to the Warres" (Lovelace), **II:** 229

"To Margot Heinemann" (Cornford), **Supp. XIII:** 91–92

"To Marguerite—Continued" (Arnold), **V:** 211

To Marry, or Not to Marry (Inchbald), **Supp. XV:** 147, 155, 160, 161

"To Mary" (Cowper), **Retro. Supp. III:** 46

"To Mary Boyle" (Tennyson), **IV:** 329, 336

"To Mr. Dryden" (Congreve), **II:** 338

To Mr. Harriot (Chapman), **I:** 241

"To Mr. Hobs" (Cowley), **II:** 196, 198

To Mistress Anne (Skelton), **I:** 83

"To My Brother George" (Keats), **IV:** 214

"To My Brothers" (Keats), **IV:** 215

"To My Daughter in a Red Coat" (Stevenson), **Supp. VI:** 254

"To my dead friend Ben: Johnson" (King), **Supp. VI:** 157

"To My Desk" (Dunn), **Supp. X:** 80

"To My Father" (Conn), **Supp. XIII:** 73

To My Fellow Countrymen (Osborne), **Supp. I:** 330

"To My Friend, Mr. Pope, . . . " (Wycherley), **II:** 322

"To My Inconstant Mistris" (Carew), **II:** 225

To My Lady Morton (Waller), **II:** 238

To My Lord Chancellor . . . (Dryden), **II:** 304; **Retro. Supp. III:** 61

"To My Lord Northumberland Upon the Death of His Lady" (Waller), **II:** 233

"To My Mother Eileen" (Delanty), **Supp. XIV:** 72, 75

To My Mother on the Anniversary of Her Birth, April 27, 1842 (Rossetti), **V:** 260

"To My Sister" (Wordsworth), **IV:** 8

"To My Wife" (Larkin), **Retro. Supp. III:** 203

"To Night" (Lovelace), **II:** 231

"To Nobodaddy" (Blake), **III:** 299

"To Olga Masson" (tr. Thomas), **Supp. IV:** 495

"To One Who Wanted a Philosophy from Me" (Russell), **VIII:** 290

"To One Who Was with Me in the War" (Sassoon), **VI:** 431

"To Penshurst" (Jonson), **Retro. Supp. I:** 164

"To Perilla" (Herrick), **II:** 113

"To P. H. T" (Thomas), **Supp. III:** 401

"To Please His Wife" (Hardy), **VI:** 20, 22

"To Poet Bavius" (Behn), **Supp. III:** 40

"To Pontilianus" (Campion), **Supp. XVI:** 100

To Present the Pretense (Arden), **Supp. II:** 30

"To President Mary Robinson" (Delanty), **Supp. XIV:** 68

"To R. B." (Hopkins), **V:** 376, 378

"To Rilke" (Lewis), **VII:** 446

"To Room Nineteen" (Lessing), **Supp. I:** 248

"To Rosa" (Tennyson), **Retro. Supp. III:** 322

"To Saxham" (Carew), **III:** 223

To Scorch or Freeze (Davie), **Supp. VI:** 113–115

"To seek each where, where man doth live" (Wyatt), **I:** 110

"To seem the stranger lies my lot" (Hopkins), **V:** 374–375

"To Sir Henry Cary" (Jonson), **Retro. Supp. I:** 154

To Sir With Love (Braithwaite), **Supp. IV:** 445

"To Sleep" (Graves), **VII:** 267

"To Sleep" (Keats), **IV:** 221

"To Solitude" (Keats), **IV:** 213–214

"To Stella, Visiting Me in My Sickness" (Swift), **III:** 31
"To Stella, Who Collected and Transcribed His Poems" (Swift), **III:** 31
"To Stella . . . Written on the Day of Her Birth . . ." (Swift), **III:** 32
To the Air, **Supp. IV:** 269
"To the Athenian Society" (Defoe), **Retro. Supp. I:** 67
"To the Author of a Poem, intitled, Successio" (Pope), **Retro. Supp. I:** 233
"To the Coffee Shop" (Kinsella), **Supp. V:** 274
"To the Evening Star" (Blake), **Retro. Supp. I:** 34
"To the fair Clarinda, who made Love to Me, imagin'd more than Woman" (Behn), **Supp. III:** 8; **Retro. Supp. III:** 8–9
"To the Future" (Soutar), **Supp. XVI:** 254–255
"To the High Court of Parliament" (Hill), **Supp. V:** 192, 193; **Retro. Supp. III:** 138–139
"To the immortal memory of the Halybutt" (Cowper), **Retro. Supp. III:** 47
"To the King" (Waller), **II:** 233
"To the King: Complane I Wald" (Dunbar), **VIII:** 117
To the King, upon His . . . Happy Return (Waller), **II:** 238
To the Lighthouse (Woolf), **V:** 281; **VI:** 275, 278; **VII:** xv, 18, 21, 26, 27, 28–29, 36, 38; **Supp. IV:** 231, 246, 321; **Supp. V:** 63; **Retro. Supp. I:** 308, 317–318
"To the Master of Balliol" (Tennyson), **IV:** 336
To the Memory of Charles Lamb (Wordsworth), **IV:** 86
"To the Memory of Mr. Oldham" (Dryden), **Retro. Supp. III:** 56–59
"To the Memory of My Beloved, the Author Mr William Shakespeare" (Jonson), **Retro. Supp. I:** 165
"To the Memorie of My Ever Desired Friend Dr. Donne" (King), **Supp. VI:** 156
"To the Merchants of Edinburgh" (Dunbar), **VIII:** 126
"To the Monument of Sha Jahan" (Delahunt), **Supp. XIV:** 59
"To the Muses" (Blake), **III:** 289; **Retro. Supp. I:** 34
"To the Name of Jesus" (Crashaw), **II:** 180
"To the Nightingal" (Finch), **Supp. IX:** 68–69
"To the Nightingale" (McGuckian), **Supp. V:** 283
To the North (Bowen), **Supp. II:** 85, 88–89
"To the Pen Shop" (Kinsella), **Supp. V:** 274
"To the Poet Coleridge" (Robinson), **Supp. XIII:** 210
"To the Queen" (Tennyson), **IV:** 337
To the Queen, upon Her . . . Birthday (Waller), **II:** 238

"To the Reader" (Jonson), **Retro. Supp. I:** 165
"To the Reader" (Webster), **I:** 246
"To the Reverend Shade of His Religious Father" (Herrick), **II:** 113
"To the Rev. W. H. Brookfield" (Tennyson), **IV:** 329
To the Right Honourable the Mayor and Aldermen of the City of London: The Humble Petition of the Colliers, Cooks, Cook-Maids, Blacksmiths, Jackmakers, Braziers, and Others (Arbuthnot), **Supp. XVI:** 25
"To the Riviera" (Wain), **Supp. XVI:** 294
"To the Royal Society" (Cowley), **II:** 196, 198
"To the Sea" (Larkin), **Supp. I:** 283, 285; **Retro. Supp. III:** 208–209
"To the Shade of Elliston" (Lamb), **IV:** 82–83
"To the Slow Drum" (Ewart), **Supp. VII:** 42
"To the Small Celandine" (Wordsworth), **IV:** 21
"To the Spirit" (Hart), **Supp. XI:** 127
"To the (Supposed) Patron" (Hill), **Supp. V:** 184
"To the Virgins, to Make Much of Time" (Herrick), **II:** 108–109
To the Wedding (Berger), **Supp. IV:** 80
To This Hard House (Friel), **Supp. V:** 115
"To Thom Gunn in Los Altos, California" (Davie), **Supp. VI:** 112
"To Three Irish Poets" (Longley), **VIII:** 167–168
"To True Soldiers" (Jonson), **Retro. Supp. I:** 154
"To Vandyk" (Waller), **II:** 233
"To Virgil" (Tennyson), **IV:** 327
"To wet your eye withouten tear" (Wyatt), **I:** 105–106
"To what serves Mortal Beauty?" (Hopkins), **V:** 372, 373
"To Whom It May Concern" (Motion), **Supp. VII:** 264
To Whom She Will (Jhabvala), **Supp. V:** 224–226
"To William Camden" (Jonson), **Retro. Supp. I:** 152
"To William Godwin" (Coleridge), **IV:** 43
"To X" (Fuller), **Supp. VII:** 74
"To Yvor Winters, 1955" (Gunn), **Supp. IV:** 261; **Retro. Supp. III:** 120
"Toads" (Larkin), **Supp. I:** 277, 278, 281
"Toads Revisited" (Larkin), **Supp. I:** 281
"Toccata of Galuppi's, A" (Browning), **IV:** 357; **Retro. Supp. III:** 25
To–Day (periodical), **VI:** 103
"Today is Sunday" (Davies), **Supp. XIV:** 36, 45
Todhunter, John, **V:** 325
"Todd" (Conn), **Supp. XIII:** 71
Todorov, Tzvetan, **Supp. IV:** 115–116
"Toft Cup, The" (Thompson), **Supp. XV:** 285
Together (Douglas), **VI:** 299–300, 304, 305
Toil & Spin: Two Directions in Modern Poetry (Wallace–Crabbe), **VIII:** 319, 325

Tolkien, J. R. R., **Supp. II: 519–535; Supp. IV:** 116
"Tollund Man, The" (Heaney), **Supp. II:** 273, 274; **Retro. Supp. I:** 128
Tolstoy (Wilson), **Supp. VI:** 304
Tolstoy, Leo, **Supp. IV:** 94, 139
"Tom Brown Question, The" (Wodehouse), **Supp. III:** 449
Tom Brown's Schooldays (Hughes), **V:** xxii, 157, 170; **Supp. IV:** 506
Tom Jones (Fielding), **III:** 95, 96–97, 100–102, 105; **Supp. II:** 194, 195; **Retro. Supp. I:** 81, 86–89, 90–91; **Retro. Supp. I:** 81, 86–89, 90–91
Tom O'Bedlam's Beauties (Reading), **VIII:** 264–265
"Tom the Porter" (Byrom), **Supp. XVI:** 81
Tom Thumb (Fielding), **III:** 96, 105
"Tom–Dobbin" (Gunn), **Supp. IV:** 267; **Retro. Supp. III:** 122
Tomlin, Eric Walter Frederick, **VII:** xv, xxxviii
"Tomlinson" (Kipling), **VI:** 202
"Tomorrow" (Conrad), **VI:** 148
"Tomorrow" (Harris), **Supp. V:** 131
"Tomorrow Is a Million Years" (Ballard), **Supp. V:** 26
Tomorrow Morning, Faustus! (Richards), **Supp. II:** 427–428
Tomorrow Never Dies (Fleming), **Supp. XIV:** 95
"Tom's Garland" (Hopkins), **V:** 376
"Tone of Time, The" (James), **VI:** 69
"Tongue in My Ear: On Writing and Not Writing *Foreign Parts*" (Galloway), **Supp. XII:** 123–124
"Tongues of Fire" (Wallace–Crabbe), **VIII:** 325
Tonight at 8:30 (Coward), **Supp. II:** 152–153
Tono–Bungay (Wells), **VI:** xii, 237–238, 244
Tonson, Jacob, **II:** 323; **III:** 69
"Tony Kytes, The Arch–Deceiver" (Hardy), **VI:** 22
"Tony White's Cottage" (Murphy), **Supp. V:** 328
"Too Dearly Bought" (Gissing), **V:** 437
Too Good to Be True (Shaw), **VI:** 125, 127, 129
Too Great a Vine: Poems and Satires, Second Series (Clarke), **Supp. XV:** 26
"Too Late" (Browning), **V:** 366, 369; **Retro. Supp. III:** 26
Too Late the Phalarope (Paton), **Supp. II:** 341, 351–353
Too Many Husbands (Maugham), **VI:** 368–369
"Too Much" (Muir), **Supp. VI:** 207
"Toot Baldon" (Motion), **Supp. VII:** 253
Tooth and Nail (Rankin), see *Wolfman*
Top Girls (Churchill), **Supp. IV:** 179, 183, 189–191, 198
Topkapi (film), **Supp. IV:** 4
"Torridge" (Trevor), **Supp. IV:** 501
"Tortoise and the Hare, The" (Dahl), **Supp. IV:** 226
Tortoises (Lawrence), **VII:** 118

Tortoises, Terrapins and Turtles (Sowerby and Lear), **V:** 76, 87
"Torturer's Apprenticeship, The" (Murray), **Supp. VII:** 280
"Tory Prime Minister, Maggie May . . . , A" (Rushdie), **Supp. IV:** 456
Totemism (Frazer), **Supp. III:** 171
"Totentanz" (Wilson), **Supp. I:** 155, 156, 157
Tottel's Miscellany, **I:** 97–98, 114
Touch (Gunn), **Supp. IV:** 257, 264, 265–266; **Retro. Supp. III:** 120, 121
"Touch" (Gunn), **Supp. IV:** 265–266
Touch and Go (Lawrence), **VII:** 120, 121
Touch of Love, A (Coe), **Supp. XV:** 50, 52, 53–54, 58, 60, 63
Touch of Love, A (screenplay, Drabble), **Supp. IV:** 230
Touch of Mistletoe, A (Comyns), **VIII:** 54–55, 56, 58–59, 65
Tour Thro' the Whole Island of Great Britain (Defoe), **III:** 5, 13; **Retro. Supp. I:** 75–76
Tour to the Hebrides, A (Boswell), see *Journal of a Tour to the Hebrides*
Tourneur, Cyril, **II:** 24, 33, **36–41**, 70, 72, 85, 97
Toward Reality (Berger), see *Permanent Red: Essays in Seeing*
"Toward the Imminent Days" (Murray), **Supp. VII:** 274
"Towards an Artless Society" (Lewis), **VII:** 76
Towards Democracy (Carpenter), **Supp. XIII:** 36, 37–40
"Towards Democracy" (Carpenter), **Supp. XIII:** 37–38
Towards the End of Morning (Frayn), **Supp. VII:** 53–54, 65
Towards the Human (Smith, I. C.), **Supp. IX:** 209
Towards the Mountain (Paton), **Supp. II:** 346, 347, 351, 359
Towards Zero (Christie), **Supp. II:** 132, 134
Tower, The (Fry), **Supp. III:** 194, 195
Tower, The (Yeats), **VI:** 207, 216, 220; **Retro. Supp. I:** 333–335
Towers of Silence, The (Scott), **Supp. I:** 267–268
Town (periodical), **V:** 22
"Town and Country" (Brooke), **VI:** 420
Town Before You, The (Cowley), **Supp. XVI:** 115, 123
"Town Betrayed, The" (Muir), **Supp. VI:** 206
"Town Itself, The" (Reed), **Supp. XV:** 255
Townley plays, **I:** 20
Townsend, Aurelian, **II:** 222, 237
Townsend Warner, George, **VI:** 485
Township Plays (Fugard), **Supp. XV:** 105
Town-Talk (periodical), **III:** 50, 53
"Trace Elements" (Wallace-Crabbe), **VIII:** 323
"Track 12" (Ballard), **Supp. V:** 21
Trackers of Oxyrhyncus, The (Harrison), **Supp. V:** 163, 164
Tract 90 (Newman), see *Remarks on Certain Passages of the 39 Articles*

"Tractor" (Hughes), **Retro. Supp. II:** 211
Tracts for the Times (Newman), **Supp. VII:** 291, 293
"Traction–Engine, The" (Auden), **Retro. Supp. I:** 3
"Trade" (Carpenter), **Supp. XIII:** 40
"Tradition and the Individual Talent" (Eliot), **VII:** 155, 156, 163, 164
"Tradition of Eighteen Hundred and Four, A" (Hardy), **VI:** 22
Tradition of Women's Fiction, The (Drabble), **Supp. IV:** 231
Tradition, the Writer and Society (Harris), **Supp. V:** 145, 146
"Traditional Prize Country Pigs" (Cope), **VIII:** 82–83
"Traditions, Voyages" (Wallace-Crabbe), **VIII:** 318
Traffics and Discoveries (Kipling), **VI:** 204; **Retro. Supp. III:** 194
"Tragedy and the Essay, The" (Brontë), **V:** 135
"Tragedy Of, The" (Scupham), **Supp. XIII:** 220–221, 223
Tragedy of Brennoralt, The (Suckling), **II:** 226
Tragedy of Byron, The (Chapman), **I:** 233, 234, 241n, 251
Tragedy of Count Alarcos, The (Disraeli), **IV:** 306, 308
Tragedy of Doctor Faustus, The (Marlowe), **Retro. Supp. I:** 200, 207–208
"Tragedy of Error, A" (James), **VI:** 25
Tragedy of Sir John Van Olden Barnavelt, The (Fletcher and Massinger), **II:** 66
Tragedy of Sophonisba, The (Thomson), **Supp. III:** 411, 422, 423, 424
Tragedy of the Duchess of Malfi, The (Webster), see *Duchess of Malfi, The*
Tragedy of Tragedies; or, The Life . . . of Tom Thumb, The (Fielding), see *Tom Thumb*
"Tragedy of Two Ambitions, A" (Hardy), **VI:** 22
Tragic Comedians, The (Meredith), **V:** 228, 234
Tragic History of Romeus and Juliet, The (Brooke), **I:** 305–306
Tragic Muse, The (James), **VI:** 39, **43–55**, 67
"Tragic Theatre, The" (Yeats), **VI:** 218
Tragical History of Doctor Faustus, The (Hope), **Supp. VII:** 160–161
Tragical History of Dr. Faustus, The (Marlowe), **III:** 344
Traherne, Thomas, **II:** 123, **189–194, 201–203**; **Supp. XI:** 263–280
Trail of the Dinosaur, The (Koestler), **Supp. I:** 32, 33, 36, 37
Traill, H. D., **III:** 80
Train of Powder, A (West), **Supp. III:** 439–440
Trained for Genius (Goldring), **VI:** 333
Traité du poeme épique (Le Bossu), **III:** 103
Traitor's Blood (Hill, R.), **Supp. IX:** 117
"Trampwoman's Tragedy, The" (Hardy), **VI:** 15; **Retro. Supp. I:** 120

Transatlantic Review (periodical), **VI:** 324; **Supp. XIII:** 190
Transatlantic Sketches (James), **VI:** 67
"Transfiguration, The" (Muir), **Supp. VI:** 207
"Transformation" (Carpenter), **Supp. XIII:** 47
"Transformation Scenes" (Scupham), **Supp. XIII:** 222
Transformed Metamorphosis, The (Tourneur), **II:** 37, 41
"Transients and Residents" (Gunn), **Supp. IV:** 271, 273; **Retro. Supp. III:** 125
transition (quarterly periodical), **Supp. I:** 43n
Transitional Poem (Day Lewis), **Supp. III:** 117, 121–123
"Translation of Poetry, The" (Morgan, E.), **Supp. IX:** 168–169
Translations (Friel), **Supp. V:** 123–124
Translations and Tomfooleries (Shaw), **VI:** 129
"Translations from the Early Irish" (Kinsella), **Supp. V:** 264
Translations of the Natural World (Murray), **Supp. VII:** 281–282
Transmission (Kunzru), **Supp. XIV:** 165, 170–172, 175, 176
"Transparencies" (Stevenson), **Supp. VI:** 262
"Transvaal Morning, A" (Plomer), **Supp. XI:** 214
Trap, The (Richardson), **Supp. XIII:** 184–186
Traps (Churchill), **Supp. IV:** 179, 180, 183–184, 188, 198
Traulus (Swift), **III:** 36
Travelers (Jhabvala), **Supp. V:** 230
"Traveling to My Second Marriage on the Day of the First Moonshot" (Nye), **Supp. X:** 202
"Traveller" (Kinsella), **Supp. V:** 263
Traveller, The (Goldsmith), **III:** 177, 179, 180, 185–186, 191; **Retro. Supp. I:** 149
"Traveller, The" (Stevenson), **Supp. VI:** 254, 265
"Travelling" (Healy), **Supp. IX:** 106
Travelling Behind Glass (Stevenson), **Supp. VI:** 256–257
"Travelling Behind Glass" (Stevenson), **Supp. VI:** 257, 261
"Travelling Companion, The" (Kinsella), **Supp. V:** 261
"Travelling Companions" (James), **VI:** 25, 69
Travelling Grave, The (Hartley), see *Killing Bottle, The*
Travelling Home (Cornford), **VIII:** 109, 111, 112
"Travelling Letters" (Dickens), **V:** 71
Travelling Sketches (Trollope), **V:** 101
Travels (Morris, J.), **Supp. X:** 172, 183
Travels in Arabia Deserta (Doughty), **Supp. II:** 294–295
Travels in Italy (Addison), **III:** 18
Travels in Nihilon (Sillitoe), **Supp. V:** 410
Travels Through France and Italy (Smollett), **III:** 147, **153–155**, 158

Travels with a Donkey in the Cevennes (Stevenson), **V:** 389, 395; **Retro. Supp. I:** 262
Travels with My Aunt (Greene), **Supp. I:** 2, 13, 16; **Retro. Supp. II:** 161
Travesties (Stoppard), **Supp. I:** 438, 445, 446, **447–449**, 451; **Retro. Supp. II:** 349–351
Trawler: A Journey Through the North Atlantic (O'Hanlon), **Supp. XI:** 196, 206–207
"A Treading of Grapes" (Brown), **Supp. VI:** 70
Treason's Harbour (O'Brian), **Supp. XII:** 256
Treasure Island (Stevenson), **V:** xxv, 383, 385, 386, 394, 395; **Retro. Supp. I:** 263
"Treasure of Franchard, The" (Stevenson), **V:** 395
"Treasure, The" (Brooke), **Supp. III:** 57, 58
"Treatise for Laundresses" (Lydgate), **I:** 58
Treatise of Civil Power in Ecclesiastical Causes . . . , The (Milton), **II:** 176
Treatise of Human Nature, A (Hume), **IV:** 138; **Supp. III:** 229, 230–231, **232–237**, 238
Treatise of the Fear of God, A (Bunyan), **II:** 253
Treatise of the Soul, A (Ralegh), **I:** 157
Treatise on Civil Power, A (Hill), **Retro. Supp. III:** 142, 143, 144–145, 146
Treatise on Method (Coleridge), **IV:** 56
Treatise on the Astrolabe, A (Chaucer), **I:** 31
Treatise on the Passion (More), **Supp. VII:** 245
Trebitsch, Siegfried, **VI:** 115
Tree, Herbert Beerbohm, **Supp. II:** 44, 46, 53–54, 55
"Tree, The" (Thomas), **Supp. I:** 180
"Tree, The" (Wallace–Crabbe), **VIII:** 317
"Tree at Dawn, The" (Pitter), **Supp. XIII:** 144
Tree House, The (Jamie), **Supp. XIV:** 129, 143
"Tree in Heaven, A" (Pitter), **Supp. XIII:** 138
Tree of Idleness and Other Poems, The (Durrell), **Retro. Supp. III:** 95
"Tree of Knowledge, The" (James), **VI:** 69
Tree of Man, The (White), **Supp. I:** 129, 131, 134, 136, 137–138, 143
Tree of Strings (MacCaig), **Supp. VI:** 192–193
Tree of the Sun, The (Harris), **Supp. V:** 139–140
Tree on Fire, A (Sillitoe), **Supp. V:** 409, 410, 414, 421, 422–423
"Tree Unleaved, The" (Warner), **Supp. VII:** 371
"Trees, The" (Larkin), **Supp. I:** 284, 285
Trelawny, Edward, **IV:** xiv, 203, 207, 209
Tremaine (Ward), **IV:** 293
Trembling of the Veil, The (Yeats), **VI:** 210

Tremendous Adventures of Major Gahagan, The (Thackeray), **V:** 22, 37
Tremor of Forgery, The (Highsmith), **Supp. V:** 175–176
Tremor of Intent (Burgess), **Supp. I:** 185, 191–192
"Tremors" (Conn), **Supp. XIII:** 73
Trench, The (Boyd), **Supp. XVI:** 32, 46–47
Trench Town Rock (Brathwaite), **Supp. XII:** 36
"Trenches St. Eloi" (Hulme), **Supp. VI:** 140
Trespass of the Sign, The: Deconstruction, Theology, and Philosophy (Hart), **Supp. XI:** 122, 128
Trespasser, The (Lawrence), **VII:** 89, 91, 93–95; **Retro. Supp. II:** 227
Tretis of the Tua Mariit Wemen and the Wedo, The (Dunbar), **VIII:** 120, 123, 124–126
Trevelyan, G. M., **I:** 375; **V:** xxiv, 223, 227, 234; **VI:** xv, 347, **383–396**; list of works, **VI:** 394–396
Trevenen (Davie), **Supp. VI:** 111
Trevisa, John, **Supp. IX:** **243–260**
Trevor, William, **Supp. IV:** **499–519**
Trevor–Roper, Hugh, **Supp. IV:** 436
Trial, The (Kafka), **III:** 340
Trial of a Judge (Spender), **Supp. II:** 488
Trial of Dedan Kimathi, The (Ngũgĩ/Mũgo), **VIII:** 223
Trial of Elizabeth Cree: A Novel of the Limehouse Murders, The (Ackroyd), **Supp. VI:** 10
Trial of the Fox, The (Henryson), **Supp. VII:** 136, 138, 139, 140
Trial of the Honourable Augustus Keppel, The (Burke), **III:** 205
Tribes of Ireland, The (tr. Mangan), **Supp. XIII:** 119
"Tribune's Visitation, The" (Jones), **Supp. VII:** 175, 179–180
"Tribute of a Legs Lover" (Dunn), **Supp. X:** 70
Tributes (Jennings), **Supp. V:** 216
Trick is to Keep Breathing, The (Galloway), **Supp. XII:** 117, 119–120, 124, 129
Trick of It, The (Frayn), **Supp. VII:** 61–62
Trick to Catch the Old One, A (Middleton), **II:** 3, 4–5, 21
"Trickster and the Sacred Clown, Revealing the Logic of the Unspeakable, The" (Belmonte), **Supp. IV:** 15–16
Trieste and the Meaning of Nowhere (Morris, J.), **Supp. X:** 171, 173, 176, 178, 186–187
Trilby (du Maurier), **Supp. III:** 134, 135, 136
Trilogy (Beckett), **Retro. Supp. I:** 18, 20–23
Trilogy of Death (James), **Supp. IV:** 328, 329, 335, 337
"Trim" (Dutton), **Supp. XII:** 88
"Trinity at Low Tide" (Stevenson), **Supp. VI:** 264
Trinity College (Trevelyan), **VI:** 383, 393

Trip to Scarborough, A (Sheridan), **II:** 334, 336; **III:** 253, 261, 270
Triple Thinkers, The (Wilson), **VI:** 164
"Triple Time" (Larkin), **Supp. I:** 279
Tristan and Iseult (Sutcliff), **Supp. XVI:** 271–272
Tristan and Iseult: A Play in Four Acts (Symons), **Supp. XIV:** 279
"Tristia" (Sisson), **Supp. XI:** 259
"Tristram and Iseult" (Arnold), **V:** 210
"Tristram and Iseult: Prelude of an Unfinished Poem" (Swinburne), **V:** 332
Tristram Shandy (Sterne), **III:** 124, 126, **127–132**, 135, 150, 153; **IV:** 183; **Supp. II:** 204, 205
Triumph and Tragedy (Churchill), **VI:** 361
Triumph of Death (Fletcher), **II:** 66
Triumph of Gloriana, The (Swinburne), **V:** 333
Triumph of Honour (Field), **II:** 66
"Triumph of Life, The" (Shelley), **IV:** xi, 197, 206–207, 209; **Retro. Supp. I:** 256
Triumph of Love (Field), **II:** 66
Triumph of Love, The (Hill), **Supp. V:** 183, 189, 198–199, 202; **Retro. Supp. III:** 133, 139–140
Triumph of the Four Foster Children of Desire (Sidney), **Retro. Supp. II:** 329–330
Triumph of Time (Fletcher), **II:** 66
"Triumph of Time, The" (Swinburne), **V:** 311, 313, 318–319, 331
"Triumphal March" (Eliot), **VII:** 152–153
Triumphs of Love and Innocence, The (Finch), **Supp. IX:** 74–76
"Triumphs of Odin, The" (Gray), **III:** 142
"Triumphs of Sensibility" (Warner), **Supp. VII:** 371
Triumphs of Truth, The (Middleton), **II:** 3
Triumphs of Wealth and Prosperity, The (Middleton), **II:** 3
Trivia (Connolly), **Supp. III:** 98
Trivia; or, The Art of Walking the streets of London (Gay), **III:** 55, 57, 67
"Troglodyte, The" (Brooke–Rose)), **Supp. IV:** 103
Troilus and Cressida (Dryden), **II:** 293, 305; **Retro. Supp. III:** 62
Troilus and Cressida (Shakespeare), **I:** 313, 314; **II:** 47, 70; **IV:** 225; **V:** 328
Troilus and Criseyde (Chaucer), **I:** 24, 30, 31, 32–34, 41, 43, 44; **IV:** 189; **Retro. Supp. II:** 40–45; **Retro. Supp. III:** 275
Trójumanna saga, **VIII:** 237
Trollope, Anthony, **II:** 172–173; **IV:** 306; **V:** x, xvii, xxii–xxv, 11, **89–103**; **VII:** xxi; **Supp. IV:** 229, 230
Trollope, Frances, **V:** 89
Trollope: A Commentary (Sadleir), **V:** 100, 102
"Trollope and His Style" (Sykes Davies), **V:** 103
Trooper Peter Halket of Mashonaland (Schreiner), **Supp. II:** 454
"Troopship" (Fuller), **Supp. VII:** 69

"Troopship in the Tropics, A" (Lewis), **VII:** 446
Trophy of Arms, A: Poems 1926–1935 (Pitter), **Supp. XIII:** 134, 135, 140–142
Tropic Seed (Waugh), **Supp. VI:** 275
Trotter, Catharine, **Supp. XVI: 277–291**
"Troubadour" (Gunn), **Retro. Supp. III:** 129
Trouble at Willow Gables and Other Fictions (Larkin), **Retro. Supp. III:** 200–201, 212
"Trouble with Lichen" (Wyndham), **Supp. XIII:** 292–294
Troubled Eden, A, Nature and Society in the Works of George Meredith (Kelvin), **V:** 221, 234
Troublesome Offspring of Cardinal Guzman, The (De Bernières), **Supp. XII:** 65, 69, 73–74
Troublesome Reign of John, King of England, The, **I:** 301
"Trout, A" (Nye), **Supp. X:** 201
"Trout Stream, The" (Welch), **Supp. IX:** 267
"Troy" (Muir), **Supp. VI:** 206
Troy Park (Sitwell), **VII:** 138
Troy-book (Lydgate), **I:** 57, 58, 59–65, 280
"Truant Hart, The" (Coppard), **VIII:** 96
"Truce of the Bear, The" (Kipling), **VI:** 203
True Born Irishman, The (Friel), **Supp. V:** 126
"True Function and Value of Criticism, The" (Wilde), **Retro. Supp. II:** 367
True Heart, The (Warner), **Supp. VII:** 370, 375
True History (Lucian), **III:** 24
True History of Squire Jonathan and His Unfortunate Treasure, The (Arden), **Supp. II:** 31
True History of the Kelly Gang (Carey), **Supp. XII:** 49, 51, 54, 57, 60, 61–62
"True Love" (Nye), **Supp. X:** 199–200, 202
True Patriot, The (Fielding), **III:** 105; **Retro. Supp. I:**
True Relation of the Apparition of . . . Mrs. Veal . . . to . . . Mrs. Bargrave . . . (Defoe), **III:** 13
True State of the Case of Bosavern Penlez, A (Fielding), **III:** 105
True Traveller, The (Davies), **Supp. XI:** 86, 91
True Travellers: A Tramps Opera in Three Acts (Davies), **Supp. XI:** 93
True Widow, The (Shadwell), **II:** 115305
True-Born Englishman, The (Defoe), **III:** 3, 12; **Retro. Supp. I:** 64, 67
Truelove, The (O'Brian), **Supp. XII:** 258–259
"Truly Great" (Davies), **Supp. XI:** 85
Trumpet (Kay), **Supp. XIII:** 99, 101–102, 103, 105–107
Trumpet-Major, The: A Tale (Hardy), **VI:** 5, 6–7, 20; **Retro. Supp. I:** 114
"Trust" (Gunn), **Retro. Supp. III:** 124
"Trustie Tree, The" (Roberts, K.), **Supp. X:** 270

"Truth" (Bacon), **III:** 39
"Truth" (Cowper), **III:** 212
Truth About an Author (Bennett), **VI:** 264–265
Truth About Blayds, The (Milne), **Supp. V:** 299
"Truth About the Navy, The" (Stead), **Supp. XIII:** 239
"Truth in the Cup" (Warner), **Supp. VII:** 381
"Truth of Imagination, The" (Beer), **Supp. XIV:** 8–9
"Truth of Masks, The" (Wilde), **Retro. Supp. II:** 368
"Truthful Adventure, A" (Mansfield), **VII:** 172
Trying to Explain (Davie), **Supp. VI:** 115
"Tryst, The" (Soutar), **Supp. XVI:** 249, 252
"Tryst at an Ancient Earthwork, A" (Hardy), **VI:** 22
Trystram of Lyoness (Swinburne), **V:** 299, 300, 314, 327–328, 332
T.S. Eliot (Raine), **Supp. XIII:** 175
"T–Song" (Delahunt), **Supp. XIV:** 51–52
Tsotsi (Fugard), **Supp. XV:** 102, 105
Tsvetayeva, Marina, **Supp. IV:** 493
Tucker, Abraham, pseud. of William Hazlitt
Tudor trilogy (Ford), **VI:** 319, 323, 325–327; *see also Fifth Queen, The; Fifth Queen Crowned, The; Privy Seal*
"Tuesday; or, The Ditty" (Gay), **III:** 56
"Tuft of Violets, The" (Pitter), **Supp. XIII:** 144
"Tulips" (McGuckian), **Supp. V:** 281
Tumatumari (Harris), **Supp. V:** 136, 137
Tumble-down Dick (Fielding), **III:** 105
"Tumps" (Cope), **VIII:** 78
Tunbridgiale (Byrom), **Supp. XVI:** 73
Tunc (Durrell), **Supp. I:** 113–118, 120; **Retro. Supp. III:** 85, 91
Tune in Tomorrow (screenplay, Boyd), **Supp. XVI:** 45–46
"Tunnel" (Barnes), **Supp. IV:** 75, 76
Tunnel, The (Richardson), **Supp. XIII:** 184, 189, 190
Tunning of Elinour Rumming, The (Skelton), **I:** 82, 86–87, 92
"Tunstall Forest" (Davie), **Supp. VI:** 110
Tuppenny Stung (Longley), **VIII:** 164, 165
Turbott Wolfe (Plomer), **Supp. XI:** 209, 210–212, 213, 214, 219, 222, 223
"Turf, The" (Sisson), **Supp. XI:** 258
Turkish Delight (Churchill), **Supp. IV:** 181
Turkish Mahomet and Hiren the Fair Greek (Peele), **I:** 205
Turkish tales (Byron), **IV:** x, 172, 173–175
"Turn for the Better, A" (Nicholson), **Supp. VI:** 217
Turn of the Screw, The (James), **III:** 334, 340, 345; **V:** xxvi, 14; **VI:** 39, **52–53**, 69; **Supp. IV:** 97, 116, 503, 511
Turn of the Years, The (Pritchett), **Supp. III:** 311
Turn Outside, A (Smith), **Retro. Supp. III:** 311

"Turn Outside, A" (Smith), **Retro. Supp. III:** 311
Turner, J. M. W., **V:** xix, xx, 174–175, 178
"Turns" (Harrison), **Supp. V:** 154–155
Turning of the Tide, The (Hill), see *Castle of the Demon, The*
"Tursac" (Dunn), **Supp. X:** 76
Tutchin, John, **III:** 3
"Tutelar of the Place, The" (Jones), **Supp. VII:** 179–180
Tuve, Rosamund, **II:** 124, 130; **Retro. Supp. II:** 174
"TV" (Smith, I. C.), **Supp. IX:** 221
"Twa Dogs, The" (Burns), **III:** 315, 316
"Twa Herds, The" (Burns), **III:** 311, 319
Twain, Mark, **IV:** 106; **V:** xix, xxiv–xxv
"Twelfth Night" (Scupham), **Supp. XIII:** 221
Twelfth Night (Shakespeare), **I:** 312, 320; **Retro. Supp. III:** 268, 269, 277
Twelfth of Never, The (Carson), **Supp. XIII:** 65–66
Twelve Adventurers and Other Stories (Brontë), **V:** 151
Twelve, and Other Poems by Aleksandr Blok, The (tr. Stallworthy), **Supp. X:** 292
Twelve Apostles (Ewart), **Supp. VII:** 40
12 Edmondstone Street (Malouf), **Supp. XII:** 217
"12 Edmondstone Street" (Malouf), **Supp. XII:** 218
Twelve Idyls and Other Poems (Abercrombie), **Supp. XVI:** 9, 11
Twelve Months in a Curatorship (Carroll), **V:** 274
Twelve Pound Look, The (Barrie), **Supp. III:** 6, 8, 9, 15–16
"Twelve Songs" (Auden), **VII:** 383, 386
"Twentieth Century Blues" (Coward), **Supp. II:** 147
Twenty five (Gregory), **VI:** 309
"Twenty Golden Years Ago" (Mangan), **Supp. XIII:** 123–124
"Twenty Pounds" (Gissing), **V:** 437
Twenty Years A-Growing (screenplay, Thomas), **Retro. Supp. III:** 348
Twenty-five Poems (Thomas), **Supp. I:** 174, 176, 180; **Retro. Supp. III:** 335, 338–341
"Twenty-four years" (Thomas), **Supp. I:** 177; **Retro. Supp. III:** 342–343
"24th March 1986" (Ewart), **Supp. VII:** 46
"29 February, 1704" (Fallon), **Supp. XII:** 114
Twenty-One Poems (Sisson), **Supp. XI:** 249
"Twenty-Seven Articles, The" (Lawrence), **Supp. II:** 287
Twenty Thousand Streets Under the Sky (Hamilton), **Supp. XVI:** 182
"26th December" (Scupham), **Supp. XIII:** 227
Twice Over (Kay), **Supp. XIII:** 100
Twice Round the Black Church: Early Memories of Ireland and England (Clarke), **Supp. XV:** 15, 16, 18, 27

Twice Through the Heart (Kay), **Supp. XIII:** 100, 101

Twilight Bar (Koestler), **Supp. I:** 25

Twilight in Italy (Lawrence), **VII:** 116

Twin Rivals, The (Farquhar), **II:** 353, 357–358, 364

"Twin Sets and Pickle Forks" (Dunn), **Supp. X:** 67–68

Twine, Laurence, **I:** 321

Twitchell, James B., **Supp. III:** 383

Twits, The (Dahl), **Supp. IV:** 205, 207, 223

'Twixt Land and Sea: Tales (Conrad), **VI:** 148

"Two Analogies for Poetry" (Davie), **Supp. VI:** 115

Two Autobiographical Plays (Arden), **Supp. II:** 31

Two Biographical Plays (Arden), **Supp. II:** 31

"Two Blond Flautists" (Fuller), **Supp. VII:** 79

Two Bookes of Ayres (Campion), **Supp. XVI:** 92, 96

"Two Chairs" (Powys), **VIII:** 251, 252

Two Cheers for Democracy (Forster), **VI:** 397, 411

"Two Chorale–Preludes" (Hill), **Supp. V:** 199

"Two Countries" (James), **VI:** 69

Two Destinies, The (Collins), **Supp. VI:** 102

"Two Drovers, The" (Scott), **IV:** 39

"Two Early French Stories" (Pater), **V:** 344

"Two Faces, The" (James), **VI:** 69

Two Faces of January, The (Highsmith), **Supp. V:** 173–174

"Two Formal Elegies" (Hill), **Retro. Supp. III:** 135

Two Foscari, The (Byron), **IV:** xviii, 178, 193

"Two Fragments: March 199–" (McEwan), **Supp. IV:** 395

"Two Frenchmen" (Strachey), **Supp. II:** 500, 502

"Two Fusiliers" (Graves), **VI:** 452

"Two Gallants" (Joyce), **VII:** 44

Two Generals, The (FitzGerald), **IV:** 353

Two Gentlemen of Verona (Shakespeare), **I:** 302, 311–312

"Two Girls Singing" (Smith, I. C.), **Supp. IX:** 213

Two Great Questions Consider'd, The (Defoe), **III:** 12

Two Guardians, The (Yonge), **V:** 253

"Two Hares and a Priest" (Beer), **Supp. XIV:** 14

Two Heroines of Plumplington, The (Trollope), **V:** 102

"Two Houses" (Thomas), **Supp. III:** 399

"Two Impromptus" (Amis), **Supp. II:** 15

"Two in the Campagna" (Browning), **IV:** 357, 369; **Retro. Supp. III:** 24

"Two Kinds of Motion" (Stevenson), **Supp. VI:** 255

"Two Kitchen Songs" (Sitwell), **VII:** 130–131

"Two Knights, The" (Swinburne), **V:** 315, 333

Two Letters on the Conduct of Our Domestic Parties (Burke), **III:** 205

Two Letters on the French Revolution (Burke), **III:** 205

Two Letters . . . on the Proposals for Peace (Burke), **III:** 205

Two Letters . . . to Gentlemen in the City of Bristol . . . (Burke), **III:** 205

Two Lives (Seth), **Supp. X:** 290

Two Lives (Trevor), **Supp. IV:** 516

Two Magics, The (James), **VI:** 52, 69

Two Mice, The (Henryson), **Supp. VII:** 136, 137, 140

Two Noble Kinsmen, The (Shakespeare), **I:** 324, 325; **II:** 43, 66, 87; **Retro. Supp. III:** 281

Two of Us, The (Frayn), **Supp. VII:** 57

"Two Old Men Outside an Inn" (Cornford), **VIII:** 113

Two on a Tower: A Romance (Hardy), **VI:** 4, 5, 20; **Retro. Supp. I:** 114

Two or Three Graces (Huxley), **VII:** 201

Two Paths, The (Ruskin), **V:** 180, 184

"Two Peacocks of Bedfont, The" (Hood), **IV:** 256, 267

Two People (Milne), **Supp. V:** 310

"Two Races of Men, The" (Lamb), **IV:** 82

"Two Spirits, The" (Shelley), **IV:** 196

Two Stories: "Come and Dine" and "Tadnol" (Powys), **VIII:** 248

"2000: Zero Gravity" (Motion), **Supp. VII:** 266

"2001: The Tennyson/Hardy Poem" (Ewart), **Supp. VII:** 40

Two Thieves, The (Powys), **VIII:** 248, 255

Two Thousand Seasons (Armah), **Supp. X:** 1–3, 6–11, 13

Two Towers, The (Tolkien), **Supp. II:** 519

Two Voices (Thomas), **Supp. IV:** 490

"Two Voices, The" (Tennyson), **IV:** 329; **Retro. Supp. III:** 321

"Two Ways of It" (MacCaig), **Supp. VI:** 187

Two Women of London: The Strange Case of Ms. Jekyll and Mrs. Hyde (Tennant), **Supp. IX:** 238–239, 240

Two Worlds and Their Ways (Compton-Burnett), **VII:** 65, 66, 67, 69

"Two Year Old" (MacCaig), **Supp. VI:** 192

Two Years Ago (Kingsley), **Supp. XVI:** 205

"Two Years Old" (Cornford), **VIII:** 113

"Two–Headed Beast, The" (Fallon), **Supp. XII:** 102

Two–Part Inventions (Howard), **V:** 418

"Two–Party System in English Political History, The" (Trevelyan), **VI:** 392

"Two–Sided Man, The" (Kipling), **VI:** 201

Twopence Coloured (Hamilton), **Supp. XVI:** 179, 182–183

Twyborn Affair, The (White), **Supp. I:** 132, 148–149

"Tyes, The" (Thomas), **Supp. III:** 401

"Tyger, The" (Blake), **III:** 296; **Retro. Supp. I:** 42–43

Tyler, F. W., **I:** 275*n*

Tylney Hall (Hood), **IV:** 254, 256, 259, 267

Tynan, Katherine, **V:** 441

Tynan, Kenneth, **Supp. II:** 70, 140, 147, 152, 155; **Supp. IV:** 78

Tyndale, William, **I:** 375–377

"Typhoon" (Conrad), **VI:** 136, 148

Tyrannicida (tr. More), **Supp. VII:** 235–236

Tyrannick Loce; or, The Royal Martyr (Dryden), **II:** 290, 294, 305

"Tyre, The" (Armitage), **VIII:** 11

"Tyronic Dialogues" (Lewis), **VII:** 82

*U*dolpho (Radcliffe), *see Mysteries of Udolpho, The*

Ugliest House in the World, The (Davies), **Supp. XIV:** 35, 36–40

"Ugliest House in the World, The" (Davies), **Supp. XIV:** 37

Ugly Anna and Other Tales (Coppard), **VIII:** 89

"Uist" (Crawford), **Supp. XI:** 81

Ukulele Music (Reading), **VIII:** 265, 268–269, 270, 271

"Ula Masondo" (Plomer), **Supp. XI:** 214

Ulick and Soracha (Moore), **VI:** 89, 95, 99

"Ultima" (Thompson), **V:** 441

"Ultima Ratio Regum" (Spender), **Supp. II:** 488

"Ultimatum" (Larkin), **Retro. Supp. III:** 199

Ultramarine (Lowry), **Supp. III:** 269, 270, **271–272,** 280, 283, 285

"Ultrasound" (Jamie), **Supp. XIV:** 141

"Ululu" (Delanty), **Supp. XIV:** 73

Ulysses (Butler), **Supp. II:** 114

Ulysses (Joyce), **V:** 189; **VII:** xv, 42, 46–47, 48–52; **Retro. Supp. I:** 169, 176–179; critical studies, **VII:** 57–58; **Supp. IV:** 87, 370, 390, 426; **Retro. Supp. III:** 165, 167, 168, 169, 170, 174–177, 179

"Ulysses" (Tennyson), **IV:** xx, 324, 328, 332–334; **Retro. Supp. III:** 317, 322

"Uma Himavutee" (Steel), **Supp. XII:** 269

"Umbra" (Campion), **Supp. XVI:** 99

"Umbrella Man, The" (Dahl), **Supp. IV:** 221

"Un Coeur Simple" (Flaubert), **Supp. IV:** 69

Un Début dans la vie (Balzac), **Supp. IV:** 123

"Unarmed Combat" (Reed), **VII:** 422–423; **Supp. XV:** 250, 251

"Unattained Place, The" (Muir), **Supp. VI:** 206

Unbearable Bassington, The (Saki), **Supp. VI: 245–248**

Unbeaten Tracks in Japan (Bird), **Supp. X:** 19, 29–30

"Unbidden Guest, The" (Powys), **VIII:** 251

Unblest, The: A Study of the Italian Poet Giacomo Leopardi as a Child and in Early Manhood (Reed), **Supp. XV:** 252

UNBU–UNSO

"Unbuilders, The" (Crawford), **Supp. XI:** 70

Uncensored (Rattigan), **Supp. VII:** 311

"Unchangeable, The" (Blunden), **Supp. XI:** 43

Unclassed, The (Gissing), **V:** 437

Unclay (Powys), **VIII:** 256

Uncle Bernac (Doyle), **Supp. II:** 159

Uncle Dottery: A Christmas Story (Powys), **VIII:** 248

"Uncle Ernest" (Sillitoe), **Supp. V:** 414

Uncle Fred in the Springtime (Wodehouse), **Supp. III:** 460–461

Uncle Silas (Le Fanu), **III:** 345; **Supp. II:** 78–79, 81

Uncle Vanya (tr. Frayn), **Supp. VII:** 61

Unclouded Summer (Waugh), **Supp. VI:** 274

Uncollected Essays (Pater), **V:** 357

Uncollected Verse (Thompson), **V:** 451

Uncommercial Traveller, The (Dickens), **V:** 72

Unconditional Surrender (Waugh), **VII:** 303, 304; see also Sword of Honour trilogy

Unconscious Memory (Butler), **Supp. II:** 107–108

Unconsoled, The (Ishiguro), **Supp. IV:** 301, 302, 304, 305, 306–307, 314–316; **Retro. Supp. III:** 156–158, 162

"Uncovenanted Mercies" (Kipling), **VI:** 175

"Under a Lady's Picture" (Waller), **II:** 234–235

"Under Ben Bulben" (Yeats), **VI:** 215, 219–220; **Retro. Supp. I:** 338

"Under Brinkie's Brae" (Brown), **Supp. VI:** 64

"Under Carn Brea" (Thomas), **Supp. IV:** 492

Under Milk Wood (Thomas), **Supp. I:** 183–184; **Retro. Supp. III:** 335, 336, 337, 343, 347, 348, 349

Under Plain Cover (Osborne), **Supp. I:** 335–336

"Under That Bag of Soot" (Constantine), **Supp. XV:** 74

Under the Dam (Constantine), **Supp. XV:** 66

Under the Deodars (Kipling), **Retro. Supp. III:** 186

Under the Greenwood Tree: A Rural Painting of the Dutch School (Hardy), **VI:** 1, 2–3, 5, 20; **Retro. Supp. I:** 112–113

Under the Hill (Beardsley), **VII:** 292

Under the Hill (Firbank), **Supp. II:** 202

Under the Ice (Conn), **Supp. XIII:** 70, 73–75

"Under the Ice" (Conn), **Supp. XIII:** 74

Under the Microscope (Swinburne), **IV:** 337; **V:** 329, 332, 333

Under the Net (Murdoch), **Supp. I:** 220, 222, 228, 229–230

Under the Sunset (Stoker), **Supp. III:** 381

Under the Volcano (Lowry), **Supp. III:** 269, 270, 273, **274–280**, 283, 285

Under the Reservoir (Redgrove), **Supp. VI:** 236

Under Twenty–five: An Anthology (ed. O'Donovan, Sanderson, and Porteous), **Supp. XII:** 51

Under Western Eyes (Conrad), **VI:** 134, 144–145, 148; **Retro. Supp. II:** 81–82

"'Under Which King, Bezonian?'" (Leavis), **VII:** 242

Under World (Hill, R.), **Supp. IX:** 120, 121

Undergraduate Sonnets (Swinburne), **V:** 333

Underhill, Charles, see Hill, Reginald

"Understanding the Ur–Bororo" (Self), **Supp. V:** 401–402

Undertones of War (Blunden), **VI:** 428, 429; **Supp. XI:** 33, 36, 38, 39–41, 47

Underwood (Jonson), **Retro. Supp. I:** 166

Underwood, Dale, **II:** 256n

Underwoods (Stevenson), **V:** 390n, 395; **Retro. Supp. I:** 267–268

Undine (Schreiner), **Supp. II:** **444–445**

"Undiscovered Planet, The" (Nicholson), **Supp. VI:** 217

"Undressing" (Nye), **Supp. X:** 198, 200

Undying Fire, The (Wells), **VI:** 242

Unequal Marriage; or, Pride and Prejudice Twenty Years Later, An (Tennant), see *Unequal Marriage: Pride and Prejudice Continued, An*

Unequal Marriage: Pride and Prejudice Continued, An (Tennant), **Supp. IX:** 237–238, 239–240

"Unfinished Draft, An" (Beddoes), **Supp. XI:** 30

Unfinished Portrait (Christie), **Supp. II:** 133

"Unfortunate" (Brooke), **Supp. III:** 55

"Unfortunate Lover, The" (Marvell), **II:** 211

Unfortunate Traveller, The (Nashe), **I:** 114, 281

"Ungratefulnesse" (Herbert), **II:** 127

Unguarded Hours (Wilson), **Supp. VI:** 299, 308

"Unhappy Families" (Carter), **Supp. IV:** 459

Unhappy Favorite, The (Banks), **II:** 305

Unhappy Penitent, The (Trotter), **Supp. XVI:** 283–284

Unholy Trade, The (Findlater), **VII:** 8–9, 14

Unicorn, The (Murdoch), **III:** 341, 345; **Supp. I:** 215, 225, 226, 228

Unicorn, The (Rosenberg), **VI:** 433

"Unicorn, The" (Soutar), **Supp. XVI:** 254

Unicorn from the Stars, The (Yeats and Gregory), **VI:** 318

"Unimportant Fire, An" (Rushdie), **Supp. IV:** 445

"Union, A" (Davies), **Supp. XIV:** 38

Union of the Two Noble and Illustre Families of Lancaster and York, The (Hall), **I:** 299

"Union Reunion" (Wilson), **Supp. I:** 153, 155, 157

Union Street (Barker), **Supp. IV:** 45, 46–50, 57

Universal English Short–hand (Byrom), **Supp. XVI:** 73

Universal Chronicle (periodical), **III:** 111

Universal Gallant, The (Fielding), **III:** 105

"University of Mainz, The" (Waugh), **Supp. VI:** 269

"University Feud, The: A Row at the Oxford Arms" (Hood), **IV:** 258

Unjust War: An Address to the Workingmen of England (Morris), **V:** 305

Unkindness of Ravens, An (Rendell), **Supp. IX:** 199

Unknown, The (Maugham), **VI:** 369

Unknown Assailant (Hamilton), **Supp. XVI:** 188, 189–190

"Unknown Bird, The" (Thomas), **Supp. III:** 402

"Unknown Man" (Conn), **Supp. XIII:** 76

Unknown Mayhew, The (Mayhew), **Supp. XVI:** 209, 211, 215, 216

Unknown Shore, The (O'Brian), **Supp. XII:** 248, 251, 252

"Unknown Shores" (Thomas), **Supp. IV:** 490

Unlikely Stories, Mostly (Gray, A.), **Supp. IX:** 80, 90

Unlimited Dream Company, The (Ballard), **Supp. V:** 28–29

Unlit Lamp, The (Hall), **Supp. VI:** 120–122, **123–125**

"Unluckily for a Death" (Thomas), **Supp. I:** 178

Unmentionable Man, An (Upward), **Supp. XIII:** 250, 260–261

"Unmentionable Man, An" (Upward), **Supp. XIII:** 260–261

Unnamable, The (Beckett), **Supp. I:** 45, 51, 52, 53–54, 55, 56, 60; **Supp. IV:** 106; **Retro. Supp. I:** 22–23

Unnatural Causes (James), **Supp. IV:** 320, 321, 324–326

Unnatural Death (Sayers), **Supp. II:** 135; **Supp. III:** 338–339, 340, 343

Unnaturall Combat, The (Massinger), **Supp. XI:** 183

Unofficial Rose, An (Murdoch), **Supp. I:** 222, 223–224, 229, 232

Unpleasantness at the Bellona Club, The (Sayers), **Supp. III:** 330, 340

Unprofessional Tales (Douglas), **VI:** 293, 305

Unpublished Early Poems (Tennyson), **IV:** 338

Unquiet Grave, The: A Word Cycle by Palinurus (Connolly), **Supp. III:** **103–105**

Unrelenting Struggle, The (Churchill), **VI:** 356

"Unremarkable Year, The" (Fuller), **Supp. VII:** 78

Unruly Times: Wordsworth and Coleridge in Their Time (Byatt), **Supp. IV:** 145

"Unseen Centre, The" (Nicholson), **Supp. VI:** 217

"Unsettled Motorcyclist" (Gunn), **Retro. Supp. III:** 116

"Unsettled Motorcyclist's Vision of His Death, The" (Gunn), **Supp. IV:** 260; **Retro. Supp. III:** 120

Unsocial Socialist, An (Shaw), **VI:** 103, 104, 105, 106, 129

"Unstable dream" (Wyatt), **I:** 103, 109
Unsuitable Attachment, An (Pym), **Supp. II: 375–377**
Unsuitable Job for a Woman, An (James), **Supp. IV:** 320, 335, 336
Unsweet Charity (Waterhouse), **Supp. XIII:** 273
Unsworth, Barry, **Supp. VII: 353–367**
"Until Eternal Music Ends" (Fallon), **Supp. XII:** 102
"Until My Blood Is Pure" (Chatwin), **Supp. IV:** 173
Until the End of the World (Wenders and Carey), **Supp. XII:** 53
Untilled Field, The (Moore), **VI:** 88, 93, 98
Untitled Sea Novel (Lowry), **Supp. III:** 280
Unto This Last (Ruskin), **V:** xii, xxii, 20, 179–180
Unusual Life of Tristan Smith, The (Carey), **Supp. XII:** 52, 53, 54, 60, 62
"Unusual Young Man, An" (Brooke), **Supp. III:** 50–51
Up Against It (Orton), **Supp. V:** 363, 366, 369–370
"Up and Awake" (Kinsella), **Supp. V:** 268
"Up and Down" (Smith), **Supp. II:** 470
"Up at a Villa—Down in the City" (Browning), **IV:** 360
Up the Rhine (Hood), **IV:** 254, 259, 267
Up to Midnight (Meredith), **V:** 234
Updike, John, **Supp. IV:** 27, 136, 480, 483
"Upon a Child That Dyed" (Herrick), **II:** 115
"Upon a Cloke Lent Him by Mr. J. Ridsley" (Vaughan), **II:** 184
"Upon a Dead Man's Head" (Skelton), **I:** 84
"Upon Ancient and Modern Learning" (Temple), **III:** 40
"Upon Appleton House" (Marvell), **II:** 208, 209–210, 211, 212–213; **Retro. Supp. II:** 261–262
Upon Cromwell's Return from Ireland (Marvell), **II:** 199
"Upon Her Majesty's New Buildings" (Waller), **II:** 238
"Upon Heroick Virtue" (Temple), **III:** 40
"Upon Julia's Clothes" (Herrick), **II:** 107
"Upon Julia's Fall" (Herrick), **II:** 107
"Upon Julia's Unlacing Herself" (Herrick), **II:** 106
"Upon Julia's Voice" (Herrick), **II:** 107
"Upon Nothing" (Rochester), **II:** 259, 270
"Upon Our Late Loss of the Duke of Cambridge" (Waller), **II:** 233
"Upon Poetry" (Temple), **III:** 40
"Upon the Death of a Gentleman" (Crashaw), **II:** 183
"Upon the Death of Mr. R. W . . . ." (Vaughan), **II:** 184
"Upon the Death of the Lord Hastings" (Dryden), **Retro. Supp. III:** 59–60
"Upon the Earl of Roscommon's Translation of Horace" (Waller), **II:** 234
"Upon the Gardens of Epicurus" (Temple), **III:** 40

"Upon the Hurricane" (Finch), **Supp. IX:** 68–71
Upon the Late Storme, and of the Death of His Highness (Waller), **II:** 238
"Upon the Lonely Moor" (Carroll), **V:** 265, 267
Upstairs Downstairs (teleplay, Weldon), **Supp. IV:** 521
Upton, John, **I:** 121
Upward, Edward, **Supp. XIII: 249–263**
Urania (Pitter), **Supp. XIII:** 135, 144
Ure, Peter, **VI:** 220
Urgent Copy (Burgess), **Supp. I:** 186, 190, 194, 197
Uriah on the Hill (Powys), **VIII:** 255, 256
Urn Burial (Hill, R.), **Supp. IX:** 117
"Urphänomen" (Burnside), **Supp. XIII:** 17–18
"Us" (Crawford), **Supp. XI:** 74
Use of Poetry and the Use of Criticism, The (Eliot), **VII:** 153, 158, 164; **Retro. Supp. II:** 65–66
Use of Weapons (Banks), **Supp. XI:** 10, 12
Useful and Instructive Poetry (Carroll), **V:** 263, 264, 273
Uses of Literacy, The (Hoggart), **Supp. IV:** 473
"Uses of the Many-Charactered Novel" (Stead), **Supp. IV:** 466
Using Biography (Empson), **Supp. II:** 180
Usk, Thomas, **I:** 2
"Usk, The" (Sisson), **Supp. XI:** 257–258
U.S. Martial (Harrison), **Supp. V:** 163
"Usquebaugh" (Cope), **VIII:** 74
"Usura Canto," see "Canto 45"
Utility Player, The (Keneally), **Supp. IV:** 347
Utopia (More), **III:** 24; **Supp. VII:** 233, 235, 236, 238–240, 243, 248
"Utter Rim, The" (Graves), **VII:** 270
Utz (Chatwin), **Supp. IV:** 159, 163, 173, 174–175; **Supp. IX:** 59–60, 61

"V." (Harrison), **Supp. V: 153, 157–160**
V. (Pynchon), **Supp. IV:** 116
V. and Other Poems (Harrison), **Supp. V:** 160
V. C. O'Flaherty (Shaw), **VI:** 119–120, 129
Vafþrúðnismál, **VIII:** 230
Vagabundi Libellus (Symonds), **Supp. XIV:** 251, 252
Vagrant Mood, The (Maugham), **VI:** 374
Vailima Letters (Stevenson), **V:** 391, 396
Vain Fortune (Moore), **VI:** 87, 91
Vainglory (Firbank), **Supp. II:** 201, 203–204, 205, 208–209
Val D'Arno (Ruskin), **V:** 184
Vala; or, The Four Zoas (Blake), see *Four Zoas, The*
Vale (Moore), **VI:** 99
Vale and Other Poems (Russell), **VIII:** 290, 291, 292
"Valediction, A: Forbidding Mourning" (Donne), **II:** 185, 197; **Retro. Supp. II:** 87–88

"Valediction, A: Of Weeping" (Donne), **II:** 196
"Valediction of my name, in the window, A" (Donne), **Retro. Supp. II:** 92
"Valentine" (Cope), **VIII:** 76
Valentinian (Fletcher), **II:** 45, 58–60, 65
Valentinian: A Tragedy . . . (Rochester), **II:** 270
Valiant Pilgrim (Brittain), **Supp. X:** 46
Valiant Scot, The (Webster), **II:** 69, 85
Valla–Ljóts saga, **VIII:** 241
Valley of Bones, The (Powell), **VII:** 349
"Valley of Couteretz" (Tennyson), **IV:** 330
Valley of Fear, The (Doyle), **Supp. II:** 162, 163, 171, 172, 173, 174
"Valley of Vain Desires, The" (Symonds), **Supp. XIV:** 252
Valmouth: A Romantic Novel (Firbank), **Supp. II:** 199, 201, 202, 205, **213–214**
Valperga; or, The Life and Adventures of Castruccio, Prince of Lucca (Shelley), **Retro. Supp. III:** 287, 289, 293, 294, 295, 296–297
"Value of Money, The" (Berger), **Supp. IV:** 92
"Values" (Blunden), **Supp. XI:** 46
Vamp Till Ready (Fuller), **Supp. VII:** 81
Vampirella (Carter), **III:** 341
Vampyre, The (Polidori), **III:** 329, 334; **Supp. III:** 385
"Van Gogh among the Miners" (Mahon), **Supp. VI:** 168
Van, The (Doyle), **Supp. V:** 78, 85–87
Van Vechten, Carl, **Supp. II:** 200, 203, 218
Vanbrugh, Sir John, **II:** 289, **323–337**, 339, 347, 360; **III:** 253, 261
Vancenza; or, The Dangers of Credulity (Robinson), **Supp. XIII:** 205
Vandaleur's Folly (Arden and D'Arcy), **Supp. II:** 35, 39
"Vanishing Twin" (Burnside), **Supp. XIII:** 23–24
"Vanitie" (Herbert), **II:** 127
"Vanities" (Conn), **Supp. XIII:** 72
Vanity Fair, (periodical), **Supp. XIII:** 191
Vanity Fair (Thackeray), **IV:** 301; **V:** xxi, 17, 19, 20, 23, **25–28**, 30, 31, 35, 38; **Supp. IV:** 238
"Vanity of Human Wishes, The" (Johnson), **III:** 109–110, 121, 280, 281; **IV:** 188; **Supp. IV:** 271; **Retro. Supp. I:** 139, 148
"Vanity of Spirit" (Vaughan), **II:** 185
"Vaquero" (Muldoon), **Supp. IV:** 415
Vargas Llosa, Mario, **Supp. IV:** 440
Variation of Public Opinion and Feelings, The (Crabbe), **III:** 286
"Variations of Ten Summer Minutes" (MacCaig), **Supp. VI:** 193
Variation on a Theme (Rattigan), **Supp. VII:** 315, 319–320
"Variations and Excerpts" (Ewart), **Supp. VII:** 43
"Variations on a Theme of Wallace Stevens" (Burnside), **Supp. XIII:** 19–20

Variations on a Time Theme (Muir), **Supp. VI:** 204
"Variations on a Time Theme" (Muir), **Supp. VI:** 205
Varieties of Parable (MacNeice), **VII:** 405
Various Haunts of Men, The (Hill), **Supp. XIV:** 116
Varma, D. P., **III:** 338, 346
Varney the Vampire (Pecket and Rymer), **Supp. III:** 385
Vasari, Georgio, **V:** 346
"Vashti" (Abercrombie), **Supp. XVI:** 2
"Vastness" (Tennyson), **IV:** 329, 330
Vathek (Beckford), **III: 327–329,** 345; **IV:** xv, 230
Vaughan, Henry, **II:** 123, 126, **184–189,** 190, **201–203,** 221; **Retro. Supp. II:** 172
Vaughan, Thomas, **II:** 184, 185
"Vauxhall Gardens by Day" (Dickens), **V:** 47n
"V.E. Day" (Scupham), **Supp. XIII:** 225
Vega and Other Poems (Durrell), **Retro. Supp. III:** 95
"Velvet Glove, The" (James), **VI:** 69
Venables, Robert, **II:** 131, 137
Vendor of Sweets, The (Naipaul), **Supp. I:** 400
Venerable Bede, The, **I:** 374–375
Venetia (Disraeli), **IV:** xix, 298, 299, 307, 308
Vengeance of Fionn, The (Clarke), **Supp. XV:** 17–18
Veni, Creator Spiritus (Dryden), **II:** 300
Venice (Morris, J.), **Supp. X:** 175–177
Venus and Adonis (Shakespeare), **I:** 291, 306, 325; **IV:** 256; **Retro. Supp. III:** 278
Venus and Tannhäuser (Beardsley), **V:** 318n
Venus and the Rain (McGuckian), **Supp. V:** 277, 282–284, 287
"Venus and the Rain" (McGuckian), **Supp. V:** 277–278
"Venus and the Sun" (McGuckian), **Supp. V:** 283
"Venus Fly-trap" (MacCaig), **Supp. VI:** 192
Venus Observed (Fry), **Supp. III:** 195, 202–203, 207, 208
"Venus Smiles" (Ballard), **Supp. V:** 26
Venusberg (Powell), **VII:** 344, 345
Vera; or, The Nihilists (Wilde), **V:** 401, 419; **Retro. Supp. II:** 362
Veranilda (Gissing), **V:** 435, 437
Verbivore (Brooke–Rose), **Supp. IV:** 100, 111–112
Vercelli Book, **Retro. Supp. II:** 301–303
"Verdict, The" (Cameron), **Supp. IX:** 27
Vergil, **II:** 292, 300, 304; **III:** 222, 311, 312; **IV:** 327; **Supp. III:** 415–416, 417
Vergil's Gnat (Spenser), **I:** 123
Vérité de la religion Chrétienne (tr. Sidney), **I:** 161
Verlaine, Paul, **V:** 404, 405
Vermeer, Jan, **Supp. IV:** 136
Vernacular Republic, The (Murray), **Supp. VII:** 270
Verne, Jules, **III:** 341; **VI:** 229

Veronese, Paolo, **V:** 179
"Vers de Société" (Larkin), **Supp. I:** 282, 285; **Retro. Supp. III:** 210
Vers d'Occasion (Day Lewis), **Supp. III:** 130
Verse (Murray), **Supp. VII:** 270
Verse (Wallace–Crabbe), **VIII:** 316
"Verse and Mathematics: A Study of the Sources of Poetry" (Caudwell), see "Illusion and Reality: A Study of the Sources of Poetry"
"Verse from an Opera—The Village Dragon" (Ewart), **Supp. VII:** 37
Verses (Rossetti), **V:** 260; **Retro. Supp. III:** 251, 253, 258, 260
Verses: Dedicated to Her Mother (Rossetti), **Retro. Supp. III:** 254
Verses of V. A. D. (Brittain), **Supp. X:** 35
"Verses for a Christmas Card" (Morgan, E.), **Supp. IX:** 161, 162
Verses, in the Character of a Corsican (Boswell), **III:** 248
Verses Lately Written upon Several Occasions (Cowley), **II:** 202
Verses on the Death of Dr. Swift (Swift), **III:** 21, 32; **Retro. Supp. I:** 274
"Verses Supposed to be Written by Alexander Selkirk" (Cowper), **Retro. Supp. III:** 35
"Verses to a Friend: On His Playing a Particular Melody. Which Excited the Author to Tears" (Mangan), **Supp. XIII:** 120–121
"Verses . . . to Sir Thomas Hanmer" (Collins), **III:** 160, 175
Versions and Perversions of Heine (Sisson), **Supp. XI:** 247
Vertical Man: Sequel to A Selected Life (Kinsella), **Supp. V:** 267
Vertigo (Sebald), **VIII:** 295, 296, 297, 298–300
"Verulam" (Roberts, K.), **Supp. X:** 275
Very Fine Clock, The (Spark), **Supp. I:** 213
Very Good Hater, A (Hill, R.), **Supp. IX:** 111
Very Great Man Indeed, A (Reed), **Supp. XV:** 253
Very Private Eye, A: An Autobiography in Diaries and Letters (Pym), **Supp. II:** 363, 374
Very Private Life, A (Frayn), **Supp. VII:** 54–56
"Very Simply Topping Up the Brake Fluid" (Armitage), **VIII:** 4
Very Woman, A (Fletcher and Massinger), **II:** 66; **Supp. XI:** 184
"Vespers" (Auden), **Retro. Supp. I:** 13
"Vespers" (Milne), **Supp. V:** 301–302
Vet's Daughter, The (Comyns), **VIII:** 53, 60, 61–62
Vexilla Regis (Jones), **Supp. VII:** 180
Vexilla Regis (Skelton), **I:** 84
Via Media, The (Newman), **Supp. VII:** 295, 302
"Via Maestranza" (Cameron), **Supp. IX:** 27
"Via Negativa" (Thomas), **Supp. XII:** 286
"Via Portello" (Davie), **Supp. VI:** 107

"Vicar, The" (Praed), **V:** 14
Vicar of Bullhampton, The (Trollope), **V:** 102
Vicar of Sorrows, The (Wilson), **Supp. VI:** 308
Vicar of Wakefield, The (Goldsmith), **III:** 177, 178, 179, 180, **181–184,** 185, 188, 191
Viceroy of Ouidah, The (Chatwin), **Supp. IV:** 158, 165–168, 173; **Supp. IX:** 55–56
"Victim" (Fallon), **Supp. XII:** 104
Victim of Circumstances, A, and Other Stories (Gissing), **V:** 437
Victim of the Aurora, A (Keneally), **Supp. IV:** 346, 352–354
Victims (Fallon), **Supp. XII:** 104
"Victor Hugo" (Swinburne), **V:** 333
Victoria, queen of England, **IV:** 303–304, 305; **V:** xvii, xix, xxv–xxvi, 77, 114, 117
Victoria Station (Pinter), **Supp. I:** 378
Victorian Age in Literature (Chesterton), **VI:** 337
Victorian Age of English Literature, The (Oliphant), **Supp. X:** 222
Victorian and Edwardian London from Old Photographs (Betjeman), **VII:** 358
"Victorian Guitar" (Cornford), **VIII:** 114
Victorian Lady Travellers (Middleton), **V:** 253
Victorian Ode for Jubilee Day, 1897 (Thompson), **V:** 451
Victorian Romantic, A: D. G. Rossetti (Doughty), **V:** 246, 297n, 307
"Victorians and Georgians" (Abercrombie), **Supp. XVI:** 6
Victory (Conrad), **VI:** 144, 146, 148; **Supp. IV:** 250; **Retro. Supp. II:** 82
Victory (Fugard), **Supp. XV:** 104
"Victory, The" (Stevenson), **Supp. VI:** 256, 264
Vidal, Gore, **Supp. IV:** 546
"Video, The" (Adcock), **Supp. XII:** 13
Vienna (Spender), **Supp. II:** 486, 487
"Vienna. Zürich. Constance" (Thomas), **Supp. IV:** 493
"Vienne" (Rhys), **Supp. II:** 388, 389–390
Viet Rock (play), **Supp. IV:** 435
"Vietnam Project, The" (Coetzee), **Supp. VI:** 76, **78–79,** 80
"View from Yves Hill, The" (Boyd), **Supp. XVI:** 3
"View of Exmoor, A" (Warner), **Supp. VII:** 380
"View of Poetry, A" (Muir), **Supp. VI:** 202–203
View of the Edinburgh Theatre . . . , A (Boswell), **III:** 247
View of the English Stage, A (Hazlitt), **IV:** 129, 139
View of the Present State of Ireland (Spenser), **I:** 139
Views and Reviews (James), **VI:** 67
Views in Rome and Its Environs (Lear), **V:** 76, 87
Views in the Seven Ionian Islands (Lear), **V:** 87

Víga–Glúms saga, **VIII:** 241
"Vigil and Ode for St. George's Day" (Sisson), **Supp. XI:** 251–252
"Vigil in Lent, A" (Symons), **Supp. XIV:** 271
"Vigil of Corpus Christi, The" (Gunn), **Supp. IV:** 266
Vigny, Alfred de, **IV:** 176
Vile Bodies (Waugh), **VII:** 289, 290–291
Villa Rubein (Galsworthy), **VI:** 277
Village, The (Crabbe), **III:** 273, 274, 275, 277–278, 283, 286
"Village, The" (Reid), **Supp. VII:** 325
"Village, The" (Smith, I. C.), **Supp. IX:** 220–221
Village and Other Poems, The (Smith, I. C.), **Supp. IX:** 220–221
Village Betrothal (Greuze), **Supp. IV:** 122
Village by the Sea (Desai), **Supp. V:** 55, 63, 68–69
Village Minstrel, and Other Poems, The (Clare), **Supp. XI:** 56–57
"Village Priest, The" (Ngũgĩ), **VIII:** 220
Village Wooing (Shaw), **VI:** 127, 129
"Villain, The" (Davies), **Supp. XI:** 98–99
Villainy of Stock-Jobbers Detected, The (Defoe), **III:** 12
"Villanelle" (Empson), **Supp. II:** 183
Villette (Brontë), **V:** xxi, 112, 125–126, 130, 132, 136, 145, **147–150,** 152; **Retro. Supp. I:** 53, 54, 60–61
Villiers, George, *see* Buckingham, duke of
Villon (Bunting), **Supp. VII:** 3, 6
Villon, François, **V:** 327, 384
Vinaver, Eugéne, **Retro. Supp. II:** 242, 246
Vindication &c., The (Dryden), **II:** 305
Vindication of a Natural Diet . . . , A (Shelley), **IV:** 208
Vindication of . . . Lord Carteret, A (Swift), **III:** 35–36
Vindication of Natural Society, A (Burke), **III:** 195, 198, 205
Vindication of . . . Some Gospel-Truths, A (Bunyan), **II:** 253
Vindication of Some Passages in . . . the Decline and Fall . . . . , A (Gibbon), **III:** 233
Vindication of the English Constitution (Disraeli), **IV:** 298, 308
Vindication of the Rights of Men, A (Wollstonecraft), **Supp. III: 467–470,** 474, 476
Vindication of the Rights of Women, A (Wollstonecraft), **IV:** xv, 118; **Supp. III:** 465, **470–473,** 476
Vindicator, **Supp. XIII:** 117, 127
Vindiciae Ecclesiae Anglicanae: Letters to Charles Butler . . . . (Southey), **IV:** 71
Vine, Barbara, *see* Rendell, Ruth
Vinegar Tom (Churchill), **Supp. IV:** 181, 184–186, 198
Vinland (Brown), **Supp. VI:** 67
Vintage London (Betjeman), **VII:** 358–359
"Vintage to the Dungeon, The" (Lovelace), **II:** 231

Violent Effigy, The: A Study of Dickens's Imagination (Carey), **V:** 73
"Violent Noon, The" (Ballard), **Supp. V:** 20
Viper and Her Brood, The (Middleton), **II:** 3, 33
Virchow, Rudolf, **V:** 348
Virgidemiarum (Hall), **II:** 25
Virgil, *see* Vergil
Virgilius Restauratus (Arbuthnot), **Supp. XVI:** 27
Virgin and the Gipsy, The (Lawrence), **VII:** 91, 115
Virgin and the Nightingale, The: Medieval Latin Lyrics (tr. Adcock), **Supp. XII:** 10
Virgin in the Garden, The (Byatt), **Supp. IV:** 139, 145–147, 149
Virgin Martyr, The (Massinger and Dekker), **Supp. XI:** 182, 183, 192–193
"Virgin Mary to the Child Jesus, The" (Browning), **IV:** 313
"Virgin Russia" (Cameron), **Supp. IX:** 19
Virgin Territory (Maitland), **Supp. XI:** 163, 166–168, 170, 171, 172
"Virgini Senescens" (Sisson), **Supp. XI:** 255–256
Virginia (O'Brien), **Supp. V:** 334
Virginia Woolf: A Biography (Bell), **VII:** 38; **Retro. Supp. I:** 305
Virginia Woolf Icon (Silver), **Retro. Supp. I:** 305
Virginians, The (Thackeray), **V:** 29, **31–33,** 38
Virginibus Puerisque and Other Papers (Stevenson), **V:** 395; **Retro. Supp. I:** 262
Virtuous Villager, The (Haywood), **Supp. XII:** 136
Viscount of Blarney, and Other Plays, The (Clarke), **Supp. XV:** 25
Vision, A (Yeats), **VI:** 209, 213, 214, 222
"Vision, The" (Burns), **III:** 315
"Vision, The" (Traherne), **Supp. XI:** 266, 267
"Vision and Prayer" (Thomas), **Supp. I:** 178; **Retro. Supp. III:** 345
Vision of Bags, A (Swinburne), **V:** 333
Vision of Battlements, A (Burgess), **Supp. I:** 185, 187, 195–196
Vision of Cathkin Braes, The (Morgan, E.), **Supp. IX:** 160–163
"Vision of Cathkin Braes, The" (Morgan, E.), **Supp. IX:** 163
"Vision of Connaught in the Thirteenth Century, A" (Mangan), **Supp. XIII:** 127
Vision of Delight, The (Jonson), **Retro. Supp. I:** 165
Vision of Don Roderick, The (Scott), **IV:** 38
Vision of Gombold Proval, The (Orton), **Supp. V:** 365–366, 370
Vision of Judgement, A (Southey), **IV:** 61, 71, 184–187
Vision of Judgment, The (Byron), **IV:** xviii, 58, 61–62, 132, 172, 178, **184–187,** 193

"Vision of Poets, A" (Browning), **IV:** 316
"Vision of the Empire, The" (Williams, C. W. S.), **Supp. IX:** 282
"Vision of the Last Judgment, A" (Blake), **III:** 299
"Vision of the Mermaids, A" (Hopkins), **V:** 361, 381
Vision of the Three T's, The (Carroll), **V:** 274
"Vision of that Ancient Man, The" (Motion), **Supp. VII:** 260, 261
Vision of William Concerning Piers the Plowman . . . , The (ed. Skeat), **I:** 17
Vision Showed . . . to a Devout Woman, A (Julian of Norwich), **Supp. XII:** 153–154, 159
"Visions Fugitives" (Boyd), **Supp. XVI:** 44
Visions of the Daughters of Albion (Blake), **III:** 307; **Retro. Supp. I:** 39–40
"Visit" (Richardson), **Supp. XIII:** 192
"Visit in Bad Taste, A" (Wilson), **Supp. I:** 157
"Visit to Grandpa's, A" (Thomas), **Supp. I:** 181; **Retro. Supp. III:** 348
"Visit to Morin, A" (Greene), **Supp. I:** 15, 18
"Visit to the Dead, A" (Cameron), **Supp. IX:** 27
"Visitation, The" (Jennings), **Supp. V:** 212
Visitation, The (Roberts), **Supp. XV:** 264–265, 266
Visitations (MacNeice), **VII:** 416
"Visiting Hour" (Conn), **Supp. XIII:** 74
"Visiting Hour" (Kinsella), **Supp. V:** 273
"Visiting Hour" (Murphy), **Supp. V:** 326
"Visiting Julia" (Hart), **Supp. XI:** 123
Visiting Mrs. Nabokov and Other Excursions (Amis), **Supp. IV:** 42, 43
"Visiting Rainer Maria" (McGuckian), **Supp. V:** 286
Visiting the Caves (Plomer), **Supp. XI:** 213, 214
"Visitor" (Richardson), **Supp. XIII:** 192
"Visitor, The" (Bowen), **Supp. II:** 81
"Visitor, The" (Blunden), **Supp. XI:** 36
"Visitor, The" (Dahl), **Supp. IV:** 219–220
Visitor, The (Orton), **Supp. V:** 363, 367
"Visitors, The" (Fuller), **Supp. VII:** 77
"Visits, The" (James), **VI:** 49, 69
"Visits to the Cemetery of the Long Alive" (Stevenson), **Supp. VI:** 264
Vita Nuova (tr. Rossetti), **V:** 238
"Vitai Lampada" (Newbolt), **VI:** 417
Vittoria (Meredith), **V:** 227–228, 234
Vivaldi and the Number 3 (Butlin), **Supp. XVI:** 53, 65–66, 67, 68
"Vivaldi Learns a New Skill" (Butlin), **Supp. XVI:** 65
Vivian (Edgeworth), **Supp. III:** 158
Vivian Grey (Disraeli), **IV:** xvii, 293–294, 297, 299, 308
"Vivien" (Tennyson), **Retro. Supp. III:** 327
Vivisector, The (White), **Supp. I:** 132, 145–146
Vizetelly (publisher), **VI:** 86

"Vocation" (Malouf), **Supp. XII:** 221
"Voice, The" (Brooke), **Supp. III:** 52
"Voice, The" (Hardy), **VI:** 18
"Voice from the Dead, A" (Connolly), **Supp. III:** 111
"Voice of Brisbane, The" (Hart), **Supp. XI:** 131
"Voice of Nature, The" (Bridges), **VI:** 79
Voice of Scotland, **Supp. XII:** 204
"Voice of the Ancient Bard, The" (Blake), **Retro. Supp. I:** 37
"Voice of Things, The" (Hardy), **Retro. Supp. I:** 121
Voice Over (MacCaig), **Supp. VI:** 194
Voice Through a Cloud, A (Welch), **Supp. IX:** 262–263; 266–267, 268
Voices in the City (Desai), **Supp. V:** 54, 59–60, 72
Voices in the Night (Steel), **Supp. XII:** 273–274
Voices of the Stones (Russell), **VIII:** 290
"Voices of Time, The" (Ballard), **Supp. V:** 22, 24, 29, 34
Volpone (Jonson), **I:** 339, 343–344, 348; **II:** 4, 45, 70, 79; **V:** 56; **Retro. Supp. I:** 163, 164
Vǫlsunga saga, **VIII:** 231
Voltaire, **II:** 261, 348; **III:** 149, 235, 236, 327; **IV:** xiv, 290, 295, 346; **Supp. IV:** 136, 221
"Voltaire at Ferney" (Auden), **Retro. Supp. I:** 8
Voltaire in Love (Mitford), **Supp. X:** 163
Vǫlundarkviða, **VIII:** 230
"Volunteer, The" (Asquith), **VI:** 417
Volunteers (Friel), **Supp. V:** 111, 112, 121–122
Vǫluspá, **VIII:** 230, 231, 235, 243
Vonnegut, Kurt, Jr., **III:** 341; **Supp. IV:** 116
Vortex, The (Coward), **Supp. II:** 139, 141–143, 144, 149
Voss (Meale and Malouf), **Supp. XII:** 218
Voss (White), **VII:** 31; **Supp. I:** 130, 131, **138–141**, 142
Vote, Vote, Vote for Nigel Barton (Potter, D.), **Supp. X:** 228, 231–232
Votive Tablets (Blunden), **IV:** 86; **Supp. XI:** 36
Vox clamantis (Gower), **I:** 48, 49–50
"Vox Humana" (Gunn), **Supp. IV:** 261–262
Voyage, The (Muir), **Supp. VI:** 204, **206–207**
Voyage In the Dark (Rhys), **Supp. II: 394–396**
Voyage of Captain Popanilla, The (Disraeli), **IV:** 294–295, 308
"Voyage of Mael Duin," **Supp. IV:** 415–416
Voyage of the Dawn Treader, The (Lewis), **Supp. III:** 248, 260
Voyage of the Destiny, The (Nye), **Supp. X:** 195–196
"Voyage Out, The" (Adcock), **Supp. XII:** 6
Voyage Out, The (Woolf), **VII:** 20, 27, 37; **Retro. Supp. I:** 307, 315–316
Voyage That Never Ends, The (Lowry), **Supp. III:** 276, 280

Voyage to Abyssinia, A (tr. Johnson), **III:** 107, 112, 121; **Retro. Supp. I:** 139
Voyage to New Holland, A (Dampier), **III:** 24
Voyage to the Island of Love, A (Behn), **Supp. III:** 37
Voyage to Venus (Lewis), **Supp. III:** 249
"Voyagers Regret, The" (Jewsbury), **Supp. XIV:** 162
Voyages (Hakluyt), **I:** 150, 267; **III:** 7
"Voyages of Alfred Wallis, The" (Graham), **Supp. VII:** 110
Vulgar Errors (Browne), *see Pseudodoxia Epidemica*
Vulgar Streak, The (Lewis), **VII:** 72, 77
"Vulgarity in Literature" (Huxley), **V:** 53; **VII:** 198
"Vulture, The" (Beckett), **Supp. I:** 44

W. B. Yeats, Man and Poet (Jeffares), **VI:** 223
W. B. Yeats: The Critical Heritage (Jeffares), **VI:** 224
"W. Kitchener" (Hood), **IV:** 267
W. Somerset Maugham and the Quest for Freedom (Calder), **VI:** 376n
Waagen, Gustav Friedrich, **III:** 328
Wager, William, **I:** 213
Waggoner, The (Blunden), **Supp. XI:** 36, 42
Waggoner, The (Wordsworth), **IV:** 24, 73
"Wagner" (Brooke), **Supp. III:** 53
Wagner the Werewolf (Reynolds), **III:** 335
Wagstaff, Simon, pseud. of Jonathan Swift
Waif Woman, The (Stevenson), **V:** 396
"Wail and Warning of the Three Khalendars, The" (Mangan), **Supp. XIII:** 125–126
Wain, John, **VI:** 209
Wain, John, **Supp. XVI: 293–309**
Wainewright, Thomas, **V:** 405
Waingrow, W., **III:** 249
Waith, Eugene, **II:** 51, 64
"Waiting" (Montague), **Supp. XV:** 220
"Waiting" (Self), **Supp. V:** 402
"Waiting at the Station" (Thackeray), **V:** 25
"Waiting for Breakfast" (Larkin), **Supp. I:** 277
"Waiting for Columbus" (Reid), **Supp. VII:** 334
Waiting for Godot (Beckett), **I:** 16–17; **Supp. I:** 51, 55–56, 57, 59; **Supp. IV:** 281, 429; **Retro. Supp. I:** 17–18, 20–21, 23–24; **Retro. Supp. II:** 344
"Waiting for J." (Ishiguro), **Supp. IV:** 303; **Retro. Supp. III:** 161
Waiting for the Barbarians (Coetzee), **Supp. VI:** 75–76, **81–82**
Waiting for the Telegram (Bennett), **VIII:** 28
"Waiting Grounds, The" (Ballard), **Supp. V:** 21, 22
"Waiting in Hospital" (Cornford), **VIII:** 113
Waiting in the Wings (Coward), **Supp. II:** 155

Waiting Room, The (Harris), **Supp. V:** 136, 137–138, 140
"Waiting Supper, The" (Hardy), **VI:** 22
"Waking Father, The" (Muldoon), **Supp. IV:** 416–417
"Waking in a Newly Built House" (Gunn), **Supp. IV:** 263
Waking of Angantýr, The, **VIII:** 232
Waldegrave, Frances, **V:** 77, 80, 81
Waldere, **Retro. Supp. II:** 306–307
Wales: Epic Views of a Small Country (Morris, J.), **Supp. X:** 185
Wales, the First Place (Morris, J.), **Supp. X:** 177, 185
Walk in Chamounix, A, and Other Poems (Ruskin), **V:** 184
Walk on the Water, A (Stoppard), **Supp. I:** 437, 439
Walker, Ernest, **IV:** 304
Walker, London (Barrie), **Supp. III:** 4
Walker, R. S., **III:** 249
Walker, Shirley, **Supp. IV:** 347
Walker and Other Stories, The (O'Brian), **Supp. XII:** 251
"Walking Home" (Delanty), **Supp. XIV:** 67
"Walking in a Newly Built House" (Gunn), **Retro. Supp. III:** 121
Walking on Glass (Banks), **Supp. XI:** 7–8
"Walking to the Cattle Place" (Murray), **Supp. VII:** 274–275, 280, 281
"Walking with God" (Cowper), **III:** 212
"Walking Wounded" (Scannell), **VII:** 423
"Wall, The" (Jones), **Supp. VII:** 175
"Wall I Built, The" (Healy), **Supp. IX:** 107
Wall of the Plague, The (Brink), **Supp. VI: 52–53**
Wallace–Crabbe, Christopher, **VIII: 311–325**
Waller, Edmund, **II:** 138, 222, **232–236**, 256, 271
Walpole, Horace, **III:** 324, **325–327**, 336, 345; **Supp. III:** 383–384
Walpole, Hugh, **VI:** 55, 247, 377; **VII:** 211
Walpole, Robert, **Retro. Supp. I:** 235–236
"Walrus and the Carpenter, The" (Carroll), **V:** 268
Walsh, William, **II:** 325, 337, 339, 347; **Retro. Supp. I:** 232
Walsingham; or, The Pupil of Nature (Robinson), **Supp. XIII:** 210–211
Walt Whitman: A Study (Symonds), **Supp. XIV:** 261
Walter Pater: A Critical Study (Thomas), **V:** 355, 358; **VI:** 424
Walter Pater: The Idea in Nature (Ward), **V:** 347, 359
Walter Savage Landor: A Biography (Forster), **IV:** 87, 100
Walton, Izaak, **I:** 178; **II:** 118, 119, 130, **131–144**; **Retro. Supp. II:** 171–172
Walton, William, **VII:** xv
Walts, Janet, **Supp. IV:** 399
Waltz: An Apostrophic Hymn by Horace Hornem, Esq. (Byron), **IV:** 192

Wanderer, The, **Retro. Supp. II:** 304
Wanderer, The (Auden), **VII:** 380
"Wanderer, The" (tr. Morgan), **Supp. IX:** 160–161
"Wanderer, The" (Smith), **Supp. II:** 465
Wanderer, The; or, Female Difficulties (Burney), **Supp. III:** 64, 67, 74, 75, 76–77
"Wandering Angus, The" (Yeats), **Supp. IV:** 424
Wandering Islands, The (Hope), **Supp. VII:** 153–156, 157, 159
Wandering Jew, The (Shelley), **IV:** 209
"Wanderings of Brendan,"**Supp. IV:** 415
Wanderings of Odysseus, The (Sutcliff), **Supp. XVI:** 273
Wanderings of Oisin, The (Yeats), **IV:** 216; **VI:** 220, 221; **Supp. V:** 36; **Retro. Supp. I:** 325
Want of Wyse Men, The (Henryson), **Supp. VII:** 146–147
Wanting Seed, The (Burgess), **Supp. I:** 186, 190, 192–193
War (Doyle), **Supp. V:** 77, 87, 88–89
War and Common Sense (Wells), **VI:** 244
"War Cemetery" (Blunden), **Supp. XI:** 35
War Crimes (Carey), **Supp. XII:** 52, 54
"War Crimes" (Carey), **Supp. XII:** 54–55
"War Death in a Low Key" (Ewart), **Supp. VII:** 44
War Fever (Ballard), **Supp. V:** 33
"War Fever" (Ballard), **Supp. V:** 33
"War Games" (Scupham), **Supp. XIII:** 225
War in Heaven (Williams, C. W. S.), **Supp. IX:** 279, 280–281
War in Samoa (Stevenson), **V:** 396
War in South Africa, The: Its Cause and Conduct (Doyle), **Supp. II:** 161
War in the Air . . . , The (Wells), **VI:** 234, 244
War Issues for Irishmen (Shaw), **VI:** 119
War of Don Emmanuel's Nether Parts, The (De Bernières), **Supp. XII:** 65, 68, 69, 70–72
War of the Worlds, The (Wells), **VI:** 226, 233–234
War Plays, The (Bond), **Supp. I:** 423, 434
"War Poets, The" (Longley), **VIII:** 173
War Speeches (Churchill), **VI:** 361
"War That Will End War, The" (Wells), **VI:** 227, 244
"War–time" (Ewart), **Supp. VII:** 38
"War Widow" (Jamie), **Supp. XIV:** 131, 133–134
Ward, A. C., **V:** xiii, xxviii, 85, 86, 347, 348, 349
Ward, Edward, **III:** 41
Ward, Mrs. Humphry, **VI:** 387
Ward, R. P., **IV:** 293
"Ward 1G" (Fuller), **Supp. VII:** 80
"Ward 9" (Self), **Supp. V:** 401
Warden, The (Trollope), **V:** xxii, 92, 93, 101
"Warden's Daughter, The" (Gissing), **V:** 437
Ware the Hawk (Skelton), **I:** 88
"Waring" (Browning), **IV:** 356; **Retro. Supp. III:** 20
Warner, Alan, **Supp. XI:** 281–296
Warner, Sylvia Townsend, **Supp. VII:** 369–383
"Warning to Children" (Graves), **VII:** 265
Warren, Austin, **II:** 155, 332n
Warrior Scarlet (Sutcliff), **Supp. XVI:** 261, 269
"Warriors of the North, The" (Hughes), **Supp. I:** 342, 350
"Warriors Soul, The" (Conrad), **VI:** 148
War's Embers (Gurney), **VI:** 425
"Wartime Childhood, A" (Scupham), **Supp. XIII:** 218
Warton, Joseph, **III:** 162, 170n
"Was He Married?" (Smith), **Supp. II:** 468; **Retro. Supp. III:** 311, 314
"Was, Is, Will Be" (Reid), **Supp. VII:** 327
Washington Square (James), **VI:** 32–33
Wasp Factory, The (Banks), **Supp. XI:** 1–3, 6
Wasp in a Wig, The (Carroll), **V:** 274
"Wasps, The" (Constantine), **Supp. XV:** 78–79
"Waste Land, The" (Eliot), **VI:** 137, 158; **VII:** xv, 143, **147–150;** **Supp. II:** 122; **Supp. IV:** 58, 249, 377; **Retro. Supp. I:** 3; **Retro. Supp. II:** 120, 121, 124–129
"Waste Land, The" (Paton), **Supp. II:** 345
Waste of Shame: The Mystery of Shakespeare and His Sonnets (Boyd), **Supp. XVI:** 46
"Wasted Day, A" (Cornford), **VIII:** 103
Wasted Years, The (Phillips), **Supp. V:** 380
"Wat o' the Cleugh" (Hogg), **Supp. X:** 110
Wat Tyler (Southey), **IV:** 59, 62, 66, 71, 185
"Watch, The" (Cornford), **VIII:** 102–103, 107
"Watch, The" (Swift), **Supp. V:** 433–434
Watch and Ward (James), **VI:** 24, 26, 67
Watch in the Night, A (Wilson), **Supp. VI:** 307
Watched Pot, The (Saki), **Supp. VI:** 250
Watching for Dolphins (Constantine), **Supp. XV:** 66, 72
"Watching for Dolphins" (Constantine), **Supp. XV:** 65, 74
"Watching People Sing" (Kay), **Supp. XIII:** 107–108
"Watching Post" (Day Lewis), **Supp. III:** 128
Watching the Perseids (Scupham), **Supp. XIII:** 226–227, 229
"Watching the Perseids: Remembering the Dead" (Scupham), **Supp. XIII:** 227
Watchman, The (periodical), **IV:** 43, 55, 56
Watchman, The (Rankin), **Supp. X:** 244
Water and Waste (Reading), **VIII:** 261, 262
Water Babies, The: A Fairy-tale for a Land Baby (Kingsley), **Supp. XVI:** 201–**Supp. XVI:** 202, 204, 205
Water Beetle, The (Mitford), **Supp. X:** 151, 167
"Water Carrier, The" (Montague), **Supp. XV:** 213
"Water Cinema" (Redgrove), **Supp. VI:** 236
"Water Diviner, The" (Beer), **Supp. XIV:** 4
"Water Lady, The" (Hood), **IV:** 255
"Water Lilies" (Jamie), *Supp. XIV:* 143
"Water Music" (MacDiarmid), **Supp. XII:** 212
Water of Life, The (Bunyan), **II:** 253
Water of the Wondrous Isles, The (Morris), **V:** 306
"Watercress Girl, The" (Coppard), **VIII:** 90, 95
"Waterfall" (Fallon), **Supp. XII:** 103
Waterfall, The (Drabble), **Supp. IV:** 230, 239–241
"Waterfall, The" (Longley), **VIII:** 177–178
"Waterfall of Winter" (Redgrove), **Supp. VI:** 234
"Watergaw, The" (MacDiarmid), **Supp. XII:** 204–205
"Waterglass, The" (Reid), **Supp. VII:** 326
Waterhouse, Keith, **Supp. XIII: 265–279**
"Waterkeeper's Bothy" (Murphy), **Supp. V:** 328
"Water–Lady" (Redgrove), **Supp. VI:** 230
Waterland (Swift), **Supp. V:** 427, 434–437
Waterlight: Selected Poems (Jamie), **Supp. XIV:** 129, 143
"Watermark" (Gunesekera), **Supp. X:** 87
Waters of Babylon, The (Arden), **Supp. II:** 21, 22, 23–24, 25, 29
"Watershed, The" (Auden), **Retro. Supp. I:** 3
"Water–Witch, Wood–Witch, Wine–Witch" (Redgrove), **Supp. VI:** 234
Watson, George L., **VI:** 152
Watson, John B., **Supp. II:** 451
Watson, John Richard, **IV:** ix, xxv, 26, 375
Watson, Peter, **Supp. III:** 102–103, 105, 109
Watson, Richard, **III:** 301
Watson, Sir William, **VI:** 415
Watson, Thomas, **I:** 193, 276
Watsons, The (Austen), **IV:** 108, 122
Watson's Apology (Bainbridge), **Supp. VI:** 23
Watt, Ian, **VI:** 144; **Retro. Supp. I:** 70
Watt (Beckett), **Supp. I:** 46, **47–49,** 50, 51; **Retro. Supp. I:** 17, 20
Watteau (Brookner), **Supp. IV:** 122
Watteau, Jean-Antoine, **Supp. IV:** 122
Watter's Mou', The (Stoker), **Supp. III:** 381
"Wattle Tent" (Murphy), **Supp. V:** 329
Watts, Isaac, **III:** 118, 211, 288, 294, 299, 300
Watts–Dunton, Theodore, **V:** 314, 334
Waugh, Alec, **Supp. VI: 267–277**
Waugh, Evelyn, **V:** 33; **VII:** xviii, xx–xxi, **289–308;** **Supp. II:** 4, 74, 199,

213, 218; **Supp. III:** 105; **Supp. IV:** 27, 281, 287, 365, 505
"Wave, The" (Delanty), **Supp. XIV:** 75
Waverly novels (Scott), **IV:** 28, 30–34, 38
Waverly; or, 'Tis Sixty Years Since (Scott), **III:** 335; **IV:** xvii, 28, 30–31, 37, 38; **Supp. III:** 151, 154
Waves, The (Woolf), **VI:** 262; **VII:** xv, 18, 22, 27, 38; **Supp. III:** 45; **Supp. IV:** 461, 557; **Retro. Supp. I:** 308, 314, 319–320
"Waves Have Gone Back, The" (Dutton), **Supp. XII:** 93
"Waxwing Winter" (McGuckian), **Supp. V:** 289
Waxwings (Raban), **Supp. XI:** 227, 228, 238–241
"Way It Was, The (Raine), **Supp. XIII:** 174
"Way It Came, The" (James), **VI:** 69
Way of All Flesh, The (Butler), **VI:** ix; **Supp. II:** 97, 98, 99, 104, **111–114,** 117, 119
Way of Being Free, A (Okri), **Supp. V:** 353, 359, 360
"Way of Imperfection, The" (Thompson), **V:** 451
"Way of Literature: An Apologia, The" (Brown), **Supp. VI:** 70
Way of Looking, A (Jennings), **Supp. V:** , 210, 211, 214
"Way of the Cross, The" (du Maurier), **Supp. III:** 147
Way of the Spirit (Haggard), **Supp. III:** 214, 222
Way of the World, The (Congreve), **II:** 339, **343–346,** 347, 350
"Way the Wind Blows, The" (Caudwell), **Supp. IX:** 36
"Way to Keep Him, The" (Robinson), **Supp. XIII:** 205
Way to the Stars, The (Rattigan), **Supp. VII:** 313, 319
"Way up to Heaven, The" (Dahl), **Supp. IV:** 218–219
Way Upstream (Ayckbourn), **Supp. V:** 3, 10, 14
Way We Live, The (Jamie), **Supp. XIV:** 129, 134–136, 143
"Way We Live, The" (Jamie), **Supp. XIV:** 135
Way We Live Now, The (Trollope), **IV:** 307; **V:** xxiv, 98–99, 100, 102
"Wayfaring Tree, The" (tr. Mangan), **Supp. XIII:** 118
Ways and Means (Coward), **Supp. II:** 153
Ways of Dying (Mda), **Supp. XV:** 199–202, 203, 205, 206
Ways of Escape (Greene), **Supp. I:** 3, 7, 11, 18
Ways of Seeing (Berger), **Supp. IV:** 79, 82, 88–90
Ways of Telling: The World of John Berger (Dyer), **Supp. IV:** 81
"Wayside Station, The" (Muir), **Supp. VI:** 206
"We All Try" (Caudwell), **Supp. IX:** 36, 37
"We Are Seven" (Wordsworth), **IV:** 8, 10

"We have a pritty witty king" (Rochester), **II:** 259
"We lying by seasand" (Thomas), **Supp. I:** 176; **Retro. Supp. III:** 341
"We Must Act Quickly" (Paton), **Supp. II:** 359
We Shall Sing for the Fatherland and Other Plays (Mda), **Supp. XV:** 196, 198–199, 202–203
We Were Dancing (Coward), **Supp. II:** 153
"We Will Not Play the Harp Backward Now, No" (Delanty), **Supp. XIV:** 71
Weak Woman (Davies), **Supp. XI:** 92
"Weal and Woe in Garveloch" (Martineau), **Supp. XV:** 188
"Wealth, The" (Dunn), **Supp. X:** 66
Wealth of Mr. Waddy, The (Wells), *see Kipps*
Wealth of Nations, The (Smith), *see Inquiry into the Nature & Causes of the Wealth of Nations*
Wearieswa': A Ballad (Swinburne), **V:** 333
Weather in Japan, The (Longley), **VIII:** 166, 177–178
"Weather in Japan, The" (Longley), **VIII:** 177
Weatherboard Cathedral, The (Murray), **Supp. VII:** 270, 272–273, 282
Weathering (Reid), **Supp. VII:** 323, 330–331
"Web, The" (Scupham), **Supp. XIII:** 229
Webb, Beatrice, **VI:** 227, 241; **Supp. IV:** 233
Webb, Mary, **Supp. IV:** 169
Webb, Philip, **V:** 291, 296
Webb, Sidney, **VI:** 102; **Supp. IV:** 233
Webber, Andrew Lloyd, **Supp. V:** 3
Webster, John, **II:** 21, 31,, 33, **68–86,** 82359, 97, 100; **Supp. IV:** 234
Webster: "The Dutchess of Malfi" (Leech), **II:** 90*n*
Wedd, Nathaniel, **VI:** 398, 399
"Wedding, The" (Smith, I. C.), **Supp. IX:** 224
"Wedding Ceilidh, The" (Burnside), **Supp. XIII:** 29
Wedding Day, The (Inchbald), **Supp. XV:** 158, 160
"Wedding Gown, The" (Moore), **VI:** 93
"Wedding Guest, A" (Plomer), **Supp. XI:** 222
Wedding of Cousins, A (Tennant), **Supp. IX:** 239
"Wedding Morning" (Kinsella), **Supp. V:** 261
"Wedding Wind" (Larkin), **Supp. I:** 277, 285
Wedding-Day, The (Fielding), **III:** 105
"Wedding-Wind" (Larkin), **Retro. Supp. III:** 210
"Weddings" (Thomas), **Supp. IV:** 491
Weddings at Nether Powers, The (Redgrove), **Supp. VI:** 235
Wedgwood, Tom, **IV:** 127–128
Wednesday Early Closing (Nicholson), **Supp. VI:** 212, 214
"Wednesday; or, The Dumps" (Gay), **III:** 56

"Wee Wifey" (Jamie), **Supp. XIV:** 138
Wee Willie Winkie (Kipling), **VI:** 204; **Retro. Supp. III:** 186
Wee Willie Winkie and Other Stories (Kipling), **Retro. Supp. III:** 186
"Weed, The" (Pitter), **Supp. XIII:** 143
"Weed Species" (Dutton), **Supp. XII:** 94–95
"Weeds" (Nicholson), **Supp. VI:** 219
"Week with Uncle Felix, A" (Galloway), **Supp. XII:** 122–123
Weekend with Claude, A (Bainbridge), **Supp. VI:** 17–19, 24
Weekly Journal (newspaper), **III:** 7
Weep Before God (Wain), **Supp. XVI:** 306
Weep Not, Child (Ngũgĩ), **VIII:** 212, 213, 214, 218–219
"Weep Not My Wanton" (Coppard), **VIII:** 88, 93
"Weeper, The" (Crashaw), **II:** 180, 181, 183
"Weighing" (Heaney), **Retro. Supp. I:** 133
"Weights" (Murray), **Supp. VII:** 278
"Weignachtsabend" (Roberts, K.), **Supp. X:** 270
Weil, Simone, **Supp. I:** 217
Weinraub, Judith, **Supp. IV:** 345
Weir of Hermiston, The (Stevenson), **V:** 383, 384, 387, 390, 392, 396; **Retro. Supp. I:** 270
Weis, C. McC., **III:** 249
Weismann, August, **Supp. II:** 108
Welch, Denton, **Supp. III:** 107, **Supp. IX: 261–270**
"Welcome, The" (Cowley), **II:** 196
"Welcome to Sack, The" (Herrick), **II:** 111
Weldon, Fay, **Supp. IV: 521–539**
"Well at the Broch of Gurness, The" (Jamie), **Supp. XIV:** 141
Well at the World's End, The (Morris), **V:** 306
Well of Loneliness, The (Hall), **VI:** 411; **Supp. VI:** 119–120, 122, **125–128,** 129, 131
Well of Lycopolis, The (Bunting), **Supp. VII:** 4
"Well of Pen–Morta, The" (Gaskell), **V:** 15
Well of the Saints, The (Synge), **VI:** 308, 311, 312–313; **Retro. Supp. I:** 297–298
"Well-Spring, The" (Nye), **Supp. X:** 195, 205
Well-Beloved, The: A Sketch of a Temperament (Hardy), **VI:** 14, 20; **Retro. Supp. I:** 114–115
"Wellington College" (Murphy), **Supp. V:** 328
Wells, H. G., **III:** 341; **V:** xxiii, xxvi, 388, 426–427, 429, 438; **VI:** x–xiii, 102, **225–246,** 287; **VII:** xiv, 197; list of works and letters, **VI:** 243–246; **Supp. II:** 295; **Supp. III:** 434; **Supp. IV:** 256
"Wells, Hitler, and the World State" (Orwell), **VII:** 274
"Wells, The" (Redgrove), **Supp. VI:** 234, 237

Well-Wrought Urn, The (Brooks), **IV:** 323n, 339
Welsh Ambassador, The, **II:** 100
"Welsh Hill Country, The" (Thomas), **Supp. XII:** 283
"Welsh History" (Thomas), **Supp. XII:** 283
Welsh, Irvine, **Supp. IV:** 26
Welsh Girl, The (Davies), **Supp. XIV:** 35, 36, 46–47
"Welsh Landscape" (Thomas), **Supp. XII:** 283
Welsh Opera, The (Fielding), **III:** 105
"Welshman to Any Tourist, A" (Thomas), **Supp. XII:** 283
"Welshness in Wales" (Morris, J.), **Supp. X:** 184–185
We're Not Going to Do Anything (Day Lewis), **Supp. III:** 118
"Werewolf, The" (Carter), **Supp. III:** 88
Werner, J., **III:** 249
Werner: A Tragedy (Byron), **IV:** 193
Werther (Goethe), see *Sorrows of Young Werther, The*
Wesker, Arnold, **VI:** 101
Wesley, Charles, **III:** 211
Wesley, John, **II:** 273
Wessex: A National Trust Book (Beer), **Supp. XIV:** 12
"Wessex Calendar" (Beer), **Supp. XIV:** 5
Wessex Poems (Hardy), **VI:** 14; **Retro. Supp. I:** 110
Wessex Tales: Strange, Lively and Commonplace (Hardy), **VI:** 20
West, Anthony, **VI:** 241, 242
West, Arthur Graeme, **VI:** 423
"West End, The" (Healy), **Supp. IX:** 107
West, Moris, **Supp. IV:** 343
West, Rebecca, **VI:** 226, 227, 252, 371; **Supp. II:** 146–147; **Supp. III:** 431–445
"West Country" (Scupham), **Supp. XIII:** 219
"West Indies, The" (Macaulay), **IV:** 278
West Indies and the Spanish Main, The (Trollope), **V:** 101
West of Suez (Osborne), **Supp. I:** 339
West Pier, The (Hamilton), **Supp. XVI:** 188, 189
West Window, The (Hartley), see *Shrimp and the Anemone, The*
Western Swing (Greig), **Supp. XVI:** 162–163
"Westland Row" (Kinsella), **Supp. V:** 263
"Westland Well" (Swinburne), **V:** 333
Westmacott, Mary (pseud., Christie), **Supp. II:** 123, 133
"Westminster Abbey" (Arnold), **V:** 208–209
Westminster Alice, The (Saki), **Supp. VI:** 239
Westminster Review, The (periodical), **V:** xviii, 189
Westward Ho! (Dekker and Webster), **II:** 68, 85
Westward Ho! or, The Voyages and Adventures of Sir Amyas Leigh, Knight of Burrough in the County of Devon, in the Reign of Her Glorious Majesty Queen Elizabeth (Kingsley), **Supp. XVI:** 198–199, 205
Westwind (Rankin), **Supp. X:** 244
Wet Fish (Arden), **Supp. II:** 28
"Wet Night, A" (Beckett), **Supp. I:** 45; **Retro. Supp. I:** 19
"Wet Snow" (MacCaig), **Supp. VI:** 186
Wetherby (Hare), **Supp. IV:** 282, 289–290
"Whale, The" (Soutar), **Supp. XVI:** 250
Whale Caller, The (Mda), **Supp. XV:** 205–206
What a Carve Up! (Coe), **Supp. XV:** 49, 50, 51, 55–57, 58, 60, 61, 62
"What a Misfortune" (Beckett), **Supp. I:** 45
What Am I Doing Here (Chatwin), **Supp. IV:** 157, 163, 173; **Supp. IX:** 52, 53, 60–61
What Became of Jane Austen? (Amis), **Supp. II:** 1, 2, 11
What D'Ye Call It, The (Gay), **III:** 58, 60, 67
"What Do Hippos Eat?" (Wilson), **Supp. I:** 156–157
"What Does It Matter?" (Forster), **VI:** 411
"What Ever" (Kay), **Supp. XIII:** 107
What Every Woman Knows (Barrie), **Supp. III:** 6, 9, **10–11**
"What Gets Lost *Lo Que Se Pierde*" (Reid), **Supp. VII:** 331
"What Happened to Blake?" (Hare), **Supp. IV:** 281, 283
What Happened to Burger's Daughter: or How South African Censorship Works (Gordimer), **Supp. II:** 237
"What I Believe" (Spender), **Supp. II:** 494
"What I Have Been Doing Lately" (Kincaid), **Supp. VII:** 221
"What I Know About Myself" (Burnside), **Supp. XIII:** 29
What I Really Wrote About the War (Shaw), **VI:** 129
What Is He? (Disraeli), **IV:** 308
"What Is the Language Using Us For?" (Graham), **Supp. VII:** 115
"What Is There to Discuss?" (Ramsey), **VII:** 240
What Lack I Yet? (Powys), **VIII:** 255
What Maisie Knew (James), **VI: 50–52,** 67
"What meaneth this?" (Wyatt), **I:** 104
What Mrs. McGillicuddy Saw (Christie), see *4.50 from Paddington*
"What rage is this" (Wyatt), **I:** 104
What the Black Mirror Saw (Redgrove), **Supp. VI:** 236
What the Butler Saw (Orton), **Supp. V:** 367, 371, 377–378
What the Hammer (Healy), **Supp. IX:** 96, 106–107
What the Public Wants (Bennett), **VI:** 263–264
"What the Shepherd Saw" (Hardy), **VI:** 22
"What the Thrush Said" (Keats), **IV:** 225
"What the Thunder Said" (Eliot), **Retro. Supp. II:** 128–129
"What Then?" (Thomas), **Supp. XII:** 290, 291
"What Then?" (Yeats), **Retro. Supp. I:** 337
"'What, Then, Does Dr. Newman Mean'? A Reply to a Pamphlet Lately Published by Dr. Newman" (Kingsley), **Supp. XVI:** 203
What Where (Beckett), **Supp. IV:** 284
"What will they do?" (Thomas), **Supp. III:** 400, 401
What You Will (Marston), **II:** 29–30, 40
Whately, Richard, **IV:** 102, 122
"Whatever Sea" (Dutton), **Supp. XII:** 92–93
What's Become of Waring? (Powell), **VII:** 346, 353
"What's Your Success?" (Smith, I. C.), **Supp. IX:** 214
Wheatcroft, Geoffrey, **Supp. IV:** 173
"Wheel of Time, The" (James), **VI:** 69
Wheels of Chance, The: A Holiday Adventure (Wells), **VI:** 231–232, 244
"Wheest, Wheest" (MacDiarmid), **Supp. XII:** 206
"When a Beau Goes In" (Ewart), **VII:** 423; **Supp. VII:** 37
"When all my five and country senses see" (Thomas), **Supp. I:** 176
"When Earth's Last Picture Is Painted" (Kipling), **VI:** 169
"When I Am Dead, My Dearest" (Rossetti), **V:** 249
"When I Have Fears" (Keats), **IV:** 221
"When I Was Thirteen" (Welch), **Supp. IX:** 268–269
When Is a Door Not a Door? (Arden), **Supp. II:** 29
"When Israel came out of Egypt" (Clough), **V:** 160
"When My Girl Comes Home" (Pritchett), **Supp. III:** 312, **321–324**
When My Girl Comes Home (Pritchett), **Supp. III:** 313, 321
When People Play People (Mda), **Supp. XV:** 196, 202
"When the Camel Is Dust it Goes Through the Needle's Eye" (Stevenson), **Supp. VI:** 264
"When the Kye Comes Hame" (Hogg), **Supp. X:** 110
When the Moon Has Set (Synge), **VI:** 310n; **Retro. Supp. I:** 294
"When the Sardines Came" (Plomer), **Supp. XI:** 215
When the Sleeper Wakes (Wells), **VI:** 234
When the Wicked Man (Ford), **VI:** 319, 332
When They Lay Bare (Greig), **Supp. XVI:** 168–170
"When They Want to Know What We Were Like" (Healy), **Supp. IX:** 107
When We Dead Awaken (Ibsen), **VI:** 269; **Retro. Supp. I:** 170, 175
"When we that were dear . . . A (Henley), **V:** 392
When We Were Orphans (Ishiguro), **Retro. Supp. III:** 149, 158–159, 162
When We Were Very Young (Milne), **Supp. V:** 295, 301–302

When William Came (Saki), **Supp. VI: 248–250**
"When Windsor walles sustained my wearied arm" (Surrey), **I:** 113
"When You Are Old" (Yeats), **Retro. Supp. I:** 329
"When You Go" (Morgan, E.), **Supp. IX:** 168
"When you see millions of the mouthless dead" (Sorley), **VI:** 422
Where Adam Stood (Potter, D.), **Supp. X:** 232–234
Where Angels Fear to Tread (Forster), **VI:** 400–401; **Retro. Supp. II:** 136–139
"Where I'm Coming From" (Ali), **Supp. XIII:** 1
"Where once the waters of your face" (Thomas), **Supp. I:** 173–174; **Retro. Supp. III:** 338
Where Shall We Go This Summer (Desai), **Supp. V:** 53, 55, 63–64, 66, 73
"Where Tawe Flows" (Thomas), **Supp. I:** 180
Where the Rivers Meet (Wain), **Supp. XVI:** 297, 301–302
Where the Wind Came (Wallace–Crabbe), **VIII:** 315–317, 318
Where There Is Darkness (Phillips), **Supp. V:** 380
"Where They Are Wrong" (Paton), **Supp. II:** 360
Where You Find It (Galloway), **Supp. XII:** 117, 126–127
"Where You Find It" (Galloway), **Supp. XII:** 126
"Whereabouts" (Carson), **Supp. XIII:** 63
Whereabouts: Notes on Being a Foreigner (Reid), **Supp. VII:** 323, 335–336
"Wherefore Lament" (Pitter), **Supp. XIII:** 143
"Whereto Art Thou Come" (Thompson), **V:** 444
Whether a Dove or Seagull (Warner), **Supp. VII:** 370, 371, 372–373, 376
Whetstone, George, **I:** 282, 313
Whibley, Charles, **II:** 259
Which Is the Man? (Cowley), **Supp. XVI:** 110
"Which New Era Would Be?" (Gordimer), **Supp. II:** 242
Whig Examiner (periodical), **III:** 51, 53
Whig Interpretations of History, The (Butterfield), **IV:** 291
While the Sun Shines (Rattigan), **Supp. VII:** 313
Whims and Oddities (Hood), **IV:** 253, 255, 257, 267
Whimsicalities (Hood), **IV:** 254, 267
Whirling (Wallace–Crabbe), **VIII:** 323–324, 325
Whirlpool, The (Gissing), **V:** 437
"Whisht" (Crawford), **Supp. XI:** 75
Whisperer, The (Nicholson), **Supp. VI:** 218
Whispering Roots, The (Day Lewis), **Supp. III:** 116, 118, 129–130
"Whispers" (Tennyson), **IV:** 332
"Whispers of Immortality" (Eliot), **VII:** 145

Whistle Down the Wind (Waterhouse and Hall), **Supp. XIII:** 274, 275
Whistlecraft (Frere), **IV:** 182–183
Whistler, James McNeill, **V:** 238, 245, 320, 407
Whit; or, Isis Amongst the Unsaved (Banks), **Supp. XI:** 14
White, Gilbert, **Supp. VI: 279–295**
White, James, **IV:** 79
White, Norman, **V:** 379n
White, Patrick, **Supp. I:** 129–152; **Supp. IV:** 343
White, Tony, **Supp. IV:** 256, 272, 273–274
"White Air of March, The" (Smith, I. C.), **Supp. IX:** 216–217
White Boats (Greig), **Supp. XVI:** 161, 162
White Bird, The (Berger), **Supp. IV:** 89
White Bird, The (MacCaig), **Supp. VI:** 192
White Chappell, Scarlet Tracings (Sinclair), **Supp. XIV:** 233, 241–242
White Cockade, The (Gregory), **VI:** 315
White Company, The (Doyle), **Supp. II:** 159, 163
White Countess, The (Ishiguro), **Retro. Supp. III:** 162
White Devil, The (Webster), **I:** 246; **II:** 68, 70, 72, 73–75, 76, 79, 80–85, 97; **Supp. IV:** 234–235
White Doe of Rylstone, The (Wordsworth), **IV:** xvii, 24
White Eagles over Serbia (Durrell), **Retro. Supp. III:** 85
White Goddess, The (Graves), **VII:** xviii, 257, 259, 261–262
"White Heliotrope" (Symons), **Supp. XIV:** 275–276
White Horseman, The (MacCaig), **Supp. VI:** 184
White Hotel, The (Thomas), **Supp. IV:** 479, 481–483, 486, 490, 493
"White Island, The; or, Place of the Blest" (Herrick), **II:** 113
White Liars (Shaffer), **Supp. I:** 322–323
White Lies (Shaffer), **Supp. I:** 322
"White Man's Burden, The" (Kipling), **Retro. Supp. III:** 187, 197
White Mercedes, The (Pullman), **Supp. XIII:** 150, 153
White Monkey, The (Galsworthy), **VI:** 274
"White Negro, The" (Mailer), **Supp. IV:** 17–18
"White Noon, The" (Smith, I. C.), **Supp. IX:** 211
White Paternoster and Other Stories, The (Powys), **VIII:** 248, 256
White Peacock, The (Lawrence), **VII:** 88, 89, 91–93; **Retro. Supp. II:** 222–223, 226
"White–Pinafored Black Cat, The" (Upward), **Supp. XIII:** 260
"White Poet, The" (Dunn), **Supp. X:** 71
"White Queen, The" (Harrison), **Supp. V:** 151
"White Seal, The" (Kipling), **Retro. Supp. III:** 190
"White Ship, The" (Rossetti), **V:** 238, 244

"White Spirits" (Delanty), **Supp. XIV:** 70
"White Stocking, The" (Lawrence), **VII:** 114
White Threshold, The (Graham), **Supp. VII:** 110–111
"White Windsor Soap" (McGuckian), **Supp. V:** 288
White Writing: On the Culture of Letters in South Africa (Coetzee), **Supp. VI: 84–85**
White–Eagles over Serbia (Durrell), **Supp. I:** 100
Whitehall, Harold, **V:** 365, 382
Whitelock, Derek, **Supp. IV:** 348
"Whitewashed Wall, The" (Hardy), **Retro. Supp. I:** 120
Whitman, Walt, **IV:** 332; **V:** 418; **VI:** 55, 63; **Supp. IV:** 163, 487
Whitsun Weddings, The (Larkin), **Supp. I:** 276, **279–281**, 285; **Retro. Supp. III:** 205–208
"Whitsun Weddings, The" (Larkin), **Supp. I:** 285; **Retro. Supp. III:** 206–207, 208
"Whitsunday" (Herbert), **II:** 125
"Whitsunday in Kirchstetten" (Auden), **VII:** 396, 397
"Who Are These Coming to the Sacrifice?" (Hill), **Supp. V:** 191
Who Are You? (Kavan), **Supp. VII:** 214
"Who Goes Home?" (Day Lewis), **Supp. III:** 130
Who Guards a Prince? (Hill, R.), **Supp. IX:** 117
Who Is Sylvia? (Rattigan), **Supp. VII:** 317
"Who Knows?" (Pitter), **Supp. XIII:** 145
"Who Needs It?" (Blackwood), **Supp. IX:** 9
"Who Speaks My Language?" (Wain), **Supp. XVI:** 306
Who was Changed and Who was Dead (Comyns), **VIII:** 53, 60–61
Who Was Oswald Fish? (Wilson), **Supp. VI: 300–301**
Whole Armour, The (Harris), **Supp. V:** 132, 134, 135
Whole Duty of Man, The (Allestree), **III:** 82
"Whole of the Sky, The" (Armitage), **VIII:** 11
"Whole Truth, The" (Motion), **Supp. VII:** 256
Whole Works of Homer, The (Chapman), **I:** 235
Whoroscope (Beckett), **Supp. I:** 43; **Retro. Supp. I:** 19
Who's the Dupe? (Cowley), **Supp. XVI:** 109–110, 112, 114–115
"Who's Who" (Auden), **Retro. Supp. I:** 2
Whose Body? (Sayers), **Supp. III:** 334, 336–338, 340, 350
"Whose Endless Jar" (Richards), **Supp. II:** 426, 429
Whose Is the Kingdom? (Arden and D'Arcy), **Supp. II:** 39, 40–41
"Whoso list to hunt" (Wyatt), **I:** 101, 109

Why Are We So Blest? (Armah), **Supp. X:** 1–2, 5–9, 13–14
"Why Brownlee Left" (Muldoon), **Supp. IV:** 409, 410, 415, 418, 426
Why Come Ye Not to Court? (Skelton), **I:** 92–93
Why Do I Write? (Bowen), **Supp. II:** 80, 81, 91
Why Don't You Stop Talking (Kay), **Supp. XIII:** 102, 109–110
"Why Don't You Stop Talking" (Kay), **Supp. XIII:** 102, 109–110
Why Frau Frohmann Raised Her Prices and Other stories (Trollope), **V:** 102
"Why Has Narrative Poetry Failed" (Murphy), **Supp. V:** 320–321
"Why I Became a Plumber" (Maitland), **Supp. XI:** 175
"Why I Have Embraced Islam" (Rushdie), **Supp. IV:** 437
"Why I Ought Not to Have Become a Dramatic Critic" (Beerbohm), **Supp. II:** 54
"Why Not Take Pater Seriously?" (Fletcher), **V:** 359
Why Scots Should Rule Scotland (Gray, A.), **Supp. IX:** 80, 85
"Why She Would Not" (Shaw), **VI:** 130
"Why Should Not Old Men Be Mad?" (Yeats), **Retro. Supp. I:** 337
"Why Should We Fear the Romish Priests?" (Kingsley), **Supp. XVI:** 203
Why So, Socrates? (Richards), **Supp. II:** 425
"Why the Novel Matters" (Lawrence), **VII:** 122
"Why We Are in Favour of This War" (Hulme), **Supp. VI:** 140
"Why Write of the Sun" (Armitage), **VIII:** 3
Wi the Haill Voice (tr. Morgan, E.), **Supp. IX:** 168
Wicked Heat (Hart), **Supp. XI:** 121, 130–133
"Wicked Stepmother's Lament, The" (Maitland), **Supp. XI:** 175
"Wicked Tunge Wille Sey Amys, A" (Lydgate), **I:** 57
Wide Sargasso Sea (Rhys), **Supp. II:** 387, 389, **398–401,** 441; **Retro. Supp. I:** 60
Wide-Awake Stories: A Collection of Tales Told by Little Children between Sunset and Sunrise, in the Punjab and Kashmi (Steel), **Supp. XII:** 266
Widow, The (Middleton), **II:** 3, 21
"Widow, The" (Smith, I. C.), **Supp. IX:** 211
"Widow at Windsor, The" (Kipling), **Retro. Supp. III:** 188
Widow; Or, A Picture of Modern Times, The (Robinson), **Supp. XIII:** 207
Widow Ranter, The (Behn), **Supp. III:** 34; **Retro. Supp. III:** 10
Widow Ranter, The (Belin), **II:** 305
"Widower in the Country, The" (Murray), **Supp. VII:** 271
Widower's Son, The (Sillitoe), **Supp. V:** 410, 414, 415, 425

Widowers' Houses (Shaw), **VI:** 104, 107, 108, 129; **Retro. Supp. II:** 310–312
"Widowhood System, The" (Friel), **Supp. V:** 113
Widowing of Mrs. Holroyd, The (Lawrence), **VII:** 120, 121
Widow's Tears, The (Chapman), **I:** 243–244, 245–246
Widow's Vow, The (Inchbald), **Supp. XV:** 147, 148, 154, 161
Widsith, **Retro. Supp. II:** 304
Wiene, Robert, **III:** 342
Wife for a Month (Fletcher), **II:** 65
Wife of Bath, The (Gay), **III:** 60, 67
Wife of Bath's Prologue, The (Chaucer), **I:** 24, 34, 39, 40
Wife of Bath's Tale, The (Chaucer), **I:** 27, 35–36
"Wife of Ted Wickham, The" (Coppard), **VIII:** 95
"Wife Speaks, The" (Day Lewis), **Supp. III:** 125
Wife's Lament, The, **Retro. Supp. II:** 305
Wigs on the Green (Mitford), **Supp. X:** 155–156
Wilberforce, William, **IV:** 133, 268; **V:** 277
Wild Ass's Skin, The (Balzac), **III:** 339, 345
"Wild Boar and the Ram, The" (Gay), **III:** 59
Wild Body, The (Lewis), **VII:** 72, 77, 78, 79
"Wild Clematis in Winter" (Hill), **Retro. Supp. III:** 144
"Wild Colonial Puzzler, The" (Wallace-Crabbe), **VIII:** 318
Wild Bird's Nest, The (tr. O'Connor), **Supp. XIV:** 220, 221, 222
Wild Blood (Thompson), **Supp. XIV:** 286, 288–289, 294
Wild Duck, The (Ibsen), **VI:** ix
"Wild Flowers" (Howard), **V:** 48
Wild Gallant, The (Dryden), **II:** 305; **Retro. Supp. III:** 60
Wild Garden, The; or, Speaking of Writing (Wilson), **Supp. I:** 153, 154–155, 156, 158, 160
Wild Girl, The (Roberts), **Supp. XV:** 265–266, 272
Wild Goose Chase, The (Fletcher), **II:** 45, 61–62, 65, 352, 357
Wild Honey (Frayn), **Supp. VII:** 61
Wild Irish Boy, The (Maturin), **VIII:** 207, 209
Wild Knight, The (Chesterton), **VI:** 336
"Wild Lemons" (Malouf), **Supp. XII:** 220
Wild Nights (Tennant), **Supp. IX:** 230, 233–234
Wild Reckoning: An Anthology Provoked By Rachel Carson's "Silent Spring" (ed. Burnside and Riordan), **Supp. XIII:** 31
"Wild Sunrise" (Sutcliff), **Supp. XVI:** 264
Wild Swans at Coole, The (Yeats), **VI:** 207, 213, 214, 217; **Retro. Supp. I:** 331

Wild Wales: Its People, Language, and Scenery (Borrow), **Supp. XII:** 17, 28–31
"Wild with All Regrets" (Owen), **VI:** 446, 452, 453
Wild Wreath (tr. Robinson), **Supp. XIII:** 213
Wilde, Oscar, **III:** 334, 345; **V:** xiii, xxi, xxv, xxvi, 53, 339, **399–422; VI:** ix, 365; **VII:** 83; **Supp. II:** 43, 45–46, 48, 50, 51, 53, 54, 141, 143, 148, 155; **Supp. IV:** 288; **Retro. Supp. II:** 314–315, **359–374**
Wilder Hope, The: Essays on Future Punishment . . . (De Quincey), **IV:** 155
"Wilderness, The" (Keyes), **VII:** 439
Wilderness of Zin (Woolley and Lawrence), **Supp. II:** 284
Wildest Dreams (Ayckbourn), **Supp. V:** 3, 10, 12, 14
"Wildgoose Chase, A" (Coppard), **VIII:** 95
"Wildlife" (Adcock), **Supp. XII:** 12
Wildtrack (Wain), **Supp. XVI:** 306, 307
"Wilfred Owen and the Georgians" (Hibberd), **VI:** 460
Wilfred Owen: Complete Poems and Fragments (Stallworthy), see *Complete Poems and Fragments of Wilfred Owen, The*
Wilfred Owen: War Poems and Others (Hibberd), **VI:** 446, 459
"Wilfred Owen's Letters" (Hibberd), **VI:** 460
Wilhelm Meister (Goethe), **IV:** 241; **V:** 214
Wilhelm Meister's Apprenticeship (tr. Carlyle), **IV:** 241, 250
Wilkes, John, **IV:** 61, 185
Wilkes, Thomas, **II:** 351, 363
Wilkie, David, **IV:** 37
Wilkins, George, **I:** 321
Wilkinson, Martin, **Supp. IV:** 168
"Will, The" (Donne), **Retro. Supp. II:** 91
Will Drew and Phil Crewe and Frank Fane . . . (Swinburne), **V:** 333
"Will Men Ever Face Fact and Not Feel Flat" (Smith), **Retro. Supp. III:** 311
"Will o' the Mill" (Stevenson), **V:** 395
"Will of the Dying Ass, The" (tr. Symonds), **Supp. XIV:** 253
Will Warburton (Gissing), **V:** 435, 437
"Will Waterproofs Lyrical Monologue" (Tennyson), **Retro. Supp. III:** 322
"Will Ye No' Come Back Again?" (Wallace-Crabbe), **VIII:** 323
Willey, Basil, **II:** 145, 157; **Supp. II:** 103, 107, 108
"William and Mary" (Dahl), **Supp. IV:** 218, 219
William B. Yeats: The Poet in Contemporary Ireland (Hone), **VI:** 223
William Blake (Chesterton), **VI:** 344
William Blake (Swinburne), **V:** 313, 314, 317, 329–330, 332
William Cobbett (Chesterton), **VI:** 341, 345
"William Cobbett: In Absentia" (Hill), **Supp. V:** 183

"William Congreve" (Swinburne), **V:** 332
William Dunbar, Selected Poems (Dunbar), **VIII:** 119
William Morris (Bloomfield), **V:** 306
William Morris, Artist, Writer, Socialist (Morris), **V:** 301, 305
"William Morris as I Knew Him" (Shaw), **VI:** 129
William Pitt . . . an Excellent New Ballad . . . (Boswell), **III:** 248
William Posters trilogy (Sillitoe), **Supp. V:** 410, 413, 421–424
William Soutar: Collected Poems (Soutar), **Supp. XVI:** 255–256
"William Tennissippi" (Morgan, E.), **Supp. IX:** 161
William Wetmore Story and His Friends (James), **VI:** 67
"William Wordsworth" (De Quincey), **IV:** 146
William Wordsworth: A Biography (Moorman), **IV:** 4, 25
Williams, Basil, **VI:** 234
Williams, Charles Walter Stansby, **Supp. IX:** 271–286
Williams, H., **III:** 15n, 35
Williams, Hugo, **Supp. IV:** 168
Williams, Iolo, **VII:** 37
Williams, Raymond, **Supp. IV:** 95, 380
Williams, William Carlos, **Supp. IV:** 257, 263
Williams Manuscript and the Temple, The (Charles), **Retro. Supp. II:** 174
Willis, W., **III:** 199n
"Willowwood" sonnets (Rossetti), **V:** 243, 259
Willy Wonka and the Chocolate Factory (film), **Supp. IV:** 203
Wilmot, John, *see* Rochester, earl of
Wilson, A. N., *see* Wilson, Angus
Wilson, Angus, **V:** 43, 72; **VI:** 165; **Supp. I:** 153–168; **Supp. II:** 92; **Supp. IV:** 229, 231, 234, 346; **Supp. VI:** 297–310
Wilson, Colin, **III:** 341
Wilson, Dover, *see* Wilson, J. Dover
Wilson, Edmund, **IV:** 27; **V:** 66, 69, 72; **VI:** 56, 62, 363; **VII:** 53; **Supp. II:** 57, 118, 124, 200, 204, 223; **Supp. III:** 95, 101, 105
Wilson, F. A. C., **VI:** 208, 220
Wilson, F. P., **I:** 286
Wilson, J. Dover, **I:** 326; **III:** 116n; **V:** 287, 290
Wilson, J. H., **II:** 257, 271
Wilson, John, **IV:** 11
Wilson, Rae, **IV:** 262
Wiltshire and Gloucestershire Standard, **Supp. XV:** 168
Wimsatt, M. K., Jr., **III:** 249
Winckelman, Johann, **V:** 341, 343, 344
"Winckelmann" (Pater), **V:** 341, 343, 344
Wind, Edgar, **I:** 237; **V:** 317n
"Wind" (Hughes), **Supp. I:** 343–344
Wind Among the Reeds, The (Yeats), **VI:** 211, 222
Wind from Nowhere, The (Ballard), **Supp. V:** 22
"Windfalls" (Fallon), **Supp. XII:** 110–111

"Windfarming" (Crawford), **Supp. XI:** 81
"Windhover, The" (Hopkins), **V:** 366, 367; **Retro. Supp. II:** 190, 191, 195–196
Winding Paths: Photographs by Bruce Chatwin (Chatwin, B.), **Supp. IX:** 62
Winding Stair, The (Yeats), **Supp. II:** 84–85; **Retro. Supp. I:** 336–337
Winding Stair, The: Francis Bacon, His Rise and Fall (du Maurier), **Supp. III:** 139
Windom's Way (Ambler), **Supp. IV:** 3
Window, (periodical), **Supp. XIII:** 191
"Window, The" (Moore), **VI:** 93
Window, The; or, The Songs of the Wrens (Tennyson), **Retro. Supp. III:** 317
Window in Thrums, A (Barrie), **V:** 392; **Supp. III:** 3
Windows (Galsworthy), **VI:** 269
"Windows, The" (Herbert), **Retro. Supp. II:** 176
Windows of Night (Williams, C. W. S.), **Supp. IX:** 274
"Wind's on the World, The" (Morris), **V:** 305
"Windscale" (Nicholson), **Supp. VI:** 218
Windsor Forest (Pope), **III:** 70, 77; **Retro. Supp. I:** 231
Wine, A Poem (Gay), **III:** 67
"Wine and Venus" (tr. Symonds), **Supp. XIV:** 253
Wine–Dark Sea, The (O'Brian), **Supp. XII:** 258–259
"Wine Fed Tree, The" (Powys), **VIII:** 251
Wine, Water and Song (Chesterton), **VI:** 340
Wine, Women, and Song: Mediaeval Latin Students' Songs (tr. Symonds), **Supp. XIV:** 253
"Wingless" (Kincaid), **Supp. VII:** 220, 221, 226
"Wings of a Dove" (Brathwaite), **Supp. XII:** 44
Wings of the Dove, The (James), **VI:** 32, 55, **59–60,** 320; **Supp. IV:** 243
"Winkie" (Dunn), **Supp. X:** 77
Winkworth, Catherine, **V:** 149
Winners and Losers (Parsons), **Supp. XV:** 228, 229
Winnie-the-Pooh (Milne), **Supp. V:** 295, 303–307
"Winning of Etain, The" (Boland), **Supp. V:** 36
"Winnowers, The" (Bridges), **VI:** 78
Winshaw Legacy, The (Coe), **Supp. XV:** 49, 55–57
Winslow Boy, The (Rattigan), **Supp. VII:** 307, 313–315
"Winter" (Blake), **Retro. Supp. I:** 34
"Winter" (Brontë), **V:** 107
"Winter" (Dunn), **Supp. X:** 69
"Winter" (Thomas), **Supp. XII:** 290
Winter (Thomson), **Supp. III:** 411, 412–413, 417, 418
Winter Apology (Bainbridge), **Supp. VI:** 22–23
"Winter Field" (Coppard), **VIII:** 98
Winter Fuel (Millais), **V:** 379

Winter Garden (Bainbridge), **Supp. VI:** 22–23, 24
Winter in the Hills, A (Wain), **Supp. XVI:** 293–294, 297, 299–300
Winter House and Other Poems, The (Cameron), **Supp. IX:** 17, 22–25
"Winter in Camp" (Fuller), **Supp. VII:** 70
"Winter in England" (Fuller), **Supp. VII:** 70
"Winter in July" (Lessing), **Supp. I:** 240
Winter in the Air (Warner), **Supp. VII:** 380
"Winter Landscape near Ely, A" (Davie), **Supp. VI:** 110
"Winter, My Secret" (Rossetti), **V:** 256
"Winter Night" (Fuller), **Supp. VII:** 72
"Winter Nosegay, The" (Cowper), **Retro. Supp. III:** 47
Winter Pilgrimage, A (Haggard), **Supp. III:** 214
Winter Pollen: Occasional Prose (Hughes), **Retro. Supp. II:** 202
Winter Quarters (Scupham), **Supp. XIII:** 221–222, 223
Winter Tales (Brown), **Supp. VI:** 68–70
"Winter with the Gulf Stream" (Hopkins), **V:** 361, 381
Winter Words, in Various Moods and Metres (Hardy), **VI:** 20
Winter Work (Fallon), **Supp. XII:** 106–108, 109, 114
"Winter Work" (Fallon), **Supp. XII:** 106
Wintering Out (Heaney), **Supp. II:** 268, 272–273; **Retro. Supp. I:** 125, 128
Winters, Yvor, **VI:** 219; **Supp. IV:** 256–257, 261; **Retro. Supp. I:** 335
"Winters and the Palmleys, The" (Hardy), **VI:** 22
"Winter's Tale, A" (Thomas), **Supp. I:** 177, 178; **Retro. Supp. III:** 345
Winter's Tale, The (Chaucer), **I:** 25
Winter's Tale, The (Shakespeare), **I:** 166n, 302, 322–323, 327; **Retro. Supp. III:** 277, 281
"Winter's Talents" (Davie), **Supp. VI:** 112
"Winter–Saturday" (Crawford), **Supp. XI:** 70–71
Winterslow: Essays and Characters Written There (Hazlitt), **IV:** 140
Winterson, Jeanette, **Supp. IV:** 541–559
Winterwood and Other Hauntings (Roberts, K.), **Supp. X:** 273
"Wintry Beauty" (Soutar), **Supp. XVI:** 254
"Wintry Manifesto, A" (Wallace–Crabbe), **VIII:** 313
"Wires" (Larkin), **Supp. I:** 278, 285
"Wisdom Literature", **Retro. Supp. II:** 304
Wisdom of Father Brown, The (Chesterton), **VI:** 338
"Wisdom of Gautama, The" (Caudwell), **Supp. IX:** 33
Wisdom of Solomon Paraphrased, The (Middleton), **II:** 2
Wisdom of the Ancients (Bacon), *see De sapientia veterum*
Wise, T. J., **V:** 150, 151

Wise Children (Carter), **Supp. III:** 90–91
Wise Man of the East, The (Inchbald), **Supp. XV:** 159, 160
Wise Virgins (Wilson), **Supp. VI:** 297, **301,** 303
Wise Wound, The (Redgrove), **Supp. VI:** 230, 233
"Wish, The" (Cowley), **II:** 195, 198
"Wish, The" (Dahl), **Supp. IV:** 206, 221
"Wish House, The" (Kipling), **VI:** 169, 193, 196, **197–199**
Wish I Was Here (Kay), **Supp. XIII:** 102, 107, 109, 110
"Wish in Spring" (Warner), **Supp. VII:** 373
"Wishes to His (Supposed), Mistresse" (Crashaw), **II:** 180
Wit at Several Weapons, **II:** 21, 66
Wit Without Money (Fletcher), **II:** 66
Witch, The (Middleton), **II:** 3, 21; **IV:** 79
Witch, The (Williams, C. W. S.), **Supp. IX:** 276–277
"Witch at Endor" (Abercrombie), **Supp. XVI:** 9–10
Witch Hunt (Rankin), **Supp. X:** 245, 252
"Witch of Atlas, The" (Shelley), **IV:** 196, 204
Witch of Edmonton, The (Dekker, Ford, Rowley), **II:** 89, 100
"Witch of Fife, The" (Hogg), **Supp. X:** 106–108
Witchcraft (Williams, C. W. S.), **Supp. IX:** 284
Witchcraft: New-Style (Abercrombie), **Supp. XVI:** 9
"Witchcraft: Old-Style" (Abercrombie), **Supp. XVI:** 9–**Supp. XVI:** 10
Witches, The (Dahl), **Supp. IV:** 204, 213, 215, 225–226
Witches, The (film), **Supp. IV:** 203
"Witches' Corner, The" (Fallon), **Supp. XII:** 108–109
"Witches of Traquair, The" (Hogg), **Supp. X:** 110
Witch's Head, The (Haggard), **Supp. III:** 213
"With Alan to the Fair" (Upward), **Supp. XIII:** 261
With My Little Eye (Fuller), **Supp. VII:** 70–71
"With my Sons at Boarhills" (Stevenson), **Supp. VI:** 260
"With Your Tongue Down My Throat" (Kureishi), **Supp. XI:** 158
Wither, George, **IV:** 81
"Withered Arm, The" (Hardy), **VI:** 22; **Retro. Supp. I:** 116
Within the Gates (O'Casey), **VII:** 7
Within the Tides: Tales (Conrad), **VI:** 148
Without a Backward Glance (Butlin), **Supp. XVI:** 52, 55, 58
"Without Benefit of Clergy" (Kipling), **VI:** 180–183
"Without Eyes" (Redgrove), **Supp. VI:** 235
"Without the Option" (Wodehouse), **Supp. III:** 456
Without Title (Hill), **Retro. Supp. III:** 142, 143–144

Witlings, The (Burney), **Supp. III:** 64, 71, 72, 75
"Witness, The" (Lessing), **Supp. I:** 244
Witness for the Prosecution (Christie), **Supp. II:** 125, 134
Wit's Treasury (Meres), **I:** 296
Wittig, Monique, **Supp. IV:** 558
Wives and Daughters (Gaskell), **V:** xxiii, 1–4, 8, 11–13, 14, 15; **Retro. Supp. III:** 100, 102, 110–112
Wives as They Were, and Maids as They Are (Inchbald), **Supp. XV:** 147, 148, 158
Wizard of Oz, The (Baum), **Supp. IV:** 450
Wizard of Oz, The (film), **Supp. IV:** 434, 443, 448, 450, 455
Wizard of Oz, The (Rushdie), **Supp. IV:** 434
Wodehouse, P. G., **Supp. III:** **447–464**
Wodwo (Hughes), **Supp. I:** 343, 346, **348–350,** 363; **Retro. Supp. II:** 205–206
Woefully Arrayed (Skelton), **I:** 84
Wog (Carey), **Supp. XII:** 52
Wolf and the Lamb, The (Henryson), **Supp. VII:** 136, 141
Wolf and the Wether, The (Henryson), **Supp. VII:** 136, 140–141
Wolf, Friedrich, **IV:** 316–317
Wolf, Lucien, **IV:** 293
Wolf Leader, The (Dumas *pére*), **III:** 339
Wolf that gat the Nekhering throw the wrinkis of the Foxe that begylit the Cadgear, The (Henryson), see *Fox, the Wolf, and the Cadger, The*
Wolfe, Tom, **Supp. IV:** 454
Wolff, S. L., **I:** 164
"Wolfhound, The" (Murphy), **Supp. V:** 323
Wolfman (Rankin), **Supp. X:** 244, 246, 248, 250
Wolfwatching (Hughes), **Retro. Supp. II:** 214
Wollstonecraft, Mary, **Supp. III:** **465–482;** **Retro. Supp. I:** 39
Wolves and the Lamb, The (Thackeray), **V:** 35
Woman (periodical), **VI:** 249; **Supp. XIII:** 135
Woman, The (Bond), **Supp. I:** 423, 434, 435
"Woman: And Her Place in a Free Society" (Carpenter), **Supp. XIII:** 41
"Woman, The Place, The Poet, The" (Boland), **Supp. V:** 35
Woman and Labour (Schreiner), **Supp. II:** 444, **454–456**
"Woman at the Shore, The" (Mansfield), **VII:** 173
Woman Beware Woman 231, 233–234, 235–236
Woman-Captain, The (Shadwell), **II:** 359
Woman Hater, The (Beaumont and Fletcher), **II:** 46, 65
Woman-Hater, The (Burney), **Supp. III:** 64
Woman in Black, The (Hill), **Supp. XIV:** 116, 118, 124–125, 126
"Woman in His Life, The" (Kipling), **VI:** 193

"Women in Jerusalem" (Jamie), **Supp. XIV:** 129
Woman in Mind (Ayckbourn), **Supp. V:** 3, 6–7, 10, 11, 13, 15
Woman in the Moon, The (Lyly), **I:** 204–205
Woman in White, The (Collins), **III:** 340, 345; **Supp. VI:** 91–94, **95–97,** 100, 102–103
Woman Killed With Kindness, A (Heywood), **II:** 19
Woman of No Importance, A (Bennett), **VIII:** 27
Woman of No Importance, A (Wilde), **V:** xxvi, 414, 419; **Retro. Supp. II:** 369
"Woman of No Standing, A" (Behan), **Supp. II:** 66
"Woman of the House, The" (Murphy), **Supp. V:** 313, 318–319
Woman of the Inner Sea (Keneally), **Supp. IV:** 347, 348, 358–360
"Woman of Three Cows, The" (Mangan), **Supp. XIII:** 126–127
"Woman out of a Dream, A" (Warner), **Supp. VII:** 373
Woman Pleased (Fletcher), **II:** 45, 65
"Woman! When I behold thee flippant, vain" (Keats), **Retro. Supp. I:** 188–189
"Woman Who Rode Away, The" (Lawrence), **VII:** 87–88, 91, 115
Woman Who Walked into Doors, The (Doyle), **Supp. V:** 78, 88, 91–92
"Woman with a Knife and Fork Disorder, The" (Kay), **Supp. XIII:** 102, 110
Womanhood, Wanton, Ye Want (Skelton), **I:** 83
"Womans constancy" (Donne), **Retro. Supp. II:** 89
"Woman's History, A" (Davies), **Supp. XI:** 99
"Woman's Last Word, A" (Browning), **IV:** 367; **Retro. Supp. II:** 24; **Retro. Supp. III:** 24
Woman's Prize, The; or, The Tamer Tamed (Fletcher), **II:** 43, 45, 65
"Woman's Song" (Warner), **Supp. VII:** 373
Woman's World (periodical), **V:** 404
Womb of Space: The Cross-Cultural Imagination (Harris), **Supp. V:** 140, 146
"Womb with a View" (Roberts), **Supp. XV:** 261–262
"Women, The" (Boland), **Supp. V:** 50–51
"Women" (Smith, I. C.), **Supp. IX:** 218
"Women, The" (Stevenson), **Supp. VI:** 254
Women at Oxford: A Fragment of History, The (Brittain), **Supp. X:** 47
"Women at Geneva" (Brittain), **Supp. X:** 37
Women: Or, Pour et Contre (Maturin), **VIII:** 207
Women Beware Women (Middleton), **II:** 1, 3, 8, **10–14,** 19
Women Fly When Men Aren't Watching (Maitland), **Supp. XI:** 170, 174, 175, 176

Women in Love (Lawrence), **IV:** 119; **VI:** 276; **VII:** 87–88, 89, 91, 98, **101–104**; **Retro. Supp. II:** 228–229
Women's Work in Modern England (Brittain), **Supp. X:** 39
"Wonder" (Traherne), **II:** 191; **Supp. XI:** 266
Wonder of Women, The; or, The Tragedie of Sophonisba (Marston), **II:** 25, 30–31, 40, 305
Wonder Stories (Wyndham), **Supp. XIII:** 281
"Wonderful Story of Henry Sugar, The" (Dahl), **Supp. IV:** 223
Wonderful Tennessee (Friel), **Supp. V:** 126–127
Wonderful Visit, The (Wells), **VI:** 226, 228, 230, 243
Wonderful Story of Aladdin and the Enchanted Lamp, The (Pullman), **Supp. XIII:** 152
Wondrous Tale of Alroy, The (Disraeli), *see Alroy*
"Wonnerfu Walrd O John Milton, The" (Butlin), **Supp. XVI:** 53–54
Wood, Anthony à, **II:** 185
Wood Beyond, The (Hill, R.), **Supp. IX:** 121
Wood Beyond the World, The (Morris), **V:** 306
"Wood Fire, The" (Hardy), **Retro. Supp. I:** 121
"Wood near Athens, A" (Gunn), **Retro. Supp. III:** 129–130
"Wooden Chair with Arms" (MacCaig), **Supp. VI:** 192
Woodhouse, Richard, **IV:** 230, 232, 233
Woodlanders, The (Hardy), **VI:** 1, 5, 7, 8, 9; **Retro. Supp. I:** 115
"Woodlands, 7 Kilnwell Road, Market Rasen" (Scupham), **Supp. XIII:** 224
Woodman, Thomas, **Supp. IV:** 364
Woods, Helen Emily, *see* Kavan, Anna
"Woods of Westermain, The" (Meredith), **V:** 221
"Woodsman" (MacCaig), **Supp. VI:** 192
"Woodspurge, The" (Rossetti), **V:** 241, 242, 314–315
Woodstock (Scott), **IV:** xviii, 27, 39
Woodward, Benjamin, **V:** 178
Woolf, Leonard, **VI:** 415; **VII:** 17
Woolf, Virginia, **I:** 169; **IV:** 107, 320, 322; **V:** xxv, 226, 256, 260, 281, 290; **VI:** 243, 252, 275, 411; **VII:** xii, xiv–xv, **17–39**; **Supp. II:** 341–342, 487, 501–502; **Supp. III:** 19, 41–42, 45, 49, 60, 103, 107, 108; **Supp. IV:** 231, 233, 246, 399, 407, 461, 542, 558; **Supp. V:** 36, 63; **Retro. Supp. I:** 59, **305–323**
"Wool-Gatherer, The" (Hogg), **Supp. X:** 111
Woolley, Hannah, **Supp. III:** 21
Woolley, Leonard, **Supp. II:** 284
"Word, The" (Hart), **Supp. XI:** 132
"Word, The" (E. Thomas), **Supp. III:** 406
"Word, The" (R.S. Thomas), **Supp. XII:** 290, 291
Word Carved on a Sill, A (Wain), **Supp. XVI:** 306

Word Child, A (Murdoch), **Supp. I:** 228
Word for the Navy, A (Swinburne), **V:** 332
Word over All (Day Lewis), **Supp. III:** 118, 128
Word-Links (Carroll), **V:** 274
"Words" (Gunn), **Supp. IV:** 267; **Retro. Supp. III:** 122
Words and Music (Beckett), **Supp. I:** 53, 60
Words and Music (Coward), **Supp. II:** 152
"Words for Jazz Perhaps" (Longley), **VIII:** 167
Words of Advice (Weldon), **Supp. IV:** 536–537
Words upon the Window Pane, The (Yeats), **VI:** 219, 222
"Wordscape: Elegy for Angus" (Greig), **Supp. XVI:** 161
Wordsworth, Dorothy, **II:** 273; **IV:** 1–4, 10, 19, 49, 128, 143, 146
Wordsworth, William, **II:** 188–189; **III:** 174; **IV:** viii–xi, **1–26**, 33, 70, 73, 95–96, 111, 137, 178, 214, 215, 281, 311, 351, 352; **V:** 287, 311, 331, 351–352; **VI:** 1; and Coleridge, **IV:** 43–45, 50, 51, 54; **Retro. Supp. II:** 62, 63–64; and DeQuincey, **IV:** 141–143, 146, 154; and Hazlitt, **IV:** 126–130, 133–134, 137, 138; and Keats, **IV:** 214, 215, 225, 233; and Shelley, **IV:** 198, 203, 207; and Tennyson, **IV:** 326, 329, 336; literary style, **III:** 304, 338; **IV:** 95–96, 154, 336; verse forms, **II:** 200; **V:** 224; **Supp. II:** 269; **Supp. IV:** 230, 252, 558
"Wordsworth" (Pater), **V:** 351–352
"Wordsworth and Byron" (Swinburne), **V:** 332
"Wordsworth's Ethics" (Stephen), **V:** 287
"Work" (Lamb), **IV:** 83
Work in Hand (Cameron), **Supp. IX:** 26–27
Work in Progress (Cameron), **Supp. IX:** 17
Work in Progress (Lowry), **Supp. III:** 280
Work in Progress (Redgrove), **Supp. VI:** 231
Work in Regress (Reading), **VIII:** 273
"Work of Art, A" (Warner), **Supp. VII:** 380
"Work of Art In the Age of Mechanical Reproduction, The" (Symons), **Supp. XIV:** 278–279
"Work of My Own, A" (Winterson), **Supp. IV:** 558
"Work of Water, The" (Redgrove), **Supp. VI:** 235
Work Suspended (Waugh), **VII:** 298–299
Work, Wealth and Happiness of Mankind, The (Wells), **VI:** 225
"Work without Hope" (Coleridge), **Retro. Supp. II:** 65
Workers in the Dawn (Gissing), **V:** 424, 435, 437
Workes of Edmund Waller in This Parliament, The (Waller), **II:** 238
"Workhouse Clock, The," (Hood), **IV:** 261, 264

Workhouse Donkey, The (Arden), **Supp. II:** 28, 30
Workhouse Ward, The (Gregory), **VI:** 315, 316
Workmen of England (Kingsley), **Supp. XVI:** 203
Working Legs: A Two-Act Play for Disabled Performers (Gray, A.), Supp. **IX:** 89–90
Working Novelist, The (Pritchett), **VI:** 290
Working of Water, The (Redgrove), **Supp. VI:** 235–236
Working with Structuralism: Essays and Reviews on Nineteenth- and Twentieth-Century Literature (Lodge), **Supp. IV:** 365, 377
"Workmen" (Crawford), **Supp. XI:** 81
Works (Congreve), **II:** 348
Works (Cowley), **II:** 195
Works (Swift), **III:** 24
Works of Art and Artists in England (Waagen), **III:** 328
Works of Charles Lamb, The, **IV:** 73, 81, 85
Works of Dr. Thomas Campion, The (Campion), **Supp. XVI:** 103
Works of Henry Fielding, The (ed. Stephen), **V:** 290
Works of Henry Vaughan, The (Martin), **II:** 184
Works of Max Beerbohm, The (Beerbohm), **Supp. II:** 45, 46, 47
Works of Morris and Yeats in Relation to Early Saga Literature, The (Hoare), **V:** 299, 306
Works of Mrs. Catharine Cockburn, Theological, Moral, Dramatic, and Poetical, The (Trotter), **Supp. XVI:** 277, 279, 282
Works of Mrs. Cowley, The: Dramas and Poems (Cowley), **Supp. XVI:** 110
Works of Ossian (Macpherson), **VIII:** 189, 192
Works of Samuel Johnson, The, **III:** 108n, 121
Works of Sir John Vanbrugh, The (ed. Dobrée and Webb), **II:** 323n
Works of Sir Thomas Malory, The (ed. Vinavier), **I:** 70, 80
Works of the English Poets (Johnson), **Retro. Supp. I:** 143
Works of Thomas Campion, The: Complete Songs, Masques, and Treatises with a Selection of the Latin Verse (Campion), **Supp. XVI:** 98, 104
Works of Thomas Lodge, The (Tyler), **VI:** 102
Works of Virgil, The (tr. Dryden), **II:** 304; **Retro. Supp. III:** 63
Works of William Blake, The (ed. Yeats), **VI:** 222
World (periodical), **VI:** 103, 104
"World, The" (Vaughan), **II:** 185, 186, 188
World Authors: 1970–1975 (ed. Wakeman), **Supp. XI:** 246, 248, 249, 253
World Bank: A Prospect, The (Morris, J.), **Supp. X:** 175

World Crisis, The (Churchill), **VI:** 353–354
World I Breathe, The (Thomas), **Supp. I:** 176, 180–181
World in the Evening, The (Isherwood), **VII:** 309, 314–315
World Is Not Enough, The (Fleming), **Supp. XIV:** 95
World of Charles Dickens, The (Wilson), **Supp. I:** 166
World of Difference, A (MacCaig), **Supp. VI:** 193–194
"World of Light, A" (Jennings), **Supp. V:** 210
World of Light, A (Sarton), **Supp. II:** 82
World of Light, The (Huxley), **VII:** 201
World of Love, A (Bowen), **Supp. II:** 77, 79, 81, 84, 94
World of Paul Slickey, The (Osborne), **Supp. I:** 333–334
World of Strangers, A (Gordimer), **Supp. II:** 227, 231, 232, 236, 243
"World of Women, The" (Fallon), **Supp. XII:** 111
World Set Free, The: A Story of Mankind (Wells), **VI:** 227, 244
"World with One Eye Shut, The" (Crace), **Supp. XIV:** 21
World Within World (Spender), **Supp. II:** 482, 483, 484, 485, 486, 487, 488, 490
Worldliness (Moore), **VI:** 95, 98
Worlds, The (Bond), **Supp. I:** 423, 434
World's Desire, The (Haggard and Lang), **Supp. III:** 213, 222
"World's End, The" (Empson), **Supp. II:** 182
World's Room, The (MacCaig), **Supp. VI:** 192
"Worlds That Flourish" (Okri), **Supp. V:** 356
"Worlds to Barter" (Wyndham), **Supp. XIII:** 281–282
Worm and the Ring, The (Burgess), **Supp. I:** 186, 187, 188, 189
Worm of Spindlestonheugh, The (Swinburne), **V:** 333
Wormwood (Kinsella), **Supp. V:** 262–263
"Wormwood" (Kinsella), **Supp. V:** 262
Worst Fears (Weldon), **Supp. IV:** 538
"Worst of It, The" (Browning), **IV:** 369
"Worstward Ho" (Beckett), **Supp. I:** 62; **Retro. Supp. I:** 29–30
Worthies of England (Fuller), **II:** 45
Worthies of Westminster (Fuller), **Retro. Supp. I:** 152
Wotton, Sir Henry, **II:** 132, 133, 134, 138, 140, 141, 142, 166
Wotton, William, **III:** 23
Wotton Reinfred (Carlyle), **IV:** 250
Woty, W., **III:** 170n
"Wound, The" (Gunn), **Supp. IV:** 259; **Retro. Supp. III:** 118, 121
"Wound, The" (Hughes), **Supp. I:** 348
Wound in My Heart, The (Ngũgĩ), **VIII:** 222
"Wounds" (Longley), **VIII:** 171
"Wowing of the King quhen he wes in Dumfermeling, The" (Dunbar), **VIII:** 118

"Wreath for Tom Moore's Statue" (Kavanagh), **Supp. VII:** 193
"Wreaths" (Hill), **Supp. V:** 186
"Wreaths" (Longley), **VIII:** 173
"Wreck" (MacCaig), **Supp. VI:** 186
Wreck of the Archangel, The (Brown), **Supp. VI:** 71
"Wreck of the Deutschland, The" (Hopkins), **V:** 361, 362, **363–366,** 367, 369, 370, 375, 379, 380, 381; **Retro. Supp. II:** 189, 191–194
"Wreck of the Deutschland, The": A New Reading (Schneider), **V:** 366, 382
Wreck of the Mary Deare, The (film, Ambler), **Supp. IV:** 3
Wrecked Eggs (Hare), **Supp. IV:** 282, 293
Wrecker, The (Stevenson), **V:** 383, 387, 396
Wrens, The (Gregory), **VI:** 315–316
"Wrestling" (Rossetti), **V:** 260
Wretched of the Earth, The (Fanon), *see Les Damnés de la terre*
Wright, William Aldis, **IV:** 343, 353
Write On: Occasional Essays, '65–'85 (Lodge), **Supp. IV:** 366
Writer and the Absolute, The (Lewis), **VII:** xv, 71, 72, 73–74, 76
Writer in Disguise, The (Bennett), **VIII:** 27
Writers and Their Work series, **VII:** xi, xxii
Writer's Britain: Landscape in Literature, A (ed. Drabble), **Supp. IV:** 230, 252
Writer's Diary, A (Woolf), **V:** 226
"Writer's Friends, A" (Stead), **Supp. IV:** 461, 466
Writers in Politics (Ngũgĩ), **VIII:** 224
Writer's Ireland: Landscape in Literature, A (Trevor), **Supp. IV:** 514
Writer's Notebook, A (Maugham), **VI:** 365, 366
"Writers Take Sides, The" (Stead), **Supp. IV:** 463, 466
"Writing" (Auden), **Retro. Supp. I:** 13
"Writing" (Motion), **Supp. VII:** 256
"Writing as a Woman" (Stevenson), **Supp. VI:** 257
Writing Game: A Comedy, The (Lodge), **Supp. IV:** 366, 381
Writing in a State of Seige (Brink), **Supp. VI:** 47, 49
Writing Left-Handed (Hare), **Supp. IV:** 282, 283
"Writing the Poem" (Scupham), **Supp. XIII:** 220, 223, 225
"Written After the Death of Charles Lamb" (Wordsworth), **IV:** 73
"Written in a Fit of Illness 1755" (Cowper), **Retro. Supp. III:** 45
"Written in a Quarrel" (Cowper), **Retro. Supp. III:** 45
"Written in My Lady Speke's Singing Book" (Waller), **II:** 234
Written on the Body (Winterson), **Supp. IV:** 542, 547, 549–551, 552, 553, 555, 557
"Wrong" (Burnside), **Supp. XIII:** 21–22
Wrong About Japan: A Father's Journey with His Son (Carey), **Supp. XII:** 54

Wrong Box, The (Stevenson and Osbourne), **V:** 387, 396
"Wrong Name, The" (Powys), **VIII:** 251
Wulf and Eadwacer, **Retro. Supp. II:** 305
Wulfstan, Archbishop, **Retro. Supp. II:** 298
Wurzel-Flummery (Milne), **Supp. V:** 298–299
Wuthering Heights (Brontë), **III:** 333, 338, 344, 345; **V:** xx, 113, 114, 127, 128, 131, 133–135, 140, **141–145,** 254; **Supp. III:** 144, 145; **Supp. IV:** 231, 452, 462, 513; **Retro. Supp. I:** 50, 52, 53, 54, 57–58
Wyatt, Sir Thomas, **I: 97–112,** 113, 115
"Wyatt resteth here, that quick could never rest" (Surrey), **I:** 115
Wycherley, William, **II: 307–322,** 343, 352, 360
Wycliffe, John, **I:** 375
Wyllard's Weird (Braddon), **VIII:** 49
Wymer, T. L., **V:** 324, 335
"Wyncote, Pennsylvania: A Gloss" (Kinsella), **Supp. V:** 274
Wyndham, Francis, **Supp. IV:** 159, 161, 304
Wyndham, John, **Supp. V:** 22; **Supp. XIII: 281–294**
Wyndham Lewis: A Memoir (Eliot), **VII:** 77
Wyndham Lewis: His Theory of Art and Communication (McLuhan), **VII:** 71n

Xanadu (Armitage), **VIII:** 1
"Xerox" (Carson), **Supp. XIII:** 63
"XL. A Lake" (Beddoes), **Supp. XI:** 29
Xorandor (Brooke-Rose), **Supp. IV:** 100, 111
X/Self (Brathwaite), **Supp. XII:** 33, 41–42, 46
XVI Revelations of Divine Love, Shewed to a Devout Servant of Our Lord, Called Mother Juliana, an Anchorete of Norwich: Who Lived in the Dayes of King Edward the Third (Julian of Norwich), **Supp. XII:** 155
XX Poems (Larkin), **Supp. I:** 277
"XX Poems" (Larkin), **Retro. Supp. III:** 204
"XXII. Life a Glass Window" (Beddoes), **Supp. XI:** 29
"XXXVIII. Rain" (Beddoes), **Supp. XI:** 29

"Yaddo Letter, The" (Mahon), **Supp. VI:** 176
Yan Tan Tethera (Harrison), **Supp. V:** 150, 164
Yangtse Incident (film, Ambler), **Supp. IV:** 3
Yangtze Valley and Beyond, The (Bird), **Supp. X:** 31
Yard of Sun, A (Fry), **Supp. III:** 191, 194, 195, 204–205
"Yardley Oak" (Cowper), **III:** 218
"Yarrow" (Muldoon), **Supp. IV:** 429–432
Yarrow Revisited, and Other Poems (Wordsworth), **IV:** 25

YATE–ZWEI

Yates, Edmund, **V:** 20
Yates, Frances M., **I:** 237
"Ye happy youths, whose hearts are free" (Etherege), **II:** 267
Yealland, Lewis, **Supp. IV:** 58–59
"Year at Ambleside, A" (Martineau), **Supp. XV:** 186
Year In, Year Out (Milne), **Supp. V:** 309, 310–311
"Year of the Foxes, The" (Malouf), **Supp. XII:** 219
"Year of the Sloes, For Ishi, The" (Muldoon), **Supp. IV:** 414
Year of the Whale, The (Brown), **Supp. VI:** 71
Year to Remember: A Reminiscence of 1931, A (Waugh), **Supp. VI:** 273
Years, The (Woolf), **VII:** 18, 22, 24, 27, 28, 36, 38; **Retro. Supp. I:** 308
Year's Afternoon, The (Dunn), **Supp. X:** 81–83
Years Between, The (Kipling), **VI:** 204
"Years Later" (Murphy), **Supp. V:** 313, 320
Years of the Young Rebels, The (Spender), **Supp. II:** 493
"Years On" (Wallace-Crabbe), **VIII:** 323
Yeast (Kingsley), **V:** 4
Yeast: A Problem (Kingsley), **Supp. XVI:** 196–197, 205
"Yeats, Berkeley, and Romanticism" (Davie), **Supp. VI:** 107
Yeats, William Butler, **II:** 78; **III:** 21, 36, 184; **IV:** 196, 216, 323, 329; **V:** xxiii, xxv, xxvi, 301, 304, 306, 311, 318, 329–330, 355, 356, 404; **VI:** ix, xiii–xiv, 55–56, 86, 88, **207–224,** 307, 308, 309, 314; **VII:** 1, 3, 42, 404; **Supp. II:** 84–85, 275, 332, 487; **Supp. III:** 102, 121, 124; **Supp. IV:** 257, 409, 412, 413, 414, 419, 423–424, 480; **Supp. V:** 36, 39; **Retro. Supp. I:** 170–171, 290, **325–339**
"Yeats in Civil War" (Boland), **Supp. V:** 36
Yellow Admiral, The (O'Brian), **Supp. XII:** 259
Yellow Book (periodical), **VI:** 248, 365
Yellow Book, The (Mahon), **Supp. VI:** 176, **177**
"Yellow Girl, The" (Sitwell), **VII:** 138
"Yellow Pages" (Raine), **Supp. XIII:** 164
"Yellow Streak, The" (Maugham), **VI:** 371
Yellow Wallpaper, The (du Maurier), **Supp. III:** 147
Yellowplush Correspondence, The (Thackeray), **V:** 21, 22, 37
"Yellowskin" (Powys), **VIII:** 251
Yes and No (Greene), **Supp. I:** 2
"Yesterday Afternoon, O'erpowered" (Mangan), **Supp. XIII:** 120
Yglesias, Jose, **Supp. IV:** 460
Yogi and the Commissar, The (Koestler), **Supp. I:** 26–27, 35

"Yoka Nikki: An Eight-Day Diary" (Plomer), **Supp. XI:** 216
Yokohama Garland (Coppard), **VIII:** 98
"Yon Toun" (Soutar), **Supp. XVI:** 254, 256
"Yongy-Bonghy-Bo" (Lear), **V:** 84–86
Yorkshire Tragedy, The, **II:** 3, 21
"You" (Armitage), **VIII:** 8
"You and Me and the Continuum" (Ballard), **Supp. V:** 21
"You Lived in Glasgow" (Smith, I. C.), **Supp. IX:** 216
You Make Your Own Life (Pritchett), **Supp. III:** 313, 316, 317
You Never Can Tell (Coward), **Supp. II:** 141
You Never Can Tell (Shaw), **VI:** 109, 111–112; **Retro. Supp. II:** 314–315
You Never Know, Do You? (Coppard), **VIII:** 89
You Only Live Twice (Fleming), **Supp. IV:** 212–213; **Supp. XIV:** 96
You Only Live Twice (screenplay, Dahl), **Supp. IV:** 212–213
"You praise the firm restraint with which they write" (Campbell), **IV:** 320
"You that in love find luck and abundance" (Wyatt), **I:** 104
"You Told Me Once" (Smith, I. C.), **Supp. IX:** 216
"You Went Away" (MacCaig), **Supp. VI:** 185
Young, Edward, **III:** 302, 307, 336; **Retro. Supp. I:** 43
Young, G. M., **IV:** 277, 290, 291, 295; **V:** 228, 262
Young, Kenneth, **IV:** xii, xxv; **VI:** xi–xii, xiii, xxxiv; **VII:** xviii, xxxix
Young, Richard B., **I:** 170
Young Adolph (Bainbridge), **Supp. VI:** 18, **21–22,** 24
"Young and Old" (Kingsley), **Supp. XVI:** 204
"Young Blades" (Ewart), **Supp. VII:** 38
"Young Dragon, The" (Southey), **IV:** 67
Young Duke, The (Disraeli), **IV:** 293, 295–296, 308
Young Emma (Davies), **Supp. XI:** 89, 91–92
Young George du Maurier, The: A Selection of His Letters, 1860–1867 (du Maurier), **Supp. III:** 135–136
"Young Ghost" (Scupham), **Supp. XIII:** 226, 227
"Young Him" (Nicholson), **Supp. VI:** 216
"Young Huntsman with Falcon" (Conn), **Supp. XIII:** 80
Young Idea, The (Coward), **Supp. II:** 141
Young King, The (Behn), **Retro. Supp. III:** 9–10
"Young King, The" (Wilde), **V:** 406
Young Lady, The (Haywood), **Supp. XII:** 136, 142
"Young Love Lies Sleeping" (Rossetti), **V:** 249

Young Men and Old Women (Inchbald), **Supp. XV:** 156–157
"Young Parson Richards" (Shelley), **IV:** 209
Young Pobble's Guide to His Toes, The (Ewart), **Supp. VII:** 45
Young Samuel Johnson (Clifford), **III:** 244n
Young Shoulders (Wain), **Supp. XVI:** 293
"Young Soldier with Bloody Spurs, The" (Lawrence), **VII:** 118
Young Visitors, The (Ashford), **V:** 111, 262
"Young Woman Visitor, The" (Murray), **Supp. VII:** 280
"Young Women in Rollers" (Dunn), **Supp. X:** 69
"Young Women with the Hair of Witches" (Redgrove), **Supp. VI:** **232–233,** 236
Younger Edda, See Snorra Edda
Your Five Gallants (Middleton), **II:** 3, 21
"Your Philosophies Trouble Me" (Paton), **Supp. II:** 360
Your Shadow (Hart), **Supp. XI:** 122, 125–128
"Your Shadow's Songs" (Hart), **Supp. XI:** 126
Youth (Conrad), **VI:** 135, 137; **Retro. Supp. II:** 73
Youth (Rosenberg), **VI:** 432
"Youth" (Tennyson), **IV:** 329
"Youth and Art" (Browning), **IV:** 369
Youth and the Peregrines (Fry), **Supp. III:** 193, 194
"Youth in Memory" (Meredith), **V:** 222, 234
"Youth of Man, The" (Arnold), **V:** 210
"Youth of Nature, The" (Arnold), **V:** 210
"Youth Revisited" (Fuller), **Supp. VII:** 73

Zaillian, Steven, **Supp. IV:** 346
Zapolya (Coleridge), **IV:** 56
Zastrozzi: A Romance (Shelley), **III:** 338; **IV:** 208
ZBC of Ezra Pound, A (Brooke-Rose), **Supp. IV:** 99, 114–115
Zea Mexican Diary, 7 Sept. 1926–7 Sept. 1986, The (Brathwaite), **Supp. XII:** 36
Zeal of Thy House, The (Sayers), **Supp. III:** 335–336, 348–349
Zee & Company (O'Brien), **Supp. V:** 334
"Zero" (Crawford), **Supp. XI:** 77
Zhdanov, Andrei, **Supp. IV:** 82
"Zoetrope" (Carson), **Supp. XIII:** 63
Zola, Émile, **V:** xxiv–xxvi, 286; **VI:** viii; **Supp. IV:** 136, 249
Zoo (MacNeice), **VII:** 403
Zoo Story, The (Albee), **Supp. IV:** 435
Zoom! (Armitage), **VIII:** 1, 2–4
Zoonomia; or, The Laws of Organic Life (Darwin), **Supp. XVI:** 128, 132–134, 137–138, 140, 141
Zuleika Dobson; or, An Oxford Love Story (Beerbohm), **Supp. II:** 43, **56–59**
Zweig, Paul, **Supp. IV:** 356